לקוטי אמרים
תניא

Likkutei Amarim
— Tanya —

BY RABBI SCHNEUR ZALMAN OF LIADI

נבג"מ

Bi-Lingual Edition

by
Kehot Publication Society
770 Eastern Parkway / Brooklyn, New York 11213
(718) 774-4000 / FAX (718) 774-2718
editor@kehot.com

Orders Department
291 Kingston Avenue / Brooklyn, New York 11213
(718) 778-0226 / FAX (718) 778-4148
www.kehot.com

LCC: 84-82007
ISBN: 978-0-8266-0400-2

Printed in the United States of America

ספרי׳ — **אוצר החסידים** — ליובאוויטש

לקוטי אמרים
תניא

יוצא לאור על ידי מערכת

„אוצר החסידים"

770 איסטערן פאַרקוויי — ברוקלין, נ.י.

שנת חמשת אלפים שבע מאות ושבעים לבריאה

שנת המאתים וחמשים להסתלקות־הילולא של הבעש״ט ז״ל

LIKKUTEI AMARIM
— TANYA —

by

Rabbi Schneur Zalman
of Liadi

Bi-Lingual Edition

הוצאה ה'תעה

KEHOT PUBLICATION SOCIETY
770 Eastern Parkway / Brooklyn, New York 11213
5770 • 2009

ספרי׳ — אוצר החסידים — ליובאוויטש
לקוטי אמרים
עם
אגרת התשובה ואגרת הקדש
ברוקלין, נ. י.
הוצאת ספרים
קרני הוד תורה
קה״ת
ליובאוויטש

מפתח כללי

COMPREHENSIVE TABLE OF CONTENTS

NOTE:

The daily MOREH SHIUR — study sections — have been incorporated into the text of the English translation.

★*The regular year is denoted by the symbol ● which signifies the beginning of the daily portion.*

★*The leap year is denoted thus ▲*

The corresponding date for each section is located at the foot of the page.

For further explanation, the reader is directed to the section entitled MOREH SHIUR on page 960.

★These symbols are placed in the margin adjacent to the line containing the sentence or phrase at which the day's section commences.

PREFACE

by the Lubavitcher Rebbe

Chassidus in general, and Chabad Chassidus in particular, is an all-embracing world outlook and way of life which sees the Jew's central purpose as the unifying link between the Creator and Creation.[1] The Jew is a creature of "heaven" and of "earth," of a heavenly Divine soul, which is truly a part of G-dliness,[2] clothed in an earthly vessel constituted of a physical body and animal soul, whose purpose is to realise the transcendency and unity of his nature, and of the world in which he lives, within the absolute Unity of G-d.

The realisation of this purpose entails a two-way correlation: one in the direction from above downward to earth; the other, from the earth upward. In fulfillment of the first, man draws holiness from the Divinely-given Torah and commandments, to permeate therewith every phase of his daily life and his environment—his "share" in this world;[3] in fulfillment of the second, man draws upon all the resources at his disposal, both created and man-made, as vehicles for his personal ascendancy and, with him, that of the surrounding world. One of these basic resources is the vehicle of human language and communication.

As the Alter Rebbe, author of the *Tanya*, pointed out in one of his other works,[4] any of the "seventy tongues" when used as an instrument to disseminate the Torah and Mitzvoth, is itself "elevated" thereby from its earthly domain into the sphere of holiness, while at the same time serving as a vehicle to draw the Torah and Mitzvoth, from above downward, to those who read and understand this language.

* * *

In the spirit of the above-mentioned remarks, the volume presented here—the first English translation of the *Tanya* (Part I) since its first appearance 165 years ago—is an event of considerable importance. It brings this basic work of Chabad philosophy and way of life to a wider range of Jews, to whom the original work presents a language problem or even a barrier. It is thus a further contribution to the "dissemination of the fountains" of Chassidus which were unlocked by Rabbi Israel Ba'al Shem Tov, who envisaged Chassidus as a stream

Notes will be found at the end of the Preface

of "living waters," growing deeper and wider, until it should reach every segment of the Jewish people and bring new inspiration and vitality into their daily lives.

The translation of such a work as the *Tanya* presents a formidable task. As a matter of fact, several unsuccessful attempts had been made at various times in the past to translate the *Tanya* into one or another of the European languages.[5] It is therefore to the lasting credit of Dr. Nissan Mindel that this task has been accomplished.

Needless to say, translations are, at best, inadequate substitutes for the original. It is confidently hoped, however, that the present translation, provided as it is with an Introduction, Glossary, Notes and Indexes, will prove a very valuable aid to students of Chassidus in general, and of Chabad in particular.

MENACHEM SCHNEERSON

Lag B'Omer, 5722

Notes to Preface

[1] *See also* Tanya, *chaps. 36–37.*
[2] Ibid., *beg. chap. 2.*
[3] Ibid., *chap. 37.*
[4] Torah Or, *Mishpatim, beg.* "Vayyiru . . . k'ma'asei livnas hasapir."
[5] A translation of all the parts of the *Tanya* into Yiddish, by the late Rabbi Uriel Zimmer ע"ה was published by Otzar Hachassidim Lubavitch and Kehot Publication Society in 1958. An English translation of the second part of the *Tanya* appears in *The Way of the Faithful,* by Raphael Ben Zion (Los Angeles, 1945), which leaves much to be desired. A new and revised English translation of it, together with the other parts of the *Tanya* is in preparation by the Kehot Publication Society.*

* Subsequently, the English translations of all five parts of *Tanya* have already been published by the Kehot Publication Society.

ב"ה.

פתח דבר

(מכ"ק אדמו"ר זי"ע להוצאה דשנת ה'תשי"ד)**

בזה הננו מו"ל את הספר **לקוטי אמרים — תניא** אשר לרבנו הזקן, בפוטוגרפיא מהתניא דפוס ווילנא שנת תרצ"ז.

על פי בקשת רבים, הדפסנו בהוצאה זו — בסוף הספר — את ה„מורה שיעור" — שיעורי לימוד התניא כפי שנחלק, על ידי כ"ק מו"ח אדמו"ר זצוקללה"ה נבג"מ זי"ע, „לימי השנה, מראש השנה לחסידות י"ט כסלו עד י"ט כסלו הבא עלינו ועל כל ישראל אחינו לטובה ולברכה בגשמיות וברוחניות".

כן באו בהוספה לבסוף: א) מפתח ענינים. ב) מפתח שמות ספרים ואנשים. ג) לוח התיקון. ד) הערות ותיקונים. ה) כתבי יד ודפוסי התניא (רשימה קצרה — ערוכים על ידי הח"מ. ו) פאקסימיליא של: 1) השער דהוצאה הראשונה של התניא. 2) עמוד מכתב יד התניא מהדורא קמא אשר קרוב לודאי שזהו גוף כתי"ק רבנו הזקן*.

מנחם מענדל בן חנה שניאורסאהן

ערב שבת קדש עשרים במנחם אב ה'תשי"ג
ברוקלין, נ.י.

---

*) ראה מכתב כ"ק מו"ח אדמו"ר אודות זה — בספר קיצורים והערות לספר לקוטי אמרים. בספר זה באו ג"כ: א) קיצורים לתניא חלק ראשון, הגהות על התניא, המאמר „להבין הקושיא הנזכרת בתחלת ספר התניא", רשימות הערות וביאורים בפרקים א־כג של התניא, הידועים בשם „ומשביעין אותו". „ונפש השנית" — כל הנ"ל לכ"ק אדמו"ר הצמח צדק נ"ע. ב) הערות מכ"ק אדמו"ר מהורש"ב נ"ע על התניא. ג) מכתב אודות התניא ורשימה ע"ד העתקת התניא מכ"ק מו"ח אדמו"ר. ד) פאקסימיליא מכתב יד התניא וביאור אודותו מכ"ק מו"ח אדמו"ר. ה) פאקסימיליא משער התניא דפוס ראשון.

**) בהוצאה זו נתקנו כמה מטעיות הדפוס שבהוצאות הקודמות, בחלקם נכנסו בפנים ובחלקם — בלוח התיקון ובהערות ותיקונים. כן נדפסו, בפאקסימיליא, כל ארבעת העמודים של הכת"י תניא מהדורא קמא וביאור כ"ק מו"ח אדמו"ר ע"ד כת"י תניא הנ"ל.

●▲ SEFER

LIKUTEI AMARIM

PART ONE

ENTITLED

SEFER SHEL BENONIM

Compiled from (sacred) books and from sages, exalted saints, whose souls are in Eden; based on the verse "For it is exceedingly near to you, in your mouth and in your heart, to do;"[1] to explain clearly how it is exceedingly near, in a lengthy and short way, with the aid of the Holy One, may He be blessed.

---

[1] Deut. *30:14*.

● 19 Kislev ▲ *19 Kislev*

קובץ
שלשלת האור

היכל שלישי — שער ראשון

ספר

לקוטי אמרים

חלק ראשון

הנקרא בשם

ספר של בינונים

מלוקט מפי ספרים ומפי סופרים קדושי עליון נ״ע מיוסד על פסוק כי קרוב אליך הדבר מאוד בפיך ובלבבך לעשותו · לבאר היטב איך הוא קרוב מאוד בדרך ארוכה וקצרה בעזה״י.

ונתוסף בו **אגרת התשובה** מאדמו״ר נ״ע בדרך ארוכה וקצרה כולל כל ענייני התשובה גם **אגרת הקודש** אשר כתב בכתב ידו הקדושה ולשונו הטהור.

כל אלה חוברו יחדיו תמים מלמעלה עיר וקדיש משמיא נחית

הוא ניהו כ״ק אדמו״ר הגדול הגאון האלקי אור עולם
מופת הדור נזר ישראל ותפארתו קדוש ה׳ מכובד

מרנא ורבנא **שניאור זלמן** נבג״מ.

ועתה הוגה היטב **התוצאה החדשה והמתקנת** בעיון נמרץ כמבואר מעל״ד.

יוצא לאור על ידי מערכת

„אוצר החסידים״

770 איסטערן פּאַרקוויי — ברוקלין, נ.י.

שנת בקדוש ישראל יגילו לפ״ק

מודעה רבה

על אודות התוצאה החדשה והמתוקנת שנעשתה בידיעת והסכמת הרבנים שליט"א נכדי אדמו"ר בעל הצ"צ נ"ע זי"ע.

בגון דא צריך לאודועי ברבים. אשר עלינו להודות לה' כי גבר עלינו חסדו עד כה שזכינו בעזר השי"ת להגיה את האגה"ת והאגה"ק על צד היותר נעלה עד מקום שידו של אדם מגעת בעיון נמרץ ע"י השתדלות עצומה וזריזות יתירה בחיפוש אחר חיפוש בכת"י ישנים הנמצאים אצל הרבנים הקדושים שליט"א נכדי אדמו"ר בעל הצ"צ ז"ל נ"ע שיש לסמוך עליהם. ונוסף ע"ז שגם אח"כ ביגיעה עצומה ומתינות גדולה הונף והוברר רבות פעמים לברר וללבן כל דבר עד שבאנו לעומק השוה והמישור לעמוד על דעת חכמים. ובאיזה מקומן זכינו לגוף כתי"ק הנמצאים ת"י הרבנים הנ"ל ואור ה' האיר עינינו להגיה מתוכם גם מעט מן המעט מן השגיאות הנמצאים בהלק"א ושער היחוד והאמונה שבדפוס סלאוויטא נתקנו כעת בעזה"י מלבד אשר בשער היחוד והאמונה הוספנו את ההשלמה מפרק ז'. ועל הטוב זו תורה יזכר לטוב החסיד המפורסם מו"ה משה ווייל"ער ז"ל מקריסלאווא אשר יגע וטרח ומצא הרבה להגיה את האגה"ק וקיבץ על יד על יד רבות ההשמטות מהאגה"ק. וכ"ז היה לנו לעינים למלאכת ההג"ה אשר ממנו לקחנו הרבה. וזכות גדול לו בזה. ואנחנו תפלה אשר פועל ידינו ירצה ה' לשמחת לבב כל הצמאים והתאבים לדבר ה' המה דברי כ"ק אדמו"ר זצוקללה"ה נ"ע זי"ע. ויספו ענוים בה' שמחה ואביוני אדם בקדוש ישראל יגילו אכי"ר.

והחובה עלי להודיע כי זכות ההדפסה של זה הספר התניא **תוצאה חדשה ומתוקנת** עם כל התיקונים וההוספות שבו, מסרתי להמדפיסים האלמנה והאחים ראם לקנין עולם. זמבלעדם וזולתם אסור לשום אדם להדפיס את הספר התניא הזה שעם התיקונים וההוספות הנ"ל הן בתבנית זה והן בתבנית אחר. וע"ז באתי עה"ח יום א' דחנוכה תר"ס לפ"ק, פה ווילנא.

נאם **אשר ב"ר מאיר ז"ל שו"ב מניקאלאייעב.**

מודעה רבה ב

אנחנו הח"מ המדפיסים האלמנה והאחים ראם מכרנו את זכות הדפסת ספר התניא תוצאה חדשה ומתוקנת דשנת חמשת אלפים ושש מאות וששים לברה"ע הלקוחה בידנו מאת ר' אשר ב"ר מאיר גראצמאן שו"ב מניקאלאייעב הבא בכח הרבנים הקדושים שליט"א נכדי אדמו"ר בעל הצ"צ זצ"ל נבג"מ זי"ע, את הזכות הזאת מכרנו עתה לכ"ק אדמו"ר הר"ר שלום דובער שליט"א מליובאוויטש ע"י בא כחו ר' אנשיל אראנאוויטש שי' מפה ווילנא לטובת המוסד תומכי-תמימים, ומעתה אין אנו רשאים להדפיס את ספר התניא, לא אנחנו ולא באי כחנו, או גם מגירא דילן עד סוף העולם, ונוסף להזכות מכרנו לכ"ק אדמו"ר שליט"א מליובאוויטש הנ"ל ע"י בא כחו הנ"ל את המאטריצין והפלאטין השיכים להדפסת התניא הנ"ל (שמעתה הוא נחשב להונו ורכושו של המוסד הנ"ל) והחובה עלינו לתת מקום לכל הנ"ל בבית דפוסנו כל אימת שירצה ר' אנשיל הנ"ל הבא בכח אדמו"ר שליט"א, וכ"ז נעשה בקנא"ס ובכל תוקף דין תורה ודינא דמלכותא וע"ז באנו עה"ח יום ד' כ"ה לחדש תמוז תרס"ט פה ווילנא:

נאום האלמנה והאחים ראם.

Approbation[1]

by the famous rabbi and chasid, G-dly man, of saintly renown, our teacher Rabbi *Meshulam Zusil* of Anipoli:[2]

I have seen the writings of this rabbi and gaon, G-dly man, saintly and pure, lucid speculum; and well he did; G-d in His wonderful kindness having put into his pure heart to accomplish all this in order to show the G-dly people His holy ways.

It was [the author's] intention not to publish these writings in print, since it is not his custom. However, because these *kuntresim*[3] have spread in the midst of all Israel in numerous copies by sundry copyists, and, as a result of the many transcriptions, the copyists' errors have multiplied exceedingly, he was impelled to bring these *kuntresim* to the printing press.

And G-d has aroused the spirit of the [two] partners, the outstanding and distinguished scholar R. Sholom Shachne,[4] the son of R. Noah, and the outstanding and distinguished scholar R. Mordechai, the son of R. Shmuel haLevi, to bring these *kuntresim* to the printing house in Slavita. So I said of this good deed, More power to you. However, they were apprehensive of the growing number of printing establishments which are wont to cause damage and ruin to the accredited ones. In view of this, we have resolved to give this approbation so that no man should dare lift his hand and foot to cause any damage, Heaven forfend, to the said printers by encroaching upon their exclusive right in any manner. It is to restrain any person from reprinting this book without the knowledge of the said printers for a period of five full years from the date below. He who will heed these my words will be blessed with good. These are the words of one who demands this for the glory of the Torah, this day, the third, twice blessed with "it is good,"[5] of the weekly portion *Tavo*, in the year פדותינו (556).[6]

The insignificant MESHULAM ZUSIL of Anipoli

by the famous rabbi and chasid, G-dly man, of saintly renown, our teacher Rabbi *Yehuda Leib haCohen*:[7]

The wisdom of the man illumines the face of the earth[8]—on seeing the work of the saintly hands of the author, rabbi and gaon, G-dly man, saintly and pure, pious and humble, whose hidden [powers] had been revealed long ago, when he dwelt in the council of the wise with *our lord, master and teacher*, the *world gaon*,[9] and drew water from the *well of living waters*. Now, *Israel*[10] shall rejoice as his saintly words are revealed in this compiled work which is about to go to press, to teach the people of G-d the ways of holiness, as anyone can see in the inwardness of [the author's] words.

That which is common knowledge requires no proof. Only because of the apprehension of a wrong, lest a loss be caused to the printers, I come to confer sanction and prohibition, that no man lift up his hand or foot to reprint this work for a period of five years from below date. Whoever will heed these my words will be blessed with good.

These are the words of one who speaks for the glory of the Torah, this third day of the weekly portion *Tavo*, 556.[11]

YEHUDA LEIB HACOHEN

הסכמת

הרב החסיד המפורסם איש אלהי קדוש יאמר לו מוהר"ר משולם זוסיל מְאניפאלי:

הנה בראותי את הכתבים של הרב האי גאון איש אלקים קדוש וטהור ואספקלריא המאירה וטוב אשר עשה ואשר הפליא ה' חסדו ונתן בלבו הטהור לעשות את כל אלה להראות עם ה' דרכיו הק'. ורצונו היה שלא להעלות את הכתבים ההם לבית הדפוס מחמת שאין דרכו בכך. רק מחמת התפשטות הקונטריסים ההם בקרב כל ישראל בהעתקות רבות מידי סופרים משונים ומחמת ריבוי העתקות שונות רבו הט"ס במאד. והוכרח להביא הקונטרסים ההם לבית הדפוס. והעיר ה' את רוח השותפים ה"ה הרבני המופלג הותיק מוהר"ר שלום שכנא במוהר"ר נח וה"ה הרבני המופלג הותיק מוהר"ר מרדכי במוהר"ר שמואל הלוי להביא הקונטרסים ההם לבית הדפוס בסלאוויטא ולפעלא טבא אמרתי יישר חילא אך עלו בלבם מגור מסביב מן הדפוסים אשר רבו שדרכן להזיק ולקלקל המאושרים אי לזאת גמרנו בלבינו ליתן הסכמה לבל ירים איש את ידו ואת רגלו לגרום להמדפיסים הנ"ל שום היזק חס ושלום בהשגת גבול בשום אופן. ואסור לשום אדם לדפוס הספר הנ"ל בלתי ידיעת המדפיסים הנ"ל עד משך חמש שנים רצופים מיום דלמטה ושומע לדברי אלה יבא עליו ברכת טוב הכ"ד הדורש זאת לכבוד התורה היום יום ג' שנכפל בו כי טוב פ' תבא שנת פדותינו לפ"ק.

הקטן **משולם זוסיל מאניפאלי.**

הרב החסיד המפורסם איש אלהי קדוש יאמר לו מהור"ר יהודא ליב הכהן:

חכמת אדם תאיר פני הארץ בראותי ידי קדש המחבר הרב הגאון איש אלקים קדוש וטהור חסיד ועניו אשר מכבר נגלה מסתריו יושב בשבת תחכמוני אצל אדונינו מורינו ורבינו גאון עולם ודלה מים מבאר מים חיים וכעת ישמח ישראל בהגלות דברי קדשו המחובר להביא לבית הדפוס ללמד לעם ה' דרכי קדש כאשר כל אחד יחזה בפנימיות דבריו והמפורסם אין צריך ראיה רק מחשש קלקול הדבר שלא יגרום היזק למדפיסים באתי ליתן תוקף ואזהרה לבל ירים איש את ידו ורגלו לדפוס עד משך חמש שנים מיום דלמטה ושומע לדברי אלה יבוא עליו ברכת טוב הכ"ד המדבר זאת לכבוד התורה היום יום ג' פרשה תבא תקנ"ו לפ"ק.

יהודא ליב הכהן.

---

[1] *Note that the name of the author was withheld both from the front cover as well as from the Approbations in the first seven editions. Only beginning with the eighth edition (Shklov '574 [1814]), the author's name was included in the title cover posthumously, when also the Approbation by the author's sons first appeared.* [2] *The author's colleague and a disciple of Rabbi Dov Ber of Miezricz.* [3] *See* Tanya, *KPS ed. (Brooklyn, N.Y., 1958), p. 407.* [4] *The author's son-in-law and father of Rabbi Menachem Mendel of Lubavitch, third leader of Chabad.* [5] Gen. *1:10, 12.* [6] *I.e. 5556; it is customary to omit the millennial.* [7] *A disciple of Rabbi Dov Ber of Miezricz, and a colleague of the author.* [8] Eccl. *8:1.* [9] *The reference is to Rabbi Dov Ber of Miezricz, hinted also by the word* "מבאר" in "מבאר מים חיים"—"*from the well of living waters.*" [10] *Alluding to Rabbi* Israel Ba'al Shem *Tov.* [11] *See n. 6, above.*

▲*Approbation*[1]

by the rabbis (long may they live), the sons of the gaon the author (of blessed memory, whose soul is in Eden).

Whereas it has been agreed by us to give authorisation and prerogative to bring to the printing press, for a remembrance unto the children of Israel, the written words of uprightness and truth, the words of the Living G–d, authored by our lord father, teacher and master, of blessed memory, recorded personally in his saintly expression, whose words are all burning coals to set the hearts aflame to bring them closer to their Father in heaven; they are entitled *Igeret hakodesh* ("Holy Epistle"), being mostly epistles sent by his holy eminence, to teach the people of G–d the way by which to walk and the deed which they should do;

And inasmuch as he has made references, in many places, to the *Sefer Likutei Amarim*, since the words of the Torah are scanty in one place and ample in another,[2] especially also as he introduced new material in the *Kuntres Acharon* on certain chapters which he wrote when he composed the *Sefer Likutei Amarim*, profound discussions on passages in the *Zohar*, *Etz Chayim* and *Peri Etz Chayim*, which [passages] appear contradictory to one another, but he, with his inspired perception, has reconciled them, each statement in its own manner, as he has written in the *Likutei Amarim*, we have seen fit and proper to join them with the *Sefer Likutei Amarim* and *Igeret hateshuvah*[3] of his saintly eminence, our lord father, teacher and master, of blessed memory;

[Therefore], we come to place a great fence and the rabbinic injunction of נח"ש[4] (excommunication) for which there is no remedy, that no man lift his hand to reprint them in their present form, or in part, for a period of five years from the date below.[5]

However, this should be made known: To our misfortune the manuscripts written by his personal saintly hand which were composed with great punctiliousness, without a superfluous or deficient letter, have become extinct; only this little has remained from the abundance, and it has been carefully collected one by one from the *copies* spread among the disciples. Should, therefore, an error be discovered (who can understand [and prevent] errors?)[6] the evident error will be identified as a scribe's error, but the meaning will be clear.

Declared by DOV BER, the son of my lord father, teacher and master, gaon and chasid, saint of Israel, our teacher and master SCHNEUR ZALMAN, of blessed memory, נבג"מ.[7]

Also declared by CHAYIM ABRAHAM, the son of my lord father, teacher and master, gaon and chasid our teacher and master SCHNEUR ZALMAN, the memory of the tzaddik be blessed, נבג"מ.[7]

Also declared by MOSHE, the son of my lord father, teacher and master, gaon and chasid, SCHNEUR ZALMAN, of blessed memory, נבג"מ.[7]

הסכמת

הרבנים שי׳ בני הגאון המחבר ז״ל נ״ע.

היות שהוסכם אצלינו ליתן רשות והרמנא להעלות על מכבש הדפוס לזכרון לבנ״י כתוב דברי יושר ואמת דברי אלקים חיים של א״א מו״ר ז״ל כתובים בכתב ידו הקדושה בעצמו ולשונו הקדוש שכל דבריו כגחלי אש בוערות ילהיבו הלבבות לקרבן לאביהן שבשמים. ובשם אגרת הקדש נקראו שרובם היו אגרת שלוח מאת כ״ק להורות לעם ה׳ הדרך ילכו בה והמעשה אשר יעשון ומחמת שבכמה מקומות הציב לו ציונים בס׳ לקוטי אמרים שלו וד״ת עניים במקום אחד ועשירים בם״א ומה גם בשביל דבר שנתחדש בו קונטרס אחרון על איזה פרקים אשר כתב בעת חיברו הס׳ לק״א פלפול ועיון עמוק על מאמרי זהר וע״ח ופע״ח שנראים כסותרים זא״ז וברוח מבינתו מישבם כל דיבור על אופניו שכתב בלק״א ראו ראינו שראוי ונכון לחברם עם ספר לקוטי אמרים ואגה״ת של כ״ק א״א מו״ר ז״ל. אי לזאת באנו להטיל גודא רבה וגזרת נח״ש דרבנן דלית לה אסוותא שלא ירים איש את ידו להדפים כתבניתם או זה בלא זה משך חמשה שנים מיום דלמטה ברם כגון דא צריך לאודועי שבעו״ה ספו תמו כתבי ידו הקדושה בעצמו אשר היו בדקדוק גדול לא חסר ולא יתר אות א׳ ולא נשאר כ״א זה המעט מהרבה אשר נלקטו אחד לאחד מהעתקות המפוזרים אצל התלמידים ואם המצא תמצא איזה טעות שגיאות מי יבין ימצא הטעות דמוכח מטעות סופר והכונה תהיה ברורה:

נאום **דוב בער** בא״א מו״ר הגאון החסיד קדוש ישראל מרנא ורבנא **שניאור זלמן** ז״ל נבג״מ.

ונאום **חיים אברהם** בא״א מו״ר הגאון החסיד מרנא ורבנא **שניאור זלמן** זצ״ל נבג״מ.

ונאום **משה** בא״א מו״ר הגאון החסיד **שניאור זלמן** ז״ל נבג״מ.

---

[1] *First published in the Shklov, '574 (1814) ed. See n.1., p. viii, above.* [2] Talmud Yerushalmi, Rosh Hashanah, *ch.* 3, hal. 5. [3] *Note that* Sha'ar ha-Yichud veha-Emunah *(part II of the* Tanya) *is not mentioned here; neither is it mentioned in the title cover.* [4] נדוי, חרם, שמתא *three forms of excommunication.* [5] *In the Shklov, '574 ed. appears the date "5[th day (Thu.)] 22nd of Iyar, '574," subsequently omitted.* [6] Ps. *19:13.* [7] נשמתו בגנזי מרומים—*"his soul rests in the hidden treasures of heaven."*

●▲*Compiler's Foreword*[1]

Being an Epistle sent to the Communities of our Faithful. May the Almighty guard them.

To you, O men, do I call. Listen to me, you who pursue righteousness, who seek the Lord; and may G-d hearken to you, both great and small, all the faithful in our land and those adjacent to it. May each in his place achieve peace and eternal life, for ever and ever. Amen. May this be His will.

Behold, it is known as a saying current among people—all our faithful—that listening to words of moral advice is not the same as seeing and reading them in books. For the reader reads after his own manner and mind, and according to his mental grasp and comprehension at that particular time. Hence, if his intelligence and mind are confused and wander about in darkness in G-d's service, he finds difficulty in seeing the beneficial light that is concealed in books, even though the light is pleasant to the eyes and [brings] a healing to the soul.

Apart from this, the books on piety which stem from human intelligence,[2] certainly have not the same appeal for all people, for not all intellects and minds are alike, and the intellect of one man is not affected and excited by what affects [and excites][3] the intellect of another. Compare with what our Rabbis, of blessed memory, have said[4] with reference to the blessing of the "Wise One in Secrets" (חכם הרזים) upon beholding 600,000 Jews,[5] because their minds are dissimilar from one another, and so on.[6] As also Rabbi Moses ben Nachman, of blessed memory, [explains the reason for this blessing] in *Milchamot*, elaborating on the commentary of the *Sifre* concerning Joshua who is described as "a man in whom there is spirit,"[7] "who can meet the spirit of each and every one,"[8] and so on.

But even the books on piety, whose basis is in the peaks of holiness, the Midrashim of our Sages, of blessed memory, through whom the spirit of G-d speaks and His word is on their tongue; and [although] the Torah and the Holy One, blessed be He, are one and the same, and all the 600,000 general [souls][9] of Israel with their individual [offshoots] down to the "spark" in the most worthless and least estimable members of our people, the children of Israel, are thus bound up with the Torah, and the Torah binds them to the Holy One, blessed be He, as is known from the holy *Zohar*[10]—this [bond] pertains [only] in a general way to the community of Israel as a whole. [As for the individual] although the Torah was given to be interpreted, in general and in particular down to the minutest detail, to [apply to] each individual soul of Israel, which is rooted in it [so that these books pertain to every person], nevertheless not every person is privileged to recognise his individual place in the Torah.

[A further difficulty is the complexity of Torah interpretation.] Even in the case of the laws governing things prohibited and permitted, which have been revealed to us and to our children,[11] we find and witness differences of opinion among Tana'im and Amora'im from one extreme to the other. Yet "these as well as these are the words of the living G-d."[12] The plural[13] is used as a reference to the source of life for the souls of Israel, which are generally divided into three categories —right, left,

הקדמת המלקט

והיא אגרת השלוחה לכללות אנשי שלומינו יצ"ו :

אליכם אישים אקרא שמעו אלי רודפי צדק מבקשי ה' וישמע אליכם אלקים למגדול ועד קטן כל אנ"ש דמדינתינו וסמוכות שלה איש על מקומו יבוא לשלום וחיים עד העולם נס"ו אכי"ר :

הנה מודעת זאת כי מרגלא בפומי דאינשי בכל אנ"ש לאמר כי אינה דומה שמיעת דברי מוסר לראייה וקריאה בספרים שהקורא קורא לפי דרכו ודעתו ולפי השגת ותפיסת שכלו באשר הוא שם ואם שכלו ודעתו מבולבלים ובחשיכה יתהלכו בעבודת ה' בקושי יכול לראות את האור כי טוב הגנוז בספרים אף כי מתוק האור לעינים ומרפא לנפש ובר מן דין הנה ספרי היראה הבנויים ע"פ שכל אנושי בוודאי אינן שוין לכל נפש כי אין כל השכלים והדעות שוות ואין שכל אדם זה מתפעל ומתעורר ממה שמתפעל שכל חבירו וכמו שארז"ל גבי ברכת חכם הרזים על ששים ריבוא מישראל שאין דעותיהם דומות זו לזו וכו' וכמ"ש הרמב"ן ז"ל במלחמות שם בפירוש הספרי גבי יהושע שנאמר בו איש אשר רוח בו שיכול להלוך נגד רוחו של כל אחד ואחד וכו'. אלא אפילו בספרי היראה אשר יסודותם בהררי קודש מדרשי חז"ל אשר רוח ה' דבר בם ומלתו על לשונם ואורייתא וקב"ה כולא חד וכל ששים רבוא כללות ישראל ופרטיהם עד ניצוץ קל שבקלים ופחותי הערך שבעמינו ב"י כולהו מתקשראן באורייתא ואורייתא היא המקשרת אותן להקב"ה כנודע בזה"ק הרי זה דרך כללות לכללות ישראל ואף שניתנה התורה לידרש בכלל ופרט ופרטי פרטות לכל נפש פרטית מישראל המושרשת בה הרי אין כל אדם זוכה להיות מכיר מקומו הפרטי שבתורה : והנה אף בהלכות איסור והיתר הנגלות לנו ולבנינו מצאנו ראינו מחלוקת תנאים ואמוראים מן הקצה אל הקצה ממש ואלו ואלו דברי אלהים חיים לשון רבים על שם מקור החיים לנשמות ישראל הנחלקות דרך כלל לשלשה קוין ימין ושמאל ואמצע

---

[1] Hakdamat ha-melaket—*for the author considers himself merely a "compiler."* [2] *As contrasted with books which the author considers divinely inspired, of which he speaks in the following part.* [3] *In the text the word* ומתעורר *is missing. See list of text emendations in the* Tanya, *KPS (Brooklyn, N.Y., 1958), ed. R. Menachem M. Schneerson, pp. 403 ff.* [4] Berachot *58a.* [5] *The reading in the text is* ששים ריבוא *("sixty ten-thousands"), corresponding to the number of adult male Israelites in the Exodus from Egypt.* (Ex. *12:37;* Num. *11:21, etc.*). [6] *The blessing praises G-d Who knows the secrets in the hearts of all men.* [7] Num. *27:18.* [8] *Cf. Rashi's commentary on said verse.* [9] *In the text the word* נשמות *is missing.* [10] *III, 73a, Cf. Rabbi Joseph I. Schneersohn,* Some Aspects of Chabad Chassidism *tr. N. Mindel pub. Machne Israel (Brooklyn, N.Y., 1944), pp. 18 ff.* [11] *The expression "revealed to us and to our children" is taken from* Deut. *29:28. The first part of this verse is quoted by the author later. Cf. also beg. ch. 44,* infra. [12] Eruvin *13b.* [13] Elokim chayim, *rather than* eloka chay.

and centre, namely, kindness (*chesed*), might (*gevurah*), and so on,[14] so that the souls, whose root originates in the category of kindness, are likewise inclined towards kindness in the leniency of their decisions, and so forth,[15] as is known. All the more, *a minori ad majus*, in the case of those things which are hidden [yet revealed only] to the Lord our G-d,[16] these being the awe and love that are in the mind and heart of each and every one according to his capacity, i.e. according to his heart's estimation,[17] as explained in the holy *Zohar*[18] on the verse, "Her husband is known in the gates (*she'arim*), . . ."[19]

●▲ I speak, however, of those who know me well, each and every one of our faithful who lives in our country and in lands adjacent to it, with whom words of affection have been frequently exchanged, and who have revealed to me all the secrets of their heart and mind in the service of G-d which is dependent on the heart.[20] May my word percolate to them, and my tongue be as the pen of the scribe in these *kuntresim* that are entitled *Likutei Amarim* ("Selected Discourses"), which have been selected from books and teachers,[21] heavenly saints, whose souls are in Eden, and who are renowned among us. [The subjects of] some of [these discourses] are hinted to the wise, in the sacred epistles of our teachers[22] in the Holy Land, may it be built and established speedily in our days, Amen; some of them I have heard from their saintly mouth when they were here with us; and all of them are responsa to many questions which all our faithful in our country have constantly asked, seeking advice, each according to his station, so as to receive moral guidance in the service of G-d, since time no longer permits of replying to everyone individually and in detail on his particular problem. Furthermore, forgetfulness is common.

I have, therefore, recorded all the replies to all the questions, to be preserved as a sign-post and to serve as a visual reminder for each and every person, so that he will no longer press for admission to private conference with me. For in these [responsa] he will find peace for his soul, and true counsel on every matter that he finds difficult in the service of G-d. His heart will thus be firmly secured in the Lord Who completes everything for us.

As for him whose mind falls short in the understanding of the counsel given in these *kuntresim*, let him discuss his problem with the foremost scholars of his town, and they will elucidate it for him. And I beg of them not to lay their hand on their mouth, to conduct themselves with false meekness and humility, G-d forbid. It is known what bitter punishment is his who withholds food [i.e. knowledge], and the greatness of the reward [in the opposite case], from the Rabbinic teaching[23] relating to the Scriptural text, "The Lord lighteneth the eyes of them both,"[24] for G-d will cause His face to shine upon them, with the light of the countenance of the King [the Source of] life. May the Giver of life to the living make us worthy to live to see the days when "no longer shall one man instruct the other . . . for all shall know Me, . . ."[25] "for the world shall be full of the knowledge of G-d, . . ."[26] Amen. May this be His will.

---

[14] *The third category is* tiferet ("*beauty*"). *See* Igeret hakodesh, *ch. 15.* [15] *See* ibid., *ch. 13 for more light on the subject.* [16] *See n. 11 above.* [17] *A reinterpretation of the word* shi'ur ("*an estimated measure*")

ואמצע שהם חסד וגבורה וכו׳ ונשמות ששרשן ממדת חסד הנהגתן גם כן להטות כלפי חסד להקל כו׳ כנודע וכ״ש וק״ו בהנסתרות לה׳ אלהינו דאינון דחילו ורחימו דבמוחא ולבא דכל חד וחד לפום שיעורא דיליה לפום מה דמשער בליביה כמ״ש בזה״ק על פסוק נודע בשערים בעלה וגו׳ :

אך ביודעיי ומכיריי קאמינא הם כל אחד ואחד מאנ״ש שבמדינותינו וסמוכות שלה אשר היה הדבור של חיבה מצוי בינינו וגילו לפני כל תעלומות לבם ומוחם בעבודת ה׳ התלויה בלב אליהם תטוף מלתי ולשוני עט סופר בקונטריסים אלו הנקראים בשם לקוטי אמרים מלוקטים מפי ספרים ומפי סופרים קדושי עליון נשמתם עדן המפורסמים אצלינו וקצת מהם נרמזין לחכימין באגרות הקדש מרבותינו שבאה״ק תובב״א . וקצתם שמעתי מפיהם הקדוש בהיותם פה עמנו וכולם הן תשובות על שאלות רבות אשר שואלין בעצה כל אנ״ש דמדינתינו תמיד כל אחד לפי ערכו לשית עצות בנפשם בעבודת ה׳ להיות כי אין הזמן גרמא עוד להשיב לכל אחד ואחד על שאלתו בפרטות וגם השכחה מצויה על כן רשמתי כל התשובות על כל השאלות למשמרת לאות להיות לכל אחד וא׳ לזכרון בין עיניו ולא ידחוק עוד ליכנס לדבר עמי ביחידות כי בהן ימצא מרגוע לנפשו ועצה נכונה לכל דבר הקשה עליו בעבודת ה׳ ונכון יהיה לבו בטוח בה׳ גומר בעדינו : ומי שדעתו קצרה להבין דבר עצה מתוך קונטריסים אלו יפרש שיחתו לפני הגדולים שבעירו והם יבוננוהו ואליהם בקשתי שלא לשום יד לפה להתנהג בענוה ושפלות של שקר ח״ו וכנודע עונש המר על מונע בר וגודל השכר ממאמר רז״ל ע״פ מאיר עיני שניהם ה׳ כי יאיר ה׳ פניו אליהם אור פני מלך חיים. ומחיה חיים יזכנו ויחיינו לימים אשר לא ילמדו עוד איש את רעהו וגו׳ כי כולם ידעו אותי וגו׳ כי מלאה הארץ דעה את ה׳ וגו׳ אכי״ר:

והנה אחר שנתפשטו הקונטריסים הנ״ל בקרב כל אנ״ש הנ״ל בהעתקות רבות מידי סופרים שונים ומשונים הנה ע״י

ריבוי

---

and sha'ar ("*gate*") *in the Biblical quotation following.* [18] *I, pp. 103a-b.* [19] Prov. *31:23.* [20] Ta'anit *2a. Cf. Bachya's Introduction to his* Duties of the Heart. [21] *On the sources of the* Tanya *see* Introduction, infra. [22] *RSZ regarded some of his senior colleagues, the disciples of R. Dov Ber of Miezricz (among whom he himself was the youngest) as his "teachers," esp. R. Mendel Horodoker.* [23] Temurah *16a.* [24] Prov. *29:13.* [25] Jer. *31:33.* [26] Isa. *11:9.*

▲ Since the said *kuntresim* have been disseminated among all our faithful, as mentioned above, by means of numerous transcriptions by the hands of various and sundry scribes, the multitude of transcriptions brought about an exceedingly great number of copyists' errors. Therefore the spirit of the noble men, named on another page, has generously moved them to a personal and financial effort to have the said *kuntresim* published, cleared of chaff and errors, and thoroughly checked. I congratulate them on this worthy deed.

And inasmuch as there is an explicit verse, "Cursed be he that removeth his neighbour's landmark"[27]—and "cursed" includes both damnation and shunning,[28] G-d forbid—therefore, "like Judah and scripture in addition"[29] I come to invoke a strict prohibition on all publishers against printing the said *kuntresim*, either themselves or through their agency without the authority of the above-named, for a period of five years from the day that this printing is completed. And it will be well with those who conform, and they will be blessed with good.

These are the words of the compiler of the said *Likutei Amarim*.

---

[27] Deut. *27:17*. [28] Shevu'ot *36a*. [29] Kiddushin *6a*.

ריבוי ההעתקות שונות רבו כמו רבו הט"ס במאוד מאוד ולזאת נדבה רוחם של אנשים אפרתים הנקובים הנ"ל מע"ל לטרוח בגופם ומאודם להביא את קונטריסים הנ"ל לבית הדפוס מנוקים מכל סיג וט"ס ומוגהים היטב ואמינא לפעלא טבא יישר חילא ולהיות כי מקרא מלא דבר הכתוב ארור מסיג גבול רעהו וארור בו קללה בו נידוי ח"ו וכו' ע"כ כיהודה ועוד לקרא קאתינא למשדי גודא רבא על כל המדפיסים שלא להדפיס קונטריסים הנ"ל לא על ידי עצמן ולא על ידי גירא דילהון בלתי רשות הנקובים הנ"ל משך חמש שנים מיום כלות הדפוס ולשומעים יונעם ותבא ברכת טוב כה דברי המלקט ליקוטי אמרים הנ"ל:

•▲*Chapter 1*

It has been taught (*Niddah*, end ch. 3): An oath is administered to him [before birth, warning him]: "Be righteous and be not wicked; and even if the whole world tells you that you are righteous, regard yourself as if you were wicked."[1]

This requires to be understood, for it contradicts the Mishnaic dictum (*Avot*, ch. 2), "And be not wicked in your own estimation."[2] Furthermore, if a man considers himself to be wicked he will be grieved at heart and depressed, and will not be able to serve G–d joyfully and with a contented heart; while if he is not perturbed by this [self-appraisal], it may lead him to irreverence, G–d forbid.[3]

However, the matter [will be understood after a preliminary discussion].

We find in the *Gemara*[4] five distinct types—a righteous man who prospers, a righteous man who suffers, a wicked man who prospers, a wicked man who suffers, and an intermediate one (*Benoni*).[5] It is there explained that the "righteous man who prospers" is the perfect *tzaddik*; the "righteous man who suffers" is the imperfect *tzaddik*. In *Ra'aya Mehemna* (*Parshat Mishpatim*)[6] it is explained that the "righteous man who suffers" is one whose evil nature is subservient to his good nature,[7] and so on. In the *Gemara* (end ch. 9, *Berachot*)[8] it is stated that the righteous are motivated by their good nature, . . . and the wicked by their evil nature, while the intermediate men are motivated by both, and so on.[9] Rabbah declared, "I, for example, am a *Benoni*." Said Abbaye to him, "Master, you do not make it possible for anyone to live," and so on.[10]

To understand all the aforesaid clearly an explanation is needed, as also to understand what Job said [*Bava Batra*, ch. 1], "Lord of the universe, Thou hast created righteous men and Thou hast created wicked men, . . ."[11] for it is not preordained whether a man will be righteous or wicked.[12]

It is also necessary to understand the essential nature of the rank of the Intermediate. Surely that cannot mean one whose deeds are half virtuous and half sinful, for if this were so, how could Rabbah err in classifying himself as a *Benoni*? For it is known that he never ceased studying [the Torah], so much so that the Angel of Death could not overpower him;[13] how, then, could he err to have half of his deeds sinful, G–d forbid?

Furthermore, [at what stage can a person be considered a *Benoni* if] when a man commits sins he is deemed completely wicked (but when he repents afterward he is deemed completely righteous)? Even he who violates a minor prohibition of the Rabbis is called wicked, as it is stated in *Yevamot*, ch. 2, and in *Niddah*, ch. 1. Moreover, even he who has the opportunity to forewarn another against sinning and does not do so is called wicked (ch. 6, *Shevuot*).[14] All the more so he who neglects any positive law which he is able to fulfil, for instance, whoever is able to study Torah and does not,

---

[1] Niddah 30*b*. *The "oath" is also explained in terms of a delegation of power to the soul so that it be able to fulfil its destiny in life on earth. Cf.* Kitzurim VeHaorot LeTanya, *ed. Rabbi Menachem Mendel of Lubavitch, KPS (Brooklyn, N.Y., 1948), pp. 66f.* [2] Avot *II.13*. [3] *The apparent contradiction between the two*

ליקוטי ספר של בינונים אמרים ה

פרק א תניא [בספ"ג דנדה] משביעים אותו

תהי צדיק ואל תהי רשע ואפי' כל
העולם כולו אומרים לך צדיק אתה היה בעיניך כרשע
וצריך להבין דהא תנן [אבות פ"ב] ואל תהי רשע בפני
עצמך וגם אם יהיה בעיניו כרשע ירע לבבו ויהיה עצב
ולא יוכל לעבו' ה' בשמחה ובטוב לבב ואם לא ירע לבבו
כלל מזה יכול לבוא לידי קלות ח"ו. אך הענין כי הנה
מצינו בגמרא ה' חלוקות. צדיק וטוב לו צדיק ורע לו רשע
וטוב לו רשע ורע לו ובינוני. ופירשו בגמרא צדיק וטוב לו
צדיק גמור צדיק ורע לו צדיק שאינו גמור וברעיא
מהימנא פ' משפטים פי' צדיק ורע לו שהרע שבו כפוף
לטוב וכו' ובגמרא ספ"ט דברכות צדיקים יצ"ט שופטן כו'
רשעים יצה"ר שופטן בינונים זה וזה שופטן וכו' אמר רבה
כגון אנא בינוני א"ל אביי לא שביק מר חיי לכל בריה
וכו' ולהבין כל זה באר היטב וגם להבין מה שאמר איוב
[ב"ב פ"א] רבש"ע בראת צדיקי' בראת רשעי' כו' והא
צדיק ורשע לא קאמר. וגם להבין מהות מדרגת הבינוני
שבודאי אינו מחצה זכיות ומחצה עונות שא"כ איך טעה
רבה בעצמו לומר שהוא בינוני ונודע דלא פסיק פומיה
מגירסא עד שאפי' מלאך המות לא היה יכול לשלוט בו
ואיך היה יכול לטעות במחצה עונות ח"ו. ועוד שהרי
בשעה שעושה עונות נקרא רשע גמור [ואם אח"כ עשה
תשובה נקרא צדיק גמור] ואפילו העובר על איסור קל
של דברי סופרים מקרי רשע כדאיתא בפ"ב דיבמות
ובפ"ק דנדה ואפילו מי שיש בידו למחות ולא מיחה נק'
רשע [בפ"ו דשבועו'] וכ"ש וק"ו במבטל איזו מ"ע שאפש'
לו לקיימה כמו כל שאפשר לו לעסוק בתורה ואינו עוסק

שעליו

---

sources is explained in ch. 13. The meaning of both the Baraita *and* Mishnah *is expounded in chs. 13, 14, 29 and 34.* [4] Berachot *7a; cf.* Rosh Hashanah *16b.* [5] *The author borrows this term for the alternative name of his work,* Sefer shel Benonim, *but he uses the term in a different sense.* [6] Zohar *II, 117b.* [7] *This is a play on the words* ורע לו *rendered literally "the evil (belongs) to him," i.e. he is master of the evil nature in him.* [8] Berachot *61b.* [9] *Cf. beg. ch. 9.* [10] *Since there was none greater than Rabbah, it would mean that there was not even one tzaddik in the world, and all who are of lesser stature than Rabbah would be placed in the "Book of the Wicked" to be condemned to immediate death (*Rosh Hashanah *16b).* [11] Bava Batra *16a.* [12] Niddah *16b. The answer to this question will be found in ch. 14.* [13] *Cf.* Bava Metzia *86a.* [14] Shevuot *39b.*

regarding whom our Sages have quoted,[15] "Because he hath despised the word of the Lord ... [that soul] shall be utterly cut off. ..."[16] It is thus plain that such a person is called wicked, more than he who violates a prohibition of the Rabbis. If this is so, we must conclude that the Intermediate man (*Benoni*) is not guilty even of the sin of neglecting to study the Torah.[17] Hence Rabbah could have mistaken himself for a *Benoni.*

Note: As for what is written in the Zohar *III, p. 231: He whose sins are few is classed as a "righteous man who suffers,"*[18] *this is the query of Rav Hamnuna to Elijah. But according to Elijah's answer,* ibid., *the explanation of a "righteous man who suffers" is as stated in* Ra'aya Mehemna *on* Parshat Mishpatim, *which is given above. And the Torah has seventy facets [modes of interpretation].*[19]

●▲And as for the general saying[20] that one whose deeds and misdeeds are equally balanced is called *Benoni*, while he whose virtues outweigh his sins is called a *Tzaddik*, this is only the figurative use of the term in regard to reward and punishment, because he is judged according to the majority [of his acts] and he is deemed "righteous" in his verdict, since he is acquitted in law. But concerning the true definition and quality of the distinct levels and ranks, "Righteous" and "Intermediate" men, our Sages have remarked[21] that the Righteous are motivated [solely] by their good nature, as it is written, "And my heart is a void within me,"[22] that is, void of an evil nature, because he [David] had slain it through fasting.[23] But whoever has not attained this degree, even though his virtues exceed his sins, cannot at all be reckoned to have ascended to the rank of the Righteous (*tzaddik*). This is why our Sages have declared in the Midrash, "The Almighty saw that the righteous were few, so He planted them in every generation, ..."[24] [for,] as it is written, "The *tzaddik* is the foundation of the world."[25]

The explanation [of the questions raised above] is to be found in the light of what Rabbi Chayim Vital wrote in *Sha'ar ha-Kedushah* (and in *Etz Chayim*, Portal 50, ch. 2) that in every Jew, whether righteous or wicked, are two souls, as it is written,[26] "The *neshamot* (souls) which I have made,"[27] [alluding to] two souls. There is one soul which originates in the *kelipah* and *sitra achra*, and which is clothed in the blood of a human being, giving life to the body, as is written, "For the life of the flesh is in the blood."[28] From it stem all the evil characteristics deriving from the four evil elements which are contained in it. These are: anger and pride, which emanate from the element of Fire, the nature of which is to rise upwards; the appetite for pleasures—from the element of Water, for water makes to grow all kinds of enjoyment; frivolity and scoffing, boasting and idle talk

---

[15] Sanhedrin *99a.* [16] Num. *15:31.* [17] *The reiteration of the sin of neglect of Torah study is due to its prevalent nature and the difficulty of avoiding it completely (cf. end ch. 25). The author emphasising that the* benoni *is innocent even of this, and certainly of transgressions more easily avoidable.* [18] *The contradiction is in the implication that "few sins" are not inconsistent with the rank of* tzaddik. [19] *Hence the reason for Rav Hamnuna's query.* Otiot d'Rabbi Akiva: *comp.* Bamidbar Rabba, *ch. 14:12.* [20] *Cf. Maimonides, Code,* Hilchot Teshuva *3:1; Rashi,* Rosh Hashanah *16b.* [21] Berachot *61b.* [22] Ps. *109:22.* [23] *Cf. beg. ch. 9.* [24] *Cf.* Yoma *38b.* [25] Prov. *10:25.* [26] *The text should read* וכדכתיב *(not* דכתיב*) as amended*

שעליו דרשו רז"ל כי דבר ה' בזה וגו' הכרת תכרת וגו' ופשיטא דמקרי רשע טפי מעובר איסור דרבנן וא"כ ע"כ הבינוני אין בו אפי' עון ביטול תורה ומש"ה טעה רבה בעצמו לומר שהוא בינוני* והא דאמרי' בעלמא דמחצ' על מחצה מקרי בינוני ורוב זכיות מקרי צדיק הוא שם המושאל לענין שכר ועונש לפי שנדון אחר רובו ומקרי צדיק בדינו מאחר שזוכה בדין אבל לענין אמיתת שם התואר והמעלה של מעלת ומדרגות חלוקות צדיקים ובינונים ארז"ל צדיקים יצ"ט שופטן שנא' ולבי חלל בקרבי שאין לו יצה"ר כי הרגו בתענית אבל כל מי שלא הגיע למדרגה זו אף שזכיותיו מרובים על עונותיו אינו במעלת ומדרגת צדיק כלל ולכן ארז"ל במדרש ראה הקב"ה בצדיקים שהם מועטים עמד ושתלן בכל דור ודור וכו' וכמ"ש וצדיק יסוד עולם: אך ביאור הענין על פי מ"ש הרח"ו ז"ל בשער הקדושה [ובע"ח שער נ' פ"ב] דלכל איש ישראל אחד צדיק ואחד רשע יש שתי נשמות דכתיב ונשמות אני עשיתי שהן שתי נפשות נפש אחת מצד הקליפה וסטרא אחרא והיא המתלבשת בדם האדם להחיות הגוף וכדכתיב כי נפש הבשר בדם היא וממנה באות כל המדות רעות מארבע יסודות רעים שבה דהיינו כעס וגאוה מיסוד האש שנגבה למעלה. ותאות התענוגים מיסוד המים כי המים מצמיחים כל מיני תענוג. והוללות וליצנות והתפארות ודברים בטלים

מיסוד

הגהה

(ומ"ש בזוהר ח"ג ד' רל"א כל שממועטין עונותיו וכו' היא שאלת רב המנונא לאליהו אבל לפי תשובת אליהו שם הפי' צדיק ורע לו הוא כמ"ש בר"מ פרשה משפטים דלעיל ושבעים פנים לתורה):

(*Cf.* Tanya, op. cit., *p. 403), because the Biblical text is here only loosely interpreted, for the word "souls" refers to the collective noun, not to two souls.* [27] Isa. *57:16.* [28] Lev. *17:11.*

from the element of Air; and sloth and melancholy—from the element of Earth. From this soul stem also the good characteristics which are to be found in the innate nature of all Israel, such as mercy and benevolence. For in the case of Israel, this soul of the *kelipah* is derived from *kelipat nogah*, which also contains good, as it originates in the esoteric "Tree of Knowledge of Good and Evil."[29] The souls of the nations of the world, however, emanate from the other, unclean *kelipot* which contain no good whatever, as is written in *Etz Chayim*, Portal 49, ch. 3, that all the good that the nations do, is done from selfish motives. So the *Gemara*[30] comments on the verse, "The kindness of the nations is sin,"[31]—that all the charity and kindness done by the nations of the world is only for their own self-glorification, and so on.

●▲ *Chapter 2*

The second soul of a Jew is truly a part of G–d above,[1] as it is written, "And He breathed into his nostrils the breath of life,"[2] and "Thou didst breathe it [the soul] into me."[3] And it is written in the *Zohar*, "He who exhales, exhales from within him," that is to say, from his inwardness and his innermost, for it is something of his internal and innermost vitality that man emits through exhaling with force.

So, allegorically speaking, have the souls of Jews risen in the [Divine] thought,[4] as it is written, "My firstborn son is Israel,"[5] and "Ye are children unto the Lord your G–d".[6] That is to say, just as a child is derived from his father's brain, so—to use an anthropomorphism—the soul of each Israelite is derived from G–d's (blessed be He) thought and wisdom. For He is wise—but not through a knowable wisdom,[7] because He and His wisdom are one; and as Maimonides says

Note: And the Sages of the Kabbalah have agreed with him as is stated in Pardess[8] *of Rabbi Moshe Cordovero. Also according to the Kabbalah of the "Ari" (Rabbi Isaac Luria) this is substantiated in the mystic principle of the "Clothing of the Light" of the* En Sof,[9] *Blessed be He, through numerous contractions within the vessels ChaBaD*[10] *of [the world of]* Atzilut *(Emanation), but no higher than that.*[11] *For, as is explained elsewhere, the* En Sof, *blessed be He, is infinitely exalted over, and transcends, the essence and level of ChaBaD, which in relation to Him are regarded as a material action,*[12] *as is written, "Thou hast made them all with wisdom."*[13]

that "He is the Knowledge and Knower, . . . and this is not within the power of any man to comprehend clearly, . . ."[14] as it is written, "Canst thou by searching find G–d?"[15] And it is also written, "For My thoughts are not your thoughts. . . ."[16]

And though there are myriads of different gradations of souls (*neshamot*), rank upon rank, *ad infinitum*,

---

[29] *Cf.* Zohar *I, 12b.* [30] Bava Batra *10b.* [31] Prov. *14:34.*

Chapter 2
[1] Job *31:2; cf. also* Ps. *16:5; 73:26;* Jer. *10:16.* [2] Gen. *2:7; comp. Nachmanides'* Commentary, ad loc. [3] Liturgy, *Morning Prayer.* Berachot *60b.* [4] *Cf.* Genesis Rabbah *1:4.* [5] Ex. *4:22.* [6] Deut. *14:1.* [7] *Introduction to* Tikunei Zohar *12b.* [8] Shaar Mehut VeHanhagah, *ch. 13.* [9] En Sof—*The Endless, or Infinite—a term frequently used in the* Zohar *and later* Kabbalah *works to indicate the Unknowable G–d.* [10] ChaBaD *is an acrostic formed of the initial letters of the Hebrew words* chochmah *("wisdom"),* binah *("understanding") and* da'at *("knowledge"), the*

מיסוד הרוח. ועצלות ועצבות מיסוד העפר. וגם מדות טובות שבטבע כל ישראל בתולדותם כמו רחמנות וג"ח באות ממנה כי בישראל נפש זו דקליפה היא מקליפ' נוגה שיש בה ג"כ טוב והיא מסוד ע"ץ הדעת טוב ורע: משא"כ נפשות אומות עובדי גלולים הן משאר קליפות טמאות שאין בהן טוב כלל כמ"ש בע"ח שער מ"ט פ"ג וכל טיבו דעבדין האומות עובדי גלולים לגרמייהו עבדין וכדאיתא בגמרא ע"פ וחסד לאומים חטאת שכל צדקה וחסד שאומות עובדי גלולים עושין אינן אלא להתייהר כו':

פרק ב ונפש השנית בישראל היא חלק אלוה ממעל ממש כמ"ש ויפח באפיו

נשמת חיים ואתה נפחת בי וכמ"ש בזוהר מאן דנפח מתוכיה נפח פי' מתוכיותו ומפנימיותו שתוכיות ופנימיות החיות שבאדם מוציא בנפיחתו בכח: כך עד"מ נשמות ישראל עלו במחשבה כדכתיב בני בכורי ישראל בנים אתם לה' אלהיכם פי' כמו שהבן נמשך ממוח האב כך כביכול נשמת כל איש ישראל נמשכה ממחשבתו וחכמתו ית' דאיהו חכים ולא בחכמה ידיעא אלא הוא וחכמתו א' וכמ"ש הרמב"ם* שהוא המדע והוא היודע כו' ודבר זה אין ביכולת האדם להבינו על בוריו כו' כדכתיב החקר אלוה תמצא וכתיב כי לא מחשבותי מחשבותיכם וגו' ואף שיש רבבות מיני חלוקי מדרגות בנשמו' גבוה על גבוה לאין קץ

הגהה

והודו לו חכמי הקבלה כמ"ש בפרדס מהרמ"ק וגם לפי קבלת האר"י ז"ל יציבא מילתא בסוד התלבשות אור א"ס ב"ה על ידי צמצומים רבים בכלים דחב"ד דאצילו' אך לא למעלה מהאצילו' וכמ"ש במ"א שא"ס ב"ה מרומם ומתנשא רוממות אין קץ למעלה מעלה ממהות ובחי' חב"ד עד שמהות ובחי' חב"ד נחשבת כעשייה גופניית אצלו ית' כמ"ש כולם בחכמה עשית:

---

first three of the Ten Sefirot. *The corresponding faculties of the soul are defined in ch. 3.* [11] *Above the World of* Atzilut *the Unknowable G–d cannot be defined.* [12] *Accordingly, in terms of the Kabbalistic scale, Maimonides had nothing to say about G–d except from the World of* Atzilut *and "down." It is in the world of* Atzilut *where Kabbalah and Maimonides first meet, so to speak.* [13] Ps. *104:24.* [14] Code, Hilchot Yesodei ha-Torah *2:10.* [15] Job *11:7.* [16] Isa. *55:8.*

as with the superiority of the souls of the Patriarchs and of Moses our Teacher above the souls of our own generations who live in the period preceding the coming of the Messiah, which are as the very soles[17] of the feet compared with the brain and head, so in every generation there are the leaders of the Jews, whose souls are in the category of "head" and "brain" in comparison with those of the masses and the ignorant. Likewise [are there distinctions between] *nefashot* and *nefashot*, for every soul consists of *nefesh*, *ruach* and *neshamah*.[18] Nevertheless, the root of every *nefesh*, *ruach* and *neshamah*, from the highest of all ranks to the lowest that is embodied within the illiterate and the most worthless, all derive, as it were, from the Supreme Mind which is *Chochmah Ila'ah* (Supernal Wisdom).[19] [The manner of this descent is] analogous to that of a son who is derived from his father's brain, in that [even] the nails of his feet come into existence from the very same drop of semen, by being in the mother's womb for nine months, descending degree by degree, changing continually, until even the nails are formed from it. Yet [after all this process] it is still bound and united with a wonderful and essential unity with its original essence and being, which was the drop [as it came] from the father's brain. And even now, in the son, the nails receive their nourishment and life from the brain that is in the head. As is written in the *Gemara* (*Niddah*, *ibid.*),[20] "From the white of the father's drop of semen are formed the veins, the bones and the nails." (And in *Etz Chayim*, *Sha'ar ha-Chashmal*, it is likewise stated, in connection with the esoteric principle of Adam's garments in the Garden of Eden, that they [the garments] were the "nails" [derived] from the cognitive faculty of the brain). So, as it were, is it actually true of the root of every *nefesh*, *ruach* and *neshamah* in the community of Israel on high: in descending degree by degree, through the descent of the worlds of *Atzilut* (Emanation), *Beriah* (Creation), *Yetzirah* (Formation) and *Asiyah* (Action) from His blessed Wisdom, as it is written, "Thou hast made them all with wisdom,"[21] the *nefesh*, *ruach* and *neshamah* of the ignorant and unworthy come into being. Nevertheless they remain bound and united with a wonderful and essential unity with their original essence and entity; namely, the extension of *Chochmah Ila'ah* (Supernal Wisdom), inasmuch as the nurture and life of the *nefesh*, *ruach* and *neshamah* of the ignorant are drawn from the *nefesh*, *ruach* and *neshamah* of the saints and sages, the heads of Israel in their generation.

This

---

[17] *A play on the word* עקבתא *"soles."* [18] *Cf.* Zohar *I, 206a; II, 141b, etc.; also Isaiah Hurwitz,* Shenei Luchot ha-Berit *I, 9b.* [19] *The doctrine that all souls are related in that they all come from the same source was given much emphasis by the founder of Chasidut, the Baal Shem Tov, and was a major issue of contention between the protagonists and antagonists of Chasidut. The author elaborates on it in ch. 32 (לב).* [20] Niddah *31a.* [21] Ps. *104:24.*

קץ כמו גודל מעלת נשמות האבות ומשה רבינו ע"ה על נשמות דורותינו אלה דעקבי משיח׳ שהם בחי׳ עקביים ממש לגבי המוח והראש וכן בכל דור ודור יש ראשי אלפי ישראל שנשמותיהם הם בחי׳ ראש ומוח לגבי נשמות ההמון וע"ה וכן נפשות לגבי נפשות כי כל נפש כלולה מנפש רוח ונשמה מכל מקום שרש כל הנפש רוח ונשמה כולם מראש כל המדריגות עד סוף כל דרגין המלובש בגוף עמי הארץ וקל שבקלים נמשך ממוח העליון שהיא חכמה עילאה כביכול כמשל הבן הנמשך ממוח האב שאפי׳ צפרני רגליו נתהוו מטפה זו ממש ע"י שהייתה תשעה חדשים בבטן האם וירדה ממדרגה למדרגה להשתנות ולהתהוו׳ ממנה צפרנים ועם כל זה עודנה קשורה ומיוחדת ביחוד נפלא ועצום במהותה ועצמותה הראשון שהיתה טפת מוח האב וגם עכשיו בבן יניקת הצפרנים וחיותם נמשכת מהמוח שבראש כדאיתא בגמ׳ [נדה שם] לובן שממנו גידים ועצמות וצפרנים [וכמ"ש בע"ח שער החשמל בסוד לבושים של אדם הראשון בגן עדן שהיו צפרנים מבחי׳ מוח תבונה] וככה ממש כביכול בשרש כל הנפש רוח ונשמה של כללות ישראל למעלה בירידתו ממדרגה למדרגה על ידי השתלשלות העולמות אבי"ע מחכמתו ית׳ כדכתיב כולם בחכמה עשית נתהוו ממנו נפש רוח ונשמה של עמי הארץ ופחותי הערך ועם כל זה עודינה קשורות ומיוחדות ביחוד נפלא ועצום במהותן ועצמותן הראשון שהיא המשכת חכמה עילאה כי יניקת וחיו׳ נפש רוח ונשמה של עמי הארץ הוא מנפש רוח ונשמה של הצדיקים והחכמים ראשי בני ישראל שבדורם: ובזה

יובן

explains the comment of our Sages on the verse, "And to cleave unto Him"[22]—"He who cleaves unto a scholar [of the Torah] is deemed by the Torah as if he had become attached to the very *Shechinah* (Divine Presence)."[23] For, through attachment to the scholars, the *nefesh, ruach* and *neshamah* of the ignorant are bound up and united with their original essence and their root in the Supernal Wisdom, He and His wisdom being one, and "He is the Knowledge. . . .[24] (As for them who willfully sin and rebel against the sages, the nurture of their *nefesh, ruach* and *neshamah* comes from behind the back,[25] as it were, of the *nefesh, ruach* and *neshamah* of the scholars).

As for what is written in the *Zohar*[26] and in *Zohar Chadash*,[27] to the effect that the essential factor is to conduct oneself in a holy manner during sexual union, which is not the case with the children of the ignorant, and so on, it is to be understood as meaning that since there is not a *nefesh, ruach* and *neshamah* which has not a garment of the *nefesh* of its father's and mother's essence, and all the commandments that it fulfils are all influenced by that garment, . . . and even the benevolence that flows to one from heaven is all given through that garment—hence, through self-sanctification, one will cause to descend for the *neshamah* of one's child a holy garment; and however great a soul it may be, it still needs the father's sanctification. . . . But as for the soul itself, it sometimes happens that the soul of an infinitely lofty person comes to be the son of a despised and lowly man. . . . All this has been explained by Rabbi Isaac Luria, of blessed memory, in *Likutei Torah*, on *Parshat Vayera*, and in *Ta'amei ha-Mitzvot* on *Parshat Bereshit*.

•▲*Chapter 3*

Now, each distinction and grade of the three—*nefesh, ruach* and *neshamah*—consists of[1] ten faculties, corresponding to the Supernal *Ten Sefirot* (Divine manifestations),[2] from which they have descended, which are subdivided into two, namely, the three "mothers" and the seven "multiples," to wit: *chochmah* (wisdom) *binah* (understanding) and *da'at* (knowledge); and the "seven days of Creation:" *chesed* (kindness), *gevurah* (power), *tiferet* (beauty), and so on.[3]

Similarly is it with the human soul, which is divided in two—*sechel* (intellect) and *middot* (emotional attributes). The intellect includes *chochmah, binah* and *da'at* (ChaBaD), whilst the *middot* are love of G-d, dread and awe of Him, glorification of Him, and so forth. ChaBaD [the intellectual faculties] are called "mothers" and source of the *middot*, for the latter are "offspring" of the former.

The explanation of the matter is as follows:

---

[22] Deut. *30:20.* [23] Ketuvot *111b.* [24] *See n. 14, above.* [25] *I.e. ungraciously, or unwillingly. The concept is more fully explained in ch. 22.* [26] *Cf.* Zohar *II, 204b f.; III, 80–82.* [27] Bereshit, *p. 11.*

Chapter 3
[1] *Elsewhere (*e.g., Likutei Torah, Bamidbar *1a; 51b;* Shir ha-Shirim *16d) the author makes it clear that the soul does not "consist" of the ten faculties, but rather manifests itself through them, since the soul itself is essentially unknowable.* [2] *The* Ten Sefirot *are more fully discussed by the author in the fourth part of the book,* Igeret ha-Kodesh, *ch. 15 and elsewhere.* [3] Ibid.

יובן מאמר רז"ל על פסוק ולדבקה בו שכל הדבק בת"ח מעלה עליו הכתוב כאלו נדבק בשכינה ממש כי ע"י דביקה בתלמידי חכמים קשורות נפש רוח ונשמה של עמי הארץ ומיוחדות במהותן הראשון ושרשם שבחכמה עילאה שהוא ית' וחכמתו א' והוא המדע כו' [והפושעים ומורדים בתלמידי חכמים יניקת נפש רוח ונשמה שלהם מבחי' אחוריים של נפש רוח ונשמת ת"ח] ומ"ש בזהר ובזהר חדש שהעיקר תלוי שיקדש עצמו בשעת תשמיש דווקא משא"כ בני עמי הארץ כו' היינו משום שאין לך נפש רוח ונשמה שאין לה לבוש מנפש דעצמות אביו ואמו וכל המצות שעושה הכל ע"י אותו הלבוש כו' ואפי' השפע שנותנים לו מן השמים הכל ע"י לבוש זה ואם יקדש את עצמו ימשיך לבוש קדוש לנשמת בנו ואפילו היא נשמה גדולה צריכה לקידוש אביו כו' אבל הנשמה עצמה הנה לפעמים נשמת אדם גבוה לאין קץ בא להיות בנו של אדם נבזה ושפל כו' כמ"ש האר"י ז"ל כל זה בליקוטי תורה פ' וירא ובטעמי מצות פ' בראשית:

פרק ג

והנה כל בחי' ומדרגה משלש אלו נפש רוח ונשמה כלולה מעשר בחי' כנגד עשר ספירות עליונות שנשתלשלו מהן הנחלקות לשתים שהן שלש אמות ושבע כפולות פי' חכמה בינה ודעת ושבעת ימי הבנין חסד גבורה תפארת כו' וכך בנפש האדם שנחלקת לשתים שכל ומדות. השכל כולל חכמה בינה ודעת. והמדות הן אהבת ה' ופחדו ויראתו ולפארו כו' וחב"ד נקראו אמות ומקור למדות כי המדות הן תולדות חב"ד: וביאור הענין כי הנה

The intellect of the rational soul, which is the faculty that conceives any thing, is given the appellation of *chochmah*—כ״ח מ״ה—the "potentiality" of "what is."[4] When one brings forth this power from the potential into the actual, that is, when [a person] cogitates with his intellect in order to understand a thing truly and profoundly as it evolves from the concept which he has conceived in his intellect, this is called *binah*. These [*chochmah* and *binah*] are the very "father" and "mother" which give birth to love of G-d, and awe and ●▲dread of Him. For when the intellect in the rational soul deeply contemplates and immerses itself exceedingly in the greatness of G-d, how He fills all worlds and encompasses all worlds,[5] and in the presence of Whom everything is considered as nothing[6]—there will be born and aroused in his mind and thought the emotion of awe for the Divine Majesty, to fear and be humble before His blessed greatness, which is without end or limit, and to have the dread of G-d in his heart. Next, his heart will glow with an intense love, like burning coals, with a passion, desire and longing, and a yearning soul, towards the greatness of the blessed *En Sof.* This constitutes the culminating passion of the soul, of which Scripture speaks, as "My soul longeth, yea, even fainteth, . . ."[7] and "My soul thirsteth for G-d, . . ."[8] and "My soul thirsteth for Thee. . . ."[9] This thirst is derived from the element of Fire, which is found in the divine soul. As students of natural science affirm, and so it is in *Etz Chayim*, the element of Fire is in the heart, whilst the source of [the element of] Water and moisture is in the brain, which is explained in *Etz Chayim*, Portal 50, to refer to the faculty of *chochmah*,[10] called "The water of the divine soul." The rest of the *middot* are all offshoots of fear and love and their derivations, as is explained elsewhere.

Da'at, the etymology of which is to be found in the verse: "And Adam knew (*yada*) Eve,"[11] implies attachment and union. That is, one binds his mind with a very firm and strong bond to, and firmly fixes his thought on, the greatness of the blessed *En sof*, without diverting his mind [from Him]. For even one who is wise and understanding of the greatness of the blessed *En Sof*, will not—unless he binds his knowledge and fixes his thought with firmness and perseverence—produce in his soul true love and fear, but only vain fancies. Therefore *da'at* is the basis of the *middot* and the source of their vitality; it contains *chesed* and *gevurah*, that is to say, love with its offshoots and fear with its offshoots.[12]

---

[4] Zohar *III, 28a; 34a. A play on the Hebrew word* חכמה—כ״ח מ״ה. *It is also to be understood as "pure" or "creative" reason in* potentia. [5] *I.e. both immanently and transcendently.* Zohar *III, 225a.* [6] Zohar *I, 11b.* [7] Ps. *84:3.* [8] Ps. *42:3.* [9] Ps. *63:2.* [10] *Water descends from high places. It is symbolically identified with* chochmah, *the highest of the* Ten Sefirot, *and also with* chesed, *the first of the* middot. [11] Gen. *4:1.* [12] *Love and fear (awe) are two basic emotions latent in the soul which are produced by contemplation. The faculty of* da'at *stimulates these higher emotions to seek an outlet through the three "garments" of the soul, discussed in the following chapter.*

● 26 Kislev ▲ *28 Kislev*

הנה השכל שבנפש המשכל׳ שהוא המשכיל כל דבר נקרא בשם חכמה כ״ח מ״ה וכשמוציא כחו אל הפועל שמתבונן בשכלו להבין דבר לאשורו ולעמקו מתוך איזה דבר חכמה המושכל בשכלו נקרא בינה והן הם אב ואם המולידות אהבת ה׳ ויראתו ופחדו כי השכל שבנפש המשכלת כשמתבונן ומעמיק מאד בגדולת ה׳ איך הוא ממלא כל עלמין וסובב כל עלמין וכולא קמיה כלא חשיב נולדה ונתעוררה מדת יראת הרוממות במוחו ומחשבתו לירא ולהתבושש מגדולתו ית׳ שאין לה סוף ותכלית ופחד ה׳ בלבו ושוב יתלהב לבו באהבה עזה כרשפי אש בחשיקה וחפיצה ותשוקה ונפש שוקקה לגדולת אין סוף ב״ה והיא כלות הנפש כדכתיב נכספה וגם כלתה נפשי וגו׳ וכתיב צמאה נפשי לאלהים וגו׳ וכתיב צמאה לך נפשי וגו׳ והצמאון הוא מיסוד האש שבנפש האלהית וכמ״ש הטבעיים וכ״ה בע״ח שיסוד האש הוא בלב ומקור המים והליחות מהמוח וכמ״ש בע״ח שער נ׳ שהיא בחי׳ חכמה שנקרא מים שבנפש האלהית ושאר המדות כולן הן ענפי היראה והאהבה ותולדותיהן כמ״ש במקום אחר. והדעת הוא מלשון והאדם ידע את חוה והוא לשון התקשרות והתחברות שמקשר דעתו בקשר אמיץ וחזק מאוד ויתקע מחשבתו בחוזק בגדולת אין סוף ב״ה ואינו מסיח דעתו כי אף מי שהוא חכם ונבון בגדולת א״ס ב״ה הנה אם לא יקשר דעתו ויתקע מחשבתו בחוזק ובהתמדה לא יוליד בנפשו יראה ואהבה אמיתית כי אם דמיונות שוא ועל כן הדעת הוא קיום המדות וחיותן והוא כולל חסד וגבורה פי׳ אהבה וענפיה ויראה וענפיה:

ועוד

•▲*Chapter 4*

In addition,[1] every divine soul (*nefesh elokit*) possesses three garments, viz., thought, speech and action, [expressing themselves] in the 613 commandments of the Torah. For, when a person *actively*[2] fulfils all the precepts which require physical action,[3] and with his power of *speech* he occupies himself in expounding all the 613 commandments and their practical application, and with his power of *thought* he comprehends all that is comprehensible to him in the *Pardes*[4] of the Torah—then the totality of the 613 "organs" of his soul[5] are clothed in the 613 commandments of the Torah.

▲ Specifically: the faculties of ChaBaD in his soul are clothed in the comprehension of the Torah, which he comprehends in *Pardes*, to the extent of his mental capacity and the supernal root of his soul. And the *middot*, namely fear and love, together with their offshoots and ramifications, are clothed in the fulfilment of the commandments in deed and in word, namely, in the study of Torah which is "The equivalent of all the commandments."[6] For love is the root of all the 248 positive commands, all originating in it and having no true foundation without it, inasmuch as he who fulfils them in truth, truly loves the name of G-d and desires to cleave to Him in truth; for one cannot truly cleave to Him except through the fulfilment of the 248 commandments which are the 248 "Organs of the King,"[7] as it were, as is explained elsewhere;[8] whilst fear is the root of the 365 prohibitive commands, fearing to rebel against the Supreme King of kings, the Holy One, blessed be He; or a still deeper fear than this—when he feels *ashamed* in the presence of the Divine greatness to rebel against His glory and do what is evil in His eyes, namely, any of the abominable things hated by G-d, which are the *kelipot* and *sitra achra*, which draw their nurture from man below and have their hold in him through the 365 prohibitive commands [that he violates].

•▲Now these three "garments," deriving from the Torah and its commandments, although they are called "garments" of the *nefesh*, *ruach* and *neshamah*, their quality, nevertheless, is infinitely higher and greater than that of the *nefesh*, *ruach* and *neshamah* themselves,[9] as explained in the Zohar,[10] because the Torah and the Holy One, blessed be He, are one. The meaning of this is that the Torah, which is the wisdom and will of the Holy One, blessed be He, and His glorious Essence are one, since He is both the Knower and the Knowledge,

---

[1] *Having outlined in ch. 3 the intrinsic faculties of the soul, the author goes on to explain how they express themselves through the three outer "garments," or instruments.* [2] *All italics are the translator's.* [3] *Note that "action" is put first.* [4] *Literally meaning "orchard," it is taken as an acrostic of the four Hebrew words,* פשט, רמז, דרוש, סוד*, meaning: plain sense, intimation, homiletical exposition and esoteric meaning, respectively, the four levels of Scriptural interpretation.* [5] *The physical organism of the human body consists of 248 members and 365 blood vessels, corresponding to the 248 positive and 365 prohibitive commands* (Tanchuma ha-Kadum, Tetzei; Makkot 24a). *The soul, contains the spiritual counterparts of these 613 "organs." (See ch.*

פרק ד ועוד יש לכל נפש אלהית שלשה לבושים שהם מחשבה דבור ומעשה של תרי"ג מצות התורה שכשהאדם מקיים במעשה כל מצות מעשיות ובדבור הוא עוסק בפירוש כל תרי"ג מצות והלכותיהן ובמחשבה הוא משיג כל מה שאפשר לו להשיג בפרד"ס התורה הרי כללות תרי"ג אברי נפשו מלובשים בתרי"ג מצות התורה ובפרטות בחי' חב"ד שבנפשו מלובשות בהשגת התורה שהוא משיג בפרד"ס כפי יכולת השגתו ושרש נפשו למעלה. והמדות שהן יראה ואהבה וענפיהן ותולדותיהן מלובשות בקיום המצות במעשה ובדבור שהוא ת"ת שכנגד כולן כי האהבה היא שרש כל רמ"ח מ"ע וממנה הן נמשכות ובלעדה אין להן קיום אמיתי כי המקיימן באמת הוא האוהב את שם ה' וחפץ לדבקה בו באמת ואי אפשר לדבקה בו באמת כי אם בקיום רמ"ח פקודין שהם רמ"ח אברין דמלכא כביכול כמ"ש במקום אחר והיראה היא שרש לשס"ה לא תעשה כי ירא למרוד במלך מלכי המלכים הקב"ה. או יראה פנימית מזו שמתבושש מגדולתו למרות עיני כבודו ולעשות הרע בעיניו כל תועבת ה' אשר שנא הם הקליפות וסטרא אחרא אשר יניקתם מהאדם התחתון ואחיזתם בו הוא בשס"ה מצות לא תעשה. והנה שלשה לבושים אלו מהתורה ומצותיה אף שנקראים לבושים לנפש רוח ונשמה עם כל זה גבהה וגדלה מעלתם לאין קץ וסוף על מעלת נפש רוח ונשמה עצמן כמ"ש בזהר דאורייתא וקב"ה כולא חד פי' דאורייתא היא חכמתו ורצונו של הקב"ה והקב"ה בכבודו ובעצמו כולא חד כי הוא היודע והוא המדע כו'

51, below.) [6] Mishnah, Peah *1:1.* [7] Tikunei Zohar, *Tikun 30.* [8] Infra, *ch. 23.* [9] *The soul itself, as the subject loving and fearing G–d, must remain apart from G–d; it is only through its "garments" that it attains true identity with G–d, as further explained in ch. 35.* [10] *Part I, 24a; II, 60a. See beg. ch. 23 below.*

and so on, as explained above in the name of Maimonides. And although the Holy One, blessed be He, is called *En Sof* ("Infinite"), and "His greatness can never be fathomed,"[11] and "No thought can apprehend Him at all,"[12] and so are also His will and His wisdom, as it is written: "There is no searching of His understanding,"[13] and "Canst thou by searching find G-d?"[14] and again: "For My thoughts are not your thoughts"[15]—nevertheless, it is in this connection that it has been said: "Where you find the greatness of the Holy One, blessed be He, there you also find His humility."[16] For the Holy One, blessed be He, has compressed His will and wisdom within the 613 commandments of the Torah, and in their laws, as well as within the combination of the letters of the Torah, the books of the Prophets and the Hagiographa, and in the exposition thereof which are to be found in the *Agadot* and *Midrashim* of our Rabbis of blessed memory. All this in order that each *neshamah*, or *ruach* and *nefesh* in the human body should be able to comprehend them through its faculty of understanding, and to fulfil them, as far as they can be fulfilled, in act, speech and thought, thereby clothing itself with all its ten faculties in these three garments.

▲ Therefore has the Torah been compared to water,[17] for just as water descends from a higher to a lower level, so has the Torah descended from its place of glory, which is His blessed will and wisdom; [for] the Torah and the Holy One, blessed be He, are one and the same and no thought can apprehend Him at all. Thence [the Torah] has progressively descended through hidden stages, stage after stage, with the descent of the worlds, until it clothed itself in corporeal substances and in things of this world, comprising almost all of the commandments of the Torah, their laws, and in the combinations of material letters, written with ink in a book, namely, the 24 volumes of the Torah, Prophets and Hagiographa; all this in order that every thought should be able to apprehend them, and even the faculties of speech and action, which are on a lower level than thought, should be able to apprehend them and be clothed in them.

● Thus, since the Torah and its commandments "clothe" all ten faculties of the soul with all its 613 organs from head to foot, it [the soul] is altogether truly bound up in the Bundle of Life with G-d,[18] and the very light of G-d envelops and clothes it from head to foot, as it is written, "G-d is my Rock, I will take refuge *in Him*,"[19]

---

[11] Ps. *145:3*. [12] *Introduction to* Tikunei Zohar *17a*. [13] Isa. *40:28*. [14] Job *11:7*. [15] Isa. *55:8*. [16] Megillah *31a*. *This is interpreted to mean that G-d combines the powers of expansion ("greatness") and contraction ("humility"), which come into play in the process of* Tzimtzum, *Cf.* Zohar *I, 140a; II, 99a; III, 58a, 159a*. [17] Bava Kama *17a*. [18] I Sam. *25:29*. [19] Ps. *18:3*.

● 29 Kislev * ▲ *2 Teveth*

*When Kislev has only 29 days, the portion for the 30th is said together with the 29th.

וכו' כמ"ש לעיל בשם הרמב"ם. ואף דהקב"ה נקרא אין סוף ולגדולתו אין חקר ולית מחשבה תפיסא ביה כלל וכן ברצונו וחכמתו כדכתיב אין חקר לתבונתו וכתי' החקר אלוה תמצא וכתיב כי לא מחשבותי מחשבותיכם הנה על זה אמרו במקום שאתה מוצא גדולתו של הקב"ה שם אתה מוצא ענותנותו וצמצם הקב"ה רצונו וחכמתו בתרי"ג מצות התורה ובהלכותיהן ובצרופי אותיות תנ"ך ודרשותיהן שבאגדות ומדרשי חכמינו ז"ל בכדי שכל הנשמה או רוח ונפש שבגוף האדם תוכל להשיגן בדעתה ולקיימן כל מה שאפשר לקיים מהן במעשה דבור ומחשבה וע"י זה תתלבש בכל עשר בחינותיה בשלשה לבושים אלו. ולכן נמשלה התורה למים מה מים יורדים ממקום גבוה למקום נמוך כך התורה ירדה ממקום כבודה שהיא רצונו וחכמתו יתברך ואורייתא וקודשא בריך הוא כולא חד ולית מחשבה תפיסא ביה כלל. ומשם נסעה וירדה בסתר המדרגות ממדרגה למדרגה בהשתלשלות העולמות עד שנתלבשה בדברים גשמיים ועניני עולם הזה שהן רוב מצות התורה ככולם והלכותיהן ובצרופי אותיות גשמיות בדיו על הספר עשרים וארבעה ספרים שבתורה נביאים וכתובים כדי שתהא כל מחשבה תפיסא בהן ואפי' בחי' דבור ומעשה שלמטה ממדרגת מחשבה תפיסא בהן ומתלבשת בהן ומאחר שהתורה ומצותיה מלבישים כל עשר בחי' הנפש וכל תרי"ג אבריה מראשה ועד רגלה הרי כולה צרורה בצרור החיים את ה' ממש ואור ה' ממש מקיפה ומלבישה מראשה ועד רגלה כמ"ש צורי אחסה בו

וכתיב

and it is also written, "With favour (*ratzon*—will) wilt Thou compass him as with a shield,"[20] that is to say, with His blessed will and wisdom which are clothed in His Torah and its commandments.

▲ Hence it has been said: "Better is one hour of repentance and good deeds in this world than the whole life of the world to come."[21] For, the world to come is that state where one enjoys the effulgence of the Divine Presence,[22] which is the pleasure of comprehension, yet no created being—even celestial—can comprehend more than some reflection of the Divine Light; that is why the reference is to "Effulgence of the Divine Presence" (*Ziv ha-Shechinah*).[23] But as for the essence of the Holy One, blessed be He, no thought can apprehend Him at all, except when it apprehends, and is clothed in, the Torah and its *Mitzvot*; only then does it truly apprehend, and is clothed in, the Holy One, blessed be He, inasmuch as the Torah and the Holy One, blessed be He, are one and the same. For although the Torah has been clothed in lower material things, it is by way of illustration, like embracing the king. There is no difference, in regard to the degree of closeness and attachment to the king, whether while embracing the king, the latter is then wearing one robe or several robes, so long as the royal person is in them. Likewise, when the king, for his part, embraces one with his arm, even though it is dressed in his robes; as it is written, "And His right hand embraces me,"[24] which refers to the Torah which was given by G-d's right hand,[25] which is the quality of *chesed* and water.[26]

•▲ Chapter 5

Let us explain further and fully elucidate the expression *tefisa* (apprehension) in the words of Elijah, "No thought can apprehend Thee."[1]

Now, when an intellect conceives and comprehends a concept with its intellectual faculties, this intellect grasps the concept and encompasses it. This concept is [in turn] grasped, enveloped and enclothed within that intellect which conceived and comprehended it.

The mind, for its part, is also clothed in the concept at the time it comprehends and grasps it with the intellect.[2] For example, when a person understands and comprehends, fully and clearly, any *halachah* (law) in the Mishnah or Gemara, his intellect grasps and encompasses it and, at the same time, is clothed in it. Consequently, as the particular *halachah* is

---

[20] Ps. *5:13*. [21] Avot *4:17*. [22] Berachot *16b*. [23] *I.e. the "glow" of the* Shechinah, *not the* Shechinah *itself. Note the author's interpretation of* זיו *in this context as a* remote *gleam, a mere reflection.* [24] Song of Songs, *8:3*. [25] Deut. *33:2*. [26] *In Kabbalah, the "right" hand or side is the side of benevolence.* Chesed *and water are synonymous of Divine benevolence. See note 10, ch. 3.*

Chapter 5

[1] *Introduction to* Tikunei Zohar *17a*. [2] *This point is demonstrated by the fact that when the mind is preoccupied with one thing, it cannot at the same time engage in another.*

וכתיב כצנה רצון תעטרנו שהוא רצונו וחכמתו יתברך המלובשים בתורתו ומצותיה. ולכן אמרו יפה שעה אחת בתשובה ומעשים טובים בעולם הזה מכל חיי עולם הבא כי עולם הבא הוא שנהנין מזיו השכינה שהוא תענוג ההשגה ואי אפשר לשום נברא אפי׳ מהעליונים להשיג כי אם איזו הארה מאור ה׳ ולכן נקרא בשם זיו השכינה אבל הקב״ה בכבודו ובעצמו לית מחשבה תפיסא ביה כלל כי אם כאשר תפיסא ומתלבשת בתורה ומצותיה אזי היא תפיסא בהן *) ומתלבשת בהקב״ה ממש דאורייתא וקב״ה כולא חד. ואף שהתורה נתלבשה בדברים תחתונים גשמיים הרי זה כמחבק את המלך ד״מ שאין הפרש במעלת התקרבותו ודביקותו במלך בין מחבקו כשהוא לבוש לבוש אחד בין שהוא לבוש כמה לבושים מאחר שגוף המלך בתוכם. וכן אם המלך מחבקו בזרועו גם שהיא מלובשת תוך מלבושיו כמ״ש וימינו תחבקני שהיא התורה שנתנה מימין שהיא בחי׳ חסד ומים:

פרק ה ולתוספת ביאור באר היטב לשון תפיסא שאמר אליהו לית מחשבה תפיסא בך כו׳. הנה כל שכל כשמשכיל ומשיג בשכלו איזה מושכל הרי השכל תופס את המושכל ומקיפו בשכלו והמושכל נתפס ומוקף ומלובש בתוך השכל שהשיגו והשכילו וגם השכל מלובש במושכל בשעה שמשיגו ותופסו בשכלו ד״מ כשאדם מבין ומשיג איזו הלכה במשנה או בגמרא לאשורה על בוריה הרי שכלו תופס ומקיף אותה וגם שכלו מלובש בה באותה שעה. והנה הלכה זו היא

*) בכ״י ליתא תיבת בהן.

חכמתו

the wisdom and will of G–d, for it was His will that when, for example, Reuben pleads in one way and Simeon in another, the verdict as between them shall be thus and thus; and even should such a litigation never have occurred, nor would it ever present itself for judgment in connection with such disputes and claims, nevertheless, since it has been the will and wisdom of the Holy One, blessed be He, that in the event of a person pleading this way and the other [litigant] pleading that way, the verdict shall be such and such—now therefore, when a person knows and comprehends with his intellect such a verdict in accordance with the law as it is set out in the *Mishnah*, *Gemara*, or *Posekim* (Codes), he has thus comprehended, grasped and encompassed with his intellect the will and wisdom of the Holy One, blessed be He, Whom no thought can grasp, nor His will and wisdom, except when they are clothed in the laws that have been set out for us. [Simultaneously] the intellect is also clothed in them [the Divine will and wisdom].

This is a wonderful union, like which there is none other, and which has no parallel anywhere in the material world, whereby complete oneness and unity, from every side and angle, could be attained.

• Hence the special superiority, infinitely great and wonderful, that is in the commandment of knowing the Torah and comprehending it, over all the commandments involving action, and even those relating to speech, and even the commandment to study the Torah,[3] which is fulfilled through speech. For, through all the commandments involving speech or action, the Holy One, blessed be He, clothes the soul and envelops it from head to foot with the Divine light. However, with regard to knowledge of the Torah, apart from the fact that the intellect is clothed in Divine wisdom, this Divine wisdom is also contained *in it*, to the extent that his intellect comprehends, grasps and encompasses, as much as it is able so to do, of the knowledge of the Torah, every man according to his intellect, his knowledgeable capacity, and his comprehension in *Pardes*.[4]

Since, in the case of knowledge of the Torah, the Torah is clothed in the soul and intellect of a person, and is absorbed in them, it is called "bread" and "food" of the soul. For just as physical bread nourishes the body as it is absorbed internally, in his very inner self, where it is transformed into blood and flesh of his flesh, whereby he lives and exists—so, too, it is with the knowledge of

[3] *As distinct from* knowledge *of the Torah.* [4] *See note 4, ch. 4.*

• 1 Teveth

חכמתו ורצונו של הקב"ה שעלה ברצונו שכשיטעון ראובן כך וכך דרך משל ושמעון כך וכך יהיה הפסק ביניהם כך וכך ואף אם לא היה ולא יהיה הדבר הזה לעולם לבא למשפט על טענות ותביעות אלו מכל מקום מאחר שכך עלה ברצונו וחכמתו של הקב"ה שאם יטעון זה כך וזה כך יהיה הפסק כך הרי כשאדם יודע ומשיג בשכלו פסק זה כהלכה הערוכה במשנה או גמרא או פוסקים הרי זה משיג ותופס ומקיף בשכלו רצונו וחכמתו של הקב"ה דלית מחשבה תפיסא ביה ולא ברצונו וחכמתו כי אם בהתלבשותם בהלכות הערוכות לפנינו וגם שכלו מלובש בהם והוא יחוד נפלא שאין יחוד כמוהו ולא כערכו נמצא כלל בגשמיות להיות לאחדים ומיוחדים ממש מכל צד ופנה. וזאת מעלה יתרה גדולה ונפלאה לאין קץ אשר במצות ידיעת התורה והשגתה על כל המצות מעשיות ואפי' על מצות התלויות בדבור ואפי' על מצות תלמוד תורה שבדבור כי ע"י כל המצות שבדבור ומעשה הקב"ה מלביש את הנפש ומקיפה אור ה' מראשה ועד רגלה. ובידיעת התורה מלבד שהשכל מלובש בחכמת ה' הנה גם חכמת ה' בקרבו מה שהשכל משיג ותופס ומקיף בשכלו מה שאפשר לו לתפוס ולהשיג מידיעת התורה איש כפי שכלו וכח ידיעתו והשגתו בפרד"ס. ולפי שבידיעת התורה התורה מלובשת בנפש האדם ושכלו ומוקפת בתוכם לכן נקראת בשם לחם ומזון הנפש כי כמו שהלחם הגשמי זן את הגוף כשמכניסו בתוכו וקרבו ממש ונהפך שם להיות דם ובשר כבשרו ואזי יחיה ויתקיים כך בידיעת התורה

the Torah and its comprehension by the soul of the person who studies it well, with a concentration of his intellect, until the Torah is absorbed by his intellect and is united with it and they become one. This becomes nourishment for the soul, and its inner life from the Giver of life, the blessed *En Sof*, Who is clothed in His wisdom and in His Torah that are [absorbed] in it [the soul].

This is the meaning of the verse, "Yea, Thy Torah is within my inward parts."[5]

It is also stated in *Etz Chayim*, Portal 44, ch. 3, that the "garments" of the soul in the *Gan Eden* (Paradise) are the commandments while the Torah is the "food" for the souls which, during life on earth, had occupied themselves in the study of the Torah for its own sake. It is [similarly] written in the *Zohar.*[6] As for the meaning of "For its own sake,"[7] it is [study with the intent] to attach one's soul to G-d through the comprehension of the Torah, each one according to his intellect, as explained in *Peri Etz Chayim*.

(The "food" [of the soul] is in the nature of Inner Light; while the "garments" are in the nature of Encompassing Light. Therefore our Rabbis, of blessed memory, have said, "The study of the Torah equals all the commandments."[8] For the commandments are but "garments" whereas the Torah is both "food" as well as "garment"[9] for the rational soul, in which a person is clothed during learning and concentration. All the more so when a person also articulates, by word of mouth; for the breath emitted in speaking [the words of the Torah] becomes something in the nature of an Encompassing Light, as is explained in *Peri Etz Chayim*.)

●▲*Chapter 6*

"The Almighty has created one thing opposite the other."[1]

Just as the divine soul consists of ten holy *Sefirot* and is clothed in three holy garments,[2] so does the soul which is derived from the *sitra achra* of the *kelipat nogah*, which is clothed in man's blood, consist of ten "crowns of impurity."[3] These are the seven evil *middot* which stem from the four evil elements mentioned above,[4] and the intellect begetting them which is subdivided into three, viz., wisdom, understanding and knowledge, the source of the *middot.*[5] For the *middot* are according to the quality of the intellect. Hence a child desires and loves petty things of inferior worth, for his intellect is too immature and deficient to appreciate things that are much more precious. Likewise is he provoked to anger and vexation over trivial things; so, too, with boasting and other *middot*.

Now these ten unclean categories, when a person meditates in them or

---

[5] Ps. *40:9.* [6] *II, p. 210a ff.* [7] *Cf.* Tanya, *chs. 39, 40 and 41, for a further elaboration. We have here a departure from the conventional concepts of* lishemah *and* shelo lishemah. [8] Mishnah, Peah *1:1.* [9] *The "food" would correspond to the knowledge absorbed and "digested"; the "garment"—to that knowledge which is not thoroughly assimilated and remains external, as it were, yet retaining the quality of the Divine precept, like all other religious acts which are conceived as "garments" of the soul.*

Chapter 6
[1] Eccl. *7:14. In general, things in the realm of holiness have their opposite in the realm of the profane, or "the other side"* (sitra achra).

התורה והשגתה בנפש האדם שלומדה היטב בעיון שכלו עד שנתפסת בשכלו ומתאחדת עמו והיו לאחדים נעשה מזון לנפש וחיים בקרבה מחיי החיים אין סוף ברוך הוא המלובש בחכמתו ותורתו שבקרבה וז"ש ותורתך בתוך מעי וכמ"ש בע"ח שער מ"ד פ"ג שלבושי הנשמות בגן עדן הן המצות והתורה היא המזון לנשמות שעסקו בעולם הזה בתורה לשמה וכמ"ש בזהר ויקהל דף ר"י ולשמה היינו כדי לקשר נפשו לה' ע"י השגת התורה איש כפי שכלו כמ"ש בפרע"ח [והמזון היא בחי' אור פנימי והלבושים בחי' מקיפים ולכן אמרו רז"ל שתלמוד תורה שקול כנגד כל המצות לפי שהמצות הן לבושים לבד והתורה היא מזון וגם לבוש לנפש המשכלת שמתלבש בה בעיונה ולימודה וכל שכן כשמוציא בפיו בדבור שהבל הדבור נעשה בחי' אור מקיף כמ"ש בפרע"ח]:

פרק ו **והנה** זה לעומת זה עשה אלהים כי כמו שנפש האלהית כלולה מעשר ספירות קדושות ומתלבשת בשלשה לבושים קדושים כך הנפש דסטרא אחרא מקליפות נוגה המלובשת בדם האדם כלולה מעשר כתרין דמסאבותא שהן שבע מדות רעות הבאות מארבע יסודות רעים הנ"ל ושכל המולידן הנחלק לשלש שהן חכמה בינה ודעת מקור המדות כי המדות הן לפי ערך השכל כי הקטן חושק ואוהב דברים קטנים פחותי הערך לפי ששכלו קטן וקצר להשיג דברים יקרים יותר מהם. וכן מתכעס ומתקצף מדברים קטנים וכן בהתפארות ושאר מדות ועשר בחי' אלו הטמאות כשאדם מחשב בהן או

מדבר

Similarly, everything in the physical world has its spiritual counterpart from which it derives its existence and vitality—a popular concept in Chabad, as in Kabbalah generally. Cf. Zohar *III, 47b.* [2] *Thought, speech and deed.* [3] *Cf.* Zohar *III, 41a; 70a.* [4] *End of ch. 1.* [5] *Here, unlike ch. 3, the* middot *precede* sechel *to indicate the secondary role of the intellect in the animal soul, where passion predominates.*

speaks them, or acts by them, his thought —which is in his brain; and his speech— which is in his mouth; and the power of action—which is in his hands, together with his other limbs—all these are called the "impure garments" of these ten unclean categories wherein the latter are clothed at the time of the action, speech or thought. It is these that constitute all the deeds that are done under the sun, which are all "vanity and striving after the wind,"[6] as interpreted in the *Zohar*, *Beshallach*,[7] in the sense of a "ruination of the spirit. . . ."[8]

▲ So, too, are all utterances and thoughts which are not directed towards G-d and His will and service. For this is the meaning of *sitra achra*—"the other side," i.e. not the side of holiness. For the holy side is nothing but the indwelling and extension of the holiness of the Holy One, blessed be He, and He dwells only on such a thing that abnegates itself completely to Him, either actually, as in the case of the angels above, or potentially, as in the case of every Jew down below, having the capacity to abnegate himself completely to the Holy One, blessed be He, through martyrdom for the sanctification of G-d.

That is why our Sages have said that "Even when a single individual sits and engages in the Torah the *Shechinah* rests on him;"[9] and "On each [gathering of] ten Jews the *Shechinah* rests"[10] always.

● However, that which does not surrender itself to G-d, but is a separate thing by itself, does not receive its vitality from the holiness of the Holy One, blessed be He, that is, from the very inner essence and substance of the holiness itself, but from "behind its back," as it were,[11] descending degree by degree, through myriads of degrees with the lowering of the worlds, by way of cause and effect, and innumerable contractions,[12] until the Light and Life is so diminished through repeated diminutions, that it can be compressed and incorporated, in a state of exile as it were, within that separated thing, giving it vitality and existence *ex nihilo*, so that it does not revert to nothingness and non-existence as it was before it was created.[13]

▲ Consequently, this world, with all its contents, is called the world of *kelipot* and *sitra achra*. Therefore all mundane affairs are severe and evil,[14] and wicked men prevail,

---

[6] Eccl. *1:14*. [7] *II, p. 59a.* [8] *A reinterpretation of* רעות רוח. [9] Avot *3:6*. [10] Sanhedrin *39a*. [11] *Cf. note 25, ch. 2.* [12] *Cf. ch. 48;* Igeret ha-Kodesh, *ch. 20.* [13] *Evil is thus conceived as a creation* ex nihilo, *like everything else, except that it was not created for its own sake; hence it is merely tolerated. The monistic aspect of creation, despite the apparent dualism in the world, is thus emphasised, particularly in ch. 24, below.* [14] *Cf. ch. 24.*

● 3 Teveth ▲ *6 Teveth* ▲ *7 Teveth*

מדבר או עושה הרי מחשבתו שבמוחו ודבורו שבפיו וכח המעשיי שבידיו ושאר איבריו נקראים לבושי מסאבו לעשר בחי' אלו הטמאות שמתלבשות בהן בשעת מעשה או דבור או מחשבה והן הם כל המעשים אשר נעשים תחת השמש אשר הכל הבל ורעות רוח וכמ"ש בזהר בשלח שהן תבירו דרוחא כו' וכן כל הדבורים וכל המחשבות אשר לא לה' המה ולרצונו ולעבודתו שזהו פי' לשון סטרא אחרא פי' צד אחר שאינו צד הקדושה וצד הקדושה אינו אלא השראה והמשכה מקדושתו של הקב"ה ואין הקב"ה שורה אלא על דבר שבטל אצלו יתב' בין בפועל ממש כמלאכים עליונים בין בכח ככל איש ישראל למטה שבכחו להיות בטל ממש לגבי הקב"ה במסירת נפשו על קדושת ה'. ולכן אמרו רז"ל שאפי' אחד שיושב ועוסק בתורה שכינה שרויה כו' וכל בי עשרה שכינתא שריא לעולם אבל כל מה שאינו בטל אצלו ית' אלא הוא דבר נפרד בפני עצמו אינו מקבל חיות מקדושתו של הקב"ה מבחי' פנימית הקדושה ומהותה ועצמותה בכבודה ובעצמה אלא מבחי' אחוריים שיורדים ממדרגה למדרגה רבבות מדרגות בהשתלשלות העולמות דרך עלה ועלול וצמצומים רבים עד שנתמעט כל כך האור והחיות מיעוט אחר מיעוט עד שיכול להתצמצם ולהתלבש בבחי' גלות תוך אותו דבר הנפרד להחיותו ולקימו מאין ליש שלא יחזור להיות אין ואפס כבתחלה מקודם שנברא ולכן נקרא עולם הזה ומלואו עולם הקליפות וסטרא אחרא ולכן כל מעשה עוה"ז קשים ורעים והרשעים גוברים
בו

as explained in *Etz Chayim*, Portal 42, end of ch. 4.

Note: To be sure, there are contained in it [this world] the ten sefirot *[of the world] of* Asiyah *(Action) of the side of holiness, as is written in* Etz Chayim, *Portal 43, and within these ten* sefirot *of* Asiyah *are the ten* sefirot *of* Yetzirah *(Formation), and in them the ten* sefirot *of* Beriah *(Creation), and in them the ten* sefirot *of* Atzilut *(Emanation), in which abides the light of the blessed* En Sof. *Thus the light of the blessed* En Sof *pervades this lower world through being clothed in the ten* sefirot *of the Four Worlds, namely those of* Atzilut, Beriah, Yetzirah *and* Asiyah, *as explained in* Etz Chayim, *Portal 47, ch. 2, and in* Sefer ha-Gilgulim, *ch. 20.*

However, the *kelipot* are subdivided into two grades, one lower than the other. The lower grade consists of the three *kelipot* which are altogether unclean and evil, containing no good whatever. In the "chariot" of [the prophet] Ezekiel they are called "whirlwind," "great cloud." . . .[15] From them flow and derive the souls of all the nations of the world, and the existence of their bodies, and also the souls of all living creatures that are unclean and unfit for consumption,[16] and the existence of their bodies, as well as the existence and vitality of all forbidden food in the vegetable kingdom, such as *orlah*[17] and "Mixed seeds in the vineyard, . . ."[18] as explained in *Etz Chayim*, Portal 49, ch. 6, as also the existence and vitality of all actions, utterances, and thoughts pertaining to the 365 prohibitions and their offshoots, as is explained *ibid.*, at the end of ch. 5.

•▲ *Chapter 7*

On the other hand,[1] the vitalising animal soul in the Jew, that which is derived from the aspect of the *kelipah*, which is clothed in the human blood, as stated above,[2] and the "souls"[3] of the animals, beasts, birds and fishes that are clean and fit for [Jewish] consumption, as also the existence and vitality of the entire inanimate and entire vegetable world which are permissible for consumption, as well as the existence and vitality of every act, utterance and thought in mundane matters that contain no forbidden aspect—being neither root nor branch of the 365 prohibitive precepts and their offshoots, either on the explicit authority of the Torah, or by Rabbinic enactment—yet are not performed for the sake of Heaven but only by the will, desire and lust of the body; and even where it is a need of the body, or its very preservation and life, but his intention is not for the sake of Heaven, that is, to serve G-d thereby

[15] Ezek. *1:4.* [16] Lev. *11;* Deut. *14.* [17] *First three years' harvest of fruit of a tree. Cf.* Lev. *19:23.* [18] Deut. *22:9.*

Chapter 7
[1] *The author continues to expound the doctrine of the* kelipot, *and his definitions of good and evil, distinguishing an intermediate category.* [2] *Ch. 1.* [3] *The quotes are the translator's. According to Lurianic doctrine* all *things, including inanimate objects, possess a "soul," which is the creative and preserving force of the Creator, the thing's reality. This doctrine was adopted and expounded by the Ba'al Shem Tov and Rabbi Schneur Zalman. Cf.* Sha'ar ha-Yichud veha-Emunah, *ch. 1 ff.*

בו כמ"ש בע"ח שער מ"ב סוף פ"ד* אלא שהקליפות הן נחלקות לשתי מדרגות זו למטה מזו המדרגה התחתונה היא שלש קליפו' הטמאות ורעות לגמרי ואין בהם טוב כלל ונקראו במרכבת יחזקאל רוח סערה וענן גדול וגו' ומהן נשפעות ונמשכות נפשות כל אומות עובדי גלולים וקיום גופם ונפשות כל בעלי חיים הטמאים ואסורים באכילה וקיום גופם וקיום וחיות כל מאכלות אסורות מהצומח כמו ערלה וכלאי הכרם כו' וכמ"ש בע"ח שער מ"ט פ"ו וכן קיום וחיות כל המעשה דבור ומחשבה של כל שס"ה לא תעשה וענפיהן כמ"ש שם סוף פ"ה:

הגהה

*עם היות בתוכו עשר ספי' דעשיה דקדושה וכמ"ש בע"ח שער מ"ג ובתוך עשר ספי' דעשיה אלו הן עשר ספי' דיצירה ובתוכן עשר ספי' דבריאה ובתוכן עשר ספי' דאצילות שבתוכן אור א"ס ב"ה ונמצא אור א"ס ב"ה מלא כל הארץ הלזו התחתונה על ידי התלבשותו בעשר ספי' דארבע עולמות אבי"ע כמ"ש בע"ח שער מ"ז פ"ב ובספר גלגולים פרק כ':

פרק ז אך נפש החיונית הבהמית שבישראל שמצד הקליפה המלובשת בדם האדם כנ"ל ונפשות בהמות וחיות ועופות ודגים טהורים ומותרים באכילה וקיום וחיות כל הדומם וכל הצומח המותר באכילה וכן קיום וחיות כל המעשה דבור ומחשבה בענייני עוה"ז שאין בהם צד איסור לא שרש ולא ענף משס"ה מצות לא תעשה וענפיהן דאורייתא ודרבנן רק שאינן לשם שמים אלא רצון הגוף וחפצו ותאותו ואפי' הוא צורך הגוף וקיומו וחיותו ממש אלא שכוונתו אינה לשם שמים כדי לעבוד את ה' בגופו לא

עדיפי

—all these acts, utterances and thoughts are no better than the vitalising animal soul itself; and everything in this totality of things flows and is drawn from the second gradation [to be found] in the *kelipot* and *sitra achra*, namely, a fourth *kelipah*, called *kelipat nogah*. For in this world, called the "World of *Asiyah* (Action),"[4] most, indeed almost all, of it [the *kelipat nogah*] is bad, and only a little good has been intermingled within it (from which come the good qualities contained in the animal soul of the Jew, as is explained above.[5])

This [*kelipat nogah*] is an intermediate category between the three completely unclean *kelipot* and the category and order of Holiness. Hence it is sometimes absorbed within the three unclean *kelipot* (as is explained in *Etz Chayim*, Portal 49, beginning of ch. 4, on the authority of the *Zohar*), and sometimes it is absorbed and elevated to the category and level of Holiness, as when the good that is intermingled in it is extracted from the bad, and prevails and ascends until it is absorbed in Holiness. Such is the case, for example, of he who eats fat beef and drinks spiced wine in order to broaden his mind for the service of G–d and His Torah; as Ravah said: "Wine and fragrance [make a man's mind more receptive],"[6] or in order to fulfil the command concerning enjoyment of the Sabbath and Festivals.[7] In such a case the vitality of the meat and wine, originating in the *kelipat nogah*, is distilled and ascends to G–d like a burnt offering and sacrifice.

So, too, when a man utters a pleasantry in order to sharpen his wit and rejoice his heart in G–d, in His Torah and service, which should be practised joyfully, as Ravah was wont to do with his pupils, prefacing his discourse with some witty remark, to enliven the students thereby.[8]

●▲On the other hand, he who belongs to those who gluttonously guzzle meat and quaff wine in order to satisfy their bodily appetites and animal nature, derived from the so-called element of water of the four evil elements contained therein, from which comes the vice of lust—in such case the energy of the meat and wine consumed by him is degraded and absorbed temporarily in the utter evil of the three unclean *kelipot*, and his body temporarily becomes a garment and vehicle for them, until the person repents and returns to the service of G–d and His Torah. For, inasmuch

---

[4] *See* Glossary and Notes. [5] *Ch. 1.* [6] Yoma *76b.* [7] *Maimonides,* Code, Hilchot Shabbat *30:7;* Hilchot Yom Tov *6:16.* *Rabbi Schneur Zalman,* Shulchan Aruch, *242:1; 529:1, 3.* [8] Pesachim *117a.*

● 5 Teveth ▲ *9 Teveth*

עדיפי מעשה דבור ומחשבות אלו מנפש החיונית הבהמית בעצמה והכל כאשר לכל נשפע ונמשך ממדרגה השנית שבקליפות וסטרא אחרא שהיא קליפה רביעית הנקראת קליפת נוגה שבעולם הזה הנקרא עולם העשיה רובו ככולו רע רק מעט טוב מעורב בתוכה [שממנה באות מדות טובות שבנפש הבהמית שבישראל כמ״ש לעיל] והיא בחי׳ ממוצעת בין שלש קליפות הטמאות לגמרי ובין בחי׳ ומדרגת הקדושה ולכן פעמים שהיא נכללת בשלש קליפות הטמאות [כמ״ש בע״ח שער מ״ט ריש פ״ד בשם הזהר] ופעמים שהיא נכללת ועולה בבחי׳ ומדרגת הקדושה דהיינו כשהטוב המעורב בה נתברר מהרע וגובר ועולה ונכלל בקדושה כגון ד״מ האוכל בשרא שמינא דתורא ושותה יין מבושם להרחיב דעתו לה׳ ולתורתו כדאמר רבא חמרא וריחא כו׳ או בשביל כדי לקיים מצות ענג שבת וי״ט אזי נתברר חיות הבשר והיין שהיה נשפע מקליפת נוגה ועולה לה׳ כעולה וכקרבן. וכן האומר מילתא דבדיחותא לפקח דעתו ולשמח לבו לה׳ ולתורתו ועבודתו שצריכים להיות בשמחה וכמו שעשה רבא לתלמידיו שאמר לפניהם מילתא דבדיחותא תחלה ובדחי רבנן. אך מי שהוא בזוללי בשר וסובאי יין למלאת תאות גופו ונפשו הבהמית שהוא בחי׳ יסוד המים מארבע יסודות הרעים שבה שממנו מדת התאוה הנה ע״י זה יורד חיות הבשר והיין שבקרבו ונכלל לפי שעה ברע גמור שבשלש קליפות הטמאות וגופו נעשה להן לבוש ומרכבה לפי שעה עד אשר ישוב האדם ויחזור לעבודת ה׳ ולתורתו כי לפי

שהיה

as the meat and wine were *kasher*, they have the power to revert and ascend with him when he returns to the service of G–d. This is implied in the terms "permissibility" and "permitted" (*mutar*),[9] that is to say, that which is not tied and bound by the power of the "extraneous forces"[10] preventing it from returning and ascending to G–d. Nevertheless, a trace [of the evil] remains in the body. Therefore the body must undergo the "Purgatory of the grave," as will be explained later.[11]

So, too, with regard to the vitality of the drops of semen emitted from the body with animal lust, by him who has not conducted himself in a saintly manner during intimacy with his wife in her state of purity.[12]

Such is not the case, however, with forbidden foods and coition, which derive from the three *kelipot* that are entirely unclean. These are tied and bound by the Extraneous Forces for ever, and are not released until the day comes when death will be swallowed up for ever, as is written: "And I will cause the unclean spirit to pass from the land;"[13] or until the sinner repents to such an extent that his premeditated sins become transmuted into veritable merits, which is achieved through "repentance out of love," coming from the depths of the heart, with great love and fervour, and from a soul passionately desiring to cleave to the blessed G–d, and thirsting for G–d like a parched desert soil. For inasmuch as his soul had been in a barren wilderness, and in the shadow of death, which is the *sitra achra*, and infinitely removed from the light of the Divine Countenance, his soul now thirsts [for G–d] even more than the souls of the righteous, as our Sages say: "In the place where penitents stand, not even the perfectly righteous can stand."[14] It is concerning the repentance out of such great love that they have said: "The penitent's premeditated sins become, in his case, like virtues,"[15] since thereby he has attained to this great love.[16]

However, repentance that does not come from such love, even though it be true repentance, and G–d will pardon him, nevertheless his sins are not transformed into merits, and they are not completely released from the *kelipah*, until the end of time, when death will be swallowed up for ever.

●▲ Yet the vitality which is in the drops of semen that issue wastefully, even though it has been degraded and incorporated in the three unclean *kelipot*, nevertheless it can ascend from there by means of true repentance and intense *kavanah*[17] during the recital of the *Shema* at bedtime, as is known from our master, Rabbi Isaac Luria, of blessed memory, and is implied in the Talmudic saying: "He who recites the *Shema* at bedtime is as if he held a double-edged sword, . . ."[18] wherewith to slay the bodies of the Extraneous Forces that have become garments

---

[9] *The Hebrew term* מותר *literally means "released."* [10] *Another term for* kelipot *and* sitra achra. [11] *Ch. 8.* [12] *The entire sentence does not appear in our published text, but has been inserted here from a reliable manuscript in the Schneersohn Library. It has also been incorporated into the Yiddish edition of the* Tanya, *published by the Kehot Publication Society (Brooklyn, N.Y., 1956).* [13] Zechariah *13:2.* [14] Berachot *34b.* [15] Rosh Hashanah *29a.* [16] *This religious experience is unknown to the perfect* tzaddik *who never sinned, and consequently has never experienced the remorse and yearning of a repentant soul. This does not mean, however, that the* tzaddik *cannot experience any kind of* teshuvah, *for in a broader and* truer *sense*

● 6 Teveth ▲ *10 Teveth*

שהיה בשר היתר ויין כשר לכך יכולים לחזור ולעלות עמו בשובו לעבודת ה' שזהו לשון היתר ומותר כלומר שאינו קשור ואסור בידי החיצונים שלא יוכל לחזור ולעלות לה' רק שהרשימו ממנו נשאר בגוף ועל כן צריך הגוף לחיבוט הקבר כמ"ש לקמן מה שאין כן במאכלות אסורות וביאות אסורות שהן משלש קליפות הטמאות לגמרי הם אסורים וקשורים בידי החיצונים לעולם ואין עולים משם עד כי יבא יומם ויבולע המות לנצח כמ"ש ואת רוח הטומאה אעביר מן הארץ או עד שיעשה תשובה גדולה כל כך שזדונות נעשו לו כזכיות ממש שהיא תשובה מאהבה מעומקא דלבא באהבה רבה וחשיקה ונפש שוקקה לדבקה בו ית' וצמאה נפשו לה' כארץ עיפה וציה להיות כי עד הנה היתה נפשו בארץ ציה וצלמות היא הסטרא אחרא ורחוקה מאור פני ה' בתכלית ולזאת צמאה נפשו ביתר עז מצמאון נפשות הצדיקים כמאמרם ז"ל במקום שבעלי תשובה עומדים כו' ועל תשובה מאהבה רבה זו אמרו שזדונות נעשו לו כזכיות הואיל ועל ידי זה בא לאהבה רבה זו אבל תשובה שלא מאהבה זו אף שהיא תשובה נכונה וה' יסלח לו מכל מקום לא נעשו לו כזכיות ואין עולים מהקליפה לגמרי עד עת קץ שיבולע המות לנצח. אך החיות שבטפות זרע שיצאו ממנו לבטלה אף שירדה ונכללה בשלש קליפות הטמאות הרי זו עולה משם בתשובה נכונה ובכוונה עצומה בקריאת שמע שעל המטה כנודע מהאר"י ז"ל ומרומז בגמרא כל הקורא קריאת שמע על מטתו כאלו אוחז חרב של שתי פיות כו' להרוג גופות החיצונים שנעשו לבוש

לחיות

(and as the Hebrew term indicates) it means "return" to the Source, which is of infinite scope. (Cf. Likutei Torah, *beg.* Haazinu.*)* [17] *"Intention," i.e. concentration and devotion in prayer, study or the performance of a ritual precept. Cf.* infra., *chs. 38, 40, and 41 for an elaboration of the term.* [18] Berachot *5a.*

for the vitality which is in the drops [of semen], so that this vitality may ascend, as is known to those who are familiar with the Esoteric Wisdom. Therefore the sin of wasteful emission of semen is not mentioned in the Torah among the list of forbidden coitions, although it is even more heinous than they; and this sin is greater because of the enormity and abundance of the uncleanness and of the *kelipot* which he begets and multiplies to an exceedingly great extent through wasteful emission of semen, even more than through forbidden coitions. Except that in the case of forbidden coitions he contributes strength and vitality to a most unclean *kelipah*, from which he is powerless to bring up the vitality by means of repentance,

Note: The reason being that this vitality has been absorbed by the "female" element of the kelipah, *which receives and absorbs the vitality from the holiness. Not so with wasteful emission of semen, where there is obviously no female element of* kelipah, *and only its powers and forces provide the garments for the vitality of the [wasteful] semen, as is known to those familiar with the Esoteric Wisdom.*

unless he repents with such great love, that his wilful wrongs are transformed into merits.

From the above, one may understand the comment of our Sages: "Which is 'a fault that cannot be rectified?'[19]—Having incestuous intercourse and giving birth to a bastard."[20] For in such a case, even though the sinner undertakes such great repentance, he cannot cause the [newly created] vitality to ascend to Holiness, since it has already descended into this world and has been clothed in a body of flesh and blood.

●▲ Chapter 8

There is an additional aspect in the matter of forbidden foods. The reason they are called *issur* ["chained"] is that even in the case of one who has unwittingly eaten a forbidden food intending it to give him strength to serve G–d by the energy of it, and he has, moreover, actually carried out his intention, having both studied and prayed with the energy of that food, nevertheless the vitality contained therein does not ascend and become clothed in the words of the Torah or prayer, as is the case with permitted foods, by reason of its being held captive in the power of the *sitra achra* of the three unclean *kelipot.* This is so even when the prohibition is a Rabbinic enactment, for the words of the Scribes are even more stringent than the words of the Torah, and so forth.[1]

Therefore, also the evil impulse (*yetzer hara*) and the force that strains after forbidden things is a demon of non-Jewish demons, which is the evil impulse of the nations

---

[19] Eccl. *1:15.* [20] *Chagigah* 9a.

Chapter 8
[1] Mishnah, Sanhedrin *11:3;* Bamidbar Rabba *14:12, etc.*

לחיות שבטפות ועולה החיות מהם כידוע לי"ח. ולכן לא הוזכר עון זרע לבטלה בתורה בכלל ביאות אסורות אף שחמור מהן וגדול עונו בבחי' הגדלות ורבוי הטומאה והקליפות שמוליד ומרבה במאד מאד בהוצאת זרע לבטלה יותר מביאות אסורות רק שבביאות אסורות מוסיף כח וחיות בקליפה טמאה ביותר עד שאינו יכול להעלות משם החיות בתשובה* אא"כ יעשה תשובה מאהבה רבה כל כך עד שזדונות נעשו לו כזכיות ובזה יובן מאמר רז"ל איזהו מעוות שלא יוכל לתקון זה שבא על הערוה והוליד ממזר שאז גם אם יעשה תשובה גדולה כל כך אי אפשר לו להעלות החיות לקדושה מאחר שכבר ירדה לעולם הזה ונתלבשה בגוף בשר ודם:

הגה"ה

(מפני שנקלטה ביסוד דנוקבא דקליפה המקבלת וקולטת החיות מהקדושה משא"כ בזרע לבטלה שאין שם בחי' נוקבא דקליפה רק שכחותיה וחיילותיה מלבישים לחיות שבטפות כידוע לי"ח):

פרק ח ועוד זאת במאכלות אסורות שלכך נקראים בשם איסור מפני שאף מי שאכל מאכל איסור בלא הודע לשם שמים לעבוד ה' בכח אכילה ההיא וגם פעל ועשה כן וקרא והתפלל בכח אכילה ההיא אין החיות שבה עולה ומתלבשת בתיבות התורה והתפלה כמו ההיתר מפני איסורה בידי הס"א משלש קליפות הטמאות ואפי' הוא איסור דרבנן שחמורים דברי סופרים יותר מדברי תורה כו' ולכן גם היצר הרע וכח המתאוה לדברים האסורים הוא שד משדין נוכראין שהוא יצר הרע של אומות עו"ג שנפשותיהם

whose souls are derived from the three unclean *kelipot.* On the other hand, the evil impulse and the craving force after permissible things to satisfy an appetite is a demon of the Jewish demons,[2] for it can be reverted to holiness, as is explained above.[3] Nevertheless, before it has reverted to holiness it is *sitra achra* and *kelipah,* and even afterwards a trace of it remains attached to the body, since from each item of food and drink are immediately formed blood and flesh of his flesh. That is why the body must undergo the "Purgatory of the grave,"[4] in order to cleanse it and purify it of its uncleanness which it had received from the enjoyment of mundane things and pleasures, which are derived from the uncleanness of the *kelipat nogah* and of the Jewish demons; only one who had derived no enjoyment from this world all his life, as was the case with our Saintly Master [Rabbi Judah the Prince], is spared this.

• As for innocent idle chatter, such as in the case of an ignoramus who cannot study, he must undergo a cleansing of his soul, to rid it of the uncleanness of this *kelipah,* through its being rolled in "The hollow of a sling,"[5] as is stated in the *Zohar, Parshat Beshallach,* p. 59.[6] But with regard to forbidden speech, such as scoffing and slander and the like, which stem from the three completely unclean *kelipot,* the hollow of a sling (alone) does not suffice to cleanse and remove the uncleanness of the soul, but it must descend into *Gehinnom* [Purgatory].

So, too, he who is able to engage in the Torah, but occupies himself instead with frivolous things, the hollow of a sling cannot itself effectively scour and cleanse his soul, but severe penalties are meted out for neglect of the Torah in particular, apart from the general retribution for the neglect of a positive commandment through indolence, namely, in the Purgatory of Snow,[7] as is explained elsewhere.[8] Likewise, he who occupies himself with the sciences of the nations of the world is included among those who waste their time in profane matters, insofar as the sin of neglecting the Torah is concerned, as is explained in the Laws Concerning Study of the Torah.[9] Moreover, the uncleanness of the science of the nations is greater than that of profane speech, for the latter informs and defiles only the *middot* which emanate from the element of the holy *ruach* within his divine soul with the contamination of the *kelipat nogah* that is contained in profane speech which is derived from the element of the evil *ruach* of this *kelipah*

[2] *Cf.* Zohar *III, 253a; 277a f.* [3] *Ch. 7.* [4] Chibbut ha-Kever. *Cf.* Zohar *II, 151a, and especially R. Chayim Vital, end of* Sefer ha-Gilgulim, *and* Sefer ha-Kavanot, *p. 55b f.* [5] *Cf.* I Sam. *25:29: "And the souls of thine enemies, them shall he sling out, as out of the hollow of a sling," eschatologically interpreted in* Shabbat *152b.* [6] Zohar *II, p. 59a.* [7] *The Purgatory, where the soul is cleansed of the "stains" acquired during lifetime so that it could then enter the* Gan Eden *(Paradise) in the presence of the Divine Glory, operates on the principle of "measure for measure," or in kind. Thus offences of commission caused by passion and lust are cleansed in a "stream of fire," while those of omission, due to indolence and coolness, are cleansed in a "Gehenna of Snow,"*

שנפשותיהם משלש קליפות הטמאות משא"כ היצה"ר וכח המתאוה לדברים המותרים למלאת תאותו הוא שד משדין יהודאין לפי שיכול לחזור לקדושה כדלעיל. אך מ"מ קודם שחזר לקדושה הוא ס"א וקליפה וגם אח"כ הרשימו ממנו נשאר דבוק בגוף להיות כי מכל מאכל ומשקה נעשה תיכף דם ובשר מבשרו ולכן צריך הגוף לחיבוט הקבר לנקותו ולטהרו מטומאתו שקיבל בהנאת עולם הזה ותענוגיו מטומאת קליפת נוגה ושדין יהודאין אא"כ מי שלא נהנה מעוה"ז כל ימיו כרבינו הקדוש. ועל דברים בטלים בהיתר כגון ע"ה שאינו יכול ללמוד צריך לטהר נפשו מטומאה זו דקליפה זו ע"י גלגולה בכף הקלע כמ"ש בזהר פ' בשלח דף נ"ט. אבל לדיבורים אסורים כמו ליצנות ולשון הרע וכיוצא בהם שהן משלש קליפות הטמאות לגמרי אין כף הקלע [לבדו] מועיל לטהר ולהעביר טומאתו מהנפש רק צריכה לירד לגיהנם. וכן מי שאפשר לו לעסוק בתורה ועוסק בדברים בטלים אין כף הקלע לבדו מועיל לנפשו למרקה ולזככה רק עונשים חמורים שמענישים על ביטול תורה בפרטות מלבד עונש הכללי לכל ביטול מ"ע מחמת עצלות בגיהנם של שלג כמבואר במ"א וכן העוסק בחכמות אומות עובדי גלולים בכלל דברים בטלים יחשב לענין עון ביטול תורה כמ"ש בהלכות תלמוד תורה ועוד זאת יתרה טומאתה של חכמת האומות עובדי גלולים על טומאת דברים בטלים שאינו מלביש ומטמא רק המדות מיסוד הרוח הקדוש שבנפשו האלהית בטומאת קליפת נוגה שבדברים בטלים הבאים מיסוד הרוח הרע שבקליפה

זו

etc. [8] *Rabbi Isaac Luria,* Likutei Torah, Shemot. *Cf. also* Zohar *I, 62b; 237b; II, 150a/b.* [9] *The first work of Rabbi Schneur Zalman was a treatise on the* Laws Concerning the Study of the Torah (Hilchot Talmud Torah), *first published in Shklov, 1794, and subsequently incorporated in his* Shulchan Aruch.

in his animal soul, as mentioned above;[10] yet he does not defile the [intellectual] faculties of ChaBaD in his soul, for they are but words of foolishness and ignorance, since even fools and ignoramuses can speak that way. Not so in the case of the nations' science whereby he clothes and defiles the intellectual faculties of ChaBaD in his divine soul with the contamination of the *kelipat nogah* contained in those sciences, whither they have fallen through the "shattering of the vessels" out of the so-called "hinder part" of *Chochmah* of *Kedushah*, as is known to those familiar with the Esoteric Wisdom. Unless he employs [these sciences] as a useful instrument, viz., as a means of a more affluent livelihood to be able to serve G–d, or knows how to apply them in the service of G–d and His Torah. This is the reason why Maimonides and Nachmanides, of blessed memory, and their adherents, engaged in them.

●▲ Chapter 9

The abode[1] of the animal soul (*nefesh habahamit*) derived from the *kelipat nogah* in every Jew, is in the heart, in the left ventricle that is filled with blood. It is written, "For the blood is the *nefesh*."[2] Hence all lusts and boasting and anger and similar passions are in the heart, and from the heart they spread throughout the whole body, rising also to the brain in the head, so as to think and meditate about them and become cunning in them,[3] just as the blood has its source in the heart and from the heart it circulates into every limb, rising also to the brain in the head.

But the abode of the divine soul is in the brains[4] that are in the head, and from there it extends to all the limbs; and also in the heart, in the right ventricle wherein there is no blood, as is written, "The heart of the wise man is on his right."[5] It is [the source of] man's fervent love towards G–d which, like flaming coals, flares up in the heart of discerning men who understand and reflect, with the [faculty of] knowledge[6] of their brain, on matters that arouse this love;[7] also [of] the gladness of the heart in the beauty of G–d and the majesty of His glory [which is aroused] when the eyes of the wise man, that are in his head,[8] i.e. in the brain harbouring his wisdom and understanding, gaze at the glory of the King and beauty of His greatness that are unfathomable and without end or limit, as explained elsewhere; as also the other holy affections (*middot*) in the heart originate from ChaBaD [wisdom, understanding, knowledge] in the brains.

●▲ It is written, however,

---

[10] *Ch. 1.*

Chapter 9
[1] *In the sense of its principal area of manifestation.* [2] Deut. *12:23. Cf.* Supra, *end of ch. 1* Nefesh *means life, and also "desire"* (Gen. *23:8*). [3] *The animal soul is mainly moved by passion, while the intelligence reacts to it.* [4] *The divine soul is essentially intellective.* [5] Eccl. *10:2.* [6] *For the term* da'at *("knowledge"), see end ch. 3, above.* [7] *In the divine soul the relation between mind and heart is reversed from that of the animal soul. (See n. 3, above.)* [8] *Comp.* Eccl. *2:14.*

זו בנפשו הבהמית כדלעיל ולא בחי' חב"ד שבנפשו מאחר שהם דברי שטות ובורות שגם השוטים וע"ה יכולים לדבר כן. משא"כ בחכמת האומות עובדי גלולים הוא מלביש ומטמא בחי' חב"ד שבנפשו האלהית בטומאת קליפת נוגה שבחכמות אלו שנפלו שמה בשבירת הכלי' מבחי' אחוריים של חכמה דקדושה כידוע ליודעי חן אלא א"כ עושה אותן קרדום לחתוך בהן דהיינו כדי להתפרנס מהן בריוח לעבוד ה' או שיודע להשתמש בהן לעבודת ה' או לתורתו וזהו טעמו של הרמב"ם ורמב"ן ז"ל וסיעתן שעסקו בהן:

פרק ט והנה מקום משכן נפש הבהמית שמקליפת נוגה בכל איש ישראל הוא בלב בחלל שמאלי שהוא מלא דם וכתיב כי הדם הוא הנפש ולכן כל התאות והתפארות וכעס ודומיהן הן בלב ומהלב הן מתפשטות בכל הגוף וגם עולה למוח שבראש לחשב ולהרהר בהן ולהתחכם בהן כמו שהדם מקורו בלב ומהלב מתפשט לכל האברים וגם עולה להמוח שבראש. אך מקום משכן נפש האלהית הוא במוחין שבראש ומשם מתפשטת לכל האברים וגם בלב בחלל הימני שאין בו דם וכמ"ש לב חכם לימינו והיא אהבת ה' כרשפי שלהבת מתלהבת בלב משכילים המבינים ומתבוננים בדעתם אשר במוחם בדברים המעוררים את האהבה. וכן שמחת לבב בתפארת ה' והדר גאונו כאשר עיני החכם אשר בראשו במוח חכמתו ובינתו מסתכלים ביקרא דמלכא ותפארת גדולתו עד אין חקר ואין סוף ותכלית כמבואר במקום אחר וכן שאר מדות קדושות שבלב הן מחב"ד שבמוחין. אך הנה כתיב ולאום

"One nation shall prevail over the other nation."[9] The body is called a "small city."[10] Just as two kings wage war over a town, which each wishes to capture and rule, that is to say, to dominate its inhabitants according to his will, so that they obey him in all that he decrees for them, so do the two souls—the Divine and the vitalising animal soul that comes from the *kelipah*—wage war against each other over the body and all its limbs. It is the desire and will of the Divine soul that she alone rule over the person and direct him, and that all his limbs should obey her and surrender themselves completely to her and become a vehicle[11] for her, as well as a robe [instrument] for her ten faculties and three garments mentioned above,[12] all of which should pervade the organs of the body, and the entire body should be permeated with them alone, to the exclusion of any alien influence, G–d forbid. That is to say, that the three brains[13] that are in the head shall be permeated with ChaBaD of the Divine soul, namely, the wisdom of G–d and the understanding of Him, by pondering on His unfathomable and infinite greatness; and from them shall be born, through the *daat* (knowledge),[14] awe in his mind and dread of G–d in his heart,[15] as well as love of G–d that shall flare up like a glowing fire in his heart, like flaming coals, so that his soul shall yearn and long, with passion and desire, to cleave to the blessed *En Sof*, with his whole heart, soul and might, from the very depths of the right ventricle of the heart. The latter would be so thoroughly permeated with love to overflowing, as to inundate the left side as well, to the extent of subduing the *sitra achra* with its element of the "evil waters," namely, the lust stemming from *kelipat nogah*, changing it and transforming it from seeking the pleasures of this world to the love of G–d. Thus it is written, "'With all thine heart'[16]—with both your natures."[17] That is to say, that the person shall steadily rise to attain to the degree of "abundant love," a supreme affection surpassing that of "ardent love" that is comparable to burning coals.[18] This ▲ is what is called in Scripture "love of delights,"[19] which is the experience of delight in G–dliness, of the nature of the world to come. This delight is in the brain of wisdom, in the intellectual pleasure of comprehending and knowing G–d, to the extent that one's intellect and wisdom can grasp [Him]. This is the element of "water," and "seed," i.e., light that is sown

---

[9] Gen. *25:23*. [10] Eccl. *9:14*; Nedarim *32b*. [11] *An instrument without independent will.* [12] *Chs. 3 and 4.* [13] *The three intellectual faculties* chochmah, binah *and* da'at—*ChaBaD—have their corresponding physical brains.* [14] *See note 6, above.* [15] *Awe is regarded as a preliminary to love. There is, however, a higher category of reverence which can be attained only after having attained love. See chs. 23, 40–43,* infra. [16] Deut. *6:5*. [17] Berachot *54a*. [18] *The author distinguishes various degrees of love:* ahavah azah *("ardent" love)—a passionate love, and* ahavah rabbah *("great" love) or* ahavah beta'anugim *("delightful" love)—a serene love of fulfilment. The first is likened to a burning flame; the second—to*

ולאום מלאום יאמץ כי הגוף נקרא עיר קטנה וכמו
ששני מלכים נלחמים על עיר אחת שכל אחד רוצה
לכבשה ולמלוך עליה דהיינו להנהיג יושביה כרצונו
ושיהיו סרים למשמעתו בכל אשר יגזור עליהם. כך
שתי הנפשות האלהית והחיונית הבהמית שמהקליפה
נלחמות זו עם זו על הגוף וכל אבריו שהאלהית חפצה
ורצונה שתהא היא לבדה המושלת עליו ומנהיגתו וכל
האברים יהיו סרים למשמעתה ובטלים אצלה לגמרי
ומרכבה אליה ויהיו לבוש לעשר בחינותיה וג' לבושיה
הנ"ל שיתלבשו כולם באברי הגוף ויהיה הגוף כולו
מלא מהם לבדם ולא יעבור זר בתוכם ח"ו דהיינו תלת
מוחין שבראש יהיו ממולאים מחב"ד שבנפש האלהית
שהיא חכמת ה' ובינתו להתבונן בגדולתו אשר עד
אין חקר ואין סוף ולהוליד מהן על ידי הדעת היראה
במוחו ופחד ה' בלבו ואהבת ה' כאש בוערה בלבו
כרשפי שלהבת להיות נכספה וגם כלתה נפשו בחשיקה
וחפיצה לדבקה בו בא"ס ב"ה בכל לב ונפש ומאד
מעומקא דלבא שבחלל הימני שיהיה תוכו רצוף אהבה
מלא וגדוש עד שתתפשט גם לחלל השמאלי לאכפיא
לס"א יסוד המים הרעים שבה שהיא התאוה שמקליפת
נוגה לשנותה ולהפכה מתענוגי עולם הזה לאהבת ה'
כמ"ש בכל לבבך בשני יצריך והיינו שיעלה ויבא
ויגיע למדרגת אהבה רבה וחיבה יתרה ממדרגת
אהבה עזה כרשפי אש והיא הנקראת בכתוב אהבה
בתענוגים להתענג על ה' מעין עולם הבא והענג הוא
במוח חכמה ושכל המתענג בהשכלת ה' וידיעתו כפי
השגת שכלו וחכמתו והוא בחי' המים וזרע אור זרוע
שבקדושת

---

calm waters. These and other distinctions of love are later discussed at greater length. Cf. chs. 15, 16, 18, 40, 41, 46, 49. [19] Song of Songs *7:7.*

in the holiness of the divine soul that converts to good the element of "water" in the animal soul, from which the lust for mundane pleasures had been previously derived.[20]

Thus it is written in *Etz Chayim*, Portal 50, ch. 3, on the authority of the *Zohar*, that the evil is converted into, and becomes, completely good, like the good nature itself, through the shedding of the soiled garments, the pleasures of this world, in which it had been clothed.

So, too, shall the other *middot* in the heart, the offshoots of awe and love, be dedicated to G–d alone; and the faculty of speech that is in his mouth, and the thought that is in his mind, shall be entirely and solely the instruments of the "garments" of thought and speech of the divine soul alone, namely, meditation on G–d and His Torah, which shall be the theme of his speech throughout the day, his mouth ceaselessly studying [it]; and the faculty of action centered in his hands, as also in the rest of the 248 organs, shall function exclusively in the performance of the commandments, which is the third garment of the divine soul.

However, the desire of the animal soul which is derived from the *kelipah* is the very opposite—and it is for the good of man, that he may prevail over her and vanquish her, as in the parable of the harlot in the holy *Zohar*.[21]

•▲ *Chapter 10*

Behold, when a person fortifies his divine soul and wages war against his animal soul to such an extent that he expels and eradicates its evil from the left part—as is written, "And thou shalt root out the evil from within you"[1]—yet the evil is not actually converted to goodness, he is called "Incompletely righteous," or "A righteous man who suffers."[2] That is to say, there still lingers in him a fragment of wickedness in the left part, except that it is subjugated and nullified by the good, because of the former's minuteness. Hence he imagines that he has driven it out and it has quite disappeared. In truth, however, had all the evil in him entirely departed and disappeared, it would have been converted into actual goodness.

The explanation of the matter is that "A completely righteous man," in whom the evil has been converted to goodness, and who is consequently called "A righteous man who prospers,"[3] has completely divested himself of the filthy garments of evil. That is to say, he utterly despises the pleasures of this world, finding no enjoyment in human pleasures

[20] *Thus the divine soul is conceived as being potentially capable of not only suppressing the evil impulse, but also completely "sublimating" it.* [21] *See also end of ch. 29. The parable: A king desired to test the moral strength of his only son. He had a most charming and clever woman brought before him. Explaining to her the purpose of the test, he ordered her to try her best to seduce the crown-prince. For the test to be valid, the "harlot" had to use all her charms and guile, without betraying her mission in the slightest way. Any imperfection on her part would mean disobedience and failure of her mission. While the "harlot" uses all her seductive powers, she inwardly desires that the crown-prince should not succumb to them. Cf.* Zohar *II, p. 163a.*

שבקדושת נפש האלהית המהפכת לטוב את בחי'
המים שבנפש הבהמית שמהם באו תאות תענוגי
עוה"ז מתחלה וכמ"ש בע"ח שער נ' פרק ג' בשם הזהר
שהרע נהפך להיות טוב גמור כמו יצר טוב ממש
בהסיר הבגדים הצואים ממנו שהם תענוגי עוה"ז שהוא
מלובש בהם וכן שאר כל המדות שבלב שהן ענפי
היראה והאהבה יהיו לה' לבדו וכל כח הדבור שבפה
והמחשבה שבמוח יהיו ממולאים מן לבושי המחשבה
והדבור של נפש האלהית לבדה שהן מחשבת ה'
ותורתו להיות שיחתו כל היום לא פסיק פומיה מגירסא
וכח המעשיי שבידי' ושאר רמ"ח אבריו יהיה במעשה
המצות לבד שהוא לבוש השלישי של נפש האלהית
אך נפש הבהמית שמהקליפה רצונה להפך ממש
לטובת האדם שיתגבר עליה וינצחנה כמשל הזונה
שבזה"ק:

פרק י והנה כשהאדם מגביר נפשו האלהית ונלחם כל כך עם הבהמית עד
שמגרש ומבער הרע שבה מחלל השמאלי כמ"ש
ובערת הרע מקרבך ואין הרע נהפך לטוב ממש נקרא
צדיק שאינו גמור וצדיק ורע לו דהיינו שיש בו עדיין
מעט מזער רע בחלל השמאלי אלא שכפוף ובטל לטוב
מחמת מיעוטו ולכן נדמה לו כי ויגרשהו וילך לו כולו
לגמרי אבל באמת אלו חלף והלך לו לגמרי כל הרע שבו
היה נהפך לטוב ממש. וביאור הענין כי הנה צדיק גמור
שנהפך הרע שלו לטוב ולכן נקרא צדיק וטוב לו הוא
ע"י הסרת הבגדים הצואים לגמרי מהרע דהיינו למאוס
מאד בתענוגי עוה"ז להתענג בם בתענוגות בני אדם
למלאת

This parable is intended to explain the ultimate function of the animal soul, with its inherent evil and complete license and independence. Yet although the forces of evil must be real enough for the purpose of which they have been created, their origin and purpose is rooted in good, and they can, in fact, be so converted. Herein lies the underlying principle of the problem of evil.

Chapter 10
[1] Deut. *21:21.* [2] צדיק ורע לו —*see n. 7, ch. 1.* [3] צדיק וטוב לו —*i.e. "possessing (only) good."*

of merely gratifying the physical appetites, instead of [seeking] the service of G-d, inasmuch as they are derived from and originate in the *kelipah* and *sitra achra*; for whatever is of the *sitra achra* is hated by the perfectly righteous man with an absolute hatred, by reason of his great love of G-d and of His Holiness with profuse affection and delight and superlative devotion, as is stated above.[4] For they are antithetical one to the other. Thus it is written, "I hate them with absolute hatred: I count them mine enemies. Search me, [O G-d,] and know my heart. . . ."[5] Hence, according to the abundance of the love toward G-d, so is the extent of the hatred towards the *sitra achra*, and the utter contempt of evil, for contempt is as much the opposite of real love as is hatred.

▲ The "Incompletely righteous" is he who does not hate the *sitra achra* with an absolute hatred; therefore he does not also absolutely abhor evil. And as long as the hatred and scorn of evil are not absolute, there must remain some vestige of love and pleasure in it, and the fouled garments have not entirely and absolutely been shed; therefore the evil has not actually been converted to goodness, since it still has some hold in the filthy garments, except that it is nullified because of its minute quantity and is accounted as nothing. Therefore such a person is called a righteous man, in whom the evil is subjugated and surrendered to him. Accordingly, his love of G-d is also not perfect, with the result that he is called "incompletely righteous."

• Now, this grade is subdivided into myriads of degrees in respect of the quality of the minute evil remaining [in him] from any of the four evil elements, as well as in relation to its proportionate abnegation by reason of its minuteness, such as, by way of example, one in sixty, or in a thousand, or in ten thousand, and the like.[6] Such are the gradations of the numerous righteous men who are to be found in every generation, as mentioned in the Gemara, viz., "Eighteen thousand righteous men stand before the Holy One, blessed be He."[7]

However, it is with regard to the superior quality of the "completely righteous," that Rabbi Simeon ben Yochai said: "I have seen superior men (*benei aliyah*), and their numbers are few. . . ."[8] The reason for their title of "superior men"[9] is that they convert evil and make it ascend to holiness, as is written in the *Zohar*, in the Introduction,[10] that when Rabbi Chiyya wished to ascend to the *hechal* (heavenly shrine) of Rabbi Simeon ben Yochai, he heard a voice come out and say, "Which of you, before coming here, has converted darkness into light

---

[4] *Ch. 9.* [5] Ps. *139:22, 23.* [6] *In* Halachah, *in cases of admixture of a non-kosher element into kosher articles of human consumption (solids or liquids), the non-kosher element is deemed non-existent if its proportion is less than 1/60th, 1/100th, etc., as the case may be. Cf., e.g.* Chullin *97b f.* [7] Sukkah *45b;* Sanhedrin *97b.* [8] Ibid. [9] *Literally, "men of ascent"*—בני עליה. [10] Zohar *I, 4a.*

למלאת תאות הגוף בלבד ולא לעבודת ה׳ מפני היותם נמשכים ונשפעים מהקליפה וס״א וכל מה שהוא מהס״א הצדיק גמור הוא שונאו בתכלית השנאה מחמת גודל אהבתו לה׳ וקדושתו באהבה רבה בתענוגים וחיבה יתרה הנ״ל כי הם זה לעומת זה כדכתיב תכלית שנאה שנאתים לאויבים היו לי חקרני ודע לבבי וגו׳ וכפי ערך גודל האהבה לה׳ כך ערך גודל השנאה לס״א והמיאוס ברע בתכלית כי המיאוס הוא הפך האהבה ממש כמו השנאה. וצדיק שאינו גמור הוא שאינו שונא הס״א בתכלית השנאה ולכן אינו מואס ג״כ ברע בתכלית וכל שאין השנאה והמיאוס בתכלית ע״כ נשאר איזה שמץ אהבה ותענוג לשם ולא הוסרו הבגדים הצואים לגמרי מכל וכל ולכן לא נהפך לטוב ממש מאחר שיש לו איזה אחיזה עדיין בבגדים הצואים אלא שהוא בטל במיעוטו וכלא חשיב ולכן נקרא צדיק ורע כפוף ובטל לו. ועל כן גם אהבתו לה׳ אינו בתכלית ולכן נקרא צדיק שאינו גמור. והנה מדרגה זו מתחלקת לרבבות מדרגות בענין בחי׳ מיעוט הרע הנשאר מאחת מארבע יסודות הרעים ובענין ביטולו במיעוטו בששים עד״מ או באלף ורבבה וכיוצא עד״מ והן הם בחי׳ צדיקים הרבים שבכל הדורות כדאיתא בגמ׳ דתמניסר אלפי צדיקי קיימי קמי׳ הקב״ה אך על מעלת צדיק גמור הוא שאמר רשב״י ראיתי בני עליה והם מועטים כו׳ שלכן נקראים בני עליה שמהפכין הרע ומעלים אותו לקדושה כדאיתא בזהר בהקדמה שכשרצה רבי חייא לעלות להיכל ר״ש בן יוחאי שמע קלא נפיק ואמר מאן מנכון די חשוכא מהפכן לנהורא

וטעמין

and bitter taste into sweetness? [Otherwise] do not approach here," and so forth. ▲ A further explanation of the title "superior men" is that their service in the category of "do good," in the fulfillment of the Torah and its commandments, is for the sake of the Above, the ultimate of the highest degrees, and not merely in order to attach themselves to G–d so as to quench the thirst of their [own] soul, which thirsts for G–d, as is written, "Ho, everyone that thirsteth, come ye to the waters,"[11] as is explained elsewhere. Rather [is their service] as explained in *Tikunei Zohar*: "Who is kind?—He who conducts himself with benevolence towards his Creator—towards His nest,[12] uniting the Holy One, blessed be He, and His *Shechinah* within those who dwell in the nethermost worlds."[13] As also explained in *Ra'aya Mehemna* on *Parshat Tetze*: "In the manner of a son who ingratiates himself with his father and mother, whom he loves more than his own body and soul . . . and is prepared to sacrifice his own life for them, to redeem them, . . ."[14] and as is explained elsewhere.[15]

(And both interpretations are complementary, for through acts of refinement of the good out of the *nogah*, one elevates the "feminine waters"[16] causing "supernal unions" to bring down the "masculine waters"[17] which are the flow of [Divine] kindness contained in each of the 248 positive precepts, all of which are in the nature of kindness and "masculine waters," that is to say, the flow of holiness of His blessed Divinity from above downward, to be clothed in those who live in the lower worlds, as explained elsewhere.)

●▲ *Chapter 11*

"One is the opposite of the other"[1]—the "wicked man who prospers" is antithetical to the "righteous man who suffers."[2] That is to say, the goodness that is in his divine soul which is in his brain and in the right part of his heart, is subservient to, and nullified by, the evil of the *kelipah* that is in the left part. This type, too, is subdivided into myriads of degrees which differ in respect of the extent and manner of the nullification and subservience of the good to the bad, G–d forbid.

There is the person in whom the said subservience and nullification are in a very minor way, and even these are not permanent or recurring at frequent intervals; but on rare occasions the evil prevails over the good and conquers the "small city," that is the body—yet not all of it, but only a part of it, subjecting it to its (evil's) discipline, to become a vehicle

---

[11] Isaiah 55:1. [12] *This homily is based on a play on the words* חסיד—חסד, קונו—קנו. *The text reads:* איזהו חסיד המתחסד עם קונו—עם קן דיליה, לייחדא קודשא בריך הוא ושכינתיה בתחתונים. [13] *Introduction to* Tikunei Zohar *1b. Cf.* Zohar *II, 114b; III, 222b; 281a.* [14] Zohar *III, 281a.* [15] *The absolute altruistic worshipper is not motivated by a desire to save his soul, or to gratify its longing for unity with the Deity, but by pure love and a desire to please G–d and make His presence felt everywhere.* [16] "*Male*" *and* "*female*" *are terms used in Kabbalah to denote* "*giver*" *and* "*recipient,*" *respectively.* "*Feminine waters*" *therefore denotes benevolent acts, self-inspired, rising from man to G–d, while* "*masculine waters*" *de-*

ומעמין מרירו למיתקא עד לא ייתון הכא וכו׳ : ועוד נקראים בני עליה מפני שגם עבודתם בבחי׳ ועשה טוב בקיום התורה ומצותיה הוא לצורך גבוה ומעלה מעלה עד רום המעלות ולא כדי לדבקה בו ית׳ בלבד לרוות צמאון נפשם הצמאה לה׳ כמ״ש הוי כל צמא לכו למים וכמ״ש במ״א אלא כדפירשו בתיקונים איזהו חסיד המתחסד עם קונו עם קן דיליה לייחדא קב״ה ושכינתי׳ בתחתונים וכמ״ש ברעי׳ מהימנא פ׳ תצא כברא דאשתדל בתר אבוי ואימיה דרחים לון יתיר מגרמיה ונפשיה ורוחיה וגשמתי׳ כו׳ ומסר גרמיה למיתה עלייהו למיפרק לון כו׳ וכמ״ש במ״א. [ושניהם עולים בקנה אחד כי ע״י הבירורים שמבררים מנוגה מעלים מיין נוקבין ונעשי׳ יחודים עליונים להוריד מיין דכורין שהם הם מימי החסדים שבכל מצוה ומצוה מרמ״ח מצות עשה שכולן הן בחי׳ חסדים ומיין דכורין דהיינו המשכת קדושת אלהותו ית׳ מלמעלה למטה להתלבש בתחתונים כמ״ש במ״א]:

פרק יא וזה לעומת זה רשע וטוב לו לעומת צדיק ורע לו דהיינו שהטוב שבנפשו האלהי׳ שבמוחו ובחלל הימני שבלבו כפוף ובטל לגבי הרע מהקליפה שבחלל השמאלי וזה מתחלק גם כן לרבבות מדרגות חלוקות בענין כמות ואיכות הביטול וכפיפת הטוב לרע ח״ו יש מי שהכפיפה והביטול אצלו מעט מזער ואף גם זאת אינו בתמידות ולא תדיר לפרקים קרובים אלא לעתים רחוקים מתגבר הרע על הטוב וכובש את העיר קטנה הוא הגוף אך לא כולו אלא מקצתו לבד שיהיה סר למשמעתו ונעשה לו מרכבה ולבוש

---

notes the flow of Divine influence and grace from G-d to man. [17] *See note, above.*

Chapter 11
[1] Eccl. *7:14.* [2] *Defined in the previous chapter.*

and a garment wherein one of the soul's three garments mentioned above[3] is clothed, namely, either in deed alone, in the commission of minor transgressions and not major ones, G-d forbid; or in speech alone, in the utterance of something that borders on slander and scoffing and the like; or in thought alone, in contemplations of sin, which are more serious than actual sin,[4] or even when he does not contemplate committing a sin but indulges in contemplation on the carnal union between male and female in general, whereby he is guilty of violating the admonition of the Torah, "Keep thee from every wicked thing,"[5] meaning that "One must not harbour impure fancies by day, . . ."[6] or, when it is a fitting time to study the Torah, but he turns his heart to vain things, as we have learned in the *Mishnah* in *Avot*, "He that wakes in the night [or that walks alone by the way], and turns his heart to vanity [is guilty against his own soul]."[7] For, by reason of any one of all these things, and their like, he is called wicked at such time that the evil in his *nefesh* prevails over him, clothing itself in his body, inducing it to sin and defiling it.

Presently, however, the good that is in his divine soul asserts itself, and he is filled with remorse, and he seeks pardon and forgiveness of G-d. Indeed, G-d will forgive him if he has repented with the appropriate penitence according to the counsel of our Sages, of blessed memory, namely, the three-fold division of atonement which is expounded by Rabbi Ishmael,[8] as is explained elsewhere.[9]

There is also the person in whom the wickedness prevails more strongly, and all three garments of evil clothe themselves in him, causing him to commit more heinous and more frequent sins. But intermittently he suffers remorse, and thoughts of repentance enter his mind, from the quality of good that is in his soul, that gathers strength now and then. However, he has not enough strength to vanquish the evil so as to rid himself entirely of his sins and be as one who confesses and abandons [his evil ways, once and for all]. Concerning such a person, the Rabbis, of blessed memory, have said, "The wicked are full of remorse."[10] These represent the majority of the wicked, in whose soul still lingers some good.

But he who never feels contrition, and in whose mind no thoughts of repentance at all ever enter, is called the "wicked who suffers,"[11] for the evil that is in his soul has alone remained in him, having so prevailed over the good that the latter has already departed from within him, standing aloof, so to speak, over him.[12] Therefore the Sages have said, "*Over* every ten Jews hovers the *Shechinah*."[13]

---

[3] *Ch. 4.* [4] Yoma *29a. Cf.* Chiddushei Aggadot *of Rabbi Shlomo Ideles,* ad loc.; Netivot Olam *of Rabbi Judah Loewe of Prague,* Netiv ha-Perishut, *ch. 2. The reason why "contemplation of sin is more serious than actual sin" is that of the three "garments" of the soul (thought, speech and act), thought is the innermost and closest to the soul; hence the contamination strikes closer to the core.* [5] Deut. *23:10.* [6] "*. . . so as not to defile himself by night*" (Ketuvot *46a*). [7] Avot *3:4.* [8] *End of Tractate* Yoma. [9] *Part III of the* Tanya: Igeret ha-Teshuva, *ch. 1.* [10] Nedarim *9b.* [11] רשע ורע לו *i.e. "possessing (only) evil."* [12] *Thus the good that is in the soul is in a state of "suspended animation" —paralysed, yet not destroyed. Hence,*

ולבוש להתלבש בו א׳ משלשה לבושיה הנ״ל דהיינו או במעשה לבד לעשות עבירות קלות ולא חמורות ח״ו או בדיבור לבד לדבר אבק לשון הרע וליצנות וכהאי גוונא או במחשבה לבד הרהורי עבירה הקשים מעבירה וגם אם אינו מהרהר בעבירה לעשותה אלא בענין זיווג זכר ונקיבה בעולם שעובר על אזהרת התורה ונשמרת מכל דבר רע שלא יהרהר ביום כו׳ או שהיא שעת הכושר לעסוק בתורה והוא מפנה לבו לבטלה כדתנן באבות הניעור בלילה כו׳ ומפנה לבו כו׳ שבאחת מכל אלה וכיוצא בהן נקרא רשע בעת ההיא שהרע שבנפשו גובר בו ומתלבש בגופו ומחטיאו ומטמאו ואח״כ גובר בו הטוב שבנפשו האלהי׳ ומתחרט ומבקש מחילה וסליחה מה׳ וה׳ יסלח לו אם שב בתשובה הראויה על פי עצת חכמינו ז״ל בשלשה חלוקי כפרה שהיה ר׳ ישמעאל דורש כו׳ כמ״ש במ״א. ויש מי שהרע גובר בו יותר ומתלבשי׳ בו כל שלשה לבושים של הרע ומחטיאו בעבירות חמורות יותר ובעתים קרובים יותר אך בינתיים מתחרט ובאים לו הרהורי תשובה מבחי׳ הטוב שבנפשו שמתגבר קצת בינתיים אלא שאין לו התגברות כל כך לנצח את הרע לפרוש מחטאיו לגמרי להיות מודה ועוזב ועל זה אמרו רז״ל רשעים מלאים חרטות שהם רוב הרשעים שיש בחי׳ טוב בנפשם עדיין. אך מי שאינו מתחרט לעולם ואין באים לו הרהורי תשובה כלל נקרא רשע ורע לו שהרע שבנפשו הוא לבדו נשאר בקרבו כי גבר כל כך על הטוב עד שנסתלק מקרבו ועומד בבחי׳ מקיף עליו מלמעלה ולכן ארז״ל כל בי עשרה שכינתא שריא:

והבינוני

even the "completely wicked" individual can, through a paramount effort, reactivate the good, and repent, for "the gates of repentance are not closed to anyone." [13] Sanhedrin *39a. That is to say, even if they are wicked, the* Shechinah *hovers over them.*

●▲ Chapter 12

The "intermediate man" (*benoni*) is he in whom evil never attains enough power to capture the "small city," so as to clothe itself in the body and make it sin. That is to say, the three "garments" of the animal soul, namely, thought, speech and act, originating in the *kelipah*, do not prevail within him over the divine soul to the extent of clothing themselves in the body—in the brain, in the mouth and in the other 248 parts[1]—thereby causing them to sin and defiling them, G–d forbid.

Only the three garments of the divine soul, they alone, are implemented in the body, being the thought, speech and act engaged in the 613 commandments of the Torah. He has never committed, nor ever will commit, any transgression; neither can the name "wicked" be applied to him even temporarily, or even for a moment, throughout his life.[2]

▲ However, the essence and being of the divine soul, which are its ten faculties,[3] do not constantly hold undisputed sovereignty and sway over the "small city," except at appropriate times, such as during the recital of the *Shema* or the *Amidah*, which is a time when the Supernal Intellect is in a sublime state;[4] and likewise below, this is a propitious time for every man, when he binds his ChaBaD (intellectual faculties) to G–d, to meditate deeply on the greatness of the blessed *En Sof*, and to arouse the burning love in the right part of his heart, to cleave to Him by virtue of the fulfillment of the Torah and its commandments out of love. This is the essential aspect of the *Shema*, the recital of which is enjoined by the Torah,[5] and of the blessings which precede and follow it, which are a Rabbineal enactment,[6] the latter being the preparation for the fulfillment of the recital of the *Shema*, as is explained elsewhere.[7] At such time the evil that is in the left part is subjected to, and nullified in, the goodness that is diffused in the right part, from the wisdom, understanding and knowledge (ChaBaD) in the brain, which are bound to the greatness of the blessed *En Sof*.[8]

However, after prayer, when the state of sublimity of the Intellect of the blessed *En Sof* departs, the evil in the left part reawakens, and he begins to feel a desire for the lusts of the world and its delights. ●▲Yet, because the evil has not the sole authority and dominion over the "city," it is unable to carry out this desire from the potential into the actual by clothing itself in the bodily limbs, in deed, speech, and persistent thought to the extent of

[1] *"Brain"*—thought; *"mouth"*—word; *"the other limbs"*—act. [2] *Though the* benoni *has never committed a sin in his life, he is still not deemed a* tzaddik, *as long as his natural impulses have not been completely sublimated, as explained further in this chapter. On the other hand, past offences need not preclude one from attaining the rank of* benoni, *if there was proper repentance. At any rate, the rank of* benoni, *as defined in the* Tanya, *is far superior to the rank of* tzaddik *as defined generally when it is applied to one whose good deeds exceed the bad. Cf.* supra, *ch. 1.* [3] Supra, *ch. 3.* [4] מוחין דגדלות *i.e. the Supernal of* Sefirot *of* chochmah, binah, da'at *(ChaBaD), are in a state of greatness.* [5] *Maimonides, Code,* Hilchot Keriat

פרק יב והבינוני הוא שלעולם אין הרע גובר כל כך לכבוש את העיר קטנ׳ להתלבש בגוף להחטיאו דהיינו ששלש׳ לבושי נפש הבהמית שהם מחשבה דבור ומעשה שמצד הקליפ׳ אין גוברים בו על נפש האלהית להתלבש בגוף במוח ובפה ובשאר רמ״ח אברים להחטיאם ולטמאם ח״ו רק שלשה לבושי נפש האלהית הם לבדם מתלבשים בגוף שהם מחשבה דבור ומעשה של תרי״ג מצות התורה ולא עבר עבירה מימיו ולא יעבור לעולם ולא נקרא עליו שם רשע אפי׳ שעה אחת ורגע אחד כל ימיו אך מהות ועצמות נפש האלהית שהן עשר בחינותיה לא להן לבדן המלוכה והממשלה בעיר קטנה כי אם בעתים מזומנים כמו בשעת קריאת שמע ותפלה שהיא שעת מוחין דגדלות למעלה וגם למטה היא שעת הכושר לכל אדם שאז מקשר חב״ד שלו לה׳ להעמיק דעתו בגדולת א״ס ב״ה ולעורר את האהבה כרשפי אש בחלל הימני שבלבו לדבקה בו בקיום התורה ומצותיה מאהבה שזהו ענין המבואר בקריאת שמע דאורייתא וברכותיה שלפניה ולאחריה שהן מדרבנן הן הכנה לקיום הק״ש כמ״ש במ״א ואז הרע שבחלל השמאלי כפוף ובטל לטוב המתפשט בחלל הימני מחב״ד שבמוח המקושרים בגדולת א״ס ב״ה. אבל אחר התפלה בהסתלקות המוחין דגדלות א״ס ב״ה הרי הרע חוזר וניעור בחלל השמאלי ומתאוה תאוה לתאות עוה״ז ותענוגיו. רק מפני שלא לו לבדו משפט המלוכה והממשלה בעיר אינו יכול להוציא תאותו מכח אל הפועל להתלבש באברי הגוף במעשה דבור ומחשבה ממש

Shema *1:1.* [6] Ibid., *1:7.* [7] *Reference is made here to the text of the blessing in the daily liturgy, which are designed to inspire surrender and ecstasy. Cf.* infra, *ch. 49.* [8] *The evil nature is then temporarily repressed, but not sublimated.*

concentrating his attention on the enjoyment of the mundane pleasures, as to how to satisfy the lust of his heart, because the brain rules over the heart (as explained in *Ra'aya Mehemna, Parshat Pinchas*)[9] by virtue of its innately created nature. For this is how man is created from birth, that each person may, with the will-power in his brain, restrain himself and control the drive of lust that is in his heart, preventing his heart's desires from expressing themselves in action, word or thought, and divert his attention altogether from the craving of his heart toward the completely opposite direction particularly in the direction of holiness.[10]

Thus it is written: "Then I saw that wisdom excelleth folly as light excelleth darkness."[11] This means that just as light has a superiority, power and dominion over darkness, so that a little physical light banishes a great deal of darkness, which is therewith inevitably superseded, as a matter of course and necessity, so is much foolishness of the *kelipah* and *sitra achra* (as, indeed, our Sages say, "A man does not sin unless a spirit of folly enters into him"[12]) inevitably driven away by the wisdom that is in the divine soul in the brain, whose desire is to rule alone in the "city" and to pervade the whole body, in the manner already mentioned,[13] by means of her three garments, namely, thought, speech and act of the 613 commandments of the Torah, as explained earlier.

●▲ Nevertheless, such a person is not deemed a *tzaddik* at all, because the superiority which the light of the divine soul possesses over the darkness and foolishness of the *kelipah*, wherewith the latter is expelled forthwith, exists only in the aforementioned three garments, but does not extend to its very essence and being in relation to those of the *kelipah*. For in the "intermediate" man (*benoni*) the essence and being of the animal soul from the *kelipah* in the left part remains entirely undislodged after prayer. For then the burning love of G-d is not in a revealed state in his heart, in the right part, but is only inwardly paved with hidden love, that is the natural adoration in the divine soul, as will be explained later. Therefore it is possible for the folly of the wicked fool to rise openly in the left part of his heart, creating a lust for all material

---

[9] *Cf.* Zohar *III, p. 224a.* [10] *The doctrine of the inherent supremacy of "intellect over emotion" is one of the basic, though not original, tenets of ChaBaD. Comp. Maimonides,* Guide *III, 8.* [11] Eccl. *2:13.* [12] Sotah *3a.* [13] Supra, *ch. 9.*

● 16 Teveth ▲ *22 Teveth*

ממש להעמיק מחשבתו בתענוגי עוה"ז איך למלאת תאות לבו כי המוח שליט על הלב [כמ"ש בר"מ פ' פינחס] בתולדתו וטבע יצירתו שכך נוצר האדם בתולדתו שכל אדם יכול ברצונו שבמוחו להתאפק ולמשול ברוח תאותו שבלבו שלא למלאת משאלות לבו במעשה דבור ומחשבה ולהסיח דעתו לגמרי מתאות לבו אל ההפך לגמרי ובפרט אל צד הקדושה כדכתיב וראיתי שיש יתרון לחכמה מן הסכלות כיתרון האור מן החושך פי' כמו שהאור יש לו יתרון ושליטה וממשלה על החושך שמעט אור גשמי דוחה הרבה מן החשך שנדחה ממנו מאליו וממילא כך נדחה ממילא סכלות הרבה של הקליפה וס"א שבחלל השמאלי [כמאמר רז"ל אלא אם כן נכנס בו רוח שטות וכו'] מפני החכמה שבנפש האלהית שבמוח אשר רצונה למשול לבדה בעיר ולהתלבש בשלשה לבושיה הנ"ל בכל הגוף כולו כנ"ל שהם מחשבה דבור ומעשה תרי"ג מצות התורה כנ"ל ואעפ"כ אינו נקרא צדיק כלל מפני שיתרון הזה אשר לאור נפש האלהית על החושך וסכלות של הקליפה הנדחה ממילא אינו אלא בשלשה לבושי' הנ"ל ולא במהותה ועצמותה על מהותה ועצמותה של הקליפה כי מהותה ועצמותה של נפש הבהמית שמהקליפה שבחלל השמאלי לא נדחה כלל ממקומו בבינוני אחר התפלה שאין רשפי אש אהבת ה' בהתגלות לבו בחלל הימני כי אם תוכו רצוף אהבה מסותרת שהיא אהבה הטבעית שבנפש האלהית כמ"ש לקמן ואזי יכול להיות סכלות הכסיל הרע בהתגלו' לבו בחלל השמאלי להתאות תאוה לכל ענייני

גשמיות

things of this world, whether permitted or, G-d forbid, prohibited, as if he had not prayed at all. Nevertheless, in regard to a forbidden matter, it does not occur to him to actually violate the prohibition, G-d forbid, and it remains in the realm of sinful thoughts, "Which are yet more heinous than sin itself,"[14] and which can be forceful enough to rise to his mind, to distract him from the Torah and Divine service, as our Sages said, "There are three sins against which a man is daily not safeguarded: sinful thoughts, distraction in prayer," and so forth.[15]

●▲ However, the impression [of prayer] on the intellect and the hidden [i.e. innate] fear and love of G-d in the right part [of the heart], enable one to prevail and triumph over this evil of passionate craving, depriving it from gaining supremacy and dominion over the "city," and from carrying out this desire from the potential into the actual by clothing itself in the bodily organs. Moreover, even in the mind alone, in so far as sinful thoughts are concerned, evil has no power to compel the mind's volition to entertain willingly, G-d forbid, any wicked thought rising of its own accord from the heart to the brain, as discussed above.[16] But no sooner does it reach there than he thrusts it out with both hands and averts his mind from it the instant he reminds himself that it is an evil thought, refusing to accept it willingly, even to let his thoughts play on it willingly; how much more so to entertain any idea of putting it into effect, G-d forbid, or even to put it into words. For he who wilfully indulges in such thoughts is deemed wicked at such time, whereas the "intermediate" person is never wicked for a single moment.

So, too, in matters affecting a person's relations with his neighbour, as soon as there rises from his heart to his mind some animosity or hatred, G-d forbid, or jealousy or anger, or a grudge and suchlike, he gives them no entrance into his mind and will. On the contrary, his mind exercises its authority and power over the spirit in his heart, to do the very opposite and to conduct himself towards his neighbour with the quality of kindness and a display of abundant love, to the extent of suffering from him to the extreme limits without becoming provoked into anger, G-d forbid, or to revenge in kind, G-d forbid; but rather to repay the offenders with favours, as taught in the *Zohar*,[17] that one should learn from the example of Joseph towards his brothers.

---

[14] *See n. 4, ch. 11.* [15] *The third item is "slanderous gossip."* Bava Batra, *164b*. [16] *Beg. ch. 9.* [17] *I, 201a f.*

גשמיות עוה״ז בין בהיתר בין באיסור ח״ו כאלו לא התפלל כלל אלא שבדבר איסור אינו עולה בדעתו לעשות האיסור בפועל ממש ח״ו אלא הרהורי עבירה הקשים מעבירה יכולים לפעול לעלות למוחו ולבלבלו מתורה ועבודה וכמארז״ל ג׳ עבירות אין אדם ניצול מהן בכל יום הרהור עבירה ועיון תפלה כו׳ רק שלזה מועיל הרשימו במוחין ויראת ה׳ ואהבתו המסותרת בחלל הימני להתגבר ולשלוט על הרע הזה המתאוה תאוה שלא להיות לו שליטה וממשלה בעיר להוציא תאותו מכח אל הפועל להתלבש באברי הגוף ואפי׳ במוח לבדו להרהר ברע אין לו שליטה וממשלה להרהר ח״ו ברצונו שבמוחו שיקבל ברצון ח״ו הרהור זה הרע העולה מאליו מהלב למוח כנ״ל אלא מיד בעלייתו לשם דוחהו בשתי ידים ומסיח דעתו מיד שנזכר שהוא הרהור רע ואינו מקבלו ברצון אפי׳ להרהר בו ברצון וכ״ש להעלותו על הדעת לעשותו ח״ו או אפי׳ לדבר בו כי המהרהר ברצון נק׳ רשע באותה שעה והבינוני אינו רשע אפי׳ שעה אחת לעולם. וכן בדברים שבין אדם לחבירו מיד שעולה לו מהלב למוח איזו טינא ושנאה ח״ו או איזו קנאה או כעס או קפידא ודומיהן אינו מקבלן כלל במוחו וברצונו ואדרבה המוח שליט ומושל ברוח שבלבו לעשות ההפך ממש להתנהג עם חבירו במדת חסד וחיבה יתרה מודעת לו לסבול ממנו עד קצה האחרון ולא לכעוס ח״ו וגם שלא לשלם לו כפעלו ח״ו אלא אדרבה לגמול לחייבים טובות כמ״ש בזהר ללמוד מיוסף עם אחיו:

ובזה

●▲ Chapter 13

Therewith will be understood the commentary of our Sages[1] that "'Intermediate' people are judged by both [the good and evil natures], for it is written, 'He stands at the right hand of the poor man, to save him from them that judge his soul.'"[2]

Note that they did not say "ruled" by both, G–d forbid, because where the evil nature gains any control and dominion over the "small city," even though but temporarily, one is at such times deemed "wicked."

The evil nature [in the *benoni*], however, is no more than, for example, a magistrate or judge who gives his opinion on a point of law, yet it is not necessarily a final decision to be implemented in deed, for there is another magistrate or judge who is contesting this opinion. It is, therefore, necessary to arbitrate between the two, and the final verdict rests with the arbitrator.

Similarly, the evil nature states its opinion in the left part of the heart,[3] which thence ascends to the brain for contemplation. Immediately it is challenged by the second judge, the divine soul in the brain[4] extending into the right part of the heart, the abode of the good nature. The final verdict comes from the arbitrator—the Holy One, blessed be He, who comes to the aid of the good nature, as our Sages said, "If the Almighty did not help him, he could not overcome his evil inclination."[5] The help comes by means of the glow radiated by the Divine light, which illuminates the divine soul that it may gain the upper hand and mastery over the folly of the fool and evil nature, in the manner of the excellence of light over darkness, as stated above.[6]

▲ Yet, inasmuch as the evil in the [heart's] left part of the *benoni* is in its innate strength, craving after all the pleasures of this world, not having been nullified in its minuteness in relation to the good, nor having been relegated from its position to any degree—except in so far as it has no authority and power to diffuse itself throughout the limbs of the body, because the Holy One, blessed be He, "Stands at the right hand of the poor man," helping him and irradiating his divine soul—such a person is likened to a "wicked man." In the words of our Sages, "Even if the whole world tells you that you are righteous, in your own eyes regard yourself *as if* you were wicked"[7]—not as *actually* wicked.[8] But one should consider oneself to be an "intermediate" person and not accept the world's opinion which would have him believe that the evil in him has been dissolved by the good, which is the category of a *tzaddik*. Rather should he consider himself in his own estimation

[1] Berachot *61b*. [2] "Them that judge"—*in the plural, allegorically interpreted to refer to the two impulses which motivate man's actions.* [3] *The "seat" of the passions. Cf.* supra, *ch. 9.* [4] *The intellect is the forte of the divine soul.* Ibid. [5] Kiddushin *30b*. [6] *Ch. 12.* [7] Niddah *30b*. [8] *Here is the answer to the question raised in the beginning of ch. 1. The clue is in the word* כרשע *(not* רשע*).*

פרק יג ובזה יובן לשון מאמרז"ל בינונים זה וזה שופטן [פי' יצר טוב ויצר הרע] דכתיב כי יעמוד לימין אביון להושיע משופטי נפשו ולא אמרו זה וזה מושלים ח"ו כי כשיש איזו שליטה וממשלה ליצר הרע בעיר קטנה אפי' לפי שעה קלה נקרא רשע באותה שעה אלא היצה"ר אינו רק עד"מ כמו שופט ודיין האומר דעתו במשפט ואעפ"כ יכול להיות שלא יהיה פסק הלכה כך למעשה מפני שיש עוד שופט ודיין החולק עליו וצריך להכריע ביניהם והלכה כדברי המכריע כך היצה"ר אומר דעתו בחלל השמאלי שבלב ומהלב עולה למוח להרהר בו ומיד חולק עליו השופט השני שהוא הנפש האלהית שבמוח המתפשט בחלל הימני שבלב מקום משכן היצר טוב והלכה כדברי המכריע הוא הקב"ה העוזרו להיצר טוב כמאמר רז"ל אלמלא הקב"ה עוזרו אין יכול לו והעזר היא ההארה שמאיר אור ה' על נפש האלהית להיות לה יתרון ושליטה על סכלות הכסיל ויצה"ר כיתרון האור מן החושך כנ"ל. אך מאחר שהרע שבחלל השמאלי בבינוני הוא בתקפו כתולדתו להתאות תאוה לכל תענוגי עוה"ז ולא נתבטל במיעוט לגבי הטוב ולא נדחה ממקומו כלל רק שאין לו שליטה וממשלה להתפשט באברי הגוף מפני הקב"ה העומד לימין אביון ועוזר ומאיר לנפש האלהית לכן נקרא כרשע כמארז"ל אפילו כל העולם כולו אומרים לך צדיק אתה היה בעיניך כרשע ולא רשע ממש אלא שיחזיק עצמו לבינוני ולא להאמין להעולם שאומרים שהרע שבו נתבטל לגבי הטוב שזו מדרגת צדיק אלא יהיה בעיניו כאלו

as if the very essence of the evil is in its full strength and might, in the left part, as from birth, and that nothing of it has ceased or departed; on the contrary, with the passing of time it has gained strength, because the man has indulged it considerably, in eating and drinking and other mundane pursuits.

● Even one whose whole aspiration is in G–d's Torah, which he studies day and night for its own sake, this is still no proof whatever that the evil has been dislodged from its place, but it may still be that its essence and substance are in their full strength and might in its abode in the left part, except that its garments—the thought, speech and act of the animal soul—are not invested in the brain, mouth and hands and the other parts of the body, because G–d has given the mind supremacy and dominion over the heart. Therefore the divine soul in the intellect rules over the [entire] "small city," i.e., all the parts of the body, making them a garment and vehicle for her three garments, wherein to be clothed, to wit, the thought, speech and act of the 613 commandments of the Torah.

However, in its essence and substance, the divine soul in the *benoni* has no preponderance over the animal soul, except at the time when his love for G–d manifests itself in his heart on propitious occasions, such as during prayer and the like. Even then it is limited to preponderance and dominion alone, as is written, "And one nation shall prevail over the other,"[9] that is, when one rises the other falls, and vice versa. Thus, when the divine soul gains strength and ascendancy over the animal soul, in the source of *gevurot* which is *binah*,[10] through pondering on the greatness of G–d, the blessed *En Sof*, thereby generating intense and flaming love of G–d in the right part of his heart—then the *sitra achra* in the left part is subdued. But it is not entirely abolished, in the case of the *benoni*; it is so only in a *tzaddik*, concerning whom it is said, "My heart is void within me."[11] The latter despises and hates evil with a consummate hatred and contempt, or without quite such complete hatred, as is explained above.[12]

But in an "intermediate" person it is, by way of example, similar to a sleeping man, who can

[9] Gen. *25:23*. [10] Chochmah *corresponds to* chesed; binah—*to* gevurah. [11] Ps. *109:22*. [12] *Ch. 10, with reference to the two types of* tzaddik.

כאלו מהותו ועצמותו של הרע הוא בתקפו ובגבורתו בחלל השמאלי כתולדתו ולא חלף והלך ממנו מאומה ואדרבה נתחזק יותר בהמשך הזמן שנשתמש בו הרבה באכילה ושתיה ושאר ענייני עוה"ז ואף מי שבתורת ה' חפצו ויהגה בה יומם ולילה לשמה אין זו הוכחה כלל שנדחה הרע ממקומו אלא יכול להיות שמהותו ועצמותו הוא בתקפו ובגבורתו במקומו בחלל השמאלי רק שלבושיו שהם מחשבה דבור ומעשה של נפש הבהמית אינן מתלבשים במוח והפה והידים ושאר אברי הגוף מפני ה' שנתן שליטה וממשלה למוח על הלב ולכן נפש האלהית שבמוח מושלת בעיר קטנה אברי הגוף כולם שיהיו לבוש ומרכבה לשלש' לבושיה שיתלבשו בהם שהם מחשבה דבור ומעשה של תרי"ג מצות התורה אבל מהותה ועצמותה של נפש האלהית אין לה שליטה וממשלה על מהותה ועצמותה של נפש הבהמית בבינוני כי אם בשעה שאהבת ה' הוא בהתגלות לבו בעתים מזומנים כמו בשעת התפלה וכיוצא בה ואף גם זאת הפעם אינה רק שליטה וממשלה לבד כדכתיב ולאום מלאום יאמץ כשזה קם זה נופל וכשזה קם כו' שנפש האלהית מתאמצת ומתגברת על נפש הבהמית במקור הגבורות שהיא בינה להתבונן בגדולת ה' א"ס ב"ה ולהוליד אהבה עזה לה' כרשפי אש בחלל הימני שבלבו ואז אתכפיא ס"א שבחלל השמאלי אבל לא נתבטל לגמרי בבינוני אלא בצדיק שנאמר בו ולבי חלל בקרבי והוא מואס ברע ושונאו בתכלית השנאה והמיאוס או שלא בתכלית השנאה כנ"ל. אבל בבינוני הוא ד"מ כאדם שישן שיכול

לחזור

awaken from his sleep. So is the evil in the "intermediate" person dormant, as it were, in the left part, during the recital of the *Shema* and the Prayer [*Amidah*], when his heart is aglow with the love of G–d, but later it can wake up again.

For this reason Rabbah considered himself as though he were a *benoni*,[13] though his mouth never ceased from study, and his desire was in G–d's Torah, day and night, with the passionate craving and longing of a soul yearning for G–d with overwhelming love, such as experienced during the reciting of the *Shema* and *Amidah*. Hence he appeared in his own eyes like an "intermediate" who prays all day, as, indeed, our Sages have said, "Would that a man prayed the whole day long!"[14]

• Now, this quality of love of which we speak in the case of the "intermediate" people which is attained at the time of prayer by virtue of the preponderance of the divine soul, etc., is, in comparison with the degree attained by the *tzaddikim* who serve G–d in perfect truth, not called "true service" at all, since it passes and disappears after prayer, and it is written, "The lip of truth shall be established *for ever*, but a lying tongue is but for a moment."[15] Nevertheless, in relation to the rank of the "intermediate" people, it is regarded as a truly perfect service in terms of *their* [level of] truth, in each man relative to his standing in the ranks of the "intermediate." For in their case, too, their love, during their prayers, may be termed "the lip of truth shall be established for ever," since their divine soul has the power to reawaken this kind of love constantly, during its preponderance in time of prayer day after day, by means of an appropriate [mental] preparation, each soul according to its intrinsic quality and rank. For Truth is the attribute of Jacob, who is called[16] the "Middle bolt which secures [everything] from end to end,"[17] from the highest gradations and degrees to the end of all grades. And in each gradation and plane it fixes its bolt through the most central point, which is the point and quality of its attribute of Truth. The attribute of Truth is an unbounded inheritance which has no limit upwards to the highest degrees, while all lower gradations and degrees are as nothing compared with those that are superior to them. (As is known to those who are familiar with the Esoteric Discipline, that the quality which is, as it were, the "head" and "intellect" of lower grades,

[13] *See ch. 1.* [14] Berachot *21a.*
[15] Prov. *12:19.* [16] Zohar *I, 1b; 224a.* [17] *Comp.* Exod. *26:28.*

• 20 Teveth

לחזור וליעור משנתו כך הרע בבינוני הוא כישן בחלל השמאלי בשעת ק"ש ותפלה שלבו בוער באהבת ה' ואח"כ יכול להיות חוזר וניעור. ולכן היה רבה מחזיק עצמו כבינוני אף דלא פסיק פומיה מגירסא ובתורת ה' חפצו יומם ולילה בחפיצה וחשיקה ותשוקה ונפש שוקקה לה' באהבה רבה כבשעת ק"ש ותפלה ונדמה בעיניו כבינוני המתפלל כל היום וכמאמר רז"ל הלואי שיתפלל אדם כל היום כולו: והנה מדת אהבה זו האמורה בבינונים בשעת התפלה ע"י התגברות הנפש האלהית כו' הנה לגבי מדרגת הצדיקים עובדי ה' באמת לאמיתו אין בחי' אהבה זו נקראת בשם עבודת אמת כלל מאחר שחולפת ועוברת אחר התפלה וכתיב שפת אמת תכון לעד ועד ארגיעה לשון שקר ואעפ"כ לגבי מדרגת הבינונים נקראת עבודה תמה באמת לאמיתו שלהם איש איש כפי מדרגתו במדרגת הבינונים והריני קורא באהבתם שבתפלתם ג"כ שפת אמת תכון לעד הואיל ובכח נפשם האלהית לחזור ולעורר בחי' אהבה זו לעולם בהתגברותה בשעת התפלה מדי יום ביום ע"י הכנה הראויה לכל נפש כפי ערכה ומדרגת' כי הנה מדת אמת היא מדתו של יעקב הנקרא בריח התיכון המבריח מן הקצה אל הקצה מרום המעלות ומדרגות עד סוף כל דרגין ובכל מעלה ומדרגה מבריח תוך נקודה האמצעית שהיא נקודת ובחי' מדת אמת שלה ומדת אמת היא נחלה בלי מצרים ואין לה שיעור למעלה עד רום המעלות וכל מעלות ומדרגות שלמטה הם כאין לגבי מעלות ומדרגות שלמעלה מהן [כידוע לי"ח שבחי' ראש ומוחין של מדרגות תחתונות

הן

is inferior to the so-called "soles" and "feet" of the grades above them. Compare the statement of our Sages, "The feet of the *chayyot* measure up to all.")[18]

•▲Chapter 14

The rank of *benoni* is one that is attainable by every man, and each person should strive after it. Every person can at any time or hour be an "intermediate," because the "intermediate" man does not revile evil[1]—for that is a feeling entrusted to the heart, and not all times are alike.[2] [His task is] only to "turn away from evil and do good," in actual practice—in deed, speech or thought, wherein the choice, ability and freedom are given to every man that he may act, speak and think even what is contrary to the desire of his heart and diametrically opposed to it.[3] Even when the heart craves and desires a material pleasure, whether permitted or, G–d forbid, prohibited, he can steel himself and divert his attention from it altogether, declaring to himself, "I will not be wicked even for a moment, because I will not be parted and separated, Heaven forefend! from the One G–d under any circumstances, being mindful of the admonition, 'Your iniquities interpose between you and G–d.'[4] Nay, my real desire is to unite my *nefesh*, *ruach* and *neshamah* with Him, through investing them in His blessed three garments, namely, in action, speech and thought dedicated to G–d, His Torah and His commandments, by virtue of the love of G–d that is hidden in my heart, as in the heart of all Jews, who are called 'lovers of Thy Name.'[5] Even the most unworthy among the worthless is capable of sacrificing himself for the sanctity of G–d; surely, I am not inferior to him. It is only that a spirit of folly has overcome him, and he imagines that committing a sin will not affect his Jewishness and his soul will not be severed thereby from the G–d of Israel, forgetting also about his love of G–d which is hidden in his heart. But as for me, I have no desire to be such a fool as he to deny the truth!"

▲ It is different, however, with something that is entrusted to the heart, namely, that the evil should actually be despised in the heart and abhorred with absolute hatred, or even not quite so absolutely.[6] This cannot be attained, truly and sincerely, except through great

---

[18] Chagigah *13a*.

Chapter 14

[1] *Cf.* supra, *chs. 11 and 12.* [2] *Prayer-time, for instance, is more propitious, as mentioned in ch. 12.* *Cf. n. 5,* ibid. [3] *Note that "thought" is also included in the ability of self-control.* [4] Isa. *59:2.* [5] Ps. *5:21.* [6] *Referring to the two categories of* tzaddik (supra, *ch. 10).*

הן למטה מבחי׳ עקביים ורגלי מדרגות עליונות מהן וכמאמר רז״ל רגלי החיות כנגד כולן]:

פרק יד והנה מדת הבינוני היא מדת כל אדם ואחריה כל אדם ימשוך שכל אדם יכול להיות בינוני בכל עת ובכל שעה כי הבינוני אינו מואס ברע שזהו דבר המסור ללב ולא כל העתים שוות אלא סור מרע ועשה טוב דהיינו בפועל ממש במעשה דבור ומחשבה שבהם הבחירה והיכולת והרשות נתונה לכל אדם לעשות ולדבר ולחשוב גם מה שהוא נגד תאות לבו והפכה ממש כי גם בשעה שהלב חומד ומתאוה איזו תאוה גשמיית בהיתר או באיסור ח״ו יכול להתגבר ולהסיח דעתו ממנה לגמרי באמרו ללבו אינני רוצה להיות רשע אפי׳ שעה אחת כי אינני רוצה להיות מובדל ונפרד ח״ו מה׳ אחד בשום אופן כדכתיב עונותיכם מבדילים וגו׳ רק אני רוצה לדבקה בו נפשי רוחי ונשמתי בהתלבשן בשלשה לבושיו ית׳ שהם מעשה דבור ומחשבה בה׳ ותורתו ומצותיו מאהבה מסותרת שבלבי לה׳ כמו בלב כללו׳ ישראל שנקראו אוהבי שמך ואפי׳ קל שבקלים יכול למסור נפשו על קדושת ה׳ ולא נופל אנכי ממנו בודאי אלא שנכנס בו רוח שטות ונדמה לו שבעביר׳ זו עודנו ביהדותו ואין נשמתו מובדלת מאלהי ישראל וגם שוכח אהבתו לה׳ המסותרת בלבו אבל אני אינני רוצה להיות שוטה כמוהו לכפור האמת. משא״כ בדבר המסור ללב דהיינו שיהא הרע מאוס ממש בלב ושנאוי בתכלית שנאה או אפי׳ שלא בתכלית שנאה הנה זה אי אפשר שיהיה באמת לאמיתו אלא ע״י גודל ותוקף

and intense love of G-d, the kind of ecstatic love and Divine bliss which is akin to the World to Come. Of this experience the Rabbis said,[7] "Thy world wilt thou see in thy life, . . ." and not every man can attain this state, for this is in the nature of a gracious reward, as is written, "I will make your priestly office a rewarding service, . . ."[8] as is explained elsewhere.[9] Therefore did Job say, "Thou didst create *tzaddikim*. . . ."[10] It is also found in *Tikunei Zohar*,[11] that in the souls of [the people of] Israel there are many kinds of gradations and distinctions—pious men, strong men who gain mastery over their nature, scholars of the Torah, prophets, . . . *tzaddikim*, and so forth. Note there.

●▲ Now we can understand the redundancy of the oath, "Be righteous (*tzaddik*) and be not wicked,"[12] which is unintelligible at first glance: Since he is warned, "Be righteous!" where is the need to put him on oath again that he shall not be wicked? The answer is, that inasmuch as not everyone is privileged to become a *tzaddik*, nor has a person the full advantage of choice in this matter to experience true delight in G-d and to actually and truly abhor evil; he is consequently adjured a second time: "Thou shalt," at any rate, "not be wicked!" Here the right of choice and freedom is extended to every person, to check the drive of his heart's desire and to conquer his nature, so that he shall not be wicked even for a moment throughout his life, whether in the realm of "turn away from evil" or in that of "do good," there being no "good" other than Torah,[13] that is the "Study of the Torah which balances them all."

Nevertheless, a person must set aside specific periods in which to commune with his soul in order to cultivate the abhorrence of evil, as, for example, reminding himself of the admonition of our Sages[14] that "Woman is a vessel full of filth, . . ."[15] and in like manner. So, too, all dainties and delicacies turn into a "vessel full of filth." Likewise in regard to all pleasures of this world, the wise man foresees what becomes of them, for in the end they rot and become worms and dung. Conversely, [let him] delight and rejoice in G-d by reflection on the greatness of the blessed *En Sof*, to the best of his capacity. He may well realise that he cannot attain to this degree with a full measure of truth except in illusion; nevertheless he should do

---

[7] Berachot *17a*. [8] Num. *18:7*. [9] *Cf.* infra, *ch. 43*. [10] *The category of* tzaddik *is therefore "created," i.e. given to a very few by Divine grace, and not easily attainable by one's own efforts. Hence it is possible to say with Job, "Thou didst* create tzaddikim." *See beg. ch. 1*. [11] Introduction, *1b*. [12] *Cf.* supra, *beg. ch. 1*. [13] Berachot *5a*. [14] Shabbat *152a*. [15] *In her menstrual period.*

ותוקף האהבה לה׳ בבחי׳ אהבה בתענוגים להתענג על ה׳ מעין עוה״ב. ועל זה אמרו רז״ל עולמך תראה בחייך כו׳ ואין כל אדם זוכה לזה כי זהו כעין קבול שכר וכדכתיב עבודת מתנה אתן את כהונתכם וגו׳ כמ״ש במ״א. ולכן אמר איוב בראת צדיקים וכו׳ וכדאיתא בתיקונים שיש בנשמות ישראל כמה מיני מדרגות ובחי׳. חסידים גבורים המתגברים על יצרם מארי תורה נביאים כו׳ צדיקים כו׳ ע״ש:

ובזה יובן כפל לשון השבועה תהי צדיק ואל תהי רשע דלכאורה תמוה כי מאחר שמשביעים אותו תהי צדיק למה צריכים להשביעו עוד שלא יהיה רשע. אלא משום שאין כל אדם זוכה להיות צדיק ואין לאדם משפט הבחירה בזה כל כך להתענג על ה׳ באמת ושיהיה הרע מאוס ממש באמת ולכן משביעים שנית אל תהי רשע עכ״פ שבזה משפט הבחירה והרשות נתונה לכל אדם למשול ברוח תאותו שבלבו ולכבוש יצרו שלא יהיה רשע אפי׳ שעה אחת כל ימיו בין בבחי׳ סור מרע בין בבחי׳ ועשה טוב ואין טוב אלא תורה דהיינו תלמוד תורה שכנגד כולן. אך אעפ״כ צריך לקבוע לו עתים גם כן לשית עצות בנפשו להיות מואס ברע כגון בעצת חכמינו ז״ל אשה חמת מלאה צואה כו׳. וכהאי גוונא. וכן כל מיני מטעמים ומעדנים נעשים כך חמת מלא כו׳. וכן כל תענוגי עוה״ז החכם רואה הנולד מהן שסופן לרקוב ולהיות רמה ואשפה וההפך להתענג ולשמוח בה׳ ע״י התבוננות בגדולת א״ס ב״ה כפי יכולתו אף שיודע בנפשו שלא יגיע למדרגה זו באמת לאמיתו כי אם בדמיונות אעפ״כ הוא יעשה את

his part in an effort to uphold the oath administered to him, "Be righteous," and G-d will do as He sees fit. Furthermore, habitude reigns supreme in any sphere and becomes second nature. Therefore if he accustoms himself to despise evil, it will to some extent become despicable in truth; similarly, when he accustoms himself to gladden his heart in G-d, through reflection on His greatness—for self-impulsion induces heavenly inspiration.[16] With all that, perhaps a spirit from above will descend upon him, and he will merit something of the spirit (*ruach*) that is rooted in some *tzaddik* that will attach itself to him, so that he may serve G-d with true joy, as is written, "Rejoice, O ye *tzaddikim*, in G-d."[17] Then will in truth be fulfilled in him the avowed oath: "Be righteous."

●▲*Chapter 15*

With the above in mind, we may now understand the text, "Then shall ye again discern between the righteous man and the wicked man; between him that is serving G-d and him that serves Him not."[1]

The difference between "One who is serving G-d" and a righteous man (*tzaddik*) is, that "One who is serving (*oved*) G-d"—in the active present—is one who is engaged in "active service," namely, the struggle against his evil nature in an effort to gain mastery over it and to banish it from the "small city," that it should not vest itself in the organs of the body. Verily it entails much effort and toil to wage constant war with it. This is the *benoni*.

The *tzaddik*, however, is designated "Servant (*eved*) of G-d," which is a title already earned, as the title "sage" or "king" is bestowed on one who has already become a sage or king. So is this person who has already effected and completely accomplished his task of waging war against the evil in him, with the result that he has expelled it and it has disappeared, and his heart has become "void within him."[2]

▲In the category of *benoni* there are also to be found two gradations, to wit, "One who is serving G-d" and "One who serves Him not."[3] Yet the latter is not wicked, for never in his life did he commit even a minor transgression and, moreover, he fulfilled all the commandments which were possible for him to fulfil, including the study of the Torah which balances everything else, his mouth never ceasing from study. The reason he is referred to as "one who serves Him not" is that he does not wage any battle against his [evil] disposition in order to vanquish it by means of the Divine light that irradiates the divine soul, whose abode is in the brain which predominates over the heart, as explained above;[4] for his disposition does not confront him at all

---

[16] Zohar *II, 135b*. [17] Ps. *97:12*.

Chapter 15
[1] Mal. *3:18*. [2] *Cf.* supra, *ch. 1*.
[3] *In the sense that he requires little or no effort, by virtue of his natural disposition, as subsequently explained.*
[4] *Ch. 12.*

את שלו לקיים את השבועה שמשביעים תהי צדיק וה׳ יעשה הטוב בעיניו. ועוד שההרגל על כל דבר שלטון ונעשה טבע שני. וכשירגיל למאס את הרע יהיה נמאס קצת באמת וכשירגיל לשמח נפשו בה׳ ע״י התבוננות בגדולת ה׳ הרי באתערותא דלתתא אתערותא דלעילא וכולי האי ואולי יערה עליו רוח ממרום ויזכה לבחי׳ רוח משרש איזה צדיק שתתעבר בו לעבוד ה׳ בשמחה אמיתית כדכתיב שמחו צדיקים בה׳ ותתקיים בו באמת השבועה שמשביעים תהי צדיק:

פרק טו ובזה יובן מ״ש ושבתם וראיתם בין צדיק לרשע בין עובד אלהים לאשר לא עבדו שההפרש בין עובד אלהים לצדיק הוא שעובד הוא לשון הוה שהוא באמצע העבודה שהיא המלחמה עם היצה״ר להתגבר עליו ולגרשו מהעיר קטנה שלא יתלבש באברי הגוף שהוא באמת עבודה ועמל גדול להלחם בו תמיד והיינו הבינוני. אבל הצדיק נקרא עבד ה׳ בשם התואר כמו שם חכם או מלך שכבר נעשה חכם או מלך כך זה כבר עבד וגמר לגמרי עבודת המלחמה עם הרע עד כי ויגרשהו וילך לו ולבו חלל בקרבו. ובבינוני יש ג״כ שתי מדרגות עובד אלהים ואשר לא עבדו ואעפ״כ אינו רשע כי לא עבר מימיו שום עבירה קלה וגם קיים כל המצות שאפשר לו לקיימן ותלמוד תורה כנגד כולם ולא פסיק פומיה מגירסא אלא שאינו עושה שום מלחמה עם היצר לנצחו ע״י אור ה׳ המאיר על נפש האלהית שבמוח השליט על הלב כנ״ל מפני שאין יצרו עומד לנגדו כלל לבטלו

in an attempt to distract him from study and prayer, and he is consequently never obliged to wage war against it. Thus, for example, is the case of one who is by nature an assiduous student because he is organically so disposed, and is likewise free from conflict with regard to sexual desire by reason of his frigid nature, and similarly with the other mundane pleasures wherein he naturally lacks any feeling of enjoyment. Hence he does not need to concentrate so much on the greatness of G–d to consciously create a spirit of knowledge and fear of G–d in his mind, in order to guard himself against violation of the prohibitive commandments; or to arouse the love of G–d in his heart to induce his attachment to Him through the fulfillment of the [positive] commandments and the study of the Torah which balances everything else. For him suffices the hidden love that is in the heart of all Jews, who are called "The lovers of His name."[5] Therefore he is in no wise called "One who is serving," inasmuch as this latent love is not of his making or accomplishment by any means, but it is our inheritance that has come down from the Patriarchs to the whole community of Israel, as will be discussed further.[6]

So, too, is one who, although by nature not an assiduous student, has yet accustomed himself to study with great diligence, so that the habit has become second nature with him; for him, too, suffices the innate love, unless he wishes to study more than his wont. This will explain the state- ●▲
ment in the *Gemara* that "One who is serving G–d" refers to him who reviews his lesson 101 times, while "One who serves him not" refers to him who repeats his lesson no more than 100 times.[7] This is because in those days it was customary to review each lesson one hundred times, as, indeed, illustrated in the *Gemara*, *ibid.*, by the example taken from the market, where donkey-drivers used to hire themselves out at a rate of ten *parasangs*[8] for a *zuz*, but for eleven *parasangs* charged two *zuzim*, because that exceeded their customary practice. For the same reason, the 101st revision, which is beyond the normal practice to which the student had been accustomed since childhood, is considered equivalent to all the previous one hundred times put together, and even surpassing them in endurance and effort, hence entitling him to be called "One who is serving G–d." For in order to change his habitual nature, he must arouse the love of G–d by means of meditation in his mind on the greatness of G–d, in order to gain mastery over the nature that is in the left part [of the heart] which is full of blood of the animal soul

---

[5] Ps. *69:37*. [6] *Chs. 18, 19, and 44*. [7] Chagigah *9b*. [8] *Persian miles.*

לבטלו מתורתו ועבודתו ואין צריך ללחום עמו כלל כגון שהוא מתמיד בלמודו בטבעו מתולדתו על ידי תגבורת המרה שחורה וכן אין לו מלחמה מתאות נשים מפני שהוא מצונן בטבעו וכן בשאר תענוגי עוה"ז הוא מחוסר הרגש הנאה בטבעו ולכן אין צריך להתבונן כל כך בגדולת ה' להוליד מבינתו רוח דעת ויראת ה' במוחו להשמר שלא לעבור על מצות ל"ת ואהבת ה' בלבו לדבקה בו בקיום המצות ות"ת כנגד כולן אלא די לו באהבה מסותרת אשר בלב כללות ישראל שנקראו אוהבי שמו ולכן אינו נקרא עובד כלל כי אהבה זו המסותרת אינה פעולתו ועבודתו כלל אלא היא ירושתנו מאבותינו לכלל ישראל וכמ"ש לקמן . וכן אף מי שאינו מתמיד בלמודו בטבעו רק שהרגיל עצמו ללמוד בהתמדה גדולה ונעשה ההרגל לו טבע שני די לו באהבה מסותרת זו אא"כ רוצה ללמוד יותר מרגילותו ובזה יובן מ"ש בגמרא דעובד אלהים היינו מי ששונה פרקו מאה פעמים ואחד ולא עבדו היינו מי ששונה פרקו מאה פעמים לבד והיינו משום שבימיהם היה הרגילות לשנות כל פרק מאה פעמים כדאיתא התם בגמרא משל משוק של חמרים שנשכרים לעשר פרסי בזוזא ולאחד עשר פרסי בתרי זוזי מפני שהוא יותר מרגילותם . ולכן זאת הפעם המאה ואחת היתרה על הרגילות שהורגל מנעוריו שקולה כנגד כולן ועולה על גביהן ביתר שאת ויתר עז להיות נקרא עובד אלהים מפני שכדי לשנות טבע הרגילות צריך לעורר את האהבה לה' ע"י שמתבונן בגדולת ה' במוחו לשלוט על הטבע שבחלל השמאלי המלא דם הנפש הבהמית

שמהקליפה

originating in the *kelipah*, whence comes his nature. This is a perfect service for a *benoni*. Or, he must awaken the hidden love in his heart to control,[9] through it, the nature that is in the left part, for this, too, is called service—the waging of war against his nature and inclination, by means of exciting the love that is hidden in his heart. However, if he wages no war at all, the said love in itself can in no way be credited to his service.

●▲Chapter 16

This, then, is the important principle regarding the Divine Service for the *benoni*: The essential thing is to govern and rule the nature that is in the left ventricle [of the heart] by means of the Divine light that irradiates the divine soul in the mind.[1] That is to say, to rule the heart by means of meditation in the mind on the greatness of the blessed *En Sof*, whereby his understanding will beget a spirit of knowledge and fear of the Lord in his mind, to make him turn away from the evil condemned by the Torah, or by the Rabbis, even from a minor Rabbinic prohibition, Heaven forbid; and [at the same time arousing] the love of G–d in his heart, in the right part, with a fervour and desire to cleave to Him through the fulfillment of the precepts of the Torah and of the Rabbis, and through the study of the Torah which is equivalent to them all.

Furthermore, one must know an additional important principle in the service of the "intermediates." This is that even if the capacity of one's intellect and the spirit of one's understanding do not attain to the level of producing a revealed love of G–d in one's heart, to make it glow like burning coals with a great desire and yearning and heartfelt passion to cleave unto Him, but the love is hidden in one's brain and in the recesses of one's heart,

Note: The reason for this is that the vitality of this person's intellect and nefesh, ruach *and* neshamah *is derived from the so-called* ibbur *("gestation") and concealment within the [Supernal] understanding, and not from the quality of birth and revelation—as it is known to those familiar with the Esoteric Discipline.*

that is to say, the heart comprehends, with the spirit of wisdom and understanding in the brain, the greatness of the blessed *En Sof*, in relation to Whom all else has absolutely no reality, for which reason it is due unto Him, blessed be He, that the soul of every living creature should yearn for Him, to cleave and be absorbed in His light; likewise is it fitting for the *nefesh* and *ruach*[2] within him to languish for Him, with a fervent desire

---

[9] *In this case—without changing his nature; only keeping it in check.*

Chapter 16

[1] *Cf.* supra, *ch. 13.* [2] Neshamah *is omitted here, for it is already alluded to in the "Hidden love in the brain and the recesses of the heart," just mentioned.*

שמהקליפה שממנה הוא הטבע וזו היא עבודה תמה לבינוני. או לעורר את האהבה המסותרת שבלבו למשול על ידה על הטבע שבחלל השמאלי שזו נקרא ג"כ עבודה להלחם עם הטבע והיצר ע"י שמעורר האהבה המסותרת בלבו משא"כ כשאין לו מלחמה כלל אין אהבה זו מצד עצמה נקראת עבודתו כלל:

פרק טז וזה כלל גדול בעבודת ה' לבינונים העיקר הוא למשול ולשלוט על הטבע שבחלל השמאלי ע"י אור ה' המאיר לנפש האלהית שבמוחו לשלוט על הלב כשמתבונן במוחו בגדולת א"ס ב"ה להוליד מבינתו רוח דעת ויראת ה' במוחו להיות סור מרע דאורייתא ודרבנן ואפילו איסור קל של דבריהם ח"ו ואהבת ה' בלבו בחלל הימני בחשיקה וחפיצה לדבקה בו בקיום המצות דאורייתא ודרבנן ות"ת שכנגד כולן. ויתר על כן צריך לידע כלל גדול בעבודה לבינונים שגם אם אין יד שכלו ורוח בינתו משגת להוליד אהבת ה' בהתגלו' לבו שיהיה לבו בוער כרשפי אש וחפץ בחפיצה וחשיקה ותשוקה מורגשת בלב לדבקה בו רק האהבה מסותרת במוחו ותעלומות לבו* דהיינו שהלב מבין ברוח חכמה ובינ' שבמוחו גדולת א"ס ב"ה דכולא קמיה כלא חשיב ממש אשר על כן יאתה לו יתב' שתכלה אליו נפש כל חי לידבק ולהכלל באורו. וגם נפשו ורוחו אשר בקרבו כך יאתה להן להיות כלות אליו בחשיקה וחפיצה לצאת

הגהה

(והסיבה לזה היא מפני היות המוחין שלו ונר"נ שלו מבחי' עיבור והעלם תוך התבונה ולא מבחי' לידה והתגלות כידוע לי"ח):

to emerge from their sheath, which is the body, in order to cleave to Him; except that they dwell perforce in the body and are bound up in it, like deserted wives;[3] and no thought of theirs can grasp Him at all, except when it grasps, and is vested in, the Torah and its commandments, as in the example of embracing the king, mentioned above;[4] therefore, it is proper for them to embrace Him with their whole heart, soul and might, which means the fulfillment of the 613 commandments in act, speech and thought, the last being the comprehension and knowledge of the Torah, as explained above.[5]

Consequently, when [the *benoni*] ponders this subject in the recesses of his heart's and mind's understanding, with a unanimity of mouth and heart, in that he upholds by word of mouth that which has been resolved in the understanding of his heart and mind, namely to direct his desire towards the Divine Torah, meditating on it day and night in oral study, while his hands and other bodily organs carry out the commandments, in accordance with the resolution of his heart's and mind's understanding, then this understanding is clothed in the act, speech and thought of the Torah and its commandments, providing for them, as it were, intelligence, vitality and "wings" wherewith to soar on high. It is the same as if he practised them with real fear and love as revealed in his heart (with a desire, fervour and passion that are felt in the heart and soul thirsting for G-d, by reason of the glowing embers of love in his heart, as mentioned above), inasmuch as it is this understanding in his brain and heart's recesses that is instrumental in leading him to engage in them, and had he not so delved in it, he would not have occupied himself with them at all, but with his physical needs alone. (And even if he is naturally disposed to be an assiduous student, nevertheless he would naturally love his body more.)

• Our Sages, of blessed memory, hinted at this when they said, "The Holy One, blessed be He, unites a good thought to the deed."[6] One would have expected them to say, that the Torah regards the good thought as if it had been put into practice.[7] The explanation, however, is that it is the revealed fear and love in the heart that are clothed in the act of the commandments, giving them vitality to soar on high, inasmuch as the heart is also corporeal, as the other parts of the body which are the instruments of the action, except that it is internal and their source of vitality; therefore it can

---

[3] *Cf.* infra, *end of ch. 50.* [4] *Ch. 4.* [5] Ibid., *and ch. 5.* [6] *Cf.* Kiddushin *40a.* [7] *As the Talmud continues, "Even if a man intended to fulfil a commandment, but was forcibly prevented, Scripture ascribes it to him as if he had performed it." The question is, why the difference in expression? The answer is that each statement conveys a different meaning.*

לצאת מנרתקן הוא הגוף לדבקה בו רק שבע"כ חיות הנה בתוך הגוף וצרורות בו כאלמנות חיות ולית מחשבה דילהון תפיסא ביה כלל כי אם כאשר תפיסא ומתלבשת בתורה ובמצותי' כמשל המחבק את המלך הנ"ל. ואי לזאת יאתה להן לחבקו בכל לב ונפש ומאד דהיינו קיום התרי"ג מצות במעשה ובדבור ובמחשבה שהיא השגת וידיעת התורה כנ"ל הנה כשמעמיק בענין זה בתעלומות תבונות לבו ומוחו ופיו ולבו שוין שמקיים כן בפיו כפי אשר נגמר בתבונת לבו ומוחו דהיינו להיות בתורת ה' חפצו ויהגה בה יומם ולילה בפיו וכן הידים ושאר אברים מקיימים המצות כפי מה שנגמר בתבונת לבו ומוחו הרי תבונה זו מתלבשת במעשה דבור ומחשבת התורה ומצותיה להיות להם בחי' מוחין וחיות וגדפין לפרחא לעילא כאלו עסק בהם בדחילו ורחימו ממש אשר בהתגלות לבו [בחפיצה וחשיקה ותשוקה מורגשת בלבו ונפשו הצמאה לה' מפני רשפי אש אהבתו שבלבו כנ"ל] הואיל ותבונה זו שבמוחו ותעלומות לבו היא המביאתו לעסוק בהם ולולי שהיה מתבונן בתבונה זו לא היה עוסק בהם כלל אלא בצרכי גופו לבד [וגם אם הוא מתמיד בלמודו בטבעו אעפ"כ אוהב את גופו יותר בטבעו] וזה רמזו רז"ל באמרם מחשבה טובה הקב"ה מצרפה למעשה והוה ליה למימר מעלה עליו הכתוב כאלו עשאה. אלא הענין כי דחילו ורחימו שבהתגלות לבו הם המתלבשים במעשה המצות להחיותם לפרחא לעילא כי הלב הוא ג"כ חומרי כשאר אברים שהם כלי המעשה אלא שהוא פנימי וחיות להם ולכן יכול

להתלבש

clothe itself in their act, to be their "wings" wherewith to ascend. However, the above-mentioned fear and love that are in the intelligence of the brain and the recesses of the heart are of an infinitely higher order than that of "action" and they cannot clothe themselves in the performance of the commandments to become their intelligence and vitality, as it were, to uplift them to soar upwards, were it not for the fact that the Holy One, blessed be He, fuses and unites them together with the action; hence they are called "good thought," for they are not actual awe and love in a revealed state in the heart, but only in the intelligence of the brain and in the recesses of the heart, as mentioned above.

Note: Thus it is also written in the Zohar *and* Etz Chayim, *that* תבונה *(intelligence) contains the letters* בן ובת *("son and daughter"), referring to awe and love;*[8] *and sometimes it descends to become the intelligence in the feminine principle of* ze'er anpin,[9] *represented in the letters of the Torah and the commandments, as the initiated will understand.*

But the Almighty produces this coalescence in order to elevate the performance of the commandments and study of the Torah—which are carried out under the influence of the said good thought—into the world of *Beriah*, the abode to which ascend the Torah and commandments that are performed through intelligent awe and love which are truly revealed in the heart. But even without this they still rise to the World of *Yetzirah*, by means of the natural fear and love which are latent in the heart of all Jews from birth, as will be later explained at length.[10]

●▲ *Chapter 17*

With the above in mind, one can understand the Scriptural text, "But the thing is very nigh unto thee, in thy mouth and in thy heart, that thou mayest do it."[1]

At first glance, the statement that "The thing is very nigh unto thee . . . in thy heart" seems to be contrary to our experience (yet the Torah is eternal[2]).[3] For it is not a "very nigh thing" to change one's heart from mundane desires to a sincere love of G-d. Indeed, it is stated in the *Gemara*, "Is fear [of Heaven] a small thing?"[4] How much more so—love. Moreover, the Rabbis also said, that only *tzaddikim* have control over their hearts.[5]

But the words "That thou mayest *do it*" refer to a love which merely leads to the performance of the commandments, this being the hidden desire of the heart (רעותא דלבא), even if it does not glow openly

---

[8] *The affections (fear and love) are "born" of the intellect (*chochmah *and* binah*). Cf.* supra, *ch. 3.* [9] *"Small Image"—a Kabbalistic term, corresponding to the seven Divine* middot *(*chesed, gevurah, *etc.). The "feminine" principle is to be understood (as in all Kabbalistic terminology) in the sense of recipient of the flow of Divine influence.* [10] *Chs. 38, 39, 44.*

Chapter 17
[1] Deut. *30:14.* [2] *Maimonides,* Hilchot Yesodei HaTorah, *ch. 9;* Hilchot Teshuvah, *3:8; Commentary on* Mishnah, Sanhedrin, *ch. 10.*

להתלבש בהם להיות להם גדפין להעלותם. אך הדחילו ורחימו שבתבונות מוחו ותעלומות לבו הנ"ל גבהו דרכיהם למעלה מעלה מבחי' המעשה ואי אפשר להם להתלבש בבחי' מעשה המצות להיות להם בחי' מוחין וחיות להעלותן לפרחא לעילא אם לא שהקב"ה מצרפן ומחברן לבחי' המעשה והן נקראות בשם מחשבה טובה כי אינן דחילו ורחימו ממש בהתגלות לבו כי אם בתבונת מוחו ותעלומות לבו כנ"ל * אך צירוף זה מצרף הקב"ה כדי להעלות מעשה המצות ועסק התורה הנעשים על ידי מחשבה טובה הנ"ל עד עולם הבריאה מקום עליית התורה והמצות הנעשים ע"י דחילו ורחימו שכליים אשר בהתגלו' לבו ממש אבל בלא"ה נמי עולים לעולם היציר' ע"י דחילו ורחימו טבעיים המסותרים בלב כל ישראל בתולדותם כמ"ש לקמן באריכות:

הגהה

(וכמ"ש בזוהר וע"ח דתבונה אותיות ב"ן וב"ת שהן דחילו ורחימו ולפעמים התבונה יורדת להיות מוחין בנוק' דזעיר אנפין שהן אותיות התורה והמצות והמשכיל יבין):

פרק יז

ובזה יובן מ"ש כי קרוב אליך הדבר מאד בפיך ובלבבך לעשותו דלכאורה הוא בלבבך נגד החוש שלנו [והתורה היא נצחית] שאין קרוב מאד הדבר להפך לבו מתאוות עוה"ז לאהבת ה' באמת וכמ"ש בגמרא אטו יראה מילתא זוטרתי היא וכל שכן אהבה. וגם אמרו רז"ל דצדיקים דוקא לבם ברשותם. אלא דלעשותו ר"ל האהבה המביאה לידי עשיית המצות בלבד שהיא רעותא דלבא שבתעלומות לב גם כי אינה בהתגלות לבו כרשפי

---

[3] *Hence it could not refer to the time of Moses only, but must hold good for our time as well.* [4] Berachot *33b;* Megillah *25a.* [5] Bereshit Rabba *34:11; 67:7.*

like flaming coals. This thing is very near, and it is easy for any person who has brains in his head, for his brain is under his control, and he is able to concentrate it on anything he wishes. If, then, he will contemplate with it on the greatness of the blessed *En Sof*, he will inevitably generate in his mind, at least, the love of G-d to cleave unto Him through the performance ▲ of His commandments and Torah. And this constitutes the whole [purpose of] man, for it is written, "This day to do them"[6]— "this day" referring specifically to the world of [physical] action,[7] while "tomorrow" [i.e., in afterlife] is the time of reward, as is explained elsewhere.

The mind, in turn, by virtue of its inherent nature, is master over the left part of the heart, and over the mouth and all the limbs which are the instruments of ● action, except in him who is completely wicked, as the Rabbis said, that the wicked are under the control of their heart, but their heart is in no wise controlled by them.[8] This is a punishment for the enormity and potency of their sin. But the Torah does not speak of these "dead" who in their life are called "dead."[9] Indeed, it is impossible for the wicked to begin to serve G-d without their first repenting for their past—in order to shatter the *kelipot*, which form a sundering curtain and an iron partition that interpose between them and their Father in Heaven—by means of contriteness of heart and bitterness of soul over their sins, as is explained in the *Zohar* on the verse, "The sacrifices of G-d are a broken spirit: a broken and contrite heart...."[10] For through breaking one's heart the spirit of uncleanliness of the *sitra achra* is broken (see *ibid.* on *Parshat Pinchas*, p. 240, and on *Parshat Vayikra*, p. 8 and p. 5, and the commentary of the "Ramaz"[11] ▲ thereon). This is the category of "lower repentance," whereby the lower [letter] "*hai*"[12] is raised up from its fall into the forces of evil, which is the mystery of the *Shechinah* in exile, as our Rabbis, of blessed memory state, "When they [the Israelites] were exiled into Edom, the *Shechinah* went with them."[13] That is to say, when a person practises the acts of "Edom"[14] he degrades and brings down thither the Divine spark which vitalises his *nefesh*, *ruach* and *neshamah* that are clothed within him in the animal soul of the *kelipah*, which is in the left part of his heart, which reigns over him as long as he remains wicked, dominating his "small city," while the *nefesh*, *ruach* and *neshamah* are forced into exile under it. But when his heart breaks within him, and the spirit of uncleanliness and of the *sitra achra* is broken, and [the forces of evil are] dispersed,

---

[6] Deut. *7:11.* [7] Eruvin *22a.* [8] *See n. 4, above.* [9] Berachot *18b.* [10] Ps. *51:18.* [11] *Rabbi Moses Zacuto (1625–1697).* [12] *Referring to the second letter* hai *of the Tetragrammaton.* Teshuvah *(spelled* תשוב-ה*) implies the return of the* hai. *Cf.* Igeret ha-Teshuvah, *chs. 4, 7, 8.* [13] Megillah *29a.* [14] *Edom is here understood allegorically as the embodiment of evil.*

כרשפי אש ודבר זה קרוב מאד ונקל לכל אדם אשר יש לו מוח בקדקדו כי מוחו ברשותו ויכול להתבונן בו בכל אשר יחפוץ וכשיתבונן בו בגדולת א"ס ב"ה ממילא יוליד במוחו על כל פנים האהבה לה' לדבקה בו בקיום מצותיו ותורתו וזה כל האדם כי היום לעשותם כתיב שהיום הוא עולם המעשה דוקא ולמחר כו' כמ"ש במ"א. והמוח שליט בטבעו ותולדתו על חלל השמאלי שבלב ועל פיו ועל כל האברים שהם כלי המעשה אם לא מי שהוא רשע באמת כמארז"ל שהרשעים הם ברשות לבם ואין לבם ברשותם כלל וזה עונש על גודל ועוצם עונם ולא דברה תורה במתים אלו שבחייהם קרוים מתים כי באמת אי אפשר לרשעים להתחיל לעבוד ה' בלי שיעשו תשובה על העבר תחלה לשבר הקליפו' שהם מסך מבדיל ומחיצה של ברזל המפסקת בינם לאביהם שבשמים ע"י שבירת לבו ומרירת נפשו על חטאיו כמ"ש בזהר על פסוק זבחי אלהים רוח נשברה לב נשבר וגו' שע"י לב נשבר נשברה רוח הטומאה דס"א [ע"ש פ' פינחס ד' ר"מ ופ' ויקרא ד' ח' ור' ה' ע"א ובפי' הרמ"ז שם] והיא בחי' תשובה תתאה להעלות ה' תתאה להקימה מנפילתה שנפלה אל החיצוני' שהוא סוד גלות השכינה כמארז"ל גלו לאדום שכינה עמהם דהיינו כשהאדם עושה מעשה אדום מוריד וממשיך לשם בחי' וניצוץ אלהות המחיה את נר"נ שלו המלובשים בו בנפש הבהמית מהקליפה שבלבו שבחלל השמאלי המולכת בו בעודו רשע ומושלת בעיר קטנה שלו ונר"נ כבושי' בגולה אצלה וכשנשבר לבו בקרבו ונשברה רוח הטומאה וס"א ויתפרדו כו'

היא

then [the *Shechinah*] rises from its fall and remains upright, as is explained elsewhere.

•▲*Chapter 18*

To explain more adequately and more precisely the word "very" in the verse, "But the thing is very nigh unto thee, . . ."[1]

It should be recognised with certainty that even the person whose understanding in the knowledge of G-d is limited, and who has no heart to comprehend the greatness of the blessed *En Sof*, to produce therefrom awe and love [of G-d] even in his mind and understanding alone[2]—however it is a "very nigh thing" for him to observe and practise all the commandments of the Torah and the "Study of the Torah which counter-balances them all," in his very mouth and heart, from the depths of his heart, in true sincerity, with fear and love; namely, the hidden love in the heart of all Jews which is an inheritance to us from our Patriarchs.

However, we must, first of all, preface a clear and precise explanation of the origin and essence of this love, how it became our inheritance, and how awe is also incorporated in it.

▲ The explanation is as follows: The Patriarchs verily constituted the "Chariot,"[3] and therefore they merited [the blessing of] transmitting to their descendants, coming after them for ever, a *nefesh*, *ruach* and *neshamah* from the ten holy *Sefirot* of the four worlds of *Atzilut*, *Beriah*, *Yetzirah* and *Asiyah*, to each according to his station and according to his works. Even the most worthless of worthless men and the sinners of Israel are thus endowed, at the time of marital union, with, at any rate, a *Nefesh d'Nefesh* of *Malchut d'Asiyah* (Royalty in world of Action), which is the lowest grade of holiness [in the world] of *Asiyah*.[4] Nevertheless, since the latter is of the ten holy *Sefirot* it is compounded of them all, including *Chochmah d'Asiyah* (Wisdom of the world of Action), wherein is clothed *Chochmah d'Malchut d'Atzilut* (Wisdom of Royalty in the world of Emanation), incorporating *Chochmah d'Atzilut* (Wisdom of the world of Emanation) which is illuminated by the light of the blessed *En Sof* itself, as is written, "The Lord hath founded the earth in wisdom,"[5] and "In wisdom hast Thou made them all."[6] Thus it comes to pass that the blessed *En Sof* is garbed, as it were, in the wisdom of the human soul, of whatever sort of a Jew he may be. [In turn,] the soul's faculty of wisdom, together with the light of the blessed *En Sof* that is vested in it, spreads throughout the entire soul, animating it "from head to foot," so to speak, as is written, "Wisdom giveth life to them that have it."[7]

---

[1] Deut. *30:14*. [2] *I.e. without emotional sway.* [3] *Being the "vehicle" and bearers of G-dliness. Cf. chs. 23, 29, 34, 37. Cf.* Bereishit Rabba *47:8;* Zohar *III, 252a;* Torah Or, op. cit., *p. 23d f.* [4] Malchut *is the lowest of the Ten Sefirot in each of the Four Worlds;* nefesh *is the lowest aspect of the soul. Thus a* nefesh *of the* nefesh *of* Malchut *is the lowest order of a soul.* [5] Prov. *3:19*. [6] Ps. *104:24*. [7] Eccl. *7:12*.

היא קמה מנפילתה וגם נצבה כמ"ש במ"א:

פרק יח ולתוספת ביאור באר היטב מלת מאד שבפסוק כי קרוב אליך הדבר

מאד וגו' צריך לידע נאמנה כי אף מי שדעתו קצרה בידיעת ה' ואין לו לב להבין בגדולת א"ס ב"ה להוליד ממנה דחילו ורחימו אפי' במוחו ותבונתו לבד אעפ"כ קרוב אליו הדבר מאד לשמור ולעשות כל מצות התורה ות"ת כנגד כולן בפיו ובלבבו ממש מעומקא דלבא באמת לאמיתו בדחילו ורחימו שהיא אהבה מסותרת שבלב כללות ישראל שהיא ירושה לנו מאבותינו רק שצריך להקדי' ולבאר תחלה באר היטב שרש אהבה זו ועניינה ואיך היא ירושה לנו ואיך נכלל בה גם דחילו. והענין כי האבות הן הן המרכבה ועל כן זכו להמשיך נר"נ לבניהם אחריהם עד עולם מעשר ספירות דקדושה שבארבע עולמות אבי"ע לכל אחד ואחד כפי מדרגתו וכפי מעשיו ועל כל פנים אפי' לקל שבקלים ופושעי ישראל נמשך בזיווגם נפש דנפש דמלכות דעשיה שהיא מדרגה התחתונה שבקדושת העשיה ואעפ"כ מאחר שהיא מעשר ספירות קדושות היא כלולה מכולן גם מחכמה דעשי' שבתוכה מלובשת חכמה דמלכות דאצילות שבתוכה חכמה דאצילות שבה מאיר אור א"ס ב"ה ממש כדכתיב ה' בחכמה יסד ארץ וכולם בחכמה עשית ונמצא כי אין סוף ב"ה מלובש בבחי' חכמה שבנפש האדם יהיה מי שיהיה מישראל ובחי' החכמה שבה עם אור א"ס ב"ה המלובש בה מתפשטת בכל בחי' הנפש כולה להחיותה מבחי' ראשה עד בחי' רגלה כדכתיב החכמה תחיה בעליה

ולפעמים

(At times sinners of Israel may even bring down very lofty souls which had been in the depths of the *kelipot*, as is explained in the *Sefer Ha-Gilgulim*.)[8]

●▲ Now, *chochmah* (wisdom) is the source of intelligence and comprehension, and it is above *binah* (understanding) which is intellectual understanding and comprehension, whereas *chochmah* is above them, and their source. Note the etymological composition of the word **חכמה**—**כ"ח מ"ה** ("the potentiality of what is"), that which is not yet comprehended and understood, or grasped intellectually;[9] consequently there is vested in it the light of the *En Sof*, blessed be He, Who can in no way be comprehended by any thought. Hence all Jews, even the women and the illiterate, believe in G–d, since faith is beyond understanding and comprehension,[10] for "The simple believeth every thing, but the prudent man understandeth. . . ."[11] But with regard to the Holy One, blessed be He, Who is beyond intelligence and knowledge, and Who can in no wise be comprehended by any thought—all men are like fools in His blessed presence, as is written, "So brutish am I, and ignorant: I am as a beast before Thee; yet I am continually with Thee, . . ."[12] meaning that "*Because* I am brutish and as a beast, I am continually with Thee."[13] Therefore even the most worthless of worthless and the transgressors of the Israelites, in the majority of cases sacrifice their lives for the sanctity of G–d's Name and suffer harsh torture rather than deny the one G–d, although they be boors and illiterate and ignorant of G–d's greatness. [For] whatever little knowledge they do possess, they do not delve therein at all, [and so] they do not give up their lives by reason of any knowledge and contemplation of G–d. Rather [do they suffer martyrdom] without any knowledge and reflection, but as if it were absolutely impossible to renounce the one G–d; and without any reason or hesitation whatever. This is because the one G–d illuminates and animates the entire *nefesh*, through being clothed in its faculty of *chochmah*, which is beyond any graspable and understood knowledge or intelligence.

●▲ Chapter 19

To elucidate still further, it is necessary to clarify the meaning of the verse, "The candle of G–d is the soul (*neshamah*) of man."[1] What it means is that the souls of Jews, who are called "man,"[2] are, by way of illustration, like the flame of the candle, whose nature it is always to scintillate upwards,

---

[8] Book on Transmigration, *by R. Chayim Vital.* [9] Supra, *ch. 3.* [10] *Where knowledge ends, faith begins.* [11] Prov. *14:15.* [12] Ps. *73:22.* [13] *Communion with G–d could never be fully attained through intellectual comprehension, because G–d is incomprehensible. It is through faith which transcends comprehension that man can feel true closeness with G–d.*

Chapter 19

[1] Prov. *20:27.* [2] Yevamot *61a.*

[ולפעמים ממשיכים פושעי ישראל נשמות גבוהות מאד שהיו בעמקי הקליפות כמ"ש בספר גלגולים]:
הנה החכמה היא מקור השכל וההבנה והיא למעלה מהבינה שהוא הבנת השכל והשגתו והחכמה היא למעלה מההבנה וההשגה והיא מקור להן וזהו לשון חכמה כ"ח מ"ה שהוא מה שאינו מושג ומובן ואינו נתפס בהשגה עדיין ולכן מתלבש בה אור א"ס ב"ה דלית מחשבה תפיסא ביה כלל ולכן כל ישראל אפילו הנשים ועמי הארץ הם מאמינים בה' שהאמונה היא למעלה מן הדעת וההשג' כי פתי יאמין לכל דבר וערום יבין וגו' ולגבי הקב"ה שהוא למעלה מן השכל והדעת ולית מחשבה תפיסא ביה כלל הכל כפתיים אצלו ית' כדכתיב ואני בער ולא ארע בהמות הייתי עמך ואני תמיד עמך וגו' כלומר שבזה שאני בער ובהמות אני תמיד עמך ולכן אפי' קל שבקלים ופושעי ישראל מוסרים נפשם על קדושת ה' על הרוב וסובלים עינוים קשים שלא לכפור בה' אחד ואף אם הם בורים ועמי הארץ ואין יודעים גדולת ה'. וגם במעט שיודעים אין מתבוננים' כלל ואין מוסרי' נפשם מחמת דעת והתבוננות בה' כלל. אלא בלי שום דעת והתבוננות רק כאלו הוא דבר שאי אפשר כלל לכפור בה' אחד בלי שום טעם וטענה ומענה כלל והיינו משום שה' אחד מאיר ומחיה כל הנפש ע"י התלבשותו בבחי' חכמה שבה שהיא למעלה מן הדעת והשכל המושג ומובן:

פרק יט ולתוספת ביאור צריך לבאר היטב מ"ש נר ה' נשמת אדם פי' שישראל

הקרוים אדם נשמתם היא למשל כאור הנר שמתנענע תמיד

for the flame of the fire intrinsically seeks to be parted from the wick in order to unite with its source above, in the universal element of fire which is in the sublunar sphere, as is explained in *Etz Chayim*. And although it would thereby be extinguished and emit no light at all below, and even above, in its source, its light would be nullified, nevertheless this is what it seeks in accordance with its nature.

In like manner does the *neshamah* of man, including the quality of *ruach* and *nefesh*, naturally desire and yearn to separate itself and depart from the body in order to unite with its origin and source in G-d, the fountain-head of all life, blessed be He, though thereby it would become null and void, completely losing its entity therein, with nothing remaining of its former essence and being.[3] Nevertheless, this is its will and desire by its nature.

"Nature" is an applied term for anything that is not in the realm of reason and comprehension. In our case, too, the inference is that this will and desire of the soul are not within the realm of reason, knowledge and intelligence that can be grasped and understood, but beyond graspable and comprehensible knowledge and intelligence; for this nature stems from the faculty of *chochmah* found in the soul, wherein abides the light of the blessed *En Sof*.

• Now this is a general principle in the whole realm of holiness—it [holiness] is only that which is derived from *chochmah* called קודש העליון ("supreme holiness"), whose existence is nullified in the light of the blessed *En Sof* which is clothed in it, so that it is not a thing apart, as is explained above; therefore it is called *koach mah* [power of humility and abnegation]. This stands in direct contrast to the so-called *kelipah* and *sitra achra*, wherefrom are derived the souls of the gentiles who work for themselves alone, demanding, "Give, give!"[4] and "Feed me!"[5] in order to become independent beings and entities, as mentioned above, in direct contrast to the category of *chochmah*. Therefore they are called "dead,"[6] for "wisdom (*chochmah*) gives life,"[7] and it is also written, "They die, without wisdom."[8] So are the wicked and transgressors of Israel before they face the test to sanctify G-d's name. For the faculty of *chochmah* which is in the divine soul, with the spark of G-dliness from the light of the blessed *En Sof* that is clothed in it, is, as it were, in exile in their body, within the animal soul coming from the *kelipah*, in the left part of the heart, which reigns and holds sway over

---

[3] *This passage does not mean extinction of the soul; only its cessation as a* distinct entity. [4] Prov. *30:15*. [5] Gen. *25:30*. [6] Berachot *18b*. [7] Eccl. *7:12*. [8] Job *4:21*.

• 3 Shevat

תמיד למעלה בטבעו מפני שאור האש חפץ בטבע ליפרד מהפתילה ולידבק בשרשו למעלה ביסוד האש הכללי שתחת גלגל הירח כמ"ש בע"ח ואף שע"י זה יכבה ולא יאיר כלום למטה וגם למעלה בשרשו יתבטל אורו במציאות בשרשו אעפ"כ בכך הוא חפץ בטבעו. כך נשמת האדם וכן בחי' רוח ונפש חפצה וחשקה בטבעה ליפרד ולצאת מן הגוף ולידבק בשרשה ומקורה בה' חיי החיים ב"ה הגם שתהיה אין ואפס ותתבטל שם במציאות לגמרי ולא ישאר ממנה מאומה ממהותה ועצמותה הראשון אעפ"כ זה רצונה וחפצה בטבעה וטבע זה הוא שם המושאל לכל דבר שאינו בבחי' טעם ודעת וגם כאן הכוונה שרצון וחפץ זה בנפש אינו בבחי' טעם ודעת ושכל מושג ומובן אלא למעלה מהדעת ושכל המושג והמובן והיא בחי' חכמה שבנפש שבה אור א"ס ב"ה. וזהו כלל בכל סטרא דקדושה שאינו אלא מה שנמשך מחכמה שנק' קודש העליון הבטל במציאות באור א"ס ב"ה המלובש בו ואינו דבר בפני עצמו כנ"ל ולכן נקרא כ"ח מ"ה והוא הפך ממש מבחי' הקליפה וס"א שממנה נפשות אומות העולם דעבדין לגרמייהו ואמרין הב הב והלעיטני להיות יש ודבר בפני עצמו כנ"ל הפך בחי' החכמה ולכן נקראים מתים כי החכמה תחיה וכתיב ימותו ולא בחכמה. וכן הרשעים ופושעי ישראל קודם שבאו לידי נסיון לקדש השם כי בחי' החכמה שבנפש האלהית עם ניצוץ אלהות מאור א"ס ב"ה המלובש בה הם בבחי' גלות בגופם בנפש הבהמית מצד הקליפה שבחלל השמאלי שבלב המולכת ומושלת

בגופם

their body; in accordance with the esoteric doctrine of the exile of the *Shechinah*, as mentioned earlier.[9]

For this reason, this love of the divine soul, whose desire and wish is to unite with G-d, the blessed fountain-head of all life, is called "hidden love," for it is hidden and veiled, in the case of the transgressors of Israel, in the sackcloth of the *kelipah*, whence there enters into them a spirit of folly to sin, as the Rabbis have said, "A person does not sin unless the spirit of folly has entered into him."[10]

• However, this exile of the faculty of *chochmah* refers only to that aspect of it which is diffused throughout the *nefesh* and animates it. Yet the root and core of this faculty of the divine soul remains in the brain and does not clothe itself in the sackcloth of the *kelipah* in the left part of the heart, in veritable exile, but it is, as it were, dormant in the case of the wicked, not exercising its influence in them so long as their knowledge and understanding are preoccupied with mundane pleasures. Nevertheless, when they are confronted with a test in a matter of faith, which transcends knowledge, touching the very soul and the faculty of *chochmah* within it, at such time it is aroused from its sleep and it exerts its influence by virtue of the Divine force that is clothed in it, as is written, "Then the Lord awaked as one out of sleep."[11] [On such occasion the sinner is inspired] to withstand the test of faith in G-d, without any reasoning, or knowledge, or intelligence that may be comprehended by him, and to prevail over the *kelipah* and temptations of this world, whether permitted or prohibited, to which he had been accustomed—even to despise them, and to choose G-d as his portion and lot, yielding to Him his soul [to suffer martyrdom] in order to sanctify His Name. For, even though the *kelipot* had prevailed over him all his life and he was impotent against them, as the Rabbis have said that "The wicked are under the control of their heart,"[12] yet when he faces a test challenging his faith in the One G-d, [a faith] which has its roots in the uppermost heights of holiness, namely, the faculty of *chochmah* of the divine soul, in which is clothed the light of the blessed *En Sof*, then all the *kelipot* are made null and void, and they vanish, as though they had never been, in the presence of the Lord. So it is written, "All the nations are as nothing before Him, . . ."[13] and "For, lo, Thine enemies, O Lord, for lo, Thine enemies shall perish; and the workers of iniquity shall be scattered,"[14] and, again, "As wax melteth before fire, so shall the wicked perish,"[15] and "The hills melted like wax."[16]

---

[9] *Ch. 17.* [10] Sotah *3a.* [11] Ps. *78:65.* [12] Bereshit Rabba *34:11.* [13] Isa *40:17.* [14] Ps. *92:10.* [15] Ps. *68:3.* [16] Ps. *97:5.*

• 4 Shevat

בגופם בסוד גלות השכינה כנ"ל. ולכן נקראת אהבה זו בנפש האלהית שרצונה וחפצה לדבק בה' חיי החיים ברוך הוא בשם אהבה מסותרת כי היא מסותרת ומכוסה בלבוש שק דקליפה בפושעי ישראל וממנה נכנס בהם רוח שטות לחטוא כמאמר רז"ל אין אדם חוטא כו' אלא שגלות הזה לבחי' חכמה אינו אלא לבחי' המתפשטת ממנה בנפש כולה להחיותה אבל שרש ועיקר של בחי' חכמה שבנפש האלהית הוא במוחין ואינה מתלבשת בלבוש שק דקליפה שבלב בחלל השמאלי בבחי' גלות ממש. רק שהיא בבחי' שינה ברשעים ואינה פועלת פעולתה בהם כל זמן שעסוקים בדעתם ובינתם בתאות העולם. אך כשבאים לידי נסיון בדבר אמונה שהיא למעלה מהדעת ונגעה עד הנפש לבחי' חכמה שבה אזי היא ניעורה משנתה ופועלת פעולתה בכח ה' המלובש בה. וכמ"ש ויקץ כישן ה' לעמוד בנסיון באמונת ה' בלי שום טעם ודעת ושכל מושג לו להתגבר על הקליפות ותאוות עוה"ז בהיתר ובאיסור שהורגל בהם ולמאוס בהם ולבחור לו ה' לחלקו ולגורלו למסור לו נפשו על קדושת שמו ואף כי הקליפות גברו עליו כל ימיו ולא יכול להם כמארז"ל שהרשעים הם ברשות לבם מ"מ כשבא לידי נסיון בדבר אמונה בה' אחד שיסודתה בהררי קודש היא בחי' חכמה שבנפש האלהית שבה מלובש אור א"ס ב"ה הרי כל הקליפות בטלים ומבוטלים והיו כלא היו ממש לפני ה' כדכתיב כל הגוים כאין נגדו וגו' וכתיב כי הנה אויביך ה' כי הנה אויביך יאבדו יתפרדו וגו' וכתיב כהמס דונג מפני אש יאבדו וגו' וכתיב הרים כדונג נמסו.

והנה

The force of the Divine light of the blessed *En Sof* that is clothed in the soul's *chochmah* is great and powerful enough to banish and repel the *sitra achra* and the *kelipot* so that they could not even touch its garments, namely, the thought, speech and act of faith in the One G–d. In other words, [it enables one] to withstand a test of self-sacrifice, to the extent of even refusing to do some single act that is contrary to the faith in the One G–d, such as, for example, to bow to an idol, even without acknowledging it in his heart at all, or to utter any false notion, Heaven forbid, regarding the unity of G–d, be it merely by way of rendering lip-service only, while his heart remains perfect in the belief in G–d. This is called "Fear that is contained in love," the natural love of the divine soul that is found in all Jews, the intrinsic desire and will of which is to be attached to its origin and source in the light of the blessed *En Sof*. For by virtue of this love and this desire, it instinctively recoils in fear and dread from touching even the fringe of the impurity of idolatry, Heaven forbid, which denies the faith in one G–d, even where such contact involves only its outer garments, namely, speech and act; without any faith whatever in the heart.

●▲ *Chapter 20*

It is well known that the commandment and admonition[1] concerning idolatry, which are contained in the first two commandments of the Decalogue—"I am"[2] and "Thou shalt not have any other gods,"[3] comprise the entire Torah.[4] For the commandment "I am" contains all the 248 positive precepts, whilst the commandment "Thou shalt not have" contains all the 365 prohibitions.[5] That is why we heard only "I am" and "Thou shalt not have" directly from the Almighty, as our Sages say,[6] "Because these two are the sum-total of the whole Torah."

In order to elucidate this matter clearly, we must first briefly refer to the subject and essence of the Unity[7] of the Holy One, blessed be He, Who is called One and Unique, and "All believe that He is All Alone,"[8] exactly as He was before the world was created, when there was naught beside Him, as is written, "Thou wast the same ere the world was created; Thou hast been the same since the world hath been created. . . ."[9] This means: exactly the same without any change, as it is written, "For I, the Lord, have not changed,"[10] inasmuch

[1] *The positive and prohibitive aspects of the injunction, respectively.* [2] Exod. *20:2.* [3] Ibid., *v. 3.* [4] *The first ("I am") is the positive, the second ("Thou shalt not") is the prohibitive aspect, both ruling out idolatry; the first implicitly, the second —explicitly.* [5] *Cf.* Shenei Luchot Habrit, *beg.* Parshat Yitro. Zohar *II, 276a.* [6] Makkot *24a. The other eight Commandments were relayed by Moses.* [7] *The discussion of this subject is carried over into the following chapter; cf. also ch. 33.* [8] Liturgy *of New Year's Day and Day of Atonement.* [9] Liturgy, *daily Morning Service.* [10] Mal. *3:6.*

והגה אור ה׳ א״ס ב״ה המלובש בחכמה שבנפש גדול ועצום כחו כל כך לגרש ולדחות הס״א והקליפות שלא יוכלו יגעו אפי׳ בלבושיו שהם מחשבה דבור ומעשה של אמונת ה׳ אחד דהיינו לעמוד בנסיון למסור נפשו אפי׳ שלא לעשות רק איזה מעשה לבד נגד אמונת ה׳ אחד כגון להשתחות לעבודה זרה אף שאינו מאמין בה כלל בלבו וכן שלא לדבר תועה ח״ו על אחדות ה׳ אף שאין פיו ולבו שוין רק לבו שלם באמונת ה׳ וזה נקרא דחילו הנכלל ברחימו שהיא אהבה הטבעית שבנפש האלהית שבכללות ישראל שחפצה ורצונה בטבעה לידבק בשרשה ומקורה אור א״ס ב״ה שמפני אהבה זו ורצון זה היא יראה ומפחדת בטבעה מנגוע בקצה טומאת ע״ז ח״ו שהיא נגד אמונת ה׳ אחד אפילו בלבושיה החיצונים שהם דבור או מעשה בלי אמונה בלב כלל:

פרק כ והנה מודעת זאת לכל כי מצות ואזהרת ע״ז שהם שני דברות הראשונים אנכי ולא יהיה לך הם כללות כל התורה כולה. כי דבור אנכי כולל כל רמ״ח מצות עשה. ולא יהיה לך כולל כל שס״ה מצות ל״ת ולכן שמענו אנכי ולא יהיה לך לבד מפי הגבורה כמארז״ל מפני שהם כללות התורה כולה. ולבאר היטב ענין זה צריך להזכיר תחלה בקצרה ענין ומהות אחדותו של הקב״ה שנקרא יחיד ומיוחד וכל מאמינים שהוא לבדו הוא כמו שהיה קודם שנברא העולם ממש שהיה הוא לבדו וכמ״ש אתה הוא עד שלא נברא העולם אתה הוא משנברא כו׳ פי׳ הוא ממש בלי שום שינוי כדכתיב אני ה׳ לא שניתי כי עוה״ז

as this world and likewise all supernal worlds do not effect any change in His blessed Unity,[11] by their having been created *ex nihilo*. For just as He was All Alone, Single and Unique, before they were created, so is He One and Alone, Single and Unique after they were created, since, beside Him, everything is as nothing, ▲verily as null and void. For the coming into being of all the upper and nether worlds out of non-being, and their life and existence sustaining them from reverting to non-existence and nought, as was before, is nothing else but the word of G-d and the breath of His blessed mouth[12] that is clothed in them.

● To illustrate from the soul of a human being:

When a man utters a word,[13] this utterance in itself is as absolutely nothing even when compared only with his general "articulate soul," which is the so-called middle "garment,"[14] namely, its faculty of speech, which can produce speech without limit or end;[15] all the more when it is compared with its so-called innermost "garment," to wit, its faculty of thought, which is the source of speech and its life-force; not to mention when it is compared with the essence and entity of the soul, these being its ten attributes mentioned above,[16] viz. *chochmah*, *binah*, *da'at* (ChaBaD), and so on, from which are derived the "letters" of thought that are clothed in the speech when it is uttered. For thought can as much be defined in terms of "letters" as speech, except that in the former they are more spiritual and ▲refined. But the ten attributes—ChaBaD, and so forth—are the root and source of thought, and, prior to their being clothed in the garment of thought, still lack the element of "letters." For example, when a man suddenly becomes conscious of a certain love or desire in his heart, before it has risen from the heart to the brain to think and meditate about it, it has not yet acquired the element of "letters"; it is only a simple desire and longing in the heart for the object of his affection. All the more so before he began to feel in his heart a craving and desire for that thing, and it is as yet confined within the realm of his wisdom, intellect and knowledge, that is, the thing is known to him to be desirable and gratifying, something good and pleasant to attain and to cling to, as, for instance, to learn some wisdom or to eat some[17] delicious food. Only

---

[11] *Not to mention His essence.* [12] *See* Ps. *33:6.* [13] *Hebrew text should read* דבור *instead of* דבר. [14] *Of the three garments: thought,* speech *and act.* [15] *Physical incapacity (or death) does not limit the soul's potential capacity for speech, which is intrinsic to it.* [16] *Ch. 3.* [17] *Text should read* איזה *instead of* איזו.

עוה"ז וכן כל העולמות העליונים אינן פועלים שום שינוי באחדותו ית' בהבראם מאין ליש שכמו שהיה הוא לבדו הוא יחיד ומיוחד קודם הבראם כן הוא לבדו הוא יחיד ומיוחד אחר שבראם משום דכולא קמיה כלא חשיב וכאין ואפס ממש כי התהוות כל העולמו' עליונים ותחתונים מאין ליש וחיותם וקיומם המקיימם שלא יחזרו להיות אין ואפס כשהיה אינו אלא דבר ה' ורוח פיו ית' המלובש בהם. ולמשל כמו בנפש האדם כשמדבר דבר אחד שדבור זה לבדו כלא ממש אפי' לגבי כללות נפשו המדברת שהוא בחי' לבוש האמצעי שלה שהוא כח הדבור שלה שיכול לדבר דבורי' לאין קץ ותכלית וכ"ש לגבי בחי' לבוש הפנימי שלה שהוא המחשבה שממנה נמשכו הדבורים והיא חיותם וא"צ לומר לגבי מהות ועצמות הנפש שהן עשר בחינותיה הנ"ל חב"ד כו' שמהן נמשכו אותיות מחשבה זו המלובשות בדבור זה כשמדבר כי המחשבה היא ג"כ בחי' אותיות כמו הדבור רק שהן רוחניות ודקות יותר אבל עשר בחי' חב"ד כו' הן שרש ומקור המחשבה ואין בהם בחי' אותיות עדיין קודם שמתלבשות בלבוש המחשבה. למשל כשנופלת איזו אהבה וחמדה בלבו של אדם קודם שעולה מהלב אל המוח לחשב ולהרהר בה אין בה בחי' אותיות עדיין רק חפץ פשוט וחשיקה בלב אל הדבר ההוא הנחמד אצלו וכ"ש קודם שנפלה התאוה והחמדה בלבו לאותו דבר רק היתה בכח חכמתו ושכלו וידיעתו שהיה נודע אצלו אותו דבר שהוא נחמד ונעים וטוב ויפה להשיגו ולידבק בו כגון ללמוד איזו חכמה או לאכול איזו מאכל ערב רק

לאחר

after the desire and craving have already found their way into the heart, through the stimulus of his wisdom, intellect and knowledge, and thence ascended once more back to the brain, to think and meditate on how to translate his craving from the potential into the practical, with a view to actually obtaining that food or acquiring that wisdom—it is here that the so-called "letters" are born[18] in his mind, such "letters" corresponding to the language of each nation, employing them in speech and thought about all things in the world.[19]

●▲ *Chapter* 21

However, "The nature of the Divine order is not like that of a creature of flesh and blood."[1] When a man utters a word, the breath emitted in speaking is something that can be sensed and perceived as a thing apart, separated from its source, namely, the ten faculties of the soul itself. But with the Holy One, blessed be He, His speech is not, Heaven forfend, separated from His blessed Self, for there is nothing outside of Him, and there is no place devoid of Him.[2] Therefore, His blessed speech is not like our speech, G–d forbid, (just as His thought is not like our thought, as is written, "For My thoughts are not like your thoughts,"[3] and "So My ways are higher than your ways, . . ."[4]). His blessed speech is called "speech" only by way of an anthropomorphic illustration, in the sense that, as in the case of man below, whose speech reveals to his audience what was hidden and concealed in his thoughts, so, too, is it on high with the blessed *En Sof*, Whose emitted light and life-force—as it emerges from Him, from concealment into revelation, to create worlds and to sustain them—is called "speech." These [emanations] are indeed, the ten fiats by which the world was created;[5] likewise also the remainder of the Torah, Prophets and Hagiographa, which the Prophets conceived in their prophetic vision.

▲ Yet His so-called speech and thought are united with Him in absolute union as, for example, a person's speech and thought whilst they are still *in potentia* in his wisdom and intellect, or in a desire and craving that are still in the heart prior to rising from the heart to the brain, where by cogitation they are formulated into the so-called "letters";[6] for at that time the "letters" of thought and speech which evolve from that longing or desire, were still *in potentia* in the heart, where they were absolutely

[18] *Text should read* נולדו *instead of* נולדה. [19] *Continued in next chapter.*

Chapter 21

[1] Berachot *40a.* [2] Tikunei Zohar, Tikun *57, p. 91b.* [3] Isa. *55:8.* [4] Ibid., *v. 9.* [5] Avot *5:1.* [6] *See previous chapter.*

לאחר שכבר נפלה החמדה והתאוה בלבו בכח חכמתו ושכלו וידיעתו ואח"כ חזרה ועלתה מהלב למוח לחשב ולהרהר בה איך להוציא תאותו מכח אל הפועל להשיג המאכל או למידת החכמה בפועל הרי בכאן נולדה בחי' אותיות במוחו שהן אותיות כלשון עם ועם המדברים והמהרהרים בהם כל ענייני העולם:

פרק כא והנה מדת הקב"ה שלא כמדת בשר ודם שהאדם כשמדבר דבור הרי הבל הדבור שבפיו הוא מורגש ונראה דבר בפני עצמו מובדל משרשו שהן עשר בחי' הנפש עצמה אבל הקב"ה אין דבורו מובדל ממנו ית' ח"ו כי אין דבר חוץ ממנו ולית אתר פנוי מיני' ולכן אין דבורו ית' כדבורינו ח"ו [כמו שאין מחשבתו כמחשבתינו כדכתיב כי לא מחשבותי מחשבותיכם וכתיב כן גבהו דרכי מדרכיכם וגו'] ולא נקרא דבורו ית' בשם דבור רק עד"מ כמו שדבור התחתון שבאדם הוא מגלה לשומעים מה שהיה צפון ונעלם במחשבתו כך למעלה בא"ס ב"ה יציאת האור והחיות ממנו ית' מההעלם אל הגילוי לברוא עולמות ולהחיותם נק' בשם דבור והן הן עשרה מאמרות שבהן נברא העולם וכן שאר כל התורה נביאים וכתובים שהשיגו הנביאים במראה נבואתם. והרי דבורו ומחשבתו כביכול מיוחדות עמו בתכלית היחוד ד"מ כמו דבורו ומחשבתו של אדם בעודן בכח חכמתו ושכלו או בתשוקה וחמדה שבלבו קודם שעלתה מהלב למוח להרהר בה בבחי' אותיות שאז היו אותיות המחשבה והדבור הזה הנמשכות מחמדה ותשוקה זו בכח בלב ומיוחדות שם בתכלית היחוד

fused with their root, namely, the wisdom and intellect in the brain, and the longing and desire in the heart.

● Verily so, by way of example, are the "speech" and "thought" of the Holy One, blessed be He, absolutely united with His blessed essence and being, even after His blessed "speech" has already become materialised in the creation of the worlds, just as it was united with Him ere the worlds were created. There is thus no manner of change in His blessed Self, but only for the created beings which receive their life-force from His blessed "word", as it were, in its revealed state at the creation of the worlds, in which it is clothed, giving them life through a process of gradual descent from cause to effect and a downward gradation, by means of numerous and various contractions,[7] until the created beings can receive their life and existence from it, without losing their ▲ entity. These "contractions" are all in the nature of "veiling of the Countenance," to obscure and conceal the light and life-force that are derived from His blessed "word," so that it shall not reveal itself in a greater radiance than the lower worlds are capable of receiving. Hence it seems to them as if the light and life-force of the word of the Omnipresent, blessed be He, which is clothed in them, were something apart from His blessed Self, and it only issues from Him, just as the speech of a human being [issues] from his soul. Yet, in regard to the Holy One, blessed be He, no concealment or delitescency hides or obscures anything from Him, to Whom darkness is like light, as is written, "Yea, the darkness obscureth not from Thee. . . ."[8] For all the "contractions" and "garments" are not things distinct from Him, Heaven forfend, but "Like the snail, whose garment is part of his body,"[9] and as is written, "The Lord, He is G–d,"[10] as is explained elsewhere.[11] Therefore, in His Presence all else is of no account whatever.

●▲ *Chapter 22*

Yet, since "The Torah employs human language,"[1] the "word" of G–d, blessed be He, is actually called "speech," like the speech of a human being, for in truth it is so, by virtue of the descent and flow of the life-force to the lower planes, by means of many and powerful contractions

[7] *The process of* tzimtzum. [8] Ps. *139:12.* [9] Bereishit Rabba *21.* [10] Deut. *4:35.* [11] *The Tetragrammaton (YHVH, usually translated "the L–rd") is conceived in Kabbalah as the transcendent creative Divine force, while* Elohim *("G–d") —the immanent Divine force concealed in nature. Cf.* Sha'ar ha-Yichud veha-Emunah, *ch. 6. The equation emphasises the absolute Unity of the Creator.*

Chapter 22
[1] Berachot *22a.*

● 8 Shevat ● 9 Shevat ▲ *16 Shevat* ▲ *17 Shevat*

היחוד בשרשן שהן החכמה ושכל שבמוח וחמדה ותשוקה שבלב. וככה ממש ד"מ מיוחדות דבורו ומחשבתו של הקב"ה בתכלית היחוד במהותו ועצמותו ית' גם אחר שיצא דבורו ית' אל הפועל בבריאות העולמות כמו שהיה מיוחד עמו קודם בריאת העולמו' ואין שום שינוי כלל לפניו ית' אלא אל הברואים המקבלים חיותם מבחי' דבורו ית' בבחי' יציאתו כבר אל הפועל בבריאת העולמות שמתלבש בהם להחיותם ע"י השתלשלו' מעלה לעלול וירידת המדרגו' בצמצומים רבים ושונים עד שיוכלו הברואים לקבל חיותם והתהוותם ממנו ולא יתבטלו במציאות וכל הצמצומים הם בחי' הסתר פנים להסתיר ולהעלים האור והחיות הנמשך מדבורו ית' שלא יתגלה בבחי' גילוי רב שלא יוכלו התחתונים לקבל ולכן ג"כ נדמה להם אור וחיות הדבור של מקום ב"ה המלובש בהם כאלו הוא דבר מובדל ממהותו ועצמותו ית' רק שנמשך ממנו ית' כמו דבור של אדם מנפשו. אך לגבי הקב"ה אין שום צמצום והסתר והעלם מסתיר ומעלים לפניו וכחשכה כאורה כדכתיב גם חשך לא יחשיך ממך וגו' משום שאין הצמצומים והלבושי' דבר נפרד ממנו ית' ח"ו אלא כהדין קמצא דלבושי' מיניה וביה כמ"ש כי ה' הוא האלהים וכמ"ש במ"א ולכן קמיה כולא כלא חשיב ממש:

פרק כב

רק שהתורה דברה כלשון ב"א ונקרא בתורה דבורו של מקו' ב"ה בשם דבור ממש כדבורו של אדם לפי שבאמת כך הוא דרך ירידת והמשכת החיות לתחתונים בצמצומים רבים

of various kinds, in order that many diverse creatures be created from them.

Indeed, so great and powerful are the contractions and concealment of the Countenance, that even unclean things, *kelipot* and *sitra achra*, can come into being and be created, receiving their life and existence from the Divine word and the breath of His blessed mouth, in concealment of His Countenance and by virtue of the downward gradations.

Therefore are [the *kelipot*] called[2] "other gods" (אלהים אחרים), for their nurture and life are not of the so-called "Countenance" but of the so-called "hinder part" (אחוריים)[3] of holiness; "hinder" exemplifying the act of a person giving something unwillingly to an enemy, when he throws it to him over his shoulder, as it were, having turned away his face from him since he hates him.

So, on high, the term "Countenance" exemplifies the inner[4] quality of the Supernal Will and true desire, in which G–d delights to dispense life from the realm of holiness to everyone who is near to Him.

But the *sitra achra*, and unholiness, is "An abomination unto G–d which He hates,"[5] and He does not give it life from His inner will and true desire as if He delighted in it, Heaven forbid, but in the manner of one who reluctantly throws something over his shoulder to his enemy; [He does so] only to punish the wicked and to give a goodly reward to the righteous who subjugate the *sitra achra*. This is [why it is] called the "hinder-part" of the Supernal Will.

• Now, the Supernal Will, of the quality of "Countenance," is the source of life which animates all worlds. But since it is in no way bestowed on the *sitra achra*, and even the so-called "hinder-part" of the Supernal Will is not actually clothed in it, but merely hovers over it from above, therefore it is the abode of death and defilement—may G–d preserve us! For the tiny amount of light and life that it derives and absorbs into itself from the so-called "hinder-part" of the supernal holiness is, as it were, in a state of actual exile in it, as an aspect of the esoteric doctrine of the exile of the *Shechinah*, referred to above.[6]

Therefore, also, it is termed "other gods," since it constitutes actual idolatry and denial of the unity of the Supreme King of kings, the Holy One, blessed be He. For inasmuch as the light and life of holiness are, as it were, in a state of exile, within it, it does not

[2] *Heb. text should read* נקראים *instead of* נקרא. [3] *A gloss based on the words* אחרים—אחוריים. [4] *A gloss based on the words* פנימיות—פנים. [5] Deut. *12:31*. [6] *Ch. 19*.

רבים ועצומים מינים ממינים שונים להבראות מהם
ברואים רבים מינים ממינים שונים וכ"כ גברו ועצמו
הצמצומים והסתר פנים העליונים עד שיוכלו להתהוות
ולהבראות גם דברים טמאים וקליפות וס"א ולקבל
חיותם וקיומם מדבר ה' ורוח פיו ית' בהסתר פנים
וירידת המדרגות ולכן נקרא אלהים אחרים מפני
שיניקתם וחיותם אינה מבחי' פנים אלא מבחי' אחוריים
דקדושה ופי' אחוריים כאדם הנותן דבר לשונאו שלא
ברצונו שמשליכו לו כלאחר כתפו כי מחזיר פניו ממנו
משנאתו אותו כך למעלה בחי' פנים הוא פנימית
הרצון העליון וחפצו האמיתי אשר חפץ ה' להשפיע
חיות לכל הקרוב אליו מסטרא דקדושה אבל הס"א
והטומאה היא תועבת ה' אשר שנא ואינו משפיע לה
חיות מפנימית הרצון וחפצו האמיתי אשר חפץ בה ח"ו
כ"א כמאן דשדי בתר כתפוי לשונאו שלא ברצונו
רק כדי להעניש את הרשעים וליתן שכר טוב לצדיקי'
דאכפיין לס"א וזה נקרא בחי' אחוריים דרצון העליון
ב"ה. והנה רצון העליון בבחי' פנים הוא מקור החיים
המחיה את כל העולמות ולפי שאינו שורה כלל על
הס"א וגם בחי' אחוריים של רצון העליון אינו מלובש
בתוכה ממש אלא מקיף עליה מלמעלה לכך היא מקום
המיתה והטומאה ה' ישמרנו כי מעט מזער אור וחיות
שיונקת ומקבלת לתוכה מבחי' אחוריים דקדושה
שלמעלה הוא בבחי' גלות ממש בתוכה בסוד גלות
השכינה הנ"ל ולכן נקרא בשם אלהים אחרים שהיא
ע"ז ממש וכפירה באחדותו של ממ"ה הקב"ה כי מאחר
שאור וחיות דקדושה הוא בבחי' גלות בתוכה אינה
בטילה

surrender itself in any degree to the holiness of the Holy One, blessed be He. On the contrary, it surges upward like an eagle, saying, "I am, and there is nothing beside me,"[7] or, as the utterance, "My river is mine own, and I have made myself."[8] That is why the Rabbis, of blessed memory, said that arrogance truly compares with idolatry,[9] for the essence and root of idolatry is that it is regarded as a thing in itself, sundered from the Divine holiness; it does not imply an outright denial of G–d, as is stated in the *Gemara* that they [the heathens] call Him "The G–d of gods,"[10] thus only presuming themselves also to be entities and independent beings. But thereby they separate themselves from the blessed Divine holiness, since they do not surrender themselves to Him. For the supernal holiness rests only on what is surrendered to Him, as is explained above.[11] Therefore they are called in the holy *Zohar*[12] "Peaks of separation." But this constitutes a denial of His true unity, where everything is as nothing compared with Him and truly nullified before Him and before His will which animates them all and constantly gives them existence out of nothing.

•▲ *Chapter 23*

In the light of all that has been said above, we can better understand and more fully and clearly elucidate the statement in the *Zohar*[1] that "The Torah and the Holy One, blessed be He, are entirely one," and the commentary in the *Tikunim* that "The 248 commandments are the 248 'organs' of the King."[2]

The commandments constitute the innermost Supreme Will and His true desire which are clothed in all the upper and nether worlds, thereby giving them life, inasmuch as their very life and sustenance is dependent upon the performance of the commandments by the [creatures], in the lower world, as is known.

It follows that the performance of the commandments and their fulfillment is the innermost garment of the innermost Supreme Will, since it is due to this performance that the light and life of the Supreme Will issue forth to be clothed in ▲the worlds. Hence they are called "organs" of the King, as a figure of speech, for just as the organs of the human body are a garment for its soul and are completely and utterly surrendered to it, as evidenced from the fact that as soon as a person desires to stretch out his hand or foot, they obey his will immediately and forthwith, without any command or instruction to them and with no hesitation whatever, but in the very instant

[7] Isa. *47:8;* Zeph. *2:15*. [8] *The quotation is a combination of* Ezek. *29:9 and 29:3*. [9] Sotah *4b*. [10] Menachot *110a*. [11] *Ch.6* [12] *I, 158a*.

Chapter 23
[1] *Cf. I, 24a; II, 60a;* Tikunei Zohar *21b*. [2] Tikunei Zohar, Tikun *30*.

בטילה כלל לגבי קדושת הקב"ה ואדרבה מגביה עצמה כנשר לומר אני ואפסי עוד וכמאמר יאור לי ואני עשיתני ולכן אמרו רז"ל שגסות הרוח שקולה כע"ז ממש כי עיקר ושרש ע"ז הוא מה שנחשב לדבר בפני עצמו נפרד מקדושתו של מקום ולא כפירה בה' לגמרי כדאיתא בגמ' דקרו ליה אלהא דאלהיא אלא שגם הם מחשיבים עצמם ליש ודבר בפני עצמו ובזה מפרידים את עצמם מקדושתו של מקום ב"ה מאחר שאין בטלים לו ית' כי אין קדושה עליונה שורה אלא על מה שבטל לו ית' כנ"ל ולכן נקראי' טורי דפרודא בזה"ק והרי זו כפירה באחדותו האמיתית דכולא קמיה כלא חשיב ובטל באמת לו ית' ולרצונו המחיה את כולם ומהוה אותם מאין ליש תמיד:

פרק כג ועם כל הנ"ל יובן ויבואר היטב בתוספ' ביאור מה שאמרו בזהר דאוריית'

וקב"ה כולא חד ובתיקוני' פירשו דרמ"ח פיקודין אינון רמ"ח אברין דמלכא לפי שהמצות הן פנימיות רצון העליון וחפצו האמיתי המלובש בכל העולמו' העליוני' ותחתוני' להחיותם כי כל חיותם ושפעם תלוי במעשה המצות של התחתוני' כנודע. ונמצא שמעשה המצות וקיומן הוא לבוש הפנימי לפנימית רצון העליון שממעשה זה נמשך אור וחיות רצון העליון להתלבש בעולמות ולכן נקרא' אברי דמלכא ד"מ כמו שאברי גוף האדם הם לבוש לנפשו ובטלים לגמרי אליה מכל וכל כי מיד שעולה ברצונו של אדם לפשוט ידו או רגלו הן נשמעות לרצונו תכף ומיד בלי שום צווי ואמירה להן ובלי שום שהייה כלל אלא כרגע ממש כשעלה

that he wills it; so, by way of example, is the life-force animating the performance of the commandments and their fulfillment completely surrendered to the Supreme Will which is clothed therein, becoming in relation to it like a body to a soul.

▲ Likewise the external garment of the divine soul in the person fulfilling and practising the commandment—this being its faculty of action—clothes itself in the vitality of the performance of the commandment, thus also becoming like a body in relation to the soul, the "soul" being the Supreme Will to which it is completely surrendered. In this way, the organs of the human body which perform the commandment—in which the divine soul's faculty of action is clothed at the time of the act and fulfillment of the commandment—truly become a vehicle for the Supreme Will; as, for example, the hand which distributes charity to the poor or performs another commandment; or the feet which carry a person towards the performance of a commandment; similarly with the mouth and tongue engaged in uttering the words of the Torah, or the brain engaged in reflecting on the words of the Torah or on the fear of Heaven, or the greatness of G-d, blessed be He.

This is what the Sages meant when they said that "The Patriarchs are truly the chariot,"[3] for all their organs were completely holy and detached from mundane matters, serving as a vehicle solely for the Supreme Will alone throughout their lives.

●▲ As for the thought and meditation—in the words of the Torah—that are in the brain, and the power of speech—engaged in the words of the Torah—that is in the mouth,[4] these being the innermost garments of the divine soul, not to mention the divine soul itself which is clothed in them—all of them are completely merged in perfect unity with the Supreme Will, and are not merely a vehicle. For the Supreme Will is identical with the very subject of the *halachah* wherein one thinks and speaks, inasmuch as all the laws are particular streams flowing from the inner Supreme Will itself, since His blessed Will willed it that a particular act be permissible, or a food ritually fit for consumption, or this [person] inculpable and that entirely innocent, or the reverse. So also are the letter combinations of the Pentateuch, Prophets and Hagiographa a promulgation of His will and wisdom which are united with the blessed *En Sof* in perfect unity, since He is the Knower and the Knowledge, and so forth. This, then, is the meaning of the above mentioned quotation that "The Torah and the Holy One, blessed be He, are altogether One," and not merely "organs" of the King

---

[3] Bereishit Rabba *47:6*. [4] *I.e. the faculties of thought and speech as distinct from action.*

כשעלה ברצונו. כך ד"מ החיות של מעשה המצות וקיומן הוא בטל לגמרי לגבי רצון העליון המלובש בו ונעשה לו ממש כגוף לנשמה. וכן הלבוש החיצון של נפש האלהית שבאדם המקיים ועושה המצוה שהוא כח ובחי' המעשה שלה הוא מתלבש בחיות של מעשה המצוה ונעשה ג"כ כגוף לנשמה לרצון העליון ובטל אליו לגמרי ועל כן גם אברי גוף האדם המקיימים המצוה שכח ובחי' המעשה של נפש האלהית מלובש בהם בשעת מעשה וקיום המצוה הם נעשו מרכבה ממש לרצון העליון כגון היד המחלקת צדקה לעניים או עושה מצוה אחרת. ורגלים המהלכות לדבר מצוה וכן הפה ולשון שמדברי' דברי תורה והמוח שמהרהר בד"ת וי"ש ובגדולת ה' ב"ה. וזהו שארז"ל האבות הן הן המרכבה שכל אבריהם כולם היו קדושים ומובדלים מענייני עוה"ז ולא נעשו מרכבה רק לרצון העליון לבדו כל ימיהם: אך המחשבה וההרהור בד"ת שבמוח וכח הדבור בד"ת שבפה שהם לבושי' הפנימים של נפש האלהית וכ"ש נפש האלהית עצמה המלובשת בהם כולם מיוחדים ממש ביחוד גמור ברצון העליון ולא מרכבה לבד כי רצון העליון הוא הוא הדבר הלכה עצמה שמהרהר ומדבר בה שכל ההלכות הן פרטי המשכות פנימיות רצון העליון עצמו שכך עלה ברצונו ית' שדבר זה מותר או כשר או פטור או זכאי או להפך וכן כל צרופי אותיות תנ"ך הן המשכת רצונו וחכמתו המיוחדו' בא"ס ב"ה בתכלית היחוד שהוא היודע והוא המדע כו' וז"ש דאורייתא וקב"ה כולא חד ולא אברין דמלכא לחוד

כפיקודין

as are the commandments.

▲ Now, since at such time as a person occupies himself with the words of the Torah, the Supreme Will, united as it is in perfect unity with the blessed *En Sof*, is completely manifest and in no way obscured in the divine soul and its innermost garments, i.e. its thought and speech—it follows that the soul and its garments are also at such time veritably united with the blessed *En Sof* in perfect unity, like the union of the "speech" and "thought" of the Holy One, blessed be He, with His essence and being, as mentioned above.[5] For there is no separate thing except through "concealment of the Countenance" as explained there. Moreover, their union is even of a higher and profounder order than the union of the blessed *En Sof* with the upper worlds, since the Supreme Will is actually manifest in the soul and its garments when they are engaged in the Torah, because it is identical with the Torah; while all the supernal worlds receive their vitality from the light and life that are derived from the Torah, which is His Will and Wisdom, as it is written, "In wisdom Thou hast made them all."[6] Thus, His Wisdom, i.e. the Torah, is above them all, and it is identical with His blessed Will which is described as "encompassing" all worlds, i.e. that aspect which cannot clothe itself within the worlds, but animates and illuminates in a transcending and encompassing manner.[7] Yet, it [this very light] does clothe itself in the human soul and its garments in a truly manifest form, when the person occupies himself with the words of the Torah, even though he does not perceive it, . . .[8] (—this is what enables him to endure it, because he does not perceive it; it is otherwise, however, in the case of the upper spheres).[9]

• With the above in mind, it becomes clear why the study of the Torah excels so much over all other commandments, including even prayer which is the unifying force of the upper spheres. (As for the ruling that one, whose study of the Torah is not his entire occupation, must interrupt his study for prayer,[10] this is only because he pauses and interrupts his studies anyway[11]).

▲ From this the intelligent man will be able to draw a sense of great awe as he occupies himself with the Torah, considering how his soul, and its "garments" in the brain and mouth, are truly merged in perfect unity with the Supreme Will and light of the blessed *En Sof*

[5] *Ch. 21.* [6] Ps. *104:24.* [7] *Further discussion on the immanent and transcending aspects of the Divine emanation will be found in chs. 41, 46, 48 and 51.* [8] *Cf.* Megillah *3a.* [9] *. . . where there is no such obscurity as in the physical world.* [10] *Seemingly indicating that prayer has priority over study.* [11] Shabbat *11a; Maimonides,* Hilchot Tefilla, *6:8; Rabbi Schneur Zalman,* Shulchan Aruch, *106:4.*

כפיקודין. ומאחר שרצון העליון המיוחד בא"ס ב"ה בתכלית היחוד הוא בגילוי לגמרי ולא בהסתר פנים כלל וכלל בנפש האלהית ולבושיה הפנימים שהם מחשבתה ודבורה באותה שעה שהאדם עוסק בדברי תורה הרי גם הנפש ולבושיה אלו מיוחדים ממש בא"ס ב"ה באותה שעה בתכלית היחוד כיחוד דבורו ומחשבתו של הקב"ה במהותו ועצמותו כנ"ל כי אין שום דבר נפרד כי אם בהסתר פנים כנ"ל ולא עוד אלא שיחודם הוא ביתר שאת ויתר עז מיחוד אור א"ס ב"ה בעולמות עליונים מאחר שרצון העליון הוא בגילוי ממש בנפש ולבושיה העוסקים בתורה שהרי הוא הוא התורה עצמה וכל העולמות העליונים מקבלים חיותם מאור וחיות הנמשך מהתורה שהיא רצונו וחכמתו ית' כדכתיב כולם בחכמה עשית וא"כ החכמה שהיא התורה למעלה מכולם והיא היא רצונו ית' הנק' סובב כל עלמין שהיא בחי' מה שאינו יכול להתלבש בתוך עלמין רק מחיה ומאיר למעלה בבחי' מקיף והיא היא המתלבשת בנפש ולבושיה בבחי' גילוי ממש כשעוסקים בד"ת ואע"ג דאיהו לא חזי כו' [ומשו' הכי יכול לסבול משום דלא חזי משא"כ בעליונים]. ובזה יובן למה גדלה מאד מעלת העסק בתורה יותר מכל המצות ואפי' מתפלה שהיא יחוד עולמות עליונים [והא דמי שאין תורתו אומנתו צריך להפסיק היינו מאחר דמפסיק ומבטל בלא"ה]. ומזה יוכל המשכיל להמשיך עליו יראה גדולה בעסקו בתורה כשיתבונן איך שנפשו ולבושיה שבמוחו ובפיו הם מיוחדי' ממש בתכלית היחוד ברצון העליון ואור א"ס ב"ה ממש

המתגלה

which are manifest in them, compared with which all the worlds, supernal and nether, are truly as nought and as a nonentity and nullity, so much so that the Divine light is not actually clothed in them, but merely surrounds all the worlds in a form of "encirclement," as it were, in order to provide their essential source of life; only some glow which they can bear is clothed in them, in order that they should not revert to nought altogether.

This is the meaning of the verse, "And G-d commanded us [to do] all these statutes, in order to fear G-d. . . ."[12] [Regarding this "great fear" it was said, "Where there is no wisdom, there is no fear,"[13] and in relation to it the Torah is called "A gateway to the dwelling,"[14] as is explained elsewhere]. However, not every mind can sustain such fear; yet even he whose mind cannot bear such fear at all, whether in whole or in part, because of the inferiority of his soul's level in its root and source in the lower [15] gradations of the ten *sefirot* of the World of *Asiyah*, nevertheless the lack of such fear is no obstacle to performance, as will be explained later.[16]

●▲ Chapter 24

Antithetically,[1] the 365 prohibitive commandments of the Torah, as well as the Rabbinic injunctions, since they are contrary to His blessed Will and Wisdom and, indeed, the very opposite thereof, represent total and complete separation from His blessed Unity and Oneness, the same as the *sitra achra* and *kelipah* which are called *avodah zarah* (idolatry) and "other gods" because of the "Hiding of the Countenance" of the Supreme Will, as is explained above.[2]

Likewise the three "garments" of the *nefesh* stemming from the *kelipat nogah* in Jews, namely, thought, speech and action, when clothed in the 365 prohibitive commands of the Torah, or in the Rabbinic injunctions, as also the essence of the *nefesh* itself which pervades these garments—all become actually united with the said *sitra achra* and *kelipah*, called *avodah zarah*. Furthermore, they become subordinate and secondary to it [the *kelipah*], and considerably inferior and more debased than it. For the *kelipah* is not clothed in a corporeal body,[3] and it knows its Master and is not rebellious against Him by any independent act of sending its evil messengers, G-d forbid, when not commissioned by the Omnipresent, blessed be He. Witness Balaam's statement, "I cannot go beyond the word of

[12] Deut. *6:24. In the quotation the word* לעשות *("to do") is missing.* [13] Avot *3:17.* [14] Shabbat *31b;* Yoma *72b.* [15] *In the text the word* תחתונים *should be amended to read* תחתונות. [16] *Ch. 41.*

Chapter 24
[1] *I.e. in contrast to the 248 positive precepts whereby the worshipper achieves unity with G-d, as explained in the previous chapter.* [2] *Ch. 22.* [3] *Hence not so "screened" from the Divine light.*

המתגלה בהם מה שכל העולמות עליונים ותחתונים כלא חשיבי קמיה וכאין ואפס ממש עד שאינו מתלבש בתוכם ממש אלא סובב כל עלמין בבחי' מקיף להחיות' עיקר חיותם רק איזו הארה מתלבשת בתוכם מה שיכולים לסבול שלא יתבטלו במציאות לגמרי. וז"ש ויצונו ה' את כל החוקים האלה ליראה את ה' וגו' [ועל יראה גדולה זו אמרו אם אין חכמה אין יראה והתורה נקראת אצלה תרעא לדרתא כמ"ש במ"א] אלא דלאו כל מוחא סביל דא יראה כזו. אך גם מאן דלא סביל מוחו כלל יראה זו לא מינה ולא מקצתה מפני פחיתות ערך נפשו בשרשה ומקורה במדרגות תחתונים דעשר ספירות דעשיה אין יראה זו מעכבת בו למעשה כמ"ש לקמן:

פרק כד וזה לעומת זה הן שס"ה מצות לא תעשה דאורייתא וכל איסורי דרבנן מאחר שהן נגד רצונו וחכמתו ית' והפכם ממש הם נפרדים מיחודו ואחדותו ית' בתכלית הפירוד ממש כמו הס"א והקליפה הנק' ע"ז ואלהים אחרים מחמת הסתר פנים של רצון העליון כנ"ל. וכן ג' לבושי הנפש שמקליפת נוגה שבישראל שהם מחשבה דבור ומעשה המלובשי' בשס"ה ל"ת דאורייתא ודרבנן וכן מהות הנפש עצמה המלובשת בלבושיה כולם מיוחדים ממש בס"א וקליפ' זו הנק' ע"ז ולא עוד אלא שבטלים וטפלים אליה וגרועים ופחותים ממנה מאד כי היא אינה מלובשת בגוף חומרי ויודעת את רבונה ואינה מורדת בו לפעול פעולתה במשלחת מלאכי רעים שלה שלא בשליחותו של מקום ב"ה ח"ו וכמאמר בלעם לא אוכל לעבור את פי ה'

G–d. . . ."[4] And even though it is called *avodah zarah*, He is, at least, acknowledged as "The G–d of gods," and the latter are utterly powerless to contravene His blessed Will, for they know and apprehend that He is their life and sustenance, since they derive their nurture from the so-called "hinder-most part" of the blessed Supreme Will which encompasses them. It is only because their sustenance and inner life-source are, as it were, in "exile" within them that they presume to regard themselves as gods, which is a denial of His unity. Nevertheless they are not so completely heretical as to deny G–d and to assert that He does not exist; only they regard Him as the "G–d of gods," recognising that their life and existence are [ultimately] derived and bestowed upon them from His blessed Will. Therefore they are never rebellious against His blessed Will.

If this be so, then the person who opposes His blessed Will is exceedingly inferior to and more debased than the *sitra achra* and the *kelipah*, called *avodah zarah* and "strange gods," and he is completely sundered from His Unity and Oneness, even more than they, as though denying His unity more radically than they, G–d forbid.[5]

Compare what is written in *Etz Chayim*, Portal 42, end of ch. 4, that the evil which is in this material world is the dregs of the coarse *kelipot*, . . .; hence the ultimate in the purifying process, and so on.[6] Therefore are all worldly things severe and evil, and the wicked prevail in it, and so forth.[7]

● This explains the commentary of our Sages, of blessed memory, on the verse, "If any man's wife turn aside,"[8] that "no person commits any transgression [unless a spirit of folly has entered into him]."[9] For even an adulterous woman, with her frivolous nature, could have controlled her passionate drive, were it not for the spirit of folly in her which covers, obscures and conceals the hidden love of her divine soul yearning to cleave to her faith in G–d, in His Unity and Oneness, and not to be parted, G–d forbid, even at the cost of her life, from His Unity, by idolatrous worship, G–d forbid, be it only by an outward acknowledgment, without any belief at all in her heart. Surely she could subdue the temptation and lust of adultery, which is lighter suffering than death, may G–d protect us! But the distinction she makes between the interdict against adultery and that against bowing to an idol is also but a spirit of folly stemming from the *kelipah* which envelops the divine soul up to, but not including, its faculty of *chochmah*,

---

[4] Num. *22:18.* [5] *Note the distinction between evil and evil-doer.* [6] *See Glossary on* Birur. [7] *Our material world being the "lowest" or grossest, evil is here at its strongest.* [8] Num. *5:12.* [9] Sotah *3a.*

● 15 Shevat

ה׳ וגו׳ ואף שנקרא ע״ז הא קרו ליה אלהא דאלהיא ואינם יכולי׳ לעבור כלל על רצונו ית׳ כי יודעי׳ ומשיגים שהוא חיותם וקיומם שיונקים מבחי׳ אחוריים דאחוריי׳ של רצון העליון ב״ה המקיף עליהם אלא שיניקתם וחיותם שבתוכם היא בבחי׳ גלות בתוכם להחשיב עצמן אלהות והרי זו כפירה באחדותו אבל מ״מ אינן כופרים וכחשו בה׳ לגמרי ולומר לא הוא אלא דקרו ליה אלהא דאלהיא דהיינו חיותם וקיומם הנמשך ויורד עליהם מרצונו ית׳ ולכן אינן עוברין רצונו ית׳ לעולם. וא״כ האדם העובר על רצונו ית׳ הוא גרוע ופחות הרבה מאד מהס״א וקליפה הנקראת ע״ז ואלהים אחרים והוא בתכלי׳ הפירוד מיחודו ואחדותו של הקב״ה יותר ממנה וכאלו כופר באחדותו יותר ממנה ח״ו. וכמ״ש בע״ח שער מ״ב סוף פ״ד שהרע שבעו״הז החומרי הוא שמרי הקליפות הגסות כו׳ והוא תכלית הבירור וכו׳ ולכן כל מעשה עו״הז קשים ורעים והרשעים גוברים בו וכו׳: ולכן אמרו רז״ל על פסוק כי תשטה אשתו אין אדם עובר עבירה וכו׳ דאפי׳ אשה המנאפת שדעתה קלה היתה מושלת ברוח תאותה לולי רוח שטות שבה המכסה ומסתיר ומעלי׳ את האהבה מסותרת שבנפשה האלהית לדבקה באמונת ה׳ ויחודו ואחדותו ולא ליפרד ח״ו מאחדותו אפי׳ נוטלים את נפשה ממנה לעבוד ע״ז ח״ו ואפי׳ בהשתחואה לבדה בלי שום אמונה בלב כלל וכ״ש לכבוש היצר ותאות הניאוף שהם יסורים קלים ממיתה ה׳ ישמרנו וההפרש שאצלה בין איסור ניאוף לאיסור השתחואה לע״ז הוא ג״כ רוח שטות דקליפה המלבשת לנפש האלהית עד בחי׳ חכמה שבה ולא עד

בכלל

because of the Divine light that is clothed in that faculty, as mentioned above.[10]

The real truth, however, is that even in the case of a minor sin, the offender transgresses against the blessed Supreme Will and is completely sundered from His blessed Unity and Oneness even more than the *sitra achra* and the *kelipah*, called "strange gods" and "idolatry," and than all things that are derived therefrom in this world, to wit, the unclean cattle and beasts, and unclean birds, and the abominable insects and reptiles. To quote: "The gnat was [created] ahead of thee [man],"[11] which means that even the gnat—which consumes but does not excrete,[12] and is the lowest *kelipah* and the most distant from holiness, which bestows benevolence even at the greatest distance—precedes the sinful man in the descending gradation and flow of life from the blessed Supreme Will. All the more so the other unclean living creatures, and even the fierce beasts, all of which do not deflect from their purpose but obey His blessed command, even though they cannot perceive it. . . .[13] To quote further, "And the fear of you and the dread of you shall be upon every beast of the earth,"[14] eliciting the commentary of our Sages, of blessed memory, that "No evil beast defies a human being unless he appears to it like an animal."[15] While confronting the righteous, from whose face the Divine image never departs, the evil beasts are humbled before them, as is stated in the *Zohar* of Daniel in the lions' den.

It is, therefore, clear that he who sins and transgresses against His blessed Will, even in a minor offence, is, at the time he commits it, more completely removed from the Supreme Holiness, namely His blessed Unity and Oneness, than all the unclean living creatures and abominable insects and reptiles which derive their sustenance from the *sitra achra* and the *kelipah* of "idolatry."

• As for the principle that saving a life overrides certain prohibitions,[16] and the circumstances when the law calls for the commission of a transgression so as to escape death[17]—this is in accordance with the explanation of our Sages, of blessed memory, that "The Torah declares, 'violate one Sabbath for him, that he may observe many Sabbaths,'"[18] and not because of the relative lenity or gravity of the sins. (This is supported by the fact that the violation of the Sabbath is extremely grave and comparable with idolatry in relation to the law of animal slaughtering by one who is a habitual transgressor of any particular Jewish precept, as codified in *Yore De'ah* Sect. II, unlike the case of one whose particular wilful sin is that of incest.[19] Nevertheless, when it is a question of saving a life, the prohibitions of the Sabbath are suspended, but never those of incest. *Ergo*, it is a decree of

---

[10] *Ch. 19.* [11] Sanhedrin *38a;* Vayikra Rabba *14.* [12] *The symbol of extreme selfishness.* [13] *Cf. Megillah 3a.* [14] Gen. *9:2.* [15] Sanhedrin *38b; i.e. debased by sin.* [16] Yoma *82a.* [17] Sanhedrin *74a.* [18] Shabbat *151b;* Yoma *85b.*

[19] *Jewish law disqualifies one who openly desecrates the Sabbath, or commits idolatry, from slaughtering animals for "kosher" consumption. But not in the case of a person guilty of any other particular transgression, including incest.*

• 16 Shevat

בכלל מפני אור ה׳ המלובש בחכמה כנ״ל. אבל באמת לאמיתו אפי׳ עבירה קלה הרי העוברה עובר על רצון העליון ב״ה והוא בתכלית הפירוד מיחודו ואחדותו ית׳ יותר מס״א וקליפה הנקרא׳ אלהים אחרי׳ וע״ז ממש ויותר מכל הדברים הנשפעים ממנה בע״הז שהם בהמות טמאות וחיות ועופות טמאים ושקצים ורמשים וכמאמר יתוש קדמך פי׳ דאף יתוש שמכנים ואינו מוציא שהיא קליפ׳ היותר תחתונה ורחוקה מבחי׳ הקדושה המשפעת בתכלית הריחוק קודמת לאיש החוטא בהשתלשלות וירידת החיות מרצון העליון ב״ה וכ״ש שאר בעלי חיים הטמאים ואפי׳ חיות רעות שכולם אינם משנים תפקידם ופקודתו ית׳ שמרה רוחם ואע״ג דאיהו לא חזי כו׳. וכמ״ש ומוראכם וחתכם יהיה על כל חית הארץ וכפי׳ רז״ל שאין חיה רעה מושלת באדם אא״כ נדמה לה כבהמה. והצדיקים שאין צלם אלהים מסתלק מעל פניהם כל חיות רעות אתכפיין קמייהו כמ״ש בזהר גבי דניאל בגוב אריות. וא״כ החוטא ועובר רצונו ית׳ אפי׳ בעבירה קלה בשעת מעשה הוא בתכלית הריחוק מקדושה העליונה שהיא יחודו ואחדותו ית׳ יותר מכל בעלי חיים הטמאי׳ ושקצי׳ ורמשים המושפעים מס״א וקליפת ע״ז ומה שפיקוח נפש דוחה שאר עבירות וגם יעבור ואל יהרג היינו כפי׳ חז״ל אמרה תורה חלל עליו שבת אחת כדי שישמור שבתות הרבה ולא משו׳ קלות העבירות וחומרן [תדע שהרי שבת חמורה ושקולה כע״ז לענין שחיטת מומר לדבר אחד בי״ד סי׳ ב׳ משא״כ במומר לגילוי עריות ואפי׳ הכי פיקוח נפש דוחה שבת ולא ג״ע אלא דגזירת הכתוב

Holy Writ.)[20]

After the sinful act, however, if it belongs to the category of sins the penalty for which is neither *karet* (spiritual extinction) nor death by Divine visitation, in which case the divine soul does not entirely perish and is not completely cut off from its root in the living G-d, except that through this sin its attachment to, and connection with, its root has been weakened somewhat—in that case his vitalising animal soul which is clothed in the body, and also his body, return and rise from the *sitra achra* and *kelipah* and draw closer to the holiness of the divine soul that pervades them, which believes in One G-d, and remains faithful to Him even at the time when the sin is committed, except that it is then in a state of veritable "exile," as it were, within the animal soul of the *sitra achra* which has caused the body to sin and has dragged it down with itself into the depths of *Sheol*, far down beneath the defilement of the *sitra achra* and *kelipah* of "idolatry"—may G-d preserve us! What greater exile can there be than this, "A plunge from a high roof to a deep pit!"—as has been previously explained,[21] that the root and source of all Jewish souls is in the Supreme Wisdom, and He and His Wisdom are one and the same, and so forth. It is comparable, by way of example, to one who seizes the king's head, drags it down and dips his face in a privy full of filth, than which there is no greater outrage, even if he does it only for a moment. For the *kelipot* and *sitra achra* are called[22] "vomit and filth,"[23] as is known.

*Note: According to the extent and specific nature of the blemish [thus caused] in the soul and in its roots in the upper spheres, are the various so-called purifying processes and retributions in Purgatory, or in this world—an appropriate retribution for each transgression and sin, in order to cleanse and remove the stain and blemish. Nor is the blemish always identical in the case of transgressions punishable by death or spiritual extinction (*karet*).*

•▲ Chapter 25

This, then, is the meaning[1] of the Scriptural text, "But the thing is very nigh unto thee. . . ."[2] For at any time and moment a person is capable and free to rid himself of the spirit of folly and forgetfulness,[3] and to recollect and awaken his love of the One G-d which is certainly latent in his heart, without any doubt. This is the meaning of the words "in thy heart."[4] Included therein is also fear, that is, the dread of separation in any wise from His blessed Unity and Oneness,

---

[20] *Hence it is not a matter of lenity or gravity of the sins in question.* [21] Supra, *ch. 2.* [22] *In the text the word* נקראים *should be amended to read* נקראות. [23] Isaiah *28:8.* *Comp.* Guide *III, 8.*

Chapter 25
[1] *The author returns to the theme begun in ch. 18.* [2] Deut. *30:14.* [3] *The "spirit of folly"—driving him to sins of commission; "forgetfulness" of the innate love of G-d—causing sins of omission.* [4] Deut. *30:14.*

הכתוב הוא] אלא שלאחר מעשה החטא אם היא מעבירות שאין בהן כרת ומיתה בידי שמים שאין נפשו האלהית מתה לגמרי ונכרתת משרשה באלהים חיים רק שנפגם קצת דביקותה ואחיזתה בשרשה בחטא זה* הרי גם נפשו החיוני' הבהמית המלובש' בגופו וכן גופו חוזרים ועולים מהס"א וקליפה זו ומתקרבים לקדושת נפש האלהית המלובשת בהם המאמינה בה' אחד וגם בשעת החטא היתה באמנה אתו ית' רק שהיתה בבחי' גלות ממש תוך נפש הבהמית מס"א המחטיאה את הגוף ומורידתו עמה בעמקי שאול למטה מטה תחת טומאת הס"א וקליפת ע"ז ה' ישמרנו ואין לך גלות גדול מזה מאיגרא רמה כו' וכמש"ל דשרש ומקור נפשו' כל בית ישראל הוא מחכמה עילאה והוא ית' וחכמתו אחד וכו' והוא כמשל האוחז בראשו של מלך ומורידו למטה וטומן פניו בתוך בית הכסא מלא צואה שאין לך עלבון גדול מזה אפי' עושה כן לפי שעה שהקליפות וס"א נקראים קיא צואה כנודע:

הגהה

(ולפי ערך וחלוקי בחי' הפגם בנפש ובשרשה בעליונים כך הם חלוקי בחי' המירוק והעונש בגיהנם או בעוה"ז לכל עון וחטא עונש מיוחד למרק ולהעביר הלכלוך והפגם וכן בחייבי מיתה וכרת אין פוגמין כולם בשוה):

פרק כה וזהו שכתוב כי קרוב אליך הדבר מאד וגו' שבכל עת ובכל שעה בידו של אדם וברשותו הוא להעבי' רוח שטות והשכחה מקרבו ולזכור ולעורר אהבתו לה' אחד המסותרת בודאי בלבבו בלי שום ספק. וז"ש ובלבבך ונכלל בה גם דחילו דהיינו שלא ליפרד בשום אופן מיחודו ואחדותו יתברך

even at the price of life itself and without reason and logic, but purely by virtue of one's divine nature. All the more so where it involves merely the suppression of one's appetites, which is easier than the pangs of death. This thing, i.e. repressing his evil inclination, is easier by far, both in the category of "turning away from evil" [and that of "doing good"],[5] even when it concerns a minor prohibition laid down by the Scribes, so as not to transgress against His blessed Will, since at the time of its commission he is thereby sundered from His Unity and Oneness just as much as committing actual idolatry. As for repenting afterwards, he can do this regarding idolatry, too.

▲ To be sure, "He who says, 'I will sin and repent afterwards,' is not given an opportunity to do so."[6] But this means that such a sinner is not granted the auspicious occasion to repent. If, however, he has seized the opportunity himself and has repented, "Nothing can stand in the way of repentance."[7]

Nonetheless every Jew is prepared and ready to suffer martyrdom for the sanctification of G-d's Name, and will not commit an idolatrous act even temporarily, with the intention of repenting afterwards. This is because of the divine light which is clothed in his soul, as explained above,[8] which does not come within the realm of time at all, but transcends it, having rule and dominion over it, as is known.

●▲Likewise in the category of "doing good,"[9]—to bestir oneself like a lion with might and stout-heartedness against the [evil] nature which weighs down his body and casts sloth over him from the so-called element of "earth" in the animal soul, restraining him from zealously exerting his body with all kinds of effort and perseverance in the service of G-d entailing effort and toil, such as labouring in the Torah with deep concentration, as well as orally, so that his mouth shall not cease from study. To quote the Rabbis, of blessed memory, "One should always submit to the words of the Torah like the ox to the yoke and the ass to the load."[10] So, too, in relation to devout prayer with the utmost intensity. Likewise with regard to serving G-d in money matters, such as ▲the duty of charity, and the like, duties which involve coming to grips with the evil nature seeking means of deception to dissuade the person from dissipating his money and physical health. It is very easy for a person to restrain and subjugate his nature when he considers deeply that to conquer his nature in all the above, and more, and even to do the very opposite, is by far less

---

[5] *The apodotic clause is expanded later; cf. n. 9.* [6] Yoma *ch. 8,* Mishnah *9.* [7] Talm. Yerush., Peah *1:1 ("in the way of repenters"); Comp. T.B.* Kiddushin *40a.* [8] *Ch. 19.* [9] *Cf. n. 5, above.* [10] Avodah Zarah *5b.*

● 18 Shevat ▲ *26 Shevat* ▲ *27 Shevat* ▲ *28 Shevat*

יתברך אפי׳ במסירת נפש ממש בלי שום טעם ושכל מושג אלא בטבע אלהי וכ״ש בשבירת התאוות הקלה מיסורי מיתה שקרוב אליו הדבר יותר לכבוש היצר הן בבחי׳ סור מרע אפי׳ מעבירה קלה של דברי סופרים שלא לעבור על רצונו ית׳ מאחר שנפרד בה מיחודו ואחדותו כמו בע״ז ממש בשעת מעשה והרי גם בע״ז יכול לעשות תשובה אח״כ. ואף שהאומר אחטא ואשוב אין מספיקין כו׳ היינו שאין מחזיקים ידו להיות לו שעת הכושר לעשות תשובה אבל אם דחק השעה ועשה תשובה אין לך דבר שעומד בפני התשובה. ואעפ״כ כל איש ישראל מוכן ומזומן למסור נפשו על קדושת ה׳ שלא להשתחוות לע״ז אפי׳ לפי שעה ולעשות תשובה אח״כ והיינו מפני אור ה׳ המלובש בנפשם כנ״ל שאינו בבחי׳ זמן ושעה כלל אלא למעלה מהזמן ושליט ומושל עליו כנודע. והן בבחי׳ ועשה טוב להתגבר כארי בגבורה ואומץ הלב נגד היצר המכביד את גופו ומפיל עליו עצלה מבחי׳ יסוד העפר שבנפש הבהמית מלהטריח גופו בזריזות בכל מיני טורח ועבוד׳ משא בעבודת ה׳ שיש בה טורח ועמל כגון לעמול בתורה בעיון ובפה לא פסיק פומיה מגירסא וכמארז״ל לעולם ישים אדם עצמו על דברי תורה כשור לעול וכחמור למשאוי וכן לתפלה בכונה בכל כחו ממש וכן בעבודת ה׳ שהוא בדבר שבממון כמו עבודת הצדקה וכיוצא באלו ממלחמות היצר ותחבולותיו לקרר נפש האדם שלא להפקיר ממונו ובריאות גופו שלעמוד נגדו ולכבשו קרוב מאד אל האדם כשישים אל לבו שלנצח היצר בכל זה ויותר מזה ולעשות הפכו ממש קל

מאד

painful than the pangs of death—may G–d preserve us! Yet he would have accepted the pangs of death—preserve us G–d!—lovingly and willingly, only not to be parted from His blessed Unity and Oneness even for a moment by an act of idolatry, G–d forbid.

All the more lovingly and willingly must he accept upon himself to cleave unto Him for ever. For by fulfilling His blessed Will by means of such service, there will be revealed in it the innermost Supreme Will of the aspect of the "Countenance" and great revelation, without obscurity whatever; and when there is no "hiding of the Countenance" of the Supreme Will, there is no separation whatever and nothing can have a separate and independent existence of its own. Thus his soul, both the divine and vivifying, together with their garments, will be united in a perfect unity with the Supreme Will and the blessed light of the *En Sof*, as has been explained above.

▲ This union is eternal in the upper spheres, for He, blessed be He, and His Will are above time, and so is His revealed Will, manifest in His word which is the Torah, eternal, as is written, "But the word of G–d shall stand for ever,"[11] and "His words are living and enduring, . . ."[12] and "He will not alter or change His Law for ever. . . ."[13]

● However, here below, [the union] is within the limits of time, persisting only during such time when one is occupied in the study of Torah, or in the performance of a commandment. For afterwards, if he engages in anything else, he is here below separated from the Higher Unity. This is so when he occupies himself with altogether vain things which are utterly useless for the Divine Service. Nevertheless, should he later repent and return to the service of G–d, to Torah and prayer, and ask forgiveness of G–d for not having engaged in the Torah when he could have done so, G–d will pardon him. To quote the Rabbis: "If one has transgressed against a positive precept, but has repented, he is pardoned on the spot."[14] Therefore they instituted the blessing of "Forgive us" to be recited three times daily[15] for the sin of neglecting the Torah, a sin which no one can escape each day. Similarly the daily burnt-offering[16] used to bring atonement for neglect of the positive precepts.

This is not the same as saying, "I will sin and repent afterwards," unless at the time he is committing the sin he relies on subsequent repentance and sins because of it, as explained elsewhere.

▲ In the light of the above, it will be understood why our teacher Moses, peace be upon him, in Deuteronomy commanded the generation

[11] Isa. *40:8.* [12] *Liturgy,* Morning Prayer. [13] *From the famous hymn* Yigdal *on the Thirteen Principles of Faith, originally formulated by Maimonides, incorporated into the liturgy of the Ashkenazic and Sephardic rites.* [14] Yoma *86a.* [15] *In the "Eighteen Benedictions" of the week-day prayers.* [16] *In the Sanctuary of old.*

מאד מיסורי מיתה ה׳ ישמרנו ויסורי מיתה ה׳ ישמרנו היה מקבל באהבה וברצון שלא ליפרד מיחודו ואחדותו ית׳ אפי׳ לפי שעה להשתחות לע״ז ח״ו וכ״ש שיש לו לקבל באהבה וברצון כדי לדבקה בו לעולם ועד דהיינו כשיעשה רצונו ית׳ בעבודה זו יתגלה בה פנימית רצון העליון בבחי׳ פנים וגילוי רב ולא בהסתר כלל וכשאין שום הסתר פנים ברצון העליון אזי אין דבר נפרד כלל וכלל להיות יש ודבר בפני עצמו ולזאת תהיינה נפשו האלהית והחיונית ולבושיהן כולן מיוחדות בתכלית היחוד ברצון העליון ואור א״ס ב״ה כנ״ל. ויחוד זה למעלה הוא נצחי לעולם ועד כי הוא ית׳ ורצונו למעלה מהזמן וכן גילוי רצונו שבדבורו שהיא התורה הוא נצחי וכמ״ש ודבר אלהינו יקום לעולם ודבריו חיים וקיימים כו׳ ולא יחליף ולא ימיר דתו לעולמים כו׳. אלא שלמטה הוא תחת הזמן ובאותה שעה לבדה שעוסק בה בתור׳ או במצוה כי אח״כ אם עוסק בדבר אחר נפרד מהיחוד העליון למטה. והיינו כשעוסק בדברים בטלים לגמרי שאין בהם צורך כלל לעבודת ה׳ ואעפ״כ כשחוזר ושב לעבודת ה׳ אח״כ לתורה ולתפלה ומבקש מחילה מה׳ על שהיה אפשר לו לעסוק אז בתורה ולא עסק ה׳ יסלח לו כמארז״ל עבר על מצות עשה ושב לא זז משם עד שמוחלין לו. ולזה תקנו ברכת סלח לנו שלש פעמים בכל יום על עון ביטול תורה שאין אדם ניצול ממנו בכל יום וכמו התמיד שהיה מכפר על מצות עשה. ואין זה אחטא ואשוב אא״כ שבשעת החטא ממש הוא סומך על התשובה ולכך חוטא כמ״ש במ״א: ובזה יובן למה צוה משה רבינו ע״ה במשנה תורה לדור

שנכנסו

that was to enter the Land of Israel to recite the *Shema* twice daily, to acknowledge the Kingdom of Heaven with self-sacrifice, although he had promised them, "The Lord your G-d shall lay your dread and fear upon all the land."[17] The reason is that the fulfillment of the Torah and its commandments is dependent on being constantly aware of one's readiness to surrender one's life to G-d for His Unity's sake, so that this awareness be permanently fixed in one's heart and not depart from one's memory night and day. For in this way is one able to face one's evil nature and vanquish it always, at any time or moment, as has been explained.[18]

●▲ *Chapter 26*

Truly this should be made known as a cardinal principle, that as with a victory over a physical obstacle, such as in the case of two individuals who are wrestling with each other, each striving to throw the other—if one is lazy and sluggish he will easily be defeated and thrown, even though he be stronger than the other, exactly so is it in the conquest of one's evil nature; it is impossible to conquer it with laziness and heaviness, which originate in sadness and in a heart that is dulled like a stone, but rather with alacrity which derives from joy and from a heart that is free and cleansed from any trace of worry and sadness in the world.

As for what is written, "In all sadness there would be profit,"[1] which means that some profit and advantage would be derived from it, the phrase, on the contrary, indicates that sadness in itself has no virtue, except that some profit is derived and experienced from it, namely, the true joy in the Lord G-d which follows from genuine anguish over one's sins, at propitious moments with bitterness of soul and a broken heart. For thereby the spirit of impurity and of the *sitra achra* is broken, as also the iron wall that separates him from his Father in Heaven, as is commented in the *Zohar* on the verse, "A broken and a contrite heart, O G-d, Thou wilt not despise;"[2] then will be fulfilled in him the preceding verses: "Make me hear joy and gladness . . . Restore unto me the joy of Thy salvation, and uphold me with Thy generous spirit."[3]

This is the simple reason why Rabbi Isaac Luria, of blessed memory, instituted the recital of this Psalm after the Midnight Prayer,[4] before commencing study, in order to study with the true joy in G-d which succeeds

---

[17] Deut. *11:25*. [18] *The recital of the* Shema—*which teaches the acceptance of martyrdom for the sanctification of G-d's Name—was instituted on the eve of the conquest of the Promised Land. Since a miraculous conquest was promised, this precept could not have been related to the imminent battle for the conquest of the Land, but was meant for all times, for the conquest of one's own nature.*

Chapter 26
[1] Prov. *14:23*. [2] Ps. *51:19*. [3] Ibid., *vs. 10, 14*. [4] Tikun Chatzot.

שנכנסו לארץ לקרות ק"ש פעמים בכל יום לקבל עליו מלכות שמים במסירת נפש והלא הבטיח להם פחדכם ומוראכם יתן ה' וגו' אלא משום שקיום התורה ומצותיה תלוי בזה שיזכור תמיד ענין מסירת נפשו לה' על יחודו שיהיה קבוע בלבו תמיד ממש יומם ולילה לא ימיש מזכרונו כי בזה יוכל לעמוד נגד יצרו לנצחו תמיד בכל עת ובכל שעה כנ"ל:

פרק כו ברם כגון דא צריך לאודעי כלל גדול כי כמו שנצחון לנצח דבר גשמי כגון שני אנשים המתאבקים זה עם זה להפיל זה את זה. הנה אם האחד הוא בעצלות וכבדות ינוצח בקל ויפול גם אם הוא גבור יותר מחבירו ככה ממש בנצחון היצר אי אפשר לנצחו בעצלות וכבדות הנמשכות מעצבות וטמטום הלב כאבן כ"א בזריזות הנמשכת משמחה ופתיחת הלב וטהרתו מכל נדנוד דאגה ועצב בעולם. ומ"ש בכל עצב יהיה מותר פי' שיהיה איזה יתרון ומעלה מזה הנה אדרבה מלשון זה משמע שהעצב מצד עצמו אין בו מעלה רק שיגיע ויבא ממנו איזה יתרון והיינו השמחה האמיתית בה' אלהיו הבאה אחר העצב האמיתי לעתים מזומנים על עונותיו במר נפשו ולב נשבר שע"י זה נשברה רוח הטומאה וס"א ומחיצה של ברזל המפסקת בינו לאביו שבשמים כמ"ש בזהר ע"פ רוח נשברה לב נשבר וגו' ואזי יקוים בו רישיה דקרא תשמיעני ששון ושמחה וגו' השיבה לי ששון ישעך ורוח נדיבה וגו' וזהו טעם הפשוט לתיקון האר"י ז"ל לומר מזמור זה אחר תיקון חצות קודם הלימוד כדי ללמוד בשמחה אמיתית בה' הבאה אחר העצב

remorse. For such joy has an excellence similar to that of a light emerging from the very darkness, as is written in the *Zohar* on the verse, "Then I saw that wisdom excelleth folly as light excelleth darkness."[5] Note there, and it will suffice for him who understands. Furthermore, Scripture states it explicitly: "Because thou didst not serve the Lord thy G-d with joyfulness, . . ."[6]—and everyone is familiar with the commentary of Rabbi Isaac Luria, of blessed memory, on this verse.

• The following is sound counsel as to how to cleanse one's heart of all sadness and of every trace of worry about mundane matters, even about "Children, Health and Sustenance." Everyone is familiar with the statement of the Rabbis that "Just as one must recite a blessing for the good, [one must also recite a blessing for misfortune]."[7] In the *Gemara* it is explained that one should accept [misfortune] with joy, like the joy of a visible and obvious benefit, For "this is also for the good," except that it is not apparent and visible to mortal eyes, because it stems from the "hidden world" which is higher than the "revealed world," the latter emanating from the letters *vav* and *hai* of the Tetragrammaton, whereas the "hidden world" represents the letters *yod—hai*. Hence the meaning of the verse, "Happy is the man whom Thou, O G-d,[8] chasteneth."[9] Therefore, the Rabbis, of blessed memory, commented[10] that it is to those who rejoice in their afflictions that the verse refers: "But they that love Him shall be as the sun going forth in its might."[11] For this is the joy of desiring the nearness of G-d more than anything in the life of this world, as is written, "Because Thy lovingkindness is better than life, . . ."[12] and the nearness of G-d is infinitely stronger and more sublime in the "hidden world," for "The concealment of His strength is there,"[13] and "The Most High abides in secrecy."[14] Therefore, [the man who accepts affliction with joy], merits [to see] the "Sun going forth in its might"—in the world to come, i.e. the sun emerging from its sheath in which it is enclosed in this world.[15] But in the world to come it will appear out of its covering, meaning that then the "hidden world" will be revealed and will shine and send forth light in a great and intense revelation to those who had taken refuge in Him in this world and had taken shelter under His "shadow"—the shadow of wisdom (*chochmah*), i.e. in the sense of "shade" as differing from light and revealed goodness. Suffice it for him who understands.

• As for the sadness which is connected with heavenly[16] matters, one must seek ways and means of freeing oneself from it, to say nothing of the time of Divine Service, when one must serve G-d with gladness and a joyful heart. But even if he is a man of commerce

---

[5] Eccl. *2:13. The emphasis is on the words* מן החשך*—literally* "from *darkness.*" [6] Deut. *28:47.* [7] Berachot, *ch. 9,* Mishnah *5.* [8] *YH*—yod-hai. *Thus the "misfortunes" are blessings in disguise, originating in the "hidden" worlds.* [9] Ps. *94:12.* [10] Yoma *23a.* [11] Jud. *5:31.* [12] Ps. *63:4.* [13] Hab. *3:4.* [14] Ps. *91:1.* [15] *Cf.* Ned. *8b.* [16] *I.e. failure in matters of the spirit.*

העצב שיש לשמחה זו יתרון כיתרון האור הבא מן החשך דוקא כמ"ש בזהר על פסוק וראיתי שיש יתרון לחכמה מן הסכלות כיתרון האור כו' ע"ש וד"ל ומקרא מלא דבר הכתוב תחת אשר לא עבדת את ה' אלהיך בשמחה וגו' ונודע לכל פי' האר"י ז"ל על פסוק זה:

והנה עצה היעוצה לטהר לבו מכל עצב ונדנוד דאגה ממילי דעלמא ואפי' בני חיי ומזוני מודעת זאת לכל מאמר רז"ל כשם שמברך על הטובה כו' ופירשו בגמ' לקבולי בשמחה כמו שמחת הטובה הנגלית ונראית כי גם זו לטובה רק שאינה נגלית ונראית לעיני בשר כי היא מעלמא דאתכסי' שלמעלה מעלמא דאתגלייא שהוא ו"ה משם הוי"ה ב"ה ועלמא דאתכסיא הוא י"ה וז"ש אשרי הגבר אשר תיסרנו י"ה וגו' ולכן ארז"ל כי השמחים ביסורים עליהם הכתוב אומר ואוהביו כצאת השמש בגבורתו כי השמחה היא מאהבתו קרבת ה' יותר מכל חיי העוה"ז כדכתיב כי טוב חסדך מחיים וגו' וקרבת ה' היא ביתר שאת ומעלה אין קץ בעלמא דאתכסיא כי שם חביון עוזו ויושב בסתר עליון ועל כן זוכה לצאת השמש בגבורתו לעתיד לבא שהיא יציאת חמה מנרתקה שהיא מכוסה בו בעוה"ז ולעתיד תתגלה מכסויה דהיינו שאז יתגלה עלמא דאתכסיא ויזרח ויאיר בגילוי רב ועצום לכל החוסים בו בעוה"ז ומסתופפים בצלו צל החכמה שהוא בחי' צל ולא אורה וטובה נראית וד"ל: אך העצבות ממילי דשמיא צריך לשית עצות בנפשו לפטר ממנה אין צריך לומר בשעת עבודה שצריך לעבוד ה' בשמחה ובטוב לבב אלא אפילו מי שהוא בעל עסקים

ורדך

and worldly affairs, should there enter into him any melancholy or anxiety about heavenly matters during the time of his business affairs, it is clearly a machination of evil impulse in order to lure him afterwards into lusts, G–d forbid, as is known. For were it not so, whence would a genuine sadness, which is one that is derived from love or fear of G–d, come to him in the midst of his business affairs?

Thus, whether the melancholy encroaches on him during Divine Service, in study or prayer, or not during Divine Service, he should tell himself that now is not the time for genuine anxiety, not even for worry over serious transgressions, G–d forbid. For, for this, one needs appointed times and a propitious occasion, with calmness of mind to reflect on the greatness of G–d, against Whom one has sinned, so that thereby one's heart may truly be rent with sincere contrition. It is explained elsewhere when this time should be, and it is there explained also that as soon as his heart has been broken during these specific occasions, he should forthwith completely remove the sorrow from his heart and believe with a perfect faith that G–d has removed his sin in His abundant forgiveness. This is the true joy in G–d which comes after the remorse, as mentioned above.

●▲ Chapter 27

Should the sadness, however, not come from worry over sins, but from evil thoughts and desires that enter his mind—if they enter not during Divine Service but whilst he is occupied with his own affairs and with mundane matters and the like, he should, on the contrary, be happy in his portion in that, though they enter his mind, he averts his mind from them in order to fulfil the injunction, "That ye seek not after your own heart and your own eyes, after which ye go astray."[1] The verse does not speak of the righteous, to refer to them as "going astray," G–d forbid, but of "Intermediates" (*benonim*) like him, in whose mind do enter erotic thoughts whether of an innocent nature, and so on;[2] when he averts his mind from them, he is fulfilling this injunction. Indeed, the Rabbis, of blessed memory, have said, "He who has passively abstained from committing a sin, receives a reward as though he had performed a precept."[3] Consequently, he should rejoice

---

[1] Num. *15:39*. [2] "*. . . or otherwise.*" [3] Kiddushin *39b*.

ודרך ארץ אם נופל לו עצב ודאגה ממילי דשמיא בשעת עסקיו בידוע שהוא תחבולת היצר כדי להפילו אח"כ בתאוות ח"ו כנודע שאל"כ מאין באה לו עצבות אמיתית מחמת אהבת ה' או יראתו באמצע עסקיו. והנה בין שנפלה לו העצבות בשעת עבודה בת"ת או בתפלה ובין שנפלה לו שלא בשעת עבודה זאת ישים אל לבו כי אין הזמן גרמא כעת לעצבות אמיתית אפי' לדאגת עונות חמורים ח"ו. רק לזאת צריך קביעות עתים ושעת הכושר בישוב הדעת להתבונן בגדול' ה' אשר חטא לו כדי שע"י זה יהיה לבו נשבר באמת במרירות אמיתית וכמבואר עת זו במ"א ושם נתבאר ג"כ כי מיד אחר שנשבר לבו בעתים קבועים ההם אזי יסיר העצב מלבו לגמרי ויאמין אמונה שלימה כי ה' העביר חטאתו ורב לסלוח וזו היא השמחה האמיתית בה' הבאה אחר העצב כנ"ל:

פרק כז ואם העצבות אינה מדאגת עונות אלא מהרהורים רעים ותאוות רעות שנופלות במחשבתו. הנה אם נופלות לו שלא בשעת העבודה אלא בעת עסקו בעסקיו ודרך ארץ וכהאי גוונא אדרבה יש לו לשמוח בחלקו שאף שנופלות לו במחשבתו הוא מסיח דעתו מהן לקיים מה שנאמר ולא תתורו אחרי לבבכם ואחרי עיניכם אשר אתם זונים אחריהם. ואין הכתוב מדבר בצדיקי' לקראם זונים ח"ו אלא בבינונים כיוצא בו שנופלים לו הרהורי ניאוף במחשבתו בין בהיתר כו' וכשמסיח דעתו מקיים לאו זה ואמרו רז"ל ישב ולא עבר עבירה נותנים לו שכר כאלו עשה מצוה ועל כן צריך לשמוח

בקיום

at his compliance with the injunction as when performing an actual positive precept.

▲ On the contrary, such sadness is due to conceit in that he does not recognise his position.[4] Hence he is sad at heart because he has not attained the rank of a *tzaddik*, inasmuch as the righteous are certainly not troubled by such foolish thoughts. For had he recognised his station, that he is very far from the rank of a *tzaddik*, and would that he be a *benoni* and not a wicked person even for a single moment throughout his life—then, surely, this is the quality of the "Intermediates" and their service: To subdue the evil impulse and thought rising from the heart to the brain, and completely to avert the mind therefrom, thrusting the temptation away with both hands, as has ▲been explained earlier.[5] And with every thrust wherewith he expels it from his mind, the *sitra achra* down below is suppressed, and, since the "Stimulus from below causes a stimulus from above,"[6] the *sitra achra* above which soars like an eagle, is also suppressed, in accordance with Scripture, "Though thou exalt thyself as the eagle, thence will I bring thee down, saith the Lord."[7] Thus the *Zohar, Parshat Terumah* (p. 128) extolls the great satisfaction before Him, blessed be He, when the *sitra achra* is subdued here below, for then the glory of the Holy One, blessed be He, rises above all, more than by any praise, and this ascent is greater than all else, and so forth.[8]

● Therefore, no person should feel depressed, nor should his heart become exceedingly troubled, even though he be engaged all his days in this conflict, for perhaps because of this was he created and this is his service—constantly to subjugate the *sitra achra*.

It is concerning this that Job said,[9] "Thou hast created wicked men"—not that they shall actually be wicked, G-d forbid, but that they shall share the temptations of the wicked in their thoughts and meditations alone and that they shall eternally wage war to avert their minds from them in order to subdue the *sitra achra*; yet they would not be able to annihilate it completely, for that is accomplished by the *tzaddikim*.

▲ For there are two kinds of gratification before Him, blessed be He: one, from the complete annihilation of the *sitra achra* and the conversion of bitter to sweet and of darkness to light, by the *tzaddikim*; the second, when the *sitra achra* is subdued whilst it is still at its strongest and most powerful and soars like an eagle, whence the Lord brings her down through the effort

---

[4] *As a* benoni, *not a* tzaddik. [5] *Ch. 12.* [6] Zohar *II, 135b.* [7] Ovad. *1:4.* [8] *Cf. at length* Zohar *II, 128b.* [9] Bava Batra *16a. See beg. ch. 1, above.*

בקיום הלאו כמו בקיום מצות עשה ממש ואדרבה העצבות היא מגסות הרוח שאינו מכיר מקומו ועל כן ירע לבבו על שאינו במדרגת צדיק שלצדיקים בודאי אין נופלים להם הרהורי שטות כאלו כי אילו היה מכיר מקומו שהוא רחוק מאד ממדרגת צדיק והלואי היה בינוני ולא רשע כל ימיו אפי' שעה אחת הרי זאת היא מדת הבינונים ועבודתם לכבוש היצר וההרהור העולה מהלב למוח ולהסיח דעתו לגמרי ממנו ולדחותו בשתי ידים כנ"ל ובכל דחיה ודחיה שמדחהו ממחשבתו אתכפיא ס"א לתתא ובאתערותא דלתתא אתערותא דלעילא ואתכפיא ס"א דלעילא המגביה עצמה כנשר לקיים מ"ש אם תגביה כנשר וגו' משם אורידך נאם ה' וכמו שהפליג בזהר פ' תרומה [דף קכח] בגודל נחת רוח לפניו ית' כד אתכפיא ס"א לתתא דאסתלק יקרא דקב"ה לעילא על כולא יתיר משבח' אחרא ואסתלקות' דא יתיר מכולא וכו'. ולכן אל יפול לב אדם עליו ולא ירע לבבו מאד גם אם יהיה כן כל ימיו במלחמה זו כי אולי לכך נברא וזאת עבודתו לאכפיא לס"א תמיד. ועל זה אמר איוב בראת רשעים ולא שיהיו רשעים באמת ח"ו אלא שיגיע אליהם כמעשה הרשעים במחשבתם והרהורם לבד והם יהיו נלחמים תמיד להסיח דעתם מהם כדי לאכפי' לס"א ולא יוכלו לבטלה מכל וכל כי זה נעשה ע"י צדיקים. ושני מיני נחת רוח לפניו ית' למעלה. א' מביטול הס"א לגמרי ואתהפכא ממרירו למתקא ומחשוכא לנהורא ע"י הצדיקים. והשנית כד אתכפיא הס"א בעודה בתקפה וגבורתה ומגביה עצמה כנשר ומשם מורידה ה' באתערותא

דלתתא

of the *benonim* below. This is indicated in the verse, "And make me delicacies such as I love."[10] The word *mata'amim* ("delicacies") is in the plural, to indicate two kinds of gratification, and the words are those of the *Shechinah* to her children, the community of Israel, as explained in the *Tikunim*. The analogy is to material food, where there are two kinds of relishes: one of sweet and luscious foods, and the other of tart or sour articles of food which have been well spiced and garnished so that they are made into delicacies to quicken the soul.

This is what is alluded to in the verse, "The Lord hath made everything for His sake; also the wicked unto the day of evil,"[11] meaning that the wicked man shall repent of his evil and turn his evil into "day" and light above, when the *sitra achra* is subdued and the glory of the Holy One, blessed be He, is brought forth on high.

●▲ Moreover, even in the case of things that are fully permissible, the more of his impulse that a man sacrifices, even if only for a while, with the intention of subduing the *sitra achra* in the left part—as for example, when he wants to eat but postpones his meal for an hour or less, and during that time he occupies himself in the Torah, as is stated in the *Gemara*[12] that the fourth hour is the time when all men eat, but the sixth hour is the time when scholars eat, because they used to starve themselves for two hours with this intention, although after the meal, also, they studied all day; so, too, if he restrains his mouth from uttering words that his heart longs to express concerning mundane matters; likewise with the thoughts of his mind, even in the least way, whereby the *sitra achra* is subdued below—the glory and holiness of the Holy One, blessed be He, ▲goes forth above to a great extent, and from this holiness issues a sublime holiness on man below, to assist him with a great and powerful aid in serving Him, Who is blessed.

This is also what the Rabbis meant, "If a man consecrates himself in a small measure down below, he is sanctified much more from above,"[13] apart from his having fulfilled the positive commandment of the Torah, "Sanctify yourselves, and be ye holy"[14] by dedicating himself [through abstemiousness] in permissible things. The meaning of "Sanctify yourselves" is "You shall *make* yourselves holy,"[15] that is to say, although in truth one is not holy and separated from the *sitra achra*, for it is at its strength

---

[10] *The words* (Gen. *27:4*) *spoken by Isaac to Esau are allegorically interpreted here according to* Tikunei Zohar. [11] Prov. *16:4*. [12] Shabbat *10a*. [13] Yoma *39a*. [14] Lev. *20:7*. [15] *The Hebrew word for "holy"* (kadosh) *means "setting apart," i.e. separating from the unholy.*

דלתתא ע"י הבינונים. וז"ש הכתוב ועשה לי מטעמים כאשר אהבתי מטעמים לשון רבים שני מיני נחת רוח והוא מאמר השכינה לבניה כללות ישראל כדפי' בתיקונים. וכמו שבמטעמים גשמיים ד"מ יש שני מיני מעדנים אחד ממאכלים ערבים ומתוקים. והשני מדברים חריפים או חמוצי' רק שהם מתובלים ומתוקני' היטב עד שנעשו מעדנים להשיב הנפש. וז"ש הכתו' כל פעל ה' למענהו וגם רשע ליום רעה פי' שישוב מרשעו ויעשה הרע שלו יום ואור למעלה כד אתכפיא ס"א ואסתלק יקרא דקב"ה לעילא. ולא עוד אלא אפי' בדברים המותרים לגמרי כל מה שהאדם זובח יצרו אפי' שעה קלה ומתכוין לאכפיא לס"א שבחלל השמאלי כגון שחפץ לאכול ומאחר סעודתו עד לאחר שעה או פחות ועוסק בתורה באותה שעה. כדאיתא בגמ' שעה רביעית מאכל כל אדם שעה ששית מאכל ת"ח. והיו מרעיבים עצמם שתי שעות לכוונה זו אף שגם אחר הסעודה היו לומדים כל היום. וכן אם בולם פיו מלדבר דברים שלבו מתאוה מאד לדברם מענייני העולם וכן בהרהורי מחשבתו אפי' במעט מזעיר דאתכפיא ס"א לתתא אסתלק יקרא דקב"ה וקדושתו לעילא הרבה ומקדושה זו נמשכת קדושה עליונה על האדם למטה לסייעו סיוע רב ועצום לעבודתו ית'. וז"ש רז"ל אדם מקדש עצמו מעט למטה מקדשין אותו הרבה מלמעלה לבד מה שמקיים מצות עשה של תורה והתקדשתם וכו' כשמקדש עצמו במותר לו ופי' והתקדשתם שתעשו עצמכם קדושים כלומר אף שבאמת אינו קדוש ומובדל מס"א כי היא בתקפה

ובגבורתה

and might, as at its birth, in the left part, yet one subdues his evil impulse and sanctifies himself—then "Shall ye be holy,"[16] that is to say, in the end one will be truly holy and separated from the *sitra achra*, by virtue of being sanctified in a great measure from above, and being helped to expel it from his heart little by little.

●▲ *Chapter 28*

Even if there occur to him lustful imaginations or other extraneous thoughts *during* Divine Service, in Torah or in devout prayer, he must not let his heart dwell on them but must immediately avert his mind from them. Nor should he be foolish by attempting to sublimate the *middot* of the extraneous thought, as is known. For such things were meant only for *tzaddikim*, in whom extraneous thoughts do not occur of their own making, but those of others. But as for him whose extraneous thought is his own, from the aspect of evil that is in the left part of his heart, how can he raise it up when he himself is bound below?

Nevertheless he must not be downcast at heart and feel dejected and despicable during Divine Service, which should be with great joy. On the contrary, he should draw fresh strength and intensify [his] effort with all his power to concentrate on the prayer with increased joy and gladness, in the realisation that the foreign thought that had invaded his heart comes from the *kelipah* in the left part, which, in the case of the *benoni*, wages war with the divine soul within him. For it is known that the way of combatants, as of wrestlers, is that when one is gaining the upper hand the other likewise strives to prevail with all the resources of his strength. Therefore, when the divine soul exerts itself and summons its strength for prayer, the *kelipah* also gathers strength at such time to confuse her and topple her by means of a foreign ●thought of its own. This refutes the error commonly held by people, who mistakenly deduce from the occurrence of the foreign thought that this proves their prayer to be worthless, for if one prayed as is fitting and proper no foreign thoughts would have occurred to him. What they say would be true

---

[16] *The imperative form used in the Pentateuch to express the commandments can be interpreted also in the simple future tense. Hence the commandments may be understood from the linguistic aspect as both a command and a promise of its fulfillment.*

● 26 Shevat ● 27 Shevat ▲ *8 Adar I*

ובגבורתה כתולדתה בחלל השמאלי רק שכובש יצרו ומקדש עצמו. והייתם קדושים כלומר סופו להיות קדוש ומובדל באמת מהס"א ע"י שמקדשים אותו הרבה מלמעלה ומסייעים אותו לגרשה מלבו מעט מעט:

פרק כח **ואפילו** אם נופלים לו הרהורי תאוות ושאר מחשבות זרות בשעת העבודה בתורה או בתפלה בכוונה אל ישית לב אליהן אלא יסיח דעתו מהן כרגע. וגם אל יהי שוטה לעסוק בהעלאת המדות של המחשבה זרה כנודע כי לא נאמרו דברים ההם אלא לצדיקים שאין נופלים להם מחשבות זרות שלהם כ"א משל אחרים. אבל מי שנופל לו משלו מבחי' הרע שבלבו בחלל השמאלי איך יעלהו למעלה והוא עצמו מקושר למטה: אך אעפ"כ אל יפול לבו בקרבו להיות מזה עצב נבזה בשעת העבודה שצריך להיות בשמחה רבה אלא אדרבה יתחזק יותר ויוסיף אומץ בכל כחו בכוונת התפלה בחדוה ושמחה יתירה בשומו אל לבו כי נפילת המחשבה זרה היא מהקליפה שבחלל השמאלי העושה מלחמה בבינוני עם נפש אלהית שבו. ונודע דרך הנלחמים וכן הנאבקים יחד כשאחד מתגבר אזי השני מתאמץ להתגבר ג"כ בכל מאמצי כחו. ולכן כשנפש האלהית מתאמצת ומתגברת להתפלל אזי גם הקליפה מתגברת כנגדה לבלבלה ולהפילה במחשב' זרה שלה ולא כטעות העולם שטועים להוכיח מנפילת המחשבה זרה מכלל שאין תפלתם כלום שאילו התפלל כראוי ונכון לא היו נופלים לו מחשבות זרות. והאמת היה כדבריהם

if there were only one single soul, the same that prays as well as thinks and fancies the foreign thoughts.

The real truth, however, is that there are two souls, waging war one against the other in the person's mind, each one wishing and desiring to rule over him and pervade his mind exclusively. Thus all thoughts of Torah and the fear of Heaven come from the divine soul, while all mundane matters come from the animal soul, except that the divine soul is clothed in it. This is like the example of a person praying with devotion, while facing him there stands a wicked heathen who chats and speaks to him in order to confuse him. Surely the thing to do in such a case would be not to answer him good or evil, but rather to pretend to be deaf without hearing, and to comply with the verse, "Answer not a fool according to his folly, lest thou also be like unto him."[1] Similarly, he must answer nothing, nor engage in any argument and counter-argument with the foreign thought, for he who wrestles with a filthy person is bound to become soiled himself. Rather should he adopt an attitude as if he neither knows nor hears the thoughts that have befallen him; he must remove them from his mind and strengthen still more the power of his concentration. However, if he finds it hard to dismiss them from his mind, because they distract his mind with great intensity, then he should humble his spirit before G–d and supplicate Him in his thought to have compassion upon him in His abundant mercies, as a father who takes pity on his children who stem from his brain;[2] so may the Lord have pity on his soul which is derived from Him Who is blessed, and deliver it from the "turbulent waters;"[3] for His sake He will do it, for verily "His people is a part of the Lord."[4]

•▲ *Chapter 29*

There is yet an additional aspect that the *benonim* must contend with, namely, that occasionally and even frequently, they experience a dullness of the heart, which becomes like a stone, and the person is unable, try as he might, to open his heart to the "Service of the heart," namely, prayer.[1] Also, at times, he is unable to wage war against the evil impulse, so as to sanctify himself in the things that are permissible,[2] because of the heaviness that is in his heart.

In this case, the advice given in the holy *Zohar* is, as the president of the Heavenly Academy said in the *Gan Eden*: "A wooden beam that will not

---

[1] Prov. *26:4*. [2] *Cf.* supra, *ch. 2*. [3] *Allusion to* Ps. *124:5*. [4] Deut. *32:9*. *Thus, by helping the divine soul, G–d helps Himself, as it were.*

Chapter 29
[1] Taanit *2a*. [2] *Cf.* supra, *ch. 27*, *where a limited form of abstemiousness is highly commended.*

כדבריהם אם היתה נפש אחת לבדה היא המתפללת והיא המחשבת ומהרהרת המחשבות זרות. אבל באמת לאמיתו הן שתי נפשות הנלחמו' זו עם זו במוחו של אדם כל אחת חפצה ורצונה למשול בו ולהיות המוח ממולא ממנה לבדה. וכל הרהורי תורה ויראת שמים מנפש האלהית וכל מילי דעלמא מנפש הבהמית רק שהאלהית מלובשת בה. והוא כמשל אדם המתפלל בכוונ' ועומד לנגדו ער"ג רשע ומשיח ומדבר עמו כדי לבלבלו שזאת עצתו בודאי שלא להשיב לו מטוב ועד רע ולעשות עצמו כחרש לא ישמע ולקיים מה שכתו' אל תען כסיל באולתו פן תשוה לו גם אתה כך אל ישיב מאומה ושום טענה ומענה נגד המחשבה זרה כי המתאבק עם מנוול מתנוול ג"כ רק יעשה עצמו כלא יודע ולא שומע ההרהורי' שנפלו לו ויסירם מדעתו ויוסיף אומץ בכח כוונתו ואם יקשה לו להסירם מדעתו מפני שטורדים דעתו מאד בחזקה אזי ישפיל נפשו לה' ויתחנן לו ית' במחשבתו לרחם עליו ברחמיו המרובים כרחם אב על בנים הנמשכים ממוחו וככה ירחם ה' על נפשו הנמשכת מאתו ית' להצילה ממים הזדונים ולמענו יעשה כי חלק ה' ממש עמו:

פרק כט

אך עוד אחת צריך לשית עצות בנפשו' הבינונים אשר לפעמים ועתים רבים יש להם טמטום הלב שנעשה כאבן ולא יכול לפתוח לבו בשום אופן לעבודה שבלב זו תפלה. וגם לפעמים לא יוכל להלחם עם היצר לקדש עצמו במותר לו מפני כבדות שבלבו וזאת היא עצה היעוצה בזהר הקדוש דאמר רב מתיבתא בגן עדן אעא דלא סליק

catch fire should be splintered . . .; a body into which the light of the soul does not penetrate should be crushed. . . ."[3]

The reference to the "Light of the soul" is that the light of the soul and of the intellect does not illuminate to such an extent as to prevail over the coarseness of the body. For, although he understands and contemplates in his mind on the greatness of G-d, this is not apprehended and implanted in his mind to a degree that would enable him to prevail over the coarseness of the heart because of [the nature of] this ▲coarseness and crassness, the cause being the arrogance of the *kelipah*, which exalts itself above the light of the holiness of the divine soul, obscuring and darkening the light thereof. Therefore one must crush it and cast it down to the ground, that is to say, by setting aside appointed times for humbling oneself and considering oneself despicable and contemptible,[4] as is written, "A broken heart, a broken spirit"[5]—this is the *sitra achra*, which is the very man himself in "intermediate" people, in whose heart the vital soul which animates the body is in its native strength; hence it is the very man himself. Whereas with regard to the divine soul within him it is said, "The soul which Thou gavest within me is pure."[6] Note the words "Which Thou gavest *within* me," implying that man himself is not [identified with] the pure soul—except in the case of *tzaddikim*, in whom the contrary is true, namely, that the "pure soul," i.e., the divine soul, is the man, while their body is called "The flesh of ▲man."[7] Compare the statement of Hillel the Elder to his disciples, who, when going to eat, used to say that he was going to perform an act of kindness to the "Lowly and poor creature,"[8] by which he meant his body, which he regarded as if it were foreign to him. Therefore he used the expression that he was "Performing an act of kindness" towards it in giving it food, because he himself was nothing else but the divine soul, since it alone animated his body and flesh, inasmuch as in the *tzaddikim* the evil that was in the vital soul pervading his blood and flesh, had been transformed into good and absorbed into the very holiness of the divine soul.

● With an "intermediate," however, since the substance and essence of the vitalising animal soul, which is derived from the *sitra achra*, and pervades his blood and flesh, has not been transformed into good, it ▲surely constitutes the man himself. If so,

[3] Zohar *III, 168a.* [4] *A play on* Ps. *15:4. Note the reinterpretation.* [5] *Comp.* Ps. *51:29.* [6] *Morning Liturgy;* Berachot *60b.* [7] Exod. *30:32.* [8] Lev. *R. 34:3.*

סליק ביה נהורא מבטשין ליה כו׳. גופא דלא סליק ביה נהורא דנשמתא מבטשין ליה כו׳ פי׳ נהורא דנשמתא שאור הנשמה והשכל אינו מאיר כל כך למשול על חומריות שבגוף. ואף שמבין ומתבונן בשכלו בגדולת ה׳ אינו נתפס ונדבק במוחו כל כך שיוכל למשול על חומריו׳ הלב מחמת חומריותן וגסותן והסיבה היא גסות הקליפה שמגביה עצמה על אור קדושת נפש האלהית ומסתרת ומחשיכה אורה. ולזאת צריך לבטשה ולהשפילה לעפר דהיינו לקבוע עתים להשפיל עצמו להיות נבזה בעיניו נמאס ככתוב ולב נשבר רוח נשברה היא הס״א שהיא היא האדם עצמו בבינונים שנפש החיונית המחיה הגוף היא בתקפה כתולדתה בלבו נמצא היא היא האדם עצמו. ועל נפש האלהית שבו נאמר נשמה שנתת בי טהורה היא שנתת בי דייקא מכלל שהאדם עצמו איננו הנשמה הטהורה כי אם בצדיקים שבהם הוא להפך שנשמה הטהורה שהיא נפש האלהית הוא האדם וגופם נקרא בשר אדם. וכמאמר הלל הזקן לתלמידיו כשהיה הולך לאכול היה אומר שהוא הולך לגמול חסד עם העלובה ועניה הוא גופו כי כמו זר נחשב אצלו ולכן אמר שהוא גומל חסד עמו במה שמאכילו כי הוא עצמו אינו רק נפש האלהית לבד כי היא לבדה מחיה גופו ובשרו שהרע שהיה בנפש החיונית המלובשת בדמו ובשרו נתהפך לטוב ונכלל בקדושת נפש האלהית ממש בצדיקים. אבל בבינוני מאחר שמהותה ועצמותה של נפש החיונית הבהמית שמס״א המלובשת בדמו ובשרו לא נהפך לטוב הרי היא היא האדם עצמו וא״כ

הוא

he is removed from G-d with utmost remoteness, for the lusting drive in his animal soul is capable of lusting also after forbidden things which are contrary to His blessed Will, even though he does not crave their actual fulfillment, G-d forbid; yet they are not truly scorned by him as by the *tzaddikim*, as explained above (ch. 12). In this he is inferior and more loathsome and abominable than unclean animals and insects and reptiles, as is mentioned above,[9] and as is written, "But I am a worm, and not a man. . . ."[10]

(Even when his divine soul gathers strength within him to arouse his love of G-d during prayer, this is not altogether genuine, since it is transient and vanishes after prayer, as has been discussed earlier, end of ch. 13.)

▲ Especially so, if he calls to mind the contamination of his soul with the sin of youth, and the blemish he has wrought in the supernal worlds—where everything is timeless, and it is as if he had caused his blemish and defilement this very day, G-d forbid. And although he had sincerely repented already, yet the essence of repentance is in the heart, and in the heart are found many distinctions and gradations, and everything is according to what kind of a man he is and according to the time and place, as is known to the knowing.

Consequently now, at this time, when he regards himself and sees that "The light of the soul does not penetrate into him," it is evident that to-day his repentance has not been accepted, and his sins [still] separate him, or that it is desired to raise him to a more sublime level of repentance, coming more deeply from the heart. Therefore King David said, "And my sin is ever before me."[11]

●▲ And even he who is innocent of the grievous sins of youth should set his heart to fulfil the counsel of the holy Zohar to be of the "masters of accounts,"[12] that is to say, he should keep a reckoning with his soul regarding all the thoughts, utterances and actions that have come and gone, since he came into being and until the present day, as to whether they all came from the direction of holiness, or from the direction of impurity—the Lord deliver us!—these being all the thoughts, utterances and actions that are not [dedicated] to G-d, and His will and service, for this is the meaning of *sitra achra*, as has been explained above (ch. 6). And it is known that every time a person thinks holy thoughts, he becomes

[9] *Ch. 24.* [10] Ps. *22:7.* [11] Ps. *51:5.* [12] *Cf.* Zohar *III, 178a.*

● 30 Shevat ▲ *13 Adar I* ▲ *14 Adar I*

הוא רחוק מה׳ בתכלית הריחוק שהרי כח המתאוה שבנפשו הבהמית יכול ג״כ להתאוות לדברי׳ האסורים שהם נגד רצונו ית׳ אף שאינו מתאוה לעשותם בפועל ממש ח״ו רק שאינם מאוסים אצלו באמת כבצדיקים כמש״ל [פ׳ יב]. ובזה הוא גרוע ומשוקץ ומתועב יותר מבעלי חיים הטמאים ושקצים ורמשים כנ״ל וכמ״ש ואנכי תולעת ולא איש וגו׳ [וגם כשמתגברת בו נפשו האלהית לעורר האהבה לה׳ בשעת התפלה אינה באמת לאמיתו לגמרי מאחר שחולפת ועוברת אחר התפלה כנ״ל ספי״ג] ובפרט כשיזכור טומאת נפשו בחטאת נעורים והפגם שעשה בעליוני׳ ושם הוא למעלה מהזמן וכאלו פגם ונטמא היום ח״ו ממש ואף שכבר עשה תשובה נכונה הרי עיקר התשובה בלב והלב יש בו בחי׳ ומדרגות רבות והכל לפי מה שהוא אדם ולפי הזמן והמקום כידוע ליודעים ולכן עכשיו בשעה זו שרואה בעצמו דלא סליק ביה נהורא דנשמתא מכלל שהיום לא נתקבלה תשובתו ועונותיו מבדילים או שרוצים להעלותו לתשובה עילאה יותר מעומקא דלבא יותר ולכן אמר דוד וחטאתי נגדי תמיד. וגם מי שהוא נקי מחטאות נעורים החמורים ישים אל לבו לקיים מאמר זה״ק להיות ממארי דחושבנא דהיינו לעשו׳ חשבון עם נפשו מכל המחשבות והדיבורים והמעשים שחלפו ועברו מיום היותו עד היום הזה אם היו כולם מצד הקדושה או מצד הטומאה ר״ל דהיינו כל המחשבות והדיבורים והמעשים אשר לא לה׳ המה ולרצונו ולעבודתו שזהו פי׳ לשון ס״א כנ״ל [בפ״ו] ומודעת זאת כי כל עת שהאדם מחשב מחשבות קדושות נעשה

מרכבה

at that time a "vehicle" for the *hechalot* (chambers) of holiness, whence these thoughts originate, and vice versa, becoming at that time an unclean "vehicle" for the *hechalot* of impurity, whence all impure thoughts originate. So, too, with speech and action.

▲ In addition, he must earnestly remember that most of his dreams are vanity and affliction of the spirit,[13] because his soul does not rise upward, as it is written, "Who shall ascend the mountain of the Lord? He that hath clean hands and a pure heart."[14] But "those originating from the evil side, come and attach themselves to him and report to him in his dreams of mundane affairs . . . and often mock him and show him false things and torment him in his dreams," and so on, as stated in the Zohar on *Vayikra* [II], (p. 25a, b). See it there discussed at length.

● The longer he will reflect on these matters in his thoughts, delving deeply also into books, in order to break down his heart within him and render himself shamed and despised in his own eyes, as is written in the Scriptures,[15] so utterly despised that he despises his very life—the more he despises and degrades thereby the *sitra achra*, casting it down to the ground and humbling it from its haughtiness and pride and self-exaltation, wherewith it exalts itself over the light of the holiness of the divine soul, obscuring its effulgence.

He must also thunder against it with a strong and raging voice in order to humble it, as the Rabbis state,[16] "A person should always rouse the good impulse against the evil impulse, as it is written, 'Rage, and sin not.'"[17] That is to say, one must rage against the animal soul, which is his evil impulse,[18] with stormy indignation in his mind, saying to it: "Thou art evil and wicked, abominable, loathsome and disgraceful, . . ." with all the epithets by which our Sages, of blessed memory, have rightly called it, ". . . How long wilt thou conceal from me the light of the blessed *En Sof*, which pervades all the worlds; which was, is, and will be the same, including also this place where I stand, just as the light of the blessed *En Sof* was alone before the world was created, without any change, as is written, 'For I, the Lord, have not changed,'[19] for He transcends time, and so forth? But thou, who is repulsive . . . , dost deny the truth, which is plain to see, by physical sight, that everything in His presence is truly like nothing at all."

---

[13] *See ch. 6, above.* [14] Ps. *24:3, 4.* [15] Ps. *15:4; see n. 4, above.* [16] Berachot *5a.* [17] Ps. *4:5.* [18] *Elsewhere (e.g.* Torah Or *38b) the author does not identify the evil impulse with the animal soul, defining the former as the attributes of the latter.* [19] Mal. *3:6.*

מרכבה בעת זו להיכלות הקדושה שמהן מושפעות מחשבות הללו וכן להפך נעשה מרכבה טמאה בעת זו להיכלות הטומאה שמהן מושפעות כל מחשבות רעות וכן בדבור ומעשה. עוד ישים אל לבו רוב חלומותיו שהם הבל ורעות רוח משום שאין נפשו עולה למעלה וכמ"ש מי יעלה בהר ה' נקי כפים וגו' ואינון סטרין בישין אתיין ומתדבקן ביה ומודעין ליה בחלמא מילין דעלמא וכו' ולזמנין דחייכן ביה ואחזיאו ליה מילי שקר וצערין ליה בחלמיה כו' כמ"ש בזהר ויקרא [ד' כ"ה ע"א וע"ב] ע"ש באריכות. והנה כל מה שיאריך בעניינים אלו במחשבתו וגם בעיונו בספרים להיות לבו נשבר בקרבו ונבזה בעיניו נמאס ככתוב בתכלית המיאוס ולמאס חייו ממש הרי בזה ממאס ומבזה הס"א ומשפילה לעפר ומורידה מגדולתה וגסות רוחה וגבהותה שמגביה את עצמה על אור קדושת נפש האלהית להחשיך אורה. וגם ירעים עליה בקול רעש ורוגז להשפילה כמאמר רז"ל לעולם ירגיז אדם יצ"ט על יצ"הר שנאמר רגזו וגו' דהיינו לרגוז על נפש הבהמית שהיא יצרו הרע בקול רעש ורוגז במחשבתו לומר לו אתה רע ורשע ומשוקץ ומתועב ומנוול וכו' ככל השמות שקראו לו חכמינו ז"ל באמת עד מתי תסתיר לפני אור א"ס ב"ה הממלא כל עלמין היה הוה ויהיה בשוה גם במקום זה שאני עליו כמו שהיה אור א"ס ב"ה לבדו קודם שנברא העולם בלי שום שינוי כמ"ש אני ה' לא שניתי כי הוא למעלה מהזמן וכו' ואתה מנול וכו' מכחיש האמת הנראה לעינים דכולא קמיה כלא ממש באמת בבחי' ראייה חושית.

והנה

In this way he will help his divine soul to enlighten her eyes with the truth of the unity of the light of the *En Sof*, with a perceptive vision and not merely by cognition alone, as it were, as is explained elsewhere that this is the core of the whole [Divine] Service. And the explanation is that in truth there is no substance whatever in the *sitra achra*, wherefore it is compared to darkness which has no substance whatever and, consequently is banished in the presence of light. Similarly the *sitra achra* which, although it possesses abundant vitality wherewith to animate all impure animals and the souls of the nations of the world; and also the animal soul of the Jew, as has been explained,[20] nevertheless has no vitality of its own, G-d forbid, but [derives it] from the realm of holiness, as has been explained above.[21] Therefore it is completely nullified in the presence of holiness, as darkness is nullified before physical light, except that in regard to the holiness of the divine soul in man, the Holy One, blessed be He, has given [the animal soul] permission and ability to raise itself against [the divine soul] in order that man should be challenged to overcome it and to humble it by means of the humility and submission of his spirit and his abhorring in himself that which is despicable. And "Through the impulse from below comes an impulse from Above," to fulfil what is written, "Thence will I bring thee down, saith the Lord,"[22] namely, depriving it of its dominion and power and withdrawing from it the strength and authority which had been given it to rise up against the light of the holiness of the divine soul; whereupon it inevitably becomes nullified and is banished, just as darkness is nullified before physical light.

Indeed, we find this explicitly stated in the Torah in connection with the Spies who, at the outset declared, "For he is stronger than we"[23]—"Read not 'than we,' but 'than He,' "etc.,[24] for they had no faith in G-d's ability. But afterwards they reversed themselves and announced, "Lo, we will readily go up. . . ."[25] Whence did their faith in G-d's ability return to them? Our teacher Moses, peace unto him, had not meanwhile shown them any sign or wonder concerning this. He had only told them that the Lord was angry with them and had sworn not to allow them to enter the Land. Why should this have influenced them, and of what avail was this to them, if they did not believe, Heaven forfend, in the Lord's ability to subdue the thirty-one kings,[26] for which reason they had no desire whatever

[20] *Ch. 6, above.* [21] Ibid. [22] Ovad. *1:4.* [23] Num. *13:31.* [24] Arachim *15a;* Sotah *35a. The Hebrew word* ממנו. *permits both interpretations.* [25] Num. *14:40.* [26] *Cf.* Joshua *12.*

● 2 Adar

והנה על ידי זה יועיל לנפשו האלהית להאיר עיניה באמת יחוד אור אין סוף ברא‌יה חושיית ולא בחי׳ שמיעה והבנה לבדה כמ״ש במ״א שזהו שרש כל העבודה והטעם לפי שבאמת אין שום ממשות כלל בס״א שלכן נמשלה לחשך שאין בו שום ממשות כלל וממילא נדחה מפני האור וכך הס״א אף שיש בה חיות הרבה להחיות כל בעלי חיים הטמאים ונפשות אומות עכו״ם וגם נפש הבהמית שבישראל כנ״ל מ״מ הרי כל חיותה אינה מצד עצמה ח״ו אלא מצד הקדושה כנ״ל ולכן היא בטלה לגמרי מפני הקדושה כביטול החשך מפני האור הגשמי רק שלגבי קדושת נפש האלהית שבאדם נתן לה הקב״ה רשות ויכולת להגביה עצמה כנגדה כדי שהאדם יתעורר להתגבר עליה להשפילה ע״י שפלות ונמיכת רוחו ונבזה בעיניו נמאס ובאתערותא דלתתא אתערותא דלעילא לקיים מ״ש משם אורידך נאם ה׳ דהיינו שמסירה מממשלתה ויכלתה ומסלק ממנה הכח ורשות שנתן לה להגביה עצמה נגד אור קדושת נפש האלהית ואזי ממילא בטילה ונדחית כביטול החשך מפני אור הגשמי. וכמו שמצינו דבר זה מפורש בתורה גבי מרגלים שמתחלה אמרו כי חזק הוא ממנו אל תקרי ממנו כו׳ שלא האמינו ביכולת ה׳ ואח״כ חזרו ואמרו הננו ועלינו וגו׳ ומאין חזרה ובאה להם האמונה ביכולת ה׳ הרי לא הראה להם משרע״ה שום אות ומופת על זה בנתיים רק שאמ׳ להם איך שקצף ה׳ עליהם ונשבע שלא להביאם אל הארץ ומה הועיל זה להם אם לא היו מאמינים ביכולת ה׳ ח״ו לכבוש ל״א מלכי׳ ומפני זה לא רצו כלל ליכנס

to enter the Land?

But undoubtedly, since the Israelites themselves are "Believers, the descendants of believers," except that the *sitra achra*—which is clothed in their bodies—had risen against the light of the holiness of their divine soul, in her impudent haughtiness and arrogance, without sense or reason—now, therefore, as soon as the Lord had become angered against them and thundered angrily, "How long shall I bear with this evil congregation. . . . Your carcasses shall fall in this wilderness. . . . I the Lord have spoken, I will surely do it unto all this evil congregation,"[27] their heart was humbled and broken within them when they heard these stern words, as is written, "And the people mourned greatly."[28] Consequently, the *sitra achra* toppled from its dominion, from its haughtiness and arrogance, leaving the Israelites to their inborn faith.

From the above, every person in whose mind enter doubts as to [his] faith, can deduce that they are nothing more than empty words of the *sitra achra*, which raises itself against his soul. But the Israelites themselves are faithful. . . .[29] Furthermore, the *sitra achra* itself entertains no doubts about faith, except that she has been given permission to confuse man with words of falsehood and deceit, in order that he may acquire greater rewards, as the harlot seeks to seduce the king's son with falsehood and deceit, with the king's approval, as [in the parable] mentioned in the holy *Zohar*.[30]

•▲ Chapter 30

This also a person must resolve in his heart, to fulfil the instruction of our Rabbis, of blessed memory: "And be humble of spirit before all men."[1] This you must *be* in true sincerity, in the presence of *any* individual, even in the presence of the most worthless of worthless men. This accords with the instruction of our Sages: "Judge not thy fellow until thou art come to his place."[2] For it is his "place" that causes him to sin, because his livelihood requires him to go to the market for the whole day and to be one of those who "Sit at the [street] corners," where his eyes behold all the temptations; the eye sees and the heart desires,[3] and his evil nature is kindled like a baker's red-hot oven, as is written in Hosea: "It burneth as a flaming fire. . . ."[4]

It is different, however, with him who goes but little to the market place, and who remains in his house for the greater part of the day; or even if he spends the whole day in the market but is possibly

---

[27] Num. *14:27, 29, 35.* [28] Ibid., *v. 39.* [29] . . . *the descendants of the faithful.* [30] *Cf. Note 18 on ch. 9.*

Chapter 30
[1] Avot *4:10.* [2] Ibid., *2:4.* [3] *Rashi*, Num. *15:39;* Bamidbar Rabbah, *10:2.* [4] Hosea *7:6.*

ליכנס לארץ אלא ודאי מפני שישראל עצמן הם מאמינים בני מאמינים רק שהס"א המלובשת בגופם הגביה עצמה על אור קדושת נפשם האלהית בגסות רוחה וגבהות' בחוצפה בלי טעם ודעת ולכן מיד שקצף ה' עליהם והרעים בקול רעש ורוגז עד מתי לעדה הרעה הזאת וגו' במדבר הזה יפלו פגריכם וגו' אני ה' דברתי אם לא זאת אעשה לכל העדה הרעה הזאת וגו' וכששמעו דברים קשים אלו נכנע ונשבר לבם בקרבם כדכתיב ויתאבלו העם מאד וממילא נפלה הס"א מממשלתה וגבהותה וגסות רוחה וישראל עצמן הם מאמינים ומזה יכול ללמוד כל אדם שנופלים לו במחשבתו ספיקות על אמונה כי הם דברי רוח הס"א לבדה המגביה עצמה על נפשו אבל ישראל עצמן הם מאמינים כו' וגם הס"א עצמה אין לה ספיקות כלל באמונה רק שניתן לה רשות לבלבל האדם בדברי שקר ומרמה להרבות שכרו כפיתויי הזונה לבן המלך בשקר ומרמה ברשות המלך כמ"ש בזה"ק:

פרק ל עוד זאת ישים אל לבו לקיים מאמר רז"ל והוי שפל רוח בפני כל האדם. והוי באמת לאמיתו בפני כל האדם ממש אפי' בפני קל שבקלים. והיינו ע"פ מארז"ל אל תדין את חבירך עד שתגיע למקומו. כי מקומו גורם לו לחטוא להיות פרנסתו לילך בשוק כל היום ולהיות מיושבי קרנות ועיניו רואות כל התאוות והעין רואה והלב חומד ויצרו בוער כתנור בוערה מאופה כמ"ש בהושע הוא בוער כאש להבה וגו'. משא"כ מי שהולך בשוק מעט ורוב היום יושב בביתו וגם אם הולך כל היום בשוק יכול להיות

not so passionate by nature—for the evil inclination of all people is not the same: there is one whose nature, . . .[5] as is explained elsewhere.

▲ In truth, however, even he whose nature is extremely passionate and whose livelihood obliges him to sit all day at the [street] corners, has no excuse whatever for his sins, and he is termed an utter evildoer (*rasha gamur*) because there is no dread of G–d before his eyes. For he should have controlled himself and restrained the impulse of his desire in his heart because of the fear of G–d Who sees all actions, as has been explained above,[6] for the mind has supremacy over the heart by nature.

▲ It is indeed a great and fierce struggle to break one's passion, which burns like a fiery flame, through fear of G–d; it is like an actual test. Therefore, each person according to his place and rank in the service of G–d must weigh and examine his position as to whether he is serving G–d in a manner commensurate with the dimensions of such a fierce battle and test—in the realm of "do good,"[7] as, for example, in the service of prayer with *kavanah* (devotion), pouring out his soul before G–d with his entire strength, to the point of exhaustion of the soul,[8] while waging war against his body and animal soul within it which impede his devotion, a strenuous war to beat and grind them like dust, each day before the morning and evening prayers. Also during prayer he needs to exert himself, with the exertion of the spirit and of the flesh, as will be explained later at length.[9]

●▲Anyone who has not reached this standard of waging such strenuous war against his body, has not yet measured up to the quality and dimension of the war waged by one's evil nature which burns like a fiery flame, that it be humbled and broken by dread of G–d.

So, too, in the matter of grace after meals, and all benedictions, whether those connected with the partaking of food or with the performance of precepts, [to be recited] with *kavanah*, to say nothing of the *kavanah* of precepts "For their own sake." So, too, in the matter of one's occupation in the study of the Torah, to learn much more than his innate or accustomed desire, and inclination, by virtue of a strenuous struggle with his body. For to study a fraction more than is one's wont is but a small tussle which neither parallels nor bears comparison with the war of one's evil impulse

---

[5] *More on this subject, e.g.* Likutei Torah, Vayikra *2d;* Va-Etchanan, *5a.* [6] *Chs. 12, 19.* [7] Ps. *34:15. That of "turn away from evil" will follow later.* [8] Sifre *on* Deut. *6:5* —עד מיצוי הנפש—*literally, to the extent of "wringing out" the soul.* [9] *Ch. 42.*

להיות שאינו מחומם כ״כ בטבעו כי אין היצר שוה בכל נפש יש שיצרו כו׳ כמ״ש במ״א. והנה באמת גם מי שהוא מחומם מאד בטבעו ופרנסתו היא להיות מיושבי קרנות כל היום אין לו שום התנצלות על חטאיו ומיקרי רשע גמור על אשר אין פחד אלהי׳ לנגד עיניו. כי היה לו להתאפק ולמשול על רוח תאוותו שבלבו מפני פחד ה׳ הרואה כל מעשיו כמש״ל כי המוח שליט על הלב בתולדתו. והנה באמת שהיא מלחמה גדולה ועצומ׳ לשבור היצר הבוער כאש להבה מפני פחד ה׳ וכמו נסיון ממש. והלכך צריך כל אדם לפי מה שהוא מקומו ומדרגתו בעבודת ה׳ לשקול ולבחון בעצמו אם הוא עובד ה׳ בערך ובחי׳ מלחמה עצומה כזו ונסיון כזה בבחי׳ ועשה טוב כגון בעבודת התפלה בכוונה לשפוך נפשו לפני ה׳ בכל כחו ממש עד מיצוי הנפש ולהלחם עם גופו ונפש הבהמית שבו המונעים הכוונה במלחמה עצומה ולבטשם ולכתתם כעפר קודם התפלה שחרית וערבית מדי יום ביום וגם בשעת התפלה לייגע עצמו ביגיעת נפש ויגיעת בשר כמ״ש לקמן באריכות. וכל שלא הגיע לידי מדה זו להלחם עם גופו מלחמה עצומה כזו עדיין לא הגיע לבחי׳ וערך מלחמת היצר הבוער כאש להבה להיות נכנע ונשבר מפני פחד ה׳. וכן בענין ברכת המזון וכל ברכת הנהנין והמצות בכונה ואצ״ל כונת המצות לשמן. וכן בענין עסק לימוד התורה ללמוד הרבה יותר מחפצו ורצונו לפי טבעו ורגילותו ע״י מלחמה עצומה עם גופו. כי הלומד מעט יותר מטבעו ה״ז מלחמה קטנה ואין לה ערך ודמיון עם מלחמת היצר

הבוער

burning like fire; he is called utterly wicked (*rasha gamur*) if he does not conquer his impulse so that it be subdued and crushed before G-d.

For, what difference is there between the category of "Turn away from evil" and that of "Do good"?[10] Both are the command of the Holy King, the One and Only, blessed be He.

So, too, with the other commandments, especially in matters involving money, as the service of charity (*tzedakah*) and the like.

▲ Even in the category of "Turn away from evil" every intelligent person can discover within himself that he does not turn aside from evil completely and in every respect where a hard battle at a level such as described above is called for, or even on a lesser level than the aforementioned: for example, to stop in the middle of a pleasant gossip, or in the middle of a tale discrediting his fellow, even though it be a very small slur, and even though it be true, and even when the purpose is to exonerate oneself—as is known from what Rabbi Simeon said to his father, our saintly teacher: "I did not write it, but Judah the tailor wrote it," when his father replied, "Keep away from slander." (Note there, in the *Gemara*, beginning of ch. 10 of *Bava Batra*.)[11]

The same applies to very many similar things which occur frequently, especially with regard to sanctifying oneself in permissible things, an enactment based on the Biblical text, "Ye shall be holy, . . ."[12] and "Sanctify yourselves, therefore. . . ."[13] Moreover, "Rabbinic enactments are even stricter than Biblical enactments,"[14] and so forth. But all these and similar ones are of the sins which a person tramples under-foot and has come to regard as permissible in consequence of repeated transgression, and so on.[15]

▲ In truth however, if he is a scholar and upholds the Law of G-d and wishes to be close to G-d, his sin is very great and his guilt is increased manifold in that he does not wage war and does not overcome his impulse in a manner commensurate with the quality and nature of the intense battle mentioned above, than the guilt of the most worthless of worthless men of the corner-squatters who are removed from G-d and His Torah, whose guilt is not as heinous—in not restraining their impulse which burns like a fiery flame by means of the dread of G-d, Who knows and sees all their deeds—as the guilt of the person who is ever so close to G-d, His Torah and His service. As the Rabbis, of blessed memory, said about "*Acher*": "For he knew My glory. . . ."[16] Therefore the Rabbis declared in regard to the illiterate that "Deliberate infringements [of the Law] are regarded, in their case, as inadvertent acts."[17]

---

[10] *Sins of omission are as reprehensible as sins of commission insofar as disobedience is concerned.* [11] Bava Batra *164b.* [12] Lev. *19:2.* [13] Lev. *20:7.* [14] Sanhedrin, *ch. 11,* Mishnah *3;* Berachot *3b;* Avodah Zarah *41a;* Rosh Hashanah *19a;* Yevamot *85b.* [15] Avodah Zarah *18a.* [16] Chagigah *15a (comp.* Chidushei ha-Bach, *ad loc).* [17] Bava Metzia *33b.*

▲ *20 Adar I* ▲ *21 Adar I*

הבוער כאש דמקרי רשע גמור אם אינו מנצח יצרו להיות נכנע ונשבר מפני ה׳. ומה לי בחי׳ סור מרע ומה לי בחי׳ ועשה טוב הכל היא מצות המלך הקדוש יחיד ומיוחד ב״ה. וכן בשאר מצות ובפרט בדבר שבממון כמו עבודת הצדקה וכה״ג. ואפי׳ בבחי׳ סור מרע יכול כל איש משכיל למצוא בנפשו שאינו סר לגמרי מהרע בכל מכל כל במקום שצריך למלחמה עצומה כערך הנ״ל ואפי׳ פחות מערך הנ״ל כגון להפסיק באמצע שיחה נאה או סיפור בגנות חבירו ואפי׳ גנאי קטן וקל מאד אף שהוא אמת ואפי׳ כדי לנקות עצמו כנודע מהא דאר״ש לאביו רבינו הקדוש לאו אנא כתבי׳ אלא יהודא חייטא כתביה וא״ל כלך מלה״ר [ע״ש בגמ׳ רפ״י דב״ב]. וכה״ג כמה מילי דשכיחי טובא ובפרט בענין לקדש עצמו במותר לו שהוא מדאוריית׳ כמ״ש קדושים תהיו וגו׳ והתקדשתם וגו׳. וגם ד״ס חמורים מד״ת וכו׳. אלא שכל אלו וכיוצא בהן הן מעוונות שהאדם דש בעקביו וגם נעשו כהיתר מחמת שעבר ושנה וכו׳. אבל באמת אם הוא יודע ספר ומחזיק בתורת ה׳ וקרבת אלקי׳ יחפץ גדול עונו מנשוא ואשמתו גדלה בכפלי כפליים במה שאינו נלחם ומתגבר על יצרו בערך ובחי׳ מלחמה עצומה הנ״ל מאשמת קל שבקלים מיושבי קרנות הרחוקים מה׳ ותורתו ואין אשמתם גדולה כ״כ במה שאינם כובשים יצרם הבוער כאש להבה מפני פחד ה׳ המבין ומביט אל כל מעשיהם כאשמת כל הקרב הקרב אל ה׳ ואל תורתו ועבודתו וכמשארז״ל גבי אחר שידע בכבודי וכו׳ ולכן ארז״ל על ע״ה שזדונות נעשו להם כשגגות:

פרק לא

•▲ *Chapter 31*

Even if by prolonging the deep concentration on the aforementioned matters for an hour or two, in order to acquire a humble spirit and a contrite heart, the individual will lapse into a profound dejection, he should not worry. For although sadness stems from the realm of *kelipat nogah* and not from that of holiness, since in regard to holiness it is written, "Strength and gladness are in His place,"[1] and "The Divine Presence (*Shechinah*) abides only in joy . . . as is the case also in the study of the law," and so on,[2] except that if the sadness comes from reflections about celestial [i.e. spiritual] things, it is derived from the realm of goodness that is in *nogah* (hence Rabbi Isaac Luria, of blessed memory, wrote that even worry about sins is only fitting during confession[3] but not during prayer and Torah study, which should be conducted with joy derived from the side of holiness, exclusively)—

Nevertheless, the method of subduing the *sitra achra* is on the latter's own ground, as the Rabbis of blessed memory have said, "From the forest itself is taken the axe wherewith to fell it,"[4] and "He met his equal."[5] With regard to this it is written, "In all sadness there is profit,"[6] the profit being the joy that follows the sadness, as will be explained later.

In truth, however, a contrite heart and the bitterness[7] of the soul because of its remoteness from the light of the Divine countenance and its being clothed in the *sitra achra*—are not called *atzvut* (dejection) in the sacred tongue, for *atzvut* implies that the heart is dull like a stone and is devoid of vitality. But in the case of *merirut* (bitterness) and a broken heart, the contrary is surely true—there is vitality in the heart fermenting agitation and bitterness, except that this vitality stems from the attribute of the holy *gevurot* (severity), whereas joy comes from the attribute of *chasadim* (kindness), for the heart is comprised of them both.

Thus it is sometimes necessary to awaken the attribute of the holy *gevurot* in order to ameliorate the stern judgments, arising from the animal soul and evil nature, when triumphing, Heaven forfend, over man. For the stern judgments can be sweetened only at their source.[8] Therefore the Rabbis, of blessed memory, said that "A person should always excite the good nature,"[9] that is, whenever he perceives in his soul that he is in need of it. But the propitious time, which is the time specifically fitting for the majority of people, is when one is in any case troubled by mundane worries, or, simply, without

---

[1] I Chron. *16:27*. [2] *Cf.* Shabbat *30b*. [3] *In the Prayer Before Retiring to Bed.* [4] Sanhedrin *39b*. [5] Shabbat *121b*. [6] Prov. *14:23*. [7] *The author makes a distinction between* עצבות *("sadness," bordering on depression or melancholy) and* מרירות *("bitterness").* [8] *See* infra, *chs. 40 and 41*. [9] Berachot *5a*.

פרק לא והנה אף אם כשיאריך הרבה להעמיק בענייני׳ הנ״ל כשעה ושתי׳ להיות בנמיכת רוח ולב נשבר יבא לידי עצבות גדולה לא יחוש ואף שעצבות היא מצד קליפת נוגה ולא מצד הקדושה כי בצד הקדושה כתיב עוז וחדוה במקומו ואין השכינה שורה אלא מתוך שמחה וכן לדבר הלכה וכו׳ אלא שאם העצבות היא ממילי דשמיא היא מבחי׳ טוב שבנוגה [ולכן כתב האר״י ז״ל שאפי׳ דאגת העונות אינה ראויה כ״א בשעת הוידוי ולא בשעת התפלה ות״ת שצ״ל בשמחה שמצד הקדושה דווקא] אעפ״כ הרי כך היא המדה לאכפיא לס״א במינה ודוגמתה. כמארז״ל מיניה וביה אבא לשדי׳ ביה נרגא ופגע בו כיוצא בו. וע״ז נאמר בכל עצב יהיה מותר והיתרון היא השמחה הבאה אחר העצב כדלקמן. אך באמת אין לב נשבר ומרירות הנפש על ריחוקה מאור פני ה׳ והתלבשותה בס״א נקראים בשם עצבות כלל בלשון הקודש כי עצבות היא שלבו מטומטם כאבן ואין חיות בלבו אבל מרירות ולב נשבר אדרבה הרי יש חיות בלבו להתפעל ולהתמרמר רק שהיא חיות מבחי׳ גבורות קדושות והשמחה מבחי׳ חסדים כי הלב כלול משתיהן. והנה לעתים צריך לעורר בחי׳ גבורות הקדושות כדי להמתיק הדינים שהם בחי׳ נפש הבהמי׳ ויצה״ר כששולט ח״ו על האדם כי אין הדינים נמתקין אלא בשרשן ולכן ארז״ל לעולם ירגיז אדם יצ״הט והיינו בכל עת שרואה בנפשו שצריך לכך אך שעת הכושר שהיא שעה המיוחדת וראויה לכך לרוב בני אדם היא בשעה שהוא עצב בלא״ה ממילי דעלמא או כך בלי

שום

apparent cause. Then is the appropriate time to transform the sadness by becoming one of those "Masters of account" mentioned earlier[10] and to act on the counsel of the Rabbis "Constantly to excite," and so on, as has been mentioned above. Thereby will he rid himself of the dejection • occasioned by mundane affairs. Following this he will attain true joy when he will reflect in his heart and gain a double measure of comfort, in view of what has been said above in truth, saying to himself: "Truly and without doubt I am far removed from G–d, and I am abominable and loathsome.... Yet all this is myself alone, that is to say, the body with its vivifying soul. Yet, there is within me a veritable part of G–d, which is found even in the most worthless of the worthless, namely, the divine soul with a spark of veritable G–dliness which is clothed in it and animates it, except that it is, as it were, in [a state of] exile. Therefore, on the contrary, the further I am separated from G–d, and the more contemptible and loathsome, the deeper in exile is my divine soul, and the more greatly is she to be pitied; therefore I shall make it my whole aim and desire to extricate her and liberate her from this exile, in order to restore her 'To her Father's house as in her youth,'[11] before she was clothed in my body, when she was absorbed in His blessed light and completely united with Him. Now she will again be thus absorbed and united with Him, may He be blessed, if I will bend my whole aim toward the Torah and the commandments, to clothe therein all her ten faculties, as mentioned above, especially in the precept of prayer, to cry unto the Lord in her distress of exile in my despicable body, to liberate her from her prison, that she may attach herself to Him, blessed be He."

This is the essence of "Repentance and good deeds,"[12] the latter being the good deeds which one performs in order to restore the portion of the Lord to the Source and Root of all the worlds.

• And this shall be his service all his life in great joy, the joy of the soul in her release from the despised body and "Returning to her Father's house as in her youth," when engaged in Torah and prayer. Indeed, the Rabbis, of blessed memory, have said, that one should be in a state of repentance throughout one's life.[13] For there is no greater joy than the escape from exile and imprisonment, as in the example of the king's son who was kept in captivity, grinding [corn], in

---

[10] *Ch. 29.* [11] Lev. *22:13.*
[12] *Comp.* Avot *4:11.* [13] Shabbat *153a.*

שום סבה אזי היא שעת הכושר להפך העצב להיות ממרי דחושבנא הנ"ל ולקיים מארז"ל לעולם ירגיז וכו' כנ"ל ובזה יפטר מהעצבות שממילי דעלמא ואח"כ יבא לידי שמחה אמיתית דהיינו שזאת ישיב אל לבו לנחמו בכפליים אחר הדברי' והאמת האלה הנ"ל לאמר ללבו אמת הוא כן בלי ספק שאני רחוק מאד מה' בתכלית ומשוקץ ומתועב כו' אך כל זה הוא אני לבדי הוא הגוף עם נפש החיונית שבו אבל מ"מ יש בקרבי חלק ה' ממש שישנו אפי' בקל שבקלים שהיא נפש האלהית עם ניצוץ אלקות ממש המלובש בה להחיותה רק שהיא בבחי' גלות וא"כ אדרבה כל מה שאני בתכלי' הריחוק מה' והתיעוב ושיקוץ הרי נפש האלהית שבי בגלות גדול יותר והרחמנות עליה גדולה מאד ולזה אשים כל מגמתי וחפצי להוציאה ולהעלותה מגלות זה להשיבה אל בית אביה כנעורי' קודם שנתלבשה בגופי שהיתה נכללת באורו ית' ומיוחדת עמו בתכלית וגם עתה כן תהא כלולה ומיוחדת בו ית' כשאשים כל מגמתי בתור' ומצות להלביש בהן כל עשר בחינותיה כנ"ל ובפרט במצות תפלה לצעוק אל ה' בצר לה מגלותה בגופי המשוקץ להוציאה ממסגר ולדבקה בו ית' וזו היא בחי' תשובה ומעשים טובים שהן מעשים טובים שעושה כדי להשיב חלק ה' למקורא ושרשא דכל עלמין. וזאת תהיה עבודתו כל ימיו בשמחה רבה היא שמחת הנפש בצאתה מהגוף המתועב ושבה אל בית אביה כנעוריה בשעת התורה והעבודה וכמארז"ל להיות כל ימיו בתשובה ואין לך שמחה גדולה כצאת מהגלות והשביה כמשל בן מלך שהיה בשביה וטוחן בבית

האסורים

prison and becoming covered with filth; then he is liberated and he returns to his father's royal house.

And although the body is still in its contemptible and abominable state—it is referred to in the *Zohar* as "The skin of the serpent"—inasmuch as the essence and substance of the animal soul have not converted to good, so as to merge into holiness, nevertheless his soul will become more precious in his eyes than the despised body, and he will rejoice in her joy, and not confound and confuse the joy of the soul with the misery of the body.[14]

This [release of the soul from her exile in the body] is in the nature of the "Exodus from Egypt," in connection with which it is written, "The people had fled."[15] At first sight it is strange that it should have happened in this way. For had Pharaoh been requested to liberate them for ever, would he not have been compelled to let them go? But because the evil in the souls of the Israelites was still in its strength in the left part—for not until the Giving of the Law did their impurity cease[16]—yet their aim and desire was to free their divine souls from the exile of the *sitra achra*, which is the "Defilement of Egypt," and cleave to Him, blessed be He, as is written, "The Lord is my strength and my fortress and my refuge in the day of affliction, . . ."[17] "my high tower and my refuge, . . ."[18] "and He is my escape, . . ."[19] [so, too, was the physical exodus from Egypt in a manner of escape]. Hence in the time to come, when the Lord will remove the spirit of impurity from the earth, it is written of it, "[ye shall not go out in haste], nor go by flight, for the Lord will go before you. . . ."[20]

• The quality of this repentance will be stronger and more intense, from the depth of the heart, and likewise the joy of the soul will be with an added measure of light and joy, when he will reflect in his heart with knowledge and understanding, to console himself from his distress and sorrow, saying, as above: "Truly and without a doubt, . . ." "but it was not I who created myself. Why, then, has G–d done such a thing, to cause a portion of His blessed light, which fills and encompasses all worlds, and before Whom everything is of no account, to descend and to be clothed in a 'serpent's skin' and in a fetid drop? It cannot be otherwise than that this descent is for the purpose of an ascent—to raise up to G–d the whole vital animal soul, which is of the *kelipat nogah*, and all her 'garments,' namely her faculties of thought, speech and action, through their being enclothed in the act, speech and thought of the Torah." (As for the meaning of this ascent—

---

[14] *Cf.* infra, *ch. 33*. [15] Exod. *14:5*. [16] Shabbat *146a*. [17] Jer. *16:19*. [18] II Sam. *22:2*. [19] *Liturgy*, Adon Olam. [20] Isa. *52:12*.

• 8 Adar

האסורים ומנוול באשפה ויצא לחפשי אל בית אביו המלך ואף שהגוף עומד בשיקוצו ותיעובו וכמ"ש בזהר דנקרא משכא דחויא כי מהותה ועצמותה של הנפש הבהמית לא נהפך לטוב ליכלל בקדושה מ"מ תיקר נפשו בעיניו לשמוח בשמחתה יותר מהגוף הנבזה שלא לערבב ולבלבל שמחת הנפש בעצבון הגוף. והנה בחי' זו היא בחי' יציאת מצרים שנאמר בה כי ברח העם דלכאור' הוא תמוה למה היתה כזאת וכי אילו אמרו לפרעה לשלחם חפשי לעולם לא היה מוכרח לשלחם אלא מפני שהרע שבנפשות ישראל עדיין היה בתקפו בחלל השמאלי כי לא פסקה זוהמתם עד מתן תורה רק מגמתם וחפצם היתה לצאת נפשם האלהית מגלות הס"א היא טומאת מצרים ולדבקה בו ית' וכדכתיב ה' עוזי ומעוזי ומנוסי ביום צרה וגו' משגבי ומנוסי וגו' והוא מנוס לי וגו' ולכן לעתיד כשיעביר ה' רוח הטומאה מן הארץ כתיב ובמנוסה לא תלכון כי הולך לפניכם ה' וגו'. ולהיות בחי' תשובה זו ביתר שאת ויתר עז מעומקא דלבא וגם שמחת הנפש תהיה בתוספת אורה ושמחה כאשר ישיב אל לבו דעת ותבונה לנחמו מעצבונו ויגונו לאמר כנ"ל הן אמת כו' אך אני לא עשיתי את עצמי. ולמה עשה ה' כזאת להוריד חלק מאורו ית' הממלא וסובב כל עלמין וכולא קמי' כלא חשיב והלבישו במשכא דחויא וטפה סרוחה אין זה כי אם ירידה זו היא צורך עליה להעלות לה' כל נפש החיונית הבהמית שמקליפת נוגה וכל לבושיה הן בחי' מחשבה דבור ומעשה שלה ע"י התלבשותן במעשה דבור ומחשבת התורה [וכמ"ש לקמן ענין

העלאה

how this is the ultimate purpose of the creation of the world—it will be later explained at length.)[21] "If this is so, there is one thing for me to do, and this will be my sole aim all the days of my earthly life, to fully occupy therein the life of my spirit and soul, as is written, 'Unto Thee, O Lord, I lift up my soul,'[22] that is to say, to bind my thought and speech with His blessed thought and speech, which are the very laws which have been set before us, and likewise my action—in the performance of the commandments."

For this reason the Torah is described as "Restoring the soul,"[23] i.e. [restoring it] to its source and root. Concerning this it is written, "The precepts of the Lord are right, rejoicing the heart."[24]

●▲ *Chapter 32*

Acting on the suggestion mentioned above—to view one's body with scorn and contempt, and finding joy only in the joy of the soul alone—is a direct and easy way to attain the fulfillment of the commandment "Thou shalt love thy fellow as thyself"[1] toward every soul of Israel, both great and small.

▲ For, whereas one despises and loathes one's body, while as for the soul and spirit, who can know their greatness and excellence in their root and source in the living G–d? Being, moreover, all of a kind and all having one Father—therefore, all Israelites are called real brothers by virtue of the source of their souls in the One G–d; only the bodies are separated. Hence in the case of those who give major consideration to their bodies while regarding their souls as of secondary importance, there can be no true love and brotherhood among them, but only [a love] which is dependent on a [transitory] thing.[2]

▲ This is what Hillel the Elder meant when he said in regard to the fulfillment of this commandment, "This is the whole Torah, whilst the rest is but commentary,"[3] and so on. For the basis and root of the entire Torah are to raise and exalt the soul high above the body, reaching unto the Source and Root of all the worlds, and also to bring down the blessed light of the *En Sof* upon the community of Israel, as will be explained later,[4] i.e. into the fountain-head of the souls of all Israel, to become "One into One."[5] This is impossible if there is, G–d forbid, disunity among the souls, for the Holy One, blessed be He, does not dwell in an imperfect place,[6] as we pray: "Bless us, O our Father, all of us together, with the light of Thy countenance,"[7] as has been explained at great length elsewhere.

●▲ As for the Talmudic statement[8] to the effect that one who sees his friend sinning should hate him and should tell his teacher

---

[21] *Chs. 35, 36, 37.* [22] Ps. *25:1.* [23] Ps. *19:8.* [24] Ps. *19:9.*

Chapter 32
[1] Lev. *19:18.* [2] Avot *5:16.* [3] Shabbat *31a.* [4] *Ch. 41.* [5] Zohar *II, 135a.* [6] Zohar *I, 216b.* [7] *Liturgy,* Amidah. [8] Shevuot *30a.*

העלאה זו באריכות איך שהיא תכלית בריאת העולם]
וא"כ איפוא זאת אעשה וזאת תהיה כל מגמתי כל ימי
חלדי לכל בהן חיי רוחי ונפשי וכמ"ש אליך ה' נפשי
אשא דהיינו לקשר מחשבתי ודבורי במחשבתו
ודבורו ית' והן הן גופי הלכות הערוכו' לפנינו וכן מעשה
במעשה המצות שלכן נקראת התורה משיבת נפש פי'
למקורה ושרשה וע"ז נאמ' פקודי ה' ישרים משמחי לב:

פרק לב

והנה ע"י קיום הדברי' הנ"ל להיות גופו נבזה ונמאס בעיניו רק שמחתו
תהיה שמחת הנפש לבדה הרי זו דרך ישרה וקלה לבא
לידי קיום מצות ואהבת לרעך כמוך לכל נפש מישראל
למגדול ועד קטן. כי מאחר שגופו נמאס ומתועב אצלו
והנפש והרוח מי יודע גדולתן ומעלתן בשרשן ומקורן
באלקי' חיים. בשגם שכולן מתאימות ואב א' לכולנה
ולכן נקראו כל ישראל אחים ממש מצד שורש נפשם
בה' אחד רק שהגופים מחולקי'. ולכן העושי' גופם עיקר
ונפשם טפלה אי אפשר להיות אהבה ואחוה אמיתית
ביניהם אלא התלויה בדבר לבדה. וז"ש הלל הזקן על
קיום מצוה זו זהו כל התורה כולה ואידך פירושא הוא
כו'. כי יסוד ושורש כל התורה הוא להגביה ולהעלו'
הנפש על הגוף מעלה מעלה עד עיקרא ושרשא דכל
עלמין וגם להמשיך אור א"ס ב"ה בכנסת ישראל כמ"ש
לקמן דהיינו במקור נשמות כל ישראל למהוי אחד
באחד דוקא ולא כשיש פירוד ח"ו בנשמות דקב"ה לא
שריא באתר פגים וכמ"ש ברכנו אבינו כולנו כאחד
באור פניך וכמ"ש במ"א באריכות: ומ"ש בגמ' שמי
שרואה בחבירו שחטא מצוה לשנאותו וגם לומר לרבו
שישנאהו

to hate him also, this applies to a companion in Torah and precepts, having already applied to him the injunction, "Thou shalt repeatedly rebuke thy friend (*amitecha*),"[9] meaning "Him who is with thee in Torah and precepts,"[10] and who, nevertheless, has not repented of his sin, as stated in *Sefer Charedim*.[11]

▲ But as for the person who is not one's colleague and is not on intimate terms with him, Hillel the Elder said, "Be of the disciples of Aaron, loving peace and pursuing peace, loving the creatures and drawing them near to the Torah."[12] This means that even in the case of those who are removed from G–d's Torah and His service, and are therefore classified simply as "creatures," one must attract them with strong cords of love, perchance one might succeed in drawing them near to the Torah and Divine service. Even if one fails, one has not forfeited the merit of the precept of neighbourly love.

▲ Even with regard to those who are close to him, and whom he has rebuked, yet they had not repented of their sins, when he is enjoined to hate them, there still remains the duty to love them also, and both are right: hatred, because of the wickedness in them; and love on account of the aspect of the hidden good in them, which is the Divine spark in them, which animates their divine soul. He should also awaken pity in his heart for [the divine soul], for she is held captive, as it were, in the evil of the *sitra achra* that triumphs over her in wicked people. Compassion destroys hatred and awakens love, as is known from the [interpretation of the] text, "To [the house of] Jacob who redeemed Abraham."[13]

(As for King David, peace unto him, who said, "I hate them with a consummate hatred,"[14] he was referring to [Jewish] heretics and atheists who have no portion in the G–d of Israel, as stated in the Talmud, Tractate *Shabbat*, beginning of ch. 16).

•▲ *Chapter 33*

This, also, will be the true joy of the soul, especially when one recognises, at appropriate times, that one needs to purify and illuminate one's soul with gladness of the heart. Let him then concentrate his mind and envisage in his intelligence and understanding the subject of His blessed true Unity: how He permeates all worlds, both upper and lower, and even the fullness of this earth is His blessed glory; and how everything is of no reality whatever in His presence; and He is One Alone in the upper and lower realms,

---

[9] Lev. *19:17*. [10] *A play on the word* עמיתך: עם-אתך. *See* Kitzurim VeHaorot LeTanya, *p. 36*. [11] *By Rabbi Eliezer Azkari (16th century)*. [12] Avot *1:12*. [13] Isa. *29:22*. [14] Ps. *139:22*.

שישנאהו. היינו בחבירו בתורה ומצות וכבר קיים בו מצות הוכח תוכיח את עמיתך עם שאתך בתורה ובמצות ואעפ"כ לא שב מחטאו כמ"ש בס' חרדים אבל מי שאינו חבירו ואינו מקורב אצלו הנה ע"ז אמר הלל הזקן הוי מתלמידיו של אהרן אוהב שלום וכו' אוהב את הבריות ומקרבן לתורה. לומר שאף הרחוקים מתורת ה' ועבודתו ולכן נקראי' בשם בריות בעלמא צריך למשכן בחבלי עבותו' אהבה וכולי האי ואולי יוכל לקרבן לתורה ועבודת ה' והן לא לא הפסיד שכר מצות אהבת ריעים וגם המקורבים אליו והוכיחם ולא שבו מעונותיהם שמצוה לשנאותם מצוה לאהבם ג"כ ושתיהן הן אמת שנאה מצד הרע שבהם ואהבה מצד בחי' הטוב הגנוז שבהם שהוא ניצוץ אלקות שבתוכם המחיה נפשם האלקית וגם לעורר רחמים בלבו עליה כי היא בבחי' גלות בתוך הרע מס"א הגובר עליה ברשעי' והרחמנות מבטלת השנאה ומעוררת האהבה כנודע ממ"ש ליעקב אשר פדה את אברהם [ולא אמר דה"ע תכלית שנאה שנאתים וגו' אלא על המינים והאפיקורסים שאין להם חלק באלהי ישראל כדאיתא בגמרא ר"פ ט"ז דשבת]:

פרק לג עוד זאת תהיה שמחת הנפש האמיתי' ובפרט כשרואה בנפשו בעתים

מזומנים שצריך לזככה ולהאירה בשמחת לבב אזי יעמיק מחשבתו ויצייר בשכלו ובינתו ענין יחודו ית' האמיתי איך הוא ממלא כל עלמין עליונים ותחתונים ואפי' מלא כל הארץ הלזו הוא כבודו ית' וכולא קמיה כלא חשיב ממש והוא לבדו הוא בעליונים ותחתונים ממש

as He was One Alone before the six days of Creation; and also in the space wherein this world was created, the heavens and earth, and all their host—He alone filled this space; and now also this is so, being One Alone without any change whatever. For all things created are nullified beside Him in their very existence, as are nullified the letters of speech and thought within their source and root, namely, the essence and substance of the soul, which are its ten faculties, *chochmah*, *binah*, *da'at*, . . . wherein the element of letters is not yet found prior to their embodiment in the garment of thought (as has been explained at length in chs. 20 and 21, note there), and as is explained elsewhere by means of an illustration from nature, namely, the nullification of the sun's radiation and light at their source, the orb of the sun in the sky. For surely its radiance and light glow and spread forth there, too, and even more strongly than in the space of the universe; but there [in the sun] the light is nullified within its source, as though it were nonextant at all.

Exactly so, figuratively speaking, is the world and all that fills it dissolved out of existence in relation to its source, which is the light of the blessed *En Sof*, as is there explained at length.

When one will deeply contemplate this, his heart will be gladdened and his soul will rejoice even with joy and singing, with all heart and soul and might, in [the intensity of] this faith which is tremendous, since this is the [experience of the] very proximity of G-d, and it is the whole [purpose] of man and the goal of his creation, as well as of the creation of all the worlds, both upper and lower, that He may have an abode here below, as will later be explained at length.[1]

Behold, how great is the joy of a common and lowly man when he is brought near to a king of flesh and blood, who accepts his hospitality and lodges under his roof! How infinitely more so is the [joy in the] abiding nearness of the Supreme King of kings, the Holy One, blessed be He. And so it is written, "For who is this that engaged his heart to approach unto Me? saith the Lord."[2]

• For this reason it was instituted to offer praise and thanks to His blessed Name each morning, and to say: "Happy are we! How goodly is our portion, and how pleasant is our lot, and how beautiful our heritage!"[3] In other words, just as a person rejoices

---

[1] *Ch. 36.* [2] Jer. *30:21.* [3] *Liturgy, Morning Prayer; introduction to* first Shema.

• 12 Adar

ממש כמו שהיה לבדו קודם ששת ימי בראשית וגם במקום הזה שנברא בו עולם הזה השמים והארץ וכל צבאם היה הוא לבדו ממלא המקום הזה וגם עתה כן הוא לבדו בלי שום שינוי כלל מפני שכל הנבראים בטלים אצלו במציאות ממש כביטול אותיות הדבור והמחשבה במקורן ושרשן הוא מהות הנפש ועצמותה שהן עשר בחינותיה חכמה בינה ודעת כו׳ שאין בהם בחי׳ אותיות עדיין קודם שמתלבשות בלבוש המחשבה [כמ״ש בפ׳ כ׳ וכ״א באריכות ע״ש] וכמ״ש ג״כ במ״א משל גשמי לזה מענין ביטול זיו ואור השמש במקורו הוא גוף כדור השמש שברקיע שגם שם מאיר ומתפשט ודאי זיוו ואורו וביתר שאת מהתפשטותו והארתו בחלל העולם אלא ששם הוא בטל במציאות במקורו וכאילו אינו במציאות כלל: וככה ממש דרך משל הוא ביטול העולם ומלואו במציאות לגבי מקורו שהוא אור א״ס ב״ה וכמש״ש באריכו׳. והנה כשיעמיק בזה הרבה ישמח לבו ותגל נפשו אף גילת ורנן בכל לב ונפש ומאד באמונה זו כי רבה היא כי היא קרבת אלהים ממש וזה כל האדם ותכלית בריאתו ובריאות כל העולמות עליונים ותחתוני׳ להיות לו דירה זו בתחתוני׳ כמ״ש לקמן באריכות. והנה כמה גדולה שמחת הדיוט ושפל אנשים בהתקרבותו למלך בשר ודם המתאכסן ודר אתו עמו בביתו וק״ו לאין קץ לקרבת ודירת ממ״ה הקב״ה וכדכתיב כי מי הוא זה אשר ערב לבו לגשת אלי נאם ה׳: ועל זה תיקנו ליתן שבח והודיה לשמו ית׳ בכל בקר ולומר אשרינו מה טוב חלקנו וכו׳ ומה יפה ירושתנו כלומר כמו שהאדם שש

ושמח

and is happy when an inheritance of an immense fortune, for which he had not toiled, falls to him, how infinitely more should we rejoice over our heritage that our fathers have bequeathed to us, namely, the true Unity of G–d: that even down here on earth there is naught else beside Him alone, and this is His abode in the lower worlds.

This is what our Rabbis, of blessed memory said,[4] "Six hundred and thirteen commandments were given to Israel. . . . Came Habakkuk and based them [all] on a single one, as it is written, 'The righteous shall live by his faith'"[5] that is to say, as if there had been no more than one commandment, namely, faith alone. For by faith alone will he come to fulfil all the 613 commandments. In other words, when his heart will exult and rejoice in his faith in G–d's Unity, in perfect joy, as though he had but this one commandment, and it alone were the ultimate purpose of his creation and that of all the worlds—then with the force and vitality of his soul which are generated by this great joy, his soul will ascend ever higher above all internal and external obstacles which hinder his fulfillment of all the 613 commandments.

This is the meaning of the words "Shall live by his faith," with the emphasis on *shall live*, as at the Resurrection of the Dead, by way of example; so will his soul revive with this great joy. This is a doubled and re-doubled joy, for apart from the joy of the soul apprehending the nearness of •G–d and His dwelling with him, he will doubly rejoice with the joy of the Lord and the tremendous gratification rendered to Him by virtue of his faith, whereby the *sitra achra* is verily subdued and darkness is changed into light, i.e. the darkness of the *kelipot* of this corporeal world, which obscure and conceal His blessed light until the End, as is written, "He setteth an end to darkness"[6] (which refers to the end of days, when the spirit of impurity will be banished from the earth,[7] and the glory of the Lord will be revealed, and all flesh shall see together;[8] as will be explained later[9]). Particularly in the diaspora, where the atmosphere is unclean and filled with *kelipot* and *sitra achra*. For there is no joy before Him, blessed be He, like the light and joy of the particular excellence of light that comes out of darkness. This is the meaning of the verse, "Let Israel rejoice in his Maker,"[10] that is to say, that everyone who is of the seed of Israel should rejoice and be happy in the joy of the Lord Who is

---

[4] Makkot *24a*. [5] Hab. *2:4*.
[6] Job *28:3*. [7] Zechariah *13:2*.
[8] Isa. *40:5*. [9] *End ch. 36* infra.
[10] Ps. *149:2*.

• 13 Adar

ושמח בירושה שנפלה לו הון עתק שלא עמל בו כן ויותר מכן לאין קץ יש לנו לשמוח על ירושתנו שהנחילנו אבותינו הוא יחוד ה' האמיתי אשר אפי' בארץ מתחת אין עוד מלבדו וזו היא דירתו בתחתונים וז"ש רז"ל תרי"ג מצות ניתנו לישראל בא חבקוק והעמידן על אחת שנאמר וצדיק באמונתו יחיה כלומר כאלו אינה רק מצוה אחת היא האמונה לבדה כי ע"י האמונה לבדה יבא לקיום כל התרי"ג מצות דהיינו כשיהיה לבו שש ושמח באמונתו ביחוד ה' בתכלית השמחה כאלו לא היתה עליו רק מצוה זו לבדה והיא לבדה תכלית בריאתו ובריאת כל העולמות הרי בכח וחיות נפשו בשמחה רבה זו תתעלה נפשו למעלה מעלה על כל המונעים קיום כל התרי"ג מצות מבית ומחוץ. וזהו שאמר באמונתו יחיה יחיה דייקא כתחיית המתים דרך משל כך תחיה נפשו בשמחה רבה זו והיא שמחה כפולה ומכופלת כי מלבד שמחת הנפש המשכלת בקרבת ה' ודירתו אתו עמו. עוד זאת ישמח בכפליים בשמחת ה' וגודל נחת רוח לפניו ית' באמונה זו דאתכפיא ס"א ממש ואתהפך חשוכא לנהורא שהוא חשך הקליפות שבעו"הז החומרי המחשיכים ומכסים על אורו ית' עד עת קץ כמ"ש קץ שם לחשך [דהיינו קץ הימין שיעביר רוח הטומאה מן הארץ ונגלה כבוד ה' וראו כל בשר יחדיו וכמ"ש לקמן] ובפרט בארצות עו"ג שאוירם טמא ומלא קליפות וס"א ואין שמחה לפניו ית' כאורה ושמחה ביתרון אור הבא מן החשך דייקא. וז"ש ישמח ישראל בעושיו פי' שכל מי שהוא מזרע ישראל יש לו לשמוח בשמחת ה' אשר

ששׂ

pleased and glad to dwell in the lower spheres, which are of the order of physical *Asiyah*. That is why the Psalmist uses the plural *osav* ["Them that made him"], referring to the corporeal world which is full of *kelipot* and the *sitra achra*, and is called "public domain"[11] and "mountains of separation." And these are transmuted to light, and become a "private domain"[12] for His blessed Unity, by means of this faith.

•▲ Chapter 34

It is well known that the Patriarchs themselves constitute the "Chariot."[1] For throughout their lives they never for a moment ceased from binding their mind and soul to the Lord of the universe, with the aforementioned absolute surrender to His blessed Unity. Likewise were all the Prophets after them, each according to the station of his soul and the degree of his apprehension, The rank of our teacher Moses, peace to him, surpassed them all, for concerning him it was said, "The *Shechinah* speaks out of Moses' throat."[2] Something of this [union] the Israelites experienced at Mount Sinai, but they could not endure it, as the Rabbis say, "At each [Divine] utterance their souls took flight, . . ."[3] which is an indication of the extinction of their existence, of which we spoke above. Therefore G-d at once commanded that a Sanctuary be made for Him, with the Holy of Holies for the presence of His *Shechinah*, which is the revelation of His blessed Unity, as will be explained later.[4]

▲ But since the Temple was destroyed, the Holy One, blessed be He, has no other sanctuary or established place for His habitation, that is, for His blessed Unity, than the "Four cubits of *halachah*,"[5] which is His blessed will and wisdom as embodied in the laws which have been set out for us. Therefore, after contemplating deeply on the subject of this self-nullification, discussed above, according to his capacity, let the person reflect in his heart as follows: "Inasmuch as my intelligence and the root of my soul are of too limited a capacity to constitute a 'chariot' and abode for His blessed Unity in perfect truth, since my mind cannot at all conceive and apprehend Him with any manner or degree of apprehension in the world, nor even an iota of the apprehension of the Patriarchs and Prophets—if this be so, I shall make for Him a tabernacle and habitation by engaging in the study of the Torah, as my time permits, at appointed times by day and by night,

---

[11] רשות הרבים *in the sense of "multiverse."* [12] רשות היחיד *in the sense of "universe."*

Chapter 34
[1] *Cf.* supra, *chs. 23 and 29.* [2] Zohar *III, 232a; cf. also* Zohar *III, 7a.* [3] Shabbat *88b.* [4] *Ch. 53.* [5] Berachot *8a.*

שש ושמח בדירתו בתחתוני' שהם בחי' עשיה גשמיית ממש. וז"ש בעושיו לשון רבים שהוא עו"הז הגשמי המלא קליפות וס"א שנק' רשות הרבים וטורי דפרודא ואתהפכן לנהורא ונעשים רשות היחיד ליחודו ית' באמונה זו:

פרק לד

והנה מודעת זאת שהאבות הן הן המרכבה שכל ימיהם לעולם לא הפסיקו אפי' שעה אחת מלקשר דעתם ונשמתם לרבון העולמים בביטול הנ"ל ליחודו ית' ואחריהם כל הנביאים כל אחד לפי מדרגת נשמתו והשגתו ומדרגת משרע"ה היא העולה על כולנה שאמרו עליו שכינה מדברת מתוך גרונו של משה ומעין זה זכו ישראל במעמד הר סיני רק שלא יכלו לסבול כמאמר רז"ל שעל כל דיבור פרחה נשמתן כו' שהוא ענין ביטול במציאות הנ"ל לכן מיד אמר להם לעשות לו משכן ובו קדשי הקדשים להשראת שכינתו שהוא גילוי יחודו ית' כמ"ש לקמן ומשחרב ב"המק אין להקב"ה בעולמו משכן ומכון לשבתו הוא יחודו ית' אלא ארבע אמות של הלכה שהוא רצונו ית' וחכמתו המלובשים בהלכות הערוכות לפנינו ולכן אחר שיעמיק האדם מחשבתו בענין ביטול הנ"ל כפי יכלתו זאת ישיב אל לבו כי מהיות קטן שכלי ושרש נשמתי מהכיל להיות מרכבה ומשכן ליחודו ית' באמת לאמיתו מאחר דלית מחשבה דילי תפיסא ומשגת בו ית' כלל וכלל שום השגה בעולם ולא שמץ מנהו מהשגת האבו' והנביאים אי לזאת אעשה לו משכן ומכון לשבתו הוא העסק בת"ת כפי הפנאי שלי בקביעות עתים ביום ובלילה

כדת

in accordance with the law which was given to each individual in the 'Laws Concerning the Study of the Torah,' and as the Rabbis stated, 'Even one chapter in the morning. . . .' "[6]

In this way his heart will be gladdened and he will rejoice and offer praise and thanks for his portion, with a joyous and happy heart, that he has merited to act as host to the Almighty twice daily, to the limit of his available time, and according to the capacity which has been generously bestowed upon him by G-d.

●▲And if G-d will lavish on him in yet a fuller measure, then "He who has clean hands will increase his effort"[7] and "a good intention. . . ."[8] And even the remainder of the day, when he is engaged in commerce, he will provide a dwelling for Him through the giving of charity out of the proceeds of his labour, which is one of the Divine qualities, "As He is compassionate, . . ."[9] and as written in the *Tikunim* that "Kindness is the right hand."[10] And even though he distributes no more than a fifth part, this fifth carries the other four parts with it up to G-d, to provide a dwelling for Him, blessed be He, as is known from the Rabbinic statement, that the commandment of charity is balanced against all the sacrifices.[11] And through the sacrifices all living creatures were elevated unto G-d through the offering of one beast, all plants through that of one tenth of a measure of fine meal mingled with oil, and so on. Apart from this, at the time of study and prayer, there ascends unto G-d everything one has eaten and drunk and enjoyed of the other four parts for the health of the body, as will be explained later.

▲ All the above mentioned particulars regarding the diverse joys of the soul do not preclude the person from considering himself shameful and loathsome, or from having a contrite heart and humble spirit, at the very time of the joy. For the sense of shame, . . . is occasioned by the aspect of the body and animal soul, whilst his joy comes from the aspect of the divine soul and the spark of G-dliness that is clothed therein and animates it, as has been discussed above (ch. 31). After this manner it is stated in the *Zohar*, "Weeping is lodged in one side of my heart, and joy is lodged in the other."[12]

●▲ *Chapter 35*

Let us elucidate further the term "to do it."[1] Let us also understand, in a very small measure, the purpose of the creation of "Intermediates" and the descent of their souls into this world, to be clothed within

[6] Menachot *99b*. [7] Job *17:9*. [8] "*. . . G-d joins unto a deed.*" Kiddushin *40a;* Zohar *I, 28a*. [9] Shabbat *133b*. [10] Tikunei Zohar, *Introduction, 17a*. [11] Sukkah *49b;* Bava Batra *9a*. [12] Zohar *II, 255a; III, 75a*.

Chapter 35
[1] *Cf.* supra, *beg. ch. 17*.

● 15 Adar ● 16 Adar ▲ *2 Adar II* ▲ *3 Adar II* ▲ *4 Adar II*

כדת הניתנה לכל אחד ואחד בהלכות תלמוד תורה וכמאמר רז"ל אפי' פרק אחד שחרית כו' ובזה ישמח לבו ויגיל ויתן הודאה על חלקו בשמחה ובטוב לבב על שזכה להיות אושפיזכן לגבורה פעמים בכל יום כפי העת והפנאי שלו כמסת ידו אשר הרחיב ה' לו: ואם ירחיב ה' לו עוד אזי טהור ידים יוסיף אומץ ומחשבה טובה כו' וגם שאר היום כולו שעוסק במשא ומתן יהיה מכון לשבתו ית' בנתינת הצדקה שיתן מיגיעו שהיא ממדותיו של הקב"ה מה הוא רחום וכו' וכמ"ש בתיקונים חסד דרועא ימינא ואף שאינו נותן אלא חומש הרי החומש מעלה עמו כל הארבע ידות לה' להיות מכון לשבתו ית' כנודע מאמר רז"ל שמצות צדקה שקולה כנגד כל הקרבנו' ובקרבנות היה כל החי עולה לה' ע"י בהמה אחת וכל הצומח ע"י עשרון סלת אחד בלול בשמן כו' ומלבד זה הרי בשעת התורה והתפלה עולה לה' כל מה שאכל ושתה ונהנה מארבע הידות לבריאות גופו כמ"ש לקמן. והנה בכל פרטי מיני שמחות הנפש הנ"ל אין מהן מניעה להיות נבזה בעיניו נמאס ולב נשבר ורוח נמוכה בשעת השמחה ממש מאחר כי היותו נבזה בעיניו וכו' הוא מצד הגוף ונפש הבהמית והיותו בשמחה הוא מצד נפש האלהית וניצוץ אלהות המלובש בה להחיותה כנ"ל [בפ' ל"א] וכה"ג איתא בזהר בכיה תקיעא בלבאי מסטרא דא וחדוה תקיעא בלבאי מסטרא דא:

פרק לה

והנה לתוספת ביאור תיבת לעשותו וגם להבין מעט מזעיר תכלית בריאת הבינונים וירידת נשמותיהם לעוה"ז להתלבש בנפש

the animal soul which is derived from the *kelipah* and *sitra achra.* Since they will not be able to banish her [the animal soul] throughout their lives, nor to dislodge her from her place in the left part of the heart, so that none of her impure fancies should rise to the brain, inasmuch as the very essence of the animal soul derived from the *kelipah* remains [in the Intermediates] in her full strength and might as at birth, except that her "garments" do not invest their bodies, as discussed above[2]—if so, why have their souls descended into this world to labour in vain, G-d forbid, to wage war throughout their lives against the [evil] nature which they cannot vanquish?

But let this be their solace, to comfort them doubly and helpfully, and to gladden their heart in G-d, Who dwells with them in their Torah and [Divine] Service:

▲ To quote, by way of preface, the comment of the *Yenuka* (*Zohar, Parshat Balak*[3]) on the verse: "The wise man's eyes are in his head":[4] "Where else are a man's eyes? . . . But the interpretation of the verse certainly is as follows: We have learned that a man must not walk four cubits bareheaded. The reason is that the *Shechinah* rests on his head; and a wise man's eyes and everything he possesses are 'in his head,' i.e. in Him Who rests and abides above his head; and if his eyes are there, he must know that the Light which shines above his head needs oil; for the body of a man is a wick, and the Light is kindled above it. And King Solomon cried, saying, 'Let there be no lack of oil above thy head.'[5] For the Light on a man's head must have oil, meaning good deeds, and this is the meaning of the phrase, 'The wise man's eyes are in his head.'" The quotation ends here.

●▲ The explanation of this figure, whereby the Light of the *Shechinah* is compared to the flame of a lamp which produces no light nor clings to the wick without oil, and likewise the *Shechinah* does not rest on a man's body, which is likened to a wick, except through good deeds alone, and it is not sufficient that his soul (*neshamah*), which is a part of G-dliness from Above, should act for him as oil to the wick—is clear and understandable to every intelligent person. It is, that the *neshamah* of a person—even if he be a perfect *tzaddik* serving G-d with fear and love of delights[6]—does not, nevertheless, completely dissolve itself out of existence, so as to be truly nullified and absorbed

---

[2] Ch. 12. [3] Zohar *III, 187a.*
[4] Eccl. *2:14.* [5] Eccl. *9:8.*
[6] *Cf.* supra, *chs. 9, 14.*

בנפש הבהמית שמהקליפה וס"א מאחר שלא יוכלו לשלחה כל ימיהם ולדחותה ממקומה מחלל השמאלי שבלב שלא יעלו ממנה הרהורים אל המוח כי מהותה ועצמותה של נפש הבהמית שמהקליפה היא בתקפה ובגבורתה אצלם כתולדתה רק שלבושיה אינם מתלבשים בגופם כנ"ל וא"כ למה זה ירדו נשמותיהם לעו"הז ליגע לריק ח"ו להלחם כל ימיהם עם היצר ולא יכלו לו ותהי זאת נחמתם לנחמם בכפליים לתושיה ולשמח לבם בה' השוכן אתם בתוך תורתם ועבודתם והוא בהקדים לשון הינוקא [בזהר פ' בלק] על פסוק החכם עיניו בראשו וכי באן אתר עינוי דבר נש כו' אלא קרא הכי הוא ודאי דתנן לא יהך בר נש בגילוי' דרישא ארבע אמות מאי טעמא דשכינתא שריא על רישיה וכל חכם עינוהי ומילוי ברישיה אינון בההוא דשריא וקיימא על רישיה וכד עינוי תמן לנדע דההוא נהורא דאדליק על רישיה אצטריך למשחא בגין דגופא דב"נ איהו פתילה ונהורא אדליק לעילא ושלמה מלכא צוח ואמר ושמן על ראשך אל יחסר דהא נהורא דבראשו אצטריך למשחא ואינון עובדאן טבאן וע"ד החכם עיניו בראשו עכ"ל. והנה ביאור משל זה שהמשיל אור השכינה לאור הנר שאינו מאיר ונאחז בפתילה בלי שמן וכך אין השכינה שורה על גוף האדם שנמשל לפתילה אלא ע"י מעשים טובים דווקא ולא די לו בנשמתו שהיא חלק אלוה ממעל להיות היא כשמן לפתיל' מבואר ומובן לכל משכיל כי הנה נשמת האדם אפי' הוא צדיק גמור עובד ה' ביראה ואהבה בתענוגי' אעפ"כ אינה בטילה במציאות לגמרי ליבטל וליכלל

באור

into the light of G-d to the extent of becoming one and the same absolutely, but the person remains an entity apart, one who fears G-d and loves Him. It is different, however, with the commandments and good deeds, which are His blessed will. His blessed will is the source of life for all the worlds and creatures, flowing down to them through many contractions (*tzimtzumim*) and the concealment of the countenance of the Supreme Will (*Ratzon Elyon*), blessed be He, and the recession of the levels, until it was made possible for creatures to come into being *ex nihilo*, separate beings that should not lose their identity, as discussed above.[7] The commandments, however, are different in that they are the inwardness of His blessed will, without any concealment of the Countenance whatever; the vitality that is in them [therefore] is in no way a separate, independent thing, but is united and absorbed in His blessed will, and they become truly one with a perfect union.

• Now, the meaning of the "indwelling" of the *Shechinah* is the revelation of His blessed Divinity and of the light of the blessed *En Sof* in any thing. That is to say, that such thing merges into the light of G-d, and its reality is completely dissolved in Him; only then does the One G-d abide and manifest Himself in it. But any thing whose reality is not completely nullified in Him, the light of G-d does not abide nor manifest itself therein, even if one be a perfect *tzaddik* who cleaves to Him with abundant love,[8] since no thought can truly apprehend Him at all. For the truth of "The Lord is the true G-d"[9] is His Unity and Oneness—that He is One Alone and there is no reality whatsoever apart from Him.[10] Hence the person who loves [G-d] and [*ipso facto*] exists [apart] and is not null and void—cannot by his thought apprehend Him at all; and the light of G-d cannot abide and reveal itself in him, except through the fulfillment of the commandments which constitute in reality His blessed will and wisdom without any concealment of Countenance.

Note: This accords with the comment and explanation which I heard from my teacher, peace to him, on a passage in Etz Chayim *stating that the light of the blessed* En Sof *does not become unified even in the world of* Atzilut, *unless it clothes itself first in the* sefirah *of Wisdom—the reason being that the blessed* En Sof *is the true One*

[Note continued on next page]

• Therefore, when a person occupies himself in the Torah, his *neshamah*, which is his divine soul, with her two innermost garments only, namely the power of speech and thought,

---

[7] *Chs. 20, 21, 22.* [8] Supra, *ch. 9.* [9] Jer. *10:10.* [10] Isa. *45:6.*

• 18 Adar • 19 Adar

באור ה׳ ממש להיות לאחדים ומיוחדים ביחוד גמור רק הוא דבר בפני עצמו ירא ה׳ ואוהבו. משא״כ המצות ומעשים טובים שהן רצונו ית׳ ורצונו ית׳ הוא מקור החיים לכל העולמות והברואים שיורד אליהם על ידי צמצומים רבים והסתר פנים של רצון העליון ב״ה וירידת המדרגות עד שיוכלו להתהוות ולהבראות יש מאין ודבר נפרד בפני עצמו ולא יבטלו במציאות כנ״ל משא״כ המצות שהן פנימית רצונו ית׳ ואין שם הסתר פנים כלל אין החיות שבהם דבר נפרד בפני עצמו כלל אלא הוא מיוחד ונכלל ברצונו ית׳ והיו לאחדים ממש ביחוד גמור. והנה ענין השראת השכינה הוא גילוי אלהותו ית׳ ואור א״ס ב״ה באיזה דבר והיינו לומר שאותו דבר נכלל באור ה׳ ובטל לו במציאות לגמרי שאז הוא ששורה ומתגלה בו ה׳ אחד אבל כל מה שלא בטל אליו במציאות לגמרי אין אור ה׳ שורה ומתגלה בו ואף צדיק גמור שמתדבק בו באהבה רבה הרי לית מחשבה תפיסא ביה כלל באמת כי אמיתת ה׳ אלהים אמת הוא יחודו ואחדותו שהוא לבדו הוא ואפס בלעדו ממש. וא״כ זה האוהב שהוא יש ולא אפס לית מחשבה דיליה תפיסא ביה כלל ואין אור ה׳ שורה ומתגלה בו אלא ע״י קיום המצות שהן רצונו וחכמתו ית׳ ממש בלי שום הסתר פנים* והנה כשהאדם עוסק בתורה אזי נשמתו שהיא נפשו האלהית עם שני לבושיה הפנימים לבדם שהם כח הדבור ומחשבה נכללות

הגהה

*(וכאשר שמעתי ממורי ע״ה פי׳ וטעם למ״ש בע״ח שאור א״ס ב״ה אינו מתייחד אפי׳ בעולם האצילות אלא ע״י התלבשותו תחלה בספי׳ חכמה והיינו משום שא״ס ב״ה הוא אחד האמת שהוא

are absorbed in the Divine light of the blessed *En Sof*, and are united with it in a

[Note continued from previous page]
Who is One Alone and apart from Whom there is nothing, and this is the level of Wisdom, and so on.

perfect union. This constitutes the resting of the *Shechinah* on his divine soul, as the Rabbis stated, "Even if one person sedulously occupies himself with the Torah, the *Shechinah* is with him."[11]

However, in order to draw the light and effulgence of the *Shechinah* also over his body and animal soul, i.e. on the vital spirit clothed in the physical body, he needs to fulfil the practical commandments which are performed by the body itself. For then the very energy of the body itself which is engaged in this action is absorbed in the Divine light and in His will, and is united with Him in a perfect union. This is the third garment of the divine soul. Thereby also the energy of the vital spirit in the physical body, originating in the *kelipat nogah*, is transformed from evil to good, and is actually absorbed into holiness like the divine soul itself, since it is this [animal soul] that carries out and performs the act of the commandment, because without it the divine soul could not have been acting through the body at all, for it is spiritual whilst the body is material and coarse. The intermediary linking them is the vital animal soul, which is clothed in the human blood, in the heart and in all the body.

• And although the essence and substance of the animal soul in his heart, namely its evil dispositions, have not yet been absorbed into holiness, nevertheless since they have submitted to holiness and, albeit unwillingly, respond "Amen" and agree and are reconciled to perform the commandment, under the preponderance of the divine soul in his brain which rules the heart, and, in the meantime, these [evil dispositions] are in a state of exile or slumber, as it were, as discussed above[12]—therefore, this is no obstacle to the suffusion of the *Shechinah* over the human body at such time. Thus the energy of the vital soul that is embodied in the performance of the commandment is actually absorbed into the Divine light and is united with it in a perfect union, thereby illuminating the totality of the vital soul throughout the body, and also the physical body itself in a manner of "Encompassing from above," from head to foot. This is what is meant by the phrase, "The *Shechinah*

---

[11] Berachot *6a*. [12] *Ch. 13*.

• 20 Adar

נכללות באור ה' א"ס ב"ה ומיוחדות בו ביחוד גמור והיא השראת השכינה על נפשו האלהית כמארז"ל שאפי' אחד שיושב ועוסק בתורה שכינה עמו. אך כדי להמשיך אור והארת השכינה גם על גופו ונפשו הבהמית שהיא החיונית המלובשת בגופו ממש צריך לקיים מצות מעשיות הנעשים ע"י הגוף ממש שאז כח הגוף ממש שבעשיה זו נכלל באור ה' ורצונו ומיוחד בו ביחוד גמור והוא לבוש השלישי של נפש האלהית ואזי גם כח נפש החיונית שבגופו ממש שמקליפת נוגה נתהפך מרע לטוב ונכלל ממש בקדושה כנפש האלהית ממש מאחר שהוא הפועל ועושה מעשה המצוה שבלעדו לא היתה נפש האלהית פועלת בגוף כלל כי היא רוחניית והגוף גשמי וחומרי והממוצע ביניהם היא נפש החיונית הבהמית המלובשת בדם האדם שבלבו וכל הגוף ואף שמהותה ועצמותה של נפש הבהמית שבלבו שהן מדותיה הרעים עדיין לא נכללו בקדושה מ"מ מאחר דאתכפין לקדושה ובע"כ עונין אמן ומסכימין ומתרצין לעשיית המצוה ע"י התגברות נפשו האלהית שבמוח ששליט על הלב והן בשעה זו בבחי' גלות ושינה כנ"ל ולכך אין זו מניעה מהשראת השכינה על גוף האדם בשעה זו דהיינו שכח נפש החיונית המלובש בעשיית המצוה הוא נכלל ממש באור ה' ומיוחד בו ביחוד גמור וע"י זה ממשיך הארה לכללות נפש החיונית שבכל הגוף וגם על הגוף הגשמי בבחי' מקיף מלמעלה מראשו ועד רגליו וז"ש ושכינתא

שריא

שהוא לבדו הוא ואין זולתו וזו היא מדרגת החכמה וכו') :

rests *on* his head;[13] the word "on" indicates this. Similarly, "On every [assembly of] ten the *Shechinah* rests."[14]

Clearly, any such diffusion of the light of the *Shechinah*, that is the revelation of the light of the blessed *En Sof*, cannot be termed mutability in Him, G-d forbid, nor multiplicity. Witness the passage in *Sanhedrin*,[15] where a heretic said to Rabban Gamliel: "You say that on every assembly of ten men the *Shechinah* rests. How many Divine Presences have you, then?" And he replied to him with an example of the light of the sun which enters through many windows.... The intelligent man will understand.

•▲ Chapter 36

It is a well-known Rabbinic statement that the purpose of the creation of this world is that the Holy One, blessed be He, desired to have an abode in the lower worlds.[1] But surely with Him the distinction of "upper" and "lower" has no validity, for He pervades all worlds equally.

The explanation of the matter, however, is as follows:

Before the world was created, He was One Alone, One and Unique, filling all space in which He created the universe. It is still the same now insofar as He is concerned. For the change relates only to those who receive His blessed life-force and light, which they receive through many "garments" which conceal and obscure His blessed light, as is written, "For no man shall see Me and live,"[2] and, as our Rabbis, of blessed memory, have explained it, that even angels, who are called *chayyot*,[3] cannot see Him.. . .[4]

This is the concept of the *Hishtalshelut* (downward gradation) of the worlds and their descent, degree by degree, through a multitude of "garments" which screen the light and life that emanate from Him, until there was created this material and gross world, the lowest in degree, than which there is none lower in the aspect of concealment of His blessed light; [a world of] doubled and redoubled darkness, so much so that it is full of *kelipot* and the *sitra achra* which oppose the very G-dhead, saying: "I am, and there is nothing else besides me."[5]

▲ Clearly, the purpose of the *Hishtalshelut* of the worlds and their descent, degree by degree, is not for the sake of the higher worlds, because for them this is a descent from the light of His blessed Countenance. But the ultimate purpose [of creation] is this lowest world, for such was His blessed will that He shall have satisfaction

---

[13] Zohar *III, 187a. See* supra, *pp. 157 and 159.* [14] Sanhedrin *39a.* [15] Ibid.

Chapter 36

[1] Midrash Tanchuma, Nasso *16.* [2] Exod. *33:20.* [3] *An interpretation of the word* חיות. [4] Sifre, *end of* Parshat Behaalotcha; Midrash Bamidbar R. *end of* Parshat Nasso. [5] Isa. *47:8, 10;* Zeph. *2:15.*

שריא על רישיה על דייקא וכן אכל בי עשרה שכינתא שריא. והנה כל בחי' המשכת אור השכינה שהיא בחי' גילוי אור א"ס ב"ה אינו נקרא שינוי ח"ו בו ית' ולא ריבוי כדאיתא בסנהדרין דאמר ליה ההוא מינא לרבן גמליאל אמריתו כל בי עשרה שכינתא שריא כמה שכינתא אית לכו והשיב לו משל מאור השמש הנכנס בחלונות רבים כו' והמשכיל יבין:

פרק לו והנה מודעת זאת מארז"ל שתכלית בריאת עולם הזה הוא שנתאוה הקב"ה להיות לו דירה בתחתונים. והנה לא שייך לפניו ית' בחי' מעלה ומטה כי הוא ית' ממלא כל עלמין בשוה. אלא ביאור הענין כי קודם שנברא העולם היה הוא לבדו ית' יחיד ומיוחד וממלא כל המקום הזה שברא בו העולם וגם עתה כן הוא לפניו ית' רק שהשינוי הוא אל המקבלים חיותו ואורו ית' שמקבלים ע"י לבושים רבים המכסים ומסתירים אורו ית' כדכתיב כי לא יראני האדם וחי וכדפי' רז"ל שאפי' מלאכים הנק' חיות אין רואין כו' וזהו ענין השתלשלות העולמות וירידתם ממדרגה למדרג' ע"י ריבוי הלבושי' המסתירים האור והחיות שממנו ית' עד שנברא עוה"ז הגשמי והחומרי ממש והוא התחתון במדרגה שאין תחתון למטה ממנו בענין הסתר אורו ית' וחשך כפול ומכופל עד שהוא מלא קליפות וס"א שהן נגד ה' ממש לומ' אני ואפסי עוד. והנה תכלית השתלשלו' העולמו' וירידתם ממדרגה למדרגה אינו בשביל עולמות העליוני' הואיל ולהם ירידה מאור פניו ית' אלא התכלית הוא עוה"ז התחתון שכך עלה ברצונו ית' להיות נחת רוח לפניו יתברך

when the *sitra achra* is subdued and the darkness is turned to light, so that the Divine light of the blessed *En Sof* shall shine forth in the place of the darkness and *sitra achra* throughout this world, all the more strongly and intensely, with the excellence of light emerging from darkness, than its effulgence in the higher worlds, where it shines through "garments" and in concealment of the Countenance, which screen and conceal the light of the blessed *En Sof*, in order that they should not dissolve out of existence.

▲ For this purpose, the Holy One, blessed be He, gave to Israel the Torah which is called "might" and "strength,"[6] as the Rabbis, of blessed memory, have said,[7] that the Almighty puts strength into the righteous in order that they may receive their reward in the hereafter, without being nullified in their very existence, in the Divine light that will be revealed to them in the hereafter without any cloak, as is written, "No longer shall thy Teacher hide Himself (literally: He will not conceal Himself from thee with robe and garment)[8] . . . but thine eyes shall see thy Teacher."[9] It is also written, "For they shall see eye to eye, . . ."[10] and, "The sun shall be no more thy light by day . . . , but the Lord shall be thine everlasting light. . . ."[11]

It is well known that the Messianic Era, and especially the time of the Resurrection of the Dead, is the fulfillment and culmination of the creation of the world, for which purpose it was originally created.

Note: The receiving of the reward is essentially in the seventh millennium, as is stated in Likutei Torah *of Rabbi Isaac Luria, of blessed memory.*

●▲ Something of this revelation has already been experienced on earth, at the time of the Giving of the Torah, as is written, "Unto thee it was showed, that thou mightest know that the Lord He is G–d; there is naught else beside Him"[12]—"It was *showed*" verily with physical vision, as is written, "And all the people saw the thunderings"[13]—"They *saw* what is [normally] heard."[14] And the Rabbis, of blessed memory, explained, "They looked eastwards and heard the speech issuing forth: 'I am,' etc., and so [turning] towards the four points of the compass, and upwards and downwards," as is also explained in the *Tikunim* that "There was no place from which He did not speak unto them. . . ." This was so because of the revelation of His blessed will in the Decalogue constituting the epitome of the whole Torah,[15] which is the inwardness of His blessed will and wisdom, wherein there is no concealment of the Countenance at all, as is written, "For in the light of Thy Countenance hast Thou given us the Law of life."[16] Therefore they [the Israelites at Sinai]

---

[6] Song of Songs Rabba, *2:10;* Zohar *II, 58a; III, 269a; cf.* Zevachim *116a.* [7] Sanhedrin *100b.* [8] יכנף—כנף. [9] Isa. *30:20.* [10] Isa. *52:8.* [11] Isa. *60:19.* [12] Deut. *4:35.* [13] *Literally: "voices."* Exod. *20:15.* [14] Mechilta, *on the verse.* [15] Rashi, Exod. *24:12;* Zohar *II, 90b.* [16] *Liturgy,* Amidah *Prayer.*

● 22 Adar ▲ *9 Adar II* ▲ *10 Adar II*

ית׳ כד אתכפיא ס״א ואתהפך חשוכא לנהורא שיאיר אור ה׳ אין סוף ב״ה במקום החשך והס״א של כל עו״הז כולו ביתר שאת ויתר עז ויתרון אור מן החשך מהארתו בעולמות עליונים שמאיר שם ע״י לבושים והסתר פנים המסתירים ומעלימים אור א״ס ב״ה שלא יבטלו במציאות. ולזה נתן הקב״ה לישראל את התורה שנקר׳ עוז וכח וכמארז״ל שהקב״ה נותן כח בצדיקים לקבל שכרם לעתיד לבא שלא יתבטלו במציאות ממש באור ה׳ הנגלה לעתיד בלי שום לבוש כדכתיב ולא יכנף עוד מוריך [פי׳ שלא יתכסה ממך בכנף ולבוש] והיו עיניך רואות את מוריך וכתיב כי עין בעין יראו וגו׳ וכתיב לא יהיה לך עוד השמש לאור יומם וגו׳ כי ה׳ יהיה לך לאור עולם וגו׳. ונודע שימות המשיח ובפרט כשיחיו המתים הם תכלית ושלימות בריאות עולם הזה שלכך נברא מתחילתו* וגם כבר היה לעולמים מעין זה בשעת מתן תורה כדכתי׳ אתה הראת לדעת כי ה׳ הוא האלהים אין עוד מלבדו הראת ממש בראיה חושיית כדכתיב וכל העם רואים את הקולות רואים את הנשמע ופי׳ רז״ל מסתכלים למזרח ושומעין את הדבור יוצא אנכי כו׳. וכן לארבע רוחות ולמעלה ולמטה וכדפי׳ בתיקונים דלית אתר דלא מליל מיניה עמהון כו׳ והיינו מפני גילוי רצונו ית׳ בעשרת הדברות שהן כללות התורה שהיא פנימית רצונו ית׳ וחכמתו ואין שם הסתר פנים כלל כמ״ש כי באור פניך נתת לנו תורת חיים ולכן היו בטלים

הגהה

(וקבלת שכר עיקרו באלף השביעי כמ״ש בלקוטי תורה מהאר״י ז״ל):

repeatedly expired out of existence, as the Rabbis have taught that "At each [Divine] utterance their soul took flight, . . . but the Holy One, blessed be He, restored it to them with the dew with which He will revive the dead."[17] This is the dew of the Torah which is called "might," as the Rabbis have said, "Everyone who occupies himself with the Torah is revived by ▲the dew of the Torah. . . ."[18] Later, however, the sin [of the Golden Calf] caused both them and the world to become gross again—until "The end of days," when the dross of the body and of the world will be purified, and they will be able to apprehend the revealed Divine light which will shine forth to Israel by means of the Torah, called "might." And, as a result of the overflow of the illumination on Israel, the darkness of the gentiles will also be lit up, as is written, "And the nations shall walk by thy light, . . ."[19] and, "O, house of Jacob, come ye, and let us walk in the light of the Lord";[20] again, "And the glory of the Lord shall be revealed, and all flesh shall see together, . . .";[21] and, "To go into the holes of the rocks, and into the clefts of the boulders, for fear of the Lord and for the glory of His majesty."[22] And as we pray, "Shine forth in the splendour and excellence of Thy might upon all the inhabitants of the world. . . ."[23]

●▲ *Chapter 37*

This culminating fulfillment of the Messianic Era and of the Resurrection of the Dead, which is the revelation of the light of the blessed *En Sof* in this material world, depends on our actions and service throughout the duration of the *galut*. For what causes the reward of a commandment is the commandment itself,[1] because by virtue of performing it the person suffuses a flood of light of the blessed *En Sof* from above downwards, to be clothed in the corporeality of the world, in something that was previously under the dominion of the *kelipat nogah*, from which it had received its vitality. These are all those things that are [ritually] clean and permissible, wherewith the precept of action is performed, viz., parchment used in the phylacteries and *Mezuzah* and the scroll of the Torah, as taught by the Rabbis that nothing is fitting for a sacred purpose which is not clean and permissible for consumption;[2] similarly an *etrog* which is not *orlah*;

Note: For orlah *is one of the three completely impure* kelipot *that can never ascend [into holiness]*

[Note continued on next page]

▲so, too, money given to charity which had not been dishonestly acquired; and similarly with other things. Thus,

[17] Shabbat *88b*. [18] Ketubot *111b*. [19] Isa. *60:3*. [20] Isa. *2:5*. [21] Isa. *40:5*. [22] Isa. *2:21*. [23] Liturgy, Amidah, *High Holidays*.

Chapter 37
[1] *Cf.* Avot *4:2*. [2] Shabbat *108a*.

● 23 Adar ▲ *11 Adar II* ▲ *12 Adar II* ▲ *13 Adar II*

בטלים במציאות ממש כמארז"ל שעל כל דיבור פרחה נשמתן כו' אלא שהחזירה הקב"ה להן בטל שעתיד להחיות בו את המתים והוא טל תורה שנקרא עוז כמארז"ל כל העוסק בתורה טל תורה מחייהו כו' רק שאח"כ גרם החטא ונתגשמו הם והעולם עד עת קץ הימין שאז יזדכך גשמיות הגוף והעולם ויוכלו לקבל גילוי אור ה' שיאיר לישראל ע"י התורה שנקר' עוז ומיתרון ההארה לישראל יגיה חשך האומות גם כן כדכתיב והלכו גוים לאורך וגו' וכתיב בית יעקב לכו ונלכה באור ה' וכתיב ונגלה כבוד ה' וראו כל בשר יחדיו וגו' וכתיב לבוא בנקרת הצורים ובסעיפי הסלעי' מפני פחד ה' והדר גאונו וגו' וכמ"ש והופע בהדר גאון עוזך על כל יושבי תבל ארצך וגו':

פרק לז והנה תכלית השלימות הזה של ימות המשיח ותחיית המתים שהוא גילוי אור א"ס ב"ה בעוה"ז הגשמי תלוי במעשינו ועבודתנו כל זמן משך הגלות כי הגורם שכר המצוה היא המצוה בעצמה כי בעשייתה ממשיך האדם גילוי אור א"ס ב"ה מלמעלה למטה להתלבש בגשמיות עוה"ז בדבר שהיה תחלה תחת ממשלת קליפת נוגה ומקבל חיותה ממנה שהם כל דברים הטהורים ומותרי' שנעשית בהם המצוה מעשיית כגון קלף התפילין ומזוזה וספר תורה וכמאמר רז"ל לא הוכשר למלאכת שמים אלא טהורים ומותרים בפיך. וכן אתרוג שאינו ערלה * ומעות הצדקה שאינן גזל וכיוצא בהם ועכשיו שמקיים

הגהה

* (שהערלה היא משלש קליפות הטמאות לגמרי שאין להם עליה לעולם

[Note continued from previous page]
as explained in Etz Chayim. *Similarly the performance of any precept involving a transgression, G–d forbid.*

when a person performs the Divine commandment and will, by means of these ["clean" things], the vitality that is in them ascends and is dissolved and absorbed into the light of the blessed *En Sof*, which is His blessed will that is clothed in them, since therein there is no concealment of Countenance whatever, to obscure His blessed light.

In like manner, the energy of the vital animal soul which is in the organs of the body of the person performing the commandment, is also clothed in this performance, and it rises from the *kelipah* and is absorbed into the holiness of the precept, which is His blessed will, and is dissolved into the light of the blessed *En Sof*.

Likewise in regard to the commandment of Torah study and the recital of *Shema* and Prayer, and similar precepts, although they do not involve physical action in the strict sense, such as would be dominated by the *kelipat nogah*. Nevertheless it has been established that meditation cannot take the place of speech,[3] and that a person does not fulfil the commandment until he has uttered [the words] with his lips. And it has been established that the articulation by the lips is deemed as "action."[4] For the divine soul cannot express itself through the lips and mouth and tongue and teeth, which are all corporeal, except through the agency of the vital animal soul, which is clothed in the organs of the physical body. Hence the more strength one puts into his speech, the more of the vital soul's energy does he introduce and invest into those words. This is the meaning of the verse, "All my bones shall declare. . . ."[5] This also is what the Rabbis meant when they said, "If the Torah reposes in all the 248 organs, it will be preserved; but if not, it will not be preserved."[6] For forgetfulness comes from the *kelipah*[7] of the body and vital animal soul, which are of the *kelipat nogah* that is sometimes absorbed into holiness, which is accomplished when one weakens their power and transfers all their strength into the holiness of the Torah or Prayer.

●▲Furthermore, the vital soul's energy which is clothed in the letters of speech in Torah study or Prayer, or the like, or in the precepts of performance, derives its entire growth and vitality from the blood, which is of the *kelipat nogah* itself, namely, all the foods and drinks which the person has eaten

---

[3] Berachot *20b*. *Cf.* Shulchan Aruch, Orach Chayim, *sec. 62, 3*. [4] Bava Metziah *90b;* Sanhedrin *65a*. [5] Ps. *35:10*. [6] Eruvin *54a*. [7] Zohar *I, 193b;* Pardes, "Erech Shikchah"; *Rabbi Chayim Vital*, "Shaar Hamitzvot", *beg. of* VaEtchanan.

שמקיים בהם מצות ה׳ ורצונו הרי החיות שבהם עולה ומתבטל ונכלל באור

לעולם כמ״ש בע״ח וכן כל מצוה הבאה בעבירה ח״ו)

א״ס ב״ה שהוא רצונו ית׳ המלובש בהם מאחר שאין שם בחי׳ הסתר פנים כלל להסתיר אורו ית׳ וכן כח נפש החיונית הבהמית שבאברי גוף האדם המקיים המצוה הוא מתלבש ג״כ בעשיה זו ועולה מהקליפה ונכלל בקדושת המצוה שהיא רצונו ית׳ ובטל באור א״ס ב״ה וגם במצות תלמוד תורה וק״ש ותפלה וכיוצא בהן אף שאינן בעשיה גשמית ממש שתחת ממשלת קליפת נוגה מ״מ הא קיימא לן דהרהור לאו כדבור דמי ואינו יוצא ידי חובתו עד שיוציא בשפתיו וקיימא לן דעקימת שפתיו הוי מעשה כי אי אפשר לנפש האלהית לבטא בשפתיים ופה ולשון ושיניים הגשמיים כי אם ע״י נפש החיונית הבהמית המלובשת באברי הגוף ממש וכל מה שמדבר בכח גדול יותר הוא מכנים ומלביש יותר כחות מנפש החיונית בדיבורים אלו וז״ש הכתוב כל עצמותי תאמרנה וגו׳ וז״ש רז״ל אם ערוכה בכל רמ״ח איברים משתמרת ואם לאו אינה משתמרת כי השכחה היא מקליפת הגוף ונפש החיונית הבהמית שהן מקליפת נוגה הנכללת לפעמים בקדושה והיינו כשמתיש כחן ומכנים כל כחן בקדושת התורה או התפלה:

זאת ועוד אחרת שכח נפש החיונית המתלבשת באותיות הדבור בת״ת או תפלה וכיוצא בהן או מצות מעשיות הרי כל גידולו וחיותו מהדם שהוא מקליפת נוגה ממש שהן כל אוכלין ומשקין שאכל ושתה

and drunk and which have become blood, having been under its dominion and having drawn their nurtures from it [the *kelipat nogah*]. But now it is converted from evil to good and is absorbed into holiness, by virtue of the energy of the vital soul that has grown from it, which has now clothed itself in these letters or in this action which constitute the very inwardness of His blessed will, without any concealment of Countenance. And their vitality is also absorbed into the light of the blessed *En Sof*, which is His blessed will. And with their vitality, the energy of the vital soul is absorbed and elevated. Thereby will ascend also the totality of the *kelipat nogah*, constituting the general vitality of this ▲ material and gross world, when the whole *neshamah* and divine soul of all Israel, which is divided into 600,000 particular offshoots, and each particular soul will fulfil all the 613 commandments of the Torah:—

The 365 prohibitions, to restrain the 365 blood vessels of the vital soul in the body, so as not to receive nurture or vitality through that sin from one of the three completely unclean *kelipot*, from which are derived the 365 prohibitions in the Torah together with their offshoots as laid down by the Rabbis; for the vital soul would no longer be able to ascend to G-d if it had been defiled with the impurity of the three unclean *kelipot*, which can never be elevated but must be completely nullified and annihilated, as is written, "And I will cause the unclean spirit to pass out of the land";[8] and

The 248 positive precepts, in order to draw the light of the blessed *En Sof* earthwards, so as to raise up to Him and bind and unite with Him, the totality of the vital soul which is in the 248 organs of the body, with a perfect union, to become truly one, as it was His blessed will that He should have an abode amongst the lowest creatures, and they become a "vehicle" (*merkavah*) for Him, as were the Patriarchs.

●▲ Thus, when the totality of the vital soul of the community of Israel will be a holy *merkavah* for G-d, then shall the general vitality of this world, now constituting the *kelipat nogah*, emerge from its impurity and filth and ascend unto holiness to become a *merkavah* for G-d, through the revelation of His glory, "And all flesh shall see together," and He will shine forth on them with the splendour of His majestic greatness, and the whole world will be filled with the glory of

---

[8] Zech. *13:2.*

ושתה ונעשו דם שהיו תחת ממשלתה ויִנקו חיותם ממנה ועתה היא מתהפכת מרע לטוב ונכללת בקדוש' ע"י כח נפש החיונית הגדל ממנה שנתלבש באותיות אלו או בעשיה זו אשר הן הן פנימיות רצונו ית' בלי שום הסתר פנים וחיותן נכלל ג"כ באור א"ס ב"ה שהוא רצונו ית' ובחיותן נכלל ועולה ג"כ כח נפש החיונית וע"י זה תעלה ג"כ כללות קליפת נוגה שהיא כללות החיות של עו"הז הגשמי והחומרי כאשר כל הנשמה ונפש האלהית שבכלל ישראל המתחלקת בפרטות לששים רבוא תקיים כל נפש פרטית כל תרי"ג מצות התורה שס"ה ל"ת להפריד שס"ה גידים של דם נפש החיונית שבגוף שלא יינקו ויקבלו חיות בעבירה זו מאחת משלש קליפות הטמאות לגמרי שמהן נשפעים שס"ה לא תעשה דאורייתא' וענפיהן שהן מדרבנן ושוב לא תוכל נפש החיונית לעלות אל ה' אם נטמאה בטומאת השלש קליפות הטמאות שאין להן עליה לעולם כ"א ביטול והעברה לגמרי כמ"ש ואת רוח הטומאה אעביר מן הארץ ורמ"ח מצות עשה להמשיך אור א"ס ב"ה למטה להעלות לו ולקשר ולייחד בו כללות הנפש החיונית שברמ"ח אברי הגוף ביחוד גמור להיות לאחדים ממש כמו שעלה ברצונו ית' להיות לו דירה בתחתונים והם לו למרכבה כמו האבות. ומאחר שכללות נפש החיונית שבכללות ישראל תהיה מרכבה קדושה לה' אזי גם כללות החיות של עו"הז שהיא קליפת נוגה עכשיו תצא אז מטומאת' וחלאתה ותעלה לקדושה להיות מרכבה לה' בהתגלות כבודו וראו כל בשר יחדיו ויופיע עליהם בהדר גאון עוזו וימלא כבוד ה'

the Lord, and Israel shall behold [it] eye to eye, as at the Giving of the Law, as is written, "Unto thee it was showed, that thou mightest know, that the Lord, He is G-d; there is nothing else beside Him."[9]

In this way, all three unclean *kelipot* will be completely destroyed and annihilated, for their present nurture and vitality from holiness comes to them through the medium of the *kelipat nogah*, which is the intermediary between them.

▲ It follows, therefore, that the whole fulfillment of the Messianic Era and of the Resurrection of the Dead—which is the revelation of His blessed glory and Divinity, and the banishment of the spirit of impurity from the world—is dependent on the suffusion of His Divinity and of the light of the blessed *En Sof* over the vital soul of the community of Israel in all its 248 organs, through its fulfillment of all the 248 positive precepts; and on the banishment of the spirit of impurity from it through its observance of all the 365 prohibitions, so that its 365 veins do not ▲ derive nurture from it. For the community of Israel, comprising 600,000 particular souls, is the [source of] life for the world as a whole, which was created for their sake.[10] And each one of them contains and is related to the vitality of one part in 600,000 of the totality of the world, which [part] depends on his vital soul for its elevation to G-d through its own [the soul's] elevation, by virtue of the individual's partaking of this world for the needs of his body and vital soul in the service of G-d, viz., eating, drinking, and the like, [his] dwelling and all his utensils.

Yet these 600,000 particular souls are roots, and each root subdivides into 600,000 sparks, each spark being one *neshamah;* and so with the *nefesh* and *ruach* in each of the four worlds—*Atzilut, Beriah, Yetzirah, Asiyah.* And each spark descended into this ●▲ world—although it is indeed a profound descent and a state of true exile, for even if one be a perfectly righteous person, serving G-d with fear and a great love of delights, he cannot attain to the degree of attachment to G-d, in fear and love, as before it came down to this gross world, not a fraction of it, and there is no comparison or similarity between them at all, as is clear to every intelligent person,

---

[9] Deut. *4:35.* [10] *Cf.* Rashi, Gen. *1:1.*

ה׳ את כל הארץ וישראל יראו עין בעין כבמתן תורה דכתיב אתה הראת לדעת כי ה׳ הוא האלהים אין עוד מלבדו ועל ידי זה יתבלעו ויתבטלו לגמרי כל השלש קליפות הטמאות כי יניקתן וחיותן מהקדושה עכשיו היא ע״י קליפת נוגה הממוצעת ביניהן ונמצא כי כל תכלית של ימות המשיח ותחיית המתים שהוא גילוי כבודו ואלהותו ית׳ ולהעביר רוח הטומאה מן הארץ תלוי בהמשכת אלהותו ואור א״ס ב״ה לנפש החיונית שבכללות ישראל בכל רמ״ח אבריה ע״י קיומה כל רמ״ח מצות עשה ולהעביר רוח הטומאה ממנה בשמירת׳ כל שס״ה מצות ל״ת שלא יינקו ממנה שס״ה גידיה כי כללות ישראל שהם ששים רבוא נשמות פרטיות הם כללות החיות של כללות העולם כי בשבילם נברא וכל פרט מהם הוא כולל ושייך לו החיות של חלק אחד מששים רבוא מכללות העולם התלוי בנפשו החיונית להעלותו לה׳ בעלייתה דהיינו במה שמשתמש מעו״הז לצורך גופו ונפשו החיונית לעבודת ה׳ כגון אכילה ושתיה ודומיהם ודירה וכל כלי תשמישיו אלא שששים רבוא נשמות פרטיות אלו הן שרשי׳ וכל שרש מתחלק לששים רבוא ניצוצות שכל ניצוץ הוא נשמה אחת וכן בנפש ורוח בכל עולם מארבע עולמות אצילו׳ בריאה יצירה עשיה וכל ניצוץ לא ירד לעו״הז אף שהיא ירידה גדולה ובחי׳ גלות ממש כי גם שיהיה צדיק גמור עובד ה׳ ביראה ואהבה רבה בתענוגים לא יגיע למעלות דביקותו בה׳ בדחילו ורחימו בטרם ירידתו לעו״הז החומרי לא מינה ולא מקצתה ואין ערך ודמיון ביניהם כלל כנודע לכל משכיל

שהגוף

for the body cannot endure, ... nevertheless [each spark] descended into this world, to be clothed in a body and vital soul, for the sole purpose of mending them and separating them from the evil of the three impure *kelipot*, through the observance of the 365 prohibitions and their offshoots, and in order to elevate his vital soul together with its portion that belongs to it of the totality of the world, so as to join and unite them with the light of the blessed *En Sof*, which the person draws into them through fulfilling all the 248 positive precepts through the agency of the vital soul, the very one that fulfils all the active commandments, as has been explained above. It has also been stated in (*Etz Chayim*, Portal 26) that the soul itself [*neshamah*] needs no *tikun* (mending) at all ... and there is no necessity for it to be embodied in this world ... except in order to bring down the light to mend them ... and this is exactly similar to the esoteric exile of the *Shechinah* for the purpose of elevating the sparks. ...

●▲ In the light of the above, one can understand why our Rabbis, of blessed memory, so strongly emphasized the virtue of charity,[11] declaring that "It balances all the other commandments,"[12] and throughout the Yerushalmi Talmud it is called simply "The Commandment," for such was the usage of the language to call charity simply "The Commandment," because it is the core of the precepts of action and surpasses them all. For all [precepts] are only intended to elevate the vital soul unto G–d, since it is she [the soul] that performs them and clothes itself in them, thereby being absorbed into the light of the blessed *En Sof* which is vested in them. Hence you can find no commandment in which the vital soul is clothed to the same extent as in the commandment of charity: for in all [the other] commandments only one faculty of the vital soul is embodied, and then only at the time of the performance of the precept, whilst in the case of charity, which a man gives out of the toil of his hands, surely all the strength of his vital soul is embodied in the execution of his work or occupation by which he earned the money; when he gives it for charity, his whole vital soul ascends to G–d. Even where one does not depend on his toil for a livelihood, nevertheless since with this [charity] money he could have purchased necessities of life, for his vivifying soul, hence he is giving his soul's life to G–d.

Therefore our Rabbis, of blessed memory, said that it [charity] brings

[11] Bava Batra *9a*. [12] Ibid.

שהגוף אינו יכול לסבול כו׳ אלא ירידתו לעולם הזה להתלבש בגוף ונפש החיונית הוא כדי לתקנם בלבד ולהפרידם מהרע של שלש קליפות הטמאות על ידי שמירת שס״ה לא תעשה וענפיהן ולהעלות נפשו החיונית עם חלקה השייך לה מכללות עו״הז ולקשרם ולייחדם באור א״ס ב״ה אשר ימשיך בהם ע״י קיומו כל רמ״ח מצות עשה בנפשו החיוני׳ שהיא היא המקיימ׳ כל מצות מעשיות כנ״ל וכמ״ש [בע״ח שער כ״ו] כי הנשמה עצמה אינה צריכה תיקון כלל כו׳ ולא הוצרכה להתלבש בעו״הז וכו׳ רק להמשיך אור לתקנם כו׳ והוא ממש דוגמת סוד גלות השכינה לברר ניצוצין וכו׳.

ובזה יובן מה שהפליגו רז״ל במאד מאד במעלת הצדקה ואמרו ששקולה כנגד כל המצות ובכל תלמוד ירושלמי היא נק׳ בשם מצוה סתם כי כך היה הרגל הלשון לקרוא צדקה בשם מצוה סתם מפני שהיא עיקר המצות מעשיות ועולה על כולנה שכולן הן רק להעלות נפש החיונית לה׳ שהיא היא המקיימת אותן ומתלבשת בהן ליכלל באור א״ס ב״ה המלובש בהן ואין לך מצוה שנפש החיונית מתלבשת בה כל כך כבמצות הצדקה שבכל המצות אין מתלבש בהן רק כח א׳ מנפש החיונית בשעת מעשה המצוה לבד אבל בצדקה שאדם נותן מיגיע כפיו הרי כל כח נפשו החיונית מלובש בעשיית מלאכתו או עסק אחר שנשתכר בו מעות אלו וכשנותנן לצדקה הרי כל נפשו החיונית עולה לה׳ וגם מי שאינו נהנה מיגיעו מ״מ הואיל ובמעות אלו היה יכול לקנות חיי נפשו החיונית הרי נותן חיי נפשו לה׳. ולכן אמרו רז״ל שמקרבת את

הגאולה

the Redemption nearer.[13] For with one act of charity a person elevates a great part of the vivifying soul, of whose powers and faculties he cannot elevate in the same measure by performing several other active precepts.

• As for the statement of our Rabbis that "The study of the Torah equals all other commandments combined,"[14] this is because Torah study is effected through the faculties of speech and thought, which are the innermost garments of the vivifying soul; also the essence and substance of the faculties of *ChaBaD* (*chochmah*, *binah*, *da'at*) of the *kelipat nogah* in the vivifying soul are integrated into holiness itself when one occupies oneself in Torah with concentration and intelligence.

And although the essence and substance of the emotion attributes (*middot*)—*chesed*, *gevurah*, *tiferet*, and so on—cannot be mastered by Intermediates so as to be converted to holiness, this is because the evil is stronger in the emotion attributes than in the intelligences, by reason of its greater nurture from the holiness of the *middot*, as is known to those familiar with the Esoteric Discipline.

Furthermore, and this is the most important aspect of all in the pre-eminence of Torah study over all other commandments, based on the above-mentioned[15] quotation from the *Tikunim*, that "The 248 commandments are the 248 'organs' of the King": Just as in the case of a human being, by way of example, there is no comparison or similitude between the vitality that is in his 248 organs and the vitality that is in the brain, i.e., the intellect which is subdivided into the three faculties of ChaBaD, exactly analogous, by way of example, yet removed by myriads of distinctions *ad infinitum*, is the illumination of the light of the blessed *En Sof* that is clothed in the active precepts, compared with the illumination of the light of the blessed *En Sof* in the ChaBaD aspects of the wisdom of the Torah, in each man according to his intelligence and mental grasp. And although his apprehension is only in its material aspects, yet the Torah is likened to water, which descends from a high level, . . . as has been explained above.[16]

• Nevertheless, the Rabbis declared, "Not learning, but doing is the essential thing."[17] It is also written, "This day to *do* them."[18] And [it has been ruled that] one should interrupt the study of the Torah in order to fulfil an active precept that cannot be performed by others.[19] For, "This is the whole man,"[20] and the purpose of his creation and his descent to this world, in order that He have an abode here below especially, to turn darkness into light, so that the glory of the Lord shall fill all of this material world, with the emphasis on *material*, and "All flesh shall see it

---

[13] Ibid., *10a*. [14] Mishnah, Peah *1:1*. [15] *Ch. 23*. [16] *Ch. 4*. [17] Avot *1:17*. [18] Deut. *7:11*. [19] Moed Katan *9b*. [20] Eccl. *12:13*.

• 28 Adar • 29 Adar

הגאולה לפי שבצדק׳ אחת מעלה הרבה מנפש החיונית מה שלא היה יכול להעלות ממנה כל כך כחות ובחי׳ בכמה מצות מעשיות אחרות. ומ״ש רז״ל שת״ת כנגד כולם היינו מפני שת״ת היא בדבור ומחשבה שהם לבושים הפנימי׳ של נפש החיונית וגם מהותן ועצמותן של בחי׳ חב״ד מקליפת נוגה שבנפש החיונית נכללות בקדושה ממש כשעוסק בתורה בעיון ושכל ואף שמהותן ועצמותן של המדות חג״ת כו׳ לא יכלו להם הבינונים להפכם לקדושה היינו משום שהרע חזק יותר במדות מבחב״ד מפני יניקתן שם מהקדושה יותר כידוע לי״ח: זאת ועוד אחרת והיא העולה על כולנה במעלת עסק ת״ת על כל המצו׳ ע״פ מ״ש לעיל בשם התיקוני׳ דרמ״ח פיקודין הן רמ״ח אברי׳ דמלכא וכמו באדם התחתון ד״מ אין ערוך ודמיון כלל בין החיות שברמ״ח איבריו לגבי החיות שבמוחין שהוא השכל המתחלק לג׳ בחי׳ חב״ד ככה ממש ד״מ להבדיל ברבבות הבדלות לאין קץ בהארת אור א״ס ב״ה המתלבשות במצות מעשיות לגבי הארת אור א״ס שבבחי׳ חב״ד שבחכמת התורה איש איש כפי שכלו והשגתו. ואף שאינו משיג אלא בגשמיות הרי התורה נמשלה למים שיורדים ממקום גבוה כו׳ כמ״ש לעיל ואעפ״כ ארז״ל לא המדרש עיקר אלא המעשה והיום לעשותם כתיב ומבטלין ת״ת לקיום מצוה מעשיית כשא״א לעשותה ע״י אחרים משום כי זה כל האדם ותכלית בריאתו וירידתו לעוה״ז להיות לו ית׳ דירה בתחתונים דוקא לאהפכא חשוכא לנהורא וימלא כבוד ה׳ את כל הארץ הגשמית דייקא וראו כל בשר יחדיו

together," as has been discussed above.

On the other hand, when the precept is one that can be performed by others, one does not interrupt the study of the Torah,[21] though the whole Torah is, after all, only an explanation of the active ordinances. The reason is that [the Torah] is, as it were, the ChaBaD of the blessed *En Sof*, and when a person is engaged in it he draws over himself the light of the blessed *En Sof*, of an infinitely higher order and splendour than the illumination and influence obtained through the commandments, which are "The organs of the King." This is what Rav Sheshet [meant when he] said, "Rejoice, O my soul! For thee did I learn Scripture; for thee did I learn Mishnah,"[22] as is explained elsewhere at length.

● This influence and illumination which man, by means of his occupation with the Torah, draws from the reflected light of the blessed *En Sof* and causes to shine on his soul and on the souls of all Israel, which is the *Shechinah*, Keneset Israel, the fount of all the souls of Israel, as will be explained later[23]—is termed "*keriah*" ("calling"); hence *kore baTorah* ["Calling *by means of* the Torah"]. This means that through one's occupation with the Torah one calls to the Holy One, blessed be He, to come to him, to use an anthropomorphism, like a person calling to his companion to come to him, or like a child calling his father to come and join him, so that he should not be separated from him and remain alone, G-d forbid. This is the meaning of the text, "The Lord is nigh to all that call unto Him; to all that call unto Him in truth,"[24] and " 'Truth' applies only to the Torah."[25] The meaning is thus rendered in the sense of calling to the Holy One, blessed be He, specifically through the Torah. It is different, however, when one does not call Him through occupation in the Torah, but merely cries: "Father! Father!" as the prophet laments over him: "And none calls by Thy name, . . ."[26] as is explained elsewhere. The intelligent person should ponder on this in order to inculcate into himself a great reverence at the time of his occupation with the Torah, as has been previously explained (ch. 23).

●▲ *Chapter 38*

In the light of all that has been said above, one will clearly understand the decision of the *Halachah*, that has been laid down in the Talmud and Codes that meditation is not valid in lieu of verbal articulation,[1] so that if one has recited the *Shema* only in his mind and heart, even with the full force of his concentration (*kavanah*), he has not fulfilled his obligation, and he is required to recite it again [orally].[2] Similarly with grace after meals,[3] which is ordained by the Torah,[4] and with other benedictions ordained by the Rabbis,[5] and with prayer.[6] On the other hand, if he has uttered them with his lips but did not intend with his heart, he has fulfilled his obligation

---

[21] Moed Katan *9b*. [22] Pesachim *68b*. [23] *Chs. 41, 52*. [24] Ps. *145:18. The word* באמת *is here translated not as an adverb, (i.e. "truthfully"), but as a noun—instrument—* "by means of *(that which is) Truth,*"

יחדיו כנ"ל משא"כ כשאפשר לעשותה ע"י אחרים אין מבטלין ת"ת אף שכל התורה אינה אלא פירוש המצות מעשיות והיינו משום שהיא בחי' חב"ד של א"ס ב"ה ובעסקו בה ממשיך עליו אור א"ס ב"ה ביתר שאת והארה גדולה לאין קץ מהארה והמשכה ע"י פקודין שהן אברי' דמלכא וז"ש רב ששת חדאי נפשאי לך קראי לך תנאי כמ"ש במ"א באריכות: והנה המשכה והארה זו שהאדם ממשיך ומאיר מהארת אור א"ס ב"ה על נפשו ועל נפשות כל ישראל היא השכינ' כנסת ישראל מקור כל נשמות ישראל כמ"ש לקמן ע"י עסק התורה נקראת בלשון קריאה קורא בתורה פי' שע"י עסק התורה קורא להקב"ה לבוא אליו כביכול כאדם הקורא לחבירו שיבא אליו וכבן קטן הקורא לאביו לבא אליו להיות עמו בצוות' חדא ולא ליפרד ממנו ולישאר יחידי ח"ו וז"ש קרוב ה' לכל קוראיו לכל אשר יקראוהו באמת ואין אמת אלא תורה דהיינו שקורא להקב"ה ע"י התורה דוקא לאפוקי מי שקורא אותו שלא על ידי עסק התורה אלא צועק כך אבא אבא וכמו שקובל עליו הנביא ואין קורא בשמך כו' וכמ"ש במ"א. ומזה יתבונן המשכיל להמשיך עליו יראה גדולה בשעת עסק התורה כמש"ל [פ' כ"ג]:

פרק לח

והנה עם כל הנ"ל יובן היטב פסק ההלכה הערוכה בתלמוד ופוסקי' דהרהור לאו כדבור דמי ואם קרא ק"ש במחשבתו ובלבו לבד בכל כח כוונתו לא יצא ידי חובתו וצריך לחזור ולקרות וכן בברכת המזון דאורייתא ובשאר ברכות דרבנן ובתפל' ואם הוציא בשפתיו ולא כיון לבו יצא ידי חובתו בדיעבד

---

namely, the Torah. [25] Tanna debei Eliyahu Zuta, *ch. 21.* [26] Isa. *64:6.* "*The Torah is His Name,*" Zohar *II, 90b; III 73a.*

Chapter 38
[1] Berachot *20b;* Shulchan Aruch, "Orach Chayim," *62:3.* [2] Shulchan Aruch, loc. cit. [3] Ibid. *185:2.* [4] Maimonides, Code, Hilchot Berachot *1:1.* [5] Shulchan Aruch, Ibid. *206:3.* [6] Ibid. *101:2.*

ex post facto, and he is not required to repeat them, except for the first verse of the *Shema*[7] and the first benediction of the *Amidah*.[8] Thus it is stated (at the beginning of ch. II of *Berachot*):[9] "Up to here the commandment of intention (*kavanah*) applies; from here on comes the commandment of recitation," and so on.

The reason is that the *neshamah* needs no *tikun* (mending)[10] for herself by means of the commandments, but has only to draw forth light to perfect the vivifying soul and body by means of the letters of speech which the *nefesh* pronounces with the aid of the five organs of verbal articulation. Similarly with the active commandments which the *nefesh* performs with the [aid of the] other bodily organs.

▲ Nevertheless, it has been said that "Prayer or other benediction [recited] without *kavanah* is like a body without a *neshamah*."[11] This means that, just as in all creatures in this world, possessing a body and a soul, namely the *nefesh* of all living, and the *ruach* of all human flesh, and the *neshamah* of all that has the spirit of life in its nostrils among all living creatures, all of which G–d animates and brings into existence *ex nihilo*, constantly, by the light and vitality which He imbues into them, for also the material body, and even the very inanimate stones and earth, have within them light and vitality from His blessed Self, so that they do not revert to naught and nothingness as they were before—there is, nevertheless, no comparison or similarity whatever between the quality of the light and vitality that illumine the body, and the quality of the light and vitality that illumine the *neshamah*, which is the soul of all living.

●▲ To be sure, in both there is an identical light, in terms of concealment of the Countenance, and [in terms of] the identical garments wherein the light hides, conceals, and clothes itself, for both [body and soul] are of this world wherein the light and vitality [issuing] from the breath of His blessed mouth is equally concealed in a general way, by virtue of the concealment of the Countenance and graded descent, in the progressive lowering of the worlds, by means of numerous and profound *tzimtzumim* (contractions) until [the light] has clothed itself in the *kelipat nogah*, in order to animate the totality of this material world, that is, all things which are permissible and clean in this world; and from it and through it, all things that are impure receive their sustenance, for it is the mediating agent, as it were, as has been explained above.[12]

Nevertheless, the illumination, i.e., the flow of vitality wherewith G–d illumines

---

[7] Ibid. *60:5*. [8] Ibid. *101:1*. [9] Berachot *13b*. [10] See *ch. 37, above*. [11] Shenei Luchot ha-Berit, op. cit., *vol. I, p. 249b*. [12] *Ch. 7*.

בדיעבד ואין צריך לחזור לבד מפסוק ראשון של ק"ש וברכה ראשונה של תפלת שמונה עשרה וכדאי' [ברפ"ב דברכות] ע"כ מצות כוונה מכאן ואילך מצות קריאה וכו'. והיינו משום שהנשמה אינה צריכה תיקון לעצמה במצות רק להמשיך אור לתקן נפש החיונית והגוף ע"י אותיות הדבור שהנפש מדברת בה' מוצאות הפה וכן במצות מעשיות שהנפש עושה בשאר אברי הגוף: אך אעפ"כ אמרו תפלה או שאר ברכה בלא כוונה הן כגוף בלא נשמה פי' כי כמו שכל הברואים שבעו"הז שיש להם גוף ונשמה שהם נפש כל חי ורוח כל בשר איש ונשמת כל אשר רוח חיים באפיו מכל בעלי חיים וה' מחיה את כולם ומהוה אותם מאין ליש תמיד באור וחיות שמשפיע בהם שגם הגוף החומרי ואפי' אבנים ועפר הדומם ממש יש בו אור וחיות ממנו ית' שלא יחזור להיות אין ואפס כשהיה ואעפ"כ אין ערך ודמיון כלל בין בחי' אור וחיו' המאיר בגוף לגבי בחי' אור וחיות המאיר בנשמה שהיא נפש כל חי ואף שבשניהם אור אחד שוה בבחי' הסתר פנים ולבושי' שוים שהאור מסתתר ומתעלם ומתלבש בו כי שניהם הם מעו"הז שבכללותו מסתתר בשוה האור והחיות שמרות פיו ית' בבחי' הסתר פנים וירידת המדרגות בהשתלשלות העולמות ממדרגה למדרגה בצמצומים רבים ועצומים עד שנתלבש בקליפת נוגה להחיות כללות עו"הז החומרי דהיינו כל דברים המותרים והטהורים שבעולם הזה וממנה ועל ידה מושפעים דברים הטמאים כי היא בחי' ממוצעת כנ"ל אעפ"כ ההארה שהיא המשכת החיות אשר ה' מאיר ומחיה

and animates by way of this garment, is not the same for all of them in the manner ●▲ of contraction and expansion. For in the corporeal body and in the actually inanimate object, like stones and earth, the illumination is one of greatest contraction which has no parallel, where the vitality is so minute as not to have even the power of vegetation. In plants the illumination is not so greatly contracted. In general, all things are subdivided into four grades—mineral, vegetable, animal and man ("speaker")—corresponding with the four letters of the blessed Name [Tetragrammaton], from which they receive their influence.

And just as the illumination and flow of vitality in the inanimate and vegetable bear no comparison or parallel with the illumination and flow of vitality which is clothed in animals and man, although in all there is one equal light in the category of concealed Countenance, which is clothed in the same garment in all of them, namely, the garment of *nogah*,[13]—so, too, there is no comparison or parallel between the illumination and flow of the light of the blessed *En Sof*—the inwardness of His blessed will, without concealment of the Countenance and without any garment whatever—which irradiates and pervades the active precepts; likewise in the case of precepts that depend on verbal articulation and utterance of the lips without *kavanah*, which [articulation] is regarded as real action, as mentioned above, by comparison with the illumination and flow of the light of the blessed *En Sof* which irradiates and pervades the *kavanah* of the active precepts that a person intends, whilst engaged in performing them, to cleave to Him, blessed be He, through fulfilling His will, inasmuch as He and His will are one and the same.[14] Similarly in the case of *kavanah* in prayer, the recital of *Shema* with its benedictions, and all other benedictions, wherein through his intention (*kavanah*) he attaches his thought and intellect to Him, may He be blessed. Not that an attachment (*devekut*) ● of the human thought and intellect to Him, blessed be He, is intrinsically superior to the attachment through the performance of the active precepts in actual practice, as will be explained further on. Rather it is also His blessed will that one should cleave to Him with one's intelligence, thought and intention in the active commandments, and with intention during the recital of *Shema*, prayer and other benedictions. And the illumination of this Supreme Will (*Ratzon Elyon*) which irradiates and pervades this *kavanah* is infinitely greater and more sublime than the illumination of the Supreme Will which irradiates and pervades

---

[13] *See chs. 7, 37, above.* [14] *The concept of* kavanah, *of far-reaching mystical implications in Lurianic and earlier Kabbalah, receives a simplified definition.*

ומחיה דרך לבוש זה אינה שוה בכולן בבחי' צמצום והתפשטות כי בגוף הגשמי והדומם ממש כאבנים ועפר ההארה היא בבחי' צמצום גדול אשר אין כמוהו והחיות שבו מועטת כל כך עד שאין בו אפי' כח הצומח ובצומח ההארה אינה בצמצום גדול כל כך. והדרך כלל נחלקות לארבע מדרגות דומם צומח חי מדבר כנגד ד' אותיות שם הוי"ה ב"ה שממנו מושפעים וכמו שאין ערך ודמיון ההארה והמשכת החיו' שבדומם וצומח להארה והמשכת החיות המלובש' בחי ומדבר אף שבכולן אור אחד שוה בבחי' הסתר פנים ומלובש בלבוש אחד בכולן שהוא לבוש נוגה כך אין ערך ודמיון כלל בין הארת והמשכת אור א"ס ב"ה שהוא פנימיות רצונו ית' בלי הסתר פנים ולבוש כלל המאירה ומלובשת במצות מעשיות ממש. וכן במצות התלויות בדבור וביטוי שפתים בלי כוונה שהוא נחשב כמעשה ממש כנ"ל לגבי ההארה והמשכת אור א"ס ב"ה המאירה ומלובשת בכוונת המצות מעשיות שהאדם מתכוין בעשייתן כדי לדבקה בו ית' ע"י קיום רצונו שהוא ורצונו אחד וכן בכוונת התפלה וק"ש וברכותיה ושאר ברכות שבכוונתו בהן מדבק מחשבתו ושכלו בו ית' ולא שדביקות המחשבה ושכל האדם בו ית' היא מצד עצמה למעלה מדביקו' קיום המצות מעשיו' בפועל ממש כמ"ש לקמן אלא מפני שזהו ג"כ רצונו ית' לדבקה בשכל ומחשבה וכוונת המצות מעשיו' ובכוונ' ק"ש ותפלה ושאר ברכות והארת רצון העליון הזה המאירה ומלובשת בכוונה זו היא גדולה לאין קץ למעלה מעלה מהארת רצון העליון המאירה ומלובשת בקיום

the performance of the commandments themselves in action and speech but without *kavanah.* It is comparable to the superiority of the light of the soul over the body, which is a vessel and garb for the soul, as the body of the commandment itself is a vessel and garb for its *kavanah.*

And although in both of them, in the commandment and in its *kavanah,* there is the same Will which is perfectly simple, without any change or multiplicity, G–d forbid, which is united with His blessed Essence and Being in perfect unity, nevertheless the illumination is not the same in respect of contraction and extension, and

Note: It is also so explained in Etz Chayim, *that the* kavanah *of the commandments and of Torah study is in the category of "light," while the commandments themselves are grades and categories of "vessels" that constitute* tzimtzum *of the light, for through the contraction of the light the vessels came into being, as is known to those who are familiar with the Esoteric Discipline.*

it, too, is differentiated into four grades. For the "body" of the commandments themselves constitute two grades, namely, the commandments involving real action and those which are performed verbally and mentally, such as the study of the Torah, reciting the *Shema,* praying, saying Grace after meals, and other benedictions. The *kavanah* of the commandments [i.e. the intention] to cleave to His blessed Self, being like the soul to the body [of the commandments], is likewise subdivided into two grades, corresponding to the two categories of soul which are present in corporeal bodies, namely in animals and in man [respectively].

●▲ In the case of a person who is intelligent enough to know G–d and to reflect on His blessed greatness, and to beget out of his understanding a lofty fear in his brain and a love of G–d in the right part of his heart, so that his soul will thirst for G–d, [seeking] to cleave unto Him through the fulfillment of the Torah and commandments, which are an extension and reflection of the light of the blessed *En Sof* onto his soul thereby to cleave to Him; and with this intention he studies [the Torah] and performs the commandments, and likewise with this intention he prays and recites the blessings—then this *kavanah* is, by way of simile, like the soul of a human being, who possesses intelligence and freedom of choice and speaks from knowledge.

But he whose intelligence is too limited to know and reflect on the greatness of the blessed *En Sof* so as to beget out of this understanding a conscious love in his heart, and also awe

● 6 Nisan ▲ *26 Adar II*

בקיום המצות עצמן במעשה ובדבור בלי כוונה כגודל מעלת אור הנשמה על הגוף שהוא כלי ומלבוש הנשמה כמו גוף המצוה עצמה שהוא כלי ומלבוש לכוונתה ואף שבשתיהן במצוה ובכוונתה מלובש רצון אחד פשוט בתכלית הפשיטות בלי שום שינוי וריבוי ח"ו ומיוחד במהותו ועצמותו ית' בתכלית היחוד אף על פי כן ההארה אינה שוה בבחינת צמצום והתפשטות * ונחלקת גם כן לארבע מדרגות כי גוף המצות עצמן ממש הן ב' מדרגות שהן מצות מעשיות ממש ומצות התלויות בדבור ומחשבה כמו תלמוד תורה וק"ש ותפלה וברכת המזון ושאר ברכות. וכוונת המצות לדבקה בו ית' שהיא כנשמה לגוף נחלקת ג"כ לשתי מדרגות כמו שתי מדרגות הנשמה שהן בגוף החומרי שהן חי ומדבר. כי מי שדעתו יפה לדעת את ה' ולהתבונן בגדולתו ית' ולהוליד מבינתו יראה עילאה במוחו ואהבת ה' בחלל הימני שבלבו להיות נפשו צמאה לה' לדבקה בו ע"י קיום התורה והמצות שהן המשכת והארת אור א"ס ב"ה על נפשו לדבקה בו ובכוונה זו הוא לומד ומקיים המצות וכן בכוונה זו מתפלל ומברך הרי כוונה זו על ד"מ כמו נשמת המדבר שהוא בעל שכל ובחירה ובדעת ידבר ומי שדעתו קצרה לידע ולהתבונן בגדולת א"ס ב"ה להוליד האהבה מבינתו בהתגלות לבו וכן היראה במוחו

הגה"ה

(וכמ"ש בע"ח שכוונת המצות ותלמוד תורה היא במדרגת אור וגוף המצות הן מדרגות ובחי' כלים שהם בחי' צמצום שע"י צמצום האור נתהוו הכלים כידוע לי"ח):

in his mind, and dread of G–d in his heart, yet he recalls and awakens the natural love that is hidden in his heart, bringing it out of the hidden recesses of the heart into the conscious mind, at least, so that his will which is in his mind and which is latent also in his heart should approve and favour, with complete willingness and truthful sincerity, that he suffer martyrdom in actual fact for the Unity of G–d, in order to attach to Him his divine soul and her garments and unite them with His Unity and Oneness, namely, the Supernal Will that is clothed in Torah study and in the performance of the commandments, as explained above; and in this [natural love] is contained also fear [wherewith] to accept His reign and not rebel against Him, G–d forbid—and with this *kavanah* he turns away from evil and does good, and studies and prays and recites benedictions, following only the plain meaning of the words without conscious fear and love in his heart and mind—this *kavanah* is, by way of the simile, like the soul of a living creature that has no intelligence and freedom of will, whose *middot*, namely its fear of harmful things and its love of pleasing things, are only natural to it, and do not originate in its understanding and knowledge. So, by way of example, are the natural love and fear which are latent in the heart of every Jew, since they are our heritage from our Patriarchs and like a natural instinct in our souls, as has been mentioned above.[15]

•▲ Chapter 39

It is also for this reason that the angels are called *chayyot* (beasts) and *behemot* (cattle), as is written, "And the face of a lion on the right side . . . and the face of an ox on the left side, . . ."[1] for they have no freedom of choice, and their fear and love are their natural instincts, as stated in *Ra'aya Mehemna* on *Parshat Pinchas*. Therefore the quality of *tzaddikim* is superior to theirs, for the abode of the souls of the righteous is in the world of *Beriah*, whereas the abode of the angels is in the world of *Yetzirah*.

Note: This refers to ordinary angels, but there are higher angels in the world of Beriah, *whose service is with intelligent fear and love, as is explained in* Ra'aya Mehemna, ibid., *that there are two kinds*

[Note continued on next page]

The difference between them is that in the world of *Yetzirah* only the *middot* of the blessed *En Sof*

---

[15] *Chs. 18, 19.*

Chapter 39
[1] Ezek. *1:10.*

במוחו ופחד ה' בלבו רק שזוכר ומעורר את האהבה הטבעית המסותרת בלבו ומוציאה מההעלם והסתר הלב אל הגילוי במוח עכ"פ שיהיה רצונו שבמוחו ותעלומות לבו מסכים ומתרצה בריצוי גמור באמת לאמיתו למסו' נפשו בפועל ממש על יחוד ה' כדי לדבק' בו נפשו האלהית ולבושיה ולכללן ביחודו ואחדותו שהוא רצון העליון המלובש בת"ת ובקיום המצות כנ"ל וגם היראה כלולה בה לקבל מלכותו שלא למרוד בו ח"ו ובכוונה זו הוא סור מרע ועושה טוב ולומד ומתפלל ומברך בפירוש המלות לבדו בלא דחילו ורחימו בהתגלות לבו ומוחו הרי כוונה זו עד"מ כמו נשמת החי שאינו בעל שכל ובחירה וכל מדותיו שהן יראתו מדברים המזיקים אותו ואהבתו לדברים הנאהבים אצלו הן רק טבעיים אצלו ולא מבינתו ודעתו וכך הן על ד"מ היראה והאהבה הטבעיות המסותרות בלב כל ישראל כי הן ירושה לנו מאבותינו וכמו טבע בנפשותינו כנז"ל:

פרק לט ומפני זה ג"כ נקראים המלאכים בשם חיות ובהמות כדכתי' ופני אריה אל הימין וגו' ופני שור מהשמאל וגו' לפי שאינם בעלי בחירה ויראתם ואהבתם היא טבעית להם כמ"ש בר"מ פ' פנחס ולכן מעלת הצדיקים גדולה מהם כי מדור נשמות הצדיקים הוא בעולם הבריאה ומדור המלאכי' בעולם היצירה* וההבדל שביניהם הוא כי בעולם היצירה מאירות שם מדותיו של א"ס ב"ה לבדן

הגה"ה

(והיינו בסתם מלאכים אבל יש מלאכים עליונים בעולם הבריאה שעבודתם בדחילו ורחימו שכליים כמ"ש בר"מ שם שיש שני מיני חיות

[Note continued from previous page]
of holy chayyot, *instinctive and intelligent, as also explained in* Etz Chayim.

shine forth, namely the love of Him, and the dread and fear of Him, . . . as is stated (in the *Tikunim*[2] and in *Etz Chayim*)[3] that the six *Sefirot* nest in [the world of] *Yetzirah*. Therefore it is the constant service of the angels, resting neither by day nor by night, to stand in fear and dread, . . . these being the whole camp of Gabriel on the left; while the service of the camp of Michael is with love.[4]. . . But in the world of *Beriah* shine forth the *chochmah, binah* and *da'at* of the blessed *En Sof* which are the source of the *Middot* and their "mother" and root, as stated in the *Tikunim*[5] that *ima ila'a* ("Supernal Mother")[6] nests in the three *Sefirot*, in the "[Divine] Throne" which is the world of *Beriah*. Therefore this is the abode of the souls of the righteous who serve G–d with fear and love, which are derived from the understanding and knowledge of the greatness of the blessed *En Sof*. For this love is called *re'uta de-libba* ("heart's desire"), as has already been mentioned.[7] And from this "heart's desire" is produced a garment for the soul in the world of *Beriah* which constitutes the Higher Garden of Eden, as will be explained later, and as is written in the *Zohar* on [*Parshat*] *Vayakhel*.

• But this applies specifically to *neshamot*, which [possess] a great cognition, as it were, of the blessed *En Sof*. As for the category of *ruach* of the righteous, as also all other souls of Israelites who have served G–d with the fear and love that are latent in the heart of all Jews, these do not ascend thither, except on the Sabbath and the New Moon by means of the pillar that rises from the Lower to the Higher Garden of Eden, i.e. the world of *Beriah* which is called the Higher Garden of Eden, wherein to take pleasure in G–d and derive enjoyment from the splendour of the *Shechinah*. For the intellect of a created being can have no enjoyment or pleasure except in what it conceives, understands, knows and apprehends, with its intellect and apprehension, what is possible for it to understand and grasp of the light of the blessed *En Sof*, by virtue of His blessed wisdom and understanding which shine forth in the world of *Beriah*.

As for the reason that these souls merit to ascend higher than the angels, even though their service has been with no more than natural fear and love, it is that through their fear

---

[2] Tikun 7. [3] "Seder ABYA" *ch. 3*. [4] Zohar *III, 118b; Tikunei Zohar*, Tikun *70*. [5] Tikun *7*. [6] *Synonymous with* Binah. [7] *See ch. 17; also ch. 44*, infra.

• 8 Nisan

לבדן שהן אהבתו ופחדו ויראתו כו׳. וכמ״ש [בתיקונים וע״ח] דשית ספירין מקננין ביצירה ולכן זאת היא עבודת המלאכים תמיד יומם ולילה לא ישקוטו לעמוד ביראה ופחד וכו׳ והיינו כל מחנה גבריאל שמהשמאל ועבודת מחנה מיכאל היא האהבה כו׳. אבל בעולם הבריאה מאירות שם חכמתו ובינתו ודעתו של א״ס ב״ה שהן מקור המדות ואם ושרש להן וכדאיתא בתיקונים דאימא עילאה מקננא בתלת ספירן בכרסיא שהוא עולם הבריאה ולכן הוא מדור נשמות הצדיקים עובדי ה׳ בדחילו ורחימו הנמשכות מן הבינה ודעת דגדולת א״ס ב״ה שאהבה זו נקרא רעותא דלבא כנ״ל ומרעותא דלבא נעשה לבוש לנשמה בעולם הבריאה שהוא גן עדן העליון כדלקמן וכמ״ש בזהר ויקהל אך היינו דווקא נשמות ממש שהן בחי׳ מוחין דגדלות א״ס ב״ה אבל בחי׳ הרוח של הצדיקים וכן שאר כל נשמות ישראל שעבדו את ה׳ בדחילו ורחימו המסותרות בלב כללו׳ ישראל אין עולות לשם רק בשבת ור״ח לבד דרך העמוד שמג״ע התחתון לג״ע העליון שהוא עולם הבריאה הנקרא ג״ע העליון להתענג על ה׳ וליהנות מזיו השכינה כי אין הנאה ותענוג לשכל נברא אלא במה שמשכיל ומבין ויודע ומשיג בשכלו ובינתו מה שאפשר לו להבין ולהשיג מאור א״ס ב״ה ע״י חכמתו ובינתו ית׳ המאירות שם בעולם הבריאה ומה שזוכות נשמות אלו לעלות למעלה מהמלאכים אף שעבדו בדחילו ורחימו טבעיים לבד היינו מפני שע״י דחילו ורחימו

חיות הקדש טבעיים ושכליים וכמ״ש בע״ח :

and love the *sitra achra* which was clothed in their body was subdued, both in the realm of "depart from evil"—by subjugating and breaking the passions, and in the realm of "do good," as discussed earlier. For they had the freedom to choose evil, G–d forbid, yet they chose the good in order to subdue the *sitra achra*, thereby elevating the glory of the Holy One, blessed be He, . . . as the excellence of light, . . . discussed above.

However, all this is concerned with the abode of the souls and their station, but their Torah and service are actually absorbed into the Ten *Sefirot* which are a category of G–dliness and with which the light of the blessed *En Sof* unites itself in perfect unison; that is to say, in the Ten *Sefirot* of *Beriah*—through intelligent fear and love, and in the Ten *Sefirot* of *Yetzirah*—through natural fear and love. In them are clothed the Ten *Sefirot* of *Atzilut* (Emanation) and are completely united with them, while the Ten *Sefirot* of *Atzilut* are absolutely united with their Emanator, the blessed *En Sof*. The souls, on the other hand, are not absorbed into the G–dliness of the Ten *Sefirot*, but are stationed in the *hechalot* (palaces) and abodes of *Beriah* or *Yetzirah*, enjoying the effulgence of the *Shechinah*, the light of the blessed *En Sof*, which is united with the Ten *Sefirot* of *Beriah* or *Yetzirah*, it being the glow of their very Torah and service (see *Zohar*, *Vayakhel*, p. 210),[8] for "the reward of a commandment is the commandment itself."[9]

●▲ The world of *Atzilut*, however, is beyond the intelligence, comprehension and understanding of a created intellect, because the *chochmah*, *binah* and *da'at* of the blessed *En Sof* are united with it therein in perfect unity, a profound and wonderful unity which infinitely excels, in degree and form, that which is found in the world of *Beriah*; for in the latter they descended to give light by means of *tzimtzum*, so that created intellects should be able to receive from them *ChaBaD* (*chochmah*, *binah*, *da'at*), to know G–d and to understand and apprehend something of the light of the blessed *En Sof*, to the extent possible for created intellects which are limited and finite, without their being dissolved in their existence and ceasing completely to exist as created beings, only to revert to their source and root, namely, G–dliness ▲itself. It is this *tzimtzum* that is the cause of the glow of *ChaBaD* of the blessed *En Sof* illuminating the souls in the world of *Beriah*.

---

[8] Zohar *II, p. 210a f.* [9] Avot *4:2.*

ורחימו שלהם אתכפיא ס"א המלובשת בגופם בין בבחי' סור מרע לכבוש התאוות ולשברן ובין בבחי' ועשה טוב כנ"ל והם היו בעלי בחירה לבחור ברע ח"ו ובחרו בטוב לאכפיא לס"א לאסתלקא יקרא דקב"ה כו' כיתרון האור כו' כנ"ל והנה כל זה הוא במדור הנשמות ומקום עמידתן אך תורתן ועבודתן נכללות ממש בי"ס שהן בחי' אלהות ואור א"ס מתייחד בהן בתכלית היחוד והיינו בי"ס דבריאה ע"י דחילו ורחימו שכליים ובי"ס דיצירה ע"י דחילו ורחימו טבעיי' ובתוכן מלובשות י"ס דאצי' ומיוחדות בהן בתכלית וי"ס דאצי' מיוחדות בתכלית במאצילן א"ס ב"ה משא"כ הנשמו' אינן נכללות באלהות די"ס אלא עומדות בהיכלות ומדורין דבריאה או יצירה ונהנין מזיו השכינה הוא אור א"ס ב"ה המיוחד בי"ס דבריאה או דיצי' והוא זיו תורתן ועבודתן ממש [ע' זהר ויקהל דר"י] כי שכר מצוה היא מצוה עצמה: ועולם האצילות שהוא למעלה מהשכל וההשגה וההבנה לשכל נברא כי חכמתו ובינתו ודעתו של א"ס ב"ה מיוחדות שם בו בתכלית היחוד ביחוד עצום ונפלא ביתר שאת ויתר עז לאין קץ מבעולם הבריאה כי שם ירדו להאיר בבחי' צמצום כדי שיוכלו שכלים נבראי' לקבל מהן חב"ד לידע את ה' ולהבין ולהשיג איזו השגה באור א"ס ב"ה כפי כח שכלים הנבראים שהם בעלי גבול ותכלית שלא יתבטלו במציאותם ולא יהיו בגדר נבראים כלל רק יחזרו למקורם ושרשם שהוא בחי' אלהות ממש. והנה צמצום זה היא סבת ההארה שמאירות שם חב"ד של א"ס ב"ה לנשמות אלו בעולם הבריאה.

משא"כ

It is different in [the world of] *Atzilut*, where they [*ChaBaD*] are not subject to the same extent of *tzimtzum;* consequently it is impossible for created intellects to apprehend them. That is why no thought of the [created intellects] can apprehend anything there. Hence it is the abode of the great *tzaddikim*, whose service supremely transcends even the quality of fear and love which are derived from the understanding and knowledge of His blessed greatness, just as the world of *Atzilut* is far beyond the understanding and knowledge of a created intellect. Indeed, their service has been truly in the nature of a "vehicle" to the blessed *En Sof*, being nullified to Him in existence and absorbed in His blessed light, they and everything they possessed, through the fulfillment of the Torah and commandments, in the way which has been said of the Patriarchs that they personally constituted the Chariot, because throughout their lives this was their service.

▲ But as for him whose soul's root is too small to contain such perfect service, so as to be nullified and absorbed in His blessed light by constant service, but only at such intervals and times which are propitious on high, viz. during the prayer of the *Amidah* which is in *Atzilut*, especially when making the genuflexions,[10] for genuflexion characterises *Atzilut* (as explained in *Peri Etz Chayim* on the prayer of the Inauguration of the Sabbath), since it symbolises self-nullification in His blessed light to be accounted as nothing at all before Him—in such a case, therefore, the principal abode of his soul is in the world of *Beriah* (and only occasionally, at propitious times, does his soul ascend to *Atzilut*, by virtue of the "feminine waters,"[11] as is known to those familiar with the Esoteric Discipline).

●▲"The reward of a commandment is the commandment itself" means that from the reward we know its essence and rank. But we do not concern ourselves with esoteric matters, which are [related to] the great *tzaddikim* who are in the category of a "vehicle." Our concern is with matters that are "revealed to us," to which every man should aspire: To know with certainty the essence and quality of Divine Service, with a conscious fear and love in one's heart, stemming from understanding and knowledge of the greatness of the blessed *En Sof*, which has its place in the Ten *Sefirot* of *Beriah;* and of service with the natural fear and love in the mind, [which is] in the Ten *Sefirot* of *Yetzirah*. But a service without the inspiration of fear and love even in the mind,

---

[10] *There are four genuflexions in the* Amidah. [11] מים נוקבין—מ"ן. *See end ch. 10, above.*

● 10 Nisan ▲ *1 Nisan* ▲ *2 Nisan*

משא"כ באצילות שאינם בבחי' צמצום כ"כ א"א לשכלים נבראים לקבל מהן ולכן לית מחשבתא דילהון תפיסא שם כלל לכן הוא מדור לצדיקי' הגדולים שעבודתם היא למעלה מעלה אפי' מבחי' דחילו ורחימו הנמשכות מן הבינה ודעת בגדולתו ית' כמו שעולם האצילות הוא למעלה מעלה מבחי' בינה ודעת לשכל נברא אלא עבודתם היתה בבחי' מרכבה ממש לא"ס ב"ה וליבטל אליו במציאות ולהכלל באורו ית' הם וכל אשר להם ע"י קיום התורה והמצות ע"ד שאמרו האבות הן הן המרכבה והיינו לפי שכל ימיהם היתה זאת עבודתם. אך מי ששרש נשמתו קטן מהכיל עבודה תמה זו ליבטל וליכלל באורו ית' בעבודתו בקביעות רק לפרקים ועתים שהם עת רצון למעלה וכמו בתפלת שמונה עשרה שהיא באצילות ובפרט בהשתחוואו' שבה שכל השתחוואה היא בבחי' אצילות [כמ"ש בפרע"ח בקבל' שבת] כי היא ענין ביטול באורו ית' להיות חשיב קמיה כלא ממש אזי ג"כ עיקר קביעות נשמתו הוא בעולם הבריאה [רק לפרקים בעת רצון תעלה נשמתו לאצילות בבחי' מ"נ כידוע לי"ח]: והנה שכר מצוה מצוה פי' שמשכרה נדע מהותה ומדרגתה ואין לנו עסק בנסתרות שהם צדיקי' הגדולים שהם בבחי' מרכבה רק הנגלו' לנו שאחריהם כל אדם ימשוך לידע נאמנה מהות ומדרגת עבודת ה' בדחילו ורחימו בהתגלות לבו הנמשכות מן הבינה ודעת בגדולת א"ס ב"ה מקומה בי"ס דבריאה ועבודה בדחילו ורחימו הטבעיים שבמוחו בי"ס דיצירה אבל עבודה בלי התעוררות דחילו ורחימו אפי' במוחו בבחי'

גילוי

in a conscious state, that is to say, without arousing the natural love which is hidden in the heart and bringing it out of the concealment and recesses of the heart into the consciousness of the mind and the latency of the heart at any rate, but it remains hidden in the heart as at birth, as it was prior to the service—such a service remains below, in the world of "separateness," called the externality of the worlds, having no power to rise and be absorbed in His blessed Unity, in the Ten Holy *Sefirot*, as is written in the *Tikunim* that "Without fear and love it cannot soar upwards nor can it ascend and stand before G–d."[12]

●▲This is so even if the service is not strictly "Not for its own sake," that is, for some ulterior motive, Heaven forfend. It also applies to the service which is described as "Their fear toward Me has become [like] a trained human precept,"[13] that is to say, it is a matter of habit to which the person has become accustomed since infancy, having been habituated and trained by his father and teacher to fear G–d and to serve Him, but he does not really do it for its own sake. For [performance] truly for its own sake cannot be without arousing at least the innate fear and love and bringing them out from the concealment of the heart into the consciousness of the mind and the latency of the heart, at any rate. For just as a person does nothing for his companion in carrying out the latter's will, unless he loves him or fears him, so one cannot truly act for His blessed Name, just to carry out His will, without recalling and arousing any love or fear for Him in his mind and thought and the latency of his heart, at least.

Nor is love alone called "service" without at least the lower fear (*yirah tattaah*), which is latent in every Jewish heart, as will be later amplified.[14]

●▲However, when a person is engaged [in service] truly not for its own sake, but for some personal motive, with a view to his own glorification, as, for example, in order to become a scholar, and the like, then that motive, which originates in the *kelipat nogah*, clothes itself in his Torah, and the Torah is temporarily in a state of exile in the *kelipah*, until he repents, since "[Repentance] brings healing to the world."[15] For with his return to G–d, his Torah also returns with him. Therefore the Rabbis of blessed memory declared, "A man should always occupy himself

---

[12] Tikunei Zohar, Tikun *10*.
[13] Isa. *29:13*. [14] *Ch. 41*. [15] Yoma *86b*.

גילוי דהיינו לעורר האהבה הטבעית המסותרת בלב להוציאה מההעלם והסתר הלב אל הגילוי אפי' במוחו ותעלומות לבו עכ"פ רק היא נשארת מסותרת בלב כתולדתה כמו שהיתה קודם העבודה הרי עבודה זו נשארת למטה בעולם הפירוד הנק' חיצוניות העולמות ואין בה כח לעלות וליכלל ביחודו ית' שהן עשר ספי' הקדושות וכמ"ש בתיקונים דבלא דחילו ורחימו לא פרחא לעילא ולא יכלא לסלקא ולמיקם קדם ה'. והיינו אפי' אם אינו עוסק שלא לשמה ממש לשום איזו פניה ח"ו אלא כמ"ש ותהי יראתם אותי מצות אנשי' מלומדה פי' מחמת הרגל שהורגל מקטנותו שהרגילו ולימדו אביו ורבו לירא את ה' ולעבדו ואינו עוסק לשמה ממש כי לשמה ממש אי אפשר בלא התעוררות דחילו ורחימו הטבעיים עכ"פ להוציאן מהסתר הלב אל הגילוי במוח ותעלומות לבו עכ"פ כי כמו שאין אדם עושה דבר בשביל חבירו למלאת רצונו אא"כ אוהבו או ירא ממנו כך אי אפשר לעשות לשמו ית' באמת למלאת רצונו לבד בלי זכרון והתעוררות אהבתו ויראתו כלל במוחו ומחשבתו ותעלומות לבו עכ"פ וגם אהבה לבדה אינה נק' בשם עבודה בלי יראה תתאה לפחות שהיא מסותרת בלב כל ישראל כמ"ש לקמן וכשעוסק שלא לשמה ממש לשום איזו פניה לכבוד עצמו כגון להיות ת"ח וכהאי גוונא אזי אותה פניה שמצד הקליפה דנוגה מתלבשת בתורתו והתורה היא בבחי' גלות בתוך הקליפה לפי שעה עד אשר יעשה תשובה שמביאה רפואה לעולם שבשובו אל ה' גם תורתו שבה עמו ולכן אמרו רז"ל לעולם יעסוק

אדם

[with Torah and precepts, even if not for its own sake], for from motives of self-interest he will come [to study and observe] for its own sake"[16]—[this they state] with certainty, for ultimately he is bound to do repentance, whether in this incarnation or in another, "Because none is rejected by Him."[17]

On the other hand, if a person acts without any particular motivation, neither "For its own sake" nor for selfish reasons, then it is not contingent upon repentance, but as soon as he, once again, learns this subject "For its own sake," then even that which he had learned without any particular intent, conjoins and attaches itself with this study and ascends on high, since it had not yet been invested with any *kelipot nogah*. Therefore "A man should always occupy himself. . . ."

The same is true of prayer without *kavanah*, as is discussed in the *Zohar.*[18]

•▲ Chapter 40

However, as long as he has not re-studied that subject "For its own sake," his study does not ascend even into the Ten *Sefirot* which shine in the worlds of *Yetzirah* and *Asiyah*. For the *Sefirot* are a category of G–dliness, and in them is clothed and united the light of the blessed *En Sof* itself, and "Without fear and love it cannot rise and stand before G–d," as is written in the *Tikunim*. But his study ascends into the *hechalot* and abodes which are the externalities of the worlds, wherein the angels stand. Thus Rabbi Chayim Vital, of blessed memory, writes in "The Gate of Prophecy," ch. 2, that from Torah studied without *kavanah* angels are created in the world of *Yetzirah*, whilst from commandments performed without *kavanah*, angels are created in the world of *Asiyah*[1]—and all angels are possessed of matter and form.[2]

However, Torah which is studied "Not for its own sake" indeed, as, for example, for the purpose of becoming a scholar, and the like, it does not at all ascend on high even to the *hechalot* and abodes of the angels of Holiness, but it remains below in this material world which is the dwelling-place of the *kelipot*—

Note: As explained in the Zohar, *Part III, pp. 31b and 121b, where note: "That word ascends and breaks through the heavens . . . and evokes what it evokes—if good—good, . . ." note there. Also page 105a: "From a word of the Torah is formed a sound*

[Note continued on next page]

as commented in the *Zohar* on the verse: "What profit hath a man of all his toil which he labours under the sun?"[3]: "Even with the toil of Torah,

[16] Pesachim *50b;* Nazir *23b.*
[17] *II* Sam. *14:14.* [18] *Cf.* Kuntress Acharon, Tanya, *section 3.*

Chapter 40
[1] Ibid. [2] *Cf. Nachmanides,* Shaar Hagemul. [3] Eccl. *1:3, with emphasis on* "his *labour*" *and on* "under *the sun.*"

אדם וכו' שמתוך שלא לשמה בא לשמה בודאי שבודאי סופו לעשות תשובה בגלגול זה או בגלגול אחר כי לא ידח ממנו נדח אך כשעושה סתם לא לשמה ולא שלא לשמה אין הדבר תלוי בתשובה אלא מיד שחוזר ולומד דבר זה לשמה הרי גם מה שלמד בסתם מתחבר ומצטרף ללימוד זה ופרחא לעילא מאחר שלא נתלבש בו עדיין שום קליפה דנוגה ולכן לעולם יעסוק אדם כו' וכן הענין בתפלה שלא בכוונה כמ"ש בזהר:

פרק מ

אך כל זמן שלא חזר ולמד דבר זה לשמה אין לימודו עולה אפי' בי"ס המאירות בעולם היצירה והעשיה כי הספירות הן בחי' אלהות ובהן מתלבש ומתייחד אור א"ס ב"ה ממש ובלא דחילו ורחימו לא יכלא לסלקא ולמיקם קדם ה' כמ"ש בתיקונים רק לימודו עולה להיכלות ומדורין שהן חיצוניות העולמות שבהן עומדים המלאכים וכמ"ש הרח"ו ז"ל בשער הנבוא' פ"ב שמהתורה שלא בכוונה נבראים מלאכים בעולם היצירה ומהמצות בלי כוונה נבראים מלאכים בעולם העשייה וכל המלאכים הם בעלי חומר וצורה אבל תורה שלא לשמה ממש כגון להיות ת"ח וכה"ג אינה עולה כלל למעלה אפי' להיכלו' ומדור המלאכים דקדושה אלא נשארת למטה בעו"הז הגשמי שהוא מדור הקליפות* וכמ"ש בזהר על פסוק מה יתרון לאדם בכל עמלו שיעמול תחת השמש דאפילו עמלא דאורייתא

אי

הגה"ה

(כמ"ש בזהר ח"ג דף ל"א ע"ב ודף קכ"א עמוד ב' עי' שם ההיא מלה סלקא ובקעא רקיעין כו' ואתער מה דאתער אי טב טב כו' ע"ש ודף ק"ה ע"א מלה דאורייתא אתעביד מיניה קלא וסליק

[Note continued from previous page]
which ascends, . . ." Also page 168b: "The voices of Torah and Prayer rend the heavens . . ."

if he does it for his own glory. . . ." This is also the meaning of the statement: "Happy is he who comes here with his learning in his hand,"[4] which means that it was not left behind in this world below.

• [The reason Torah requires *kavanah* to ascend on high] albeit the Torah and the Holy One, blessed be He, are altogether One, for He and His will are One [is as follows.] Although the Holy One, blessed be He, fills all worlds alike, nevertheless the worlds are not all of equal rank. The difference is due to the recipients in two respects: Firstly, in that the higher worlds receive a radiance infinitely greater than the lower; and, secondly, in that they receive it without as many "garments" and "screens" as the lower. And this world is the lowest world in both aspects, for the radiance that is in it is greatly contracted unto the utmost limit; hence it is corporeal and material. And even this [contracted radiance] comes in many "garments" and "screens" until it is clothed in the *kelipat nogah*, to animate all clean things in this world, including the vivifying, articulate soul in man. [Consider,] therefore, [this animal soul] as it utters words of Torah and prayer without *kavanah*. These are holy letters, of course, and the *kelipat nogah* in the vivifying soul constitutes no separating curtain in any degree concealing and covering His blessed Holiness clothed in them, as it conceals and covers His blessed Holiness in the vivifying soul when it speaks idle words, or as in the vivifying soul of any of the other living creatures that are clean. And though there is no place that is void of Him,[5] yet He is the "Most hidden One of all the hidden,"[6] and is called the "Hidden G–d."[7] So too, the radiance and extension of vitality from Him, may He be blessed, is hidden in the many dense "garments" and "screens" until it is clothed and concealed in the garment of *nogah*. This is not, however, the case with the holy letters in the words of Torah and Prayer, wherein, on the contrary, the *kelipat nogah* is converted to good and is absorbed into this Holiness, as is discussed above.[8] Nevertheless the glow of His blessed Holiness that is in them is in a state of *tzimtzum* to the utmost limit,

[4] Pesachim *50a*. [5] Tikunei Zohar, Tikun *57, p. 91b*. [6] Ibid., *Introd.* [7] Isa. *45:12*. [8] *Chs. 35, 37; cf. end ch. 53.*

• 14 Nisan

אי עביד בגין יקריה כו׳ וז״ש אשרי מי שבא לכאן ותלמודו בידו פי׳ שלא נשאר למטה בעו״הז. ואף דאורייתא וקב״ה כולא חד שהוא ורצונו אחד הרי קב״ה איהו ממלא כל עלמין בשוה ואעפ״כ אין העולמות שוים במעלתם והשינוי הוא מהמקבלים בב׳ בחי׳ הא׳ שהעליונים מקבלים הארה יותר גדולה לאין קץ מהתחתונים והשנית שמקבלים בלי לבושים ומסכים רבים כ״כ כבתחתונים ועו״הז הוא עולם השפל בב׳ בחי׳ כי ההארה שבו מצומצמת מאד עד קצה האחרון ולכן הוא חומרי וגשמי וגם זאת היא בלבושים ומסכים רבים עד שנתלבשה בקליפת נוגה להחיות כל דברים הטהורים שבעו״הז ובכללם הוא נפש החיונית המדברת שבאדם ולכן כשמדברת דברי תורה ותפלה בלא כוונה אף שהן אותיות קדושות ואין קליפת נוגה שבנפש החיונית מסך מבדיל כלל להסתיר ולכסות על קדושתו ית׳ המלובשת בהן כמו שהיא מסתרת ומכסה על קדושתו ית׳ שבנפש החיונית כשמדברת דברים בטלי׳ ושבנפש החיונית שבשאר בעלי חיים הטהורים דאף דלית אתר פנוי מיני׳ מ״מ איהו סתימו דכל סתימין ונק׳ אל מסתתר וגם ההארה והתפשטות החיות ממנו ית׳ מסתתרת בלבושים ומסכים רבים ועצומים עד שנתלבשה ונסתתרה בלבוש נוגה משא״כ באותיות הקדושות של דברי תורה ותפלה דאדרבה קליפת נוגה מתהפכת לטוב ונכללת בקדושה זו כנ״ל מ״מ ההארה שבהן מקדושתו ית׳ היא בבחי׳ צמצום עד קצה האחרון
מאחר

וסליק כו׳ וד׳ קס״ח ע״ב קלין דאורייתא וצלותא בקעין רקיעין כו׳):

since the voice and speech are material.

● But in the case of prayer with *kavanah* and Torah with *kavanah* "For its own sake," the *kavanah* is clothed in the letters of the speech because it is their source and root, since by reason and cause of it he speaks these letters. Therefore it elevates them to its level in the Ten *Sefirot* of *Yetzirah* or *Beriah*, according to whether the *kavanah* is inspired by intelligent or natural fear and love, . . . as has been discussed above. There the light of the blessed *En Sof*, namely, the blessed Higher Will which is clothed in the letters of the Torah which he studies and in their *kavanah*, or in the prayer and its *kavanah*, or in the commandment and its *kavanah*, shines forth and is revealed with a great and infinite brightness that cannot shine forth and be revealed at all in any manner or form as long as the letters and the commandment are still in this material world, until the era of the end of days, when the world will be uplifted from its materiality, "And the glory of the Lord will be revealed, . . ." as has been previously discussed at length.

▲*Note: And there* [*in the Ten* Sefirot] *shines forth and is revealed also the Supernal Union* (Yichud Elyon) *that is produced by each commandment and by Torah study, this being the union of His blessed attributes which coalesce into one another,* Gevurot *(the "stern" attributes) are sweetened by* Chasadim *(benevolent attributes) through the Supernal Propitious Time of the blessed* En Sof *which shines forth and reveals itself in a manner of a great and intense manifestation by reason of the "impulse" from below, namely, the performance of the commandment, or the occupation in Torah, wherein the Higher Will of the blessed* En Sof *is clothed.*

But the essential Union takes place far higher, in the world of Atzilut, *where the core and essence of His blessed attributes are united with their Emanator, the blessed* En Sof, *and there is the core and essence of the Supreme Will of the blessed* En Sof, *while only a glow from them shines in* Beriah, Yetzirah *and* Asiyah, *in each of these worlds according to its rank. And although the soul of the person who occupies himself in the Torah and in the commandment does not derive from* Atzilut, *nevertheless the Higher Will that is clothed in this commandment and which is identical with the very* halachah *or word of the Torah in which he is occupied, is G-dliness and light of the blessed* En Sof, *the Emanator, for He and His will are One, and by His blessed will He has caused His attributes to emanate from Him yet they are united with Him, may He be blessed. By the*

[Note continued on next page]

▲ In the light of the above it will be clearly understood why fear and love are figuratively called "wings," as is written: "And with twain did he fly,"[9] (and as Rabbi Chayim Vital, of blessed memory, explained in *Sha'ar ha-Yichudim*, ch. 11), that the wings are to a bird what arms are

[9] Isa. *6:2.*

מאחר שהקול והדבור הוא גשמי אבל בתפלה בכוונה ותורה בכוונה לשמה הרי הכוונה מתלבשת באותיות הדבור הואיל והיא מקור ושרש להן שמחמתה ובסיבתה הוא מדבר אותיות אלו לכן היא מעלה אותן עד מקומה בי"ס דיצירה או דבריאה לפי מה שהיא הכוונה בדחילו ורחימו שכליים או טבעיים כו' כנ"ל ושם מאיר ומתגלה אור א"ס ב"ה שהוא רצון העליון ב"ה המלובש באותיות התורה שלומד ובכוונתן או בתפלה ובכוונתה או במצוה ובכוונתה בהארה גדולה לאין קץ מה שלא יכול להאיר ולהתגלות כלל בעוד האותיות והמצוה בעוה"ז הגשמי לא מינה ולא מקצתה עד עת קץ הימין שיתעלה העולם מגשמיותו ונגלה כבוד ה' וגו' כנ"ל באריכות * ובזה יובן היטב הא דדחילו ורחימו נקראי' גדפין ד"מ כדכתי' ובשתים יעופף [וכמ"ש הרח"ו ז"ל בשער היחודים פי"א] שהכנפים בעוף הן זרועות האדם

הגהה

(ושם מאיר ומתגלה ג"כ היחוד העליון הנעשה בכל מצוה ות"ת שהוא יחוד מדותיו ית' שנכללות זו בזו ונמתקות הגבורות בחסדים ע"י עת רצון העליון א"ס ב"ה המאיר ומתגלה בבחי' גילוי רב ועצום באתערותא דלתתא היא עשיית המצוה או עסק התורה שבהן מלובש רצון העליון א"ס ב"ה אך עיקר היחוד הוא למעלה מעלה בעולם האצילות ששם הוא מהות ועצמות מדותיו ית' מיוחדו' במאצילן א"ס ב"ה ושם הוא מהות ועצמות רצון העליון א"ס ב"ה והארתן לבד היא מאירה בבי"ע בכל עולם מהן לפי מעלתו ואף שנפש האדם העוסק בתורה ומצוה זו אינה מאצילות מ"מ הרי רצון העליון המלובש במצוה זו והוא הוא עצמו הדבר הלכה והתורה שעוסק בה הוא אלהות ואור א"ס המאציל ב"ה שהוא ורצונו אחד וברצונו ית' האציל מדותיו המיוחדות בו ית' וע"י גילוי

[Note continued from previous page]
revelation of His will, which becomes manifest through this occupation with the Torah and the particular commandment they [the attributes] coalesce into one another and the Gevurot *are sweetened by* Chasadim *at this propitious moment.*

to a man.... And in *Tikunim* it is explained that they who occupy themselves with Torah and commandments in fear and love are called "children"; otherwise they are called "fledglings" that cannot fly.

Note: In Tikun 45 *it is written that the [figure of a] bird represents Metatron.*[10] *His head is the letter* yod, *and the body is the letter* vav *and the two wings are the two [letters]* hai,[11] *and so forth. This refers to the world of* Yetzirah *which is identified with Metatron, wherein are the "bodies" of the* halachot *of the* Mishnah; *his head symbolises the intellectual aspects, the* chochmah, binah, da'at *(ChaBaD), that is the inwardness of the* halachot, *their esoteric meaning and their reasons; whilst the two wings—fear and love—refer to the higher* hai, *which is love, and the lower* hai, *which is the lower fear (*yirah tattaah*), namely, the yoke of the Kingdom of Heaven and the dread of G–d, like the awe one feels in the presence of a king, for example; for this is an external and exposed fear, unlike the higher fear* (yirah ilaah), *which is a feeling of shame, which is of "The hidden things belonging to the Lord our G–d," and it is found in the Higher Wisdom* (chochmah ilaah), *symbolising the letter* yod *of the blessed Name [Tetragrammaton], as is explained in* Ra'aya Mehemna.

▲ For just as the wings of a bird are not the essential parts of it, and its vitality does not depend on them at all—as we have learned, that "If its wings have been removed, it is *kasher*" (ritually clean),[12] the essential parts being its head and entire body, while the wings merely serve the head and body, enabling it to fly with their aid—so, by way of example, are the Torah and commandments the essential aspect of the Higher Union through the manifestation of the Higher Will that is revealed through them, while the fear and love raise them to that place where the Will, the light of the blessed *En Sof*, and the union (*Yichud*), are revealed, namely, the worlds of *Yetzirah* and *Beriah*.

Note: Or even in [the world of] Asiyah, *in the ten* Sefirot *of holiness, the abode of the active commandments and also of [the study of] Holy Writ. But in the case of the Mishnah, the* Yichud *and light of the blessed* En Sof *are revealed in [the world of]* Yetzirah; *and, in the case of Talmud, in [the world of]* Beriah. *This means that when one studies Holy Writ, the* Yichud *and light of the blessed* En Sof *are diffused from* Atzilut *to* Asiyah; *and in [the study of] Mishnah [they reach] to* Yetzirah *only; and in [the case of] Talmud—to* Beriah *only. For they are all in* Atzilut.

[Note continued on next page]

●▲And although fear and love also form part of the 613 commandments,[13] nevertheless they are called "wings," for the consummation of love is the service out of love, and love without service is a "love of delights"[14]

---

[10] *The highest ranking angel.* [11] *Referring to the Tetragrammaton.* [12] Chullin *56b.* [13] *Cf. Maimonides,* Sefer Hamitzvot, *Precepts 3 & 4.* [14] *Cf. chs. 9, 14, above.*

האדם כו׳ ובתיקונים פי׳ שהעוסקים בתורה ומצות בדחילו ורחימו נקראים בנים ואם לאו נק׳ אפרוחים דלא יכלין לפרחא * כי כמו שכנפי העוף אינם עיקר העוף ואין חיותו תלוי בהם כלל כדתנן ניטלו אגפיה כשרה והעיקר הוא ראשו וכל גופו והכנפיי׳ אינם רק משמשים לראשו וגופו לפרחא בהון וכך ד״מ התורה ומצות הן עיקר היחוד העליון ע״י גילוי רצון העליון המתגלה על ידיהן והדחילו ורחימו הם מעלים אותן למקום שיתגלה בו הרצון אור אין סוף ברוך הוא והיחוד שהן יצירה ובריאה * והנה אף דדחילו ורחימו הם ג״כ מתרי״ג מצות אעפ״כ נקראין גדפין להיות כי תכלית האהבה היא העבודה מאהבה ואהבה בלי עבודה היא אהבה

בתענוגים

גילוי רצונו המתגלה ע״י עסק תורה ומצוה זו הן נכללות זו בזו ונמתקות הגבורות בחסדים בעת רצון זו):

הגהה

(ובתיקון מ״ה דעופא הוא מט״ט רישא דיליה י׳ וגופא וא״ו ותרין גדפין ה׳ ה׳ כו׳ והיינו עולם היצירה שנקרא מט״ט ובו הן גופי הלכות שבמשנה ורישא דיליה הן המוחין ובחי׳ חב״ד שהן פנימיות ההלכות וסודן וטעמיהן ותרין גדפין דחילו ורחימו הן ה׳ עילאה שהיא רחימו וה׳ תתאה היא יראה תתאה עול מלכות שמים ופחד ה׳ כפחד המלך ד״מ שהיא יראה חיצונית ונגלית משא״כ יראה עילאה יראו בושת היא מהנסתרות לה׳ אלהינו והיא בחכמה עילאה יו״ד של שם הוי״ה ב״ה כמ״ש בר״מ):

הגהה

(או אפילו בעשיה בי״ס דקדושה מקום מצות מעשיות וכן מקרא אבל במשנה מתגלה היחוד ואור אין סוף ברוך הוא ביצירה ובתלמוד בבריא׳ דהיינו שבלימוד מקרא מתפשט היחוד ואור א״ס ב״ה מאצילו׳ עד העשיה ובמשנה עד היצירה לבדה ובתלמוד עד הבריאה לבדה כי כולן באצילות

אבל

[Note continued from previous page]
As for Kabbalah, it is not diffused at all from Atzilut *to* Beriah, Yetzirah *and* Asiyah, *as is explained in* Peri Etz Chayim.

delighting in G–d, which is of the nature of the world to come and the receiving of reward, as it is written, "This day—to do them," "and tomorrow" [in the world to come] — to receive one's reward.[15] But he who has not attained this dimension of savouring the nature of the world to come, but whose soul still yearns and thirsts for G–d and goes out to Him all day, yet he does not quench his thirst with the water of the Torah that is in front of him—such a man is like one who stands in a river and cries: "Water! Water to drink!" Thus the prophet laments over such a man: "Ho, every one that thirsteth, go ye to the waters."[16] For in its simple meaning the verse makes no sense: Surely, he who is thirsty and longs to learn will study of his own accord; why, then, does the prophet need to rebuke him "Ho?" This is explained at length elsewhere.

●▲*Chapter 41*

One must, however, constantly bear in mind the beginning of the service and its core and root. By this is meant that, although fear is the root of "Depart from evil" and love—of "Do good," nevertheless it is not sufficient to awaken the love alone to do good, but one must at least first arouse the innate fear which lies hidden in the heart of every Jew not to rebel against the Supreme King of kings, the Holy One, blessed be He, as has been stated above,[1] so that this [fear] shall manifest itself in his heart or, at least, his mind. This means that he should at least contemplate in his thought on the greatness of the blessed *En Sof*, and on His Kingship, which extends to all worlds, both higher and lower, and that "He fills all worlds and encompasses all worlds," as is written: "Do I not fill heaven and earth?"[2] Yet He leaves both the higher and lower [worlds] and uniquely bestows His Kingdom upon His people Israel, in general, and upon him in particular, as, indeed, a man is obliged to say: "For my sake was the world created."[3] And on his part, he accepts His Kingdom upon himself, that He be King over him, to serve Him and do His will in ▲all kinds of servile work. "And, behold, G–d stands over him,"[4] and "The whole world is full of His glory,"[5] and He looks upon him and "Searches his reins and heart"[6] [to see] if he is serving Him

---

[15] Eruvin *22a*. [16] Isa. *55:1*.

Chapter 41
[1] *Ch. 4; see also end of chs. 19, 38.*
[2] Jer. *23:24*. [3] Sanhedrin *ch.* *4*, Mishnah *5*. [4] *Allusion to* Gen. *28:13*. [5] Isa. *6:3*. [6] Jer. *11:20*.

בתענוגים להתענג על ה׳ מעין עוה״ב וקבלת שכר והיום לעשות׳ כתי׳ ולמחר לקבל שכרם ומי שלא הגיע למדה זו לטעום מעין עוה״ב אלא עדיין נפשו שוקקה וצמאה לה׳ וכלתה אליו כל היום ואינו מרוה צמאונו במי התורה שלפניו הרי זה כמי שעומד בנהר וצועק מים מים לשתות כמו שקובל עליו הנביא הוי כל צמא לכו למים. כי לפי פשוטו אינו מובן דמי שהוא צמא ומתאווה ללמוד פשיטא שילמוד מעצמו ולמה לו לנביא לצעוק עליו הוי וכמ״ש במ״א באריכות:

אבל קבלה אינה מתפשטת כלל מאצילות לבי״ע כמ״ש בפרע״ח):

פרק מא ברם צריך להיות לזכרון תמיד ראשית העבודה ועיקרה ושרשה. והוא כי אף שהיראה היא שרש לסור מרע והאהבה לועשה טוב. אעפ״כ לא די לעורר האהבה לבדה לועשה טוב ולפחות צריך לעורר תחלה היראה הטבעית המסותרת בלב כל ישראל שלא למרוד בממ״ה הקב״ה כנ״ל שתהא בהתגלות לבו או מוחו עכ״פ דהיינו להתבונן במחשבתו עכ״פ גדולת א״ס ב״ה ומלכותו אשר היא מלכות כל עולמים עליונים ותחתונים ואיהו ממלא כל עלמין וסובב כל עלמין וכמ״ש הלא את השמים ואת הארץ אני מלא ומניח העליונים ותחתונים ומייחד מלכותו על עמו ישראל בכלל ועליו בפרט כי חייב אדם לומר בשבילי נברא העולם והוא גם הוא מקבל עליו מלכותו להיות מלך עליו ולעבדו ולעשות רצונו בכל מיני עבודת עבד. והנה ה׳ נצב עליו ומלא כל הארץ כבודו ומביט עליו ובוחן כליות ולב אם עובדו כראוי

as is fitting. Therefore he must serve in His presence with awe and fear like one standing before the king.

One must meditate profoundly and at length on this thought according to the capacity of apprehension of his brain and thought and according to the time available to him, before he occupies himself with Torah or a commandment, such as prior to ●▲putting on his *Tallit* or phylacteries. He should also reflect how the light of the blessed *En Sof*, which encompasses all worlds and pervades all worlds, which is identical with the Higher Will, is clothed in the letters and wisdom of the Torah and in the *tzitzit* (Fringes) and the phylacteries, and through his study or donning these latter he draws over himself His blessed light, that is, over "The portion of G-dliness from above" which is within his body,[7] that it may be absorbed and nullified in His blessed light. Specifically, in the case of the phylacteries, [he should intend] that the attributes of wisdom and understanding which are in his divine soul may be nullified and absorbed into the attributes of wisdom and understanding of the blessed *En Sof*, which are clothed, in particular, in the chapters of קדש and והיה כי יביאך.[8] That is to say, that he should use his wisdom and understanding that are in his soul, only for G-d alone. Similarly that the attribute of *da'at* that is in his soul, which includes both *chesed* (kindness) and *gevurah* (sternness), i.e., fear and love, in his heart, be nullified and absorbed into the attribute of the Higher Knowledge, which contains *chesed* and *gevurah* which is clothed in the chapters of שמע and והיה אם שמע.[9] This is what is written in the *Shulchan Aruch*:[10] "That he make his heart and brain ▲subservient to Him. . . ." And whilst putting on the *tzitzit* he should bear in mind, what is written in the Zohar, namely, to draw over himself His blessed Kingdom, which is the Kingdom over all worlds, . . . to bestow it particularly upon us through this commandment. And this corresponds to the subject of: "Thou shalt surely set a king over thee."[11]

In such a case, even though after all this [contemplation] no fear or dread descends upon him in a manifest manner in his heart, nevertheless since he accepts upon himself the Kingdom of Heaven and draws fear of Him, blessed be He, over himself in his conscious thought and rational volition, and this submission is beyond doubt a sincere one—for it is the nature of all Jewish souls not to rebel against the blessed Holy King—then the Torah he studies or the commandment he performs because of this submission and because of this inspired fear in his mind, are termed "perfect service,"

---

[7] *See beg. ch. 2.* [8] *Two of the four parchment scrolls contained in the* Tefillin *(phylacteries) are inscribed with the portions* Ex. *13:1–10 and* Ex. *13:11–16; the other two are mentioned below.* [9] Deut. *6:4–8 and* Deut. *11:13–21. See note above.* [10] Orach Chayim, *sec. 25, 5.* [11] Deut. *17:15.*

כראוי . ועל כן צריך לעבוד לפניו באימה וביראה כעומד לפני המלך ויעמיק במחשבה זו ויאריך בה כפי יכולת השגת מוחו ומחשבתו וכפי הפנאי שלו לפני עסק התורה או המצוה כמו לפני לבישת טלית ותפילין וגם יתבונן איך שאור אין סוף ב"ה הסובב כל עלמין וממלא כל עלמין הוא רצון העליון הוא מלובש באותיו' וחכמת התורה או בציצית ותפילין אלו ובקריאתו או בלבישתו הוא ממשיך אורו ית' עליו דהיינו על חלק אלוה ממעל שבתוך גופו ליכלל וליבטל באורו יתברך ודרך פרט בתפילין ליבטל וליכלל בחי' חכמתו ובינתו שבנפשו האלהית בבחי' חכמתו ובינתו של א"ס ב"ה המלובשות הדך פרט בפ' קדש והיה כי יביאך דהיינו שלא להשתמש בחכמתו ובינתו שבנפשו בלתי לה' לבדו וכן ליבטל ולכלול בחי' הדעת שבנפשו הכולל חו"ג שהן יראה ואהבה שבלבו בבחי' דעת העליון הכולל חו"ג המלובש בפ' שמע והיה אם שמוע והיינו כמ"ש בש"ע לשעבד הלב והמוח כו' ובעטיפת ציצית יכוין כמ"ש בזהר להמשיך עליו מלכותו ית' אשר היא מלכות כל עולמים וכו' לייחדה עלינו ע"י מצוה זו והוא כענין שום תשים עליך מלך ואזי אף אם בכל זאת לא תפול עליו אימה ופחד בהתגלות לבו מ"מ מאחר שמקבל עליו מלכות שמים וממשיך עליו יראתו ית' בהתגלות מחשבתו ורצונו שבמוחו וקבלה זו היא אמיתית בלי שום ספק שהרי היא טבע נפשות כל ישראל שלא למרוד במלך הקדוש ית' הרי התורה שלומד או המצוה שעושה מחמת קבלה זו ומחמת המשכת היראה שבמוחו נקראות בשם עבודה שלימה ככל

like all service [performed] by a slave to his master or to his king.

▲ On the other hand, if one studies and performs the commandment with love alone, in order to cleave to Him through His Torah or commandments, it is not termed "Service of a servant," which is what the Torah demands, viz., "And ye shall serve the Lord your G–d, . . ."[12] and "Him shall ye serve, . . ."[13] as explained in the *Zohar* (*Parshat Behar*): "Just like the ox on which one first places a yoke in order to make it useful to the world . . . so too must a human being first of all submit to the yoke of the Kingdom of Heaven . . . and if this submission is not found in him, holiness cannot rest on him. . . ."[14] (See also *Ra'aya Mehemna*, ibid., 111b) that every man must be of two categories and levels, namely, the category of a servant and that of a son. And although there is a son who is also a servant, it is not possible to attain to this degree without the prerequisite of *yirah ilaah*, as is known to the initiated.

●▲ Furthermore, even in the case of him who in his mind and thought feels no fear or shame on account of the poor capacity of his soul, originating in the lower degrees of the Ten *Sefirot* of *Asiyah*, nevertheless since he is intent in his service to serve the King, it is a complete service, for fear and service are accounted as two commandments of the total of 613, and they do not deter each other. But as a matter of fact, he also fulfils the commandment of fear in that he introduces the fear into his thought, for at this hour and moment, at any rate, there rests on him the fear of Heaven, at least like the fear in the presence of an ordinary mortal, even not a king, who is watching him, when he would restrain himself from doing anything unbecoming in the other's eyes. This is termed fear, as Rabbi Yochanan ben Zakkai said to his disciples: "May it be G–d's will that the fear of Heaven be upon you like the fear of a human being . . . for you know that when a person commits a sin, he says [to himself], 'May no-one see me.'. . ."[15] However, such fear is termed *yirah tattaah* ("lower fear") and *yirat chet* ("fear of sin") which precedes wisdom,[16] while the higher fear is the fear of shame. . . .[17] For there are two kinds of fear. . . .

---

[12] Ex. *23:25*. [13] Deut. *13:5*. [14] Zohar *III, p. 108a, with slight changes*. [15] Berachot *28b*. [16] Avot *3:9*. [17] *See ch. 3, above.*

ככל עבודת העבד לאדונו ומלכו משא"כ אם לומד ומקיים המצוה באהבה לבדה כדי לדבקה בו על ידי תורתו ומצותיו אינה נקראת בשם עבודת העבד והתורה אמרה ועבדתם את ה' אלהיכם וגו' ואותו תעבודו וגו' וכמ"ש בזהר [פ' בהר] כהאי תורא דיהבין עליה עול בקדמיתא בגין לאפקא מיניה טב לעלמא כו' הכי נמי אצטריך לב"נ לקבלא עליה עול מלכות שמים בקדמיתא כו' ואי האי לא אשתכח גביה לא שריא ביה קדוש' כו' [וברע"מ שם ד' ק"א ע"ב] שכל אדם צ"ל בשתי בחי' ומדרגות והן בחי' עבד ובחי' בן ואף דיש בן שהוא ג"כ עבד הרי אי אפשר לבא למדרגה זו בלי קדימת היראה עילאה כידוע ליודעים: והנה אף מי שגם במוחו ובמחשבתו אינו מרגיש שום יראה ובושה מפני פחיתות ערך נפשו ממקור חוצבה ממדרגות תחתונו' דו"ם דעשיה אעפ"כ מאחר שמתכוין בעבודתו כדי לעבוד את המלך הרי זו עבודה גמורה כי היראה והעבודה נחשבות לשתי מצות במנין תרי"ג ואינן מעכבות זו את זו. ועוד שבאמת מקיים גם מצות יראה במה שממשיך היראה במחשבתו כי בשעה ורגע זו עכ"פ מורא שמים עליו עכ"פ כמורא בשר ודם הדיוט לפחות שאינו מלך המביט עליו שנמנע בעבורו מלעשות דבר שאינו הגון בעיניו שזו נק' יראה כמו שאמר רבן יוחנן בן זכאי לתלמידיו יהי רצון שיהא מורא שמים עליכם כמורא בשר ודם כו' תדעו כשאדם עובר עבירה אומר שלא יראני אדם כו' רק שיראה זו נקראת יראה תתאה ויראת חטא שקודמת לחכמתו ויראה עילאה הוא ירא בושת כו' דאית יראה ואית יראה כו'

אבל

Without any fear at all, however, it does not soar on high through love alone, just as a bird cannot fly with one wing, for fear and love are the two wings (as has been explained in the *Tikunim*). Similarly, fear alone is but one wing, and one's service cannot ascend on high with it, although it is termed the "Service of a servant," for there must also be the filial quality, in order to awaken, at least, the natural love that is hidden in his heart, to become conscious of it in his mind at any rate, to be aware of his love of the One G–d in his thought and desire to cleave to Him, may He be blessed. This should be his *kavanah* when occupying himself with the Torah or the particular commandment, that his divine soul as well as his vivifying soul, together with their "garments," shall cleave to Him, as has been explained above.[18]

●▲ Yet in fact the Rabbis, of blessed memory, have said that a man should never separate himself from the community.[19] Therefore he should intend to unite and attach to Him, blessed be He, the fount of his divine soul and the fount of the souls of all Israel, being the spirit of His blessed mouth, called by the name *Shechinah*,[20] because it dwells and clothes itself in all worlds, animating them and giving them existence, and is that which imbues him with the power of speech to utter the words of Torah, or with the power of action to perform the particular commandment.

This union is attained through the drawing forth of the light of the blessed *En Sof* here below by means of occupation in the Torah and the commandments wherein [the light of the *En Sof*] is clothed. And he should be intent on drawing His blessed light over the fount of his soul and of the souls of all Israel to unite them. The meaning of this union will be discussed at length later on, note there.[21] This is the meaning of "For the sake of the Union of the Holy One, blessed be He, with His *Shechinah*, in the name of all Israel."[22]

Note: Thereby the Gevurot *will, of themselves, also be sweetened by the* Chasadim *through the coalescence of the* Middot *and their union by means of the revelation of the blessed Higher Will which is revealed on high through the impulsion from below, namely, its revelation here below in the occupation in the Torah and commandment which are His blessed will. Thus it is written in*

[Note continued on next page]

● And although in order that this *kavanah* should be sincere in his heart, so that his heart should truly desire this *Yichud Elyon* (Higher Union), there needs to be in his heart the "great love" (אהבה רבה) for G–d alone, to do what is gratifying only to Him and not [even] for the purpose of satiating his own soul

[18] *Chs. 23, 35, 37. See also ch. 14.* [19] Berachot *49b; here in a figurative sense.* [20] *See ch. 37, above.* [21] *Ch. 46,* infra. [22] *Text of this declaration, introducing the Morning Prayer, is to be found in the Prayer Books following the Lurianic rite (*Peri Etz Chayim; Mishnat Chasidim, *etc.).*

אבל בלי יראה כלל לא פרחא לעילא באהבה לבדה כמו שהעוף אינו יכול לפרוח בכנף אחד דדחילו ורחימו הן תרין גדפין [כמ"ש בתיקונים] וכן היראה לבדה היא כנף אחד ולא פרחא בה לעילא אף שנק' עבודת עבד וצריך להיות ג"כ בחי' בן לעורר האהבה הטבעית עכ"פ המסותרת בלבו שתהא בהתגלות מוחו עכ"פ לזכור אהבתו לה' אחד במחשבתו וברצונו לדבקה בו ית' וזאת תהיה כוונתו בעסק התורה או המצוה הזו לדבקה בו נפשו האלהית והחיונית ולבושיהן כנ"ל. אך אמנם אמרו רז"ל לעולם אל יוציא אדם עצמו מן הכלל לכן יתכוין ליחד ולדבקה בו ית' מקור נפשו האלהית ומקור נפשות כל ישראל שהוא רוח פיו ית' הנק' בשם שכינה על שם ששוכנת ומתלבשת תוך כל עלמין להחיותן ולקיימן והיא היא המשפעת בו כח הדבור הזה שמדבר בדברי תורה או כח המעשה הזה לעשות מצוה זו ויחוד זה הוא ע"י המשכת אור א"ס ב"ה למטה ע"י עסק התורה והמצות שהוא מלובש בהן ויתכוין להמשיך אורו ית' על מקור נפשו ונפשות כל ישראל לייחדן וכמ"ש לקמן פי' יחוד זה באריכות ע"ש. וזהו פי' לשם יחוד קב"ה ושכינתיה בשם כל ישראל* ואף שלהיות כוונה זו אמיתית בלבו שיהיה לבו חפץ באמת יחוד העליון הזה צריך להיות בלבו אהבה רבה לה' לבדו לעשות נחת רוח לפניו לבד ולא לרוות נפשו

הצמאה

הגהה

(וגם על ידי זה יתמתקו גם כן הגבורות בחסדים ממילא בהתכללות המדות ויחודם על ידי גילוי רצון העליון ב"ה המתגלה למעלה באתערותא דלתתא הוא גילויו למטה בעסק התורה והמצוה שהן רצונו ית' וכמ"ש באדרא

[Note continued from previous page]
Idra Rabba *and in* Mishnat Chassidim, *tractate* Arich Anpin, *ch. 4, that the 613 commandments of the Torah are derived from the "whiteness" of* Arich Anpin,[23] *which is the Higher Will, the source of the* Chasadim. *

which thirsts for G–d, but he must be "Like a son who strives for the sake of his father and mother, whom he loves more than his own body and soul, . . ." (as explained above[24] in the name of *Ra'aya Mehemna*), nevertheless every man should habituate himself to this *kavanah.* For though it may not be in his heart in perfect and complete truth, so that he should long for it with all his heart, nevertheless his heart does genuinely desire it to some small extent, because of the natural love in every Jewish heart to do whatever is the blessed Higher Will. And this union is his true desire, namely the Higher Union in *Atzilut,* which is produced by the impulsion from below, through the union of the divine soul and its absorption into the light of G–d which is clothed in the Torah and commandments in which it occupies itself so that they become One in reality, as has been explained above.[25] For by reason of this, are also united the source of Torah and commandments, i.e., the Holy One, blessed be He, with the source of his divine soul which is called *Shechinah.* These are the two categories of "filling all worlds" and of "encompassing all worlds,"[26] as is explained elsewhere at length.

• But the union of the soul with, and its absorption into, the light of G–d, making them one, this is what every member of Israel desires in very truth, utterly, with all his heart and all his soul, because of the natural love that is hidden in every Jewish heart to cleave to G–d and not, under any circumstances, to be parted or sundered or separated, G–d forbid, from His blessed Unity and Oneness, even at the cost of his very life. And occupation in the Torah and commandments and prayer is also a matter of actual surrender of the soul, as when it leaves the body at the end of seventy years, for it no longer thinks of bodily needs, but its thought is united with, and clothed in, the letters of the Torah and prayer, which are the word and thought of the blessed G–d, and they truly become one. This is [also] the whole occupation of the souls in the Garden of Eden, as is stated in the *Gemara* and in the *Zohar,*

---

[23] *See* Glossary. [24] *Ch. 10.* [25] *Chs. 5, 23.* [26] *The immanent and transcending Divine attributes are thus brought into unity through the agency of man.*

• 22 Nisan

*The daily portion for the 20th Nisan ends here.

הצמאה לה׳ אלא כברא דאשתדל בתר אבוי ואמי׳ דרחים לון יתיר מגרמיה ונפשיה כו׳ [כמ״ש לעיל בשם רעיא מהימנא]. מ״מ יש לכל אדם להרגיל עצמו בכוונה זו כי אף שאינה באמת לאמיתו לגמרי בלבו שיחפוץ בזה בכל לבו מ״מ מעט מזער חפץ לבו בזה באמת מפני אהבה הטבעית שבלב כל ישראל לעשות כל מה שהוא רצון העליון ב״ה ויחוד זה הוא רצונו האמיתי והיינו יחוד העליון שבאצילות הנעשה באתערותא דלתתא ע״י יחוד נפש האלהית והתכללותה באור ה׳ המלובש בתורה ומצות שעוסקת בהן והיו לאחדי׳ ממש כמש״ל כי ע״ז מתיחדים ג״כ מקור התורה והמצות שהוא הקב״ה עם מקור נפשו האלהית הנקרא בשם שכינה שהן בחי׳ ממלא כל עלמין ובחי׳ סובב כל עלמין כמ״ש במ״א באריכות. אבל יחוד נפשו והתכללותה באור ה׳ להיות לאחדים בזה חפץ כל אדם מישראל באמת לאמיתו לגמרי בכל לב ובכל נפש מאהבה הטבעית המסותרת בלב כל ישראל לדבקה בה׳ ולא ליפרד ולהיות נכרת ונבדל ח״ו מיחודו ואחדותו ית׳ בשום אופן אפי׳ במסירת נפש ממש ועסק התורה ומצות והתפלה הוא ג״כ ענין מסירת נפש ממש כמו בצאתה מן הגוף במלאת שבעים שנה שאינה מהרהרת בצרכי הגוף אלא מחשבתה מיוחדת ומלובשת באותיות התורה והתפלה שהן דבר ה׳ ומחשבתו ית׳ והיו לאחדים ממש שזהו כל עסק הנשמות בג״ע כדאיתא בגמרא ובזהר אלא

באדרא רבא ובמשנת חסידים מסכת א״א פ״ד שתרי״ג מצות התורה נמשכות מחיוורתא דא״א שהוא רצון העליון מקור החסדים):

except that there they find delight in their apprehension of, and absorption into, the light of G–d.

This is why it was ordained to recite at the beginning of the morning blessings before the prayer: "O my G–d, the soul which Thou gavest me is pure . . . Thou didst breathe it into me . . . and Thou wilt take it from me. . . ." Meaning: Inasmuch as Thou didst breathe it into me and Thou wilt take it from me, I therefore as of now hand it over and return it to Thee to unite it with Thy Oneness, as is written: "Unto Thee, O Lord, do I lift up my soul,"[27] that is, through the binding of my thought with Thy thought, and of my speech with Thy speech, by means of the letters of the Torah and of prayer; and, especially, when one speaks to G–d in the second person, as "Blessed art *Thou*," and the like.

●▲ With this preparedness to surrender his soul to G–d, he should begin [to recite] the morning benedictions: "Blessed art Thou. . . ." Similarly, with this preparedness he should also begin to learn a regular course of study immediately after prayer. So, also in the course of the day, such preparation is necessary at least before he begins to study, as is known that the essential preparation [of intent] "for its own sake," where it is *sine qua non*, is before the beginning of study in the case of Intermediates. This is the same as in the case of [writing] a bill of divorce or a scroll of the Torah, requiring *sine qua non* "for their own sake," and it is sufficient if at the commencement of writing he says: "I am now about to write for the sacred purpose of the scroll of the Law,"[28] or [in the case of a bill of divorce] "For him and for her. . . ."[29] However, when he studies for a number of consecutive hours he should reflect on the preparedness referred to above, at least at hourly intervals. For in each hour there is a different flow from the higher worlds to animate those who dwell here below, while the flow of vitality of the previous hour returns to its source (in accordance with the esoteric principle of the "Advance and Retreat" in *Sefer Yetzirah*) together with all the Torah and good deeds of those who dwell here below [performed within that hour]. For in each hour of the twelve hours of the day, there rules one of the twelve combinations of the blessed Tetragrammaton, whilst the combinations of the name A-D-N-Y rule at night, as is known.[30]

▲ Now, all his intent in the surrender of his soul to G–d through Torah and prayer, to elevate the spark of G–dliness therein back to its source, should be solely for the purpose of bringing gratification before Him, may He be blessed, as, for example, the joy of a king when his only son returns to him, being released from captivity

---

[27] Ps. *25:1*. [28] Shulchan Aruch, Yoreh Deah *274:1*. [29] Ibid., Even HaEzer *131:1, 8*. [30] *Re: doctrine of* tzerufei otiot *("letter combinations") in the process of Creation, see* Sha'ar ha-Yichud veha-Emunah, *ch. 1*.

אלא ששם מתענגים בהשגתם והתכללותם באור ה׳ וזהו שתקנו בתחלת ברכות השחר קודם התפלה אלהי נשמה וכו׳ ואתה נפחתה כו׳ ואתה עתיד ליטלה ממני כו׳ כלומ׳ מאחר שאתה נפחתה בי ואתה עתיד ליטלה ממני לכן מעתה אני מוסרה ומחזירה לך לייחדה באחדותך וכמ״ש אליך ה׳ נפשי אשא והיינו על ידי התקשרות מחשבתי במחשבתך ודיבורי בדיבורך באותיות התורה והתפלה ובפרט באמירה לה׳ לנכח כמו ברוך אתה וכה״ג והנה בהכנה זו של מסירת נפשו לה׳ יתחיל ברכות השחר ברוך אתה כו׳ וכן בהכנה זו יתחיל ללמוד שיעור קבוע מיד אחר התפלה וכן באמצע היום קודם שיתחיל ללמוד צריכה הכנה זו לפחות כנודע שעיקר ההכנה לשמה לעכב הוא בתחל׳ הלימוד בבינונים וכמו בגט וס״ת שצריכים לשמה לעכב ודיו שיאמר בתחלת הכתיבה הריני כותב לשם קדושת ס״ת או לשמו ולשמה כו׳ וכשלומד שעות הרבה רצופות יש לו להתבונן בהכנה זו הנ״ל בכל שעה ושעה עכ״פ כי בכל שעה ושעה היא המשכה אחרת מעולמות עליונים להחיות התחתונים והמשכת החיות שבשעה שלפניה חוזרת למקורה [בסוד רצוא ושוב שבס׳ יצירה] עם כל התורה ומעשים טובים של התחתונים כי בכל שעה שולט צירוף אחד מי״ב צירופי שם הוי״ה ב״ה בי״ב שעות היום וצירופי שם אדנ״י בלילה כנודע. והנה כל כוונתו במסירת נפשו לה׳ ע״י התורה והתפלה להעלות ניצוץ אלהות שבתוכה למקורו תהא רק כדי לעשות נחת רוח לפניו ית׳ כמשל שמחת המלך בבוא אליו בנו יחידו בצאתו מן השביה

ובית

or imprisonment, as has been mentioned above.[31]

This *kavanah* is genuinely and truly sincere in every Jewish soul at every season and every hour, by virtue of the natural love which is a heritage bequeathed to us from our ancestors. Nevertheless one needs to establish set periods for reflecting on the greatness of G-d in order to attain intelligent fear and love, and with all that, perhaps one may succeed, as has been stated previously.

•▲ Chapter 42

In the light of what has already been said on the subject of the lower kind of fear, one will clearly understand the Talmudic comment on the verse: "And now, O Israel, what doth the Lord thy G-d require of thee, but to fear the Lord thy G-d."[1] [The *Gemara* asks:] "Is fear, then, such a small thing?" [And the *Gemara* replies:] "Yes, in the case of Moses it was a small thing," and so forth.[2]

At first glance the answer is incomprehensible, for it is written: "What doth the Lord require of *thee*?" [not of Moses]. The explanation, however, is as follows: Each and every soul of the house of Israel contains within it something of the quality of our teacher Moses, peace unto him, for he is one of the "seven shepherds"[3] who cause vitality and G-dliness to flow to the community of Jewish souls, for which reason they are called "shepherds." Our teacher, Moses, peace unto him, is the sum of them all, and he is called "the faithful shepherd." This means that he brings down the quality of *da'at* (knowledge) to the community of Israel that they may know the Lord, each according to the capacity of his soul and its root above, and its nurture from the root of the soul of our teacher Moses, peace unto him, which is rooted in the *Da'at Elyon* (Higher Knowledge) of the Ten *Sefirot* of *Atzilut*, which are united with their blessed Emanator, for He and His Knowledge are One, and He is the Knowledge. . . .[4]

In addition and beyond this [general influence to the community as a whole] there descend, in every generation, sparks from the soul of our teacher Moses, peace unto him, and they clothe themselves in the body and soul of the sages of that generation, the "eyes" of the congregation,[5] to impart knowledge to the people that they may know the greatness of G-d and serve Him with heart and soul. For the service of the heart is according to the *da'at* (knowledge) as is written: "Know thou the G-d of thy father, and serve Him with a perfect heart and with a willing mind."[6] But regarding the future [Messianic Era] it is written: "And they shall teach no more every man his neighbour, and every man his brother, saying, Know the Lord: for they shall all know Me. . . ."[7]

However, the essence of knowledge is not the knowing alone, that people should know the greatness of G-d from

[31] *Ch. 31.*

Chapter 42
[1] Deut. *10:12*. [2] Berachot *33b*. [3] Sukkah *52b*; *another version in* Tikunim, *end*; Zohar Chadash (*104a*). [4] *Ref. to Maimonides' statement already quoted in chs. 2, 4, 23.* [5] *See* Taanit *24a and* Rashi, loc. cit.; Num. *16:24*. [6] *I* Chron. *28:9*. [7] Jer. *31:33*.

ובית האסורים כנ"ל. והנה כוונה זו היא אמיתית באמת לאמיתו לגמרי בכל נפש מישראל בכל עת ובכל שעה מאהבה הטבעית שהיא ירושה לנו מאבותינו. רק שצריך לקבוע עתים להתבונן בגדולת ה' להשיג דחילו ורחימו שכליים וכולי האי ואולי וכו' כנ"ל:

פרק מב

והנה במ"ש לעיל בענין יראה תתאה יובן היטב מ"ש בגמ' על פסוק ועתה ישראל מה ה' אלהיך שואל מעמך כי אם ליראה את ה' אלהיך אטו יראה מילתא זוטרתי היא אין לגבי משה מילתא זוטרתי היא וכו' דלכאורה אינו מובן התירוץ דהא שואל מעמך כתיב. אלא הענין הוא כי כל נפש ונפש מבית ישראל יש בה מבחי' משרע"ה כי הוא משבעה רועים הממשיכים חיות ואלהות לכללו' נשמות ישראל שלכן נקראים בשם רועים ומשרע"ה הוא כללו' כולם ונקרא רעיא מהימנא דהיינו שממשיך בחי' הדעת לכללות ישראל לידע את ה' כל אחד כפי השגת נשמתו ושרשה למעלה ויניקתה משרש נשמת משרע"ה המושרשת בדעת העליון שבי"ס דאצילות המיוחדות במאצילן ב"ה שהוא ודעתו אחד והוא המדע כו'. ועוד זאת יתר על כן בכל דור ודור יורדין ניצוצין מנשמת משרע"ה ומתלבשין בגוף ונפש של חכמי הדור עיני העדה ללמד דעת את העם ולידע גדולת ה' ולעבדו בלב ונפש כי העבודה שבלב היא לפי הדעת כמ"ש דע את אלהי אביך ועבדהו בלב שלם ונפש חפיצה ולעתיד הוא אומר ולא ילמדו איש את רעהו לאמר דעו את ה' כי כולם ידעו אותי וגו' אך עיקר הדעת אינה הידיעה לבדה שידעו גדולת ה' מפי סופרים

authors and books; but the essential thing is to immerse one's mind deeply into the the greatness of G–d and fix one's thought on G–d with all the strength and vigour of the heart and mind, until his thought shall be bound to G–d with a strong and mighty bond, as it is bound to a material thing that he sees with his physical eyes and concentrates his thought on it. For it is known that *da'at* connotes union, as in the phrase "And Adam *yada* (knew) ●▲Eve. . . ."[8] This capacity and this quality of attaching one's "knowledge" to G–d is present in every soul of the House of Israel by virtue of its nurture from the soul of our teacher Moses, peace unto him. Only, since the soul has clothed itself in the body, it needs a great and mighty exertion, doubled and redoubled:—First is the wearying of the flesh, the crushing of the body and its submission, so that it shall not obscure the light of the soul, as has been mentioned above[9] in the name of the *Zohar*, that "A body into which the light of the soul does not penetrate should be crushed," which is accomplished by means of penitential reflections from the depths of the heart, as is explained there.

▲ Next is the exertion of the soul, that the service shall not be burdensome to it, to exert its thought to delve into and reflect upon the greatness of G–d for a long and uninterrupted period, the measure of which is not the same for every soul. There is the naturally refined soul which, immediately it considers the greatness of G–d, attains a fear and dread of G–d. As is written in the *Shulchan Aruch, Orach Chayim*, sec. I, that "When a man reflects that the great King, the Supreme King of kings, the Holy One, blessed be He, with Whose glory the whole world is full, stands over him and sees his actions, he will immediately be overcome with fear. . . ." There is a soul that is of lowly nature and origin, coming from the lower gradations of the Ten *Sefirot* of *Asiyah*, which cannot discover G–dliness by contemplation except with difficulty and forcefulness, especially if it had been contaminated by the sin of youth, for the sins interpose, . . . (as is explained in *Sefer Chasidim*, ch. 35). Nevertheless, by dint of forceful effort, when his thought greatly exerts itself with much vigour and toil and intense concentration, immersing in [contemplation of] the greatness of G–d for a considerable time, there will certainly come to him, at any rate, the lower fear

---

[8] Gen. *4:1*. [9] *Ch. 29*.

סופרים ומפי ספרים אלא העיקר הוא להעמיק דעתו בגדולת ה' ולתקוע מחשבתו בה' בחוזק ואומץ הלב והמוח עד שתהא מחשבתו מקושרת בה' בקשר אמיץ וחזק כמו שהיא מקושרת בדבר גשמי שרואה בעיני בשר ומעמיק בו מחשבתו כנודע שדעת הוא לשון התקשרות כמו והאדם ידע וגו' וכח זה ומדה זו לקשר דעתו בה' יש בכל נפש מבית ישראל בניקתה מנשמת משרע"ה רק מאחר שנתלבשה הנפש בגוף צריכה ליגיעה רבה ועצומה כפולה ומכופלת. האחת היא יגיעת בשר לבטש את הגוף ולהכניעו שלא יחשיך על אור הנפש כמש"ל בשם הזהר דגופא דלא סליק ביה נהורא דנשמתא מבטשין ליה והיינו על ידי הרהורי תשובה מעומק הלב כמ"ש שם. והשנית היא יגיעת הנפש שלא תכבד עליה העבודה ליגע מחשבתה להעמיק ולהתבונן בגדולת ה' שעה גדולה רצופה כי שיעור שעה זו אינו שוה בכל נפש יש נפש זכה בטבעה שמיד שמתבוננת בגדולת ה' יגיע אליה היראה ופחד ה' כמ"ש בש"ע א"ח סימן א' כשיתבונן האדם שהמלך הגדול ממ"ה הקב"ה אשר מלא כל הארץ כבודו עומד עליו ורואה במעשיו מיד יגיע אליו היראה וכו' ויש נפש שפלה בטבעה ותולדתה ממקור חוצבה ממדרגות תחתונות די"ס דעשיה ולא תוכל למצוא במחשבתה האלהות כ"א בקושי ובחזקה ובפרט אם הוטמאה בחטאת נעורי' שהעוונות מבדילים כו' [כמ"ש בס"ח סי' ל"ה] ומ"מ בקושי ובחזק' שתתחזק מאד מחשבתו באומץ ויגיעה רבה ועומק גדול להעמיק בגדולת ה' שעה גדולה בודאי תגיע אליו עכ"פ היראה תתאה

referred to above, and as the Rabbis, of blessed memory, have said: ["If a man says] 'I have laboured and I have found'—believe him."[10] It is also written: "If thou seekest her as silver and searchest for her as for hidden treasures: Then shalt thou understand the fear of the Lord."[11] This means, in the manner of a man seeking a hidden treasure or the wealth buried in the depths of the earth, for which he digs with tireless toil, so must one delve with unflagging energy in order to bring to light the treasure of the fear of Heaven, which lies buried and concealed in the understanding of the heart of every Jewish individual, this being of a quality and level transcending the limitations of time, and this is the natural, hidden fear referred to above. However, in order that it should be translated into action, in the sense of "fear of sin," namely, to turn away from evil in deed, word and thought, one needs to bring it to light from the hidden depths of the understanding of the heart where it transcends time, and to place it within the realm of the actual thought that is in the brain. [This means] immersing his thought in it for a lengthy period of time until its activity shall emerge from the potential into the actual, namely, turning away from evil and doing good in thought, speech and act because of G-d, Who looks and sees, hears and listens and perceives all his deeds and searches his reins and heart. As the Rabbis, of blessed memory, said: "Reflect upon three things, and thou wilt not come within the power of sin: The Eye sees, and the Ear hears. . . ."[12] And ●▲ although He has no bodily likeness, yet, on the contrary, everything is revealed and known to Him infinitely more than, for example, through the medium of physical sight or hearing. It is, by way of illustration, like a man who knows and feels within himself all that is happening to and being experienced by each and all of his 248 organs, such as cold and heat, feeling the heat even in his toe-nails, for example, as when he is scorched by fire; so also their essence and substance and all that is done to them, he knows and senses in his brain.

Corresponding to this knowledge, by way of example, the Holy One, blessed be He, knows all that befalls all created beings, both higher and lower, because they all receive their flow of life from Him, may He be blessed, as is written: "For all things come of Thee."[13] And this is the meaning of what we say: "Verily also nothing that is formed is withheld from Thee."[14] And as Maimonides has said (and this has been accepted by the scholars of the *Kabbalah*,

---

[10] Megillah *6b*. [11] Prov. *2:4–5*. [12] Avot *II, 1*. [13] *I* Chron. *29:14*. [14] Liturgy, Musaf *for the New Year.*

● 26 Nisan ▲ *22 Nisan*

תתאה הנ"ל וכמשארז"ל יגעתי ומצאתי תאמין וכדכתי' אם תבקשנה ככסף וכמטמונים תחפשנה אז תבין יראת ה' פי' כדרך שמחפש אדם מטמון ואוצר הטמון בתחתיות הארץ שחופר אחריו ביגיעה עצומה כך צריך לחפור ביגיעה עצומה לגלות אוצר של יראת שמים הצפון ומוסתר בבינת הלב של כל אדם מישראל שהיא בחי' ומדרגה שלמעלה מהזמן והיא היראה הטבעית המסותרת הנ"ל רק שכדי שתבא לידי מעשה בבחי' יראת חטא להיות סור מרע במעשה דבור ומחשבה צריך לגלותה ממצפוני בינת הלב שלמעלה מהזמן להביאה לבחי' מחשבה ממש שבמוח להעמיק בה מחשבתו משך זמן מה ממש עד שתצא פעולתה מהכח אל הפועל ממש דהיינו להיות סור מרע ועשה טוב במחשבה דבור ומעשה מפני ה' הצופה ומביט ומאזין ומקשיב ומבין אל כל מעשהו ובוחן כליותיו ולבו וכמאמר רז"ל הסתכל בשלשה דברים כו' עין רואה ואוזן שומעת כו' וגם כי אין לו דמות הגוף הרי אדרבה הכל גלוי וידוע לפניו ביתר שאת לאין קץ מראיית העין ושמיעת האזן עד"מ רק הוא עד"מ כמו אדם היודע ומרגיש בעצמו כל מה שנעשה ונפעל באחד מכל רמ"ח איבריו כמו קור או חום ואפי' חום שבצפרני רגליו עד"מ אם נכוה באור וכן מהותם ועצמותם וכל מה שמתפעל בהם יודע ומרגיש במוחו וכעין ידיעה זו עד"מ יודע הקב"ה כל הנפעל בכל הנבראים עליונים ותחתונים להיות כולם מושפעי' ממנו ית' כמ"ש כי ממך הכל וז"ש וגם כל היצור לא נכחד ממך וכמ"ש הרמב"ם [והסכימו לזה חכמי הקבלה כמ"ש

as Rabbi Moses Cordovero writes in *Pardess*), that "Knowing Himself, as it were, He knows all created things that exist by virtue of His true existence. . . ."

Nevertheless this parallel is only an appeal to the ear. In truth, however, the analogy bears no similarity whatever to the object of the comparison. For the human soul, even the rational and the divine, is affected by the accidents of the body and its pain, by reason of its being actually clothed within the vivifying soul which is clothed in the body itself.

The Holy One, blessed be He, however, is not, Heaven forbid, affected by the accidents of the world and its changes, nor by the world itself, for they do not affect any change in Him, G–d forbid. In order to help us perceive this well with our intelligence, the Scholars of Truth have already treated of it at length in their books. But all Jews are "Believers descended from believers,"[15] without human intellectual speculation whatever, and they declare: "Thou wast the same ere the world was created," and so forth,[16] as has been explained above in ch. 20.

●▲Now, therefore, each individual Jew, whoever he may be, when he ponders upon this for some considerable time each day—how the Holy One, blessed be He, is truly omnipresent in the higher and lower [worlds], and in reality fills the heavens and the earth, and that the whole world is truly full of His glory, and that He looks and regards and searches his reins and his heart and all his actions and words, and counts his every step—then fear will be implanted in his heart throughout the day; and when he again meditates on this, even with a superficial reflection, at any time or moment, he will turn away from evil and do good, in thought, speech and deed, so as not to rebel, G–d forbid, in the sight of His glory whereof the whole world is full. This is in accord with the instruction of Rabbi Yochanan ben Zakkai to his disciples, quoted above.[17]

This, then, is what the verse means: "But to fear the Lord thy G–d, to walk in all His ways."[18] For this is the fear that leads to the fulfillment of His blessed commandments through turning away from evil and doing good. This is the "lower fear" which has been discussed earlier. As it applies to "Moses," that is to say, in relation to the quality of *da'at* that is in each divine Jewish soul, this is a minor thing, as has been stated above. (For *da'at* is [the faculty] which binds the hidden understanding of the heart with that which is actually revealed

---

[15] Shabbat *92a*. [16] Liturgy. Cf. Yalkut, Va-etchanan *836*, *quoting a Talmud Yerushalmi source.* [17] *Ch. 41*. [18] Deut. *10:12*.

כמ"ש הרמ"ק בפרד"ס] שבידיעת עצמו כביכול יודע כל הנבראים הנמצאים מאמיתת המצאו וכו' רק שמשל זה אינו אלא לשכך את האזן אבל באמת אין המשל דומה לנמשל כלל כי נפש האדם אפי' השכלית והאלהית היא מתפעלת ממאורעי הגוף וצערו מחמת התלבשותה ממש בנפש החיונית המלובשת בגוף ממש אבל הקב"ה אינו מתפעל ח"ו ממאורעי העולם ושינוייו ולא מהעול' עצמו שכולם אינן פועלים בו שום שינוי ח"ו והנה כדי להשכיל זה היטב בשכלנו כבר האריכו חכמי האמת בספריהם אך כל ישראל מאמינים בני מאמיני' בלי שום חקירת שכל אנושי ואומרי' אתה הוא עד שלא נברא העולם וכו' כנ"ל פ"כ: והנה כל אדם מישראל יהיה מי שיהיה כשיתבונן בזה שעה גדולה בכל יום איך שהקב"ה מלא ממש את העליונים ואת התחתונים ואת השמים ואת הארץ ממש מלא כל הארץ כבודו ממש וצופה ומביט ובוחן כליותיו ולבו וכל מעשיו ודבוריו וכל צעדיו יספור אזי תקבע בלבו היראה לכל היום כולו כשיחזור ויתבונן בזה אפילו בהתבוננות קלה בכל עת ובכל שעה יהיה סור מרע ועשה טוב במחשבה דבור ומעשה שלא למרות ח"ו עיני כבודו אשר מלא כל הארץ וכמאמר רבן יוחנן בן זכאי לתלמידיו כנ"ל וז"ש הכתוב כי אם ליראה את ה' אלהיך ללכת בכל דרכיו שהיא יראה המביאה לקיום מצותיו ית' בסור מרע ועשה טוב. והיא יראה תתאה הנ"ל ולגבי משה דהיינו לגבי בחי' הדעת שבכל נפש מישראל האלהית מילתא זוטרתי היא כנ"ל [שהדעת הוא המקשר מצפוני בינת הלב אל בחי' גילוי

במחשבה

in thought, as is known to those who are familiar with the Esoteric Discipline).

●▲ In addition to this, one should remember that, as in the case of a mortal king, the essence of fear [of him] relates to his inner nature and vitality and not to his body—for when he is asleep, there is no fear of him—and, surely, his inner character and vitality are not perceived by physical eyes but only by the vision of the mind, through the physical eyes beholding his stature and robes, and making the beholder aware of the vitality that is clothed in them. If this be so, he must likewise truly fear G–d when gazing with his physical eyes at the heavens and earth and all their host wherein is clothed the light of the blessed *En Sof* that animates them.

Note: And it is also seen with the glance of the eye that they are nullified to His blessed light by the fact that they "prostrate" themselves every day towards the west at the time of their setting. As the Rabbis, of blessed memory, commented on the verse: "And the host of heaven worship Thee,"[19] *that the* Shechinah *abides in the west, so that their daily orbit westwards is a kind of prostration and self-nullification.*[20] *Even he who has never seen the king and does not recognise him at all, nevertheless when he enters the royal court and sees many honourable princes prostrating themselves before one man, there falls on him a fear and awe.*

And although many garments are involved in this investment, there is no difference or distinction at all in the fear of a mortal king, whether he be naked or robed in one or in many garments.

The essential thing, however, is the [mental] training to habituate one's mind and thought continuously, that it ever remain fixed in his heart and mind, that everything one sees with one's eyes—the heavens and earth and all that is therein—constitutes the outer garments of the King, the Holy One, blessed be He. In this way he will constantly be aware of their inwardness and vitality. This is also implicit in the word *emunah* ("faith"), which is a term indicating "training," to which a man habituates himself, like a craftsman who trains his hands, and so forth.

▲ There should also be a constant remembrance of the dictum of the Rabbis, of blessed memory, "Acceptance of the yoke of the Kingdom of Heaven," which parallels the injunction "Thou shalt surely set a king over thee,"[21] as has been explained elsewhere, and so on. For the Holy One, blessed be He, forgoes the higher and lower worlds and uniquely bestows His Kingdom upon us, . . . and we

---

[19] Neh. *9:6.* [20] Sanhedrin *91b;* Bava Batra *25a.* [21] Deut. *17:15.*

במחשבה ממש כידוע לי"ח] ועוד זאת יזכור כי כמו שבמלך בשר ודם עיקר היראה היא מפנימיותו וחיותו ולא מגופו שהרי כשישן אין שום יראה ממנו. והנה פנימיותו וחיותו אין נראה לעיני בשר רק בעיני השכל על ידי ראיית עיני בשר בגופו ולבושיו שיודע שחיותו מלובש בתוכם וא"כ ככה ממש יש לו לירא את ה' ע"י ראיית עיני בשר בשמים וארץ וכל צבאם אשר אור א"ס ב"ה מלובש בהם להחיותם* ואף שהוא ע"י התלבשות בלבושים רבים הרי אין הבדל והפרש כלל ביראת מלך בשר ודם בין שהוא ערום ובין שהוא לבוש לבוש אחד ובין שהוא לבוש בלבושים רבים אלא העיקר הוא ההרגל להרגיל דעתו ומחשבתו תמיד להיות קבוע בלבו ומוחו תמיד אשר כל מה שרואה בעיניו השמים והארץ ומלואה הכל הם לבושים החיצונים של המלך הקב"ה וע"י זה יזכור תמיד על פנימיותם וחיותם וזה נכלל ג"כ בלשון אמונה שהוא לשון רגילות שמרגיל האדם את עצמו כמו אומן המאמן ידיו וכו'. וגם להיות לזכרון תמיד לשון חז"ל קבלת עול מלכות שמים שהוא כענין שום תשים עליך מלך כמ"ש במ"א וכו' כי הקב"ה מניח את העליונים והתחתונים ומייחד מלכותו עלינו וכו' ואנחנו מקבלים

הגה"ה

*(וגם נראה בראיית העין שהם בטלים לאורו ית' בהשתחוואתם כל יום כלפי מערב בשקיעתם כמארז"ל ע"פ וצבא השמים לך משתחוים שהשכינה במערב ונמצא הילוכם כל היום כלפי מערב הוא דרך השתחוואה וביטול והנה גם מי שלא ראה את המלך מעולם ואינו מכירו כלל אעפ"כ כשנכנס לחצר המלך ורואה שרים רבים ונכבדים משתחוים לאיש א' תפול עליו אימה ופחד):

accept it. . . . And this is the significance of the obeisances in the prayer of the Eighteen Benedictions, following the verbal acceptance of the yoke of the Kingdom of Heaven in the recital of the *Shema*, whereby one accepts it once again in actual deed, with a [positive] act, and so forth, as is explained elsewhere.

•▲ Chapter 43

Concerning this *yirah tattaah* ("lower fear"), which is directed toward the fulfillment of His commandments, in both areas of "Depart from evil and do good," it was said, "Where there is no fear [of G–d], there is no wisdom."[1] It comprises a quality of "smallness"[2] and a quality of "greatness." The latter being the quality of fear that has its origin in contemplation on the greatness of G–d—that He fills all worlds, and from the earth to the heavens is a distance of 500 years, . . . and the distance from one heaven to the next, . . . the feet of the "*Chayyot*" measure up to them all, . . .[3] and similarly on the evolvement of all the worlds, one above the other to the topmost heights—nevertheless this fear is called an "external" and "inferior" fear, because it is derived from the worlds which are "garments" of the King, the Holy One, blessed be He, Who conceals and hides and clothes Himself in them, to animate them and give them existence, that they may exist *ex nihilo*, . . . yet [this fear] is the gate and entrance[4] to the fulfillment of the Torah and commandments.

As for the *yirah ilaah* ("higher fear"), however, a fear stemming from a sense of shame, an inner fear that derives from the inward aspects of G–dliness within the worlds, it was said concerning it that "Where there is no wisdom, there is no fear,"[5] for חכמה is [made up of the letters] כ"ח מ"ה,[6] and "*Chochmah* comes from *ayin*" (Nothing),[7] and "Who is wise? He who sees that which is born."[8] That is to say, he sees how everything originates and comes into being *ex nihilo* by means of the word of G–d and the breath of His blessed mouth. As is written: "And all their host by the breath of His mouth."[9] Therefore, the heavens and the earth and all their host are truly nullified in reality, within the word of G–d and the breath of His mouth, and are accounted as nothing at all, as nought and nothingness indeed, just as the light and brightness of the sun are nullified within the body of the sun itself. And let not man regard himself as an exception to this principle, for also his body and *nefesh* and *ruach* and *neshamah* are nullified in reality in the word of G–d, Whose blessed word is united with His thought, . . . as has been explained above at length (chs. 20 and 21), taking as an example

---

[1] Avot *III:17*. [2] *Referring to the "natural" fear defined in chs. 41 and 42.* [3] Chagigah *13a*. [4] *I.e. a preliminary and prerequisite.* [5] Avot *III:17*. [6] *Cf. ch. 19, above.* [7] *A paraphrase of Job 28:12.* [8] Tamid *32a. Note the reinterpretation.* [9] Ps. *33:6*.

מקבלים וכו׳ וזהו ענין ההשתחוואות שבתפלת י״ח אחר קבלת עול מלכות שמים בדבור בק״ש לחזור ולקבל בפועל ממש במעשה וכו׳ כמ״ש במ״א:

פרק מג והנה על יראה תתאה זו שהיא לקיום מצותיו ית׳ בבחי׳ סור מרע ועשה טוב אמרו אם אין יראה אין חכמה ויש בה בחי׳ קטנות ובחי׳ גדלות דהיינו כשנמשכת בחי׳ יראה זו מההתבוננות בגדולת ה׳ דאיהו ממלא כל עלמין ומהארץ לרקיע מהלך ת״ק שנה וכו׳ ובין רקיע לרקיע כו׳ רגלי החיות כנגד כולן וכו׳ וכן השתלשלות כל העולמות למעלה מעלה עד רום המעלות אעפ״כ נקרא יראה זו יראה חיצונית ותתאה מאחר שנמשכת מהעולמות שהם לבושים של המלך הקב״ה אשר מסתתר ומתעלם ומתלבש בהם להחיותם ולקיימם להיות יש מאין וכו׳ רק שהיא השער והפתח לקיום התורה והמצות. אך היראה עילאה ירא בשת ויראה פנימית שהיא נמשכת מפנימית האלהות שבתוך העולמות עליה אמרו אם אין חכמה אין יראה דחכמה היא כ״ח מ״ה והחכמה מאין תמצא ואיזהו חכם הרואה את הנולד פי׳ שרואה כל דבר איך נולד ונתהוה מאין ליש בדבר ה׳ ורוח פיו ית׳ כמ״ש וברוח פיו כל צבאם ואי לזאת הרי השמים והארץ וכל צבאם בטלים במציאות ממש בדבר ה׳ ורוח פיו וכלא ממש חשיבי ואין ואפס ממש כביטול אור וזיו השמש בגוף השמש עצמה ואל יוציא אדם עצמו מהכלל שגם גופו ונפשו ורוחו ונשמתו בטלים במציאות בדבר ה׳ ודבורו ית׳ מיוחד במחשבתו כו׳ וכנ״ל [פ׳ כ׳ וכ״א] באריכות בר״מ מנפש

the human soul, one utterance of whose speech and thought are veritably as nothing. . . . This is what is meant by the verse: "Behold, the fear of the Lord, that is wisdom."[10]

However, one cannot attain to this fear and wisdom except in the fulfillment of the Torah and commandments through the lower, external fear. And this is what is meant by the statement: "Where there is no fear, there is no wisdom."[11]

• Now, in love, too, there are two grades —*ahavah rabbah* ("great love") and *ahavat olam* ("eternal love").[12] "Great love" is an ecstatic love, and it is "A fiery flame that rises of itself." It comes from above in a manner of a "gift" to him who is perfect in fear, as is known from the saying of the Rabbis, of blessed memory: "The way of a man is to search for a woman."[13] For love is called "man" or "male," as is written: "He hath remembered His loving kindness";[14] whilst a woman [symbolises] "fear of G–d," as is known.[15] Without the prerequisite of fear, it is impossible to attain to this "great love," for this love originates from the realm of *Atzilut*, wherein are no sundering or separateness, G–d forbid.

Ahavat olam, however, is that which comes from the understanding and knowledge of the greatness of G–d, the blessed *En Sof*, Who fills all worlds and encompasses all worlds and before Whom everything is accounted as nothing at all, like the nullity of one utterance within the intelligent soul while it still remains in its thought or in the desire of the heart, as has been explained earlier.[16] For as a result of such contemplation, the attribute of love that is in the soul will be divested of its garments, i.e., it will not clothe itself in anything of pleasure or enjoyment, whether physical or spiritual, to love it, and will not desire anything whatever in the world other than G–d alone, the Source of the vitality of all enjoyments, for they are all nullified in reality and are accounted as nothing at all, compared with Him, there being no manner of comparison or similitude between them, G–d forbid, just as there is no comparison between that which is absolutely nought and nothing—and everlasting life. As is written: "Whom have I in heaven [but Thee]? And there is nothing upon earth that I desire with Thee. My flesh and my heart yearn, O Rock of my heart. . . ."[17] And as will be explained later.[18]

Also he, whose soul's quality of love is not clothed at all in any physical or spiritual enjoyment, is able to kindle his soul as with burning coals and an intense fire

---

[10] Job *28:28.* [11] Avot *3:17.* [12] *Lit. "worldly" love, i.e. of this world, a love of G–d derived from contemplation of G–d in nature, as explained later on.* [13] Kiddushin *2b.* [14] Ps. *98:3; a play on the word* זכר *("remembered") which can be read by merely changing one vowel as* זכר *("male").* [15] *A reference to* Prov. *31:30. Cf.* Zohar *III, 42b, where the whole ch. 31 of* Prov. *is interpreted* allegorically. *"Male seeking female" is here metaphorically explained as "love seeking fear" in order to fulfil itself.* [16] *Ch. 20.* [17] Ps. *73:25–26.* [18] *Ch. 48.*

• 30 Nisan

מנפש האדם שדבור אחד מדבורו ומחשבתו כלא ממש כו׳ וזש״ה הן יראת ה׳ היא חכמה. אך אי אפשר להשיג ליראה וחכמה זו אלא בקיום התורה והמצות ע״י יראה תתאה החיצונית וז״ש אם אין יראה אין חכמה. והנה באהבה יש ג״כ שתי מדרגות אהבה רבה ואהבת עולם. אהבה רבה היא אהבה בתענוגי׳ והיא שלהבת העולה מאליה ובאה מלמעלה בבחי׳ מתנה למי שהוא שלם ביראה כנודע על מאמר רז״ל דרכו של איש לחזר אחר אשה שאהבה נקראת איש וזכר כמ״ש זכר חסדו ואשה יראת ה׳ כנודע ובלי קדימת היראה אי אפשר להגיע לאהבה רבה זו כי אהבה זו היא מבחי׳ אצילות דלית תמן קיצוץ ופירוד ח״ו אך אהבת עולם היא הבאה מהתבונה ודעת בגדולת ה׳ א״ס ב״ה הממלא כל עלמין וסובב כל עלמין וכולא קמיה כלא ממש חשיב וכביטול דבור אחד בנפש המשכל׳ בעודו במחשבתה או בחמדת הלב כנ״ל אשר ע״י התבוננו׳ זו ממילא תתפשט מדת האהבה שבנפש מלבושיה דהיינו שלא תתלבש בשום דבר הנאה ותענוג גשמי או רוחני לאהבה אותו ולא לחפוץ כלל שום דבר בעולם בלתי ה׳ לבדו מקור החיים של כל התענוגים שכולם בטילים במציאות וכלא ממש קמיה חשיבי ואין ערוך ודמיון כלל בינידם ח״ו כמו שאין ערוך לאין ואפס המוחלט לגבי חיים נצחיים וכמ״ש מי לי בשמים ועמך לא חפצתי בארץ כלה שארי ולבבי צור לבבי וגו׳ וכמ״ש לקמן וגם מי שאין מדת אהבה שבנפשו מלובשת כלל בשום תענוג גשמי או רוחני יכול להלהיב נפשו כרשפי אש ושלהבת עזה

ולהב

and a flame that strives heavenwards through the contemplation referred to ●▲ above, as will be enlarged upon later. This quality of love sometimes precedes fear, according to the quality of the *da'at* which fathers it, as is known. (For *da'at* incorporates both *chasadim* and *gevurot*, which are love and fear; and sometimes the *chasadim* descend and manifest themselves first.) Therefore it is possible for a wicked and a sinful person to repent by virtue of the love that is born in his heart at the time he remembers the Lord his G-d. At any rate, fear, too, is included therein [in the love], as a matter of course, except that it is in a stage of "minuteness" and "concealment," namely, the fear of sin, of rebelling against Him, G-d forbid, while the love is in a revealed state in his heart and mind. However, such a case is but an accidental and spontaneous occurrence, or an "emergency prescription" through G-d's particular providence as the occasion requires, as happened with Rabbi Eliezer ben Durdaya.[19]

However, the order of service, which is determined by and depends on man's choice, is to begin with the fulfillment of the Torah and commandments through the "lower" fear in its state of "minuteness" at least, to depart from evil and do good, so as to illuminate his divine soul with the light of the Torah and its commandments, whereupon the light of love will also shine forth upon it (for the word ואהבת—"And thou shalt love"—has a numerical value twice that of אור—"light"[20]—as is known to those who are familiar with the Esoteric Discipline).

●▲ Chapter 44

Each of the said two grades of love—the "great love" and the "eternal love"—is subdivided into many shades and gradations without limit, in each individual according to his capacity. As is written in the holy *Zohar*[1] on the verse: "Her husband is known in the gates,"[2] that "This refers to the Holy One, blessed be He, Who makes Himself known and attaches Himself to every one according to the extent which one measures in one's heart. . . ."[3] Therefore fear and love are called "The secret things known to the Lord our G-d,"[4] while the Torah and commandments are those things which are "Revealed to us and to our children to do. . . ."[5] For we have all one Torah and one law, in so far as the fulfillment of all the Torah and commandments in actual performance is concerned. It is otherwise with fear and love, which vary according to the knowledge of G-d in the mind and heart, as has been mentioned above.[6]

Yet there is one love which incorporates something of all the distinctions and gradations of both "great love"

---

[19] Avodah Zarah *17b*. [20] *Alluding to the light of Torah and its commandments which arouses the light of love.*

Chapter 44
[1] Zohar *I, 103b*. [2] Prov. *31:23*. *Cf. Note 17*, Compiler's Foreword. [3] *Note the reinterpretation of this verse.* [4] Deut. *29:28*. [5] Ibid. [6] *Chs. 42, 43*.

ולהב העולה השמימה ע״י התבוננו׳ הנ״ל כמ״ש לקמן והנה בחי׳ אהבה זו פעמים שקודמת ליראה כפי בחי׳ הדעת המולידה כנודע [שהדעת כולל חסדים וגבורות שהם אהבה ויראה ופעמים שהחסדים קודמים לירד ולהתגלות] ולכן אפשר לרשע ובעל עבירות שיעשה תשובה מאהבה הנולדה בלבו בזכרו את ה׳ אלהיו ומ״מ היראה ג״כ כלולה בה ממילא רק שהיא בבחי׳ קטנות והעלם דהיינו יראת חטא למרוד בו ח״ו והאהבה היא בהתגלות לבו ומוחו אך זהו דרך מקרה והוראת שעה בהשגחה פרטית מאת ה׳ לצורך שעה כמעשה דר״א בן דורדייא · אבל סדר העבודה הקבועה ותלויה בבחירת האדם צריך להקדים תחלה קיום התורה והמצות ע״י יראה תתאה בבחי׳ קטנות עכ״פ בסור מרע ועשה טוב להאיר נפשו האלהית באור התורה ומצותיה ואח״כ יאיר עליה אור האהבה [כי ואהבת בגימטריא ב״פ אור כידוע לי״ח]:

פרק מד

והנה כל מדרגת אהבה מב׳ מדרגות אלו אהבה רבה ואהבת עולם נחלקת לכמה בחי׳ ומדרגות לאין קץ כל חד לפום שיעורא דיליה כמ״ש בזה״ק ע״פ נודע בשערים בעלה דא קב״ה דאיהו אתידע ואתדבק לכל חד לפום מה דמשער בלביה וכו׳ ולכן נקראי׳ דחילו ורחימו הנסתרות לה׳ אלהינו ותורה ומצות הן הנגלות לנו ולבנינו לעשות כו׳ · כי תורה אחת ומשפט אחד לכולנו בקיום כל התורה ומצות בבחי׳ מעשה משא״כ בדחילו ורחימו שהם לפי הדעת את ה׳ שבמוח ולב כנ״ל · אך אחת היא אהבה הכלולה מכל בחי׳ ומדרגות אהבה רבה ואהבת

and "eternal love," and equally belongs in every Jewish soul, as our inheritance from our Patriarchs. And that is what the *Zohar* says on the verse: "[Thou art] my soul; I desire Thee in the night, . . ."[7] that "One should love the Holy One, blessed be He, with a love of the soul and the spirit, as these are attached to the body, and the body loves them," and so forth.[8] This is the interpretation of the verse: "My soul, I desire Thee," which means "Since Thou, O Lord, art my true soul and life, therefore do I desire Thee." That is to say, "I long and yearn for Thee like a man who craves the life of his soul, and when he is weak and exhausted he longs and yearns for his soul to revive in him; and also when he goes to sleep he longs and yearns for his soul to be restored to him when he awakens from his sleep. So do I long and yearn to draw the light of the blessed *En Sof*, the Life of true life, within me through occupation in the Torah when I awaken during the night from my sleep;" for the Torah and the Holy One, blessed be He, are one and the same. So the *Zohar* says, *ibid.*, "Out of love for the Holy One, blessed be He, a man should rise each night and exert himself in His service until the morning. . . ."

●▲ A great and more intense love than that—one which is likewise concealed in every soul of Israel as an inheritance from our ancestors—is that which is defined in *Ra'aya Mehemna*: "Like a son who strives for the sake of his father and mother, whom he loves even more than his own body, soul and spirit, . . ."[9] for "have we not all one Father?"[10]

And although [one may ask], who is the man and where is he, who dares presume in his heart to approach and attain even a thousandth part of the degree of love of "The Faithful Shepherd" [Moses]? Nevertheless a minute portion and particle of his great goodness and light illumines the community of Israel in each generation, as is stated in the *Tikunim*[11] that "An emanation from him is present in every generation", "To illumine them,"[12] and so forth. Only, this glow is in a manner of great occultation and concealment in the souls of all Israel. But to bring forth this hidden love from its delitescence and concealment to [a state of] revelation, to be manifest in his heart and mind, this is "Not beyond reach nor is it afar off, but the word is very nigh unto thee, in thy mouth and in thy heart."[13]

[7] Isa. *26:9*. [8] Zohar *III, 67a*. *This love of G–d is equated with the love of life itself—somewhat less altruistic than the love defined further on.* [9] *Cf. end ch. 10 and ch. 43.* [10] Mal. *2:10*. [11] Tikun *69, pp. 112a; 114a*. *Cf.* Igeret Hakodesh, *end ch. 27*. [12] *Cf.* Zohar *III, 216b; 273a*. [13] Deut. *30:11–12*.

ואהבת עולם והיא שוה לכל נפש מישראל וירושה לנו מאבותינו · והיינו מ"ש הזהר ע"פ נפשי איותיך בלילה וגו' דירחים לקב"ה רחימותא דנפשא ורוחא כמה דאתדבקו אילין בגופא וגופא רחים לון וכו' · וז"ש נפשי איותיך כלומר מפני שאתה ה' נפשי וחיי האמיתים לכך איותיך פי' שאני מתאוה ותאב לך כאדם המתאוה לחיי נפשו וכשהוא חלש ומעונה מתאוה ותאב שתשוב נפשו אליו וכן כשהוא הולך לישן מתאוה וחפץ שתשוב נפשו אליו כשיעור משנתו כך אני מתאוה ותאב לאור א"ס ב"ה חיי החיים האמיתיים להמשיכו בקרבי ע"י עסק התורה בהקיצי משנתי בלילה דאורייתא וקב"ה כולא חד · כמ"ש הזהר שם דבעי בר נש מרחימותא דקב"ה למיקם בכל לילא לאשתדלא בפולחניה עד צפרא כו' · ואהבה רבה וגדולה מזו והיא מסותרת ג"כ בכל נפש מישראל בירושה מאבותינו היא מ"ש בר"מ כברא דאשתדל בתר אבוי ואימיה דרחים לון יתיר מגרמיה ונפשיה ורוחיה כו' כי הלא אב אחד לכולנו · ואף כי מי הוא זה ואיזהו אשר ערב לבו לגשת להשיג אפי' חלק אחד מני אלף ממדרגת אהבת רעיא מהימנא · מ"מ הרי אפס קצהו ושמץ מנהו מרב טובו ואורו מאיר לכללות ישראל בכל דור ודור כמ"ש בתיקונים דאתפשטותיה בכל דרא ודרא לאנהרא לון וכו' רק שהארה זו היא בבחי' הסתר והעלם גדול בנפשות כל בית ישראל ולהוציא אהבה זו המסותרת מההעלם וההסתר אל הגילוי להיות בהתגלות לבו ומוחו לא נפלאת ולא רחוקה היא אלא קרוב הדבר מאד בפיך ובלבבך

דהיינו

That is to say, it should be habitual on his tongue and voice to arouse the intention of his heart and mind, so as to immerse his thought in the Life of life, the blessed *En Sof*, for He is literally our true Father and the Source of our life, and to awaken our love for Him like the love of a son for his father. And when he accustoms himself to this continually, habit will become nature.

●▲Even if it appears to him at first sight that this is an illusion, he need not be concerned, because it is intrinsically the absolute truth by virtue of the "hidden love." But the purpose of its emergence into the open is in order to translate it into action, namely, the occupation in the Torah and commandments which he studies and performs as a result of it, with the intention to bring gratification before Him, may He be blessed, like a son serving his father.

Concerning this it was said that "A good thought is united by the Holy One, blessed be He, to a deed,"[14] providing the "wings" to soar upwards, as explained earlier.[15] As for the "gratification," it is akin, by way of the illustration used earlier,[16] to the joy of a king whose son returns to him after liberation from captivity; or from the fact that it has been made possible for Him to have a habitation down here, as already mentioned.[17]

But even in regard to the above-mentioned [love, in the] category of "My soul, I desire Thee," the thing is very nigh to be brought out of [its] concealment into the open through constant practice, with mouth and heart in full accord.

However, even if he cannot bring it into a revealed state in his heart, nevertheless he can occupy himself in the Torah and commandments "for their own sake" through portraying the idea of this love in the contemplation of his mind, and "A good thought is united by the Holy One, blessed be He. . . ."

●▲The said two distinctions of love—though they are an inheritance unto us from our Patriarchs, and like a natural instinct in our souls, and so, too, is the fear that is contained in them, which is the fear of being sundered, G–d forbid, from the Source of our life and our true Father, blessed be He—are, nevertheless, not termed "natural" fear and love unless they be in the mind and thought alone and in the latency of the heart. Then their station is in the Ten *Sefirot* of *Yetzirah* whither they bring up with them the Torah and commandments of which they have been the inspiration and cause.

But when they are in a manifest state in the heart, they are called in the *Zohar* *re'uta d'libba* ("heart's desire") and they are stationed in the Ten *Sefirot* of *Beriah*, whither they bring up

---

[14] Kiddushin *40a*. [15] *Ch. 39; cf. also ch. 16*. [16] *Ch. 31*. [17] *End ch. 41, and ch. 31*.

דהיינו להיות רגיל על לשונו וקולו לעורר כוונת לבו ומוחו להעמיק מחשבתו בחיי החיים א"ס ב"ה כי הוא אבינו ממש האמיתי ומקור חיינו ולעורר אליו האהבה כאהבת הבן אל האב· וכשירגיל עצמו כן תמיד הרי ההרגל נעשה טבע· ואף אם נדמה לו לכאורה שהוא כח דמיוני לא יחוש מאחר שהוא אמת לאמיתו מצד עצמו בבחי' אהבה מסותרת רק שתועלת יציאתה אל הגילוי כדי להביאה לידי מעשה שהוא עסק התורה והמצות שלומד ומקיים ע"י זה כדי לעשות נחת רוח לפניו ית' כבן העובד את אביו· ועל זה אמרו מחשבה טובה הקב"ה מצרפה למעשה להיות גדפין לפרחא כנ"ל· והנחת רוח הוא כמשל שמחת המלך מבנו שבא אליו בצאתו מבית האסורים כנ"ל או להיות לו דירה בתחתונים כנ"ל והנה גם לבחי' נפשי אויתיך הנ"ל קרוב הדבר מאד להוציאה מההעלם אל הגילוי ע"י ההרגל תמיד בפיו ולבו שוין· אך אם אינו יכול להוציאה אל הגילוי בלבו אעפ"כ יכול לעסוק בתורה ומצות לשמן ע"י ציור ענין אהבה זו במחשבה שבמוחו ומחשבה טובה הקב"ה מצרפה כו': והנה ב' בחי' אהבות אלו אף שהן ירושה לנו מאבותינו וכמו טבע בנפשותינו וכן היראה הכלולה בהן שהיא ליראַ מליפרד ח"ו ממקור חיינו ואבינו האמיתי ב"ה אעפ"כ אינן נקראות בשם דחילו ורחימו טבעיים אלא כשהן במוחו ומחשבתו לבד ותעלומות לבו ואז מקומן בי"ס דיצירה ולשם הן מעלות עמהן התורה והמצות הבאות מחמתן ובסיבתן· אבל כשהן בהתגלות לבו נק' רעותא דלבא בזוהר ומקומן בי"ס דבריאה ולשם הן מעלות עמהן

with them the Torah and commandments which have been induced by them. For their emergence from the latency and concealment of the heart into a state of "revelation" comes through the faculty of *da'at*, i.e. through a powerful fixation of the mind and an intense concentration—touching the depth of the heart pre-eminently and continuously—on the blessed *En Sof*, as to how He is our very life and our blessed true Father. And it is well known, what is written in the *Tikunim*,[18] that "There in the world of *Beriah* nests the 'Supernal Mother,'"[19] which is the contemplation of the light of the blessed *En Sof*, the Giver of life, which is in accordance with the teaching of Elijah: "*Binah* is the heart, and with it does the heart understand."[20]

Furthermore, these two distinctions of love, that have been referred to above, contain a quality of love which is greater and more sublime than the intelligent fear and love, the love termed above as *Ahavat* ●▲ *Olam* ("eternal love"). Nonetheless a person must strain his intellect to apprehend and attain also the distinction of "eternal love" referred to above,[21] which stems from understanding and knowledge of the greatness of G–d, in order thereby to fan the blaze of the fiery love, with glowing coals and an intense fire and a flame that rises heavenwards, so that "not even many waters can extinguish it . . ., nor rivers quench it. . . ."[22] For there is a superiority and excellence in the quality of love burning like fiery coals and an intense flame, . . . which comes from the understanding and knowledge of the greatness of the blessed *En Sof* over the two distinctions of love referred to above, when they are not like fiery coals and a blaze, . . . similar to the superiority and excellence of gold over silver, and so forth, as will be explained later.[23]

Besides, this is the whole man and his *raison d'être*, that one may know the glory of the Lord and the majestic splendour of His greatness, each according to the limit of his capacity, as is written in *Ra'aya Mehemna, Parshat Bo*: "In order that they may know Him," and so forth,[24] and as is known.

●▲ Chapter 45

There is yet another direct road open to man, namely, to occupy himself with the Torah and commandments for their own sake through the attribute of our Patriarch Jacob, peace unto him, this being the attribute of mercy.[1] It is first to arouse in his mind great compassion before G–d for the Divine spark which animates

[18] Tikun *6.* [19] *The attribute of* Binah *of the world of* Atzilut. [20] *Introduction to* Tikunei Zohar *p. 17a.* [21] *Ch. 43.* [22] Songs *8:7. The Hebrew text should read* 'וגו' *instead of* 'וכו' *as the quotations refer to a Scriptural text.* [23] *Ch. 50.* [24] Zohar *II, p. 42b.*

Chapter 45
[1] Pardess, *Gate 23, ch. 10.*

עמהן התורה והמצות הבאות מחמתן· מפני שיציאתן מההעלם והסתר הלב אל בחי׳ גילוי היא ע״י הדעת ותקיעת המחשבה בחוזק והתבוננות עצומה מעומקא דלבא יתיר ותדיר בא״ס ב״ה איך הוא חיינו ממש ואבינו האמיתי ב״ה ומודעת זאת מ״ש בתיקונים כי בעולם הבריאה מקננא תמן אימא עילאה שהיא ההתבוננות באור א״ס חיי החיים ב״ה וכמאמר אליהו בינה לבא ובה הלב מבין. ולא עוד אלא שב׳ בחי׳ אהבות אלו הנ״ל הן כלולות מן בחי׳ אהבה רבה וגדולה ומעולה מדחילו ורחימו שכליים אשר האהבה נק׳ לעיל בשם אהבת עולם רק שאעפ״כ צריך לטרוח בשכלו להשיג ולהגיע גם לבחי׳ אהבת עולם הנ״ל הבאה מהתבונה ודעת בגדולת ה׳ כדי להגדיל מדורת אש האהבה ברשפי אש ושלהבת עזה ולהב העולה השמימה עד שמים רבים לא יוכלו לכבות וכו׳ ונהרות לא ישטפוה וכו׳ כי יש יתרון ומעלה לבחי׳ אהבה כרשפי אש ושלהבת עזה וכו׳ הבאה מהתבונה ודעת בגדולת א״ס ב״ה על שתי בחי׳ אהבה הנ״ל כאשר אינן כרשפי אש ושלהבת כו׳ כיתרון ומעלת הזהב על הכסף וכו׳ כמ״ש לקמן וגם כי זה כל האדם ותכליתו למען דעת את כבוד ה׳ ויקר תפארת גדולתו איש איש כפי אשר יוכל שאת כמ״ש בר״מ פ׳ בא בגין דישתמודעון ליה וכו׳ וכנודע:

פרק מה עוד יש דרך ישר לפני איש לעסוק בתורה ומצות לשמן ע״י מדתו של יעקב אע״ה שהיא מדת הרחמי׳ לעורר במחשבתו תחלה רחמים רבים לפני ה׳ על ניצוץ אלהות המחיה נפשו

his soul that has descended from its Source, the Life of life, the blessed *En Sof*, Who pervades all worlds and transcends all worlds and in comparison with Whom everything is accounted as nothing. Yet it [this spark] has been clothed in a "serpent's skin" which is far removed from the light of the King's countenance, at the greatest possible distance, since this world is the nadir of the coarse *kelipot*. . . .

And especially when he will recall all his actions and utterances and thoughts since the day he came into being, unworthy as they were, causing the King to be "Fettered by the tresses"[2]—"By the impetuous thoughts of the brain,"[3] for "Jacob is the cord of his inheritance,"[4] as in the illustration of one pulling a rope, and so forth.[5] This is the esoteric doctrine of the "Exile of the *Shechinah*." Concerning this it is written: "And let him return unto the Lord, and have mercy upon Him,"[6] arousing great compassion towards G–d Who dwells among us, as is written: "Who dwelleth among them in • the midst of their uncleanness."[7] This is the meaning of the verse: "And Jacob kissed Rachel and lifted up his voice and wept."[8] For "Rachel" represents *Knesset Israel*,[9] the community of Israel, the fount of all souls; and "Jacob"—with his supernal attribute, the attribute of Mercy in *Atzilut*—is the one who arouses great compassion for her. "And he lifted up his voice"—upwards to the fount of the Higher Mercies, called the "Father of Mercies," and their source; "and he wept"—to awaken and draw from there abundant compassion upon all the souls and upon the fount of the community of Israel, to raise them from their exile and to unite them in the *Yichud Elyon* (Higher Unity) of the light of the blessed *En Sof*, on the level of "kisses," which is "The attachment of spirit with spirit," as is written: "Let him kiss me with the kisses of his mouth,"[10] which means the union of the word of man with the word of G–d, namely, the *halachah*. So, too, are coupled thought with thought, act with act, the latter referring to the active observance of commandments and, in particular, the act of charity and loving-kindness. For "*chesed* (kindness) is the [Divine] right arm,"[11] and this is, as it were, an actual "embrace," as it is written: "And his right arm doth embrace me,"[12] while the occupation in the Torah by word of mouth and concentrated thought constitute, as it were, actual "kisses."

In this way, a person is able to attain the distinction of *Ahavah Rabbah* ("great love") in the consciousness of his heart, as is written: "Of Jacob, who redeemed Abraham,"[13] as has been explained elsewhere.[14]

---

[2] Songs *7:6*. [3] *Another meaning of* רהטים *is "gutters" (comp.* Gen. *30:38). Thus* מלך אסור ברהטים *could be rendered "The King bound in the gutters." Cf.* Lev. Rabba, *sec. 31:4*. [4] Deut. *32:9. Note the interpretation of the word* חבל *usually translated in this verse by "lot."* [5] *Tugging at a rope at one end vibrates the other—a figure to illustrate how every action below causes a corresponding reaction On High. See* Iggeret ha-Teshuvah, *ch. 5*. [6] *Note the deviation from the standard translation ("that* He *may have mercy upon* him"*). The ambiguity of the word* וירחמהו *permits both renditions.* [7] Lev. *16:16*. [8] Gen. *29:11*. [9] *Comp.* Gen. R. *71, 3; 82, 11*. [10] Songs *1:2*. [11] Tikunei Zohar, *Introduction, p. 17a*. [12] Songs *2:6*. [13] Isa.

נפשו אשר ירד ממקורו חיי החיים א״ס ב״ה הממלא
כל עלמין וסובב כל עלמין וכולא קמיה כלא חשיב
ונתלבש במשכא דחויא הרחוק מאור פני המלך
בתכלית ההרחק כי העו״הז הוא תכלית הקליפו׳ הגסות
כו׳ ובפרט כשיזכור על כל מעשיו ודבוריו ומחשבותיו
מיום היותו אשר לא טובים המה ומלך אסור ברהטים
ברהיטי מוחא כי יעקב חבל נחלתו. וכמשל המושך
בחבל וכו׳ והוא סוד גלות השכינה. וע״ז נאמר וישוב
אל ה׳ וירחמהו לעורר רחמים רבים על שם ה׳ השוכן
אתנו כדכתיב השוכן אתם בתוך טומאתם · וזש״ה
וישק יעקב לרחל וישא את קולו ויבך. כי רחל היא
כנסת ישראל מקור כל הנשמות · ויעקב במדתו
העליונה שהיא מדת הרחמים שבאצילות הוא המעורר
רחמים רבים עליה · וישא את קולו למעלה למקור
הרחמים העליונים הנק׳ אב הרחמים ומקורם · ויבך
לעורר ולהמשיך משם רחמים רבים על כל הנשמות
ועל מקור כנסת ישראל להעלותן מגלותן ולייחדן
ביחוד העליון אור א״ס ב״ה בבחי׳ נשיקין שהיא
אתדבקות רוחא ברוחא כמ״ש ישקני מנשיקות פיהו
דהיינו התקשרות דבור האדם בדבר ה׳ זו הלכה וכן
מחשבה במחשבה ומעשה במעשה שהוא מעשה
המצות · ובפרט מעשה הצדקה וחסד · דחסד דרועא
ימינא והוא בחי׳ חיבוק ממש כמ״ש וימינו תחבקני ·
ועסק התורה בדבור ומחשבת העיון הן בחי׳ נשיקין
ממש · והנה ע״י זה יכול לבוא לבחי׳ אהבה רבה
בהתגלות לבו כדכתיב ליעקב אשר פדה את אברהם
כמ״ש במ״א:

פרק מו

29:22. [14] *Cf. end ch. 32 above. See* Torah Or *51a.*

●▲ Chapter 46

There is yet another good way for a man, which is suitable for all and "very nigh" indeed, to arouse and kindle the light of the love that is implanted and concealed in his heart, that it may shine forth with its intense light, like a burning fire, in the consciousness of the heart and mind, to surrender his soul to G-d, together with his body and [material] possessions, with all his heart, and all his soul and all his might, from the depth of the heart, in absolute truth, especially at the time of the recital of the *Shema* and its blessings, as will be explained.

This [way] is: to take to heart the meaning of the verse: "As in water, face answereth to face, so does the heart of man to man."[1] This means that as [in the case of] the likeness and features of the face which a man presents to the water, the same identical face is reflected back to him from the water, so indeed is also the heart of a man who is loyal in his affection for another person, for this love awakens a loving response for him in the heart of his friend also, cementing their mutual love and loyalty for each other, especially as ▲each sees his friend's love for him. Such is the common nature in the character of every man even when they are equal in status. How much more so when a great and mighty king shows his great and intense love for a commoner who is despised and lowly among men, a disgraceful creature cast on the dunghill, yet he [the king] comes down to him from the place of his glory, together with all his retinue, and raises him and exalts him from his dunghill and brings him into his palace, the royal palace, in the innermost chamber, a place such as no servant nor lord ever enters, and there shares with him the closest companionship with embraces and kisses and spiritual attachment[2] with all heart and soul—how much more will, of itself, be aroused a doubled and redoubled love in the heart of this most common and humble individual for the person of the king, with a true attachment of spirit, heart and soul, and with infinite heartfelt sincerity. Even if his heart be like a heart of stone, it will surely melt and become water, and his soul will pour itself out like water, with soulful longing for the love of the king.

●▲In a manner corresponding in every detail to the said figure and image

[1] Prov. 27:19. [2] "*Embraces*"—*performance of the precepts; "kisses"—precepts performed orally (esp. prayer); "spiritual attachment" (lit. "attachment of spirit to spirit")—meditation and comprehension. In other words, complete communion by thought, word and deed.*

פרק מו ויש דרך ישר לפני איש שוה לכל נפש וקרוב הדבר מאד מאד לעורר ולהאיר אור האהבה התקועה ומסותרת בלבו להיות מאירה בתוקף אורה כאש בוערה בהתגלות לבו ומוחו למסור נפשו לה׳ וגופו ומאודו בכל לב ובכל נפש ומאד מעומקא דלבא באמת לאמיתו ובפרט בשעת ק״ש וברכותיה כמו שיתבאר· והוא כאשר ישים אל לבו מ״ש הכתו׳ כמים הפנים לפנים כן לב האדם אל האדם פי׳ כמו שכדמות וצורת הפנים שהאדם מראה במים כן נראה לו שם במים אותה צורה עצמה ככה ממש לב האדם הנאמן באהבתו לאיש אחר הרי האהבה זו מעוררת אהבה בלב חבירו אליו ג״כ להיות אוהבים נאמנים זה לזה בפרט כשרואה אהבת חבירו אליו· והנה זהו טבע הנהוג במדת כל אדם אף אם שניהם שוים במעלה ועל אחת כמה וכמה אם מלך גדול ורב מראה אהבתו הגדולה והעצומה לאיש הדיוט ונבזה ושפל אנשים ומנוול המוטל באשפה ויורד אליו ממקו׳ כבודו עם כל שריו יחדיו ומקימו ומרימו מאשפתו ומכניסו להיכלו היכל המלך חדר לפנים מחדר מקום שאין כל עבד ושר נכנס לשם ומתייחד עמו שם ביחוד וקירוב אמיתי וחיבוק ונישוק ואתדבקות רוחא ברוחא בכל לב ונפש עאכ״ו שתתעורר ממילא האהבה כפולה ומכופלת בלב ההדיוט ושפל אנשים הזה אל נפש המלך בהתקשרות הנפש ממש מלב ונפש מעומקא דלבא לאין קץ· ואף אם לבו כלב האבן המס ימס והיה למים ותשתפך נפשו כמים בכלות הנפש ממש לאהבת המלך: והנה ככל הדברים האלה וככל החזיון הזה וגדול

but to an infinitely greater degree, has the Lord our G–d dealt with us. For His greatness is beyond comprehension, and He pervades all worlds and transcends all worlds; and from the holy *Zohar*, as also from our Master Rabbi Isaac Luria of blessed memory, it is known of the infinite multitude of *hechalot* and worlds, and of the countless myriads of angels in each world and *hechal*. So does the *Gemara* note, "It is written: 'Is there any numbering of His hosts?'[3] Yet, it is also written: 'A thousand thousands minister unto Him, and ten thousand times ten thousand stand before Him.'. . ."[4] The discrepancy is explained by the answer, "A thousand thousands, . . . is the quota of one 'troop' but His troops are innumerable."[5] Yet, before Him, all of them are accounted as nothing at all and are nullified in their very existence, just as one word is truly nullified in relation to the essence and being of the articulate soul whilst the utterance was still held in its [faculty of] thought, or in the will and desire of the heart, as has been explained above at length.[6]

▲ All these [angels] ask: "Where is the place of His glory?" And they answer: "The whole earth is full of His glory,"[7] that is, His people, Israel. For the Holy One, blessed be He, forsakes the higher and lower creatures choosing none of them but Israel His people, whom He brought out of Egypt—"The obscenity of the earth,"[8] the place of filth and impurity—"Not through the agency of an angel, nor of a *saraf*, . . . but the Holy One, blessed be He, Himself in His glory"[9] descended thither, as is written: "And *I* am *come down* to deliver them, . . ."[10] in order to bring them near to Him in true closeness and unity, with a truly soulful attachment on the level of "kisses" of mouth to mouth, by means of uttering the word of G–d, namely, the *halachah*, and the fusion of spirit to spirit, namely, the comprehension of the Torah and the knowledge of His will and wisdom, all of which is truly one [with G–d]; also with a form of "embrace," namely, the fulfillment of the positive precepts with the 248 organs, for the 248 ordinances are the 248 "organs" of the King, as has been explained.[11] These, in a general way, are divided into three categories—right, left, and centre—namely, *chesed* (kindness), *din* (stern justice) and *rachamim* (mercy)—the two arms and the body, and so forth.[12]

● This is the meaning of [the text of the benedictions] "Who hath sanctified us by His commandments": like one who betrothes[13] a wife that she may be united with him with a perfect bond, as is written: "And he shall cleave to his wife, and they shall be one flesh."[14] Exactly so, and even infinitely surpassing,

---

[3] Job *25:3*. [4] Dan. *7:10*. [5] Chagigah *13b*. [6] *Ch. 20*. [7] Isa. *6:3* [8] Gen. *42:9*. [9] Passover Haggadah. [10] Exod. *3:8*. [11] *Ch. 23*. [12] Tikunei Zohar. *Introduction*. [13] *The word* קדשנו *("who sanctified us") may be rendered "who has betrothed us"* (קדושין—*betrothal)*. [14] Gen. *2:24*.

וגדול יתר מאד בכפלי כפליים לאין קץ עשה לנו אלהינו כי לגדולתו אין חקר ואיהו ממלא כל עלמין וסובב כל עלמין ונודע מזה"ק והאר"י ז"ל ריבוי ההיכלות והעולמות עד אין מספר ובכל עולם והיכל ריבוא רבבות מלאכים לאין קץ ותכלית · וכמ"ש בגמ' כתיב היש מספר לגדודיו וכתיב אלף אלפין ישמשוניה וריבו רבבן קדמוהי כו' ומשני אלף אלפין וכו' מספר גדוד אחד אבל לגדודיו אין מספר וכולם קמיה כלא ממש חשיבי ובטלים במציאות ממש כביטול דבור א' ממש לגבי מהות הנפש המדברת ועצמותה בעוד שהיה דיבורה עדיין במחשבתה או ברצון וחמדת הלב כנ"ל באריכות: וכולם שואלים איה מקום כבודו ועונים מלא כל הארץ כבודו הם ישראל עמו · כי הניח הקב"ה את העליונים ואת התחתונים ולא בחר בכולם כי אם בישראל עמו והוציאם ממצרים ערות הארץ מקום הזוהמא והטומאה לא ע"י מלאך ולא ע"י כו' אלא הקב"ה בכבודו ובעצמו ירד לשם כמ"ש וארד להצילו וגו' כדי לקרבם אליו בקירוב ויחוד אמיתי בהתקשרות הנפש ממש בבחי' נשיקין פה לפה לדבר דבר ה' זו הלכה ואתדבקות רוחא ברוחא היא השגת התורה וידיעת רצונו וחכמתו דכולא חד ממש · וגם בבחי' חיבוק הוא קיום המצות מעשיות ברמ"ח אברים דרמ"ח פיקודין הן רמ"ח אברין דמלכא כנז"ל · ודרך כלל נחלקין לשלש בחי' ימין ושמאל ואמצע שהן חסד דין רחמים תרין דרועין וגופא וכו' · וז"ש אשר קדשנו במצותיו כאדם המקדש אשה להיות מיוחדת עמו ביחוד גמור כמ"ש ודבק באשתו והיו לבשר אחד · ככה ממש ויתר על כן

לאין

is the union of the divine soul that is occupied in Torah and commandments, and of the vivifying soul, and their garments referred to above, with the light of the blessed *En Sof*.

▲ Therefore did Solomon, peace unto him, in the *Song of Songs* compare this union with the union of bridegroom and bride in attachment, desire, and pleasure, embrace and kissing. This is also the meaning of "Who hath sanctified us by His commandments," by means of which He has raised us to the heights of the blessed Supreme Holiness, which is the holiness of the Holy One, blessed be He, Himself. *Kedushah* ("holiness") is a term indicating aloofness, in that the Holy One, blessed be He, is apart from the worlds, namely, His quality of "encompassing all worlds," which cannot be clothed within them.

For through the union of the soul with, and its absorption into, the light of the blessed *En Sof*, it attains the quality and degree of the holiness of the blessed *En Sof* Himself, since it unites itself with, and is integrated into, Him, may He be blessed, and they become One in reality. This is the meaning of the verse: "And ye shall be holy unto Me, for I the Lord am holy, and I have separated you from other peoples that ye should be Mine;"[15] and, "Ye shall do all My commandments and be holy unto your G–d; I am the Lord your G–d. . . "[16] The meaning is that through fulfillment of the commandments I become *your* G–d, [in the same sense] as "The G–d of Abraham," "The G–d of Isaac," and so on, called thus because the Patriarchs were, as it were, a "vehicle" unto Him, may He be blessed, and they were nullified and absorbed into His light.

So it is with the soul of every Israelite at the time he occupies himself with Torah and commandments. Therefore the Rabbis, of blessed memory, made it obligatory for us to rise and remain standing in the presence of every one who is engaged in a commandment, even if the latter is uncultured and illiterate.[17] This is because the Lord dwells and clothes Himself in this man's soul at such time, though his soul is unconscious of it because of the barrier of the bodily grossness which has not been purified and which dims the eyes of the soul [preventing it] from seeing Divine visions, as experienced by the Patriarchs and others of their stature, who "Saw their world during their lifetime."[18]

●▲ This is also the meaning of what Asaf said, under Divine inspiration, on behalf of the whole community of Israel in exile: "So foolish was I and ignorant, I was as a beast before Thee. Yet am I continually with Thee."[19] This means that even though I am as a "beast" when I am with Thee, being unaware of, and insensitive to, this union

---

[15] Lev. *20:26.* [16] Num. *15:40–41.* [17] Kiddushin *33a.* [18] *Cf. ch. 14, above.* [19] Ps. *73:22–23.*

● 12 Iyar ▲ *8 Iyar* ▲ *9 Iyar*

לאין קץ הוא יחוד נפש האלהית העוסקת בתורה ומצות ונפש החיונית ולבושיהן הנ"ל באור א"ס ב"ה · ולכן המשיל שלמה ע"ה בשיר השירים יחוד זה ליחוד חתן וכלה בדביקה חשיקה וחפיצה בחיבוק ונישוק. וז"ש אשר קדשנו במצותיו שהעלנו למעלת קודש העליון ב"ה שהיא קדושתו של הקב"ה בכבודו ובעצמו וקדושה היא לשון הבדלה מה שהקב"ה הוא מובדל מהעולמות והיא בחי' סובב כל עלמין מה שאינו יכול להתלבש בהן. כי ע"י יחוד הנפש והתכללותה באור א"ס ב"ה הרי היא במעלת ומדרגת קדושת א"ס ב"ה ממש מאחר שמתייחדת ומתכללת בו ית' והיו לאחדים ממש. וז"ש והייתם לי קדושים כי קדוש אני ה' ואבדיל אתכם מן העמים להיות לי ואומר ועשיתם את כל מצותי והייתם קדושים לאלהיכם אני ה' אלהיכם וגו' פי' כי ע"י קיום המצות הריני אלוה שלכם כמו אלהי אברהם אלהי יצחק וכו' שנקרא כן מפני שהאבות היו בחי' מרכבה לו ית' ובטלים ונכללים באורו · וככה הוא בכל נפש מישראל בשעת עסק התורה והמצות ולכן חיבו רז"ל לקום ולעמוד מפני כל עוסק במצוה אף אם הוא בור ועם הארץ והיינו מפני ה' השוכן ומתלבש בנפשו בשעה זו רק שאין נפשו מרגשת מפני מסך החומר הגופני שלא נזדכך ומחשיך עיני הנפש מראות מראות אלהים כמו האבות וכיוצא בהן שראו עולמם בחייהם. וז"ש אסף ברוח הקדש בעד כל כנסת ישראל שבגולה ואני בער ולא אדע בהמות הייתי עמך ואני תמיד עמך · כלומר שאע"פ שאני כבהמה בהיותי עמך ולא אדע ולא ארגיש בנפשי יחוד זה

in my soul, which should bring down on it fear and awe first, followed by a great love of delights, or a burning [love] like fiery coals, similar to the quality of the *tzaddikim*, whose corporeality has been purified; for, as is known, *da'at*[20] connotes a sensitivity of the soul, comprising *chesed* (kindness) and *gevurah* (sternness)[21]—Yet "I am continually with Thee," for the corporeality of the body does not prevent the union of the soul with the light of the blessed *En Sof*, Who fills all worlds, and as is written: "Yea, the darkness hideth not from Thee."[22]

Thereby will be understood the severity of the punishment for transgressing the prohibition of work on the Sabbath or that of unleavened bread on Passover, which [prohibition] equally applies to all. For even in the soul of an uncultured and completely illiterate person shines the light of the sanctity of Sabbath or Festival; hence he faces capital punishment by *karet*[23] or stoning, for the profanation of this sanctity.

Similarly, [transgression involving] the slightest amount of leaven, or the handling of *muktzeh*[24] tarnishes the sanctity which rests on his soul, just as it would the sanctity of the soul of a *tzaddik*, for we have all one Torah.

(And as for the use of the plural form "*behemot*,"[25] this is an intimation that before Him, may He be blessed, even the so-called *Da'at Elyon* ["Supernal Knowledge"]—which comprises *chesed* and *gevurah*—is like "beasts" i.e. a physical creation, when compared with the light of the *En Sof*, as is written: "In wisdom hast Thou made them all,"[26] and this is called *Behemah rabbah* ["a great beast"], as is explained elsewhere. And this is the Name of ב"ן,[27] with the numerical equivalent of בהמה [beast], preceding *Atzilut*.)

•▲ Chapter 47

"In every generation and every day a person is obliged to regard himself as if he had that day come out of Egypt."[1] This refers to the release of the divine soul from the confinement of the body, the "serpent's skin," in order to be absorbed into the Unity of the light of the blessed *En Sof*, through occupation in the Torah and commandments in general, and in particular through accepting the Kingdom of Heaven during the recital of the *Shema*, wherein the person explicitly accepts and draws over himself His blessed Unity, when he says: "The Lord is our G-d, the Lord is One."[2]

It has previously been explained[3] that "our G-d" is understood in the same way as "The G-d of Abraham," and so forth,[4] because he became nullified and absorbed into the Unity of the light of the blessed *En Sof*, except that Abraham merited this by reason of his works and his advancing in holiness from degree to degree, as is written: "And Abram journeyed, going on and on. . . ."[5] In our case, however, it is a heritage and a gift, in that He has given

[20] *Implicit in the words* ולא ארע. [21] *I.e. love and fear.* [22] Ps. *139:12, here interpreted* "hideth (me) *not from Thee.*" [23] "*Cutting off*" *of the soul; Divine punishment through premature or sudden death.* [24] *Anything forbidden to be used or handled on Sabbath.* [25] *In* Ps. *73:22, quoted earlier.* [26] Ps. *104:24.* [27] *The Tetragrammaton spelled out fully (each of the four letters—phonetically) in Hebrew letters, produces four variations,*

זה שתפול עליה אימתה ופחד תחלה ואח"כ אהבה רבה בתענוגים או כרשפי אש כמדת הצדיקי' שנזדכך חומרם וכנודע שרעת הוא לשון הרגשה בנפש והוא כולל חסד וגבורה. אעפ"כ אני תמיד עמך כי אין החומר מונע יחוד הנפש באור א"ס ב"ה הממלא כל עלמין וכמ"ש גם חושך לא יחשיך ממך· ובזה יובן חומר עונש איסור מלאכה בשבתות וחמץ בפסח השוה לכל נפש לפי שאף בנפש בור ועם הארץ גמור מאיר אור קדושת שבת וי"ט ונידון בנפשו בכרת וסקילה על חילול קדושה זו. וגם משהו חמץ או טלטול מוקצה פוגם בקדושה שעל נפשו כמו בקדושת נפש הצדיק כי תורה אחת לכולנו· [ומ"ש בהמות לשון רבים לרמז כי לפניו ית' גם בחי' דעת העליון הכולל חו"ג נדמה כבהמות ועשייה גופנית לגבי אור א"ס כמ"ש כולם בחכמה עשית ונק' בהמה רבה כמ"ש במ"א. והוא שם ב"ן בגימ' בהמ"ה שלפני האצילות]:

פרק מז והנה בכל דור ודור וכל יום ויום חייב אדם לראות עצמו כאילו הוא יצא היום ממצרים. והיא יציאת נפש האלהית ממאסר הגוף משכא דחויא ליכלל ביחוד אור א"ס ב"ה ע"י עסק התורה והמצות בכלל ובפרט בקבלת מלכות שמים בק"ש שבה מקבל וממשיך עליו יחודו ית' בפירוש באמרו ה' אלהינו ה' אחד. וכמש"ל כי אלהינו הוא כמו אלהי אברהם וכו' לפי שהיה בטל ונכלל ביחוד אור א"ס ב"ה רק שאברהם זכה לזה במעשיו והילוכו בקודש ממדרגה למדרגה. כמ"ש ויסע אברם הלוך ונסוע וגו': אבל אנחנו ירושה ומתנה היא לנו שנתן לנו

---

or Names, corresponding to the numbers 45 (שם מ"ה), *52* (שם ב"ן), *63* (שם ס"ג), *and 72* (שם ע"ב).

Chapter 47
[1] *The* Mishnah (Pesachim *10, M.5*) *does not contain the words "and every day" and "that day," which the author inserts.* [2] Deut. *6:4.* [3] *Ch. 46.* [4] "*. . . the G-d of Isaac, and the G-d of Jacob*"—Liturgy (Amidah). *Cf.* Mechilta *on* Ex. *3:15.* [5] Gen. *12:9.*

us His Torah and has clothed in it His blessed will and wisdom, which are united with His blessed Essence and Being in perfect unity; and surely this is as if He gave us His very self, as it were. In this sense the *Zohar*[6] commented on the verse: "That they bring Me an offering." (For the expression לי ["to Me"] has the same meaning as אותי ["Me"]; and hence the text should have read "Me *and* an offering,"[7] except that both are one and the same. Study it well there.)

This is the interpretation of "And Thou hast given to us, O Lord, our G–d, in love, . . ." [and] "For by the light of Thy countenance hast Thou given us, O Lord our G–d. . . ."[8] Therefore the only thing that precludes us from the attachment of the soul to His blessed Unity and light is the will, that is, if the human being does not will it at all, G–d forbid, to cleave to Him. . . . But immediately he does so desire, and he accepts and draws upon himself His blessed G–dliness and declares: "The Lord is our G–d, the Lord is One." then surely is his soul spontaneously absorbed into His blessed Unity, for "Spirit evokes spirit, and draws forth spirit."[9] This is a form of "Exodus from Egypt." Therefore it was ordained that the paragraph concerning the Exodus from Egypt be read specifically during the recital of the *Shema*,[10] although it is a commandment by itself, and not appertaining to the commandment of the recital of the *Shema*, as is stated in the Talmud and Codes;[11] for they are actually the same thing. Likewise, at the end of the paragraph referring to the Exodus from Egypt, it is concluded also, "I am the Lord your G–d."[12] This also accords with what has been explained earlier.

•▲ *Chapter 48*

Contemplating on the greatness of the blessed *En Sof*, the intelligent person [will realise] that as His name indicates, so is He—there is no end or limit or finitude at all to the light and vitality that diffuse from Him, may He be blessed, by His simple[1] will, and which is united with His blessed essence and being in perfect unity. Had the worlds descended from the light of the blessed *En Sof* without "contractions,"[2] but according to a gradual descent, from grade to grade by means of cause and effect—this world would not, in such case, have ever been created in its present form, in a finite and limited order, [viz.] "From the earth to heaven there being a journey of five hundred years,"[3] and similarly between heaven and heaven, and so also the diameter of each heaven. Even the World to Come and the Supreme Garden of Eden—the habitation of the souls of the great *tzaddikim*—and the souls themselves and, needless to add, the angels—are all in the realm of bounds and limitation, for

---

[6] *II, 140b* [7] *Literally* ". . . take *Me and an offering*." [8] Liturgy. *The emphasis is on* "*Thou hast* given *us* . . . our G–d." [9] *I.e. bestows an extra measure of spirituality*. Zohar *II, 162b*. [10] *Cf.* Berachot, *13a; Rabbi Schneur Zalman of Liadi*, Shulchan Aruch, Orach Chayim *58:1*. [11] Berachot *21a;* Ibid. *67:1–2*. [12] Num. *15:41*.

Chapter 48

[1] *I.e. uncaused.* [2] *The doctrine of* tzimtzum *has already been referred to previously in chs. 21 and 38. Here and in the next chapter, it is further expounded.* [3] Chagigah *13a*.

לנו את תורתו והלביש בה רצונו וחכמתו ית' המיוחדים במהותו ועצמותו ית' בתכלית היחוד והרי זה כאלו נתן לנו את עצמו כביכול. כמ"ש בז"הק ע"פ ויקחו לי תרומה [דלי כלומר אותי והל"ל ותרומה אלא משום דכולא חד ע"ש היטב]: וז"ש ותתן לנו ה' אלהינו באהבה כו' כי באור פניך נתת לנו ה' אלהינו כו' ולזה אין מונע לנו מדביקות הנפש ביחודו ואורו ית' אלא הרצון שאם אין האדם רוצה כלל ח"ו לדבקה בו כו'. אבל מיד שרוצה ומקבל וממשיך עליו אלהותו ית' ואומר ה' אלהינו ה' אחד הרי ממילא נכללת נפשו ביחודו ית' דרוח אייתי רוח ואמשיך רוח והיא בחי' יציאת מצרים ולכן תקנו פ' יציאת מצרים בשעת ק"ש דווקא. אף שהיא מצוה בפני עצמה ולא ממצות ק"ש כדאיתא בגמרא ופוסקים אלא מפני שהן דבר אחד ממש. וכן בסוף פ' יציאת מצרים מסיים ג"כ אני ה' אלהיכם והיינו גם כן כמש"ל:

פרק מח

והנה כאשר יתבונן המשכיל בגדולת א"ס ב"ה כי כשמו כן הוא א"ס ואין קץ ותכלית כלל לאור וחיות המתפשט ממנו ית' ברצונו הפשוט ומיוחד במהותו ועצמותו ית' בתכלית היחוד ואילו היתה השתלשלות העולמות מאור א"ס ב"ה בלי צמצומי' רק כסדר המדרגות ממדרגה למדרגה בדרך עלה ועלול לא היה העוה"ז נברא כלל כמו שהוא עתה בבחי' גבול ותכלית מהארץ לרקיע מהלך ת"ק שנה וכן בין כל רקיע לרקיע וכן עובי כל רקיע ורקיע ואפי' עו"הב וג"ע העליון מדור נשמות הצדיקי' הגדולים והנשמו' עצמן ואצ"ל המלאכי' הן בבחי' גבול ותכלית כי יש

there is a limit to their apprehension of the light of the blessed *En Sof*, which shines on them through being clothed in *ChaBaD*, etc., hence, there is also a boundary to their enjoyment derived from the splendour of the *Shechinah*, and to their pleasure in the light of G–d; for they cannot absorb enjoyment and delight of an infinite order, without being nullified out of their existence and returned to their source.

●▲ Now, as for the intricate details of the "contractions"—this is not the place for their explanation.[4] But in general they are something in the nature of "occulation and concealment" of the flow of the light and vitality, so that only an extremely minute portion of light and vitality should illuminate and reach the lower creatures in a revealed manner, as it were, pervading them and acting in them and animating them so that they might receive existence *ex nihilo*, and be in a state of finitude and limitation. This constitutes an exceedingly contracted illumination, and it is considered as virtually nothing at all compared with the quality of the limitless and infinite illumination, and there is no reference or relationship between them, as the term "reference" is understood in values, where the figure 1 has a relevancy with the number 1,000,000, for it is one millionth part of it; but as regards a thing which is in the realm of infinity, there is no number that can be considered relative to it, for a billion or trillion do not attain the relevancy of the figure 1 in comparison with a billion or trillion, but is veritably accounted as nothing.

▲ So, indeed, is the quality of the contracted illumination which informs the higher and lower worlds, acting in them and animating them—compared with the quality of the hidden and concealed light that is of an infinite order and does not clothe itself or exercise its influence in the worlds, to animate them in a revealed manner, but it "encompasses" them from above and is called *sovev kol almin* (the "Encompasser of all Worlds"). The meaning of this is not that it encircles and encompasses from above spatially, G–d forbid, for in spiritual matters the category of space is in no way applicable. But the meaning is that it "Encircles and encompasses from above" insofar as the so-called "revealed" influence is concerned, for influence which is in the category of "revelation" in the worlds, is referred to as "investiture", being "clothed"

---

[4] *See* Torah Or, *p. 27a;* Likutei Torah, "Vayikrah," *p. 101 ff.;* "Ekev," *p. 33 ff. See also Translator's Introduction to* Likutei Amarim, *Part II.*

יש גבול להשגתן באור א״ס ב״ה המאיר עליהן בהתלבשות חב״ד כו׳. ולכן יש גבול להנאתן שנהנין מזיו השכינה ומתענגין באור ה׳ כי אין יכולין לקבל הנאה ותענוג בבחי׳ א״ס ממש שלא יתבטלו ממציאותן ויחזרו למקורן. והנה פרטיות הצמצומים איך ומה אין כאן מקום ביאורם. אך דרך כלל הן הם בחי׳ הסתר והעלם המשכת האור והחיות שלא יאיר ויומשך לתחתונים בבחי׳ גילוי להתלבש ולהשפיע בהן ולהחיותם להיות יש מאין. כי אם מעט מזער אור וחיות בכדי שיהיו בבחי׳ גבול ותכלית שהיא הארה מועטת מאד וממש כלא חשיבי לגבי בחי׳ הארה בלי גבול ותכלית ואין ביניהם ערך ויחס כלל כנודע פי׳ מלת ערך במספרים שאחד במספר יש לו ערך לגבי מספר אלף אלפים שהוא חלק אחד מני אלף אלפים אבל לגבי דבר שהוא בבחי׳ בלי גבול ומספר כלל אין כנגדו שום ערך במספרים שאפי׳ אלף אלפי אלפים וריבוא רבבות אינן אפי׳ כערך מספר אחד לגבי אלף אלפי אלפים ורבוא רבבות אלא כלא ממש חשיבי. וככה ממש היא בחי׳ ההארה מועטת זו המתלבשת בעולמות עליונים ותחתונים להשפיע בהם להחיותם לגבי ערך אור הגנוז ונעלם שהוא בבחי׳ א״ס ואינו מתלבש ומשפיע בעולמות בבחי׳ גילוי להחיותם אלא מקיף עליהם מלמעלה ונקרא סובב כל עלמין. ואין הפי׳ סובב ומקיף מלמעלה בבחי׳ מקום ח״ו כי לא שייך כלל בחי׳ מקום ברוחניות. אלא ר״ל סובב ומקיף מלמעלה לענין בחי׳ גילוי השפעה כי ההשפעה שהוא בבחי׳ גילוי בעולמו׳ נקראת בשם הלבשה שמתלבשת

בעולמות

within the worlds, for the influence that they receive is clothed and comprehended by them; whereas the influence which does not come within the category of "revelation," but remains in occultation and concealment and is not apprehended by the worlds, is not described as being "invested" but as "encircling and encompassing." Therefore, since the worlds belong in the order of the finite and limited, it follows that only an extremely minute and contracted reflection of the flow of the light of the blessed *En Sof* clothes and reveals itself in them in a revealed form, and this, only to animate them in a finite and limited state. But the principal light without contraction to such an extent, is called *makif* ("encircler") and *sovev* ("encompasser"), since its influence is not revealed within them, inasmuch as they belong in the order of the finite and the limited.

●▲ To illustrate this point, consider this material world. Even though "The whole world is full of His glory,"[5] namely, the light of the blessed *En Sof*, as is written: "Do not I fill heaven and earth? saith the Lord,"[6] nevertheless only a very small vitality, of the category of inanimate and vegetable worlds, is clothed therein in the form of "revealed" influence, while all the light of the blessed *En Sof* is termed as "encompassing" it, even though it actually pervades it, since its influence is no more revealed in it, but is active in it in a hidden and concealed manner; and any influence of a concealed nature is referred to as "Encircling from above," for the "hidden world" is on a higher plane than the "revealed world."

Let us make it more intelligible by means of an example. When a man forms an image in his mind of something that he has seen or sees—although the entire body and essence of that thing, both its exterior and interior and its very core, are completely mirrored in his mind and thought, for he has seen it or is seeing it in its entirety—this is expressed by saying that his mind encompasses that object completely, and that thing is enveloped by his mind and thought. But it is not encompassed in actual fact, only in the imagination of the man's thought and mind.

▲ The Holy One, blessed be He, however, of Whom it is written: "For My thoughts are not your thoughts, . . ."[7] surely

[5] Isa. *6:3*. [6] Jer. *23:24*. [7] Isa. *55:8*.

בעולמות כי הם מלבישים ומשיגים ההשפעה שמקבלים משא״כ ההשפעה שאינה בבחי׳ גילוי אלא בהסתר והעלם ואין העולמות משיגים אותה אינה נקראת מתלבשת אלא מקפת וסובבת הלכך מאחר שהעולמות הם בבחי׳ גבול ותכלית נמצא שאין השפעת אור א״ס מתלבש ומתגלה בהם בבחי׳ גילוי רק מעט מזער הארה מועטת מצומצמת מאד מאד והיא רק כדי להחיותם בבחי׳ גבול ותכלית. אבל עיקר האור בלי צמצום כ״כ נק׳ מקיף וסובב מאחר שאין השפעתו מתגלית בתוכם מאחר שהם בבחי׳ גבול ותכלית. והמשל בזה הנה הארץ הלזו הגשמיות אף שמלא כל הארץ כבודו. והיינו אור א״ס ב״ה כמ״ש הלא את השמים ואת הארץ אני מלא נאם ה׳. אעפ״כ אין מתלבש בתוכה בבחי׳ גילוי ההשפעה רק חיות מעט מזער בחי׳ דומם וצומח לבד וכל אור א״ס ב״ה נק׳ סובב עליה אף שהוא בתוכה ממש. מאחר שאין השפעתו מתגלית בה יותר רק משפיע בה בבחי׳ הסתר והעלם וכל השפעה שבבחי׳ הסתר נקרא מקיף מלמעלה כי עלמא דאתכסי׳ הוא למעלה במדרגה מעלמ׳ דאתגליא ולקרב אל השכל יותר הוא בדרך משל. כמו האדם שמצייר בדעתו איזה דבר שראה או שרואה הנה אף שכל גוף עצם הדבר ההוא וגבו ותוכו ותוך תוכו כולו מצוייר בדעתו ומחשבתו מפני שראהו כולו או שרואהו הנה נקראת דעתו מקפת הדבר ההוא כולו. והדבר ההוא מוקף בדעתו ומחשבתו רק שאינו מוקף בפועל ממש רק בדמיון מחשבת האדם ודעתו. אבל הקב״ה דכתיב ביה כי לא מחשבותי מחשבותיכם כו׳ הרי

מחשבתו

His Thought and Mind knowing all created things, encompass each and every created being from its beginning to its end and its inside and very core, all in actual reality.

● For example, in the case of the orb of this earth, His blessed knowledge encompasses the entire diameter of the globe of the earth, together with all that is in it and its deepest interior to its lowest depths, all in actual reality. For this knowledge constitutes the vitality of the whole spherical thickness of the Earth and its creation *ex nihilo*. However, it would not have come into being as it now is, as a finite and limited thing, with an exceedingly minute vitality sufficient for the categories of inorganic matter and vegetation, were it not for the many powerful contractions which have condensed the light and vitality that is clothed in the orb of the earth, so as to animate it and sustain it in its finite and limited status and in the categories of inorganic and vegetable matter alone.

▲ But His blessed knowledge which is united with His essence and being—for "He is the Knowledge, the Knower, and the Known, and knowing Himself, as it were, He knows all created things, but not with a knowledge that is external to Himself, like the knowledge of a human being, for all of them [the created things] are derived from His blessed Reality, and this thing is not within the power of human beings to comprehend clearly," and so forth[8]—

Note: As Maimonides, of blessed memory, has written—and the scholars of Kabbalah subscribed to his views—as is stated in Pardess *of Rabbi Moshe Cordovero, of blessed memory. This also accords with the Kabbalah of our Master Rabbi Isaac Luria, of blessed memory, in the mystery of* tzimtzum *and the clothing of the lights in vessels, as has been mentioned previously in ch. 2.*

—this knowledge, since it is of an infinite order, is not described as clothing itself in the orb of the earth, which is finite and limited, but as encircling and encompassing it, although this knowledge embraces its entire thickness and interior in actual reality, thus giving it existence *ex nihilo*, as is explained elsewhere.

●▲ *Chapter 49*

Even though the particular aspects of the nature of the occultation and concealment of the light of the blessed *En Sof* in the descent of the worlds—until this material world was created—are too numerous to count

---

[8] Maimonides, *Code*, hilchot Yesodei ha-Torah *2:10; cf.* Tanya, *beg. ch. 2.*

מחשבתו ודעתו שיודע כל הנבראים מקפת כל נברא ונברא מראשו ועד תחתיתו ותוכו ותוך תוכו הכל בפועל ממש. למשל כדור הארץ הלזו הרי ידיעתו ית' מקפת כל עובי כדור הארץ וכל אשר בתוכו ותוך תוכו עד תחתיתו הכל בפועל ממש שהרי ידיעה זו היא חיות כל עובי כדור הארץ כולו והתהוותו מאין ליש רק שלא היה מתהוה כמות שהוא עתה בעל גבול ותכלית וחיות מועטת מאד כדי בחי' דומם וצומח. אם לא ע"י צמצומים רבים ועצומים שצמצמו האור והחיות שנתלבש בכדור הארץ להחיותו ולקיימו בבחי' גבול ותכלית ובבחי' דומם וצומח בלבד אך ידיעתו ית' המיוחדת במהותו ועצמותו. כי הוא המדע והוא היודע והוא הידוע ובידיעת עצמו כביכול יודע כל הנבראים ולא בידיעה שחוץ ממנו כידיעת האדם. כי כולם נמצאים מאמיתתו ית'. ודבר זה אין ביכולת האדם להשיגו על בוריו וכו'* הרי ידיעה זו מאחר שהיא בבחי' א"ס אינה נקרא' בשם מתלבשת בכדור הארץ שהוא בעל גבול ותכלית אלא מקפת וסובבת. אף שידיעה זו כוללת כל עביו ותוכו בפועל ממש ומהווה אותו ע"ז מאין ליש וכמ"ש במ"א:

הגהה

*(כמ"ש הרמב"ם ז"ל והסכימו עמו חכמי הקבלה כמ"ש בפרד"ס מהרמ"ק ז"ל וכ"ה לפי קבלת האר"י ז"ל בסוד הצמצו' והתלבשות אורות בכלים כמש"ל פ"ב):

פרק מט

והנה אף כי פרטי בחי' ההסתר וההעלם אור א"ס ב"ה בהשתלשלות העולמות עד שנברא עו"הז הגשמי עצמו מספר ומינים ממינים

and are of many diverse kinds, as is known to those who have tasted of the Tree of Life,[1] yet in general there are three levels of powerful and comprehensive "contractions," giving rise to three comprehensive worlds, each category consisting of myriads upon myriads of particulars. These are the three worlds of *Beriah*, *Yetzirah* and *Asiyah*, for the world of *Atzilut* is G-dliness itself.

In order to create the world of *Beriah*, which consists of the higher souls and angels, whose service to G-d is in the sphere of ChaBaD [the intellectual faculties] which are clothed in them and are apprehended by them and from which they receive influence, there preceded a powerful "contraction," as mentioned above.

So, too, from *Beriah* to *Yetzirah*. For the minute portion of light which clothes itself in the world of *Beriah* is still in a category of infinity in relation to the world of *Yetzirah*, and is unable to clothe itself in the latter except through a contraction and occulation. So, too, from *Yetzirah* to *Asiyah*.

(An elaborate explanation of these three "contractions," in order to make them more accessible to our poor intellect is given elsewhere.[2])

The purpose of all the "contractions" is the creation of the material human body and the subjugation of the *sitra achra*, to bring about the pre-eminence of light supplanting darkness—when a person elevates his divine soul and his vivifying soul together with their garments[3] and all the powers of the body, to G-d alone, as has been discussed earlier at length,[4] for this is the purpose of the descent of the worlds.

To quote [again] "As water mirrors the reflection of a face": As the Holy One, blessed be He, has, as it were, laid down and set aside, figuratively speaking, His great infinite light, and has stored it away and concealed it by means of three different kinds of "contractions"—and all this because of His love for lowly man, in order to raise him up to G-d, for "Love impels the flesh,"[5] how much more, and an infinite number of times more, is it fitting that a man also should relinquish and set aside all he possesses, both spiritually and physically, and renounce everything in order to cleave to Him, may He be blessed, with attachment, desire and longing, without any hindrance, within or without, neither of body nor soul, nor money, nor wife and children.

• Thereby will be understood the true reason and meaning of the Rabbinical enactment, ordaining the recitations of the blessings of the *Shema*: two preceding it. . . .[6]

---

[1] *The Kabbalah.* [2] *The doctrine of* tzimtzum *is more fully discussed in the second part of the* Tanya (Sha'ar ha-Yichud veha-Emunah). [3] *The text should read* ולבושיהן *instead of* ולבושיה, *as it refers to both souls.* [4] *Chs. 35–37.* [5] Bava Metziah *84a.* [6] Berachot, *ch. 1,* Mishnah *4.*

• 19 Iyar

ממינים שונים כידוע לטועמים מעץ החיים: אך דרך כלל הם שלשה מיני צמצומים עצומים כלליים. לשלשה מיני עולמות כלליים. ובכל כלל יש רבוא רבבות פרטיים. והם שלשה עולמות בי״ע. כי עולם האצילו׳ הוא אלהות ממש. וכדי לברוא עולם הבריא׳ שהן נשמות ומלאכים עליונים אשר עבודתם לה׳ בבחי׳ חב״ד המתלבשים בהם והם משיגים ומקבלים מהם היה תחלה צמצום עצום כנ״ל. וכן מבריאה ליצירה. כי אור מעט מזער המתלבש בעולם הבריא׳ עדיין הוא בבחי׳ א״ס לגבי עולם היצירה. ואי אפשר להתלבש בו אלא ע״י צמצום והעלם וכן מיצירה לעשיה [וכמ״ש במ״א ביאור שלשה צמצומים אלו באריכות לקרב אל שכלינו הדל] ותכלית כל הצמצומים הוא כדי לברוא גוף האדם החומרי ולאכפייא לס״א ולהיות יתרון האור מן החושך בהעלות האדם את נפשו האלהית והחיונית ולבושיה וכל כחות הגוף כולן לה׳ לבדו כנ״ל באריכות. כי זה תכלית השתלשלות העולמות. והנה כמים הפנים לפנים כמו שהקב״ה כביכול הניח וסילק לצד אחד דרך משל את אורו הגדול הבלתי תכלית וגנזו והסתירו בג׳ מיני צמצומים שונים. והכל בשביל אהבת האדם התחתון להעלותו לה׳. כי אהבה דוחקת הבשר. עאכ״ו בכפלי כפליים לאין קץ כי ראוי לאדם ג״כ להניח ולעזוב כל אשר לו מנפש ועד בשר ולהפקיר הכל בשביל לדבקה בו ית׳ בדביקה חשיקה וחפיצה ולא יהיה שום מונע מבית ומבחוץ לא גוף ולא נפש ולא ממון ולא אשה ובנים. ובזה יובן טוב טעם ודעת לתקנת חכמים שתקנו ברכות ק״ש שתים לפניה כו׳

For it would appear, at first glance, that they have no connection whatever with the recital of the *Shema*, as "Rashba"[7] and other codifiers have stated. Why, then, were they termed "Blessings of the *Shema?*" And why were they ordained to to be recited specifically before it?

But the reason is that the essence of the recital of the *Shema* is to fulfil the injunction "With all thine heart, . . ." to wit, "With both thy natures, . . ."[8] that is to say, to overcome anything that deters from the love of G–d. For "thine heart" alludes to the wife and children, to whom a man's heart is, by his very nature, bound. So have the Rabbis, of blessed memory, commented on the verses: "For He spake, and it came to pass,"[9] that this refers to the wife; "He commanded, and it stood fast,"[10] that this refers to the children;[11] and by "Thy soul and thy might" is understood, literally, your life and sustenance—renouncing everything for the love of G–d. ▲ But how can physical man attain to this level? It is, therefore, to this end that the blessing of *yotzer or* was introduced first, for [in this blessing] there is said and repeated at length the account and order of the angels "standing at the world's summit" in order to proclaim the greatness of the Holy One, blessed be He—how all of them are nullified in His blessed light and "Pronounce in fear, . . ." "and sanctify, . . ." and "Declare in fear, 'Holy,' . . ."[12] [13] meaning that He is apart from them, and He does not clothe Himself in them in a "revealed" state, but "The whole *earth* is full of His glory," namely, the community of Israel above and Israel below, as has been explained earlier.

So, too, "The *Ofanim* and holy *Chayyot* with great thunder . . . [declare] 'Blessed be the glory of the Lord from His place,' "[14] for they neither know, nor do they apprehend His place, as we say, "For He alone is exalted and holy."[15]

▲ Then follows the second blessing, "With an everlasting love hast Thou loved us, O Lord, our G–d."[16] That is to say, that He set aside all the supernal, holy hosts and caused His *Shechinah* to dwell upon us, so that He be called "Our G–d," in the same sense that He is called "The G–d of Abraham," as explained earlier.[17] This is because "love impels the flesh." Therefore it is called *ahavat olam* ("worldly love"), for this is the so-called "contraction" of His great and infinite light, taking on the garb of finitude, which is called *olam* ("world"), for the sake of the love of His people Israel, in order to bring them near to Him, that they might be absorbed into His blessed Unity and Oneness.

This is also the meaning of "With great and exceeding pity [hast Thou pitied us],"[18] namely, exceeding the nearness of G–d towards all the hosts above; ". . . and us hast Thou chosen

---

[7] *Rabbi Solomon ibn Aderet, 13th cent. Spanish Talmud exegete and codifier.* [8] Berachot *54a.* [9] Ps. *33:9.* [10] Ibid. [11] Shabbat *152a.* [12] Isa. *6:3.* [13] Liturgy. [14] Ezek. *3:12.* [15] Liturgy. [16] *According to the Lurianic rite*—אהבת עולם. *In the Ashkenazic rite the text reads*—אהבה רבה. [17] *Chs. 46 and 47.* [18] Liturgy.

כו׳ דלכאורה אין להם שייכות כלל עם קריאת שמע כמ״ש הרשב״א ושאר פוסקי׳. ולמה קראו אותן ברכות ק״ש ולמה תקנו אותן לפניה דווקא. אלא משום שעיקר ק״ש לקיים בכל לבבך כו׳ בשני יצריך כו׳ דהיינו לעמוד נגד כל מונע מאהבת ה׳. ולבבך הן האשה וילדיה. שלבבו של אדם קשורה בהן בטבעו. כמשארז״ל ע״פ הוא אמר ויהי זו אשה הוא צוה ויעמוד אלו בנים. ונפשך ומאדך כמשמעו חיי ומזוני להפקיר הכל בשביל אהבת ה׳. ואיך יבא האדם החומרי למדה זו לכך סידרו תחלה ברכות יוצר אור. ושם נאמר ונשנה באריכות ענין וסדר המלאכים העומדים ברום עולם להודיע גדולתו של הקב״ה איך שכולם בטלים לאורו ית׳ ומשמיעים ביראה כו׳ ומקדישים כו׳ ואומרים ביראה קדוש כו׳ כלומר שהוא מובדל מהן ואינו מתלבש בהן בבחי׳ גילוי אלא מלא כל הארץ כבודו היא כנסת ישראל למעלה וישראל למטה כנ״ל. וכן האופנים וחיות הקודש ברעש גדול וכו׳ ברוך כבוד ה׳ ממקומו לפי שאין יודעים ומשיגים מקומו וכמ״ש כי הוא לבדו מרום וקדוש. ואח״כ ברכה שניה אהבת עולם אהבתנו ה׳ אלהינו. כלומר שהניח כל צבא מעלה הקדושים והשרה שכינתו עלינו להיות נקרא אלהינו. כמו אלהי אברהם כו׳ כנ״ל. והיינו כי אהבה דוחקת הבשר ולכן נקרא אהבת עולם שהיא בחי׳ צמצום אורו הגדול הבלתי תכלית להתלבש בבחי׳ גבול הנקרא עולם בעבור אהבת עמו ישראל כדי לקרבם אליו ליכלל ביחודו ואחדותו ית׳. וז״ש חמלה גדולה ויתירה פי׳ יתירה על קרבת אלהים שבכל צבא מעלה. ובנו בחרת מכל

from every people and tongue," which refers to the material body which, in its corporeal aspects, is similar to the bodies of the gentiles of the world; "And Thou hast brought us near . . . to give thanks, . . ."—the interpretation of "thanks" will be given elsewhere; ". . . and proclaim Thy Unity, . . ."[19]—to be absorbed into His blessed Unity, as has been explained above.

●▲ When the intelligent person will reflect on these matters in the depths of his heart and brain, then—as [surely as] water mirrors the image of a face—his soul will spontaneously be kindled and it will clothe itself in a spirit of benevolence, willingly to lay down and resolutely to abandon all he possesses, in order only to cleave unto Him, may He be blessed, and to be absorbed into His light with an attachment and longing, and so forth, in a manner of "osculation" (נשיקין) and the attachment of spirit to spirit, as has been explained earlier.

But how does the attachment of spirit to spirit take place? To this end it is stated [further on]: "And these words shall be . . . upon thine heart. And thou shalt speak of them. . . ."[20] As is explained in *Etz Chayim* that the union of "osculation" is essentially the union of ChaBaD with ChaBaD,[21] that is, concentration in the Torah; while the mouth, as the outlet of the breath and its emergence into a revealed state, represents the category of speech engaged in ▲words of the Torah, for "By the word that proceedeth out of the mouth of G-d doth man live."[22] However, one does not fulfil one's duty by meditation and deliberation alone, until one expresses the words with his lips, in order to draw the light of the blessed *En Sof* downwards [even] unto the vivifying soul which dwells in the blood of man—which is produced by [the intake of food from] the mineral, vegetable and animal [worlds]—thus to raise them all to G-d, together with the entire Universe and to cause them to be absorbed in His blessed Unity and Light, which will illumine the world and its inhabitants in a revealed manner—"And the glory of G-d shall be revealed, and all flesh shall see it together. . . ."[23] For this is the purpose of the descent of all the worlds, that the glory of the Lord may pervade this world especially, in a revealed manner, to "change darkness to light and bitterness to sweetness," as has been explained above at length.[24] And this is the essence of man's *kavanah* in his service: to draw the light of the blessed *En Sof* down below. However, the initiative must come through the elevation of the מ"ן[25] to surrender to Him his soul and possessions, as has been explained above.

●▲ Chapter 50

All the distinctions and gradations of love, that have been mentioned above, derive from the "right side," from the distinction of "Priest, man of

---

[19] Ibid. [20] *From the first portion of the* Shema (Deut. *6:4–9)*. [21] *The attachment of the intellectual faculties of man to those of G-d embodied in the Torah.* [22] Deut. *8:3*. [23] Isa. *40:5*. [24] *Chs. 36, 37.* [25] מים נוקבין. *See end ch. 10, above.*

מכל עם ולשון הוא הגוף החומרי הנדמה בחומריותו לגופי אומות העולם. וקרבתנו וכו׳ להודות וכו׳ ופי׳ הודאה יתבאר במ״א. וליחדך כו׳ ליכלל ביחודו ית׳ כנ״ל והנה כאשר ישים המשכיל אלה הדברים אל עומקא דלבא ומוחא אזי ממילא כמים הפנים לפנים תתלהט נפשו ותתלבש ברוח נדיבה להתנדב להניח ולעזוב כל אשר לו מנגד ורק לדבקה בו ית׳ וליכלל באורו בדביקה חשיקה וכו׳ בבחי׳ נשיקין ואתדבקות רוחא ברוחא כנ״ל. אך איך היא בחי׳ אתדבקות רוחא ברוחא לזה אמר והיו הדברים האלה כו׳ על לבבך ודברת בם כו׳ וכמ״ש בע״ח שיחוד הנשיקין עיקרו הוא יחוד חב״ד בחב״ד והוא עיון התורה והפה הוא מוצא הרוח וגילויו בבחי׳ גילוי והיינו בחי׳ הדבור בד״ת. כי על מוצא פי ה׳ יחיה האדם ומ״מ לא יצא ידי חובתו בהרהור ועיון לבדו עד שיוציא בשפתיו כדי להמשיך אור א״ס ב״ה למטה עד נפש החיונית השוכנת בדם האדם המתהוה מדומם צומח חי כדי להעלות כולן לה׳ עם כל העולם כולו ולכללן ביחודו ואורו ית׳ אשר יאיר לארץ ולדרים בבחי׳ גילוי ונגלה כבוד ה׳ וראו כל בשר וכו׳ שזהו תכלית השתלשלות כל העולמות להיות כבוד ה׳ מלא כל הארץ הלזו דוקא בבחי׳ גילוי לאהפכא חשוכא לנהורא ומרירא למיתקא כנ״ל באריכות. וזהו תכלית כוונת האדם בעבודתו להמשיך אור אין סוף ברוך הוא למטה רק שצריך תחלה העלאת מ״ן למסור לו נפשו ומאודו כנ״ל:

פרק נ **והנה** כל בחי׳ ומדרגות אהבה הנ״ל הן מסטרא דימינא ובחי׳ כהן איש

חסד

grace"[1] and are called *kesef ha-kodoshim* ("longing for holy things")[2] etymologically as in "Thou sore longedst[3] after thy father's house."[4]

There is, however, yet another distinction of love which excels them all, as gold is superior to silver, and this is a love like fiery coals from the distinction of the "Supernal *Gevurot*" from *Binah ilaah* ("Supernal Understanding").[5] This is when, through contemplation on the greatness of the blessed *En Sof*, before Whom everything is truly accounted as nought, the soul is kindled and flares up towards the glory of the splendour of His greatness, in order to gaze on the glory of the King, like glowing coals of a mighty flame which surges upwards, striving to be parted from the wick and the wood on which it has taken hold. This is brought on by the preponderance of the element of Divine fire that is in the divine soul. In consequence of this it develops a thirst, as is written: "My soul thirsteth for Thee";[6] next it attains the distinction of "love-sickness";[7] and then it reaches a state of very rapture of the soul (כלות הנפש) as is written: "Yea, my soul is enraptured."[8]

From here [supernal *Gevurot*] issues forth the root of the Levites[9] [on earth] below (and in the World to Come, when the world will be exalted, they will become the priests, as our Master Rabbi Isaac Luria, of blessed memory, commented on the verse, "But the priests, the Levites,"[10] that the Levites of to-day will become the priests of the future). The service of the Levites was to raise the voice of melody and thanksgiving, with song and music, with tunefulness and harmony, in a manner of "advance and retreat"[11] which is the distinction of the intense love resembling the flame that flashes out of the lightning, as is mentioned in the *Gemara* (*Chagigah*, ch. II).[12]

It is impossible to elucidate this matter clearly in writing. Yet every warm-hearted and intelligent person gifted with understanding, who deeply binds his mind and contemplation to G–d, will discover the goodness and light which are treasured up in his intelligent soul, each according to his capacity—("There is one who is affected [in one way] . . ., and there is one who is affected [in another],")—prefacing it with the fear of sin, in order to be completely parted from evil, that the iniquities may not interpose, . . ., G–d forbid.

●▲ The order of the service in occupying oneself with the Torah and commandments, a service derived from the category of the said intense love, is in the manner of "retreat" alone, as is written in *Sefer Yetzirah*: "And if thy heart hastens, return to the One."[13] The interpretation of [the phrase] "If thy heart hastens" is the craving of the soul that is in the right side of the heart

---

[1] Zohar *I, 256b; 258b.* [2] כסף הקדשים—*lit. "holy silver" (cf. II* Kings, *12:5).* [3] נכסף נכספתה—*from the same root as* כסף. [4] Gen. *31:30.* [5] Chochmah *and* Binah *in the intellect have their counterparts* chesed *and* gevurah *in the* middot. [6] Ps. *63:2.* [7] Song of Songs *2:5.* [8] Ps. *84:3.* [9] *Whereas the priest is the man of* chesed, *the Levite symbolises* gevurah, *as explained in many sources of Kabbalah and Chasidut. Cf. e.g.* Likutei Torah, Bamidbar, *1c;* Korach *54a f;* Va-Etchanan *8b.* [10] Ezek *44:15.* [11] *The counterpart of the ecstatic worship by the angels (*chayyot*); cf.* Ezek. *1:14.* [12] Chagigah *13b.* [13] *1:8 Cf. Introduction to* Tikunei Zohar *7a.*

חסד ונק׳ כסף הקדשים מלשון נכסוף נכספת לבית אביך. אך יש עוד בחי׳ אהבה העולה על כולנה כמעלת הזהב על הכסף והיא אהבה כרשפי אש מבחי׳ גבורות עליונות דבינה עילאה דהיינו שע״י התבוננות בגדולת א״ס ב״ה דכולא קמיה כלא ממש חשיב תתלהט ותתלהב הנפש ליקר תפאר׳ גדולתו ולאסתכל׳ ביקרא דמלכא כרשפי אש שלהבת עזה העולה למעל׳ וליפרד מהפתילה והעצים שנאחזת בהן והיינו על ידי תגבורת יסוד האש אלהי שבנפש האלהית ומזה באה לידי צמאון וכמ״ש צמאה לך נפשי ואח״כ לבחי׳ חולת אהבה ואח״כ באה לידי כלות הנפש ממש כמ״ש גם כלתה נפשי והנה מכאן יצא שורש הלוים למטה [ולעתיד שהעולם יתעלה יהיו הם הכהנים וכמ״ש האר״י ז״ל ע״פ והכהנים הלוים שהלוים של עכשיו יהיו כהנים לעתיד] ועבודת הלוים היתה להרים קול רינה ותודה בשירה וזמרה בניגון ונעימה בבחי׳ רצוא ושוב שהיא בחי׳ אהבה עזה זו כשלהבת היוצא מן הבזק כדאיתא בגמ׳ [פ״ב דחגיגה] ואי אפשר לבאר ענין זה היטב במכתב רק כל איש נלבב ונבון המשכיל על דבר ומעמיק לקשר דעתו ותבונתו בה׳ ימצא טוב ואור הגנוז בנפשו המשכלת כל חד לפום שיעורא דיליה [יש מתפעל כו׳ ויש מתפעל כו׳] אחרי קדימת יראת חטא להיות סור מרע בתכלית שלא להיות עונותיכם מבדילים כו׳ ח״ו. והנה סדר העבודה בעסק התורה והמצות הנמשכת מבחי׳ אהבה עזה זו היא בבחי׳ שוב לבד כמ״ש בספר יצירה ואם רץ לבך שוב לאחד פי׳ ואם רץ לבך היא תשוקת הנפש שבלב בחלל הימני

כשמתגברת

—when it gains sway[14] and bursts into flame and grows so exceedingly enraptured that the very soul is consumed with a desire to pour itself out into the embrace of its Father, the blessed Life of life, and to leave its confinement in the corporeal, physical body, in order to attach itself to Him, may He be blessed—then one must take to heart the teaching of the Rabbis, of blessed memory: "Despite thyself thou livest"[15] in this body, animating it for the purpose of drawing downwards the higher life from the blessed Life of life, through the life-giving Torah, that there may be a dwelling in the lower world for His blessed Oneness in a revealed state. As has been explained above, and as is explained in the holy *Zohar*,[16] "That there be 'One in One,' the meaning of which is that the *yichud hane'elam* (hidden Unity) shall become a category of the 'revealed world.'"

And this is the interpretation of the text: "Come, my beloved," and so on.[17] From this will be understood the adage of the Rabbis: "Despite thyself thou livest, and despite thyself. . . ."[18] As for what shall one's will be indeed? The answer will be found elsewhere in the lengthy explanation of this Mishnah:[19] "Despite thyself thou livest"—with the aid of the blessed Life of life.

•▲ *Chapter 51*

To return to, and further to elucidate, the expression of the *Yenuka*, mentioned earlier,[1] it is necessary first to explain—so that one may understand a little—the subject of the indwelling of the *Shechinah*, which rested in the Holy of Holies and likewise, all other places where the *Shechinah* rested.—What is the meaning of this? Is not the whole world full of His glory? And surely there is no place void of Him.

The [clue to the] understanding of this is to be found in the text: "From my flesh I see G-d."[2] The analogy is from the soul of a human being which pervades all the 248 organs of the body, from head to foot, yet its principal habitation and abode is in his brain, whence it is diffused throughout all the organs, each of which receives from it vitality and power appropriate to it, according to its composition and character: the eye for seeing, the ear for hearing, the mouth for speaking, and the feet for walking—as we clearly sense that in the brain one is conscious of everything that is affected in the 248 organs and everything that is experienced by them.

Now, the variation in the acquisition of powers and vitality by the organs of the body from the soul, is not due to the [soul's] essence and being, for this would make its core and essence divisible into 248 diverse parts, vested in 248 *loci* according to the various forms and locations of the organs of the body. If this were so, it would follow

[14] . . . *over the left part, i.e. over the natural desires of the animal soul.* [15] Avot *IV, 22.* [16] *II, 135a.* [17] "*. . . let us go out into the field,*" *etc., alluding to the consummation of love in the "field," i.e. this material world. Or perhaps it refers to the well-known Sabbath hymn, "Come my Beloved to meet the Bride."* [18] Avot *IV, 22.* [19] *See* Torah Or *2a; 25b, etc.*

Chapter 51
[1] *Ch. 35.* [2] Job *19:26.*

כשמתגברת ומתלהבת ומתלהטת במאד מאד עד כלות הנפש ממש להשתפך אל חיק אביה חיי החיים ב"ה ולצאת ממאסרה בגוף הגופני וגשמי לדבקה בו ית' אזי זאת ישיב אל לבו מארז"ל כי ע"כ אתה חי בגוף הזה להחיותו כדי להמשיך חיים עליוני' מחיי החיים ב"ה למטה ע"י תורת חיים להיות דירה בתחתוני' לאחדותו ית' בבחי' גילוי כמש"ל וכמ"ש בז"הק למהוי אחד באחד פי' שהיחוד הנעלם יהיה בבחי' עלמא דאתגליא וז"ש לכה דודי וכו' ובזה יובן מארז"ל ע"כ אתה חי וע"כ וכו' ואלא איך יהיה רצונו וכמ"ש במ"א באריכות על משנה זו ע"כ אתה חי בעזרת חיי החיים ב"ה:

פרק נא

והנה לתוספת ביאור לשון הינוקא דלעיל צריך לבאר תחלה להבין קצת ענין השראת השכינה שהיתה שורה בבית ק"ק וכן כל מקום השראת השכינה מה עניינו הלא מלא כל הארץ כבודו ולית אתר פנוי מיניה. אך הענין כדכתיב ומבשרי אחזה אלוה שכמו שנשמת האדם היא ממלאה כל רמ"ח אברי הגוף מראשו ועד רגלו ואעפ"כ עיקר משכנה והשראתה היא במוחו ומהמוח מתפשטת לכל האברים וכל אבר מקבל ממנה חיות וכח הראוי לו לפי מזגו ותכונתו העין לראות והאזן לשמוע והפה לדבר והרגלים להלוך כנראה בחוש שבמוח מרגיש כל הנפעל ברמ"ח אברים וכל הקורות אותם. והנה אין שינוי קבלת הכחות והחיות שבאברי הגוף מן הנשמה מצד עצמה ומהותה שיהיה מהותה ועצמותה מתחלק לרמ"ח חלקי' שונים מתלבשי' ברמ"ח מקומו' כפי ציור חלקי מקומו' אברי הגוף שלפי זה נמצא עצמותה

that its essence and core are fashioned in a material design, in a likeness and form resembling the shape of the body, Heaven forfend! Rather, it is entirely a single and simple spiritual entity, which, by its intrinsic essence, is divested of any corporeal shape and of any category and dimension of space, size, or physical limitation. It is, therefore, impertinent to say, in relation to its core and essence, that it is located in the brain of the head more than it is in the feet, since its core and essence are not subject to the dimensions and categories of physical limitation. But there are contained in it, in its intrinsic essence, 613 kinds of powers and vitalities to be actualised and to emerge from concealment in order to animate the 248 organs and 365 veins of the body, through their embodiment in the vivifying soul, which also possesses the corresponding 248 and 365 powers and vitalities.

• It is with reference to the flow of all the 613 kinds of powers and vitalities from the concealment of the soul into the body in the process of animating it, that it has been said that the principal dwelling place and abode of this flow of life and of this manifestation is situated entirely in the brains of the head. Therefore they first receive the power and vitality appropriate to them acccording to their disposition and character, namely, *ChaBaD* (*chochmah, binah, da'at*) and the faculty of thought, and all that pertains to the brains; and not only this, but also the sum-total of all the streams of vitality flowing to the other organs is also contained and is clothed in the brain that is in the head. It is there that the core and root of the said manifest flow of the light and vitality of the whole soul are to be found. From there a radiation is diffused to all the other organs, each of which receives the power and vitality appropriate to it in accordance with its disposition and character: the faculty of sight reveals itself in the eye, and the faculty of hearing manifests itself in the ear, and so forth. But all the powers flow from the brain, as is known, for therein is located the principal dwelling-place of the whole soul, in its manifest aspect, since the sum-total of the vitality that is diffused from it is revealed there. Only, the [individual] powers of the said general vitality shine forth and are radiated from there into all the organs of the body, much in the same manner as light radiates from the sun and penetrates rooms within rooms. (Even the heart receives vitality from the brain; hence the brain has an intrinsic supremacy over it, as has been explained above.[3])

---

[3] *Ch. 12.*

• 24 Iyar

עצמותה ומהותה מצוייר בציור גשמי ודמות ותבנית כתבנית הגוף ח"ו אלא כולה עצם אחד רוחני פשוט ומופשט מכל ציור גשמי ומבחי' וגדר מקום ומדה וגבול גשמי מצד מהותה ועצמות' ולא שייך במהות' ועצמותה לומר שהיא במוחין שבראש יותר מברגלים מאחר שמהותה ועצמותה אינה בגדר ובחי' מקום וגבול גשמי רק שתרי"ג מיני כחות וחיות כלולים בה במהותה ועצמותה לצאת אל הפועל והגילוי מההעלם להחיות רמ"ח אברין ושס"ה גידין שבגוף ע"י התלבשותם בנפש החיונית שיש לה ג"כ רמ"ח ושס"ה כחות וחיות הללו. והנה על המשכת כל התרי"ג מיני כחות וחיות מהעלם הנשמה אל הגוף להחיותו עליה אמרו שעיקר משכנה והשראתה של המשכה זו וגילוי זה הוא כולו במוחין שבראש ולכן הם מקבלים תחלה הכח והחיות הראוי להם לפי מזגם ותכונתם שהן חכ"ד וכח המחשבה וכל השייך למוחין ולא זו בלבד אלא גם כללות כל המשכות החיות לשאר האברים ג"כ כלולה ומלובשת במוחין שבראש ושם הוא עיקרה ושרשה של המשכ' זו בבחי' גילוי האור והחיו' של כל הנשמ' כולה ומשם מתפשטת הארה לשאר כל האברים ומקבל כל א' כח וחיו' הראוי לו כפי מזגו ותכונתו כח הראיה מתגלה בעין וכח השמיעה באוזן וכו'. וכל הכחות מתפשטים מהמוח כנודע כי שם הוא עיקר משכן הנשמה כולה בבחי' גילוי שנגלית שם כללו' החיות המתפשט ממנה. רק כחותיה של כללות החיות מאירים ומתפשטים משם לכל אברי הגוף כדמיון האור המתפשט ומאיר מהשמש לחדרי חדרים [ואפילו הלב מקבל מהמוח ולכן המוח שליט עליו בתולדתו כנ"ל]:

וככה

●▲ In a truly like manner, figuratively speaking, does the blessed *En Sof* fill all worlds and animate them. And in each world there are creatures without limit or end, myriads upon myriads of various grades of angels and souls, . . . and so, too, is the abundance of the worlds without end or limit, one higher than the other. . . .

Now, the core and essence of the blessed *En Sof* is the same in the higher and lower worlds, as in the example with the soul given above, and as is written in the *Tikunim* that "He is the Hidden One of all the hidden."[4] This is to be understood that even in the higher, hidden worlds He is hidden and concealed within them, just as He is hidden and concealed in the lower, for no thought can apprehend Him at all even in the higher worlds. Thus as He is to be found there, so is He found in the very lowest.

▲ The difference between the higher and lower worlds is with regard to the stream of vitality which the blessed *En Sof* causes to flow and illumine in a category of "revelation out of concealment" (which is one of the reasons why the influence and stream of this vitality is figuratively called "light"), thereby animating the worlds and the creatures therein. For the higher worlds receive, in a somewhat more "revealed" form, than do the lower; and all creatures therein receive each according to its capacity and nature, which is the nature and the form of the particular flow with which the blessed *En Sof* imbues and illumines it.

But the lower [worlds], even the spiritual ones, do not receive [the light] in quite such a "revealed" form, but only by means of many "garments," wherein the blessed *En Sof* invests the vitality and light which He causes to flow and shine on them in ▲order to animate them. These garments, wherein the blessed *En Sof* invests and conceals the light and vitality, are so numerous and powerful that thereby He created this very corporeal and physical world. He gives it existence and animates it by the vitality and light which He causes to flow and shine forth unto it—a light that is clothed, hidden and concealed within the numerous and powerful garments, which hide and screen the light and vitality, so that no light or vitality whatever is visibly revealed, but only

[4] Tikunei Zohar, *Introd. 17a.*

וככה ממש עד"מ א"ס ב"ה ממלא כל עלמין להחיותם ובכל עולם יש בריאים לאין קץ ותכלית רבוא רבבות מיני מדרגות מלאכים ונשמות כו' וכן ריבוי העולמות אין לו קץ וגבול גבוה על גבוה כו'. והנה מהותו ועצמותו של א"ס ב"ה שוה בעליונים ותחתונים כמשל הנשמה הנ"ל וכמ"ש בתיקונים דאיהו סתימו דכל סתימין פי' דאפי' בעלמין סתימין דלעילא הוא סתום ונעלם בתוכם כמו שהוא סתום ונעלם בתחתוני' כי לית מחשבה תפיסא ביה כלל אפי' בעולמות עליונים. ונמצא כמו שמצוי שם כך נמצא בתחתונים ממש. וההבדל שבין עולמו' עליונים ותחתונים הוא מצד המשכת החיות אשר א"ס ב"ה ממשיך ומאיר בבחי' גילוי מההעלם [שזה אחד מהטעמי' שההשפעה והמשכות החיות מכונה בשם אור עד"מ] להחיות העולמות והברואים שבהם שהעולמו' העליוני' מקבלים בבחי' גילוי קצת יותר מהתחתוני' וכל הברואי' שבהם מקבלים כל א' כפי כחו ותכונתו שהיא תכונת ובחי' המשכה הפרטית אשר א"ס ב"ה ממשיך ומאיר לו. והתחתונים אפי' הרוחניים אינם מקבלים בבחי' גילוי כ"כ רק בלבושים רבים אשר א"ס ב"ה מלביש בהם החיות והאור אשר ממשיך ומאיר להם להחיותם וכ"כ עצמו וגברו הלבושים אשר א"ס ב"ה מלביש ומסתיר בהם האור והחיות עד אשר ברא בו עוה"ז החומרי והגשמי ממש ומהווהו ומחיידו בחיות ואור אשר ממשיך ומאיר לו אור המלובש ומכוסה ומוסתר בתוך הלבושים הרבים והעצומים המעלימים ומסתירי' האור והחיות עד שאין נראה ונגלה שום אור וחיות רק

דברים

corporeal and physical things that appear lifeless. Yet they contain light and vitality which constantly give them existence *ex nihilo*, that they shall not revert and become nothing and nought as they had been. This light comes from the blessed *En Sof*, except that it is clothed in many garments, as is written in *Etz Chayim*, that the light and vitality of the physical orb of Earth, which is seen by mortal eyes, is derived from *Malchut d'Malchut d'Asiyah*[5] and in it is contained *Malchut d'Yetzirah*, and so on, so that in all of them are contained the Ten *Sefirot* of *Atzilut* which are united with their Emanator, the blessed *En Sof*.

•▲*Chapter 52*

Now, just as in the human soul the principal manifestation of the general vitality is in the brain, while all the organs receive merely a light and potency which shines to them from the source of the manifestation of the said vitality in the brain, so indeed, figuratively speaking, is the essential manifestation of the general stream of vitality, animating the worlds and the creatures therein, clothed and contained in His blessed will, wisdom, understanding and knowledge, which are called the "intelligence," and these are those which are clothed in the Torah and its commandments.

The manifestation of this general flow of life is the source of the vitality which the worlds receive, each one in particular. Only a glow is diffused and shines forth from this source in a similar manner as the light radiates from the sun, by way of example, or as the powers of the organs of the body derive from the brain, as discussed above.[1]

It is this source which is called the "world of manifestation" or "matron," or "nether matriarch," or "*Shechinah*,"[2] from the scriptural phrase: "That I may dwell among them."[3] For this source is the beginning of the revelation of the light of *En Sof*, which extends to and illumines the worlds in a "revealed" manner. From this source there extends to each individual thing the particular light and vitality suitable for it, and it [the light] dwells and is clothed in them, thereby animating them. Therefore it is figuratively called "mother of the children," and "community of Israel," for from this source have emanated the souls of *Atzilut* and have been created the souls of *Beriah*, and so forth, all of them being derived only from the extension of the vitality and light from this source which is called "*Shechinah*," resembling the radiation of light

---

[5] *The lowest of all the* sefirot; *for* Malchut *is the tenth* sefirah, *and* Asiyah—*the fourth of the Four Worlds.*

Chapter 52

[1] *In the previous chapter.*

[2] *Literally "indwelling," from the word* ושכנתי *in the quoted verse.*

[3] Exod. *25:8.*

דברים חומריים וגשמיים ונראים מתים אך בתוכם יש אור וחיות המהוה אותם מאין ליש תמיד שלא יחזרו להיות אין ואפס כשהיו ואור זה הוא מא"ס ב"ה רק שנתלבש בלבושים רבים וכמ"ש בע"ח שאור וחיות כדור הארץ החומרי הנראה לעיני בשר הוא ממלכות דמלכות דעשיה ובתוכה מלכות דיצירה *) וכו' עד שבתוך כולן י"ס דאצילות המיוחדות במאצילן א"ס ב"ה:

פרק נב וכמו שבנשמת האדם עיקר גילוי כללות החיות הוא במוחין וכל האברים מקבלים אור וכח לבד המאיר להם ממקור גילוי החיות שבמוחין ככה ממש עד"מ עיקר גילוי כללות המשכת החיות להחיות העולמות והברואים שבהם הוא מלובש ונכלל ברצונו וחכמתו ובינתו ודעתו ית' הנק' בשם מוחין והן הן המלובשים בתורה ומצותיה וגילוי כללות המשכה זו הוא מקור החיות אשר העולמות מקבלי' כל א' בפרטות רק הארה מתפשטת ומאירה ממקור זה כדמיון אור המתפשט מהשמש עד"מ וכחות אברי הגוף מהמוח הנ"ל ומקור זה הוא הנקרא עלמא דאתגליא ומטרונית' ואימא תתאה ושכינה מלשון ושכנתי בתוכם על שם שמקור זה הוא ראשית התגלות אור א"ס אשר ממשיך ומאיר לעולמות בבחי' גילוי וממקור זה נמשך לכל א' האור וחיות פרטי הראוי לו ושוכן ומתלבש בתוכם להחיותם ולכן נקרא אם הבנים עד"מ וכנסת ישראל שממקור זה נאצלו נשמות דאצי' ונבראו נשמות דבריאה וכו' וכולן אינן רק מהתפשטות החיות והאור מהמקור הזה הנק' שכינה כהתפשטות האור מהשמש

*) [ברפוסים הקודמים הי' כתוב „מלכות דמלכות דעשיה" ונ"ל דצ"ל „מלכות דיצירה" וכ"ה באגה"ק סי' כ"ה המתחיל להבין אמרי בינה כו'. אשר נמצא לפנינו גוף כתי"ק].

from the sun.

●▲But as for the *Shechinah* itself, namely, the origin and core of the manifestation whereby the blessed En Sof illumines the worlds in a "revealed" form and which is the source of all streams of vitality in all the worlds (their entire vitality being no more than the light which is diffused from it like the light radiated from the sun), the worlds cannot endure or receive the light of this *Shechinah*, that it might actually dwell and clothe itself in them—without a "garment" to screen and conceal its light from them, so that they may not become entirely nullified and lose their identity within their source, like the nullification of the light of the sun in its source, namely, in the sun itself, where this light cannot be seen, but only the integral mass of the sun itself.

▲ But what is this "garment" which is able to conceal and clothe [the *Shechinah*] yet will not [itself] be completely nullified within its light? This is His blessed will and wisdom, and so forth, which are clothed in the Torah and its commandments that are revealed to us and to our children, for "The Torah issues from wisdom,"[4] which is *chochmah ilaah* ("Supernal Wisdom") that is immeasurably higher than the world of manifestation, for "He is wise, but not with a knowable wisdom," and so forth. And as has previously been explained, the light of the blessed *En Sof* is clothed in and united with the Supernal Wisdom, and He, may He be blessed, and His wisdom are One, only that it has descended by means of obscuring gradations, from grade to grade, with the descent of the worlds, until it has clothed itself in material things, namely, the 613 commandments of the Torah.

●▲As [this Wisdom] came down by descents from world to world, the *Shechinah*, too, came down and clothed itself in it in each world. This is the shrine of the "Holy of Holies," which is contained in each world. So also has it been stated in the Zohar and *Etz Chayim*, that the *Shechinah* —which is *Malchut d'Atzilut* (being the manifestation of the light and vitality of the blessed *En Sof*, which illumines the worlds, wherefore it is called the "word of G–d" and the "breath of His mouth," as it were, as in the case of human beings, by way of example, speech reveals to the hearers the speaker's secret and hidden thought)—clothes itself in the shrine of the Holy of Holies of *Beriah*, namely, the *ChaBaD* (*Chochmah, Binah, Da'at*) of *Beriah*. Through the latters' clothing themselves in the *Malchut d'Beriah*, there have been created the souls and the angels which exist in the world of *Beriah*.

---

[4] Zohar *II, 85a and 121a.*

מהשמש אבל השכינה עצמה שהיא ראשית הגילוי ועיקרו מה שא"ס ב"ה מאיר לעולמות בבחי' גילוי והיא מקור כל המשכות החיות שבכל העולמות [שכל החיו' שבהם אינו רק אור המתפשט ממנה כאור המתפשט מהשמש] א"א לעולמות לסבול ולקבל אור שכינתה שתשכון ותתלבש בתוכם ממש בלא לבוש המעלים ומסתיר אורה מהם שלא יתבטלו במציאות לגמרי במקורם כביטול אור השמש במקורו בגוף השמש שאין נראה שם אור זה רק עצם גוף השמש בלבד.

ומהו הלבוש שיוכל להסתירה ולהלבישה ולא יתבטל במציאות באורה הוא רצונו ית' וחכמתו וכו' המלובשים בתורה ומצותיה הנגלית לנו ולבנינו דאורייתא מחכמה נפקת היא חכמה עילאה דלעילא לעילא מעלמא דאתגליא דאיהו חכים ולא בחכמה ידיעה וכו' וכמש"ל שאור א"ס ב"ה מלובש ומיוחד בחכמה עילאה והוא ית' וחכמתו אחד רק שירדה בסתר המדרגות ממדריגה למדריגה בהשתלשלות העולמות עד שנתלבשה בדברים גשמיים שהן תרי"ג מצות התורה. ובירידתה בהשתלשלו' מעולם לעולם גם השכינה ירדה ונתלבשה בה בכל עולם ועולם וזהו היכל ק"ק שבכל עולם ועולם וכמ"ש בזהר וע"ח שהשכינה שהיא מלכות דאצילות [שהיא בחי' גילוי אור א"ס ב"ה וחיות שמאיר לעולמות ולכן היא נקראת דבר ה' ורוח פיו כביכול עד"מ כמו שבאדם הדבור הוא מגלה מחשבתו הסתומה ונעלמה להשומעים] היא מתלבשת בהיכל ק"ק דבריאה שהיא חב"ד דבריאה ובהתלבשותן במלכות דבריאה נבראו הנשמות והמלאכי' שבבריאה

וגם

From there also descends the [wisdom of the] Talmud that we possess. It has already been previously explained in the name of *Tikunim*, that in the world of *Beriah* there shine and flow forth the *Chochmah*, *Binah* and *Da'at* (*ChaBaD*) of the blessed *En Sof*, in a powerfully contracted manner, in order that the souls and the angels, which are limited and finite beings, shall be able to receive the influence from these categories of *ChaBaD*. Therefore thence also originates the Talmud, which is also a category of *ChaBaD*, for the Talmud consists of the reasons and interpretations of the *halachot* in clearly defined terms. These reasons and interpretations are a category of *ChaBaD*, while the *halachot* themselves derive from the *middot* of the blessed *En Sof*, namely, kindness, justice, mercy, . . . from which originate permission and prohibition, license and restriction, liability and blamelessness, as is explained in the *Tikunim*.

• By virtue of the clothing of *Malchut d'Atzilut* in *Malchut d'Beriah* it clothes itself in the shrine of the Holy of Holies of *Yetzirah*, this being the *ChaBaD* of *Yetzirah*. When the latter are clothed in the *Malchut d'Yetzirah*, there are formed the *Ruchot*[5] and the angels which belong in [the world of] *Yetzirah*. Thence, too, comes the *Mishnah* that we possess, which comprises the legal decisions that are likewise derived from *ChaBaD* of the blessed *En Sof*. Only that the categories of *ChaBaD*, that is, the reasons and interpretations of the *halachot*, are clothed and hidden within the laws themselves and are not in a revealed form, while the elements of the *halachot* [themselves], which are in a revealed form, are the very reflection of the attributes of the blessed *En Sof* in their revealed form. Thus, it has been explained above in the name of the *Tikunim*, namely, that six *Sefirot* nest in *Yetzirah*. They comprise, in general, two extensions—right and left—acting either with forbearance from the aspect of kindness, that is to say, to permit a thing to ascend to G–d, or acting forbiddingly.[6] . . . And all this is according to the *Chochmah Ilaah d'Atzilut* ("Higher Wisdom of Emanation"); in which *Binah* and *Da'at* are contained, and they are united with the blessed *En Sof*, for in all of them are clothed *ChaBaD* of *Atzilut* with which the light of the blessed *En Sof* is united in a perfect union.

In a like manner the *Shechinah* descended and clothed itself in the shrine of the Holy of Holies of *Asiyah*.

Each of those three worlds is subdivided into myriads of gradations, which are also called particular worlds, and *Malchut d'Atzilut* which is clothed in the *Malchut*

---

[5] *Sing.* Ruach, *the second of the three grades comprising the human soul* (Nefesh, Ruach, Neshamah). [6] *Things permitted ("unchained" or "released") are said to be determined by the aspect of* chesed, *while the things forbidden ("chained") are determined by the aspect of* gevurah. *Cf. ch. 7.*

• 29 Iyar

וגם משם נמשך התלמוד שלפנינו וכמש״ל בשם התיקונים שבעולם הבריאה מאירות ומשפיעות שם חכמתו ובינתו ודעתו של א״ס ב״ה בבחי׳ צמצום עצום בכדי שיוכלו הנשמות והמלאכים שהם בעלי גבול ותכלית לקבל השפעה מבחי׳ חב״ד אלו ולכן נמשך משם התלמוד שהוא ג״כ בחי׳ חב״ד שהתלמוד הוא טעמי ההלכות על בוריין והטעמים הם בחי׳ חב״ד וההלכות עצמן הן ממדותיו של א״ס ב״ה שהן חסד דין רחמים כו׳ שמהן נמשך ההיתר והאיסור והכשר והפסול והחיוב והפטור כמ״ש בתיקוני׳. ובהתלבשות מלכות דאצי׳ במלכות דבריאה מתלבשת בהיכל ק״ק דיצי׳ שהוא חב״ד דיצירה ובהתלבשותן במלכות דיצירה נוצרו הרוחות והמלאכים שביצירה וגם משם היא המשנה שלפנינו שהיא הלכות פסוקות הנמשכות ג״כ מחב״ד של א״ס ב״ה רק שבחי׳ חב״ד שהם טעמי ההלכות הם מלובשים וגנוזי׳ בגופי ההלכות ולא בבחי׳ גילוי וגופי ההלכו׳ שהן בבחי׳ גילוי הן הן הארת מדותיו של א״ס ב״ה בבחי׳ גילוי כמש״ל בשם התיקוני׳ דשית ספירן מקננין ביצירה שהן דרך כלל שני קוין ימין ושמאל להקל מסטרא דחסד דהיינו להתיר שיוכל לעלות אל ה׳ או להחמיר כו׳ והכל ע״פ חכמה עילאה דאצי׳ ובינה ודעת כלולות בה ומיוחדות בא״ס ב״ה כי בתוך כולן מלובשות חב״ד דאצילות שאור א״ס ב״ה מיוחד בהן בתכלית היחוד וכן בדרך זה ירדה השכינה ונתלבשה בהיכל ק״ק דעשיה וכל עולם מג׳ עולמות אלו מתחלק לרבבות מדריגות הנקראות גם כן עולמות פרטים ומלכות דאצילו׳ מלובשת במלכות

של

Note: Thereby will be understood the text of the verse: "Thy kingdom (Malchutecha) *is the kingdom of all worlds."*[7]

of each particular world—descends and clothes itself in the shrine of the Holy of Holies, namely, the *ChaBaD*, which is in the world below it in rank.

It is from the *Shechinah* which is clothed in the shrine of the Holy of Holies of each and every general or particular world that light and vitality are extended and diffused to the whole world and the creatures contained therein, the souls, angels, and so forth, for all of them were created by the ten fiats in the act of Creation, these being the "word" of G-d which is termed "*Shechinah.*"

●▲*Chapter 53*

At the time the First Temple stood, in which the Ark and Tables [of the Decalogue] were housed in the Holy of Holies, the *Shechinah*, i.e. *Malchut d'Atzilut*, that is, the aspect of the "revealed" light of the blessed *En Sof*, dwelled there and was clothed in the Ten Commandments, far higher and stronger, and with a greater and mightier revelation, than its revelation in the shrines of the Holy of Holies above in the upper worlds. For the Ten Commandments are the "All-embracing principles of the whole Torah," which comes from the Higher Wisdom,[1] that is far higher than the world of manifestation. In order to engrave them on material tablets of stone it (the *Shechinah*) did not descend degree by degree, parallel to the order of descent of the worlds down to this material world. For this material world functions through the garment of material nature, while the Tables [of the Decalogue] are "The work of G-d, and the writing is the writing of G-d,"[2] beyond the nature of this material world which is derived from the effulgence of the *Shechinah* in the shrine of the Holy of Holies of *Asiyah* ("Action"), whence issues light and vitality to the world of *Asiyah*, in which this our world also is contained.

But the category of the Higher Wisdom of *Atzilut*, consisting of the totality of the Torah as it is epitomized in the Decalogue, has clothed itself in *Malchut* of *Atzilut* and of *Beriah* alone, and they alone, united as they are with the light of the blessed *En Sof* that is within them, are referred to as the "*Shechinah*" which rested in the Holy of Holies of the First Temple, through

---

[7] Ps. *145:13.*

Chapter 53
[1] Zohar *II, 85a; 121a.* [2] Exod. *32:16.*

* של כל עולם פרטי יורדת ומתלבשת בהיכל ק"ק שהוא חב"ד שבעולם שלמטה ממנו במדרגה. והנה מהשכינה המלובשת בהיכל ק"ק של כל עולם ועולם כללי או פרטי נמשך ומתפשט ממנה אור וחיות לכל העולם והברואים שבו נשמות ומלאכים וכו' כי כולם נבראו בעשרה מאמרות שבמעשה בראשית שהם דבר ה' הנקרא בשם שכינה:

הגה"ה
(ובזה יובן לשון הכתוב מלכותך מלכות כל עולמים):

פרק נג והנה כשהיה בית ראשון קיים שבו היה הארון והלוחות בבית ק"ק היתה השכינה שהיא מלכות דאצילות שהיא בחי' גילוי אור א"ס ב"ה שורה שם ומלובשת בעשרת הדברות ביתר שאת ויתר עז בגילוי רב ועצום יותר מגילויה בהיכלות ק"ק שלמעלה בעולמות עליונים כי עשרת הדברות הן כללות התורה כולה דנפקא מגו חכמה עילאה דלעילא לעילא מעלמא דאתגליא וכדי להקקן בלוחות אבנים גשמיים לא ירדה ממדרגה למדרגה כדרך השתלשלות העולמות עד עוה"ז הגשמי כי עוה"ז הגשמי מתנהג בהתלבשות הטבע הגשמי והלוחות מעשה אלהים המה והמכתב מכתב אלהים הוא למעלה מהטבע של עוה"ז הגשמי הנשפע מהארת השכינה שבהיכל ק"ק דעשיה שממנה נמשך אור וחיות לעולם העשיה שגם עוה"ז בכללו אלא בחי' חכמה עילאה דאצילות שהיא כללות התורה שבי' הדברות נתלבשה במלכות דאצי' ודבריא' לבדן והן המיוחדות באור א"ס שבתוכן הן הנקראות בשם שכינה השורה בק"ק דבית ראשון ע"י התלבשותה

its clothing itself in the Ten Commandments, which were engraved in the Tables [reposing] in the Ark, by miraculous means and by the work of the Living G–d (this being the "hidden" world which nests in the world of *Beriah* as is known to those familiar with the Esoteric Discipline). ●▲ As for the Second Temple, in which did not repose the Ark and Tables [of the Decalogue],[3] our Rabbis, of blessed memory, said that the *Shechinah* did not abide there.[4] This refers to the category of the *Shechinah* which used to abide in the First Temple—which was not of the ordinary descent of the worlds. But in the Second Temple it abided according to the order of gradual descent, of *Malchut d'Atzilut* vested in *Malchut d'Beriah* and the latter in *Malchut d'Yetzirah*, and the latter in the shrine of the Holy of Holies of *Asiyah* which in turn was clothed in the Holy of Holies of the Temple here below. In it rested the *Shechinah*, i.e. *Malchut d'Yetzirah* which was clothed in the Holy of Holies of *Asiyah*.

Therefore no man was permitted to enter there, except the High Priest on the Day of Atonement. However, since the Temple was destroyed, there remains to the blessed Holy One but "The four cubits of *Halachah* alone."[5] Hence each individual who sits by himself and occupies himself in the Torah, the *Shechinah* is with him, as is stated in the first chapter of *Berachot*.[6] The phrase "The *Shechinah* is *with* him" means in the order of the gradual descent and investment of *Malchut d'Atzilut* in *Malchut d'Beriah*, and *Yetzirah* and *Asiyah*. For the 613 commandments of the Torah are by and large active precepts, as are also those which are fulfilled by word and thought, such as Torah study and Grace after meals and the recital of the *Shema* and Prayer, for it has been ruled that contemplation has not the validity of speech, and one has not fulfilled one's obligation by contemplation and *kavanah* alone, until he gives utterance with his lips; and it has been ruled that the motion of the lips is considered an "action."

The 613 commandments of the Torah, together with the seven commandments of our Rabbis, combine to total the numerical equivalent of כתר ("crown") which is the blessed *Ratzon Elyon* (the "Supernal Will"), which is clothed in His blessed Wisdom, and they are united with the light of the blessed *En Sof* in a perfect union. "The Lord by wisdom hath founded the earth,"[7] which refers to the Oral Law that is derived from the Higher Wisdom, as is written in the Zohar, "The Father [*chochmah*] begat the daughter[8] [i.e. *Malchut*, the Oral Law]."

●▲And this is what the *Yenuka* meant when he said that "The Supernal light that is kindled on one's head, namely,

---

[3] Yoma *21b*. [4] Ibid. *9b*. [5] Berachot *6a*. [6] Ibid. [7] Prov. *3:19*. [8] Zohar *III, 248a; 256b*.

התלבשותה בי׳ הדברות החקוקות בלוחות שבארון בנס ומעשה אלהים חיים [הוא עלמא דאתכסיא המקנן בעולם הבריאה כנודע לי״ח] ובבית שני שלא היה בו הארון והלוחות אמרז״ל שלא היתה שכינה שורה בו. פי׳ מדרגת שכינה שהיתה שורה בבית ראשון שלא כדרך השתלשלות העולמות אלא בבית שני היתה שורה כדרך השתלשלות והתלבשות מלכות דאצי׳ במלכות דבריאה ודבריא׳ במלכו׳ דיצירה ודיצי׳ בהיכל ק״ק דעשי׳ וק״ק דעשי׳ היה מתלבש בק״ק שבבהמ״ק שלמטה ושרתה בו השכינה מלכות דיצירה המלובשת בק״ק דעשיה. ולכן לא היה רשאי שום אדם ליכנס שם לבד כהן גדול ביה״כ ומשחרב בית המקדש אין לו להקב״ה בעולמו אלא ד״א של הלכה בלבד ואפילו אחד שיושב ועוסק בתורה שכינה עמו כדאית׳ בברכו׳ פ״ק פי׳ שכינה עמו כדרך השתלשלות והתלבשות מלכות דאצילות במלכות דבריאה ויצירה ועשיה כי תרי״ג מצות התורה רובן ככולן הן מצות מעשיות וגם התלויות בדבור ומחשבה כמו ת״ת ובהמ״ז וק״ש ותפלה הא קיימא לן דהרהור לאו כדבור דמי ואינו יוצא ידי חובתו בהרהור וכוונה לבד עד שיוציא בשפתיו וקי״ל דעקימת שפתיו הוי מעשה ותרי״ג מצות התורה עם שבע מצות דרבנן בגימטריא כת״ר שהוא רצון העליון ב״ה המלובש בחכמתו יתברך המיוחדות באור א״ס ב״ה בתכלית היחוד וה׳ בחכמה יסד ארץ היא תורה שבעל פה דנפקא מחכמה עילאה כמ״ש בזהר דאבא יסד ברתא. וז״ש הינוקא דנהורא עילאה דאדליק על רישיה היא

שכינתא

the *Shechinah*, requires oil,"[9] that is, to be clothed in wisdom, which is called "oil from the holy anointing,"[10] as is explained in the *Zohar*, that "these are the good deeds," namely, the 613 commandments, which derive from His blessed wisdom. Thereby the light of the *Shechinah* can cling to the wick, i.e. the vivifying soul in the body, which is metaphorically called a "wick." For just as in the case of a material candle, the light shines by virtue of the annihilation and burning of the wick turning to fire, so does the light of the *Shechinah* rest on the divine soul as a result of the annihilation of the animal soul and its transformation "From darkness to light and from bitterness to sweetness" in the case of the righteous, or at least through the destruction of its garments, which are thought, speech and action, and their transformation from the darkness of the *kelipot* to the Divine light of the blessed *En Sof*, which is clothed and united in the thought, speech and action of the 613 commandments of the Torah, in the case of *benonim*. For as a result of the transformation of the animal soul, originating from the *kelipat nogah*, [a transformation] from darkness to light, and so forth, there is brought about the so-called "ascent of the feminine waters"[11] to draw the light of the *Shechinah*, i.e. the category of the "revealed" light of the blessed *En Sof*—over one's divine soul [principally dwelling] in the brain of the head. Thereby will also be clearly understood the text "For the Lord Thy G–d is a consuming fire"[12] as is explained elsewhere.[13]

CONCLUSION OF THE FIRST PART WITH THE HELP OF G–D, MAY HE BE BLESSED AND EXALTED.

---

[9] Zohar *III. 187a. Cf.* Tanya, *chs. 35, 51.* [10] Exod. *30:31.* [11] *See end ch. 10, above.* [12] Deut. *4:24.* [13] Likutei Torah, Shelach *40b;* Reeh *34c;* Haazinu *78d, etc.*

שכינתא אצטריך למשחא פי׳ להתלבש בחכמה הנק׳
שמן משחת קדש כמ״ש בזהר ואינון עובדין טבין הן
תרי״ג מצות הנמשכות מחכמתו ית׳ כדי לאחוז אור
השכינה בפתילה היא נפש החיונית שבגוף הנקראת
פתילה עד״מ כי כמו שבנר הגשמי האור מאיר ע״י
כליון ושריפת הפתילה הנהפכת לאש כך אור השכינה
שורה על נפש האלהית על ידי כליון נפש הבהמית
והתהפכותה מחשוכא לנהורא וממרירו למתקא בצדיקים
או לפחות ע״י כליון לבושיה שהן מחשבה דבור ומעשה
והתהפכותן מחשך הקליפות לאור ה׳ א״ס ב״ה המלובש
ומיוחד במחשבה דבור ומעשה תרי״ג מצות התורה
בבינונים כי ע״י התהפכות נפש הבהמית הבאה מקליפ׳
נוגה מחשוכא לנהורא וכו׳ נעשה בחי׳ העלאת מ״ן
להמשיך אור השכינה היא בחי׳ גילוי אור א״ס ב״ה על
נפשו האלהית שבמוחין שבראשו ובזה יובן היטב מ״ש
כי ה׳ אלהיך אש אוכלה הוא וכמ״ש במ״א:

נשלם חלק ראשון בעז״ה ית׳ וית׳

•▲ Likutei Amarim[1]

PART TWO

Called[2] "*Chinuch Katan*"[3]

Compiled from books and from Sages, exalted saints, whose souls are in Eden. Based on the first section of the Recitation of the *Shema.*[4]

"Educate the child according to his way, even when he will be old he will not depart from it."[5] Since it is written "According to *his* way," it is understood that it is not the path of perfect truth, hence of what merit is it that "Even when he will be old he will not depart from it?"

It is well-known that Fear (Awe) and Love are the roots and foundations of the service of G–d.[6] Fear is the root and basis of "Refrain from evil,"[7] and Love—of "and do good"[8] and the observance of all the positive commandments of the Torah and the Rabbis, as will be explained in their proper place.[9] (The commandment of educating a child includes also [training in the performance of] the positive precepts,[10] as is stated in *Orach Chayim*, section 343.[11])

Concerning the love [of G–d] it is written at the end of the portion *Ekev*, "Which I command you to *do* it, to love G–d. . . ."[12] It is necessary to understand how an expression of doing can be applied to love, which is in the heart. The explanation, however, is that there are two kinds of love of G–d. One is the natural[13] yearning of the soul to its Creator. When the rational soul prevails over the grossness [of the body],[14] subdues and subjugates it, then [the love of G–d] will flare and blaze with a flame which ascends of its own accord, and will rejoice and exult in G–d its Maker and will delight in Him with wondrous bliss. Those who merit this state of *Ahavah Rabbah* ("great" love) are the ones who are called *Tzaddikim*[15] as it is written, "Rejoice in G–d, ye *Tzaddikim.*"[16] Yet, not everyone is privileged to attain this state, for it requires a very great refinement of one's physical grossness, and in addition a great deal of Torah and good deeds in order to merit a lofty *Neshamah* which is above the level of *Ruach* and *Nefesh*,[17] as explained in *Reishit Chochmah*,[18] *Shaar HaAhavah.*[19]

The second is a love which every man can attain when he will engage in profound contemplation in the depths of his heart on matters that arouse the love of G–d which is in the heart of every Jew.[20] Be it in a general way, that He is our very life,[21] and just as one loves his soul and his life, so he will love G–d when he will meditate and reflect in his heart that G–d is his true soul and actual life, as the *Zohar*[22] comments on the verse, "[You are] my soul, I desire You;"[23] or in a particular way, when he will understand and comprehend the greatness of the King of kings, the Holy One, blessed be He, in detail, to the extent that his intellect can grasp and even beyond. Then he will contemplate G–d's great and wondrous love to us to descend to Egypt, the "Obscenity of the earth,"[24] to bring our souls out of the "iron crucible,"[25] which is the *sitrah achrah*,[26] may the All-Merciful spare us, to bring us close to Him and to bind us to His very Name,[27] and He and His Name are One.[28] That is to say, He elevated us from the nadir of degradation

ליקוטי אמרים חלק שני

הנקרא בשם חינוך קטן

מלוקט מפי ספרים ומפי סופרים קדושי עליון נ״ע מיוסד על פרשה ראשונה של קריאת שמע :

לנער על פי דרכו גם כי יזקין לא יסור ממנה הנה מרכתיב על פי דרכו משמע שאינה דרך האמת לאמיתו וא״כ מאי מעליותא שגם כי יזקין לא יסור ממנה. אך הנה מודעת זאת כי שרשי עבודת ה׳ ויסודותיה הן דחילו ורחימו היראה שרש ויסוד לסור מרע והאהבה לועשה טוב וקיום כל מ״ע דאורייתא׳ ודרבנן כמו שיתב׳ במקומן (ומצות החינוך היא ג״כ במ״ע כמ״ש בא״ח סימן שמ״ג) : והנה באהבה כתיב בס״פ עקב אשר אנכי מצוה אתכם לעשותה לאהבה את ה׳ וגו׳ וצריך להבין איך שייך לשון עשייה גבי אהבה שבלב אך הענין הוא דיש שני מיני אהבת ה׳ האחת היא כלות הנפש בטבעה אל בוראה כאשר תתגבר נפש השכלית על החומר ותשפילהו ותכניעהו תחתיה אזי תתלהב ותתלהט בשלהבת העולה מאליה ותגל ותשמח בה׳ עושה ותתענג על ה׳ תענוג נפלא והזוכים למעלת אהבה רבה זו הם הנקראים צדיקים כדכתיב שמחו צדיקים בה׳ אך לא כל אדם זוכה לזה כי לזה צריך זיכוך החומר במאד מאד וגם תורה ומעשים טובים הרבה לזכות לנשמה עליונה שלמעלה ממדרגת רוח ונפש כמ״ש בר״ח שער האהבה. והשנית היא אהבה שכל אדם יוכל להגיע אליה כשיתבונן היטב בעומקא דלבא בדברים המעוררים את האהבה לה׳ בלב כל ישראל. הן דרך כלל כי הוא חיינו ממש וכאשר האדם אוהב את נפשו וחייו, כן יאהב את ה׳ כאשר יתבונן וישים אל לבו כי ה׳ הוא נפשו האמיתית וחייו ממש כמ״ש בזהר ע״פ נפשי אויתיך וגו׳. והן דרך פרט. שכשיבין וישכיל בגדולתו של ממ״ה הקב״ה דרך פרטית כאשר יוכל שאת בשכלו ומה שלמעלה משכלו ואח״כ יתבונן באהבת ה׳ הגדולה ונפלאה אלינו לירד למצרים ערות הארץ להוציא נשמותינו מכור הברזל שהוא הס״א ר״ל לקרבנו אליו ולדבקנו בשמו ממש והוא ושמו אחד דהיינו שרוממנו מתכלית השפלות והטומאה

---

[1] *Collected Discourses.* [2] *The following is the author's introduction which is called* "Chinuch Katan." *The complete work is referred to as* Shaar HaYichud VeHaemunah. [3] *The Education of the Child.* [4] *The* Shema *consists of three sections of the Torah:* Deut. *6:4–10, 11:13–22, and* Num. *15:37–42. Following the first verse of the first section, our Sages have instituted the recital of the verse,* "Baruch Shem K'vod," *etc. See* Pesachim *56a.* [5] Prov. *22:6.* [6] *Cf.* "*Commentary*" *on Maimonides,* Yad Hachazakah, "Hilchot Yesodei Hatorah" *2:10;* Reishit Chochmah, *beginning of* Shaar HaAhava; Shulchan Aruch HaRav, *by Rabbi Schneur Zalman of Liadi,* "Hilchot Talmud Torah" *4:6.* [7] Ps. *34:15; i.e., the fulfillment of the negative injunctions.* [8] Ibid. [9] Likutei Amarim (Tanya), *Part I, chs. 4, 41. Originally, Rabbi Schneur Zalman intended to arrange* Shaar HaYichud VeHaemunah *before the first part of* Likutei Amarim. *See* "*List of Notes and Text Emendations to* Tanya." [10] *I.e., in addition to the negative precepts. Therefore we are to educate a child in the fear and love of G–d which will be the inspiration for the performance of all the commandments.* [11] *See Commentators* ad locum *and* Shulchan Aruch HaRav, Orach Chayim, *section 343:2–3.* [12] Deut. *11:22.* [13] *Cf.* Tanya, *ch. 19.* [14] *The natural*

(Notes cont. at end of Hebrew Text)

and defilement to the acme of holiness and to His infinite greatness, may He be blessed. Then, "As in water, face reflects face,"[29] love will be aroused in the heart of everyone who contemplates and meditates upon this matter in the depths of his heart —to love G-d with an intense love and to cleave unto Him, heart and soul, as was explained at length in its place.[30]

• It is this love which Moses, our teacher, peace unto him, wished to implant in the heart of every Jew, in the section "And now Israel, . . ."[31] in the verse, "Behold, the heavens belong to G-d, your Lord[32] . . . only in your fathers did He delight . . . you shall circumcise . . . with seventy souls . . . [Therefore] you shall love. . . ."[33] Hence he concluded his words concerning this love "Which I command you, to *do* it,"[34] which is love that is produced in the heart through the understanding and knowledge of matters which inspire love. And this he had commanded previously [in the verse]: "And these words, which I command you this day, shall be upon your heart"[35] so that through this [meditation] you will come to love G-d, as is stated in the *Sifri* on this verse.

Thus, there can be applied to this second type of love an expression of charge and command, namely, to devote one's heart and mind to matters which stimulate love. However, an expression of command and charge is not at all applicable to the first kind of love which is a flame that ascends of its own accord. Furthermore, it is the reward of the *Tzaddikim* to savour of the nature of the World to Come in this world. That is the meaning of the verse, "I will give you the priesthood as a service of gift,"[36] as will be explained in its proper place.[37]

• Now, those who are familiar with the esoteric meaning of Scripture know [the explanation of] the verse, "For a *Tzaddik* falls seven times and rises up again."[38] Especially since man is called "mobile"[39] and not "static," he must ascend from level to level and not remain forever at one plateau. Between one level and the next, before he can reach the higher one, he is in a state of decline from the previous level.[40] Yet, it is written, "Though he falls, he shall not be utterly cast down."[41] It is considered a decline only in comparison with his former state, and not, G-d forbid, in comparison with all other men, for he is still above them in his service [of G-d], inasmuch as there remains in it an impression of his former state. The root of his service, however, is from the love of G-d to which he has been educated and trained from his youth before he reached the level of *Tzaddik*. This, then, is the meaning of "Even when he will be old, . . ." And the first thing which arouses Love and Fear, and their foundation,[42] is the pure and faithful belief in His Unity and Oneness, may He be blessed and exalted.

---

[29] Prov. *27:19*. "*. . . so does the heart of man to man.*" *I.e., the love of one man for another awakens a loving response towards himself in the heart of his friend. How much more so will reflection upon the manifestation of G-d's love towards us inspire love for Him.* [30] Tanya *I, ch. 46*. [31] Deut. *10:12*. [32] *V.* Infra., *ch. 1, n. 5*. [33] Deut. *10:14–11:1*. [34] Ibid. *11:22*. [35] Ibid. *6:6*. [36] Num. *18:7*. *The priesthood symbolises the state of* Ahavah Rabbah *which is granted as a Divine gift to the perfectly righteous. Hence it is within the reach of every Jew and is not limited to those born of the priestly class. Cf. Maimonides,* Yad Hachazakah, "Hilchot Shemitah and Yovel," *11:13*. [37] *V.* Tanya *I, chs. 14, 43;* Likutei Amarim, *Part*

והטומאה לתכלית הקדושה וגדולתו ית׳ שאין לה קץ ותכלית אזי כמים הפנים אל פנים תתעורר האהבה בלב כל משכיל ומתבונן בענין זה בעומקא דלבא לאהוב את ה׳ אהבה עזה ולדבקה בו בלב ונפש כמו שיתבאר במקומה באריכות. והנה ענין אהבה זו רצה מרע״ה ליטע בלב כל ישראל בפרשה ועתה ישראל וגו׳ בפסוק הן לה׳ אלהיך השמים וגו׳ רק באבותיך חשק וגו׳ ומלתם וגו׳ בשבעים נפש וגו׳ ואהבת וגו׳. ולכן סיים דבריו על אהבה זו אשר אנכי מצוה אתכם לעשותה שהיא אהבה עשויה בלב ע״י הבינה והדעת בדברים המעוררים את האהבה וע״ז צוה כבר תחלה והיו הדברים האלה אשר אנכי מצוך היום על לבבך כדי שעי״ז תבא לאהבה את ה׳ כדאיתא בספרי ע״פ זה. והנה על אהבה זו השנית שייך לשון מצוה וצווי דהיינו לשום לבו ודעתו בדברים המעוררים את האהבה אבל באהבה ראשונ׳ שהיא שלהבת העולה מאליה לא שייך לשון צווי ומצוה כלל ולא עוד אלא שהיא מתן שכרן של צדיקים לטעום מעין עו״הב בעה״ז שעליה נאמר עבודת מתנה אתן את כהונתכם כמו שיתב׳ במקומה אך הנה ידוע ליודעים טעמא דקרא מאי דכתיב כי שבע יפול צדיק וקם ובפרט שהאדם נקרא מהלך ולא עומד וצריך לילך ממדרגה למדרגה ולא לעמוד במדרגה אחת לעולם ובין מדרגה למדרגה טרם שיגיע למדרגה עליונה ממנה הוא בבחי׳ נפילה ממדרג׳ הראשונ׳ אך כי יפול לא יוטל כתיב ואינה נקראת נפילה אלא לגבי מדריגתו הראשונה ולא לגבי שאר כל אדם ח״ו שאעפ״כ הוא למעלה מכל האדם בעבודתו כי נשאר בה בחי׳ רשימו ממדריגתו הראשונה אך עיקרה מאהבה שנתחנך והורגל בה מנעוריו בטרם שהגיע למדרגת צדיק וז״ש גם כי יזקין וגו׳. והנה ראשית הדברים המעוררים האהבה והיראה ויסודן היא האמונה הטהורה ונאמנה ביחודו ואחדותו יתברך ויתּ׳:

IV "Iggeret Hakodesh," *ch. 18.* [38] Prov. *24:16. For further elaboration of this subject see* Pelech Harimon *by Rabbi Hillel ben Meir, Kehot Publication Society (Brooklyn, 1954), Part I, p. 302.* [39] *Cf.* Zech. *3:7. See also* Torah Or, "Vayeshev," *pp. 59–60;* Likutei Torah *by Rabbi Schneur Zalman of Liadi, Vol. II,* "Bechukotay," p. *89b; III,* "Shelach," *p. 76b, ff.—Man has been endowed with an unrestricted capacity for spiritual progress. All other creatures have a prescribed level which they cannot surpass.* [40] *V.* Pelech Harimon, loc. cit. [41] Ps. *37:24.* [42] *The root and foundation of the observance of all the positive and negative precepts are Love and Fear of G–d, as explained above.*

(Notes cont. at end of Hebrew Text)

●▲Shaar Hayichud Vehaemunah[1]

Let us understand [at least] in a small measure, the statement in the *Zohar*[2] that *Shema Yisrael, . . .*[3] is *Yichudah Ilaah* ("higher level Unity") and *Baruch Shem K'vod Malchuto Leolam Vaed*[4] is *Yichudah Tataah* ("lower level Unity").

Chapter 1

"Know this day and take unto your heart that *Hava'ye* is *Elokim* (G-d is the Lord)[5] in the heavens above and upon the earth below; there is no other."[6] This requires explanation. For would it occur to you that there is a god dwelling in the waters beneath the earth that it is necessary to negate it so strongly [as to say,] "Take unto your heart?"[7]

It is written: "Forever, O G-d, Your word stands firm in the heavens."[8] The Baal Shem Tov,[9] of blessed memory, has explained that "Your word" which you uttered, "Let there be a firmament in the midst of the waters . . .",[10] these very words and letters[11] stand firmly forever within the firmament of heaven and are forever clothed within all the heavens to give them life, as it is written, "The word of our G-d shall stand firm forever"[12] and "His words live and stand firm forever. . . ."[13] For if the letters were to depart [even] for an instant, G-d forbid, and return to their source, all the heavens would become naught and absolute nothingness, and it would be as though they had never existed at all, exactly as before the utterance, "Let there be a firmament." And so it is with all created things, in all the upper and lower worlds, and even this physical earth, which is the "Kingdom of the silent" (inanimate).[14] If the letters of the Ten Utterances[15] by which the earth was created during the Six Days of Creation were to depart from it [but] for an instant, G-d forbid, it would revert to naught and absolute nothingness, exactly as before the Six Days of Creation.

This same thought was expressed by the Ari,[16] of blessed memory, when he said that even in completely inanimate matter, such as stones or earth or water, there is a soul and spiritual life-force—that is, the enclothing of the "Letters of speech"[17] of the Ten Utterances which give life and existence to inanimate matter that it might arise out of the naught and nothingness which preceded the Six Days of Creation.

●Now, although the name *even* (stone) is not mentioned in the Ten Utterances recorded in the Torah, nevertheless, life-force flows to the stone through combinations and substitutions of the letters which are transposed in the "Two hundred and thirty-one gates,"[18] either in direct or reverse order, as is explained in the *Sefer Yetzirah*,[19] until the combination of the name *even* descends[20] from the Ten

---

[1] *The Gate to [the Understanding of] G-d's Unity and the Faith.* [2] *I, 18b. The* Zohar *is the most basic Kabbalistic work consisting of the mystical interpretation of the Pentateuch. It was written by Rabbi Shimon Bar Yochai in the Mishnaic period.* [3] Deut. *6:4. "Hear, O Israel."* [4] *"Blessed be His Name Whose Glorious Kingdom is for ever and ever."* [5] *The Ineffable Name or the Tetragrammaton—the Name of four letters, Y-H-V-H—is pronounced in conversation* Hava'ye. *The prescribed traditional reading in Scripture and Prayer is* Ad-nay. *Hence, the usual English rendition of Lord. However, the name* Hava'ye *refers to G-d the Infinite, transcending creation and nature, omnipresent, omnipotent and omniscient. Therefore, it is here trans-*

להבין מעט מזער מ"ש בזהר דשמע ישראל כו' הוא יחודא עילאה ובשכמל"ו הוא יחודא תתאה:

פרק א וידעת היום והשבות אל לבבך כי ה' הוא האלהים בשמים ממעל ועל הארץ מתחת אין עוד. וצריך להבין וכי תעלה על דעתך שיש אלהים נשרה במים מתחת לארץ שצריך להזהיר כ"כ והשבות אל לבבך. הנה כתיב לעולם ה' דברך נצב בשמים ופי' הבעש"ט ז"ל כי דברך שאמרת יהי רקיע בתוך המים וגו' תיבות ואותיות אלו הן נצבות ועומדות לעולם בתוך רקיע השמים ומלובשות בתוך כל הרקיעים לעולם להחיותם כדכתיב ודבר אלהינו יקום לעולם ודבריו חיים וקיימים לעד כו' כי אילו היו האותיות מסתלקות כרגע ח"ו וחוזרות למקורן היו כל השמים אין ואפס ממש והיו כלא היו כלל וכמו קודם מאמר יהי רקיע כו' ממש וכן בכל הברואים שבכל העולמות עליונים ותחתונים ואפי' ארץ הלזו הגשמית ובחי' דומם ממש אילו היו מסתלקות ממנה כרגע ח"ו האותיות מעשרה מאמרות שבהן נבראת הארץ בששת ימי בראשית היתה חוזרת לאין ואפס ממש כמו לפני ששת ימי בראשית ממש וז"ש האר"י ז"ל שגם בדומם ממש כמו אבנים ועפר ומים יש בחי' נפש וחיות רוחנית דהיינו בחי' התלבשות אותיות הדבור מעשרה מאמרו' המחיות ומהוות את הדומם להיות יש מאין ואפס שלפני ששת ימי בראשית ואף שלא הוזכר שם אבן בעשרה מאמרות שבתורה אעפ"כ נמשך חיות לאבן ע"י צירופים וחילופי אותיו' המתגלגלות ברל"א שערים פנים ואחור כמ"ש בס' יצירה עד שמשתלשל מעשרה מאמרות

lated "G-d." The name Elokim *emphasises G-d's justice and rulership, (See* Rashi's *Commentary* Genesis *2:5, 6:2.) therefore it is translated "Lord," instead of the usual rendition of G-d. The original Hebrew readings of both names, rather than their translations, are retained throughout this text as their definition and explanation form a basic part of this treatise and are fully explained in chs. 4 and 6, infra.* [6] Deut. *4:39.* [7] *A simple negative statement would suffice to repudiate the absurd poly-theistic notion of a deity inhabiting the waters. Obviously, the emphasis upon the importance of meditation and contemplation that "there is no other" points to a rejection of something far more subtle. The answer to this question will be*

(Notes cont. at end of Hebrew Text)

Utterances, and is derived from them, and this is the life-force of the stone. And so it is with all created things in the world—their names in the Holy Tongue are the very "letters of speech" which descend, degree by degree, from the Ten Utterances recorded in the Torah, by means of substitutions and transpositions of letters through the "two hundred and thirty-one gates," until they reach and become invested in that particular created thing to give it life. [This descent is necessary] because individual creatures are not capable of receiving their life-force directly from the Ten Utterances of the Torah, for the life-force issuing directly from them is far greater than the capacity of the individual creatures. They can receive the life-force only when it descends and is progressively diminished, degree by degree, by means of substitutions and transpositions of the letters and by *Gematriot*, their numerical values,[21] until the life-force can be condensed and enclothed and there can be brought forth from it a particular creature. And the name by which it is called in the Holy Tongue is a vessel for the life-force[22] condensed into the letters of that name which has descended from the Ten Utterances in the Torah, that have power and vitality to create being *ex nihilo* and give it life forever. For the Torah and the Holy One, blessed be He, are one.[23]

•▲Chapter 2

From the foregoing [exposition] the answer to the heretics [is deduced], and the root of the error of those who deny individual Divine Providence and the signs and miracles recorded in the Torah is revealed. They err, making a false analogy, in comparing the work of G–d, the Creator of heaven and earth, to the work of man and his schemes. For, when a goldsmith has made a vessel, that vessel is no longer dependent upon the smith, and even when his hands are removed from it and he goes away, the vessel remains in exactly the same image and form as when it left the hands of the smith. In the same way, these fools conceive the creation of heaven and earth. But their eyes are covered [and they fail] to see the great difference between the work of man and his schemes—which consists of making one thing out of another which already exists,[1] merely changing the form and appearance

tzimtzum = condensation

[21] *Each Hebrew letter has its own numerical value, e.g.,* א *equals 1,* ב *equals 2, and so forth.* Gematria *is the calculation of the numerical values of Hebrew words—for example* אחד *equals 13.* Gematria *represents even a greater descent and dimunition of the light and life-force than the combination, substitution etc., of the Divine letters, for here the relationship between the two words is only a numerical one. See end of ch. 7,* infra. [22] *Thus, a name is not merely an arbitrary method of distinguishing one person or object from another, but is actually related to one's soul. This elucidates the statement in the Talmud* (Yoma *83b,* Tanchuma Bereishit) *that Rabbi Meir recognised the character and nature of a person merely by knowing his name. For further explanation see*

מאמרות ונמשך מהן צירוף שם אבן והוא חיותו של האבן וכן בכל הנבראים שבעולם השמות שנקראים בהם בלשון הקדש הן הן אותיות הדבור המשתלשלו' ממדרגה למדרגה מעשרה מאמרות שבתורה ע"י חילופים ותמורות האותיות ברל"א שערים עד שמגיעות ומתלבשות באותו נברא להחיותו לפי שאין פרטי הנבראים יכולים לקבל חיותם מעשרה מאמרות עצמן שבתורה שהחיות הנמשך מהן עצמן גדול מאד מבחי' הנבראים פרטיים ואין כח בהם לקבל החיות אלא ע"י שיורד החיות ומשתלשל ממדרגה למדרגה פחותה ממנה ע"י חילופים ותמורות האותיות וגימטריאות שהן חשבון האותיות עד שיוכל להתצמצם ולהתלבש ולהתהוות ממנו נברא פרטי וזה שמו אשר יקראו לו בלה"ק הוא כלי לחיות המצומצם באותיות שם זה שנשתלשל מעשרה מאמרות שבתורה שיש בהם כח וחיות לברוא יש מאין ולהחיותו לעולם דאורייתא וקב"ה כולא חד:

פרק ב והנה מכאן תשובת המינים וגילוי שורש טעותם הכופרים בהשגחה פרטית

ובאותו' ומופתי התורה שטועי' בדמיונם הכוזב שמדמין מעשה ה' עושה שמי' וארץ למעשה אנוש ותחבולותיו כי כאשר יצא לצורף כלי שוב אין הכלי צריך לידי הצורף כי אף שידיו מסולקות הימנו והולך לו בשוק הכלי קיים בתבניתו וצלמו ממש כאשר יצא מידי הצורף כך מדמין הסכלים האלו מעשה שמים וארץ אך טח מראות עיניהם ההבדל הגדול שבין מעשה אנוש ותחבולותיו שהוא יש מיש רק שמשנה הצורה והתמונה מתמונת חתיכת

Likutei Torah "Behar," *p. 82;* "Mayim Rabbim," *by Rabbi Shmuel of Lubavitch, ch. 22;* Sefer Ha-Maamarim Tov Shin Chet, *p.154–7.*
[23] *Cf.* Zohar *I, 24a; II, 60a. See also* Tikunim *6, 22. This is more fully explained by the author in* Tanya, *chs. 23, 4.*

Chapter 2
[1] *In Hebrew:* yesh mi-yesh.

from an ingot of silver to a vessel—and the making of heaven and earth, which is *creatio ex nihilo.*[2]

Indeed, this is an even greater miracle than, for example, the splitting of the Red Sea. For then, G–d drove back the sea by a strong east wind all the night and the waters were divided and stood upright as a wall.[3] If G–d had stopped the wind, the waters would have instantly flowed downward, as is their way and nature, and undoubtedly they would not have stood upright as a wall, even though this nature of water [to flow downward] is also created *ex nihilo*, for a stone wall stands erect by itself without [the assistance of] the wind, ▲but the nature of water is not so. [Thus, if for the miracle of the splitting of the Red Sea the continuous action of G–d was necessary] how much more so is it in the creation of being out of nothing which transcends nature and is far more miraculous than the splitting of the Red Sea, that with the withdrawal of the power of the Creator from the thing created, G–d forbid, it would revert to naught and complete non-existence. Rather, the Activating Force of the Creator must *continuously* be in the thing created to give it life and existence. [These Forces] are the "letters of speech" of the Ten Utterances by which [beings] were created.

And that is the meaning of the verse: **ואתה מחי' את כולם**.[4] Read not **מחי'**, give life, but **מהוה** bring into being, i.e., *ex nihilo.*[5] The word **אתה**, You, indicates all the letters from *Aleph* to *Tav*,[6] and the letter *Hai*,[7] the five organs of verbal articulation,[8] the sources of the letters.[9] Although He has no bodily likeness,[10] yet, Scripture itself ascribes to Him [anthropomorphic terms[11] such as] "And G–d spoke" or "And G–d said," which denote the revelation of the twenty-two Supernal Letters to the Prophets and the enclothing [of the letters] in their intellect and comprehension in the prophetic vision, as well as in their thought and speech, as it is written, "The spirit of G–d spoke in me, and His word is upon my tongue,"[12] as has been explained by the Ari, of blessed memory, (in the *Shaar HaNevuah*). Similar to this is the investment of the letters in created things—as it is written, "By the word of G–d were the heavens made, and by the breath of His mouth all their host,"[13]—only [the enclothing of the letters in created beings] is through numerous and powerful descents until [the letters] reach the corporeal [world of] *Asiyah*;[14] whereas the comprehension of the Prophets is in [the world of] *Atzilut*[15] as it becomes clothed in the world of *Beriah.*[16]

---

[2] *In Hebrew:* yesh mi-ayin. [3] Ex. *14:21–22; 15:8.* [4] VeAtah Mechaye et Kulam, "*And You give life to them all.*" Neh. *9:6.* [5] *I.e., the life-force which in every created being not only gives it life and vivifies it, but* continuously *brings it into existence* ex nihilo. *The verse is thus interpreted for the phrase "to give life" does not necessarily imply "to create," as for example, the soul which gives life to and vivifies the body, yet does not bring it into being. Whereas in Creation the life-force not only vivifies but also creates and must continuously flow into the created being, for without it, it would revert to* nothingness. *By giving life, He actually creates it* ex nihilo. *Hence, He constantly renews the existence of the world and all the creatures, creating them anew from*

חתיכת כסף לתמונת כלי למעשה שמים וארץ שהוא
יש מאין והוא פלא גדול יותר מקריעת ים סוף עד"מ
שהוליך ה' את הים ברוח קדים עזה כל הלילה ויבקעו
המים ונצבו כמו נד וכחומה ואילו הפסיק ה' את הרוח
כרגע היו המים חוזרים וניגרים במורד כדרכם וטבעם
ולא קמו כחומה בלי ספק אף שהטבע הזה במים גם כן
נברא ומחודש יש מאין שהרי חומת אבנים נצבת
מעצמה בלי רוח רק שטבע המים אינו כן וכ"ש וק"ו
בבריאת יש מאין שהיא למעלה מהטבע והפלא ופלא
יותר מקריעת ים סוף עאכ"ו שבהסתלקו' כח הבורא מן
הנברא ח"ו ישוב הנברא לאין ואפס ממש אלא צריך
להיות כח הפועל בנפעל תמיד להחיותו ולקיימו והן הן
בחי' אותיות הדבור מעשרה מאמרות שבהם נבראו
וע"ז נאמר ואתה מחיה את כולם אל תקרי מחיה אלא
מהוה דהיינו יש מאין ואתה הן בחי' האותיות מאל"ף
ועד תי"ו והה"א היא ה' מוצאות הפה מקור האותיות
ואף שאין לו דמות הגוף הרי מקרא מלא דבר הכתוב
וידבר ה' ויאמר ה' והיא בחי' התגלות הכ"ב אותיות
עליונות לנביאי' ומתלבשות בשכלם והשגתם במראה
הנבואה וגם במחשבתם ודיבורם כמ"ש רוח ה' דבר בי
ומלתו על לשוני וכמ"ש האר"י ז"ל [בשער הנבואה]
וכעין זה היא התלבשות האותיות בברואים כדכתיב
בדבר ה' שמים נעשו וברוח פיו כל צבאם רק שהיא
ע"י השתלשלות רבות ועצומות עד שיורדות לעשיה
גופנית משא"כ השגת הנביאי' היא באצילו' המתלבשת
בעולם הבריאה:

והנה

nothing at every moment, just as at the beginning of Creation. So, in reality, "to give life" and to "bring into being" are identical. See Pardes, "Shaar Vav," *ch. 8;* Reishit Chochmah, "Shaar HaKedusha," *end of ch. 7;* Shaloh, "Shaar HaOtiot, *pp. 48b, 70a.* [6] *The letter* aleph *is the first, and* tav *is the last of the letters in the Hebrew alphabet.* [7] *The numerical value of* hai *is 5. See n. 21, ch. 1,* supra. [8] *I.e., the larynx, palate, tongue, teeth and lips.* [9] *The meaning of this verse is that "You" create, i.e., the Divine power which issues through the twenty-two letters of the alphabet, indicated in the word* Atah. *For there could not emerge from G–d, the Infinite, a limited and finite world.* [10] *Maimonides,* Yad *(Notes cont. at end of Hebrew Text)*

●▲ *Chapter 3*

Now, following these words and the truth [concerning the nature of the Creation], every intelligent person will understand clearly that each creature and being is actually considered naught and absolute nothingness in relation to the Activating Force and the "Breath of His mouth"[1] which is in the created thing, continuously calling it into existence and bringing it from absolute non-being into being. The reason that all things created and activated appear to us as existing[2] and tangible, is that we do not comprehend nor see with our physical eyes the power of G–d and the "Breath of His mouth" which is in the created thing. If, however, the eye were permitted to see[3] and to comprehend the life-force and spirituality which is in every created thing, flowing into it from "That which proceeds out of the mouth of G–d"[4] and "His breath," then the materiality, grossness and tangibility of the creature would not be seen by our eyes at all, for it is completely nullified in relation to the life-force and the spirituality which is within it, since without the spirituality it would be naught and absolute nothingness, exactly as before the Six Days of Creation. The spirituality which flows into it from "That which proceeds out of the mouth of G–d" and "His breath"—that alone continuously brings it forth from naught and nullity into being, and gives it existence. Hence, there is truly nothing besides Him.

●▲ An illustration of this is the light of the sun which illumines the earth and its inhabitants. [This illumination] is the radiance and the light which spreads forth from the body of the sun and is visible to all as it gives light to the earth and the expanse of the universe. Now, it is self-evident that this light and radiance is also present in the very body and matter of the sun-globe itself in the sky, for if it can spread forth and shine to such a great distance, then certainly it can shed light in its own place. However, there in its own place, this radiance is considered naught and complete nothingness, for it is absolutely non-existent in relation to the body of the sun-globe which is the source of this light and radiance, inasmuch as this radiance and light is merely the illumination which shines from the body of the sun-globe itself. It is only in the space of the universe, under the heavens and on the earth, where the body of the sun-globe is not present, that this light and radiance appears to the eye to have actual existence. And here, the term *YESH* ("existence") can truly be applied to it,

---

[1] *Allusion to* Ps. *33:6, quoted above. This does not negate the reality of the universe or imply that the physical world is illusory. What is meant here is that the world does not possess* independent *existence; its true reality is the Divine force which continuously brings it into being.* [2] *I.e. Self-subsisting.* [3] *In Time to Come, however, even man's corporeal eyes will see G–dliness and the Divine force in every created thing. See* Isa. *40:5, 52:8;* Rosh Hashanah *31a.* Likutei Torah, "Bechukotay," p. *94;* Tanya *I, ch. 37.* [4] Deut. *8:3; cf.* Zohar *III, 47b.*

פרק ג והנה אחרי הדברי' והאמת האלה כל משכיל על דבר יבין לאשורו איך שכל נברא ויש הוא באמת נחשב לאין ואפס ממש לגבי כח הפועל ורוח פיו שבנפעל המהוה אותו תמיד ומוציאו מאין ממש ליש ומה שכל נברא ונפעל נראה לנו ליש וממשו' זהו מחמת שאין אנו משיגים ורואים בעיני בשר את כח ה' ורוח פיו שבנברא אבל אילו ניתנה רשות לעין לראות ולהשיג את החיות ורוחניות שבכל נברא השופע בו ממוצא פי ה' ורוח פיו לא היה גשמיות הנברא וחומרו וממשו נראה כלל לעינינו כי הוא בטל במציאות ממש לגבי החיות והרוחניות שבו מאחר שמבלעדי הרוחניו' היה אין ואפס ממש כמו קודם ששת ימי בראשי' ממש והרוחניות השופע עליו ממוצא פי ה' ורוח פיו הוא לבדו המוציאו תמיד מאפס ואין ליש ומהוה אותו א"כ אפס בלעדו באמת והמשל לזה הוא אור השמש המאיר לארץ ולדרים שהוא זיו ואור המתפשט מגוף השמש ונראה לעין כל מאיר על הארץ ובחלל העולם והנה זה פשוט שאור וזיו הזה ישנו ג"כ בגוף וחומר כדור השמש עצמו שבשמים שאם מתפשט ומאיר למרחוק כ"כ כ"ש שיוכל להאיר במקומו ממש רק ששם במקומו ממש נחשב הזיו הזה לאין ואפס ממש כי בטל ממש במציאות לגבי גוף כדור השמש שהוא מקור האור והזיו הזה שהזיו והאור הזה אינו רק הארה מאירה מגוף ועצם כדור השמש רק בחלל העולם תחת כל השמים ועל הארץ שאין כאן גוף כדור השמש במציאות נראה כאן האור והזיו הזה ליש ממש לעין כל ונופל עליו כאן שם יש באמת משא"כ

whereas, when it is in its source, in the body of the sun, the term *YESH* ("existence") cannot be applied to it at all, and it can only be called naught and non-existent. There it is indeed naught and absolutely non-existent, for there, only its source, the body of the sun, gives light, and there is nothing besides it.

▲ The exact parallel to this illustration is the relationship between all created things and the Divine flow [of the life-force] from the "Breath of His mouth," which flows upon them and brings them into existence. G-d is their source, and they themselves are merely like a diffusing light and effulgence from the flow and spirit of G-d, which issues forth and becomes clothed in them and brings them from naught into being. Hence, their existence is nullified in relation to their source, just as the light of the sun is nullified and is considered naught and complete nothingness and is not [even] referred to as "existing" at all when it is in its source; only beneath the heavens, where its source is not present [can it be called "existing"]. In the same manner, the term *YESH* ("existence") can be applied to all created things only [as they appear] to our corporeal eyes, for we do not see nor comprehend at all the source, which is the spirit of G-d, that brings them into existence. Therefore, it appears to our eyes that the materiality, grossness and tangibility of the created things actually exist, just as the light of the sun appears to have actual existence when it is not within its source.

But in the following, the illustration is apparently not completely identical with the object of comparison. For in the illustration, the source [the sun] is not present at all in the space of the universe and upon the earth where its light is seen as actually existing. Whereas, all created things are always within their source, and it is only that the source is not visible to our physical eyes. [If so], why are they not nullified in their source? To understand this, some prefatory remarks are necessary.

•▲ *Chapter 4*

It is written: "For a sun and a shield is *Hava'ye Elokim.*"[1] The explanation of this verse [is as follows]: "Shield" is a covering for the sun, to protect the creatures so that they should be able to bear [its heat]. As our Sages, of blessed memory, have said, "In Time to Come,[2] the Holy One, blessed be He, will take out the sun from its sheath, the wicked will be punished by it. . . ."[3] Now, just as the covering shields [i.e., conceals] the sun, so does the name *Elokim* shield [i.e., conceal] the name *Hava'ye*, blessed be He.

---

[1] Ps. *84:12.* [2] *I.e., the Messianic Era.* [3] Nedarim *8b.*

● 12 Sivan ▲ *12 Sivan* ▲ *13 Sivan*

משא"כ כשהוא במקורו בגוף השמש אין נופל עליו שם יש כלל רק שם אין ואפס כי באמת הוא שם לאין ואפס ממש שאין מאיר שם רק מקורו לבדו שהוא גוף השמש המאיר ואפס בלעדו וכדברים האלה ממש בדמותם כצלמם הם כל הברואים לגבי שפע האלהי מרוח פיו השופע עליהם ומהוה אותם והוא מקורם והם עצמם אינם רק כמו אור וזיו מתפשט מן השפע ורוח ה' השופע ומתלבש בתוכם ומוציאם מאין ליש ולכן הם בטלים במציאות לגבי מקורם כמו אור השמש שבטל במציאות ונחשב לאין ואפס ממש ואינו נקרא בשם יש כלל כשהוא במקורו רק תחת השמים שאין שם מקורו כך כל הברואי' אין נופל עליהם שם יש כלל אלא לעיני בשר שלנו שאין אנו רואים ומשיגים כלל את המקור שהוא רוח ה' המהוה אותם. ולכן נראה לעינינו גשמיות הנבראים וחומרם וממשם שהם יש גמור כמו שנרא' אור השמש יש גמור כשאינו במקורו רק שבזה אין המשל דומה לנמשל לגמרי לכאורה שבמשל אין המקור במציאות כלל בחלל העולם ועל הארץ שנראה שם אורו ליש גמור משא"כ כל הברואי' הם במקורם תמיד רק שאין המקור נראה לעיני בשר ולמה אינן בטלים במציאות למקורם אך להבין זה צריך להקדים:

פרק ד כי הנה כתיב כי שמש ומגן ה' אלהים פי' מגן הוא נרתק לשמש להגן שיוכלו הבריות לסבלו כמארז"ל לעתיד לבא הקב"ה מוציא חמה מנרתקה רשעים נידונין בה כו' וכמו שהנרתק מגין בעד השמש כך שם אלהים מגין לשם הוי"ה ב"ה

דשם

The meaning of the name *Hava'ye* is "That which brings everything into existence *ex nihilo*." The prefix י [added to the stem הוה], modifies the verb, indicating that the action is present and continuous—as Rashi[4] comments on the verse, "In this manner does Job do יעשה all the days"[5]—i.e., the life-force which flows at every instant into all things created, from "that which proceeds out of the mouth of G–d" and "His breath," and brings them into existence *ex nihilo* at *every moment*. For the fact that they were created during the Six Days of Creation is not sufficient for their continued existence, as explained above.[6]

In the enumeration of the praises of the Holy One, blessed be He, it is written, "*Hagadol*" (the Great), "*Hagibor*"[7] (the Mighty), etc. "*Hagadol*" refers to the attribute of *Chesed* (Kindness) and the spreading forth of the life-force into all the worlds and created things without end or limit[8] so that they shall be created *ex nihilo* and exist through *Chesed Chinom* (gratuitous kindness). And [the attribute of *Chesed*] is called *Gedulah* (Greatness) for it comes from the greatness of the Holy One, blessed be He, in His Glory and Essence, for "G–d is great and His greatness is unsearchable,"[9] and therefore, He also causes life-force and existence *ex nihilo* to issue forth for an unlimited number of worlds and creatures, for "It is the nature of the beneficient to do good."[10]

●▲Now, this attribute [of *Chesed*] is the praise of the Holy One, blessed be He, alone, for no created thing can create a being out of naught and give it life.[11] This attribute is also beyond the cognition of all creatures and their understanding. For it is not within the power of the intellect of any creature to understand and comprehend this quality and its ability to create a being out of nothing and vivify it. For *creatio ex nihilo* is a matter which transcends the intellect of the creatures inasmuch as it stems from the Divine attribute of *Gedulah*. And the Holy One, blessed be He, and His attributes are a perfect unity, as the Holy *Zohar* states, "He and His attributes are One,"[12] and just as it is not possible for any creature's mind to comprehend his Creator, so it is impossible for him to comprehend His attributes.

And just as it is impossible for any creature's mind to apprehend His attribute of *Gedulah*, which is the ability to create a being out of nothing and give it life, as it is written, "The world is built by kindness,"[13] exactly so it is not possible for him to apprehend the Divine attribute of *Gevurah* (Might, Restraint), which is the quality of *Tzimtzum* (condensation, contraction, concentration) and restraint of the spreading forth of

[4] *Acronym for Rabbi Shlomo Yitzchaki, the most famous Biblical and Talmudic commentator.* [5] Job *1:5.* [6] *Ch. 2*, supra. [7] Deut. *10:17;* Liturgy, Amidah *Prayer.* [8] *The characteristic of* Chesed *is to bestow boundlessly.* [9] *See* Ps. *145:3.* [10] *See* Chacham Tzvi *(Responsa)*, *18, by Rabbi Tzvi Hirsch Ben Jacob Ashkenazi;* Shomer Emunim, *2, 14, by Rabbi Joseph Irgas, quoting the Kabbalists.* [11] "*Even if all mankind were to gather they could not create even a small mosquito and vivify it,*" (Bereishit Rabbah *39:14*). [12] *Introduction to* Tikunei Zohar. *Cf.* Likutei Amarim, *Part IV*, "Igeret Hakodesh," *ch. 20.* [13] Ps. *89:3.*

דשם הוי"ה פירושו שמהוה את הכל מאין ליש והיו"ד משמשת על הפעולה שהיא בלשון הוה ותמיד כדפרש"י ע"פ ככה יעשה איוב כל הימים והיינו החיות הנשפע בכל רגע ממש בכל הברואים ממוצא פי ה' ורוחו ומהוה אותם מאין ליש בכל רגע כי לא די להם במה שנבראו בששת ימי בראשית להיות קיימים בזה כמ"ש לעיל. והנה בסידור שבחיו של הקב"ה כתיב הגדול הגבור כו' ופי' הגדול היא מדת חסד והתפשטות החיות בכל העולמות וברואים לאין קץ ותכלית להיות ברואים מאין ליש וקיימים בחסד חנם ונקראת גדולה כי באה מגדולתו של הקב"ה בכבודו ובעצמו כי גדול ה' ולגדולתו אין חקר ולכן משפיע ג"כ חיות והתהוות מאין ליש לעולמות וברואים אין קץ שטבע הטוב להטיב והנה כמו שמדה זו היא שבחו של הקב"ה לבדו שאין ביכולת שום נברא לברוא יש מאין ולהחיותו וגם מדה זו היא למעלה מהשכלת כל הברואים והשגתם שאין כח בשכל שום נברא להשכיל ולהשיג מדה זו ויכלתה לברוא יש מאין ולהחיותו כי הבריאה יש מאין הוא דבר שלמעלה משכל הנבראים כי היא ממדת גדולתו של הקב"ה והקב"ה ומדותיו אחדות פשוט כדאיתא בזה"ק דאיהו וגרמוהי חד וכשם שאין ביכולת שום שכל נברא להשיג בוראו כך אינו יכול להשיג מדותיו וכמו שאין ביכולת שום שכל נברא להשיג מדת גדולתו שהיא היכולת לברוא יש מאין ולהחיותו כדכתיב עולם חסד יבנה כך ממש אין ביכלתו להשיג מדת גבורתו של הקב"ה שהיא מדת הצמצום ומניעת התפשטות

החיות

the life-force from His [attribute of] *Gedulah* preventing it from descending upon and manifesting itself to the creatures, to give them life and existence in a revealed manner, but rather with His Countenance concealed.[14] For the life-force conceals itself in the body of the created being and [it appears] as though the body of the created being has independent existence and is not [merely] a spreading forth of the life-force and spirituality—as the diffusion of the radiation and light from the sun—but an independently existing entity. Although, in reality, it has no independent existence, and is only like the diffusion of the light from the sun, nevertheless, this [concealment] is the very Restraining Power of the Holy One, blessed be He, Who is Omnipotent, to condense the life-force and spirituality which issues from the "Breath of His mouth" and to conceal it, so that the body of the created being shall not become nullified.[15]

And it is not within the scope of the intellect of any creature to comprehend the essential nature of the *Tzimtzum* and concealment [of the life-force] and that nonetheless the body of the creature be created *ex nihilo*—just as it is not within the capacity of any creature's intellect to comprehend the essential nature of the creation of being out of nothing.

●▲ [The *Tzimtzum* and concealing of the life-force is called *Kelim* ("vessels") and the life-force itself is called "Light."[16] For just as a vessel covers that which is within it, so does the *Tzimtzum* cover and conceal the light and the flowing life-force. And the *Kelim* are the [Divine] letters[17] whose roots are the five [terminal] letters מנצפ״ך, which are the five restraining forces[18] that divide and separate the breath and voice in the five organs of speech, in order that the twenty-two letters shall be formed. The source of the five restraining forces is *Botzinah D'kardunita* "(Light from Dark")[19] which is the Supernal *Gevurah* of *Atik Yomin* ("Ancient of Days");[20] and the source of the kindnesses is also *Chesed* of *Atik Yomin*, as is known to those well-versed in the Esoteric Wisdom.[21]][22]

●▲ *Chapter 5*

Concerning this our Sages of blessed memory said, "Originally it arose in [G–d's] thought to create the world with the attribute of stern judgement;[1] He saw, however, that the world could not endure, [so] He combined with it the attribute of mercy,"[2] that is, the revelation of G–dliness through the *Tzaddikim*

---

[14] *See* Tanya *I, ch. 22.* [15] *The vitality emanating from* Chesed *is too abundant and powerful for finite creatures to exist without its concealment and contraction.* [16] Kelim *and Light together comprise the* Sefirot *They are, respectively, the finite and infinite aspects of the* Sefirot. *The* Kelim *limit the Infinite Light, causing it to be revealed in proportion to the capacity of the finite beings. The* Kelim, *then, perform the function of concealing and at the same time, revealing the Divine Light.* [17] *In the same way, letters serve to reveal thought, yet at the same time, limit it. For speech cannot convey all that is in the mind of the thinker.* [18] *These five letters terminate a word and no other letters may follow them. Inasmuch as this is an act of limitation, it*

החיות מגדולתו מלירד ולהתגלות על הנבראים להחיותם ולקיימם בגילוי כ"א בהסתר פנים שהחיות מסתתר בגוף הנברא וכאילו גוף הנברא הוא דבר בפני עצמו ואינו התפשטות החיות והרוחניות כהתפשטות הזיו והאור מהשמש אלא הוא דבר בפני עצמו ואף שבאמת אינו דבר בפני עצמו אלא כמו התפשטות האור מהשמש מכל מקום הן הן גבורותיו של הקדוש ברוך הוא אשר כל יכול לצמצם החיות והרוחניות הנשפע מרוח פיו ולהסתירו שלא יבטל גוף הנברא במציאות וזה אין בשכל שום נברא להשיג מהות הצמצו' וההסתר ושיהיה אעפ"כ גוף הנברא נברא מאין ליש כמו שאין יכולת בשכל שום נברא להשיג מהות הבריאה מאין ליש. [והנה בחי' הצמצום והסתר החיות נקרא בשם כלים והחיות עצמו נקרא בשם אור שכמו שהכלי מכסה על מה שבתוכו כך בחי' הצמצום מכסה ומסתיר האור והחיות השופע והכלים הן הן האותיות ששרשן ה' אותיות מנצפ"ך שהן ה' גבורות המחלקות ומפרידות ההבל והקול בה' מוצאות הפה להתהוות כ"ב אותיות ושרש הה' גבורות הוא בוצינא דקרדוניתא שהיא גבורה עילאה דעתיק יומין ושרש החסדים הוא ג"כ חסד דעתיק יומין כידוע לי"ח:

פרק ה והנה על זה אמרו רז"ל בתחלה עלה במחשבה לברוא את העולם

במד"הד ראה שאין העולם מתקיים שתף בו מדת רחמים דהיינו התגלות אלהות על ידי צדיקים ואותות

---

is an act of Gevurah. [19] *I.e., Light which has been condensed and concealed through* Tzimtzum. *It is the Supernal limiting force which determines the quantity and quality of light and life-force in each world,* Sefirah *and being—thereby imposing all the limitations and differentiations inherent in Creation.* [20] *The realm which transcends all worlds including* Atzilut. [21] *I.e., Kabbalah.* [22] *Brackets are the author's.*

Chapter 5

[1] *I.e., with the attribute of* Tzimtzum, *complete concealment of the Divine light. Judgement signifies an act of negation and an imposition of limits. Therefore, in Kabbalah it is a*

(Notes cont. at end of Hebrew Text)

and the signs and miracles recorded in the Torah.[3] And regarding this, it was stated in the *Zohar*, "Above, in the 'Side of Supernal Holiness,' there is right and left," namely, *Chesed* and *Gevurah*. This means that both are attributes of G–dliness, above the intellect and comprehension of the creatures, for "He and His attributes are One in the world of *Atzilut*."[4] Even the comprehension of Moses, our teacher, peace unto him, in his prophetic vision, was not in the world of *Atzilut* [itself], but only as it [*Atzilut*] becomes clothed in the world of *Beriah*;[5] and even then, was not of these two attributes, *Chesed* and *Gevurah*, but only as they become clothed in attributes which are of lower levels than they, viz. the attributes of *Netzach* (victory, eternity), *Hod* (majesty), *Yesod* (foundation)[6] [as is explained in *Shaar HaNevuah*].[7]

It is only the *Tzaddikim* in *Gan Eden* who are granted the reward of comprehending the spreading forth of the life-force and light which issues from these two attributes, *Chesed* and *Gevurah*. And this [comprehension] is the "food"[8] of the souls of the *Tzaddikim* who, in this world, occupied themselves with the study of Torah for its own sake.[9] For from the spreading forth of these two attributes, a firmament[10] is spread over the souls in *Gan Eden*, and this firmament is called *Razah D'Oraytah* ("The secret of the Torah"). In it is the secret of the twenty-two letters of the Torah which was given from these two attributes, as it is written, "From His right hand He gave unto them a fiery Law."[11] And from this firmament drops dew[12] as "food" for the souls, i.e., the knowledge of the secret of the twenty-two letters of the Torah. For this firmament is the "Secret of knowledge," and the Torah is the "food" of the souls in *Gan Eden*, and the precepts are "garments" [of the souls],[13] as all this is explained [in *Zohar Vayakhel*, pp. 209–210 and in *Etz Chayim*, *Shaar* 44, ch. 3].[14]

•▲Chapter 6

Now, the name *Elokim* is the name which indicates the attribute of *Gevurah* and *Tzimtzum*, hence it is also numerically equal to *hateva*[1] (nature), for it [*Elokim*] *conceals* the Supernal Light which brings the world into existence and gives it life, and it appears as though the world exists

---

[3] *Miracles are evidence of G–d's "hand" in nature and demonstrate that He is the Master of all; all cosmic and natural powers are subservient to Him.* [4] *Introduction to* Tikunei Zohar. [5] *See ch. 2, n. 16,* supra. [6] *See* Likutei Amarim, *Part IV,* "Igeret HaKodesh," *ch. 15.* [7] *Brackets are the author's.* [8] *Just as food is absorbed by the body and transformed into flesh and blood, so the light of* Atzilut *is comprehended and absorbed by the soul and united with it. This Divine light is the "food" or inner life of the soul. Cf.* Tanya *I, ch. 5.* [9] *From pure and disinterested motives—to fulfil G–d's command—and not for the purpose of reward or self-aggrandisement. In* Tanya *I,* ibid., *it is interpreted as "study with the intent to attach one's*

ואותות ומופתים שבתורה. והנה על זה אמרו בזהר דלעילא בסטרא דקדושה עילאה אית ימינא ואית שמאלא דהיינו חסד וגבורה פי' דשתיהן הן מדות אלהות למעלה משכל הנבראים והשגתם דאיהו וגרמוהי חד בעולם האצילות ואף השגת משה רבינו עליו השלום בנבואתו לא היתה בעולם האצילות אלא על ידי התלבשותו בעולם הבריאה ואף גם זאת לא בשתי מדות אלו חו"ג אלא על ידי התלבשותן במדות שלמטה מהן במדרגה שהן מדות נצח הוד יסוד [כמ"ש בשער הנבואה] רק שמתן שכרם של צדיקים בגן עדן הוא השגת התפשטות החיות ואור הנמשך משתי מדות אלו חו"ג והוא מזון נשמות הצדיקים שעסקו בתורה לשמה בעו"הז כי מהתפשטות שתי מדות אלו נמתח רקיע על הנשמות שבגן עדן ורקיע זה נקרא רזא דאורייתא ובו סוד כ"ב אותיות התורה הנתונה משתי מדות אלו כדכתיב מימינו אש דת למו ומרקיע זה נוטף טל למזון הנשמות דהיינו ידיעת סוד כ"ב אותיות התורה כי הרקיע הזה הוא סוד הדעת והתורה היא מזון הנשמות בג"ע והמצות הן לבושים כמבואר כל זה [בזהר ויקהל דף ר"ט ור"י ובע"ח שער מ"ד פרק ג']:

פרק ו

והנה שם אלהים הוא שם מדת הגבורה והצמצום ולכן הוא גם כן בגימטריא הטבע לפי שמסתיר האור שלמעלה המהוה ומחיה העולם ונראה כאילו העולם עומד ומתנהג

---

soul to G–d through the comprehension of the Torah, each one according to his intellect." [10] Shamayim, *the Hebrew word for heaven, is a combination of* esh *(fire) and* mayim *(water) which symbolise* Gevurah *and* Chesed *respectively.* [11] Deut. 33:2. "*Right hand*" *indicates* Chesed, "*Fiery*" *indicates* Gevurah. *It was necessary for the Torah, whose source is* Chesed*—i.e., the issuing forth of the Infinite Light—to descend and become condensed through* Tzimtzum *and* Gevurah *until it could become clothed in the corporeal, material things of this world and could be comprehended and fulfilled by created beings. Cf.* Likutei Amarim *I, chapter 4, Part IV,* "Igeret HaKodesh," *ch. 10.* [12] *The Torah is likened to dew*

(Notes cont. at end of Hebrew Text)

and conducts itself in a natural way.[2] And this name *Elokim* is a shield and a covering for the name *Hava'ye*, to conceal the light and life-force which flows from the name *Hava'ye* and brings creation into existence from naught, so that it [the light and life-force] should not be revealed to the creatures, who thereby would become absolutely nullified.[3]

This quality of *Gevurah* and *Tzimtzum* is also a quality of *Chesed* for through it [*Tzimtzum* and *Gevurah*] the world is built. And this is the quality of *Gevurah* ●▲ which is included in *Chesed*. From the inclusion of the attributes one in the other, it is evident that "He and His attributes are One," for since they are in a complete unity with Him, they therefore unite with each other and are comprised of each other.[4] As Eliyahu said, "And You are He who binds [the attributes] together and unites them . . .; and aside from You there is no unity among those above . . ."[5]

This, then, is the meaning of that which is written "And take unto your heart that *Hava'ye* is *Elokim*"[6]—that is, these two names are *actually one*, for even the name *Elokim*, which contracts and conceals the light is a quality of *Chesed*, just as the name *Hava'ye*. For the attributes of the Holy One, blessed be He, unite with Him in a complete unity, and "He and His Name are One,"[7] for His attributes are His Names.[8] Since this is so, you will consequently know that "In the heavens above and on the earth below, *en od*—there is nothing else [besides G–d]."[9] This means that even the material earth, which appears to the eyes of all to be actually existing is naught and complete nothingness in relation to the Holy One, blessed be He. For the name *Elokim* conceals and contracts [the light and life-force] only for the lower [creatures], but not for the Holy One, blessed be He, since He and His Name *Elokim* are One. Therefore, even the earth and that which is below it are naught and complete nothingness in relation to the Holy One, blessed be He, and are not called by any name at all, not even the name *od* (else) which is an expression indicating a secondary, subordinate status, as the statement of our Sages of blessed memory, "*Yehudah v'od likrah*;"[10] [unlike] the body which is subordinate to the soul and life-force within it [and is referred to as *od*]. [And this is the meaning of the verse: "I will praise *Hava'ye* with my life (soul) and will sing to *Elokim b'odi*"[11]

---

[2] *I.e., according to fixed, immutable laws, in no way dependent upon or influenced by anything supernatural. Divinity is not readily evident in nature.* [3] *Since the light and life-force is too abundant and powerful for finite creatures to exist without its concealment and contraction.* [4] *The attributes, or* sefirot *are interconnected with each other and function harmoniously together. They are also mutually inclusive—each attribute contains all the others—and are differentiated only by the predominance of the particular quality which gives each its name. Cf.* Pardess, "Shaar *8*," *ch. 2.* [5] *Introduction to* Tikunei Zohar. [6] Deut. *4:39*. *Here follows the answer to the question raised at the beginning of ch. 1*, supra. [7] *Cf.* Zohar *II, 19b.* [8] *The attri-*

ומתנהג בדרך הטבע ושם אלהים זה הוא מגן ונרתק לשם הוי"ה להעלים האור והחיות הנמשך משם הוי"ה ומהוה מאין ליש שלא יתגלה לנבראים ויבטלו במציאות והרי בחי' גבורה זו וצמצום הזה הוא גם כן בחי' חסד שהעולם יבנה בו וזו היא בחי' גבורה הכלולה בחסד והנה מהתכללות המדות זו בזו נראה לעין דאיהו וגרמוהי חד שהן מדותיו כי מאחר שהן ביחוד גמור עמו לכן הן מתייחדות זו בזו וכלולות זו מזו כמאמר אליהו ואנת הוא דקשיר לון ומיחד לון וכו' ובר מינך לית יחודא בעילאי כו' וז"ש והשבות אל לבבך כי ה' הוא האלהים פירוש ששני שמות אלו הם אחד ממש שגם שם אלהים המצמצם ומעלים האור הוא בחי' חסד כמו שם הוי"ה משום שמדותיו של הקדוש ברוך הוא מתיחדות עמו ביחוד גמור והוא ושמו אחד שמדותיו הן שמותיו ואם כן ממילא תדע שבשמים ממעל ועל הארץ מתחת אין עוד פי' שגם הארץ החומרית שנראית יש גמור לעין כל היא אין ואפס ממש לגבי הקדוש ברוך הוא כי שם אלהים אינו מעלים ומצמצם אלא לתחתונים ולא לגבי הקב"ה מאחר שהוא ושמו אלהים אחד ולכן גם הארץ ומתחת לארץ הן אין ואפס ממש לגבי הקב"ה ואינן נקראות בשם כלל אפילו בשם עוד שהוא לשון טפל כמאמר רז"ל יהודה ועוד לקרא וכגוף שהוא טפל לנשמה וחיות שבתוכו [וז"ש אהללה ה' בחיי אזמרה לאלהי בעודי שהחיים

---

butes correspond to the specific Names of the Deity, to wit—Hava'ye *corresponds to Kindness and Mercy,* Elokim *to Might,* Ad-nay *to Sovereignty, etc. Cf.* Zohar *III, 10b, 11a.* [9] Deut. ibid. *Thus, the unity of G–d does not mean only that there are no other gods, but that there is nothing apart from Him, i.e., there is no existence whatsoever apart from His existence; the whole Creation is nullified within Him as the rays of the sun within the orb of the sun. This is the meaning of* Yichudah Ilaah *(higher level Unity) which will be further explained in ch. 7,* infra. [10] Kiddushin 6*a*. "*Does a verse in the Torah require additional or secondary substantiation from the customs of the Land of Judah?*" [11] Ps. 146:2.

(with my body). For the soul is derived from the name *Hava'ye* and the *od*, which is the body, the subordinate (of the soul), from the name *Elokim*.][12] For the soul does not bring the body into existence *ex nihilo*, [hence it can be called *od* in relation to the soul], but the Holy One, blessed be He, Who brings everything into existence *ex nihilo*—everything is absolutely nullified in relation to Him, just as the light of the sun [is nullified] in the sun.

●▲Therefore, it was necessary for Scripture to warn, "And know this day and take unto your heart . . .",[13] so that it should not enter your mind that the heavens and all their host and the earth and all therein are separate entities in themselves, and that the Holy One, blessed be He, fills the whole world—in the same way as the soul is invested in the body—and causes the flow of the "vegetative force" into the earth, and the force of motion into the celestial spheres, and moves them and directs them according to His Will, just as the soul moves the body and directs it according to its will. In truth, however, the analogy bears no similarity whatsoever to the object of comparison since the soul and the body are actually separate from each other in their very sources. The source of the body and its essence comes into being not from the soul, but from the seed of his father and mother; and even afterwards, his growth is not from the soul alone, but through his mother's eating and drinking all the nine months [of gestation], and subsequently through his own eating and drinking. This is not so, however, in the case of heaven and earth, for their very being and essence was brought into existence from naught and absolute nothingness, solely through the "Word of G–d" and the "Breath of His mouth," may He be blessed. And the word of G–d still stands forever [in all created things], and flows into them continuously at every instant and continuously brings them into existence from nothing, just as, for example, the coming into existence of the light from the sun within the very globe of the sun. Hence, in reality, they [heaven and earth] are completely nullified in relation to the "Word of G–d" and the "Breath of His mouth," may He be blessed, which are unified with His Essence and Being, may He be blessed, as will be explained later,[14] just as the light of the sun is nullified in the sun.

Yet these are

---

[12] *Brackets are the author's.* [13] Deut. ibid. [14] *Ch. 7*, infra.

שהחיים נמשכים משם הוי"ה והעור שהוא הגוף הטפל משם אלהים] לפי שהנשמה אינה מהוה הגוף מאין ליש אבל הקב"ה המהוה את הכל מאין ליש הכל בטל במציאות אצלו כמו אור השמש בשמש. ולכן הוצרך הכתוב להזהיר וידעת היום והשבות אל לבבך וגו' שלא תעלה על דעתך שהשמים וכל צבאם והארץ ומלואה הם דבר נפרד בפני עצמו והקדוש ברוך הוא ממלא כל העולם כהתלבשות הנשמה בגוף ומשפיע כח הצומח בארץ וכח התנועה בגלגלים ומניעם ומנהיגם כרצונו כמו שהנשמה מניעה את הגוף ומנהיגתו כרצונה. אך באמת אין המשל דומה לנמשל כלל כי הנשמה והגוף הם באמת נפרדי' זה מזה בשרשם כי אין התהוות שרש הגוף ועצמותו מנשמתו אלא מטפות אביו ואמו וגם אחרי כן אין גידולו מנשמתו לבדה אלא על ידי אכילת ושתיית אמו כל תשעה חדשים ואחר כך על ידי אכילתו ושתייתו בעצמו מה שאין כן השמים והארץ שכל עצמותם ומהותם נתהוה מאין ואפס המוחלט רק בדבר ה' ורוח פיו ית' וגם עדיין נצב דבר ה' לעולם ושופע בהם תמיד בכל רגע ומהוה אותם תמיד מאין ליש כהתהוות האור מהשמש בתוך גוף כדור השמש עצמו דרך משל ואם כן הם בטלים באמת במציאות לגמרי לגבי דבר ה' ורוח פיו ית' המיוחדים במהותו ועצמותו ית' כמו שיתבאר לקמן כביטול אור השמש בשמש רק שהן הן גבורותיו

His Restraining Powers, to hide and conceal, through the attribute of *Gevurah* and *Tzimtzum*, the life-force which flows into them, so that heaven and earth and all their host should appear as if they were independently existing entities. However, the *Tzimtzum* and concealment is only for the lower [worlds], but in relation to the Holy One, blessed be He, "Everything before Him is considered as actually naught,"[15] just as the light of the sun in the sun. And the attribute of *Gevurah* does not, Heaven forfend, conceal for Him, may He be blessed, for it is not an independent entity—since *Hava'ye* is *Elokim*.

•▲*Chapter 7*

With the above in mind, we may now understand[1] the statement in the holy *Zohar*, that the verse *Shema Yisrael* is *Yichudah Ilaah* ("higher level Unity"), and *Baruch Shem K'vod Malchuto Leolam Vaed* is *Yichudah Tataah* ("lower level Unity").[2] For *Vaed* is *Echad* through the substitution of letters.[3]

The cause and reason for this *Tzimtzum* and concealment that the Holy One, blessed be He, obscured and hid the life-force of the world, to make the world appear as an independently existing entity [is as follows]: It is known to all that the purpose of the creation of the world is for the sake of the revelation of His kingdom, may He be blessed, for "There is no King without a nation."[4] The word *am* (nation), is related etymologically to the word *ommemot* (concealed, dimmed),[5] for they are separate entities, distinct and distant from the level of the king. For, even if the king had very many sons, the name kingdom would not apply to them, nor even to nobles alone. Only "In a multitude of *people* is the glory of the king."[6]

The name which indicates the attribute of His *Malchut* (Kingship, Royalty), may He be blessed, is the name *Adnut* (Lordship), for He is the "Lord of the whole earth."[7] Thus, it is this attribute and this Name which bring into existence and sustain the world so that it should be as it is now, a completely independent and separate entity, and not absolutely nullified. For with the withdrawal of this attribute

[15] Zohar *I, 11b.*

Chapter 7

[1] *Rabbi Schneur Zalman here returns to elucidate the opening statement of the treatise.* [2] Zohar *I, 18b.* [3] Zohar *II, 134a. According to the rules of Hebrew grammar, the letters in the alphabet are divided into various groups, i.e. according to their source in the organs of speech; and the letters in each group are interchangeable. The letters* aleph, hai, vav, *and* yud *fall into one group. Therefore,* aleph *may be interchanged with* vav. *The letters* aleph, chet, hai *and* ayin *fall into another category. Thus,* chet *may be interchanged with* ayin. *Hence* echod *becomes* vaed. [4] Sefer HaChayim, "Geulah," *ch. 2; Emek HaMelech,* "Shaar HaMitzvot," *beginning of*

גבורותיו במדת הגבורה והצמצום להסתיר ולהעלים
החיות השופע בהם שיהיו נראים השמים והארץ
וכל צבאם כאילו הם דבר בפני עצמו אך אין
הצמצום וההסתר אלא לתחתונים אבל לגבי הקדוש
ברוך הוא כולא קמיה כלא ממש חשיבי כאור
השמש בשמש ואין מדת הגבורה מסתרת חס ושלום
לפניו יתברך כי איננה דבר בפני עצמו אלא ה׳
הוא האלהים:

פרק ז ובזה יובן מ״ש בזוהר הקדוש דפסוק
שמע ישראל הוא יחודא עילאה
וברוך שם כבוד מלכותו לעולם ועד הוא יחודא
תתאה כי ועד הוא אחד בחלופי אתוון כי הנה
סיבת וטעם הצמצום וההסתר הזה שהסתיר והעלים
הקדוש ברוך הוא את החיות של העולם כדי שיהיה
העולם נראה דבר נפרד בפני עצמו הנה הוא ידוע
לכל כי תכלית בריאת העולם הוא בשביל
התגלות מלכותו יתברך דאין מלך בלא עם פי׳ עם
מלשון עוממות שהם דברים נפרדים וזרים ורחוקים
ממעלת המלך כי אילו אפילו היו לו בנים רבים
מאד לא שייך שם מלוכה עליהם וכן אפילו על
שרים לבדם רק ברוב עם דווקא הדרת מלך ושם
המורה על מדת מלכותו יתברך הוא שם אדנות
כי הוא אדון כל הארץ ונמצא כי מדה זו ושם
זה הן המהוין ומקיימין העולם להיות עולם כמות
שהוא עכשיו יש גמור ודבר נפרד בפני עצמו
ואינו בטל במציאות ממש כי בהסתלקות מדה
זו

---

ch. 1; Rabbenu Bachya, "Vayeshev," *38:2. Cf.* Pirkei D'Rebbe Eliezer, *ch. 3.* [5] *Cf.* Rashi, Judges *5:14. The nature of Kingship requires the separation and concealment of the King from his subjects. He must stand aloof from them or the relationship of sovereignty is destroyed. In the same way, the Infinite concealed Himself and the world appears as a separate and independent entity; thus He can exercise sovereignty over it.* [6] Prov. *14:28.* [7] Josh. *3:11, 13.*

and this Name, G–d forbid, the world would revert to its source "In the word of G–d" and "The breath of His mouth" and would be completely nullified there, and the name "world" could not be applied to it at all.

●▲ The term "world" can be applied solely to that which possesses the dimensions of space and time; "space" referring to east, west, north, and south, upward and downward, and "time," to past, present and future. All these dimensions have no relation to the holy supernal attributes.[8] Only concerning the attribute of His *Malchut*, may He be blessed, is it possible to say that He, may He be blessed, is King "Above without end and below without limit," and likewise in all four directions. The same is true concerning the dimensions of time, [as it is written,] "G–d reigns, G–d reigned and G–d will reign."[9] Thus, the life-force of space, and likewise of time, and their coming into being from nothingness,[10] and their existence as long as they shall exist, is from the attribute of His *Malchut*, may He be blessed, and the name *Adnut*, blessed be He. Now, since the attribute of His *Malchut*, may He be blessed, is united with His Essence and Being in an absolute union, as will be explained,[11] therefore, space and time are also completely nullified in relation to His Essence and Being, may He be blessed, as the light of the sun is nullified in the sun.

And this is the [meaning of] the intertwining of the [letters of the] name *Adnut* with the [letters of the] name *Hava'ye*. The name *Hava'ye* indicates that He transcends time, for "He was, He is, and He will be at the same instant," as is explained [in *Ra'aya Mehemna*.[12] on the Portion of *Pinchas*];[13] and likewise [is He] above space, for He continuously brings into existence all the dimensions of space everywhere, from the uppermost to the lowermost [regions] and in the four directions.[14] Now, although He is supra- ●▲ spatial and supra-temporal, nevertheless, He is also found below in space and time, that is, He unites with His attribute of *Malchut* from which space and time are derived and come into existence.[15] And this is *Yichudah Tataah*, [the intertwining of (the letters of the name) *Hava'ye* with

---

[8] *I.e., the nine higher attributes or* Sefirot. Malchut *is the tenth and lowest attribute. See ch. 9, n. 7,* infra. [9] Liturgy, *Morning Prayer. The quotation is a combination of* Ps. *93:1, Ibid. 10:16,* Ex. *15:18.* [10] *Time is a creation* ex nihilo *for it depends on the motion of created things; and whatever is inseparable from things created must likewise be created. Cf.* Moreh Nevuchim *II, ch. 13. Furthermore, time, which is divisible into finite parts, e.g., seconds, minutes etc., cannot be infinite for Infinity is indivisible. Since it is finite it must be created* ex nihilo. *Cf.* Derech Mitzvotecha *by Rabbi Menachem Mendel of Lubavitch, Kehot Publication Society (Brooklyn, 1953), p. 113–114.* [11] *Ch. 8,* infra. [12] Zohar *III, 257b.* Ra'aya Mehem-

זו ושם זה ח"ו היה העולם חוזר למקורו בדבר ה' ורוח פיו ית' ובטל שם במציאות ממש ולא היה שם עולם עליו כלל והנה גדר ובחי' שם עולם נופל על בחי' מקום ובחי' זמן דוקא בחי' מקום הוא מזרח ומערב צפון דרום מעלה ומטה בחי' זמן עבר הוה ועתיד. והנה כל בחי' אלו אין להן שייכות במדות הקדושות העליונות כי אם במדת מלכותו ית' לבדה שייך לומר שהוא ית' מלך למעלה עד אין קץ ולמטה עד אין תכלית וכן לד' סטרין וכן בבחי' זמן ה' מלך ה' מלך ה' ימלוך ונמצא שחיות המקום וכן חיות הזמן והתהוותם מאין ליש וקיומם כל זמן קיומם הוא ממדת מלכותו ית' ושם אדנות ב"ה ולפי שמדת מלכותו ית' מיוחדת במהותו ועצמותו ית' בתכלית היחוד כמו שיתבאר הלכך גם בחי' המקום והזמן בטילים במציאות ממש לגבי מהותו ועצמותו ית' כביטול אור השמש בשמש וזהו שילוב שם אדנות בשם הוי"ה כי שם הוי"ה מורה שהוא למעלה מן הזמן שהוא היה הוה ויהיה ברגע א' כמ"ש [בר"מ פרשת פנחס] וכן למעלה מבחי' מקום כי הוא מהוה תמיד את כל בחי' המקום כולו מלמעלה עד למטה ולד' סטרין. והנה אף על פי שהוא ית' למעלה מהמקום והזמן אף על פי כן הוא נמצא גם למטה במקום וזמן דהיינו שמתייחד במדת מלכותו שממנה נמשך ונתהווה המקום והזמן וזהו יחודא תתאה [שילוב הוי"ה

באדנות

---

na *is a part of the* Zohar *which explains the esoteric meaning of the precepts.* [13] *Brackets are the author's.* [14] *In the intertwining letters of the name* Adnut *into the letters of the name* Hava'ye, *the* Yud *of* Hava'ye *is the first letter, and therefore this name predominates. This indicates that time and space are nullified in relation to Him. This is* Yichudah Ilaah. *See also ch. 6, n.* 9, supra. *It is this Unity which is affirmed in the recital of* "Shema Yisrael . . . *G–d is One," i.e., One and Alone for there is nothing apart from Him.* [15] *I.e. He is both transcendent and immanent. Through* Malchut *He becomes immanent in creation.*

(the letters of the name) *Adnut*,[16] blessed be He],[17] i.e., His Essence and Being, may He be blessed, which is called by the name *En Sof* ("Infinite"), completely fills the whole earth temporally and spatially. In the heavens above and on the earth [below] and in the four directions, all are equally permeated with the light of the *En Sof*, blessed be He, for He is on the earth below exactly as in the heavens above. For all, [heaven and earth] are within the dimensions of space which are completely nullified in the light of the *En Sof*, blessed be He, which clothes itself in it through the attribute of His *Malchut* that is united with Him, may He be blessed. However, the attribute of His *Malchut* is the attribute of *Tzimtzum* and concealment, to hide the light of the *En Sof*, blessed be He, so that the existence of time and space should not be completely nullified and there will be no dimensions of time and space whatsoever, even for the lower [worlds].

●▲ Now, from the foregoing exposition the verse, "I, *Hava'ye*, have not changed,"[18] will be understood. This means: there is no change [in Him] at all; just as He was alone prior to the creation of the world, so is He alone after it was created. And thus it is written, "You were the same before the world was created; You have been the same, . . ."[19] without any change in His Essence, nor in His Knowledge, for by knowing Himself, He knows all created things, since all come from Him and are nullified in relation to Him. And as Maimonides, of blessed memory, stated, that He is the Knower, He is the Known, and He is Knowledge itself—all are one. This is beyond the power of speech to express, beyond the capacity of the ear to hear, and of the heart of man to apprehend clearly. For the Holy One, blessed be He, His Essence and Being, and His Knowledge are all absolutely one, from every side and angle, and every form of unity. His Knowledge is not superadded to His Essence and Being as it is in the soul of man, whose knowledge is added to his essence and is compounded with it. For when man studies a subject and knows it, his rational soul was already within him

---

[16] *In the intertwining of the letters of the name* Hava'ye *into the letters of the name* Adnut, *the* Aleph *of* Adnut *is first, and therefore this name prevails. This indicates that time and space exist, but they are permeated with* Hava'ye, *the Infinite. Therefore, the* Zohar *states that* "Baruch Shem . . . *Blessed be His Name Whose Glorious* Kingdom *is for ever and ever" is the expression of* Yichudah Tataah. "*Kingdom*" *points to finite, material existence yet filled with His Essence.* [17] *Brackets are the author's.* [18] Mal. *3:6.* [19] Liturgy, *Morning Prayer;* Yalkut VaEtchanan, *835.*

באדנות ב"ה] דהיינו שמהותו ועצמותו יתברך הנקרא בשם אין סוף ברוך הוא מלא את כל הארץ ממש בזמן ומקום כי בשמים ממעל ובארץ ולד' סטרין הכל מלא מאור א"ס ב"ה בשוה ממש כי כך הוא בארץ מתחת כמו בשמים ממעל ממש כי הכל הוא בחי' מקום הבטל במציאות באור אין סוף ברוך הוא המתלבש בו על ידי מדת מלכותו המיוחדת בו ית' רק שמדת מלכותו היא מדת הצמצום וההסתר להסתיר אור אין סוף ב"ה שלא יבטלו הזמן והמקום ממציאותם לגמרי ולא יהיה שום בחי' זמן ומקום במציאות אפילו לתחתונים. והנה במ"ש יובן מ"ש אני ה' לא שניתי פי' שאין שום שינוי כלל כמו שהיה לבדו קודם בריאת העולם כך הוא לבדו אחר שנברא וז"ש אתה הוא עד שלא נברא העולם אתה הוא כו' בלי שום שינוי בעצמותו ולא בדעתו כי בידיעת עצמו יודע כל הנבראים שהכל ממנו ובטל במציאות אצלו וכמ"ש הרמב"ם ז"ל שהוא היודע והוא הידוע והוא הדיעה עצמה הכל אחד ודבר זה אין כח בפה לאמרו ולא באזן לשמעו ולא בלב האדם להכירו על בוריו כי הקב"ה מהותו ועצמותו ודעתו הכל אחד ממש מכל צד ופינה בכל דרך יחוד ואין דעתו דבר נוסף על מהותו ועצמותו כמו שהוא בנפש האדם שדעתה דבר נוסף על מהותה ומורכב בה שהרי כשהאדם לומד ויודע איזה דבר כבר היתה בו נפשו

before he studied and knew it, and afterwards, this knowledge was added to his soul. And so, day after day, "Days speak, and a multitude of years teach wisdom."[20] This is not a perfect unity, but a composite.

The Holy One, blessed be He, however, is a perfect unity, without any composition and plurality at all. Hence, perforce, His Essence and Being and His Knowledge are all absolutely one, without any composition. Therefore, just as it is impossible for any creature in the world to comprehend the Essence of the Creator and His Being, so it is impossible to comprehend the essence of His Knowledge; only to believe, with a faith which transcends intellect and comprehension,[21] that the Holy One, blessed be He, is completely One and Unique. He and His Knowledge are all absolutely one, and knowing Himself, He perceives and knows all the higher and lower beings [even] unto a small worm in the sea and a minute mosquito which will be in the centre of the earth; there is nothing concealed from Him. This knowledge does not add multiplicity and composition to Him at all, since it is merely knowledge of Himself; and His Being and His Knowledge are all one.

Inasmuch as this is very difficult to envisage, therefore, the Prophet said, "For as the heavens are higher than the earth so are My ways higher than your ways, and My thoughts than your thoughts;"[22] and it is written, "Can you by searching find G–d? . . .";[23] and it is written, "Have You eyes of flesh, or do You see as man sees?"[24] —for man sees and knows everything with a knowledge that is external to himself, and the Holy One, blessed be He, by knowing Himself. These are the words of Maimonides. [See *Hilchot Yesodei Hatorah*,[25] and the Sages of the *Kabbalah* have agreed with him, as is explained in *Pardess*[26] of Rabbi Moses Cordovero,[27] of blessed memory.][28]

●▲ In the light of what has been said above[29] it is possible to understand the error of some, scholars in their own eyes, may G–d forgive them, who erred and misinterpreted in their study of the writings of the Ari, of blessed memory, and understood the doctrine of *Tzimtzum*, which is mentioned therein literally—that the Holy One, blessed be He, removed Himself and His Essence, G–d forbid, from this world, and only guides

---

[20] Job *32:7*. [21] *True belief implies pure faith which transcends the realm of the intellect. First one must strive to understand to the extent of one's intellectual capacities. Beyond that limit, he is to believe with simple faith. Simply stated, "where knowledge ends, faith begins."* [22] Isa. *55:9*. [23] Job *11:7*. [24] Ibid. *10:4*. [25] *Ch. 2:9–10, paraphrased and elucidated.* [26] Shaar Mehut VeHanhagah, *ch. 13*. [27] *One of the most famous Kabbalists of the sixteenth century.* [28] *Brackets are the author's.* [29] *I.e., The Unity of G–d and His knowledge.*

נפשו המשכלת בטרם שלמד וידע ואחר שלמד וידע ניתוספה ידיעה זו בנפשו וכן מידי יום ביום ימים ידברו ורוב שנים יודיעו חכמה ואין זו אחדות פשוטה אלא מורכבת אבל הקב"ה הוא אחדות פשוט בלי שום הרכבה וצד ריבוי כלל ואם כן ע"כ מהותו ועצמותו ודעתו הכל דבר אחד ממש בלי שום הרכבה ולפיכך כשם שאי אפשר לשום נברא בעולם להשיג מהות הבורא ועצמותו כך אי אפשר להשיג מהות דעתו רק להאמין באמונה שהיא למעלה מהשכל ומהשגה שהקב"ה יחיד ומיוחד הוא ודעתו הכל אחד ממש ובידיעת עצמו מכיר ויודע כל הנמצאים עליונים ותחתונים עד שלשול קטן שבים ועד יתוש קטן שיהיה בטבור הארץ אין דבר נעלם ממנו ואין ידיעה זו מוסיפה בו ריבוי והרכבה כלל מאחר שאינה רק ידיעת עצמו ועצמותו ודעתו הכל אחד ולפי שזה קשה מאד לצייר בשכלנו ע"כ אמר הנביא כי גבהו שמים מארץ כן גבהו דרכי מדרכיכם ומחשבותי ממחשבותיכם וכתיב החקר אלוה תמצא וגו' וכתיב העיני בשר לך אם כראות אנוש תראה שהאדם רואה ויודע כל הדברים בידיעה שחוץ ממנו והקב"ה בידיעת עצמו עכ"ל [ע"ש בה' יסודי התורה והסכימו עמו חכמי הקבלה כמבואר בפרדס מהרמ"ק ז"ל]:

והנה מכאן יש להבין שגגת מקצת חכמים בעיניהם ה' יכפר בעדם ששגו וטעו בעיונם בכתבי האריז"ל והבינו ענין הצמצום המוזכר שם כפשוטו שהקב"ה סילק עצמו ומהותו ח"ו מעוה"ז רק שמשגיח מלמעלה

from above, with individual Providence, all the created beings which are in the heavens above and on the earth below. Now, aside from the fact that it is altogether impossible to interpret the doctrine of *Tzimtzum* literally, [for then it] is a phenomenon of corporeality, concerning the Holy One, blessed be He, who is set apart from them [i.e., phenomena of corporeality], many myriads of separations *ad infinitum*, they also did not speak wisely, since they are "Believers, the sons of believers"[30] that the Holy One, blessed be He, knows all the created beings in this lower world and exercises Providence over them, and perforce His knowledge of them does not add plurality and innovation to Him, for He knows all by knowing Himself. Thus, as it were, His Essence and Being and His Knowledge are all one.[31]

▲ And this is stated in *Tikunim*, *Tikun* 57: "There is no place devoid of Him, not in the upper worlds nor in the lower worlds;" and in *Ra'aya Mehemna*, on the Portion of *Pinchas*: "He grasps all and none can grasp Him. . . . He encompasses all worlds, . . . and no one goes out from His domain; He fills all worlds, . . . He binds and unites a kind to its kind, upper with lower, and there is no closeness in the four elements[32] only through the Holy One, blessed be He, as He is within them."[33]

The meaning of "None can grasp Him," is that there is no one [even] amongst all the "Supernal Intelligences"[34] who can grasp with his intellect the Essence and Being of the Holy One, blessed be He; as it is written in *Tikunim*, "Hidden One of all the hidden and no thought can grasp You at all."[35] And even in the lower worlds, although "He fills all worlds," He is not as the soul of man within his body, which is grasped within the body to the extent that it is affected and is influenced by bodily changes and its pain, [as] from blows or cold or the heat of fire and the like. The Holy One, blessed be He, however, is not affected by the changes of this world, from summer to winter and from day to night, as it is written, "Even the darkness does not obscure for You, and the night shines as the day,"[36] for He is not grasped within the worlds at all even though He fills them.

●▲ And this is also the meaning of "He encompasses all worlds." For example, when a man reflects upon

---

[30] Sabbath *97a. Faith is a legacy from the Patriarchs and comes naturally to their children.* [31] *Hence it is contradictory to assert that He is absent from a place where His knowledge and providence function.* [32] *Fire, air, water, and dust, the basic elements of which all created things are composed.* [33] Zohar *III, 225a.* [34] *I.e., Angels, who, according to Maimonides* (Moreh Nevuchim, *I, ch. 49) are incorporeal and occupy no space. They are distinguished one from the other only by the extent and level of their comprehension, and hence are called "Intelligences." Nachmanides in* Shaar Ha Gemul *(quoted in* Torah Or *4:2) holds that they do have bodily existence but their bodies are formed only of the* spiritual *elements of "fire" and "air." They are*

מלמעלה בהשגחה פרטית על כל היצורים כולם
אשר בשמים ממעל ועל הארץ מתחת והנה מלבד
שא"א כלל לומר ענין הצמצום כפשוטו שהוא ממקרי
הגוף על הקב"ה הנבדל מהם ריבוא רבבות הבדלות
עד אין קץ אף גם זאת לא בדעת ידברו מאחר
שהם מאמינים בני מאמינים שהקב"ה יודע כל
היצורים שבעוה"ז השפל ומשגיח עליהם וע"כ אין
ידיעתו אותם מוסיפה בו ריבוי וחידוש מפני שיודע
הכל בידיעת עצמו הרי כביכול מהותו ועצמותו
ודעתו הכל א' וז"ש בתקונים תיקון נ"ז דלית אתר
פנוי מיניה לא בעילאין ולא בתתאין ובר"מ פ' פנחס
איהו תפיס בכולא ולית מאן דתפיס ביה כו' איהו
סוכ"ע כו' ולית מאן דנפיק מרשותי' לבר איהו
ממכ"ע כו' איהו מקשר ומיחד זונא לזיניה עילא
ותתא ולית קורבא בד' יסודין אלא בקב"ה כד איהו
בינייהו עכ"ל. ור"ל לית מאן דתפיס בי' שאין מי
שיתפוס בהשגת שכלו מכל שכלים העליונים במהותו
ועצמותו של הקב"ה כמ"ש בתקונים סתימא דכל
סתימין ולית מחשבה תפיסא בך כלל וגם בתחתונים
אע"ג דאיהו ממכ"ע אינו כנשמת האדם תוך גופו
שהיא נתפסת תוך הגוף עד שמתפעלת ומקבלת
שינויים משינויי הגוף וצערו מהכאות או קרירות או
חמימות האש וכיוצא משא"כ בהקב"ה שאינו מקבל
שום שינוי משינויי עוה"ז מקיץ לחורף ומיום ללילה
כדכתיב גם חשך לא יחשיך ממך ולילה כיום יאיר
לפי שאינו נתפס כלל תוך העולמות אע"ג דממלא
לון וזהו ג"כ ענין סוכ"ע פי' ד"מ כשאדם מתבונן
באיזה

"Intelligences" in that despite their bodily existence, their conceptions are non-spatial and non-temporal, while man's conceptions are circumscribed by the limitations of time and space. See Torah Or, ibid.; Likutei Torah, "Shelach," *46:1.* [35] *Introduction to* Tikunei Zohar. [36] Ps. *139:12.*

an intellectual subject in his mind or upon a physical matter in his thoughts, then his intellect and thought encompass that subject whose image is formed in his thought or in his mind, but they do not encompass that subject in actual fact. The Holy One, blessed be He, however, of Whom it is written, "For My thoughts are not your thoughts. . . ."[37] His Thought and Knowledge of all created beings actually encompass each and every creature; for [His Knowledge] is indeed its life-force and that which brings it into existence from nothingness into being in actual reality.[38]

▲ And "He fills all worlds" is the life-force which clothes itself within the created being. It is powerfully contracted within it according to the intrinsic nature of the created being which is finite and limited in quantity and quality, i.e., its significance and importance. As for example, the sun whose body is finite and limited quantitatively being approximately one hundred and sixty-seven times the size of the globe of the earth;[39] and whose quality and significance, namely, its light, is also limited as to the extent that it can give light, for it cannot illuminate indefinitely since it is a created being. Likewise, all created beings are finite and limited, for "From the earth to the heaven is a journey of five hundred years. . . ."[40]

Hence, the life-force which is invested in them is greatly and powerfully contracted, for it must undergo numerous and powerful contractions until there are brought into existence from its power and light created beings, as they are finite and limited. For the source of the life-force is ●▲ the "Breath of the mouth" of the Holy One, blessed be He, which clothes itself in the Ten Utterances of the Torah. And the "Breath of His mouth," may He be blessed, could have diffused without end and limit and created worlds infinite in their quantity and quality and given them life forever, and this world would not have been created at all. (For just as the Holy One, blessed be He, is called "Infinite," so are all His attributes and actions [infinite], for "He and His attributes are One,"[41]—i.e., the life-force which emanates from His attributes, namely, Kindness and Mercy and His other holy attributes,

---

[37] Isa. *55:8.* [38] *Cf.* Tanya, *ch. 48.* [39] *See Maimonides,* Yad HaChazakah, "Hilchot Yesodei HaTorah," *3:8; and Introduction to his* "*Commentary* on Mishnayot." *As to the seeming contradiction between this view and that of present day astronomy that the sun is 5/4 million* or more *times greater than the earth, the Lubavitcher Rebbe, Rabbi Menachem M. Schneerson* שליט"א, *has explained as follows: The view of astronomy applies to the* volume *of the sun, and that of Maimonides to its* diameter. *The diameter of the sun, based on present-day astronomy, is about one hundred and ten times that of the earth (not 170), but this measurement takes into consideration only specific layers of the sun and* not all of them. *For the outermost layers of the*

באיזה דבר חכמה בשכלו או דבר גשמי במחשבתו אזי שכלו ומחשבתו מקיפים על הדבר ההוא המצויר במחשבתו או בשכלו אך אין מקיפים על הדבר ההוא ממש בפועל ממש. אבל הקב"ה דכתיב ביה כי לא מחשבותי מחשבותיכם וגו' מחשבתו וידיעתו שיודע כל הנבראים מקפת כל נברא ונברא בפ"מ שהרי היא היא חיותו והתהוותו מאין ליש בפועל ממש. וממלא כל עלמין היא בחי' החיות המתלבשת תוך עצם הנברא שהיא מצומצמת בתוכו בצמצום רב כפי ערך מהות הנברא שהוא בעל גבול ותכלית בכמותו ואיכותו דהיינו מעלתו וחשיבותו כגון השמש שגופו יש לו גבול ותכלית בכמותו שהוא כמו קס"ז פעמים כגודל כדור הארץ ואיכותו ומעלתו הוא אורו ג"כ יש לו גבול עד כמה יוכל להאיר כי לא יאיר לבלתי תכלית מאחר שהוא נברא וכן כל הנבראים הם בעלי גבול ותכלית כי מהארץ לרקיע מהלך ת"ק שנה כו'. וא"כ החיות המלובשת בהם היא בבחי' צמצום רב ועצום כי צריכה תחלה להתצמצם צמצומים רבים ועצומים עד שיתהוה מכחה ואורה עצם הנבראים כמות שהם בעלי גבול ותכלית כי מקור החיות הוא רוח פיו של הקב"ה המתלבש בעשרה מאמרות שבתורה ורוח פיו ית' היה יכול להתפשט לאין קץ ותכלית ולברוא עולמות אין קץ ותכלית לכמותם ואיכותם ולהחיותם עדי עד ולא הי' נברא עוה"ז כלל (שכמו שהקב"ה נקרא א"ס כך כל מדותיו ופעולותיו דאיהו וגרמוהי חד היינו החיות הנמשכת ממדותיו שהן חסד ורחמים ושאר מדותיו

הקדושות

---

sun contract and expand greatly from time to time, and not all the layers are visible to the eye (only their effects are visible). Hence, it is difficult to measure them. Likewise, the protuberance is not taken into account. It has been measured and found that the sun has expanded to the extent that its diameter was more *than 170 times the diameter of the earth and later contracted.* [40] Hagigah *13a.* [41] *Introduction to* Tikunei Zohar.

by means of their clothing themselves in the "Breath of His mouth," "For He spoke and it was"[42] and "The world is built through kindness"[43] by "The word of G-d and the breath of His mouth,"[44] which becomes a vessel and "garment" for this kindness, "Like the snail whose garment is part of his body."[45])

The Holy One, blessed be He, however, contracted the light and life-force in order that it should be able to diffuse from the "Breath of His mouth," and invested it in the combinations of the letters of the Ten Utterances and their combinations of combinations, by substitutions and transpositions of the letters themselves and their numerical values and equivalents.[46] For each substitution and transposition indicates the descent of the light and life-force degree by degree, so that it will be able to create and give life to creatures whose quality and significance is lower than the quality and significance of the creatures created from the letters and words of the Ten Utterances themselves, in which the Holy One, blessed be He, in His Glory and Essence, is clothed, for [the Ten ▲Utterances] are His attributes.[47] And the numerical value indicates the progressive diminution of the light and life-force until there remains from it only the final level which is that of the sum and number of kinds of powers and grades contained in the light and life-force invested in a particular combination of a particular word.

(It is only after all these contractions and others like them, as His Wisdom, may He be blessed, has ordained, that the light and life-force could invest itself even in the lower [created things], such as inanimate stones and dust. Stone, for example, its name *even*, אבן, indicates that its source is in the [Divine] Name which numerically equals fifty-two ב"ן,[48] with an א, one, added to it from another Name,[49] for a reason known to its Creator. Now the name ב"ן is itself of very high worlds, yet through numerous and powerful contractions, degree by degree, there descended from it a life-force very greatly condensed, until it could clothe itself in a stone. And this is the soul of the inanimate being, which gives it life and brings it into existence *ex nihilo* at every instant, as has been explained previously.[50] This is the principle of

[42] Ps. *33:9*. [43] Ibid. *89:3*. [44] Ibid. *33:6*. [45] *Cf.* Bereishit Rabbah *21:5*. [46] *See ch. 1, notes 18 and 21* supra. [47] Pardess, "Shaar" *2:3–6. See ch. 11*, infra. [48] *The four letters of the name* Hava'ye *may be spelled phonetically in four different ways by using different vowels. Each spelling yields a different numerical value. The numerical value of Hava'ye when spelled out thus* יוד הה וו הה *is 52 or* ב"ן. [49] *See* Likutei Torah *by Rabbi Schneur Zalman of Liadi*, "*Reay*," *p. 54 col. 1*. [50] *Chs. 1, 2*, supra.

הקדושות ע"י התלבשותן שמתלבשות ברוח פיו כי הוא אמר ויהי ועולם ע"י חסד יבנה בדבר ה' ורוח פיו הנעשה כלי ולבוש לחסד זה כהדין קמצא דלבושיה מיניה וביה) אלא שצמצם הקב"ה האור והחיות שיוכל להתפשט מרוח פיו והלבישו תוך צירופי אותיות של עשרה מאמרות וצירופי צירופיהן בחילופי ותמורות האותיות עצמן ובחשבונן ומספרן שכל חילוף ותמורה מורה על ירידת האור והחיות ממדרגה למדרגה דהיינו שיוכל לברוא ולהחיות ברואים שמדרגות איכותם ומעלתם היא פחותה ממדרגות איכות ומעלת הברואים הנבראים מאותיות ותיבות עצמן שבעשרה מאמרות שבהן מתלבש הקב"ה בכבודו ובעצמו שהן מדותיו והחשבון מורה על מיעוט האור והחיות מיעוט אחר מיעוט עד שלא נשאר ממנו אלא בחי' אחרונה שהוא בחי' החשבון ומספר כמה מיני כחות ומדרגות כלולות באור וחיות הזה המלובש בצירוף זה של תיבה זו (ואחר כל הצמצומי' האלה וכיוצא בהן כאשר גזרה חכמתו ית' הוא שהי' יכול האור והחיות להתלבש גם בתחתוני' כמו אבנים ועפר הדומם כי אבן ד"מ שמה מורה כי שרשה משם העולה ב"ן במספרו ועוד אלף נוספת משם אחר (לישעם) [נר' דצ"ל לטעם] הידוע ליוצרה. והנה שם ב"ן בעצמו הוא בעולמות עליונים מאד רק שע"י צמצומי' רבים ועצומים ממדרגה למדרגה ירד ממנו חיות מועט במאד מאד עד שיוכל להתלבש באבן וזו היא נפש הדומם המחי' ומהוה אותו מאין ליש בכל רגע וכמש"ל וזו היא בחי' ממכ"ע

"He fills all worlds" which differs from the principle of "He encompasses all worlds.")

And each power and grade [of the life-force] can create beings according to its level, even unlimited in quantity and quality, to give them life forever, since it is the power of G–d which issues and emanates from the "Breath of His mouth" and there is no restraint [to Him]. But, their quality will not be on a level as high as the quality and level of the creatures which could be created from the power and degree of the letters themselves.

•▲ *Chapter 8*

Now, what Maimonides, of blessed memory, has said that the Holy One, blessed be He, His Essence and Being, and His Knowledge are completely one, a perfect unity and not a composite at all,[1] applies equally to all the attributes of the Holy One, blessed be He, and to all His holy names and the designations which the Prophets and Sages, of blessed memory, have ascribed to Him, such as Gracious, Merciful, Beneficient, and the like. This is also true with respect to His being called Wise, as it is written, "And He is also wise, . . ."[2]; and with respect to His Will, [as it is written] "G–d desires those who fear Him,"[3] and "He wishes to do kindness,"[4] and "He desires the repentence of the wicked and does not wish their death and wickedness,"[5] and "Your eyes are too pure to behold evil."[6] His Will and His Wisdom and His attribute of Kindness and His Mercy and His other attributes do not add plurality and composition, G–d forbid, to His Essence and Being, but His Essence and Being and His Will and Wisdom and Understanding and Knowledge and His attribute of Kindness and His Might and Mercy and Beauty—which is composed of His Kindness and Might[7] —and likewise His other holy attributes, are all an absolutely perfect unity, which is His very Essence and Being.

And as Maimonides of blessed memory, stated: "This is beyond the power of speech to express, beyond the capacity of the ear to hear, and of the heart of man to apprehend clearly,"[8] for man visualises in his mind all the concepts which he wishes to conceive and understand—all as they are within himself. For instance, if he wishes to envisage the essence of Will or the essence of Wisdom or of Understanding

---

[1] Yad HaChazakah, "Hilchot Yesodei HaTorah" *2:10*. [2] Isa. *31:2*. [3] Ps. *147:11*. [4] Micah *7:18*. [5] *Cf.* Ezek. *18:23;* Liturgy, Musaf *High Holy Days*. [6] Habak. *1:13*. [7] *"Beauty" is the combination of the qualities of Kindness and Might, with Kindness predominating. Kindness, or* Chesed *is the unrestrained flow of the life-giving force. This in itself is too strong to allow finite creatures to exist. So the attribute of Might or* Gevurah *limits and controls the abundance of light, while* Chesed *tempers the severity of* Gevurah. *The result is* Tiferet *or Beauty—the harmonious balance between stark severity and the overabundance of love.* [8] Loc. cit.

ממכ"ע משא"כ בחי' סוכ"ע) וכל כח ומדרגה יכול לברוא ברואים כפי בחי' מדרגה זו גם כן לאין קץ ותכלית בכמותם ואיכותם להחיות עדי עד מאחר שהוא כח ה' המתפשט ונאצל מרוח פיו ואין מעצור כו'. אך שלא יהי' איכותם במעלה גדולה כ"כ כאיכות ומעלת ברואים שיוכלו להבראות מבחי' כח ומדריגת האותיות עצמן:

פרק ח והנה מ"ש הרמב"ם ז"ל שהקב"ה מהותו ועצמותו ודעתו הכל אחד ממש אחדות פשוטה ולא מורכבת כלל כן הענין ממש בכל מדותיו של הקב"ה ובכל שמותיו הקדושים והכינויים שכינו לו הנביאים וחז"ל כגון חנון ורחום וחסיד וכיוצא בהן וכן מה שנקרא חכם דכתיב וגם הוא חכם וגו' וכן רצונו כי רוצה ה' את יראיו וחפץ חסד הוא ורוצה בתשובתם של רשעים ואינו חפץ במיתתם וברשעתם וטהור עינים מראות ברע אין רצונו וחכמתו ומדת חסדו ורחמנותו ושאר מדותיו מוסיפים בו ריבוי והרכבה ח"ו במהותו ועצמותו אלא עצמותו ומהותו ורצונו וחכמתו ובינתו ודעתו ומדת חסדו וגבורתו ורחמנותו ותפארתו הכלולה מחסדו וגבורתו וכן שאר מדותיו הקדושות הכל אחדות פשוטה ממש שהיא היא עצמותו ומהותו וכמ"ש הרמב"ם ז"ל שדבר זה אין כח בפה לאמרו ולא באזן לשמעו ולא בלב האדם להכירו על בוריו כי האדם מצייר בשכלו כל המושכלות שרוצה להשכיל ולהבין הכל כמות שהם בו כגון שרוצה לצייר בשכלו מהות הרצון או מהות חכמה או בינה או

or of Knowledge or the essence of the attribute of Kindness and Mercy and the like, he visualises them all as they are within himself. But in truth, the Holy One, blessed be He, is "High and exalted"[9] and "Holy is His Name,"[10] that is to say, He is Holy and separated[11] many myriads of degrees of separations *ad infinitum*, above the quality, type or kind of praises and exaltations which creatures could grasp and conceive in their intellect.

• For the first[12] quality and rank of creatures is wisdom, hence it is called "The beginning."[13] For indeed, it is the beginning and fountainhead of all the life-force in creatures, for from wisdom are derived understanding and knowledge and from them flow all the emotion attributes of the rational soul, such as love and kindness and mercy and the like. As is seen clearly that the child, having no wisdom, is always angry and unkind. And even his love is for trivial things which are not worthy to be loved, because he has no wisdom to love things which are worthy of love, for [the quality of] love is according to [the level of] wisdom.

And from the emotion attributes of the soul words and letters of thought issue forth, for the soul thinks of that which it loves or [of] how to perform [deeds] of kindness and mercy. And so it is with the other emotion attributes. In every thought in the world, there is clothed some emotion attribute which brings it [the soul] to think that thought, and this attribute is the vivifying force of that thought. And from the letters of thought proceed letters of speech, and they [the letters of thought] are their very vivifying force. And speech brings to action, [as] of charity and kindness, e.g., the king who commands his servants to give [charity]. And even when a man himself performs some deed, the power of the soul and its life-force which clothes itself in this deed, is as absolute nothingness in relation to the power of the soul and its life-force which clothes itself in the speech of man; [they are to each other] as the relation and comparison of the body to the soul. Likewise is the relation of the letters of speech to the letters of thought; and likewise is the relation

---

[9] Liturgy, *Morning Prayer*. [10] Ibid., *Sabbath Morning Prayer*. [11] *The Hebrew word for "holy" means "set apart," separated from the unholy. When applied to G–d it indicates His sublime exaltedness and transcendence over the worlds.* [12] *I.e., highest.* [13] Ps. *111:10*. *See also* Targum Yerushalmi, Gen. *1:1*.

• 27 Sivan

או דעת או מהות מדת חסד ורחמים וכיוצא בהן הוא מצייר כולן כמות שהן בו אבל באמת הקדוש ב"ה הוא רם ונשא וקדוש שמו כלומר שהוא קדוש ומובדל ריבוא רבבות עד אין קץ ותכלית מדרגות הבדלות למעלה מעלה מערך וסוג ומין כל התשבחות והמעלות שיוכלו הנבראים להשיג ולצייר בשכלם כי המעלה ומדרגה הראשונה אצל הנבראים היא החכמה שלכן נקראת ראשית כי באמת היא ראשית ומקור כל החיות בנבראים כי מהחכמה נמשכות בינה ודעת ומהן נמשכות כל המדות שבנפש המשכלת כמו אהבה וחסד ורחמים וכיוצא בהן וכנראה בחוש שהקטן שאין בו דעת הוא בכעס תמיד ואכזרי וגם אהבתו היא לדברים קטנים שאין ראוי לאהבם מפני שאין בו דעת לאהוב דברים הראויים לאהבם שהאהבה כפי הדעת ומהמדות שבנפש נמשכות בה תיבות ואותיות המחשבה שהנפש מחשבת בדבר שאוהבת או איך לפעול החסד ורחמים וכן בשאר מדות ובכל מחשבה שבעולם מלובשת בה איזו מדה המביאה לחשוב מחשבה זו ומדה זו היא חיותה של מחשבה זו ומאותיות המחשבה נמשכות אותיות הדבור והן חיותן ממש והדבור מביא לידי מעשה הצדקה וחסד כגון המלך שמצוה לעבדיו ליתן וגם כשהאדם עושה בעצמו איזה דבר הרי כח הנפש וחיותה המתלבש בעשיה זו הוא כאין ממש לגבי כח הנפש וחיותה המתלבש בדבור האדם וכערך ומשל הגוף לנשמה וכן ערך אותיות הדבור לאותיות המחשבה וכן ערך אותיות

of the letters of thought to the essence of the emotion attribute which is clothed in it and vivifies it; and likewise the relation of the essence and life-force of the emotion attribute in comparison with the wisdom, understanding and knowledge which together constitute the intellect from which this attribute was derived. All this applies to the soul of man and the souls of all the created beings in all the higher and lower worlds. In all of them, wisdom is the beginning and source of the life-force.

•▲ *Chapter 9*

In regard to the Holy One, blessed be He, however, the quality of Wisdom—which [in all created beings] is the beginning of thought and its genesis—is to Him the completion of action; i.e., in relation to the Holy One, blessed be He, it [Wisdom] is considered as if it were the quality and level of action, as it is written, "You have made them all with wisdom."[1] That is to say, [Wisdom relative to Him is] as the quality of the life-force in physical and material action is in relation to the quality of the life-force in Wisdom, the beginning and source of the life-force in man and all the physical creatures. [The life-force in physical action] is as nothing in comparison with the life-force in the letters of speech, which [in turn] is of no account in comparison with the life-force in the letters of thought, which [in turn] is as nothing compared to the life-force and level of the emotion attributes from which this thought is derived, which [again] is as nothing relative to the life-force and level and degree of Wisdom, Understanding and Knowledge, the source of the attributes. Exactly so is the quality and level of Wisdom, the beginning and source of the life-force in all the worlds, in relation to the Holy One, blessed be He, in His Glory and Essence, Who is sublimated and exalted many myriads of degrees of elevations more than the elevation of the quality of Wisdom over the quality of the life-force in action which is only an elevation of five degrees, namely, the qualities of action, speech, thought, emotion attributes, and intellect. The Holy One, blessed be He however, is "High and exalted" above the level of Wisdom myriads of degrees like these *ad infinitum*. •▲But inasmuch as it is within the power of created beings to comprehend only the descent from the level of Wisdom which is their beginning, to the level of

[1] Ps. 104:24.

אותיות המחשבה למהות המדה המלובשת בה ומחיה אותה וכן ערך מהות וחיות המדה לגבי החכמה ובינה ודעת שכללותן הוא השכל שממנו נמשכה מדה זו וכל זה בנפש האדם ונפש כל הברואים שבכל העולמות עליונים ותחתונים שבכולם החכמה היא ראשית ומקור החיות:

פרק ט אבל לגבי הקדוש ברוך הוא מדרגת החכמה שהיא תחלת מחשבה וראשיתה היא סוף מעשה אצלו דהיינו שנחשבת כאילו היא בחי' ומדרגת עשייה לגבי הקדוש ב"ה כדכתיב כולם בחכמה עשית והיינו לומר שכערך החיות שבעשיה גופנית וגשמיית לערך חיות החכמה שהיא ראשית ומקור החיות באדם וכל הברואים גשמיים שהוא כאין לגבי חיות שבאותיות הדבור שהוא כאין לגבי החיות שבאותיות המחשבה שהוא כאין לגבי חיות ומעלת המדות שמהן נמשכה מחשבה זו שהוא כאין לגבי חיות ומעלת ומדרגת החכמה בינה ודעת מקור המדות כן ממש ערך מדרגת ומעלת החכמה שהיא ראשית ומקור החיות שבכל העולמות לגבי הקדוש ב"ה בכבודו ובעצמו המרומם והמתנשא ריבוא רבבות מדרגות רוממות יותר מרוממות מדרגת החכמה על בחי' חיות שבעשייה שהיא רוממות חמש מדרגות לבד שהן מדרגות בחי' עשייה ודבור ומחשבה ומדות ושכל אבל הקדוש ב"ה רם ומתנשא ממדרגת החכמה רבבות מדרגות כאלו עד אין קץ רק מפני שאין בנבראים כח להשיג רק ההשתלשלות ממדרגת חכמה שהיא ראשיתם למדרגת עשיה

action which is the lowermost [of levels], therefore, we say that in relation to the Holy One, blessed be He, the level of Wisdom is considered exactly as the level of action.

That is to say, He is "High and exalted" and very greatly elevated above the level of Wisdom, and it is not at all proper to ascribe to Him anything that is appurtenant to Wisdom even in a very lofty and sublime form, as to say of Him that it is beyond the capacity of any higher or lower creature to comprehend His Wisdom or His Essence. For comprehension pertains and applies to a matter of knowledge and wisdom [about which one can] say that it can or cannot be understood because of the profundity of the concept. But, it is not at all proper to say concerning the Holy One, blessed be He, Who transcends intellect and wisdom, that it is impossible to apprehend Him because of the depth of the concept, for He is not within the realm of comprehension at all. And one who states that it is not possible to apprehend Him, is as one who says concerning some lofty and profound wisdom that it cannot be touched with the hands because of the depth of the concept, for whoever hears it will mock him because the sense of touch refers and applies only to physical objects which may be grasped by the hands. Exactly so, the quality of intellect and comprehension in relation to the Holy One, blessed be He, is considered as actual physical action. Even the comprehension of the Intelligences[2] in the upper worlds, and even the quality of Supernal Wisdom[3] which gives life to them all [is considered so in relation to the Holy One, blessed be He], as it is written, "You have *made* them all in *wisdom*."[4]

As for the Holy One, blessed be He, being called "Wise" in Scripture,[5] and our Sages, of blessed memory, also designating to Him the quality and level of Wisdom,[6] the reason is that He is the source of wisdom, for from Him, may He be blessed, issues and emanates the essence of the quality of *Chochmah Ilaah* (Supernal Wisdom) which is in the world of *Atzilut*. And likewise [is He called] Merciful and Kind because He is the source of mercy and kindness; and likewise the other attributes, for they all proceeded and emanated from Him, may He be blessed. The manner and nature of the flow and emanation—how and what—is known

---

[2] *See ch. 7, n. 34,* supra. [3] *I.e., the* Sefirah *of Wisdom in the world of* Atzilut. [4] Ps. *104:24*. [5] Isa. *31:2*. Jer. *10:12*. et al. [6] Berachot *58a*. Sanhedrin *104b* et al.

עשיה השפלה לכך אנו אומרים שלגבי הקדוש ב"ה נחשבת מדרגת החכמה כמדרגת עשיה ממש דהיינו לומר שהוא רם ונשא ונעלה עילוי רב מאד מאד ממדרגת החכמה ולא שייך כלל לייחס אצלו שום ענין המתייחס לחכמה אפילו בדרך מעלה ועילוי רב כגון לומר עליו שא"א לשום נברא עליונים ותחתונים להשיג חכמתו או מהותו כי ענין ההשגה מתייחס ונופל על דבר חכמה ושכל לומר שאפשר להשיגו או אי אפשר להשיגו מפני עומק המושג אבל הקדוש ברוך הוא שהוא למעלה מן השכל והחכמה לא שייך כלל לומר בו שאי אפשר להשיגו מפני עומק המושג כי אינו בבחי' השגה כלל והאומר עליו שאי אפשר להשיגו הוא כאומר על איזו חכמה רמה ועמוקה שאי אפשר למששה בידים מפני עומק המושג שכל השומע יצחק לו לפי שחוש המישוש אינו מתייחס ונופל אלא על עשיה גשמית הנתפסת בידים וככה ממש נחשבת לגבי הקב"ה מדרגת השכל וההשגה כעשייה גשמית ממש ואפילו השגת שכלים שבעולמות עליונים ואפילו מדרגת חכמה עילאה המחיה את כולם כדכתיב כולם בחכמה עשית. ומה שהקדוש ברוך הוא נקרא חכם בכתוב וגם חז"ל כינו לו מדרגת ומעלת החכמה היינו משום שהוא מקור החכמה שממנו ית' נמשך ונאצל מהות מדרגת חכמה עילאה שבעולם האצילות וכן רחום וחסיד על שם שהוא מקור הרחמים והחסדים וכן שאר המדות שכולן נמשכו ונאצלו ממנו יתברך ודרך וענין ההמשכה והאצילות איך ומה ידוע למשכילים

to the intellectuals [versed in the teachings of Kabbalah].

●▲ *Note: (The*[7] *mystical principle of the* Tzimtzum *of the light of the* En Sof, *blessed be He, and the* Tzimtzum *of A"K,*[8] *and the esoteric doctrine of the* Diknah.[9] *For the underlying purpose of all contractions is to condense the light in order that it become clothed within the vessels of the Ten* Sefirot[10] *It is only after the light of* En Sof *was clothed within the vessels of* ChaBaD[11] *that it can be stated [concerning the Holy One, blessed be He] what Maimonides said: "He is the Knower, and He is the Knowledge, and He is the Known, and by knowing Himself, . . ."*[12] *for the vessels of* Atzilut *become the soul and life-force of* Beriah,[13] Yetzirah,[14] Asiyah,[15] *and of all that is therein. Without the aforesaid* Tzimtzum *and investiture, however, it is not at all proper to say that "He is the Knower and He is the Knowledge, . . ." for He is not within the realm and limitation of knowing and knowledge at all, G–d forbid, but infinitely elevated above even the quality and limitation of wisdom to the extent that the quality of wisdom is considered in relation to Him, may He be blessed, as the quality of physical action.)*

Now, we are not concerned with esoteric matters, but it is incumbent upon us to believe with complete faith, matters that are revealed to us—that He and His attributes are One, i.e., the attributes of the Holy One, blessed be He, and His Will and Wisdom and Understanding and Knowledge [are One] with His Essence and Being, Who alone is exalted, infinite elevations above the quality of wisdom and intellect and comprehension. Hence, His unity with the attributes which He emanated from Himself, may He be blessed, is also beyond the realm of comprehension, [i.e., it is not possible] to understand how He unites with them. And therefore, the attributes of the Holy One, blessed be He, which are the *Sefirot*, are called in the Holy *Zohar*, "the secret of faith," which is the faith that transcends intellect.

●▲Chapter 10

However, since "The Torah speaks the language of man"[1] in order "To enable the ear to hear what it can understand,"[2] therefore, permission has been granted to Scholars of Truth[3] to speak allegorically of the *Sefirot*. And they called them "lights," so that by means of this illustration, the nature of the unity of the Holy One, blessed be He, and His attributes, will be somewhat understood by us. It is, by way of illustration, as the unity of the light of the sun within its orb, with the solar globe, which is called "luminary," as it is written, "The greater luminary. . . ."[4] And the radiation and the beam which spreads forth and shines from it is called "light," as it is written, "And G–d called the light—day."[5] When the light is in its source in the orb of the sun, it is united with it in absolute unity, for

[7] *Here follows a brief description of the emanation of the attributes from the Infinite.* [8] *Acrostic for* Adam Kadmon, *the first and highest state of existence in which the Infinite manifests Himself after the* Tzimtzum. *It is the source of all subsequent emanations and creations.* [9] *The realm following* A"K *and preceding* Atzilut *is called* Keter *(Crown). The powerfully contracted light which issues from it into* Atzilut *to bring forth the* Sefirot *or attributes is denoted in Kabbalistic works as* Diknah. *For a fuller elaboration of this concept see* Likutei Torah, "Masay," *p. 148–149;* "Ki Tetzeh," *p. 76;* "Nitzavim," *p. 103.* [10] *I.e., the ten Divine qualities or attributes which are the channels through which the Infinite Light issues forth and becomes*

למשכילים * והנה אין לנו עסק בנסתרו' אך הנגלות לנו להאמין אמונה שלימה דאיהו וגרמוהי חד דהיינו מדותיו של הקדוש ב"ה ורצונו וחכמתו ובינתו ודעתו עם מהותו ועצמותו המרומם לבדו רוממות אין קץ מבחי' חכמה ושכל והשגה ולכן גם יחודו שמתייחד עם מדותיו שהאציל מאתו ית' ג"כ אינו בבחי' השגה להשיג איך מתייחד בהן ולכן נקראו מדותיו של הקדוש ב"ה שהן הספירות בזה"ק רזא דמהימנותא שהיא האמונה שלמעלה מן השכל:

הגה"ה

(סוד הצמצום באור א"ס ב"ה וצמצום א"ק וסוד הדיקנא שסוד כל הצמצומים לצמצם האור שיתלבש בבחי' כלים די"ס והנה אחר שנתלבש אור א"ס בבחי' כלים דחב"ד אז שייך לומר מ"ש הרמב"ם הוא היודע והוא המדע והוא הידוע ובידיעת עצמו וכו' לפי שבחי' כלים דאצילות נעשים נשמה וחיות לבי"ע ולכל אשר בהם אבל בלי צמצום והלבשה הנ"ל לא שייך כלל לומר הוא היודע והוא המדע וכו' כי אינו בבחי' וגדר דעת ומדע כלל ח"ו אלא למעלה מעלה עילוי רב עד אין קץ אפי' מבחי' וגדר חכמה עד שבחי' חכמה נחשבת אצלו ית' כבחי' עשיה גשמית):

פרק י אך מכל מקום הואיל ודברה תורה כלשון בני אדם לשכך את האזן מה שהיא יכולה לשמוע לכך ניתן רשות לחכמי האמת לדבר בספירות בדרך משל וקראו אותן אורות כדי שעל ידי המשל הזה יובן לנו קצת ענין היחוד של הקדוש ב"ה ומדותיו שהוא בדרך משל כענין יחוד אור השמש שבתוך גוף כדור השמש עם גוף השמש שנקרא מאור כמ"ש את המאור הגדול וגו' והזיו והניצוץ המתפשט ומאיר ממנו נקרא אור כמ"ש ויקרא אלהים לאור יום וכשהאור הוא במקורו בגוף השמש הוא מיוחד עמו בתכלית היחוד כי אין

---

contracted to create and act in the universe. The ten Sefirot *are:* Chochmah *(Wisdom)*, Binah *(Understanding)*, Da'at *(Knowledge)*, Chesed *(Kindness)*, Gevurah *(Might)*, Tiferet *(Beauty, Mercy)*, Netzach *(Eternity, Victory)*, Hod *(Majesty)*, Yesod *(Foundation)*, Malchut *(Sovereignty)*. *See* Likutei Amarim, *Part IV*, "Igeret HaKodesh," *ch. 15.* [11] *Acrostic formed from the initial letters of the words* Chochmah, Binah, Da'at, *the first three of the ten* Sefirot. [12] Loc. cit. [13] *See ch. 2, n. 14,* supra. [14] *Lit., "formation," the third of the four worlds, the chief domain of the Angels.* [15] *See ch. 2, n. 16,* supra.

(Notes cont. at end of Hebrew Text)

there is only one entity, namely, the body of the luminary which emits light; for there the radiation and light is absolutely one being with the body of the luminary which illuminates, and it has no existence by itself at all.

Precisely in this manner, and even more so, [is the unity of] the attributes of the Holy One, blessed be He, and His Will and Wisdom in the world of *Atzilut*, with His Essence and Being, as it were, Who becomes clothed in them and unites with them in perfect unity, since they were derived and emanated from Him, may He be blessed, as for example, the spreading of the light from the sun. However, [His unity with His attributes] is not exactly in this manner, but in a manner which is remote and concealed from our comprehension, for His ways are higher than our ▲ways.[6] Nevertheless, from the illustration which is given in order "To enable the ear to hear what it can understand," we can perceive and comprehend that just as the light of the sun which is united with and nullified in its source has no name by itself at all, only the name of the source, so all the attributes of the Holy One, blessed be He, and His Will and Wisdom are not designated and called by these names at all [relative to Him] only in relation to the higher and lower creatures who are brought into existence and given life and guided in their conduct by the Holy One, blessed be He, through His Will and Wisdom and Understanding and Knowledge which clothe themselves in His holy attributes. As it is stated in the Midrash,[7] "By means of ten things was the world created: by Wisdom, by Understanding and by Knowledge, . . . as it is written, 'G–d by Wisdom founded the earth, by Understanding He established the heavens, by His Knowledge the depths were split,'. . .";[8] and as expressed by Elijah, "You have brought forth ten *Tikunim* ("garments"), and we call them ten *Sefirot*,[9] wherewith to direct hidden worlds unrevealed, and worlds revealed, and You conceal Yourself in them. . . ."[10]

●▲For example, on the first day of the Six Days of Creation, the attribute of Kindness—comprised of all His holy attributes,[11] with His Will and Wisdom and Understanding and Knowledge clothed in it—was revealed, and He created with it the light, through the Utterance, "Let there be light,"[12] which is the spreading forth and flow of the light from above into the world, and its diffusion in the world from one end to the other. This [creation of light] is the quality

---

[6] *Cf.* Isa. *55:9*. [7] Hagigah *12a*. Midrash *is the Homiletic exegesis of the Torah.* [8] Prov. *3:19–20*. [9] *The* Sefirot *are called "garments" for they clothe and hide G–d's essence.* [10] *Introduction to* Tikunei Zohar. [11] *Each attribute includes all the others. The specific designation denotes the dominant quality of the attribute.* [12] Gen. *1:3*.

אין שם רק עצם אחד שהוא גוף המאור המאיר כי הזיו והאור שם עצם אחד ממש עם גוף המאור המאיר ואין לו שום מציאות כלל בפני עצמו וכדברים האלה ממש ויותר מזה הן מדותיו של הקב"ה ורצונו וחכמתו בעולם האצילות עם מהותו ועצמותו כביכול המתלבש בתוכם ומתייחד עמהם בתכלית היחוד מאחר שנמשכו ונאצלו מאתו ית' ע"ד משל כדרך התפשטות האור מהשמש אך לא ממש בדרך זה רק בדרך רחוקה ונפלאה מהשגתינו כי גבהו דרכיו מדרכינו ומ"מ לשכך האזן נשמע ונתבונן ממשל אור השמש המיוחד ובטל במקורו ואינו עולה בשם כלל בפ"ע רק שם המקור לבדו כך כל מדותיו של הקדוש ב"ה ורצונו וחכמתו אינן עולות ונקראות בשמות אלו כלל אלא לגבי הנבראים עליונים ותחתונים שהווייתם וחיותם והנהגתם שהקב"ה מהוה ומחיה אותם ומנהיגם הוא ברצונו וחכמתו ובינתו ודעתו המתלבשות במדותיו הקדושות כדאיתא במדרש בעשרה דברים נברא העולם בחכמה בתבונה ובדעת וכו' דכתיב ה' בחכמה יסד ארץ כונן שמים בתבונה בדעתו תהומות נבקעו וגו' וכמאמר אליהו דאפיקת עשר תיקונין וקרינן להון עשר ספירן לאנהגא בהון עלמין סתימין דלא אתגליין ועלמין דאתגליין ובהון אתכסיאת כו' עד"מ ביום ראשון משֵשת ימי בראשית נגלית מדת החסד כלולה מכל מדותיו הקדושות ורצונו וחכמתו ובינתו ודעתו מלובשין בה ובה ברא בה את האור במאמר יהי אור שהיא בחי' התפשטות והמשכת האור לעולם מלמעלה והתפשטותו בעולם מסוף העולם עד סופו שהיא בחי'

מדת

of Kindness, yet, because it also includes the attribute of Might, therefore, it [the light] was not spiritual as the actual Supernal Light, and also became clothed in this world, which is finite and limited, for "It is a journey of five hundred years from the earth to the heaven and from east to west."[13]

In like manner, on the second day, the attribute of Might, which is composed of the other attributes and His Will, . . . was revealed and He created with it the firmament through the Utterance, "Let there be a firmament in the midst of the waters and let it divide the waters from the waters."[14] This [separation of the waters] is the quality of *Tzimtzum* and restraints, to conceal the upper spiritual waters from the lower waters. Through this separation from the upper waters, the lower waters became material. And the attribute of Kindness is included in it [Might] as "The world is built with Kindness,"[15] for all this [the division of the waters] is in order that dry land appear and man upon it to worship G–d. And similarly, each [of the other attributes of the Holy One, blessed be He, was revealed on each subsequent day of creation].

And it is this thought that Elijah expressed in *Tikunim, loc. cit.*, "To show how the world is conducted with righteousness and justice, . . . righteousness is law, justice is mercy . . . ; all [the revelation of the attributes] is to show how the world is conducted, but it is not that You have a knowable righteousness—which is law, and not a knowable justice—which is mercy, nor any of these other attributes at all."

●▲ *Chapter 11*

The Ten Utterances are also designated "utterances" only in relation to the creatures. For just as the emotion attributes of the human soul, when they come to be revealed in action, come clothed in the letters of thought, [so do the attributes of the Holy One, blessed be He]. For example, the attribute of kindness and mercy of the soul cannot become revealed in deed unless one thinks about and contemplates doing an act of charity and kindness in actuality, for one cannot act without thought. And if one commands others to perform [an act of kindness], as the king, then the attribute of kindness and also the letters of thought clothe themselves in the letters of speech. [And likewise is it when one speaks words of kindness and compassion to his friend.][1]

So, figuratively speaking, when the attributes of the Holy One, blessed be He, reach the level of the revelation of their action in the lower [worlds]; this revelation

---

[13] Hagigah *13a*. [14] Gen. *1:6*.
[15] Ps. *89:3*.

Chapter 11
[1] *Brackets are the author's.*

מדת חסד רק מפני שכלולה גם ממדת גבורה לכן לא היה רוחני כאור של מעלה ממש וגם נתלבש בעה"ז שהוא בבחי' גבול ותכלית שהוא מהלך ת"ק שנה מהארץ לרקיע וממזרח למערב וכן ביום שני נגלית מדת גבורה כלולה משאר מדות ורצונו כו' וברא בה הרקיע במאמר יהי רקיע בתוך המים ויהי מבדיל בין מים למים שהיא בחי' צמצום וגבורות להעלים מים העליונים הרוחניים ממים התחתונים ועל ידי זה נתגשמו התחתונים בהבדלם מהעליונים ומדת חסד כלולה בה כי עולם חסד יבנה שהכל כדי שתראה היבשה ואדם עליה לעבוד ה' וכן כולן וז"ש אליהו בתיקונים שם לאחזאה איך אתנהיג עלמא בצדק ומשפט כו' צדק איהו דין משפט איהו רחמי כו' כולא לאחזאה איך אתנהיג עלמא אבל לאו דאית לך צדק ידיעא דאיהו דין ולא משפט ידיעא דאיהו רחמי ולאו מכל אינון מדות כלל:

פרק יא והנה גם עשרה מאמרות ג"כ נקראו בשם מאמרו' לגבי הנבראי' בלבד כי כמו שהמדות שבנשמת האדם כשבאות להתגלו' במעשה הן באות מלובשות באותיות המחשבה כגון מדת חסד ורחמים שבנשמה א"א לבא לידי התגלות בפועל ממש כ"א ע"י שמחשב בדעתו ומהרהר מעשה הצדקה וחסד לעשותה בפ"מ כי א"א לעשות בלי מחשבה ואם מצוה לאחרים לעשות כמו המלך אזי מתלבשת מדת החסד וגם אותיות המחשבה באותיות הדבור [וכן כשמדבר דברי חסד ורחמים לרעהו] כך עד"מ מדותיו של הקב"ה כשבאות לבחי' התגלות פעולתן בתחתוני' נקרא גילוי זה והמשכת

and the flow of this action is called "utterance" and combination of letters, for there can be no action proceeding from His attributes without [the intermediacy of] combinations which are called "letters." For instance, for the creation of light from the attribute of Kindness, there issued from it a flow of action and a power with which to produce and create the light. And the flow of this power and this life-force is designated "utterance" and [combination of] the letters "Let there be Light."[2] Although they are not like our letters of thought, G-d forbid, nevertheless, they are a phenomenon which indicates the bringing into existence of the light from nothing. Hence, the light was created from this flow of action, and not other things which were also created from the attribute of Kindness, such as water and the like, because there were clothed in them powers in other combinations which indicate the bringing into existence of water and the like. Thus it follows that all life-forces and powers which issue from His holy attributes to the lower worlds, to create them *ex nihilo* and to give them life and to sustain them, are given the appellation "Holy Letters," which are the flow of the life-force from His Will and His Wisdom and His attributes, to bring worlds into being and give them life.

And these worlds are of two kinds: "Hidden worlds unrevealed,"[3] which come into existence and live and are sustained from concealed powers and life-forces, as, for example, the letters of thought in the human soul; and "Worlds revealed,"[3] which were created and live from the revelation of the hidden powers and life-forces called "Letters of thought," which, when they are in the state of revelation in order to give life to the revealed worlds, are called "utterances" and "The word of G-d" and the "Breath of His mouth," as, for example, the letters of speech in man which reveal to his listeners what was concealed and hidden in his ●▲heart. In truth, however, the Supernal Letters of Speech are exceedingly higher than the level and essence of the wisdom and intellect of the created beings. For from the utterance and letters "Let us make man in our image, . . ."[4] was created Man, possessor of wisdom and intellect; or even by the Divine breath

---

[2] Gen. *1:3*. [3] *Introduction to* Tikunei Zohar. [4] Gen. *1:26*.

והמשכת פעולה זו בשם מאמר וצירוף אותיו׳ שהרי א״א שתהיה שום פעולה נמשכת ממדותיו הקדושות בלי צירופים הנקרא׳ בשם אותיות כגון לבריאת האור ממדת החסד נמשך ממנה המשכת פעולה וכח לפעול ולברוא בו את האור והמשכת כח זה וחיות זו נקראת בשם מאמר ואותיות יהי אור כי אף שאינן כאותיות מחשבה שלנו ח״ו מ״מ הם ענין המורה על התהוו׳ האור מאין ליש שלכן נברא האור מהמשכת כח זה ולא נבראו ממנו דברים אחרים שנבראו ג״כ ממדת חסד כמו מים וכיוצא בהם מפני שנתלבשו בהם כחות בבחי׳ צירופים אחרים המורים על התהוות המים וכיוצא ונמצא כי כל חיות וכחות הנמשכות ממדותיו הקדושות לתחתונים לבראם מאין ליש ולהחיות׳ ולקיימם נקראו׳ בשם אותיו׳ הקדושות שהן בחי׳ המשכת החיות מרצונו וחכמתו ומדותיו להתהוות עולמות ולהחיותם והם שני מיני עולמות עלמין סתימין דלא אתגליין הם המתהוים וחיים וקיימים מכחות והמשכות נעלמות כמו אותיו׳ המחשבה שבנשמת האדם עד״מ ועלמין דאתגליין נבראו וחיים מהתגלות שנתגלו כחות והמשכות הנעלמות הנקראות בשם אותיו׳ המחשב׳ וכשהן בבחי׳ התגלות להחיו׳ עלמין דאתגליין נקראות בשם מאמרות ודבר ה׳ ורוח פיו כמו אותיות הדבור באדם עד״מ שהן מגלות לשומעים מה שהיה צפון וסתום בלבו אבל באמת בחי׳ אותיות הדבור של מעלה היא למעלה מעלה ממדרגות ומהות חכמה ושכל הנברא׳ שהרי במאמר ואותיו׳ נעשה אדם בצלמינו וגו׳ נברא האדם בעל חכמה ושכל או אפי׳ בהבל העליון לבד

alone [was he created], as it is written, "And He breathed into his nostrils a soul of life."[5] Hence, the Divine Speech and Breath is the source of wisdom and intellect in the soul of Adam, which contains all the souls of the *Tzaddikim*,[6] who are superior to the ministering angels.[7] The reason for [the transcendence of the Supernal Letters over the soul] is that the letters of His speech, may He be blessed, are effluences of powers and life-forces from His attributes, may He be blessed, which are united with His Essence and Being in a perfect unity that is infinitely higher than the level of wisdom in created beings. And they are called by the name "letters" not in relation to the created beings, but only relative to His attributes themselves.

Now, there are twenty-two kinds of effluences of life-forces and powers, differing one from the other, by which all the higher and lower worlds and all the creatures in them were created. For so it arose in His Will and Wisdom, may He be blessed, to create the world with exactly twenty-two kinds of different effluences, neither less nor more, and these are the twenty-two letters which are fixed in the mouth and tongue, as we have learned in the *Sefer Yetzirah*.[8] [And their written shape indicates the form of the flow, as will be explained later.][9] For the letters of speech and thought in the human soul are also outflows from the essence and being of the intellect and emotion attributes, as is explained elsewhere.[10]

•▲ Chapter 12

[Although there are only twenty-two letters,] the creatures are divided into their general and particular kinds by changes in the combinations, substitutions, and transpositions [of the letters] as was explained above,[1] for every letter is a flow of a life-force and an individual, particular power. And when many letters were combined to form a word, then aside from the numerous kinds of powers and life-forces which issue forth according to the number of letters in the word, there is, in addition, the one which transcends them all, [viz.,] the flow of a higher power and general life-force which contains and is equivalent to all the various powers and individual life-forces of the letters and transcends them all, and it unites them and combines them to give power and life-force to the world which was created

[5] Ibid. *2:7.* [6] Shaar HaMitzvot, "Ki Tetzeh"; Shaar HaPesukim "Bereishit" *3;* Shaar HaGilgulim *6, 7, 12. Cf.* Shemot Rabbah *40:3.* [7] *Cf.* Likutei Torah, "Behar," *p. 81.* [8] *Chs. 1:2, 2:2,* et al. [9] *Brackets are the author's.* [10] *See* Tanya *I, ch. 20.*

Chapter 12
[1] *Chs. 1, 7, 10,* supra.

לבד כדכתי' ויפח באפיו נשמת חיים וא"כ הדבור והבל העליון הוא מקור החכמה והשכל שבנשמת אדם הראשון הכוללת כל נשמות הצדיקים שהם גדולים ממלאכי השרת והיינו לפי שאותיות דיבורו ית' הן בחי' המשכות כחות וחיות ממדותיו ית' המיוחדות במהותו ועצמותו בתכלית היחוד שהוא למעלה מעלה לאין קץ ממדרגת חכמה שבנבראים ולא נקראו בשם אותיות לגבי הנבראים אלא לגבי מדותיו ית' בכבודן ובעצמן והנה הן כ"ב מיני המשכות חיות וכחות שונים זה מזה שבהן נבראו כל העולמות עליונים ותחתונים וכל הברואים שבתוכם שכך עלה ברצונו וחכמתו ית' לברוא העולם בכ"ב מיני המשכות שונות דוקא לא פחות ולא יותר והן הן כ"ב אותיות הקבועות בפה ולשון כדתנן בס' יצירה [ותמונתן בכתב היא מורה על ציור ההמשכה כמ"ש לקמן] שגם אותיות הדבור והמחשבה שבנפש האדם הן המשכות מהשכל והמדו' שבנפש ממהותן ועצמותן כמ"ש במ"א:

פרק יב רק שהברואים מתחלקים למינידם בכללות ובפרטות ע"י שינויי הצירופים וחילופים

ותמורות כנ"ל כי כל אות היא המשכת חיות וכח מיוחד פרטי וכשנצטרפו אותיות הרבה להיות תיבה אזי מלבד ריבוי מיני כחות וחיות הנמשכים כפי מספר האותיות שבתיבה עוד זאת העולה על כולנה המשכת כח עליון וחיות כללית הכולל' ושקולה כנגד כל מיני הכחו' והחיות פרטיות של האותיות ועולה על גביהן והיא מחברתן ומצרפתן יחד להשפיע כח וחיות לעולם הנברא

בתיבה

in general and in its individual [parts] with this word.

Note: (Inasmuch as each and every letter of the twenty-two letters of the Torah is a flow of a life-force and an individual, particular power, which does not flow through any other letter, therefore, the written shape of each letter is in a specific, distinctive form, which indicates the pattern of the flow and the manifestation of the light and the life-force and the power which is revealed and flows through this letter, [i.e.,] how it flows and is revealed from the attributes of the Holy One, blessed be He, and His Will and His Wisdom. . . .)

As, for example, through the words of the utterance "Let there be a firmament, . . ."[2] the seven heavens and all their celestial hosts were created. As our Sages, of blessed memory, stated, "*Shechakim*, in which millstones stand and grind manna for the *Tzaddikim* . . . , *Z'vul*, in which [the heavenly] Jerusalem and the Holy Temple and the Altar [are built] . . . , *Machon*, in which there are the stores of snow and the stores of hail. . . ."[3] The heavens as a whole were created and live and exist through the aggregate words of the utterance "Let there be a firmament, . . ." and each individual created being in the seven heavens was created and lives and exists from some combination of the letters of these words, or their substitutions and transpositions, according to the quality of the life-force of that particular creature. For every change in a combination is an intermixing and interweaving of the powers and life-forces in a different form, since each letter antecedent in the combination dominates and it is the essential [force] in this created being, while the others are subordinate to it and are included in its light, and thereby a new being is created. Likewise, through the substitution of letters or their transpositions, new creatures of lower levels in comparison with the beings created from the letters themselves are created. For they ●▲ [the changes in the letters], by way of illustration, are as the light which shines upon the earth at night from the moon—and the moonlight is from the sun—hence, the light which is on the earth is a [reflected] light from the light of the sun.

Exactly so, allegorically speaking, the letters of the Utterances are the aggregate flow of the life-force and the light and the power from the attributes of the Holy One, blessed be He, to create the worlds from nothingness and to give life and sustain them as long as it shall be His Will, may He be blessed.

---

[2] Gen. 1.6. [3] Hagigah 12b.

בתיבה זו לכללו ולפרטיו * כגון ד"מ בתיבו' שבמאמר יהי רקיע וגו' שנבראו בהן ז' רקיעים וכל צבא השמים אשר בהם כמאמר רז"ל שחקים שבו רחיים עומדות וטוחנות מן לצדיקים וכו' זבול שבו ירושלים ובה"מק ומזבח וכו' מכון שבו אוצרות שלג ואוצרות ברד וכו' שכללות הרקיעים נבראו וחיים וקיימים בכללות תיבות אלו שבמאמר יהי רקיע וכו' ופרטי הברואים שבז' רקיעים נברא כל פרט מהם וחי וקיים מאיזה צירוף אותיות מתיבות אלו או חילופיהן ותמורותיהן שהן כפי בחי' חיות הנברא הפרטי ההוא כי כל שינוי צירוף הוא הרכבת ואריגת הכוחו' והחיות בשינוי שכל אות הקודמת בצירוף היא הגוברת והיא העיקר בבריאה זו והשאר טפילות אליה ונכללות באורה ועי"ז נבראת בריה חדשה וכן בחילופי אותיות או תמורותיהן נבראות בריאות חדשו' פחותי המעלה בערך הנבראים מהאותיות עצמן כי הן ד"מ דוגמת אור המאיר בלילה בארץ מן הירח ואור הירח הוא מהשמש ונמצא אור שעל הארץ הוא אור האור של השמש וככה ממש ד"מ האותיות שבמאמרות הן כללות המשכת החיות והאור והכח ממדותיו של הקב"ה לברוא העולמו' מאין ליש ולהחיותן ולקיימן כ"ז משך רצונו ית' ומכללות

הגהה

(ולפי שכל אות ואות מכ"ב אותיות התורה היא המשכת חיות וכח מיוחד פרטי שאינו נמשך באות אחרת לכך גם תמונתן בכתב כל אות היא בתמונה מיוחדת פרטית המורה על ציור ההמשכה והתגלות האור והחיו' והכח הנגלה ונמשך באות זו איך הוא נמשך ונתגלה ממדותיו של הקב"ה ורצונו וחכמתו וכו') :

From this aggregate flow and great radiation, G–d caused to shine and issue forth its derivations similar to it, and its offshoots, which are derivations and effluences of the light from the letters. And these are the substitutions of letters and their transpositions, and He created with them the particular creatures in each world. In like manner, G–d again projected [the light] and caused to issue forth and descend a radiation of the radiation of the radiation from the effulgences of the letters; and likewise He again caused it to issue forth and to descend to the lowest [level] in the category of descents, until the completely inanimate, such as stones and dust were created. And their names *even* and *afar* are substitutions of substitutions, . . . and transpositions of transpositions, . . . as explained above.

CONCLUDED PART TWO WITH THE HELP OF G–D, MAY HE BE BLESSED AND EXALTED.

ומכללות המשכה והארה גדולה הזו האיר ה' והמשיך ממנה תולדותיה כיוצא בה וענפיה שהן תולדות והמשכת האור מהאותיות והן הן חילופי אותיות ותמורותיהן וברא בהן ברואים פרטים שבכל עולם וכן האיר ה' עוד והמשיך והוריד הארה דהארה מהארות האותיו' וכן המשיך עוד והוריד עד למטה מטה בבחי' השתלשלות עד שנברא הדומם ממש כאבנים ועפר ושמותיהן אבן ועפר הם חילופים דחילופים כו' ותמורות דתמורות כו' כנ"ל:

נשלם חלק שני

בעז"ה יתברך ויתעלה

•▲ *Chapter 1*

TANYA, It has been taught in a Beraita at the end of Tractate Yoma:[1] There are three types of atonement, and repentance accompanies each. If one neglects a positive commandment and repents, he is forgiven forthwith. If one violates a prohibition and repents, his repentance is tentative, and Yom Kippur atones.

[This means that though, in terms of fulfillment, positive commandments are superior and supersede[2] prohibitions, this is because by performing a positive command one precipitates an illumination and flow into the higher worlds[3] from the reflected Infinite Light, blessed be He, (in Zohar[4] we find the 248 positive commandments equated with the 248 "organs[5] of the King") and also onto his Divine soul,[6] as we declare in the blessings, "Who has hallowed us with His commandments."[7]

But concerning repentance, though the punishment for rebelling against His rule and not performing the King's word is commuted, nonetheless, that illumination is withheld . . .[8] Our Sages[9] apply the verse, "A misdeed that cannot be corrected,"[10] to neglecting the evening reading of *Shema* or . . .[11] Though he will be scrupulous henceforth about reading the morning and evening *Shema* forevermore, his repentance is ineffectual in correcting what he once neglected.

By violating a prohibition, evil cleaves to his soul, he impairs its root and origin (in the garbs of the Ten Sefirot[12] of Asiyah,[13] as Tikunei Zohar[14] writes, "You have fashioned garbs for them,[15] from which souls for mankind fly forth . . .") Therefore there is no atonement for his own soul or higher until Yom Kippur, as is written, "He will atone for the holy place for the impurities of Israel and their sins . . . before G-d will you be purified."[16] *Before G-d* is stressed.[17] Hence one dare not infer any leniency from this, G-d forbid, in the positive commandments, particularly in Torah study. On the contrary, our Sages assert, "G-d has pardoned idolatry . . ."[18]—though excision and capital punishment are involved,—"and did not pardon neglect of Torah study."]

If one commits a sin of excision[19] or execution, repentance and Yom Kippur are tentative and sufferings scour (i.e., they complete the atonement. *M'markin*, the expression here, denotes scouring and rinsing to "polish" the soul. *Kapara*, atonement, is the term for cleaning, removing the impurities of the sin), as we find, "I shall remember with a rod their sins, and with afflictions their misdeeds."[20]

---

[1] *86a.* [2] Yevamot *3b.* [3] *Kabbala and Chassidut explain the difficulty in creating a finite physical universe by an infinite Creator with the concept of tzimtzum, or contraction, concealment. There was a series of concealments of the presence and infinitude of the Creator, resulting ultimately, in our physical universe, in the virtually total obscuring of G-d. The non-corporeal intermediate steps between Creator and this material world are called "Worlds," four in general terms, with innumerable subgradations within each of these Worlds. The highest World is Atzilut, "Emanation," a state of proximity and relative unity with G-d. Lower Worlds appear to be independent, entities apart from the Creator. In the fourth, Asiyah or "Action," there*

פרק א תניא בסוף יומא שלשה חלוקי כפרה הם ותשובה עם כל אחד. עבר על מ"ע ושב אינו זז משם עד שמוחלין לו עבר על מל"ת ושב תשובה תולה ויוה"כ מכפר. (פי' דאע"ג דלענין קיום מ"ע גדולה שדוחה את ל"ת. היינו משום שע"י קיום מ"ע ממשיך אור ושפע בעולמות עליונים מהארת אור א"ס ב"ה (כמ"ש בזהר דרמ"ח פקודין אינון רמ"ח אברין דמלכא) וגם על נפשו האלקית כמ"ש אשר קדשנו במצותיו. אבל לענין תשובה אף שמוחלין לו העונש על שמרד במלכותו ית' ולא עשה מאמר המלך. מ"מ האור נעדר וכו' וכמארז"ל ע"פ מעוות לא יוכל לתקן זה שביטל ק"ש של ערבית או וכו'. דאף שנזהר מעתה לקרות ק"ש של ערבית ושחרית לעולם אין תשובתו מועלת לתקן מה שביטל פ"א. והעובר על מל"ת ע"י שנדבק הרע בנפשו עושה פגם למעלה בשרשה ומקור חוצבה (בלבושי' די"ס דעשי' כמ"ש בת"ז לבושין תקינת לון דמנייהו פרחין נשמתין לב"נ וכו') לכך אין כפרה לנפשו ולא למעלה עד יוה"כ כמ"ש וכפר על הקדש מטומאות בנ"י ומפשעיהם וכו' לפני ה' תטהרו לפני ה' דייקא ולכן אין ללמוד מכאן שום קולא ח"ו במ"ע ובפרט בת"ת. ואדרבה ארז"ל ויתר הקב"ה על ע"ז וכו' אף שהן כריתות ומיתות ב"ד ולא ויתר על ביטול ת"ת). עבר על כריתות ומיתות ב"ד תשובה ויוה"כ תולין ויסורין ממרקין (פי' גומרין הכפרה והוא מלשון מריקה ושטיפה לצחצח הנפש. כי כפרה היא לשון קינוח שמקנח לכלוך החטא) שנאמר ופקדתי בשבט פשעם ובנגעים עונם.
עכ"ל

---

is the spiritual plane where physical matter does not yet exist, and the final corporeal World we inhabit. "Higher" and "lower" refer to stages closer or more distant from the Creator, with a deeper or lesser awareness of Him, hence a greater or lesser awareness of their own being. (There is no implication of physical distance, an obviously irrelevant concept.) Through performance of mitzvot, positive commandments, subordinating the physical world and specific objects at hand to a higher, Divine purpose, all stages (or Worlds) experience a clearer apprehension of the Creator, become "closer" to Him, His presence and being become more evident. This "illumination" extends also to the individual soul performing the mitz-

(Notes cont. at end of Hebrew Text)

Thus far the Beraita.

●▲ The commandment of repentance as required by the Torah is simply the abandonment of sin (cf. *Sanhedrin*,[21] ch. 3; *Choshen Mishpat*, end of sect. 34, regarding witnesses). He must resolve in perfect sincerity never again to revert to folly to rebel against His rule, may He be blessed; he will never again violate the King's command, G-d forbid, neither a positive command nor a prohibition.

This is the basic meaning of the term *teshuvah*, repentance, to *return* to G-d with all his heart and soul, to serve Him, and to keep all His commandments. "Let the wicked abandon his way, and the sinful his thoughts, and return to G-d . . ."[22] Such statements abound: "Return unto the Lord your G-d and hearken to His voice . . . with all your heart . . ."[23] and "Return O Israel until the Lord your G-d . . ."[24] and "Bring us back, Lord, unto You . . ."[25]

This is not at all the common conception that repentance is synonymous with fasting. Even where sufferings are the completion of atonement, as in the case of sins of excision or execution, G-d brings the sufferings on the sinner. ("I shall remember with a rod," clearly specifies *I*.) When the repentance is acceptable before Him, as he returns to G-d with all his heart and soul out of love, then following the initiative undertaken from below,[26] and "As water reflects the countenance . . ."[27] there is an awakening Above, arousing the love and kindness of G-d, to scour his sin through affliction in this physical world. "For whom the Lord loves He chastises . . ."[28]

Therefore Maimonides and *Sefer Mitzvot Gadol* make no mention of fasting in the mitzvah of teshuvah, even for sins of excision or capital sins. They cite only confession and the plea for forgiveness—"They shall confess their sin . . ."[29]

But then we find in Joel,[30] "Return to Me with all your hearts, with fasting and weeping . . ." However this was to nullify the Heavenly decree that had already been issued, to expunge the sin of the generation through the affliction of locust. This is the justification for all fasts undertaken for any trouble threatening the community, as in the Book of Esther.

There are descriptions in the Musar literature,[31] particularly the *Rokeach* and *Sefer Chassidim*,

[21] *25b.* [22] Isaiah *55:7.* [23] Deut. *30:2.* [24] Hosea *14:2.* [25] Lamentations *5:22.* [26] *Kabbala and Chassidut frequently refer to the dual concepts of "arousal (or stimulation, awakening, initiative) from below," meaning man, and "arousal from Above," by G-d. Either may be the cause of the other. For example, the Exodus was the result of G-d's initiative, arousal from above, for the people had not "earned" redemption. The hurried escape, the arousal below, followed. During the Rosh Hashana repentance period, initiative must come from below, repentance, followed by an arousal Above, forgiveness. The initial stimulation awakens a dormant reaction. (The terms are found in* Zohar *II, 135b.)* [27] Proverbs *27:19.* [28] *Ibid.,*

עכ"ל הברייתא: והנה מצות התשובה מן התורה היא עזיבת החטא בלבד (כדאי' בגמ' פ"ג דסנהדרין ובח"מ סס' ל"ד לענין עדות) דהיינו שיגמור בלבו בלב שלם לבל ישוב עוד לכסלה למרוד במלכותו ית' ולא יעבור עוד מצות המלך ח"ו הן במ"ע הן במל"ת. וזהו עיקר פי' לשון תשובה לשוב אל ה' בכל לבו ובכל נפשו לעבדו ולשמור כל מצותיו כמ"ש יעזוב רשע דרכו ואיש און מחשבותיו וישוב אל ה' וכו'. ובפ' נצבים כתיב ושבת עד ה' אלקיך ושמעת בקולו וכו' בכל לבבך וכו' שובה ישראל עד ה' אלקיך וכו' השיבנו ה' אליך וכו'. ולא כדעת ההמון שהתשובה היא התענית. ואפי' מי שעבר על כריתות ומיתות ב"ד שגמר כפרתו היא ע"י יסורים. היינו שהקב"ה מביא עליו יסורים (וכמ"ש ופקדתי בשבט וכו' ופקדתי דייקא) והיינו כשתשובתו רצויה לפניו ית' בשובו אל ה' בכל לבו ונפשו מאהבה אזי באתערותא דלתתא וכמים הפנים וכו' אתערותא דלעילא לעורר האהבה וחסד ה' למרק עונו ביסורים בעוה"ז וכמ"ש כי את אשר יאהב ה' יוכיח וכו'. ולכן לא הזכירו הרמב"ם והסמ"ג שום תענית כלל במצות התשובה אף בכריתות ומיתות ב"ד. רק הוידוי ובקשת מחילה כמ"ש בתורה והתודו את חטאתם וכו'. ומ"ש ביואל שובו עדי בכל לבבכם בצום ובבכי כו' היינו לבטל הגזרה שנגזרה למרק עון הדור ע"י יסורי' בארבה. וזהו הטעם בכל תעניות שמתענין על כל צרה שלא תבא על הצבור וכמ"ש במגלת אסתר. ומ"ש בספרי המוסר ובראשם ספר הרוקח וס' חסידים הרבה

3:12. [29] Deut. 5:7. [30] 2:12. [31] *For a description of the approaches of* Musar *(ethical teachings)*, chakira *(philosophical speculation)*, *and* Chassidut, *see "On the Teachings of Chassidus."*

of numerous fasts and mortifications for excision and capital sins. The same is true of sins punished by death by divine agency,[32] like wasteful emissions of semen, as the Torah recounts of Er and Onan.[33] In this sense their judgment is identical. These fasts and mortifications are intended to avoid the punishment of suffering at the hand of Heaven, G-d forbid, and also to urge on and expedite the conclusion of his soul's atonement. Also, perhaps he does not return to G-d with all his heart and soul out of love, but only out of fear.

•▲*Chapter 2*

However, all this refers to atonement and forgiveness of the sin—he is pardoned completely for having violated the command of the King when he has done a full repentance. No charge or semblance of accusation is made against him on the day of judgment to punish him for his sin, G-d forbid, in the World to Come. He is completely exonerated from the judgment to come.

Nonetheless, that he may be acceptable before G-d, as beloved of Him as before the sin, that his Creator may derive delight from his service—in past times he would bring an *olah*[1] offering. This offering was brought even for an ordinary positive commandment that involves no excision or execution. In *Torat Kohanim* there is a comment on the verse, "It shall be accepted for him,"[2] and we find in the Talmud, *Zevachim*[3] chapter I, that the *olah* offering atones for positive commandments; it is a "gift" after he has done penance and the punishment was commuted.

If one displeases his king and appeases him through an intercessor, and the king does forgive him, still he will send an appropriate gift to the king that the king might agree that he appear again before his sovereign. (The expression "atones" we quoted from the Talmud, and in the verse, "It will be accepted for him to *atone* for him,"[2] does not refer to the soul's atonement for the sin, but rather his "restoration" before G-d. Now the Creator may derive delight from him, as the Talmud remarks there, and as the verse, "It shall be perfect, to be desired.")[4]

Today we have no offerings to call forth G-d's pleasure; fasting replaces the offering. The Talmud says, "May my loss of fat and blood be regarded as though I had offered before You . . ."[5]

Therefore there are many cases of Talmudic sages, who for some trivial fault underwent a great many fasts. Rabbi Elazar ben Azariah contended that

---

[32] Ex. *21:29 and Rashi for an example.* [33] Genesis *38:7–10.*

Chapter 2
[1] Lev. *1:3.* [2] Ibid., *1:4.* [3] *7b.* [4] Lev. *22:21.* [5] Berachot *17a.*

הרבה תעניות וסיגופים לעובר על כריתות ומיתות ב"ד וכן למוציא זרע לבטלה שחייב מיתה בידי שמים כמ"ש בתורה גבי ער ואונן ודינו כחייבי כריתות לענין זה. היינו כדי לינצל מעונש יסורי' של מעלה ח"ו. וגם כדי לזרז ולמהר גמר כפרת נפשו. וגם אולי אינו שב אל ה' בכל לבו ונפשו מאהבה כ"א מיראה:

פרק ב אך כל זה לענין כפרה ומחילת העון שנמחל לו לגמרי מה שעבר על מצות המלך כשעשה תשובה שלימה ואין מזכירין לו דבר וחצי דבר ביום הדין לענשו ע"ז ח"ו בעוה"ב ונפטר לגמרי מן הדין בעוה"ב. אמנם שיהי' לרצון לפני ה' ומרוצה וחביב לפניו ית' כקודם החטא להיות נחת רוח לקונו מעבודתו. היה צריך להביא קרבן עולה אפי' על מ"ע קלה שאין בה כרת ומיתת ב"ד כמו שדרשו רז"ל בת"כ ע"פ ונרצה לו וכדאיתא בגמ' פ"ק דזבחים דעולה מכפרת על מ"ע והיא דורון לאחר שעשה תשובה ונמחל לו העונש. וכאדם שסרח במלך ופייסו ע"י פרקליטין ומחל לו. אעפ"כ שולח דורון ומנחה לפניו שיתרצה לו לראות פני המלך (ולשון מכפרת וכן מ"ש בתורה ונרצה לו לכפר עליו אין זו כפרת נפשו אלא לכפר לפני ה' להיות נחת רוח לקונו כדאי' שם בגמ' וכמ"ש תמים יהי' לרצון). ועכשיו שאין לנו קרבן להפיק רצון מה' התענית הוא במקום קרבן כמ"ש בגמרא שיהא מיעוט חלבי ודמי שנתמעט כאלו הקרבתי לפניך וכו'. ולכן מצינו בכמה תנאים ואמוראי' שעל דבר קל היו מתענים תעניות הרבה מאד כמו ראב"ע שהי' מתיר שתהא

פרה

a cow may go out (wearing) its strap between its horns on Shabbat while his colleagues prohibited it. Once a neighbour's cow went out with its strap and R. Elazar did not hinder her. Because he did not support his colleagues, he fasted so long that his teeth were blackened.[6] Rabbi Joshua once remarked, "I am ashamed of your words, Beit Shammai."[7] His teeth too turned black through fasting. Rav Huna, because his tefilin strap once turned over, endured forty fasts.[8] There are many such incidents.

With this precedent, the Ari[9] taught his disciples, according to Kabbala principles, the number of fasts for many transgressions, though they entail no excision or death by divine agency. Examples: for anger—151 fasts; even for a Rabbinic prohibition like *stam yainam*[10]—seventy-three fasts; for neglecting a positive Rabbinic enactment like worship—sixty-one fasts.

In general, the mystery of the fast is remarkably effective for the revelation of the Supreme Will, similar to the offering, of which it is said, "An aroma pleasing to G-d."[11] In Isaiah[12] we find, "Do you call this a fast and a day desirable to G-d!" Obviously, an acceptable fast is a "desirable day."

•▲*Chapter 3*

The latter Musar sages were divided about one who repeated a sin several times. Some contend that he must fast the number of fasts appropriate to that sin according to the number of transgressions. For example, the number of fasts prescribed in the penances of the Ari for wasteful emission of semen is eighty-four. If someone commits this sin ten or twenty times, say, he must fast ten or twenty times eighty-four, and so on in all instances. These sages compare the fasts to the *chatat*[1] offering required for every instance of violation.

Others compare fasts to the *olah* offering brought for neglect of a positive command. Violation of a number of positive commands is atoned for by one *olah*, as the Talmud explains in *Zevachim*, ch. I.

The accepted decision

[6] Yerushalmi Betza *2:8*. [7] Chagiga *22b*. [8] Moed Katan *25a; R. Huna fasted forty days for slighting a colleague* (Bava Metzia *33a*). [9] *Rabbi Isaac Luria (1534–1572), a Kabbalist with a profound influence on Rabbi Schneur Zalman.* [10] *Wine used in idolatrous libations are Biblically prohibited. The Rabbinic prohibition is extended to any "ordinary" non-Jewish wine. See* Kitzur Shulchan Aruch *(Code of Jewish Law, Abridged)* sect. *47*. [11] Lev. *1:13*. [12] *58:5*.

Chapter 3
[1] Lev. *4*.

פרה יוצאה ברצועה שבין קרניה בשבת וחכמים אוסרי׳ ופ״א יצאה כן פרתו של שכנתו ולא מיחה בה והושחרו שיניו מפני הצומות על שלא קיים דברי חביריו. וכן ר׳ יהושע שאמר בושני מדבריכם ב״ש והושחרו שיניו מפני הצומות. ורב הונא פעם אחת נתהפכה לו רצועה של תפילין והתענה מ׳ צומות. וכהנה רבות. ועל יסוד זה לימד האריז״ל לתלמידיו עפ״י חכמת האמת מספר הצומות לכמה עונות וחטאים אף שאין בהן כרת ולא מיתה בידי שמים כמו על הכעס קנ״א תעניות וכו׳. ואפי׳ על איסור דרבנן כמו סתם יינם יתענה ע״ג תעניות וכו׳ וכן על ביטול מ״ע דרבנן כמו תפלה יתענה ס״א תעניות וכו׳ והדרך כלל סוד התענית היא סגולה נפלאה להתגלות רצון העליון ב״ה כמו הקרבן שנא׳ בו ריח ניחוח לה׳. וכמ״ש בישעי׳ הלזה תקרא צום ויום רצון לה׳ מכלל שהצום הנרצה הוא יום רצון:

פרק ג והנה חכמי המוסר האחרונים נחלקו במי שחטא חטא א׳ פעמים רבות. דיש אומרים שצריך להתענות מספר הצומות לאותו חטא פעמים רבות כפי המספר אשר חטא. כגון המוציא זרע לבטלה שמספר הצומות המפורש בתיקוני תשובה מהאריז״ל הן פ״ד תעניות ואם חטא בזה עשר או עשרים פעמים עד״מ צריך להתענות עשר או עשרים פעמים פ״ד וכן לעולם. דומיא דקרבן חטאת שחייב להביא על כל פעם ופעם. ויש מדמין ענין זה לקרבן עולה הבאה על מ״ע דאפי׳ עבר על כמה מ״ע מתכפר בעולה אחת כדאי׳ בגמ׳ פ״ק דזבחים. והכרעה המקובלת

in this dispute is to fast three times the number of fasts prescribed for that specific sin, i.e. 252 for emission, and similarly for other sins. This is based on an observation in Zohar, end of Noach; as soon as mortal man is guilty one time before the Holy One, blessed be He, he makes an impression . . . the third time the stain penetrates from one side through the other . . . Therefore the number of fasts ought also be three . . .

●▲ However, all this applies to the strong and healthy, whose physical vigour would not be sapped at all by repeated fasts, as in the generations of yore. But whoever would be affected by many fasts, and might suffer illness or pain, G-d forbid, as in contemporary generations, is forbidden to engage in many fasts. This ban concerns even sins of excision or execution, and certainly the positive and prohibitory commands that do not involve excision. Instead the measure of fasting is the personal estimate of what he can tolerate without doubt.

For even in those early Talmudic generations, only the robust who could mortify themselves fasted so frequently. But whoever cannot fast and does, is called "sinner" in *Taanit*,[2] ch. I. This applies even to one who fasts for specifically known sins, as Rashi explains there, and we find in *Zevachim*,[3] ch. I, that there is no one of Israel who is not guilty of a positive commandment . . .

It goes without saying that a student of Torah who fasts, sins and is doubly punished, for the weakness resulting from his fast prevents him from studying Torah properly.

What then is his alternative? "Your sin redeem with charity."[4] The codifiers of Torah law specified for each fast day of repentance approximately eighteen (coins) . . .[5] The wealthy shall add according to his means . . . See *Magen Avraham* on laws of Fasts.[6]

* * *

●▲ Nonetheless, every man of spirit who desires to be close to G-d, to repair his soul, to return it to G-d with the finest and most preferred repentance, shall be stringent with himself. He should complete, at least once during his life span,

---

[2] *11b.* [3] *7a.* [4] Daniel *4:24.* [5] Shulchan Aruch Orach Chayim *334:26 and commentaries.* [6] ibid. *568:12.*

המקובלת בזה להתענות ג"פ כפי מספר הצומות דחטא זה. דהיינו רנ"ב צומות על הוצאות שז"ל וכן בשאר חטאים ועונות. והטעם הוא עפ"י מ"ש בזוה"ק ס"פ נח כיון דחב ב"נ קמי קודב"ה זמנא חדא עביד רשימו כו' זמנא תליתאה אתפשט ההוא כתמא מסטרא דא לסטרא דא כו'. לכך צריך מספר הצומות ג"כ ג"פ וכו'. אכן כל זה באדם חזק ובריא שאין ריבוי הצומות מזיק לו כלל לבריאות גופו וכמו בדורות הראשונים. אבל מי שריבוי הצומות מזיק לו שאפשר שיוכל לבא לידי חולי או מיחוש ח"ו כמו בדורותינו אלה. אסור לו להרבות בתעניות אפי' על כריתות ומיתות ב"ד ומכ"ש על מ"ע ומל"ת שאין בהן כרת. אלא כפי אשר ישער בנפשו שבודאי לא יזיק לו כלל. כי אפי' בדורות הראשונים בימי תנאים ואמוראים לא היו מתענין בכה"ג אלא הבריאים דמצו לצעורי נפשייהו ודלא מצי לצעורי נפשיה ומתענה נקרא חוטא בגמ' פ"ק דתענית. ואפי' מתענה על עבירות שבידו כדפרש"י שם וכדאיתא בגמ' פ"ק דזבחים שאין לך אדם מישראל שאינו מחוייב עשה וכו'. ומכ"ש מי שהוא בעל תורה שחוטא ונענש בכפליים כי מחמת חלישות התענית לא יוכל לעסוק בה כראוי. אלא מאי תקנתי' כדכתיב וחטאך בצדקה פרוק. וכמ"ש הפוסקים ליתן בעד כל יום תענית של תשובה ערך ח"י ג"פ וכו' והעשיר יוסיף לפי עשרו וכו' כמ"ש המ"א הלכות תענית:

ומ"מ כל בעל נפש החפץ קרבת ה' לתקן נפשו להשיבה אל ה' בתשובה מעולה מן המובחר. יחמיר על עצמו להשלים עכ"פ פעם א' כל ימי חייו

מספר

the number of fasts for every grave sin incurring death at least, if only death by divine agency. For example, for wasteful emission he should undergo the series of eighty-four fasts once in his life. He may postpone the fasts until the shorter winter days and fast some ten days or less, for example, in one winter, and complete the series of eighty-four in nine or more years according to his stamina. (Besides, he may also eat a little about three hours before sunrise, and this would still be considered a fast, if he so stipulated.)

For the completion of the mentioned 252, he may fast another four times eighty-four until past noon, which the Talmud Yerushalmi considers a fast. In this context, two half-days are reckoned as one full day. Naturally, this approach applies to any other sins, for each heart knows its own anguish and desires its vindication.

* * *

▲ There still remain the fasts in excess of the 252, or whatever amount, that he ought to fast in deference to the more stringent opinion insisting on the appropriate number of fasts for every violation committed, as noted. These may be redeemed with charity, approximating eighteen (coins) for each fast day. Charity may redeem all other fasts that he should have undergone for sins not entailing death, and even for neglecting a positive command, Torah or Rabbinic, and neglect of "Torah study which equals them all,"[7] according to the number of fasts prescribed by the Ari's penances. (Most of these are noted in *Mishnat Chassidim*, Tractate *Teshuvah*.) All of these fasts he may redeem with charity if he cannot mortify himself, as noted.

Though this might amount to a considerable sum, he need not fear for the injunction, "Do not distribute more than one fifth."[8] These circumstances are not "distribution" for charity, since he does this to release himself from fasting and affliction. This is no less necessary than medicine for his body or his other needs.

The number of fasts enumerated in the above-mentioned penances is exceedingly great. Therefore all who revere

---

[7] Peah *1:1*. [8] Ketuvot *50a. This is one of the enactments of the Conclave of Usha about a century after the destruction of the Beit Hamikdash by the Romans.*

מספר הצומות לכל עון ועון מעונות החמורים שחייבין עליהם מיתה עכ"פ ואפי' בידי שמים בלבד כגון להוצאות ז"ל פ"ד צומות פ"א בימי חייו. ויכול לדחותן לימים הקצרים בחורף ויתענה כעשר תעניות עד"מ בחורף א' או פחות ויגמור מספר הפ"ד צומות בט' שנים או יותר כפי כחו (וגם יכול לאכול מעט כג' שעות לפני נ"ה ואעפ"כ נחשב לתענית אם התנה כן) ולתשלום רנ"ב צומות כנ"ל יתענה עוד ד' פעמים פ"ד עד אחר חצות היום בלבד דמיחשב ג"כ תענית בירושלמי. וב' חצאי יום נחשבים לו ליום א' לענין זה. וכן לשאר עונות כיוצא בהן אשר כל לב יודע מרת נפשו וחפץ בהצדקה:

אכן מספר הצומות העודפי' על רנ"ב וכה"ג שהיה צריך להתענות לחוש לדעת המחמירי' להתענות מספר הצומות שעל כל חטא וחטא כפי מספר הפעמים שחטא כנ"ל. יפדה כולן בצדקה ערך ח"י ג"פ בעד כל יום. וכן שאר כל תעניות שצריך להתענות על עבירות שאין בהן מיתה ואפי' על ביטול מ"ע דאוריי' ודרבנן ות"ת כנגד כולם כפי המספר המפורש בתיקוני התשובה מהאר"י ז"ל (ורובם נזכרים במשנת חסידים במס' התשובה) הכל כאשר לכל יפדה בצדקה כנ"ל אי לא מצי לצעורי נפשי' כנ"ל. ואף שיעלה לסך מסויים אין לחוש משום אל יבזבז יותר מחומש. דלא מקרי בזבוז בכה"ג מאחר שעושה לפדות נפשו מתעניות וסיגופים. ולא גרעא מרפואת הגוף ושאר צרכיו. ולפי שמספר הצומות המוזכרי' בתקוני תשובה הנ"ל רבו במאד מאד לכן נהגו עכשיו כל החרדים לדבר

the word of G-d are now accustomed to being unstintingly generous with charity, for the prevalent lack of hardihood prevents them from mortifying themselves over much. (A comment is made elsewhere on this subject on the verse, "The kindnesses of G-d, for they are not concluded.")[9]

•▲*Chapter 4*

However, all we have said refers to the culmination of the atonement and the "polishing" of the soul before G-d after repentance, as cited from *Zevachim*, where the *olah* offering is described as a presentation after the intercessor's successful plea . . . But the beginning of the mitzvah of teshuvah, its fundament, is the return to G-d in truth and with a complete heart. We must explain this fully and discuss it comprehensively.

Let us begin with the Zohar's[1] statement interpreting teshuvah according to *sod*,[2] the mystical approach. "Teshuvah is *tashuv hai*, returning the *hai*;[3] the latter hai is teshuvah tata'a, inferior teshuvah; the upper hai is teshuvah ila'a, superior teshuvah." We must also note that the Zohar states several times that teshuvah is ineffective for violation of the covenant[4] and for wasteful emission. This is rather surprising, for "Nothing can withstand teshuvah, even idolatry and immorality . . ."[5] The *Reishit Chochmah* explains that the intention of the Zohar is that inferior teshuvah is ineffective, but superior teshuvah . . .

To comprehend even a mite of this let us see what the Scripture and our Sages say about excision and death by divine agency. A violator of an excision sin would actually die before his fiftieth[6] year. In the case of death by divine agency he actually dies before sixty,[6] like Chananiah ben Azur in Jeremiah.[7] (Indeed, there were instances when the punishment of death by divine agency was meted out instantly, as with Er and Onan.) But, in every generation there are so many guilty of excision and death who enjoy extended and pleasant days and years!

•▲The key will be found in the passage, "For part of G-d is His people . . ."[8] a part of the Tetragrammaton, the Ineffable Name. We find, "He breathed into his nostrils the breath of life,"[9] and, we are told, "Who exhales, does so from within . . ."[10] Though He has no bodily form . . .,[11] G-d forbid, the Torah does "Speak

---

[9] Lam. *3:22. In* Igeret Hakodesh *Sect. 10, Rabbi Schneur Zalman states that the source of Torah is in the infinite attribute of* Chesed, *kindness. Only when mitzvot descend to the finite world of mortal man do they undergo tzimtzum, contraction, and acquire dimension. Thus almost all mitzvot have dimension*—Succah, tzitzit *etc., dimension in time or space, minimum and maximum in quantity, etc. Charity too has its limitations—ten percent for the ordinary and twenty percent for the generous. However this last standard applies only when one has not violated the mitzvot; his religious equilibrium, we might say, is undisturbed. If one has committed a sin, then atonement, reparation of the defect, must come from a higher source,* Kindness, *the infinite, superior to the*

לדבר ה׳ להרבות מאד מאד בצדקה. מחמת חלישות הדור דלא מצו לצעורי נפשם כולי האי (וכמ״ש במ״א ע״פ חסדי ה׳ כי לא תמנו):

פרק ד ואולם כל הנ״ל הוא לגמר הכפרה ומירוק הנפש לה׳ אחר התשובה כמ״ש לעיל מהגמ׳ פ״ק דזבחים דעולה דורון היא לאחר שריצה הפרקליט וכו׳. אמנם התחלת מצות התשובה ועיקרה לשוב עד ה׳ באמת ובלב שלם. ההכרח לבאר היטב בהרחבת הביאור. בהקדים מ״ש בזוה״ק בביאור מלת תשובה ע״ד הסוד. תשוב ה׳. ה׳ תתאה תשובה תתאה. ה׳ עילאה תשובה עילאה. וגם מ״ש בזוה״ק בקצת מקומות שאין תשובה מועלת לפוגם בריתו ומוציא ז״ל. והוא דבר תמוה מאד שאין לך דבר עומד בפני התשובה ואפי׳ ע״ז וג״ע וכו׳. ופי׳ בר״ח שכונת הזהר שאין מועלת תשובה תתאה כ״א תשובה עילאה וכו׳. הנה להבין זאת מעט מזעיר צריך להקדים מה שמבואר מהכתוב ומדברי רז״ל ענין הכרת ומיתה בידי שמים כשעבר עבירה שחייבי׳ עלי׳ כרת הי׳ מת ממש קודם חמשים שנה. ובמיתה בידי שמים מת ממש קודם ששים שנה כחנניה בן עזור הנביא בירמי׳ (ולפעמי׳ גם במיתה בידי שמים נפרעין לאלתר כמו שמצינו בער ואונן) והרי נמצאו בכל דור כמה וכמה חייבי כריתות ומיתות והאריכו ימיהם (ושניהם) [ושנותיהם] בנעימים. אך הענין יובן עפ״י מ״ש כי חלק ה׳ עמו וכו׳ חלק משם הוי׳ ב״ה כדכתיב ויפח באפיו נשמת חיים ומאן דנפח מתוכו נפח וכו׳. ואף שאין לו דמות הגוף וכו׳ ח״ו. אך דברה תורה כלשון

---

state of tzimtzum. To elicit infinite pardon man must exceed ordinary bounds, being charitable beyond the limitations of a specified percentage. Rabbi Schneur Zalman interprets the verse rather ingeniously: "The kindnesses of G-d"—if we are to call forth the attribute of Kindness, *infinite pardon, through our unbounded deeds, it is because "lo tamnu"—we are not perfect. The last word, tamnu, may mean either "They are not concluded," as is the usual rendition, or "We are not perfect."*

Chapter 4

[1] Raya Mehemna *122a.* [2] *Torah is interpreted on four planes, the first is* pshat, *or simple meaning; the second is* remez, *or allusion, hint; the third is* drush, *or homily; and the*

(Notes cont. at end of Hebrew Text)

in the language of men."[12]

There is a vast difference in the case of mortal man between the breath issuing from his mouth while speaking and the breath of forceful blowing. When speaking there is embodied within the breath only the smallest amount of the speaker's power and life-force, and even that is only of the superficial aspect of the soul that dwells within him. But when he blows with force, he blows from deep within himself. That breath embodies the internal power and life-force of the vivifying soul . . .

▲ Precisely so in the analogy of Creation, allowing for the infinite differentiations involved, these two profoundly different states exist. All the hosts of heaven, even the spiritual beings like angels,[13] were created *ex nihilo*. They derive their existence from the external aspect of the life-force issuing from the Infinite (*En Sof*) to vitalise creation. This external aspect of the life-giving power is called the "Breath of His mouth," as it were, in the verse "By the breath of His mouth all their hosts."[14] This is the creative power embodied in the Ten Utterances[15] (that are instruments for this power and the extension of the power . . . as explained in *Likutei Amarim* II, ch. 11).

In contrast, the soul of man derives initially from the internal of the life-force and flow issuing from the Infinite, as in the verse quoted above, "He breathed . . ." Subsequently it descended through ever more concealing planes, also through the letters in the Utterance, "Let us make man . . ."[16] in order that the soul could eventually be invested in a body in this inferior physical world.

The Scripture calls the angels "Elokim," as in "For the Lord your G–d is the G–d of G–ds (Elokim) . . ."[17] and "Praise the G–d of G–ds (Elokim) . . ."[18] and "The sons of G–d (Elokim) came to present themselves . . ."[19] They derive their nurture from the external of the life-force, which is merely the state of letters. Similarly the name Elokim is an external state compared to the Tetragrammaton.

But the soul of man, deriving its being from the internal of the vivifying power is a "Part of G–d (Tetragrammaton)." For the Tetragrammaton indicates the internal of the life-giving power, which far transcends the state of letters, or articulation.

●▲ To explain: there is a passage in *Tikunei Zohar*, Maamar Eliahu. "You are He Who elicited the ten *tikunim* called the Ten Sefirot, to conduct by them the concealed[20] worlds.

---

[12] Berachot *31b*. [13] *The "Worlds" mentioned above describe states and existences at different removes from G–d, each accordingly less conscious of His presence and infinity. The last three (*Beriah *or Creation,* Yetzirah *or Formation, and* Asiyah *or Action) parallel thought, speech, and deed respectively as manifestations of man's soul. Thought is internal, united with the thinker; speech is intermittent and directed outward, to another; deed is farther from the performer, and his works exist independently of him. On each of these planes, or Worlds, there are beings, for example, the soul before it inhabits a body and after the death of the body. Another example is what we commonly call "angels." These are spiritual beings with spiritual dimensions, for*

כלשון בנ"א. כי כמו שיש הפרש והבדל גדול באדם התחתון עד"מ בין ההבל שיוצא מפיו בדיבורו להבל היוצא ע"י נפיחה. שביוצא בדיבורו מלובש בו כח וחיות מעט מזעיר והוא בחי' חיצוניות מנפש החיה שבקרבו. אבל ביוצא בכח הנופח דמתוכו נפח מלובש בו כח וחיות פנימי' מבחי' הנפש החיה וכו'. ככה ממש עד"מ המבדיל הבדלות לאין קץ. יש הפרש עצום מאד למעלה בין כל צבא השמים ואפי' המלאכי' שנבראו מאין ליש וחיים וקיימי' מבחי' חיצוניות החיות והשפע שמשפיע א"ס ב"ה להחיות העולמות ובחי' זו נקראת בשם רוח פיו עד"מ כמ"ש וברוח פיו כל צבאם והיא בחי' חיות המלובשת באותיות שבעשרה מאמרות (שהן בחי' כלים והמשכות וכו' כמ"ש בלק"א ח"ב פי"א). ובין נשמת האדם שנמשכה תחלה מבחי' פנימי' החיות והשפע שמשפיע א"ס ב"ה כמ"ש ויפח וכו' ואח"כ ירדה בסתר המדרגה ג"כ ע"י בחי' האותיות שבמאמר נעשה אדם וכו' כדי להתלבש בגוף עוה"ז התחתון. ולכן נקראו המלאכי' בשם אלקים בכתוב וכמ"ש כי ה' אלקיכם אלקי האלקי' כו' הודו לאלקי האלקי' כו' ויבאו בני האלקי' להתייצב כו'. לפי שיניקת חיותם היא מבחי' חיצוניות שהיא בחי' האותיות לבד ושם אלקים הוא בחי' חיצוניות לגבי שם הוי' ב"ה. אבל נשמת האדם שהיא מבחי' פנימי' החיות היא חלק שם הוי' ב"ה. כי שם הוי' מורה על פנימי' החיות שהיא למעלה מבחי' האותיות. וביאור הענין כנודע ממאמר אליהו אנת הוא דאפיקת עשר תיקונין וקרינן להון עשר ספירן לאנהגא בהון עלמין סתימין וכו'

---

instance intellectual or emotion characteristics that define and bound them. (The three-fold Holy Holy Holy in Isaiah *6:3 indicate different apprehensions of His abstract being. See also the blessing preceding the Morning Shema.) In terms of absolute comprehension of the Creator they are superior to mortals. In terms of potential, of volition, man is the superior. They are bounded, foreordained. Man can choose—and grow. As the text will note, all beings, including the most exalted spiritual beings, are inferior in their source to man.* [14] Psalm *33:6.* [15] Avot *5; "Speech" indicates the existence of some being besides the speaker, for speech is communication directed to another, reveals to another.*

(Notes cont. at end of Hebrew Text)

... You are Wise, and not by the known wisdom. You understand, and not by the known understanding ..." All the attributes, the Ten Sefirot, are included and represented in their source, the Tetragrammaton.

The Tetragrammaton is composed of four letters: *yud*, *hai*, *vav*, and *hai*.

The *yud*, a simple point, symbolizes His Wisdom,[21] the state of concealment and obscurity, before it develops into a state of expansion and revelation in comprehension and understanding. (The "thorn" on the yud indicates the Supreme Will, far superior to the level of *chochmah ila'a*, the higher wisdom, as is known.)

When the "point" evolves into a state of expansion and revelation of comprehension and understanding in the concealed worlds, it is then contained and represented in the letter *hai*. The shape of the letter has dimension, expansion in breadth, which implies the breadth of explanation and understanding, and expansion in length, to indicate extension and flow downward into the concealed worlds.

In the next stage this extension and flow are drawn still lower into the revealed worlds. This may be compared to one who wishes to reveal his thoughts to another through his speech, for example. This stage of extension is contained and represented in the final letters *vav* and *hai*.

Vav, in shape a vertical line, indicates downward extension. Also, this flow downward is effected through the divine traits of benevolence and goodness and His other sacred traits, included in general terms in the six attributes in the verse, "Yours O G-d is the greatness ..." until "Yours O G-d is the dominion ...",[22] until, but not inclusive. His seventh attribute, *malchut* or dominion, is called the "Word of G-d," as in the verse, "Wherever the word of the king holds sway."[23]

This attribute of dominion is contained and represented in the final *hai* of the Tetragrammaton. The internal aspect and the source of speech is the breath that rises from the heart, then is molded by the five oral articulations[24]—*alef*, *chet*, *hai*, and *ayin* from the throat ... The *hai* implies this internal aspect of speech, for it is the pristine unvocalised breath, "A light letter without substance."[25] Though He has no corporeal form, G-d forbid, the Torah speaks in the language of men. The word of G-d, with its twenty-two letters, would separate into the five

---

[21] *See the Explanatory Notes to "On Learning Chassidus" for the Chabad exposition of the process of development of intellect and emotion.* [22] *I* Chronicles *29:11.* [23] Kohelet *8:4; see "The Tzemach Tzedek and the Haskalah Movement," P. 110, Note 3.* [24] Sefer Yetzirah *2:3.* [25] Akdamot.

וכו׳. אנת חכים ולא בחכמה ידיעא אנת מבין ולא בבינה ידיעא וכו׳. וכל הי׳ ספירות נכללות ונרמזות בשם הוי׳ ב״ה. כי היו״ד שהיא בחי׳ נקודה לבד מרמזת לחכמתו ית׳ שהיא בבחי׳ העלם והסתר קודם שבאה לבחי׳ התפשטות וגילוי ההשגה וההבנה (והקוץ שעל היו״ד רומז לבחי׳ רצון העליון ב״ה שלמעלה מעלה ממדרגת בחי׳ חכמה עילאה כנודע). ואחר שבאה לבחי׳ התפשטות וגילוי ההשגה וההבנה לעלמין סתימין נכללת ונרמזת באות ה״א שיש לה בחי׳ התפשטות לרוחב המורה ומרמז על הרחבת הביאור וההבנה וגם לאורך המורה על בחי׳ ההמשכה וההשפעה מלמעלה למטה לעלמין סתימין. ואח״כ כשנמשכת המשכה והשפעה זו יותר למטה לעלמין דאתגליין. וכמו האדם שרוצה לגלות חכמתו לאחרים ע״י דיבורו עד״מ. נכללת ונרמזת המשכה זו באותיות ו״ה. כי הוי״ו מורה על ההמשכה מלמעלה למטה. וגם המשכה זו היא ע״י מדת חסדו וטובו ושאר מדותיו הקדושות הנכללות בדרך כלל במספר שש שבפסוק לך ה׳ הגדולה וכו׳ עד לך ה׳ הממלכה וכו׳ ולא עד בכלל. כי מדת מלכותו ית׳ נק׳ בשם דבר ה׳ כמ״ש באשר דבר מלך שלטון ונכללת ונרמזת באות ה״א אחרונה של שם הוי׳. כי פנימי׳ ומקור הדיבור הוא ההבל העולה מן הלב ומתחלק לה׳ מוצאות הפה אחה״ע מהגרון וכו׳. וגם הברת הה״א היא בחי׳ הבל לבד כמ״ש אתא קלילא דלית בה משש. ואף שאין לו דמות הגוף ח״ו. אך דברה תורה כלשון בני אדם. בשגם שגם דבר ה׳ כ״ב אותיות המתחלקות לה׳

חלקי

articulations and thus were all beings created. (For a discussion of these letters, see Likutei Amarim II, ch. 11.)

• Analogously, again considering the infinite separation between the two cases, these same four stages apply to the soul of man, i.e., the divine soul that "He blew from within Himself." There is the initial state of hidden concept symbolised in the letter *yud*, with its potential of being revealed, thus understanding and conceiving of His true being and His greatness . . . each person according to his measure, according to the breadth of his intellect and understanding.

As man deepens his intelligence, as he broadens his mind and comprehension, to contemplate His greatness, his now-developed understanding is indicated in the letter *hai*, that has breadth. The *hai* also has length to indicate downward extension, that from his understanding and contemplation of G–d's majesty, he arouses love and fear and their ramifications in his mind and in the recesses of his heart.

In the following stage these emotions would actually become manifest in his heart. This leads to the true service of G–d, in Torah study and mitzvah observance, with voice and speech or with deed. This is the import of the letters *vav hai* . . .

Another meaning behind the four letters as applied to man: the contemplation endeavouring to understand and conceive of His true being, derives also from Torah, for Torah proceeds from *chochmah*,[26] Wisdom, represented by the *yud* of the Tetragrammaton . . .

•▲ *Chapter 5*

Bringing the divine soul down into the physical world to invest itself within a human body, derives from the internal aspect, the source, of speech. This is the "breath" of the Supreme One, indicated in the latter *hai* mentioned above. "He *breathed* into his nostrils the breath of life and man became a living soul."[1] Whoever breathes with force . . .

Let us return to a verse cited earlier. "For part of G–d is His people; Jacob is the cord of His possession."[2] Jacob is compared to a rope, the upper end bound above and the lower end below.

The simple meaning of the verse "He breathed" is to show us that just as, for example, if one blows in some direction, and there is any separation or obstruction there, then the exhaled breath will not reach that place at all

---

[26] Zohar *II 85a, 121a.*

Chapter 5
[1] Gen. *2:7.* [2] Deut. *32:10.*

חלקי המוצאות ובהן נברא כל היצור (וכמ"ש בלק"א ח"ב פי"א ביאור ענין אותיות אלו). וככה ממש עד"מ המבדיל הבדלות לאין קץ בנשמת האדם שהיא בחי' נפש האלקי' דמתוכיה נפח יש בה בחי' שכל הנעלם המרומז באות יו"ד שבכחו לצאת אל הגילוי להבין ולהשכיל באמתתו ית' ובגדולתו וכו' כל חד וחד לפום שיעורא דילי' לפי רוחב שכלו ובינתו. וכפי אשר מעמיק שכלו ומרחיב דעתו ובינתו להתבונן בגדולתו ית' אזי מרומזת בינתו באות ה"א שיש לה רוחב וגם אורך המורה ההמשכה מלמעלה למטה להוליד מבינתו והתבוננותו בגדולת ה' אהבה ויראה ותולדותיהן במוחו ותעלומות לבו ואח"כ בבחי' התגלות לבו. ומזה נמשכה עבודה האמיתית בעסק התורה והמצות בקול ודבור או מעשה הן אותיות וא"ו ה"א וכו'. וגם ההתבוננות להבין ולהשכיל באמתתו וגדולתו ית' נמשכה ג"כ מהתורה דאורייתא מחכמה נפקא היא בחי' יו"ד של שם הוי' וכו':

פרק ה והנה המשכת וירידת הנפש האלקי' לעוה"ז להתלבש בגוף האדם נמשכה מבחי' פנימי' ומקור הדיבור הוא הבל העליון המרומז באות ה"א תתאה כנ"ל וכמ"ש ויפח באפיו נשמת חיים ויהי האדם לנפש חיה ומאן דנפח וכו'. וז"ש כי חלק ה' עמו יעקב חבל נחלתו פי' כמו חבל עד"מ שראשו א' קשור למעלה וקצהו למטה. כי הנה פשט הכתוב מ"ש ויפח הוא להורות לנו כמו שעד"מ כשהאדם נופח לאיזה מקום אם יש איזה דבר חוצץ ומפסיק בינתיים אין הבל הנופח עולה ומגיע כלל לאותו

—so precisely, if anything separates and obstructs between man's body and the "breath" of the Supreme One.

The truth is though that nothing material or spiritual is a barrier before Him—"Do I not fill heaven and earth!"[3] "All the world is full of His glory."[4] "There is no place devoid of Him."[5] "In the heavens above and on the earth below there is none else."[6] "He fills all worlds . . ."[7]

But Isaiah declares, "Only your sins separate you from your G-d."[8] The reason is that sins oppose the Supreme Will Who gives life to all,[9] as in the verse, "Whatever G-d wills He did in heaven and earth."[10] (It has been noted above, that the Supreme Will is the source of the benevolence issuing from His Name, the Tetragrammaton, and is represented in the "thorn" atop the letter *yud.*)

This is the significance of excision, the consequence of certain grave sins. The "cord," the soul—or as the verse has it—Jacob, drawn from the final *hai* in G-d's Name, the Tetragrammaton, is severed, cut off. "That soul shall be cut off from before Me, I am the Lord."[11] The soul is cut off from *before Me.*

Other sins that do not incur excision do cause at least a defect in the soul, a "defect" being similar to the "defect" or nick that invalidates a blade for ritual slaughter.

Returning to the analogy of the cord—a thick rope woven of 613 thin strands parallels the Scriptual "cord," the downward flow from G-d mentioned above, comprising 613 mitzvot. When man violates one of them, G-d forbid, a thin strand is severed . . .

But even if one has incurred excision or death, there yet remains an impression within him of his divine soul, and through this he may live until fifty or sixty years and no more. (The statement attributed to the Ari, that the Encompassing enters him . . . is irrelevant to the life of the physical body, and applies until fifty years, or to the contemporary period, as will be noted.)

•▲*Chapter 6*

However all this pertained when Israel was on a higher plane, when the Divine Presence dwelt among Israel in the Beit Hamikdash. Then the vitality of the body came only through the divine soul, from the internal of the life-giving power

---

[3] Jeremiah *23:24.* [4] Is. *6:3.* [5] Tikunei Zohar *51.* [6] Deut. *4:39. Likutei Amarim II explains this rendition, rather than "there is no other."* [7] Zohar *III 255a.* [8] *59:2.* [9] Nehemiah *9:6.* [10] Psalm *135:6.* [*11*] Lev. *22:3.*

לאותו מקום ככה ממש אם יש דבר חוצץ ומפסיק בין גוף האדם לבחי' הבל העליון. אך באמת אין שום דבר גשמי ורוחני חוצץ לפניו ית' כי הלא את השמים ואת הארץ אני מלא ומלא כל הארץ כבודו ולית אתר פנוי מיני' בשמים ממעל ועל הארץ מתחת אין עוד ואיהו ממלא כל עלמין וכו' אלא כמ"ש בישעי' כי אם עוונותיכם היו מבדילים ביניכם לבין אלקיכם. והטעם לפי שהם נגד רצון העליון ב"ה המחי' את הכל כמ"ש כל אשר חפץ ה' עשה בשמים ובארץ (וכמש"ל שהוא מקור השפעת שם הוי' ונרמז בקוצו של יו"ד). וזהו ענין הכרת. שנכרת ונפסק חבל ההמשכה משם הוי' ב"ה שנמשכה מה"א תתאה כנ"ל. וכמ"ש בפ' אמור ונכרתה הנפש ההיא מלפני אני ה'. מלפני דייקא. ובשאר עבירות שאין בהן כרת עכ"פ הן פוגמין הנפש כנודע. ופגם הוא מלשון פגימת הסכין והוא עד"מ מחבל עב שזור מתרי"ג חבלים דקים ככה חבל ההמשכה הנ"ל כלול מתרי"ג מצות וכשעובר ח"ו על אחת מהנה נפסק חבל הדק וכו'. אך גם בחייב כרת ומיתה נשאר עדיין בו הרשימו מנפשו האלקי' ועי"ז יכול לחיות עד נ' או ס' שנה ולא יותר (ומ"ש בשם האריז"ל שנכנסה בו בחי' המקיף וכו' אינו ענין לחיי גשמיות הגוף ומיירי עד נ' שנה או בזמן הזה כדלקמן):

פרק ו

אמנם זהו בזמן שהיו ישראל במדרגה עליונה כשהיתה השכינה שורה בישראל בבהמ"ק. ואז לא היו מקבלים חיות לגופם רק ע"י נפש האלקי' לבדה מבחי' פנימי' השפע שמשפיע

issuing from the Infinite, through the Tetragrammaton, as described above.

But after that they had fallen from their estate, and through their actions caused the mystery of the exile of the Divine Presence.[1] "By your sins was your mother expelled,"[2] meaning that the benevolence flowing forth from the latter *hai* as mentioned descended far down, from plane to plane, until it entered into the Ten Sefirot of *nogah.*[3] The benevolence and vitality proceed through the hosts of heaven and those charged over them to every living physical being in this world, even to vegetation. "There is no blade of grass that has no spirit above . . ."[4]

Thus even the sinful and deliberate transgressors of Israel may receive vitality for their bodies and animal souls, exactly as other living beings do, for "They are compared and equal to beasts."[5] In fact their nurture is granted them with even greater emphasis and force,[6] as explained in Zohar, Pkudai. Every benevolence and vitality granted mortal man while he commits evil in the eyes of G–d, in deed or speech, or by musing on sin . . . all issues to him from the chambers of the *sitra achra* described there in the Zohar.

Man possesses choice, whether he shall derive his nurture from the chambers of the *sitra achra* or from the chambers of holiness, from whom flow all good and holy thoughts . . .

For "One opposing the other did G–d make . . ."[7] The chambers of the *sitra achra* derive their vitality from the embodiment within them and the descent within them of the issue of the Ten Sefirot of nogah comprising "good and evil," the Tree of Knowledge . . .[8] as known to the initiate.

●▲ "Jacob is the cord of His possession."[9] The analogy is to a cord whose one end is above and its other end below. When one pulls the lower end he will move and pull after it the higher end as well, as far as it can be pulled.

The root of the soul of man and its source is in the latter *hai,* as we have explained earlier. Through his evil deeds and thoughts he "pulls" and draws down the life-force issuing from the *hai* into

---

[1] Megilla *29a.* [2] Is. *50:1.* [3] Nogah *(brightness or shining) is found in* Ezekiel *1:4. Kabbala and Chassidut tell of the "three kelipot" (husks or shells) that are evil,* sitra achra, *the "other side" in opposition to purity and holiness.* Nogah, *an intermediate stage between holiness and defilement, is composed of good and evil and can be directed either way. The prohibited (forbidden food, say), the evil, derive from the three impure kelipot, and the permitted from* nogah. *A* nogah *"neutral" (like food) may satisfy a gross physical appetite and be degraded, or it might be consumed for a higher purpose and be elevated. (See Likutei Amarim I, ch. 7, etc.) In our text the life-force that had issued from a state of purity and holiness now descends to this* nogah *state, and can*

● 19 Tammuz ▲ *24 Tammuz*

שמשפיע א"ס ב"ה ע"י שם הוי' ב"ה כנ"ל. אך לאחר שירדו ממדרגתם וגרמו במעשיהם סוד גלות השכינה כמ"ש ובפשעיכם שולחה אמכם דהיינו שירדה השפעת בחי' ה"א תתאה הנ"ל ונשתלשלה ממדרגה למדרגה למטה מטה עד שנתלבשה השפעתה בי"ס דנוגה המשפיעות שפע וחיות ע"י המזלות וכל צבא השמים והשרים שעליהם לכל החי הגשמי שבעוה"ז וגם לכל הצומח כמארז"ל אין לך כל עשב מלמטה שאין לו מזל וכו'. ואזי יכול גם החוטא ופושעי ישראל לקבל חיות לגופם ונפשם הבהמיות כמו שאר בע"ח ממש כמ"ש נמשל כבהמות נדמו. ואדרבה ביתר שאת ויתר עז עפ"י המבואר מזוה"ק פ' פקודי שכל שפע וחיות הנשפעת לאדם התחתון בשעה ורגע שעושה הרע בעיני ה' במעשה או בדיבור או בהרהורי עבירה וכו' הכל נשפע לו מהיכלות הסט"א המבוארים שם בזוה"ק. והאדם הוא בעל בחירה אם לקבל השפעתו מהיכלות הסט"א או מהיכלות הקדושה שמהם נשפעות כל מחשבות טובות וקדושות וכו'. כי זה לעו"ז עשה האלקי' וכו'. והיכלות הסט"א מקבלים ויונקים חיותם מהתלבשות והשתלשלות השפע די"ס דנוגה הכלולה מבחי' טו"ר היא בחי' עה"ד וכו' כנודע לי"ח. והנה יעקב חבל נחלתו כתיב. עד"מ כמו החבל שראשו א' למעלה וראשו השני למטה אם ימשוך אדם בראשו השני ינענע וימשך אחריו גם ראשו הראשון כמה שאפשר לו להמשך. וככה ממש בשרש נשמת האדם ומקורה מבחי' ה"א תתאה הנ"ל הוא ממשיך ומוריד השפעתה ע"י מעשיו הרעים ומחשבותיו עד תוך

היכלות

---

fall even further, as we shall see. [4] Bereshit Rabba *10:6.* [5] Psalm *49:12.* [6] *A play on* Gen. *49:3.* [7] Kohelet *7:14.* [8] *Before Adam partook of the forbidden fruit, good and evil were distinct, black-and-white. The demarcation became blurred, a grey state ensued, with no pure good or pure evil in the world. Through his service of G–d, overcoming temptation to sin for example, man separates good from evil, "purifying" the material world.* [9] *Deuteronomy 32:9.*

the chambers of the *sitra achra*, as it were, from which he receives his thoughts and deeds. Because he, the sinful person, draws the flow of vitality into the *sitra achra*, he receives his "share" of vitality first.[9] This will suffice for the understanding.

Hence the statement,[10] "Not within our hands is the reason for either the tranquility of the wicked . . ."—in *our* hands, in this time of exile after the destruction. This is the sense of the "Exile of the Shechinah," as it were, His granting benevolent life-force to the chambers of the *sitra achra* that He despises.

But when the sinner performs the appropriate penance, then he removes from them the life-force he brought to them originally through his deeds and thoughts. By his repentance he returns the flow issuing from the Shechinah to its proper place.

This then is "*tashuv hai tata'a*," returning the latter *hai* from its state of exile. "G-d will return those of you who return,"[11] meaning *with* those who return. Our Sages have commented on this verse, "He shall *bring back* is not said . . ."[12]

•▲Chapter 7

In the true and direct path to the lower teshuvah, returning the latter *hai* noted above, there are two general elements. The first is to awaken supreme compassion from the source of mercy for his spirit (*neshama*)[1] and divine soul (*nefesh*) that has fallen from a lofty peak, the true Life, into a deep pit, the chambers of defilement and *sitra achra*. Divine compassion is also to be aroused for the source of the soul in the source of life, the Name of G-d, the Tetragrammaton. "He shall return to G-d and He will grant him mercy."[2] "Him" would refer to G-d here, arousing mercies on the life-giving power issuing from His Name, that has descended into the chambers of the impure *sitra achra*, to give them vitality. This was brought about through the deeds of man, his scheming and evil thoughts. "The king is bound with tresses,"[3] is interpreted as "Bound with the tresses of the mind . . ."[4] The King is "bound" by man's improper thoughts, the Divine Presence is in exile, as noted above.

The auspicious time for this arousal of mercies is *Tikun Chatzot*, the midnight prayers, as noted in the Siddur,[5] see there at length. We find there, "The crown of our head is fallen; woe to us, for we have sinned."[6] Therefore the Holy One is called the "humiliated King" in *Pirkei Hechalot*, as R. Moshe Cordovero wrote,

---

[9] *and thus "receive their nurture with greater force."* [10] Avot *4:15*. [11] Deut. *30:3*. [12] Megilla *29a*. ". . . *but 'He shall return,' to teach us that the Holy One, blessed be He, returns with them from the exiles.*"

Chapter 7
[1] *There are three elements in the soul, and it may be known by any of these names according to the context*—nefesh, ruach, *and* neshama. *Likutei Amarim I, ch. 1 describes the "animal nefesh" and ch. 2 the "Divine (or G-dly) nefesh."* (Devarim Rabba *2 notes two more discussed at length in Chassidut*—chaya *and* yechida.) [2] Is. *55:7*. [3] Song of Songs *7:6*. [4] cf. Tikunei Zohar 21:b; 124:b. [5]

היכלות הסט"א כביכול שמשם מקבל מחשבותיו ומעשיו. ומפני שהוא הממשיך להם ההשפעה לכן הוא נוטל חלק בראש וד"ל. וזהו שאמרו רז"ל אין בידינו לא משלות הרשעים וכו' בידינו דוקא כלומר בזמן הגלות אחר החורבן. וזוהי בחי' גלות השכינה כביכול להשפיע להיכלות הסט"א אשר שנאה נפשו ית'. וכשהאדם עושה תשובה נכונה אזי מסלק מהם ההשפעה שהמשיך במעשיו ומחשבותיו. כי בתשובתו מחזיר השפעת השכינה למקומה. וזהו תשוב ה"א תתאה מבחי' גלות וכמ"ש ושב ה' אלקיך את שבותך כלומר עם שבותך וכמאמר רז"ל והשיב לא נאמר וכו':

פרק ז ואולם דרך האמת והישר לבחי' תשובה תתאה ה"א תתאה הנ"ל הם ב' דברים דרך כלל. הא' הוא לעורר רחמים העליונים ממקור הרחמים על נשמתו ונפשו האלקי' שנפלה מאיגרא רמה חיי החיים ב"ה לבירא עמיקתא הן היכלות הטומאה והסט"א. ועל מקורה במקור החיים הוא שם הוי' ב"ה וכמ"ש וישוב אל הוי' וירחמהו. פי' לעורר רחמים על השפעת שם הוי' ב"ה שנשתלשלה וירדה תוך היכלות הסט"א הטמאים להחיותם ע"י מעשה אנוש ותחבולותיו ומחשבותיו הרעות וכמ"ש מלך אסור ברהטים ברהיטי מוחא וכו' היא בחי' גלות השכינה כנ"ל. וזמן המסוגל לזה הוא בתיקון חצות כמ"ש בסידור בהערה עש"ב. וז"ש שם נפלה עטרת ראשינו אוי נא לנו כי חטאנו. ולכן נקרא הקדב"ה מלך עלוב בפרקי היכלות כמ"ש הרמ"ק ז"ל כי

Siddur Im Dach 302, Kehot, *1965*.
[6] Lam. *5:16*.

for there is no humiliation deeper than this. Especially when the thoughtful meditate on the greatness of the Infinite, who encompasses[7] all worlds and permeates all worlds, each person according to the range of his intellect and understanding, will they be extremely grieved over this.

The second element is to crush and subdue evil, the husk and *sitra achra*, whose entire being is simply grossness and arrogance. "If you exalt yourself like the eagle . . ."[8] This crushing and subjugation is to be literally into the ground, for this is its death and nullification. Evil is crushed through a broken and shattered heart, a sense of personal unworthiness, repugnance . . . This is described in the Zohar on the verse, "The offerings of G-d (Elokim) are a broken spirit, a heart broken and shattered . . ."[9] All animal offerings are dedicated to G-d (the Tetragrammaton), the attribute of mercies. To Elokim, the Name indicating the attribute of justice, no animal offering is brought. Instead the offering is the sundering and removing of the spirit of defilement and *sitra achra*. This is the meaning of a "broken spirit."

●▲ How is the spirit of the *sitra achra* broken? When the heart is broken and crushed . . . And how is the heart to be broken and crushed? Only a minor part of this can be through mortifications and fasts in our generations. We cannot fast as did King David. Our sages remark on the verse, "My heart is a void within me"[10] —he destroyed it with fasts.[11]

But the true humbling of the heart, that it be broken and crushed, and the removal of the spirit of impurity and *sitra achra*, is achieved through being a "master of accounting"[12] with all the profundity of the mind. He must concentrate his intellect and understanding deeply for a period every day, or at night before *Tikun Chatzot*, to realise that through his sins he wrought the exile of the *Shechinah*, as noted above. He will also ponder that he [caused] the uprooting of his spirit and divine soul from the true Life, and demeaned it to a place of defilement and death, the chambers of the *sitra achra*. He must become deeply aware that his soul has become a vehicle for them, receiving from them vitality to endow his body, as noted above.

Our Sages declared that "The wicked while alive are dead."[13] Their ability to live is derived from the site of death and defilement. (Hence, the verse,

---

[7] *See Explanatory Notes, "On Learning Chassidus."* [8] Ovadiah *4;* Jer. *49:16.* [9] Psalm *51:19.* [10] Psalm *109:22.* [11] Berachot *61b;* Likutei Amarim *I, ch. 1, 13, etc.: David utterly destroyed the evil impulse within him.* [12] cf. Zohar *III 178a.* [13] Berachot *18b.*

כי אין לך עלבון גדול מזה. ובפרט כאשר יתבונן המשכיל בגדולת א"ס ב"ה ממכ"ע וסכ"ע כל א' וא' לפי שיעור שכלו והבנתו יתמרמר ע"ז מאד מאד: והב' לבטש ולהכניע הקליפה וסט"א אשר כל חיותה היא רק בחי' גסות והגבהה כמ"ש אם תגביה כנשר וכו'. והביטוש וההכנעה עד עפר ממש זוהי מיתתה וביטולה. והיינו ע"י לב נשבר ונדכה ולהיות נבזה בעיניו נמאס וכו'. וכמ"ש בזוה"ק ע"פ זבחי אלקי' רוח נשברה לב נשבר ונדכה וכו'. כי כל קרבן מן הבהמה הוא לשם הוי' היא מדת הרחמים. אבל לשם אלקים היא מדת הדין אין מקריבין קרבן בהמה כ"א לשבר ולהעביר רוח הטומאה והסט"א וזהו רוח נשברה. והאיך נשברה רוח הסט"א. כשהלב נשבר ונדכה וכו'. והאיך נשבר הלב ונדכה. הנה מעט מזעיר הוא ע"י סיגופים ותעניות בדורותינו אלה שאין לנו כח להתענות הרבה כדוד המלך כמאמר רז"ל ע"פ ולבי חלל בקרבי שהרגו בתענית. אך עיקר הכנעת הלב להיות נשבר ונדכה והעברת רוח הטומאה וסט"א הוא להיות ממארי דחושבנא בעומק הדעת להעמיק דעתו ובינתו שעה אחת בכל יום או לילה לפני תיקון חצות להתבונן במה שפעל ועשה בחטאיו בחי' גלות השכינה כנ"ל וגם [גרם] לעקור נשמתו ונפשו האלקי' מחיי החיים ב"ה והורידה למקום הטומאה והמות הן היכלות הסט"א ונעשית בבחי' מרכבה אליהם לקבל מהם שפע וחיות להשפיע לגופו כנ"ל. וזהו שאמרו רז"ל רשעים בחייהם קרויים מתים כלומר שחייהם נמשכים ממקום המות והטומאה (וכן מ"ש לא

"The dead will not praise . . ."[14] is no mockery of the impoverished,[15] G-d forbid. Rather, the reference is to the wicked who, while living, are called dead, for they are confused with alien thoughts while in their wickedness, and do not desire repentance, as is known.)

●▲ One who has never violated a sin of excision or a sin incurring death by divine agency, for example vain emission and the like, but other less severe sins, nonetheless suffers a defect in the spirit and divine soul, as in the analogy of the defects and severance of the fine strands of cord, as noted above. Through an accumulation of sins there can eventually be a defect as grave as from one prohibition involving excision or death. This would be true even when a single sin is repeated numerous times.

The prophet[16] compares sins to a cloud that dims the light of the sun. "I have wiped away like a cloud your transgressions"—these are the grave sins [that are barriers] between the internal of the power flowing forth from G-d and the divine soul. This barrier is like the separation of a thick cloud that stands between the sun and the earth with its inhabitants. "And like a cloud your sins"—these are the lesser sins that man tramples under heel,[17] sins that separate as does a thin and wispy cloud.

In the illustration, if one obscures the sunlight streaming through a window with many fine and lacy curtains, they will darken as much as one thick curtain will, and even more. Exactly so is the parallel, all those sins man tramples indifferently, and certainly those sins our Sages stormed against, that are actually like idolatry, immorality, and bloodshed.

Examples of these are sins like ignoring the needy[18]—"Beware lest there be in your heart something *belia'al*, unworthy . . ."[19] *Belia'al*, unworthy, is used in reference to idolatry . . .[20] Or tale-bearing,[21] the evil tongue that is equated with idolatry, immorality, and bloodshed. The vile-tempered[22] is like the idolatrous, and so is the arrogant.[23] There are many such described in the Talmud. Torah study equals them all,[24] as our Sages assert, "G-d has pardoned idolatry . . ."[25]

For this reason the order of *Kriat Shema* at

---

[14] Psalm *115:7*. [15] Proverbs *17:5*. Berachot *18a* *applies the verse to wearing tefillin in a cemetery, etc., a "mockery of the impoverished" who cannot perform the mitzvah.* [16] Is. *44:12*. *A discourse on this verse by Rabbi Menachem Mendel (1789–1866), author of Tzemach Tzedek, has been translated as a Supplement to "The Tzemach Tzedek and the Haskalah Movement," p. 100. The reader is warmly urged to study that discourse, for it treats much of the material in this Igeret Hateshuvah. It was originally delivered before Jewish troops in 1843* (ibid. *p. 55*). [17] Avodah Zara *18a; Rashi* on Deut. *7:12*. [18] cf. Avot *5:13*. [19] Deut. *15:9*. [20] Berachot *31b*. [21] cf. Shabbat *33;* Bava Batra *164b;* Erchin *15*. [22]

לא המתים יהללו כו׳ אינו כלועג לרש ח״ו אלא הכוונה על הרשעים שבחייהם קרויים מתים שמבלבלים אותם במחשבות זרות בעודם ברשעם ואינם חפיצים בתשובה כנודע). ואף מי שלא עבר על עון כרת וגם לא על עון מיתה בידי שמים שהוא הוצאת ז״ל וכה״ג אלא שאר עבירות קלות. אעפ״כ מאחר שהן פוגמים בנשמה ונפש האלקית וכמשל פגימת ופסיקת חבלים דקים כנ״ל. הרי בריבוי החטאים יכול להיות פגם כמו בלאו אחד שיש בו כרת או מיתה. ואפי׳ בכפילת חטא אחד פעמים רבות מאד. כמו שהמשיל הנביא החטאים לענן המאפיל אור השמש כמ״ש מחיתי כעב פשעיך הם עבירות חמורות [המבדילים] בין פנימית השפעת שם הוי׳ ב״ה לנפש האלקית. כהבדלת ענן עב וחשוך המבדיל בין השמש לארץ ולדרים עליה עד״מ. וכענן חטאתיך הן עבירות קלות שאדם דש בעקביו המבדילים כהבדלת ענן קל וקלוש עד״מ. והנה כמו שבמשל הזה אם משים אדם נגד אור השמש בחלון מחיצות קלות וקלושות לרוב מאד הן מאפילות כמו מחיצה אחת עבה ויותר. וככה ממש הוא בנמשל בכל עונות שאדם דש בעקביו ומכ״ש המפורסמות מדברי רז״ל שהן ממש כע״ז וג״ע וש״ד. כמו העלמת עין מן הצדקה כמ״ש השמר לך פן יהי׳ דבר עם לבבך בליעל כו׳ ובליעל היא ע״א וכו׳. והמספר בגנות חבירו היא לה״ר השקולה כע״ז וג״ע וש״ד וכל הכועס כאלו ע״ז וכן מי שיש בו גסות הרוח. וכהנה רבות בגמרא. ות״ת כנגד כולן כמארז״ל ויתר הקב״ה על ע״ז וכו׳. ולכן סידרו בק״ש שעל

המטה

---

cf. Shabbat *105b; Avot 2:10.* [23] Sotah *4b.* [24] Peah *1.* [25] *See above ch. 1 and Note 18.*

the bedside includes acceptance of the four executions of the Court... Besides, according to the mystical interpretation of *sod*, impairing the *yud* of the Name (Tetragrammaton) is like incurring lapidation; impairing the *hai* is like incurring burning; impairing the *vav* is like incurring the sword, and the latter *hai*, is like incurring strangulation. Neglecting the *Shema* impairs the *yud*, and tefillin the *hai*, tzitzit the *vav*, and worship the latter *hai*...

From this the intelligent can infer for other sins and transgressions, and for neglect of Torah, which equals them all.

•▲ Chapter 8

After deeply considering all this, he can truly plead, from the inmost heart, "In Your great mercies, wipe away my sins..."[1] By then his heart is thoroughly impressed with the pathetic state of the spark of divinity within him, and above, as noted. This plea is to arouse supreme mercies, of the Thirteen Traits of Compassion,[2] which come from the Supreme Will, symbolised in the "thorn" atop the *yud*, far transcending the flow issuing from the letters of His Name.

Because of their lofty origin these Attributes of Compassion correct all defects, as in the passage, "He bears sin and transgression, and cleanses."[2] With this awakening of mercies following the contrition, there is no further nurture for evil and *sitra achra* from the life-force emanating from the lower *hai*, as noted. (The latter *hai* returns to its proper place, united as before with the *yud-hai-vav*. This will suffice for the knowing.)

As there is a "restoration" of the *hai* above, so too below in the divine soul within man, no more do "your sins divide."[3] It is said, "He cleanses"—those who come back to Him,[4] to lave and cleanse their souls of the soiled garments, the "externals" that the Talmud describes as "encrusting..."[5]

• After the cleansing spirit passes over and purifies them, then their souls are enabled to return unto G-d Himself, literally, to ascend the greatest heights, to their very source, and cleave to Him with a remarkable unity. This is the original unity, the ultimate in union, that existed before the soul was blown by the breath of His mouth to descend and be incorporated

Chapter 8

[1] Psalm *51:3*. [2] cf. Ex. *34:6–7*. *In Likutei Sichot IV (Kehot, 1964), p. 1058, Note 14, the Lubavitcher Rebbe makes this observation: The original verse (*Ex. *34:7) quoted here includes the word "v'chata'a," the unintentional sin, as well as the other two, intentional sins. Igeret Hateshuvah omits this one word. The reason for the omission is that in our text the Thirteen Traits of Compassion are called forth to "correct all defects," referring to deliberate sins for which no offering is provided. Supreme mercies alone can avail the sinner. The chata'a, unintentional sin, does have the chatat offering, and is commuted without calling upon "supreme" mercies. On the other hand, the verse describing the Thirteen Traits does include*

המטה לקבל עליו ד׳ מיתות ב״ד וכו׳. מלבד שעפ״י הסוד כל הפוגם באות יו״ד של שם הוי׳ כאילו נתחייב סקילה והפוגם באות ה״א כאילו נתחייב שריפה ובאות וי״ו כאילו נתחייב הרג ובאות ה״א אחרונה כאילו נתחייב חנק. והמבטל ק״ש פוגם באות יו״ד ותפילין באות ה״א וציצית באות וי״ו ותפלה באות ה״א וכו׳. ומזה יכול המשכיל ללמוד לשאר עונות וחטאי׳ וביטול תורה כנגד כולן:

פרק ח והנה אחרי העמקת הדעת בכל הנ״ל יוכל לבקש באמת מעומקא דלבא כרוב רחמיך מחה פשעי וכו׳. כי אזי תקבע בלבו באמת גודל הרחמנות על בחי׳ אלקות שבנפשו ושלמעלה כנ״ל. ובזה יעורר רחמים העליונים מי״ג מדה״ר הנמשכות מרצון העליון ב״ה הנרמז בקוצו של יו״ד שלמעלה מעלה מבחי׳ ההשפעה הנשפעת מאותיות שם הוי׳. ולכן הי״ג מדות הרחמים מנקים כל הפגמים וכמ״ש נושא עון ופשע ונקה. ושוב אין יניקה להחיצונים והסט״א מהשפעת ה״א תתאה כנ״ל (ובזה תשוב ה״א תתאה למקומה להתייחד ביה״ו וד״ל). וכן ממש למטה בנפש האלקית שבאדם שוב אין עונותיכם מבדילים וכמ״ש ונקה מנקה הוא לשבים לרחוץ ולנקות נפשם מלבושים הצואים הם החיצונים כמ״ש בגמ׳ מלפפתו וכו׳. ומאחר שרוח עברה ותטהרם אזי תוכל נפשם לשוב עד הוי׳ ב״ה ממש ולעלות מעלה מעלה למקורה ולדבקה בו ית׳ ביחוד נפלא. כמו שהיתה מיוחדת בו ית׳ בתכלית היחוד בטרם שנפחה ברוח פיו ית׳ לירד למטה ולהתלבש

בגוף

---

chata'a, because of the following words —"He cleanses, and cleanses not," meaning that He forgives those who return, but not the recalcitrant, as our text will shortly note. Even for unintentional sins, the verse declares, "return" is required. [3] Is. *59:2.* [4] Yoma *86a.* [5] Sotah *3b. Man's good works precede him in the Coming World and his sins encrust him.*

within the body of man. (To illustrate this unity: before one exhales, the breath is united with the person; he and his breath are not separable yet.) This is the perfect return, teshuvah.

This state of unity and this return are called *teshuvah ila'a*, the superior return, that follows *teshuvah tata'a*, the inferior return. The Zohar, in *Raya Mehemna* on Nasso, explains that *teshuvah ila'a* is being occupied with Torah study, in reverence and fear of the Holy One . . . for this is *ben yud-hai* or *binah* . . .[6] (Here the superiority of the penitent over the perfectly saintly, as the Zohar states in *Chayei Sara*, is that "They draw onto themselves with a more intense longing of the heart, and with greater forcefulness, to approach the King . . .")[7]

•▲Chapter 9

The explanation of this subject is discussed frequently in Zohar and *Tikunim*. Binah is the superior teshuvah—"The mother crouching over the chicks . . ."[1] He is to meditate profoundly and with concentration on the greatness of G–d, and through his intellectual comprehension arouses a sense of intellectual reverence and love, rationally, intelligently. This love is that of the verse, "To love the Lord your G–d" for "He is your life . . ."[2] He will not be content with the endowed,[3] latent love alone . . . So too with fear of G–d, and terror or shame . . . as is known. This is the import of "The mother crouching over the chicks . . ."

Ahava, love, is primarily the cleaving of spirit to spirit, as "He kisses me with the kisses of his mouth . . ."[4] as is known. This cleaving of spirit is the meaning of "With all your soul,"[5] with every aspect of your soul, with intellect, emotions and their garbs of thought, speech and deed. All cleave to Him. Man's emotional faculties are bound up with His—"As He is merciful . . ."[6] Man's intellect adheres to His intellect and wisdom, assiduous Torah study, for "Torah issues from Wisdom."[7] Man's thought is devoted to G–d's, and his speech is the word of G–d, the Halacha,[8] as in the passages, "I have placed My word in your mouth,"[9] and "My words that I have placed in your mouth."[10] Man's deeds shall be works of charity, to revive the spirit of the fallen,[11] thus cleaving to G–d's actions, as in, "For six days G–d wrought . . ."[12]

---

[6] *As noted earlier,* yud *or* chochmah *is the germ of the idea and* hai *or* binah *is its amplification and development. In* binah *there is the beginning of an emotive response to the intellectual comprehension, even before the emotions are actually manifest. This state of "intellectual" love and fear is* ben yud-hai, *the "offspring" of intellect, the same Hebrew letters as* binah. [7] Zohar *I 129b;* Berachot *34b.*

Chapter 9

[1] Deut. *22:6.* Binah *is the "mother" and emotions the "offspring," or as the verse has it, the "chicks." These emotions are man's creations, the product of his efforts. They are results of intellectual endeavour, not gift or heritage.* [2] Deut. *30:20.* [3] *See* Likutei Amarim *I, ch. 44, etc., and*

בגוף האדם (וכמו עד"מ באדם הנופח ברוח פיו בטרם שיוצא הרוח מפיו הוא מיוחד בנפשו) וזו היא תשובה שלימה. והנה בחי' יחוד זה ותשובה זו היא בחי' תשובה עילאה שלאחר תשובה תתאה וכמ"ש בזוה"ק בר"מ פ' נשא דתשובה עילאה היא דיתעסק באוריי' בדחילו ורחימו דקדב"ה וכו' דאיהו בן י"ה בינה וכו' (ומעלת בעלי תשובה על צדיקים גמורים בזה היא כמ"ש בזוה"ק פ' חיי שרה דאינון משכי עלייהו ברעותא דלבא יתיר ובחילא סגי לאתקרבא למלכא וכו'):

פרק ט וביאור הענין כמ"ש בזוה"ק ותיקוני' בכמה מקומות. דבינה איהי תשובה עילאה והאם רובצת על האפרוחים וכו'. דהיינו שע"י שמתבונן בגדולת ה' בהעמקת הדעת ומוליד מרוח בינתו דו"ר שכליים ובטוב טעם ודעת כענין שנא' לאהבה את ה' אלקיך משום כי הוא חייך וכו' ולא די לו באהבה טבעית המסותרת לבד וכו'. וכן ביראה ופחד או בושה וכו' כנודע. אזי נקראת האם רובצת על האפרוחי' וכו'. והנה עיקר האהבה היא אתדבקות רוחא ברוחא כמ"ש ישקני מנשיקות פיהו וכו' כנודע. וע"ז נאמר ובכל נפשך שהם הם כל חלקי הנפש שכל ומדות ולבושיהם מחשבה דיבור ומעשה לדבקה כולן בו ית' דהיינו המדות במדותיו ית' מה הוא רחום וכו'. והשכל בשכלו וחכמתו ית' הוא עיון התורה דאורייתא מחכמה נפקא. וכן המחשבה במחשבתו ית' והדיבור בדבר ה' זו הלכה וכמ"ש ואשים דברי בפיך ודברי אשר שמתי בפיך. והמעשה הוא מעשה הצדקה להחיות רוח שפלים כמ"ש כי ששת ימים עשה ה' וכו'

II, pg. 283, on the concealed and created love. [4] Song of Songs *1:2.* [5] Deut. *6:5.* [6] Yerushalmi Peah *1:1;* Sotah *14a;* Shabbat *133b;* Rambam Yad "Deot" *1:5 and 6.* [7] Zohar *II 85a.* [8] cf. Shabbat *138b.* [9] Is. *51:16.* [10] Ibid., *59:* 12. [11] Ibid., *57:15.* [12] Ex. *20:11.*

as is known elsewhere.

This is the cleaving of spirit to spirit—the ultimate attachment and union as a result of love . . . Since the violation of the covenant through wasteful emission, to say nothing of stark immorality or unions prohibited by Torah or the Sages (for the words of the Sages are more grave . . .),[13] causes a blemish in the mind, therefore his rectification is that he occupy himself with Torah that derives from Wisdom.

In *Tanna Dvai Eliahu* we find, "A man commits a sin and is liable to death before the Almighty, what shall he do and live? If he was accustomed to studying one page, he shall study two, to studying one chapter, he shall study two chapters . . ." This parallels the illustration of the cord severed and then reknotted—the place of the knot is so much thicker than the unaffected portion. So it is with the "Cord of His possession."

"With kindness and truth is sin forgiven . . ."[14] and "There is no 'truth' but Torah . . ."[15]

Similarly, "The sin of the house of Eli will not be remitted by offerings"[16] Only offerings are ineffective, but they will be pardoned through Torah and good deeds, as explained in *Rosh Hashana* end of Ch. I.[17]

•▲ Chapter 10

This superior form of teshuvah, the cleaving of spirit to spirit through intellectual study of Torah and physical performance of acts of kindness, is a matter of eliciting from Above—that the word of G-d shall actually be in his mouth, as in "I place my words in your mouth,"[1] and "His right hand embraces me"[2] because of man's acts of kindness since "Kindness is the right arm . . ."[3]

But the mortal man must move from stage to stage, ascending gradually until he attains this superior teshuvah and cleaving of spirit to spirit. He ascends through the heart's devoted worship, particularly during *Shema* and its blessings, that he might in perfect truth say, "You shall love . . . with all your heart and with all your soul . . ."[4] and "These words shall be . . . speak of them . . ."[5] The word of G-d must truly be in his mouth, and there is no truth . . .[6]

Then he must assiduously perform all the mitzvot, for "He has sanctified us with His commandments." This sanctification is identical with "You are sanctified unto me."[7] This is the highest degree of sacredness, an expression of separation and apartness, that cannot

[13] cf. Berachot *4b;* Eruvin *22b;* Sanhedrin *88b.* [14] Prov. *16:6.* [15] cf. Berachot *5b.* [16] *I* Samuel *3:4.* [17] *18a.*

Chapter 10
[1] Is. *51:16.* [2] Song of Songs *2:6.* [3] Tikunei Zohar, *Introduction.* [4] Deut. *6:5.* [5] *6:6–7.* [6] . . . *but Torah.* [7] Kiddushin *5b; formula declaring betrothal.*

וכו׳ כנודע במ״א. וזו היא אתדבקות דרוחא ברוחא בתכלית הדביקות והיחוד כשהיא מחמת אהבה וכו׳. ולפי שפגם הברית בהוצאת ז״ל ואצ״ל בעריות או שאר איסורי ביאה דאורייתא או דרבנן (כי חמורים ד״ס וכו׳) פוגם במוח לכן תיקונו הוא דיתעסק באורייתא דמחכמה נפקא. וז״ש בתנא דבי אליהו אדם עבר עבירה ונתחייב מיתה למקום מה יעשה ויחיה אם היה רגיל לקרות דף אחד יקרא ב׳ דפים לשנות פרק א׳ ישנה ב׳ פרקים וכו׳. והיינו כמשל חבל הנפסק וחוזר וקושרו שבמקום הקשר הוא כפול ומכופל. וככה הוא בחבל נחלתו וכו׳. וזש״ה בחסד ואמת יכופר עון וכו׳ ואין אמת אלא תורה וכו׳. ועון בית עלי בזבח ומנחה הוא דאינו מתכפר אבל מתכפר בתורה וגמ״ח כדאי׳ בספ״ק דר״ה:

פרק י **והנה** תשובה עילאה זו דאתדבקותא דרוחא ברוחא ע״י תורה וגמ״ח. היא בבחי׳ המשכה מלמעלה למטה להיות דבר ה׳ ממש בפיו וכמ״ש ואשים דברי בפיך. וימינו תחבקני בגמ״ח דחסד דרועא ימינא וכו׳. אבל אדם התחתון צריך לילך ממדרגה למדרגה ממטה למעלה היא בחי׳ תשובה עילאה ואתדבקות רוחא ברוחא בכוונת הלב בתפלה ובפרט בק״ש וברכותיה. כדי לומר ואהבת כו׳ בכל לבבך ובכל נפשך וכו׳ באמת לאמיתו. וכן והיו הדברים האלה וכו׳ ודברת בם וכו׳ להיות דבר ה׳ בפיו באמת ואין אמת וכו׳. וכן לקיים כל המצות כמ״ש אשר קדשנו במצותיו כמו הרי את מקודשת לי היא בחי׳ קדש העליון לשון פרישות והבדלה שאינו

יכול

be contained within Creation since "All are considered as naught before Him."[8] This sacredness attains to the state of Encompassing all worlds, the Supreme Will . . . as discussed in Likutei Amarim, ch. 46.

After worship again we say, "To You, O G-d, I lift my soul,"[9] that spirit cleave to spirit all through the day . . . All this is brought about through meditation on the greatness of the Infinite, concentrating the mind deeply in the two blessings preceding *Shema* and in *Psukai d'zimra*,[10] as is known.

●▲ Since the *tefilla*[11] is the state of *teshuvah ila'a*, the higher return, it must be preceded by *teshuvah tata'a*, the lower return. This is what the Sages intended in the Mishna,[12] "One embarks on worship only with earnestness." Rashi explains, "Humility." This is the state of *teshuvah tata'a*, to arouse divine compassion, as noted above, and as the Talmud infers from the passage, "She was embittered."[13]

At the same time we must note the Beraita[14] there, "Our Sages taught, 'One embarks on worship only with joy.'" In our bereaved generation, when not all are capable of turning their hearts instantly from the extreme of humility to joy, it is advised that the time for *teshuvah tata'a* be designated at *Tikun Chatzot*, as we noted above. Whoever cannot do this nightly should maintain an absolute minimum of once every week, before the Shabbat. It is familiar to the initiates that Shabbat is on the order of *teshuvah ila'a*, and the very letters of the word Shabbat[15] spell *tashev*, as in, "You return man."[16] On Shabbat all the worlds ascend to their source . . . The Shabbat worship particularly is on the order of *teshuvah ila'a*. This will suffice for the knowledgeable.

(We can now understand the verse, "Return to Me, for I have redeemed you."[17] Since "I have wiped away your sins like a cloud"[18]—removing the *sitra achra*, and "I have redeemed you" from evil through the arousal of the Supreme Compassion following the initiative taken by man below in his *teshuvah tata'a*, as explained above—therefore, "Return to Me"—with *teshuvah ila'a*.)

●▲ Chapter 11

This subject, harbouring contrary emotions simultaneously in the heart, humility—the state of *teshuvah tata'a* as explained, and gladness as well, has already been discussed in Likutei Amarim, end of ch.

---

[8] Zohar. [9] Psalm *86:4*. [10] *The verses of praise drawn mainly from the Psalms, which expound on G-d's greatness as Creator, the beauty and magnitude of His works. Then in the blessings before Shema we find the exalted fervour of the angels, their reverence and love of G-d. These are introductions to Shema and the Shemona Esrai following.* [11] Tefilla, *"prayer" properly refers to Shemona Esrai, and is the fulfillment of the mitzvah of prayer.* [12] Berachot *30b*. [13] *I* Samuel *1:10*. [14] Berachot *31a*. [15] Bereishit Rabba *22*. [16] Psalm *90:3*. [17] Is. *44:22*. [18] Is. *44:22*.

יכול להתלבש תוך עלמין משום דכולא קמיה כלא חשיב אלא בבחי׳ סובב כ״ע הוא רצון העליון ב״ה וכו׳ כמ״ש בלק״א פמ״ו. וגם אחר התפלה אומרים אליך ה׳ נפשי אשא דהיינו לאתדבקא רוחא ברוחא כל היום וכו׳. וכל זה ע״י ההתבוננות בגדולת א״ס ב״ה בהעמקת הדעת בשתים לפניה ובפסוקי דזמרה כנודע. ומאחר שהתפלה היא בחי׳ תשובה עילאה צריך להקדים לפניה בחי׳ תשובה תתאה. וז״ש רז״ל במשנה אין עומדין להתפלל אלא מתוך כובד ראש ופרש״י הכנעה והיא בחי׳ תשובה תתאה לעורר רחמים כנ״ל וכדיליף התם בגמ׳ מקרא דכתיב והיא מרת נפש. אכן בברייתא שם ת״ר אין עומדין להתפלל אלא מתוך שמחה. ועכשיו בדור יתום הזה שאין הכל יכולין להפוך לבם כרגע מן הקצה. אזי עצה היעוצה להקדים בחי׳ תשובה תתאה בתיקון חצות כנ״ל. ומי שא״א לו בכל לילה עכ״פ לא יפחות מפעם א׳ בשבוע לפני יום השבת כנודע ליודעים שהשבת היא בחי׳ תשובה עילאה ושב״ת אותיות תש״ב אנוש כי בשבת היא עליות העולמות למקורם כו׳ ובפרט תפלות השבת וד״ל. (ובזה יובן מ״ש שובה אלי כי גאלתיך פי׳ כי מאחר שמחיתי כעב פשעיך היא העברת הסט״א וגאלתיך מן החיצונים בהתעוררות רחמים עליונים באתערותא דלתתא בתשובה תתאה כנ״ל אזי שובה אלי בתשובה עילאה):

פרק יא ואמנם להיות בלבו ההכנעה היא בחי׳ תשובה תתאה כנ״ל וגם השמחה בה׳ שתיהן ביחד. כבר מילתא אמורה בלק״א ס״פ ל״ד

34. It has been illuminated by the Zohar,[1] "Joy is lodged in one side of my heart . . ." Joined to this is the faith and confidence, the heart being firm and certain in G–d that He desires goodness,[2] and is gracious and merciful[3] and generously forgiving[4] the instant one pleads for forgiveness and atonement of Him. ("According to Your great mercies wipe away my sins; lave me, purify me, wipe away all my sins . . .")[5] Not the faintest vestige of doubt dilutes this absolute conviction.

For this reason, in every Shemona Esrai, the moment we plead, "Forgive us . . ." we conclude, "Blessed are You, O G–d, gracious and generous in pardon." Without the certainty of pardon this would be a case of doubtful blessing, which we do not recite lest it be a blessing in vain.[6] But there is no doubt here whatsoever, for we have asked, "Forgive us, pardon us." Furthermore, were we not to repeat our transgressions we would be immediately redeemed,[7] in accordance with the blessing we recite, "Blessed are You, O G–d, Who redeems Israel."

Even by human standards this certainty of pardon is legitimate. One must forgive as soon as he is asked for pardon. He must not be cruel and vindictive, even when one mutilates another, as we find in *Bava Kama*,[8] end of ch. 8. If one has asked his fellow for forgiveness three times and has been rebuffed, he need not apologise further.

When King David[9] asked the Gibeonites to forgive King Saul who had killed Gibeonites, they refused to pardon him. David decreed that they shall not enter the Congregation of G–d, who are merciful . . . See *Yevamot*,[10] end of ch. 8.

As a divine trait, forgiveness is as swift, and infinitely more so.

●▲ The praise and blessing addressed to G–d, "Gracious and generous in forgiveness," emphasises the word *marbeh*, "generous," implying multiplicity. This term is used in Ezra, "Generous in pardon." It is characteristic of men, that if one injures another and asks his pardon which is granted, and then repeats the misdeed, it becomes more difficult to grant pardon again, and certainly a third and fourth time.

But by the standard of G–d, there is no difference between once and a thousand times. Pardon is a manifestation of the attribute of mercy. Divine attributes are not bounded and finite; they are infinite

---

Chapter 11
[1] *II 255a; III 75a.* [2] Micha *7:18.* [3] Nehemiah *9:17.* [4] cf. Is. *55:7.* [5] Psalm *51:3, 4, 11.* [6] Berachot *33a.* [7] cf. Sanhedrin *97b.* [8] *92a.* [9] *II* Samuel *21.* [10] *78b and 79a.*

ל״ד. כמ״ש בזוה״ק חדוה תקיעא בלבאי מסטרא דא וכו׳ ובצירוף עוד האמונה והבטחון להיות נכון לבו בטוח בה׳ כי חפץ חסד הוא וחנון ורחום ורב לסלוח תיכף ומיד שמבקש מחילה וסליחה מאתו ית׳ (כרוב רחמיך מחה פשעי כבסני טהרני וכל עוונותי מחה וכו׳) בלי שום ספק וס״ס בעולם. וכמו שאנו מברכין בכל תפלת י״ח תיכף שמבקשים סלח לנו כו׳ ברוך אתה ה׳ חנון המרבה לסלוח והרי ספק ברכות להקל משום חשש ברכה לבטלה אלא אין כאן שום ספק כלל מאחר שבקשנו סלח לנו מחל לנו. ואילו לא היינו חוזרים וחוטאים היינו נגאלין מיד כמו שאנו מברכין בא״י גואל ישראל. והרי אפי׳ במדת ב״ו כן שצריך האדם למחול תיכף ומיד שמבקשים ממנו מחילה ולא יהא אכזרי מלמחול ואפי׳ בקוטע יד חבירו כדאי׳ בגמ׳ בספ״ח דב״ק. ואם ביקש ממנו ג״פ ולא מחל לו שוב א״צ לבקש ממנו. והגבעונים שביקש דוד המלך ע״ה מהם מחילה בעד שאול שהמית את הגבעונים ולא רצו למחול גזר דוד עליהם שלא יבאו בקהל ה׳ שהם רחמנים וכו׳ כדאי׳ בפ״ח דיבמות. ובמדת הקב״ה עאכ״ו לאין קץ. ומה שמשבחים ומברכים את ה׳ חנון המרבה לסלוח המרבה דייקא וכמ״ש בעזרא ורב לסלוח. דהיינו שבמדת ב״ו אם יחטא איש לאיש וביקש ממנו מחילה ומחל לו ואח״כ חזר לסורו קשה מאד שימחול לו שנית ומכ״ש בשלישית ורביעית. אבל במדת הקב״ה אין הפרש בין פעם א׳ לאלף פעמים כי המחילה היא ממדת הרחמים ומדותיו הקדושות אינן בבחי׳ גבול ותכלית אלא בבחי׳ א״ס כמ״ש

as in the verse, "For His mercies have not ended."[11] In terms of infinity there is no difference whatsoever between a small number and a large one. Before Him all are considered as naught,[12] and He makes equal the small and the great . . .[13]

Therefore "He removes our sins every year."[14] All the sins confessed in the *Al Chet* annually, though repeatedly violated, are again confessed on Yom Kippur in the coming year, and so on always. "Every year" is not necessarily a yearly pardon, for three times every day we pronounce, "Blessed are You, O G–d, gracious and generous in forgiveness."

The Talmud[15] tells us that the prayers were introduced in place of the regular altar offerings. The daily morning offering was to atone for the sins of the previous night, and the regular evening sacrifice atoned for the sins of the past day, and so on day by day constantly. "Every year" means only that Yom Kippur atones for the grave sins, while the regular offerings, the *olah*, atoned only for violations of positive commands.[16] In our time, worship with repentance replaces offerings, as noted above.

But this is not an attitude of "I will sin and later repent."[17] That is relevant only if while committing the sin he could have overcome his impulse to evil, but depended in his heart on repenting later. Since the opportunity to repent caused him to sin, "He is not granted an opportunity . . ."[17] Withal he is not *granted* an opportunity. But if he pressed forcefully and overpowered his evil impulse and did repent, then his repentance is accepted.[18]

But we who plead daily, "Forgive us," preface that prayer with "Bring us back with a perfect repentance before You," that is, that we revert no more to folly. On Yom Kippur too we ask, "May it be Your will that I sin no more."[19] For us opportunity is granted, freely. "Whoever comes to purify himself is given assistance."[20] Whoever *comes*, as soon as he comes, and the pardon and forgiveness are also granted forthwith.

●▲ "My sin is before me always,"[21] does not imply that one ought constantly be melancholy, humiliated, G–d forbid, for a following verse declares, "Let me hear gladness and joy . . . and the free spirit shall uphold me . . ."[22] He ought all his days experience *teshuvah ila'a*,

---

[11] Lam. *3:22.* [12] cf. Daniel *4:32.* [13] *V'chol maaminim in Rosh Hashana and Yom Kippur prayers.* [14] Yom Kippur Machzor. [15] Berachot *26a.* [16] *See ch. 2 above.* [17] Yoma *85a.* [18] Yoma *87a;* Shulchan Aruch Orach Chaim *606:1.* [19] Machzor. [20] Shabbat *104a.* [21] Psalm *51:5.* [22] Psalm *51:10, 14.*

כמ"ש כי לא כלו רחמיו. ולגבי בחי' א"ס אין הפרש כלל בין מספר קטן לגדול דכולא קמי' כלא ממש חשיב ומשוה קטן וגדול וכו'. ולכן מעביר אשמותינו בכל שנה ושנה וכל החטאי' שמתוודים בעל חטא מדי שנה אף שחזר ועבר עליהם חוזר ומתודה עליהם ביוה"כ בשנה הבאה וכן לעולם. ובכל שנה ושנה לאו דוקא אלא כמו כן בכל יום ויום ג"פ מברכי' בא"י חנון המרבה לסלוח וכמארז"ל תפלה כנגד תמידין תקנוה. ותמיד של שחר הי' מכפר על עבירות הלילה ותמיד של בין הערביים על של יום וכן מדי יום ביום לעולם. אלא שיוה"כ מכפר על עבירות חמורות. והתמיד שהוא קרבן עולה מכפר על מ"ע בלבד. וכן התפלה בזמן הזה עם התשובה כנ"ל. ואין זה אחטא ואשוב. כי היינו דוקא שבשעת החטא היה יכול לכבוש יצרו אלא שסומך בלבו על התשובה ולכן הואיל והתשובה גורמת לו לחטוא אין מספיקין וכו'. ואף גם זאת אין מספיקין דייקא. אבל אם דחק ונתחזק ונתגבר על יצרו ועשה תשובה מקבלין תשובתו. אבל אנו שמבקשים בכל יום סלח לנו אנו מקדימין לבקש והחזירנו בתשובה שלימה לפניך דהיינו שלא נשוב עוד לכסלה וכן ביוה"כ מבקשים יהי רצון מלפניך שלא אחטא עוד מספיקין ומספיקין כמארז"ל הבא לטהר מסייעין אותו הבא דייקא מיד שבא ואי לזאת גם הסליחה והמחילה היא מיד. ומ"ש וחטאתי נגדי תמיד אין המכוון להיות תמיד עצב נבזה ח"ו דהא כתיב בתרי' תשמיעני ששון ושמחה וכו' ורוח נדיבה תסמכני וכו' ומשום שצ"ל כל ימיו בתשובה עילאה

שהיא

which is marked by great joy, as we noted above. "Before me" is the term *negdi*, as in "Stand *mineged*,"[23] and "*Mineged* around the Tent of Assembly shall they camp."[24] Rashi defines the term as "at a distance." The intention of our verse is merely that his heart does not become haughty,[25] that he be of humble spirit before all men,[26] for the remembrance is between his eyes[27] that he has sinned before G–d.

In fact, as far as gladness is concerned, the remembrance will be especially effective in encouraging happiness in the face of whatever misfortunes threaten to overtake him, whether from Heaven or caused by man, whether in speech or in deed. (This constant awareness of one's sins is good counsel to be immune to anger or any sort of resentment . . .) The Talmud[28] declares, "Those humiliated who do not humiliate in turn, who hear their insult and do not retort, who perform out of love and are happy in affliction . . ." Whoever passes over his feelings, all his sins are passed over.[29]

•▲*Chapter 12*

The reason for "Happiness in the afflictions"[1] of the body is that they are a great and potent favour for the sinning soul, to cleanse it in This World and to redeem it from purification in the next. (This is particularly true in our generations, when it is not possible to fast in accordance with the prescriptions in the penances of the Ari, fasts imperative for the cleansing of the soul, to rescue it from cleansing in Gehinnom.)

Nachmanides, in his Introduction to the *Commentary* on Job, writes that even the sufferings of Job for seventy years have absolutely no comparison to the suffering of a soul even briefly in Gehinnom, for fire is one part of sixty . . . It is only that the world is built by kindness,[2] and through mild suffering in This World one is saved from severe judgments in the Coming World.

The movement of a shadow on earth of a few inches equals the sun's movement in the heaven of thousands of miles . . . Infinitely more so is this true in the parallel, in the descent of the worlds, from the most exalted heights until this physical world. We see this in the Zohar's comments on the subject of the elevation of the higher worlds

---

[23] *II* Samuel *18:13*. [24] Numbers *2:2*. [25] cf. Deut. *17:20*. [26] cf. Avot *4:10 and 4*. [27] cf. Ex. *13:9*. [28] Shabbat *88b*. "*. . . they are meant in the verse: Those who love Him (shall be) like the sun rising in full strength (*Judges *5:31).*" [29] Rosh Hashana *17a*.

Chapter 12

[1] *Quoted end of last chapter.* [2] Psalm *89:3*.

שהיא בשמחה רבה כנ"ל אלא נגדי דייקא כמו ואתה תתיצב מנגד מנגד סביב לאהל מועד יחנו ופרש"י מרחוק. והמכוון רק לבלתי רום לבבו ולהיות שפל רוח בפני כל האדם כשיהיה לזכרון בין עיניו שחטא נגד ה'. ואדרבה לענין השמחה יועיל זכרון החטא ביתר שאת בכדי לקבל בשמחה כל המאורעות המתרגשות ובאות בין מן השמים בין ע"י הבריות בדיבור או במעשה (וזו עצה טובה להנצל מכעס וכל מיני קפידא וכו') וכמארז"ל הנעלבים ואינן עולבין שומעי' חרפתם ואין משיבי' עושים מאהבה ושמחי' ביסורי' וכו' וכל המעביר על מדותיו מעבירי' לו על כל פשעיו:

פרק יב וטעם השמחה ביסורי הגוף לפי שהיא טובה גדולה ועצומה לנפש החוטאת למרקה בעה"ז ולהצילה מהמירוק בגיהנם (בפרט בדורותינו אלה שאין ביכולת להתענות כפי מספר כל הצומות שבתיקוני תשובה מהאר"י ז"ל הצריכות למירוק הנפש להצילה ממירוק בגיהנם) וכמ"ש הרמב"ן ז"ל בהקדמה לפי' איוב שאפי' יסורים של איוב ע' שנה אין להן ערך כלל ליסורי הנפש שעה אחת בגיהנם כי אש א' מששים וכו'. אלא לפי שעוה"ז חסד יבנה וביסורין קלין בעוה"ז ניצול מדיני' קשים של עוה"ב כמשל הילוך והעתקת הצל בארץ טפח לפי הילוך גלגל השמש ברקיע אלפים מילין וכו'. ויתר על כן לאין קץ הוא בנמשל בבחי' השתלשלות העולמות מרום המעלות עד עוה"ז הגשמי. וכנודע ממ"ש בזוה"ק מענין עליות עולמות העליוני'

as a result of the initiative taken by man below. The Zohar describes the effects of the offering of one fowl, a dove or pigeon, or a handful of meal, on the altar. Such are the effects of all the mitzvot of performance, as known from the Ari.

This too is our Sages' comment on the verse, "Sanctify yourselves and you shall be holy"[3]—man sanctifies himself only a little below, and he becomes sanctified in great measure from above...[4] (It was noted above in reference to "Who sanctified us with His commandments..." that Israel's sanctification through mitzvot is bound up with the Infinite, that Encompasses all worlds...)

Precisely so is it in reference to reward and punishment, as our Sages[5] say, "The reward of a mitzvah is a mitzvah..." as discussed elsewhere. This knowledge is elementary to the understanding, and those with intelligence in this matter will discover good.

---

[3] Lev. *11:44*. [4] Yoma *39a*.
[5] Avot *4:2*.

העליוני׳ באתערותא דלתתא בהקרבת עוף אחד בן יונה או תור ע״ג המזבח או קומץ מנחה. וכן הוא בכל המצות מעשיות כנודע מהאריז״ל. וז״ש רז״ל ע״פ והתקדשתם והייתם קדושים אדם מקדש עצמו מעט מלמטה מקדשין אותו הרבה מלמעלה וכו׳ (וכמ״ש לעיל בענין אשר קדשנו במצותיו וכו׳ בחי׳ סוכ״ע וכו׳) וככה ממש הוא בענין שכר ועונש כמארז״ל שכר מצוה מצוה וכו׳ וכמ״ש במ״א. ודעת לנבון נקל ומשכיל על דבר ימצא טוב:

●▲ I. We begin with a benediction,[1] to bless and to give thanks to the Lord, for He is good:[2] my soul has heard and was revived[3] by a good tiding—there is no Good but Torah,[4] the Torah of the Lord is whole[5]—referring to the completion of the whole Talmud in most cities and congregations of our followers.[6] Gratitude for the past, and a request for the future: may G–d grant and continue to strengthen their hearts among the mighty[7] with the might of Torah[8] in like manner from year to year, and make known to mankind the might of the Oral Torah[9] and its strong (עוז) power.[10]

King Solomon, peace be to him, explained: "She girds her loins with strength (עוז) . . ."[11] The "loins" are the faculty[12] which supports the whole body, with the head that was put and stands over them; and they are the ones that take and bring (the body) to its desired destination. And just as it is with the corporeality of the body, so it is with [the aspect of] the spiritual of the Divine soul. The true belief in the One G–d, the blessed En Sof—

[Who permeates all worlds and encompasses all worlds,[13] and there is no place void of Him[14] above to no end and below to no limit, and likewise in all four directions, truly in a state of infinitude, and likewise in the aspects of "year" and "soul",[15] as known.]

Now, this belief is referred to as the faculty of the "loins" which upholds and sustains[16] the "head," meaning the intellect that contemplates and cogitates on the greatness of the blessed En Sof in the aspects of "world," "year," "soul,"[17] and on the magnitude of His kindness and His wonders with us, that we are "A people near unto Him"[18] and truly "To cleave unto Him."[19] (Thus it is) known from the saying:[20] "One hour of repentance and good deeds in this world is better than all the life of the world to come." For the world to come is but a gleam and reflection of the [aspect called] Shechinah,[21] "Who dwells" . . .,[22] and was created by the single *yud* of His blessed Name.[23] . . . Repentance and good deeds, however, truly bring Israel nigh unto their Father in Heaven, unto His Being and Essence, as it were, [the aspect of infinitude, indeed], and as it is written:[24] "His splendour is over the earth and the heaven, and He exalts the horn of His people" . . .; "Who has sanctified us (to Himself) through His commandments, and commanded us."[25] . . . And as waters (reflect) the face . . .[26] from this contemplation are born the intellectual or the natural awe and love,[27]

---

[1] *This letter was written in reply to the* "good tiding . . . *referring to the completion of the whole Talmud" etc.; the author, therefore, responds firstly with a benediction, in accordance with the Talmudic precept (Berachot 59b) that one is to laud G–d for glad tidings.* Cf. Shulchan Aruch, Orach Chayim, 221:1; Seder Birchot Hanehenin, *by the author, ch. 12.* [2] Par. *Psalms 106:1; etc.* [3] Par. *Isaiah 55:3.* [4] *Avot VI:3; Berachot 5a.* [5] Par. *Psalms 19:8.* [6] אנשי שלומים (שלומינו), lit. "*men of (our) persuasion" (brotherhood); a term used to denote particular groups in general, and especially in frequent use among Chassidim, when referring to their own group(s). The term is of Biblical origin,* cf. *Jer. 38:22; Obadiah 1:7;* cf. *also Gen 34:21. The study of the*

א פותחין בברכה לברך ולהודות לה׳ כי
טוב. שמועה טובה שמעה
ותחי נפשי. אין טוב אלא תורה. תורת ה׳ תמימה.
זו השלמת כל הש״ס כולו ברוב עיירות ומנינים
מאנ״ש. הודאה על העבר ובקשה על העתיד. כה
יתן וכה יוסיף ה׳ לאמץ לבם בגבורים מדי שנה
בשנה בגבורה של תורה. ולהודיע לבני אדם גבורתה
של תורה שבע״פ וכחה עוז. פי׳ שלמה המלך ע״ה
חגרה בעוז מתניה כו׳. מתנים הם דבר המעמיד
כל הגוף עם הראש הנצב ועומד עליהם. והם
המוליכים ומביאים אותו למחוז חפצו. וכמו שהוא
בגשמיות הגוף כך הוא בבחי׳ רוחניות הנפש
האלהית האמונה האמיתית בה׳ אחד א״ס ב״ה דאיהו
ממכ״ע וסוכ״ע ולית אתר פנוי מיניה למעלה עד אין
קץ ולמטה עד אין תכלית וכן לד׳ סטרין בבחי׳ א״ס
ממש. וכן בבחי׳ שנה ונפש כנודע. הנה אמונה זו
נק׳ בשם בחי׳ מתנים דבר המעמיד ומקיים את הראש
הוא השכל המתבונן ומעמיק דעת בגדולת א״ס ב״ה
בבחי׳ עולם שנה נפש. וברוב חסדו ונפלאותיו עמנו
להיות עם קרובו ולדבקה בו ממש כנודע ממאמר
יפה שעה אחת בתשובה ומע״ט בעוה״ז מכל חיי
עוה״ב שהוא רק זיו והארה מבחי׳ הנק׳ שכינה השוכן
כו׳ ונברא ביו״ד א׳ משמו ית׳ כו׳ אבל תשובה
ומעשים טובים מקרבין ישראל לאביהם שבשמים
ממש למהותו ועצמותו כביכול בחי׳ א״ס ממש וכמ״ש
הודו על ארץ ושמים וירם קרן לעמו כו׳ אקב״ו כו׳
וכמים הפנים כו׳ להוליד מתבונה זו דו״ר שכליים או
טבעיים

---

complete Talmud, to which this letter refers, was not an incidental occasion. R. Shneur Zalman demanded of his followers that this should be done annually, in every city and, where so applicable, by every congregation; see Kuntress Acharon, *sect. IX.* [7] Par. *Amos 2:16, though relating it to Avot de R. Natan 23:1: "The mighty are none others than the mighty in Torah."* [8] *See Derech Eretz Zutah, ch. 4: "There is no might but in Torah." See also Numbers Rabba, 10:8.* [9] *See previous note; also, in the scheme of the Sefirot the Oral Torah is related to the Sefirah* gevurah—cf. *Zohar I:253a;* ibid. *III:257a;* et passim. [10] Lit.: וכחה עוז—*"and her strong power." The Torah is referred to as "power"*

(Notes cont. at end of Hebrew Text)

that there be a state of "Their heart cried unto the Lord,"[28] or a state of "Flashes of fire, a mighty flame"[29]—on a level of "advance" (*ratzo*), and, afterwards, on a level of "retreat" (*shov*)[30]—due to the fear of G-d in his heart and being abashed by His greatness . . . This is the aspect of "the left hand parries,"[31] as it is written of the Giving of the Torah:[32] "The people saw and they trembled, and they stood from afar . . ." And these are the faculties of the arms[33] and the body of the soul.[34]

●▲ But what gives the power and strength to the faculty of the loins—to support and sustain the head and the arms? It is the occupation with, and the study of the *halachot*[35] in the Oral Torah—which is the [state of] manifestation of the Supreme Will (*ratzon ha'elyon*).[36] For though "The Torah derives from *chochmah*,"[37] its source and [its] root surpasses exceedingly the rank of *chochmah*, and is [that which is] referred to as the blessed Supreme Will,[38] as it is written:[39] "As with a shield *ratzon ta'etrenu* (You encompass him with favour)"—as a crown[40] which is *over* the brains that are in the head, [and as known from what has been explained on the verse "A woman of valour is the crown of her husband"—and "whoever repeats *halachot* every day . . ."[41]].

This is the meaning of "She girds her loins with *strength*": there is no *strength* but Torah,[42] for it gives power and strength to the faculty of the loins—which are girded and embodied in it[43] to strengthen and fortify its "arms," namely the intellectual or natural awe and love, each one according to his measure. ([44]As regards supporting and sustaining the faculty of the "head" of the soul, i.e. the intellect that contemplates . . . [Solomon] said:[45] "She perceives that her trade is good," as explained elsewhere.)

However, the occasion and time for the strengthening and fortification of the "arms" and the "head" is the time of the morning-prayer. For above that is the time of compassion and a time of Supreme favour.[46] And, therefore, that I will seek after from those who seek the Lord: let them both contemplate and ponder, and have as a reminder between their eyes,[47] all that I wrote them last year in general, and especially with respect to the devotion of prayer from the depth of the heart.[48] Day after day they should seek the Lord with all their heart and with all their soul,[49] to pour out their soul as water in the presence of the Lord,[50] and as the saying of our sages, of blessed memory, in *Sifre*:[51] "To the extent of pressing out the soul . . ."

---

[28] Par. *Lament. 2:18.* [29] Par. *Song 8:6;* cf. Likutei Torah *III: 66b, and references cited there;* infra, *sect. XXIX.* [30] *See Ezek. I:14. "Advance" and "retreat" are two levels in the worship of G-d which—in their natural sequence—follow one upon the other, in this order.* Ratzo, *lit. running, signifies a fierce love and passion for G-d: "running" (advancing) toward G-d, in order to cleave unto Him.* Shov, *lit. returning, which follows upon, and is a still higher level than* ratzo, *signifies the occupation with Torah and* Mitzvot, *thus bringing the "advance" to its proper conclusion. By the "retreat" the Divine abundance is elicited and drawn earthwards, in, and through the fulfillment of the Torah and the commandments. While* advance *signi-*

טבעיים להיות בחי' צעק לבם אל ה' או בחי' רשפי אש ושלהבת עזה בבחי' רצוא ואח"כ בבחי' שוב להיות פחד ה' בלבו וליבוש מגדולתו כו' והוא בחי' שמאל דוחה כמ"ש במ"ת וירא העם וינועו ויעמדו מרחוק כו' והן בחי' הזרועות והגוף שבנפש:

אך מי הוא הנותן כח ועוז לבחי' מתנים להעמיד ולקיים הראש והזרועות הוא עסק ולימוד הלכות בחורה שבע"פ שהיא בחי' גילוי רצון העליון דאורייתא מחכמה היא דנפקת אבל מקורה ושרשה הוא למעלה מעלה מבחי' חכמה והוא הנקרא בשם רצון העליון ב"ה וכמ"ש כצנה רצון תעטרנו כעטרה שהיא על המוחין שבראש וכנודע ממ"ש ע"פ אשת חיל עטרת בעלה. וכל השונה הלכות בכל יום כו'. וזהו חגרה בעוז מתניה אין עוז אלא תורה שהיא נותנת כח ועוז לבחי' מתנים החגורים ומלובשים בה לחזק ולאמץ זרועותיה הן דו"ר שכליים או טבעיים כל חד לפום שיעורא דיליה. (ועל העמדת וקיום בחינת הראש שבנפש הוא השכל המתבונן כו' אמר טעמה כי טוב סחרה כו' ומבואר במ"א): אך עת וזמן החיזוק ואימוץ הזרועות והראש היא שעת תפלת השחר שהיא שעת רחמים ועת רצון העליון למעלה. ולזאת אותה אבקש ממבקשי ה' יבינו וישכילו יחדיו ולהיות לזכרון בין עיניהם כל מה שכתבתי אליהם אשתקד בכלל. ובפרט מענין כוונת התפלה מעומקא דלבא יום יום ידרשון ה' בכל לבם ובכל נפשם ונפשם תשתפך כמים נוכח פני ה' וכמארז"ל בספרי עד מיצוי הנפש כו':

ועתה

---

fies "love," retreat *includes "awe."* (Cf. Torah Or, *1d-2a, 25b)* In Likutei Torah *(IV: 19d), the author applies these two levels to Deut. 13:5: "You should go after the Lord your G-d"*—ratzo; *"Him you shall fear, His commandments you shall keep" etc.*—shov. [31] *See Sotah 47a.—An aspect of* gevurah; *withdrawal* (cf. *Introduction*). [32] *Exodus 20:15.* [33] *"Love" and "awe"; advance and retreat.* [34] I.e. *the counterpart of the physical body in the soul; the harmony between love and awe.* (*See Introduction.)* [35] *Legal rulings.* [36] *G-d's Will is expressed in the Torah. The legal rulings of the "Oral Torah" define and explicate (manifest) in detail the Divine Will as expressed in the Torah.—See* infra, *sect.*
(Notes cont. at end of Hebrew Text.)

●▲And now once more I put forth my hand a second time to an additional explanation and twofold request, extended and laid out before all like-minded people,[52] those nigh and those afar, to take upon themselves (the following):

On all week-days, businessmen, who do not have so much time, should not descend before the Ark.[53] Only from those who have the time [either teachers, or such as are supported by their parents] who are able to prolong the morning-prayer to at least about an hour and a half—on all week-days, shall one descend before the Ark, according to lot or by consent of the majority. And he should gather about him all those who are supported by their parents, or teachers, who are able to prolong like himself. This (arrangement) is not to be changed, I beg and beseech you!

On the Sabbaths and Festivals, however, when all the businessmen, too, have the time and opportunity to prolong their prayers with the devotion of their heart and soul to the Lord. Moreover, theirs is the duty to do so with exceeding uplifting and abundant strength, as stated in *Shulchan Aruch, Orach Chayim*,[54] and as it is written in the Torah of Moses:[55] "Six days you shall work . . . and the seventh day is a Sabbath *unto the Lord your G-d*," stating expressly that (the Sabbath) is wholly unto the Lord.[56] On a Sabbath or Festival, therefore, they too can descend before the Ark, according to lot or by assent of the majority, as I wrote last year.

And it should be made known that, G-d willing, it is my intention to send spies secretly to all congregations,[57] to find out and to inform about anyone that is able, and about anyone that has the time to prolong and meditate on prayer but is slothful. He shall be punished by estrangement, to be pushed away with both hands when he comes hither to hear the "Words of the living G-d."[58] And from the negative you can infer the positive.[59] But with those that shall obey it will be well, and the blessing of goodness shall come unto them—"There is no Good but Torah. . ."

[52] Cf. *above, note 6.* [53] *That is, to lead the congregation in prayer.* [54] *Section 290:2 (glosses of R. Moses Isserles).* [55] *Exodus 20:9, 10.* [56] *See.* Shulchan Aruch *of R. Shneur Zalman,* Orach Chayim *290:5.* [57] Lit.: minyanim—*i.e. groups of ten or more men (the legally required quorum) gathered for the purpose of prayer etc. In colloquial use the term denotes not only the numbered groups but, where these gather regularly in a fixed place, to the congregation in general.* [58] *A locution for the teachings of Chassidism.* [59] *A Talmudic proposition;* cf. *Nedarim 11a.*

ועתה הפעם הנני יוסיף שנית ידי בתוספת ביאור ובקשה כפולה שטוחה ופרושה לפני כל אנשי שלומים הקרובים והרחוקים לקיים עליהם שכל ימי החול לא ירדו לפני התיבה הבעלי עסקים שאין להם פנאי כ"כ. רק אותם שיש להם פנאי או המלמדים או הסמוכים על שולחן אביהם שיכולים להאריך בתפלת השחר ערך שעה ומחצה לפחות כל ימות החול מהם יהיה היורד לפני התיבה ע"פ הגורל או ע"פ ריצוי הרוב. והוא יאסוף אליו בסביב לו כל הסמוכים על שולחן אביהם או מלמדים שיוכלו להאריך כמוהו בבל ישונה נא ונא:

אך בשבתות וימים טובים שגם כל בעלי עסקים יש להם פנאי ושעת הכושר להאריך בתפלתם בכוונת לבם ונפשם לה'. ואדרבה עליהם מוטל ביתר שאת ויתר עז כמו שכתוב בשולחן ערוך אורח חיים וכמו שכתוב בתורת משה ששת ימים תעבוד כו' ויום השביעי שבת לה' אלהיך דייקא כולו לה'. ולזאת גם הם ירדו לפני התיבה בשבת ויום טוב על פי הגורל או בריצוי הרוב כמ"ש אשתקד:

וכגון דא צריך לאודועי שבדעתי אי"ה לשלוח לכל המנינים מרגלים בסתר לידע ולהודיע כל מי שאפשר לו וכל מי שיש לו פנאי להאריך ולעיין בתפלה ומתעצל יהי' נידון בריחוק מקום להיות נדחה בשתי ידים בבואו לפה לשמוע דא"ח ומכלל לאו אתה שומע הן ולשומעים יונעם ותבא עליהם ברכת טוב ואין טוב אלא תורה וכו':

אחר

Upon his arrival from Petersburg[1]

●▲ II. "I have become small from all the favours and from all . . ."[2] This means that by every favour (*chesed*) that G-d bestows upon man, (man) is to become very humble. For "*chesed*[3] is the right arm,"[4] and "His right arm embraces me,"[5]—which refers to the state of G-d actually bringing him close (to Himself), far more intensely than before. And whoever is close to G-d, with ever exceeding uplifting and elevation, must be ever more humble—to the lowliest plane,[6] as it is written: "From afar the Lord has appeared to me."[7] And as known, "All that are *before Him* are esteemed as nothing."[8] Hence, whoever is more "before Him" is that much more as nothing, naught, and non-existent.

And this is the rank of the "right side" of holiness, and of "*chesed* unto Abraham"[9] who said:[10] "And I am dust and ashes."[11] This (humility) is also the trait of Jacob, and therewith he justified himself for his fear of Esau and did not rely on the promise given to him—"And, behold, I am with you . . ."[12] (That is), because Jacob regarded himself as utterly insignificant[13] [because of the multitude of favours, "for with my staff . . ."[14]], and as unfit and unworthy to be saved . . . and as the saying of our sages, of blessed memory, "maybe sin will cause . . .," for it appeared to him that he had sinned.[15]

It is different, though, with the corresponding opposite,[16] i.e. Ishmael—"*chesed of kelipah*"[17]: the more kindness (manifested to him), the more he grows in pride, haughtiness and self-satisfaction.[18]

Therefore I come with a general announcement to inform all our followers regarding the multitude of favours—"The great things that the Lord has done with us"[19]: to hold on to the attributes of Jacob, the "remnant of His people"[20] and the "remainder of Israel,"[21] who regards himself truly as remnants and excess that is of no use.[22] They are not to become haughty-minded in relation to their brethren . . . not to speak defiantly against them or hiss at them,[23] Heaven forfend. A strict warning: hold your peace! No mention is to be made![24] Rather, they are to subdue their spirit and heart before everyone[25] according to the attribute of "Truth (*emet*) unto Jacob,"[26] with humility and a "Soft answer that turns

---

[1] *This letter the author sent to all his followers upon his release from imprisonment brought about by calumnies instigated by the opponents of Chassidism. The history of this letter, and the events of that important phase in the annals of Chassidism, form the contents of* The Arrest and Liberation of Rabbi Shneur Zalman of Liadi, tr. *J. I. Schochet (Kehot: New York, 1964).* [2] *Genesis 32:11.* [3] *Grace, favour, kindness.* [4] In *the "Man-Image" of the Sefirot* (cf. *Introduction).—Tikunei Zohar, Intr.: 17a.* [5] *Song 2:6.* [6] *See* Kitzurim Vehe'arot Lesefer Likutei Amarim, ed. *R. Menachem M. Schneerson, pp. 40 and 149.* [7] *Jer. 31:2.* [8] *Zohar I:11b, (the emphasis is the author's).* [9] *Micha 7:20. Abraham signifies the attribute*

אחר ביאתו מפ"ב.

ב קטנתי מכל החסדים ומכל כו'. פי' שבכל חסד וחסד שהקדוש ב"ה עושה לאדם צריך להיות שפל רוח במאד. כי חסד דרועא ימינא. וימינו תחבקני. שהיא בחי' קרבת אלהים ממש ביתר שאת מלפנים. וכל הקרוב אל ה' ביתר שאת והגבה למעלה מעלה. צריך להיות יותר שפל רוח למטה מטה כמ"ש מרחוק ה' נראה לי. וכנודע דכולא קמי' דווקא כלא חשיב. וא"כ כל שהוא קמי' יותר הוא יותר כלא ואין ואפס וזו בחי' ימין שבקדושה וחסד לאברהם שאמר אנכי עפר ואפר. וזו היא ג"כ מדתו של יעקב. ובזאת התנצל על יראתו מפני עשו ולא די לו בהבטחתו והנה אנכי עמך כו'. מפני היות קטן יעקב במאד מאד בעיניו מחמת ריבוי החסדים כי במקלי כו'. ואינו ראוי וכדאי כלל להנצל כו'. וכמארז"ל שמא יגרום החטא שנדמה בעיניו שחטא. משא"כ בזלע"ז הוא ישמעאל חסד דקליפה. כל שהחסד גדול הוא הולך וגדל בגובה וגסות הרוח ורוחב לבו. ולזאת באתי מן המודיעים מודעה רבה לכללות אנ"ש על ריבוי החסדים אשר הגדיל ה' לעשות עמנו לאחוז במדותיו של יעקב שאר עמו ושארית ישראל שמשים עצמו כשיריים ומותרות ממש שאין בו שום צורך. לבלתי רום לבבם מאחיהם כו' ולא להרחיב עליהם פה או לשרוק עליהם ח"ו. הס מלהזכיר באזהרה נוראה רק להשפיל רוחם ולבם במדת אמת ליעקב מפני כל אדם בנמיכות רוח ומענה רך משיב חימה

---

of chesed; *see Sefer Habahir 48 (131); Zohar I:41a, II:51b; Zohar Chadash 27a;* et passim.—*The "right side," too, signifies* chesed; *see the Introduction.* [10] *Genesis 18:27.* [11] Cf. *Chulin 89a.* [12] *Genesis 28:6.* [13] Lit.: *was very, very small in his (own) esteem.* [14] *Genesis 32:11.* [15] *Berachot 4a.* [16] *See Eccles. 7:14: G-d has made* one thing opposite the other. *This verse is interpreted to mean that everything in one realm has its corresponding opposite in another realm. Thus every factor in the realm of "holiness" has a corresponding opposite in the "other side," in the realm of the profane or evil.—See Sefer Habahir 9 (11); Zohar I:160a;* ibid., *III:282a; Tikunei Zohar 70:125b;* et passim.

(Notes cont. at end of Hebrew Text)

away anger,"[27] and with a restrained spirit . . . And,[28] maybe, through all that G-d will put into the heart of their brethren that "as waters (reflect) the face . . ."[29]

●▲ III. "And he garbed himself with *tzedakah*[1] as a coat of mail, and a helmet of salvation upon his head."[2] (On this verse) our sages, of blessed memory, commented: "Just as with chain mail each scale adds up to form a large mail, so it is with charity; each coin adds up to a large amount."[3] This means, just as the mail is made of scales over gaps, and these shield against any arrow entering through the gaps, so it is with the act of charity.

The meaning of this is (as follows). Charity is greater than all the commandments.[4] (The performance of the commandments) produces "garments" for the soul.[5] (These garments) are elicited from the light of the blessed En Sof, from the level of *sovev kolalmin*[6] ([7]as the meaning of *memale kolalmin*[8] and *sovev kolalmin* has been explained in *Likutei Amarim*, see there[9]), by the "arousal from below,"[10] i.e. the (performance of the) command of G-d and the will of the blessed Supreme Being. The essence of this efflux from the light of the blessed En Sof is a garment and encompassing light (*or makif*) for the ten Sefirot of Atzilut, Beriah, Yetzirah and Asiyah [which evolve from cause to cause and from rung to rung . . .] referred to as *memale kolalmin*. This means that the light of the blessed En Sof vests Itself and radiates within the whole evolution of the ten Sefirot of Atzilut, Beriah, Yetzirah and Asiyah, and it emanates the ten Sefirot of Atzilut which evolve into Beriah, Yetzirah and Asiyah, by means of an immense contraction (*tzimtzum*) [explained in *Etz Chayim*[11]], and is referred to as the inner light (*or pnimi*).[12]

Now, by the fulfillment of the commandments the above-mentioned *or makif* is elicited and radiates within the ten Sefirot of Atzilut, Beriah, Yetzirah and Asiyah, thereby uniting Itself with the *or pnimi*. This is referred to as the unification of the Holy One, blessed is He, and His Shechinah, as explained elsewhere.[13] And from a reflection of a reflection from the above-mentioned *or makif* [by means of a great contraction] a garment is made in the lower and upper Garden of Eden for the *nefesh–ruach–neshamah*[14] of man, enabling them to derive pleasure and attain some apprehension and illumination from the light of the blessed En Sof, as explained elsewhere.[15] And this is what our sages, of blessed memory, said: "In this world there is no reward for the commandments."[16] For in this world, which is physical, and in a state of limitation and a great, and most immense contraction, it is impossible that any reflection of the light of the blessed En Sof should become invested, except by means of the ten Sefirot, which, in the sacred *Zohar*,[17] are referred to as the "body": "*Chesed*

---

[27] *Proverbs 15:8.* [28] *The following words did not appear in the original epistle, and were added later by the author. See R. Menachem M. Schneerson,* Hayom Yom, *p. 77.* [29] *Proverbs 27:19; see* supra, *section I, note 26.*

Section III

[1] צדקה *has two interrelated meanings: a) righteousness and b) charity* (cf. Moreh Nevuchim *3:53). Though these two meanings are strictly interrelated, the emphasis in these writings is chiefly on the latter. As a scriptural term it is, therefore, left untranslated (in this, and subsequent sections) to avoid confusion.* [2] *Isaiah 59:17.* [3] *Bava Batra 9b.* [4] *"Charity is equal to all the commandments (together)"—Bava Batra 9a;* Tosefta, *Peah, end of ch. 4. See* Tanya *I, ch. 37.*

● 7 Av ▲ *11 Av*

חימה. ורוח נכאה כו׳. וכולי האי ואולי יתן ה׳ בלב אחיהם כמים הפנים וגו׳:

ג **וילבש** צדקה כשריון וכובע ישועה בראשו. ודרשו רז״ל מה שריון זה כל קליפה וקליפה מצטרפת לשריון גדול אף צדקה כל פרוטה ופרוטה מצטרפת לחשבון גדול. פי׳ שהשריון עשוי קשקשים על נקבים והם מגינים שלא יכנס חץ בנקבים. וככה הוא מעשה הצדקה:

וביאור הענין כי גדולה צדקה מכל המצות שמהן נעשי׳ לבושי׳ להנשמה הנמשכי׳ מאור א״ס ב״ה מבחי׳ סובב כל עלמין (כמבואר הפי׳ ממכ״ע וסובב כ״ע בלק״א ע״ש) באתערותא דלתתא היא מצות ה׳ ורצון העליון ב״ה. ועיקר המשכה זו מאור א״ס ב״ה הוא לבוש ואור מקיף לי״ס דאבי״ע המשתלשלות מעילה לעילה וממדרגה למדרגה כו׳ הנקראות בשם ממלא כ״ע. פי׳ כי אור א״ס ב״ה מתלבש ומאיר בתוך כל השתלשלו׳ הע״ס דאבי״ע והוא המאציל הע״ס דאצילות המשתלשלו׳ לבי״ע ע״י צמצום עצום המבואר בע״ח ונקרא אור פנימי. וע״י קיום המצות נמשך אור מקיף הנ״ל ומאיר תוך הע״ס דאבי״ע ומתייחד עם האור פנימי ונקרא יחוד קוב״ה ושכינתי׳ כמ״ש במ״א. ומהארה דהארה מאור מקיף הנ״ל ע״י צמצום רב נעשה לבוש לבחי׳ נר״ן של האדם בג״ע התחתון והעליון שיוכלו ליהנות ולהשיג איזה השגה והארה מאור א״ס ב״ה כמ״ש במ״א. וזה שאמרו רז״ל שכר מצוה בהאי עלמא ליכא. כי בעוה״ז הגשמי ובעל גבול וצמצום רב ועצום מאד מאד א״א להתלבש שום הארה מאור א״ס ב״ה כ״א ע״י י״ס הנקראים גופא בזוה״ק. חסד

דרועא

---

[5] *The reward for observing Torah and Mitzvot is the soul's delighting in the splendour of the Shechinah. In the world to come the soul will actually apprehend, in a manifest way, the very essence of the Divine vivification, thus Divinity Itself, as it were. The problem is that the soul is finite. Though its source is in Divinity, as it evolves and descends to become vested in the body, the soul becomes a created and distinct, thus finite entity. How then can this created entity apprehend creative Divinity which is infinite and essentially inapprehensible? The mediating factor, which enables the soul to apprehend Divinity, is* Torah *and* Mitzvot.

Torah *and* Mitzvot *are essentially Divine; their source is in the Supreme Will and the Divine* chochmah—

(Notes cont. at end of Hebrew Text)

is the right arm, . . ." For just as there is no comparison between the physical body and the soul, so there is no comparison whatever between the ten Sefirot of Atzilut and the Supreme Emanator, the blessed En Sof. For in relation to the blessed En Sof even the Supreme *chochmah*,[18] which is the first (of the Sefirot), is on the plane of a material action, as explained in *Likutei Amarim*.[19]

Therefore, by the act of charity and the performance of kindness [the fruits of which man enjoys in this world[20]] there appear, metaphorically speaking, gaps in the supernal garment that encompasses the Body—[the *kelim* (vessels) of the ten Sefirot[21]]—through which to irradiate and to diffuse light and abundance: from "*chesed*, the right arm"[22]—longevity in this physical world;[23] and from "the left arm"[24]—wealth and honour,[25] and likewise with beauty,[26] grandeur and majesty, and gladness.[27]

But to prevent the *chitzonim*[28] from drawing, above, from the light and abundance which evolves and descends netherwards to this physical world, and likewise, below, to shield man, and to guard him and to save him from all physical and spiritual harm, the *or makif* reflects the light, and, figuratively speaking, fills the breach. For it is of the category of Infinitude and *sovev kolalmin*, as mentioned above. And this is what our sages, of blessed memory, said: "Adds up to a *great* amount,"[29] for "Great is the Lord and exceedingly glorified"[30]—without end, limit, and restriction [[31]Heaven Forfend].

●▲ But what causes the descent to this physical world of the light and abundance from the ten Sefirot [which are referred to as the "body"]? It is the above-mentioned union; for it is an additional radiation and effluence from the level of the light of the En Sof, the blessed Supreme Emanator, in a measure exceeding the radiation and effluence at the beginning of the emanation and evolution . . . And the additional radiation and effluence starts at the beginning of the ten Sefirot.

That is the meaning of "And a helmet of salvation upon his head": *yeshu'ah*[32] is of the etymon of *vayisha'*—"And the Lord *had regard* to Abel and his gift,"[33] which refers to the descent of the light and abundance of the "three-hundred-and-seventy lights" mentioned in the sacred *Zohar*,[34] and as it is written:[35] "May the Lord make His Face radiate toward you"; "May He make His face radiate with us forever"[36]—*with us*,[37] that is, through the act of charity.

---

[18] Chochmah 'ilaah. [19] *Part II (*Sha'ar Hayichud*), ch. 9; cf. also part I: ch. 2, in the author's marginal gloss.* [20] Mishnah, *Peah I:1.* [21] *See Introduction for the meaning of this term.* [22] *That is, from the Sefirah* chesed. [23] *See Proverbs 3:16: Length of days in her right arm.* [24] *That is, from the Sefirah* gevurah. [25] *Proverbs 3:16: and in her left arm, riches and honour.* [26] I.e. *beauty (as implied by the term* tiferet*) emanates from the Sefirah* tiferet. [27] Par. *I Chron. 16:27.—The Hebrew terms are:* Hod *and* Hadar, *and* Chedvah. Hod *and* Hadar *correspond to the Sefirot* netzach *and* hod *(see Zohar II:98a, and* Hagahot R. Chaim Vital, ad loc.—*in the light of Zohar I:262a); grandeur and majesty thus*

דרועא ימינא כו'. לפי שכמו שאין ערוך לו להגוף הגשמי לגבי הנשמה כך אין ערוך כלל לי"ס דאצילות לגבי המאציל העליון א"ס ב"ה. כי אפי' ח"ע שהיא ראשיתן היא בבחי' עשיה גופנית לגבי א"ס ב"ה כמ"ש בלק"א. ואי לזאת במעשה הצדקה וגמ"ח שאדם אוכל מפירותיהן בעוה"ז יש נקבים עד"מ בלבוש העליון המקיף על גופא הם הכלים די"ס. להאיר מהם ולהשפיע אור ושפע מחסד דרועא ימינא אורך ימים בעוה"ז הגשמי ועושר וכבוד מדרועא שמאלא. וכן בתפארת. והוד והדר וחדוה וכו': אך כדי שלא ינקו החיצונים למעלה מאור ושפע המשתלשל ויורד למטה מטה עד עוה"ז הגשמי. וכן למטה להגין על האדם ולשמרו ולהצילו מכל דבר רע בגשמיות וברוחניות. לזאת חוזר ומאיר אור המקיף וסותם הנקב עד"מ. כי הוא מבחי' א"ס וסובב כ"ע כנ"ל. וזהו שאמרו רז"ל מצטרפת לחשבון גדול דייקא כי גדול ה' ומהולל מאד בלי סוף ותכלית וגבול [ח"ו]: אך מי הוא הגורם לירידת האור והשפע לעוה"ז הגשמי מי"ס הנקראים גופא הוא היחוד הנ"ל שהיא תוספת הארה והשפעה מבחי' אור א"ס המאציל העליון ב"ה ביתר שאת על ההארה וההשפעה שבתחילת האצילות וההשתלשלות וכו'. וראשית תוספת ההארה וההשפעה היא לראשית הי"ס וזה הוא וכובע ישועה בראשו ישועה הוא מלשון וישע ה' אל הבל ואל מנחתו. והוא ירידת האור והשפע דש"ע נהורין שבזוה"ק. וכמ"ש יאר ה' פניו אליך. יאר פניו אתנו סלה. אתנו הוא ע"י מעשה הצדקה.

וזה

---

emanate from the fourth and fifth attributes. Chedvah *corresponds to the Sefirah* yesod *(see Zohar I:206b and III:5a); gladness thus emanates from the sixth attribute.—Cf. the interpretation of this verse in R. Chayim Vital,* Sha'ar Hakavanot, s.v. דרוש ענין תפלת חשחר (ed. *Tel Aviv 1962, vol. I: p. 107a).* [28] *Extraneous forces;* i.e. *extraneous (the furthest removed) in relation to holiness; thus, the forces of evil and impurity.* [29] *The author puts emphasis on the word "great";* cf. infra, *section XXX.* [30] *Psalms 48:2 (*ibid. *145:3).—This effect of the* or makif, *in reward for the performance of kindness, stems from the infinite Greatness* (chesed) *of G-d.* [31] *Brackets appear in the text.* [32] *Salvation.* [33] *Genesis*

(Notes cont. at end of Hebrew Text)

And this is the meaning of "He who sows *tzedakot* (charities), brings forth *yeshu'ot*."[38] "So may the Lord make His Face radiate towards them," "their tzedakah shall stand forever;"[39] and may their horn be exalted by the *yeshu'ah* of "He who causes to sprout the horn of *yeshu'ah*,"[40] the sprout of *tzedakah* from the "helmet of *yeshu'ah*"—mentioned above, as is the wish (of he) who seeks it.[41]

●▲ IV. Israel shall be redeemed only through *tzedakah*, as it is written:[1] "*Veshaveha*—and her repatriates,[2] through *tzedakah*."[3] It is written:[4] צדק לפניו יהלך.[5] Now, it should really say: ילך.[6] But the idea is according to what is written:[7] "My heart said for You 'Seek *panay* (My face)',"[8] that is: "Seek the *pnimiyut*[9] of the heart." For in the heart [[10] the element of the Divine fire that is in the heart][11] there are two aspects: the aspect of *chitzoniyut*,[12] and the aspect of *pnimiyut*. The *chitzoniyut* of the heart is the enthusiasm that flares up on account of the understanding (*binah*) and the knowledge (*da'at*) of the greatness of the Lord, the blessed En Sof, by contemplating[13] on His greatness, and from this contemplation giving birth to a strong love like unto "flashes of fire . . ."[14] The *pnimiyut* of the heart is that "point" in the inwardness [of the heart] and depth of the heart which transcends the aspect of the knowledge and the contemplation that man can contemplate in his heart on the greatness of the Lord; and as it is written:[15] "From the depths I call unto You, O Lord," i.e. from the depth of the heart.[16] ([17] It is for example, so with worldly matters: sometimes there is an extremely important matter upon which the whole vitality of man hinges and touches him as far as, and including the innermost point of the heart, and it causes him to perform acts and say things without any reason whatever.[18] And "The one corresponds to the other,"[19] it is precisely so with the "service of the heart."[20] This is because the faculty of the innermost point of the heart transcends the faculty of reason (*da'at*)—which extends and vests itself in the attributes born of wisdom - understanding - knowledge (*ChaBaD*), as known.[21] It is,[22] rather, an aspect of the radiation from the Supreme *chochmah*, which transcends *binah* and *da'at*,[23] and in which there is vested and concealed the actual light of G-d, as it is written:[24] "The Lord by *chochmah* . . ."[25] And this precisely is the aspect of the spark of Divinity in every soul of Israel.)

● The reason that not every person merits this rank [of the service of the heart from the depth of the heart in a state

---

[38] Liturgy, *Morning-prayers*. [39] *Psalms 112:3*. [40] Liturgy, *weekday* 'Amidah. [41] Par. *Lament. 3:25*.

Section IV

[1] *Isaiah 1:27*. [2] *See below, note 55*. [3] *Shabbat 139a; Sanhedrin 98a*. [4] *Psalms 85:14*. [5] Tzedek *(righteousness; here in the sense of charity) shall go before Him*. [6] *The proper grammatical form for the conventional translation and sense, rather than the causative* יהלך. [7] *Psalms 27:8*. [8] I.e., "*my heart said in Your (G-d's) name: Seek My Face*"; *see comment.* a.l. [9] *Inwardness; the innermost point, identical with essence (see Introduction* s.v.; *and* infra, *note 26).*—פנים *(face) is etymologically related to* פנים *(interior)*; cf. *Maimonides,*

וזה הוא זורע צדקות מצמיח ישועות. וככה יאר ה' פניו
אליהם צדקתם עומדת לעד וקרנם תרום בישועת
מצמיח קרן ישועה צמח צדקה מהכובע ישועה הנ"ל.
כנפש תדרשנו:

ד אין ישראל נגאלין אלא בצדקה שנא' ושביה
בצדקה. כתיב צדק לפניו יהלך והול"ל
ילך. אך הענין עפ"י מ"ש לך אמר לבי בקשו פני פי' בקשו
פנימית הלב כי הנה בלהב יסוד האש האלקית שבלב
(נ"א הנה בהלב [יסוד האש האלקית שבלב]) יש ב' בחי'.
בחי' חיצוניות ובחי' פנימיות. חיצוני' הלב היא התלהבות
המתלהבת מבחי' הבינה והדעת בגדולת ה' א"ס ב"ה
(להתבוננן) [להתבונן] בגדולתו ולהוליד מתבונה זו אהבה
עזה כרשפי אש וכו'. ופנימי' הלב היא הנקודה שבפנימיות
הלב ועומקא דליבא שהיא למעלה מעלה מבחי' הדעת
והתבונה שיוכל האדם להתבונן בלבו בגדולת ה'. וכמ"ש
ממעמקים קראתיך ה' מעומקא דליבא (ועד"מ כמו במילי
דעלמא לפעמים יש ענין גדול מאד מאד שכל חיות
האדם תלוי בו ונוגע עד נקודת פנימיות הלב ועד
בכלל וגורם לו לפעמים לעשות מעשים ולדבר דברים
שלא בדעת כלל) וזלע"ז ככה הוא ממש בעבודה
שבלב. והיינו לפי שבחי' נקודת פנימית הלב היא
למעלה מבחי' הדעת המתפשט ומתלבש במדות
שנולדו מחב"ד כנודע. רק היא בחי' הארת חכמה
עליונה שלמעלה מהבינה והדעת ובה מלובש וגנוז
אור ה' ממש כמ"ש ה' בחכמה כו' והיא היא בחי'
ניצוץ אלקות שבכל נפש מישראל. ומה שאין כל אדם
זוכה למדרגה זו לעבודה שבלב מעומקא דלבא בבחי'
פנימיות

Hilchot Yesodei Hatorah *I:10.* [10] *Brackets appear in the text.* [11] V. L.: *for in the flame, the element etc.; (reading* בלהב *instead of* בהלב*).* [12] *Outwardness, externality; the antonym of* pnimiyut*; the degree furthest removed from* pnimiyut, *the essence. See Introduction,* s.v. [13] V. L.: *to cause them to contemplate.* [14] Par. *Song 8:6;* cf. supra, *sect. I, note 29.* [15] *Psalms 130:1.* [16] *Zohar II: 63b.* [17] *Brackets appear in the text.* [18] *In most texts the brackets close here. But it would appear quite obviously from the context that the passage to be enclosed by the brackets ends further on. R. Menachem M. Schneerson notes in* H. V. *that in the Shklov edition of the* Tanya *(1814) there do not appear any*

(Notes cont. at end of Hebrew Text)

of *pnimiyut*] is because this aspect is with him in a state of exile and captivity.[26] And this is actually the state of the exile of the Shechinah, for this precisely is the aspect of the spark of Divinity that is in his divine soul. The cause of the exile is as our sages, of blessed memory, said:[27] "They were exiled to Babylon, and the Shechinah went with them;" i.e. (man) has vested the aspect of the innermost point of his heart in the corresponding opposite,[28] namely in the soiled garments of mundane matters and worldly desires, which are referred to as "Babylon,"[29] and is the aspect of the prepuce that covers the covenant and the innermost point of the heart. Of this it was said:[30] "And you shall excise the prepuce of your heart."

Now, in circumcision there are two grades: *milah*[31] and *peri'ah*,[32] which (apply respectively to) the coarse prepuce and the thin membrane. With respect to the prepuce of the heart there are likewise coarse and delicate desires. These require *milah* and *peri'ah*, and "Having circumcised and not having uncovered is tantamount to not having circumcised,"[33] because, after all, the innermost point of the heart is still covered in a garment of thin sack-cloth: in a state of exile and captivity.[34] Now, concerning the excision of the prepuce itself it is written: "And you shall excise the prepuce of your heart," i.e., *you*, by yourselves. But the removal of the thin membrane is a difficult matter for man, and of this it was said that with the coming of the Messiah "*the Lord, your G–d*, will circumcise your heart . . . to love the Lord your G–d with all your heart and all your soul, *for the sake of your life*,"[35] i.e., because the Lord alone is literally your whole life.[36] That is why this love[37] stems from the depth of the heart, from the truly innermost point, as mentioned above, and transcends the faculty of *da'at*. Therefore, too, the Messiah will come when generally "unexpected[38] by Israel,"[39] which is the manifestation of the general innermost point, and the emergence of the general Shechinah from the exile and captivity forever more. Similarly, every individual spark of the Shechinah, inherent in the soul of every one of Israel, emerges for the moment from the exile and captivity during the "momentary life—meaning prayer,"[40] and the service of the heart from the depth of the heart, (i.e.) from the aspect of the innermost point [which becomes revealed from the prepuce and soars upwards to cleave unto Him with a fierce passion,

---

[26] Pnimiyut *is the innermost point; the essence. (See Introduction,* s.v.*) Intellect and emotion are external to soul; they are its expression and manifestation.* Chochmah, *a state of nascence rather than an external entity, is as close to essence of soul as is attainable. Its revelation is the expression of the soul's essence and is naturally uncommon. As the text explains, it is in a "state of exile", the spark of Divinity within it prevented from manifesting itself, remaining more potential than effective in ordering actual life.* [27] *Megilah 29a.* [28] I.e. *in the corresponding opposite of the love and worship of G–d.* [29] Cf. Tanya *I, ch. 17, with respect to Edom.* [30] *Deut. 10:16. ("Excise" in Hebrew is the same term used for "circumcise".)* [31] *Excision.* [32]

פנימיות היינו לפי שבחינה זו היא אצלו בבחי׳ גלות ושביה והיא בחינת גלות השכינה ממש כי היא היא בחינת ניצוץ אלהות שבנפשו האלהית וסבת הגלות הוא מאמר רז״ל גלו לבבל שכינה עמהם דהיינו מפני שהלביש בחינת פנימית נקודת לבבו בזה לעומת זה דהיינו בלבושים צואים דמילי דעלמא ותאות עוה״ז הנקרא בשם בבל והיא בחינת ערלה המכסה על הברית ונקודה הפנימית שבלב ועל זה נאמר ומלתם את ערלת לבבכם. והנה במילה יש שני בחינות מילה ופריעה שהן ערלה גסה וקליפה דקה וכן בערלת הלב יש ג״כ תאות גסות ודקות מילה ופריעה ומל ולא פרע כאלו לא מל מפני שסוף סוף עדיין נקודת פנימית הלב היא מכוסה בלבוש שק דק בבחינת גלות ושביה. והנה על מילת הערלה ממש כתי׳ ומלתם את ערלת לבבכם אתם בעצמכם אך להסיר הקליפה הדקה זהו דבר הקשה על האדם וע״ז נא׳ בביאת המשיח ומל ה׳ אלהיך את לבבך כו׳ לאהבה את ה׳ אלהיך בכל לבבך ובכל נפשך למען חייך כלומר למען כי ה׳ לבדו הוא כל חייך ממש. שלכן אהבה זו היא מעומקא דלבא מנקודה פנימית ממש כנ״ל ולמעלה מבחינת הדעת ולכן משיח בא בהיסח הדעת לכללות ישראל והיא גילוי בחינת נקודה פנימית הכללית ויציאת השכינה הכללית מהגלות והשביה לעד ולעולמי עולמים וכן כל ניצוץ פרטי מהשכינה שבנפש כל אחד מישראל יוצאת מהגלות והשביה לפי שעה בחיי שעה זו תפלה ועבודה שבלב מעומקא דלבא מבחינת נקודה הפנימית הנגלית מהערלה ועולה למעלה לדבקה בו בתשוקה עזה

בבחינת

Uncovering (as in Num. 5:18; see Ibn Ezra ad loc.*).* [33] *Shabbat 137b.* [34] *See* Pardess Rimonim, *23:17,* s.v. פריעה. [35] *Deut. 30:6. See the commentary of Nachmanides,* ad loc. [36] *This unique interpretation may be better understood by quoting a passage from* Kuntress Hahitpa'alut, *by the author's son, R. Dov Ber of Lubavitch, where this oft-quoted principle is elucidated: "It is written (Deut. 30:20):* 'to love the Lord your G-d, for He is your life.' *It is impossible to explain that* 'for הוא your life' *refers to* 'to love the Lord'*—i.e. that this love is your life. For if so, it would have to say* 'for היא *(the feminine gender, as opposed to the masculine* הוא; ahavah—love—*is a feminine word)' etc. Why then*

(Notes cont. at end of Hebrew Text)

in a mode of "for the sake of your life"]. And this, too, is considered a state of *hessech da'at*[41] of man. For that rank[42] transcends the *da'at* of man and his contemplation on the greatness of the Lord; it is, though, a sort of gift given by the Lord from Heaven from the radiation of the [aspect of the] Supreme Countenance (*panim*), as it is written:[43] "May the Lord make His *panim* radiate toward you," and as it is written:[44] "And the Lord, your G-d, will circumcise . . ."

• But it is well-known that an arousal from above comes only in response to an arousal from below,[45] in the mode of an elevation of *mayin nukvin*,[46] as our sages, of blessed memory, said: "No drop descends from above . . ."[47] It is, therefore, necessary that man perform first the *milah* by himself, to remove the prepuce of the heart and the coarse and thin husks which clothe and cover the innermost point of the heart [i.e. the aspect of the love of the Lord in a mode of "for the sake of your life," which is in exile among the desires of this world, which are also in a mode of "for the sake of your life" by way of "the one corresponding to the other,"[48] as mentioned above]. And this is done by the giving of charity to G-d from his money which is his vitality, especially with him whose substance is limited and who is very hard pressed at the time, for he gives of his very life;[49] and more specifically, when he earns by the toil of his hands. For it is not possible that one does not work oftentimes in a mode of "the innermost point of the heart," i.e. from the depth of the heart, as is the way of the world in their occupations with business and the like. Thus, now, at the time that he disburses the fruits of his toil and gives unto the Lord with joy and gladness, he, thereby, redeems his soul from the pit.[50] That is, (he redeems) the innermost point of his heart which was in a state of exile and captivity within the coarse or thin husk (*kelipah*), as it is written: "Guard your heart from every *mishmar*"[51]—the meaning of *mishmar* being a prison.[52] Thus, now, through this charity, it was redeemed from the *chitzonim*.[53] This is also *peri'ah*, a notion of "removing a debt,"[54] for he had become indebted and subjected to the *chitzonim* that ruled in him over the innermost point of his heart. And this is the meaning of "and her captives (*shaveha*)[55] through *tzedakah*."

•▲ And this is the meaning of צדק לפניו יהלך: לפניו is of the etymon of *pnimiyut*, and יהלך has a connotation of הולכה.[56] For it[57] leads the innermost (point)

---

[41] *Absentmindedness; see above, note 38.* [42] *The revelation of this inmost spark, the Shechinah residing within man in concealment.* [43] *Numbers 6:25; see above, note 9.* [44] *Deut. 30:6.* [45] "Arousal—*(or: stimulation, initiative)*—from below" *refers to an act undertaken by man, a human effort, while* "arousal from above" *refers to the Divine efflux, issuing from Above. Generally, to elicit this Heavenly effusion one needs to* "*arouse*" *it. This is done by an appropriate, benevolent act on earth.* Cf. *Zohar I:77b, 86b, 88a;* ibid., *III:110b,* et passim. *See also below, notes 46 and 47, and* infra, *section V, notes 83–90 (and the text to which these notes apply).* [46] *Feminine waters.—See Zohar I:29b: "The earth is fed from the waters of the*

בבחינת למען חייך והוא גם כן בבחי' היסח דעת האדם כי בחינה זו היא למעלה מדעת האדם והתבוננותו בגדולת ה' רק היא בחינת מתנה נתונה מאת ה' מן השמים מהארת בחי' פנים העליונים כמ"ש יאר ה' פניו אליך וכמ"ש ומל ה' אלקיך כו'. אך מודעת זאת כי אתערותא דלעילא היא באתערותא דלתתא דוקא בבחינת העלאת מ"נ כמשארז"ל אין טפה יורדת מלמעלה כו'. ולכן צריך האדם לעשות בעצמו תחלת מילה זו להסיר ערלת הלב וקליפה הגסה ודקה המלבישות ומכסות על בחינת נקודת פנימית הלב שהיא בחינת אהבת ה' בחינת למען חייך שהיא בגלות בתאוות עוה"ז שהם ג"כ בבחי' למען חייך בזלע"ז כנ"ל והיינו ע"י נתינת הצדקה לה' ממונו שהוא חיותו ובפרט מי שמזונותיו מצומצמים ודחיקא ליה שעתא טובא שנותן מחייו ממש ובפרטות אם נהנה מיגיע כפיו שא"א שלא עסק בהם פעמים רבות בבחי' נקודת פנימית הלב מעומקא דלבא כמנהג העולם בעסקיהם במו"מ וכה"ג והרי עתה הפעם כשמפזר מיגיעו ונותן לה' בשמחה ובטוב לבב הנה בזה פודה נפשו משחת דהיינו בחינת נקודת פנימית לבבו שהיתה בבחי' גלות ושביה בתוך הקליפה גסה או דקה כמ"ש מכל משמר נצור לבך משמר פי' בית האסורים ועתה נפדה מהחיצונים בצדקה זו וזה גם כן לשון פריעה ענין פריעת חוב שנתחייב ונשתעבד לחיצונים שמשלו בו על נקודת פנימיות לבבו וזהו ושביה בצדקה. וזהו צדק לפניו יהלך לפניו הוא מלשון פנימיות ויהלך הוא מלשון הולכה שמוליך את פנימית הלב

---

*heaven, and its waters are poured into it. However, these waters are mascu*line, *and the nether ones are* feminine; *and the nether ones are fed from the masculine ones. The nether waters call unto the upper, like a female that receives the male" etc., see there and* ibid. *60b. The essentially Lurianic concept of the elevation of the feminine waters* (מ"ן) *is the "arousal from below" (see previous note), which consequently elicits the masculine waters* (מ"ד, mayin duchrin)*—the "arousal from above," to issue and effuse netherwards, "to feed, and be received by the category of the feminine." See* Etz Chayim *39:1* Seq. *and Tanya, end of ch. 10 and end of ch. 53;* supra, [47] *Zohar III:247b; Ta'anit 25b.*
[48] *See*

(Notes cont. at end of Hebrew Text)

of the heart unto G–d, and then "It sets his steps towards the way of G–d,"[58] as it is written: "And you shall walk in His ways:"[59] "You shall go after the Lord your G–d,"[60]—with every performance of the commandments, and the study of Torah which is equivalent to them all.[61] For they all ascend unto G–d through the inwardness of the heart with greater uplifting, and exceedingly surpassing their ascent unto G–d through the externality of the heart[62] [which is born of contemplation and knowledge alone, without an illumination of the face[63] from above, but in a state of "concealment of the face"[64]]. For the Supernal *panim* does not radiate downwards except through an arousal from below, through the act of charity which is called "peace."[65] And this is the meaning of what is written: "He has redeemed my soul[66] in peace,"[67] stating expressly "my soul."[68] This is also the reason why charity is called "peace" (*shalom*), because according to the saying of our sages, of blessed memory,[69] peace is made between Israel and their Father in Heaven, through the redemption of their souls [which are truly a part of G–d] from the hands of the *chitzonim*. This is especially the case with charity for the Land of Israel, for it is truly the charity of the Lord,[70] as it is written: "The eyes of the Lord your G–d are constantly upon it;"[71] "And My eyes and My heart will be there at all times."[72] And it[73] has stood by us to redeem the life of our soul from the counsel of those who intend to repel our steps, and it will stand by us forever to establish our soul in the true life of the Fountainhead of life,[74] to be enlightened with the light of life[75] which the Lord "will make His Face radiate, with us, Selah,"[76] amen—may this be (His) will.

●▲ V. "And David made a name."[1] In the sacred *Zohar* this is interpreted in relation to the verse "and David performed justice and *tzedakah* with all his people . . ."[2]: "Rabbi Shimon wept and said: Who makes the Holy Name, every day? He who gives charity unto the poor, . . ."[3]

This will be understood by first explaining the comment of our sages, of blessed memory, on the verse[4] "For by *Yud-Hai*,[5] the Lord is the *tzur*[6] of the worlds": "This world was created by the *hai*,[7] the world to come was created by the *yud*[8]."[9] This means that the delight which the souls of the righteous derive and enjoy from the splendour of the Shechinah[10] which radiates in the upper and lower Gardens of Eden, consists of their delighting in their apprenhension and conception, for they conceive, know and attain some apprehension of the light and vitality which effuses there—in a state of manifestation—from the blessed En Sof to their soul and their spirit of

[58] *Psalms 85:14 (conclusion of* צדק לפניו יהלך*).* [59] *Deut. 28:9.* [60] *Deut. 13:5.* [61] *Peah I:1.* [62] Cf. *Zohar II:210b.* [63] Heorat Panim. [64] Hesster Panim. [65] Tossefta, *Peah, end of ch. 4; Bava Batra 10a.* [66] *Or:* "through peace." [67] *Psalms 55:19.* [68] I.e. *the* pnimiyut, *the innermost point.* [69] *See above, note 65.* [70] *See* infra, *section XVII.* [71] *Deut. 11:12.* [72] *I Kings 9:3.* [73] *This charity.* [74] Lit.: *the Life of life;—(*cf. *Yoma 71a; Tikunei Zohar 19:41b, and 69:115a; and see* infra, *end of sect. XXIIa).* [75] Par. *Job 33:30;* cf. *Psalms 56:14.* [76] *Psalms 67:2;* cf. supra, *end of section III.*

Section V

[1] *II Samuel 8:13.* [2] Ibid., 15.

הלב לה׳ ואחר כך ישים לדרך ה׳ פעמיו כמ״ש והלכת בדרכיו אחרי ה׳ אלהיכם תלכו בכל מעשה המצות ות״ת כנגד כולן שכולן עולין לה׳ על ידי פנימית הלב ביתר שאת ומעלה מעלה מעלייתן לה׳ ע״י חיצונית הלב הנולד מהתבונה והדעת לבדן בלי הארת פנים מלמעלה אלא בבחינת הסתר פנים כי אין הפנים העליונים מאירים למטה אלא באתערותא דלתתא במעשה הצדקה הנקרא שלום. וז״ש פדה בשלום נפשי נפשי דייקא. וזהו ג״כ הטעם שנקרא הצדקה שלום לפי שנעשה שלום בין ישראל לאביהם שבשמים כמארז״ל דהיינו על ידי פדיון נפשותיהן הם חלק ה׳ ממש מידי החיצונים ובפרט צדקת א״י שהיא צדקת ה׳ ממש כמ״ש תמיד עיני ה׳ אלהיך בה והיו עיני ולבי שם כל הימים והיא שעמדה לנו לפדות חיי נפשנו מעצת החושבים לדחות פעמינו ותעמוד לנו לעד לשום נפשנו בחיים אמיתים מחיי החיים לאור באור החיים אשר יאר ה׳ פניו אתנו סלה אכי״ר:

ה ויעש דוד שם ופי׳ בזוה״ק משום שנאמר ויהי דוד עושה משפט וצדקה לכל עמו כו׳ בכה ר״ש ואמר מאן עביד שמא קדישא בכל יומא מאן דיהיב צדקה למסכני כו׳. ויובן בהקדים מאמר רז״ל ע״פ כי ביה ה׳ צור עולמים בה׳ נברא עוה״ז ביו״ד נברא עוה״ב. פי׳ שהתענוג שמתענגים נשמות הצדיקים ונהנין מזיו השכינה המאיר בג״ע עליון ותחתון הוא שמתענגים בהשגתם והשכלתם שמשכילים ויודעים ומשיגים איזה השגה באור וחיות השופע שם מא״ס ב״ה בבחינת גילוי לנשמתם ורוח בינתם

---

[3] *Zohar III: 113a, b.* [4] *Isaiah 26:4.* [5] *These two letters combined form a name of G-d, reading: For in G-d, the Lord etc.* [6] Tosafot *on Berachot 51a (*s.v. זוכה*) enlightens this interpretation, by quoting a version which does not appear in our text of the* Talmud: "*do not read* צור *(rock)*, but צר *(formed, designed).*" *This version does appear in the Zohar, II: 22b, though emending* צור *to* צייר *(former, designer), an emendation that appears elsewhere in the* Talmud *(relating to other verses),* e.g. *Berachot 10a, etc.* [7] *The letter* hai *(second letter of* Yud-hai*).* [8] *The letter* yud *(first letter of* Yud-Hai*).* [9] *Menachot 29b; Medrashim on Genesis 2:4.* [10] *See* supra, *section I, note 21.*

understanding, so that each and every one can understand and attain some perception according to his level and his deeds.[11] That is why in the sacred *Zohar*[12] the world to come (*olam habah*) is referred to as *binah* (understanding). And this flow issues from the plane of the Supreme *chochmah*, which is the source of the conception and apprehension referred to as *binah*.[13] For *chochmah* is the primordium of the intellect, antecedent to apprehension and understanding becoming manifest, rather, still in a state of hiding and concealment,[14] except for some trifle here and there flowing forth and issuing thence to the faculty of *binah*, making it possible to understand and to apprehend the hidden intellect. In the sacred *Zohar*, *chochmah* is, therefore, referred to as "the dot in the palace;"[15] and this is the form of the *yud* of the blessed Tetragrammaton (*Havayah*),[16] and is called Eden[17]—of which it is said:[18] "No eye has seen it . . ."[19] And it is referred to as "The Father (*abba*)[20] who founded the Daughter (*barta*)[21]."[22] This means:

The formation of the letters of speech which issue from the five organs of articulation[23] is not an intellectual capacity. It is also not inherent in the nature of these organs to pronounce the letters—[by means of the breath and the sound that strikes them]—by either a natural faculty or by an intellectual faculty. With the lips, for example, through which are uttered the letters B-V-M-P,[24] neither nature nor the intellect compels the utterance of the four varying types of pronunciation of these letters in accordance with the variations in the movement of the lips—which are moved by the same breath and the same sound that strikes them equally. On the contrary: the change in the movements of the lips depends on the difference in pronunciation of the letters the soul wishes to utter by means of the lips—when it is (the soul's) will to speak the letters ב, or ו, or מ, or פ.[24] It is not the other way around, that it is the will and intention of the soul to make a change in the motions of the lips—as they are moving now in the utterances of these four letters, as is empirically evident that the soul does not intend or know to intend at all the change in the motions of the lips, of those changes. This is even more evident with the utterance of the vowels. For when it is the wish of the soul to articulate the vowel *o*, then, of themselves, the lips become compressed; and with the *a*—the lips are opened.[25] Thus, it is definitely not because of the will

---

[11] Cf. *Zohar I: 129b, and 135b.* [12] *Zohar II: 158a; Zohar Chadash 93a (beg. of* Tikunim Chadashim*).* Cf. infra, *sect. XXIX.* [13] Chochmah *is the first, and as such the source of all succeeding Sefirot.* Binah *is merely the elucidation and expansion of* chochmah; *the comprehensive knowledge following upon the conceptual wisdom of* chochmah. *Thus*, binah *is referred to as "understanding (or: deriving) one thing out of another"* (i.e. *out of the* chochmah, *the original concept*). *See Introduction*, s.v. Chochmah Binah. [14] *Consciousness, and thus comprehension, is still concealed.* [15] *Zohar I: 6a; Tikunei Zohar Introd.: 12b;* et passim. Cf. *also Zohar I: 15a* ff. "*Dot*"—chochmah; "*palace*"—binah; *see Introduction.* [16] I.e. *a simple, non-*

בינתם להבין ולהשיג איזה השגה כאו"א לפי מדרגתו ולפי מעשיו ולכן נקרא עולם הבא בשם בינה בזוה"ק והשפעה זו נמשכת מבחי' ח"ע שהוא מקור ההשכלה וההשגה הנקרא בשם בינה והוא קדמות השכל קודם שבא לכלל גילוי השגה והבנה רק עדיין הוא בבחי' העלם והסתר רק שמעט מזעיר שם זעיר שם שופע ונמשך משם לבחינת בינה להבין ולהשיג שכל הנעלם ולכן נקרא בשם נקודה בהיכלא בזוה"ק וזו היא תמונת יו"ד של שם הוי' ב"ה ונקרא עדן אשר עליו נאמר עין לא ראתה כו' ונקרא אבא יסד ברתא. פי' כי הנה התהוות אותיות הדבור היוצאות מה' מוצאות הפה אינן דבר מושכל ולא מוטבע בטבע מוצאות הללו להוציא מבטא האותיות ע"י ההבל והקול המכה בהן עפ"י דרך הטבע ולא על פי דרך השכל כגון השפתים עד"מ שאותיות בומ"פ יוצאות מהן אין הטבע ולא השכל נותן ליציאת מבטא ארבע חלקי שינויי ביטוי אותיות אלו על פי שינויי תנועת השפתים שמתנועעות בהבל אחד וקול אחד הפוגע בהן בשוה ואדרבה שינוי התנועות שבשפתים הוא לפי שינוי ביטוי האותיות שברצון הנפש לבטא בשפתים כרצונה לומר אות ב' או ו' או מ' או פ' ולא להיפך שיהיה רצון הנפש וכונתה לעשות שינוי תנועות השפתים כמו שהן מתנענעות עתה בביטויי ד' אותיות אלו. וכנראה בחוש שאין הנפש מתכוונת ויודעת לכוין כלל שינוי תנועות השפתים בשינויים אלו ויותר נראה כן בביטוי הנקודות שכשהנפש רצונה להוציא מפיה נקודת קמץ אזי ממילא נקמצים השפתים ובפתח נפתחים השפתים ולא שרצון

הנפש

---

dimensional point.—The letters of the Tetragrammaton (HaVaYaH; *the ineffable* Nomen Proprium*) signify the 10 Sefirot:* Yud—chochmah; *(the first)* Hai—binah; Vav—tiferet, *or/and the totality of the six attributes (*chesed *to* yesod*); (the latter)* Hai—malchut. *(The thorn of the letter* yud *signifies* keter, *which precedes* chochmah *and is often counted as one of the ten Sefirot instead of* da'at; *see Introduction.)* Cf. *Zohar III: 17a, 258a;* et passim. *See* Tanya, *III: 4.* [17] *Zohar III: 290a; see also Zohar II: 90a.*—Eden (chochmah*) is to be distinguished from* olam. habah *(*binah*).* [18] *Isaiah 64: 3* [19] *See Berachot 34b; Tikunei Zohar, Intr.: 12a.* [20] Chochmah. [21] Malchut. [22] *Zohar III: 248a,* *(Notes cont. at end of Hebrew Text)*

of the soul to compress or to open, and there is no need to go any further into this matter which is simple, comprehensible, and intelligible to every intelligent person, namely, that the pronunciation of the letters and vowels transcends the apprehended and comprehended intellect, and is, rather, from the hidden intellect, and the primordium of the intellect which is in the articulate soul. That is why an infant cannot speak, even though it understands everything.[26]

●▲However, the letters are on planes of "matter" and "form", referred to as "internal" and "external."[27] Their source in the primordium of the intellect and the will of the soul is but the "form" of the change in pronunciation which there is among the twenty-two letters. The aspect of the "matter" and "body" of their formation, however, i.e. the aspect of their "externality," is the breath issuing from the heart. For from this breath is formed the simple sound that issues from the throat,[28] and is consequently divided into the twenty-two enunciations, and the expression of the twenty-two letters through the five known organs [*aleph-chet-hai-'ayin*[29] through the throat; *gimmel-yud-kaf-kuf* through the palate etc.], while the breath (itself) is uttered by the letter *hai*—"the light letter . . .",[30] which is the source of the "matter" and "body" of the letters prior to their division into twenty-two. And that is why our sages, of blessed memory, said that "This world[31] was created by the *hai*."

● Now, though this is the "lower *hai*" [the latter *hai* of the Tetragrammaton[32]], while our sages, of blessed memory, related this to the verse "For by *Yud-Hai*,"[33] this is because its source, and the beginning of its egression into a state of manifestation from the concealment of the *yud*,[34] is influenced and issued forth from the rank of the "upper *hai*."[35] This *hai* has dimensions of "length" and "width" to indicate the faculty of *binah*,[36] which is the expansion of the "concealed intellect"[37] into a state of manifestation and apprehension, with an extension of *da'at*,[38] and its diffusion culminates in the heart, as mentioned in the *Tikunim*[39] that "*binah*—that is the heart, and therewith the heart understands."[40] And from there issues the breath, the original manifestation of the "body" of the letters of speech[41] which become revealed from the concealment of the *yud* through the five organs. The form of the "lower *hai*",[42] which, in its written form, also has dimensions of length and width, indicates the extension of the aspect of His blessed Sovereignty,[43] "The sovereignty of all worlds"[44]—above and below, and in the four directions, which extend

---

[26] *The following passage by the author's grandson and disciple, R. Menachem Mendel of Lubavitch, will illuminate the above: "With respect to the formation* (i.e. *coming into being) of the letters of thought and speech, we see that they are born and issue from the (emotive) attributes that are in the heart; for from the heart (a desire) ascends to the mind to meditate and think with respect to the desire and passion that are in one's heart, or with respect to the fear and fright (that are in one's heart), and as explained in* Tanya *I, end of ch. 20. And from this it issues, afterwards, in the letters of speech: to speak of that matter. On the other hand, one does not think or speak at all pertaining to something to which one has no wish and will in his*

הנפש לקמוץ ולא לפתוח כלל וכלל ואין להאריך בדבר הפשוט ומובן ומושכל לכל משכיל שמבטא האותיות והנקודות הוא למעלה מהשכל המושג ומובן אלא משכל הנעלם וקדמות השכל שבנפש המדברת ולכן אין התינוק יכול לדבר אף שמבין הכל:

אך האותיות הן בבחינת חומר וצורה הנקרא פנימית וחיצונית כי הגם שמקורן הוא מקדמות השכל ורצון הנפש זו היא בחינת צורת שינוי המבטא שבכ"ב אותיות אבל בחינת החומר וגוף התהוותן והוא בחי' חיצוניותן הוא ההבל היוצא מהלב שממנו מתהוה קול פשוט היוצא מהגרון ואח"כ נחלק לכ"ב הברות וביטוי כ"ב אותיות בה' מוצאות הידועות אחה"ע מהגרון גיכ"ק מהחיך כו' ומבטא ההבל הוא אות ה' אתא קלילא כו' והוא מקור החומר וגוף האותיות טרם התחלקותן לכ"ב ולכן ארז"ל שעוה"ז נברא בה':

והנה הגם שהיא ה' תתאה ה' אחרונה שבשם הוי' ורז"ל דרשו זה על פסוק כי ביה היינו לפי שמקורה וראשיתה לבא לבחי' גילוי מהעלם היו"ד הוא מושפע ונמשך מבחינת ה' עילאה שיש לה התפשטות אורך ורוחב להורות על בחינת בינה שהיא התפשטות השכל הנעלם בבחי' גילוי והשגה בהרחבת הדעת והשפעתה מסתיימת בלב וכמ"ש בתיקונים דבינה לבא ובה הלב מבין ומשם יוצא ההבל מקור גילוי גוף האותיות הדבור המתגלות בה' מוצאות מהעלם היו"ד ותמונת ה' תתאה בכתיבתה גם כן בהתפשטות אורך ורוחב מורה על התפשטות בחי' מלכותו יתברך מלכות כל עולמים למעלה ולמטה ולד' סטרין המתפשטות ונמשכות

---

heart. Conclusively we see that speech is subject to the emotive attributes, for thence it flows and issues.

In fact, however, we see also a contradiction to this, viz. that the formation of speech, and its root, is not only from the emotive attributes alone. Rather, its root is of a higher (source), namely— issuing from the very intellect in the articulate soul, and as empirically evident that a suckling child is unable to speak, even though it possesses emotions; moreover, its emotive attributes are stronger than those of an adult, for when it has a desire there is no stopping whatever of its spirit, and it screams and becomes angry. Nevertheless, the child cannot articulate what is in its heart, but merely screams and cries with a simple voice (non-intelligible

(Notes cont. at end of Hebrew Text)

and issue from the letters of the "word of the Lord,"[45] as it is written in *Kohelet*:[46] "Wherever the king's word is regnant," as explained elsewhere.[47] [[48]As for understanding somewhat the concept and nature of "letters of speech" in relation to Divinity, inasmuch as He has no form of a body, nor of soul, Heaven forfend, this was already explained in a more or less elaborate way ([49] in *Likutei Amarim*, part II: chs. 11 and 12, see there)].

●▲ As for an exposition of the idea why our sages, of blessed memory, said that *this* world was created by the *hai*: it is known to all the wise of heart that the multitude of the worlds and *hechalot*[50] [which are innumerable, as it is written: "Is there then a number unto His hosts?",[51] and in every *hechal* and host there are a thousand thousands and myriad myriads of angels,[52] and also *nefesh-ruach-neshamah-chayah-yechidah*,[53] rungs to no end, and (likewise) in every world; and (moreover) *hechalot* from the multitude of the *hechalot* that are in Atzilut, Beriah, Yetzirah].

Now, all these multitudes, one multitude after another *ad infinitum*,[54] all this issues and effuses from the multitude of combinations of the twenty-two letters[55] of the "word of the Lord,"[56] which, in turn, divide into many (more) combinations, truly *ad infinitum*, as stated in *Sefer Yetzirah*:[57] "Seven stones build five thousand and forty houses; from here onwards go and count what the mouth is not able to express ..."[58] Though there are among the rungs and levels of the angels and souls so many different kinds of levels and rungs *ad infinitum*, one surpassing the other, all issues according to the permutations in combinations, and the substitutions of *aleph-tav*, *bet-shin*,[59] ...[60] ([61]as mentioned in ch. 12[62]). But in a general way they all possess wisdom and knowledge, and they know their Creator, because their vivification stems from the "inwardness" of the letters which issue from the rank of the Supreme *chochmah*, as men- ▲tioned above. This lowly world, however, with its vivification, is too small[63] to contain and endure the light and vivification from the aspect of the "form" of the letters and their "inwardness"—radiating and diffusing in it without any garment and concealment as they shine and effuse to the souls and angels. Rather, the radiation and diffusion comes and effuses to this world

[45] *Psalms 33:6—the "Word of G-d" (*malchut*; see Introduction) by which the universe was created; see* infra *(esp.* notes 75ff.*).* [46] *Eccles. 8:4.* [47] Tanya *III:4.* [48] *Brackets appear in the text.* [49] *Brackets appear in the text.* [50] *Shrines, palaces.—Worlds, shrines, hosts, etc., all refer to the different levels of the Divine emanations that are brought about by means of* tzimtzum. *Cf. the Introduction.* [51] *Job 25:3.* [52] *See Daniel 7:10;* cf. *Hagigah 13b, and* Tanya *I, ch. 46.* [53] *Scripture uses these five terms for the soul. (See Genesis Rabba 14:9; Deut. Rabba 2:37.) They are not synonyms, but every term denotes a different gradation of soul.* Nefesh, *the lowest grade, is the natural soul, the simple life of man.* Ruach, *the next*

ונמשכות מאותיות דבר ה׳ כמ״ש בקהלת באשר דבר מלך שלטון כמ״ש במ״א. [ולהבין מעט מזעיר ענין ומהות אותיות הדבור באלהות שאין לו דמות הגוף ולא הנפש ח״ו כבר נתבאר בדרך ארוכה וקצרה (בלק״א ח״ב פי״א וי״ב ע״ש)]:

אך ביאור הענין למה אמרו רז״ל שעוה״ז דוקא נברא בה׳. הנה ידוע לכל חכמי לב כי ריבוי העולמות וההיכלות אשר אין להם מספר כמ״ש היש מספר לגדודיו ובכל היכל וגדוד אלף אלפין ורבוא רבבן מלאכים וכן נרנח״י מדרגות לאין קץ ובכל עולם והיכלות מריבוי היכלות שבאצי׳ בריאה יצירה הנה כל ריבויים אלו ריבוי אחר ריבוי עד אין קץ ממש הכל נמשך ונשפע מריבוי צירופי כ״ב אותיות דבר ה׳ המתחלקות ג״כ לצירופים רבים עד אין קץ ותכלית ממש כמ״ש בספר יצירה שבעה אבנים בונות חמשת אלפים וארבעים בתים מכאן ואילך צא וחשוב מה שאין הפה יכול לדבר כו׳ והגם שיש במעלות ומדריגות המלאכים ונשמות כמה וכמה מיני מעלות ומדריגות חלוקות לאין קץ גבוה על גבוה הנה הכל נמשך לפי חילופי הצירופים והתמורות בא״ת ב״ש כו׳ (וכמ״ש בפ״ב) אך דרך כלל הנה כולם בעלי חכמה ודעת ויודעים את בוראם מפני היות חיותם מפנימיות האותיות הנמשכות מבחי׳ ח״ע וכנ״ל. אך העולם הזה השפל עם החיות שבתוכו קטן מהכיל ולסבול אור וחיות מבחינת צורת האותיות ופנימיותן להאיר ולהשפיע בו בלי לבוש והסתר כמו שמאירות ומשפיעות לנשמות ומלאכים רק ההארה וההשפעה באה ונשפע לעוה״ז

מבחינת

---

grade, is the spiritual life of man. Neshamah, *still higher, is the soul proper, the Divine soul. Still higher grades are* chayah *(living) and* yechidah *(single, or unique). Generally we speak only of the lower three grades (*nefesh, ruach, *and* neshamah*), sometimes of* chayah, *and hardly ever of* yechidah. *This will be understood by the analogy to the five worlds, the ten Sefirot (and the letters of the Tetragrammaton), to which these five grades correspond.* Yechidah *corresponds to Adam Kadmon, the Sefirah* keter *(the thorn of the* yud*). It is the actual Divine spark, thus totally concealed and hidden.* Chayah *corresponds to Atzilut, the Sefirah* chochmah *(the* yud*), thus the beginning of Divine manifestation and*

(Notes cont. at end of Hebrew Text)

from the level of the "matter" and "body" of the letters, and of their "externality" [which is the aspect of the breath which divides into the seven "breaths"[64] of *Kohelet*[65] on which the world stands, as mentioned in the sacred *Zohar*[66]]. And this is the "Utterance from the mouth of the Lord"[67] which vests itself in this world and all its hosts to animate them; but in it is vested the aspect of the "form" of the letters of speech and thought, (emanating) from His holy attributes, and His will and wisdom . . ., which are totally united in the blessed En Sof. ([68]And this is what Rabbi Isaac Luria, of blessed memory, stated[69] that the aspect of the *chitzoniyut* of the vessels of *malchut* of Atzilut[70]—[alluded to by the *hai* of the blessed Tetragrammaton]—descended and became the soul for the world of Asiyah). And thus it is stated in the *Tikunim*,[71] that the *yud*[72] is in Atzilut . . ., and the lower *hai*[73] nests in Asiyah.

●▲ Now, with terrestrial man, for example, when one who is so great a sage as to comprehend the wonders of wisdom contracts his intellect and thought to a single letter of his speech, this is an immense contraction (*tzimtzum*) and a great descent for his wondrous wisdom. Metaphorically speaking, precisely so, and infinitely more so, there was an immensely great and mighty contraction (*tzimtzum*)[74] when during the six days of creation "The heavens were made by the word of the Lord, and all their hosts by the breath of His mouth"[75]—i.e. by the letter *hai* of the blessed Tetragrammaton [the "easy letter"] as it is written:[76] "בהבראם," (which means): בה' בראם ("when He created them," He created them, by the *hai*).[77] It[78] is the source of the nine fiats which issued from the first fiat:[79] בראשית[80]—which is also a fiat,[81] (and identical with) the aspect of *chochmah* which is called ראשית.[82] But at that time this efflux and descent was without any arousal from below whatever[83]—"For there was no man to work . . .,"[84] but solely "Because He delights in *chesed*,"[85] and "The world was built by *chesed*."[86] And this is the meaning of בהבראם: באברהם (when He created them—because of Abraham),[87] for "*chesed* is to Abraham."[88]

▲ But after the creation of "man to work on it . . .,"[89] every arousal from above, to arouse the attribute of the Supreme *chesed*, depends on an arousal from below,[90] i.e. the charity and kindness which Israelites perform in this world. That is why our sages, of blessed memory, said: [91]"Whoever says that he has nothing but Torah—thus no deeds of kindness—he has not even Torah; rather, one is to busy himself with Torah and the performance of kindness."[92] For

---

[64] הבלים *(conventionally translated: vanities)*. [65] *Eccles 1:2:* Vanity *(1) of* vanities *(plural, thus 2)* . . . vanity *(1) of* vanities *(2), all is* vanity *(1), thus altogether seven. See Eccles. Rabba on this verse, and comment.* ad loc. [66] *Zohar I: 146b; III: 47b.* [67] *Deut. 8:3;* cf. *Zohar III: 47b.* [68] *Brackets appear in the text.* [69] Cf. Etz Chayim *47:2, and* Yefeh Sha'ah *(comment. on the* Etz Chayim*; Tel Aviv 1960), by R. Solomon Hakohen, on this chapter;* cf. *also* Etz Chayim *4:1, 2.* [70] *See Introduction for the meaning of this phrase and the statement* in toto. [71] Cf. *Tikunei Zohar VI: 23a, in the light of* Etz Chayim *42: end of ch. 4 (where this phrase appears in these very words).* [72] *Supreme* chochmah. [73] Malchut *of Atzilut,*

מבחינת חומר וגוף האותיות וחיצוניותם שהוא בחינת ההבל המתחלק לז' הבלים שבקהלת שעליהם העולם עומד כמ"ש בזוה"ק והוא מוצא פי ה' המתלבש בעולם הזה וכל צבאיו להחיותם ובתוכו מלובשת בחינת צורת אותיות הדבור והמחשבה ממדותיו הקדושות ורצונו וחכמתו וכו' המיוחדות בא"ס ב"ה בתכלית (וז"ש האר"י ז"ל שבחינת חיצוניות הכלים דמל' דאצילות המרומזות בה' של שם הוי' ב"ה הם ירדו ונעשו נשמה לעולם העשיה) וכ"כ בתקונים שהיו"ד הוא באצי' כו' וה' תתאה מקננת בעשיה:

והנה באדם התחתון למשל מי שהוא חכם גדול להשכיל נפלאות חכמה ומצמצם שכלו ומחשבתו באות אחד מדבורו הנה זה הוא צמצום עצום וירידה גדולה לחכמתו הנפלאה ככה ממש עד"מ ויתר מזה לאין קץ הי' צמצום גדול עצום ורב כאשר בדבר ה' שמים נעשו בששת ימ"ב וברוח פיו כל צבאם היא אות ה' של שם הוי' ב"ה אתא קלילא כמ"ש בהבראם בה' בראם היא מקור הט' מאמרות שנמשכו ממאמר ראשון בראשית דנמי מאמר הוא היא בחינת חכמה הנקראת ראשית אך אז היתה המשכה וירידה זו בלי אתדל"ת כלל כי אדם אין לעבוד כו' רק כי חפץ חסד הוא ועולם חסד יבנה וזהו בהבראם באברהם כי חסד לאברהם כו'. אך אחר בריאת האדם לעבדה כו' אזי כל אתדל"ע לעורר מדת חסד עליון הוא באתדל"ת בצדקה וחסד שישראל עושין בעולם הזה לכן אמרו רז"ל כל האומר אין לו אלא תורה בלי גמ"ח אפילו תורה אין לו אלא לעסוק בתורה ובגמ"ח כי

הנה

---

which ultimately vests itself in Asiyah. [74] *See Introduction.* [75] *Psalms 33:6;* cf. *note 67.* [76] *Genesis 2:4.* [77] *The word* בהבראם *(when He created them) is divisible into two parts, forming these two words.—Menachot 29b; Midrashim on Gen. 2:4.* [78] *The* hai, malchut *of Atzilut, in which* chochmah *of Atzilut is vested.* [79] *"The universe was created by ten fiats"*—(Mishnah, *Avot V:1;* cf. *Zohar I:256b; Tikunei Zohar, Intr.: 10b; Zohar Chadash, beg. of Medrash Hane'elam) the first of which is generally all-inclusive.* [80] *The initial word of the Torah,* בראשית, *may mean* in, *or* with ראשית *(the beginning).* [81] *Rosh Hashana 32a; Zohar I:15a; see also Zohar I:16b.*

(Notes cont. at end of Hebrew Text)

though the "Torah derives from *chochmah*,"[93] and the world subsists by virtue of the Torah[94] and those who discourse in it,[95] because by their speech they elicit illuminations and effusions[96] from the Supreme *chochmah* [the source of Torah] to the plane of the letters of speech [wherewith the world was created, as our sages, of blessed memory, said:[97] "Do not read בניך (your children) but בוניך (your builders)"], this efflux, however, is really of the category of a great descent. Therefore it is necessary to arouse the Supreme *chesed* which, like water, is drawn from a high place to a low place[98] by means of an arousal from below: through charity and the nether *chesed*,[99] diffusing life and kindness "To revive the spirit of the humble and downcast."[100]

And this is the meaning of the verse: "Let not the wise glorify himself in his *chochmah* . . ., but in this let him glory . . . for I am the Lord who does *chesed*. . . ."[101] For it is *chesed* that causes the vitality of *chochmah* to issue downwards, and without that it is called "*His chochmah*" only—without any efflux of life from it, Heaven forfend.[102]

• Hereby will be understood the statement of R. Isaac Luria, of blessed memory, that there are two kinds of souls among Israel: the souls of Torah scholars—who occupy themselves with Torah all their lives; and the souls of those who perform the commandments—who occupy themselves with charity and the performance of kindness.[103] Now it would seem that scholars, too, need to occupy themselves with the performance of kindness, as our sages, of blessed memory, said that (otherwise) "He has not even Torah." However, as regards scholars of Torah whose study of the Torah is their principal (occupation) [and most of their time is spent in it, and but a small part of their time with the performance of kindness], the effect of their arousal from below, to arouse the Supreme *chesed* to call forth and bring downward the infinite light vested in the Supreme *chochmah* [the source of G-d's Torah which is in their mouths], extends only to the realm of the souls that are in Beriah [through their occupation with *Gemara*], and to the angels that are in Yetzirah [through their occupation with *Mishnah*]. For the vivifications of the souls and angels effuse from the combinations of the letters of speech, i.e. the Oral Torah.[104] But the origin of the letters is in the Supreme *chochmah*, as mentioned above. Thus in order to call forth and bring downward an illumination and vivification from the level of the Supreme Breath [the "lower *hai* "[105]] to this lowly world, which implies an extremely great contraction (*tzimtzum*), the arousal from below by the scholars of Torah [who for but a small part of their time occupy themselves with charity and the performance of kindness] is not sufficient. (This is effected) only through the arousal by those who perform the commandments,

[93] *Zohar II:121a; etc. (see* supra, *section I, note 37).* [94] *Zohar II:200a;* cf. *Avot I:2; Shabbat 88a.* [95] *Zohar I:47a, III:35a.* [96] V. L.: *"inspirations," or: "indwellings."* [97] *Berachot 64a; Yevamot 122b; etc.* Cf. *above, note 58.* [98] *Water, the nature of which is to flow downwards, is symbolic of* chesed.—*See* infra, *section VIII, and notes 14f* ad loc. [99] I.e., *the kindness expressed and performed below, by man.* [100] Par. *Isaiah 57:15.* [101] *Jer. 9:22f.* [102] *When man performs* chesed *he elicits the "lights and inspirations of the supreme* chochmah", *thus sharing, as it were, in the supreme* chochmah. *When there is no human act of kindness, the supreme* chochmah *remains so to speak passive and will not issue downwards:*

• 18 Av

הנה הגם דאורייתא מחכמה נפקת ובאורייתא מתקיים עלמא ובאינון דלעאן בה כי בדבורם ממשיכים הארות והשפעות (נ"א והשראות) ח"ע מקור התורה לבחינת אותיות הדבור שבהן נברא העולם כמארז"ל א"ת בניך אלא בוניך הרי המשכה זו היא בחינת ירידה גדולה ולזה צריך לעורר חסד עליון הנמשך כמים ממקום גבוה למקום נמוך באתדל"ת בצדקה וחסד תתאה שממשיכי' חיים וחסד להחיות רוח שפלים ונדכאים. וז"ש אל יתהלל חכם בחכמתו כו' כ"א בזאת יתהלל כו' כי אני ה' עושה חסד כו' כי החסד הוא הממשיך חיי החכמה למטה וא"ל הרי נקראת חכמתו לבדו בלי המשכת חיים ממנה ח"ו. ובזה יובן מ"ש האריז"ל שיש ב' מיני נשמות בישראל נשמות ת"ח העוסקים בתורה כל ימיהם ונשמות בעלי מצות העוסקים בצדקה וגמ"ח. דלכאורה הרי גם ת"ח צריכים לעסוק בגמ"ח כמארז"ל שאפילו תורה אין לו אלא שהת"ח שתורתן עיקר ורוב ימיהם בה ומיעוט ימיהם בגמ"ח הנה פעולת אתערותם דלתתא לעורר חסד עליון להמשיך ולהוריד אוא"ס המלובש בחכ"ע מקור תורת ה' שבפיהם הוא רק לעולם הנשמות שבבריאה ע"י עסק התלמוד ולמלאכים שביצירה ע"י לימוד המשנה יען היות חיות הנשמות והמלאכים נשפעות מצירופי אותיות הדיבור היא תורה שבע"פ ומקור האותיות הוא מח"ע כנ"ל אך להמשיך ולהוריד הארה וחיות מבחינת הבל העליון ה' תתאה לעולם הזה השפל שהוא צמצום גדול ביתר עז לא די באתעדל"ת של ת"ח העוסקים מיעוט ימיהם בצדקה וגמ"ח אלא על ידי אתערותא דבעלי מצות העוסקים

---

*it remains "His (*i.e. *G–d's) chochmah" only. See* Maamarei Admur Hazaken, MS-R. Pinchas Reises *(New York, 1957), p. 78f.* Cf. *Ta'anit 7a (on Proverbs 5:17), and see also Tikunei Zohar, 22:65a.* [103] Cf. Biurei Hazohar, Vayeshev, *pp. 25a–b (on Zohar I:182a).* [104] *That is, the Torah which is studied and transmitted by word of mouth, referring to the Talmud and Rabbinic writings.—The influence of the Oral Torah extends only as far as Yetzirah:* Gemara *as far as Beriah,* and Mishna *as far as Yetzirah; see* Tanya *I, end of ch. 40, and ch. 52;* infra, *sect. XXVI.* [105] Malchut *of Atzilut, the recipient and channel of the Supreme* chochmah.

i.e. they who are occupied with charity and the performance of kindness for the major part of their life[106] ([107]and as explained in *Likutei Amarim*, part I: ch. 34). That is why they are called the "supporters of Torah."[108] They are the categories and levels of *netzach* and *hod*,[109] because they cause the light of Torah to issue downwards to the world of Asiyah.[110]

Now it is clear why charity is referred to as an "act," as it is written: "And the *act* of *tzedakah* will be peace."[111] For the effect (of charity) is to elicit the light of G–d to the world of Asiyah.[112] And that is the meaning of the subtle phraseology of the sacred *Zohar*—"He who makes the Holy Name," expressly saying "who makes." For by an arousal from below [through charity and the nether *chesed*] one arouses the Supreme *chesed* to elicit an infinite light from the rank of the Supreme *chochmah* [the *yud* of the Name], to the *hai* of the Name [the aspect of "speech" and "breath" of His blessed mouth]—to diffuse to the world of Asiyah. And, analogously speaking, though not to be compared in the least, just as a human being speaks only to others ([113]and not when he is alone), and then [when speaking to them] he contracts his intellect and thought.[114] And the intelligent will understand.

●▲VI. "But he who sows *tzedakah* has a reward of truth." (Proverbs XI)[1] This means that the attribute of truth is the reward for the sowing of *tzedakah*.[2]

It is also written:[3] "You give truth unto Jacob,"—and the prophet engages in extolling the Holy One, blessed is He, as mentioned in the sacred *Zohar*.[4] This means that it is the Holy One, blessed is He, who gives the attribute of truth unto Jacob.[5] Now this needs to be understood. Is there then no truth in Jacob, Heaven forfend, until the Holy One, blessed is He, gives it to him from above? However, it is well-known that the attribute of Jacob is the attribute of *rachamim* (compassion).[6] And the service of G–d in a mode of compassion derives from arousing in the heart of man a great compassion for the Divine spark in his soul, which is removed from the light of G–d's Countenance when (man) goes about in the darkness of the vanities of the world. And this arousal of compassion itself derives from the contemplation on, and cognition of the greatness of G–d: how even the most infinitely sublime worlds are esteemed as truly naught before Him. For all their bounty and vitality is

---

[106] *In other words, their* principal *occupation is with the performance of kindness. But they, too, have to appoint and set aside times for the study of Torah (just as the scholars of Torah have to perform commandments as well)*; cf. Hilchot Talmud Torah *by the author, ch. III, and* Kuntress Acharon ad loc. [107] *Brackets appear in the text.* [108] *Zohar I: 8a (cf. Proverbs 3:18 and Levit. Rabba 25:1).* [109] *Zohar III: 53b.—In the "Man Image" of the Sefirot,* netzach *and* hod *signify the "thighs" and the "loins"—which support the "body" (Torah); see Tikunei Zohar, Intr.: 17a, and* supra, *sect. I. (Cf. Introduction.)* [110] Cf. *Zohar I: 8a, III: 53b.* [111] *Isaiah 32:17;* cf. infra, *sect. XII.* [112] Cf. infra, *sect. IX.—*Asiyah *means an act, or*

העוסקים רוב ימיהם בצדקה וגמ"ח (וכמ"ש בלק"א בח"א פל"ד) ולכן נקראו תמכי אורייתא והן בחינות ומדרגות נו"ה להיותן ממשיכין אור התורה למטה לעולם העשיה. ובזה יובן למה נקרא הצדקה בשם מעשה כמ"ש והיה מעשה הצדקה שלום ע"ש שפעולתה להמשיך אור ה' לעולם העשיה. וזהו דקדוק לשון זוה"ק מאן דעביד שמא קדישא דעביד דייקא כי באתערותא דלתתא בצדקה וחסד תתאה מעורר חסד עליון להמשיך אור א"ס מבחינת חכמה עילאה יו"ד של שם לה' של שם בחינת הדבור ורוח פיו יתברך כדי להשפיע לעולם העשי' ועד"מ להבדיל הבדלות אין קץ כמו שאדם אינו מדבר אלא לאחרים (ולא כשהוא בינו לבין עצמו) ואז מצמצם שכלו ומחשבתו בדבורו אליהם והמשכילים יבינו:

ו **זורע** צדקה שכר אמת (במשלי י"א). פי' ששכר זריעת הצדקה היא מדת אמת וכתיב תתן אמת ליעקב ושבחא דקוב"ה מסדר נביא כו' כמ"ש בזוה"ק פירוש שהקב"ה הוא הנותן מדת אמת ליעקב וצריך להבין וכי אין אמת ביעקב ח"ו עד שהקב"ה יתן לו מלמעלה:

אך הנה מודעת זאת דמדת יעקב היא מדת רחמנות ועבודת ה' במדת רחמנות היא הבאה מהתעוררות רחמים רבים בלב האדם על ניצוץ אלקות שבנפשו הרחוקה מאור פני ה' כאשר הולך בחשך הבלי עולם והתעוררות רחמנות זו היא באה מהתבונה והדעת בגדולת ה' איך שאפילו העולמות העליונים למעלה מעלה עד אין קץ כלא ממש חשיבי קמיה כי כל שפעם וחיותם אינו רק

deed. [113] *Brackets appear in the text.* [114] *Speech is the outer manifestation of mind, of intellect and thought; it reveals the inner thought. Thought itself is self-containing; it exists in isolation. Speech reveals nothing to the speaker, for he knows already, he has the original thought of which speech is a mere manifestation. Thus speech reveals to* others. *It is a communication directed to another.*

At the same time, speech is of necessity a limitation on thought. On the pre-verbalising level one must seek the right letters, words and expressions to reveal the inner thought. The intuitive concept, as it is in itself in the inner thought, cannot be expressed; it is too compact and concentrated. It needs to "come down," to be analysed and

(Notes cont. at end of Hebrew Text)

but from a gleam and reflection of a single letter of His blessed Name, as it is stated:[7] "The world-to-come was created by the *yud*. . . ."

Now, it is in this radiation and reflection [which is an extension of vivification from His blessed Name to animate the upper and lower beings]—that there is a distinction and difference with respect to upper and lower beings. For "This world was created by the *hai*. . . ."[8] Also, all the differences in the details in every world are according to the differences in the combinations of the letters.[9] The differences in the temporal dimensions of past, present and future, and the differences in all the events throughout the differing times, all of these, too, came about from the variations in the combinations of the letters. For (the letters) are the conduits of the vivification from His attributes, His Name be blessed ([10]as explained in *Likutei Amarim*, part II: ch. 11).

But as for His blessed Being and Essence, it is written:[11] "I, the Lord, I have not changed;" neither in terms of changes of the development from the uppermost of levels to the nethermost [for just as He, blessed be He, is found in the upper worlds, so He is in precisely that measure in the nether worlds ([12]and as explained in *Likutei Amarim*, part I: ch. 51)], nor in terms of temporal changes [for just as He was alone, one and unique, before the six days of creation, so He is now after the creation]. This is so because everything is absolutely as nothing and naught in relation to His being and essence,[13] just as, metaphorically speaking [to appease the ear,[14] while in fact "There is no comparison unto You," it is written[15]], a single letter of the speech, or even of the thought of man is in relation to the general being and essence of the rational soul; and as explained elsewhere ([16]in *Likutei Amarim*, part II: ch. 9), see there.[17]

That is why we say[18] "The King Who is exalted, alone from aforetime." This means, just as aforetime, before the creation, He was alone, so now, too, "He is exalted . . . and elevated beyond the days of the world;"[19] that is, He is exalted and elevated, transcending the dimension of time—which is referred to as "*the days of the world*." This is so because the life-force of all the days derives solely from the aspect of "the King . . .", as explained elsewhere.[20]

It follows then that the compassion for the spark that dwells in the dark and gloomy body—the "hide of the snake,"[21]

---

[7] *Menachot 29b. See* supra, *section V.* [8] Ibid.—*The radiation from the* hai *is different than that of the* yud, *(more contracted, concealed etc.). Thus there is a difference between the "upper" world (the world-to-come) and the "nether" world (this world). Likewise with the effects of all the other emanations.* [9] *The letters of G-d's fiats (by which everything was created), each of which designates a specific emanation.—See* supra, *section V (and note 54* ad loc.). [10] *Brackets appear in the text.* [11] *Malachi 3:6.* [12] *Brackets appear in the text.* [13] Cf. *Zohar I:11b.* [14] I.e. "*to make it intelligible to man*" *(cf.* Mechilta, Yitro, s.v. בחדש: *ch. 4).* [15] *Psalms 40:6.* [16] *Brackets appear in the text.* [17] Cf. *also* Tanya *I, ch. 20.* [18]

רק מזיו והארה מאות אחד משמו יתברך כמאמר ביו"ד נברא עוה"ב כו'. והנה בזיו והארה זו שהוא התפשטות החיות משמו יתברך להחיות עליונים ותחתונים הוא שיש הבדל והפרש בין עליונים לתחתונים שעולם הזה נברא בה' וכו' וכן כל שינויי הפרטים שבכל עולם ועולם הוא לפי שינויי צירופי האותיות וכן שינויי הזמנים בעבר הוה ועתיד ושינויי כל הקורות בחילופי הזמנים הכל משינויי צירופי האותיות שהן הן המשכת החיות ממדותיו ית"ש (כמ"ש בלק"א ח"ב פי"א) אבל לגבי מהותו ועצמותו יתברך כתיב אני ה' לא שניתי בין בבחינת שינויי ההשתלשלות מרום המעלות עד למטה מטה שכמו שהוא יתברך מצוי בעליונים כך הוא ממש בשוה בתחתונים (וכמ"ש בלק"א ח"א פנ"א) ובין בבחינת שינויי הזמן שכמו שהיה הוא לבדו הוא יחיד ומיוחד לפני ששת ימי בראשית כך הוא עתה אחר הבריאה והיינו משום שהכל כאין ואפס ממש לגבי מהותו ועצמותו וכמו אות אחד מדבורו של אדם או אפילו ממחשבתו לגבי כללות מהות הנפש השכלית ועצמותה עד"מ לשבך את האזן ובאמת אין ערוך אליך כתיב וכמ"ש במ"א (בלק"א ח"ב פ"ט) ע"ש. וזהו שאומרים המלך המרומם לבדו מאז פירוש כמו שמאז קודם הבריאה היה הוא לבדו הוא כך עתה הוא מרומם כו' ומתנשא מימות עולם פי' שהוא רם ונשא למעלה מעלה מבחינת זמן הנקרא בשם ימות עולם והיינו לפי שחיות כל ימות עולם הוא רק מבחינת המלך כו' וכמ"ש במ"א. ואי לזאת הרחמנות גדולה מאד מאד על הניצוץ השוכן בגוף החשוך והאפל משכא דחויא

העלול

Liturgy, *Morning-prayers.* [19] Ibid. *(in the same passage).* [20] *See* Tanya, *part II: ch. 7.* [21] *See Tikunei Zohar, Intr.: 10b; 58:92b;* Etz Chayim *49:4.* Cf. *Pirke de R. Eliezer, ch. 20, and Midrash Tehilim, XCII:6.*

is overwhelming. For it is liable to contract impurity and to become defiled by all the lusts, the Merciful save us, were it not for G-d being a shield unto it, and giving it strength and might to wage war with, and triumph over the body and its passions.[22] And this is the meaning of "Lord of our strength . . ., shield of our salvation . . ."[23]

●▲ Now it is well-known that there are two types of awe and love (respectively).[24] The first ones are born from the contemplation on, and cognition of the greatness of G-d, and those matters that lead to a love of G-d and the fear of Him. The latter[25] ones are those that come afterwards, from above, as a gift, [as explained elsewhere[26] in comment on the verse[27] "I will make your priesthood a rewarding service"—that it refers to the attribute of (the supreme) love; and it is likewise in regard to awe]. Now there is surely no comparison between the first ones—which are the products of the created intellect, and the latter ones—which are from the Creator, blessed be His Name.[28] That is why *these* (the latter) are referred to as "truth," for the seal of the Holy One, blessed is He, is truth,[29] for He is the true Truth,[30] and all the truth among the creatures is esteemed as nothing before Him.[31]

But which is the way whereby man merits the "truth of G-d"? It is by arousing, before G-d, great compassion for the spark in his soul. And this is the attribute of Jacob—who[32] "Bolts from one end to the other end,"[33] that is, from the uppermost of all levels to the nethermost,[34] to cause the "truth of G-d" to issue to this lowly dark world, and as it is written: "When I sit in darkness, the Lord is a light unto me."[35] And this is the meaning of "For His *chesed* has prevailed over us. . . . "[36]

However, the arousal of great compassion before G-d also needs to be in truth. But even when it is true in mortal terms,[37] how can one arouse [through (relative) truth] the supernal compassion from the truth of G-d? The advice for this is the trait of charity—which is the attribute of compassion for one who has nothing of his own, to "Revive the spirit of the humble . . ."[38] And the arousal from below elicits an arousal from above:[39] the Lord arouses the sleeping and awakens the unconscious,[40] that is, the concealed, great compassion and Supernal graces,[41] to emerge from concealment into manifestation and a great illumination, to radiate with the light of life[42]—"The truth of G-d into the world."[43]

And this is the meaning of the idiom of "sowing" related to charity: to make sprout

---

[22] Cf. *Sukah 52b.* [23] *See above, note 18.* [24] I.e. *two general types of awe:* yirah tataah, *and* yirah ila'ah *(or:* yirat haromemut*), and two general types of love:* ahavah zutta, *and* ahavah rabba *(or:* ahavah beta'anugim*). See* Tanya *I, ch. 40* ff., *esp. ch. 43;* infra, *sect XV (and notes 89* ff. a.l.*); and sect. XVIII. See also Author's Introduction to* Tanya *I, part II; and* Hilchot Talmud Torah, *IV:6.* [25] *The second sorts of awe and love.* [26] Tanya *I, ch. 14; see* infra *sect. XVIII.* [27] *Numbers 18:7.* [28] I.e. *the lower levels of awe and love are the sort of service that is earned through man's efforts. The higher levels are the type of service that is granted as a gift from above.* [29] *Shabbat 55a; see also Zohar I:2b.* [30] Cf. *Jer. 10:10, and* Yerushalmi,

העלול לקבל טומאה ולהתגאל בכל התאוות ר״ל לולי שהקב״ה מגן לו ונותן לו עוז ותעצומות ללחום עם הגוף ותאותיו ולנצחן וז״ש ארון עוזנו כו׳ מגן ישענו כו׳. והנה מודעת זאת דיש ב׳ מיני דו״ר הראשונות הן הנולדות מהתבונה והדעת בגדולת ה׳ ובדברים המביאין לידי אהבת ה׳ ויראתו והאחרונות הן הבאות אחר כך מלמעלה בבחי׳ מתנה וכמ״ש במ״א ע״פ עבודת מתנה אתן את כהונתכם שהיא מדת אהבה וכן הוא ג״כ ביראה. והנה ודאי אין ערוך כלל בין הראשונות שהן תולדות השכל הנברא לגבי האחרונות שהן מהבורא ית״ש. ולכן הן הן הנקראות בשם אמת כי חותמו של הקב״ה אמת שהוא אמת האמיתי וכל האמת שבנבראים כלא חשיבי קמיה אך איזה הדרך שיזכה האדם לאמת ה׳ הנה הוא על ידי שיעורר רחמים רבים לפני ה׳ על הניצוץ שבנפשו שהיא מדתו של יעקב מבריח מהקצה אל הקצה דהיינו מרום המעלות עד למטה מטה להמשיך אמת ה׳ לעולם השפל הזה החשוך וכמ״ש כי אשב בחשך ה׳ אור לי וזהו כי גבר עלינו חסדו כו׳. אך התעוררות ר״ר לפני ה׳ צ״ל ג״כ באמת וגם כשהוא באמת שלו איך יוכל על ידי אמת שלו לעורר רחמים עליונים מאמת ה׳. אך העצה לזה היא מדת הצדקה שהיא מדת הרחמים על מאן דלית ליה מגרמיה להחיות רוח שפלים כו׳ ובאתעדל״ת אתעדל״ע ה׳ מעורר ישנים ומקיץ נרדמים הם בחי׳ רחמים רבים וחסדים עליונים הנעלמים לצאת מההעלם אל הגילוי והארה רבה לאור באור החיים אמת ה׳ לעולם (וזה) [וזהו] לשון זריעה הנאמר בצדקה להצמיח אמת

Sanhedrin I:1. [31] *See Maimonides,* Hilchot Yesodei Hatorah *I:3, 4.—G-d is* emet leamito, *absolute truth. All other truth is but relative.* [32] *See above note 6.* [33] *Exodus 26:28.* [34] Cf. *Zohar I:1b;* cf. *also* supra, *note 6.* [35] *Micha 7:8.* [36] *Psalms 117:2: For His* chesed *has prevailed over us, and the truth of G-d (issues) to the world.—By means of the attribute of* rachamim (tiferet), chesed *prevails over* gevurah *and issues to us, drawing forth the truth of G-d into this world.* Cf. *Tikunei Zohar, Additions: 139a.* [37] Lit.: *When one is in his own truth.* [38] Par. *Isaiah 57:15.* [39] *See* supra, *sect. IV note 45.* [40] Par. Liturgy (Nishmat Kol Chay). [41] *The Supreme* chesed. [42]

(Notes cont. at end of Hebrew Text)

the Supreme truth of G-d, especially through the charity and the true kindness performed with the Holy Land [may it be built and established speedily in our days, amen] to realise the verse: "Truth shall sprout forth from the land"[44]—from the sowing of charity in it.[45] And the kindness and great compassion that are gathered and gleaned into it, they arouse—correspondingly—the Supreme graces[41] that are hidden and concealed,[46] as it is written: "Which You have hidden . . .,"[47] to establish it and to set it up firmly. Of this it is written: "Through *tzedakah* shall you be established."[48]

●▲VII. "Happy are we, how goodly is our portion and how pleasant is our lot. . . ."[1] "The Lord is the share of my portion and my cup . . . Portions have fallen unto me . . ."[2]

To understand the phraseology "our portion," and "our lot," it is necessary to explain properly a common expression in the sayings of our sages, of blessed memory, viz.: "He has no part in the G-d of Israel."[3] It would seem that a term like "part" cannot possibly be applied to the blessed Divinity, because He is not divisible into parts, Heaven forfend. However, the idea is, as it is written about Jacob: "And he called Him *E-l*, G-d of Israel."[4] The meaning of this is as follows.

In truth, G-d, as His Name is so is He.[5] Though He permeates all the upper and lower worlds, from the peak of all levels to this lowly physical world [as it is written: "Do I not fill the heavens and the earth,"[6] *I* Myself, indeed, meaning, His Being and His Essence, as it were, and not only His glory], even so, He is *kadosh* (holy)[7] and distinct from the upper and nether worlds, and is not at all contained in them, Heaven forfend, in the way, for example, that the soul of man is contained in the body, as explained elsewhere at length.[8] And for this reason they could not receive their vivification from His Being and Essence in itself, as it were. Rather, the extension of the vivification wherewith the Holy One, blessed is He, animates the upper and nether worlds, is, metaphorically speaking, as a radiation shining from His blessed Name, for He and His Name are One,[9] and as it is written: "For His Name alone is exalted, [only His reflection and] His splendour are on the earth and the heavens. . . ."[10]

This radiation actually vests itself in the upper and lower worlds in order to animate them. It is contained in them by means of many intermediaries and numerous, immense contractions, in a development

---

[44] *Psalms 85:12. "Land" refers to the Holy Land, the subject of this Psalm.* [45] Cf. *the comment of Rashi* a.l.; cf. *also* infra, *sect. VII, note 36.* [46] V. L.: *concealed in it.* [47] *Psalms 31:20; see* infra, *sect. XIII.* [48] *Isaiah 54:14.*

Section VII

[1] Liturgy, *Morning Prayers.* [2] *Psalms 16:5* f. Cf. Sifre, *Deut. 53 (on Deut. 11:26).* [3] E.g., *Berachot 63b; Zohar II:3b; etc.* [4] *Genesis 33:20; commentaries* a.l. [5] *For He and His Name are entirely one (see below, note 9). G-d's appellates are His attributes. The Divine attributes are of the Divine essence, and G-d is absolutely one with His essence.* Cf. Tanya *II:8* f. *See also* Kuzary *II:2, and* Moreh Nevuchim *I:51* ff. [6] *Jer. 23:24.* [7] *De-*

אמת העליון אמת ה׳ ובפרט בצדקה וחסד של אמת שעושים עם אה״ק תובב״א לקיים מ״ש אמת מארץ תצמח על ידי זריעת הצדקה בה וחסד ור״ר הנאספים ונלקטים לתוכה הם מעוררים ג״כ חסדים עליונים הצפונים ונעלמים (כנ״א בה) כמ״ש אשר צפנת כו׳ לכוננה ולהקימה וז״ש בצדקה תכונני:

ז **אשרינו** מה טוב חלקנו ומה נעים גורלנו כו׳ ה׳ מנת חלקי וכוסי וגו׳. חבלים נפלו לי וגו׳. להבין לשון חלקנו וגורלנו צריך לבאר היטב לשון השגור במארז״ל אין לו חלק באלהי ישראל כי הגם דלכאורה לא שייך לשון חלק כלל באלקות יתברך שאינו מתחלק לחלקים ח״ו. אך הענין כמ״ש ביעקב ויקרא לו אל אלהי ישראל פירוש כי הנה באמת הקב״ה כשמו כן הוא כי אף דאיהו ממכ״ע עליונים ותחתונים מרום המעלות עד מתחת לארץ הלזו החומרית כמ״ש הלא את השמים ואת הארץ אני מלא אני ממש דהיינו מהותו ועצמותו כביכול ולא כבודו לבד אעפ״כ הוא קדוש ומובדל מעליונים ותחתונים ואינו נתפס כלל בתוכם ח״ו כתפיסת נשמת האדם בגופו עד״מ כמ״ש במ״א באריכות. ולזאת לא היו יכולים לקבל חיותם ממהותו ועצמותו לבדו כביכול רק התפשטות החיות אשר הקב״ה מחיה עליונים ותחתונים הוא עד״מ כמו הארה מאירה משמו יתברך שהוא ושמו אחד וכמ״ש כי נשגב שמו לבדו רק זיוו והודו על ארץ ושמים וגו׳. והארה זו מתלבשת ממש בעליונים ותחתונים להחיותם ונתפסת בתוכם על ידי ממוצעים רבים וצמצומים רבים ועצומים בהשתלשלות המדרגות

---

noting separateness; cf. Mechilta, Yitro, s.v. בחדש*: ch. 2 (on Ex. 19:6)*, *and* Sifra, *beg. of* Kedoshim *(on Levit. 19:2)*. [8] Cf. Tanya *I, ch. 42.* [9] *Zohar I: 7b; II: 86a. See also* ibid., *II: 90b.*—Cf. Pirke de R. Eliezer, *ch. 3.* [10] *Psalms 148:13.*

of levels by way of cause and effect . . . ●▲Now, this radiation [though above it radiates and extends itself in unlimited and infinite fashion to animate innumerable, concealed worlds, as mentioned in the *Idra Rabba*,[11] nevertheless] as it descends netherwards, by way of numerous contractions, to animate those that were created, formed and made, it is generally divided into 613 in number.[12] These 613 gradations correspond to the 613 commandments of the Torah, which are the 613 kinds of conduits of this radiation from the light of the blessed En Sof to illumine man's soul [which is made up of 248 "organs" and 365 "sinews"[13]]. For the principal aim of the descent and efflux of this radiation, netherwards, to all those created, formed and made, is for (the soul's) sake; for the purpose of them all is man, as known.[14]

Now this number is in a general way. More specifically, every single commandment sub-divides into infinite details, which are the essentials of the detailed rulings of every commandment [which are without number, as it is written:[15] "sixty are the queens"—these are the sixty tractates . . ., "and maidens without number"—these are the rulings . . .[16]]. For they are the efflux from the Supreme Will . . .[17] It is precisely so with man's soul. For all the souls in the world were contained in Adam.[18] In a general way his soul was divisible into the number 613: 248 "organs" and 365 "sinews"; but in a more specific way his soul was divisible into innumerable sparks[19]—which are the souls of all of Israel from the days of the Patriarchs and the tribes, to, and including the coming of the Messiah, when Scripture will be fulfilled: "And the number of the children of Israel will be as the sand of the sea that cannot be measured nor counted"[20]—"Because of the great quantity."[21]

●▲ Now "The beauty of Jacob is a reflection of the beauty of Adam,"[22] for he rectified the sin of Adam.[23] His soul, too, was composed of all the souls of Israel, in all times. And he was a vehicle for the Torah as it is above, which is referred to

[11] *Zohar III: 127b–145a, see there.* [12] *See Zohar III: 129a.* [13] *The 248 operational precepts correspond to the 248 organs, and the 365 prohibitory precepts correspond to the 365 sinews.* Cf. *Zohar I:170b; Macot 23b; see also Zohar II: 25a.* [14] *Man—created last, was first in intent (G-d's thought)—Tikunei Zohar, Introd.: 6a; that is, the whole creation is for the purpose of man who, in turn, is to serve G-d in, and with the creation.—See also Genesis Rabba I: 4 and comment.* ad loc.; *Zohar II: 108b, 275b, and III:306b. R. Saadiah Gaon,* Emunot Vedeot, *IV: Intr. and ch. I.* [15] *Song 6: 8.* [16] *Zohar III: 216a; Tikunei Zohar, Intr.: 14b; Zohar Chadash, Tik.: 98a;* et passim. Cf. *Numbers Rabba 18: 21, and Song Rabba 6: 14.* [17] Cf.

המדרגות דרך עלה ועלול וכו׳. והנה הארה זו אף שלמעלה היא מאירה ומתפשטת בבחי׳ בלי גבול ותכלית להחיות עולמות נעלמים לאין קץ ותכלית כמ״ש באדרא רבא אעפ״כ ברדתה למטה ע״י צמצומים רבים להחיות הנבראים והיצורים והנעשים היא נחלקת דרך כלל למספר תרי״ג כנגד תרי״ג מצות התורה שהן הן תרי״ג מיני המשכות הארה זו מאור א״ס ב״ה להאיר לנשמת האדם הכלולה מרמ״ח אברים ושס״ה גידים אשר בעבודה הוא עיקר תכלית ירידת והמשכת הארה זו למטה לכל הנבראים והיצורים והנעשים שתכלית כולן הוא האדם כנודע:

והנה מספר זה הוא בדרך כלל. אבל בדרך פרט הנה כל מצוה ומצוה מתחלקת לפרטים רבים לאין קץ ותכלית והן הן גופי הלכות פרטיות שבכל מצוה שאין להם מספר כמ״ש ששים המה מלכות הן ס׳ מסכתות כו׳ ועלמות אין מספר הן ההלכות כו׳ שהן המשכת רצון העליון כו׳ וכן הוא ממש בנשמת האדם כי הנה כל הנשמות שבעולם היו כלולות באדה״ר ודרך כלל היתה נשמתו נחלקת למספר תרי״ג רמ״ח אברים ושס״ה גידים אך דרך פרט נחלקת לניצוצות אין מספר שהן נשמות כל ישראל מימות האבות והשבטים עד ביאת המשיח ועד בכלל שיקוים אז מ״ש והיה מספר בנ״י כחול הים אשר לא ימד ולא יספר מרוב. והנה שופריה דיעקב מעין שופריה דאדה״ר שתיקן חטא אדה״ר והיתה נשמתו ג״כ כלולה מכל הנשמות שבישראל מעולם ועד עולם והיה מרכבה לתורה שלמעלה שנק׳ בשם

infra, *sect. XXIX.* [18] *See Exodus Rabba 40,2; 3, and* Tanchuma, Ki Tissa*: 12, as explained by R. Isaac Luria in* Sha'ar Hapessukim, Bereishit*: III,* et passim *in his other writings.* [19] Cf. Sha'ar Hagilgulim, *VI and XI.* [20] *Hosea 2:1.* [21] *See Genesis 16:10.* [22] *Bava Metzia 84a; see also Zohar I:35b, 168a, 222a, etc., and* ref. *in following note.* [23] *See Zohar III:111b; also, Zohar II:141b, and* Nitzutzei Orot ad loc.; cf. *further Zohar I:142b, and* Derech Emet ad loc.; *and Zohar II:275b–276a. R. Nathan Nata Schapiro, in his* Megaleh Amukot, *section* Toldot *(on Gen. 27:33; ed. Lublin 1912, p. 41a), explains how the rectification of Adam's sin is implied in this saying by*

(Notes cont. at end of Hebrew Text)

as *Adam*, as it is written:[24] "And on the likeness of the throne there was a likeness as the appearance of *Adam* . . .";[25] also, it is written:[26] "And *zot* was within,[27] in Israel"—and "*Zot* refers only to the Torah . . ."[28] For the Torah was contained and vested in the soul of Israel the Patriarch[29]—which compounded all the souls.

And this is the meaning of "And he called Him *E-l*, G-d of Israel": *E-l*[30] denotes the elicitation of the radiation from the light of the blessed En Sof from concealment to manifestation, to radiate manifestly in his soul, and as it is written:[31] "*E-l* is the Lord, and He gives us light."[32] And after Jacob, the light of the blessed En Sof shines openly in all the upright of heart who occupy themselves with the Torah and the commandments.

Now, this manifestation in their mind and heart with an exceeding uplifting and abundant strength,[33] occurs at the time of ●▲ prayer, as explained elsewhere. Though this manifestation through the occupation with Torah and the commandments is, generally, equal in every one of Israel [for we all have one Torah and one law[34]], nevertheless, in a more specific way not all the souls (*nefesh*) or spirits (*ruach*) and souls (*neshamah*) are equal in this regard, depending on the occurrence and time of their reincarnation and their coming into this world; and as our sages, of blessed memory, said:[35] "With what was your father more heedful? He answered him—with the *Tzitzit*. . . ."[36] Likewise not all the generations are the same. For just as with the organs of man every organ has its own, special and particular function [the eye to see and the ear to hear], so, too, through every commandment there radiates a special and particular light from the light of the blessed En Sof. And though every soul of Israel needs to be reincarnated in order to fulfil *all* the 613 commandments,[37] even so, this special care with a particular *Mitzvah* is necessary only for the sake of an increase, and prudence, and additional zeal—with exceeding uplifting and strength, doubly and manifold, surpassing the zeal for the other commandments. And that is what he meant when he said "With what was he *more* careful?"[38]

Now, the advantage of this individual light to the individual souls is not in the category of apprehensible reason and knowledge, but transcends the faculty of knowledge. For thus it rose in the Mind before Him, blessed be He. And its model below is truly the notion of the "lot."[39]

---

[24] *Ezekiel 1:26.* [25] *See Zohar I:71b–72a; and* cf. ibid., *97a.* [26] *Ruth 4:7.* [27] *The conventional translation of* לפנים *is* aforetimes, *but the author emphasises here its etymological meaning of* within *(*cf. *Zohar III:180a, and the commentary of R. Moses Zacuto,* ad loc.*; see also* Pardess Rimonim, *16:4). Thus the verse now reads: "And* zot *(this,* i.e. *the Torah) was within, in Israel (*i.e. *Jacob),"* i.e. *engraved and marked in Israel.* [28] *Zohar III:81b; Zohar Chadash, Ruth, 88d; see Menachot 53b.* [29] *Zohar Chadash, Ruth: 88c* f.; cf. *R. Menachem Mendel of Lubavitch,* Reshimot al Rut, *p. 224.—A literal translation should read:* Israel the Old (ישראל סבא)*; a Midrashic term (*cf. *Gen. Rabba 68:11, 74:11; etc.), apparently to*

בשם אדם כמ"ש ועל דמות הכסא דמות כמראה אדם וכו' וכמ"ש וזאת לפנים בישראל כו' אין זאת אלא תורה כו' שהיתה כלולה ומלובשת בנשמת ישראל סבא הכלולה מכל הנשמות וזהו ויקרא לו אל אלקי ישראל. אל לשון המשכת ההארה מאור א"ס ב"ה מההעלם אל הגילוי להאיר בבחי' גילוי בנשמתו וכמ"ש אל ה' ויאר לנו ואחריו כל ישרי לב העוסקים בתורה ובמצות מאיר אור ה' א"ס ב"ה בבחינת גילוי בנשמתם וזמן גילוי זה ביתר שאת ויתר עז ההארה במוחם ולבם הוא בשעת התפלה כמ"ש במ"א. והנה אף שגילוי זה ע"י עסק התורה והמצות הוא שוה לכל נפש מישראל בדרך כלל כי תורה אחת ומשפט א' לכולנו אעפ"כ בדרך פרט אין כל הנפשות או הרוחות והנשמות שוות בענין זה לפי עת וזמן גלגולם ובואם בעוה"ז וכמארז"ל אבוך במאי הוי זהיר טפי א"ל בציצית כו' וכן אין כל הדורות שוין כי כמו שאברי האדם כל אבר יש לו פעולה פרטית ומיוחדת העין לראות והאזן לשמוע כך בכל מצוה מאיר אור פרטי ומיוחד מאור א"ס ב"ה ואף שכל נפש מישראל צריכה לבוא בגלגול לקיים כל תרי"ג מצות מ"מ לא נצרכה אלא להעדפה וזהירות וזריזות יתירה ביתר שאת ויתר עז כפולה ומכופלת למעלה מזהירות שאר המצות. וזהו שאמר במאי הוי זהיר טפי דייקא. והנה יתרון האור הזה הפרטי לנשמות פרטיות אינו בבחינת טעם ודעת מושג אלא למעלה מבחינת הדעת שכך עלה במחשבה לפניו יתברך ודוגמתו למטה הוא בחינת הגורל ממש:

ח זורע

---

distinguish between the general term Israel, and Israel the Patriarch (where the Scriptural reference can be interpreted either way). In Cabbalistic writings, though, a distinction is made between **ישראל סבא** *and what the Zohar calls* **ישראל זוטא** *(Israel the Young, or Small); see e.g.,* Zohar *II:43a, 216a; etc. See* Torah Or, Shemot, *p. 50d.* [30] *This Divine Name is related to* chesed, *denoting G–d's grace and benevolence (Zohar III:30b–31a, 65a; Tikunei Zohar 67a; cf. also* Mechilta, Beshalach, *on Exodus 15:2, and see* Pardess Rimonim *1:10),* chesed *being the determinative motive "to diffuse without limit, even where compassion is not applicable at all" (see* infra, *section XV, and note 33* ad loc.*).* [31]

(Notes cont. at end of Hebrew Text)

●▲VIII. "He sows *tzedakot* and causes *yeshu'ot* to sprout."[1] The usage of an idiom of "sowing" in relation to the commandment of charity [and as it is written in the verse "Sow then for yourselves for *tzedakah* . . ."[2]] will be understood by what our sages, of blessed memory, said:[3] "Rabbi Eliezer gave a coin unto a poor person, and then prayed; as it is written:[4] through *tzedek* I will see Your face."[5] This means that the manifestation of His blessed Divinity, which becomes revealed in the thought of man and in his devotion during prayer,[6] each according to his own measure,[7] is by way of the charity and the "*Chesed* of the Lord eternally upon those who fear Him . . ."[8] This means, the light of the Lord, the blessed En Sof, which radiates with a great illumination above in the upper worlds [which are the *hechalot* with the angels and souls in them, explained in the sacred *Zohar*[9] by their names according to their places in the order of prayer arranged for us by the Men of the Great Assembly] is in a state of so great and immense a manifestation that they are truly in a state of self-dissolution, and esteemed as truly naught before Him, absorbed in His blessed light. Now, this "Light—which is good"[10] radiates from there to this lowly world upon those that fear the Lord and esteem His Name, who desire to worship Him by the "Service of the heart—meaning prayer,"[11] and as it is written[12]: "And the Lord will enlighten my darkness." Now, the descent of this illumination downwards to this world, is called the "*Chesed* of the Lord"[13]—referred to as water,[14] which descends from a high place to a low place . . .[15]

● Now it is well-known that above there is also an attribute of *gevurah*, and *tzimtzum*, to contract and conceal His blessed light to prevent it from becoming revealed unto the lower worlds.[16] However, everything depends on the arousal from below.[17] For if man conducts himself with kindness, by bestowing life and *chesed* . . ., he arouses the same above, as our sages, of blessed memory, said: "With the measure a man metes, it shall be measured to him."[18] Though it would appear that this is not of the (same) measure: (man deserves) only that the life of the world-to-come be granted to him, corresponding to his bestowal of life in this world; but not that the life from the illumination of the actual light of G-d[19]

Section VIII
[1] Liturgy, *Morning-prayers*. Cf. Boneh Yerushalayim, *sect. 131 (p. 135 ff) for an exposition of this section.* [2] *Hosea 10:12.* [3] *Bava Batra 10a.* [4] *Psalms 17:15.* [5] Cf. *R. Shmuel Schneersohn*, Maamar Shoftim Veshotrim—*5633 (New York, 1956), pp. 4 ff.* [6] *Which is called the "service of his heart" (see below, note 11)*; cf. Or Zarua', *by R. Isaac bar Moses of Vienna, beg. of* Hilchot Keriat Shema'*: par. 7 (*s.v. אמר רבין*; ed. Zitomir 1862, I: p. 21a).* [7] *Tikunei Zohar 70:135b; Zohar I:103b.* [8] *Psalms 103:17.* [9] *Zohar I:38a–ff;* ibid., *41a–ff; II: 244b–ff.* [10] Par. *Genesis I:4.* [11] Sifre, *Deuter.: 42 (on Deut. 11:13); Ta'anit 2a.* [12] *II Samuel 22:29 (Psalms 18:29).* [13] *See*

ח זורע צדקות מצמיח ישועות הנה מ״ש לשון זריעה במצות הצדקה וכמ״ש בפסוק זרעו לכם לצדקה כו׳. יובן ע״פ מה שארז״ל ר״א יהיב פרוטה לעני והדר מצלי דכתיב אני בצדק אחזה פניך פי׳ כי גילוי אלקותו יתברך המתגלה במחשבתו של אדם וכונתו בתפלתו כל חד לפום שיעורא דיליה הוא בתורת צדקה וחסד ה׳ מעולם ועד עולם על יראיו כו׳ כלומר שאור ה׳ א״ס ב״ה המאיר למעלה בעולמות עליונים בהארה רבה בבחי׳ גילוי רב ועצום עד שבאמת הן בטלין במציאות וכלא ממש חשיבי קמיה ונכללין באורו ית׳ והן הן ההיכלות עם המלאכים והנשמות שבהן המבוארים בזוה״ק בשמותם למקומותם בסדר התפלה שסדרו לנו אנשי כנה״ג הנה משם מאיר האור כי טוב לעולם השפל הזה על יראי ה׳ וחושבי שמו החפצים לעבדו בעבודה שבלב זו תפלה וכמ״ש וה׳ יגיה חשכי והנה ירידת הארה זו למטה לעוה״ז נקראת בשם חסד ה׳ המכונה בשם מים היורדים ממקום גבוה למקום נמוך כו׳:

והנה מודעת זאת שיש למעלה גם כן מדת הגבורה והצמצום לצמצם ולהסתיר אורו יתברך לבל יתגלה לתחתונים אך הכל תלוי באתעדל״ת שאם האדם מתנהג בחסידות להשפיע חיים וחסד כו׳ כך מעורר למעלה כמשארז״ל במדה שאדם מודד בה מודדין לו אלא דלכאורה זו אינה מן המדה כ״א להשפיע לו חיי העוה״ב לבד כנגד מה שהוא משפיע חיי עוה״ז אבל לא להשפיע לו חיי הארת אור ה׳ [נ״א

above, note 7. [14] Zohar II: 175b; III: 255a and 257a; see also Pardess Rimonim XXIII: 13, s.v. מים, and note 15, below. [15] Cf. Tikunei Zohar 69: 105a (and cf. ibid., 25: 70b). See infra, sect. XII, and Torah Or, Vayera: 14c. [16] See infra, section XV. [17] See supra, section V, note 83. [18] Mishnah, Sotah I: 7. [19] V.L.: the actual light of the blessed En Sof.

be diffused to him to illumine and enlighten his darkness in "The service of the heart—which is prayer." For the latter is a grade and level of "superior repentance" (*teshuvah ilaah*),[20] as is well-known, inasmuch as it surpasses exceedingly all the life of the world to come, as our sages, of blessed memory, said: "Better one hour of repentance and good deeds . . ."[21] as explained elsewhere at length[22] that the world to come is but a gleam and reflection . . .[23]

• However, metaphorically speaking, the idea is like sowing seeds or planting kernels—the spike that sprouts from the seed, and the tree with its fruits from the kernel, their nature and essence are not that of the seed and kernel at all. For their[24] nature and essence has been spent and is decayed in the soil. It is the vegetative property in the soil itself which brings out and makes grow the spike, the tree and its fruit; it is merely that it does not bring out and manifest its power outwardly, from potential to actuality, except through the seed and the kernel that are decayed in the soil and whose whole power has been consumed by the vegetative property in the soil—and they united and became one. And that is how the vegetative property actualises its potential and effuses vitality to make grow a spike of the kind of the seed, though with a very great increase in every single spike, and likewise, many fruits on every single tree. Moreover, the very nature and essence of the fruits, too, excels in a great and immense magnitude over the nature and essence of the planted kernel. And it is likewise with the produce of the earth which grows from seeds just like kernels, as cucumber, and the like. All this is so because the stem and root of the vitality of the fruits effuses from the vegetative property in the soil—which includes the vitality of all fruits; while the kernels that are sown in the ground are but like the arousal from below, which in the writings of Rabbi Isaac Luria, of blessed memory, is referred to as the "elevation of the *mayin nukvin*."[25]

• Now, metaphorically speaking, precisely like this, every act of charity that Israelites perform, ascends in the sense of an "elevation of the *mayin nukvin*," upwards—to the root of their souls above which, in the phraseology of the *Zohar*, is referred to as *Knesset Yisrael*, and *imma tataah*

---

[20] *For an explanation of this term see* Tanya *III: ch, 8 ff. (esp. ch. 10).* [21] *Avot IV: 17.* [22] Tanya *I, end of ch. 4.* Cf. *also* supra, *section I, note 22.* [23] *See Berachot 17a, and Maimonides,* Hilchot Teshuvah, *ch. 8.—See* supra, *sect. I note 22, and* Likutei Torah *IV: 83d. While* teshuvah tataah *(inferior* teshuvah*) corresponds to* malchut, teshuvah ila'ah *transcends this level and corresponds to the higher Sefirah* binah. *(See Zohar III: 122a ff., and Tikunei Zohar 6: 22a;* Tanya *III: 9.) He who stands in a mode of* teshuvah *is called* ba'al teshuvah; *the Zohar interprets this term literally as "possessed of* teshuvah," *signifying an absolute unification with* teshuvah *and the level it represents. See Zohar II: 106b, and comm.* a.l.; cf. *R.*

• 27 Av • 28 Av

[נ"א א"ס ב"ה] ממש שאיר ויגיה חשכו בעבודה שבלב זו תפלה שהוא בחינת ומדרגת תשובה עילאה כנודע שהרי היא למעלה מעלה מכל חיי עוה"ב כמשארז"ל יפה שעה אחת בתשובה ומע"ט כו' וכמ"ש במ"א באריכות דעוה"ב אינו אלא זיו והארה וכו':

אך הענין הוא עד"מ כמו שזורעין זרעים או נוטעין גרעין שהשבולת הצומחת מהזרע והאילן ופירותיו מהגרעין אינן מהותן ועצמותן של הזרע והגרעין כלל כי מהותם ועצמותם כלה ונרקב בארץ וכח הצומח שבארץ עצמה [נ"א עצמו] הוא המוציא והמגדל השבולת והאילן ופירותיו רק שאינו מוציא ומגלה כחו לחוץ מהכח אל הפועל כי אם על ידי הזרע והגרעין שנרקבין בארץ וכלה כל כחם בכח הצומח שבארץ ונתאחדו והיו לאחדים וע"י זה מוציא כח הצומח את כחו אל הפועל ומשפיע חיות לגדל שבולת כעין הזרע אבל בריבוי הרבה מאד בשבולת אחת וכן פירות הרבה על אילן א' וגם מהותן ועצמותן של הפירות מעולה בעילוי רב ועצום למעלה מעלה ממהותו ועצמותו של הגרעין הנטוע וכן כה"ג בפירות הארץ הגדלים מזרעונין כעין גרעינין כמו קשואים וכה"ג והכל הוא מפני שעיקר ושרש חיות הפירות נשפע מכח הצומח שבארץ הכולל חיות כל הפירות. והגרעינין הזרועים בארץ אינן אלא כעין אתערותא דלתתא הנקראת בשם העלאת מ"נ בכתבי האריז"ל:

וככה ממש עד"מ כל מעשה הצדקה שעושין ישראל עולה למעלה בבחינת העלאת מ"נ לשורש נשמותיהן למעלה הנקרא בשם כנ"י ואימא תתאה בלשון

Judah Loewe, Derech Chayim *on Avot 4:17.* [24] I.e. *of the seed and kernel.* [25] *See* supra, *section IV, note 46.*

and in the phraseology of the Talmud—as *Shechinah.*[26] The Shechinah compounds, and is totally united with all the attributes of the Holy One, blessed is He, the first of which is the attribute of *chesed.* Now, through this elevation, the actual "*chesed* of the Lord" is aroused, i.e., a revelation of His blessed light, to descend and radiate in a great and immense state of manifestation to the souls of Israel below, at least during the time of prayer.[27] For though "His greatness is unfathomable"[28]—to the extent that "All are esteemed as naught before Him,"[29] even so, "Where you find His greatness, there you find His humility,"[30] as "waters, which descend . . ."[31]

And this is the meaning of the verse: "He shines in the darkness as a light unto the upright, he that is gracious, and merciful, and *tzadik.*"[32] For man by being gracious and merciful, and "*tzadik*—fond of *tzedakot,*"[33] causes the light of G-d to shine to his soul which is vested in his body—which stands in darkness, being the "hide of the snake."[34] And this, when darkness is converted to light, is referred to as salvation (*yeshu'ah*).[35]

And this is the meaning of "He causes *yeshu'ot* to sprout." For this salvation sprouts from [the sowing of] the charity sown in the "upper land,"[36] "the land of delight"[37]—which is the Shechinah,[38] and *Knesset Yisrael,*[39] so called because it[40] vests itself in the lower worlds to animate them, as it is written:[41] "Your sovereignty[42] is the sovereignty of all worlds."[43] And this applies most particularly when one sows in the nether Holy Land, which truly corresponds to it.[44] For then the seed is immediately absorbed in the upper land without any obstacle and hindrance whatever, because there is nothing whatsoever that divides and interrupts between the lands of life;[45] for it is the gate of Heaven.[46] It is not so, however, outside the Holy Land, and suffice this for the initiated.

●▲IX. My beloved, brethren and friends—who are to me as my soul: I come as one who reminds and awakens those who sleep the slumber of the vanities of vanities, and to open the eyes of the blind. Let them consider and see[1] that throughout their life all their striving, longing and aiming for all in which there is the "life of their spirit"[2] be in "the source of the living waters"[3] [the Fountainhead of all life[4]], with respect to the soul, as well as to the flesh[5] [i.e., all mundane matters and occupations for livelihood]. Be not like those

[26] *In the* Zohar, *the terms* Knesset Yisrael *and* Imma Tataah *are synonymous with* Malchut *and* Shechinah. *(See* Pardess Rimonim, *23:1, and 11,* s.v. אם הבנים, *and* כנ"י; Tanya *I, ch. 52;* infra, *sect. XXV). There are some instances where this would not seem to be so, but see* Nitzutzei Orot, *by R. Chaim David Azulay, on Zohar II: 85a (and* ibid., *on Zohar II:90a). See also R. Joseph Gikatilla,* Sha'are Orah, *end of ch. 1.* [27] *See above, beginning of this section, and* cf. supra, *end of section IV.* [28] *Psalms 145:3.* [29] *Zohar I:11b.* [30] *Megilah 31a [according to the versions of Pessikta Zutr.* (Midrash Lekach Tov) *on Deut. X:17, and* Yalkut Shimoni, *Psalms 794 (on Ps. 68:5)].* [31] *As waters descend*

בלשון הזהר ושכינה בלשון הגמרא הכלולה מכל
מדותיו של הקב"ה ומיוחדת בהן בתכלית וראשיתן
היא מדת החסד וע"י העלאה זו מתעורר חסד ה' ממש
שהוא גילוי אורו יתברך לירד ולהאיר למטה לנשמות
ישראל בבחי' גילוי רב ועצום בשעת התפלה עכ"פ
כי אף שלגדולתו אין חקר עד דכולא קמיה כלא חשיבי
הרי במקום שאתה מוצא גדולתו שם אתה מוצא
ענותנותו כמים שיורדין כו'. וז"ש זרח בחשך אור
לישרים חנון ורחום וצדיק דע"י שהאדם חנון ורחום
וצדיק צדקות אהב גורם לאור ה' שיורח לנשמתו
המלובשת בגופו העומד בחשך שהוא משכא דחויא
וזה נקרא בשם ישועה כד אתהפכא חשוכא לנהורא
וזהו מצמיח ישועות שישועה זו צומחת מזריעת הצדקה
שזורעין בארץ העליונה ארץ חפץ היא השכינה וכנ"י
שנקראת כן ע"ש שמתלבשת בתחתונים להחיותם
כמ"ש מלכותך מלכות כל עולמים ובפרט מן הפרט
כשזורעין באה"ק התחתונה המכוונת כנגדה ממש
שהזריעה נקלטת תיכף ומיד בארץ העליונה בלי שום
מניעה ועיכוב בעולם מאחר שאין שום דבר חוצץ
ומפסיק כלל בין ארצות החיים כי זה שער השמים
משא"כ בחו"ל וד"ל:

ט אהוביי אחיי ורעיי אשר כנפשי באתי
כמזכיר ומעורר ישנים בתרדמת
הבלי הבלים ולפקוח עיני העורים יביטו לראות להיות
כל ישעם וחפצם ומגמתם לכל בהם חיי רוחם במקור
מים חיים חיי החיים כל ימי חייהם מנפש ועד בשר
דהיינו כל מילי דעלמא ועסקי פרנסה לא יהיה כאלו
דעברין

---

*from a high place to a low place; a simile signifying humility (*cf. Ta'anit *7a). In relation to G-d, the whole creation, all creatures, are insignificant, truly naught and nothing. His greatness, therefore, is not expressed through creation* per se. *Rather, His humility, that G-d created them nevertheless, and cares for them by means of an intense and particular providence, this Divine humility expresses His greatness. Therefore, in the place where you find His greatness, there you find His humility:* His humility being His greatness. *(See* Likutei Torah, *V:4 od;* cf. *also* Tanya *I, ch. 4).* [32] *Psalms 112:4.* [33] Par. *Psalms XI:7; see* Tanchuma, ed. *Buber, Noach:4, and* cf. *(see* Yalkut Shimoni, *Deut., end of 873).* [34] *(Notes cont. at end of Hebrew Text)*

that do everything for their own sake! Let not the house of Israel be like unto all the nations[6] that feed, provide and esteem their wives and children out of love.[7] For it is written: "Who is like unto Your people Israel, a unique nation on earth;"[8] this means that even in mundane matters they will not, Heaven forfend, separate[9] from the True One,[10] to bear false witness, Heaven forfend, by reciting the *Shema* every evening and morning with closed eyes: "the Lord is One"[11]—in the four directions, and in the Heavens above and on earth below,[12] while, as the eyes of the blind are opened "You cause your eyes to close upon Him, and He is no more,"[13] Heaven forfend. Only that shall be befitting us when[14] all our engagements with mundane affairs are not for their *own* sake but in order to vivify the souls, the portions of G-d, and to supply what they lack out of gratuitous kindness. For thereby we give the form[15] a semblance to its Former[16]—"the Lord is One"; for the *chesed* of G-d endures at all time,[17]—a true *chesed*[18]—to animate the universe and all that fills it, every single moment. It is just that according to the Torah a man's wife and children take precedence over all others,[19] except[20] for the saints of that generation—who take precedence over one's children and the saints of the Land of Israel take precedence over the saints in the diaspora,[21] [aside of the fact that they did not leave anyone in the diaspora comparable to themselves],[22] and suffice this for the initiated.

●▲ Therefore, my beloved, my brethren: set your hearts to these words expressed in great brevity ([23] and, please G-d, personally I will speak to them at length)—how in these times, with the advent of the Messiah,[24] the principal service of G-d is the service of charity, as our sages, of blessed memory, said: "Israel will be redeemed only through charity."[25] Our sages, of blessed memory, did not say that the study of Torah is equivalent to the performance of loving-kindness[26] except in their own days. For with them the principal service was the study of Torah and, therefore, there were great scholars: Tannaim and Amoraim. However, with the advent of the Messiah,[27] as "the Hut of David has fallen"[28] to a level of "feet" and "heels"—which is the level of "Action" there is no way of truly cleaving unto it[29] and to convert the darkness into its light, except through a corresponding category of action, namely the act of charity.[30] For, as known to the intelligent, the plane of action with reference to Divinity is the notion of a diffusion and efflux of vitality to the nethermost—to him who has nothing of his own. And whoever sacrifices his impulse in this respect and opens his hand and heart subdues the *sitra achra*[31] and "converts the darkness into the light"[32]

---

[6] L.H. [7] I.e., *out of egocentric motivation.* [8] *I Chronicles 17:21.* [9] V. L.: *to become separated.* [10] Cf. *Zohar II:155b and III:81a.* [11] *Deut. 6:4.* [12] *See Berachot 13b; Zohar I:12a;* ibid., *158a; II:216b.* [13] Par. *Proverbs 23:5.* [14] V. L.: *for . . . to be not.* [15] *The creature (man).* [16] *The Creator.*—Cf. *Genesis Rabba 27:1.* [17] *Psalms 52:3 (*cf. *Rashi* a.l.*).* [18] חסד של אמת—*signifying a gratuitous kindness (*cf. *Rashi on Genesis 47:29), continuous, ceaseless, and absolute (*cf. Likutei Torah, *III: 93b–c).* [19] *See* Shulchan Aruch, Yoreh De'ah*: 251.* [20] *From here to end of paragraph inserted according to* L. H. [21] *See* Sifre, *Deut. 116;* Shulchan Aruch, Yoreh De'ah*:251 (see also* Pitche Teshuvah, *by R.*

דעבדין לגרמיהו ולא יהיה בית ישראל כעוע״ג דזנין ומפרנסין ומוקרין לנשיהו ובנייהו מאהבה כי מי כעמך ישראל גוי אחד בארץ כתיב דהיינו שגם בעניני ארץ לא יפרידו [נ״א יפרדו] מאחד האמת ח״ו להעיד עדות שקר ח״ו בק״ש ערב ובוקר בעינים סגורות ה׳ אחד בד׳ רוחות ובשמים ממעל ובארץ מתחת ובפקוח עיני העורים התעיף עיניך בו ואיננו ח״ו אך בזאת יאות לנו להיות [נ״א בהיות] כל עסקינו במילי דעלמא לא לגרמיהו כי אם להחיות נפשות חלקי אלקות ולמלאות מחסוריהם בחסד חנם שבזה אנו מדמין הצורה ליוצרה ה׳ אחד אשר חסד אל כל היום חסד של אמת להחיות העולם ומלואו בכל רגע ורגע רק שאשתו ובניו של אדם קודמין לכל על פי התורה. ע״כ אהוביי אחיי שימו נא לבבכם לאלה הדברים הנאמרים בקצרה מאד (ואי״ה פא״פ אדבר בם בארוכה) איך היות כל עיקר עבודת ה׳ בעתים הללו בעקבות משיחא היא עבודת הצדקה כמ״ש רז״ל אין ישראל נגאלין אלא בצדקה ולא ארז״ל ת״ת שקול כנגד גמ״ח אלא בימיהם שת״ת היה עיקר העבודה אצלם וע״כ היו חכמים גדולים תנאים ואמוראים. משא״כ בעקבות משיחא שנפלה סוכת דוד עד בחי׳ רגלים ועקביים שהיא בחי׳ עשיה אין דרך לדבקה בה באמת ולהפכא חשוכא לנהורא דילה [נ״א דיליה] כ״א בבחי׳ עשיה ג״כ שהיא מעשה הצדקה כידוע למשכילים שבחי׳ עשיה באלקות היא בחי׳ השפעת והמשכת החיות למטה מטה למאן דלית ליה מגרמיה כלום וכל הזובח את יצרו בזה ופותח ידו ולבבו אתכפיא ס״א ומהפך חשוכא לאור השי״ת

Abraham Tsvi Eisenstadt, ad loc., *par. 4.)* [22] *While the previous seems to be a general Halachic statement, these latter words appear to refer specifically to the Chassidic leaders (including the author's master and colleague, R. Menachem Mendel of Vitebsk) who ascended to the Holy Land accompanied by their families and numerous followers.* [23] *Brackets appear in the text.* [24] *See infra, note 27.* [25] *Shabbat 139a; Sanhedrin 98a; (see glossary notes,* a.l.*).* [26] *See* Mishnah, *Peah I:1: "The study of Torah is equivalent to them all" (including the performance of kindness).—*Cf. *R. Menachem M. Schneerson,* Sichat Chai Elul *5722 (*Sefer Hamaamarim *5702; New York 1964, pp. 143* ff.*),*

(Notes cont. at end of Hebrew Text)

of G-d, blessed be He, Who, with the advent of the Messiah, dwells over us in a state of action; and he will merit to behold "Eye to eye, the Lord returning to Zion . . ."[33]

●▲ X. After greetings of peace and life, "may the opening of my words rouse"[1] the ear that hears the admonition of life[2] which the Lord of life[3] admonished through His Prophets and said: "The graces of the Lord are surely not concluded (תמנו) . . ."[4] Now, it should really have said תמו, as it is written elsewhere: "For your graces are not concluded (תמו) . . ."[5] But this will be understood when considering the statement in the sacred *Zohar*:[6] "There are various types of *chesed*: there is *chesed olam*[7] . . ., and there is *chesed ila'ah*[8]—i.e. *rav chesed*[9] . . ."

Now, it is well-known that the Torah is called *oz* (strength),[10] which is an expression of *gevurah* (might),[11] and as our sages, of blessed memory, said—"The 613 commandments were declared unto Moses at Sinai"[12] from the Mouth of *Gevurah*,[13] and as it is written: "From His right side a fiery law unto them."[14] This means: the source and root of the Torah consists solely of the "graces of the Lord"[15] which are referred to as the "right side".[16] That is, the elicitation of His blessed Divinity, and of a radiation from the light of the blessed En Sof to the upper and lower worlds, is effected by man who elicits the light upon himself by the fulfillment of the 248 operational precepts—which are the "248 organs of the King,"[17] i.e. the 248 vessels and garments for the radiation from the light of the blessed En Sof that is vested in them ([18] and as known, with every commandment there issues forth to him awe and love—from this light).[19] However, this efflux was first vested in the attribute of the *gevurah* of the Holy One, blessed is He,[20] referred to as "fire."[21] (*Gevurah*) is the aspect of the contraction (*tzimtzum*) of the light and vivification that issue from the light of the blessed En Sof,[22] so that it will be able to become vested in the performance of the commandments, practically all of which involve material things—as *Tzitzit*, phylacteries, sacrifices, and charity. And even commandments that involve man spiritually—as awe and love—are in a mode of limitation and measure,[23] and by no means in a mode of infinitude. For not even for a moment could man sustain in his heart so intense a love of G-d as is without end and limitation and still remain in existence in his body, and as the saying of our sages, of blessed memory, that at the time of the giving of the Torah [which was

---

[33] *Isaiah 52:8. The original letter ends here with a concluding salutation. In some versions of this letter there appear slight variations; see* Igrot Ba'al Hatanya, *pp. 93* f.

Section X

[1] Par. *Psalms 119:130.* [2] Par. *Proverbs 15:31.* [3] Lit.: *the living Lord. (The translation used seeks to retain the poetic spirit of the text.)* [4] *Lament. III:22.* [5] Liturgy, *concluding benedictions of the* Amidah. [6] *See Zohar III:133b;* ibid., *140b. See also Zohar I:219a, and III:21a.* [7] *"Grace of the world," or "perpetual grace."* [8] *Supreme* chesed. [9] *Abundant, or magnanimous* chesed *(cf. Exodus 34:6).* [10] Sifre, *Deut. 343 (on Deut. 32:2); Song Rabba I,* s.v. משכני*:1;* Tanchuma,

השי"ת השוכן עלינו בבחי' עשיה בעקבות משיחא ויזכה לראות עין בעין בשוב ה' ציון כו':

י אד"ש וחיים פתח דברי יעיר און שומעת תוכחת חיים אשר הוכיח ה' חיים ע"י נביאו ואמר חסדי ה' כי לא תמנו וגו' והל"ל כי לא תמו כמ"ש כי לא תמו חסדיך וגו'. ויובן עפ"י מ"ש בזוה"ק אית חסד ואית חסד אית חסד עולם כו' ואית חסד עילאה דהוא רב חסד כו'. כי הנה מודעת זאת התורה נקראת עוז שהוא לשון גבורה וכמו שאמרו חז"ל תרי"ג מצות נאמרו למשה מסיני מפי הגבורה וכדכתיב מימינו אש דת למו פי' שהתורה מקורה ושרשה הוא רק חסדי ה' המכונים בשם ימין דהיינו המשכת בחי' אלהותו ית' והארה מאור א"ס ב"ה אל העולמות עליונים ותחתונים ע"י האדם הממשיך האור על עצמו בקיום רמ"ח מ"ע שהן רמ"ח אברים דמלכא. פי' רמ"ח כלים ולבושים להארה [נ"ר דצ"ל להארה] מאור א"ס ב"ה המלובש בהן (ומאור זה יומשך לו דו"ר בכל מצוה כנודע) רק שהמשכה זו נתלבשה תחלה במדת גבורתו של הקב"ה המכונה בשם אש שהיא בחי' צמצום האור והחיות הנמשכות מאור אין סוף ב"ה כדי שתוכל להתלבש במעשה המצות שרובן ככולן הם בדברים חומריים כציצית ותפילין וקרבנות וצדקה ואף מצות שהן ברוחניות האדם כמו יראה ואהבה אעפ"כ הן בבחי' גבול ומדה ולא בבחי' א"ס כלל כי אהבה רבה לה' בלי קץ וגבול ומדה אין האדם יכול לסובלה בלבו ולהיות קיים בגופו אפילו רגע וכמארז"ל שבשעת מ"ת שהיתה התגלות

Beracha: *4; see* supra, *section I, note 10.* [11] *See* supra, *section I, note 10.* [12] *Macot 23b (acc. to various versions,* e.g. Ayin Ya'akov, *etc.);* Tanchuma, Shoftim: *9; etc.* [13] Lit. "*Might,*" *a frequent rabbinic expression denoting Divine Majesty (the Lord), and in Cabbalistic-Chassidic literature related to the equally-named attribute of* gevurah. *This term is also used with respect to the Giving of the Torah (see Macot 24a;* et passim*).—Whereas I could not find any rabbinic saying as our text would seem to suggest—"the 613 commandments of the Gevurah"—(*though see Zohar *II:116b), I divided it under the assumption that the author added it on his own to the original expression. Thus the proof-text from Deut. is also*

(Notes cont. at end of Hebrew Text)

a manifestation of His blessed Divinity, and of the light of the blessed En Sof, on a plane of speech and revelation[24]]—"their souls took flight . . ."[25]

●▲ Now, because the commandments were given to us by way of investment in the attribute of *gevurah* and a contraction (*tzimtzum*) of the radiation . . ., most commandments have a delimited measure. For instance, the length of *Tzitzit* (must be) twelve times the width of the thumb;[26] the phylacteries—two fingers by two fingers,[27] and necessarily square;[28] the *Lulav*—four handbreadths;[29] the *Succah*—seven handbreadths;[30] the *Shofar*—one handbreadth;[31] the *Mikveh*—forty Seahs.[32] The sacrifices, too, have a delimited measure as regards age, as for instance—"sheep of one year old," and "rams of two years old," and "oxen . . ."

The same applies also to the act of charity and the performance of kindness with one's money [even though that is one of the pillars upon which the world stands,[33] and as it is written:[34] "The world was built by *chesed*,"[35] nevertheless]—it has a set measure of preferably one fifth, and of one tenth for an average measure. . . .[36] And this is what is called *chesed olam*: the "*chesed* of G-d enduring continually"[37] that vests itself in the upper and lower worlds through the arousal from below—i.e. the precept of the charity and kindness which people perform among each other.

But because the world is in a state of finitude and measure ["From the earth to the heavens there are 500 years, and also from one heaven to another . . ."[38]; and "Six thousand years shall the world exist . . ."[39]] the Torah's commandment of charity and kindness is also given a limit and measure, just like the other com-●mandments of the Torah. However, this[40] applies only to one who observes the Torah and does not stray from it right or left, even as much as a hair's breadth. But he who has strayed from the path, Heaven forfend, whereas he has perverted his way [thus causing deficiencies in the *kodesh ha'elyon*,[41] that is, he has diminished his value as regards the efflux he could have elicited from the aspect of His Divinity and the radiation from the light of the blessed En Sof by observing the Torah and fulfilling her as behoves[42]]—such perversion cannot be rectified save by an efflux of the Supreme light which transcends the worlds and does not vest itself in them. This is what is called *chesed*

---

[24] *See Exodus 20:15, and* Mechilta, Yitro, ad loc. *(*s.v. בחודש, *ch. 9)*; Pirkei de R. Eliezer *ch. 41; Exodus Rabba, 29:3.* [25] *Exodus Rabba 29:3; Shabbat 88b.* [26] Shulchan Aruch, Orach Chayim, *XI:4;* cf. Shulchan Aruch *of the author,* ibid., *par. 5 (and 7).* [27] Ibid., *XXXII:41,* Magen Avraham a.l., *and* cf. Sh.A. *of the author,* ibid., *par. 63.* [28] *Menachot 35a;* Sh.A., Orach Chayim, *XXXII:39, and* cf. Sh.A. *of the author,* ibid. *par. 59.* [29] *Succah 32b;* Sh.A. Orach Chayim, *650:1.* [30] Sh.A., Orach Chayim, *634:1.* [31] *Nidah 26a;* Sh.A., Orach Chayim *586:9.* [32] Mishna, *Mikvaot I:7;* Sh.A., Yoreh De'ah *201.* [33] Pirkei de R. Eliezer, *ch. 12.* [34] *Psalms 89:3.* [35] *See Avot de R. Natan, ch. 4;*

החגלות אלהותו ית׳ ואא״ס ב״ה בבחי׳ דיבור והתגלות פרחה נשמתן כו׳:

והנה לפי שהמצות ניתנו לנו ע״י התלבשות במדת גבורה וצמצום ההארה כו׳ לכן רוב המצות יש להן שיעור מצומצם כמו אורך הציצית י״ב גודלין והתפילין אצבעים על אצבעים ומרובעות דוקא והלולב ד״ט והסוכה ז״ט והשופר טפח והמקוה מ׳ סאה וכן בקרבנות יש להן שיעור מצומצם לזמן כמו כבשים בני שנה ואילים בני שתים ופרים כו׳ וכן במעשה הצדקה וגמ״ח בממונו אף שהוא מהעמודים שהעולם עומד עליהם וכדכתיב עולם חסד יבנה אפ״ה יש לה שיעור קצוב חומש למצוה מן המובחר ומעשר למדה בינונית כו׳ וזה נק׳ חסד עולם פי׳ חסד אל כל היום המתלבש בעולמות עליונים ותחתונים ע״י אתערותא דלתתא היא מצות הצדקה וחסד שעושים בני אדם זה עם זה ולפי שהעולם הוא בבחי׳ גבול ומדה מהארץ עד לרקיע ת״ק שנה וכן מרקיע לרקיע כו׳ ושית אלפי שני הוי עלמא כו׳ לכן ניתן שיעור ומדה גם כן למצות הצדקה והחסד שבתורה כמו לשאר מצות התורה אך היינו דוקא לשומר התורה ולא סר ממנה ימין ושמאל אפילו כמלא נימא אבל מי שהעביר עליו הדרך ח״ו מאחר שהעוה דרכו לתת מגרעות בקדש העליון שגרע ערכו בחי׳ המשכתו מה שהיה יכול להמשיך מבחי׳ אלהותו והארת האור מאור א״ס ב״ה אילו היה שומר התורה ומקיימה כהלכתה הרי מעוות זה לא יוכל לתקן כ״א בהמשכת האור העליון שלמעלה מהעולמות ואינו מתלבש בהן הנק׳ חסד עילאה

Yalkut Shimoni, Psalms, *839 (on Ps. 89)*. [36] *Maimonides*, Hilchot Matnot 'Aniyim, *VII: 5;* Shulchan Aruch, Yoreh De'ah, *249: 1.* [37] *Psalms 52: 3.* [38] *Hagigah 13a.* [39] *Sanhedrin 97a.* [40] *The limited amount for charity.* [41] Cf. *Zohar III: 66a; also,* ibid., *II: 85b, 155b, 162b and III: 16b;* et passim.—קדש העליון *(Supreme Holiness) refers to the Supreme* chochmah; *see Zohar II: 121a;* Tanya *I, ch. 19. See also* infra, *sect. XVII, note 34.* [42] Cf. Tanya *III: 1.*

ilaah, and *rav chesed*, because it radiates and extends in a state of infinitude, without limit and measure [whereas it is not contracted within the worlds but is in a state of encompassing over them, from aloft, from the peak of all rungs to the end . . .].

Now, when man draws it downwards, through his deeds and the arousal from below, this Supreme light will then radiate and expand within the worlds and rectify all perversions and deficiencies caused in the *kodesh ha'eylon*, renewing their light and goodness with exceeding uplifting and strength, on the level of a truly new light. That is why they said that "In the place where penitents stand . . ."[43]

●▲ Now the essence of penitence (*teshuvah*) is in the heart,[44] for through contrition from the depth of the heart one arouses the depth of this Supreme light. But in order to elicit (this light) so that it will radiate in the upper and lower worlds, it is essential that there be truly an arousal from below, in the mode of an action, i.e. an act of charity and kindness that is without limit and measure. For just as man diffuses *rav chesed* [i.e. ח"ס דלי"ת (he is concerned with him who has not)[45]]—namely to the poor and destitute who has nothing of his own, without setting a limit and measure to his giving and diffusion, the Holy One, blessed is He, likewise diffuses His light and benignity in the mode of *chesed ilaah*, referred to as *rav chesed*, which radiates within the upper and lower worlds in a mode of infinitude, without limit and measure. For in relation to Him, blessed be He, all are in a state of דלי"ת, whereas they have nothing at all of their own, and all that are before Him are esteemed as naught.[46] And all the blemishes that man caused above, in the upper and the lower worlds, through his iniquities, are rectified hereby. And this is the meaning of what is written: "unto the Lord, to exercise *tzedakah* and justice is preferable to sacrifice."[47] Because the sacrifices are in a mode of quantity, measure and limit, while charity can be dispersed without limit for the purpose of rectifying one's iniquities. As for the ruling[48] that he who expends should not expend more than one fifth, this applies only to him who has not sinned, or has rectified his sins by means of self-mortification and fasts, as behoves to rectify all the blemishes above. But he who still needs to remedy his soul, surely the healing of the soul is not inferior

[43] *In the place where penitents stand, not even the perfectly righteous can stand, (Berachot 34b) because the penitents elicit the supreme light in greater strength and measure than the righteous. See Zohar I:39a, and III:16b.* Cf. *also* supra, *sect. VIII, note 23.* [44] *See Isaiah 6:10 (Megilah 17b); Zohar II:150a; also* ibid., *I:41a.*—Cf. *also*, "teshuvah *is* binah" *(Zohar I:79b, III:122a and 255b), "which is the heart" (Tikunei Zohar, Intr.: 17a).* [45] *Division of the word* חס"ד *into* חס *and the final letter* דלי"ת *(*cf. *Tikunei Zohar 22:67b). The* דלי"ת *(which written out fully spells the word meaning* "has not"*), signifies the poor and destitute for which one is to care—see Shabbat 104a; Zohar I:3a, and III:273b. See*

עילאה ורב חסד לפי שמאיר ומתפשט בבחי' א"ס בלי גבול ומדה מאחר שאיננו מצומצם תוך העולמות אלא בבחי' מקיף עליהן מלמעלה מריש כל דרגין עד סוף וכו' וכשהאדם ממשיכו למטה במעשיו ואתעדל"ת אזי אור עליון זה מאיר ומתפשט תוך העולמות ומתקן כל מעוות וכל מגרעות שניתנו בקדש העליון ומחדש אורן וטובן ביתר שאת ויתר עז בבחי' אור חדש ממש לכן אמרו במקום שבע"ת עומדין וכו'. והנה עיקר התשובה הוא בלב כי על ידי החרטה מעומקא דלבא מעורר עומק אור העליון הזה אך כדי להמשיכו להאיר בעולמות עליונים ותחתונים צריך אתעדל"ת ממש בבחי' מעשה דהיינו מעשה הצדקה וחסד בלי גבול ומדה דכמו שהאדם משפיע רב חסד פי' ח"ס דלי"ת דהיינו לדל ואביון דלית ליה מגרמי' כלום ואינו נותן גבול ומדה לנתינתו והשפעתו. כך הקב"ה משפיע אורו וטובו בבחי' חסד עילאה הנק' רב חסד המאיר בבחי' א"ס בלי גבול ומדה תוך העולמות עליונים ותחתונים שכולם הם בבחי' דלי"ת אצלו יתברך דלית להון מגרמיהון כלום וכולא קמיה כלא חשיבי ועי"ז נתקנו כל הפגמים שפגם האדם בעונותיו למעלה בעולמות עליונים ותחתונים. וז"ש עשה צדקה ומשפט נבחר לה' מזבח לפי שהקרבנות הן בבחי' שיעור ומדה וגבול. משא"כ בצדקה שיוכל לפזר בלי גבול לתקן עונותיו. ומ"ש המבזבז אל יבזבז יותר מחומש היינו דוקא במי שלא חטא או שתקן חטאיו בסיגופים ותעניות כראוי לתקן כל הפגמים למעלה. אבל מי שצריך לתקן נפשו עדיין פשיטא דלא גרעה רפואת

הנפש

---

also Netivot Olam, s.v. צדקה, *ch.* 2. [46] *Zohar I:11b.* [47] *Proverbs 21:3.* [48] *Ketuvot 50a.*

to the healing of the body where money does not count, "And all that a man has he will give on behalf of his soul"—states Scripture.[49]

●▲ Now, this type of unlimited[50] kindness is called by the Name of the Holy One, blessed is He, "The graces of the Lord," as it is written: "and the *chesed* of the Lord is everlasting . . ."[51] For though "All of Israel are compassionate and performers of kindness,"[52] nevertheless there is a limit and measure to man's compassion. But the Holy One, blessed is He, is called the blessed *En Sof*,[53] and to His attributes there is no end, as it is written:[54] "For His compassions are not exhausted."[55]

And this is the meaning of what the prophet said, after the destruction and the exile: "The graces of the Lord—**כי לא תמנו**."[56] That is: "Because *we are not perfect*[57] [for we are not whole and perfect without any sin and blemish in the soul and the upper worlds]—that is why we need to conduct ourselves in accordance with "*The graces of the Lord*" which are without limit and end, in order to elicit unto ourselves[58] compassion and *chesed ilaah*, i.e. *rav chesed*, and unlimited, infinite compassion, as it is written: "For His compassion is not exhausted . . ."[59]

And this is what our sages, of blessed memory, meant by saying: "Israel will be redeemed only through charity[60]—which they will perform even when they are legally not obligated, for "The son of David will not come until . . ."[61]

●▲ XI. To make you skillful of understanding[1] that this is not the way in which the light of the Lord dwells,[2] i.e. in there being a desire for the "life of flesh,"[3] and children, and sustenance, for on this our sages, of blessed memory, said: "make naught your will . . ."[4] That is, one's will should be nullified so that one has absolutely no will in any worldly matters that are implied by "children, life, and sustenance,"[5] and as our sages, of blessed memory, said that "Despite yourself, do you live."[6]

This means: there is to be only an absolute belief in the *Yotzer Bereishit*[7]; that is, that the creation of being *ex nihilo* (*yesh meayin*) [which is called *reishit-chochmah*,[8] i.e. His wisdom which is not apprehensible to any creature]—this creation occurs constantly and every moment,[9] by all creatures coming into being [as a substance *ex nihilo* (*yesh meayin*)] from His blessed wisdom which animates everything.[10] And when man will contemplate in the profundity of his understanding, and will imagine in his mind his coming to be

---

[49] *Job 2:4.* Cf. Tanya *III: end of ch. 3. See also Maimonides,* Hilchot De'ot *II:2, and* ibid., *I:5 (in which he obviously includes the disbursement of charity* exceeding *one fifth, and as he states explicitly in his commentary on the* Mishnah, *Peah I:1; according to the above-mentioned this cannot be regarded as contradicting his ruling—based on Ketuvot 50a and 67b—in* Hilchot 'Erchin *VIII:13).* Cf. *R. Chaim David Azulay,* Birkei Yoseph, *on* Yoreh De'ah*: 249, and* idem., Chomat Anoch, *on Proverbs XI. See also* Meah She'arim, *I:28 (p. 9a), and III:3 (p. 18a).* [50] Lit.*: without limit and measure.* [51] *Psalms 103:17.* [52] *Yevamot 79a.* [53] *Infinite.* [54] *Lament. 3:22.* [55] *Text adds* etc., *but omitted according to* H. V. [56] *See note 55*

הנפש מרפואת הגוף שאין כסף נחשב וכל אשר לאיש יתן בעד נפשו כתיב. והנה מדת חסד זו בלי גבול ומדה נקראת על שמו של הקב"ה חסדי ה' כדכתיב וחסד ה' מעולם ועד עולם כו' כי הגם שכל ישראל הם רחמנים וגומלי חסדים ברם יש גבול ומדה לרחמי האדם. אבל הקב"ה נק' א"ס ב"ה ולמדותיו אין סוף כדכתיב כי לא כלו רחמיו וכו'. וז"ש הנביא אחר החורבן והגלות חסדי ה' כי לא תמנו וגו'. פי' לפי שלא תמנו שאין אנו תמימים ושלמים בלי שום חטא ופגם בנפש ובעולמות עליונים ע"כ צריכין אנו להתנהג בחסדי ה' שהם בלי גבול ותכלית כדי לעורר עלינו רחמים וחסד עילאה שהוא רב חסד ורחמים בלי גבול ותכלית כמ"ש כי לא כלו רחמיו וגו'. וזהו שארז"ל אין ישראל נגאלין אלא בצדקה שיעשו גם אם יהיו פטורים מדינא כי אין בן דוד בא כו':

יא להשכילך בינה כי לא זו הדרך ישכון אור ה' להיות חפץ בחיי בשרים ובני ומזוני כי ע"ז ארז"ל בטל רצונך כו' דהיינו שיהי' רצונו בטל במציאות ולא יהיה לו שום רצון כלל בעניני עולם הזה כולם הנכללים בבני חיי ומזוני וכמארז"ל שע"כ אתה חי:

וביאור הענין הוא רק אמונה אמיתית ביוצר בראשית דהיינו שהבריאה יש מאין הנק' ראשית חכמה והיא חכמתו שאינה מושגת לשום נברא הבריאה הזאת היא בכל עת ורגע שמתהוים כל הברואים יש מאין מחכמתו ית' המחיה את הכל וכשיתבונן האדם בעומק הבנתו ויצייר בדעתו הווייתו מאין

---

[57] **לא תמנו** *is usually translated "they are not concluded," but may also mean, as the author translates—interprets now "we are not perfect."* [58] Lit.: *to arouse over us.* [59] *Our verse reads now: (We need to perform kindness in a mode of) "the graces of the Lord, because we are not perfect"; (this enables us to draw forth the infinite Divine compassion) "for His compassion is not exhausted."* [60] *Shabbat 139a; Sanhedrin 98a; (see glossary note* ad loc.*).* [61] *"—until the* perutah *(the smallest coin) has gone from the purse," Sanhedrin 97a; see also Pessikta Zutr. on Deut. 32:36.—The implication is a total disbursement, without regard to any limit or measure.*

(Notes cont. at end of Hebrew Text)

ex nihilo—truly every moment, how can he possibly think he has ever suffered, or had any afflictions related to "children, life, and sustenance," or whatever other worldly sufferings. For the naught (*ayin*) which is His blessed wisdom[11] is the source of life, welfare and delight. It[12] is the Eden which transcends the world to come,[13] except that, because it is not apprehensible, one imagines to have sufferings, or afflictions. In fact, however, no evil descends from above[14] and everything is good, though it is not apprehended because of its immense and abundant goodness. And this is the essence of the faith for which man was created: to believe that "There is no place void of Him"[15] and "In the light of the King's countenance there is life,"[16] and, conclusively, "Strength and gladness are in His place,"[17] because He is but good all the • time. Therefore, first of all, man ought to be happy and joyous at all times, and truly live by his faith in the Lord who animates him and is benignant with him every moment. But he who is grieved and laments makes himself appear as if he has it somewhat bad, and (is) suffering, and lacking some goodness; he is like a heretic, Heaven forfend. That is why the Cabbalists strongly rejected the trait of sadness.[18]

The faithful, however, is not indisposed by any afflictions whatever, and with respect to all mundane matters "yes" and "no" are all the same to him, in a true equation.[19] But he to whom they are not the same, shows of himself that he is of the *erev rav*[20] who act but for themselves, and loves himself to the extent of removing himself from under the hand of the Lord and to live the life of heathens—because of his self-love; that is why he desires the "life of the flesh," and "children and sustenance"—for that is his good. It would have been better for him had he not been created. For the purpose of man's creation in this world is to test him by these trials, to ascertain what is in his heart:[21] whether he will turn his heart towards the other gods, namely the passions of the body which evolve from the *sitra achra*, and desire these, or whether his desire and wish is to live the true life which evolves from the living G-d.[22]

---

[11] *See Tikunei Zohar 42:81b;* ibid., *70:127a and 133b. See also Zohar I:246b; II:43b and 64b;* et passim. Cf. Pardess Rimonim, *23:1,* s.v. אין. *(See* Kitzurim Veha'orot, *p. 100, par. 7).* [12] Ayin, chochmah. [13] *See* supra, *section V, and notes 17* f ad loc.; *(Eden is* chochmah, *and the world-to-come is* binah*).* [14] *Genesis Rabba 51:3.* [15] *Tikunei Zohar 57:91b;* ibid., *70:122b. See Exodus Rabba 2:9.* [16] *Proverbs 16:15.* [17] *I Chronicles 16:27.* [18] *See* Tanya *III:12 (*cf. Tanchuma, Yitro*:16;* Likutei Torah *of R. Isaac Luria, beg. of* 'Ekev*); also,* ibid., *ch. 11, and* Tanya, *ch. 26* f, *31, and 33.—With respect to the Cabbalists' emphasis on joy, and rejection of sadness, see Zohar II:184b, and* Hagahot R.

מאין בכל רגע ורגע ממש האיך יעלה על דעתו כי רע לו או שום יסורים מבני חיי ומזוני או שארי יסורין בעולם הרי האין שהיא חכמתו יתברך הוא מקור החיים והטוב והעונג והוא העדן שלמעלה מעוה"ב רק מפני שאינו מושג לכן נדמה לו רע או יסורים אבל באמת אין רע יורד מלמעלה והכל טוב רק שאינו מושג לגודלו ורב טובו וזהו עיקר האמונה שבשבילה נברא האדם להאמין דלית אתר פנוי מיני' ובאור פני מלך חיים וע"כ עוז וחדוה במקומו הואיל והוא רק טוב כל היום וע"כ ראשית הכל שישמח האדם ויגל בכל עת ושעה ויחיה ממש באמונתו בה' המחיה ומטיב עמו בכל רגע ומי שמתעצב ומתאונן מראה בעצמו שיש לו מעט רע ויסורין וחסר לו איזה טובה והרי זה ככופר ח"ו וע"כ הרחיקו מדת העצבות במאד חכמי האמת. אבל המאמין לא יחוש משום יסורין בעולם ובכל עניני העולם הן ולאו שוין אצלו בהשוואה אמיתית ומי שאין שוין לו מראה בעצמו שהוא מערב רב דלגרמייהו עבדין ואוהב א"ע לצאת מתחת יד ה' ולחיות בחיי עו"ג בשביל אהבתו א"ע וע"כ הוא חפץ בחיי בשרים ובני ומזוני כי זה טוב לו ונוח לו שלא נברא כי עיקר בריאת האדם בעוה"ז הוא בשביל לנסותו בנסיונות אלו ולדעת את אשר בלבבו אם יפנה לבבו אחרי אלהים אחרים שהם תאוות הגוף המשתלשלים מס"א ובהם הוא חפץ או אם חפצו ורצונו לחיות חיים אמיתים המשתלשלים מאלקים חיים אף שאינו יכול (צ"ע. ובאיזה כת"י ליתא תיבות אלו [אף שאינו יכול] ובנוסחא אחרת מצאנו כך. „או אם חפצו ורצונו

Chayim Vital, ad loc.; *Zohar II:218a, and the commentaries* Derech Emet, *and* Nitzutzei Orot, ad loc.; Pardess Rimonim, *23:16*, s.v. **עצב ועצבון**. *See also* Reishit Chochmah, Sha'ar Ha'ahava, *ch. 10 (also quoting R. Isaac Luria's celebrated comment. on Deut. 28:47)*; *R. Chaim Vital*, Sha'are Kedushah, *II:4. See further:* Likutei Torah, *II:20c;* Maamare Admur Hazaken *—5562, p. 77* ff, *and p. 305.* [19] Cf. Tzavaat Ribash, *at the beg.*, *in* comment *on Psalms 16:8.* [20] "*Mixed multitude*"—*(Exodus XII: 38), thus not of the truly faithful*, *the* "*believers, descendants of believers*"; *(*cf. *also Zohar I:25a;* ibid., *28b;* et passim*).* [21] Cf. *Deut. 8:2; II Chronicles 32:31.* [22] *In the text*

(Notes cont. at end of Hebrew Text)

One must believe that he really lives in it,[23] and all his needs, and everything related to himself, truly evolve in all their details [not from the *sitra achra*, but] "From the Lord by whom the steps of man are established,"[24] "and there is not a word . . ."[25]; conclusively, everything is absolutely good, except that it is not apprehended.[26]

By believing this truly, everything becomes good even in appearance. For by such a faith, that one believes that the very substance of what manifestly seems to be evil is (in fact) of the Supreme Good [i.e. His blessed *chochmah* which is non-apprehensible, and is the Eden which transcends the world to come], through this faith the imagined evil is truly absorbed and sublimated in the concealed Supreme Good.[27]

●▲XII. "And the act of *tzedakah* will effect peace, and the service of *tzedakah*—quietness and surety forever."[1] The difference between "act" and "service," and between "peace" and "quietness and surety,"[2] will be understood by what our sages, of blessed memory, said on the verse "He makes peace in His high places"[3]: "Michael is the prince of water and Gabriel is the prince of fire, yet they do not extinguish one another."[4] That is, Michael is the prince of *chesed*—which is called water[5] because it descends from a high place to a low place,[6] i.e. the aspect of the effusion and extension of vivification from the upper to the lower worlds. The aspect of fire [the nature of which is to soar upwards] is the category of *gevurah*,[7] of a withdrawal of the effusion of vivification [from below upwards], in order not to effuse except by way of a great and immense contraction (*tzimtzum*). Now these are conflicting attributes, opposing one another, that is when they are in a ▲mode of separate attributes. But the Holy One, blessed is He, makes peace between them, namely by means of a revelation, that a great illumination and an immense effusion from the light of the blessed En Sof becomes revealed in them. [For as His Name so is He.[8] He is not, Heaven forfend, on the plane of a measure, but transcends exceedingly—*ad infinitum*—even the rank of *chabad*,[9] which is the source

[23] I.e., *the* "true life." [24] *Psalms 37:23.* [25] *Psalms 139:4; see Medrash Tehilim*, ad loc., *and Genesis Rabba IX:3.* [26] Cf. Tanya *I, ch. 26.* [27] *The original letter concludes here with a lengthy appeal for charity (see* Igrot Ba'al Hatanya, *p. 94 f.).*

Section XII
[1] *Isaiah 32:17.* [2] *Text adds here* etc., *but omitted according to* H. V. [3] *Job 25:2.* [4] *See* Tanchuma, Vayigash: *6;* cf. *Sefer Habahir, par. 9 (11) (quoted in Zohar I:263a); Zohar III:225a; Tikunei Zohar, 70:132a. See also Deut. Rabba V:12.* [5] *Zohar II:175b; etc. See* supra,

ורצונו אף שאינו יכול לחיות חיי אמיתים כו'".
ולפי נוסחא זו נראה שתיבות [אף שאינו יכול] הוא מאמר מוסגר).
ויאמין שבאמת הוא חי בהם וכל צרכיו וכל ענייניו משתלשלים באמת בפרטי פרטיותיהם שלא מס"א כי מה' מצעדי גבר כוננו ואין מלה כו' ואם כן הכל טוב בתכלית רק שאינו מושג ובאמונה זו באמת נעשה הכל טוב גם בגלוי שבאמונה זו שמאמין שהרע הנדמה בגלוי כל חיותו הוא מטוב העליון שהיא חכמתו יתברך שאינה מושגת והיא העדן שלמעלה מעוה"ב הרי באמונה זו נכלל ומתעלה באמת הרע המדומה בטוב העליון הגנוז:

יב והיה מעשה הצדקה שלום ועבודת הצדקה השקט ובטח עד עולם. להבין ההפרש שבין מעשה לעבודה ובין שלום להשקט ובטח כו' ע"פ מה שארז"ל ע"פ עושה שלום במרומיו כי מיכאל שר של מים וגבריאל שר של אש ואין מכבין זה את זה כלומר שמיכאל שר של חסד הנק' בשם מים היורדים ממקום גבוה למקום נמוך והוא בחי' ההשפעה והתפשטות החיות מעולמות עליונים לתחתונים ובחי' אש שטבעה לעלות למעלה היא בחי' הגבורה והסתלקות השפעת החיים ממטה למעלה שלא להשפיע רק בצמצום עצום ורב והן מדות נגדיות והפכיות זו לזו והיינו כשהן בבחי' מדות לבדן. אך הקב"ה עושה שלום ביניהם דהיינו ע"י גילוי שמתגלה בהן הארה רבה והשפעה עצומה מאד מאור א"ס ב"ה אשר כשמו כן הוא שאינו בבחי' מדה ח"ו אלא למעלה מעלה עד אין קץ אפילו מבחי' חב"ד מקור המדות

---

section VIII, note 14. [6] *See* supra, *section VIII, note 15.* [7] *Zohar III: 255a;* ibid., *257a; Tikunei Zohar 69: 105a.* [8] *En Sof, Infinite.—See* supra, *section VII, note 5.* [9] *Acronym for* chochmah, binah, da'at.

of the attributes.[10]] And thus the opposing attributes of Michael and Gabriel are absorbed in their source and root, and they become truly unified and dissolve in His blessed light which radiates to them in a manifest way. The *gevurot*, thus, are tempered and sweetened in the *chassadim* by a mediary—the factor which harmonises and leans towards *chesed*, i.e. the attribute of *rachamini*.[11] In the terminology of the Cabbalists[12] (this attribute) is called *tiferet*, because it is made up of the two colours white and red, which allude to *chesed* and *gevurah*.[13] The blessed name *Havayah* (the Tetragrammaton), as it appears unqualified throughout the Torah, therefore, indicates the attribute of *tiferet*, as mentioned in the sacred *Zohar*.[14] For here the degree of the manifestation of the light of the blessed En Sof is of an immense illumination, surpassing that of His other blessed attributes.

●▲ Now, the arousal from above [to arouse a manifestation of said great illumination and immense effusion from the light of the blessed En Sof] to bring about the said peace is effected by the arousal from below, by the act of charity and the effusion of "life, favour, kindness and compassion"[15] to him who has nothing of his own, and "To revive the spirit of the humble . . ."[16]

It is well-known that our sages, of blessed memory, said of him who busies himself with Torah *lishmah*[17] that "he sets peace among the attendants of above and among the attendants of below."[18] The "attendants of above" are the princes[19] and attributes mentioned above. For these are the upper *hechalot*[20] in the world of Beriah, mentioned in the sacred *Zohar*.[21] The "attendants of below" are the lower *hechalot*, and especially this base world which, due to the sin of Adam, is mingled good and evil, and the evil rules over the good as it is written "While man rules in man . . ."[22], and "Nation will overpower nation."[23] This is empirically evident with terrestrial man who is called a microcosm,[24] for sometimes the good prevails, and sometimes the reverse, Heaven forfend. Therefore there will be no peace in the world until the time of the end, when the good shall be disencumbered from the evil[25] to become attached to its root and source, the blessed Source of Life. For then all the workers of iniquity[26] shall be scattered[27] and the spirit of impurity shall pass from the earth,[28]

---

[10] *See* Sha'ar Hayichud, *ch. 9.* [11] *See* infra, *section XV.* [12] חכמי האמת—lit. *the "savants of the truth"* (i.e. *of the true science, the Cabbalah).* [13] *Zohar III:248b; Tikunei Zohar, Intr.: 1a (text, and the inserted gloss which appears also in Zohar Chadash,* Tikunim, *117c) and 19:39b; see also Zohar Chadash 34a–b, and Zohar I:18b.* Pardess Rimonim, *X:1 ff.* Cf. *Sefer Habahir, 49 (137).* [14] *Zohar III:11a (see* Sha'are Orah, *ch. V;* Pardess Rimonim, *I:10).* Cf. Sifre, *Deut. 27 (on Deut. 3:24), Exodus Rabba 3:6, Zohar III:65a: "The Tetragrammaton always denotes* rachamim." [15] Par. Liturgy, *concluding benediction of the* Amidah. [16] Par. *Isaiah 57:15.* [17] *For its own sake, as a command of G-d,*

המדות ואזי המדות נגדיות של מיכאל וגבריאל
נכללות במקורן ושרשן והיו לאחדים ממש ובטלים
באורו יתברך המאיר להם בבחי' גילוי ואזי מתמזגים
ומתמתקים הגבורות בחסדים ע"י בחי' ממוצעת קו
המכריע ומטה כלפי חסד היא מדת הרחמים הנק'
בשם תפארת בדברי חכמי האמת לפי שהיא כלולה
מב' גוונין לובן ואודם המרמזים לחו"ג ולכן סתם שם
הוי' ב"ה שבכל התורה מורה על מדת התפארת
כמ"ש בזוה"ק לפי שכאן הוא בחי' גילוי אור א"ס
ב"ה הארה רבה ביתר שאת משאר מדותיו הקדושות
יתברך. והנה אתערותא דלעילא לעורר גילוי הארה
רבה והשפעה עצומה הנ"ל מאור א"ס ב"ה לעשות
שלום הנ"ל היא באתערותא דלתתא במעשה הצדקה
והשפעת חיים חן וחסד ורחמים למאן דלית ליה
מגרמי' כלום ולהחיות רוח שפלים כו'. ומודעת זאת
מה שאמרו רז"ל על העוסק בתורה לשמה משים
שלום בפמליא של מעלה ובפמליא של מטה. פמליא
של מעלה הם השרים והמדות הנ"ל שהן ההיכלות
עליונים בעולם הבריאה שבזוה"ק ופמליא של מטה
הן ההיכלות התחתונים ובפרט עוה"ז השפל המעורב
טוב ורע מחטא אדם הראשון והרע שולט על הטוב
כמ"ש אשר שלט האדם באדם כו' ולאום מלאום
יאמץ וכנראה בחוש באדם התחתון הנקרא בשם
עולם קטן שלפעמים הטוב גובר ולפעמים להיפך ח"ו
ואין שלום בעולם עד עת קץ שיתברר הטוב מהרע
לידבק בשרשו ומקורו מקור החיים ב"ה ואזי יתפרדו
כל פועלי און ורוח הטומאה יעבור מן הארץ כשיתברר
מתוכו

---

without any ulterior motives. See Tanya *I, end of ch. 5.* [18] *Sanhedrin 99b.* [19] *Guardian-angels.* [20] *Shrines; realms.* [21] *Zohar II: 245a* ff. *(see* Nitzutzei Orot, a.l.*).* [22] *Ecclesiastes 8:9; see* Etz Chayim, *XLIX:4 (quoted in* Hadrat Melech *on Zohar II:95b).* [23] *Genesis 25:23; see Rashi* a.l. *(Pessachim 42b, Rashi* a.l., *and cf. Zohar II:236a and 240a).* [24] Tanchuma, Pekude*:3; see Avot de R. Natan ch. 31.* [25] Cf. Tanchuma, Tetze*:11 (Rashi on Exodus 17:16, and* Tossafot, *Berachot 3a,* s.v. ועונין*) and Zohar II:67a (end of* Beshallach*).* [26] *The forces of evil.* [27] Par. *Psalms 92:10.* [28] Par. *Zechar. 13:2.*

i.e. when the element of the good which sustains it shall be extracted from its ▲midst.[29] This disencumberment (*birur*) itself will also be through a manifestation of His Divinity below, with a great illumination and immense effulgence, as it is written: "For the earth shall be full of the knowledge of the Lord,"[30] and "The glory of the Lord shall be revealed . . ."[31] Now, this is as regards the future of the world, in general. But as regards terrestrial man, at every "time of finding,"[32] meaning prayer,[33] or at other times designated to seclude oneself with one's Maker, each one, commensurate to his actions, merits a reflection of this *birur* by means of engagement with Torah *lishmah*, and likewise by means of charity, as it is related:[34] R. Eliezer gave a coin to a poor man, and then he prayed, as it is written:[35] "Through *tzedek* I will behold Your countenance"—i.e. the rank of a manifest illumination and effusion of knowledge and reason, to contemplate on the greatness of G–d, thereof to beget the intellectual awe and love, as known.[36] And through this we extract the good for G–d, and separate the evil, as it is written: "The crucible is for silver, and the furnace for gold, and man according to מהללו."[37] This means, "according to his praising G–d"[38]—with profound knowledge, to beget awe and love, that is how we disencumber the good and separate the evil, analogous to the extraction and separation of the drosses from the silver and gold in the crucible and furnace.

●▲ Now, it is well known that Israelites are by their very nature compassionate and performers of kindness.[39] This is so because their souls issued from His blessed attributes in which *chesed* prevails over the attribute of *din*, *gevurah*, and *tzimtzum*,[40] and as it is written:[41] "His *chesed* prevails over them who fear[42] Him." The *neshamah*,[43] therefore, is called "daughter of the priest,"[44] as mentioned in the sacred *Zohar*.[45] Now, the charity that issues from this aspect is referred to as "the *act* of charity," for the term act (*ma'aseh*) applies to that which is already done, or which is in constant action of itself, thus, something existent and usually constant. So here, too, the trait of kindness and compassion is implanted in the souls of the whole House of Israel from aforetimes, from the time of their creation and evolution from His blessed attributes, as it is written: "And He breathed into his nostrils . . ."[46], and "You did breathe it into me,"[47] and "He who exhales . . ."[48] Furthermore, "In His goodness He renews the act of creation every day,"[49] and "They are new every morning . . ."[50]

An idiom of *avodah* (service), however applies only

[29] *See* infra, *section XXVI, and* cf. *Introduction* (s.v. Shevirat Hakelim). [30] *Isaiah 11:9.* [31] *Isaiah 40:5.* [32] *Psalms 32:6.* [33] *See the beginning of this verse, and* cf. *Zohar III:79b.* [34] *Bava Batra 10a.* [35] *Psalms 17:45.* [36] *See* supra, *section VIII.* [37] *Proverbs 27:21.* [38] מהללו *may mean* "the praise of him" *(Rashi Metzudot); or* "that which he praises" *(Ibn Ezra), resp.* "his praising of Him" *(the interpretation in our context, which the author often uses in the same context; see* Torah Or, *65b, and 111c;* Likutei Torah, *III:28c;* Siddur, *p. 30d* Cf. J. I. *Schochet, "An Exposition of Prayer,"* Di Yiddishe Heim *V:2, p.7.)* [39] *Yevamot 79a.* Cf. Yerushalmi, *Kidushin 4:1; Numbers Rabba 8:4; Maimonides,* Hilchot Issurei Biah

מתוכו בחי' הטוב המחייהו ובירור זה יהיה ג"כ ע"י גילוי אלקותו למטה בהארה רבה והשפעה עצומה כמ"ש כי מלאה הארץ דעה את ה' ונגלה כבוד ה' כו' וזהו בכללות העולם לעתיד אך באדם התחתון בכל עת מצוא זו תפלה או שאר עתים מזומנים להתבודד עם קונו כ"א לפי מעשיו זוכה למעין בירור זה ע"י עסק התורה לשמה וכן ע"י הצדקה כמ"ש ר"א יהיב פרוטה לעני והדר מצלי דכתיב אני בצדק אחזה פניך היא בחי' גילוי הארה והשפעת הדעת והתבונה להתבונן בגדולת ה' ולהוליד מזה דו"ר שכליים כנודע ועי"ז נברר הטוב לה' ונפרד הרע כמ"ש מצרף לכסף וכור לזהב ואיש לפי מהללו. פי' לפי הילולו את ה' בעומק הדעת להוליד דו"ר ככה נברר הטוב ונפרד הרע כבירור ופירוד הסיגים מכסף וזהב במצרף וכור. והנה מודעת זאת שישראל בטבעם הם רחמנים וגומ"ח מפני היות נפשותיהם נמשכות ממדותיו ית' אשר החסד גובר בהן על מדת הדין והגבורה והצמצום וכמ"ש גבר חסדו על יריאיו שלכן נקראת הנשמה בת כהן כמ"ש בזוה"ק. והנה הצדקה הנמשכת מבחי' זו נק' בשם מעשה הצדקה כי שם מעשה נופל על דבר שכבר נעשה או שנעשה תמיד ממילא והיא דבר ההווה ורגיל תמיד ואף כאן הרי מדת החסד והרחמנות הוטבעה בנפשות כל בית ישראל מכבר מעת בריאותן והשתלשלותן ממדותיו ית' כמ"ש ויפח באפיו כו' ואתה נפחת בי ומאן דנפח כו' וגם בכל יום ויום בטובו מחדש מעשה בראשית וחדשים לבקרים כו'. אך לשון עבודה אינו נופל אלא

19:17, and Hilchot Matnot Aniyim *10:2.* [40] *Synonymous terms; see Introduction.* [41] *Psalms 103:11.* [42] *Denoting the attribute of* gevurah. [43] *The soul proper (see* supra, *sect. V, note 53).* [44] *Leviticus 22:12* f. [45] *Zohar II:95a* f. *(*ibid., *101a)*; ibid., *III:7a.* —*The* kohanim *(priests) are of the category of* chesed *(see Zohar I:256b; III:121b, and 145b).* [46] *Genesis 2:7.* [47] Liturgy, *Morning prayers.* [48] *See* Tanya *I, ch. 2;* cf. *Nachmanides on Genesis 2:7; Zohar III:46b;* Kitzurim Vehe'arot, *p. 74.* —*All these quotations imply the Divine origin of the* neshamah. [49] Liturgy, *Morning-prayers.* Cf. supra, *section XI, note 9.* [50] *Lament 3:23.*

to what man does with immense toil: it is contrary to is natural inclination, but he abnegates his nature and will before the blessed Supreme Will; as, for example, to exhaust himself in Torah and prayer "To the extent of pressing out the soul . . ."[51] And in our case, too, as regards the commandment of charity, he gives exceedingly more than the nature of his compassion and will, and as our sages, of blessed memory, commented[52] on the verse[53] "Give, you shall give": "even a hundred times."[54]

●▲ And this is the meaning of "And *the act of charity* [shall be]"—i.e. even with that type of charity which is called an "act" [and not "service"], the arousal from below will elicit an arousal from above. One arouses a manifestation of the light of the blessed En Sof by way of a great illumination and immense effulgence, and peace is made in His high places and also among the attendants of below. Though in this base world, the peace and the *birur* and separation of the evil from the good will not be manifest until the time of the end [but not during the time of the exile, as mentioned above], except in the microcosm, i.e. man, at every "time of finding"—meaning prayer, as it is written: "Through *tzedek* I will behold Your countenance," as mentioned above. Even so, after prayer it is possible that the evil will easily reawaken and become intermingled with the good as one walks in the darkness of this world. But through the charity which is in a mode of *avodah*, whereas its rank is extremely glorious and great [because one abnegates his nature and bodily will before the blessed Supreme Will, and "Subdues the *sitra achara*, and then rises the glory of the Holy One, blessed is He . . ."[55], and just "Like the excellence of light over darkness,"[56] as known[57]], the evil can no longer reawaken so easily of itself, unless, Heaven forfend, man would arouse it and draw it upon himself.

And this is the meaning of "quietness and surety forever." השקט (*quietness*) is of the etymon of "שוקט—(*he rests*) on his dregs,"[58] meaning that the dregs are completely separated from the wine and fall completely netherwards, while the wine above is wholly pure and clear. In an analogous manner it is with the *avodah* of charity: the dregs are the aspect of the mixture of evil in his soul which is gradually extricated and separated until it falls netherwards

[51] *See* Sifre, *Deut. 32 (on Deut. 6:5).* [52] Sifre, *Deut. 117.* [53] *Deut. 15:10.* [54] *Text adds here* etc., *but omitted according to* H. V. [55] *Zohar II:128b.* [56] *Eccles. 2:13.* [57] *See Zohar III: 47b; see also* ibid., *II: 187a, and* Tanya *I, ch. 12.* [58] *Jeremiah 48:11; (*cf. *Kitzurim Vehe'arot, p. 76* f.*).*

אלא על דבר שהאדם עושה ביגיעה עצומה נגד טבע נפשו רק שמבטל טבעו ורצונו מפני רצון העליון ב"ה כגון לייגע עצמו בתורה ובתפלה עד מיצוי הנפש כו'. ואף כאן במצות הצדקה ליתן הרבה יותר מטבע רחמנותו ורצונו וכמ"ש רז"ל ע"פ נתן תתן אפילו מאה פעמים וכו'. וז"ש והיה מעשה הצדקה שגם הצדקה הנק' בשם מעשה ולא בשם עבודה אעפ"כ באתעדל"ת אתערותא דלעילא מעורר גילוי אור א"ס ב"ה בהארה רבה והשפעה עצומה ונעשה שלום במרומיו וגם בפמליא של מטה רק שבעוה"ז השפל לא יתגלה השלום והבירור ופירוד הרע מהטוב עד עת קץ ולא בזמן הגלות כנ"ל רק בעולם קטן הוא האדם בכל עת מצוא זו תפלה כמ"ש בצדק אחזה פניך כנ"ל אך אחר התפלה יוכל להיות הרע חוזר וניעור בקל ולהתערב בטוב כאשר יתהלך בחשכת עוה"ז. אך הצדקה בבחי' עבודה הנה מאשר יקרה וגדלה מעלתה במאד מאד בהיותו מבטל טבעו ורצונו הגופני מפני רצון העליון ב"ה ואתכפיא ס"א ואזי אסתלק יקרא דקוב"ה כו' וכיתרון האור מן החשך דוקא כנודע. אי לזאת אין הרע יכול להיות עוד חוזר וניעור בקלות כ"כ מאליו רק אם האדם יעוררנו וימשיכנו ע"ע ח"ו. וז"ש השקט ובטח עד עולם. השקט הוא מלשון שוקט על שמריו דהיינו שהשמרים נפרדים לגמרי מן היין ונופלין למטה לגמרי והיין למעלה זך וצלול בתכלית. ועד"ז הוא בעבודת הצדקה השמרים הן בחי' תערובת רע שבנפשו נברר ונפרד מעט מעט עד שנופל למטה למקורו

to its root and source, and as it is written: "And You will cast all their sins into the depths of the sea."[59]

●▲ XIII. "How abundant is Your goodness which You have treasured up for them that fear You . . ."[1]

In the class of the "servants of the Lord" there are two degrees and levels which, depending on the root of their souls above, are distinct in relation to the categories of the *right*[2] and the *left*.[3] That is, the characteristic of the *left* is the trait of contraction (*tzimtzum*) and concealment in the service of the Lord, as it is written: "and to walk secretly . . ."[4]; "in secret places cries . . ."[5]; "whoever busies himself with Torah in secret . . ."[6] From this attribute derives also the aspect of contraction (*tzimtzum*) and limitation in the service of G-d; for example, with charity—to judge according to the means, "And he who expends, should not expend more than one fifth;"[7] and, likewise, as regards the study of Torah and the other commandments—he suffices in discharging his duty, the definite duty to which the Torah obliges him, "to appoint times . . ."[8] From it derives also what our sages, of blessed memory, said[9]: "Cast a scare upon the pupils . . ."[10] On the other hand, the characteristic of the *right* is the attribute of grace (*chesed*) and extension in the service of G-d by way of expansion, without any contraction and concealment whatever, as it is written: "And I will walk in an expanse . . ."[11], without any contraction and limitation whatever. There is no restraint to the spirit[12] of his generosity—whether it be with respect to charity, the study of Torah, or other commandments. He does not suffice in discharging his obligation only, but to the extent of "never sufficient . . ." ● Now, every one of Israel needs to comprise both these traits, for "There is no thing that has not its place."[13] Thus we find various matters that are of the leniencies of Bet Shammai and of the stringencies of Bet Hillel.[14] This comes to teach us that Bet Shammai, the root of whose soul is of the category of the supernal *left*[15]—[that is why they always decided stringently as regards all the prohibitions of the Torah; but Bet Hillel, who were of the supernal *right*,[16] would find favourable arguments to be lenient and to permit the injunctions of Bet Shammai so that these should become *muttarim*[17] from their *issur*,[18] and able to ascend upwards. Nevertheless]—in several matters, even Bet Shammai are lenient. This is so because of the inclusiveness of their soul's root, which compounds the *right* as well. And, likewise, the root of Bet Hillel's soul

---

[59] *Micha 7:19.*

Section XIII
[1] *Psalms 1:20.* [2] Chesed. [3] Gevurah. [4] *Micha 6:8.* [5] *Jeremiah 13:17.* [6] Cf. Yerushalmi, *Berachot V:1 (Maimonides,* Hilchot Talmud Torah *3:12); cf. also Mo'ed Katan 16b.* [7] *Ketuvot 50a (*cf. supra, *section X, note 36).* [8] *See the author's* Hilchot Talmud Torah, *III:4* ff. *and IV:6;* cf. Tzemach Tzedek-Chidushim 'al Hashass, *on Peah I:1.* [9] *Ketuvot 103b.* [10] *This last sentence appears in the text* after *the following one, which would render the passage rather difficult. A parenthesis inserted in the text already notes this difficulty, and suggests that it might belong here (as in our translation).* [11] *Psalms*

למקורו ושרשו וכמ"ש ותשליך במצולות ים כל חטאתם:

יג מה רב טובך אשר צפנת ליראיך וגו'. הנה בכלל עובדי ה' יש ב' בחי' ומדרגות חלוקות מצד שורש נשמתם למעלה מבחי' ימין ושמאל דהיינו שבחי' שמאל היא מדת הצמצום וההסתר בעבודת ה' כמ"ש והצנע לכת כו' במסתרים תבכה כו' כל העוסק בתורה בסתר כו'. והנה ממדה זו נמשכה ג"כ בחי' הצמצום והגבול בעבודת ה' כמו בצדקה להיות נידון בהשג יד והמבזבז אל יבזבז יותר מחומש וכה"ג בת"ת ושארי מצות די לו שיוצא י"ח מחיוב מפורש שחייבתו התורה בפי' לקבוע עתים כו'. אך בחי' ימין היא מדת החסד וההתפשטות בעבודת ה' בהתרחבות בלי צמצום והסתר כלל כמ"ש ואתהלכה ברחבה כו' וממנה נמשך ג"כ מ"ש רז"ל זרוק מרה בתלמידים כו' (צ"ע. ונראה שצ"ל קודם אך בחי' ימין כו') וגם בלי צמצום וגבול כלל ואין מעצור לרוח נדבתו בין בצדקה ובין בת"ת ושארי מצות ולא די לו לצאת י"ח בלבד אלא עד בלי די כו':

והנה כל איש ישראל צ"ל כלול מב' בחי' אלו ואין לך דבר שאין לו מקום ולכן מצינו כמה דברים מקולי ב"ש ומחומרי ב"ה ללמדנו שאף ב"ש ששרש נשמתם מבחי' שמאל העליון ולכן היו דנין להחמיר תמיד בכל איסורי התורה. וב"ה שהיו מבחי' ימין העליון היו מלמדין זכות להקל ולהתיר איסורי ב"ש שיהיו מותרים מאיסורם ויוכלו לעלות למעלה אעפ"כ בכמה דברים היו ב"ש מקילין מפני התכללות שרש נשמתם שהוא כלול גם מימין וכן שורש נשמת

ב"ה

119:45. [12] Par. *Proverbs 25:28.* [13] *Avot IV:3—Both* chesed *and* gevurah *are essential.* [14] Mishnah, *'Eduyot, ch. IV;* ibid., *V:1–5; Oholot, XI:3–6.* [15] Gevurah.—*Zohar III:245a. See* Sha'ar Hagilgulim, *ch. 36.* [16] Chesed.—*See references in note 15 above.* [17] *Permitted.* [18] *Prohibition.—That which is* assur *(bound) to the* sitra achra. *To be* muttar *(permitted) means to be* muttar *(released, free) from the* sitra achra. *See* Tanya *I, ch. 7, and* infra, *sect. XXVI.*

compounds the *left* also. For, as known of the mode and attributes of the *kodesh ha'elyon*,[19] there is no cleavage and division there,[20] Heaven forfend, and all the traits compound each other. Thus, they are united one with the other,[21] as known to the Cabbalists.[22] Thus it is written of Abraham, who is the attribute of *chesed* and love:[23] "Now I know that you are fearful of G-d,"[24]—for he had donned the attribute of *gevurah*[25] "And bound Isaac his son . . . and took the knife . . ."[26] As for Scripture stating "Abraham who loved Me,"[27] and "the *Fright* of Isaac,"[28] this difference and distinction is with respect to manifestation and concealment. In the attribute of Isaac, *fright* is in a state of manifestation, while *love* is hidden, in a state of concealment and hiding. The opposite is with the trait of our father Abraham, peace be to him.

• And this is the meaning of what King David, peace be to him, said: "How abundant is Your goodness . . ." That is to say that the attribute of goodness and *chesed*, which is in a state of concealment and hiding with everyone the root of whose soul is of the category of the *left*, referred to as "those that fear You"[29] [as is the trait of Bet Shammai], now, though this is a concealed and hidden goodness, it is nevertheless truly as abundant and immense as the attribute of *gedulah*[30] and *chesed*, which is of the *right*, and both are of the category of a manifestation that is without limit, measure and size.

And this is the meaning of Scripture: "How abundant is Your goodness,"[31] i.e. without limit and measure; whether it be the goodness "*Which You have hidden for them who fear You*," or that which "*You have wrought for them that trust in You*"—i.e. the hopeful that are of the category of the right,[32] and whose kindness and goodness are also in a state of manifestation and expansion "*before the children of man*," and by no means in a state of contraction and concealment. ([33] The reason it says "*For* them that fear You" rather than "*In* them that fear You," is because with every soul whatever is in a state of concealment is not vested within the body—in his mind and heart. It is, rather, in a state of "encompassing from above," and thence it radiates to his mind and heart at those times when an arousal of this aspect becomes necessary i.e. to be aroused and to illumine his mind and heart in order to result in a real act.)

He, therefore, said that whereas the "abundance of goodness" of the House of Israel [that which is hidden and that which is manifest]

---

[19] *See* supra, *section X, note 41.* [20] *Zohar III: 70a; also* ibid., *83a, and 109a.* [21] *See* Tanya, Sha'ar Hayichud, *ch. 6.* [22] Lit.: *the savants of the esoteric science.* —*The Sefirot are not truly separate and distinct from each other; they proceed from, and succeed each other. Thus we speak of* chesed *of* chesed, gevurah *of* chesed, *etc.;* chesed of gevurah, gevurah *of* gevurah, *etc.* Cf. *Introduction.* [23] *See* supra, *section II, note 9, and see below, note 27.* [24] *Genesis 22: 14.* [25] *See* Likutei Torah *of R. Isaac Luria,* Vayera *(on this, and the preceding passage), and* cf. *the commentary of Nachmanides on this verse, and Zohar I: 119b.* [26] *Genesis 22: 10, 11.* [27] *Isaiah 41: 8—distinctly relating* chesed to *Abraham;*

• 14 Ellul

ב"ה כלול גם משמאל כידוע דרך ומדות קדש העליון דלית תמן קיצוץ ופירוד ח"ו וכל המדות כלולות זו מזו. ולכן הם מיוחדות זו בזו כידוע לי"ח וכדכתיב באברהם שהוא מדת החסד והאהבה עתה ידעתי כי ירא אלהים אתה ע"י שלבש מדת הגבורה ויעקוד את יצחק בנו ויקח את המאכלת כו'. ומה שאמר הכתוב אברהם אוהבי ופחד יצחק הנה ההפרש וההבדל הזה הוא בבחי' גילוי והעלם שבמדת יצחק הפחד הוא בבחי' גילוי והאהבה מסותרת בבחי' העלם והסתר וההיפך במדת א"א ע"ה וזהו שאמר דהע"ה מה רב טובך וגו' כלומר שמדת הטוב והחסד אשר היא בבחינת העלם והסתר אצל כל מי ששורש נשמתו מבחי' שמאל הנק' בשם יראיך כמדת ב"ש. הנה אף שהוא טוב הגנוז וצפון אעפ"כ הוא רב וגדול מאד כמו מדת הגדולה והחסד ממש שמבחי' ימין ושתיהן הן מבחי' גילוי בלי גבול ומדה ושיעור. וז"ש מה רב טובך כלומר בלי גבול ומדה בין הטוב אשר צפנת ליראיך ובין אשר פעלת לחוסים בך שהם בעלי הבטחון שמבחי' ימין וחסדם וטובם הוא ג"כ בבחי' גילוי והתפשטות נגד בני אדם ולא בבחינת צמצום והסתר כלל. (ומ"ש ליראיך ולא ביראיך היינו משום שכל מה שהוא בבחינת העלם בכל נשמה הנה בחי' זו אינה מלובשת תוך הגוף במוחו ולבו אלא הוא בבחינת מקיף מלמעלה ומשם היא מאירה למוחו ולבו לעתים הצריכים להתעוררות בחי' זו שתתעורר ותאיר למוחו ולבו כדי לבא לידי מעשה בפועל ממש).
ואמר ע"כ אשר רב טוב לבית ישראל הצפון והגלוי

הוא

---

see Pardess Rimonim, *23:11*, s.v. אהבה. [28] *Genesis 31:42, distinctly relating* gevurah *to Isaac; see* Pardess Rimonim, *23:17*, s.v. פחד *(cf. Zohar III:12b;* ibid., *18a and 302b).* [29] Cf. Likutei Torah *III:16b;* Likutei Torah—Torat Shmuel, *ch. 49: "The* gimatriya *(numerical value) of* yirah *(awe; fear) is equivalent to that of* gevurah." [30] *The term* gedulah *(greatness) denotes the Divine* chesed; *see* Tikunei Zohar, *22:67b;* Tanya *II: ch. 4;* Likutei Torah *IV:17c* ff.; Likutei Torah—Torat Shmuel, *vol. III, ch. 46* ff. [31] *Psalms 31:20 How abundant is Your goodness which You have treasured up for them that fear You, which You have wrought for them that trust in You,*

(Notes cont. at end of Hebrew Text)

is in a state of "without limit and measure" [according to the category of their soul vested in the body], therefore "You, too, Oh Lord, treat them with the attribute of Your unlimited and infinitely great *chesed* which is called *rav chesed*." For there are different types of *chesed*:[34] there is *chesed olam*, the corresponding opposite of which is the attribute of *din*,[35] Heaven forfend, which[36] serves to diminish and contract His *chesed* and goodness. But the *chesed elyon*,[37] which is called *rav chesed*, does not have an attribute of *din* opposed to it [to diminish and contract the abundance of His grace from extending unlimited and infinitely]. For it derives from the rank of *sovev kol almin*,[38] and *temira dechol temirin*,[39] called *keter elyon*.[40] This, then, is the meaning of "You hide them in the covert of Your countenance . . . You conceal them in a pavilion . . ."[41]

●▲ XIV.[1] To arouse the ancient love and the fondness for our Holy Land,[2] that it flame as flashes of fire from the inmost of man and with a profound heart[3] as if but this very day[4] did the Lord set His spirit upon us, a spirit of generosity, when the people volunteer to consecrate themselves unto the Lord[5] with a full and liberal hand, with one increase after another, from year to year, rising over the head, like unto the measure of *kodesh ha'elyon*[6]—which radiates to the Holy Land and is constantly renewed and increased, as it is written: "Forever are the eyes of the Lord your G-d upon it, from the beginning of the year to the end of the year."[7]

Now, (the phrase) "*to the end* . . ." is apparently incomprehensible, for at the end of one year begins the second year. Thus it should have said: *for everlasting!*

However, this matter will be understood by considering the Scripture[8]—"The Lord by *chochmah* founded the earth." That is, the foundation of the *eretz ha'elyonah*[9] [i.e. the aspect of *memale kol almin*], and of the nether (land) [i.e. the *eretz chefetz*[10] which truly corresponds to it, and is called by its[11] name—*eretz hachayim*[12]], issues from the efflux and radiation from the Supreme *chochmah* which is the source of the supernal life, as it is written:[13] "*Chochmah* animates those who have it . . ."[14] This radiation and efflux is renewed annually by a truly new light. For He, blessed is He, and His *chochmah* are one, in an absolute unity[15] and it is called the "light of the blessed En Sof"

---

[34] *See* supra, *sect. X, notes 6–9.* [35] *Judgment (identical with* gevurah; *see Introduction* s.v.*).* [36] I.e., din. [37] *Supreme* chesed. [38] *Encompassing*, i.e. *transcending all worlds.* [39] *The most hidden of all hidden.* [40] *Supreme* keter.—*See Zohar I:147a (Toss.); also Zohar II:42b, and III:288b; Tikunei Zohar, Intr.: 12a; Zohar Chadash, Tik., 96d;* cf. Pardess Rimonim, *5:4.* [41] *Psalms 31:21.*

Section XIV

[1] *This letter appears in* Boneh Yerushalayim, *sect. 31 (repr. in* Igrot Ba'al Hatanya, *pp. 45 f.), with additional parts at the beginning and end which do not appear in our text here.* [2] V. L. *in* Boneh Yerushalayim*: and to renew it as aforetimes, that it . . .* [3] Par.

הוא בבחי' בלי גבול ומדה לפי ערך נפשותם המלובשת בגוף לכן גם אתה ה' תתנהג עמהם במדת חסדך הגדול בלי גבול ותכלית הנק' רב חסד. דאית חסד ואית חסד. אית חסד עולם שיש כנגדו ולעומתו מדה"ד ח"ו למעט ולצמצם חסדו וטובו. אבל חסד עליון הנק' רב חסד אין כנגדו מדה"ד למעט ולצמצם רוב חסדו מלהתפשט בלי גבול ותכלית כי הוא נמשך מבחי' סוכ"ע וטמירא דכל טמירין הנק' כתר עליון וז"ש תסתירם בסתר פניך וגו' תצפנם בסוכה וגו':

יד **לעורר** את האהבה הישנה וחבת אה"ק להיות בוערת כרשפי אש מקרב איש ולב עמוק כאלו היום ממש נתן ה' רוחו עלינו רוח נדיבה בהתנדב עם למלאות ידם לה' ביד מלאה ורחבה בריבוי אחר ריבוי מדי שנה בשנה הולך ועולה למעלה ראש כמדת קדש העליון המאיר לאה"ק המתחדש ומתרבה תמיד כדכתיב תמיד עיני ה' אלהיך בה מרשית השנה ועד אחרית שנה דהאי ועד אחרית כו' אינו מובן לכאורה שהרי באחרית שנה זו מתחלת שנה שניה וא"כ הל"ל לעולם ועד:

אך הענין יובן ע"פ מ"ש ה' בחכמה יסד ארץ שיסוד הארץ העליונה היא בחי' ממלא כ"ע והתחתונה היא ארץ חפץ המכוונת כנגדה ממש ונק' על שמה ארץ החיים הנה הוא נמשך מהמשכת והארת חכמה עילאה מקור החיים העליונים כדכתיב החכמה תחיה בעליה וכו' והארה והמשכה זו היא מתחדשת באור חדש ממש בכל שנה ושנה כי הוא יתברך וחכמתו אחד בתכלית היחוד ונק' בשם אוא"ס ב"ה

Psalms 64:7. [4] V. L. *in* B. Y.*: as if but that very day did the Lord begin to show us His grace and enlighten our eyes in the darkness with the light of the Lord that radiates to the Holy Land and to those that dwell in it; and (the light) radiates and shines within our confines ever more, so that our soul be bound to (the Holy Land) with the thick ropes of a magnanimous love, and the bond becomes stronger and renewed every morning by a new light, as our sages, of blessed memory, said on the verse* "*which I command you this day*" *(Deut. 6:6)*: "*Every day they are to be in your eyes as truly new, as if the Torah was given but this very day.*" *(Pessikta Zutr.*, a.l.; cf. *also* Sifre, *and* Rashi, a.l., *and* Tanchuma, *ed.*

(Notes cont. at end of Hebrew Text)

because there is no limit and no end to the quality and greatness[16] of the light and vitality that issues forth from Him, blessed is He, and from His *chochmah*, by way of elevation upon elevation to no end and ▲limit, to the peak of the highest levels. And every year there descends and radiates a new and renewed light which never yet shone, from the Supreme *chochmah* to the *eretz ha'elyonah*. For the light of every year withdraws to its source on the eve of every *Rosh Hashana* "When the moon is covered."[17] Afterwards, by means of the blowing of the *Shofar* and of the prayers, a new, supernal light [of a yet higher rank in the sphere of the Supreme *chochmah*] is elicited to radiate to the *eretz ha'elyonah* and them that dwell upon it, i.e. all the upper and lower worlds that receive their vitality from it [i.e. from the light of the blessed En Sof, and[18] His *chochmah* which is vested in it, as it is written: "For with You is the source of life, in Your light we see light"[19]—which refers to the light that radiates from the Supreme *chochmah*, the source of life]. ([20] And as known to the savants of the esoteric science, that every *Rosh Hashana* there is the *nessirah*,[21] and it receives new, more sublime *mochin* . . .[22])

In a very specific way this takes place every day. More sublime *mochin* are elicited by every morning-prayer,[23] and these are not the original *mochin* that withdrew after the prayer, but more sublime ones.[24] In a general way, with respect to the world as a whole during[25] the six thousand years,[26] this occurs every *Rosh Hashana*. ●And this is the meaning of the Scripture—"Forever are *the eyes* of the Lord your G-d upon it" [for the eyes are an epithet for the efflux and radiation of the light of *chochmah*,[27] wherefore the sages are referred to as the "eyes of the congregation"[28]], and "The atmosphere of the Land of Israel makes wise."[29] Now, this radiation and efflux, though it is continuous, nevertheless, it is not on one plane and level only since the beginning of the world. For every year there is a new, supernal light, because the light that was generated and shone on this *Rosh Hashana* withdraws to its source on the eve of the following *Rosh Hashana*. And this is the meaning of the Scripture "From the beginning of the year *to the end of the year*" only. And that is why מרשית (from the beginning) is written without an *aleph*, alluding

[16] V. L. *in* B. Y.: *the quality and increase of.* [17] *Rosh Hashana 8a–b.* [18] V. L. *in* B. Y.: *and from His* chochmah. [19] *Psalms 36:10.* [20] *Brackets appear in the text.* [21] V. L. *in* B. Y.: nessirah *etc.*—Nessirah, *of the root* נסר *(*to saw, to plane*), is the Cabbalistic term generally referring to the withdrawal of the "old light" and the egression of the "new" one. This term, abounding in (Lurianic) Cabbalistic and Chassidic literature dealing with the period of* Rosh Hashana, *relates to the theme of Genesis 2:21* f. *[the removal of Adam's rib (to which the Zohar applies the term* nessirah; cf. *I:34b, and* Derech Emet a.l.; *II:55a; III:19a, and 44b) and the formation of Eve*]. [22] *Brains, intellectual faculties, referring to*

ב"ה שאין סוף ואין קץ למעלת וגדולת האור והחיות הנמשך ממנו יתברך ומחכמתו בעילוי אחר עילוי עד אין קץ ותכלית לרום המעלות למעלה מעלה ובכל שנה ושנה יורד ומאיר מחכמה עילאה אור חדש ומחודש שלא היה מאיר עדיין מעולם לארץ העליונה כי אור כל שנה ושנה מסתלק לשרשו בכל ער"ה כשהחדש מתכסה בו ואח"כ ע"י תקיעת שופר והתפלות נמשך אור חדש עליון מבחי' עליונה יותר שבמדרגת חכמה עילאה להאיר לארץ עליונה ולדרים עליה הם כל העולמות העליונים והתחתונים המקבלים חיותם ממנה דהיינו מן האור א"ס ב"ה וחכמתו המלובש בה כדכתיב כי עמך מקור חיים באורך נראה אור דהיינו אור המאיר מחכמה עילאה מקור החיים (וכנודע לי"ח שבכל ר"ה היא הנסירה ומקבלת מוחין חדשים עליונים יותר כו') ובפרטי פרטיות כן הוא בכל יום ויום נמשכין מוחין עליונים יותר בכל תפלת השחר ואינן מוחין הראשונים שנסתלקו אחר התפלה רק גבוהין יותר ודרך כלל בכללות העולם בשית אלפי שנין כן הוא בכל ר"ה ור"ה. וז"ש תמיד עיני ה' אלהיך בה שהעינים הם כינוים להמשכת והארת אור החכמה שלכן נקראו חכמים עיני העדה ואוירא דא"י מחכים והארה והמשכה זו אף שהיא תמידית אעפ"כ אינה בבחי' ומדרגה אחת לבדה מימי עולם אלא שבכל שנה ושנה הוא אור חדש עליון כי האור שנתחדש והאיר בר"ה זה הוא מסתלק בער"ה הבאה לשרשו. וז"ש מרשית השנה ועד אחרית שנה לבדה ולכן כתיב מרשית חסר א' רומז על

---

chochmah, binah, *and* da'at. [23] *See* Shulchan Aruch *of R. Isaac Luria, beg. of* כונת התפילה; Likutei Torah *I:2d, III:5d.* [24] V. L. *in* B. Y.: *more sublime ones etc.* [25] V. L. *in* B. Y.: *as regards the world of the six thousand years as a whole.* [26] *Of the world's existence (Sanhedrin 97a).* [27] *See Zohar II: 218a;* Etz Chayim *8:1.* [28] *Numbers 15:24; Song Rabba I, 15:2. See also Levit. 4:13, Horiyot 5a, and Zohar III:20a.* Cf. *also* Sifre, *Deut. 41. and Ta'anit 24a.* [29] *Bava Batra 158b; see Zohar III:245b.*—I.e., *it radiates* chochmah, *emanating to it from the "Eyes" of G-d.*

to the withdrawal of the light[30] [which withdraws on the night of *Rosh Hashana*] until after the order of the blowing of the *Shofar*[31]—when a new, more sublime light descends, so sublime a light as has never shone yet since the beginning of the world. And it vests itself and conceals itself in the *eretz hachayim* of above and of below, in order to animate all the worlds for the duration of that year.[32] However, its manifestation—from this concealment—depends on the action of those below, and on their merit and penitence during the ten days of penitence, and suffice this for the initiated.

●▲XV. "To understand the allegory and metaphor, the words of the wise and their riddles"[1]—with respect to the Sefirot.

To make the verse "And from my flesh I shall behold G-d"[2] more intelligible, it is known throughout[3] [in tradition from the supreme saints, may their souls rest in Eden] that it refers to understanding somewhat of His blessed Divinity (by reflecting on) the soul which is vested in the flesh of man, in accordance with the saying of our sages, of blessed memory, on the verse "give praise, my soul . . .":[4] "Just as the Holy One, blessed is He, . . ., the soul also . . .";[5] and in accordance with the saying of the *Zohar* on the verse "And He breathed into his nostrils a breath of life"[6]: "He who exhales, exhales from within himself."[7] For even a soul (*nefesh*) of Asiyah[8] derives from the *conjunctio* of the masculine and feminine (זיווג זו"ן)[9] of Asiyah and of their *mochin*[10] [which are the aspects of the *chayah* and *neshamah* of the masculine and feminine[11]]—which in turn, are the *achurayim*[12] of the *kelim*[13] of the masculine and feminine of Atzilut.[14] (The latter)[15] are truly divine, because in them radiates the light of the blessed En Sof which is vested and concealed in the *chochmah* of Atzilut, and "He and His causations are one—in Atzilut."[16] Thus it follows that the light of the blessed En Sof radiates in the soul (*neshamah*) of man as well, vested and concealed in the light of its *chochmah* in order to animate man.[17] And from (the soul) man is able to understand somewhat of the supernal Sefirot, for they all radiate in his soul—which compounds them. But it is necessary to state ●▲
first what I heard from my master,[18] peace be to him, on the verse "And I am dust and ashes."[19]

Our father Abraham, peace be to him, said this[20] of the illumination of his soul which in his body radiates from the light of the Supreme *chesed*;[21] and that is his attribute: the attribute of magnanimous love (*ahavah rabba*).[22] For[23] he loved

---

[30] *Signified by the* aleph (cf. *Zohar II:54a;* ibid., *123a).* [31] *By which the* aleph, *the new sublime light, is elicited; see* Siddur 'im Pirush Hamilot, Sha'ar Hateki'ot, *p. 244b* ff. [32] *From the* eretz hachayim *the light effuses to all the other worlds. On the terrestrial plane it effuses from the* eretz hachayim *(the Holy Land) to all the other countries (see* Sifre, *Deut. 40, and Nachmanides, on Deut. 11:22;* cf. *Ta'anit 10a, and see also Zohar I:255b; II:22b and 152b; III:209a–b; Zohar Chadash, 87d. See also* Sha'are Orah, *ch. V).*

Section XV

[1] *Proverbs 1:6.* [2] *Job 19:26.*—Cf. Likutei Torah, *II:31b;* Boneh Yerushalayim, *30. See also* Pardess Rimonim, *IV:6.* [3] Par. *Isaiah*

על הסתלקות האור שמסתלק בליל ר"ה עד אחר התקיעות שיורד אור חדש עליון יותר שלא היה מאיר עדיין מימי עולם אור עליון כזה והוא מתלבש ומסתתר בארץ החיים שלמעלה ושלמטה להחיות את כל העולמות כל משך שנה זו אך גילויו מההסתר הזה תלוי במעשה התחתונים וזכותם ותשובתם בעשי"ת וד"ל:

טו להבין משל ומליצה דברי חכמים וחידותם בענין הספירות מודעת זאת בארץ מפי קדושי עליון נ"ע לקרב קצת אל השכל מאי דכתיב ומבשרי אחזה אלוה שהכוונה היא להבין קצת אלהותו יתברך מנפש המלובשת בבשר האדם וע"פ מארז"ל ע"פ ברכי נפשי וגו' מה הקב"ה כו' אף הנשמה כו' וע"פ מאמר הזהר ע"פ ויפח באפיו נשמת חיים מאן דנפח מתוכי' נפח ואפי' נפש דעשיה היא באה מזיווג זו"נ דעשיה והמוחין שלהם שהם בחי' חיה ונשמה דזו"נ שהן הן אחוריים דכלים דזו"נ דאצילות שהם אלהות ממש שבתוכם מאיר אור א"ס ב"ה המלובש וגנוז בחכמה דאצי' דאיהו וגרמוהי חד באצילות וע"כ גם בנשמת האדם מאיר אור א"ס ב"ה מלובש וגנוז באור החכמה שבה להחיות את האדם וממנה יוכל האדם להבין קצת בספירות העליונות שכולן מאירות בנשמתו הכלולה מהן. אך צריך להקדים מה ששמעתי ממורי ע"ה ע"פ ואנכי עפר ואפר שאמר אברהם אבינו ע"ה על הארת נשמתו המאירה בגופו מאור חסד עליון והיא מדתו מדת אהבה רבה (נ"א שבה הי') שהיה אוהב את

12:5. [4] *Psalms 103:1.* [5] *Berachot 10a; Tikunei Zohar 13:28a. See also Midrash Tehilim (*ed. *Buber), 103:4, 5, and notes* a.l. Cf. Shomer Emunim, *II:9.* [6] *Genesis 2:7.* [7] *See* supra, *sect. XII, note 48.* [8] *The lowest type of soul from the lowest of the cosmic realms;* cf. supra, *sect. V, note 53.* [9] *Cabbalistic literature abounds with allegorical anthropomorphisms, and references to categories represented by symbolic terms as "masculine" (generally: the emanating, influencing aspect), and "feminine" (generally, the recipient aspect); see Zohar I:157b;* cf. *Bava Batra 74b;* Shomer Emunim, *I:26f. These terms apply generally to the Sefirot:* chochmah *is* abba *(father);* binah *is* imma

(Notes cont. at end of Hebrew Text)

the Holy One, blessed is He, with so great and sublime a love, that he became a chariot unto the Holy One, blessed is He.[24] Now, one might possibly assume that the type of *chesed* and love as it is above in the supernal Sefirot is of a similar nature to the attribute of abundant love of our father Abraham, peace be to him, though exceedingly greater and more marvelous *ad infinitum* than the (latter). [For it is known of the Supernal attributes that they are essentially without end and limit, because the light of the blessed En Sof actually radiates and is vested within them, and "He and His causations are one." As regards the soul of man, however, which is vested in matter, its attributes are finite and limited. But, in any case, one might possibly assume that its attributes are of the same type as the Supernal attributes.] Therefore he said: "I am dust and ashes," that is, just as ashes, which are the essence and substance of the burned wood. (For the wood) was composed of the four elements fire-air-water-earth, and the three elements of fire-water-air passed away and were consumed in the smoke that came about through their compound, as known. The fourth element of the wood, namely the earth which goes netherwards and over which the fire has no dominion, it remains in existence, and it forms the ashes. Now the whole of the essence of the wood, its substantiality and matter, and its form in terms of length, width and density [visible to the eye, before it was burned], was basically from its element of earth, though the fire, water and air were contained in it. For earth is the most material of them all. It has (dimensions of) length, width and density, which is not the case with the fire, and air, and even water, of which there is but very little in the wood. And all (the wood's dimensions of) length, width and density, "All is of the earth, and all returns to earth"[25]—i.e. the ashes that remain after the fire, water and air have been separated from it. Now, there is neither a quantitative nor a qualitative resemblance and proportion between the ashes and the essence of the wood [which, prior to being burned, had sizeable dimensions of length, width and density], even though (the ashes)[26] are its very essence and substance, and of them did (the wood) come into being. Precisely so, metaphorically speaking, our father Abraham, peace be to him, said of his attribute [the attribute of grace and love radiating

---

[24] *Genesis Rabba 47:6. This expression signifies absolute self-abnegation and submission to G-d and the Divine Will (just as the chariot is totally submitted to the will of the charioteer), and thereby becoming a vehicle for Divinity on earth. See* Tanya *I, ch. 23, and 34;* cf. *R. Chaim Vital,* Sha'arei Kedushah, *I: end of 1. See also* infra, *sect. XXV, and notes 31f.* a.l. [25] Par. *Ecclesiastes 3:20.* [26] I.e. *the element of earth.*

את הקב"ה אהבה גדולה ועליונה כ"כ עד שנעשה מרכבה להקב"ה וסד"א שבחי' חסד ואהבה שלמעלה בספירות העליונות היא מעין וסוג מהות מדת אהבה רבה של א"א ע"ה רק שהיא גדולה ונפלאה ממנה למעלה מעלה עד אין קץ ותכלית כנודע ממדות העליונות שאין להם [נ"א קץ] סוף ותכלית מצד עצמן כי אור א"ס ב"ה מאיר ומלובש בתוכם ממש ואיהו וגרמוהי חד. משא"כ בנשמת האדם המלובשת בחומר שיש למדותיה קץ וגבול. אבל מ"מ סד"א שמדותיה הן מעין וסוג מדות העליונות ולז"א ואנכי עפר ואפר דכמו שהאפר הוא מהותו ועצמותו של העץ הנשרף שהיה מורכב מד' יסודות ארמ"ע וג' יסודות אמ"ר חלפו והלכו להם וכלו בעשן המתהוה מהרכבתן כנודע ויסוד הד' שהיה בעץ שהוא העפר שבו היורד למטה ואין האש שולטת בו הוא הנשאר קיים והוא האפר והנה כל מהות העץ וממשו וחומרו וצורתו באורך ורוחב ועובי שהיה נראה לעין קודם שנשרף עיקרו היה מיסוד העפר שבו רק שאמ"ר כלולים בו כי העפר הוא חומרי יותר מכולן ויש לו אורך ורוחב ועובי משא"כ באש ורוח וגם המים הם מעט מזעיר בעץ וכל ארכו ורחבו ועוביו הכל היה מן העפר והכל שב אל העפר שהוא האפר הנשאר אחרי שנפרדו ממנו אמ"ר והנה כמו שהאפר אין לו דמיון וערך אל מהות העץ הגדול באורך ורוחב ועובי קודם שנשרף לא בכמותו ולא באיכותו אף שהוא [הוא] מהותו ועצמותו וממנו נתהוה כך עד"מ אמר אאע"ה על מדתו מדת החסד והאהבה המאירה בו

in him and vested in his body]: "Though it is the attribute of the love and Supreme *chesed* of Atzilut that radiates in his soul [which was a supernal chariot], nevertheless, as (the soul) descended netherwards, [by the evolution of the worlds from one level to another, by means of many contractions] in order to become vested in his body, there is no semblance and proportion between the essence of the light of the love that radiates in him, and the essence of the light of the love and Supreme *chesed* of Atzilut, except of the sort of proportion and semblance as there is between the essence of the earth which became ashes, and its essence and core as it was (originally) in the "Tree, pleasant to the sight and good for food."[27] (But even this is only) metaphorically speaking, and, moreover, not at all comparable,[28] except that the Torah speaks in human phraseology[29] by way of allegory and metaphor.

●▲ Now, as regards the totality of the ten Sefirot as they are in the soul of man, it is known to all[30] that the attributes are generally divided into seven (emotive) attributes (*midot*),[31] and all the detailed traits in man derive from one of these seven attributes. For they are the root of all the traits, and their generality, namely: the attribute of *chesed*—to diffuse without limit; the attribute of *gevurah*—to withhold from diffusing so much, or from diffusing altogether; the attribute of *Rachamim*—to pity whoever is in need of compassion. It[32] is the mediating attribute between *gevurah* and *chesed*, (the latter of) which seeks to diffuse to all, even where compassion is not applicable at all[33] [inasmuch as he lacks nothing and is in no state of trouble whatever]. Because (*rachamim*) is the mediating attribute, it is called *tiferet.*[34] It is, by way of analogy, like beautiful garments, that is, garments dyed[35] with many colours blended in such a way that there is beauty and embellishment.[36] To a garment dyed in one colour, however, one cannot apply a term as "beauty" (*tiferet*).[37]

Now, afterwards, as the diffusion is realised, that[38] is, at the time of the actual diffusion, it is necessary to deliberate how to diffuse in such a way that the recipient be able to absorb the effusion. For example, when one wishes to convey a matter of

---

[27] Par. *Genesis 2:9.* [28] Lit.: *separate by thousands of separations.* [29] *Berachot 31b;* Sifra, Kedoshim, parsha *X.* [30] V.L.: *It is known, in a general way.* [31] *Generally speaking there are seven classes of* midot: hesed, gevurah, tiferet, *etc. More specifically, these classes subdivide into numerous details:* chesed *of* chesed, gevurah *of* chesed, tiferet *of* chesed, *etc. (*Cf. supra, *sect. XIII, note 22.)* [32] Rachamim. [33] *See* Pardess Rimonim, *23:8,* s.v. מים, *and* cf. Moreh Nevuchim *3:53.* [34] *Beauty.* [35] *See* H.V. [36] *See* supra, *section XII, note 13.* [37] Cf. Likutei Torah—Torat Shmuel, *vol. III, ch. 51.*—Chesed, gevurah, *and* tiferet, *are the generality* (i.e. *the principal classes) of the* midot. *The*

בו ומלובשת בגופו דאף שהיא [היא] מדת האהבה וחסד העליון שבאצילות המאיר בנשמתו שהיתה מרכבה עליונה אעפ"כ בירידתה למטה להתלבש בגופו ע"י השתלשלות העולמות ממדרגה למדרגה על ידי צמצומים רבים אין דמיון וערך מהות אור האהבה המאיר בו אל מהות אור אהבה וחסד עליון שבאצילות אלא כערך ודמיון מהות העפר שנעשה אפר אל מהותו ואיכותו כשהיה עץ נחמד למראה וטוב למאכל עד"מ ויותר מזה להבדיל באלפים הבדלות רק שדברה תורה כלשון בני אדם במשל ומליצה:

והנה כללות הי"ס שבנשמת האדם נודע לכל [בדרך כלל. בכ"י ליתא] שהמדות נחלקות בדרך כלל לז' מדות וכל פרטי המדות שבאדם באות מאחת מז' מדות אלו שהן שורש כל המדות וכללותן שהן מדת החסד להשפיע בלי גבול ומדת הגבורה לצמצם מלהשפיע כ"כ או שלא להשפיע [נ"א כל עיקר] כלל ומדת הרחמים לרחם על מי ששייך לשון רחמנות עליו והיא מדה ממוצעת בין גבורה לחסד שהיא להשפיע לכל גם למי שלא שייך לשון רחמנות עליו כלל מפני שאינו חסר כלום ואינו שרוי בצער כלל ולפי שהיא מדה ממוצעת נקראת תפארת כמו בגדי תפארת עד"מ שהוא בגד צבוע בגוונים הרבה מעורבי' [בו בכ"י ליתא] בדרך שהוא תפארת ונוי. משא"כ בגד הצבוע בגוון אחד לא שייך בו לשון תפארת ואח"כ בבוא ההשפעה לידי מעשה דהיינו בשעת ההשפעה ממש צריך להתיעץ איך להשפיע בדרך שיוכל המקבל לקבל ההשפעה כגון שרוצה להשפיע דבר חכמה

other, successive attributes are branches or derivatives of these three. (Cf. Introduction.) [38] *In one version* [Or Hatorah-Bereishit, *by Tzemach Tzedek,* s.v. כי ידעתיו, *par. 13, (New York, 1966; p. 196)*] *this phrase "that is . . . diffusion," does not appear. See* H.V.

wisdom to teach it to his son, if he will tell it to him in its totality, just as it is in his own mind, the son will be unable to understand and to absorb it. Rather, one needs to arrange it in a different order and context, "Every word spoken in a proper manner,"[39] gradually. This deliberation is referred to (by the terms) *netzach* and *hod.* They[40] are the kidneys that advise,[41] and also[42] the two testicles that prepare the spermatozoon,[43] i.e. the drop that issues from the brain.[44] That is (they adapt) a matter of wisdom and intelligence deriving from the father's intellect in such a way that it will not issue as it is in itself [i.e. a very subtle intellection in his brain and intellect], but that it change somewhat from the subtlety of his intelligence and become an intellection not quite so subtle, so that the son will be able to absorb it in his mind and understanding. Metaphorically speaking, it is truly as with the (seminal) drop which descends from the brain; for it is extremely tenuous, and, through the kidneys and the two testicles, it becomes truly coarse and corporeal. *Netzach* and *hod* are also referred to as "pounders" and "grindstones," because "They pound the *manah* for the righteous."[45] Just as, by way of example, he who mills [[46]wheat] with grindstones crumbles the wheat into very fine parts, so, too, the father needs to taper the insight and the wisdom he wishes to convey to his son and to divide them into many parts, relating (them) to him by gradual process, with devices and knowledge. The aspect of *netzach* also entails to prevail[47] and stand up against anything that withholds the influence and study from his son—from within and from without; ["from within"—means to strengthen himself against the attribute of *gevurah* and *tzimtzum*[48] existent in the father himself, for it[49] arouses in his will contentions against his son, saying "He is not yet fit for this"].[50]

The aspect of *yesod* is, by way of example, the bond[51] by which the father binds his intellect to the intellect of his son while teaching him with love and willingness, for he wishes his son to understand. Without this (bond), even if the son would hear the very same words from the mouth of his father [[52]as he speaks and studies to himself],[53] he would not understand them as well

---

[39] Par. *Proverbs 25:11.* [40] *The attributes of* netzach *and* hod. [41] *Berachot 61a.* [42] V.L.: *and they are* (i.e. netzach *and* hod). *In the* Zohar *(see next note) the passage reads: "the two kidneys and the two testicles."* [43] *Zohar III:296a. See* Sha'are Orah, *ch. III IV.*, *and* Pardess Rimonim *8:24*, s.v. כליות, *and* ibid., *11*, s.v. עצה; *cf.* Mevoh She'arim *III:ii:7.* [44] *See* Tanya *I, ch. 2.* [45] *Zohar III:236a (*cf. *Hagigah 12b).* [46] *Brackets appear in the text.* [47] *The root of the word* netzach *means to prevail, to be enduring, victorious. See Tikunei Zohar 13:28b; see also Zohar III:223b.* Cf. Likutei Torah—Torat Shmuel, *vol. III, ch. 52.* [48] Netzach *is bound to the "right side," the side of* chochmah *and*

חכמה ללמדה לבנו אם יאמרנה לו כולה כמו שהיא בשכלו לא יוכל הבן להבין ולקבל רק שצריך לסדר לו בסדר וענין אחר דבר דבור על אופניו מעט מעט ובחינת עצה זו נקראת נצח והוד שהן כליות יועצות וגם [נ"א והן] תרין ביעין המבשלים הזרע שהיא הטפה הנמשכת מהמוח דהיינו דבר חכמה ושכל הנמשך משכל האב שלא יומשך כמו שהוא שכל דק מאד במוחו ושכלו רק ישתנה קצת מדקות שכלו ויתהווה שכל שאינו דק כ"כ כדי שיוכל הבן לקבל במוחו והבנתו והוא ממש עד"מ כטפה היורדת מהמוח שהיא דקה מאד [מאד] ונעשית גסה וחומרית ממש בכליות ותרין ביעין וגם נו"ה נקרא שחקים ורחיים ששוחקים מן לצדיקים כמו הטוחן [חטים] ברחיים עד"מ שמפרר החטים לחלקים דקים מאד כך צריך האב להקטין השכל ודבר חכמה שרוצה להשפיע לבנו ולחלקם לחלקים רבים ולומר לו מעט מעט במועצות ודעת וגם בכלל בחינת נצח הוא לנצח ולעמוד נגד כל מונע ההשפעה והלימוד מבנו מבית ומחוץ. מבית היינו להתחזק נגד מדת הגבורה והצמצום שבאב עצמו שהיא מעוררת דינים ברצונו על בנו לומר שאינו ראוי לכך עדיין (בכ"י נרשם חסר) ובחי' יסוד היא עד"מ ההתקשרות שמקשר האב שכלו בשכל בנו בשעת למודו עמו באהבה ורצון שרוצה שיבין בנו ובלעדי זה גם אם היה הבן שומע דבורים אלו עצמם מפי אביו [שמדבר בעדו ולומר לעצמו. בבי"ק אדמו"ר בעל צ"צ נ"ע (בדרוש כי ידעתיו סעי' י"ג שהועתק שם לשון זה) ליתא תיבות אלו] לא היה מבין כ"כ כמו

עכשיו

---

chesed—*(Tikunei Zohar 22:68b; ibid., 30:74a; see also Zohar III:153b)—and seeks to have* "white" (chesed) *rule over* "red" *(*gevurah; *to which* hod *is related); Zohar III:223b.* Cf. Likutei Torah—Torat Shmuel, ibid. [49] *The attribute of* gevurah. [50] *A parenthesis in the text states that according to some manuscripts there is an omission here in the text. The omission probably deals with an explanation of the function of the attribute* hod. [51] *I Chron. 29:11 alludes to the seven lower Sefirot* (chesed, *or* gedulah, *to* malchut). *The allusion to the first five and the seventh of these is quite explicit.* Yessod, *the sixth, is expressed by the words* כי כל בשמים ובארץ *(*lit.: *for all that is in*

(Notes cont. at end of Hebrew Text)

as now when his father ties his intellect unto him and speaks with him face to face—with love and desire, because he desires very much that his son understand. And the greater the desire and delight (of the father) the greater is the influence and the study, because then the son is able to absorb more and the father influences more. For through the desire and delight his (own) insight becomes greater and more abundant,[54] with a contented disposition[55] to influence and teach his son ([56]just as, metaphorically speaking, in the sphere of the truly physical, an amplification of spermatozoon derives from an abundance of desire and delight, and, thereby, he elicits much from the brain. That is why the Cabbalists drew a comparison with the physical *conjunctio*,[57] as will be explained).

▲ Now, these attributes are the external aspects[58] of the soul. In them are vested the inner attributes, i.e. the faculties of love and awe . . ., analogous to the father who influences his son because of his love (for the son), and withholds his influence because of his dread and fear that (his son) might come to some downfall, Heaven forfend. The source and root of these internal and external attributes, is of the *chabad*[59] of his soul, for corresponding to a person's intellect are his traits. This is empirically evident, (as in the case of) a child, the *ChaBaD* of which are in a state of pettiness (*katnut*), all its traits, too, are related to insignificant things. With adults, too, "According to his intelligence is a man praised,"[60] for corresponding to the quantity of wisdom is the quantity of his love and kindness; and also his other internal and external traits have their source from his *ChaBaD*. Most important is one's *da'at*, which derives from one's *chochmah* and *binah*. This is empirically evident, for corresponding to the difference from one to the other in the opinions[61] of people, is the difference in their traits.

●▲ Now all this is only by way of allegory, for all this applies to the rational soul,[62] which is the lower one in man and derives from *kelipat nogah*.[63] But in true fact,[64] in the higher, *divine* soul, which is a part of G-d above,[65] all the internal and external attributes are to G-d alone. For because of the love of G-d and of one's great desire to cleave unto Him, "One takes delight in *chesed*"[66] in order

[54] Cf. Eliyahu Rabba, *ch. 27; Ta'anit 7a ("I have learnt from my disciples more than from any other").* [55] Lit.: *with an expansion of* da'at. [56] *Brackets appear in the text.* [57] *See Introduction, ch. I, note 6.* [58] *The* chitzoniyut. [59] *The intellectual faculties:* chochmah, binah *and* da'at. [60] *Proverbs 12:8.* [61] De'ot *(plural of* da'at*).* [62] *The rational soul (*nefesh hasichlit*) is the mediary between the natural soul* (nefesh) *and the soul proper* (neshamah), *see* Kitzurim Vehe'arot, *pp.* 86ff., *and the references cited there.* [63] *See* Etz Chayim *49:3;* Tanya *I, ch. 7. (Cf. Maimonides, Introd. to* Commentary *on Avot, end of ch. 1.)*—Kelipat nogah *is the mediary between the realms of absolute evil and impurity,*

עכשיו שאביו מקשר שכלו אליו ומדבר עמו פא״פ באהבה וחשק שחושק מאד שיבין בנו וכל מה שהחשק והתענוג גדול כך ההשפעה והלימוד גדול שהבן יוכל לקבל יותר והאב משפיע יותר כי ע״י החשק והתענוג מתרבה ומתגדל שכלו בהרחבת הדעת להשפיע וללמד לבנו (וכמו עד״מ בגשמיות ממש רבוי הזרע הוא מרוב החשק והתענוג וע״ז ממשיך הרבה מהמוח ולכן המשילו חכמי האמת לזווג גשמי כמו שית׳). והנה מדות אלו הן בחי׳ חיצוניות שבנפש ובתוכן מלובשות מדות פנימיות שהן בחי׳ אהוי״ר כו׳ דהיינו עד״מ באב המשפיע לבנו מחמת אהבתו ומונע השפעתו מפחדו ויראתו שלא יבא לידי מכשול ח״ו. ומקור ושרש מדות אלו הפנימיות והחיצוניות הוא מחב״ד שבנפשו כי לפי שכל האדם כך הן מדותיו כנראה בחוש שהקטן שהחב״ד שלו הן בבחי׳ קטנות כך כל מדותיו הן בדברים קטני הערך וגם בגדולים לפי שכלו יהולל איש כי לפי רוב חכמתו כך הוא רוב אהבתו וחסדו וכן שאר כל מדותיו פנימיות וחיצוניות מקורן הוא מחב״ד שבו והעיקר הוא הדעת שבו הנמשך מבחי׳ החו״ב שבו כנראה בחוש כי לפי שינוי דעות בני אדם זה מזה כך הוא שינוי מדותיהם. והנה כ״ז הוא רק עד״מ לבד כי כ״ז הוא בנפש השכלית התחתונה שבאדם הבאה מקליפת נוגה אך באמת לאמיתו בנפש העליונה האלהית שהיא חלק אלוה ממעל כל המדות פנימיות וחיצוניות הן לה׳ לבדו כי מחמת אהבת ה׳ ומרוב חפצו לדבקה בו הוא חפץ חסד כדי

לדבוק

---

and absolute good and holiness; see Introduction, s.v. Kelipot. [64] Lit.: *In absolute truth.* [65] *Job 31:2; see* Tanya *I, beg. of ch. 2.* [66] Par. *Micha 7:18—denoting G-d's attribute of* chesed *which man is to imitate (see* infra, *esp. note 68).*

to cleave to His attributes, as the saying of our sages, of blessed memory, on the verse[67] "And to cleave unto Him": "cleave unto His attributes."[68] It is likewise with the attribute of *gevurah*: to punish and chastise the wicked with the punishments of the Torah; and, also, to prevail[69] over his inclination and to "Sanctify himself in that which is permitted to him,"[70] and to "Put up a fence and a hedge for the Torah,"[71] because of the dread of G-d and his fear[72] lest he might come to sin, Heaven forfend.[73] And, likewise, to glorify[74] G-d and His Torah by all means of glory, and to cleave unto His praises with all the faculties of his soul, that is, with the contemplation of the intellect and thought even when he speaks.[75] Likewise, to prevail triumphantly[76] against anything that would restrain from the service of G-d and from cleaving unto Him, and against anything that would restrain having the "Glory of G-d filling all the earth,"[77] just as the wars for G-d fought by King David, peace to him.[78] And, likewise, to prostrate oneself and *to laud*[79] the Lord who animates and makes all there is, and with Him everything is essentially non-existent "And all that are before Him are esteemed as naught,"[80] truly as nothing and null. Though we cannot apprehend just how everything is truly as null before Him, nevertheless, we *acknowledge*, with a sincere admission,[81] that in absolute truth such is the case. This also includes *to thank*[82] the Lord for all the favours He has bestowed upon us, and not to be ungrateful, Heaven forfend; and this includes (further) to thank for all His praises, attributes and workings in the emanation and creation of the upper and lower worlds, for they are praiseworthy to no end, and are becoming and befitting to Him, blessed and exalted be He—which is (the sense of *hod* as) etymologically related to *hod vehadar*.[83] And likewise with the attribute of *tzadik yessod olam*,[84] that his soul be bound up in the Lord, the Fountainhead of life,[85] to cleave to Him by an attachment and desire out of a wondrous love and delight. And as for the attribute of *malchut*—to receive upon himself the yoke of His sovereignty and of His service, as the service of any servant to his master, i.e. out of awe and fear.[86]

● Now, the source and root of all the attributes are of the *ChaBaD*. That is, *chochmah* is the source of the intellect which apprehends the Lord and His wisdom, His greatness and His holy attributes wherewith He conducts and animates all the upper and lower worlds. *Binah* is the contemplation

---

[67] *Deut. 11:22.* [68] *See* Sifre, a.l. *(Deut. 49); Sotah 14a; Maimonides,* Sefer Hamitzvot *I:8,* Hilchot De'ot *I:6, and* Moreh Nevuchim *I:54.—By "imitating" the Divine attributes* (imitatio De-i) *one cleaves unto G-d. To practise* chesed *(kindness) is an imitation of the Divine attribute of* chessed. *Thus this practice is "unto G-d alone," a service of G-d.* [69] גבר*—to prevail.* [70] *Yevamot 20a;* Sifre, *Deut. 104.* [71] *Avot I:1.* [72] Cf. supra, *sect. XIII, note 29.* [73] *All these are modes of attitude or behaviour utilising the attribute of* gevurah *in the service of G-d.* [74] *The attribute of* tiferet *(*פאר*—to glorify, beautify).* [75] *These are the modes of attitude or behaviour utilising the attribute of* tiferet *in the service of G-d.* [76] *The attri-*

לדבוק במדותיו כמארז"ל ע"פ ולדבקה בו הדבק
במדותיו וכן במדת הגבורה להפרע מן הרשעים
ולענשם בעונשי התורה וכן להתגבר על יצרו ולקדש
א"ע במותר לו ולעשות גדר וסייג לתורה מפני פחד
ה' ויראתו פן יבא לידי חטא ח"ו וכן לפאר את ה'
ותורתו בכל מיני פאר ולדבקה בשבחיו בכל בחי'
נפשו דהיינו בהתבוננות שכלו ומחשבתו גם בדיבורו
וכן לעמוד בנצחון נגד כל מונע מעבודת ה' ומלדבקה
בו ונגד כל מונע מלהיות כבוד ה' מלא את כל הארץ
כמלחמות ה' אשר נלחם דהע"ה וכן להשתחוות
ולהודות לה' אשר מחיה ומהוה את הכל והכל בטל
במציאות אצלו וכולא קמיה כלא חשיב וכאין ואפס
ממש ואף שאין אנו משיגים איך הוא הכל אפס
ממש קמיה אעפי"כ מודים אנחנו בהודאה אמיתית
שכן הוא באמת לאמיתו ובכלל זה ג"כ להודות לה'
על כל הטובות אשר גמלנו ולא להיות כפוי טובה
ח"ו ובכלל זה להודות על כל שבחיו ומדותיו ופעולותיו
באצי' ובריאות עליונים ותחתונים שהם משובחים עד
אין תכלית [נ"א חקר] ונאים וראוים אליו ית' וית' והוא
מלשון הוד והדר וכן במדת צדיק יסוד עולם להיות
נפשו קשורה בה' חיי החיים ולדבקה בו בדביקה
וחשיקה בחשק ותענוג נפלא ובמדת מל' לקבל עליו
עול מלכותו ועבודתו כעבודת כל עבד לאדונו באימה
וביראה ומקור ושורש כל המדות הן מחב"ד דהיינו
החכמה היא מקור השכל המשיג את ה' וחכמתו
וגדולתו ומדותיו הקדושות שמנהיג ומחיה בהן כל
העולמות עליונים ותחתונים ובינה היא ההתבוננות
בהשגה

---

bute of netzach *(see above, note 47).* [77] Par. *Isaiah 6:3.* [78] *See* Sha'arei Orah, *ch. III/IV,* s.v. נצח.—*These are the modes of attitude or behaviour utilising the attribute of* netzach *in the service of G-d.* [79] *The attribute of* hod. Hod *is etymologically related to* הודה, *to laud, thank, acknowledge; see Zohar III:223a; Tikunei Zohar 13:28b;* Sha'are Orah, *ch. III/IV,* s.v. הוד. *Prostration before G-d is coupled with the expression of gratitude (see Berachot 34a–b; Bava Kama 16a;* cf. Sha'arei Orah, a.l.c.).—*See also* Likutei Torah—Torat Shmuel, *vol. III, ch. 53.* [80] *Zohar I:11b.* [81] *See note 79,* supra. [82] Ibid. [83] *Majesty and splendour (Psalms 104:1; see* Sha'arei Orah, *ch, III/IV,*

(Notes cont. at end of Hebrew Text)

on this apprehension in the length, width, and depth of his understanding: "To understand one matter out of another,"[87] and to beget from this apprehension its offsprings, i.e. the attributes of love and awe, and the other attributes born in the Divine soul which cogitates and contemplates on the greatness of the Lord, how His greatness is unfathomable.[88] There is an aspect of the greatness of the Lord through the Divine soul's contemplation on which a fear and dread will befall it. This (type of fear) is the *yirah tataah*,[89] an aspect of *malchut*.[90] There is another aspect of the greatness of the Lord whereof derives the *yirah ilaah*,[91] i.e., *yare boshet*.[92] There is (also) an aspect whereof derives the *ahavah rabba*,[93] and still another aspect, whereof derives the *ahavah zutta*.[94] The same applies to the external attributes, i.e. *chesed* . . .

Now, with all these it is necessary that the faculty of *da'at* be vested in them. For (*da'at*) is the aspect of the bond of the soul which is bound and thrust into this apprehension, of apprehending some aspect of the greatness of the Lord whereof some trait of these attributes is born in (the soul). For by a momentary removal of *da'at* from this apprehension, the trait begotten thereof is also withdrawn from it, that is, from its manifestation in the soul (back) into concealment, to be there *in potentia* but not in act. That is why the term *da'at* is applied to coition,[95] for it signifies a bond. Now, this is the faculty of *da'at tachton*,[96] which extends to the attributes and vests itself in them to animate and sustain them. There is also a faculty of *da'at elyon*[97] which is the faculty of the bond and joiner of the *source* of the intellect [which apprehends the profoundness of the apprehended notion which is a point and a flash flashing over his intellect] so that it extends downwards. Thereby the profoundness of the apprehended notion will come to be understood in the expansion of the elucidation, in length and breadth, which is the faculty of *binah*, referred to as *rechovot hanahar*,[98] as will be explained in its place.

XVI

●▲ To the members of the community of . . .

My beloved, my brethren and friends, who are (to me) as my (own) soul. Behold, I am aware[1] of the hardships of these times, that

[87] *Hagigah 14a; Zohar Chadash 4a.* Cf. Sifre, *Deut. 13 (on Deut. 1:13; see Rashi* a.l., *and on Exodus 31:3).* [88] *Psalms 145:3.* [89] *The "lower," or "inferior awe." On this, and the following terms see* supra, *sect. VI, and* infra, *note 94.* [90] *Tikunei Zohar 33:76b* f. *(*Cf. *Zohar I:11b).* [91] *The "upper," or "superior awe."* [92] *"Awed out of bashfulness"—before the infinite greatness of the Lord (see Zohar III:257a; Tikunei Zohar, Intr.: 5b,* ibid., *6:24a, 7:24a,* et passim*). This type of awe is also called* yirat haromemut, *the awe before the majesty of G-d.* [93] *The "magnanimous," or "superior love"* (ahavah beta'anugim). [94] *The "small," or "inferior love." —On the gradations of all these levels see: Zohar I:11b; Tikunei Zohar,*

בהשגה זו באורך ורוחב ועומק בינתו להבין דבר מתוך דבר ולהוליד מהשגה זו תולדותיה שהן מדות אהוי"ר ושארי מדות הנולדות בנפש האלהית המשכלת ומתבוננת בגדולת ה' כי לגדולתו אין חקר ויש בחי' גדולת ה' שע"י התבוננות הנפש האלהית בה תפול עליה אימתה ופחד שהיא יראה תתאה שהיא בחינת מלכות ויש בחי' גדולת ה' שממנה באה יראה עילאה יראה בושת ויש בחינה שממנה באה אהבה רבה ויש בחינה שממנה באה אהבה זוטא וכן במדות החיצוניות שהן חסד כו' ובכולן צריך להיות מלובש בהן בחינת הדעת שהוא בחינת התקשרות הנפש הקשורה ותקועה בהשגה זו שמשגת איזה ענין מגדולת ה' שממנה נולדה בה איזה מדה מהמדות כי בהיסח הדעת כרגע מהשגה זו מסתלקת ג"כ המדה הנולדה ממנה מהגילוי בנפש אל ההעלם להיות בה בכח ולא בפועל ולכן נקרא הזיווג בלשון דעת מפני שהוא לשון התקשרות וזהו בחי' דעת תחתון [נ"א הדעת התחתון] המתפשט במדות ומתלבש בהן להחיותן ולקיימן ויש בחינת דעת העליון שהוא בחינת התקשרות וחיבור מקור השכל המשיג עומק המושג שהוא כנקודה וכברק המבריק על שכלו שיתפשט למטה ויבא עומק המושג לידי הבנה בהרחבת הביאור באורך ורוחב שהיא בחינת בינה הנק' רחובות הנהר כמו שיתבאר במקומו:

לאנשי ק' וכו'

טז אהוביי אחיי ורעיי אשר כנפשי הנה לא נעלם ממני צוק העתים אשר נתדלדלה

Intr.: 5a ff., and 30:73b. See also Chovot Halevovot, Sha'ar Ahavat Hashem, *esp. the Introd. and ch. 2* f.; *Maimonides,* Hilchot Yessodei Hatorah, *II:2, and IV:12;* Ikkarim, *III:32;* Tanya *I, ch. 40ff. (esp. ch. 43); and* infra, *sect. XVIII.* [95] E.g. *Genesis 4:1, 17, 25;* et passim.—*See Tikunei Zohar 69:99a.* [96] *The "lower," or "inferior* da'at." *It proceeds from and succeeds* chochmah *and* binah, *channelling them to the lower Sefirot. See note following.* [97] *The "upper," or "superior* da'at."—*In the Sefirot scheme of* yosher, *in which the Sefirot form three parallel triads* (chochmah-chesed-netzach; binah-gevurah-hod; keter-tiferet-yesod; *see Introduction,* s.v. Body of the Sefirot) da'at *does not*

(Notes cont. at end of Hebrew Text)

the means for livelihood have declined, and especially among those known to me from your ranks whose hand has wavered; (they are) without any assistance and support, and they literally borrow in order to eat. May the Lord show them compassion and speedily bring them respite from their straits.[2]

Nonetheless, they are not acting rightly unto their soul according to the reports that they close their hand which all their life long, to this very day, was open to give with a full hand and benevolence towards all essential necessities to satisfy the needs of the innocent destitutes whose eyes are lifted unto us.[3] If, Heaven forfend, we will not have mercy on them, who then will show them compassion? And it is written: "That your brother may live with you!"[4] (The rule) "Your life takes precedence"[5] applies only in the case of "One has a pitcher of water . . .",[6] that is, when the same thing is equally essential to both to drink in order to restore their soul from thirst. But when the poor needs bread for the mouths of babes, and wood and clothes against the cold, and the like, then all these take precedence over any fine clothes and family-feasts, meat and fish, and all the delicacies of man and any members of his household. The rule "your life takes precedence" does not apply in such a case, because all these are not really essential to life, as are (the needs) of the poor, to make them[7] truly equal,[8] as mentioned in *Nedarim*, folio 80.[9]

●▲Now, (all) this is according to the strict measure of the law. In fact, however, even in the case where such reasoning does not apply, it behoves everyone not to be particular in insisting on the law, but to set aside his own life and to go far beyond the measure of the law. One should be concerned, for his own sake, with the statement of our sages, of blessed memory, that he who is exacting in a matter "Will eventually be brought to it,"[10] Heaven forfend. And, after all, all of us need, at all times, the mercies of Heaven, which are (elicited) only through an arousal from below, by arousing at all times, and every moment, our compassion for those who are in need of compassion. But he who hardens his heart and suppresses his compassion [for whatever reason there may be], he causes the same above—to suppress . . .,[11] Heaven forfend.

(One should especially consider that) after all "There is not a righteous person upon earth that does good—always—and does not sin,"[12] and charity atones[13] and protects against misfortune . . .[14] (Charity) thus is an actual cure

---

[2] Lit.: *and broaden (a space) for them in the straits (*cf. *Ps. 4:2; 118:5).* [3] Par. *Deut. XV:7, 8, and Jeremiah 2:34.* [4] *Levit. 25:36. See the commentaries by Nachmanides, and R. Obadya Seforno* a.l. [5] *Bava Metzia 62a, in comment on Lev. 25:36 ("that your brother may live* with you"*—thus: your own life takes precedence).* [6] See *ibid.* [7] *The needs of the destitute with the luxuries of the wealthy.* [8] *Needs, therefore, take precedence to luxuries.* [9] *Nedarim 80b. See also* Tossefta, *Bava Metzia XI:14;* Yerushalmi, *Shevi'it VIII:5 and Nedarim XI:1.* [10] *Bava Metzia 33a; see the commentaries by Rashi, and R. Samuel Edelis,* ad loc. *See also* Tossefta, *Bava Metzia XI:14, and the comment.* Minchat Bikurim, a.l. [11] Cf.

נתדלדלה הפרנסה ובפרט הידועים לי ממחניכם אשר מטה ידם בלי שום משען ומשענה וממש לווים ואוכלים ה׳ ירחם עליהם וירחיב להם בצר בקרוב ועם כל זה לא טוב הם עושים לנפשם לפי הנשמע אשר קפצו ידם הפתוחה מעודם עד היום הזה ליתן ביד מלאה ועין יפה לכל הצטרכות ההכרחיים לדי מחסורי האביונים נקיים אשר עיניהם נשואות אלינו ואם אנו לא נרחם עליהם ח״ו מי ירחם עליהם וחי אחיך עמך כתיב ולא אמרו חייך קודמין אלא כשביד אחד קיתון של מים וכו׳ שהוא דבר השוה לשניהם בשוה לשתות להשיב נפשם בצמא. אבל אם העני צריך לחם לפי הטף ועצים וכסות בקרה וכה״ג כל דברים אלו קודמין לכל מלבושי כבוד וזבח משפחה בשר ודגים וכל מטעמים של האדם וכב״ב ולא שייך בזה חייך קודמין מאחר שאינן חיי נפש ממש כמו של העני שוה בשוה ממש כדאיתא בנדרים דף פ׳. והנה זהו עפ״י שורת הדין גמור. אבל באמת גם אם הוא ענין דלא שייך כ״כ ה״ט ראוי לכל אדם שלא לדקדק להעמיד על הדין רק לדחוק חייו וליכנס לפני ולפנים משורת הדין ולדאוג לעצמו ממארז״ל שכל המדקדק בכך סוף בא לידי כך ח״ו וגם כי כולנו צריכים לרחמי שמים בכל עת באתערותא דלתתא דוקא בכל עת ובכל שעה לעורר רחמינו על הצריכים לרחמים וכל המאמץ לבבו וכובש רחמיו יהיה מאיזה טעם שיהיה גורם כך למעלה לכבוש וכו׳ ח״ו ומה גם כי אדם אין צדיק בארץ אשר יעשה טוב תמיד ולא יחטא והצדקה מכפרת ומגינה מן הפורענות וכו׳ ולזאת היא רפואת

הגוף

Mishna, *Sota I:7.* [12] *Eccles. VII:20.* [13] *See Deut. Rabba V:3 (cf. Sukah 49b). See also* Sefer Chassidim, *sect. 61 and 170;* Netivot Olam, s.v. גמ״ח, *beg. of ch. 1, and* ibid., s.v. צדקה, *end of ch. 4.* Cf. Tanya *III:ch. 3.* [14] *See Levit. Rabba 27:1.*

for the body and soul,[15] with respect to which—"Skin for skin, and all that a man has he will give for his *nefesh*."[16]

This applies especially as we are believers, the descendants of believers[17] (in the fact) that charity is naught but a loan to the Holy One, blessed is He,[18] as it is written: "He who is gracious unto the poor, lends unto the Lord, and He will repay him his good deed"[19]—manifold, in this world.[20] For none of the commandments is the reward given in this world except for charity, because it is beneficial to the creatures, as mentioned at the end of the first chapter of *Kidushin*.[21]

Also, one should be concerned about punishment, Heaven forfend, when one's companions are associated for the sake of a *Mitzvah* (commandment) and he is not associated with them, as known from the words of our sages, of blessed memory.[22] But it will be well with those who give heed, and upon them shall come the blessing of goodness[23]—"of the best of all things." Do good, O Lord, unto the good and the upright,[24] as is their wish and the wish of he who seeks their welfare, from the whole heart and soul.

●▲ XVII.[1] It is known that an arousal from below, when man arouses in his heart the trait of kindness and compassion for all those in need of compassion, this elicits an arousal from above, i.e. an arousal of great compassion upon him from the source of compassion,[2] to effuse unto him the "Fruits in this world, while the principal remains for the world to come."[3] This means: "the fruits" refers to the effluence effusing from the Source of compassion and Fountainhead of life,[4] blessed is He. It issues netherwards, in the mode of the evolution of the worlds from above downwards . . ., until it vests itself in this world in children, life and sustenance . . .[5] The "principal" is, as it is written: "*Mitzvatecha* (Your commandment) is very wide."[6] Now it should say *mitzvotecha*—in plural form![7] ([8]The phraseology of "is wide" is also not comprehensible.)

However, the express form of *mitzvatecha* refers to the precept of charity, which is truly the *Mitzvah* of the Lord, which the Holy One, blessed is He, Himself, in all His majesty, performs at all times by animating the worlds, and will do so in the future with exceeding uplifting and force.[9] And thus it is written:[10] "And they shall observe the way of the Lord, to do *tzedakah*' . . ."[11] Metaphorically speaking, like unto a road on which one goes from one city to another,[12] so, too, charity is a capacity for a manifestation and radiation of the light of the blessed En Sof which encompasses all worlds,[13] so that in the future, at the resurrection of the dead, it will radiate, and become manifest, even to this world, through the arousal from below as an expression of charity and gratuitous kindness,

---

[15] Cf. *Midrash Tehilim 41:4;* Tanchuma, Mishpatim: *15.* [16] *Soul, or life.—Job II:4.* Cf. supra, *section X (note 49).* [17] *Shabbat 97a.* [18] *Bava Batra, end of 10a, see Rashi, and* Chidushei Agadot, *by R. Judah Loewe,* ad loc., *and* Netivot Olam, s.v. צדקה, *ch. 4. See also* Tanchuma, Mishpatim: *15.* [19] *Proverbs 19:17.* [20] *See note following.* [21] *Kidushin 39b–40a (see Rashi,* a.l., s.v. רבי אידי*).* [22] *Hagiga 9b.* [23] Par. *Proverbs 24:25.* [24] *Psalms 125:4.*

Section XVII

[1] *See* Bitaon Chabad, *no. 31 (Kfar Chabad 1970), p. 7 for the opening paragraphs of this section.* [2] *See* supra, *section IV, note 44.* [3] *The principal and the fruits of the good deeds.*—Mishnah, *Peah I:1.*

הגוף ונפש ממש אשר עור בעד עור וכל אשר לאיש יתן בעד נפשו בשגם אנו מאמינים בני מאמינים כי הצדקה אינה רק הלואה להקב"ה כדכתיב מלוה ה' חונן דל וגמולו ישלם לו בכפליים בעולם הזה דשכר כל המצות ליכא בעוה"ז לבד מצדקה לפי שהוא טוב לבריות כדאיתא בקדושין ס"פ קמא וגם יש לחוש לעונש ח"ו כשחבריו נמנים לדבר מצוה והוא לא נמנה עמהם כנודע ממארז"ל ולשומעים יונעם ותבוא עליהם ברכת טוב בכל מילי דמיטב הטיבה ה' לטובים וישרים כנפשם ונפש הדו"ש מכל לב ונפש:

יז נודע דבאתערותא דלתתא שהאדם מעורר בלבו מדת החסד ורחמנות על כל הצריכים לרחמים אתערותא דלעילא לעורר עליו רחמים רבים ממקור הרחמים להשפיע לו הפירות בעוה"ז והקרן לעוה"ב. פי' הפירות היא השפעה הנשפעת ממקור הרחמים וחיי החיים ב"ה ונמשכת למטה מטה בבחינת השתלשלות העולמות מלמעלה למטה כו' עד שמתלבשת בעוה"ז הגשמי בבני חיי ומזוני כו' והקרן הוא כמ"ש רחבה מצותך מאד והל"ל מצותיך לשון רבים (וגם לשון רחבה אינו מובן) אלא מצותך דייקא היא מצות הצדקה שהיא מצות ה' ממש מה שהקב"ה בכבודו ובעצמו עושה תמיד להחיות העולמות ויעשה לעתיד ביתר שאת ויתר עז וכמ"ש ושמרו דרך ה' לעשות צדקה כו' כמו דרך שהולכים בה מעיר לעיר עד"מ. כך הצדקה היא בחי' גילוי והארת אור א"ס ב"ה סובב כל עלמין שיאיר ויתגלה עד עוה"ז באתערותא דלתתא בתורת צדקה וחסד חנם לעתיד בתחיית

---

[4] Lit.: *The Life of life (*cf. *Yoma 71a; Tikunei Zohar 19:41b;* ibid., *69:115a; and see* infra, *end of sect. XXIIa).* [5] *See* supra, *section XI, note 5.* [6] *Psalms 119:96.* [7] Cf. *Rashi*, a.l. [8] *Brackets appear in the text.* [9] Par. *Genesis 49:3.* [10] *Genesis 18:19.* [11] *See Zohar III:113b.* [12] Tzedakah *is called the "way of the Lord" because it is like a road-way that enables man to travel from one place to another.* [13] *The* or sovev, *or* or makif*; see* supra, *sect. III, note 12.*

[with an uplifting and force infinitely exceeding the state of manifestation of the radiation in the upper and lower Gardens of Eden]. For in the future all the souls of the *tzadikim*, and of the Tannaim and the prophets that are now in the upper Garden of Eden, at the peak of levels, will become vested in their bodies, and they will arise at the time of the resurrection to derive pleasure from the splendour of the Shechinah.

That is, the manifestation and the radiation as it is in the Garden of Eden is of the level of *memale kol almin.*[14] This is a level of the evolution from one rung to another by means of immense contractions,[15] and as the saying of our sages, of blessed memory: "The world to come was created by the *yud*"[16]—the sphere of the Supreme *chochmah*,[17] referred to as the upper Eden,[18] and evolving and vesting itself in all the worlds, as it is written: "You have made them all with *chochmah* . . ."[19] and "*chochmah* animates . . ."[20] In the Garden of Eden (the sphere of *chochmah*) is in a state of manifest apprehension to each according to his measure.[21] For as known, the delight of the souls in the Garden of Eden derives from the apprehension of the secrets of the Torah with which one busied oneself in this world with the revealed (parts of Torah) [as mentioned in the sacred *Zohar*, section *Shlach*,[22] and in the *Gemara*[23] with reference to the occurrence with Rabba bar Nachmeni].

The manifestation of the radiation at the time of the resurrection, however, will be from the level of *sovev kol almin*,[24] which is not in a state of contraction (*tzimtzum*), measure and limit, but without limit and end [as the concept of *sovev kol almin* has been explained in *Likutei Amarim*, ch. 48, not to be in its literal sense—like unto a circle, Heaven forfend, but only that it is not in a state of investment . . ., note there carefully].

●▲And this is the meaning of what our sages, of blessed memory, said: "And their crowns on their heads, and they take delight . . ."[25] A crown (*atarah*) is something that encompasses and encircles, and is called *keter*[26] [an idiom of *koteret*[27]]. It is the aspect of the intermediary which joins the radiation of the Emanator, the blessed En Sof, to the emanated,[28] and in the future it will radiate and become revealed in this world[29] unto all the righteous who will rise with the resurrection ([30]"And Your people, they are all righteous . . ."[31]). And this is the meaning of what our sages, of blessed memory, said: "In the future the righteous will be addressed as *holy*."[32] Holy is a rank of being separated;[33] it is not subject to apprehension and knowledge, because it transcends the rank of the wisdom and knowledge which there is in the Garden of Eden.[34] Thus Scripture states: "*Chochmah*

---

[14] *Permeating all worlds (thus the* or pnimi*); see* supra, *sect. III, note 12.* [15] *This radiation of the Divine immanence, the* or pnimi, *is an immensely screened derivative of the* or makif, *the radiation of the Divine transcendence. As the worlds develop from higher to lower, the* or pnimi *is contracted ever more.* [16] *Menachot 29b.—See* supra, *sect. V.* [17] Supra, *sect. V, note 16.—The* yud, *by its very form as a simple point, indicates the immense contraction of the Divine Light contained in it. The* or pnimi *thus is related to the Sefirah* chochmah *(cf.* supra, *sect. III, note 12).* [18] Ibid., *note 17.* [19] *Psalms 104:24.* [20] *Eccles. 7:12.—See Introduction,* s.v. Chochmah *(cf.* supra, *beg. of sect. V; sect. XI, note 10; sect. XIV, note 14).*

בתחיית המתים ביתר שאת ויתר עז לאין קץ מבחינת גילוי (הארה) [ההארה] בג"ע התחתון והעליון שהרי כל נשמות הצדיקים והתנאים והנביאים שהם עתה בג"ע העליון ברום המעלות יתלבשו בגופותיהם לעתיד ויקומו בזמן התחיה ליהנות מזיו השכינה לפי שההארה והגילוי שבג"ע היא בחינת ממלא כל עלמין שהוא בחינת השתלשלות ממדרגה למדרגה ע"י צמצומים עצומים וכמארז"ל ביו"ד נברא עוה"ב והיא בחינת חכמה עילאה הנקראת עדן העליון המשתלשלת ומתלבשת בכל העולמות כמ"ש כולם בחכמה עשית כו' והחכמה תחי' כו' ובג"ע היא בבחינת גילוי ההשגה לכל חד לפום שיעורא דילי' כנודע שעונג הנשמות בג"ע הוא מהשגת סודות התורה שעסק בעוה"ז בנגלה כדאיתא בזוה"ק פ' שלח ובגמ' בעובדא דרבה בר נחמני. אבל גילוי ההארה שבתחה"מ יהי' מבחינת סובב כל עלמין שאינה בבחינת צמצום ושיעור וגבול אלא בלי גבול ותכלית כמ"ש בלק"א פמ"ח ביאור ענין סוכ"ע שאינו כמשמעו כמו עיגול ח"ו אלא שאינו בבחי' התלבשות וכו' וע"ש היטב. וזהו שארז"ל ועטרותיהם בראשיהם ונהנין כו' עטרה היא בחינת מקיף וסובב ונקרא כתר מלשון כותרת והוא בחי' ממוצע המחבר הארת המאציל א"ס ב"ה להנאצלים ולעתיד יאיר ויתגלה בעוה"ז לכל הצדיקים שיקומו בתחייה (ועמך כולם צדיקים כו'). וזה שארז"ל עתידים צדיקים שיאמרו לפניהם קדוש כי קדוש הוא בחי' מובדל שאינו בגדר השגה ודעת כי הוא למעלה מעלה מבחינת החכמה ודעת שבג"ע כי החכמה

מאין

---

[21] *See Zohar I:129b;* ibid., *135b* (Medrash Hane'elam). [22] *See Zohar III:169b;* cf. ibid., *159b* ff. [23] *See Bava Metzia 86a* [24] "*Encompassing all worlds,*" *thus the* or makif; *see* supra, *sect. III, note 12.* [25] *Berachot 17a; Maim.*, Hilchot Teshuvah *V:2.* Cf. *Tikunei Zohar 36:78a, and Zohar Chadash, Tik., 120b.* [26] *Crown; garland.* Cf. Tikunei Zohar *70:135a on the subtle distinction between* keter *and* Atarah. [27] *Capitol.—See* Etz Chayim *23:2, and* cf. *Pardess Rimonim 23:11.* s.v. כתר. Cf. infra, *sect. XXIX (note 34* a.l.*).* [28] *See* Etz Chayim *42:1;* cf. Pardess Rimonim *III:1*ff.—*See Introduction,* s.v. Keter. [29] *The* or makif *thus is related to the Sefirah* keter, trans-

(Notes cont. at end of Hebrew Text)

shall be found from *ayin*"[35]—i.e. (from) the rank of the Supreme *keter*[36] which, in the sacred *Zohar*,[37] is called *ayin*;[38] its effluence and radiation are in a state of manifestation only when [after the resurrection] the soul is vested in a pure and clear body. For "Their beginning is wedged—expressly—in their end,"[39] and "The result of the act is first in thought . . .",[40] as known. But it is impossible to reach this level until one has been first in the Garden of Eden, to apprehend the aspect of the Supreme *chochmah*[41] according to his measure, and "The dew of Torah revives him"[42]—"And when you will awaken[43] it[44] will speak for you . . ."[45] and suffice it for the initiated. ● And this is the meaning of "And *mitzvatecha* is very wide," i.e. the precept of charity, which is a vessel and a very wide area in which the radiation from the light of the blessed En Sof is invested ([46] and as it is written: His garment is *tzedakah*[47]) which in the future will radiate without limit and end, because of the gratuitous kindness in the arousal from below, called "the way of the Lord." And that is the meaning of the phraseology "very (wide)," because it is without limit and end.[48] But "To every *tichlah* I have seen an end:"[49] *tichlah* is an idiom of *kalot hanefesh*, the yearning of the soul in the Garden of Eden, for there it is in a mode of end, limit and contraction, as mentioned above. And (the reason it says) "to every *tichlah*," is because there are numerous levels and rungs of Gan Eden, one higher than the other, to the topmost of levels,[50] as mentioned in *Likutei Hashass* by R. Isaac Luria, of blessed memory, in explanation of the saying of our sages, of blessed memory: "Scholars (of Torah) have no rest . . .,"[51] because they rise constantly—from level to level—in the apprehension of the Torah, which had no end . . ., until after the resurrection, when they will have rest. . . .

●▲ XVIII. It is written: "How fair and how pleasant are you, oh love *beta'anugim*."[1]

There are two kinds of love.[2] One is *ahavah beta'anugim* (love with delights), meaning that one is in a state of wondrous delight over G-d, with a great and immense joy [the joy of the soul and its yearning as it discerns that the Lord is good[3] and delightful as wondrously sweet delights]. It is truly in the mode of the world to come where "they take delight . . ."[4] And of this it is written:[5] "Rejoice, *tzadikim*,[6] in the Lord," and not everyone merits this.[7] This is the rank the sacred *Zohar*[8] refers to as *kahana bire'uta*

---

[35] *Job 28:12.* [36] *See Zohar II:42b;* ibid., *121a;* ibid., *III:290a; and note following.* [37] *Zohar III: end of 256b;* cf. *also references cited above, note 36, and* supra, *section XI, note 11.* [38] *Naught;* cf. supra, *section XIII, note 40.* [39] Sefer Yetzirah *1:7.* [40] Liturgy, *Hymn of* Lecha Dodi. [41] *In the text appears here (in brackets):* etc. *A parenthesis suggests instead:* each one. [42] *Tikunei Zohar, Intr. 12a;* ibid., *19:38b (see Ketuvot 111b;* cf. *Shabbat 88b: Chagigah 12b;* et passim*).* [43] *At the ressurection of the dead.* [44] *The Torah, which is called* keter *(*cf. *Avot IV:13, and* infra, *sect. XXIX).* [45] *Proverbs 6:22. Enabling man to reach a level he could not attain previously; Zohar I:185a; and* Nitzutzei Orot, ad loc. *See also*

מאין תמצא כתיב הוא בחינת כתר עליון הנקרא אין בזוה"ק והשפעתו והארתו בבחינת גילוי הוא דוקא כשהנשמה תתלבש בגוף זך וצח אחר התחי' כי נעוץ תחלתן בסופן דוקא וסוף מעשה במחשבה תחלה כו' כנודע. אך א"א להגיע למדרגה זו עד שיהא בג"ע תחלה להשיג בחינת חכמה עילאה (כו') [אפשר צ"ל כל חד] כפום שיעורא דיליה וטל תורה מחייהו והקיצות היא תשיחך כו' וד"ל. וזהו רחבה מצותך מאד היא מצות הצדקה שהיא כלי ושטח רחב מאד להתלבש בה הארת אור א"ס ב"ה (וכמ"ש לבושו צדקה) אשר יאיר לעתיד בבחינת בלי גבול ותכלית בחסד חנם באתערותא דלתתא זו הנק' דרך ה' וזהו לשון מאד שהוא בלי גבול ותכלית. אבל לכל תכלה ראיתי קץ תכלה היא מלשון כלות הנפש שבג"ע שהיא בבחי' קץ ותכלית וצמצום כנ"ל ולכל תכלה הוא לפי שיש כמה וכמה מעלות ומדרגות ג"ע זה למעלה מזה עד רום המעלות כמ"ש בלקוטי הש"ס מהאריז"ל בפי' מארז"ל ת"ח אין להם מנוחה כו' שעולים תמיד ממדרגה למדרגה בהשגת התורה שאין לה סוף כו' עד אחר התחי' שיהיה להם מנוחה כו':

יח כתיב מה יפית ומה נעמת אהבה בתענוגים. הנה ב' מיני אהבות הן הא' אהבה בתענוגים דהיינו שמתענג על ה' עונג נפלא בשמחה רבה ועצומה שמחת הנפש וכלותה בטעמה כי טוב ה' ונעים נעימות עריבות עד להפליא מעין עוה"ב ממש שנהנין כו' וע"ז כתיב שמחו צדיקים בה' ולא כל אדם זוכה לזה וזו היא בחינת כהנא ברעותא דלבא

Zohar I:175b; and cf. *Avot VI:9; Sotah 21a; Tikunei Zohar 31:75b–76a.* [46] *Brackets appear in the text.* [47] Piyut אתה הוא אלקינו (Machzor, Rosh Hashanah and Yom Kippur). [48] *See Targum on Psalms 119:96; Eruvin 21a,* and *Rashi* ad loc. [49] *Beginning of the verse (Psalms 119:96).* [50] *See* Zohar Chadash *Bereishit 18a.* [51] *Berachot 64a.*

Section XVIII

[1] *Song 7:7.* [2] *Zohar I:12a. See also* supra, *sect. VI (notes 24ff.), and end of sect. XV.* [3] Par. *Psalms 34:9.* [4] *Berachot 17a; Maimonides,* Hilchot Teshuvah, *ch. 8.* [5] *Psalms 97:12.* [6] *The righteous* [*in the sense of saints (see*

(Notes cont. at end of Hebrew Text)

deliba,[9] and of which it is said:[10] "A service of gift ...[11] and the stranger that comes nigh ..."[12] For there is no way to attain it by human efforts as (there is with) the awe (of G-d), of which it is asked "Did you labour with awe?", and "Woe unto the person that did not labour with awe," as mentioned in *Reishit Chochmah*. Of awe is also written[13]—"If you will seek it as silver ..."; this shows that it requires a great and immense exertion, as when one searches for fortunes. But this great love [[14]the *ahavah beta'anugim*] comes to man by itself, from above, without him preparing and attuning himself for it; rather, only after he has exerted himself in *yirat haromemut*,[15] and has attained the maximum he is able to attain of that according to the level of his soul, then, of itself, the *ahavah beta'anugim* comes from above to dwell, and to become united with the *yirah*.[16] For "It is the way of man to go ...",[17] as explained in *Likutei Amarim*.[18]

●▲ The second (type)[19] is a love and desire that the soul desires, loves and wishes to cleave unto the Lord, "To be bound up in the bundle of life."[20] The proximity to G-d is very dear to her, and that is what she desires.[21] It is most grievous unto her to become, Heaven forfend, removed from Him, blessed be He, by having an iron partition of the *chitzonim*[22] separating, Heaven forfend. This love is latent in the heart of all Israel, even in the wicked ones, and from it derives their remorse.[23]

Though, because it is latent and concealed, in a state of exile in the body, it is possible for the *kelipah*[24] to dominate over it; and that is the "spirit of folly" which causes man to sin.[25] Therefore man's service to his Maker needs to be in strengthening himself and to prevail over the *kelipah* by all means. That is, first to expel it completely from the body—from the (faculties of) thought, speech and action that are in the brain,[26] tongue,[27] and the 248 organs.[28] After that he will also be able to "Bring out the captive from prison"[29] with a strong hand. That is, "His heart is strong and steadfast among the valiant,"[30] so that the love will become revealed in a state of great manifestation in all the powers of the parts of the soul in his body, i.e. mainly in the mind and in the (faculty of) thought of the brain, so that corresponding to its intellect and understanding the mind will constantly think and contemplate on the blessed Creator

---

[9] *(The service of) the priest is with the devotion of the heart.* [10] *Numbers 18:7.* [11] I.e. *a service* (avodah) *which comes by way of a gift. See comments of Rashi and Nachmanides,* ad loc. *See* Tanya *I, ch. 14.* [12] *Priesthood symbolises the level of special proximity to, and love of G-d (cf.* Sifre, *Numbers, sect. 119), and an elevated position of sanctity (see R. Judah Loewe,* Derech Chayim, *on Avot IV:13), thus the state of* ahavah rabba, *or* ahavah beta'anugim, which *follows as a Divine gift and reward to the* tzadikim *that are on this level.* [13] *Proverbs 2:4;* cf. Tanya *I, ch. 42.* [14] *Brackets appear in the text.* [15] *Awe and bashfulness before the Majesty of G-d (as contrasted with the lower level of the dread of the*

דלבא שבזוה"ק וע"ז נאמר עבודת מתנה וגו' והזר הקרב וגו' כי אין דרך להשיגה ע"י יגיעת בשר כמו היראה ששואלין עליה יגעת ביראה ואוי לבשר שלא נתייגע ביראה כמ"ש בר"ח וכתיב ביראה אם תבקשנה ככסף וגו' מלמד שצריכה יגיעה רבה ועצומה כמחפש אחר אוצרות. אבל אהבה רבה זו [אהבה בתענוגים] נופלת לאדם מאליה מלמעלה בלי שיכין ויכוון לה אך ורק אחר שנתייגע ביראת הרוממות והגיע לתכלית מה שיוכל להשיג ממנה לפי בחינת נשמתו אזי ממילא באה האהבה בתענוגים מלמעלה לשכון ולהתייחד עם היראה כי דרכו של איש לחזר כו' כמ"ש בלק"א. והשנית היא אהבה ותאוה שהנפש מתאוה ואוהבת וחפיצה לדבקה בה' לצרור בצרור החיים וקרבת אלהים טוב לה מאד ובו תחפוץ ורע לה מאד להתרחק ממנו ית' ח"ו להיות מחיצה של ברזל מהחיצונים מפסקת ח"ו ואהבה זו היא מוסתרת בלב כלל ישראל אפילו ברשעים וממנה באה להם החרטה אך מפני שהיא מוסתרת ונעלמה בבחינת גלות בגוף הרי הקליפה יכולה לשלוט עליה וזהו רוח שטות המחטיא לאדם וע"כ עבודת האדם לקונו היא להתחזק ולהתגבר על הקליפה בכל מכל כל דהיינו מתחלה לגרשה מהגוף לגמרי ממחשבה דו"מ שבמוח ולשון ורמ"ח אברים ואח"כ יוכל ג"כ להוציא ממסגר אסיר בחוזק יד דהיינו להיות חזק ואמיץ לבו בגבורים להיות האהבה המסותרת נגלית בגילוי רב בכל כחות חלקי הנפש שבגוף דהיינו העיקר בשכל ובמחשבה שבמוח שהשכל יחשב ויתבונן תמיד כפי שכלו והשכלתו בבורא

יתברך

---

punishment of G–d; see ref. *cited* supra, *note 2); cf. Zohar I:11b; Maim.*, Hilchot Yesodei Hatorah *II:2, and IV:12; R. Joseph Albo,* Ikkarim *III:32.* [16] *See* Chovot Halevovot, Sha'ar Ahavat Hashem, *Introd., ch. 3, and end of ch. 4.* [17] The way of a man [i.e. *love; according to Psalms 98:3:* זכר חסדו*—reading* זכר *(male) for* זכר *(remembered)*] to search for a woman [i.e. *fear, awe; according to Proverbs 31:30:* אשה יראת ה'*; cf. Zohar III:27a*).—*Kidushin 2b; see next note.—Love, thus, comes where awe is to be found already.* Cf. *Zohar III:145a–b.* [18] Tanya *I, ch. 43. See also* Likutei Torah *IV:7d;* Siddur 'im Pirush Hamilot, *p. 188a.* [19] *The inferior type:* ahavah zutta. [20] *(Notes cont. at end of Hebrew Text)*

how He is the Fountainhead of life[31] in general, and of the life of his soul in particular. Consequently, he will yearn and desire to become attached to Him, and near to Him, by an intrinsic yearning as that of a child that yearns to be constantly near his father, and as fire which by its very nature always rises upwards to its source. And the more he continues to set his mind on this yearning, this yearning becomes correspondingly stronger, and will extend even unto his mouth and all his organs—to occupy himself with Torah and the commandments in order to cleave, through these, verily unto the Lord, for "The Torah and the Holy One, blessed is He, are entirely one."[32]

Of this yearning, as it is in a state of great manifestation, it is written: "My soul thirsts . . .",[33] like a person who thirsts for water, and, as yet, has no delight whatever.[34] Also, of this yearning and of this love concealed in us we pray to G-d to aid us in bringing it out from imprisonment, and that the heart be full of it alone; and that its "rival-wife," i.e. the mundane desires, do not enter its house.[35] Rather, (this yearning and love) be the mistress of the house, to rule over her "rival-wife" and to expel her at least from one's thought, speech and action. Though one cannot expel her altogether from one's heart, she should at least be hidden, in a state of exile and servitude to the mistress of the house, her mistress to make use of her for her own essentials only, as eating and drinking, as it is written:[36] "In all your ways, know Him."[37]

●▲ XIX. "He wraps (Himself with) light as (with) a garment . . . "[1] In *Likutei Torah*, by R. Isaac Luria, of blessed memory, section *Ki Tissa* and section *Vayikra*, it is stated that the apprehension of Moses our Master, peace to him, was not in the rank of the *pnimiyut*[2] of the Supreme *chochmah*—which is called *abba*[3] *of Atzilut*, and, *à fortiori*, not in the Sefirah of *keter*, called *arich anpin*,[4] which transcends (*chochmah*). Rather, it was in the rank of the *achurayim*[5] of *chochmah*[6] which vest themselves[7] in *binah*,[8] which (in turn) vests itself in the seven lower Sefirot,[9] called *z'eyr anpin*[10]—the principium of the Torah,[11] and extends to the end of the four lowest Sefirot: *netzach*, *hod*, *yesod*, *malchut* (*nhy'm*). There the apprehension of his prophecy was in the rank of the *pnimiyut*, i.e. in the rank of the *pnimiyut* of *nhy'm*. But (on the levels) beyond *nhy'm* he had no apprehension

---

[31] Lit.: *the Life of life*—(cf. supra, *sect. XVII, note 4*). [32] *Zohar II:90b; see also* ibid., *60a, and* Kitzurim Vehe'arot, *p. 104f.* Cf. Tanya *I:23*. [33] *Psalms 42:3. See* Hilchot Talmud Torah, *IV:6.* [34] *The thirst is so overpowering that he is unable to delight in anything.* [35] *See* Likutei Torah *VI: 37d* ff. *for this homily of the "two wives" as corresponding to the divine and the natural souls.* [36] *Proverbs 3:6.* [37] *Maimonides,* Hilchot De'ot *III:2f.*: *"Whether engaged in commerce or in manual labour for profit, one's heart should not be solely set on the accumulation of wealth, but he should do these things in order to obtain therewith his bodily needs . . . So too, when he eats or drinks, his purpose should not be to secure physical*

יתברך איך שהוא חיי החיים בכלל וחיי נשמתו בפרט וע"כ יכסוף ויתאוה להיות דבוק בו וקרוב אליו כוסף טבעי כבן הכוסף להיות תמיד אצל אביו וכמו אש העולה למעלה תמיד בטבעה למקורה וכל מה שיתמיד לחשוב בשכלו כוסף זה ככה יתגבר ויתפשט כוסף זה גם בפיו ובכל אבריו לעסוק בתורה ומצות לדבקה בהם בה' ממש דאורייתא וקוב"ה כולא חד ועל כוסף זה שבגילוי רב כתיב צמאה נפשי וגו' כאדם הצמא למים ואין לו תענוג עדיין כלל וגם על כוסף זה ואהבה זו המוסתרת בנו אנו מעתירים לה' להיות בעזרנו להוציאה ממסגר ושיהיה הלב מלא ממנה לבדה ולא תכנס צרתה בביתה שהיא תאות עוה"ז רק שתהיה היא עקרת הבית למשול בצרתה ולגרשה החוצה ממחדו"מ עכ"פ הגם שלא יוכל לשלחה לגמרי מלבו עכ"פ תהיה היא מוסתרת בבחי' גלות ועבדות לעקרת הבית גברתה להשתמש בה לדברים הכרחים לה לבד כאכילה ושתיה כדכתיב בכל דרכיך דעהו:

יט עוטה אור כשלמה וגו'. הנה בלקוטי תורה של האריז"ל פ' כי תשא ופ' ויקרא כתב כי השגת מרע"ה לא היתה בבחינת פנימיות דחכמה עילאה הנקרא אבא דאצי' וכ"ש בספירת הכתר שלמעלה ממנה הנקרא א"א כ"א בבחי' אחוריים דחכמה המלובשת בבינה המתלבשת בז' ספירות תחתונות שנק' ז"א סוד התורה ומתפשטת עד סוף ד' ספירות התחתונות שהן נהי"מ ושם היתה השגת נבואתו בבחי' פנימיות דהיינו מבחי' פנימיות דנהי"מ. אבל למעלה מנהי"מ לא היתה לו שום השגה

בפנימיות

---

gratification, etc., but solely to maintain his body in health and vigour etc. Man should aim to maintain physical health and vigour in order that his soul may be upright, in a condition to know G–d, . . . by all your ways know Him."—*See also the comment, by R. Levi Gersonides, and* Tzavaat Ribash, *on this verse.*

Section XIX

[1] *Psalms 104:2.* [2] *Inwardness, the highest and most profound levels (see Introduction,* s.v. Pnimiyut*).* [3] *Father;* i.e. *the* partzuf *of* abba*; (see below, note 10).* [4] Macroprosopus *(long, or extended countenance; see below, note 10).* [5] *Hinder, or extraneous sides; the lowest and most extraneous levels (see*

(Notes cont. at end of Hebrew Text)

in the *pnimiyut*, but only in the rank of the *achurayim* of the *chochmah* which are vested[12] in *binah*, which (in turn) is vested and extends itself within the *pnimiyut* of *nhy'm*. This is the principium of "The Torah is (merely) a shade of Supernal *chochmah*[13]," [14] on the level of *z'eyr anpin*. Thus it is written:[15] "You shall see *achoray*,[16] but *panay*[17] shall not be seen;" see there, and in *Sha'ar Hanevuah*, ch. 1.[18]

Now this seems rather surprising. After all, it is said: "And there did not rise another prophet in Israel as Moses."[19] How then did R. Isaac Luria, of blessed memory, apprehend more than he, and expound many themes dealing with the *pnimiyut*, even of many Sefirot and levels that transcend *chochmah* and *keter* of Atzilut?

●▲But the matter is (as follows).

It is plain and clear to all that there is a great difference between the apprehension of the Cabbalists, as R. Shimon bar Yochai and R. Isaac Luria, of blessed memory, an apprehension by wisdom and knowledge, and the prophetic apprehension of Moses our Master, peace to him, and the other prophets, to which Scripture refers as an actual vision: "You shall see *achoray*;"[20] "And I saw the Lord;"[21] "And the Lord appeared to him."[22] Now, though this is in a metaphorical sense and does not mean actual sight by the physical eye composed of flesh, nevertheless, the subject (of a metaphor) needs to resemble the metaphor, and as the *Targum*[23] (translates) וירא אליו 'ה: "And (the Lord) became revealed unto him . . ., thus a mode of revelation, that *De-us absconditus*,[24] blessed is He, became revealed to him in a state of manifestation. It is different, though, with the apprehension of the Cabbalists.[25] To them the Lord[26] does not become revealed in the mode of manifestation; rather, they apprehend the secrets of wisdom, that which is hidden and concealed from them. They[27] therefore said:[28] "A wise man is better than a prophet;"[29] because by his wisdom he can apprehend exceedingly beyond the levels that can descend netherwards in a mode of revelation to the prophets in the vision of their prophecy.[30] For only the lowest ranks can descend and become revealed to them, namely *nhy'm*. (The ranks of *nhy'm*) are the ones that always descend and become revealed from the emanator to the recipient, as a faculty of *mochin* (brains) and life-force. Thus it is known to the savants of the esoteric science that the *nhy'm* of the higher (realm) vest themselves in the lower, in order to vivify it.[31] For they are the *kelim* of the effluence and of the descent of the vivification from the higher to the lower, with respect to all

---

[12] *Text corrected according to* L. H. [13] *Thus, deriving from, but not* chochmah *as it is itself.* [14] *Genesis Rabba 17:5 (the Midrashic equivalent of the Zoharic statement "the Torah derives from the Supreme* chochmah"; infra, *note 34*. [15] *Exodus 33:23.* [16] *My hinderside (the aspect of* achurayim*).* [17] *My face (the aspect of* pnimiyut; cf. suprà, *sect. IV, note 8).* [18] Cf. *Maimonides,* Hilchot, Yessodei Hatorah *I:10.* [19] *Deut 34:10.* [20] *Exodus 33:23.* [21] *Isaiah 6:11.* [22] *Genesis 18:1.* [23] *On Genesis 18:1.* [24] *The Lord who is hidden (inserted acc. to* H.V.*).* [25] Lit.: *the savants of the truth.* [26] *Text reads here too:* De-us absconditus, *but omitted acc. to* L.H. [27] *The sages of the* Talmud. [28] *Bava*

בפנימיות כ"א בבחי' אחוריים דחכמה המלובשת בבינה המלובשת ומתפשטת תוך פנימיות דנה"מ בסוד נובלות חכמה שלמעלה תורה שהיא בבחי' ז"א וכדכתיב וראית את אחורי ופני לא יראו ע"ש ובשער הנבואה פ"א. ולכאורה יש להפליא הרי נאמר ולא קם נביא עוד בישראל כמשה ואיך השיג האריז"ל יותר ממנו ודרש כמה דרושים בבחי' פנימיות אפילו בספירות ומדרגות רבות שלמעלה מהחכמה וכתר דאצילות. אך הענין הוא פשוט ומובן לכל שיש הפרש גדול בין השגת חכמי האמת כרשב"י והאריז"ל שהיא השגת חכמה ודעת ובין השגת מרע"ה ושאר הנביאים בנבואה המכונה בכתוב בשם ראיה ממש וראית את אחורי וארא את ה' וירא אליו ה' ואף שזהו דרך משל ואינה ראיית עין בשר גשמי ממש. מ"מ הנמשל צ"ל דומה למשל וכתרגום וירא אליו ה' ואתגליא ליה וכו' שהוא בחי' התגלות שנגלה אליו הנעלם ב"ה בבחי' התגלות משא"כ בהשגת חכמי האמת שלא נגלה אליהם הוי' הנעלם ב"ה בבחי' התגלות רק שהם משיגים תעלומות חכמה הנעלם [נ"א בנעלם] ומופלא מהם ולכן אמרו חכם עדיף מנביא שיכול להשיג בחכמתו למעלה מעלה ממדרגות שיוכלו לירד למטה בבחי' התגלות לנביאים במראה נבואתם כי לא יוכלו לירד ולהתגלות אליהם רק מדרגות התחתונות שהן נהי"מ שהן הן היורדות תמיד ומתגלות מהמשפיע להמקבל בבחי' מוחין וחיות כידוע לי"ח שהנהי"מ של העליון מתלבשים בתחתון להחיותו שהן הן כלי ההשפעה והורדת החיות מהעליון לתחתון בכל העולמות

Batra 12a. [29] *See* Likutei Hashass *of R. Isaac Luria,* a.l.; *see also* Boneh Yerushalayim, *sect.* 95, *and* 114. [30] Cf. *also* Shulchan Aruch Arizal, s.v. קריאה בחכמת הקבלה, *par.* 6. [31] *See* Etz Chayim *8:2, and* infra, *sect. XX.*

the worlds and levels. Hence they also become revealed to the prophets in a mode of an actual revelation. Within these is vested the light of *binah*, the aspect of the understanding of Divinity and[32] the light of the blessed En Sof.

And in it are vested the *achurayim* of *chochmah*, a level transcending the conception and comprehension of the blessed Divinity, as the term *chochmah* denotes the source of conception and comprehension.[33] That is why they said in the *Zohar*[34] that "The Torah derives from *chochmah*".[35] For the reasons for the commandments were not revealed and transcend conception and comprehension.[36] And even the occasional places where some apparently intelligible reason was revealed and explained, this, to our intelligible reason, is not the full and absolute reason;[37] rather, within it is vested the *pnimiyut* and principium of *chochmah*, transcending conception and comprehension. It is likewise with respect to every word that was emitted from the mouth of the Holy One, blessed is He, to the prophets, as recorded in *Tnach*,[38] whether they be words of admonishment or tales of events. In them is vested an aspect of the Divine *chochmah* transcending conception and comprehension.[39] This is empirically evident from the principle of *kri* and *ktiv*.[40] The *kri* relates to the comprehension as revealed to us. The *ktiv* transcends conception and comprehension; that is, this word in its written form has no garment subject to comprehension, but in its oral reading form it does have a garment.[41] The same applies to the large letters in the *Tnach*;[42] they are from a supremely sublime world and radiate thence openly, not with a garment like the other letters.[43]

●▲Now, the aspect of the blessed Divine *chochmah*, vested in the 613 commandments of the Torah, is referred to as the category of the *achurayim* of *chochmah*. For all the *achurayim* in the Sefirot are the external and lower levels in the gradation of that Sefirah. That is why they can descend and extend below, to become vested in the creatures in order to vivify them. The aspect of the *panim* is the Sefirah itself. It is united with its Emanator, the blessed En Sof, by an absolute union. As, for example, the Sefirah of *chochmah*: it is united with its Emanator,

---

[32] V.L.: *from (instead of* and*)*. [33] *Thus itself beyond it.* [34] *Zohar II:121a;* ibid., *85a; III:81a.* [35] *The Torah as revealed to man only originates in, but is not* chochmah *in itself.* [36] Cf. *Sanhedrin 21b, comment. by R. Menachem Meiri, and R. Samuel Edelis,* a.l. *(see also the latter's comment. on Pessachim 119);* Moreh Nevuchim *III:26.* [37] *See* ref. *cited above, note 36, and cf.: Berachot 33b and Rashi* a.l. *(*s.v. מדותיו*), and* Yerushalmi, *Berachot 5:3.* [38] Torah-Neviim-Ketuvim *(the Bible).* [39] Cf. *Zohar III:149b;* ibid., *152a;* Moreh Nevuchim *III:50.* [40] *The textual reading of Scripture (kri) sometimes differs from the textual writ* (ktiv). [41] Cf. *Pessachim 50a, and Rashi* a.l.*; Zohar III:230a.* [42]

העולמות והמדרגות ולכן ג"כ הן הן המתגלות לנביאים בבחי' התגלות ממש ובתוכן מלובש אור הבינה שהיא בחי' הבנת האלהות מאור [נ"א ואור] א"ס ב"ה ובתוכה מלובשים אחוריים דחכמה שהיא מדרגה שלמעלה מהשכל וההבנה באלהות ב"ה כי שם חכמה מורה על מקור השכל וההבנה ולכן אמרו בזהר דאורייתא מחכמה נפקת כי טעמי מצות לא נתגלו והם למעלה מהשכל וההבנה. וגם באיזהו מקומן שנתגלה ונתפרש איזה טעם המובן לנו לכאורה אין זה הטעם המובן לנו לבדו תכלית הטעם וגבולו אלא בתוכו מלובש פנימיות ותעלומות חכמה שלמעלה מהשכל וההבנה וכן בכל דיבור ודיבור שיצא מפי הקב"ה לנביאים הכתובים בתנ"ך הן דברי תוכחה והן סיפורי מעשיות מלובש בתוכם בחינת חכמת אלהות שלמעלה מהשכל וההבנה כנראה בחוש מענין הקרי והכתיב כי הקרי הוא לפי ההבנה הנגלית לנו והכתיב הוא למעלה מהשכל וההבנה שתיבה זו ככתיבתה אין לה לבוש בבחינת ההבנה ובקריאתה בפה יש לה לבוש וכן הענין באותיות גדולות שבתנ"ך שהן מעלמא עילאה ומאירות משם בגילוי בלי לבוש כשאר האותיות. והנה בחי' חכמת אלהות ב"ה המלובשת בתרי"ג מצות התורה נק' בשם בחינת אחוריי' דחכמה כי כל אחוריים שבספירות הן מדרגות החיצונות והתחתונות במעלה שבספירה זו מה שיוכלו לירד ולהתפשט למטה להתלבש בברואים להחיותם ובחי' הפנים היא הספירה עצמה המיוחדת במאצילה א"ס ב"ה בתכלית היחוד כגון ד"מ ספירת חכמה שהיא מיוחדת במאצילה

א"ס

Some letters in Scripture are written larger than others. Cf. Encyclopaedia Talmudit, *Vol. I.* s.v. אותיות, *p. 190ff.* [43] Cf. *Zohar II: 132a and III: 2a. See also Zohar I: 3b, and ref. cited in* Derech Emet a.l.

the blessed En Sof, in an absolute unity, for the Holy One, blessed is He, and His wisdom, are one[44] ([45]as explained above[46]). But that which radiates and extends from His blessed *chochmah*, below [among the limited and finite nether beings, and becomes vested in them], is called *achurayim*, and is also called the aspect of Asiyah of Atzilut.[47] Metaphorically speaking, this will be understood by the analogy with terrestrial man. There are five ranks in his soul, one lower than the other. These are the faculties of the intellect, the (emotive) attributes, thought, speech, and action.[48] Action is the lowest of them all. For the vivification that extends from the soul and is vested in the power of action, is as nothing compared to the vivification that extends from it and is vested in the power of speech. The latter (in turn) is as nothing compared to the vivification that extends from (the soul) and is vested in thought, the (emotive) attributes, and the intellect. ▲In a precisely like manner (with respect to) the category of His blessed *chochmah*, that which can become extended from it to become vested[49] in all the nether beings is[50] as nothing compared to the category of the *panim*, which is united with the blessed Emanator. For "All that are before Him are esteemed as naught."[51] But the effluence to all limited and finite nether beings is regarded, so to speak, as a descent and contraction (*tzimtzum*) with respect to the Emanator, the blessed En Sof, just as, metaphorically speaking, it would be regarded as a descent and contraction for the intellect of an intelligent person to be contracted to some purely physical and material act.

Moses our Master, peace to him, who apprehended up to the *achurayim* of *chochmah*, therefore merited that through him was given the Torah—"the outflowings of the supernal *chochma*," i.e. that which flows off from it and descends netherwards and becomes vested in our physical Torah.[52] Its principal object and purpose is the upkeep of the operative and prohibitory commandments, in true actuality and performance,[53] in accord with the saying: "To do them this day;"[54] and "Study (of Torah) is greater because it leads to performance;"[55] and "He who learns with the intent of not doing, it would have been better for him if his after-birth had been turned over, . . ."[56] And every person needs to become reincarnated until he has actually observed all the 613 commandments, as known from R. Isaac Luria, of blessed memory.[57]

* * *

[44] *Maimonides*, Hilchot Yesodei Hatorah *2:10;* Moreh Nevuchim *III:20. See* Tanya *I, ch. 2.* [45] *Brackets appear in the text.* [46] *This reference* ("above") *is not clear;* cf. H.V. a.l. [47] *The lowest realm within the world of Atzilut.—The four worlds (see Introduction* s.v.*) compound not only the order of the ten Sefirot but also the general levels denoted by the names of the worlds. Thus Atzilut is divisible into Atzilut of Atzilut, Beriah of Atzilut, etc.; the same applies to the lower three realms (Atzilut of Beriah, etc.) R. Moses Cordovero illustrates this with an analogy to a silversmith who classifies his silver into four groups according to the purity of the metal: the first type is the most pure silver, free of base metals; the second type is less pure than the first; the third*

▲*28 Ellul*

א"ס ב"ה בתכלית היחוד כי הקב"ה וחכמתו אחד (כמ"ש לעיל) ומה שמאיר ומתפשט מחכמתו ית' למטה בתחתונים שהם בעלי גבול ותכלית ומתלבש בהם נק' אחוריים ונק' ג"כ בחי' עשיה שבאצי' פי' עד"מ כמו שבאדם התחתון שיש בנשמתו ה' מדרגות זו למטה מזו שהן בחי' השכל והמדות ומחשבה ודבור ומעשה והמעשה היא התחתונה שבכולם שהחיות המתפשט מהנשמה ומלובש בכח המעשה הוא כאין לגבי החיות המתפשט ממנה ומלובש בכח הדבור שהוא כאין לגבי החיות המתפשט ממנה ומלובש במחשבה ומדות ושכל כן עד"ז ממש היא בחי' חכמתו ית' מה שיוכל להתפשט ממנה (להשפיע) [להתלבש] בתחתונים כולם הם כאין לגבי בחינת פנים המיוחד במאציל ב"ה דכולא קמיה כלא חשיב וההשפעה לכל הנבראים כולם שהם בעלי גבול ותכלית נחשבת ירידה וצמצום כביכול לגבי המאציל א"ס ב"ה עד"מ כמו שנחשבת ירידה וצמצום לשכל האדם המשכיל המצומצם באיזה עשיה גשמיות וחומרית ממש ולכן משה רבינו ע"ה שהשיג עד אחוריים דחכמה זכה שתנתן ע"י התורה שהיא נובלות חכמה שלמעלה פי' מה שנובל ממנה ויורד למטה ומתלבש בתורה גשמיות שלנו שעיקרה ותכליתה הוא קיום המצות ל"ת ועשה בפועל ומעשה ממש כמאמר היום לעשותם וגדול תלמוד שמביא לידי מעשה והלומד שלא לעשות נוח לו שנהפכה שלייתו וכו' וכל אדם מוכרח להתגלגל עד שיקיים כל התרי"ג מצות בפועל ממש כנודע מהאריז"ל:

האותיות

---

*is about half pure and half impure; and the fourth contains more base metals than silver. Now, even the first class of silver cannot be wholly and absolutely pure. There always are some drosses that cannot be removed. Thus even this first class can be subdivided into more and less "wholly pure," truly, into these four general categories. And the same applies also to the other three classes, one category differing from the other in the degree of purity. (*Pardess Rimonim *XXIV: 10).* [48] *See* Tanya *I: 3f., and II: 8.* [49] V.L.: *to emanate.* [50] *Emended according to* H.V. [51] *Zohar I: 11b. The* panim *of* chochmah *thus is completely absorbed in the Emanator.* [52] Cf. Etz Chayim, Sha'ar Hakelalim, *end of ch. 1;*

(Notes cont. at end of Hebrew Text)

●▲ [58]The letters that are revealed to us are in action, speech, and thought. Pertaining to action are the forms[59] of the letters as they are in the Assyrian script of the Torah-scroll. The letters pertaining to speech are engraved in the breath and voice which is divided into twenty-two parts. One differs from the other with respect to their form, i.e. the enunciation and utterance of the twenty-two letters in any language. For there is no difference between the sacred tongue and the other languages with respect to the nature of the letters' enunciation, only as regards their combinations. The letters pertaining to thought are [again, in any language a person may think] the words and letters of the language, which are twenty-two only. Though, in thought there are three kinds of [the aspect of] letters. When one sees in the Torah-scroll the form of the letters, they are pictured in his thought. This is referred to as the rank of "the action[60] in thought." Likewise, when one hears the letters of speech, they become inscribed in his thought and he meditates upon them. This is referred to as the rank of the "speech in thought," and as the rank of *Yetzirah*.[61] The letters of thought only, without any meditation on the letters of speech, are referred to as the "thought in thought," the rank of *Beriah*.[62]

Now, the letters of actual speech come about and receive their vivification from those very same letters that are in the thought. Though sometimes a person may speak while thinking of another matter, he can, then, speak only such words and combinations that he has already spoken (previously) and that were in his thought a great many times. Thus in those words and combinations there is left the vestige of the thought that entered into them many times. And this is the rank of the *achurayim* and externality of the *nh'y* of the *partzuf* of the higher (realm), which enters into the lower one to be unto it a faculty of *mochin* and life-force, as known.

●▲ XX. "He and His vivifications are one, He and His causations are one—in them"[1] ([2]that is, (in) the ten Sefirot of Atzilut.[3] "His vivifications"—these are the lights [*orot*],[4] and "His causations"—these are the vessels [*kelim*].[5] They are all Divinity. But this is not so in Beriah, Yetzirah, and Asiyah; etc.) Now, it needs to be understood well how the En Sof is One with His causations, i.e.

---

[58] *This part, to the end, does not seem to be part of the preceding, though the content is somewhat related.* [59] *Emended according to* H.V. [60] *Or: making (*Asiyah*).* [61] *Formation.* [62] *Creation.*

Section XX

[1] *Tikunei Zohar, Intro.: 3b (Cf. n. 3 for full quotation).* [2] *Brackets appear in the text.* [3] "*. . . for in the ten Sefirot of Atzilut (is vested) the King (the light of the En Sof). He (*i.e. *His essence) and His causations are one in them (*i.e. *in the ten Sefirot of Atzilut); He and His vivifications are one in them. This is not so in the ten Sefirot of Beriah. There they are not one with their vivification, nor are they one with their causations. But the Cause of all radiates in the ten Sefirot of Atzilut,*

האותיות הנגלות לנו הן במעשה דבור ומחשבה. דמעשה הן תמונת האותיות שבכתב אשורי שבס"ת. ואותיות הדבור נחקקות בהבל וקול המתחלק לכ"ב חלקים שונים זה מזה בצורתן. שהיא הברת ומבטא הכ"ב אותיות בכל לשון. כי אין הפרש בין להה"ק ובין שאר לשונות במהות הברת האותיות כ"א בצירופן. ואותיות המחשבה הן ג"כ בכל לשון שאדם מחשב תיבות ואותיות הלשון שהן כ"ב לבד. רק שבמחשבה יש בה ג' מיני בחי' אותיות. שהרי כשרואה בס"ת תמונת האותיות הן מצטיירות במחשבתו וזה נקרא בחינת עשי' שבמחשבה. וכן כאשר שומע אותיות הדבור הן נרשמות במחשבתו ומהרהר בהן וזה נקרא בחינת דבור שבמח' ובחי' יצירה. ואותיות המחשבה לבדה בלי הרהור אותיות הדבור נק' מח' שבמחשבה. בחי' בריאה. והנה אותיות הדבור ממש הן מתהוות ומקבלות חיותן מאותיות אלו עצמן שבמח'. ואף שלפעמים מדבר אדם ומהרהר בדבר אחר. הרי אינו יכול לדבר כ"א אותן דבורים וצירופים שכבר דברם והיו במחשבתו פעמים רבות מאד ונשאר בדיבורים וצירופים אלו הרשימו מהמחשבה שנכנסה בהם פעמים רבות. וזהו בחי' אחוריים וחיצוניות נה"י מפרצוף העליון שנכנס בתחתון להיות לו בחי' מוחין וחיות כנודע:

כ איהו וחיוהי חד איהו וגרמוהי חד בהון. (פי' ע"ס דאצילות חיוהי הן האורות וגרמוהי הן הכלים שכולן אלקות משא"כ בבי"ע כו'). וצריך להבין היטב איך הא"ס חד עם גרמוהי הן הכלים

---

*and in the ten Sefirot of Beriah; and He radiates among the ten classes of angels (*i.e. *the world of Yetzirah) and the ten heavenly constellations (*i.e. *the world of Asiyah), and does not become changed anywhere." (Tikunei Zohar,* ad loc. cit.*)* [4] I.e., *the infinite Divine effusions and emanations.* [5] *The qualitatively (but not quantitatively) finite vessels that "contain" the* orot. *See* supra, *section XV, note 13.—Elsewhere it is said that* חיוהי *(His vivifications) refers to the first three Sefirot* (chabad) *in their totality* (i.e. orot *and* kelim), *while* גרמוהי *(His causations) refers to the seven lower Sefirot in totality; see* Kitzurim Vehe'arot, *p. 105, and ref. cited there, and cf.* Likutei Torah—Torat Shmuel, *vol. III: ch. 32 and 151.*

the *kelim*. For, the *kelim* are in a mode of limitation and finitude, as mentioned in *Etz Chayim*.[6] However, the intention is to say that they are Divinity with respect to creating something out of nothing (*yesh meayin*), just like the En Sof, and not merely by way of an evolution from cause to effect.[7] As for the statement of R. Moses Cordovero[8] that the (creative) development is by way of cause and effect [and it is so stated in the sacred *Zohar*, section *Bereishit*[9]], this refers to the evolution of the Sefirot within the Sefirot themselves[10] ([11]with respect to the *kelim*). [Thus in *Sefer Yetzirah*[12] (the Sefirot) are called '*beli-mah*' (without anything), because they are not in the category of a substance and apprehensible nature,[13] just like the En Sof "Whom thought cannot grasp at all,"[14] and as it is written: "And My Face shall not be seen."[15] As for the prophecy and apprehension of Moses our Master, peace to him, it was of the upper rank of *netzach* of *z'eyr anpin*.[16]] And in the evolution the effect is encompassed by the cause, in relation to which it is essentially non-existent, just as a ray of the sun is (absorbed) in the sun, as stated in *Pardess* by R. Moses Cordovero.[17] Thus even numerous contractions will not avail to there being matter as dense as earth, by way of an evolution from the spirituality of the separate intelligences,[18] (not) even (that) of the angels,[19] except to there being the spirit of animal from the "Face of the Ox,"[20] as explained elsewhere, see •there.[21] The coming about of substantiality *ex nihilo* (*yesh meayin*), is in ▲Hebrew[22] called בריאה (creation).[23] (Such) created substance, in fact, is also esteemed as naught before Him;[24] that is, it is essentially non-existent in relation to the force and light that effulges in it from the *kelim* of the ten Sefirot of Atzilut, Beriah, Yetzirah, and Asiyah [in which the gleam (*kav*) of the light of the blessed En Sof[25] radiates], and just as the ray of the sun in the sun, as explained in *Likutei Amarim*, part II.[26] However, this is so only "before Him," relating to His blessed knowledge, from above netherwards. But in relation to the knowledge from below upwards, created substance is [in such knowledge and apprehension from below] an altogether separate thing. For the force that effuses in it is not apprehended at all. Also, there is no approximation whatever from the one to the other, neither to the whole nor to part of the relation between the effect and cause. For the effect knows and has some apprehension of its cause and becomes nullified in relation to it through this knowledge and apprehension. Even with respect to their nature and essence there is not such a great distinction (between cause and effect)

---

[6] Cf. Etz Chayim *II: 3*, et passim. [7] I.e., *they are not simply some cause from which beings evolve of themselves (in a causal process). The* kelim *of Atzilut, though qualitatively finite, are a rank in Divinity which can be described as creative Divinity in the literal sense of the term.* [8] Pardess Rimonim, *6, esp. ch. 6f.* Cf. Boneh Yerushalayim, *sect. 75.* [9] *Zohar I: 19b–20a.* [10] I.e., *each Sefirah is comprised of the grades of all the Sefirot (*chochmah of chochmah; binah of chochmah; *etc.).* Cf. supra, *sect. XIII, note 22.* [11] *Brackets appear in the text.* [12] Sefer Yetzirah *I: 2–9, 14.* [13] *See* Pardess Rimonim *I: 1*; Shomer Emunim *I: 61.* [14] *Tikunei Zohar, Intr.: 17a.* [15] *Exodus 33: 23.* [16] *See* supra, *section XIX.* [17]

הכלים הרי הכלים הן בבחי' גבול ותכלית כמ"ש בע"ח. אמנם הכוונה היא לומר שהן אלקות לברוא יש מאין כמו הא"ס ולא בבחי' השתלשלות עילה ועלול לבד ומ"ש הרמ"ק ענין השתלשלות עילה ועלול וכ"ה בזוה"ק פ' בראשית היינו בהשתלשלות הספירות בספירות עצמן (בבחי' הכלים) שנקראות בלי מה בס"י שאינן בבחי' יש ומהות מושג וכמו הא"ס דלית מחשבה תפיסא ביה כלל וכמ"ש ופני לא יראו ונבואת משה רבינו ע"ה והשגתו היתה מפרק עליון דנצח דז"א ובהשתלשלות העלול הוא מוקף מהעילה ובטל במציאות אצלו כזיו השמש בשמש כמ"ש בפרדס מהרמ"ק ואף גם צמצומים רבים מאד לא יועילו להיות גשם עב כעפר מהשתלשלות הרוחניות משכלים נבדלים אפילו של המלאכים אלא להיות רוח הבהמה מפני שור כמ"ש במ"א וע"ש ויש מאין נקרא בריאה בלה"ק והגם שהיש הנברא הוא ג"כ כלא חשיב קמיה דהיינו שבטל במציאות לגבי הכח והאור השופע בו מהכלים די"ם דאבי"ע שהקו אור א"ס ב"ה מאיר בהם וכזיו השמש בשמש כמ"ש בלק"א ח"ב. היינו קמיה דוקא שהיא ידיעתו ית' מלמעלה למטה. אבל בידיעה שממטה למעלה היש הנברא הוא דבר נפרד לגמרי בידיעה והשגה זו שממטה כי הכח השופע בו אינו מושג כלל וכלל וגם אין ערוך זה לזה כלל וכלל לא מיניה ולא מקצתיה מהערך שמהעלול אל העילה שהעלול יודע ומשיג איזה השגה בעילתו ובטל אצלו ע"י ידיעה והשגה זו וגם במהותם ועצמותם אין הפרש גדול כ"כ

רק

Pardess Rimonim, 6: end of ch. 6; see also ibid., *beg. of ch. 3.* [18] *Or:* abstract intelligences. *This is a common term in philosophical works referring to the supernal creatures or creations, devoid of any material content. They are pure spirit and, therefore, distinguishable (or separated) from one another only by their differing degrees of intellectual apprehension. (Cf. Moreh Nevuchim I: 49;* Ikkarim *II: 12).*—Cf. infra, *notes 19 and 33.* [19] I.e., *not even the most subtle and formal matter composing the bodies of the angels, could have evolved from the spirit of the abstract intelligences. According to R. Shneur Zalman, and the Cabbalists in general, the angels, too, are composed of body and soul, matter and form; see below,* *(Notes cont. at end of Hebrew Text)*

except that one is a cause and the other is an effect; but nothing whatever of the distinction there is between the nature of a created substance and the nature of the force and light that effuses in it to make it *ex nihilo* into substantiality. That is why (creation) is called precisely *yesh meayin*.[27]
● Now, the *kelim* of the ten Sefirot of Beriah, Yetzirah and Asiyah, and also the *orot* [*nefesh, ruach*[28]] are the first stage and the beginning of created substantiality (*yesh*). They are created from the category of the *neshamah* of the ten Sefirot of Beriah, Yetzirah and Asiyah, which is Divinity.[29] And these are the thirty *kelim* of *malchut of Atzilut*.[30] It is likewise in Atzilut. From the *chitzoniyut* of the *kelim* of the ten Sefirot of Atzilut [which are Divinity] were created the *hechalot*[31] of Atzilut in which the category of the *iggulim*[32] of the ten Sefirot vests itself, and also the bodies of the angels of Atzilut[33]—which are a form of substantiality (*yesh*) [as it is written:[34] "And His angels He charges with deficiency"[35]—because they are not wholly in a state of nullification as the effect
●▲ is in relation to its cause]. But the souls of the angels that emerged by the *zivvug neshikin*,[36] and also the souls[37] of man that emerged by the *zivvug zu'n* of Atzilut,[38] they, prior to their descending to Beriah, Yetzirah and Asiyah, are not a level of substantiality (*yesh*) and a distinct entity on its own. On the contrary, they are of the category of Divinity in immense contraction. They are like the *kelim* of the ten Sefirot of Atzilut which are in a category of limitation on account of the contraction of the light of the En Sof, i.e. the *kav* is vested in their *nefesh-ruach-neshamah*, and just like the original *tzimtzum* to bring about a void etc.

([39]And even after the *nefesh-ruach-neshamah* of Atzilut descended to this world to the erstwhile *tzadikim*, their essence possibly did not change to become an entity distinct from Divinity. That is why they withdrew when they wanted to sin, before they sinned.[40] It is feasible to assume that also the thousands and myriads of worlds that are in the *gulgalta* [skull] of *arich anpin* and *z'eyr anpin*,[41] are not really worlds, like the *hechalot* of Atzilut, and a category of substantiality, but are like the souls of the angels that emerged from the *zivvug neshikin*, and are called worlds in relation to the rank of the "skull" and the "beard".[42])

They are not, however, truly Divinity—able to create something *ex nihilo*, because they already emerged and became separated from the *kelim* of the ten Sefirot wherein the *kav* of the light of the En Sof is vested.

For the light is like its source,[43] i.e. the nature and essence

---

[27] *Substantiality out of nothingness. From the viewpoint of creation these are two absolutely distinct and non-related categories.* [28] Nefesh-ruach-neshamah *are the three general categories of the soul, the animating life-force of man, and the worlds as a whole (*cf. supra, *section V, note 53). Thus they are called* orot. [29] *The five soul-categories (see* supra, *section V, note 52), correspond to the five worlds (see Introduction,* s.v. Worlds*): Adam Kadmon contains all five categories, and the highest,* yechidah, *is manifest and determinative here. In Atzilut* yechidah *is submerged and concealed in the lower four ranks. Thus only the four lower categories are manifest there, with the highest among these,* chayah, *determinative. (At the same time, Atzilut,*

רק שזה עילה וזה עלול ולא מיניה ולא מקצתיה מההפרש שבין מהות היש הנברא למהות הכח והאור השופע בו להוותו מאין ליש ולכן נקרא יש מאין דוקא והנה ראשית היש הנברא ותחילתו הן הכלים די"ם דבי"ע וגם האורות נפש רוח ונבראו מבחי' הנשמה די"ם דבי"ע שהוא אלקות והן הלמ"ד כלים דמל' דאצילות וכן באצילות מחיצוניות הכלים די"ם דאצי' שהן אלקות נבראו ההיכלות דאצילות שמתלבש בהן בחי' העיגולים די"ם וגם גופות המלאכים דאצי' שהן בחי' יש וכמ"ש ובמלאכיו ישים תהלה. שאינן בבחי' ביטול לגמרי כעלול לגבי עילתו אך נשמות המלאכים שיצאו מזיווג הנשיקין וכן נשמת האדם שיצאו מזיווג דזו"נ דאצי' קודם שירדו לבי"ע אינן בכלל יש ודבר נפרד בפ"ע אלא הן מעין בחי' אלקות בצמצום עצום וכעין הכלים די"ם דאצי' שהן בבחי' גבול ע"י צמצום אור הא"ס הוא הקו המלובש בנר"נ שלהם וכמו צמצום הראשון להיות חלל וכו' (ואף גם לאחר שירדו הנר"נ דאצי' לעולם הזה לצדיקים הראשונים אפשר שלא נשתנה מהותן להיות דבר נפרד מאלקות ולכן היו מסתלקות כשרצו לחטוא בטרם יחטאו וקרוב לומר שגם האלפים ורבבות עלמין דיתבא בגולגלתא דא"א וז"א אינן עלמין ממש כעין ההיכלות דאצי' ובחינת יש אלא כעין נשמות המלאכים שיצאו מזיווג הנשיקין ונקראו עלמין לגבי בחי' הגולגלתא ודיקנא) אך אינן אלקות ממש לברוא יש מאין מאחר שכבר יצאו ונפרדו מהכלים די"ם שבהן מלובש הקו מאור א"ס שהאור הוא כעין המאור הוא מהותו ועצמותו

של

like all the worlds, is again divisible into these five *soul-categories; cf.* supra, *sect. XIX note 47). In Beriah only the three lower categories are manifest, with* neshamah *determinative; and so forth. While in Atzilut the* orot *and* kelim *are still non-corporeal and, indeed, Divine, from Beriah downwards, the* kelim *take on corporeality, but, of course, not the* orot *(the Divine effusions of a life-force). As one world serves as the conduit for the* orot *to the lower world(s), so the* nefesh-ruach *(of Yetzirah and Asiyah, respectively), emanate from the* neshamah *(of Beriah). But below* neshamah *(of Beriah), the light of the blessed En Sof is no longer manifest, but concealed. (See* Mevoh She'arim *VI:* 2, drush

(Notes cont. at end of Hebrew Text)

of the blessed Emanator, whose Being is of His essence, and He is not, Heaven forfend, caused by some other cause preceding Himself. He alone, therefore, has it in His power and ability to create something out of an absolute naught and nothingness, without this "something" having any other cause preceding it.

In order that this *yesh*, created by the power of the En Sof, should have a limit and measure, the light of the En Sof was vested in the *kelim* of the ten Sefirot of Atzilut, and becomes united in them in so absolute a unity that "He and His causations are one" to create with and through them [especially through their investment in Beriah, Yetzirah and Asiyah] creatures ●▲ that have limitation and finitude. However, it is known that the principal coming to be of the *yesh* and the totally distinct entity, is through *malchut* of Atzilut,[44] which becomes the *atik*[45] of Beriah,[46] for "There is no king without a people . . ."[47] The multitude of creatures, and their division, that were created by the force of the One and absolutely Unique[48] En Sof, it, too, is from the multitude of letters that issue from *malchut*—"The mouth of the Lord" and "All their hosts by the breath of His mouth."[49] The five organs of speech[50] are of the five *gevurot*[51] of *nukva*.[52] Thus (*malchut*) is called *alma deitgalya* (the manifest world), because through it is manifested the power of the light of the En Sof to create something out of nothing—without recourse to cause and effect.[53] The first nine Sefirot, however, emanated by a causal evolution, while the light of the En Sof is vested in *chochmah* only. And that is the meaning of "Their beginning[54] is wedged in their end."[55] For *keter* is the mediator between the Emanator and the emanated,[56] and the lowest level of the En Sof is contained in it. That is why (*keter*) is called *keter malchut* (crown of sovereignty);[57] for a crown is but for a king, and, also, the lowest level of the En Sof is the *malchut* of En Sof.[58] Consequently, from below upwards,[59] *malchut* of Atzilut, too, is called *keter*,[60] and especially since through it is the creation of the souls which are *yesh*, separate entities [in the world of Beriah]. This[61] is referred to as *lidah*,[62] just as the splitting of the Red Sea—which "depended on *atika*;"[63] also, the whole growth of the souls, throughout the seven months from the *conjunctio* of *Shmini Atzeret* to the Seventh Day of Passover, is like unto the growth of *zu'n*[64]

---

[44] *See* supra, *section VIII, note 43.* [45] *The highest level, also referred to as* keter. [46] *The lowest level of the higher realm comprises the highest level of the succeeding, lower realm; see* Etz Chayim *III:1*, et passim; *(cf. Tikunei Zohar, Intr.: 11b)*. Cf. supra, *sect. XVII, note 28, and* infra. [47] Zohar *III: 271b; see Pirke de R. Eliezer, ch. 3; and* cf. Tosafot, *Berachot 40b*, s.v. אמר אביי.—*Only where the king has subjects can one speak of kinghood in any real and meaningful way. Thus by the causations of* malchut, *the attribute of* malchut *realises itself and comes in its own right;* cf. *Introduction.* [48] Lit.: absolutely unified *(as opposed to composite)*. [49] *Psalms 33:6—The "Mouth of the Lord," the "Breath of His Mouth" etc.,*

● 8 Tishri ▲ *4 Tishri*

של המאציל ב"ה שמציאותו הוא מעצמותו ואינו עלול מאיזה עילה שקדמה לו ח"ו ולכן הוא לבדו בכחו ויכלתו לברוא יש מאין ואפס המוחלט ממש בלי שום עילה וסיבה אחרת קודמת ליש הזה וכדי שיהיה היש הזה הנברא בכח הא"ס בעל גבול ומדה נתלבש אור א"ס בכלים די"ם דאצילות ומתייחד בתוכן בתכלית היחוד עד דאיהו וגרמוהי חד לברוא בהן ועל ידן ברואים בעלי גבול ותכלית ובפרט ע"י התלבשותן בבי"ע. אמנם מודעת זאת שעיקר התהוות היש ודבר נפרד לגמרי הוא ממל' דאצילות שנעשה עתיק דבריאה כי אין מלך בלא עם וכו' וגם ריבוי הנבראים והתחלקותן שנבראו בכח הא"ס יחיד ומיוחד בתכלית הוא ע"י ריבוי האותיות היוצאין ממל' פי ה' וברוח פיו כל צבאם וה' מוצאות הפה הן מה"ג דנוק' ולזאת נקראת עלמא דאתגליא כי בה נגלה כח אור אין סוף לברוא יש מאין שלא ע"י עילה ועלול אבל ט' ספירות הראשונות נאצלו בהשתלשלות עילה ועלול ואור הא"ס הוא מלובש בחכמה לבדה. וז"ש נעוץ תחלתן בסופן כי כתר הוא ממוצע בין המאציל לנאצלים ויש בו בחי' האחרונה של הא"ס ולכן נקרא כתר מלכות כי אין כתר אלא למלך וגם כי בחי' אחרונה דא"ס היא מל' דאין סוף ולכן גם המל' דאצי' נקרא כתר ממטה למעלה ומה גם כי בריאת הנשמות ממנה להיות יש ודבר נפרד בפ"ע בעולם הבריאה ונקרא בשם לידה בקריעת י"ס דבעתיקא תליא וגם כל גידול הנשמות כל ז' חדשים מזיווג של שמיני עצרת עד שביעי של פסח הוא כמו גידול זו"נ בבטן

---

through which the universe came into being, all signify malchut—*"the architect of creation." The issues from the mouth or the breath, i.e., the multitude of articulated letters, thus correspond to the emanations that issue into manifest being through* malchut. *(*Cf. *Introduction; and* supra, *sect. V, note 22.)* [50] *See* supra, *section V, note 23.* [51] *The five* gevurah-*aspects limit, withhold, and differentiate the effusive outflowings. The organs of articulation, too, limit and make distinctions in the pristine breath of speech. This allows meaningful speech rather than the non-intelligible outflow of letters of speech as they are in their totality in the basic "matter" or breath of speech.*—Cf. Tanya, *II: 3;* supra, *sect. V, note 113.* [52] *The*

(Notes cont. at end of Hebrew Text)

in the womb of *imma ilaah*[65]—by means of the Supernal *orot* of the *imma ilaah*, and of yet higher, to the En Sof which vests itself in (*imma ilaah*) throughout the nine or seven months of pregnancy.[66] Thus it is with the creation of the souls and angels in the world of Beriah. Also, the very essence and root of the "(seminal) drop" which she[67] receives and (through which) she is impregnated by the *z'eyr anpin*, is of the *mochin* of *abba* and *imma*,[68] and issues forth to *abba* and *imma* with every *conjunctio*, from *arich anpin* and *atik yomin*,[69] and still higher—up to the En Sof. Everything is concealed, though, in the *mochin*, until the *nukva* gives birth to the souls, and the angels and the *hechalot* for the world of Beriah. Thus it follows that by means of the *ibbur* and *lidah*,[70] there is truly a manifestation of the light of the En Sof.[71]

●▲ Now it will be clear why the *Mitzvot* (commandments) are in *malchut*, the *hai* of the Tetragrammaton,[72] while the Torah is in *z'eyr anpin*, the *vav* of the Tetragrammaton.[73] Above, in *arich anpin*, the *Mitzvot* are in the "Whiteness of the *gulgalta*, i.e. the path (formed) by the parting of the hairs which divide into the 613 paths of the Torah as it is in *z'eyr anpin*."[74] The root of the Torah [which derives from the Supreme *chochmah*[75]] is in the concealed *mochin*[76] of *arich anpin*, which is the wisdom behind the reasons for the commandments.[77] However, it is like a seal in reverse.[78]

Thus "Their beginning is wedged in their end,"[79] i.e. the power of the blessed En Sof,[80] in order to create substantiality *ex nihilo*. (Creation) is not by way of a causal development[81] in which the effect would be encompassed by its cause, and essentially non-subsistent, but (in such a way) that the *yesh* is an entity distinct from Divinity so that the blessed Emanator can be a King over all separate entities by their fulfilling the commandments which He enjoins upon them, and "The end-result of the act is first in intent."[82] That is why they said in *Yerushalmi*:[83] "Is then R. Shimon not of the opinion that one interrupts[84] for *Lulav*, . . ."[85]; and "If one learns with the intention not to practise, it were better for him had his after-birth been turned over his face . . .,"[86] for the after-birth was formed first, by the (seminal) drop, and until the fortieth day, when the embryo begins to take on form, it alone was the essential substance of the embryo. In like manner, the commandments are the essence and root of the Torah, even though a commandment is corporeal[87] and the Torah is wisdom.[88] Only one is in the *chitzoniyut*,[89] and the other is in the *pnimiyut*,[90] and as (will be explained) further on.[91]

●▲ Now, in like manner,

---

[65] *The Supernal mother*, binah. [66] Lit.: *months of the* lidah. [67] *The nether mother*, malchut. [68] *Of the brains (the highest levels) of the configurations of* abba *and* imma; *thus analogous to the physical seminal drop which derives from the parental brain (cf.* supra, *section XV).* [69] *The* partzuf *corresponding to the sphere of the Supreme* keter. [70] *Pregnancy and birth.* [71] *On this profoundly mystical section see* Likutei *Torah, II: 16b* ff., *and the discourses dealing with* Shmini Atzeret. *See also the Zoharic and Lurianic interpretations of Numbers 29:35.* [72] *See* supra, *section V note 16.* [73] Ibid.; *see also*, supra, *section XIX.—The* Mitzvot, *thus, appear inferior to the Torah itself, just as* malchut *is inferior to* z'eyr anpin. [74] *Zohar*

בבטן אימא עילאה שהוא ע״י אורות עליונים מאימא עילאה ולמעלה למעלה עד אין סוף המתלבש בה כל ט׳ או ז׳ ירחי לידה. וככה הוא בבריאת נשמות ומלאכים לעולם הבריאה וגם כל עיקר ושרש הטיפה שמקבלת ומתעברת מז״א הוא ממוחין דאו״א ובכל זיווג נמשכת לאו״א מא״א וע״י ולמלמעלה למעלה עד אין סוף רק שהכל בהעלם במוחין עד לידת הנוק׳ הנשמות והמלאכים וההיכלות לעולם הבריאה. נמצא שזהו גילוי אור א״ס ממש ע״י העיבור והלידה. ובזה יובן היות המצות במל׳ ה׳ של שם הוי׳ והתורה בז״א וא״ו של שם הוי׳. הגם שלמעלה בא״א המצות הן בגולגלתא בלבנונית היא האורחא דבפלגותא דשערי דמתפלגא לתרי״ג אורחין דאורייתא שבז״א ושרש התורה דנפקא מח״ע הוא במו״ס דא״א והיינו החכמה דטעמי המצות אלא שהוא כחותם המתהפך ונעוץ תחלתן בסופן הוא כח הא״ס ב״ה לברוא יש מאין ולא ע״י עילה ועלול שיהיה העלול מוקף מעילתו ובטל במציאות רק יהיה היש דבר נפרד מאלקות בכדי שיהיה המאציל ב״ה מלך על כל הנפרדים ע״י שיקיימו מצותיו שיצוה עליהם וסוף מעשה במחשבה תחלה ולכן אמרו בירושלמי ולית ליה לר״ש שמפסיק ללולב וכו׳ וכל הלומר שלא לעשות נוח לו שנתהפכה שלייתו ע״פ וכו׳ כי השליא נוצרה תחלה מהטיפה והיא לבדה היתה עיקר הולד עד מ׳ יום שהתחילה צורת הולד. וככה המצות הן עיקר התורה ושרשה הגם שהמצוה היא גופנית והתורה היא חכמה רק שזה בחיצוניות וזה בפנימיות וכדלקמן. והנה כמ״ש מזיווג

III: 129a; ibid., *136a; (see* Tanya *I, ch. 41, author's glossary note). The "hairs of the head" refer to concealed worlds or levels which serve as conduits for the supreme emanations. Cf.* Zohar Chadash, *34a* f.*;* Derech Emet *on Zohar II: 122b;* infra, *beg. of sect. XXIX.* [75] *See* supra, *section XIX, note 34.* [76] *The brain-faculties (*chochmah, binah*) contained within the skull, thus lower in rank than the skull* (keter) *itself.* Cf. Etz Chayim. *25:5.* [77] *The* Mitzvot *are, in fact, superior to the Torah.* [78] *The stamp of an engraved seal leaves an impression which is just the opposite of the way the seal is made. What is engraved in the seal (high in the seal) appears protruding (more tangible and ma-*

(Notes cont. at end of Hebrew Text)

by the *zivvug zu'n* of Beriah, Yetzirah, and Asiyah, are created, *ex nihilo* into substantiality, all that were created, formed and made by the light of the *neshamah* within them. For (the *neshamah*) is Divinity, of the *kelim* of the ten Sefirot of *malchut* of Atzilut. In it is also contained the radiation of the *kav* from the light of the En Sof that is vested in Atzilut as far as the *prassa* (curtain)[92] This radiation of the *kav*, that radiated in the *kelim* of the ten Sefirot of *malchut*, pierced the *prassa* along with them,[93] and radiates in them in Beriah, Yetzirah and Asiyah, just as in Atzilut itself. The same is also with the very *kav* that is vested in the culmination and end of the *nh'y* of Adam Kadmon,[94] i.e. the end of the "feet" of its *yosher*[95] which culminate in the *malchut* of Asiyah: a radiation from the *kav* radiates from there and vests itself in the light of the *neshamah* of the ten Sefirot of Beriah, Yetzirah and Assiyah, which is Divinity. A radiation from (this) radiation vests itself in the *nefesh-ruach* of the ten Sefirot of Beriah, Yetzirah and Asiyah, and also in all their *kelim*, while a radiation of (that) radiation of the (original) radiation is (immanent) in all that were created, formed and made, as it is written: "The seas, and all there is in them, and You animate them all."[96]

Now, all this is by way of an extension of the vital force to animate them.▲ However, the essence and nature of the light of the En Sof is in no way subject to space and encompasses all worlds equally: "And I fill the heavens and the earth"[97] in one equal fashion, and "There is no place void of Him"[98] even in this physical world.[99] However, this is by way of "encompassing" and "encircling,"[100] and as the meaning of this was explained in *Likutei Amarim*.[101] It is not in a mode of extension and investment of the vital force to vivify them and make them come into being, *ex nihilo* into substantiality. (This is) only by a radiation from a radiation of the radiation etc. from the *kav*, as mentioned above. Also, the radiation from the light of the En Sof which encircles and encompasses the four worlds Atzilut, Beriah, Yetzirah and Asiyah in equal fashion, to the inner gleam (*kav*), is by way of the *kelim* of the ten Sefirot of Beriah, Yetzirah and Asiyah. By its radiation within the *kelim* it confers unto them the power and force to create substantiality *ex nihilo* (*yesh meayin*). Now, because the creation is by means of the *kelim*, the creatures are in a category of multifariousness and division, limitation and finitude, and especially so by means of the letters,[102] as mentioned above. Further- ●▲ more, [in addition to all that was mentioned above,] the radiation of the radiation [and all

[92] *Between Atzilut and Beriah (and likewise between the other worlds) there is a* prassa *(curtailing the higher world) which needs to be pierced in order for the light and vivification of the higher to penetrate and descend to the lower. See* Etz Chayim, *42:4 (*ibid., *ch. 13 f. of* Klalut ABYA—*I)*; ibid., *44:1*. [93] *With the* kelim. [94] *The lower three Sefirot (*netzach, hod, yesod*) of Adam Kadmon.* [95] I.e., *the end of the scheme of* yosher, *which culminates in the centre of the primordial space, the point corresponding to* malchut *of* Asiyah. *See above note 32.* [96] *Nehemiah 9:6.* [97] *Jeremiah 23:24.* [98] *Tikunei Zohar 57:91b;* ibid., *70:122b.* [99] Cf. *Exodus Rabba II:9.*

מזיווג זו"ן דבי"ע נבראו מאין ליש כל הנבראים והנוצרים והנעשים ע"י אור הנשמה שבתוכן שהיא אלקות מהכלים דו"ס דמל' דאצי' וגם בתוכה הארת הקו דאור א"ס המלובש באצי' עד הפרסא והארת הקו שהיה מאיר בכלים דו"ס דמל' בקע הפרסא עמהם ומאיר בהם בבי"ע כמו באצילות ממש וכן גם הקו בעצמו המלובש בסיום וסוף נה"י דא"ק שהוא סוף רגלי היושר שלו המסתיימים במל' דעשיה הנה הארת הקו מאירה משם ומתלבשת באור הנשמה דו"ס דבי"ע שהוא אלקות והארה דהארה מתלבשת בנפש רוח דו"ס דבי"ע ואף גם בכל הכלים שלהם והארה דהארה הוא בכל הנבראים ונוצרים ונעשים כמ"ש הימים וכל אשר בהם ואתה מחיה את כולם וכל זאת בבחינת התפשטות החיות להחיותם אמנם מציאותו ומהותו של אור הא"ס אינו בגדר מקום כלל וסובב כל עלמין בשוה ואת השמים ואת הארץ אני מלא בהשוואה אחת ולית אתר פנוי מיניה אף בארץ הלזו הגשמית רק שהוא בבחי' מקיף וסובב וכמ"ש הפי' בלק"א ולא התפשטות והתלבשות החיות להחיותם ולהוותם מאין ליש כ"א ע"י הארה דהארה דהארה וכו' מהקו כנ"ל וגם מאור א"ס הסובב ומקיף לארבע עולמות אבי"ע בשוה מאיר אל הקו הפנימי דרך הכלים דו"ס דבי"ע ובהארתו תוך הכלים נותן בהם כח ועוז לברוא יש מאין ומאחר שהבריאה היא ע"י הכלים לזאת הם הנבראים בבחינת ריבוי והתחלקות וגבול ותכלית ובפרט ע"י האותיות כנ"ל. ועוד זאת יתר על כן על כל הנ"ל הארה דהארה וכל הנ"ל

---

[100] *See Zohar III: 225a.* [101] Tanya *I: 48; see* supra, *section I, note 13.* [102] *The letters of speech.*

that was said above] manifests its power and ability in the element of the physical earth in an immense manifestation, surpassing the elements transcending it, and even the hosts of heaven. For they do not have it in their power and ability constantly to bring forth something out of nothing (*yesh meayin*), like the element of earth. (The latter) constantly makes sprout something out of nothing (*yesh meayin*), namely the herbs and trees—from the vegetative property it possesses, which is nonsubstantial (*ayin*) and spiritual, while (the growths) are physical. ([103]As for the *mazal*[104] that strikes (the herb) and says "grow,"[105]—this takes place after the herb has already sprouted. He does not tell it to sprout *ex nihilo* into substantiality, but only from small to big, and which kind of fruit, to bear, in all its details. For[106] prior to its sprouting, to whom would every herb's *mazal* ordain all the details?) Now all this is so only because the "feet" of Adam Kadmon culminate at the bottom of Asiyah,[107] and "below His feet"[108] radiates the light of the blessed En Sof which encircles all worlds without any great interruption between them, except for the *iggulim* of Adam Kadmon only.[109] Also, the *kav* of the light of the En Sof, culminating at the ending of the "feet" of Adam Kadmon, radiates from below upwards, in a mode of *or chozer*,[110] just as the investment in *arich anpin*, *abba* and *imma*, and *zu'n* of Atzilut, radiates as an *or chozer* from *malchut* of Atzilut, and *malchut* of Atzilut, from below upwards, is a category of *keter*, and "Their beginning is wedged in their end."[111] It is likewise at the culmination of the *kav* of the light of the En Sof, culminating at the ending of the *yosher* of the "feet" of Adam Kadmon: it radiates from below upwards[112] to the category of the light of the *neshamah* of the *malchut* of *malchut* of Asiyah, which is actual Divinity [(originating in) the *chitzoniyut* of the *kelim* of *malchut* of Atzilut]. ▲According to that which is stated in ch. 20 of *Sefer Hagilgulim*, cited in *Likutei Amarim*,[113] this radiation from the *kav* of the light of the En Sof vests itself first in the light of Atzilut in Asiyah, and from there to the Beriah and Yetzirah in Asiyah, and from these to the category of the light of the *neshamah* of the *malchut* of the *malchut* of Asiyah. And hence is the (creative) power and force in the culmination of the *keli* of the *malchut* of *malchut* of Asiyah within the element of earth.

This is the constant and everlasting effect, throughout the earth, of the fiat "Let the earth bring forth herbs . . ."[114]

([115]in a mode of infinitude, and not during the six days of

---

[103] *Brackets appear in the text.* [104] *The individual star, or angel of destiny.* [105] *Genesis Rabba 10:6; see* Moreh Nevuchim *II:10.* [106] *See* H.V. [107] I.e., *at the lowest level, at* malchut of Asiyah*; see above, notes 32 and 95.* [108] *In the other half of the primordial space.* [109] *Unlike the* yosher, *the* iggulim *take in the whole void (see above, note 32). The central point in the primordial space is not only the end-point of* yosher, *but also the lowest level of the* iggulim. [110] *A returning (reflecting) light. Thus there is a constant stream of light flowing both ways: from the highest to the lowest level, and back, from the lowest to the highest. See at the end of this section.* [111] Malchut *is an aspect of* keter, *not only relatively*

הנ"ל היא מראה כחה ויכלתה ביסוד העפר הגשמי בגילוי עצום ביתר עז מיסודות העליונים ממנו וגם מצבא השמים שאין בכחם ויכלתם להוציא יש מאין תמיד כיסוד העפר המצמיח תמיד יש מאין הם עשבים ואילנות (והמזל המכה ואומר גדל היינו לאחר שכבר צמח העשב ואינו אומר לו לצמוח מאין ליש אלא מקוטן לגודל ולשאת פרי כל מין ומין בפרטי פרטיות. אבל בטרם יצמח למי יאמר כל מזל ומזל לכל עשב ועשב בפרטי פרטיות) מהכח הצומח שבו שהוא אין ורוחני והם גשמיים ואין זאת אלא משום דרגלי א"ק מסתיימים בתחתית עשי' ותחת רגליו מאיר אור א"ס ב"ה הסובב כל עלמין בלי הפסק רב ביניהם רק עיגולי א"ק לבדו וגם הקו מאור א"ס המסתיים בסיום רגלי א"ק מאיר ממטה למעלה בבחי' אור חוזר כמו שהמלובש בא"א ואו"א וזו"נ דאצי' מאיר באור חוזר ממל' דאצי' ומל' דאצי' היא בחי' כתר ממטה למעלה ונעוץ תחלתן בסופן. וככה הוא בסיום הקו דאור א"ס המסתיים בסיום היושר דרגלי א"ק מאיר ממטה למעלה לבחי' אור הנשמה דמל' דמל' דעשיה שהוא אלקות ממש מחיצוניות הכלים דמל' דאצי'. ולפמ"ש בס' הגלגולים פ"כ הובא בלק"א מתלבשת תחלה הארה זו של הקו דאור א"ס באור האצי' שבעשיה וממנה לבריאה ויצירה שבעשיה ומהן לבחי' אור הנשמה דמל' דמל' דעשיה ועי"ז יש כח ועוז בסיום הכלי דמל' דמל' דעשיה שביסוד העפר והוא מאמר תדשא הארץ וכו' להיות פועל בקרב הארץ תמיד לעולם ועד (בחי' אין סוף ולא בלבד בששת ימי בראשית

---

speaking because as the lowest stage of the higher realm it is the highest of the successive, lower realm; but the keter *of its own realm is vested and wedged in it, and it reflects back into its own* keter. *Thus, their beginning (*keter*) is truly wedged in their end (*malchut*).*

[112] *In a mode of* or chozer. [113] Tanya *I, ch, 6, author's glossary note* ad loc. [114] *Genesis I:11.* [115] *Brackets appear in the text.*

creation only [as is the case with the fiat "Let the waters bring forth an abundance of creeping things,"[116] and the fiat "Let the earth bring forth living being"[117]—from the *chochmah* of the *malchut* of the *malchut* of Asiyah]. For during the Seven Days of the Beginning there shone in this world a radiation from the light of the En Sof in a mode of gratuitous *chesed*, without any (prior) elevation of *mayin nukvin*[118] at all.[119])

To make herbs and trees, and fruits, sprout *ex nihilo* into substantiality, constantly, from year to year. This is a kind of degree of infinity; for if this world will subsist for myriads of myriads of years, they will still sprout forth from year to year. There are, though, some (plants) which require a (prior) elevation of *mayin nukvin* [namely those which are sown and implanted]. But these (too, come about) like *yesh meayin*;[120] for the implanted kernel is of no estimation whatever in relation to the fruit, nor in relation to the whole tree with the branches and leaves. The same applies to the various sorts of garden-herbs and vegetables, and also to the various sorts of produce: that hundreds of kernels will come about from a single kernel is like unto *yesh meayin*, and *a fortiori*, with respect to the chaffs and spikes. Now, these fruits (that come about) by means of an elevation of *mayin nukvin*, i.e. by sowing and implanting, they are, by far, superior to those that rise independently from the vegetative property in the soil only. And from this we can understand (the notion of) the elicitations of the supernal *orot* in Atzilut, Beriah, Yetzirah, and Asiyah ([121]which is the purpose for the creation of man[122]), as explained elsewhere.[123]

●▲ And from this we can understand clearly the subject of the order of levels pertaining to the inorganic, vegetative, animal and articulate [which correspond to the aspects of earth, water, fire, and air]. Though the animal is more sublime than the vegetative, and the articulate is more sublime than the animal, nevertheless, the animal is nurtured and lives by the vegetative, and the articulate receives his vitality from both, even wisdom and knowledge. For "A child does not know how to call 'father' and 'mother' until it has tasted grain;"[124] and "I had not yet eaten the meat of oxen . . ."[125] This is the aspect of the *or chozer*: from *below*, from the bottom[126] of Asiyah [where there is an exceedingly strong manifestation of the radiation of the radiation . . . from the light of the En Sof which encircles all worlds, and from the *kav* from the light of the En Sof at the culmination of the "feet" of the *yosher* of Adam Kadmon] *upwards*, in a mode of *or chozer*, as mentioned above.

And it will be clearly understood from this the best of discernment and knowledge,

---

[116] *Genesis I: 20.* [117] Ibid., *I: 24.* [118] *Feminine waters—The initial stimulus of an appropriate act by man (see* supra, *section IV, note 46).* [119] *See* supra, *section V, and note 87* ad loc. [120] *Not truly* yesh meayin, *for there is some initial substance. Thus strictly speaking it is* yesh meyesh *(as opposed to* ayin, *naught). But the final product is so inproportionate to its source that the vegetative process is somehow analogous to* creatio ex nihilo. [121] *Brackets appear in the text.* [122] *See* Likutei Torah *IV: 2a.* [123] Cf. Likutei Torah *IV: 50d–51a; see also* supra, *section VIII.* [124] *Berachot 40a;* cf. *Zohar I: 157b, and Genesis Rabba 15: 7.* [125] *And was, there-*

בראשית כמאמר ישרצו המים ומאמר תוצא הארץ נפש חיה מחכמה דמל׳ דמל׳ דעשיה שבז׳ ימי בראשית האיר בעולם הזה הארה מאור אין סוף בחסד חנם בלי העלאת מיין נוקבין כלל) להצמיח עשבים ואילנות ופירות מאין ליש תמיד מדי שנה בשנה שהוא מעין בחי׳ א״ס שאם יתקיים עוה״ז ריבוי רבבות שנים יצמיחו מדי שנה בשנה אלא שיש מהן ע״י העלאת מ״נ והם הזרועים והנטועים ואעפ״כ הם כמו יש מאין שהגרעין הנטוע אין לו ערך כלל לגבי הפרי וגם נגד כל האילן עם הענפים והעלין וכן במיני זרעונים וירקות וגם במיני תבואה להתהוות מאות גרעינין מגרעין א׳ הוא כמו יש מאין ומכ״ש הקשין והשבלים והנה הפירות שע״י העלאת מ״נ היא הזריעה והנטיעה הם משובחים מאד מאד מהעולים מאליהן מכח הצומח לבדו שבארץ ומזה נשכיל המשכות אורות עליונים באבי״ע (שהוא תכלית בריאת האדם) כמ״ש במ״א. ומזה יובן היטב בענין סדר מדרגות דצח״מ שהן בחי׳ עפר מים אש רוח שאף שהחי הוא למעלה מהצומח והמדבר למעלה מהחי אעפ״כ החי ניזון וחי מהצומח והמדבר מקבל חיותו משניהם וגם חכמה ודעת שאין התינוק יודע לקרות אבא ואימא עד שיטעום טעם דגן כו׳ ועדיין לא אכילנא בישרא דתורא כו׳ כי הוא בחי׳ אור חוזר ממטה למעלה מתחתית העשיה שמתגלית שם ביתר עז הארה דהארה כו׳ מאור א״ס הסובב כ״ע ומהקו אור א״ס שבסיום רגלי היושר דא״ק בבחי׳ אור חוזר כנ״ל. ויובן היטב בזה טוב טעם ודעת

מה

---

fore, unable to examine the problem properly.—Bava Kama 71b–72a; see commentaries ad loc. [126] Malchut.

how it is that the supreme angels of the *Merkavah*—"The Face of the Oxen, and the Face of the Eagle"—[127] derive great enjoyment, and are nurtured and content from the spirit of the cattle and fowl that ascends to them from the sacrifices on the altar, and as the sacred *Zohar* expresses it subtly:[128] "And they derive enjoyment from their *element* and *essence*."[129] Now, after these words and this truth,[130] knowledge comes easy to the discerning[131] to understand from all the above the great advantage of the operational commandments.[132] For they are the purpose for the descent of the souls to this physical world, as it is written: "To practice them this day;"[133] and "Better one hour of repentance and good deeds in this world, than all the life of the world to come."[134]

Until here we found of his holy writing.[135]

●▲XXI. Upon enquiring after their welfare as is becoming to those who love His Name—"May my word drop and my speech trickle as dew"[1] to those who offer themselves willingly among the people[2] to practise the righteousness of the Lord (*tzidkat Hashem*) with His Holy Land,[3] by giving every year a set sum of monies for our Holy Land, may it be rebuilt and re-established speedily, in our days. (I call upon you,) to bestir the alert[4] and to strengthen weak hands, to contribute monies for the Land of Israel every week, or at least every month, of the amount assigned as the year's apportionment, as well as all the "dedicated money" that one was inspired to donate annually, without a vow,[5] for the support of our brethren who live in the Holy Land.

For, note, besides that it is known to all the great virtue of alertness with respect to all commandments—

[Thus it is mentioned repeatedly in the sayings of our sages, of blessed memory: "At all times one should try to be first when it comes to a commandment."[6] Also, it is the alertness of our father Abraham, peace to him, that stands by us and our children, for everlasting. For the *akedah*[7] itself is not really regarded as so great a test in relation to the level of our father Abraham, peace to him, especially as *G–d* said to him "please take your son, . . ."[8] After all, there are numerous saints who gave their lives for the sanctification of the Lord even though that G–d did not speak to them. However, our father Abraham, peace to him, did this with a wondrous alertness,[9] to show his joy and desire to fulfil the will of his Master, and to cause

---

[127] *Ezekiel I:10.* [128] *Zohar III:241a.* [129] *The form and essence, as opposed to the physical aspects of the animal sacrifices. The animal spirit, the "animalhood," originally deriving from these angels of the* Merkavah *(see* supra, *notes 20), thus is refracted and reflects back to its source in a mode of* or chozer. [130] Par. *2 Chron. 32:1.* [131] Par. *Proverbs 14:6.* [132] *On the revelatory plane the* Mitzvot *are but in* malchut; *their origin thus is exceedingly sublime. It is to that exceedingly high and sublime source to which the* or chozer *(effected by the fulfillment of the* Mitzvot*) reflects. Hence, the elicitations effected by the performance of* Mitzvot *are also that much more sublime (*cf. infra, *sect. XXIX; also,* supra, *sect III, note 5).* [133] *Deut.*

מה שמלאכים עליונים שבמרכבה פני שור ופני נשר נהנים מאד וניזונים ומסתפקים מרוח הבהמה והעוף העולה אליהם מהקרבנות שע"ג המזבח וכדקדוק לשון הזוה"ק ואתהניין מיסודא ועיקרא דילהון . ואחרי הדברים והאמת האלה דעת לנבון נקל להבין ע"י כל הנ"ל גודל מעלת המצות מעשיות אשר הן תכלית ירידת הנשמות לעוה"ז הגשמי כמ"ש היום לעשותם ויפה שעה א' בתשובה ומעשים טובים בעוה"ז מכל חיי עוה"ב. ע"כ מצאנו מכיה"ק :

כא אד"ש כמשפט לאוהבי שמו אל המתנדבים בעם לעשות צדקת ה' עם ארצו הקדושה לתת מדי שנה בשנה חוק הקצוב מעות אה"ק תוב"ב אליהם תטוף מלתי ותזל כטל אמרתי לזרז לזריזים ולחזק ידים רפות במתן דמים מעות א"י מדי שבת בשבתו ולפחות מדי חדש בחדשו מערכו הקצוב לערך שנה וכל כסף הקדשים אשר עלה על לב איש להתנדב בלי נדר לפרנסת אחינו יושבי אה"ק מדי שנה בשנה. כי הנה מלבד הידוע לכל גודל מעלת הזריזות בכל המצות הנאמר ונשנה בדברי רז"ל לעולם יקדים אדם לדבר מצוה כו' וזריזותי' דאברהם אבינו ע"ה היא העומדת לעד לנו ולבנינו עד עולם כי העקדה עצמה אינה נחשבה כ"כ לנסיון גדול לערך מעלת א"א ע"ה בשגם כי ה' דיבר בו קח נא את בנך כו' והרי כמה וכמה קדושים שמסרו נפשם על קדושת ה' גם כי לא דיבר ה' בם רק שא"א ע"ה עשה זאת בזריזות נפלאה להראות שמחתו וחפצו למלאות רצון קונו ולעשות נחת

7:11; cf. *Eruvin 22a.* [134] *Avot IV:17; see* supra, *section I.* [135] *R. Menachem Mendel of Lubavitch, grandson and disciple of the author, writes that his grandfather wrote this discourse a few days before his passing; see* Derech Mitzvotecha, *p. 170a, and* Kitzurim Vehe'orot, *p. 40.*

Section XXI

[1] Par. *Job 29:22 and Deut. 32:2.* [2] Par. *Judges 5:9.* [3] Cf. supra, *sect. XIV and XVII.* [4] Cf. *Macot 23a:* Sifre, *Numbers, sect. 1.* [5] *See* Shulchan Aruch, Yoreh De'ah: *203;* cf. Likutei Torah *III:82b.* [6] *Nazir 23b; Bava Kama 38b;* etc.; cf. *note 10, below.* [7] *The binding of Isaac for sacrificial purposes (Genesis XXII).* [8] *Genesis 22:2.* [9] *See Genesis 22:3, and Midrashim* ad loc.

gratification to his Maker. And from him our sages, of blessed memory, derived (the requirement of alertness) with respect to the keeping of all the commandments in general;[10] and in particular with respect to the act of charity which is superior to them all, protecting and saving by its "fruits" in this world[11] from all kinds of calamities that may come about, as it is written: "And *tzedakah* saves from death,"[12] thus, *a fortiori*, from other kinds of suffering that are lighter than death. It is, thus, certainly to our benefit, even in this world, to be as zealous with it as possible, for, after all, "Man is judged every day."[13]]

●▲Indeed, we also found and noted in the service of charity a particularly great and wondrous advantage, without parallel: the act of charity is performed in numerous times, and whoever performs it frequently is praiseworthy. This is in contrast to performing it in one time and all at once, even when the total sum is the same, as R. Moses Maimonides, of blessed memory, wrote in (his) *Commentary* on the Mishnah taught by the sages, of blessed memory: "And everything according to the quantity of the act."[14]

Now, besides that, R. Moses Maimonides, of blessed memory, explained well this reason and motive ["In order to refine the soul by means of the quantitative action"], there is an explicit verse in Scripture that "The effect of *tzedakah* is for life."[15] This means, its effect and affection is to elicit supreme life from the Fountainhead of life,[16] the blessed En Sof, to the Land of Life,[17] the Abode (*Shechinah*) of our strength[18] of which it is said[19] "And You animate them all."[20] It[21] is the hut of David that has fallen[22] even unto the dust, and as the saying of our sages, of blessed memory:[23] "When they were exiled to Edom, the Shechinah went with them . . ." (This effect of *tzedakah* is brought about) because the arousal from below, to revive the spirit of the humbled who has nothing at all of his own,[24] elicits an arousal from above; and especially so when the people offer voluntarily to sustain the inhabitants of the actual Land of Life,[25] and suffice this for the initiated.

Now, whoever is enlightened as to so great and wondrous a matter, will find to the best of discernment and knowledge how profound are the words of the sages, of blessed memory, when they said "Everything according to the quantity of the act." This refers to the act of charity which is performed at numerous times to elicit supreme life in order to bring about a Supreme Unification (*yichud*)—many times. This is also similar to what R. Moses Maimonides wrote "to refine the soul;" as is known from the sacred *Zohar*

---

[10] *Pessachim 4a; Rosh Hashana 32b;* etc. [11] Cf. *Peah I:1; see* supra, *beg. of sect. XVII.* [12] *Proverbs 10:2; see Rosh Hashana 16b, and Zohar I:104a.* [13] *Rosh Hashana 16a.* [14] *Avot 3:15; see R. Menachem Mendel of Lubavitch,* Maamarim, *pp. 7* ff. [15] *See Proverbs 10:16, and 11:19.* [16] Lit., *Life of life; see* supra, *sect. XVII, note 4.* [17] *See* supra, *sect. VIII, note 45.* [18] Ibid., *note 36.* [19] *Nehemiah 9:6.* [20] *See* supra, *sect. XIV, and note 29* a.l. [21] *The Land of Life, the Shechinah.* [22] *See* supra, *sect. IX, notes 27* f. [23] *Megilah 29a (*v.s. *of* Ayin Ya'akov, a.l.*);* Mechilta *on Exodus 12:41; see* infra, *sect. XXV, note 48.*—Cf. Tanya *I, end of ch. 17.* [24] *The "poor who has nothing of his own"*

נחת רוח ליוצרו וממנו למדו רז"ל לקיום כל המצות בכלל ובפרט מעשה הצדקה העולה על כולנה המגינה ומצלה בפירותיה בעוה"ז מכל מיני פורעניות המתרגשות כדכתיב וצדקה תציל ממות וכ"ש משאר מיני יסורים הקלים ממות כ"ש שטוב לנו גם בעוה"ז להקדימה כל מה דאפשר שהרי אדם נידון בכל יום:

אך גם זאת מצאנו ראינו בעבודת הצדקה מעלה פרטיות גדולה ונפלאה אין ערוך אליה להיות מעשה הצדקה נעשית בפעמים רבות וכל המרבה ה"ז משובח ולא בפעם א' ובבת אחת גם כי הסך הכולל אחד הוא כמ"ש הרמב"ם ז"ל בפירוש המשנה ששנו חכמים ז"ל והכל לפי רוב המעשה:

והנה מלבד כי הרמב"ם ז"ל ביאר היטב טעמו ונימוקו כדי לזכך הנפש ע"י רבוי המעשה הנה מקרא מלא דיבר הכתוב פעולת צדקה לחיים דהיינו שפעולתה וסגולתה להמשיך חיים עליונים מחיי החיים א"ס ב"ה לארץ החיים היא שכינת עוזינו שעליה נאמר ואתה מחיה את כולם והיא סוכת דוד הנופלת עד עפר וכמארז"ל גלו לאדום שכינה עמהם כו' כי באתערותא דלתתא להחיות רוח שפלים דלית ליה מגרמיה כלום אתערותא דלעילא ובפרט בהתנדב עם להחיות יושבי ארץ החיים ממש ור"ל. וכל משכיל על דבר גדול ונפלא כזה ימצא טוב טעם ודעת כמה גדולים דברי חכמים ז"ל שאמרו הכל לפי רוב המעשה דהיינו מעשה הצדקה הנעשה בפעמים רבות להמשיך חיים עליונים ליחד יחוד עליון פעמים רבות. והיינו נמי כעין מ"ש הרמב"ם לזכך הנפש כנודע מזוה"ק דשכינה

---

corresponds to the Shechinah, the Sefirah malchut*—which has "nothing of its own but what is given to it by others" (*cf. *Zohar I:249b;* Etz Chayim *6:5, and 8:5;* et passim*). See Zohar III:113b.* [25] I.e., *the terrestrial Land of Life, the Land of Israel; see* supra, *sect. VIII, note 45.*

that the *Shechinah* is called *nefesh* (soul)[26]—because she is our life and our soul. And it is written:[27] "Our soul is bent low, to the dust."[28] And that is why our sages, of blessed memory, said: "Great is charity, for it brings close the redemption"[29]—to raise (the Shechinah) from the dust, gradually,[30] "until Shilo will come."[31]

●▲ XXII(a).[1] My beloved, my brethren and friends:

An open rebuke out of a love concealed:[2] come now and let us adjudge,[3] remember the days of old, consider the years of every generation.[4] Has such ever happened since the days of the world, and where, oh where have you found such a custom in any one of the books of the early and latter sages of Israel, that it should be usage and regulation to ask for advice in mundane matters[5]—what one is to do in matters pertaining to the physical world. (Such was not asked) even of the greatest of the erstwhile sages of Israel, as the Tannaim and Amoraim "For whom no secret is hidden"[6] and "All the paths of heaven are clear unto them,"[7] except for the real prophets that were aforetimes in Israel, as Samuel the Seer to whom Saul went to enquire of G-d about the asses that were lost to his father.[8] For in fact, all matters pertaining to man, except for the words of Torah[9] and the fear of Heaven, are apprehended by prophecy only "And there is no bread unto the wise,"[10] as our sages, of blessed memory, said: "Everything is in the hands of Heaven except for the fear of Heaven;"[11] and "Seven things are hidden . . ., man does not know how he will profit, and when the Kingdom of David will return . . ."[12] Note, these are likened one to the other![13]

As for what is written in *Isaiah*[14] "A counsellor and a wise one who silences all," and also, as for the statement of our sages, of blessed memory,[15] "That one is benefitted by him[16] with *etzah* (counsel) and *toshiyah* (salvation),"—this refers to matters of the Torah, called *toshiyah*.[17] Thus the sages, of blessed memory, said:[18] "A counsellor is he who knows to intercalcate the years and to determine the months;"[19] for in Torah-terminology the principium of intercalcation is called *etzah*[20] and *sod*,[21] as mentioned in *Sanhedrin* folio 87,[22] see there in the commentary of Rashi.

●▲ However, I shall relate the truth[23] to those who listen to me: "Love upsets the natural order of conduct,"[24] for it is a covering of the eyes not to see

---

[26] Cf. Zohar Chadash, *Ruth, 84a;* cf. ibid., *78c;* et passim. [27] *Psalms 44:26.* [28] Cf. supra, *(note 22), and see Midrash Tehilim 44:2.* [29] *Bava Batra 10a.* [30] *See* Yerushalmi, *Yoma III:2.* [31] *Genesis 49:7.*

Section XXII

[1] *This section is but an excerpt from a lengthy epistle, the complete version of which appears in* Hatamim *I:2 (Warsaw, 1935; pp. 32 ff.) and in* Igrot Ba'al Hatanya, *sect. 39 (pp. 60 ff). See* supra, *Introduction, note 21.* [2] Par. *Proverbs 27:5.* [3] Par. *Isaiah I:18.* [4] Par. *Deut. 32:7.* [5] *See* H.V. [6] Par. *Daniel 4:6; see Chulin 59a.* [7] *Berachot 58b.* [8] *See I Samuel: ch. 9.* [9] Cf. *Bava Metziah 59b; Temurah 16a; Maimonides,* Hilchot

● 15 Tishri ● 16 Tishri ▲ *13 Tishri* ▲ *14 Tishri*

דשכינה נקראת נפש כי היא חיינו ונפשנו וכתיב כי שחה לעפר נפשנו. ולכן ארז"ל גדולה צדקה שמקרבת את הגאולה להקימה מעפר מעט מעט עד כי יבא שילה:

כב אהובי אחיי ורעיי מאהבה מסותרת תוכחת מגולה לכו נא ונוכחה זכרו ימות עולם בינו שנות דור ודור ההיתה כזאת מימות עולם ואיה איפוא מצאתם מנהג זה באחד מכל ספרי חכמי ישראל הראשונים והאחרונים להיות מנהג ותיקון לשאול בעצה גשמיות כדת מה לעשות בעניני העולם הגשמי אף לגדולי חכמי ישראל הראשונים כתנאים ואמוראים אשר כל רז לא אנס להו ונהירין להון שבילין דרקיע כ"א לנביאים ממש אשר היו לפנים בישראל כשמואל הרואה אשר הלך אליו שאול לדרוש ה' על דבר האתונות שנאבדו לאביו כי באמת כל עניני אדם לבד מדברי תורה וי"ש אינם מושגים רק בנבואה ולא לחכמים לחם כמארז"ל הכל בידי שמים חוץ מיראת שמים ושבעה דברים מכוסים כו' אין אדם יודע במה משתכר כו' ומלכות בית דוד מתי תחזור כו' הנה הושוו זה לזה ומ"ש בישעיה יועץ וחכם חרשים וכן משארז"ל ונהנין ממנו עצה ותושיה היינו בד"ת הנקרא תושיה כמארז"ל יועץ זה שיודע לעבר שנים ולקבוע חדשים כו' שסוד העיבור קרוי עצה וסוד בלשון תורה כדאיתא בסנהדרין דף פ"ז ע"ש בפרש"י:

אך האמת אגיד לשומעים לי כי אהבה מקלקלת השורה והנה היא כסות עינים שלא לראות האמת

Yesodei Hatorah *IX: 1, and Introd. to his Commentary on the* Mishnah. [10] *Eccles. 9: 11.* [11] *Berachot 33b.* [12] *Pessachim 54b.* [13] I.e., "*how he will profit,*" *and* "*when the Kingdom of David will return*"; *(see the commentary of R. Samuel Edelis,* ad loc.*).* [14] *Isaiah 3: 3.* [15] *Avot 6: 1.* [16] *The Scholar of Torah, who studies* lishmah. [17] *Midrash Tehilim VII: 3; Sanhedrin 26b; Zohar Chadash: 5d.* [18] *Hagigah 14a.* [19] *Emended according to* H.V. [20] *Counsel.* [21] *Mystery.* [22] *Sanhedrin 87a.* [23] Par. *Daniel 11: 2.* [24] *Genesis Rabba 55: 8;* cf. *Sanhedrin 105b.*

the truth. Because of their great love for the life of the body—[for the sake of Heaven, to worship G-d with it in a mode of flashes of fire and a great flame[25] because of their soul's love for G-d],[26] they are properly angry with the agony of the body, Heaven forfend; may G-d show compassion. Thus they are not able to bear it at all, to the point that it drives them out of their mind[27] to tramp about from city to city to seek advice from afar, and they did not implore G-d by returning unto Him with humble spirit and submission of the body to accept His chastisement with love, "for He whom He loves . . ."[28]

▲ It is analogous to a compassionate, wise and righteous father who punishes his son. Surely the wise son should not "turn his back"[29] to escape and find himself help, or even an intercessor before his father, who is compassionate, righteous and merciful. Rather, he should have his face looking straight[30] at his father, face to face, to endure his strikes with love "For weal unto him all the days."

Now, above, the aspect of *panim* (face) is that of willingness and pleasure.[31] That is, our Father in Heaven effuses unto His children all the good of the worlds, and life for the soul and body, out of love and willingness, pleasure and delight, through the Torah of Life,[32] His blessed Will, which He gave unto us, as it is written:[33] "For in the light of *panecha* (Your Face),[34] You gave us the Torah of Life . . ." to carry out His will with it.[35] And of this it was said: "For in the light of the King's Face there is life, and His will . . ."[36]

To the heathens, however, He effuses the life of their bodies without willingness, pleasure, and delight. This, therefore, is referred to as *elohim acherim*;[37] for they draw from the aspect of *achurayim*.[38]

It is likewise with man: willingness and pleasure are an aspect of *panim* (face). When one does not accept[39] with love and willingness, it is as if "he turns his neck"[40] and *achor* (back), Heaven forfend.

● The suggested advice (to be able) to accept with love, is the counsel of the Lord in the mouth of our sages, of blessed memory: "to examine one's conduct."[41] Thus one will find with himself sins that require the purgation through afflictions.[42] Then one will see clearly His great love towards himself which "upsets the natural order of conduct," as in the simile of the great and awesome king who, out of his great love, personally washes the filth from his only son, as it is written: "When the Lord will wash the filth off the daughters of Zion . . .

---

[25] Par. *Song 8:6. Cf. supra, section I note 29.* [26] Cf. supra, *end of sect. XVIII. The author does not accuse his followers of seeking physical comfort for its own sake. He views them with compassion and judges their motives to be noble. However, he admonishes them to find a profound lesson in their hardship.* [27] *See Eruvin 41b;* cf. *Zohar* Chadash *49a.* [28] *Proverbs 3:12.* [29] Par. *Joshua 7:8.* [30] Par. *Ps. 11:7.* [31] *The term* panim *denotes* pnimiyut, *the inner essence, the core. Correlative it expresses willingness. To give in a mode of* pnimiyut *implies most profound willingness and favour, stemming from the very essence of the giver.* Cf. Tanya *I, ch. 22.* [32] Cf. *Proverbs 3:8.* [33] Liturgy, *concluding benediction of the* Amidah.

האמת מרוב אהבתם לחיי הגוף לש״ש לעבוד בו את ה׳ ברשפי אש ושלהבת גדולה מאהבת נפשם את ה׳ וע״כ היטב חרה להם בצער הגוף ח״ו ה׳ ירחם ואין יכולין לקבל כלל עד שמעבירים על דעתם לכתת רגליהם מעיר לעיר לשאול עצות מרחוק ולא שעו אל ה׳ לשוב אליו ברוח נמוכה והכנעת הגוף לקבל תוכחתו באהבה כי את אשר יאהב ה׳ וכו׳:

וכמו אב רחמן חכם וצדיק המכה בנו שאין לבן חכם להפוך עורף לנוס למצוא לו עזרה או אפילו מליץ יושר לפני אביו הרחמן והצדיק וחסיד רק להיות ישר יחזו פנימו עם אביו פנים בפנים לסבול הכאותיו באהבה לטוב לו כל הימים. והנה למעלה בחי׳ פנים הוא הרצון והחשק אשר אבינו שבשמים משפיע לבניו כל טוב עולמים וחיי נפש וגוף באהבה ורצון חשיקה וחפיצה ע״י תורת חיים שהיא רצונו ית׳ אשר נתן לנו כמ״ש כי באור פניך נתת לנו תורת חיים כו׳ לעשות בה רצונו וע״ז נאמר באור פני מלך חיים ורצונו כו׳. משא״כ לעו״ג משפיע חיי גופם שלא ברצון וחשיקה וחפיצה לכך נק׳ אלהים אחרים שיונקים מבחי׳ אחוריים וכך הוא באדם הרצון והחשק הוא בחי׳ פנים ואם אינו מקבל באהבה ורצון כאלו הופך עורף ואחור ח״ו. ועצה היעוצה לקבל באהבה היא עצת ה׳ בפי חז״ל לפשפש במעשיו וימצא לו עונות הצריכין מירוק יסורים ויראה לעין גודל אהבתו אליו המקלקלת השורה כמשל מלך גדול ונורא הרוחץ בכבודו ובעצמו צואת בנו יחידו מרוב אהבתו כמ״ש אם רחץ ה׳ צואת בנות ציון כו׳ ברוח

---

[34] I.e., *out of love and willingness.* [35] *By observing the Torah and the commandments.* [36] *Proverbs 16:15.* [37] Lit.: *other gods.—G-d sustains the heathens without favour. Thus He does so by means of various intermediaries. These appear to the heathens as independent entities and forces, as "other gods"; see* Tanya *I, ch. 22;* infra, *sect. XXV.* Cf. *Tikunei Zohar 32:76b.* [38] Achurayim *(hindersides; as opposed to* panim, *the face, or frontside) denotes the most extraneous aspect, as far removed from* pnimiyut *as possible. Correlative it expresses a lack of willingness. To give in a mode of* achurayim *implies a contemptuous and strictly formal gift;* cf. Tanya *I, ch. 22.* [39] *The chastisements of G-d.* [40] Par. *Joshua*

(Notes cont. at end of Hebrew Text)

with a spirit of justice..."[43] And "As waters (reflect) face to face,"[44] there will be an arousal of love in the heart of everyone who perceives and understands the preciousness of the nature of G-d's love for the nether beings; it is dearer and better than all the life of all the worlds, as it is written: "How precious is Your *chesed*..."[45] "For Your *chesed* is better than life..."[46] For *chesed* [which is the aspect of love] is the Fountainhead of the life[47] prevalent in all the worlds, as it is written: "He sustains life through *chesed*."[48]

And then[49] G-d, too, will give weal and make His Face shine towards him in the mode of a manifestation of the love which at first was clothed and hidden in a manifestation of admonition,[50] and the *gevurot* shall be sweetened at their source and the judgments become nullified, forevermore.

●▲(XXIIb[51]). My beloved, my brethren and friends:

Due to the immensity of my preoccupations which all together surround me and "Encircle me like water all day and all night, never holding their peace,"[52]—I am unable to bear[53] the burden to state in writing all that is in my heart. Briefly, however, I come as one who reminds and repeats erstwhile matters[54] in general, and in particular to those of the people who offer themselves willingly—to stand by the (Divine) service, i.e. prayer,[55] with a loud voice:[56] to strengthen themselves very much with all might and power[57] against any internal or external obstacle, with, literally, a strong hand. This refers to the "will of those who fear Him,"[58]—transcending the wisdom and understanding G-d gave into them in order to know to exercise all that G-d commanded with intelligence and knowledge. There should be but a simple will and a spirit of voluntary offering in every one whose heart prompts him to serve "a whole service,"[59] thus to cause gratification unto his Maker. Of this it is said: "For it is a stiff-necked people, and You pardon;"[60] for pardon, too, transcends wisdom, as "they asked wisdom..."[61] Thus Moses our Master, peace to him, invoked "measure for measure,"[62] and suffice this for the initiated.

● Furthermore, I ask of you not to cast aside my words, the plea I issued for everyone to be upright and walking with integrity[63] just as "G-d made man upright; not to seek numerous calculations"[64] of the pretexts of

---

[43] *Isaiah 4:4.* [44] *Proverbs 27:19 see* supra, *section I note 26.* [45] *Psalms 36:8.* [46] *Psalms 63:4.* [47] Lit.: *the Life of the life (*cf. supra, *section XVII note 4).* [48] Liturgy, *opening-benedictions of the* Amidah. [49] *When a man accepts upon himself with love* etc. [50] *Chastisement.*—Cf. supra, *section XI, and* Tanya *I, ch. 26.* [51] *The following is obviously not a continuation of the preceding (*cf. supra, *note 1).* [52] Par. *Psalms 88:18 and Isaiah 62:6.* [53] *Emended according to* L.H. [54] *Keritot 8a.* [55] *See Judges 5:9, and commentaries* ad loc.; *Ta'anit 2a;* Sifre, *Deut., sect. 41.* [56] *See Nachmanides, end of his comment. on Exodus 13:16;* cf. Sefer Chassidim, *sect. 820.* Shulchan Aruch, Orach Chayim, *sect.*

ברוח משפט כו' וכמים הפנים אל פנים תתעורר האהבה בלב כל משכיל ומבין יקר מהות אהבת ה' אל התחתונים אשר היא יקרה וטובה מכל חיי העולמים כולם כמ"ש מה יקר חסדך וכו' כי טוב חסדך מחיים כו' כי החסד שהוא בחי' אהבה הוא חיי החיים שבכל העולמות כמ"ש מכלכל חיים בחסד ואז גם ה' יתן הטוב ויאר פניו אליו בבחי' אהבה מגולה אשר היתה תחלה מלובשת ומסותרת בתוכחה מגולה ויתמתקו הגבורות בשרשן ויתבטלו הדינין נס"ו:

אהובי אחיי ורעיי מגודל טרדתי אשר הקיפו עלי יחד וסבוני כמים כל היום וכל הלילה תמיד לא יחשו. לא אוכל משא לאמר עם הספר כל אשר בלבבי. אך בקצרה באתי כמזכיר ומחזיר על הראשונות בכלל ובפרט אל המתנדבים בעם לעמוד על העבודה זו תפלה בקול רם להתחזק מאד בכל עוז ותעצומות נגד כל מונע מבית ומחוץ ביד חזקה כמשמעו שהוא רצון יריאיו אשר למעלה מן החכמה והתבונה אשר נתן ה' בהמה לדעת לעשות את כל אשר צוה ה' בהשכל ודעת. רק רצון פשוט ורוח נדיבה בכל איש אשר ידבנו לבו לעבוד עבודה תמה לעשות נ"ר ליוצרו. ועז"נ כי עם קשה עורף הוא וסלחת. כי הסליחה היא ג"כ למעלה מן החכ'. כי שאלו לחכמה כו' ומשה רבינו ע"ה ביקש מדה כנגד מדה ור"ל. ועוד זאת אדרוש ממעל' שלא להשליך דברי אחריכם אשר ערכתי שיח להיות כל איש ישר והולך בתומו כאשר עשה האלקי' את האדם ישר ולא לבקש חשבונות רבים מעלילות

מצעדי

101, and comment. ad loc. [57] *See Berachot 34b, Rashi* ad loc. (s.v. **צריכיך**). [58] *Psalms 145:19.* [59] Cf. *Yoma 24a.* [60] *Exodus 34:9—Stiff-neckedness denotes simple will, will as it is in itself, transcending the faculties of reason; see* infra, *sect. XXIX, note 24.* Cf. Likutei Torah, *III:67d, and 71b.* [61] Yerushalmi, *Macot II:6 (see comment.* Pneh Moshe, ad loc.*); Pessikta de R.* Cahana, *(ed. Buber) sect. XXV.—Wisdom demands that sin go paired with appropriate judgment. The possibility of* teshuvah *or simple pardon (thereby avoiding judgment), thus, transcends wisdom, and is due solely to Divine grace.* [62] *Nedarim 32a.* [63] Par. *Proverbs 19:1*; etc. [64] Par. *Eccles. 7:29.*

man's steps and a person's thoughts and devices.[65] For that is the work of Heaven and not an occupation for human beings. Rather, (every one is) to believe with absolute faithfulness in the precept of our sages, of blessed memory:[66] "And be humble of spirit before every person"—in general.[67] For it is a set matter and an established proverb that each one becomes better through his fellow-being.[68] Thus it is written[69]—"All the men of Israel . . . as one man associated together"[70] just as one man is composed of many limbs; but when they become separated this affects the heart.[71] "For out of it are the issues of life."[72] With us, therefore, by all of us being as truly one man, the service (of G–d) will be established in the heart. And from the affirmative . . .[73] That is why it was said:[74] "To serve Him as *one part.*"[75]

Therefore, my beloved and dear ones: I beg of you to make an effort with all the heart and soul to drive into the heart the love for one's fellow-man, "And none of you should consider in your hearts what is evil to his fellow-man"—it is written.[76] Such (consideration) should never rise in the heart, and if it does rise one is to push it away from his heart "as smoke is driven away,"[77] and truly like an idolatrous thought. For to speak evil is as grave as idolatry, incest, and shedding of blood together.[78] If this be so with speech . . .;[79] and the advantage of the adjustment of thought over speech, whether for the good or for the better, is already known to all the wise of heart.[80]

May the good Lord, who blesses His people with peace,[81] set among you peace and life, forevermore, as is the wish of him who loves you faithfully from heart and soul.

●▲XXIII. "The matter is by the decree of the watch-angels and the say of the holy ones"[1]—the sages of the *Mishnah*, may peace be on them, who taught in their *Mishnah*: "Ten that sit and busy themselves with Torah, the Shechinah dwells amongst them."[2] This is the whole of man.[3] Moreover, (man's) very descent to this world was for the purpose of this ascent, of which there is none higher. For the Indwelling of His Might (*shechinat uzo*) which is in the heights of the upper realms,[4] and whose dread the heavens and the heavens of the heavens cannot contain,[5] dwells and becomes magnified among the children of Israel. Thus it is written: "For I, the Lord, dwell among (*toch*) the children of Israel"[6]—through the occupation with Torah and the commandments *by ten*, expressly,

---

[65] I.e. *to calculate on the motives of other people, and to criticise them.* [66] *Avot 4:10.* [67] I.e. *any one.* [68] *Whereas all of Israel together form a single stature every one complements the other, thereby improving and perfecting him;* cf. *Zohar I:234a (also,* ibid., *167b)*; Kuzary, *III:19; R. Moses Cordovero,* Tomer Devorah *I:4.—*Cf. *also Avot IV:1; Zohar III:85b.* [69] *Judges 20:11;* cf. *Hagigah 26a.* [70] Cf. Mechilta de R. Shimon bar Yochai, *(*ed. *Epstein-Melamed) on Exodus XIX:6 (Jerusalem, 1955; p. 139): "as one body, and one soul."* [71] Ibid., *(also,* Mechilta de R. Yishmael, ad loc.*); Leviticus Rabba IV:6.—See also* infra, *section XXXI.* [72] *Proverbs 4:23—On the theme of the innate unity of Israel see also:*

מצעדי גבר ומחשבות אדם ותחבולותיו. כי זו מלאכת שמים היא ולא מלאכת ב"ו. ולהאמין באמונה שלימה במצות חז"ל והוי שפל רוח בפני כל אדם בכלל כי יציבא מלתא ותקין פתגמא שכ"א מתוקן מחבירו. וכתיב כל [איש] ישראל כאיש אחד חברים. כמו שאיש א' מחובר מאברים רבים ובהפרדם נוגע בלב כי ממנו תוצאות חיים. א"כ אנחנו היות כולנו כאיש א' ממש תיכון העבודה בלב ומכלל הן כו'. וע"כ נאמר ולעבדו שכם אחד דוקא. וע"כ אהוביי ידידיי נא ונא לטרוח בכל לב ונפש לתקוע אהבת רעהו בלבו. ואיש את רעת רעהו אל תחשבו בלבבכם כתיב ולא תעלה על לב לעולם ואם תעלה יהדפנה מלבו כהנדוף עשן וכמו מחשבת ע"ז ממש. כי גדולה לה"ר כנגד ע"ז וג"ע וש"ד. ואם בדבור כך כו' וכבר נודע לכל חכם לב יתרון הכשר המח' על הדבור הן לטוב והן למוטב. וה' הטוב המברך את עמו בשלום ישים עליכם שלום וחיים עד העולם כנפש או"נ מלו"נ:

כג בגזירת עירין פתגמא ומאמר קדישין חכמי המשנה ע"ה ששנו במשנתם עשרה שושבין ועוסקין בתורה שכינה שרויה ביניהם כי זה כל האדם ואף גם זאת היתה כל ירידתו בעוה"ז לצורך עליה זו אשר אין עליה למעלה הימנה כי שכינת עוזו אשר בגבהי מרומים והשמים ושמי השמים לא יכלכלו אימתה. תשכון ותתגדל בתוך בני ישראל כמ"ש כי אני ה' שוכן בתוך בנ"י ע"י עסק התורה והמצות בעשרה דוקא כמ"ש

Yerushalmi, *Nedarim IX:4, and comment.* ad loc.; Likutei Torah of *R. Isaac Luria, on Levit. 19:18;* Likutei Torah *IV:44a; R. Menachem M. Schneerson, "Responsa,"* Kovetz Lubavitch *III:1 (New York, 1946), pp. 4* f. Cf. *J. I. Schochet, "Ahavat Yisrael,"* Di Yiddishe Heim *VIII:3* seq. *(New York, 1966–7), section VIII* et seq. [73] *You may infer the negative;* Sifre, *Deut., sect. 46.* [74] *Zephania 3:9.* [75] *One* part *(see Rashi on Genesis 48:22), or: one* shoulder *(see Targum Yonatan,* ad loc., *and* Likutei Torah *IV:80d), the meaning for both being:* with one consent. [76] *Zechariah 8:17.* [77] Par. *Psalms 68:3.* [78] Yerushalmi, *Peah I:1; Midrash Tehilim XII:2.*

(Notes cont. at end of Hebrew Text)

as our sages, of blessed memory, said: "We compare *toch-toch* . . .";[7] of this it was said: "The Holy One in your midst;"[8] and "There is no matter of holiness with less than ten."[9]

Therefore, too, our sages, of blessed memory, need to derive from Scripture whence we know that even one who sits occupied with Torah . . .[10] And even so they did not find from Scripture support for that, but only for the allotment of a reward to the individual, proportionate to himself and in proportion[11] to the many.[12] But as to causing an indwelling (*hashraah*) of G-d's Holiness, (the individual) cannot be compared to (the multitude) at all.

▲ The difference between causing an indwelling (*hashraah*) and the allotment of a reward is explicit to those who discern ● knowledge. For the "allotment of a reward" is when G-d irradiates the soul that seeks Him with the light of Torah, which is truly the wrapping of His garment—[wherefore the Torah is called "light"[13]], as it is written:[14] "He wraps (Himself in) light, as (with) a garment."[15] But because the soul is limited and finite in all its powers, the light of G-d that radiates in it is also limited, contracted, and vests itself in (the soul). That is why the heart of those who seek the Lord is in a mode of ecstasy at the time of prayer, or the like. For their heart rejoices in Him and exults "Even with exultation and song,"[16] and their soul delights in the pleasantness of the Lord[17] and His light as it becomes revealed from the wrapper of His garment—the Torah; "And His arrow comes forth like lightning."[18] This is the allotment of the reward for Torah, which is always fixed in the soul that labours in (Torah).

▲ The indwelling (*hashraah*), however, is an immense radiation from the light of G-d that radiates in (the soul) without limit and end. It cannot become vested in a finite soul, but encompasses it from above, from "its head to its foot,"[19] as our sages, of blessed memory, said: "The Shechinah hovers over every gathering of ten,"[20] i.e. —over them, from above.[21] Thus it is written: "May the pleasantness of the Lord our G-d be upon us, and the work of our hands establish upon us."[22] This is to say that the pleasantness of the Lord which shone forth through the work of our hands in the occupation with Torah and the commandments [for "The Torah and the Holy One, blessed is He, are entirely one"[23]] become established and "Dwell upon us from above"; for it is without limit and end, and does not become vested

---

[7] *An anology to two occurrences of the word* toch, *from which we derive the minimum of ten participants for a quorum; Berachot 21b; Megilah 23b.* [8] *Isaiah 12:6.* [9] *See* supra, *note 7; cf. Zohar II: 129b; Tikunei Zohar 18:35b;* et passim. [10] *The Shechinah dwells with him.—Avot 3:6; Berachot 6a.* [11] V.L. *omits "and."* [12] I.e. *the reward for his singular efforts is in proportion to communal study of Torah.* [13] *Ta'anit 7b; see also Megilah 16b, and Sefer Habahir 50 (149).* [14] *Psalms 104:2.* [15] Cf. *Zohar III: 245b.* [16] Par. *Isaiah 35:2.* [17] V.L.: *over the Lord.* [18] *Zechariah 9:14.* [19] *The totality of the soul.* [20] *Sanhedrin 39a.* [21] Cf. Tanya *I, end of ch. 11.* [22] *Psalms 90:17.* [23] *Zohar II:90b; see also Zohar, II: 60a,*

כמ"ש רז"ל אתיא תוך תוך כו' וע"ז נאמר בקרבך קדוש ואין דבר שבקדושה בפחות מעשרה ומשום הכי נמי אצטריך להו לרז"ל למילף מקרא מנין שאפילו אחד שיושב ועוסק בתורה כו' ואף גם זאת לא מצאו לו סמך מן המקרא אלא לקביעת שכר בלבד ליחיד לפי ערכו לפי [נ"א ולפי] ערך המרובים אבל לענין השראת קדושת הקב"ה אין לו ערך אליהם כלל וההפרש שבין השראה לקביעות שכר מובן למביני מדע. כי קביעת שכר הוא שמאיר ה' לנפש תדרשנו באור תורתו שהוא מעטה לבושו ממש ולכן נקראת התורה אור שנאמר עוטה אור כשלמה והנפש היא בעלת גבול ותכלית בכל כחותיה לכן גם אור ה' המאיר בה הוא גבולי מצומצם ומתלבש בתוכה וע"כ יתפעל לב מבקשי ה' בשעת התפלה וכיוצא בה כי בו ישמח לבם ויגיל אף גילת ורנן ותתענג נפשם בנועם ה' [נ"א על ה'] ואורו בהגלותו ממעטה לבושו שהיא התורה ויצא כברק חצו וזו היא קביעת שכר התורה הקבועה תמיד בנפש עמלה בה. אבל ההשראה היא הארה עצומה מאור ה' המאיר בה בלי גבול ותכלית ואינו יכול להתלבש בנפש גבולית כ"א מקיף עליה מלמעלה מראשה ועד רגלה כמו שאמרו חז"ל אכל בי עשרה שכינתא שריא כלומר עליהם מלמעלה כמ"ש ויהי נועם ה' עלינו ומעשה ידינו כוננה עלינו כלומר כי נועם ה' אשר הופיע במעשה ידינו בעסק התורה והמצות דאורייתא וקוב"ה כולא חד יתכונן וישרה עלינו מלמעלה להיותו בלי גבול ותכלית ואינו מתלבש

בנפשנו

and *III: 73a.* Cf. Kitzurim Vehe'arot, *p. 104* f. *See* Tanya *I: 4, and 23.*

in our soul and intellect. That is why we do not apprehend with our intellect the delightfulness and sweetness of the unlimited and infinite pleasantness of the Lord, and the splendour of the Shechinah, established and dwelling upon us through the work of our hands in Torah and the commandments (performed) specifically en masse.[24] And of this our sages, of blessed memory, said: "In this world there is no reward for the commandments."[25] For it is impossible for the world to attain it [the reward] but by divesting the soul from the body; and even then by way of grace, as it is written: "Also unto You, O Lord, belongs the mercy, for You render to each according to his work."[26] Thus our sages, of blessed memory, said that the Holy One, blessed is He, gives unto the righteous a capacity . . .[27] It is not so, however, with the angels, as I heard from my masters that if there were an angel standing in the presence of a gathering of ten Israelites [even if there are no words of Torah between them], an unlimited and infinite fear and awe would then befall him from the Shechinah that dwells over them that he would become totally nullified.[28]

•▲ Therefore, evil in my eyes is the behaviour that takes place under the sun[29] in general, and especially among my brethren and friends that draw near unto the Lord, "drawing near means prayer:"[30] after prayer or before it there is formed a "seat of scoffers," the Merciful save us, as our sages, of blessed memory, said: "Two who sit together, and there are no words of Torah between them. . . ."[31] And if a "seat of scoffers" is formed by ten, over which the Shechinah dwells, there is no greater insult and shaming of the Shechinah than that, the Merciful save us. And when our sages, of blessed memory, said of him who commits a transgression in secret that "He repulses the feet of the Shechinah,"[32] Heaven forfend, he who commits a transgression in public repulses the whole measure of the stature of the Creator, as it were, as our sages, of blessed memory, said: "It is impossible for Me and him . . ."[33] except that "The King is held captive in the tresses . . ."[34] But woe unto him who repulses the Shechinah when G–d will raise (the Shechinah) and say to her:[35] "Awake, arise from the dust . . .";[36] and "For three things Israel is kept back in exile: because they repulse the Shechinah, and because they shame the Shechinah . . .", as mentioned in the sacred *Zohar.*[37]

•▲ Therefore, my beloved ones, my brethren

---

[24] *As opposed to singular, individual activity.* [25] *Kidushin 39b.* [26] *Psalms 62:13.* [27] *To receive their reward. Sanhedrin 100b.* Cf. supra, *sect. III, note 5.* [28] *Thus, unlike the soul, an angel is unable to apprehend and endure the manifestation of the Shechinah.* [29] Par. *Eccles. 2:17;* etc. [30] Tanchuma, Vayera: *8; see also Genesis Rabba 49:8, and 93:6; Agadat Bereishit 22:2.* [31] *Avot 3:2.* [32] *Kidushin 31a.* [33] *Sotah 5a.* [34] *Song 7:6. The Shechinah is bound to Israel, regardless; thus, by their improper acts the Shechinah is drawn into exile with them, per force, as it were; see Levit. Rabba 31:4;* Tanchuma, Nitzavim: *3; Tikunei Zohar 6:21b;* Tanya *I, ch. 45.* [35] *Isaiah 52:2.* [36] Cf. *Zohar II:7a.* [37] *Zohar III:75b.*

בנפשנו ושכלנו ועי"כ אין אנו משיגים בשכלנו הנעימות והעריבות מנועם ה' וזיו השכינה בלי גבול ותכלית אשר מתכונן ושורה עלינו במעשה ידינו בתורה ומצות ברבים דוקא. ועי"ז ארז"ל שכר מצוה בהאי עלמא ליכא כי אי אפשר לעולם להשיגו כי אם בהתפשטות הנפש מהגוף ואף גם זאת על דרך החסד כמ"ש ולך ה' חסד כי אתה תשלם לאיש כמעשהו וכמו שארז"ל שהקב"ה נותן כח בצדיקים כו'. משא"כ במלאכים כמו ששמעתי מרבותי כי אילו נמצא מלאך אחד עומד במעמד עשרה מישראל ביחד אף שאינם מדברים בדברי תורה תפול עליו אימתה ופחד בלי גבול ותכלית משכינתא דשריא עלייהו עד שהיה מתבטל ממציאותו לגמרי ועי"כ רע בעיני המעשה אשר נעשה תחת השמש בכלל ובפרט בין אחיי ורעיי הנגשים אל ה' הגשה זו תפלה ואחר התפלה או לפניה נעשה מושב לצים ר"ל כמו שארז"ל שנים שיושבין ואין ביניהם ד"ת כו' ואם נעשה מושב לצים בעשרה דשכינתא שריא עלייהו אין לך עלבונא וקלנא דשכינתא גדול מזה רחמנא ליצלן ואם אמרו רז"ל על העובר עבירה בסתר שדוחק רגלי השכינה ח"ו העובר עבירה ברבים דוחק כל שיעור קומה של יוצר בראשית כביכול כמ"ש רז"ל אין אני והוא וכו' אלא שמלך אסור ברהטים כו'. אבל ווי למאן דדחקין לשכינתא כד יוקים לה קודשא ב"ה ויימא לה התנערי מעפר קומי וגו' ועל תלת מילין מתעכבי ישראל בגלותא על דדחקין לשכינתא ועל דעבדין קלנא בשכינתא וכו' כמ"ש בזוה"ק. על כן אהוביי אחיי ורעיי

and friends: do not commit this great evil and "Give glory unto the Lord your G-d before it grows dark,"[38] i.e., between *Mincha*[39] and *Ma'ariv*,[40] by studying every week-day in groups of ten the *pnimiyut*[41] of Torah, i.e. the Aggada contained in the work *Ayin Ya'akov*. For most of the secrets of the Torah are concealed in it,[42] and it atones man's sins, as explained in the writings of R. Isaac Luria, of blessed memory.[43] The revealed parts therein[44] are the ways of G-d wherein man is to walk, and (enable him) to devise counsels in his soul[45] pertaining to matters of heaven[46] and matters of the world,[47] as is known to all the wise of heart.[48] (They are) also to learn somewhat in *Shulchan Aruch-Orach Chayim*, the laws that are essential to every person. Of this our sages, of blessed memory, said: "Whoever repeats *halachot* every day . . ."[49]—referring to the clarified and adjudged rulings that are of practical relevance, as explained ▲in the commentary of Rashi, *ad loc.* On the holy Sabbath, towards the time of *Mincha*, they should occupy themselves with the laws of the Sabbath. For "The law of the Sabbath is important."[50] It is easy for man to stumble in it, Heaven forfend, even in the matter of a prohibition involving extirpation and stoning, because of a lack of knowledge, and "Error in teaching amounts to intentional sin,"[51] Heaven forfend. No need to mention (that the same applies to) the rabbinic injunctions which are ever so numerous, and especially with respect to the prohibitions of *muktzah*,[52] of which there are many; and as our sages, of blessed memory, said: "The words of the Sopherim[53] are more severe than the words of Torah."[54] For whoever transgresses the words of the sages, even but a light injunction of theirs [as, for instance, he who eats before the evening-prayer, and the like] is guilty of death,[55] just as one who transgresses the severe matters of the Torah. And let no individual separate himself from the congregation, even to learn something else; rather, (each one is to participate) in whatever the congregation busies itself with. There is no need to mention that one should not leave if there are not ten without him; to him I apply the verse "And those that leave the Lord shall be consumed . . .",[56] as our sages, of blessed memory, said with respect to every sacred matter.[57] For there is no holiness as the holiness of the Torah[58]—whereas "The Torah and the Holy One, blessed is He, are entirely one."[59] Thus, whoever separates himself from the community . . .[60] But he that will listen to me shall dwell securely,[61] and in his and in our own days Judah shall be saved and Jerusalem shall dwell securely,[62]—amen, may this be (His) will.

---

[38] *Jeremiah 13:16.* [39] *Afternoon-prayer.* [40] *Evening-prayer.* [41] *The "inner part," the "soul," of the Torah: the esoteric teachings of the Torah.* [42] *In the* Aggada. [43] *See* Hilchot Talmud Torah, *II:2 (and notes* ad loc., *in* ed. *N.Y. 1965); cf. Foreword to the commentary on* Shir Hashirim *attributed to Nachmanides.* [44] I.e. *the non-mystical parts.* [45] Par. *Psalms 13:3.* [46] *Religious affairs.* [47] *Secular affairs.* [48] Cf. Sifre *on Deut. 11:22; Avot de R. Natan 29:7.* [49] *Megilah 28b.* [50] *Shabbat 12a; see Rashi* ad loc. [51] *Avot 4:13.* [52] *That which is forbidden for use or handling on the Sabbath and Holy Days.* [53] *The Scribes,* i.e., *the rabbis.* [54] Yerushalmi, *Berachot I:4; Eruvin 21b.* [55] *Berachot 4b.*

ורעיי אל נא תרעו הרעה הגדולה הזאת ותנו כבוד להי אלהיכם בטרם יחשך דהיינו בין מנחה למעריב כל ימות החול ללמוד בעשרה פנימיות התורה שהיא אגדה שבש׳ ע״י שרוב סודות התורה גנוזין בה ומכפרת עונותיו של אדם כמבואר בכהאריז״ל והנגלות שבה הן דרכי ה׳ שילך בהם האדם וישית עצות בנפשו במילי דשמיא ובמילי דעלמא וכידוע לכל חכמי לב וגם ללמוד מעט בשו״ע או״ח הלכות הצריכות לכל אדם וע״ז ארז״ל כל השונה הלכות בכל יום כו׳ שהן הלכות ברורות ופסוקות הלכה למעשה כמבואר בפרש״י ז״ל שם ובשבת קדש בעלות המנחה יעסקו בהל׳ שבת כי הלכתא רבתא לשבתא ובקל יכול האדם ליכשל בה ח״ו אפילו באיסור כרת וסקילה מחסרון ידיעה ושגגת תלמוד עולה זדון ח״ו ואצ״ל באיסורי דברי סופרים שרבו כמו רבו למעלה ובפרט באיסורי מוקצה דשכיחי טובא וחמורים ד״ס יותר מד״ת כמ״ש רז״ל שכל העובר על דברי חכמים אפילו באיסור קל של דבריהם כמו האוכל קודם תפלת ערבית וכה״ג חייב מיתה כעובר על חמורות שבתורה וכל יחיד אל יפרוש עצמו מן הציבור אפילו ללמוד ענין אחר כ״א בדבר שהציבור עסוקין בו ואצ״ל שלא יצא החוצה אם לא יהיו עשרה מבלעדו ועליו אני קורא הפסוק ועוזבי ה׳ יכלו כו׳ כמשארז״ל על כל דבר שבקדושה. כי אין קדושה כקדושת התורה דאורייתא וקוב״ה כולא חד. וכל הפורש מן הציבור כו׳ ושומע לי ישכון בטח ובימיו ובימינו תושע יהודה וירושלים תשכון לבטח אמן כן יהי רצון:

כד אהוביי

---

[56] *Isaiah I: 28.* [57] Yerushalmi, *Megilah 4: 4;* cf. *Berachot 8a.* [58] *Zohar III: 81a.* [59] Supra, *note 23.* [60] *Semachot II: 10; Maimonides,* Hilchot Evel *I: 10.* [61] *Proverbs I: 33.* [62] Par. *Jeremiah 23: 6, and 33: 16.*

●▲XXIV. My beloved, my brethren:

I beg you, do not act wickedly, friends that are beloved unto their Maker and hateful unto their inclination.[1] Let no one make himself wicked before the Omnipresent the one hour[2] He has chosen of all day in which to gather and stand before Him [during that hour]. It is an auspicious time before Him to become revealed, to come into the miniature sanctuary[3] to attend to the Abode (*Shechinah*) of His Glory, "He who dwells with them in the midst of their impurity,"[4] and to be available to those who seek and beseech Him and them that hope for Him.

Now, he who recounts his needs[5] shows of himself that he does not desire to contemplate and to see the manifestation of His majestic glory. Thus he becomes an impure chariot[6] to the "supernal fool" (*ch'sil ha'elyon*)[7] of whom it is said "The fool does not desire understanding . . .",[8] as mentioned in the *Zohar* and by R. Isaac Luria, of blessed memory.[9] This means, he does not desire to contemplate and to see the preciousness of the splendour of the greatness of the King of all kings, the Holy One, blessed is He, which becomes revealed in that hour above, and also below, to those who desire to look to His glory and greatness which wraps and vests itself in the words of the liturgy [which has been properly arranged for everyone] and becomes revealed to each according to his intellect and the root of his soul, as it is written:[10] "Man *yeholel* (is praised) according to his intellect," the *ktiv*[11] being: *yehalel* (praises).[12]

Now, the kingdom of heaven is similar to a kingdom on earth.[13] It is customary for a king to have the hiding-place of his strength in the innermost chambers, with several guards at the doors, [[14]so] that many people await for days and years to see his might and glory. And when he wishes to become revealed to all, he[15] proclaims throughout his kingdom to gather and to stand before him, in order to show them his majestic glory and the precious splendour of his greatness. Now, whoever will stand before him not caring to see him, and busies himself with his needs, how inferior, foolish and simple is he; "He is like the beasts that speak not"[16] in the eyes of all creatures. Moreover, it is a dishonour to the king, by demonstrating before him that to have pleasure and delight from looking at his glory and beauty is of no more esteem in his eyes than busying himself with his (own) needs. Also, he forfeits

---

Section XXIV

[1] *The inclination towards evil.—* [*The Hebrew passage is a play on words (*יוצרי—יצרי*),* cf. *Berachot 61a; Ruth Rabba 3:1.*] [2] Par. *Eduyot 5:6.* [3] *The Synagogue;* cf. *Megilah 19a.* [4] *Levit. 16:16;* cf. *Yoma 56b.* [5] *He who focuses his prayers on his wants and needs.* [6] *See* supra, *sect. XV, note 24, for the connotation of the word "chariot." This notion applies to the realm of impurity as well as to the realm of holiness; see* supra, *sect. II, note 16.* [7] *The principal aspect and source of the forces of evil; see* infra, *note 9;* Torah Or, *p. 102c.* [8] *"—but only that his heart may lay itself bare"; Proverbs 18:2.* Cf. Chovot Halevovot, Avodat Elokim, *ch. 4.* [9] *See Zohar I: 179a* f., *and the comment.*

כד אהוביי אחיי אל נא תרעו ריעים האהובים ליוצרם ושנואים ליצרם ואל יעשה אדם עצמו רשע שעה אחת לפני המקום אשר בחר בה מכל היום להקהל ולעמוד לפניו בשעה זו שהיא עת רצון לפניו להתגלות לבוא אל המקדש מעט לפקוד לשכינת כבודו השוכן אתם בתוך טומאותם ולהמצא לדורשיו ומבקשיו ומייחליו והמספר בצרכיו מראה בעצמו שאינו חפץ להתבונן ולראות בגילוי כבוד מלכותו ונעשה מרכבה טמאה לכסיל העליון שנאמר עליו לא יחפוץ כסיל בתבונה כו' כמ"ש הזהר והאריז"ל דהיינו שאינו חפץ להתבונן ולראות ביקר תפארת גדולתו של מלך מה"מ הקב"ה הנגלות למעלה בשעה זו וגם למטה אל החפצים להביט אל כבודו וגדלו המתעטף ומתלבש בתוך תיבות התפלה הסדורה בפי כל ומתגלה לכל אחד לפי שכלו ושורש נשמתו כדכתיב לפי שכלו יהולל איש יהלל כתיב ומלכותא דרקיע כעין מלכותא דארעא שדרך המלך להיות חביון עוזו בחדרי חדרים וכמה שומרים על הפתחים (עד) אשר כמה וכמה מצפים ימים ושנים לראות עוזו וכבודו וכשעלה רצונו להתגלות לכל והעביר קול בכל מלכותו להקהל ולעמוד לפניו להראותם כבוד מלכותו ויקר תפארת גדולתו מי שעומד לפניו ואינו חושש לראותו ומתעסק בצרכיו כמה גרוע וסכל ופתי הוא ונמשל כבהמות נדמה בעיני כל הבריות וגם הוא בזיון המלך בהראותו לפניו שאינו ספון בעיניו לקבל נחת ושעשועים מהביט אל כבודו ויפיו יותר מעסק צרכיו וגם הוא מתחייב בנפשו

---

of R. Moses Zacuto a.l. [10] *Proverbs 12:8.* [11] *The textual writ, as opposed to the textual reading* (cf. supra, *sect. XIX*). [12] *Thus reading: man praises (or prays) according to his intellect. The content of one's prayer reflects one's intellect and, correspondingly, the extent of revelation elicited by that prayer;* cf. supra, *sect. XII, and note 38* a.l., *for a similar interpretation.* [13] *See Berachot 58a; Zohar I:197a.* [14] *Brackets appear in the text.* [15] *For the allegory following, see Zohar II:131a–b (Zohar I:256a, sect. 22).* [16] Par. *Psalms 49:13, 21.*—I.e. *irrational.*

his life unto the king by demonstrating how he insults and dishonours the king before all who see. Of this it was said: "And the fools raise the insult."[17] This means to say that though he is a fool, he should not "raise the insult," that the insult becomes ▲ apparent to all. Our sages, of blessed memory, therefore, ordained that with prayer one should be "As standing before the King."[18] At least he should make himself appear as if he stands etc. to the sight of all who look with physical eyes at his actions and words, even though the fool has no thought. That is why all the prayers were ordained for the one that will contemplate on them properly. But he that does not show this, makes himself guilty, at the risk of his life, and of him it was said in the sacred *Zohar*[19] that "He causes an insult against the Supernal Arrangement and shows that he is separate and has no part in the G–d of Israel," the Merciful save us.

Therefore,[20] I come to act as an agent of our sages, of blessed memory, to enact a decree to apply equally to every one: No idle talk is to be spoken[21] from the moment the deputy of the congregation[22] begins to recite the prayer until the end of the last *Kadish*,[23] at *Shacharit*, *Mincha*, and *Arvit*.[24] And he who will disobey wittingly shall sit on the ground and beg of three people to release him from the supernal excommunication. "As he will repent, he will be healed,"[25] and fully retro-actively, no excommunication will apply to him. For, from the very outset it applies only to those that rebel and revolt, who do not care at all to seek atonement from Heaven and from the creatures for this sin which calls for judgment. Also, (this applies) only when they speak deliberately, with contempt, but not to one who forgets, or unwittingly uttered some words, for he does not require a release at all; "And G–d who is righteous, examines the hearts and the kidneys."[26] Do good, O Lord, unto the good and unto those that are upright in their hearts.[27]

●▲ XXV. "To comprehend the words of understanding"[1] stated in the sacred book called *Tzavaat Ribash*[2]—[though in fact it is not at all his testament,[3] and he did not ordain anything before his passing; they are mere gleanings of his pure sayings that were gathered, "gleanings upon gleanings,"[4]

---

[17] *Proverbs 3:35.* [18] *Berachot 33a.* [19] *Zohar II: 131b;* cf. *Zohar I: 256a.* [20] Par. *Bava Kama 84b.* [21] *See references cited* supra, *note 19, and commentary* Mikdash Melech, ad loc.; Sefer Chassidim, *sect. 18. See also* Mikdash Melech *on Zohar III: 75b.* [22] *Who leads the congregation in prayer.* [23] *Prayer of sanctification of G–d's Name.* [24] *Emended according to* H.V. [25] Par. *Isaiah 6:10.* [26] *Psalms 7:10.* [27] *Psalms 125:4.*

Section XXV
[1] Par. *Proverbs 1:2.* [2] Lit.: *Testament of R. Israel Ba'al Shem.* [3] *Emended according to the glosses of Tzemach Tzedek (*Kitzurim Vehe'arot, *p. 40);* L.H. [4] Par. *Ta'anit 6b.*

בנפשו למלך על הראות קלונו ובזיונו את המלך לעין כל רואה וע"ז נאמר וכסילים מרים קלון כלומר אף שהוא כסיל לא יהי' מרים קלון שיהי' נראה הקלון לעין כל. וע"כ קבעו חז"ל בתפלה כאלו עומד לפני המלך עכ"פ יהי' מראה בעצמו כאלו עומד כו' לעין כל רואה בעיני בשר אל מעשיו ודיבוריו אף שאין לו מחשבה לכסיל וע"ז הענין נתקן כל התפלות למתבונן בהם היטב ומי שאינו מראה כן מתחיב בנפשו ועליו אמרו בזהר הק' דאנהיג קלנא בתקונא עילאה ואחזי פרודא ולית ליה חולקא באלהא דישראל ר"ל ע"כ שליחותייהו דרז"ל קא עבידנא לגזור גזירה שוה לכל נפש שלא לשוח שיחה בטלה משיתחיל הש"ץ להתפלל התפלה עד גמר קדיש בתרא שחרית ערבית ומנחה וכו'. והעובר ע"ז בזדון ישב על הארץ ויבקש מג' אנשים שיתירו לו נידוי שלמעלה ושב ורפא לו ולא חל עליו שום נידוי למפרע כל עיקר כי מתחלתו לא חל כ"א על המורדים והפושעים שאינם חוששים כלל לבקש כפרה מן השמים ומן הבריות על העון פלילי הזה. וגם דוקא כשמדברים בזדון בשאט נפש ולא על השוכח או שנזרקו מפיו כמה תיבות בלא מתכוין שא"צ התרה כלל ובוחן לבות וכליות אלקים צדיק. הטיבה ה' לטובים ולישרים בלבותם:

כה להבין אמרי בינה מ"ש בספר הנק' צוואת ריב"ש הגם שבאמת אינה צוואתו ולא ציוה כלל לפני פטירתו רק הם לקוטי אמרותיו הטהורות שלקטו לקוטי בתר לקוטי ולא

and (the compilers) did not know how to determine the phraseology exactly in its proper fashion. The connotation, however, is absolutely true.]—we shall precede[5] with the saying of our sages, of blessed memory: "Whoever is in a rage is as if he worships idols."[6] The reason is clear to those that have understanding, because at the time of his anger faith has departed from him. For were he to believe that what happened to him is of the Lord's doing, he would not become angry at all. And though it is a person possessed of free choice cursing him, or hitting him, or causing damage to his money, and therefore guilty according to the laws of man and the laws of Heaven for having chosen evil, nevertheless, as regards the person harmed—this was already decreed from Heaven, and "The Omnipresent has many deputies."[7] And not only this, but even at that particular time when he hits or curses him, there is vested in him a force from G-d and "The breath of His mouth,"[8] blessed be He, which animates and sustains him, and as it is written: "For the Lord told him: 'curse!'."[9] Now, where did He say (so) to Shimi? But this thought, that occurred in Shimi's heart and mind, descended from G-d, and the "*Breath of His mouth*—which animates—*all their hosts*" animated the spirit of Shimi at the time he spoke those words to David.[10] For if the "Breath of His mouth," blessed be He, had departed from the spirit of Shimi for a single moment, he could not have spoken at all.

▲ ([11]And that is the meaning of "For the Lord told him—[at that very moment, indeed]—*curse David*, who then shall say ●. . ." And as known what the Baal Shem Tov, of blessed memory, said[12] on the verse[13] "Forever, Oh Lord, Your word stands in the heavens": The combinations of the letters wherewith the heavens were created, i.e. the fiat "Let there be a firmament . . .",[14] stand and remain vested in the Heavens forever, to vivify and sustain them. Thus unlike the theory of the philosophers who deny individual providence.[15] They, in their false imagination, compare the work of G-d, the Maker of Heaven and Earth, to the work of man and his schemes: when the metal-smith has completed a vessel, the vessel no longer needs the hands of the smith. For though his hands are removed from it, it remains intact by itself. But their eyes are bedaubed so that they cannot see[16] the great difference between man's work and schemes—[which is (the production of) something out of something (*yesh meyesh*), except that he changes the form and the image]—and the making

[5] *For the passage in question see* infra, *note 81*. [6] *Zohar I:27b; III:179a, and 234b; Zohar Chadash 21a; Maimonides,* Hilchot De'ot *II:3*. Cf. *Shabbat 105b; Nedarim 22b*. [7] *Zohar III:36b; Rashi on Exodus 16:32.—See Ta'anit 18b;* Mechilta, *and Rashi on Exodus 21:13;* Emunot Vedeot, *by R. Saadiah Gaon, IV:5. See also Numbers Rabba 18:22;* etc. Boneh Yerushalayim, *sect. 122*. [8] *Psalms 33:6*. [9] *II Samuel 16:10*. [10] *See* Sefer Hachinuch, *sect. 241 (*cf. Minchat Chinuch, ad loc., *and* Tanchuma, Vayikra*:7)*: Reshit Chochmah, Sha'ar Ha'anavah, *ch. 3*. Cf. *references cited* supra, *note 7*. [11] *Brackets appear in the text*. [12] *See* Tanya *II:1, and* cf. *Midrash Tehilim, 119:36. (See* Hayom Yom, ed. *R. Mena-*

ולא ידעו לכוין הלשון על מתכונתו. אך המכוון הוא אמת לאמיתו. והוא בהקדים מארז"ל כל הכועס כאילו עובד עכו"ם וכו'. והטעם מובן ליודעי בינה לפי שבעת כעסו נסתלקה ממנו האמונה כי אילו היה מאמין שמאת ה' היתה זאת לו לא היה בכעס כלל ואף שבן אדם שהוא בעל בחירה מקללו או מכהו או מזיק ממונו ומתחייב בדיני אדם ובדיני שמים על רוע בחירתו אעפ"כ על הניזק כבר נגזר מן השמים והרבה שלוחים למקום ולא עוד אלא אפילו בשעה זו ממש שמכהו או מקללו מתלבש בו כח ה' ורוח פיו ית' המחייהו ומקיימו וכמ"ש כי ה' אמר לו קלל והיכן אמר לשמעי אלא שמחשבה זו שנפלה לשמעי בלבו ומוחו ירדה מאת ה' ורוח פיו המחי' כל צבאם החיה רוחו של שמעי בשעה שדיבר דברים אלו לדוד כי אילו נסתלק רוח פיו ית' רגע אחד מרוחו של שמעי לא יכול לדבר מאומה (וזהו כי ה' אמר לו בעת ההיא ממש קלל את דוד ומי יאמר לו וגו' וכנודע מ"ש הבעש"ט ז"ל ע"פ לעולם ה' דברך נצב בשמים שצירוף אותיות שנבראו בהן השמים שהוא מאמר יהי רקיע כו' הן נצבות ועומדות מלובשות בשמים לעולם להחיותם ולקיימם ולא כהפלוסופים שכופרים בהשגחה פרטית ומדמין בדמיונם הכוזב את מעשה ה' עושה שמים וארץ למעשה אנוש ותחבולותיו כי כאשר יצא לצורף כלי שוב אין הכלי צריך לידי הצורף שאף שידיו מסולקות הימנו הוא קיים מעצמו וטח מראות עיניהם ההבדל הגדול שבין מעשה אנוש ותחבולותיו שהוא יש מיש רק שמשנה הצורה והתמונה למעשה שמים

chem M. Schneerson, p. 99).—*See also the anthology* Sefer Ba'al Shem Tov, *section* Bereshit: *par. 48–51.* [13] *Psalms 119:89.* [14] *Genesis I:6;* cf. Likutei Torah-Torat Shmuel, *vol. III, ch. 20.* [15] *See* Moreh Nevuchim, *III:17.* [16] Par. *Isaiah 44:18.*

of heaven and earth [which is *creatio ex nihilo* (*yesh meayin*)]. (The latter) is a wonder much greater than, for example, the splitting of the Red Sea—which the Lord caused to go back "By a strong east-wind all that night . . . and the waters were divided."[17] If the wind had ceased but for a moment, the waters would again have flowed downward, as is their way and nature. They would not have stood upright as a wall, even though this characteristic of the water,[18] too, was created and innovated *ex nihilo* (*yesh meayin*). A wall of stones stands erect by itself, without any wind, but this is not of the nature of water. Now, *a fortiori*, and *a minori ad majus*, with respect to the creation of substantiality *ex nihilo* [which transcends nature and is more wondrous than the splitting of the Red Sea], how much more so would a withdrawal, Heaven forfend, of the force of the Creator [(bringing about) substantiality *ex nihilo*] from the creature, cause the creature to revert to absolute naught and nothingness! The operative force[19] thus needs to remain constantly in the effect,[20] to vivify and sustain it.[21] This aspect is the "word of the Lord" and the "breath of His mouth" of the ten fiats wherewith the universe was created.[22] And even this material world, and the inorganic class in it, their vivification and sustenance is the "word of the Lord" of the ten fiats that has become vested in them and sustains them to be inorganic matter and substantiality *ex nihilo*, so that they will not revert to the absolute naught and nothingness they had been. And this is the meaning of the statement of R. Isaac Luria, of blessed memory,[23] that there is a type of soul and spiritual vivification even in inorganic matter as stones, and dust, and water.[24]

●▲ Now it is known to those adept in the esoteric science that the "word of the Lord" is referred to as Shechinah, in the terminology of our sages, of blessed memory, and as *imma tataah* and *matrunita*, in the terminology of the *Zohar* [especially at the beginning of section *Vaeyra*], because it dwells and vests itself in the creatures to vivify them.[25] In the terminology of the Cabbalists it is called *malchut*, relating to "The word of the king is regnant,"[26] because the king conducts his kingdom through his edict; and also for other reasons known to those adept in the esoteric science.[27]

Now it is known that there is a rank and level of *malchut* of Atzilut, and a rank of *malchut* of Beriah, . . . *Malchut* of Atzilut is the "word of the Lord" which vivifies and brings into being the great souls that are of the rank of Atzilut, as the soul of Adam of whom it is said "And He blew into his nostrils a soul of life;"[28] and as the souls of the patriarchs, and the prophets, and the like ([29]who were

---

[17] *Exodus 14:2.* [18] *To flow downwards.* [19] *The force of the Creator.* [20] *The creature.* [21] Cf. Kuzary *III:11.* [22] *Avot IV:1; see* supra, *sect. V, note 79.* [23] Etz Chayim *39:3; see also* ibid., *50: et passim.* Cf. Tanya *I:38, and II:1.* [24] *This whole section (from "what the Ba'al Shem Tov said" onwards) is a résumé of the first two chapters of the* Sha'ar Hayichud. [25] *See Introduction,* s.v. Malchut; cf. supra, *sect. VIII. See also* Pardess Rimonim *23:4.* [26] *Eccles 8:4; see comment.* a.l. [27] Cf. supra, *sect. XX, notes 47 and 49.* [28] *(Emended according to* Kitzurim Vehe'arot *p. 40, and* L.H.*).—Genesis 2:7; see* supra, *section XII, note 48.* [29] *Brackets appear in the text.*

שמים וארץ שהוא יש מאין והוא פלא גדול יותר מקריעת ים סוף עד"מ אשר הוליך ה' ברוח קדים עזה כל הלילה ויבקעו המים ואילו פסק הרוח כרגע היו המים חוזרים וניגרים במורד כדרכם וטבעם ולא קמו כחומה אף שטבע זה במים הוא ג"כ נברא ומחודש יש מאין שהרי חומת אבנים נצבת מעצמה בלי רוח רק שטבע המים אינו כן וכ"ש וק"ו בבריאת יש מאין שהיא למעלה מהטבע והפלא ופלא יותר מקריעת י"ס עאכ"ו שבהסתלקות ח"ו כח הבורא יש מאין מן הנברא ישוב הנברא לאין ואפס ממש אלא צ"ל כח הפועל בנפעל תמיד להחיותו ולקיימו ובחי' זה הוא דבר ה' ורוח פיו שבעשרה מאמרות שבהן נברא העולם ואפילו ארץ הלזו הגשמית ובחי' דומם שבה חיותן וקיומן הוא דבר ה' מי' מאמרות המלובש בהן ומקיימן להיות דומם ויש מאין ולא יחזרו לאין ואפס ממש כשהיו וז"ש האריז"ל שגם בדומם כאבנים ועפר ומים יש בהם בחי' נפש וחיות רוחניית. והנה נודע לי"ח כי דבר ה' נק' בשם שכינה בלשון רז"ל ואימא תתאה ומטרוניתא בלשון הזהר ובפרט בר"פ וארא לפי ששוכן ומתלבש בנבראים להחיותם ובלשון המקובלים נק' בשם מלכות ע"ש דבר מלך שלטון כי המלך מנהיג מלכותו בדיבורו ועוד טעמים אחרים ידועים לי"ח ומודעת זאת כי יש בחי' ומדריגת מל' דאצילות ובחי' מל' דבריאה וכו'. ופי' מל' דאצילות הוא דבר ה' המחי' ומהוה נשמות הגדולות שהן מבחי' אצילות כמו נשמת אדה"ר שנא' בו ויפח באפיו כו' וכמו נשמות האבות והנביאים וכיוצא בהן (שהיו מרכבה

truly a "chariot unto G–d" and in a state of self-abnegation in relation to Him.[30] Thus our sages, of blessed memory, said:[31] "The Shechinah speaks from the throat of Moses;"[32] and likewise with all the prophets and those possessed of the Holy Spirit: the Supernal Voice and Speech vested itself in their actual voice and speech, as mentioned by R. Isaac Luria, of blessed memory).

Malchut of Beriah is the "word of the Lord" which vivifies and brings into being the souls and angels in the realm of Beriah, whose level is not like the level of Atzilut. . . . And *malchut* of Asiyah is the "word of the Lord" which vivifies and brings into this world, in its totality, including the element of dust, and the water that is below ●▲the earth. [[33]However, in the countries of the heathens[34] the vivification is by way of an investment of the extraneous patron-angels (*sarim hachitzonim*) that are appointed over the seventy nations.[35] That is, a spark from the "word of the Lord," called *malchut* of Asiyah, descends and radiates over the supernal patron-angels in a way of encompassing from aloft, but does not truly vest itself in them. Rather, the vivification issues to them from this radiation shining over them from aloft, in a mode of encompassment. And from the patron-angels vivification issues to the heathens, and to the cattle, beasts, and fowl that are in their lands, and to the physical earth, and to the physical heavens, i.e. the planets.[36] ([37]However, the heavens and the earth, and the cattle, beasts, and fowl that are pure, are influenced by the *kelipat nogah*.[38] The impure (animals) and the souls of the heathens, however, are (influenced) by the other *kelipot*).[39] Now, in the lands of the heathens, the heavens and the earth and all they contain, are all esteemed as truly nothing in relation to the patron-angels—which are their vivification and sustenance. The patron-angels themselves are esteemed as truly nothing in relation to the vivification issuing to them from the spark of the "word of the Lord" which radiates over them from aloft. And even so, the vivification issuing to them from this radiation is in them in a state of exile. That is why they are called *elohim acherim* (other gods)[40] [while they call *Him* —"G–d of the gods"[41]], as if they, too, are in the category of Divinity. The heathens who are influenced by them, therefore, are truly idolaters, until the time of the end when death and the *sitra achara*[42] will be swallowed up,[43] and "Then I shall turn to the nations

---

[30] *See* supra, *section XV, note 24.* [31] *See Zohar III: 232a;* ibid., *036b.* Cf. *Exodus Rabba 3:15, and comment. by R. David Luria* ad loc.; *Zohar III: 7a, and 265a.* [32] I.e. *Moses was but a passive tool for the speech of the Shechinah, as if he himself did not exist as a separate entity.* Cf. Tanya *I: 34.* [33] *Brackets appear in the text.* [34] L.H. *substitutes* nations, *for this, and all subsequent instances of* heathens. [35] Cf. *Zohar III: beg. of 244a* (R'ayah Mehemma); *Tikunei Zohar 24: 69a.* [36] Cf. *Tikunei Zohar 32: 76b.* [37] *Brackets appear in the text.* [38] *See note following.* [39] *G–d has made one thing opposite the other. (Eccles. 7: 14; see* supra, *sect. II note 16). Everything in one realm has a corresponding opposite in another*

מרכבה לה׳ ממש ובטלים ממש במציאות אליו
כמארז״ל שכינה מדברת מתוך גרונו של משה וכן
כל הנביאים ובעלי רוה״ק היה קול ודבור העליון
מתלבש בקולם ודבורם ממש כמ״ש האריז״ל) ומל׳
דבריאה הוא דבר ה׳ המחיה ומהוה הנשמות והמלאכי׳
שבעולם הבריאה שאין מעלתם כמעלת האצי׳ וכו׳
ומלכות דעשיה הוא דבר ה׳ המחיה ומהוה את עוה״ז
בכללו עד יסוד העפר והמים אשר מתחת לארץ.
(אלא שבארצות העו״ג החיות הוא על ידי התלבשות
שרים החיצוני׳ הממוני׳ על ע׳ אומות דהיינו שיורד
ניצוץ מדבר ה׳ הנקרא בשם מלכות דעשיה ומאיר
על השרים של מעלה בבחי׳ מקיף מלמעלה אך אינו
מתלבש בהם ממש אלא נמשך להם חיות מהארה
זו שמאיר עליהם מלמעלה בבחי׳ מקיף ומהשרים
נשפע חיות לעו״ג ולבהמות חיות ועופות שבארצותיהם
ולארץ הגשמית ולשמים הגשמיים שהם הגלגלים
(אלא ששמים וארץ ובהמות וחיות ועופות טהורים
נשפעי׳ מקליפת נוגה והטמאים ונפשות העו״ג
משאר קליפות). והנה שמים וארץ וכל אשר בהם
בארצות עו״ג כולם כלא ממש חשיבי לגבי השרים
שהם חיותם וקיומם. והשרים כלא ממש חשיבי לגבי
החיות הנמשך להם מהניצוץ מדבר ה׳ המאיר עליהם
מלמעלה ואעפ״כ החיות הנמשך לתוכם מהארה זו
הוא בבחי׳ גלות בתוכם שלכן נקראי׳ בשם אלקי׳
אחרים וקרו ליה אלהא דאלהיא שגם הם הן בחי׳
אלקות ולכן העו״ג הנשפעים מהם הם עע״ז ממש עד
עת קץ שיבולע המות והסט״א ואז אהפוך אל עמים
כו׳

---

realm. The realm of holiness, sanctity, and purity, thus is opposed by a realm of impurity. The realm of impurity itself is subdivided into two principal classes: the three altogether impure kelipot, *containing no good whatever in themselves, and* kelipat nogah, an *intermediate category between the three* kelipot *mentioned and the order of holiness. Dependent on the motives and actions of man,* kelipat nogah *is absorbed in one or the other of these two realms. It is a sort of potential* kelipah, *which can be sublimated and developed, or may fall among the wholly impure* kelipot. *See Introduction,* s.v. Kelipot. [40] *See* supra, *sect. XXII, note 37.* [41] *Menachot 110a; see comment. by R. Samuel Edelis* a.l. [42] *The other*

(Notes cont. at end of Hebrew Text)

... that they may all call by the Name of the Lord."[44] This is also referred to as the "exile of the Shechinah." For this vivification, in a state of exile within them, stems from the radiation issuing to them from the spark of the "word of the Lord" called Shechinah. ([45]And this exile stems from the sin of the Tree of Knowledge and onwards,[46] and is a rank of mere *achurayim* of holiness. But when the Israelites were exiled to be among the nations—and the attachment and root of the Israelites is in the rank of the Supernal Face (*panim*)[47]—this became a total exile. Of this our sages, of blessed memory, said: "When they were exiled to Edom, the Shechinah went with them."[48])

●▲ Now, though "The Lord is one, and His Name is one"[49] [that is, His speech and the "breath of His mouth," which in the sacred *Zohar*[50] is referred to as His Name, is singularly and uniquely one], nevertheless, the radiation and efflux of vivification, issuing forth from the breath of His blessed mouth, divides into four different levels. These are the four worlds Atzilut, Beriah, Yetzirah, and Asiyah. The difference is due to ([51]many) contractions and curtailments—screening and concealing the light and vivification so that it will not radiate in the world of Beriah as much as in the world of Atzilut; and in the world of Yetzirah it is by means of further contractions and curtailments...[52] However, there is no change whatever, Heaven forfend, in the essence of the Shechinah, i.e. the "word of the Lord" and the "breath of His mouth." Also, as regards the radiation and efflux of vivification, the radiation which is in Atzilut pierces the curtailment and vests itself in Beriah. Likewise from Beriah to Yetzirah, and from Yetzirah to Asiyah.[53] Thus it follows that the light of the blessed En Sof which is in Atzilut is also in Asiyah and in this material world, through its investment in the *malchut* of Beriah, Yetzirah, and Asiyah, as everything is explained in the writings of R. Isaac Luria, of blessed memory.[54]

●▲Now, it is known to all that the soul of man is compounded of the ten Sefirot: *chochmah, binah, da'at*....[55] Though they are all of the breath of His blessed mouth [as it is written: "And He blew into his nostrils ..."[56]], nevertheless, more specifically the *ChaBaD*[57] in his soul are analogous to the *ChaBaD* in the ten Sefirot, referred to as *abba* and *imma*;[58] and the attributes

---

[44] *Zephaniah 3:9.* [45] *Brackets appear in the text.* [46] Cf. *Genesis Rabba 19:7 (and its parallel instances).* [47] Pnimiyut; *see* supra, *sect. IV, note 9.* [48] Mechilta *on Exodus 12:41;* Sifre *on Numb. 10:35, and 35:34; Megilah 29a (acc. to* v.s. *of* Ayin Ya'akov a.l.*).* Cf. Yerushalmi *Ta'anit I: end of 1.* [49] *Zechariah 14:9.* [50] Cf. *Tikunei Zohar 22:66b.* [51] *Brackets appear in the text.* [52] *See Introduction,* s.v. *Worlds.* [53] *See* supra, *section XX, and note 92* ad loc. [54] *See references cited* supra, *sect. XX, note 92.* [55] *See* supra *section XV.* [56] *Genesis 2:7; see* supra, *sect. XII, note 46.* [57] Chochmah, binah, da'at. [58] *See Introduction,* s.v. Partzufim; supra, *sect. XV, note 9.*

כו' לקרוא כולם בשם ה' ונקרא גם כן בשם גלות השכינה מאחר שחיות זה אשר בבחי' גלות בתוכם הוא מהארה הנמשכת להם מהניצוץ מדבר ה' הנקרא בשם שכינה (וגלות זה נמשך מחטא עה"ד ואילך והוא בחי' אחוריים לבד דקדושה אך כשגלו ישראל לבין האומות ואחיזת ישראל ושרשם הוא בבחי' פנים העליונים הנה זו היא גלות שלימה וע"ז ארז"ל גלו לאדום שכינה עמהם)):

והנה אף כי ה' אחד ושמו אחד דהיינו דבורו ורוח פיו המכונה בזוה"ק בשם שמו הוא יחיד ומיוחד אעפ"כ ההארה והמשכת החיות הנמשכת מרוח פיו יתברך מתחלקת לד' מדרגות שונות שהן ד' עולמות אבי"ע והשינוי הוא מחמת צמצומים ומסכים (רבים) לצמצם האור והחיות ולהסתירו שלא יהא מאיר כ"כ בעולם הבריאה כמו בעולם האצילות ובעולם היצי' הוא ע"י צמצומים ומסכים יותר וכו' אבל אין שום שינוי ח"ו בעצמות השכינה שהיא דבר ה' ורוח פיו וגם בבחי' ההארה והמשכת החיות הנה ההארה שבאצילות בוקעת המסך ומתלבשת בבריאה וכן מבריאה ליצירה ומיצירה לעשיה ולכן אור א"ס ב"ה שבאצילות הוא ג"כ בעשיה ובעוה"ז החומרי ע"י התלבשותו במלכות דבי"ע כמבואר הכל בכתבי האר"י ז"ל:

והנה נפש האדם ידוע לכל שהיא כלולה מי"ס חב"ד וכו' ואף שכולן מרוח פיו ית' כדכתיב ויפח באפיו כו' מ"מ דרך פרט חב"ד שבנפשו הן דוגמא לחב"ד שבי"ס המכונות בשם או"א ומדות אהבה

of love and fear . . . in his soul are analogous to the *midot* in the ten Sefirot, referred to as *z'eyr anpin*;[59] and the faculty of speech in his soul is analogous to the Supernal Speech, referred to as *malchut*, and Shechinah. Hence, when speaking words of Torah one arouses the Supernal Speech to unify the Shechinah.[60] That is why it is established that for the reading of the *Shema*, the grace after meals, and words of Torah, one has not discharged his duty by meditation without speech.[61]

●▲Now, with one corresponding to the other,[62] there are "ten crowns of impurity."[63] From these issue the souls of the heathens, also comprised of truly those ten ranks. And it is common knowledge that[64] which has been stated in *Sefer Hagilgulim*[65] on the verse "That man rules in man, to his evil,"[66] that it refers to the mystery of the Shechinah's exile in the *kelipot* "In order to vivify them, and to empower them to rule, now,[67] in the time of the exile; but it is 'to his evil. . . .'" And that is why the heathens dominate now[68] over Israel. For the souls of the heathens are of the *kelipot* in which the Shechinah is vested in a state of exile. Though this requires extensive exposition (as to) how and what, it is, nevertheless, fact. Despite this, the *kelipot* and heathens receive their nurture and vivification only from an aspect extended to them, of the *Achurayim* of holiness, "As with one that casts away behind his shoulders."[69] And even that is by way of numerous and immense contractions and curtailments until this radiation became vested in the materiality of this world and diffuses wealth and honour, and all physical pleasures, unto the heathens. The Israelites, however, elicit from the aspect of the Supernal Face,[70] as it is written: "May the Lord cause His Face to radiate unto you,"[71] in each one according to the root of his soul, even unto the peak of levels.

●▲After these words and this truth,[72] manifest and known to all, we shall return to our original subject with respect to anger—that one is as an idolater. This is so with respect to mundane matters, because "Everything is in the hands of Heaven except for the fear of Heaven."[73] Hence, with respect to matters of Heaven, "To warn off from wrong-doing,"[74]

---

[59] Ibid. [60] *See Zohar III: 105a; cf.* ibid., *31b.* [61] Hilchot Talmud Torah *II: 12;* Shulchan Aruch, Orach Chayim *(of the author) 62: 3, and 185: 3.* Shulchan Aruch, Yoreh De'ah *246: 22.* [62] *Eccles 7: 14; see* supra, *sect. II, note 16.* [63] *Corresponding to the ten holy Sefirot. Zohar III: 41b;* ibid., *70a.* Cf. *Zohar I: 167a;* Tanya *I, ch. 6.* [64] Par. *Isaiah 12: 5.* [65] *Ch. 2; quoted by R. Jacob of Lissa,* Ta'alumot Chochmah *on Eccles. 8: 9; see also, R. Menachem Mendel of Lubavitch,* Reshimot 'al Kohelet, a.l. *(p. 254 f.).* [66] *Ecclesiastes 8: 9.* [67] *Emended according to* L.H. [68] *Emended according to* L.H. [69] *See* supra, *sect. XXII, note 38;* Tanya *I, ch. 22.* [70] Panim *(as opposed to* achurayim*).* [71] *Numbers 6: 25.*

אהבה ויראה וכו׳ שבנפשו הן דוגמא למדות שבי״ס הנקראות בשם ז״א וכח הדבור שבנפשו דוגמא לדבור העליון הנקרא בשם מלכות ושכינה ולכן כשמדבר ד״ת מעורר דבור העליון ליחד השכינה ומשום הכי קיי״ל בק״ש ובהמ״ז וד״ת לא יצא בהרהור בלא דבור:

והנה זלעו״ז יש עשרה כתרי דמסאבותא ומהן נמשכות נפשות העו״ג ג״כ כלולות מעשר בחי׳ אלו ממש ומודעת זאת בארץ מ״ש בספר הגלגולים ע״פ אשר שלט האדם באדם לרע לו שהוא סוד גלות השכינה בתוך הקליפות להחיותם ולהשליטם בזמן הגלות אבל הוא לרע לו וכו׳ ולכן העו״ג היו שולטין על ישראל להיות נפשות העו״ג מהקליפות אשר השכינה מתלבשת בבחי׳ גלות בתוכם והנה אף שזה צריך ביאור רחב איך ומה מ״מ האמת כן הוא אלא שאעפ״כ אין הקליפות והעו״ג יונקים ומקבלים חיות אלא מהארה הנמשכת להם מבחי׳ אחוריים דקדושה כמאן דשדי בתר כתפי׳ ואף גם זאת ע״י צמצומים ומסכים רבים ועצומים עד שנתלבשה הארה זו בחומריות עולם הזה ומשפעת לעו״ג עושר וכבוד וכל תענוגים גשמיים. משא״כ ישראל יונקים מבחי׳ פנים העליונים כמ״ש יאר ה׳ פניו אליך כל אחד ואחד לפי שרש נשמתו עד רום המעלות:

ואחר הדברים והאמת האלה הגלוים וידועים לכל נחזור לענין ראשון בענין הכעס שהוא כעובד ע״ז והיינו במילי דעלמא כי הכל בידי שמים חוץ מי״ש ולכן במילי דשמיא לאפרושי מאיסורא לא שייך

---

[72] Par. *2 Chron. 32:1.* [73] *Berachot 33b.* [74] *Shabat 40b.*

the reason stated does not apply, and as it is written[75]: "And Moses was enraged."[76] This is different because G-d caused him to encounter this *mitzvah*[77] of "Warning off from wrong-doing" in order to make him meritorious.[78]

But this applies (only) when he is able to prevent[79] by his wrath and anger against his fellow-man.[80] However, when he is unable to prevent, as in the case of[81] the heathen speaking and disturbing him in his prayer, then "What is this that G-d has done to him? It is but in order that he prevail and strengthen himself ever more in his prayer, in the profundity of the heart, and with so great a concentration that he will not hear the words of the heathen." However, for such a level one needs a great and immense arousal. And the counsel suggested for such an arousal is from the subject matter itself. He should consider and contemplate on the idea of the descent of the Shechinah, as it were: "She descended in wondrous fashion"[82] to have a spark of her radiation invested. Thus she is in a state of exile among the *kelipot*, in a general way, in order to animate them. And now again, a spark of her radiation vests itself in a state of exile, in a particular way, in the speech of this heathen who speaks words that disturb the service of the Lord, i.e. the devotion of prayer. And as explained above, one corresponding to the other..., thus the Supernal Speech vests itself in the nether speech, ... Now this is truly "That man rules in man, to his evil;" that is, *because of this* man is aroused to pray with greater devotion, from the profundity of the heart, until he will not hear his words.

As for the compiler[83] writing "*sharta*" (dwelled), he did not know to determine the precise term. For the Ba'al Shem Tov, of blessed memory, used to deliver Torah-discourses in the Yiddish tongue, and not in the sacred tongue. He meant to say: "*nitlabsha*" (became vested)—that is, in a state of exile. And that is the meaning of "And especially when he is a heathen...", for then there is so much more of a state of exile.

There is no need to wonder at a spark of the Shechinah's illumination being referred to as Shechinah. Thus we find that even a created angel is referred to as G-d: in the section of *Vayera*,[84] according to the commentary of R. Moses Nachmanides; and as it is written: "And she called the name of the Lord who spoke to her...";[85] and many more (passages) like this.

●▲ It would seem to me that their seizing

---

[75] *Numbers 31:14.* [76] *See Zohar I:184a; II:182a–b; Zohar Chadash 21a; Maimonides,* Hilchot De'ot *I:4; comment. of R. Yonah, on Avot 5:11.* [77] *Leviticus 19:17; see Shabbat 54b; Maimonides,* Sefer Hamitzvot *I:205, and* Hilchot De'ot *6:7.* [78] Cf. *Mishnah, Macot 3:16.* [79] *Wrong-doing.* [80] Cf. *Yevomot 65b, Rashi (*s.v. *לומר), and comm. by R. Samuel Edelis,* ad loc. [81] *The author now passes over to the original subject of the letter,* i.e. *the passage in* Tzavaat Ribash: "... *and likewise when he hears someone talking while he prays, he is to say: 'why did G-d bring him hither to talk while I am praying; after all, all this is by the individual (Divine) Providence?! However: "speech is the Shechinah," and the*

שייך האי טעמא דאמרן וכמ"ש ויקצוף משה והיינו משום כי ה' הקרה לפניו מצוה זו לאפרושי מאיסורא כדי לזכותו:

אך זהו כשיש בידו למחות בקצפו וכעסו על חבירו אבל כשאין בידו למחות כגון עו"ג המדבר ומבלבלו בתפלתו א"כ מה זאת עשה ה' לו אין זאת כ"א כדי שיתגבר ויתאמץ יותר בתפלתו בעומק הלב ובכוונה גדולה כ"כ עד שלא ישמע דבורי העו"ג אך שלמדרגה זו צריך התעוררות רבה ועצומה. ועצה היעוצה להתעוררות זו היא מענין זה עצמו כשישים אל לבו ויתבונן ענין ירידת השכינה כביכול ותרד פלאים להתלבש ניצוץ מהארתה אשר היא בבחי' גלות בתוך הקליפות דרך כלל להחיותם ועתה הפעם ניצוץ הארתה מתלבש בבחי' גלות דרך פרט בדבור עו"ג זה המדבר דברים המבלבלים עבודת ה' היא כוונת התפלה וכמש"ל כי זה לעומת זה וכו' ודבור העליון מתלבש בדבור התחתון וכו' וזהו ממש אשר שלט האדם באדם לרע לו דהיינו שעי"ז מתעורר האדם להתפלל יותר בכוונה מעומקא דלבא עד שלא ישמע דיבוריו. ומ"ש המלקט שרתה לא ידע לכוין הלשון בדקדוק כי הבעש"ט ז"ל היה אומר ד"ת בל"א ולא בלה"ק ור"ל נתלבשה והיינו בבחי' גלות וזהו ובפרט אם הוא עו"ג כו'. שאז היא בחי' גלות ביותר ואין לתמוה אם ניצוץ מן הארת שכינה נקרא בשם שכינה דהא אשכחן שאפילו מלאך נברא נקרא בשם ה' בפ' וירא לפי' הרמב"ן וכמ"ש ותקרא שם ה' הדובר אליה וכו' וכה"ג טובא וכמדומה לי שתפיסתם

אינה

---

*Shechinah dwells in the mouth of that person in order that I strengthen myself for the worship (of G-d). Just how much must I strengthen myself in the "service—*id est *prayer," and especially when the person talking is a gentile or a child.' Hence, inasmuch as the Shechinah is, as it were, in a person like that, how much then is it proper to act with zeal."*—Tzavaat Ribash, *near the end,* s.v. **שמעתי מריב"ש ע"ה**, cf. *also,* Tanya *I, ch. 28.* [82] Par. *Lament. I:9.* [83] *Of* Tzavaat Ribash. [84] *Genesis 18:3.* [85] *Genesis 16:13 (see preceding verses).*

(this passage) is not because of the accuracy of the phraseology, but with respect to the very idea of the investment of the Shechinah in the *kelipot*. For they do not believe what R. Isaac Luria, of blessed memory, wrote in *Sefer Hagilgulim*.[86] Should they want to distinguish between the spiritual *kelipot* and the physical idolaters, you have nothing more physical than the dust of the earth; nevertheless, the *malchut* of *malchut* of Asiyah vests itself in it, and within that the *malchut* of Yetzirah . . ., and as mentioned above.[87] And should it be because of the impurity of the souls of the heathens, verily, their souls are from the *conjunctio* of the masculine and feminine (*zivvug zu'n*)[88] of the spiritual *kelipot*, as mentioned in the writings of R. Isaac Luria, of blessed memory. Hence it follows that the spiritual (*kelipot*) are the source of their impurity! But in truth, this requires extensive elucidation regarding this investment. But this complaint does not apply to us, but to the writings of R. Isaac Luria, of blessed memory. And let not he who hears (this) suspect me that I imagine to have understood the words of R. Isaac Luria, of blessed memory, to divest them from their physical connotation. I came but to explain the words of the Ba'al Shem Tov, of blessed memory, and of his disciples, according to the Cabbalah of R. Isaac Luria, of blessed memory, especially since this matter is not of the science of the Cabbalah and of the things "Secret unto the Lord our G-d,"[89] but of the "Things revealed unto us and unto our children"[90]—to believe in full faith in the explicit verse, spoken by Scripture: "Do I, then, not fill the heavens and the earth, says the Lord."[91] For Scripture does not lose its plain meaning.[92] Also, it is a simple article of faith among the general totality of Israel, handed down to them by their saintly ancestors, who walked in wholeness with the Lord without searching the concept of Divinity by means of the human intellect; for it is infinitely beyond the intellect to know how He fills the earth. But new ones have recently come[93] to examine this problem, and it is impossible to make them understand except by means of premises taken from the writings of R. Isaac Luria, of blessed memory, divested from their physical connotation, and according to what I heard from my masters, may their souls rest in Eden. However, it is impossible to explain this clearly in writing, only orally to "The ear that hears,"[94] to adept individuals,

[86] Supra, *note 65*. [87] Cf. *also* Tanya *I, chs. 6 and 51 (and references cited there)*. [88] Cf. supra, *sect. XX, note 38*. [89] Par. *Deut. 29:28*. [90] Ibid. [91] *Jeremiah 23:24*. [92] *Shabbat 63a*. [93] Par. *Deut. 32:17*. [94] *See Proverbs 15:31, and 25:12.*

אינה מצד דקדוק הלשון אלא מעיקר ענין התלבשות השכינה בקליפות שאין להם אמונה במ"ש האריז"ל בס' הגלגולים שאם ירצו לחלק בין קליפות הרוחניים לעו"ג הגשמיים אין לך גשמי כעפר הארץ ואף על פי כן מתלבשת בו מלכות דמלכות דעשיה ובתוכה מלכות דיצירה כו' וכנ"ל. ואם משום טומאת נפשות העו"ג הרי נפשותיהם מזיווג זו"ן דקליפות הרוחניים כמ"ש בכהאריז"ל. נמצא שהרוחניים מקור טומאתם אך באמת צריך ביאור רחב איך הוא התלבשות זו אבל לא עלינו תלונתם כ"א על כהאריז"ל. ואל יחשדני שומע שאני בעיני שהבנתי דברי האריז"ל להפשיטן מגשמיותן כי לא באתי רק לפרש דברי הבעש"ט ז"ל ותלמידיו עפ"י קבלת האריז"ל בשגם שענין זה אינו מחכמת הקבלה ומהנסתרות לה' אלקינו כי אם מהנגלות לנו ולבנינו להאמין אמונה שלימה במקרא מלא שדבר הכתוב הלא את השמים ואת הארץ אני מלא נאם ה' שאין מקרא יוצא מידי פשוטו וגם היא אמונה פשוטה בסתם כללות ישראל ומסורה בידם מאבותיהם הקדושים שהלכו בתמימות עם ה' בלי לחקור בשכל אנושי ענין האלקות אשר הוא למעלה מהשכל עד אין קץ לידע איך הוא מלא כל הארץ רק שחדשים מקרוב באו לחקור בחקירה זו וא"א לקרב להם אל השכל אלא דוקא עפ"י הקדמות לקוחות מכאריז"ל מופשטות מגשמיותן וכפי ששמעתי מרבותי נ"ע אך א"א לבאר זה היטב במכתב כי אם מפה לאזן שומעת ליחידי סגולה ולשרידים

and to "The remnants whom the Lord calls,"[95] as it is written: "And they who seek the Lord understand all;"[96] and from the affirmative you may infer . . .[97]

You have now seen an explanation of a single passage from the well-known books, as a sample and token that indeed all "astonishing passages" have an explanation and meaningfulness for those adept in the esoteric science. However, let them not hope for me to explain everything in writing. That is a hard and extensive labour, and absolutely impossible. But if you so desire, send from amongst you one that is "outstanding in the congregation,"[98] and, G-d willing, I will talk to him "face to face." And may the Lord be with my mouth when my words will flow, and may the utterances of my mouth find favour.[99]

●▲XXVI. In *R'aya Mehemna*, section of *Nasso*,[1] (it is stated): "And they that are wise, shall shine as the splendour of the firmament"[2] with this work of yours,[3] which is the Book of Splendour (*Sefer haZohar*)—of the splendour of the *imma ilaah*, repentance;[4] with these no trial is needed. Because in time to come Israel will taste of the Tree of Life, which is the book of the *Zohar*, and through which they will leave their exile with mercy. And through them shall be realised that "The Lord alone will lead him, and there is no strange god with Him."[5] And the Tree of Good and Evil,[6] i.e. proscription and permission, impurity and purity, will no longer domineer over Israel. Their sustenance will be from the side of the Tree of Life alone. There, there is no question from the side of evil and no disagreement from the spirit of impurity,[7] as it is written: "And the spirit of impurity I shall remove from the earth."[8] Thus the scholars of Torah will no longer be sustained by illiterate persons (*amey haaretz*), but from the side of the good, by those who consume what is pure, *Kasher*, permitted; nor[9] by the mixed multitude (*erev rav*)—who consume what is impure, unfit, prohibited. . . . But while the Tree of Good and Evil domineers . . ., these sages, who are compared to the Sabbaths and Festivals,[10] have nothing save what is given to them by those profane ones, analogous to the day of the Sabbath which has but what has been prepared for it on a week-day.[11]

"However, when the Tree of Life will dominate, the Tree of Good and Evil will be suppressed and

---

[95] *Joel 3:5.* [96] *Proverbs 28:5.* [97] *The negative (*Sifre, *Deut., sect. 46).* [98] *(*Cf. *Sanhedrin 13b).* [99] *Psalms 19:15.*

Section XXVI

[1] *Zohar III: 124b–125a.* [2] *Daniel 12:3.* [3] *Of R. Shimon bar Yochai.* [4] Imma 'ilaah *(the sphere of* binah*) corresponds to* teshuvah 'ilaah; *see* supra, *sect. VIII, note 23.* [5] *Deut. 32:12.* [6] *The Tree of Knowledge of Good and Evil (contrasted with the Tree of Life;* cf. *Genesis 2:9).* [7] *All problems and disagreements are due to the forces of evil which becloud the issue.* [8] *Zechariah 13:2.* [9] *Will they be sustained.* [10] *See Zohar III: 29a–b.* [11] Cf. *Avodah Zarah 3a.— (Week-day;* lit. *a day of the profane, as opposed to holy.)*

ולשרידים אשר ה׳ קורא כדכתיב ומבקשי הוי׳ יבינו כל ומכלל הן אתה שומע כו׳.

הנה אתם ראיתם פי׳ מאמר אחד מספרים הידועים לדוגמא ולאות כי גם כל המאמרים התמוהים יש להם פי׳ וביאור היטב לי״ח. אך לא יקוו מעלתם אלי לבאר להם הכל במכתב כי היא מלאכה כבידה ומרובה וא״א בשום אופן. רק אם תרצו שלחו מכם אחד ומיוחד שבעדה. ופא״פ אדבר בו אי״ה. וה׳ יהי׳ עם פי בהטיפי. ויהיו לרצון אמרי פי:

כו בר״מ פ׳ נשא והמשכילים יזהירו כזהר הרקיע בהאי חבורא דילך דאיהו ספר הזהר מן זהרא דאימא עילאה תשובה באילין לא צריך נסיון ובגין דעתידין ישראל למטעם מאילנא דחיי דאיהו האי ספר הזהר יפקון ביה מן גלותא ברחמים ויתקיים בהון ה׳ בדד ינחנו ואין עמו אל נכר ואילנא דטוב ורע דאיהו איסור והיתר טומאה וטהרה לא ישלטו על׳ ישראל יתיר דהא פרנסה דלהון לא להוי אלא מסטרא דאילנא דחיי דלית תמן לא קשיא מסטרא דרע ולא מחלוקת מרוח הטומאה דכתיב ואת רוח הטומאה אעביר מן הארץ דלא יתפרנסון ת״ח מע״ה אלא מסטרא דטוב דאכלין טהרה כשר היתר ולא מערב רב דאכלין טומאה פסול אסור כו׳ ובזמנא דאילנא דטוב ורע שלטא כו׳ אינון חכמים דדמיין לשבתות ויו״ט לית להון אלא מה דיהבין להון אינון חולין כגוונא דיום השבת דלית ליה אלא מה דמתקנין ליה ביומא דחול ובזמנא דשלטא אילנא דחיי אתכפייא אילנא דטוב ורע ולא יהא

the illiterate persons will have but what the scholars of Torah give them. They will be subjugated to them as if they did not exist in the world. Accordingly, the proscribed, the permitted, the impure and the pure will not be removed from the illiterate persons. As regards them—"There is no difference between the exile and the days of the Messiah, except for the (delivery from) servitude to the nations."[12] For they did not taste of the Tree of Life, and will require the teachings of proscription and permission, impurity and purity." Until here from the *R'aya Mehemna*.[13]

▲ Now, at first glance, what appears evident to those unfamiliar with the subject matter[14] from the contents of this passage is that the study of *issur* and *hetter*,[15] and of the Order of *Taharot*,[16] relates only to the Tree of Good and Evil. This is greatly surprising in itself, and contradicts the plain meaning of Scripture and the expositions of our sages, of blessed memory. For the *whole* Torah that has been revealed unto us and unto our children, is called "A tree of life unto those that lay hold on her,"[17] and not only the Book of the *Zohar*. Moreover, it[18] was concealed in their days; also,[19] the whole science of the Kabbalah was hidden in their days and concealed from all the scholars of Torah, except for a select few, and even then in a mode of "walking hiddenly"[20] and not publicly, as mentioned in the *Gemara*.[21] Thus R. Isaac Luria, of blessed memory, wrote that it is only in these latter generations that it is permitted and a duty to reveal this science, but not so in the earlier generations.[22] R. Shimon bar Yochai, too, stated in the sacred *Zohar* that the permission to reveal was given to him and his associates only.[23] Now, this itself, too, is a wondrous marvel. For if so, then the study of *issur* and *hetter*, and, *a fortiori*. of civil laws, should not defer the precept of prayer [which is arranged according to the secrets of the *Zohar* and the supreme unifications (*yichudim*)] for the savants as R. Shimon bar Yochai and his associates. But this is not the case, as mentioned in the *Gemara*[24]: R. Shimon bar Yochai and his associates, and everyone whose study of Torah is his profession,[25] do not interrupt (their study) for prayer. (This applies) even when dealing with civil laws, like Rav Yehuda, all of whose studies dealt with *Nezikin*;[26] nevertheless, he prayed but every thirty days when reviewing his studies, as mentioned in the *Gemara*.[27] Also, in *Yerushalmi*,

---

[12] *See Berachot 34b.—Thus merely a physical, and not a spiritual redemption.* [13] *On this quotation from the Zohar, and on the subject-matter which follows, see at length: R. Moses Cordovero,* Or Ne'erav, *esp. pts. IV and V; R. Chayam Vital's Introduction to* Sha'ar Hahakdamot *(published in all recent editions as Introduction to* Etz Chayim, *and reproduced in* Kuntress Etz Chayim, *by R. Sholom Dov Ber of Lubavitch (N.Y. 1956), p. 61 ff.); R. Dov Ber of Lubavitch's Introduction to* Biurei Hazohar; Kuntress Etz Chayim, op. cit. supra, *ch. 13 ff. (pp. 41 ff.), and R. Sholom Dov Ber encyclical,* ibid., *(pp. 82 ff.). See also* Likutei Torah, *II:3d ff.* [14] Lit.: *those lacking knowledge.* [15] *Proscription and permission.* [16] *The sixth*

יהא לעמי הארץ אלא מה דיהבין להון ת"ח ואתכפיין תחותייהו כאלו לא הוו בעלמא והכי איסור היתר טומאה וטהרה לא אתעבר מע"ה דמסטרייהו לית בין גלותא לימות המשיח אלא שעבוד מלכיות בלבד דאינון לא טעמי מאילנא דחיי וצריך לון מתניתין באיסור והיתר טומאה וטהרה ע"כ בר"מ:

והנה המובן מהשקפה ראשונה לכאורה מלשון זה המאמר לחסירי מדע שלימוד איסור והיתר וסדר טהרות הוא מאילנא דטוב ורע מלבד שהוא פלא גדול מחמת עצמו וסותר פשטי הכתובים ומדרשי רבותינו ז"ל שכל התורה הנגלית לנו ולבנינו נקרא עץ חיים למחזיקים בה ולא ספר הזהר לבד ובפרט שהיה גנוז בימיהם וגם כל חכמת הקבלה היתה נסתרה בימיהם ונעלמה מכל תלמידי חכמים כ"א ליחידי סגולה ואף גם זאת בהצנע לכת ולא ברבים כדאיתא בגמרא וכמ"ש האריז"ל דדוקא בדורות אלו האחרונים מותר ומצוה לגלות זאת החכמה ולא בדורות הראשונים וגם רשב"י אמר בזוה"ק שלא ניתן רשות לגלות רק לו ולחביריו לבדם ואף גם זאת פליאה נשגבה דלפי זה לא היה לימוד איסור והיתר וכ"ש דיני ממונות דוחין מצות תפלה שנתקנה ע"פ סודות הזהר ויחודים עליונים לידעים כרשב"י וחביריו וזה אינו כדאיתא בגמ' דר"ש בן יוחאי וחביריו וכל מי שתורתו אומנתו אין מפסיקין לתפלה ואפילו כשעוסק בדיני ממונות כרב יהודה דכולהו תנויי בנזיקין הוי ואפ"ה לא הוי מצלי אלא מתלתין יומין לתלתין יומין כד מהדר תלמודא כדאי' בגמ' ובירושלמי

פ"ק

---

order of the Mishnah, *dealing with the laws of purity and impurity.* [17] *Proverbs 3:18.* [18] *The Zohar.* [19] I.e. *not only the Zohar, but etc.* [20] Par. *Micha 6:8.* [21] *Hagigah 11b, and 13a. Pessachim 119a; and* cf. *Kiddushin 71a.* [22] *See Introduction to* Etz Chayim *(*cit. supra, *note 13)*; Sha'ar Hagilgulim, *end of* hakd. *16; see also* ibid., hakd. *17; Introd. to* Sha'ar Hamitzvot; Shulchan Aruch *of R. Isaac Luria*, s.v. קריאה בחכמת הקבלה, *par. 3;* Hilchot Talmud Torah *(of the author)*, *I:4, and II:10.* [23] *Zohar III:159a. See also* ibid., *II:149a, and III:79a; and* Tikunei Zohar, *Intr. 1a.* [24] *Shabath 11a.* Cf. Nitzutzei Orot *(by R. Chaim David Azulay) on Zohar II:188a, and* Hilchot Talmud

(Notes cont. at end of Hebrew Text)

first chapter of *Berachot*,[28] R. Shimon bar Yochai is of the opinion that even for the reading of the *Shema* one interrupts only (the study of) Scripture, but not of *Mishnah* [(the study of) which is more than (the study of) Scripture, according to R. Shimon bar Yochai]. And he did not differentiate between the Order of *Zera'im*, *Mo'ed* and *Kodshim*, and *Taharot* and *Nezikin*.[29] ([30]Actually he contradicts his own opinion, given in several instances in *R'aya Mehemna*, that *Mishnah* is the *shifcha*[31] . . . And Scripture, the Torah of Moses, surely excells the Cabbalah, which is the *matrunita*,[32] (as stated) in the *R'aya Mehemna*, *ad loc.*, while the Written Torah is the *malka*[33] ([34]that is, the *yesod* of *abba* vested in *z'eyr anpin*, as stated by R. Isaac Luria, of blessed memory[35]).)[36] Also, we find that R. Shimon bar Yochai dealt a great deal with the argumentation of problems and solutions which are of the side of evil and of the spirit of impurity,[37] even when he was in the cave. Moreover, he merited this by virtue of the affliction of the cave, as it is stated in the *Gemara*[38] that he gave R. Pinchas ben Yair twenty-four solutions to every query, and said to him: "If you had not seen me like this . . ." ([39]In fact, their principal occupation in the cave must have been with the teachings of the *Mishnayot*, i.e. the six hundred Orders extant in those days,[40] until (the time of) our holy Master.[41] The *Zohar* and the *Tikunim* he could have finished in two or three months; for surely he did not repeat the same thing twice.) Also, our sages, of blessed memory, said, that since the day the Temple was destroyed, the Holy One, blessed is He, has but the four cubits of *Halacha*.[42]

●▲There is yet further cause to be exceedingly amazed. How is it possible that in the days of the Messiah they will no longer need to know the laws of *issur* and *hetter*, and of impurity and purity? How will they slaughter the sacrifices, and also (the animals) for common use, when they will not know the laws of *drassa*,[43] *chalada*,[44] and *shehiya*[45] [which render the slaughtering unfit],[46] and of a defective knife?[47] Will there then be born a man who by his very nature will slaughter without *shehiya* and *drassa*? Will the knife also be the way it should be, and remain forever without a defect? (There are) also many more laws (relating to) fat, and blood, and other prohibitions. They will also need to know about the impurity of a corpse, as it is written: "The youth of a hundred years old, will die."[48] It will be further necessary to know about the impurity of a woman in confinement

---

[28] *End of sect. 2; also* ibid., *Shabbat I: 2.* [29] *See* H.V. ad loc. [30] *Brackets appear in the text.* [31] *Maid-servant.* [32] *Matron.* [33] *King.* [34] *Brackets appear in the text.* [35] Sha'ar Hamitzvot, Vaetchanan: *sect. 1.* [36] *See Zohar I: 27b–28a; III: 29b; Tikunei Zohar, Intr.: 14a–b. See Intr. to* Etz Chayim. [37] *See* supra, *note 7. See also Tikunei Zohar, Add. 9: 147a;* ibid., *10: 147b;* et passim, *and* cf. *Zohar III: 27b (*R'aya Mehemna*).* [38] *Shabbat 33b.* [39] *Brackets appear in the text.* [40] *See Chagigah 14a;* cf. Teshuvot Hageonim—Sha'are Teshuvah, *sect. 20 and 187;* Machzor Vitry, ed. *Hurwitz, II: p. 484;* Yalkut Reubeni, Beracha *(*s.v. מימות משה*).* [41] *R. Judah the Prince, editor of the* Mishnah.

פ"ק דברכות ס"ל לרשב"י דאפי' לק"ש אין מפסיקין כ"א ממקרא ולא ממשנה דעדיפי ממקרא לרשב"י ולא חילק בין סדר זרעים ומועד וקדשים טהרות לנזיקין (וסותר דעת עצמו בר"מ בכמה מקומות דמשנה איהי שפחה כו' והמקרא שהוא תורת משה ודאי עדיפא מקבלה דאיהי מטרוניתא בר"מ שם ותורה שבכתב הוא מלכא (דהיינו יסוד אבא המלובש בז"א כמ"ש האריז"ל)). וגם פלפול הקושיות ותירוצים דמסטרא דרע ורוח הטומאה אשכחן ברשב"י דעסק בי' טובא גם בהיותו במערה ואדרבה בזכות צער המערה זכה לזה כדאיתא בגמ' דאמר לר' פנחס בן יאיר אכל קושי' כ"ד פירוקי וא"ל אילו לא ראיתני בכך כו' (וגם באמת ע"כ עיקר עסקיהם במערה הי' תורת המשניות ת"ר סדרי שהיה בימיהם עד רבינו הקדוש דאילו ספר הזהר והתיקונים היה יכול לגמור בב' וג' חדשים כי בודאי לא אמר דבר אחד ב' פעמים) גם אמרו רבותינו ז"ל מיום שחרב בהמ"ק אין לו להקב"ה אלא ד' אמות של הלכה בלבד.

ועוד יש להפליא הפלא ופלא איך אפשר שלימות המשיח לא יצטרכו לידע הלכות איסור והיתר וטומאה וטהרה כי איך ישחטו הקרבנות וגם חולין אם לא ידעו הלכות דרסה וחלדה ושהי' הפוסלים השחיטה ופגימת הסכין וכי יולד איש בטבעו שיהא שוחט בלי שהי' ודרסה וגם הסכין תהי' בריאה ועומדת בלי פגימה לעולם ועוד הרבה הלכות חלב ודם ושאר איסורין וגם טומאת המת יהי' צריכין לידע כדכתיב הנער בן מאה שנה ימות וגם טומאת יולדת צריך

לידע

---

[42] *Berachot 8a.* [43] *Pressing* i.e. *making the cut by pressing upon the knife.* [44] *Passing* i.e. *passing the knife under cover by making the incision from behind the pipes outwardly, rather than in the reverse manner.* [45] *Pausing* i.e. *pausing or interrupting the act of slaughter.* [46] *These are three of the five procedural invalidations of* Shechitah *against which the slaughterer must guard (the other two being* hagramah*—cutting in a slanting direction, and* ikkur*—the severing of the pipes by a tearing action);* Chulin *9a and 27a.* [47] *Which also renders the slaughtering unfit (Chulin 17b; etc).* [48] *Isaiah 65:20.*

as it is written: "A pregnant woman, and one that gives birth together"[49] thus a woman may bear children every day, from one relationship,[50] nevertheless, the law with respect to the prohibition of her impurity does not change. There is no need to dwell on something so obvious. The reverse[51] is well-known from throughout the Talmud and the Midrashim: [that] "An objection was raised that the law is the same for the time of the Messiah;"[52] and Elijah comes to clarify all doubts;[53] and "This section, Elijah will expound in the future . . .".[54]

The statement that "the scholars of Torah will no longer be sustained by the illiterate (*amey haaretz*) . . . nor by the mixed multitude (*erev rav*), who consume what is unfit, impure, and prohibited," Heaven forfend, is also not understandable. Even[55] during the time of the second Temple they were not sustained by the "Illiterate persons who consume what is unfit and prohibited," Heaven forfend. For the scholars of Torah had fields and vineyards just like the illiterate persons, but nevertheless busied themselves with the study of *issur* and *hetter*, and of impurity and purity [all the pairs[56] that lived at the time of the second Temple], and they raised disciples in the thousands and myriads, but the study of the esoteric was in secret. . . .

●▲ But, in truth, when you will examine closely the above quoted text of the *R'ayah Mehemna*—"And the Tree of Good and Evil, which is *issur* and *hetter* . . ." (you will note that) he did not say "the *teaching* of *issur* and *hetter*" or "the *laws* of *issur* and *hetter*." Rather, he meant to say that "that which is proscribed," and "that which is permitted" is of the Tree of Good and Evil, i.e. of *kelipat nogah*,[57] as stated in *Etz Chayim*.[58] That, too, is the etymological meaning of *assur*:[59] the *kelipah* hovers over it and it cannot rise upwards like that which is *muttar*,[60] i.e. it is not tied and bound (*assur*) to the *kelipah*, and is able to ascend by means of the person consuming it with his mind on G–d,[61] or by any person serving G–d.[62] For it is with the energy from this consumption that he studies and prays to G–d. Thus, from the energy extracted from that food are formed the the letters of Torah and of the prayer which ascend to G–d. This is so during the week. But on the Sabbath, the *kelipat nogah* itself has an uplifting along with the *chitzoniyut* of all the worlds.[63] On the Sabbath it is, therefore, a duty to eat all delightful things, and to consume much meat and wine,[64] even though during the week[65] he would be called a glutton and drunkard.[66] It is otherwise with a proscribed matter. It cannot ascend,

---

[49] *Jeremiah 31:7.* [50] Cf. *Shabbat 30b. (See* Likutei Sichot *vol. 12 pg. 178.* [51] *The reverse of the proposition that the laws will no longer be relevant.* [52] *Sanhedrin 51b.* [53] *See Eduyot 8:7, and commentaries* a.l. [54] *Menachot 45a.* [55] *Emended according to* Kitzurim Vehe'arot, *p. 40;* L.H. [56] *The pairs of the leading scholars (see Avot, ch. 1).* [57] *The potential* kelipah. [58] Etz Chayim *49:2* ff. [59] *Prohibited;* lit.: *bound.* [60] *Permitted;* lit.: *released.* [61] Cf. supra, *sect. XVIII, note 37.* [62] *See* Tanya *I, chs. 7 and 8;* supra, *sect. XXV, note 39.* [63] Etz Chayim *50:6;* ibid., *40:8 (*et passim*); the Lurianic works dealing with devotions (*Sha'ar Hakavanot*;* Pri Etz Chayim*; etc.),* s.v. *the Eve of Sabbath;* cf. Pardess

לידע כדכתיב הרה ויולדת יחדיו אם תלד אשה בכל יום מביאה אחת אעפ"כ דין איסור טומאתה לא ישתנה ואין להאריך בדבר הפשוט ומפורסם הפכו בכל הש"ס ומדרשים דפריך הלכתא למשיחא ואליהו בא לפשוט כל הספיקות ופרשה זו עתיד אליהו לדורשה כו': ועוד אינו מובן מ"ש דלא יתפרנסון ת"ח מעמי הארץ כו' ולא מערב רב דאכלין פסול טמא ואסור ח"ו שהרי ת"ח שבזמן בית שני לא היו מתפרנסין מע"ה דאכלין פסול אסור ח"ו שהיה להם שדות וכרמים כע"ה ואפ"ה היו עוסקין בלימוד איסור והיתר וטומאה וטהרה כל הזוגות שהיו בימי בית שני והעמידו תלמידים לאלפים ורבבות ולימוד הנסתר בהסתר כו':

אך באמת כשתדקדק בלשון ר"מ דלעיל ואילנא דטוב ורע דאיהו איסור והיתר כו' ולא אמר תורת איסור והיתר או הלכות או"ה אלא ר"ל דגוף דבר האסור ודבר המותר הוא מאילנא דטוב ורע שהוא קליפת נוגה כמ"ש בע"ח. וזהו לשון אסור שהקליפה שורה עליו ואינו יכול לעלות למעלה כדבר המותר דהיינו שאינו קשור ואסור בקליפה ויוכל לעלות ע"י האדם האוכלו בכוונה לה' וגם בסתם כל אדם העובד ה' שבכח האכילה ההיא לומד ומתפלל לה' ונמצא שנעשה אותיות התורה והתפלה העולה לה' מכח הנברר מהמאכל ההוא וזהו בחול אבל בשבת שיש עליה לקליפת נוגה בעצמה עם החיצוניות שבכל העולמות לכן מצוה לאכול כל תענוגים בשבת ולהרבות בבשר ויין אף שבחול נקרא זולל וסובא. משא"כ בדבר איסור שאינו יכול לעלות לא

Rimonim *XVI: 4, 5. See also,* Tanya *III: end of ch. 10.* [64] Shulchan Aruch, *Orach Chayim 250:2; ed. of the author, 242:12.* [65] *When consuming much meat and wine during the week (for no sacred purpose). See Sanhedrin 70a ff.; Proverbs 23:20, and* Metzudot David a.l. [66] *See Zohar II: 218a, and* Mikdash Melech ad loc.; Tanya *I, ch. 7 f.*

either on the Sabbath or during the week-days, even if one were to pray and study with that energy [unless one ate to save an endangered life, which is permitted by our sages, of blessed memory,[67] and becomes permissible (*hetter*)[68]. But the study of Torah, even the laws of *issur* and *hetter*, impurity and purity [i.e. the *Mishnayot*, and the *Beraytot* in the *Gemara*, and the codifiers, which expound and clarify their words for practical application] these, precisely these are the fundamentals of the Oral Torah which is the Sefirah *malchut* of Atzilut, as mentioned in innumerable places in the sacred *Zohar*, and at the beginning of the *Tikunim*:[69] "*Malchut*—that is the Mouth, and we call it the Oral Torah." And in Atzilut "He and His causations are one in them,"[70] that is, the light of the blessed En Sof unites itself in Atzilut in an absolute unity, so that He, and His will and wisdom [vested in His speech, which is called *malchut*[71]] are entirely one.

●▲ R. Isaac Luria, of blessed memory, in stating[72] that the *Mishnayot* are in *malchut* of Yetzirah, meant to say the garment of *malchut* of Yetzirah in which *malchut* of Atzilut is vested.[73] And *malchut* of Yetzirah is called *shifcha*[74] in relation to *malchut* of Atzilut, while *malchut* of Beriah is called *amma.*[75] You can know this from what R. Isaac Luria, of blessed memory, stated[76] that Scripture, i.e. the Written Torah, is in Asiyah, even while it is explicit in innumerable places in the *Zohar* and the writings of R. Isaac Luria, of blessed memory, that it is *tiferet*, the *z'eyr anpin* of Atzilut! But (this means that) it vests itself in Asiyah. Thus it is stated explicitly in *Sefer Hakavanot* that Scripture, *Mishnah*, Talmud and Cabbalah are all in Atzilut; but Scripture vests itself as far as Asiyah, *Mishnah* as far as Yetzirah, and Talmud as ●far as Beriah. Now, when *malchut* of Atzilut vests itself in *kelipat nogah* in order to extract the sparks[77] that fell with the sin of Adam, and also the 288 sparks that fell with the *shevirat hakelim*,[78] *malchut* of Atzilut, too, is then referred to as "Tree of Knowledge of Good and Evil" in relation to the *z'eyr anpin* of Atzilut [which does not descend there and is referred to as Tree of Life].

Now, the investment of *malchut* in *kelipat nogah* is the mysterium of the "Exile of the Shechinah," "That man rules

---

[67] *Yoma 82a; see* Shulchan Aruch, Orach Chayim, *sect. 617* and *618.* [68] *Our text reads:* "(fully) permissible,"*—though this bracketed word does not appear in some of the earlier editions, and should probably be omitted; see Responsa by R. Menachem M. Schneerson of Lubavitch, in* Kovetz Lubavitch *I:4 (N.Y. 1944), p. 64a–b (cited in* Likutei Sichot, *vol. III: p. 985, note 16).* [69] *Introduction: 17a.* [70] *Tikunei Zohar, Intr.: 3b; see* supra, *beg. of sect. XX.* [71] *See* supra, *sect. XX, note 49.* [72] *See* Shulchan Aruch of Ari, s.v. כונת ת"ח, *par. 3;* Sha'ar Hamitzvot, Vaetchanan. [73] *The* Mishnayot, *the Sefirah* malchut *of Atzilut, are vested in* malchut *of Yetzirah.* Malchut *of Yetzirah serves as a garment for*

לא בשבת ולא בחול גם כשמתפלל ולומד בכה ההוא אם לא שאכל לפיקוח נפש שהתירו רז"ל ונעשה היתר [גמור]. אבל הלימוד בתורה אף הלכות איסור והיתר טומאה וטהרה שהם המשניות ובריתות שבגמרא ופוסקים המבארים ומבררים דבריהם להלכה למעשה הן הן גופי תורה שבע"פ שהיא ספי' מלכות דאצילות כדאי' בזוה"ק במקומות אין מספר ובריש תיקונים מלכות פה תורה שבע"פ קרינן לה ובאצי' איהו וגרמוהי חד בהון דהיינו שאור א"ס ב"ה מתייחד באצילות בתכלית היחוד שהוא ורצונו וחכמתו המלובשים בדבורו שנקרא מלכות הכל אחד:

ומ"ש האריז"ל שהמשניות הן במלכות דיצירה ר"ל לבוש מלכות דיצירה שנתלבשה בה מלכות דאצילות ומלכות דיצירה נקרא שפחה לגבי מלכות דאצילות ומלכות דבריאה נקרא אמה ותדע ממ"ש האריז"ל דמקרא דהיינו תושב"כ הוא בעשי' והרי מפורש בזהר ובכתבי האריז"ל מקומות אין מספר שהיא תפארת שהוא ז"א דאצילות אלא שמתלבשת בעשי' וכן הוא בהדיא בספר הכוונות שמקרא ומשנה ותלמוד וקבלה כולם באצילות אלא שמקרא מתלבש עד עשיה ומשנה עד היצירה ותלמוד בבריאה. והנה כשהמלכות דאצי' מתלבשת בקליפת נוגה כדי לברר הניצוצות שנפלו בחטא אדה"ר וגם הרפ"ח ניצוצין שנפלו בשבירת הכלים אזי גם המלכות דאצי' נקרא בשם עץ הדעת טוב ורע לגבי ז"א דאצילות שאינו יורד שם ונקרא עץ חיים והנה התלבשות המלכות בקליפת נוגה הוא סוד גלות השכינה אשר שלט האדם

---

malchut *of Atzilut.* [74] *Maidservant.* Cf. supra, *note 36.* [75] *Maid; a level transcending the level of* **shifcha.** [76] *See* supra, *note 72.* [77] *Of holiness.* [78] *Breaking of the vessels (see* Introduction, s.v.*).*

The sparks of Divinity are encumbered in the fragments of the broken vessels, thus, in the kelipot. *When these sparks are extracted, the* kelipot *are deprived of their vivification and cease to exist.*

in man . . ."[79] And this is the meaning of the statement in *R'aya Mehemna*: "But at the time that the Tree of Good and Evil dominates . . ., they . . ." . . . That is, at the time of the exile of the Shechinah [who effuses to the *chitzonim* that are in *kelipat nogah*, whence the mixed multitude (*erev rav*) elicits; and from their extract the scholars of Torah are supported in the exile], the principal service of man, and the purpose of the occupation with Torah and the commandments, is to disencumber the sparks, as known from R. Isaac Luria, of blessed memory.[80] Therefore, the principal mode of study is in the deliberation and argumentation of the law of *issur* and *hetter*, impurity and purity, in order to disencumber the permitted and pure from the proscribed and impure by means of the deliberation and argumentation of the law—with wisdom, understanding and knowledge. For as known, the Torah derives from *chochmah*.[81] Thus it is only through *chochmah* that they shall be disencumbered,[82] i.e. the Supreme *chochmah* of Atzilut which is vested in *malchut* of Atzilut [the principium of the Oral Torah[83] ([84]according to the principium of *abba*[85] founded *barta'*[86])]—which (in turn) is vested in *malchut* of Yetzirah, the[87] principium of the *Mishnayot* ([88]and the *Beraytot* that are vested in the *kelipat nogah* which corresponds to the world of Yetzirah; for there begins the aspect of the evil[89] inherent in the *nogah*),[90] as known from R. Isaac Luria, of blessed memory.

● Now, the intelligent will understand something yet more amazing, namely, what happens in Heaven above through the deliberation and elucidation of an adjudged ruling (*halacha*) of the *Gemara* and earlier and latter codifiers [which prior to this deliberation was in a state of concealment]: by means of this (deliberation) one elevates this ruling from the *kelipot* that were hiding and concealing it in such a way that it was not known at all, or that its reasoning was not clearly understood.[91] For the reason (of the *halacha*) is the principium of the Sefirah of the Supreme *chochmah*[92] whence [by the breaking of the vessels] sparks fell into the *kelipot*. (These sparks) are there in a state of exile because the *kelipot* domineer over them and hide the wisdom of the Torah from the upper and lower beings. That is why it is stated in *R'aya Mehemna* that "The problematic query is of the side of evil."

●▲ Now, the celestial beings do not have the power to disencumber

---

[79] *Eccles. 8:9; see* supra, *sect. XXV, and note 65* a.l. [80] *See* ref. *cited in the Introduction*, s.v. Shevirat Hakelim*; also:* Sha'ar Hamitzvot, Vaetchanan; Shulchan Aruch *of R. Isaac Luria*, כונת ח"ח, *par. 2.* [81] *Zohar II: 85a, 121a, III:81a.* [82] *Zohar II: end of 254b* (Nitzutzei Orot, ad loc.) *explained in* Etz Chayim *18:5 and 39:1;* Mevoh She'arim, *V:1:2. See* Torah Or, Bereishit*:5d, and* Esther*:96b.* [83] *See* supra *(note 69).* [84] *Brackets appear in the text.* [85] Chochmah. [86] Malchut.—*Zohar III:248a;* ibid., *256b, and 258a.* Cf. supra, *sect. V, notes 22 and 26.* [87] V.L.: *and the.* [88] *Brackets suggested by* H.V. [89] V.L.: *of the* da'at. [90] V.L.: *and* Beraytot *that are vested in the* kelipat nogah—*which corres-*

האדם באדם כו׳ וז״ש ברע״מ ובזמנא דאילנא דטו״ר שלטא כו׳ אינון כו׳ דהיינו בזמן גלות השכינה שמשפעת לחיצונים שהם בקליפת נוגה שהערב רב יונקים משם ומתמציתן ניזונין תלמידי חכמים בגלות ואז עיקר עבודת האדם ועיקר עסק התורה והמצות הוא לברר הניצוצות כנודע מהאריז״ל לכן עיקר ענין הלימוד הוא בעיון ופלפול הלכה באיסור והיתר טומאה וטהרה לברר המותר והטהור מהאסור והטמא ע״י עיון ופלפול הלכה בחכמה בינה ודעת כנודע דאוריי׳ מחכמה נפקת ובחכמה דייקא אתברירו והיינו חכמה עילאה דאצילות המלובשת במלכות דאצי׳ סוד תורה שבע״פ (בסוד אבא יסד ברתא) המלובשת במלכות דיצירה (וסוד) [סוד] המשניות וברייתות המלובשות בקליפת נוגה שכנגד עולם היצירה ששם מתחיל בחי׳ הדעת [נ״א הרע] שבנוגה [נ״א והברייתות המלובשות בק״נ שכנגד עולם העשיה ששם מתחיל בחי׳ הרע שבנוגה] כנודע מהאריז״ל. והמשכיל יבין ענין פלא גדול מזה מאד מה נעשה בשמים ממעל ע״י עיון ובירור הלכה פסוקה מן הגמרא ופוסקים ראשונים ואחרונים מה שהיה בהעלם דבר קודם העיון הלז כי ע״י זה מעלה הלכה זו מהקליפות שהיו מעלימים ומכסים אותה שלא היתה ידועה כלל או שלא היתה מובנת היטב בטעמה שהטעם הוא סוד הספי׳ חכמה עילאה שנפלו ממנה ניצוצי׳ בקליפות בשבה״כ והם שם בבחי׳ גלות שהקליפות שולטים עליהם ומעלימי׳ חכמת התורה מעליונים ותחתונים וז״ש בר״מ שהקושי׳ היא מסטרא דרע. והנה העליונים אין בהם כח לברר ולהעלות

ponds to the world of Asiyah—for there begins the aspect of the evil inherent in the nogah. [91] *See references cited* supra, *note 80.* [92] Cf. supra, *sect. XIX (note 37), and sect. XX (note 7).*

and elevate that which is in *kelipat nogah* because of the breaking (of the vessels). Only the terrestrial beings (can do that); for they are vested in a material body—"hide of the snake," which is of the *kelipat nogah.*[93] They weaken its strength by crushing the passions and suppressing the *sitra achra* so that "all the workers of evil[94] are dispersed."[95] That is why the celestial beings come to hear novelties of Torah from the terrestrial beings,[96] what they discover and reveal of the secrets of wisdom which until then were in bondage in the exile. And every one of Israel is able to reveal secrets of wisdom, ([97]to reveal) and to discover a new insight, whether it be in laws[98] or in homiletics,[99] in the revealed or in the esoteric parts (of Torah), according to the level of his soul's root.[100] Indeed, one is obliged to do so in order to perfect his soul by elevating all the sparks that fell to its part and lot, as known.[101] ([102]And every word of Torah, especially one of *halacha*, is a spark of the Shechinah, the word of the Lord.[103] Thus it is stated in the *Gemara*: "The 'word of the Lord'—that refers to the *halacha*,"[104] the principium of *malchut* of Atzilut which garbs the *chochmah* of Atzilut, and they are (both) vested in *malchut* of Yetzirah, and by the breaking of the vessels descended into the *kelipat nogah*). And to this pertains what is stated in the *Gemara*: "The Holy One, blessed is He, says: whoever occupies himself with Torah . . . I account it to him as if he had redeemed Me and My children from among the nations of the world."[105]

●▲ But when the Shechinah will emerge from the *kelipat nogah*[106] [after the extraction of the sparks shall be completed and the evil shall be separated from the good, "And all the workers of evil will be dispersed," and the Tree of Good and Evil will not domineer because the good shall depart from it], then the occupation with the Torah and commandments will not be for the purpose of disencumbrance, but to consolidate more sublime *yichudim*,[107] in order to elicit more *orot*, transcending Atzilut, as mentioned by R. Isaac Luria, of blessed memory. And everything will be by means of the *pnimiyut* of Torah,[108] by performing the commandments with supreme devotions directed towards supreme *orot*. For the root of the commandments is ever so high, in the blessed En Sof.[109]

([110]As for the statement of our sages, of blessed memory, that the commandments will be abrogated in the future,[111] this refers to the time of the resurrection of the dead. In the days

---

[93] Etz Chayim *49:4; see* supra, *section VI, note 21.* [94] *The forces of evil; the* kelipot. [95] *Psalms 92:10.* [96] *See Zohar III:173a;* cf. *Zohar I:4b.* [97] *Brackets appear in the text.* [98] Halacha. [99] Aggada. [100] Sha'ar Ruach Hakodesh, s.v. יחודים על קברי צדיקים: hakdama *3 (*ed. *Tel Aviv 1963, p. 108b);* cf. Sha'ar Hagilgulim, hakd. *17. See also* Sefer Chassidim, *sect. 530, and the comment. of R. Chaim David Azulay* ad loc.; *R. Jacob of Marvege, Responsa* Min Hashamayim, *no. 32; and* infra, *note 101.* [101] *Zohar I:4b;* Hilchot Talmud Torah *I:4 (see also* ibid., *II:2).* [102] *Brackets appear in the text.* [103] *See* supra, *section XXV (note 25),* [104] *Shabbat 138b.* [105] *Berachot 8a;* cf. *Zohar*

ולהעלות מהשבירה שבקליפת נוגה אלא התחתונים לבד לפי שהם מלובשים בגוף חומרי משכא דחויא מקליפת נוגה והם מתישים כחה בשבירת התאוות ואתכפיא ס"א ויתפרדו כל פועלי און. ולכן באים העליונים לשמוע חידושי תורה מהתחתונים מה שמחדשים ומגלים תעלומות החכמה שהיו כבושים בגולה עד עתה וכל איש ישראל יוכל לגלות תעלומות חכמה (לגלות) ולחדש שכל חדש הן בהלכות הן באגדות הן בנגלה הן בנסתר כפי בחי' שרש נשמתו ומחויב בדבר להשלים נשמתו בהעלאת כל הניצוצות שנפלו לחלקה ולגורלה כנודע (וכל דברי תורה ובפרט דבר הלכה היא ניצוץ מהשכינה שהיא היא דבר ה' כדאיתא בגמרא דבר ה' זו הלכה סוד מלכות דאצילות המלבשת לחכמה דאצילות ומלובשים במלכות דיצירה וירדו בקליפת נוגה בשבירת הכלים). וז"ש בגמרא כל העוסק בתורה אמר הקב"ה מעלה אני עליו כאלו פדאני ואת בני מבין האומות עו"ג. אבל בצאת השכינה מקליפת נוגה [נ"א מהקליפות] אחר שיושלם בירור הניצוצות ויופרד הרע מהטוב ויתפרדו כל פועלי און ולא שלטא אילנא דטוב ורע בצאת הטוב ממנה אזי לא יהיה עסק התורה והמצות לברר בירורין כ"א ליחד יחודים עליונים יותר להמשיך אורות עליונים יותר מהאצילות כמ"ש האר"י ז"ל והכל ע"י פנימיות התורה לקיים המצות בכוונות עליונות שמכוונות לאורות עליונים כו' כי שרש המצות הוא למעלה מעלה בא"ס ב"ה (ומ"ש רז"ל דמצות בטילות לע"ל היינו בתחיית המתים אבל לימות המשיח

III: 281a. (106) V.L.: *from the* kelipot. [107] *Unifications.* [108] *The inner or esoteric part of the Torah.* [109] *See* supra, *latter part of sect. XX, and the notes* ad loc. [110] *Brackets appear in the text.* [111] *Nidah 61b.*

of the Messiah, however, prior to the resurrection of the dead, they will not be abrogated).

And that is why the principal occupation with Torah will also be with the *pnimiyut* of the commandments, and their hidden reasons. The revealed aspects, however, will be manifest and known to every one of Israel, by an innate knowledge, without oblivion. Only the mixed multitude (*erev rav*) will have to deal with these, because they will not merit to taste from the Tree of Life, i.e. the *pnimiyut* of the Torah and the commandments. They will need to occupy themselves with *Mishnah*,[112] in order to weaken (by the occupation with Torah)[113] the power of the *sitra achra* which cleaves unto them, so that it will not dominate them—causing them to sin. Thus it is written: "And the sinner at the age of a hundred years old, will be cursed;"[114] this refers to the sinners of the mixed multitude.[115] Also, on the practical level, they will need the detailed rulings of proscription and impurity more than Israel. For (the latter) nothing shall occur that is unfit, impure, and proscribed, as "there shall not befall . . ."[116] It is also possible, and would appear so, that (the Israelites) will know all the fundamentals of the revealed part of the Torah from the *pnimiyut* of the Torah, like our father Abraham, peace be to him.[117] Thus they will not need to occupy themselves therewith at all. At the time of the second Temple, however, they needed to occupy themselves (therewith), not just for the practical application of the law, but, and this is the principal purpose of the Divine service, to weaken the power of the *sitra achra* and to elevate the sparks of holiness by means of Torah and worship, as explained elsewhere.[118]

After these words and this truth,[119] the above passage from the *R'ayah Mehemna* dealing with "the Tree of Good and Evil . . ." [i.e. the *kelipat nogah*, which is basically this world, as mentioned in *Etz Chayim*[120]], will be well understood with additional elucidation, and suffice this for the initiated.

XXVII.

What he wrote to the Chassidic community[1] to console them doubly for salvation[2] over the passing of the Rabbi, famous *Gaon*, holy man of G-d,[3] "Lamp of Israel, pillar of the right hand, mighty hammer,"[4] our master R. *Menachem Mendel*,[5] may his soul rest in Eden.

●▲ My beloved, my brethren and friends, who are (to me) as my soul . . .[6]

The Lord be over them, they should live[7] a life forevermore,[8] and their offspring with them, a seed of truth[9]—

[112] V.L.: *with Torah.* [113] *These words, which appear in the text in brackets, do not appear in some* MSS. [114] *Isaiah 65:20.* [115] *See Zohar I:114b* (Medrash Hane'-elam); cf. *Pessachim 68a.* [116] *No iniquity shall befall the righteous; Proverbs 12:21. See Zohar III:276a.* Cf. *Nachmanides on Deut. 30:6.* [117] *See Yoma 28b; Kiddushin 82a (cf. Zohar I:264b): Abraham observed the whole Torah etc. This statement appears rather difficult, because many of the commandments are related directly to later events, (*e.g. *the phylacteries need contain excerpts from the Torah, dealing with the* Exodus; *etc.), how then could Abraham have observed the whole Torah? But this is explained to mean that he observed it with respect to the* pni-

המשיח קודם תחה"מ אין בטלים) ולכן יהי' גם עיקר עסק התורה גם כן בפנימיות המצות וטעמיהם הנסתרים. אבל הנגלות יהיו גלוים וידועים לכל איש ישראל בידיעה בתחלה בלי שכחה וא"צ לעסוק בהם אלא לערב רב שלא יזכו למטעם מאילנא דחיי שהוא פנימיות התורה והמצוה וצריכים לעסוק [בתורה] במשנה להתיש כח הס"א הדבוק בהם (ע"י עסק התורה. בכ"י ליתא) שלא תשלוט בהם להחטיאם כדכתיב והחוטא בן מאה שנה יקולל שיהיו חוטאים מערב רב וגם למעשה יהיו צריכים לפרטי הלכות אסור וטומאה יותר מישראל שלא יארע להם פסול וטומאה ואסור כי לא יאונה כו' וגם אפשר וקרוב הדבר שידעו מפנימיות התורה כל גופי התורה הנגלית כמו אברהם אבינו ע"ה ולכן א"צ לעסוק בהם כלל. מה שאין כן בזמן בית שני היו צריכים לעסוק גם כי לא בשביל הלכה למעשה בלבד אלא שזהו עיקר עבודה להתיש כח הס"א ולהעלות ניצוצי הקדושה ע"י התורה והעבודה כמ"ש במ"א. ואחר הדברים והאמת יובן היטב בתוס' ביאור הר"מ דלעיל במה שאמר אילנא דטוב ורע כו' ר"ל קליפת נוגה שהוא עולם הזה העיקר כמ"ש בע"ח וד"ל:

כז

מה שכתב ליושבי אה"ק תובב"א לנחמם בכפליים להושיה על פטירת הרב הגאון המפורסם איש אלקים קדוש נ"י ע"ה פ"ה מהור"ר מנחם מענדל נ"ע.

אהובי אחיי ורעיי אשר כנפשי כו' ה' עליהם יחיו חיים עד העולם וצאצאיהם אתם זרע אמת ברוכי

---

miyut *of Torah,* i.e. *the esoteric part composed of the deeper and sublime reasons of Torah and the commandments (as they are in their root, prior to becoming vested in directives that require specific physical objects and actions).—See* Torah Or, Lech-Lacha: *11d;* Boneh Yerushalayim, *end of sect. 7; cf. also* Likutei Torah, *II: 18c.* [118] *The period of the Second Temple was not one of Messianic redemption. The return from the Babylonian exile, and the rebuilding of the Temple, did not constitute a restoration of pre-exilic conditions (cf. Yoma 9a f. and 21b; Sotah 48b, etc.). On the contrary, there was an increasing spiritual decline which, thus, required to be countered by means of Torah and worship; see*

(Notes cont. at end of Hebrew Text)

the blessed of the Lord are they[10] from now to everlasting.

Following the enquiry after their welfare as is becoming those that love His Name, I have come to comfort the smitten "that sigh and groan,"[11] and to console them doubly for salvation with what my ear has heard and noted for itself[12] on the saying of our sages, of blessed memory, that "He has left life unto all the living."[13]

The righteous lives by his faith,[14] and by the fear of the Lord which leads to life,[15] and by the flashes of fire of the flame[16] of his love (of G–d, which to him) supercedes life, to absorb therein the life of his *ruach*[17] all the days of his duration. And when it comes about that the Lord takes up[18] (and) gathers unto Himself his *ruach* and *neshamah,*[19] and he ascends from one elevation to another—to the peak of levels, he, then, leaves the life of his *ruach,* his effectuation on which he has laboured[20] previously among Israel [the labour of the righteous is unto the living[21]], to every living being. That is, (he leaves it to) the soul of every living being bound to his soul by the thick ropes of a magnanimous love, and an eternal love,[22] that will not be moved forevermore. For he who is the man that desires life[23] to become attached unto the Lord of life, his soul will become attached through his service; (his soul) will be bound up in the bundle of life with the Lord,[24] in the life of "The breath (*ruach*) of our nostrils of whom we said: in his *tzel* we shall live among the nations."[25] (This) he left unto us, in each and every one corresponding to the degree of his genuine alliance and his pure love, a pure love of truth from "The inward of man and a profound heart."[26] For "As waters (reflect) the face . . .";[27] and "spirit (*ruach*) rouses spirit, and brings forth spirit."[28] Thus his *ruach* remains truly in our midst, when he sees his children, the work of his hands, in his midst sanctifying His blessed Name.[29] For (His name) is magnified and sanctified when we walk in the right way that he has shown us of his ways, and we will walk in his paths[30] forevermore.

●▲And this is the meaning of the statement in the sacred *Zohar*[31] that "When the *tzadik* departs he is to be found in all worlds more than in his life-time." That is, he is to be found more even in this world of action ["this day to do them"[32]], because the action keeps growing growths of the second degree from the "Light implanted for the righteous"[33] in the field which the Lord blessed;[34] (this light) radiates to the earth and the outside places,[35] and also to us—those that are here this day, all of us that live in his ways, "The holy way shall it be called."[36]

This is as regards the service of G–d,

---

[10] Par. *Isaiah 65:23.* [11] Par. *Ezekiel 9:4.* [12] *Job 13:1.* [13] *A frequent expression in rabbinic literature; cf. e.g. R. Isaac Alfassi* (RIF), *and Maimonides, in their versions of documents-texts (resp. Yevamot, end of ch. 12, and* Hilchot Yibum Vechalitza, *end of ch. 4).* [14] *Habakuk 2:4.* [15] *Proverbs 19:23.* [16] Par. *Song 8:6.* [17] Par. *Isaiah 38:16.*—V.L.: *of his* ruach *and his* neshamah. *See* supra, *sect. V, note 53 on the terms* nefesh, ruach, neshamah. [18] Par. *II Kings 2:1.* [19] Par. *Job 34:14.* [20] Par. *Ezekiel 29:20.* [21] *Proverbs 10:16.* [22] Ahavah rabba *and* ahavat olam. *On these terms see Zohar III:263b;* Torah Or, Vayechi, *p. 47b.* [23] Par. *Psalms 34:13.* [24] *I Samuel 25:29;* see Likutei Torah *III:51d,*

ברוכי ה׳ המה מעתה ועד עולם. אחד״ש כמשפט לאוהבי שמו באתי לדבר על לב נדכאים הנאנחים והנאנקים ולנחמם בכפליים לתושיה אשר שמעה אזני ותבן לה על מארז״ל דשבק חיים לכל חי כי צדיק באמונתו יחיה וביראת ה׳ לחיים וברשפי אש שלהבת אהבתו מחיים לכל בהן חיי רוחו [נ״א ונשמתו] כל ימי חלדו ויהי בהעלות ה׳ רוחו ונשמתו אליו יאסוף ויעלה בעילוי אחר עילוי עד רום המעלות שבק חיי רוחו פעולתו אשר עבד בה לפנים בישראל פעולת צדיק לחיים לכל חי היא נפש כל חי הקשורה בנפשו בחבלי עבותות אהבה רבה ואהבת עולם כל תמוט לנצח אשר מי האיש החפץ חיים לדבקה בה׳ חיים בעבודתו תדבק נפשו והיתה צרורה בצרור החיים את ה׳ בחיי רוח אפינו אשר אמרנו בצלו נחיה בגוים אשר שבק לנו בכל אחד ואחד כפי בחי׳ התקשרותו באמת ואהבתו אהבת אמת הטהורה מקרב איש ולב עמוק כי כמים הפנים וכו׳ ורוח אייתי רוח ואמשיך רוח ורוחו עומדת בקרבינו ממש כי בראותו ילדיו מעשה ידיו בקרבו יקדישו שמו יתברך אשר יתגדל ויתקדש כאשר נלך בדרך ישרה אשר הורנו מדרכיו ונלכה באורחותיו נס״ו. וז״ש בזוה״ק דצדיקא דאתפטר אשתכח בכלהו עלמין יתיר מבחיוהי דהיינו שגם בזה העולם המעשה היום לעשותם אשתכח יתיר כי המעשה (גדול) [גדל] והולך גידולי גידולין מן אור זרוע לצדיק בשדה אשר ברכו ה׳ המאיר לארץ וחוצות וגם אנחנו אלה פה היום כולנו חיים בדרכיו דרך הקדש יקרא לה. זאת בעבודת ה׳ במילי

---

and infra. *sect. XXIX.* [25] Par. *Lament. 4:20. The context suggests that this is not a mere paraphrase.* Tzel *(shadow) is a term associated with the soul and related to the sublime rank of* chayah *(cf.* supra, *sect. V, note 53)—the "soul of soul," transcending not only the rank of* ruach *but also that of* neshamah. *The phrase, thus, appears to mean: in the life (or essence) of the* ruach *(of the* tzadik*) of which we said: "in his* tzel *we shall live" . . . This he left unto us, etc.—On the meaning and significance of* tzel, *see R. Menachem Mendel,* Tehilim Yohel Or, *on Ps. 39:7 (pp. 148 ff.).* [26] Par. *Psalms 64:7.* [27] *Proverbs 27:19; see* supra, *sect. I, note 26.* [28] *Zohar II:162b.* [29] Par.

(Notes cont. at end of Hebrew Text)

with respect to heavenly matters.[37] As for mundane matters, it is stated explicitly in the sacred *Zohar* that the *tzadikim* shield the world, and after their death even more than in their life.[38] Were it not for the prayer of the *tzadikim* in that world, the world would not endure a single moment.[39] And whoever is closer unto the habitation of the Lord,[40] during his life-time, has precedence to the blessing.[41]

(XXVII b). *An elucidation of the above.* ●▲ It is stated in the sacred *Zohar*[42] that when the *tzadik* departs he is to be found in all worlds more than in his life-time . . . Now this needs to be understood. For, granted that he is to be found increasingly in the upper worlds, because he ascends to there; but how can he be found more in this world?

This may be explained along the lines of what I received on the saying of our sages, of blessed memory, that "He has left life unto all the living."[43]

As is known, the life of the *tzadik* is not a physical life[44] but a spiritual life, consisting of faith, awe, and love. Thus of faith it is written: "And the *tzadik* lives by his faith."[45] Of awe it is written: "The awe of the Lord is for life."[46] And of love it is written:[47] "He who pursues *tzedakah*[48] and *chesed*, will find life," and *chesed* refers to love.[49]

These three attributes are prevalent in every world to the topmost of levels, all proportionate to the levels of the worlds—one higher than the other by way of cause ●▲ and effect, as known. Now, while the *tzadik* was alive on earth, these three attributes were contained in their vessel and garment on the plane of physical space. This is the aspect of the *nefesh* bound to his body. All his disciples receive but a radiation from these attributes, and a ray [from them] radiating beyond this vessel by means of his holy utterances and thoughts. That is why our sages, of blessed memory, said that a person cannot comprehend his master . . .[50] But after his passing, as the *nefesh* [which remains in the grave] is separated from the *ruach* [i.e. these three attributes] which is in the Garden of Eden,[51] whoever is nigh unto him can receive a part

[37] *Religious matters.* [38] *Zohar III:71b.* [39] *See* ibid., *III:70b* ff.; cf. *Zohar II:16b.* [40] I.e. *to the* tzadik. [41] *The original letter continues with a lengthy appeal for charity in general, and for the support of R. Mendel of Vitebsk's family in particular. (Reproduced, with slight variations, in* Igrot Ba'al Hatanya, *no. 24, p. 38 f.)* [42] *III:71b.* [43] Supra, *note 13.* [44] Par. *Proverbs 14:30.* [45] *Habakuk 2:4.* [46] *Proverbs 19:23.* [47] *Proverbs 21:21.* [48] *The* tzadik. [49]. Chesed *is synonymous with love;* cf. supra, *sect. XIII, note 27.* [50] *Rashi on Deut. 29:6; Avodah Zarah 5b;* cf. Tossafot, *Sotah 22b (*s.v. ורעד*).* I.e. *only a radiation and a mere ray are apprehended.* [51] *See Zohar I:81a;* ibid., *II:142a.*

במילי דשמיא. ובמילי דעלמא בפירוש אתמר בזוה"ק דצדיקייא מגינין על עלמא ובמיתתהון יתיר מבחייהון ואלמלא צלותא דצדיקייא בההוא עלמא לא אתקיים עלמא רגעא חדא וכל הקרוב קרוב אל משכן ה' בחייו קודם לברכה:

ביאור על הנ"ל:

איתא בזוה"ק דצדיקא דאתפטר אשתכח בכלהו עלמין יתיר מבחיוהי כו' וצריך להבין תינח בעולמות עליונים אשתכח יתיר בעלותו שמה אבל בעוה"ז איך אשתכח יתיר. וי"ל ע"ד מה שקבלתי על מאמר חז"ל דשבק חיים לכל חי כנודע שחיי הצדיק אינם חיים בשרים כ"א חיים רוחניים שהם אמונה ויראה ואהבה כי באמונה כתיב וצדיק באמונתו יחיה וביראה כתיב ויראת ה' לחיים ובאהבה כתיב רודף צדקה וחסד ימצא חיים וחסד הוא אהבה ושלשה מדות אלו הם בכל עולם ועולם עד רום המעלות הכל לפי ערך בחי' מעלות העולמות זע"ז בדרך עילה ועלול כנודע. והנה בהיות הצדיק חי על פני האדמה היו שלשה מדות אלו בתוך כלי ולבוש שלהם בבחי' מקום גשמי שהיא בחי' נפש הקשורה בגופו וכל תלמידיו אינם מקבלים רק הארת מדות אלו וזיון המאיר חוץ לכלי זה ע"י דבוריו ומחשבותיו הקדושים. ולכן ארז"ל שאין אדם עומד על דעת רבו וכו' אבל לאחר פטירתו לפי שמתפרדים בחי' הנפש שנשארה בקבר מבחי' הרוח שבג"ע שהן שלש מדות הללו לפיכך יכול כל הקרוב אליו לקבל חלק מבחי'

from the aspect of his *ruach* [which is in the Garden of Eden], because it is no (longer) within a vessel, nor on the plane of physical space. Thus is known the saying of our sages, of blessed memory, with reference to our father Jacob, peace be to him, that "The Garden of Eden entered with him."[52] Likewise it is stated in the book *Assarah Maamarot* that the sphere of the Garden of Eden spreads itself around every person, and in this sphere are recorded all his good thoughts and utterings of Torah and Divine worship; ([53] and likewise to the contrary, Heaven forfend: they[54] are recorded in the sphere of the Gehenna, which spreads itself around every person[55]). Thus it is very easy for his disciples to receive their part of the essential aspects of their master's *ruach*, i.e. his faith, his awe and his love wherewith he served the Lord, and not merely a ray thereof which radiates beyond the vessel. For the essential aspect of his *ruach* is raised, elevation upon elevation, to become absorbed in his *neshamah* which is in the upper Garden of Eden, in the supreme worlds.

Now it is known that something sacred is never wholly and totally uprooted from its place and original level, even after it has reached the highest point.[56] Thus it is this original aspect, remaining below, in the lower Garden of Eden, in its place and original level, which extends itself among his disciples; each one according to the level of his alliance and closeness to (the *tzadik*) during his lifetime and after his death out of a magnanimous love. For the efflux of anything spiritual is but by means of a magnanimous love. Thus it is stated in the sacred *Zohar*[57] that the spirit (*ruach*) in a mode of the willingness of the heart (*re'uta deliba*)[58] elicits a spirit from above; thus only when he will prepare himself towards his G-d[59] with a great preparation and immense effort to receive these attributes[60] in the way that his master taught him, and as the saying of our sages, of blessed memory: "If you have laboured and (claim to have) found—believe it."[61]

●▲Now, there is yet another type of radiation to his disciples. However, it does not vest itself truly in their mind—as is the case with the first one, but radiates over them, from aloft. It stems from the ascent of his *ruach* and his *neshamah* to the source whence it was hewn, that is to the "orchard of the holy apples" (*chakal tapuchin kadishin*).[62] (This ascent) effects a unification there (*yichud*) by means of the elevation of the *mayin nukvin*[63] of all his doings, his Torah, and the Divine Service which he served all the days of

---

[52] *Genesis Rabba 65:22;* Tanchuma *(ed. Buber)* Toldot: *10, and 22. Zohar III:84a.* [53] *Brackets appear in the text.* [54] I.e. *evil thoughts and utterings.* [55] Cf. *Genesis Rabba 65:22;* Tanchuma *(ed. Buber)* Toldot: *10, and 22.* [56] Pardess Rimonim *14:1 (where this principle is explained at length);* Etz Chayim *34:3;* Mevoh She'arim *VI:I:I. See also* Etz Chayim *6:5, 47:6* et passim. [57] *Zohar II: 162b.* [58] I.e. *the mode of* ahavah rabba *(magnanimous love). See* supra, *sect. XVIII, and notes 8–9* ad loc. [59] Par. *Amos 4:12.* [60] *The faith, awe, and love of the* tzadik. [61] *Megilah 6b.* [62] *The Garden of Eden; Zohar III: 84a.* Cf. *Rashi on Genesis 27:27; see also Zohar I: 142b. More on this term see* Aspaklarya

מבחי' רוחו שבג"ע הואיל ואינה בתוך כלי ולא בבחי' מקום גשמי כנודע מארז"ל על יעקב אבינו ע"ה שנכנס עמו ג"ע וכ"כ בספר עשרה מאמרות שאויר ג"ע מתפשט סביב כל אדם ונרשמים באויר זה כל מחשבותיו ודבוריו הטובים בתורה ועבודת ה' (וכן להיפך ח"ו נרשמים באויר המתפשט מגיהנם סביב כל אדם) הלכך נקל מאד לתלמידיו לקבל חלקם מבחי' רוח רבם העצמיית שהם אמונתו ויראתו ואהבתו אשר עבד בהם את ה' ולא זיום בלבד המאיר חוץ לכלי לפי שבחי' רוחו העצמית מתעלה בעילוי אחר עילוי להכלל בבחי' נשמתו שבג"ע העליון שבעולמות העליונים ונודע שכל דבר שבקדושה אינו נעקר לגמרי מכל וכל ממקומו ומדרגתו הראשונה גם לאחר שנתעלה למעלה ובחי' זו הראשונה שנשארה למטה בגן עדן התחתון במקומו ומדרגתו הראשונה היא המתפשטת בתלמידיו כל אחד כפי בחי' התקשרותו וקרבתו אליו בחייו ובמותו באהבה רבה כי המשכת כל רוחניות אינה אלא ע"י אהבה רבה כמ"ש בזוה"ק דרוח דרעותא דלבא אמשיך רוח מלעילא רק אם יכון לקראת אלהיו בהכנה רבה ויגיעה עצומה לקבל שלש מדות הללו כדרך שהורהו רבו וכמארז"ל יגעת ומצאת תאמין. והנה יש עוד בחי' הארה לתלמידיו רק שאינה מתלבשת בתוך מוחם ממש כבראשונה רק מאירה עליהם מלמעלה והיא מעליית רוחו ונשמתו למקור חוצבו דהיינו לחקל תפוחין קדישין ועי"ז נעשה שם יחוד ע"י העלאת מ"נ מכל מעשיו ותורתו ועבודתו אשר עבד כל ימי חייו

Hameirah *on Zohar III: 142b, par. 23.*
[63] *Feminine waters; see* supra, *sect. IV, note 46; Introd., note 199.*

his life. And in the *chakal tapuchin kadishin* are implanted most sublime lights corresponding to the nether ones, i.e. his Torah and worship. The illumination of these supernal lights radiates over all his disciples who became servants of the Lord through his Torah and worship. And this radiation, which is over them from aloft, instills in their heart thoughts of repentance and good deeds. And all the good deeds born from this radiation [radiating from the lights implanted in the orchard mentioned above] are called "growths of the second degree." But this radiation is in great latency and concealment, just like the sun radiating to the stars from below the earth. Thus it is stated in the *Tikunim*,[64] in reference to Moses our Master, peace to him, that after his passing his radiation extends in every generation to the sixty myriad souls,[65] just like the sun radiating to the sixty myriad stars from below the earth.

XXVIII.

What he wrote to his relative-by-marriage, the Rabbi, famous *Gaon*, G-dly and holy man of the Lord, "Lamp of Israel, pillar of the right hand, mighty hammer,"[1] our master *R. Levi Yitzchak*,[2] may his soul rest in Eden, head of the *Bet Din* of the holy community of Berdichev, to console him on the passing of his son, the pious rabbi, *R. Meir*,[3] may his soul rest in Eden.

●▲"Why was the section of Miriam[4] adjoined to the section of the heifer?[5] To teach you that just as the heifer effects atonement . . ."[6]

Now it needs to be understood why it was adjoined precisely to the "red heifer" ([7]which was prepared outside the three camps;[8] it is just that the Torah calls it a sin-offering[9]),[10] and it was not adjoined to the section of the sin-offering that was prepared within, on the actual altar of atonement.

However, it is known from the sacred *Zohar*, and from R. Isaac Luria, of blessed memory,[11] that the principium of the sacrifices brought on the altar is that they are an aspect of the elevation of *mayin nukvin*:[12] from the animal soul, which is in (the class of) *nogah*,[13] to their root and source, i.e. the forms of the four Animals of the Chariot bearing the Throne:[14] the Face of the Ox, and the Face of the Eagle . . .,[15] Thereby

---

[64] *Tikunei Zohar 69:112a; Zohar III:273a. See* H.V. a.l., *and the* ref. *cited there.* [65] *The sixty myriad general souls of Israel that exist in every generation; see* ibid., (supra, *note 44*), *and Eccles. Rabba I:5.*

Section XXVIII

[1] *See* supra, *sect. XXVII, notes 3 and 4.* [2] *R. Levi Yitzchak of Berdichev (1740–1810), author of* Kedushat Levi. *R. Levi Yitzchak was of the leading disciples of R. Dov Ber, the* Maggid *of Mezeritch, and a close friend and associate of R. Schneur Zalman.* [3] *Author of* Keter Torah. [4] *Numbers 20:1.* [5] *Numbers, ch. 19.* [6] *Mo'ed Katan 28a.* [7] *Brackets suggested by* H.V.

חייו ונזרעו בחקל תפוחין קדישין אורות עליונים מאד לעומת תחתונים אשר הם תורתו ועבודתו והארת אורות עליונים אלו מאירה על כל תלמידיו שנעשו עובדי ה׳ על ידי תורתו ועבודתו והארה זו שעליהם מלמעלה מכנסת בלבם הרהורי תשובה ומעשים טובים וכל המעשים טובים הנולדים מהארה זו שמאירה מאורות הזרועים בשדה הנ״ל נקרא גידולי גידולין והארה זו היא בהעלם והסתר גדול כמו שמש המאיר לכוכבים מתחת לארץ כדאיתא בתיקונים על משה רבינו ע״ה שאחר פטירתו מתפשטת הארתו בכל דרא ודרא לששים רבוא נשמות כמו שמש המאיר מתחת לארץ לששים רבוא כוכבים :

כח

מה שכתב למחותנו הרב הגאון המפורסם איש אלקים קדוש ה׳ נ״י ע״ה פ״ה מו״ה לוי יצחק נ״ע אב״ד דק״ק בארדיטשוב לנחמו על פטירת בנו הרב החסיד מו״ה מאיר נ״ע :

למה נסמכה פ׳ מרים לפ׳ פרה לומר לך מה פרה מכפרת וכו׳. וצריך להבין למה נסמכה דוקא לפרה אדומה הנעשה חוץ לשלש מחנות אלא דחטאת קריי׳ רחמנא [בכת״י הנוסחא הנעשה בחוץ. ומן תיבת לשלש עד תיבת רחמנא ליתא בכת״י] ולא נסמכה לפ׳ חטאת הנעשה בפנים על גבי המזבח כפרה ממש. אמנם נודע מזוה״ק והאריז״ל סוד הקרבנות שעל גבי המזבח הן בחי׳ העלאת מ״נ מנפש הבהמית שבנוגה אל שרשן ומקורן הן בחי׳ ד׳ חיות שבמרכבה הנושאות את הכסא פני שור ופני נשר וכו׳. ועי״ז נמשכים

---

[8] *Numbers 19:3; Rashi* ad loc.; *Yoma 68a.* [9] *Numbers 19:9; Rashi* ad loc. *Avodah Zarah 23b; Chulin 11a. The red heifer as such is not a sacrifice proper. It was not sacrificed on the altar but outside the camps of the Priests, Levites, and Israelites. However, Scripture terms it a sin-offering thus subjecting it to Halachic rulings applying to sacrifices.* [10] V.L.: (which was prepared outside) and . . . [11] Cf. *Zohar I: 64b* f.; *II: 268b* f.; *III: 240a* ff. Likutei Torah *of R. Isaac Luria*, Vayikra. [12] *Feminine waters; see* supra, *sect. IV, note 46.* [13] *See* supra, *sect. XV, note 63.* [14] *See Ezekiel, ch. 1.* [15] *See* supra, *end of sect. XX.*

the *mayin duchrin*[16] are elicited and descend from the aspect of the "Man upon the Throne,"[17] referred to as *malka*,[18] and *z'eyr anpin*.[19] As for the burning of the red heifer, however, by throwing in the cedar-wood, and the hyssop . . ., and the placing of running waters into the ashes, the *Mishnah*[20] refers to this as the *sanctification* (*kidush*) of the waters of lustration. This is the aspect of *kodesh ha'elyon*,[21] referred to as *tala dibedulcha*,[22] as mentioned in the sacred *Zohar*,[23] the aspect of the supreme *chochmah* and the *mocha setimaah* of *arich anpin*.[24] Of it is said in many places in the sacred *Zohar* that through *chochmah* they are disencumbered[25] and darkness is converted to light.[26] That is, by means of the *mocha setimaah* of *arich anpin* the world of *tikun*[27] is disencumbered and corrected from the world of *tohu*[28] and the breaking of the vessels[29] that fell into Beriah, Yetzirah and Asiyah . . ., as known. That is why (the red heifer) purifies from the defilement by a corpse, even though such is the highest degree of impurity, and much lower than *nogah*.[30]

●▲Now,[31] it is known that *abba*[32] draws from the eighth *mazal* . . .,[33] the tuft of *notzer chesed*.[34] *Notzer* is (composed of the same) letters (as) *ratzon*.[35] It is the *et ratzon*[36] that becomes revealed and radiates in a manifest way, from above downwards, at the time of the passing of the great *tzadikim*[37] who serve the Lord out of love, surrendering their soul to the Lord during their life-time every evening and morning when reading the *Shema*.[38] For thereby they elevate the *mayin nukvin* to *abba* and *imma*, as known. ([39]The same applies to (their) study of the Torah[40] which derives from *chochmah*.[41]) Thus, the aspects of the *mayin duchrin* were elicited thereby and descended from the tuft of *notzer chesed*; and they, indeed, radiate in a manifest way at the time of their passing. For as known, all the effort of man, which his soul toiled[42] during his life-time, is above in a hidden and concealed state. It becomes revealed and radiates in a manifest way from above downwards at the time of his passing.[43]

Now, by the manifestation of the illumination of the tuft of *notzer chesed* at the time of their passing, the *chesed* of the Lord radiates from world to world, over those who fear Him,[44] and effects salvations in the midst of the earth[45] to atone for the sin of the generation, even for the deliberate sins which are of the three impure *kelipot* [which are inferior to *nogah*]. For the *mazal* of *notzer* is of the *mochin setimin* of *arich anpin*, the source of the extractions (*birurim*).

---

[16] *The masculine waters, the supernal effusions; see* supra, *section IV, note 46.* [17] *Ezekiel I:26.—See Zohar III:217a.* [18] *King.*—Cf. *Zohar III:10a.* [19] Microprosopus *(see* supra, *sect. XIX, note 10)*.—Cf. *Zohar III:66b and 227a. The emanation elicited by the sacrifices proper thus stems from* malka, *and* z'eyr anpin, *corresponding to* tiferet. [20] *Parah, ch. 6;* et passim. [21] *Supreme holiness.* [22] *The Dew of Bdellium (*par. *Numbers 11:7), referring to the emanations from* arich anpin. *See commentary of R. Isaac Luria on* Sifra Detzniyuta *(Zohar II beg. of 176b), in* Sha'ar Ma'amarei Rashby *(ed. Tel Aviv 1961), p. 111b.* [23] *See Zohar III:49a., 128b and 135b.* [24] *The Concealed Brain; the aspect of* chochmah *in the*

נמשכים ויורדים מ"ד מבחי' אדם שעל הכסא הנקרא בשם מלכא וז"א. אכן בשריפת הפרה אדומה הנה ע"י השלכת עץ ארז ואזוב וכו' ונתינת מים חיים אל האפר נקרא בשם קידוש מי חטאת במשנה והיא בחי' קדש העליון הנקרא בשם טלא דבדולחא כמ"ש בזוה"ק שהיא בחי' חכמה עילאה ומוחא סתימאה דא"א ועלה איתמר בדוכתי טובא בזוה"ק בחכמה אתבררו ואתהפכא חשוכא לנהורא דהיינו עולם התיקון שנתברר ונתתקן ע"י מוחא סתימאה דא"א מעולם התהו ושבירת הכלים שנפלו בבי"ע וכו' כנודע. ולזאת מטהרת טומאת המת אף שהוא אבי אבות וכו' ולמטה מטה מנוגה:

והנה מודעת זאת דאבא יונק ממזל השמיני כו' והוא תיקון ונוצר אותיות רצון והיא ג"כ עת רצון המתגלה ומאיר בבחי' גילוי מלמעלה למטה בעת פטירת צדיקי עליון עובדי ה' באהבה במסירת נפשם לה' בחייהם ערבית ושחרית בק"ש שעי"ז היו מעלים מ"נ לאו"א בק"ש כידוע. (וכן בת"ת דמחכמה נפקא) ועי"ז היו נמשכים ויורדים בחי' מ"ד מתיקון ונוצר חסד והם הם המאירים בבחי' גילוי בפטירתם כנודע שכל עמל האדם שעמלה נפשו בחייו למעלה בבחי' העלם והסתר מתגלה ומאיר בבחי' גילוי מלמעלה למטה בעת פטירתו והנה ע"י גילוי הארת תיקון ונוצר חסד בפטירתן מאיר חסד ה' מעולם עד עולם על יראיו ופועל ישועות בקרב הארץ לכפר על עון הדור אף גם על הזדונות שהן מג' קליפות הטמאות שלמטה מנוגה לפי שמזל דנוצר ממו"ס דא"א מקור הבירורים ואתהפכא

---

partzuf *of* arich anpin.—*See* supra, *sect. X, note 41.* [25] *See* supra, *sect. XXVI, and the references cited there in note 82.* [26] *Zohar I:4a; Tikunei Zohar 21:50a.* [27] *The World of Correction (or Restitution). See Introduction,* s.v. Tohu and Tikun. [28] *The World of Chaos (or Disorder). See Introduction,* s.v. Tohu and Tikun. [29] *See Introduction,* s.v. Shevirat Hakelim. [30] *The sacrifices proper, brought on the altar, elicit from the rank of* z'eyr anpin *and sublimate the class of* nogah. *The red heifer, however, elicits from the supreme rank of* arich anpin. *Its effect, therefore, is that much greater, and it is able to sublimate even ranks far below* nogah. [31] *This paragraph emended accord-*

(Notes cont. at end of Hebrew Text)

Thus the darkness of the *shevirat hakelim* is converted into the light of the world of *tikun*. This is not the case, though, with the sacrifices that are upon the altar. They atone only for inadvertent sins which come about because of the strengthening of the animal soul which is of *nogah*, as mentioned in *Likutei Torah*, section of *Vayikra*.

That is why (the section of Miriam) was adjoined expressly to the section of the heifer: "just as the heifer . . ." Indeed, in the *Yalkut*, section of *Shemini*, the version is "the waters of lustration . . ."[46]

●▲ XXIX. "A woman of valour is the crown (*atarah*) of her husband . . ."[1]

In the *Gemara*, fourth chapter of *Megilah*,[2] it is stated: "He that makes use of the crown, passes away[3] . . . this applies to him who makes use of one who can repeat *halachot*, the crown (*keter*) of the Torah . . . It was taught in the academy of Elijah: whoever repeats *halachot*, is assured . . ."

Now it needs to be understood why the *halachot* are referred to as "crown," and "the crown of the Torah," and, also, why expressly he who repeats the *halachot* is assured . . ., and not other subjects of Torah. Furthermore, one needs to understand the saying of our sages, of blessed memory, in the eleventh chapter of *Menachot*,[4] that even if one learned but a single chapter in the morning . . ., one has fulfilled one's duty. Why is one's duty not fulfilled by other subjects of Torah?

However, it is well-known that R. Isaac Luria, of blessed memory, stated that every person of Israel needs to be reincarnated many times, until he has fulfilled all 613 commandments of the Torah in thought, speech and action.[5] This is in order to complete the garments of his soul and to correct them, so that there will not be a missing garment . . .[6] [Excepted are the commandments incumbent upon the king, because he discharges all of Israel, as he is the omneity of them all.] The reason is in order to garb all the 613 aspects and powers in one's soul, so that "Not one of them shall be lacking."[7]

An explanation for the necessity and need of these garments is given in the *Zohar*,[8] and is understood by every intelligent person. For the *nefesh*, *ruach*, and *neshamah*[9] in man, are of the genre of creatures, and it is impossible for any creature to attain any apprehension of the Creator and Former of all, the blessed En Sof. Even after G-d had already radiated of His blessed light, and caused an emanation in the form of an evolution of

---

[46] *Just as the waters of lustration effect atonement etc., thus alleviating the difficulty raised at the beginning of this letter.*

Section XXIX

[1] *Proverbs 12:4.* [2] *Folio 28b.* [3] *Avot I:13.* [4] *Folio 99b.* [5] *See* supra *section VII, note 37.* [6] *See* supra, *section III, note 5, on the "garments" of the soul.* [7] Par. *Isaiah 34:16.* [8] *Zohar II:210a–b, and 229a–b.* [9] *See* supra, *sect. V, note 53, on these terms.*

ואתהפכא חשוכא דשבירת הכלים לנהורא דעולם התיקון. משא״כ בקרבנות שע״ג המזבח שאינן מכפרים אלא על השגגות שהן מהתגברות נפש הבהמית שמנוגה כמ״ש בלקוטי תורה פ׳ ויקרא ולכן נסמכה לפ׳ פרה דוקא מה פרה וכו׳ ובילקוט פ׳ שמיני הגי׳ מי חטאת וכו׳:

כט אשת חיל עטרת בעלה כו׳. איתא בגמ׳ פ״ד דמגילה ודאשתמש בתגא חלף כו׳ זה המשתמש במי ששונה הלכות כתרה של תורה כו׳ תנא דבי אליהו כל השונה הלכות מובטח לו כו׳. וצריך להבין למה נקראו ההלכות בשם תגא וכתרה של תורה וגם למה השונה הלכות דוקא מובטח לו כו׳ ולא שאר ד״ת. וכן להבין מארז״ל בפ״א דמנחות אפי׳ לא שנה אדם אלא פרק אחד שחרית כו׳ יצא י״ח ולמה אינו יוצא י״ח בשאר ד״ת:

אך מודעת זאת מ״ש האריז״ל שכל אדם מישראל צריך לבא בגלגולים רבים עד שיקיים כל תרי״ג מצות התורה במחשבה דיבור ומעשה להשלים לבושי נפשו ולתקנם שלא יהא לבושא דחסרא כו׳ לבד מצות התלויות במלך שהוא מוציא כל ישראל כי הוא כללות כולם כו׳ והטעם הוא כדי להלביש כל תרי״ג בחי׳ וכחות שבנפשו אחת מהנה לא נעדרה כו׳. וביאור ענין הכרח וצורך לבושים אלו מבואר בזהר ומובן לכל משכיל כי להיות שנפש רוח ונשמה שבאדם הן בחי׳ נבראים וא״א לשום נברא להשיג שום השגה בבורא ויוצר הכל א״ס ב״ה וגם אחרי אשר האיר ה׳ מאורו ית׳ והאציל בבחי׳ השתלשלות מדרגות

numerous levels [level upon level], by way of immense contractions and numerous, immense garments [known to those adept in the esoteric science; in the *Idra Rabba* they are referred to as "hairs,"[10] and as written in *Daniel*: "And the hair of his head as pure wool . . ."[11]], nevertheless, neither the *nefesh*, nor the *ruach* and *neshamah* can endure the light. For the light is good and sweet . . .,[12] as it is written: "To behold the *no'am* of the Lord."[13] (*No'am*) expresses pleasantness, agreeableness, sweetness, and an infinitely immense delight, as it is written: "Then you will delight yourself in the Lord,"[14] "And He will satisfy with *tzachtzachot* . . ."[15] an idiom of *tziphey tzama*,[16] as stated in the *Zohar*.[17] It is not in (the soul's) power to absorb the pleasantness and agreeableness of the *tzachtzachot* without leaving its husk and becoming existentially nullified just like the flame in the torch, were it not that from the aspect of this very light there will evolve and issue forth some minute radiation, by way of an evolution of level after level, with many contractions, until a single garment is created thereof, a creation like the nature of this light, to garb the *nefesh*, *ruach*, and *neshamah*. By way of this garment [which is like this light], (the soul) can derive enjoyment from the ray of this light, and apprehend it, without becoming existentially nullified. It is analogous to someone looking at the sun through a fine and lucid speculum. Thus it is written: "And Moses entered into the midst of the cloud, and he ascended . . .";[18] that is, he vested himself in the cloud and ascended, and saw by way of the cloud . . . Thus it is explained[19] in the *Zohar*, volume II, folios 210 and 229.

●▲Now this light, kept concealed for the righteous in the future,[20] is termed the "pleasantness of the Lord," and the "*Tzachtzachot* to delight in the Lord," and the "400 worlds of longing" (*almin diksufin*)[21] in which the *tzadikim* delight . . . [as it is written:[22] "400 shekalim of *kessef* . . ."]. In (this light) there are very many rungs and levels, one superior to the other. But the minute radiation, which descends level after level to create this garment, is of the rank of the lowest level in this light. Metaphorically speaking, it is referred to as the external level, and *achurayim*, as stated in the *Zohar*, folio 208b ([23]*cf.* in the commentary *Mikdash Melech*), and 210b: "And that

---

[10] *Zohar III: 128b* ff. Cf. supra, *sect. XX, note 74*. [11] *Daniel 7:9*. [12] Par. *Eccles. 11:7*. [13] *Psalms 27:4*. [14] *Isaiah 58:14*. [15] Ibid., *11. The* Zohar *(II: 209a) quotes these two verses in this order*. [16] *Parched with thirst (Isaiah 5:13)*; *see comment.* a.l. [17] *Zohar II: 210b*. [18] *Exodus 24:18; see Zohar II: 229a, and I: 66a*. [19] *The preceding discourse dealing with the garments of the soul*. [20] *See Hagigah 12a; Zohar I: 45b, and II: 148b (*supra, *sect. XXVII, and notes 33 and 34* ad loc.*)*. [21] *Zohar I: 123b; III: 128b, and 288a*. [22] *Genesis 23:15.*—כסף *(silver) is etymologically related to* כסף *(to long; to desire)*. [23] *Brackets appear in the text.*

מדרגות רבות מדרגה אחר מדרגה בבחי' צמצומים עצומים ולבושים רבים ועצומים הידועים לי"ח ונקראים באד"ר בשם שערות וכדכתיב בדניאל ושער רישיה כעמר נקא כו' אעפ"כ לא יכלה הנפש או הרוח ונשמה למסבל האור כי טוב ומתוק האור וכו' כמ"ש לחזות בנועם ה' לשון נעימות ועריבות ומתיקות ותענוג עצום לאין קץ כמ"ש אז תתענג על ה' והשביע בצחצחות כו' לשון צחה צמא כמ"ש בזהר ואין בכחה לקבל הנעימות ועריבות הצחצחות שלא תצא מנרתקה ותתבטל ממציאותה כנר באבוקה אם לא שמבחי' אור זה עצמו תשתלשל ותמשך ממנו איזו הארה מועטת בדרך השתלשלות מדריגה אחר מדרגה בצמצומים רבים עד שיברא ממנה לבוש אחד נברא מעין מהות אור זה להלביש הנפש רוח ונשמה ודרך לבוש זה שהוא מעין אור זה תוכל ליהנות מזיו אור זה ולהשיגו ולא תתבטל ממציאותה וכמשל הרואה בשמש דרך עששית זכה ומאירה וכו' וכמ"ש ויבא משה בתוך הענן ויעל כו' שנתלבש בענן ועלה וראה דרך הענן וכו' כמ"ש בזח"ב דר"י ורכ"ט. והנה אור זה הגנוז לצדיקים לע"ל הנק' בשם נועם ה' וצחצחות להתענג על ה' וד' מאות עלמין דכסופין דמתענגי בהון צדיקייא כו' כמ"ש ארבע מאות שקל כסף כו' הנה יש בו מעלות ומדרגות רבות מאד גבוה מעל גבוה אך הארה מועטת היורדת מדרגה אחר מדרגה לברוא לבוש זה היא מבחי' מדרגה האחרונה שבאור זה ונקראת בשם מדרגה החיצונה ואחוריים דרך משל כמ"ש בזהר דר"ח ע"ב (עיין בס' מק"מ) ור"י ע"ב ומה

ראשתאר

which is left . . ."

Now, in the soul of man there is a faculty for delight: for (the soul) delights in what is delightful to it, as, for example, in the conception of a new insight, or the like. The aspect of the *chitzoniyut* and *achurayim* of the (soul's) capacity and state of delight is the aspect of the faculty of its will: (the soul) wills that which it wills, i.e. something that is not painful [for pain is the opposite of delight].[24] Metaphorically speaking, it is the same with the light of the blessed En Sof, as it were. The blessed Supreme will is the aspect of the *chitzoniyut* and *achurayim* of the aspect of the Supreme delight, the "pleasantness of the Lord," the *tzachtzachot*, and the "worlds of longing," mentioned above. Though these are unified in an absolute unity, for He, blessed be He, and His will, are one [and not like the will of man, Heaven forfend, neither wholly nor partially; there is no comparison whatever between them], nevertheless, the Torah speaks in human idiom,[25] to appease the ear with what it is able to hear,[26] with allegory and metaphor relating to the soul of man[27] which compounds the faculty of delight, will, wisdom, understanding. . . . (This composition of the soul) is empirically evident. For when a person conceives some wondrous new insight then, at least, at that very moment, there is born in his mind a wondrous delight. Thus it follows that the (faculty of) delight surpasses exceedingly the faculty of the intellect and wisdom, except that it is vested in the faculty of the intellect and wisdom. Thus when man senses the intellect and wisdom, that is, he apprehends and understands it well, he, then, also senses the faculty of delight which is vested in the wisdom. That is why in the sacred *Zohar*[28] the aspect of *binah* is referred to as *olam habah* (the world to come). For it is the state of the manifestation of the *chochmah*, and the delight vested in it, which the righteous apprehend in the Garden of Eden, and perceive in the *pnimiyut* of the Torah. For the Torah derives from *chochmah*,[29] and the Torah and the Holy One, blessed is He, are entirely one.[30]

●▲Now, the Cabbalists[31] term, and refer to the Supreme Will as *keter elyon*, the Supreme Crown. In it there are 620[32] pillars of light . . .[33] That is, by way of analogy, just as in a large brick house

---

[24] *The above may be summarised as follows: In the soul there is a faculty of delight. This faculty is most deep-seated and innate to the soul, beyond any apprehension. The propensity to like or dislike, that something will appeal to a person or not, is a natural disposition and innate part of the soul. In fact, it is the most basic faculty of the soul. Based on it is man's will. By nature man wills that which is agreeable to him; what he likes; that which realises his capacity for delight. Will itself expresses itself on two levels. Most often it is subject to reason. Man wills what reason dictates to him as being most agreeable. First he reasons what would be in his best interest and best agrees with his natural disposition for delight. Then he focuses his will on this rational goal.*

דאשתאר כו׳ והנה כמו שבנשמת האדם יש בה כח התענוג שמתענגת ממה שיש לה ענג ממנו כמו מהשכלת שכל חדש וכה״ג ובחי׳ חיצוניות ואחוריים של כח ובחי׳ התענוג שבה היא בחי׳ כח הרצון שבה שהוא רוצה מה שהוא רוצה דהיינו דבר שאינו צער שהצער היפך תענוג. וככה עד״מ באור א״ס ב״ה ג״כ כביכול הרצון העליון ב״ה היא בחי׳ חיצוניות ואחוריים לבחי׳ ענג העליון ונועם ה׳ וצחצחות ועלמין דכסופין הנ״ל הגם שהם מיוחדים בתכלית היחוד שהוא ית׳ ורצונו אחד ולא כרצון האדם ח״ו לא מיניה ולא מקצתיה ואין דמיון ביניהם כלל אעפ״כ דברה תורה כלשון בנ״א לשכך האזן מה שיכולה לשמוע במשל ומליצה מנשמת האדם הכלולה מכח התענוג והרצון והחכמה והבינה וכו׳ וכנראה בחוש שכשאדם משכיל איזה שכל חדש נפלא אזי באותה רגע עכ״פ נולד לו תענוג נפלא בשכלו מכלל שהתענוג הוא למעלה מעלה מבחי׳ השכל והחכמה רק שמלובש בבחי׳ שכל וחכמה וכשהאדם מרגיש השכל וחכמה דהיינו שמשיגה ומבינה היטב אזי מרגיש ג״כ בחי׳ התענוג המלובש בחכמה ולכן נקראת בחי׳ בינה בשם עוה״ב בזוה״ק שהיא בחי׳ התגלות החכמה עם התענוג המלובש בה שמשיגים הצדיקים בג״ע ומשכילים בפנימיות התורה דאורייתא מחכמה נפקא ואורייתא וקב״ה כולא חד:

והנה רצון העליון ב״ה מכונה ונקרא בפי חכמי האמת בשם כתר עליון ובו תר״ך עמודי אור וכו׳. פי׳ דרך משל כמו שיש עמודים בבית חומה גדול

This is the "lower" or "inferior" will (so-called because it is dependent on, thus lower than reason). The second type of will is not subject to reason. It does not express itself after a rational calculation but transcends it. It is supra-rational and may even act against the dictates of reason (stubbornness would be an example; see supra, *sect. XXII, note 60). This second type of will, the "superior" or "supreme" will, is the very basic or natural disposition of willing; the "will of will," or the "will to will," as it were.* (Cf. *also* Siddur im Pirush Hamilot, *pp. 161a ff.).* [25] *Berachot 31b.* [26] Mechilta, *and* Tanchuma, *on Exodus 19:18.* [27] *See* supra, *beg. of sect. XV, and notes* ad loc. [28] *Zohar II:158a; Zohar Chadash,* *(Notes cont. at end of Hebrew Text)*

there are pillars standing in the ground, and their apex is connected with the ceiling, precisely so, metaphorically speaking, the blessed Supreme *keter* transcends the aspect of the level of *chochmah*. *(Keter)* is an idiom of *koteret* (capitol), for it surrounds and encompasses above the brains in the head [i.e. the faculties of *chochmah*, *binah*, and *da'at* (chabad)].[34]

This (Supreme) Will is vested in the 613 commandments of the Torah and the seven precepts of the Rabbis,[35] practically all of which are operative commandments [even those related to speech, for we maintain that the motioning of the lips is regarded as an act;[36] and also those relating to thought or the heart. For the commandment is given only to physical man in this world,[37] because he has the choice to turn his heart to good . . .[38] The soul without a body, however, need not be enjoined about this[39]]. Thus it follows that the commandments, metaphorically speaking, are as the pillars that stand from the peak of rungs, i.e. the blessed Supreme Will, to this material world. Metaphorically speaking, they are as the hollow pillars which encompass and garb man's *neshamah*, or *ruach*, or *nefesh*, when he fulfils the commandments. By way of these pillars his *nefesh*, *ruach* and *neshamah* ascend to the peak of rungs, to be bound up in the bundle of life with the Lord,[40] that is, to be bound up and vested in the light of *keter*, the blessed Supreme Will. And by means of this garment they are able to behold the "pleasantness of the Lord," and the *tzachtzachot*, which transcend the rank of *keter* and, metaphorically speaking, are His *pnimiyut*. ([41]Though it is explained elsewhere that the commandments are the *pnimiyut* of the blessed Supreme Will,[42] those adept in the esoteric science are well acquainted with the multitude of aspects and levels within every aspect and level of the levels of holiness. There are several aspects of "*panim* to *panim*;" and several aspects of "*achurayim* to *achurayim*;"[43] to no end . . .)

Now, the seven precepts of the Rabbis are not regarded as commandments in themselves, for it was already said: "You shall not add."[44] Rather, they derive and issue from the commandments of the Torah and are included in them, in the sum of 613, to garb the 613 aspects and powers in the *nefesh*, *ruach*, and *neshamah* of man. ●▲This is the meaning of the statement in the sacred *Zohar*, section of *Pekudei* (folio 229b), that

---

[34] *See* Etz Chayim *23:1, 2;* ibid., *25:5;* supra, *sect.* XVII *(note 27* ad loc*)*. [35] *Thus 620 precepts corresponding to the 620 pillars of light.* [36] *Sanhedrin 65a.* [37] *See Eruvin 22a.* [38] *Or to evil.* [39] *See* Etz *Chayim 26:1;* Tanya *I, ch. 37.* [40] *I Samuel 25:29; see* Likutei Torah *III:51d.* [41] *Brackets appear in the text.* [42] *See* Tanya *I, ch. 23.* [43] Cf. ref. *cited* supra, *sect. XX, note 36.* [44] *Deut. 13:1; Maimonides,* Hilchot Yesodei Hatorah *IX:1.*

גדול נצבים בארץ וראשם מחובר בתקרה. ככה ממש עד"מ כתר עליון ב"ה הוא למעלה מבחי' מדרגת החכמה והוא מלשון כותרת שהוא מכתיר ומקיף על המוחין שבראש שהם בחי' חב"ד ורצון זה נתלבש בתרי"ג מצות התורה וז' מצות דרבנן שרובם ככולם הן מצות מעשיות וגם התלויות בדבור הא קיי"ל דעקימת שפתיו הוי מעשה וגם התלויות במחשבה או בלב הרי המצוה ניתנה לאדם הגשמי שבעוה"ז דוקא שהוא בעל בחירה להטות לבבו לטוב וכו'. משא"כ הנשמה בלא גוף א"צ לצותה ע"ז. ונמצא שהמצות הן עד"מ כמו העמודים נצבים מרום המעלות הוא רצון העליון ב"ה עד הארץ הלזו החומרית והן עד"מ כמו העמודים חלולין שמקיפין ומלבישין נשמת האדם או רוחו או נפשו כשמקיים המצות ודרך עמודים אלו עולין הנר"ן שלו עד רום המעלות לצרור בצרור החיים את ה'. פי' להיות צרורות ומלובשות באור הכתר הוא רצון העליון ב"ה וע"י לבוש זה יוכלו לחזות בנועם ה' וצחצחות שלמעלה ממעלת הכתר והן פנימיותו עד"מ (והגם שנתבאר במ"א שהמצות הן פנימיות רצון העליון ב"ה הנה מודעת זאת לי"ח ריבוי בחי' ומדרגות שיש בכל בחי' ומדרגה ממדרגות הקדושה כמה בחי' פנים לפנים וכמה בחי' אחוריים לאחוריים לאין קץ וכו'). והנה ז' מצות דרבנן אינן נחשבות מצות בפני עצמן שהרי כבר נאמר לא תוסף אלא הן יוצאות ונמשכות ממצות התורה וכלולות בהן במספר תרי"ג להלביש תרי"ג בחי' וכחות שבנר"ן האדם. וז"ש בזוה"ק פ' פקודי (דרכ"ט ע"ב) דאינון

עובדין

"The good deeds which man does elicit a garment from the light of the Supreme splendour . . ., and they see . . . the pleasantness of the Lord . . ." Though there it speaks of the lower Garden of Eden where the garments are of the truly operational commandment, while in the upper Garden of Eden the garments are of the love and devotion of the heart with respect to Torah and prayer [as mentioned in the *Zohar ad loc.* (folio 210[45])], however, this devotion refers to the devotion of one's occupation with Torah for its own sake (*lishmah*),[46] out of the love for God. [The commandment to study Torah also belongs to the class of operational commandments, for the motion of the lips is an act, and meditation is not the same as speech;[47] thus one does not discharge his duty by meditation alone.[48] The same applies to prayer.[49]] And certainly so, considering that the advantage of devotion over speech and deed is not of itself . . ., but because of the radiation from the Supreme Will . . ., as explained at length in *Likutei Amarim*, part I, ch. 38, see there.

●▲ Now, it is known that the blessed Supreme Will vested in the 613 commandments of the Written Torah, is hidden and covered, secreted and concealed. It is manifest only in the Oral Torah. For example, the precept of *Tefillin*: in the Written Torah it is stated "And you shall bind them for a sign on your hand, and they shall be for frontlets between your eyes."[50] This is an indistinct and concealed statement, for Scripture did not explain how, and what to bind, and what frontlets are; and where is "between your eyes" and "on your hand;" until the Oral Torah explicates that one needs to bind a single box on the hand, and four boxes on the head, and four portions of Scripture within them. Also, the boxes are to be made of prepared leather, and of necessity square, and to be tied by means of leather straps which need to be black; and all the other detailed rulings of making the *Tefillin* that were said orally. Also, "on your hand" refers only to the arm, and not to the palm of the hand; and "between your eyes" refers to the scalp, and not to the forehead. It is likewise with *all* the commandments of the Torah, whether they be operational precepts or prohibitory precepts; they are not revealed, and known, and explicated, except through the Oral Torah. For instance, the prohibitory precept that was said with respect to the Sabbath—"You shall do no work"[51]:

---

[45] *210b.* [46] *See* supra, *sect. XII, note 17.* [47] *Sanhedrin 65a; Berachot 20b.* [48] Hilchot Talmud Torah *II:12; see Eruvin 54a.* [49] *See* supra, *sect. XXV, note 61.* [50] *Deut. 6:8.* [51] *Exodus 20:10; Deut. 5:14.*

עובדין טבין דעביד בר נש משכי מנהורא דזיווא עילאה לבושא כו׳ וחמי כו׳ בנועם ה׳ וכו׳. והגם דהתם מיירי בג״ע התחתון שהלבושים שם הם ממצות מעשיות ממש אבל בג״ע העליון הלבושים הם מרעותא וכוונה דלבא באורייתא וצלותא כמ״ש בזהר שם (דר״י) הרי הכוונה היא כוונת עסקו בתורה לשמה מאהבת ה׳ ומצות ת״ת היא ג״כ מכלל מצות מעשיות דעקימת שפתיו הוי מעשה והרהור לאו כדבור דמי ואינו יוצא י״ח בהרהור לבדו וכן בתפלה ומה גם כי מעלת הכוונה על הדבור ומעשה אינה מצד עצמה כו׳ אלא מצד הארת רצון העליון כו׳ כמ״ש בלק״א ח״א פל״ח באריכות ע״ש. והנה מודעת זאת כי הנה רצון העליון ב״ה המלובש בתרי״ג מצות שבתורה שבכתב הוא מופלא ומכוסה טמיר ונעלם ואינו מתגלה אלא בתורה שבע״פ כמו מצות תפילין עד״מ שנאמר בתושב״כ וקשרתם לאות על ידך והיו לטוטפות בין עיניך והוא מאמר סתום ונעלם שלא פירש הכתוב איך ומה לקשור ומהו טוטפות והיכן הוא בין עיניך ועל ידך עד שפירשה תורה שבע״פ שצריך לקשור בית אחד על היד וד׳ בתים על הראש ובתוכם ד׳ פרשיות והבתים יהיו מעור מעובד ומרובעים דוקא ומקושרים ברצועות של עור שחורות דוקא וכל שאר פרטי הלכות עשיית התפילין שנאמרו בע״פ ועל ידך היא הזרוע דוקא ולא כף היד ובין עיניך זה קדקוד ולא המצח. וכן כל מצות שבתורה בין מ״ע בין מצות ל״ת אינן גלויות וידועות ומפורשות אלא ע״י תורה שבע״פ כמצות ל״ת שנאמר בשבת לא תעשה מלאכה

ולא

it does not explain what is regarded as work. In the Oral Torah, however, it is explicated to refer to the well-known 39 forms of work,[52] and not to the carrying of stones or heavy beams. And as it is with these, so it is with all the commandments, whether they be operational precepts or prohibitory precepts: they are indistinct, and are explicated, revealed, and known only through the Oral Torah. That is why Scripture says of the Oral Torah: "And you shall not cast off the teaching of your mother,"[53] as stated in the *Zohar*.[54] Metaphorically speaking, just as all the limbs of the child are included, in great concealment, in the sperm of the father,[55] and the mother brings this out into a state of manifestation [when giving birth to a child that is whole, with 248 limbs and 365 sinews], so, in precisely like fashion, the 248 operational precepts and the 365 prohibitory precepts emerge from concealment to manifestation through the Oral Torah. And the beginning of the verse—"Heed my son the instruction of your father"—refers to the Written Torah,[56] which derives from the Supreme *chochmah*[57] which is called "father."[58]

Now this is the meaning of "A woman of valour is the crown of her husband." For the Oral Torah is termed the "woman of valour" who gives birth to, and raises many valiant hosts, as it is written[59] "And *alamot* without number": do not read *alamot*[60] but *olamot*,[61] referring to the *halachot* which are without number, as stated in the *Tikunim*.[62] They all are the aspect of the manifestation of the blessed Supreme Will concealed in the Written Torah. And the blessed Supreme Will is exceedingly more sublime than the rank of the Supreme *chochmah*, just as a crown (*keter*) and wreath (*atarah*) is above the brains in the head.[63] The *halachot*, therefore, are referred to as "crown", and "crown of the Torah"; and "Whoever repeats *halachot* is assured that he will come to *olam habah*," by investing his *nefesh*, *ruach* and *neshamah* in the blessed Supreme Will, as stated above.

●▲XXX. It is known that our sages, of blessed memory, said[1]: "Whoever is accustomed to come to the Synagogue, and one day did not come, the Holy One, blessed is He, makes inquiry about him; for it is said[2] 'who among you fears the Lord. . . .' "

The same applies to all the commandments, and especially the precept of charity, "Which is balanced against all the commandments."[3] Though it is without a vow,[4] Heaven forfend, nevertheless, it is not becoming to the divine soul of all the men of valour

---

[52] *See* Mishnah, *Shabbat VII:2.* [53] *Proverbs 1:8.* [54] *See Zohar II:276b. See also* ibid., *238b, and* cf. ibid., *85a. (This verse is explicitely interpreted thus, in Midrash Mishle I:8.)* [55] *See Zohar III:93a;* cf. *Nidah 31a.* [56] *See* ref. *cited* supra, *note 54, and* Yalkut *Shim'oni* on *Proverbs (*ad loc.*; sect. 929).* [57] Supra, *note 29.* [58] *See* supra, *section XV, note 9.* [59] *Song 6:8.* [60] *Maidens.* [61] *Worlds.* [62] *Tikunei Zohar, Intr.: 14b.* [63] *See* supra, *note 34.*

Section XXX
[1] *Berachot 6b.* [2] *Isaiah 50:10.* [3] Yerushalmi, *Peah I:1.* [4] *See* Shulchan Aruch, Yoreh De'ah: *203;* cf. Likutei Torah *III:82b.*

ולא פי׳ מה היא מלאכה ובתורה שבע״פ נתפרש שהן ל״ט מלאכות הידועות ולא טלטול אבנים וקורות כבידות וכיוצא בהן הן כל המצות בין מ״ע בין מל״ת הן סתומות ולא מפורשות וגלויות וידועות אלא ע״י תורה שבע״פ ומשום הכי כתיב על תושבע״פ אל תטוש תורת אמך כמ״ש בזהר משום שעד״מ כמו שכל אברי הולד כלולים בטיפת האב בהעלם גדול והאם מוציאתו לידי גילוי בלידתה ולד שלם ברמ״ח אברים ושס״ה גידים ככה ממש כל רמ״ח מ״ע ושס״ה מל״ת באים מההעלם אל הגילוי בתושבע״פ ופירש׳ דקרא שמע בני מוסר אביך קאי אתורה שבכתב דנפקא מחכמה עילאה הנק׳ בשם אב. וז״ש אשת חיל עטרת בעלה כי התורה שבע״פ הנק׳ אשת חיל המולידה ומעמדת חיילות הרבה כמ״ש ועלמות אין מספר אל תקרי עלמות אלא עולמות אלו הלכות דלית לון חושבנא כמ״ש בתיקונים וכולן הן בחי׳ גילוי רצון העליון ב״ה הנעלם בתושב״כ ורצון העליון ב״ה הוא למעלה מעלה ממעלת חכמה עילאה וכמו כתר ועטרה שעל המוחין שבראש לכן נקראו ההלכות בשם תגא וכתרה של תורה והשונה הלכות מובטח לו שהוא בן עוה״ב ע״י התלבשות נר״נ שלו ברצון העליון ב״ה כנ״ל:

למודעת זאת משארז״ל כל הרגיל לבא לבהכ״נ ויום א׳ לא בא הקב״ה שאל עליו שנאמר מי בכם ירא ה׳ וכו׳ וכן בכל המצות ובפרט מצות הצדקה ששקולה כנגד כל המצות הגם שהיא בלי נדר ח״ו אעפ״כ כל הרגיל

אשר

whose hearts the fear of the Lord has touched[5] to make a dimunition in what is holy, relative to what they were accustomed to set aside, annually, from their wealth, to revive the spirit of the humble and downcast[6] who have nothing of their own. It is "The Hut of David that is fallen . . .,"[7] to raise and to exalt . . . "That it be united in the One . . ."[8] And everything is according to the quantity of the deed . . .,[9] and according to the amount (*cheshbon*). Thus our sages, of blessed memory, said "Every coin adds up to a great amount (*cheshbon*),"[10] and as the saying of our sages, of blessed memory:[11] "When is the Lord great? When He is 'in the city of our G–d. . . ."[12] It is the aspect and place of the *cheshbon*,[13] as it is written: "Your eyes are wells in *Cheshbon*."[14]

The meaning is that, as known, an arousal from below [the issuance of life, grace and kindness by an act of charity out of a good will and a friendly countenance[15]] elicits an arousal from above:[16] "The Lord will make His Countenance shine,"[17] i.e. a radiation and issue of grace, *chesed*, and Supreme favour,[18] from the Fountainhead of life,[19] the blessed En Sof [to whose greatness[20] there is no searching and apprehension whatever], to the aspect of "Your *malchut* is the *malchut* of all worlds,"[21] the "world of manifestation" (*alma deitgalya*).[22] It[23] animates all the creatures [that are in all the upper and lower *hechalot*[24]] which are in a category of number and amount (*cheshbon*), as it is written: "A thousand thousands minister unto Him."[25]

This is the meaning of the "great amount," because the quantitative act of charity brings about peace.[26] The meaning of "peace" is to join and conciliate two opposite extremes. (In our context) these are the extremity of the superior heaven, the aspect of "And to His greatness there is no searching"[27] and the extremity of the inferior heaven[28]—which vests itself in Beriah, Yetzirah and Asiyah, (that is, in) a category of limitation and number, and suffice this for the initiated.

●▲XXXI. Well-known throughout[1] is the statement in the *Tikunim* that the "Shechinah is suffering in the exile"—as it were.[2] Metaphorically speaking, it is like a bodily ailment ["Who makes a distinction between holy . . ."[3]]. The cause of illness or health lies in the extension and flow of the life-force vested in the blood of life[4] which flows from the heart to all the limbs; and turning round and around, goes the spirit of life[5] and the blood

---

[5] Par. *I Samuel 10:26.* [6] Par. *Isaiah 57:15.* [7] *Amos 9:11, referring to the Shechinah (see* supra, *sect. IX, note 29). The poor are the aspect of the Fallen Hut—the Shechinah, the Sefirah* malchut *which "has nothing of its own." See* supra, *sect. XXI, note 24.* [8] *Zohar II:135a. By giving charity one raises and reinstates the fallen "Hut," thereby effecting the ultimate goal of the unity of the Holy One, blessed is He, and His Shechinah. See also Zohar III:113b.* Cf. Tanya *I, end of ch. 50;* Boneh Yerushalayim, *sect. 76.* [9] *Avot 3:15. See* supra, *sect. XXI.* [10] *Bava Batra 9b.* [11] *Zohar II:235a; III:5a; Zohar Chadash: 44a.* [12] *Psalms 48:2.—"In the city" may also be read "[when He is] with the city." The "city of G–d" signifies*

אשר נגע יראת ה' בלבם לא יאתה לנפשם האלקית לתת מגרעות בקדש מאשר כבר הורגלו מדי שנה להפריש ממאודם להחיות רוח שפלים ונדכאים דלית להון מגרמיהון היא בחי' סוכת דוד הנופלת וכו' לקומם ולרומם וכו' למהוי אחד באחד וכו' והכל לפי רוב המעשה וכו' ולפי החשבון כמארז"ל כל פרוטה ופרוטה מצטרפת לחשבון גדול וכו' על דרך מארז"ל אימתי גדול הוי' כשהוא בעיר אלהינו וכו' היא בחי' ומקום החשבון כמ"ש עיניך ברכות בחשבון והמכון כנודע כי באתערותא דלתתא המשכת חיים חן וחסד במעשה הצדקה ברצון הטוב וסבר פנים יפות אתערותא דלעילא יאר הוי' פניו הוא הארת והמשכת חן וחסד ורצון עליון מחיי החיים א"ס ב"ה אשר לגדולתו אין חקר והשגה כלל אל בחי' מלכותך מלכות כל עולמים עלמא דאתגליא המחיה כל הברואים שבכל ההיכלות עליונים ותחתונים שהן בבחי' מספר וחשבון כמ"ש אלף אלפים ישמשוניה וזהו חשבון גדול שע"י רוב מעשה הצדקה שלום. כי פי' שלום הוא דבר המחבר ומתווך ב' קצוות הפכיים שהן קצה השמים לעילא בחי' ולגדולתו אין חקר וקצה השמים לתתא המתלבש בבי"ע בחי' גבול ומספר וד"ל:

לא נודע בשערים מ"ש בתיקונים דשכינתא איהי מרעא בגלותא כבי'. פי' עד"מ כמו חולי הגוף המבדיל בין קדש וכו' שסיבת החולי והבריאות היא התפשטות והילוך החיות מהלב אל כל האברים המלובשת בדם הנפש היוצא מהלב אל כל האברים וסובב סובב הולך הרוח חיים והדם תוך

---

malchut. *The ultimate goal, the "greatness of the Lord," will thus be achieved when this unity is effected; see Zohar III: 5a, and Zohar Chadash, 51d.* [13] *The "city of our G-d" is the aspect and place of* Cheshbon. Cheshbon, *too, signifies* malchut; *see Zohar III: 220b, and* Likutei Torah *III: 66d* f. [14] *Song 7:5.* [15] *See* Yerushalmi, *Peah 8:9; Levit. Rabba 34:1; Avot de R. Natan, ch. 13;* cf. *Bava Batra 9b. See also* infra, *sect. XXXII.* [16] Supra, *section IV, note 45.* [17] *Numbers 6:25.* [18] *Signified by Countenance* (panim); *see* supra, *section XXII,* note *31.* [19] Lit.: *the Life of life (see* supra, *sect. XVII, note 4).* [20] *The aspect* of chesed; *see* supra, *sect. XIII, note 30.* [21] *Psalms*

(Notes cont. at end of Hebrew Text)

into all the limbs, through the veins[6] that are absorbed in them, and returns to the heart. Now, when the circulation and flow of this spirit of life is always as it should be, in its proper order arranged for it by the blessed Fountainhead of life,[7] man is perfectly healthy. For all the limbs are bound together and receive their proper vitality from the heart through this circulation. But if there is any disorder in any place, restraining, hindering or reducing the circulation of the blood with the spirit of life vested in it, then this bond [which binds all the limbs to the heart through this circulation] is broken or diminished, man will fall ill and sick, may the Lord have mercy.

Precisely so, metaphorically speaking, all the souls of Israel are regarded as the limbs of the Shechinah[8] which is called the "heart," as it is written:[9] "The Rock of my heart;"[10] and as it is written: "And I will dwell amongst them."[11] That is, the term Shechinah denotes that the light of the Lord dwells in the worlds Beriah, Yetzirah and Asiyah, in order to vivify them.

The issue of this vivification is by means of a prior investment in the souls of Israel. This is so because none of the creatures are in any approximation to the blessed Creator; for all that are before Him are esteemed as truly naught.[12] Thus it is impossible for them to receive vivification from His blessed light and effluence, to become creatures *ex nihilo* into substantiality, and to be living and subsisting.[13] (This is made possible) only through the souls that rose in His thought[14] and preceded the creation of the worlds by the aspect of Speech.[15] Thus our sages, of blessed memory, said: "With whom did the Holy One, blessed is He, take counsel ...",[16] as was made known elsewhere. And it is well-known throughout[17] that the whole issuance of vivification and effluence from the upper worlds to those lower than them, are, as stated in the *Sefer Yetzirah*: "Their beginning is wedged in their culmination, and their culmination is wedged in their beginning."[18] In the writings of R. Isaac Luria, of blessed memory, this is referred to as *or yashar* (direct light), and *or chozer* (reflective light),[19] and as it is written: "And the animals advanced and retreated (*ratzo veshov*)."[20]

Thus, according to these words and this truth[21]—which it is not possible to explain properly in writing, it follows that the Shechinah is referred to as "heart," and the souls as "limbs." This teaches us that when all the souls are attached and bound together,

---

[6] *Emended according to* H.V. [7] Lit.: *the Life of life (see* supra, *sect. XVII, note 4).* [8] *Zohar III:17a;* ibid., *231b* (R'aya Mehemna)*; Tikunei Zohar 21:52a.* [9] *Psalms 73:26.* [10] *See Song Rabba 5:2 (1); Zohar I:59a* (cf. Nitzutzei Orot, ad loc.)*; Zohar II:128b. See also Tikunei Zohar 21:52a.* [11] *Exodus 25:8.* [12] *Zohar I:11b.* [13] Cf. supra, *section XX.* [14] *See Genesis Rabba I:4.* [15] *The creation of the world was by means of the Divine fiats; see Avot V:1;* cf. supra, *sect V, and XXV.* [16] *Genesis Rabba 8:7; Ruth Rabba 2:3; see Zohar Chadash, Tik.: 121c.* [17] *See* supra, *note 1.* [18] Sefer Yetzirah *I:7;* cf. *the commentary attributed to R. Abraham ibn Daud,* ad loc.—*The primordial souls in the*

תוך תוך כל האברים והגידים המובלעי' בהם וחוזר אל הלב ואם סיבוב והילוך הרוח חיים הלז הוא כהלכתו תמידי כסדרו המסודר לו מחיי החיים ב"ה אזי האדם בריא בתכלית כי כל האברים מקושרים יחד ומקבלים חיותם הראוי להם מהלב ע"י סיבוב הלז אך אם יש איזה קלקול באיזהו מקומן המונע ומעכב או ממעט סיבוב והילוך הדם עם הרוח חיים המלובש בו אזי נפסק או מתמעט הקשר הלז המקשר כל האברים אל הלב ע"י סיבוב הלז ואזי נופל האדם למשכב וחולי ה"י. וככה ממש עד"מ הנה כל נשמות ישראל נקראים בחי' אברי דשכינתא הנקראת בשם לב כמ"ש וצור לבבי וכמ"ש ושכנתי בתוכם פי' כי לשון שכינה הוא שאור הוי' שוכן בעולמות בי"ע להחיותם והמשכת חיות זו היא ע"י התלבשות תחלה בנשמות ישראל לפי שכל הנבראים אין ערוך להם אל הבורא ית' דכולא קמי' כלא ממש חשיבין וא"א להם לקבל חיות מאורו ושפעו ית' להיות נבראים מאין ליש וחיים וקיימים כ"א ע"י הנשמות שעלו במחשבה וקדמו לבריאות עולמות שע"י בחי' הדבור כמארז"ל במי נמלך הקב"ה וכו' כנודע במ"א. ונודע בשערים כי כל המשכת החיות וההשפעה מעליונים לתחתונים מהם הן כמ"ש בס"י נעוץ תחלתן בסופן וסופן בתחלתן ובכתבי האריז"ל מכונה בשם אור ישר ואור חוזר וכמ"ש והחיות רצוא ושוב אשר ע"כ ע"פ הדברים והאמת האלה אשר א"א לבאר היטב במכתב נקראת השכינה בשם לב והנשמות בשם אברים להורות לנו כי כאשר כל הנשמות דבוקות ומקושרות יחד אזי סיבוב

"original thought" of G–d thus are the conduit for the Divine issuance and effluence. [19] *See* supra, *sect. XX.* [20] *Ezekiel I:14.* [21] Par. 2. *Chron. 32:1.*

the circulation and flow of the vivification and of the effluence "turns around and around," and "their culmination is wedged in their beginning" to bind and join them all to "the Lord (who) is One," to be attached unto Him, blessed be He. And thus it is written:[22] "You are standing this day, all of you, before the Lord your G-d —[stating expressly: "all of you," and stating expressly: "before"]—your heads . . ., from the hewer of your wood . . ."[23]

And hereby will be understood the saying of our sages, of blessed memory, that the destruction of the Second Temple and the Fall of Israel into exile, and the withdrawal of the Shechinah and its descent to Edom,[24] into a state of exile, as it were; all this was because of the sin of groundless hate and a division of hearts,[25] the Merciful save us. And that is why (the Shechinah) is referred to as ailing, metaphorically speaking. As[26] for—"He raises the fallen, and heals the sick,"[27] in plural form, these are all the limbs. . . .

●▲ XXXII. May the Lord bless their substance, and may the work of their hand be acceptable,[1] that they may be accepted before the Lord at all times.[2] So may the Lord give and do so yet further to encourage them amongst the valiant.[3] And he that is noble should ever persist by noble things,[4] to be great in causing others to do[5]—in every city and congregation,[6] and it will be accounted to him for righteousness (*tzedakah*).[7] And of him who does (himself) it is said[8] "His *tzedakah omedet* (stands) forever;" *omedet*, in feminine gender, because he receives[9] the arousal of his pure heart from the one that is "greater—who causes others to do."[10] Nevertheless, it stands forever. This means:

All the acts of charity and kindness the Israelites perform in this world out of the generosity of their pure hearts, are alive and subsist in this physical world until the time of the resurrection. Then there will be a time of manifestation of Divinity and of the light of the blessed En Sof, from the rank of *sovev kol almin*,[11] in this world, and as explained at length in the letter of last year.[12] But there needs to be a vessel and an abode wherein the light of the blessed En Sof can vest itself, just as the body is (a vessel) to the soul, metaphorically speaking. Thus it is written:[13] "Is not My word like fire;" just as fire does not radiate in this world except when it is attached to, and vests itself in the wick . . ., as explained elsewhere.[14]

The body and the vessel for His blessed light is the attribute of kindness and the generosity of the heart to give and effuse vitality to him who has not. . . . Thus it is stated in the *Tikunim*:[15] "And many bodies You have prepared for them, and in this preparation they are called: *chesed*—the right arm,"

---

[22] *Deut. 29:9, 10.* [23] Cf. supra, *sect. XXIIb, and the notes* ad loc. [24] *See* supra, *section XXV, note 48.* [25] *Yoma 9b.* [26] *Emended according to* H.V. [27] Liturgy, *opening benedictions of the* Amidah.

Section XXXII
[1] Par. *Deut. 33:11.* [2] Par. *Exodus 28:38.* [3] Par. *Amos 2:16.* [4] Par. *Isaiah 32:8.* [5] *See* infra, *note 10.* [6] Lit.: Minyan; *see* supra, *sect. I, note 55.* [7] Par. *Psalms 106:31.* [8] *Psalms 112:9.* [9] *The feminine is the recipient aspect, while the masculine is the emanating aspect;* cf. supra, *sect. IV, note 46, and sect. XV, note 9.* [10] *He who causes others to do is greater than the doer.—Bava Batra 9a. See* Shulchan Aruch, Yoreh De'ah *249:5, and*

סיבוב והילוך החיות וההשפעה סובב סובב ונעוץ סופן בתחלתן לקשר ולחבר כולן להוי' אחד ולדבקה בו ית' וכמ"ש אתם נצבים היום כולכם לפני הוי' אלקיכם כולכם דייקא ולפני דייקא ראשיכם כו' מחוטב עציך כו'. ובזה יובן מארז"ל כי חורבן בית שני ונפילת ישראל בגלות והסתלקות השכינה וירידתה לאדום בבחי' גלות כבי' הכל הי' בעון שנאת חנם ופירוד לבבות ר"ל ולכן נקראת חולה עד"מ כמ"ש סומך נופלים ורופא חולים לשון רבים הם כל האברים וכו':

לב ברך ה' חילם ופועל ידם ירצה לרצון להם לפני ה' תמיד כה יתן וכה יוסיף ה' לאמץ לבם בגבורים ונדיב על נדיבות יקום להיות גדול המעשה בכל עיר ומנין ותחשב לו לצדקה ועל העושה נאמר צדקתו עומדת לעד עומדת לשון נקבה שמקבל התעוררות לבו הטהור מגדול המעשה אעפ"כ עומדת לעד. פי' שכל הצדקה והחסד שישראל עושין בעוה"ז מנדבת לבם הטהור הן הנה חיות וקיימות בעוה"ז הגשמי עד זמן התחיי' שאז הוא זמן גילוי אלקות ואור א"ס ב"ה מבחי' סובב כל עלמין בעוה"ז וכמ"ש באריכות במכתב דאשתקד וצריך להיות כלי ומכון להתלבש בו אור א"ס ב"ה כמו הגוף לנשמה עד"מ כמ"ש הלא כה דברי כאש מה אש אינה מאירה בעוה"ז אלא כשנאחזת ומתלבשת בפתילה כו' כמ"ש במ"א. והגוף והכלי לאורו ית' היא מדת החסד ונדיבת הלב ליתן ולהשפיע חיות למאן דלית ליה כו' כמ"ש בתיקונים וכמה גופין תקינת לון ואתקריאו בתיקונא דא חסד דרועא ימינא וכל

Turei Zahav, ad loc. [11] *Encompassing (transcending) all worlds. See* supra, *sect. III, note 12.* [12] *See* supra, *sect. XVII.* [13] *Jeremiah 23:29.* [14] *See* Tanya *I, ch. 35, 52, and 53 (in comment. on Zohar III: 187a).* [15] *Tikunei Zohar Intr.: 17a.*

and the whole body is included in the right side. And thus said the composer: "His garment is *tzedakah*."[16] This is the meaning of what our sages, of blessed memory, said:[17] "Charity is recompensed only according to the kindness in it, as it is written:[18] sow to yourselves for *tzedakah*, reap according to the kindness." For the harvest is the manifestation of the seed hidden in the soil. It is likewise with the charity and kindness the Israelites perform in the time of the exile: it is hidden and concealed until the time of the resurrection when the light of the blessed En Sof will vest itself and radiate in this physical world. And (when) He is one with His causations, i.e. the aspects of the *kelim* of the ten Sefirot of Atzilut,[19] thus *a fortiori*, and *a minori ad majus*, (He is one) with the light of the blessed En Sof which encompasses all worlds from exceedingly higher than the sphere of Atzilut.

That is why (charity) is referred to as *tzedakah*, a feminine gender ["his *tzedakah omedet* forever"]. For it receives a radiation from the light of the En Sof that encompasses all worlds, which vests itself in it in this physical world at the time of the resurrection. "*Tzedek* shall go before him,"[20] however, is a masculine gender. It is the attribute of kindness that is aroused in the heart of man of itself, through the arousal of the love of G-d when reading the *Shema*—to cleave unto Him[21] and to surrender his soul at *echad*;[22] and "with all your wealth"[23]—in the literal sense, . . .[24] And the arousal from below ["As waters (reflect) the face to face, so is the heart of—*the Supernal*—man . . ."[25]] elicits an arousal from above,[26] i.e. an effulgence of the light of the blessed En Sof that encompasses all worlds, to the nethermost in this physical world, in a state of manifestation, at the time of the resurrection, as explained at length in last year's letter.[27]

And this is the meaning of *yehalech* before Him."[28] For (*tzedek*) leads[29] and elicits the Supernal Countenance (*panim*) from higher than Atzilut to the world of 'Asiyah.[30] But now is a time to be brief, and may He not restrain from them all the good.[31] Do good, O Lord, unto the good, and unto those that are upright in their heart,[32] as is the wish of him who seeks it.[33]

KUNTRESS ACHARON ON SEVERAL CHAPTERS

Essay 1

SEE LIKUTEI AMARIM I, CHAPTER 40

•▲ To understand how reading narratives in Torah binds one with chochmah ila'a, the supernal wisdom.[1]

Kavanot, p. 16b,

---

[16] *The composer of the liturgical hymn* אתה הוא אלקינו (Machzor, Rosh Hashana and Yom Kippur). [17] *Sukah 49b;* cf. ref. *cited* supra, *sect. XXX, note 15.* [18] *Hosea 10:12.* [19] *Tikunei Zohar, Intr.: 3b; see* supra, *beg. of sect. XX.* [20] *Psalms 86:14.* [21] *Deut. 11:22;* (ibid., *30:22*). [22] I.e. *to be in a mode of readiness for self-sacrifice for the sanctification of G-d's Name, when uttering the word* echad *(the Lord is* One—*Deut. 6:4*). *See the writings of R. Isaac Luria dealing with devotions* (Sha'ar Hakavanot; Pri Etz Chayim *etc.)* s.v. Keriat Shema; cf. *Tikunei Zohar, Intr.: 10b; R. Joel Sirkis,* Bach on Tur Orach Chayim *LXI* (s.v. ויקראנה). *See also* Likutei Torah *II:5a;* and cf. supra, *sect. XXVIII, note 38.* [23] *And you*

וכל הגוף נכלל בימין וכך אמר הפייט לבושו צדקה. וזהו שארז״ל אין הצדקה משתלמת אלא לפי חסד שבה שנאמר זרעו לכם לצדקה קצרו לפי חסד שהקציר הוא גילוי הזריעה הטמונה בארץ וכך הוא הצדקה והחסד שישראל עושין בזמן הגלות היא טמונה ונסתרת עד זמן התחיה שיתלבש ויאיר אור א״ס ב״ה בעוה״ז הגשמי ואיהו וגרמוהי חד הם בחי׳ הכלים דע״ס דאצי׳ וכ״ש וק״ו אור א״ס ב״ה הסובב כל עלמין מלמעלה מבחי׳ אצי׳ ולפיכך נקראת צדקה לשון נקבה צדקתו עומדת לעד שמקבלת הארה מאור א״ס סובב כל עלמין המתלבש בתוכה בעוה״ז הגשמי בזמן התחיה. אבל צדק לפניו יהלך הוא לשון זכר היא מדת החסד המתעוררת בלב האדם מעצמו ע״י התעוררות אהבת ה׳ בקריאת שמע ולדבקה בו ולמסור נפשו באחד ובכל מאדך כפשוטו וכו׳ ובאתערותא דלתתא וכמים הפנים לפנים כן לב אדם העליון כו׳ אתערותא דלעילא הוא המשכת אור א״ס ב״ה הסוכ״ע למטה מטה בעוה״ז הגשמי בבחי׳ גילוי בזמן התחיה כמבואר במכתב דאשתקד באריכות. וזהו לפניו יהלך שמוליך וממשיך פנים העליונים מלמעלה מהאצי׳ עד עולם העשי׳ וכעת עת לקצר וכל טוב מהם לא יבצר הטיבה ה׳ לטובים ולישרים בלבותם כנפש תדרשנו:

קונטרס אחרון על כמה פרקים

עיין בלק״א ח״א פ״מ

להבין איך הקורא בסיפורי מעשיות שבתורה הוא מקושר בח״ע ע״פ מ״ש בכוונות דט״ז ע״ב כמו

---

shall love the Lord with all your wealth; Deut. 6:5. [24] See Berachot 54a, and 61b. [25] Proverbs 27:19; see supra, sect. I, note 26. (The "Supernal Man"—see Ezek. I:26.). [26] See supra, section IV, note 45. [27] See supra, note 12. [28] Supra, note 20. [29] Yehalech is an active form of the causative stem of the verb הלך; see supra, section IV. [30] See supra, end of sect. IV; cf. also end of sect. XXX. [31] In Hebrew this sentence is a play on rhyming words. [32] Psalms 125:4. [33] Par. Lament. 3:25.

Essay I

—It is suggested that the reader examine chs. 16, 38, 39, and 44 in Tanya I before studying this section of Kuntress Acharon—[1] Torah is the

(Notes cont. at end of Hebrew Text)

says that just as man occupies himself below, so is the likeness, supernal Man,[2] above . . . This might also apply to contemplating written words. But uttered speech, we may say, pierces and ascends to Atzilut[3] itself, or to Beriah through intellectual love and fear, or to Yetzirah through innate fear and love. Through Scripture[4] it rises from This World to the Ten Sefirot[5] of Asiyah, for "it pierces atmospheres . . ." In contrast, thought[6] (affects only)[7] the "likeness," the source of his soul . . .

But then we find in Zohar III:105 that simply thinking achieves nothing . . ., meaning that it does not have even a beneficient effect,[8] see there and page 31b. But this refers only to eliciting reaction Above, to call forth from there downward.[9] The thought simply remains there, increasing additional great illumination there. The increase in illumination in Atzilut is through study and practice of mitzvot of action in Asiyah, for the Union[10] is primarily above. Only the fruits reach This World, through calling forth illumination in minute measure here below by speech and deed. However, through mere thinking nothing is called forth. Hence he has not fulfilled the purpose of the soul's descent into This World, which is only to draw into the lower world supernal illuminations, as *Etz Chayim* XXVI says, "To call forth illumination."

But to elevate, from below upward, proper thought is imperative for without awe and love it does not fly upward,[11] as explained in *Shaar Hanevuah*, ch. 2. "And the good thought . . ."[12]

But the expression, "pierces firmaments . . ."[13] means even without awe and love—by a fortiori reasoning from the case of idle words, since the measure of good is more generous.[14] This, however, refers only to "firmaments," meaning the chambers and abodes, but not the body of Supernal Man.[15] It certainly does not apply to *nefesh*, *ruach*, and *neshama*,[16] even of Man of Asiyah,[17] meaning the Ten Sefirot, lights and vessels.[18] This is the intention of *Tikunim*, that without fear and love it cannot ascend or stand before G–d, stressing before *G–d*.[19]

Essay 2

•▲Examine *Etz Chayim*, *Shaar Hanekudot* 8:6, the statement that there can be no "turning of face to face"[1] except through mitzvot requiring action[2] exclusively. The reason is

---

[2] *The infinitude of G–d, in its ultimate degree, precludes any form or description; it is utter simplicity, unitary, with no composition or division. Adjectives are irrelevant; there can be no comprehending Him. In bringing about the existence of Creation with finite beings, at a certain stage aspects of G–d became discreet, at least in potential. These aspects, or attributes, reveal G–d, manifest Him. Where these aspects assume the form of intellect-emotion, or Sefirot, we may describe them as Adam Elyon, supernal man. "Man" comprises the attributes of intellect and emotion, which derive from the parallel Divine attributes. Mortal man's configuration is "in the image" of Higher Man's. "Higher Man" exists on each of the Four Worlds, on each plane there is the*

כמו שהאדם עוסק למטה כך דיוקן האדם העליון למעלה כו׳ וכן י״ל בהרהור באותיות הכתובות. אבל הדבור י״ל דבוקע וסליק לאצי׳ ממש או לבריאה בדו״ר שכליים או ליצי׳ בדו״ר טבעיים ובמקרא סליק מעוה״ז לי״ס דעשי׳ משום דבקע אוירין וכו׳. משא״כ בהרהור אלא הדיוקן שהוא שרש נשמתו וכו׳. ומ״ש בזהר ח״ג דק״ה דהרהור לא עביד מידי כו׳ והיינו אפי׳ לטב ע״ש ובדל״א ע״ב י״ל דהיינו לאתערא לעילא שיומשך משם לתתא רק מהשבתו נשארה שם ומוסיפה שם אור גדול בתוספת וריבוי האור באצי׳ ע״י מקרא ומצות מעשיות שבעשי׳ שעיקר היחוד הוא למעלה רק הפירות בעוה״ז ע״י המשכת אור מעט מזעיר למטה ע״י הדבור ומעשה משא״כ בהרהור לא נמשך כלום ולכן לא יצא ידי חובתו מה שירדה נשמתו לעוה״ז רק להמשיך אורות עליונים למטה כמ״ש בע״ח שכ״ו להמשיך אור אבל להעלות ממטה למעלה הוא דוקא ע״י מחשבה טובה דבלא דו״ר לא פרחא לעילא וכמ״ש בשער הנבואה פ״ב והמחשבה טובה כו׳ ומ״ש דבקע רקיעין וכו׳ והיינו אפילו בלא דו״ר במכש״כ מדברים בטלים [ז״א דגם שם יש איזו תאוה. בנ״א ליתא תיבות אלו] דמדה טובה מרובה היינו רקיעין דוקא שהן ההיכלות והבתים ולא בגוף האדם העליון וכש״כ בנר״ן אפי׳ באדם דעשיה שהן י״ס אורות וכלים וז״ש בתקונים דבלא דו״ר לא יכלא לסלקא ולמיקם קדם ה׳ דוקא:

עיין ע״ח שער הנקודות ש״ח פ״ו שאין החזרת פב״פ כ״א ע״י מצות מעשיות דוקא. וטעם הדבר כי

ע״י

---

appropriate revelation of G–d. (See end of note 3 for references on Four Worlds.) Adam Elyon is identical with m'maleh kol almin, *the permeating Light of G–d that suffuses all existence, adapting itself to the receptivity and absorptive capacities of the existence. On the plane of "intellect" He manifests Himself and is apprehended through intellect; on the plane of "emotion" through emotion, etc. Intellect and emotion vary, and within each there are different stages—corresponding "levels" of G–d are revealed in Supernal Man. (The term "man" as applied to G–d is found in Ezekiel 1:26). Parenthetically, in reference to Supernal Man "reflecting" mortal man, a Chassidic interpretation of the passage in Avot 2:1, says,*

(Notes cont. at end of Hebrew Text)

that good deeds cause the supernal union . . .

The understanding of why mitzvot which require action specifically have this effect lies in the statement in *Shaar Ma'n Uma'd*, that the first step must be elevation of *mayin nukvin*[3] of *nukva* of the Minor Visage,[4] and the *mayin nukvin* of *nukva* is the state of action,[5] as explained there, ch. 1.

Good deeds are described as trimming and hacking off the thistles that attach themselves to the hinderpart, the state of deed, as written in *Shaar* 47:5. This pruning is effected through elevating the element of good concealed in them, that is enclothed in mitzvot of action, elevating it to its source, to the sanctity of Atzilut that has already been purified.

The statement there that Adam made rectification through prayer as well, means through the utterances of speech, for the movement of the lips is also deemed a deed.[6] Utterances are from the vivifying soul[7] in the body and his blood, whose source is in *nogah*.[8]

The purifications of Asiyah[5] ascend to Yetzirah[5] through the name of *ba'n*,[9] and from Yetzirah to Beriah and Atzilut, as noted in *Shaar Ma'n*, *Drush* 11:7.

Thus we can understand why mere thought accomplishes nothing,[10] for without elevating *mayin nukvin*[3] from the "kings of *nogah*," it is impossible to draw forth drops from above to effect the union of *zu'n*,[11] for its desire is to seek it nurture from its "mother" rather than giving forth for the lower realms, as written in *Shaar Ma'n*, *Drush* 2. See also Zohar *parshat Pekudei*, 244b, that there is an order . . . to gaze upon . . . These are the intentions in worship, and the supernal unions, for those who know and understand how to "gaze upon . . ." For their very own *nefesh-ruach-neshama*[12] are *ma'n*, with selfless devotion for the Torah, and during the Tach'nun prayer, as is known.

Essay 3

[The reader is referred to Tanya I, chs. 39 and 40.]

●▲ To understand the statement in *Shaar Hayichudim*, ch. 2, that through Torah without proper intention (kavana) angels are created in the World[1] of Yetzirah: There he quotes Zohar *Shlach*, "There is no voice lost . . . except the voice of Torah and worship that ascends and pierces . . ."

Through[2] intention in worship angels are created in the World of Beriah, as with intention in Torah. Without intention it is repelled, hurled down utterly. So it is stated in Zohar *Pekudei* 245b, "In the lowest firmament . . . that are called invalid prayers . . ."

---

[3] *See Tanya I,* Glossary. Nukva *(pl. nukvin), "feminine," describes man the recipient, who must in this context take the initiative to arouse the "donor," the "masculine," or G–d.* Mayin nukvin *(feminine waters) in transliterated abbreviation is* ma'n. *Tanya IV, ch. 8, notes that "arousal from below" is identical with* haaloat ma'n, *"elevation of the feminine waters," the term employed by the Ari, Rabbi Isaac Luria. (On the Ari, see Introduction to Tanya I.)* [4] *Essay III, note 8.* [5] *Essay I, note 3; Only in the lower worlds, apparently from their Creator, is the labour of purification necessary.* [6] *Cf. Sanhedrin 45a.* [7] *Cf. Glossary and notes,* Nefesh ha-bahamit. [8] *Ibid., Glossary,*

*When Cheshvan has only 29 days, the portion for the 30th is said together with the 29th.

ע״י מע״ט גורם זיווג העליון וכו׳. ולהבין אמאי מעשיות דוקא יובן ממ״ש בשער מ״ן ומ״ד כי צריך תחלה להעלות מ״ן דנוק׳ דז״א ומ״ן דנוק׳ הן בחי׳ עשיה כמש״ש פ״א. והנה המע״ט נק׳ כסוח וקיצוץ הקוצים הנאחזים באחוריים שהן בחי׳ עשיה כמ״ש בשער מ״ז פ״ה והיינו ע״י העלאת הטוב הגנוז בהם המלובש במצות מעשיות למקורו לקדושת האצי׳ שכבר הובררה. ומ״ש שם שאדה״ר תיקן ג״כ ע״י תפלה היינו ע״י אותיות הדבור דעקימת שפתיו הוי מעשה כי הן מנפש החיונית שבגוף ודמו אשר שרשן מנוגה. והנה הבירורים דעשי׳ עולין ליצי׳ ע״י שם ב״ן ומיצי׳ לבריאה ולאצי׳ כמ״ש בשער מ״ן דרוש י״א סי׳ ז׳. ובזה יובן דהרהור לא עביד מידי כי בלי העלאת מ״ן מהמלכים שבנוגה א״א להמשיך טיפי׳ מלמעלה לזווג זו״נ כי רוצה לינק מאמו ולא להשפיע למטה כמ״ש בשער מ״ן דרוש ב׳ ועיין זהר פ׳ פקודי דרמ״ד ע״ב דאית סדורא כו׳ לאסתכלא כו׳ והן כוונות התפלה ויחודים עליונים ליודעים ומשיגים לאסתכלא כו׳ כי נר״ן שלהם עצמן הן מ״ן במס״נ על התורה ובנפילת אפים כנודע:

להבין מ״ש בשער היחודים פ״ב דע״י תורה שלא בכוונה נבראים מלאכים בעולם היצירה ושם הביא מהזהר פ׳ שלח דלית קלא דאתאביד כו׳ בר קלא דאורייתא וצלותא דסליק ובקע כו׳ והנה מכוונת התפלה נבראו מלאכים בעולם הבריאה כמו מכוונת התורה ובלא כוונה נדחית למטה לגמרי כמ״ש בזהר פ׳ פקודי דרמ״ה ע״ב גו רקיע תתאה כו׳ דאקרין צלותין פסילאן

Kelipat nogah. [9] *See Tanya II Ch. 7, note 48.* [10] *Essay I.* [11] *Essay VI, note 7.* [12] *Glossary; note 1; Essay 1, note 16.*

Essay III
[1] *See Essay VI, note 3 for references to Four Worlds.* **[2] *Here a contradictory statement is offered. First we learn that lack of kavana does not completely inhibit Torah, for it attains to Yetzirah. Then we are told that worship without kavana is repelled.***

See also *Vayakhel* 201b, "If it is a seemly word . . ."

● However the difference between Torah and worship without intention is obvious. For in the study of Torah he knows and comprehends what he is learning, for otherwise it is not called study at all. It is only that he is learning simply, without intention "for its sake,"[3] out of the manifest love of G-d in his heart, but only out of the latent natural love.[4] But he does not study with an actual negative purpose, for his aggrandisement . . .[5] "For this does not ascend higher than the sun," as stated in *Vayechi* 223b. That is because his thought and intention are clothed within the utterances of speech and prevent them from ascending.

So, too, with worship without intention, where he entertains alien thoughts. (But since his intention is for Heaven[6] therefore it is easily corrected, that it may still rise when he worships with proper intention, even one full prayer gathered piece-meal from the prayers of the entire year. See *Mikdash Melech* on *Pekudei*.)

●▲ To return to the quotation from Zohar *Pekudei*, "In the lowest firmament," while in *Vayakhel* the implication is that only if it is a "Seemly word does it ascend with it to the atmosphere of the firmaments above . . ." This seeming contradiction is no problem. The expression in *Pekudei*, "The inferior firmament of those firmaments that conduct the world," refers to *Malchut*[7] of Asiyah. In *Vayakhel* the reference is to the Minor Visage of Asiyah.[8] This is supported by *Etz Chayim*, *Shaar Hashemot*, ch. 3, in reference to the Minor Visage of Asiyah, check there.

The apparent reference may be drawn from *Pekudei* that even invalid prayer ascends to the First Chamber,[9] whence it is hurled down, but it does attain to the Minor Visage of Beriah. This is no difficulty, for even palpable sins, minor and grave, ascend to there, even to the Fourth Chamber, as noted on page 252a. It is certain, therefore, that the ascensions are not identical, and there can be no comparison or similarity between them except for the common name. This will suffice for the knowing.

This will also aid us in grasping the passage on page 247 that in the Second Chamber are the garments

---

[3] *In Tanya I, ch. 5, Torah "for its sake" is defined as the intention of binding one's soul with G-d through comprehension of Torah, each man according to his capacities. In ch. 39 we find three categories of intention: a) improper intention, for ulterior motives like becoming a scholar, b) "neutral" intention, resulting from ingrained habit for example, and c) "for its sake," through arousing at least the natural love and reverence. (On "natural" love, see note 3 to Essay I.) The reparation of the first sort of Torah study is effected through repentance. The second is elevated when he studies again with the proper intention, but repentance is not needed.* [4] *See Essay I, note 3.* [5] *This is the first category in note 3. See note 11 below.* [6] *His mind*

*When Cheshvan has only 29 days, the portion for the 30th is said together with the 29th.

פסילאן כו' וע"ש פ' ויקהל דר"א ע"ב אי היא מלה כדקא יאות כו'. אך ההפרש בין תורה לתפלה שלא בכוונה מובן מאליו כי לימוד התורה הוא מבין ויודע מה שלומד דבלא"ה לא מיקרי לימוד כלל רק שלומד סתם בלא כוונה לשמה מאהבת ה' שבלבו בבחי' גילוי רק מאהבה המסותרת הטבעית אך אינו לומד שלא לשמה ממש להתגדל כו' דהא לא סליק לעילא מן שמשא כמ"ש בפ' ויחי דרכ"ג ע"ב והיינו משום שמחשבתו וכוונתו הן מתלבשות באותיות הדבור ואינן מניחות אותן לסלקא לעילא וה"נ בתפלה שלא בכוונה שמחשב מ"ז (אלא מפני שכוונתו לשמים לכך יש לה תיקון בקל לחזור ולעלות כשמתפלל בכוונה אפי' תפלה אחת מלוקטת מתפלות כל השנה כמ"ש במק"מ פ' פקודי) ומ"ש בפ' פקודי גו רקיע תתאה ובפ' ויקהל משמע דדוקא אי איהי מלה כדקא יאות סלקין עמה עד אוירא דרקיע דלעילא כו'. לק"מ דרקיע תתאה מאינון רקיעי' דמדברי גו עלמא שבפ' פקודי הן דמלכות דעשי' ודפ' ויקהל הן דז"א דעשי' כמ"ש בע"ח שער השמות פ"ג גבי ז"א דעשייה ע"ש. והא דמשמע לכאורה בפ' פקודי דגם תפלה פסולה עולה עד היכל הראשון שממנו נדחית למטה והוא בז"א דבריאה. לק"מ שהרי אפי' כל העוונות ממש קלות וחמורות עולות לשם אפי' עד היכל הד' כמ"ש דרנ"ב ע"א אלא ודאי שאין מהות העליות שוות ואין ערוך ודמיון ביניהם אלא בשיתוף השם בלבד וד"ל. ובזה יובן ג"כ מש"ש דרמ"ז שבהיכל הב' [אולי צ"ל אוזמן הממונה. ואולי צ"ל קיימין הלבושים] ממונה על הלבושים

---

wanders during worship, but he prays only to G–d. [7] *Each of the Divine Attributes (Kindness, Severity, etc.) has its unique nature and functions, and each manifests G–d differently. His bounty, for example, is an expression of the attribute of Chesed, Kindness. The particular attribute is the source of the bounty, to be sure, but the actual performance of the attribute is through Malchut (the seventh of the emotive attributes, lit. "Sovereignty"). The manifestation of G–d in terms apprehensible to us, i.e. the physical conduct of the world, is through the attribute Malchut of the World of Asiyah, our mundane universe. For more discussion of Malchut, see "The Tzemach Tzedek and the Haskalah Movement," p. 110. note 3.*

(Notes cont. at end of Hebrew Text)

that clothe the soul as a result of performance of mitzvot, though they are in the Lower Gan Eden[10] of Asiyah, as stated on page 210.

▲ Invalid worship is superior to Torah studied with distinctly improper intention, for such Torah attains to a position lower than the sun,[11] while worship is "On the firmament . . ." But simple Torah, without negative intention but merely of the latent innate love, is not inferior to the "Breath of the mouths of studying children"[12] which ascends because it is "Breath untainted by sin." It ascends though it may be of clearly negative intention, fear of punishment by the teacher. Examine 255b: the angels elevate the breath of studying children to Atzilut.

Essay 4

●▲To understand the passage in *Pri Etz Chayim*, that in the contemporary period the primary purification[1] is only through worship, though Torah study is superior to worship. The explanation is:

Through Torah and mitzvot additional Light[2] is drawn forth into Atzilut . . . This means that through Torah study the blessed Infinite Light is drawn into the vessels of Atzilut, into the inner aspect of the vessels. This Light is an extension and revelation of the Divine Intellect. Through mitzvah observance the Light is drawn into the external aspect of the vessels, meaning *netzach-hod-yesod* of the Ten Sefirot of the Minor Visage of Atzilut.[3] Subsequently they clothe themselves in Beriah, Yetzirah, and Asiyah,[4] in the physical Torah and mitzvot in This World.

However, worship calls forth the blessed Infinite Light, specifically into Beriah, Yetzirah and Asiyah, not merely through "garbs,"[5] but the Light itself, to modify the state of creatures. The ill will be cured, for example, the rain will fall earthward that vegetation may sprout forth.

On the other hand, through Torah and mitzvot there is no modification in the parchment of the tefillin through donning them on head and arm. Even those mitzvot that are fulfilled through making the object—that change is effected by man, and not by Heaven, as is the case with worship. The latter calls forth the vivifying power from the Infinite, blessed be He, Who alone is all-capable. Hence, calling forth the blessed Infinite Light into the lower world is impossible without the "Elevation of *Mayim nukvin*"[6] from below specifically.

By contrast, Torah study affects Atzilut, which is united in any case with the Emanator, blessed be He.

---

[10] *After the death of the body, the soul continues to live as a spiritual entity, quite apart from all corporeality. Its earlier mortal life did affect it profoundly though, whether his life was exemplary or not. If man sinned, G–d forbid, his soul suffers a concomitant defect or contamination, and must undergo a process we call punishment or purification or correction. Any discussion of this must be cautious, for our experiences and conceptions are physical. We cannot truly conceive the nature of an abstract disembodied spiritual being, nor have we any inkling into its experience of what we would call pleasure or pain. Thus we can declare, that the soul cannot remain in this state of imperfection, bearing the stains and scars of evil. When the puri-*

הלבושים שמלבישים הנשמה ממעשה המצות אף שהן בג"ע התחתון דעשי' כמש"ש דר"י. והנה תפלה פסולה עדיפא מתורה שלא לשמה ממש שהיא תחת השמש והתפלה היא גו רקיע כו'. אבל תורה סתם שאינה שלא לשמה רק מאהבה מסותרת טבעי' לא גרעא מהבל פיהן של תינוקת של בית רבן דסליק לעילא מפני שהוא הבל שאין בו חטא וסליק לעילא אף אם הוא שלא לשמה ממש מיראת הרצועה שביד הסופר וע"ש דרנ"ה ע"ב שהמלאכים הם מעלים ההבל של תינוקת שב"ר עד האצי':

להבין מ"ש בפע"ח דבזמן הזה עיקר הבירור ע"י התפלה דוקא אף שתלמוד תורה למעלה מהתפלה. הענין הוא שע"י תו"מ מוסיפין אור באצי' כו'. פי' אור א"ס ב"ה בכלים דאצי' ע"י ת"ת בפנימית דהיינו המשכות המוחין ובקיום המצות בחיצונית הכלים שהם בחי' נה"י שבי"ס ז"א שבאצי' רק שמתלבשים בבי"ע בתורה ומצות הגשמיים שבעוה"ז. אבל התפלה היא המשכת אור א"ס ב"ה לבי"ע דוקא לא בדרך התלבשות בלבד רק האור ממש לשנות הנבראים מכמות שהם שיתרפא החולה וירד הגשם משמים לארץ ויולידה ויצמיחה. משא"כ בתו"מ שאין שינוי בקלף התפילין ע"י הנחתן בראש ובזרוע וגם במצות שעשייתן הוא גמר מצותן השינוי הוא ע"י אדם ולא בידי שמים כבתפלה שהיא המשכת החיות מא"ס ב"ה שהוא לבדו כל יכול והלכך כדי להמשיך אור א"ס ב"ה למטה א"א בלי העלאת מ"ן מלמטה דוקא. משא"כ לת"ת שבאצי' המיוחדת בלא"ה במאציל ב"ה והעלאת

---

fication is completed, the soul enters into Gan Eden (the term is taken from Genesis, the Paradise of Adam). Here the soul enjoys the pleasant consequences of its good deeds in its physical life. Unconstricted by body, the soul can now have an awareness, an apprehension, of G–d's being and propinquity, an experience the Talmud describes as "enjoying the radiance of G–d's presence." This consciousness of G–d will vary according to the soul and the life it led. A life of intellect, Torah study, will result in an intellectual appreciation of G–d; a life of fervent worship will establish an emotion-relationship; a life of social endeavour will bring its consonant effects, and so on. Then too the soul's relationship with G–d is not static, for

(Notes cont. at end of Hebrew Text)

The "Elevation of *mayim nukvin*" in the mind and heart of man is a state of boundless flames of fire, and described as "m'odecha," to arouse the state of Infinite.[7] This is through the Severities of *Sa'g*,[8] which constitute the 288 sparks . . .[9]

For this reason worship is called "Life of the moment,"[10] for it is Malchut[11] descending into Beriah, Yetzirah and Asiyah. Torah is called "eternal life,"[10] or the "Minor Visage,"[12] for the 248 commandments divide into the ten vessels of the Ten Sefirot of the Minor Visage . . .

●▲ Now, in one place we find that the 248 positive commandments are in the Five Kindnesses[13] and the 365 prohibitions are in the Five Severities . . . Elsewhere we find that there are 613 paths from one path . . . which is the pristine Whiteness (*lavnunit*) . . .[14]

The explanation is: all mitzvot are designed to "repair" the 248 organs[15] of the Minor Visage through drawing the blessed Infinite Light into the Intellect as contained within the Five Kindnesses and Five Severities. The source of Intellect is the *lavnunit* . . ., the supreme delight and desire to bring the light down into the 248 organs of the Minor Visage. The Light drawn forth divides into 613 individual streams according to the respective level of the mitzvot. For instance, through charity and kindness the blessed Infinite Light is drawn into the external aspect of the vessel of the Kindness of the Minor Visage, while through observing a prohibition into the external aspect of Severity, and through mercy . . .

The passage of the issuing Light is through the internality of the vessels and their Intellects, which are love and reverence, intellectual or innate,[16] meaning major or minor intellect.

This is the reason for Moses' fervent plea to fulfil the mitzvot of performance contingent on the Land,[17] for these are the ultimate purpose in the gradual descent [i.e. Creation]—to call forth the blessed Infinite Light, to purify the vessels of the Minor Visage of Beriah, Yetzirah and Asiyah.[18] These worlds are the site of the 288 sparks. The purification is effected exclusively through Torah study and mitzvot requiring action in Beriah, Yetzirah and Asiyah.

●▲ To perform a mitzvah that cannot be delegated to another, one foregoes Torah study,[19] even that of the *maaseh merkava*,[20] and beyond question one forgoes worship which is the state of intellect and intellectual love and awe.[21] The reason is as we have noted.

In addition: the magnitude of the quality of mitzvot requiring action and their study, far transcends the quality of intellect, meaning intellectual love and fear. For though the verse declares, "to cleave to Him"[22] through

---

[7] M'odecha *(Deut. 6:5) refers to absolute devotion, unrestrained and without reservation. It is the state of infinity in mortal terms, and can thus arouse the true Infinite.* [8] *Tanya I, ch. 4. Each Name denotes another aspect of G-d.* [9] *Ibid., nitzotzot.* [10] *Shabbat 10a.* [11] *Essay III, note 7.* [12] *Ibid., note 8.* [13] *"Severities" are limitations, withholding; "Kindnesses" are beneficence, granting. In their source, before they are translated into tangible forms of human kindness or sternness, they are quite abstract, removed from human context. Revelation proceeds by the stages of intellect, emotion, etc. Verbalisation of the abstract thought is a limitation on the thought. The "Five Severities" are the five articulations (Tanya II, ch. 4) that clothe the dis-*

והעלאת מ"ן במוחו ולבו של אדם היא בחי' רשפי אש בלי גבול ונק' מאדך כדי לעורר בחי' א"ס והיינו ע"י גבורות דס"ג שהן הן הרפ"ח ניצוצין כו' ולכן נק' התפלה חיי שעה היא מלכות היורדת בבי"ע ותורה חיי עולם הוא ז"א כי רמ"ח פקודין הן מתחלקין בי' כלים דע"ס דז"א כו'. והנה במ"א כתב שרמ"ח מ"ע הן בה' חסדים ושס"ה ל"ת בה"ג וכו' ובמ"א כתב שהן תרי"ג ארחין נמשכין מחד ארחא כו' שהוא לבנונית וכו'. אך הענין שכל המצות לתקן רמ"ח אברי ז"א ע"י המשכת אור א"ס ב"ה במוחין הכלולין בה"ח וה"ג ומקור המוחין הוא לבנונית כו' הוא הענג וחפץ העליון להמשיך האור למטה לרמ"ח אברין דז"א ומתחלקת ההמשכה לתרי"ג המשכות פרטיות לפי בחי' ערך המצות כגון בצדקה וגמ"ח נמשך אור א"ס ב"ה לחיצוני' הכלי דחסד דז"א ובקיום הדינין בחיצונית גבורה וברחמים כו'. ודרך ומעבר ההמשכה הוא ע"י פנימי' הכלים ומוחותיהן שהן דו"ר שכליים או טבעיים שהן בחי' מוחין דקטנות וגדלות ולזה ביקש משה רבינו ע"ה מאד לקיים המצות מעשיות התלויות בארץ שהן תכלית ההשתלשלות להמשיך אור א"ס ב"ה לברר הכלים דז"א דבי"ע שבהן הן הרפ"ח ניצוצין ע"י תו"מ מעשיות שבבי"ע דוקא. והנה לקיום מצוה שא"א לעשות ע"י אחרים מבטלין ת"ת ואפי' מעשה מרכבה וכש"כ תפלה שהיא בחי' מוחין ודו"ר שכליים והטעם כנ"ל. ועוד זאת שבאמת מאד גדלה וגבהה מעלת המצות מעשיות וכן לימודם על מעלת המוחין שהן דו"ר שכליים כי הגם דכתיב ולדבקה בו ע"י מדותיו

---

embodied thought in "letters." This is a limitation, placing bounds on the idea. In turn, only through verbalisation can the recipient, the lower plane, absorb the idea. For the inferior, then, the limitation is beneficence, or the "Five Kindnesses." Translator's Notes to "On Learning Chassidus"; Tanya III, p. 23, note 15. [14] The "Whiteness" refers to the source of mitzvot in the Divine Will, where there is as yet no "colouration" or inclination toward any particular deed. The emotive attributes (love, fear, etc.), intense and powerful as they may be, are defined, hence limited. Even intellect at its most abstract already has some definition. The soul proper transcends all its powers, and is relatively "boundless." Will, particularly

(Notes cont. at end of Hebrew Text)

His traits, still one does not cleave to the essence of the Supreme traits but only unto their state of existence,[23] in conformity with, "I am dust and ashes."[24]

This is all the more true in terms of the blessed Infinite Light, for no thought can apprehend Him in His radiance[25] or the extension of the Life-force issuing from Him. One can grasp His existence, that He gives life to all, but not His essence.[23] This applies even to the supernal beings,[26] as we find, "Holy holy holy is the Lord of hosts . . ."[27] Only "effects,"[28] emanations, may conceive their "cause," according to the order in *Etz Chayim* in the investment of the visages.

However, creatures are denied this apprehension, even the souls of Atzilut, as we find regarding Moses, "You may see my hinderpart . . ."[29]

●▲But the performance of mitzvot—"These are the works of G–d."[30] In the process of gradual descent[18] from the vessels of Atzilut to Beriah, Yetzirah and Asiyah, from the very nature[23] and essence[18] of their external aspect, as for example within the etrog and its "kinds,"[31] the Holy One, blessed be He, clothed of the very essence[32] of the internal Kindnesses of the Minor Visage, meaning from their outward state, as is known in the case of all mitzvot of action.

In contrast, man, even possessing a soul of Atzilut,[33] since it is clothed in a body, cannot detect and apprehend within his soul the character and essence of the inward Kindnesses of the Minor Visage of Atzilut. (For Atzilut is the state of *Chaya*[34] in the general Four Worlds, an encompassing[18] state from above, and does not clothe itself within any vessel at all.) Man's capacity for apprehension is limited to their existence through intellectual love and fear. The statement, "You shall see my hinderpart," is by means of prophecy only. (Prophecy entails divestment of the physical,[35] as explained in *Raya Mehemna, parshat Mishpatim.*)

This then is the reason. No creature is capable of grasping anything whatsoever of the essence[23] of G–dliness, the Creator. Without comprehension there is no investing, or grasp,[36] or cleaving in the true sense. However, the etrog by way of example, its life is drawn and descends from the very essence of the outer aspect of the vessels of *nukva* of the Minor Visage of Atzilut, which is a state of G–dliness, as stated in *Etz Chayim* that all the fruits are

---

[23] *"On the Teachings of Chassidus," p. 21, note 6, defining knowledge of "existence" and knowledge of "essence" or "character."* [24] *Gen. 18:27. See Tanya IV, sec. 15, for an explanation of the verse.* [25] *The term "radiance" and similar expressions indicate that it is not G–d's essence but only an emanation from Him, comparable to the body of the sun and its light (radiance) or "extension."* [26] *The angels, whose intellectual comprehension far exceeds the mortal's. "On the Teachings of Chassidus," p. 23; Tanya III, p. 357, note 13.* [27] *Isaiah 6:3.* [28] *Orderly progression involves the process of cause and effect, with a measurable relationship between them. The "cause" contains the "effect" in potential; the "effect" bears the impress*

מדותיו מ"מ איננו דבק אפי' במדות העליונות אלא במציאותן ולא במהותן וכמ"ש ואנכי עפר ואפר וכש"כ באור א"ס ב"ה דלית מחשבה תפיסא בי' באורו והתפשטות החיות ממנו ית' כ"א במציאותו שהוא שמחיה את כולם ולא במהותו אפי' לעליונים כמ"ש קדוש ק' ק' ה' צבאות כו' לבד עלולים הנאצלים משיגים כ"א בעילתו כפי הסדר שבע"ח בהתלבשות הפרצופים אבל לא בנבראים אפי' בנשמות דאצי' כמ"ש במשה רבינו ע"ה וראית את אחורי כו'. משא"כ מעשה המצות מעשה אלקים המה הנה בדרך השתלשלות מכלים דאצי' לבי"ע ממהותן ועצמותן דחיצוניותן כמו עד"מ אתרוג ומיניו הלביש בהן הקב"ה ממהותן ועצמותן דחסדים [פנימית] [פנימים] דז"א והיינו מבחי' חיצוניותן כנודע בכל מצות מעשיות משא"כ האדם אפי' יש לו נשמה דאצי' מאחר שמלובשת בגוף לא יוכל למצוא בנפשו ולהשיג מהותן ועצמותן של פנימית החסדים דז"א דאצי' (כי האצי' היא בחי' חיה בכללות העולמות אבי"ע שהיא בחי' מקיף מלמעלה ואינה מתלבשת בכלי כלל) כ"א מציאותן ע"י דחילו ורחימו שכליים. ומ"ש וראית את אחורי הוא בדרך נבואה דוקא. (שהוא התפשטות הגשמיות כמ"ש בר"מ פ' משפטים). והיינו הטעם לפי שא"א לנברא להשיג כלום במהות האלקות שהוא הבורא ובלי השגה אין זו הלבשה ותפיסא ודביקות אמיתית. משא"כ האתרוג עד"מ חיותו נמשכה ונשתלשלה ממהות חיצונית דכלים דנוק' דז"א דאצי' שהוא בחי' אלקות כמ"ש בע"ח שכל הפירות הן

באצי'

---

of the "cause." Intellect and emotion (see note 18) are examples. Creation ex nihilo *is not an "orderly" process. The created is a "thing", while its antecedent is "nothing." The gap is absolute. The final three of the Four Worlds are "creatures," while Atzilut is "emanation," united with the Emanator, G–d.* [29] *Exodus 33:23. See note 33.* [30] *A play on Ex. 32:16, referring to the Tablets of the Ten Commandments. The Decalogue embodies all 613 precepts. See Tanya I, ch. 36; Rashi on Exodus 24:12.* [31] *Leviticus 23:40.* [32] *The "palpability," to use a grossly inappropriate term, of G–d's presence in the object of a performed mitzvah (etrog or tefillin, say) is far superior to the awareness of G–d that is possible*

(Notes cont. at end of Hebrew Text)

in Atzilut. For the thirty vessels[37] of Atzilut descended into Beriah, Yetzirah and Asiyah (they are the Ten Utterances[38] by which the world was created) through enclothement in *nukva* of Asiyah, essence in essence.[39] For the vessels of Atzilut became the soul of Asiyah, which is actually a state of G-dliness. In Atzilut "He and the vessels are one,"[40] Emanator and Emanation. Through clothing the essence of soul in the essence of the vessels of *nukva* of Asiyah the etrog came into being. The result is that in seizing the etrog and waving it as the Halacha requires, he is actually seizing the life-force clothed within it of the *nukva* of Atzilut which is united with the Infinite Light, the Emanator, blessed be He.

The reverse is true concerning his *kavana*, intention. Here he does not grasp and seize essence even though initiated into the esoteric.[41] Only the existence aspect is within reach.

However, by learning the laws of etrog he does attain and grasp the etrog proper and its mitzvah appropriately, by speech and thought.[42] Even more so he who learns ▲the *sod* aspect of the law. Here we speak of studying the *sod* aspect of the mitzvah specifically, which is not inferior to the study of its laws proper—quite the contrary . . .—though he does not apprehend ●the essence. This does not apply to study of the order of *hishtal'sh'lut*, the orderly downward progression.[18] Even if he does comprehend the existence state, it is not intrinsically as worthy as study of the mitzvot, where he comprehends and grasps the essential nature.[43] This is considered the equivalent of actual performance, as we find "This is the Torah . . ."[44]

Be it noted that knowledge of existence aspects of *hishtal'sh'lut* is also a lofty mitzvah and an exalted one. On the contrary it outweighs them all, as we find, "Know this day . . ."[45] and "Know the G-d of your fathers . . ."[46] and it develops into a "whole heart . . ."[47] which is the essential thing. Comprehension of existence is to divest the physical . . . However, this is but one mitzvah of the 613, and man must fulfil all 613, for they descend from the essence of the external aspect of the vessels of Atzilut. Hence one must abundantly learn all 613 and fulfil them fully in practice in thought, speech, and deed. These are parallel to Beriah, Yetzirah and Asiyah, to purify whatever needs purification within those worlds.

●▲In addition: the truth is that the purifications in Beriah, Yetzirah and Asiyah of the 288 sparks[9] through Torah and mitzvot in thought

---

[37] *The vessels of Atzilut "contain" the Infinite Light, a stage in its descent into finiteness. The lower stage of the superior plane becomes the higher stage (soul) of the lower plane, roughly in the manner of a chain of links. The "thirty" vessels invest the three inferior finite worlds—the ten (analogous to the Ten Sefirot) internal vessels in Beriah, the ten intermediate in Yetzirah, the ten externals in Asiyah.* [38] Avot 5; *Tanya III p. 358, note 15.* [39] *In his Comments and Corrections to Tanya (ed. 1963), Rabbi Menachem Schneerson, the Lubavitcher Rebbe* שליט"א, *suggests that the parenthesis ends here.* [40] *Tanya IV, ch. 20.* [41] Sod, *the esoteric or mystic interpretation of Torah, including Kabbala. The initiated may be conversant and knowledgeable*

באצי׳ כי למ״ד כלים דאצי׳ ירדו לבי״ע (והן יו״ד מאמרות שבהן נברא העולם) ע״י התלבשות בנוק׳ דעשי׳ מהות במהות כי הכלים דאצי׳ נעשו נשמה בעשי׳ שהיא בחי׳ אלקות ממש לפי שבאצי׳ איהו וגרמוהי חד המאציל והנאצל וע״י התלבשות מהות הנשמה במהות הכלים דנוק׳ דעשיה נתהוה האתרוג נמצא כשתופס האתרוג ומנענעו כהלכתו ה״ז תופס ממש חיותו המלובש בו מנוק׳ דאצי׳ המיוחדת באור א״ס המאציל ב״ה. משא״כ בכוונתו אינו משיג ותופס אף היודע הסוד. אלא מציאותה ולא מהותה אך בלימוד הלכות אתרוג משיג ותופס האתרוג ממש ומצותו כהלכה בבחי׳ דבור ומחשבה וכש״כ הלומד הסוד אבל דוקא סודות המצוה דלא גרע מלימוד הלכותיה ואדרבה כו׳ אף שאינו משיג המהות. משא״כ בסדר ההשתלשלות אף אם משיג המציאות לא עדיף מצד עצמו כלימוד המצות שמשיג ותופס המהות ומעלה עליו כאילו קיים בפועל ממש כמ״ש זאת התורה כו׳ אלא שידיעת המציאות מההשתלשלות היא ג״כ מצוה רבה ונשאה ואדרבה עולה על כולנה כמ״ש וידעת היום כו׳ דע את אלקי אביך כו׳ ומביאה ללב שלם כו׳ שהוא העיקר והשגת המציאות הוא להפשיט מגשמיות כו׳ רק שזו היא מצוה אחת מתרי״ג והאדם צריך לקיים כל תרי״ג לפי שהן השתלשלות המהות החיצונית דכלים דאצי׳ לכך צריך להרבות בלימוד כל התרי״ג וקיומן בפועל ממש במחדו״מ שהן בי״ע לברר בירורין אשר שם. ועוד זאת שבאמת הבירורין שבבי״ע מרפ״ח ע״י תורה ומצות במחשבה דבור

---

with the terms and concepts, but he cannot in this manner penetrate beyond "existence" in "essence." [42] *Here speech and thought are the fulfillment of the mitzvah of learning. This is not comparable to* kavana *of a mitzvah without the mitzvah.* [43] *In studying the law one can fully comprehend the theoretical, legal aspects, and the practical aspects, the nature of the subject he studies. See "On Learning Chassidus," p. 37 ff.* [44] *Lev. 7:37;* Menachot *110a.* [45] *Deut. 4:39.* [46] *I Chronicles 28:9.* [47] Ibid.

speech, and deed, are superior in their source to the *nefesh-ruach-neshamah*[34] of man. They are of *sa'g*[8] of the internal aspect of Adam Kadmon,[48] while *nara'n*[34] that has already been corrected through *ma'h*[8] issues from the "forehead" in the form of a mere reflection. Hence the verse, "Before a king ruled . . ."[49] For this reason man sustains himself on foods of the inorganic, vegetative, and living classes, and purifies them by the *ma'h*[8] within him, and lives through them because they are of *sa'g*.[8]

Furthermore, as we find, "My face shall not be seen,"[50] meaning that the inwardness of the Most High cannot descend below, only the external and the hinderpart, which are shades[51] of the Supreme Wisdom.

Another point:[52] Verbalising any phrase of the Supreme Wisdom does not cause birth. The drop drawn from the vessel of the Supreme Wisdom has the power to cause birth and bring about existence *ex nihilo*. Besides, something of the Supreme Wisdom is included within it. The reason is that into it is drawn something of the essence[18] and nature[23] of the Supreme Wisdom.

In contrast, in thought and speech, even in intellectual conception[53] in any field of wisdom, the thought is a mere reflection, an extension[54] of the essence of intellect of the soul. Then, too, this radiance is a mere garment for the essence of the intellect. In turn the intellect is a radiance and a garment for the soul proper. However, the drop has drawn into it also of the very essence of the soul which is clothed within the brain. Hence it gives birth to offspring precisely similar to itself.

This is the difference between the service of angels who are produced by "osculation"[55] and that of souls who issue from the vessels. But the vessels of Atzilut become the soul of Beriah, Yetzirah and Asiyah, and therefore intellectual love and awe are comparable to the angels of the "osculation," of the external aspect of Chabad[56] in Beriah, Yetzirah and Asiyah. The reason is that the inwardness of Chabad and the essential nature of the inward Light cannot be revealed except through the radiance of the vessels exclusively, that descend as does the seminal drop of man issuing from the brain. Thus the verse, "My face cannot be seen."[50]

●▲Besides all this, even a soul (neshamah) of Atzilut, though it is of the vessels of Atzilut, and equally in the case of nefesh-ruach[34] of the vessels of Yetzirah-Asiyah—their intellectual love and fear too, arouse

---

[48] *See "On Learning Chassidus."*
[49] *Gen. 36:31. "Before" (not in time but on a preceding plane) the Condensation (*Tzimtzum *see Translator's Explanatory Notes to "On Learning Chassidus"), the Infinite Light shone forth "abundantly," in greater measure than the absorptive capacities of the vessels. The "shattering of the vessels" took place, and the "sparks" scattered. This intolerable and unviable situation is called* tohu *(after Gen. 1:2) and refers to the period in the verse, "Before a king ruled."* Tikun *took the place of* tohu, *a sharp diminution of Light and an increase in vessels, the process of downward progression with all the Worlds involved, culminating in our world. The mission of man is to call forth increased Divine Light into the world,*

דבור ומעשה גבוהין בשרשן מנר"ן שבאדם כי הן מס"ג שבפנימית א"ק ונר"ן שכבר נתקנו ע"י מ"ה הוא יוצא מהמצח הארה בעלמא. וז"ש לפני מלוך מלך כו' וה"ט שהאדם חי במזונות דצ"ח ומבררן במ"ה שבו וחי בהם לפי שהם מס"ג. ועוד זאת כמ"ש ופני לא יראו שפנימית העליון אינו יכול לירד למטה רק חיצוניותו ובחי' אחוריים שהוא נובלות חכמה עילאה ועוד זאת שהרי הדבור מדברי חכמה עילאה אינו מוליד והטפה שנמשכה מהכלי דח"ע יש בה כח המוליד ומהווה יש מאין וגם המשכת ח"ע כלולה בה והטעם מפני שבה נמשך מהותה ועצמותה דח"ע. משא"כ בדבור ומחשבה ואפי' בהשכלת השכל באיזו חכמה הרי חכמה זו רק הארה מתפשטת ממהות השכל שבנפש ועצמותו והארה זו היא רק לבוש למהותו ועצמותו של השכל והשכל הוא הארה ולבוש למהות הנפש. משא"כ הטפה נמשך בה גם ממהות הנפש ועצמותה המלובשת במוחין ולכן מולידה בדומה לה ממש. וזהו ההפרש בין עבודת המלאכים היוצאין מנשיקין להנשמות היוצאין מהכלים אך הכלים דאצי' נעשו נשמה לבי"ע והלכך דחילו ורחימו שכליים הן כמלאכים דנשיקין מהארת חיצונית דחב"ד בבי"ע והטעם משום דפנימית חב"ד ומהותו ועצמותו של אור פנימי אינו יכול להתגלות אלא ע"י הארת הכלים דוקא היורדים למטה כטיפת האדם ממוחין וכמ"ש ופני לא יראו. וכבר מן כל דין אפי' בנשמה דאצי' אף שהיא מכלים דאצי' וכן בנפש רוח מכלים דיצי' עשי' הנה רחימו [אולי צ"ל דו"ר] שכליי' שלהם מעוררים ג"כ

---

the "vessels." Man is to elevate the fallen sparks, by utilising the material world for Divine purpose (performance of mitzvot, etc.) rather than indulgence, and by rejecting what G-d has forbidden him. [50] *Ex. 33:23. The Hebrew word* panai *(my face) implies* pnimiyut *(inwardness).* [51] *Essay VI, note 12.* [52] *In the innate shortcoming of speech and thought. The contrast is with the seminal "drop" that has the generative power, the offspring similar to the parent. The "drop" is drawn from the brain, the seat of intellect (see Tanya I, ch. 2). If the extension of the "brain" (Supreme Wisdom) is merely thought or speech, then the generative power is lacking.* [53] *Original, creative thinking, the intellectual activity closest to*

(Notes cont. at end of Hebrew Text)

the vessels of Yetzirah-Asiyah the state of elevation from below upward, through an arousal from below.[57] However this is the state of departure[58] alone, G-d forbid.

But eliciting from above downward is of necessity through mitzvot of performance to draw Light into the vessels, and into the external aspect of the vessels, be it emphasised. The external aspect of the superior descends, while the internal of the inferior rises higher. This is the intent of Zohar *parshat P'kudai* cited above, that there is an order . . .

Both of these are needed for the Divine purpose, the elevation,[59] and the elicitation[60] through elevation of *mayin nukvin*[6] from *sa'g*[8] by deed and speech. This is the ultimate purpose of the downward progression[18]—to reveal the Higher Light below, and not to elevate the inferior. This elevation can only be momentary. Even so specifically the elevation of the vessels to the Higher Lights is the quality of Shabbat and Yom Kippur, but not the elevations and departure[58] of the Lights, G-d forbid, as written in *Pri Etz Chayim*.

The *nefesh-ruach-neshamah*[34] of man compared to his physical body in This World is considered as lights compared to vessels. So too are intellectual fear and love compared to mitzvot of action. Therefore Moses offered prayers equivalent in number to *Va'et'chanan*,[61] for the fulfillment of mitzvot requiring action specifically. So too[62] for the physical utterance of their laws.

•▲We must understand how an etrog, which is of the 288 sparks that have not yet been purified, and the parchment of the tefillin, can elicit Light into the vessels of *zu'n*[63] of Atzilut, that have already been so purified and rectified through the Name *ma'h*,[8] that they are a state of G-dliness.

An illustration for this could be the process of planting. The seed stimulates the power of growth within the soil, which is G-d's command, "Let the earth sprout forth . . . fruit trees . . ."[64] through elevation of *mayin nukvin*[6] to its source. In this manner the parchment and etrog arouse unto the loftiest heights, meaning the Name *sa'g*[8] which is above the shattering of the vessels,[65] which is the very essence of the Lights in Adam Kadmon,[66] and not merely a radiance,[25] as is the Name *ma'h*[8] which issues from the "forehead."

Similarly the study and careful examination of their[67] laws arouses the *Chabad*[56] of the Ten Sefirot of the vessels of *zu'n*,[63] and upward to the greatest heights, including *Chabad* of *sa'g* of the internal

---

[57] *Tanya III, p. 345, note 26.* [58] *The author will shortly contrast two elevations, of vessels and of lights, the former alone being desirable. He will cite examples of light-vessel relationships, like soul and body, or emotion and deed. The soul must invest the body to give it life; emotion must inspire the deed. When the vessel "rises" to receive the light, the purpose is fulfilled. When the light "rises" it removes itself from the vessel or instrument. Then soul does not vivify body, and emotion does not engender deed. In terms of the Divine Light, the ascent of the vessel is its receptive ability fulfilled; ascent of light is the obscuring of G-d.* [59] *Of the inferior, the vessel or instrument, the recipient.* [60] *Drawing the light, the superior, downward.* [61] *Deut.*

ג"כ בכלים דיצי' עשי' בחי' העלאה ממטה למעלה באתערותא דלתתא וזהו בחי' הסתלקות לבד ח"ו. אבל בחי' המשכה מלמעלה למטה הוא ע"י מצות מעשיות דוקא להמשיך אור בכלים ובחיצונית הכלים דוקא שחיצוניות העליון יורד למטה ופנימיות התחתון עולה למעלה וז"ש בזהר פ' פקודי הנ"ל דאית סדורא כו' ושתיהן צורך גבוה העלאה והמשכה ע"י העלאת מ"ן מס"ג בבחי' עובדא ומלולא וזהו תכלית ההשתלשלו' להתגלות אור עליון למטה ולא לעלות התחתון למעלה שזה אינו אלא לפי שעה ואף גם זאת דוקא עליות הכלים לאורות עליונים היא מעלת השבת ויוה"כ. אבל לא עליות והסתלקות האורות ח"ו כמ"ש בפע"ח ונר"ן של האדם לגבי גופו בעוה"ז חשיבי כאורות לגבי כלים וכן דו"ר שכליים לגבי מצות מעשיות דוקא ולכן התפלל משרע"ה תפלות כמנין ואתחנן על קיום מצות מעשיות דוקא וה"ה לדבור גשמי של הלכותיהן. אך להבין איך האתרוג שהוא מרפ"ח שלא נבררו עדיין וכן קלף התפילין ימשיך אור בכלים דזו"ן דאצי' שכבר נבררו ונתקנו ע"י שם מ"ה להיות בחי' אלקות. הנה המשל לזה היא הזריעה והנטיעה שהגרעין מעורר כח הצומח שבארץ שהוא דבר ה' תדשא הארץ כו' עץ פרי כו' ע"י העלאת מ"ן לשרשו ככה מעוררי' הקלף והאתרוג עד רום המעלות שהוא שם ס"ג שלפני השבירה שהוא מהות ועצמות אורות שבא"ק ולא הארה בעלמא כמו שם מ"ה שממצחו וכן בלימוד ועיון הלכותיהן מעורר בחי' חב"ד שבע"ס דכלים דזו"ן ועד רום המעלות ג"כ בחי' חב"ד שבס"ג דפנימית א"ק

3:23 and commentary Daat Zekenim. [62] *These, too, are considered vessels.* [63] *Essay VI, note 7.* [64] *Gen. 1:11.* [65] *See note 49.* [66] *See "On Learning Chassidus," p. 15 ff.* [67] *Tefillin and etrog, the examples cited here.*

of Adam Kadmon issuing through the "eyes . . ."

All the foregoing concerns positive commandments, but not the study of particulars of the prohibitions it would seem, particularly those that do not occur in practice at all, for example the detailed laws of *pigul*[68] and the like.

●▲ There is yet a common characteristic, that all intellectual fear and love of the angels are considered created *ex nihilo*, and are *nefesh-ruach* of Beriah, Yetzirah and Asiyah. But the detailed laws are drawn from the Supreme Wisdom of the Emanator, blessed be He, which is clothed in the physical object. This investment is not similar to that of the Supreme Wisdom in intellectual fear and love, for there the garment conceals and completely obscures, just as the gross earth thoroughly conceals the Supreme Wisdom clothed within it, as it is written, "All of them you made with wisdom,"[69] that is the externality of the externality of the vessels of *Malchut* of Atzilut found in Asiyah, is absolutely hidden in the *ruach-nefesh* of Asiyah. So too in Beriah it is completely hidden in the *ruach-nefesh*; they are creatures, and Creator is concealed from the created.

▲ This is not so, however, with regard to the laws—a radiance of Wisdom illuminates them openly. The garment of Asiyah is merely by way of passage,[70] as on holy days when *Chesed* of Atzilut which is completely clothed in *Chesed* of Beriah vivifies the physical world through passage by way of *Chesed* of Yetzirah and Asiyah. This, too, is properly called investment for otherwise it could not affect the physical aspects of This World.

Now although the physical nature of This World unquestionably conceals completely even the *Chesed* of Asiyah, still the law proper is not actually physical; it is the Will, drawn from the Supreme Wisdom for leniency or severity in the verdict. It does descend and illuminate in revealed fashion in the realm of the physical as water descends from a high place . . . The physical object itself which the law discusses really does utterly obscure, as for example the law of exchanging a cow for a donkey,[71] or flesh that is *pigul*,[68] or is not *pigul* and is kasher. Just the law itself and its revealed rationale are *Malchut* of Beriah

---

[68] *Lev. 7:18.* [69] *Psalm 104:24. "All" includes the highest stage to the lowest.* Chochmah, *the Divine Wisdom, invests even the lowliest; even the most exalted is considered as trivial as the lowliest (Asiyah, deed) before Him.* [70] *In descent from plane to plane, there may be adaptation, acquisition of the traits of the lower. The subject manifests itself through its newly acquired "garments" in which it is now clothed. Another sort of descent involves no adaptation. It is merely a "passage" through the lower plane, without adopting "garments." See note 33.* [71] Bava Metzia *100a.*

א"ק היוצא דרך העינים כו' וכל הנ"ל הוא במ"ע אבל לא בלימוד פרטי הלכות איסורי ל"ת לכאורה ובפרט בדלא שכיחי כלל כמו פרטי הלכות פיגול וכה"ג. אך עוד זאת השוה בכל כי כל דחילו ורחימו שכליים של המלאכים הן בחי' נבראים מאין ליש והן בחי' נפש רוח דבי"ע. אבל פרטי ההלכות הן המשכות ח"ע דהמאציל ב"ה המלובשת בגשמיות והלבשה זו אינה כהלבשת ח"ע בדו"ר שכליים דהתם הלבוש הוא מעלים ומסתיר לגמרי כהסתר והעלם הארץ החומריית לגבי ח"ע המלובשת בה כמ"ש כולם בחכמה עשית והיינו חיצוניות דחיצוניות דכלים דמל' דאצי' שבעשיה שהיא מסותרת לגמרי ברוח נפש דעשיה וכן בבריאה היא מסותרת לגמרי ברוח נפש שהם בחי' נבראים בהסתר והעלם הבורא מהנברא. משא"כ ההלכות הרי הארת החכמה מאירה בהן בגילוי ולבוש העשי' הוא דרך מעבר לבד כמו ביום טוב שחסד דאצי' המלובש לגמרי בחסד דבריאה מחיה עוה"ז הגשמי ע"י מעבר חסד דיצי' ועשי' הנק' ג"כ התלבשות שאל"כ לא הי' פועל בגשמיות עוה"ז ואף שגשמיות עוה"ז ודאי מסתיר לגמרי אפילו החסד דעשיה מ"מ ההלכה עצמה אינה גשמיות ממש שהיא בחי' רצון הנמשך מח"ע להקל או להחמיר רק שיורד ומאיר בבחי' גילוי בגשמיות כמים היורדים ממקום גבוה כו' והדבר הגשמי עצמו שבו מדברת ההלכה באמת הוא מסתיר לגמרי כמו המחליף פרה בחמור וכן בשר הפיגול או לא פיגול וכשר רק ההלכה בעצמה עם הטעם הנגלה היא מבחי' מלכות דבריאה ויצי'

and Yetzirah, of the state of *neshamah*, which is G-dliness that vivifies and brings into being *ex nihilo*, the nefesh-ruach of the Beriah, Yetzirah and Asiyah, which are the awe and love of angels and souls and their *chabad*.

Hence it[72] slakes their thirst before its descent into This World like waters falling . . . Even after descending into Asiyah it is far above *chabad* of Asiyah, even the ●▲ state of *neshamah* which is G-dliness. The reason is that *chabad* of Asiyah of the state of *neshamah* is the source of life of *Chabad* of *nefesh-ruach* and their offspring, and their existence *ex nihilo* with their offspring unto the ultimate stage of Asiyah, namely the earth and all its hosts.

But *chabad* of the laws with their rationales are in *malchut* of Beriah-Yetzirah. The aim of the *chochmah* is the rectification of the visages of Atzilut, upon whom are dependent all the rationales of the positive commandments in the Five Kindnesses, and of the prohibitions in the Five Severities. Therefore, even when they descend to be clothed in creatures, they are in *malchut* of Beriah-Yetzirah of the state of *neshamah* specifically, which is of the vessels of Atzilut, and not of *nefesh-ruach*.

Now although *chabad* of Beriah-Yetzirah of the *neshamah* state are far superior in quality over *malchut* of Beriah-Yetzirah of *neshamah*, still they are the source for *chabad* of Beriah-Yetzirah of the state of *nefesh-ruach*, namely the angels. How is this? The angels and souls are only of a drop drawn from *chabad* of the *neshamah* to the attribute of *Yesod* in the Minor Visage, then transmitted to *nukva*, and from there going forth in a state of "birth." For even if it is proposed that they are created from the radiance of the vessels of *nukva* of Atzilut, they themselves descend and become *neshamah*.

But the essence of *chabad* of *neshamah* extends into the "six sides"[73] of *zu'n*[63] and there they are the Six Orders of Mishnah and the Gemara. As to the statement ●▲ in *Etz Chayim* (and in *Shaar Hayichudim*) that through *Kavana* (intention) there is formed a garment for *neshamah* and through Torah study—a garment for ruach-of-ruach of Yetzirah through Mishnah, and for ruach-of-neshamah of Beriah through Gemara. This can be understood as referring only to Torah studied by man in This World that ascends above. But Talmud

---

[72] *The law.* [73] *The four compass points, above and below.*

ויצי׳ דבחי׳ נשמה שהוא אלקות המחיה ומהוה נפש רוח דבי״ע שהן דחילו ורחימו של המלאכים והנשמות וחב״ד שלהם מאין ליש ולכן היא מרוה צמאונם קודם שירדה לעוה״ז כמים היורדים כו׳ וגם אחר שירדה לעשי׳ היא למעלה מעלה מבחי׳ חב״ד דעשי׳ אפי׳ דבחי׳ נשמה שהיא אלקות והטעם משום דחב״ד דעשי׳ דבחי׳ נשמה הוא מקור החיות דחב״ד דנפש רוח ותולדותיהן והתהוותן מאין ליש עם תולדותיהן עד סוף העשיה היא הארץ וכל צבאה. אבל חב״ד דהלכות בטעמיהן שבמל׳ דבריאה ויצי׳ ענין החכמה היא בתיקון פרצופי האצי׳ שבהן תלוין כל טעמי המצות מ״ע בה׳ חסדים ומל״ת בה״ג ומשר״ה נמי כשירדו להתלבש בנבראים הן במל׳ דבריאה ויצי׳ דבחי׳ נשמה דוקא שהוא מכלים דאצי׳ ולא בבחי׳ נפש רוח. ואף דחב״ד דבריאה יצירה דבחי׳ נשמה שגבהה מאד מעלתן על בחי׳ מלכות דבריאה יצירה דנשמה ואעפ״כ הן מקור לחב״ד דבריאה יצירה של בחי׳ נפש רוח שהן המלאכים. לק״מ דבאמת המלאכים והנשמות אינן אלא מטפה הנמשכת מחב״ד דנשמה ליסוד ז״א וניתן לנוק׳ ומשם יצאו בבחי׳ לידה כי אף את״ל שנבראו מהארת הכלים דנוק׳ דאצי׳ הרי הם היורדים ונעשים נשמה. אבל עצמות חב״ד דנשמה מתפשט בו״ק דזו״ן ושם הם שיתא סדרי משנה וגמרא ומ״ש בע״ח (ושער היחודים) שע״י הכוונה נעשה לבוש נשמה וע״י התורה לבוש רוח דרוח ע״י משנה דיצי׳ ורוח דנשמה דבריאה ע״י הגמ׳ י״ל דהיינו דוקא ע״י תורת האדם בעוה״ז העולת למעלה. אבל התלמוד

עצמו

itself that was given on Sinai is in *neshamah*. Therefore it purifies *ruach*. So too with Mishnah of Yetzirah.

If it be suggested that even what was given at Sinai is in *ruach* of Beriah-Yetzirah, it is known that every angel, as an emissary from On High, is called by the Name of G-d[74] literally, for He dwells within the angel. However, when he is not a messenger he has some other name according to his function. Then he proclaims, "Holy holy holy is G-d . . ."[27] meaning, that the name of G-d is removed, distant from him. So it is actually in the state of investment of the Talmud, in the *ruach* state of Beriah, and the Mishnah in the *ruach* of Yetzirah—they are messengers of G-d, meaning vessels of *nukva* of Atzilut: the external state in Talmud, the intermediate state in Mishnah.

Thus Mishnah and Talmud contain issue of *Yesod Abba* which receives from *chochmah stima'a* of the Major Visage, in which is clothed the blessed Infinite Light. The result is that the Infinite Light, namely the Name of G-d, dwells in *ruach* of Beriah, Yetzirah and Asiyah in Scripture, Mishnah, and Talmud. When man studies he draws forth the blessed Infinite Light into This World, that it be included and nullified in His Light, blessed be He. For this is all of man.[75] This was the service of Rabbi Shimon bar Yochai and all the Tannaim and Amoraim in the revealed Torah[76]—to call forth His Light, blessed be He, and to make these purifications of *nogah*[77] all through the period of the exile. Exile is the time of dominion of the Tree of Good and Evil,[78] as we find, "The time that man dominates man . . ."[79] For this is the purpose of the descent, that the Higher descend below, and there be an "abode for Him among the lowly,"[80] in order to elevate them to become one in one.[81]

In contrast, the service of the angels with intellectual fear and love does not call forth at all; rather there is departure[58] alone . . . Thus we may understand how angels are created *ex nihilo* through study of Torah, even without *kavana*, which is a state of *ruach* alone, which is not G-dliness at all. Still, nevertheless, the name of G-d does dwell . . . This will suffice for the knowing.

---

[74] Cf. Sanhedrin *38b*. [75] *Kohelet 12:13*. [76] "*On the Teachings of Chassidus*," *p. 17*. [77] *Glossary (Kelipat nogah); Tanya III Ch. 6, note 3*. [78] *ibid. note 8*. [79] *Kohelet 8:89*. [80] "*On the Teachings of Chassidus*," *note 13*. [81] *Zohar* Truma.

עצמו שניתן בסיני הוא בנשמה ולכן הוא מברר הרוח וכן במשנה דיצי' ואף את"ל שגם הניתן מסיני הוא ברוח דבריאה יצירה הרי נודע שכל מלאך שהוא שליח מלמעלה אזי נק' בשם ה' ממש השוכן בקרבו משא"כ כשאינו שליח יש לו שם אחר כפי עבודתו ואזי קורא קדוש ק' ק' ה' כו' כלומר ששם ה' מובדל ממנו וכן הוא ממש בבחי' התלבשות התלמוד בבחי' רוח דבריאה והמשנה ברוח דיצי' הם שלוחי ה' דהיינו כלים דנוק' דאצי' החיצונים בתלמוד והאמצעי' במשנה אשר המשנה והתלמוד שבהם נמשכים מיסוד אבא המקבל מח"ס דא"א שבו מלובש אור א"ס ב"ה ונמצא שאור א"ס הוא שם ה' שוכן ברוח דבי"ע במקרא ומשנה ותלמוד וכשהאדם לומד ממשיך אור א"ס ב"ה בעוה"ז להיות נכלל ובטל באורו ית' כי זה כל האדם וזאת היתה עבודת רשב"י וכל התנאים ואמוראים בנגלה להמשיך אורו ית' ולברר בירורי נוגה כל משך זמן הגלות דשלטא אילנא דטו"ר כמ"ש עת אשר שלט האדם באדם כו' כי זהו תכלית ההשתלשלות שירד העליון למטה ויהיה לו דירה בתחתונים כדי להעלותן למהוי אחד באחד. משא"כ עבודת המלאכים דו"ר שכליים אינה בבחי' המשכה כלל וכלל רק הסתלקות כו'. ובזה יובן מה שנבראים מלאכים מאין ליש ע"י עסק התורה אפי' שלא בכוונה שהוא בחי' רוח בלבד שאינה אלקות כלל אלא לפי שאעפ"כ שם ה' שוכן וכו' וד"ל:

ולהבין

Essay 5

●▲ To understand the details of the laws that never occur at all, and probably never actually existed, and certainly will not come to pass in the Time To Come, for example the detailed laws of *pigul*[1] and the like.

It is known that every prohibited thing in this world has a source and root of life in *Kelipot*.[2] Otherwise, it could not exist in this world, without the flow (of life) from above. Even one who dandifies his hair, and the like, receives his life-force at that moment from the chambers of *kelipot*, as explained in Zohar. Therefore even the particular prohibitions that never became practical issues in this physical world, still the source of their life does actually exist in the chambers of the *kelipot*.

There are instances that possibly never did and can never actually occur, for instance errors and unwitting misdeeds like erroneously calling the ninth "tenth . . ."[3] and the like, eventualities that cannot be deliberate so that the *kelipah* may inhabit it. Possibly in these circumstances it does not exist in the chambers of the *kelipot*. [It appears to me that his use of the word "possibly," implying uncertainty, is because unwitting errors come from *nogah*.[4] Therefore it may be that their origin is in the chambers of *nogah*.—This gloss was inserted into the text by the Tzemach Tzedek.] In any event it does exist *lehavdil*[5] in the Supreme Wisdom and issued and descended in this detail to Moses on Sinai, [as the expression, "Whatever] any valid student will originate . . ."[6] and all the detailed queries of R. Yirmiah, "If she wrapped him . . ." in ch. 4 of *Chulin*.[7]

For the extension of the Supreme Wisdom is Infinite, since the Infinite is actually clothed in it. Every particular of the law is a "hair"[8] drawn from the Supreme Wisdom that "established the daughter,"[9] and is clothed in it, and is drawn from it to be invested in Beriah, Yetzirah and Asiyah. It is known that the nurture of the *kelipot* is from the backpart of the Ten sacred Sefirot, and more precisely from the garments of the Ten Sefirot of Beriah, Yetzirah and Asiyah, and more precisely, from Yetzirah-Asiyah that are intermingled with *kelipot*, as is known that their nurture is from the state of garments.

Through the study of the laws, in speech and in thought,

---

[1] *Leviticus 7:18.* [2] *Tanya I, Glossary, Kelipot.* [3] *Lev. 27:32;* Bechorot *59a.* [4] *Note 2; Tanya III Ch. 6, note 3.* [5] *"To separate," a demarcation between the sacred and the profane.* [6] *". . . was revealed to Moses on Sinai."* Yeru-shalmi Peah *2:4.* [7] *70a.* [8] *Essay VI, note 10.* [9] *"Father" is* chochmah, *wisdom. "Daughter" is* malchut *of Atzilut.*

ולהבין פרטי ההלכות דלא שכיחי כלל ואפשר שלא היו מעולם במציאות מכש"כ שלא יהיו לע"ל כמו פרטי דיני פיגול וכה"ג. הנה מודעת זאת שכל איסור שבעולם יש לו שרש ומקור חיים בקליפות שאל"כ לא הי' יכול להיות במציאות בעולם בלתי השפעה עליונה. ואפי' המסלסל בשערו וכה"ג מקבל חיותו ברגע זו מהיכלות הקליפות כמ"ש בזהר. והלכך גם פרטי האיסורים שלא באו לידי מעשה מעולם בעוה"ז הגשמי מ"מ שרשי הויותם הן במציאות בפו"מ בהיכלות הקליפות. וגם הפרטים שיוכל להיות שלא היו ולא יהיו לעולם במציאות כגון טעות ושגגות שטעה וקרא לתשיעי עשירי כו' וכה"ג דלא שייך במזיד להיות קליפה שורה ע"ז. ויוכל להיות דכה"ג אינו במציאות בהיכלות הקליפות [הגה"ה מאדמו"ר בעל צ"צ ז"ל נ"ע. נ"ל מ"ש ויוכל להיות אלמא דלא ברירא לי' היינו משום שהשגגות באות מנוגה א"כ י"ל דיש להם שרש בהיכלות דנוגה]. מ"מ עכ"פ ישנו במציאות להבדיל בחכ"ע שנתפשטה בפרט זה למשרע"ה בסיני [כמאמר מה] שכל תלמיד ותיק עתיד לחדש כו' וכל פרטי האבעיות דר' ירמי' וכרכתו כו' פ"ד דחולין. כי התפשטות חכ"ע היא בבחי' א"ס המלובש בה בפועל ממש. וכל פרט הלכה הוא שער נמשך מחכ"ע דיסד ברתא ומלובש בה וממנה נמשך ומתלבש בבי"ע. ונודע כי יניקת הקליפות מאחוריים די"ס דקדושה ובפרט מלבושים די"ס דבי"ע ובפרט דיצי' עשיה המעורבים בקליפות כנודע שיניקתם מבחי' הלבושים. וע"י עסק ההלכות בדבור ומחשבה

מתפרטים

they[10] become separated and distinct from the sacred. It is so stated in *Tikunim* and *Raya Mehemna*, "To separate [. . .]." As noted in the comment, "For they did not recite the Torah blessing before . . ."[11] This is effected by calling forth the Infinite Light into the Supreme Wisdom clothed in them (the laws). "Through *chochmah* (wisdom) are they purified"[12]—through the Infinite Light that is within it.

This Light is drawn into the Supreme Wisdom by the supernal "likeness"[13] of man who is also occupied with these laws above in his source in *nukva* of the Minor Visage[14] of Beriah, Yetzirah and Asiyah.

Thus we can understand the requirement that every *nefesh-ruach-neshamah*[15] fulfil all 613 commandments in thought, speech, and deed, meaning all the details of the laws. They must again descend into the mundane world to fulfil the Torah in all four Pardess[16] aspects, in order to purify all that pertain to them of the 288.[17] This constitutes the complete structure of man, the 613 categories, general and particular.

But in the Time to Come, when the purification is culminated, then the study of Torah will be in the form of "Do good"[18] alone. Its purpose will be to elevate *nefesh-ruach-neshama* ever and infinitely higher; and also in the 365 prohibitions, to elevate them to their source, the Sacred Severities, and to "sweeten" them with Kindnesses of the 248 positive commandments and to unite them.

Thus is the entire Torah eternal in general and in detail. Even the individual laws of the 365 prohibitions are branches of the generalities. All of them have a source above in the Five Severities[19] of sanctity, just as the 365 prohibitions themselves as they are above in the state of "blood" that vivifies the vessels of the Minor Visage.

Essay 6

●▲ "David! Do you call them songs!"[1] In Zohar we find, "The praise of Torah and its song." We must understand, what is the praise of G-d in forbidding or permitting an object.

A similar concept is implicit in "How great are Your works, O G-d, Your thoughts are very deep."[2] It is known that all worlds,[3] the exalted and the lowly, are dependent on the precise and meticulous performance of a single mitzvah. For example, if the altar offering was valid then the Supernal Union[4] is effected, and all worlds are elevated to receive their life-force[5] and sustenance. However, if there is an aberration, if the celebrant received

---

[10] *The* kelipot. [11] Nedarim *81a.* [12] *Tanya IV, ch. 21, quoting Zohar;* Sefer Maamorim *5708, p. 206, note 11.* [13] *Essay I.* [14] *Essay III, note 8.* [15] *Glossary; Tanya III, Ch. 7, note 1.* [16] *Tanya I, Ch. 4, note 4.* [17] *Sparks. Glossary, Nitzotzot.* [18] *Psalm 34: 15, "Turn from evil and do good."* [19] *Essay IV, note 13.*

Essay VI

[1] *When David brought the Ark back from the Philistine captivity (II Samuel 6; I Chronicles 13) it was borne in a wagon. David had forgotten the verse. "The sacred service is theirs; on the shoulder shall they bear it" (Numbers 7:9). This forgetfulness was a rebuke for David's declaring, "Your statutes were songs for me in my*

מתפרטים ומתפרדים מהקדושה. כמ״ש בתיקונים ור״מ לאפרשא [כו׳] והיינו כנודע ממה שאמרו על שלא ברכו בתורה תחלה כו׳ שהוא ע״י המשכת אוא״ס בח״ע המלובשת בהן. ובחכמה אתברירו באוא״ס שבה. והמשכה זו נעשה ע״י דיוקן העליון של האדם העוסק ג״כ בהלכות אלו למעלה בשרשו בנוק׳ דז״א דבי״ע. ובזה יובן חיוב כל נר״ן להשלים כל התרי״ג במחדו״מ שהן פרטי ההלכות וצריכות לבא בגלגול להשלים התורה בפרד״ס כדי לברר כל הבירורין הנוגעות להם מכל הרפ״ח שהיא קומת אדם שלמה. תרי״ג בחינות כלליות ופרטיות. אבל לע״ל כשיושלם הבירור יהי׳ עסק התורה בבחי׳ עשה טוב לבד. להעלות הנר״ן מעלה מעלה עד א״ס וגם בשס״ה ל״ת בשרשן למעלה שהן גבורות קדושות ולהמתיקן בחסדים ברמ״ח מ״ע ולכללן יחד. וע״כ התורה כולה נצחית בכללה ובפרטה. שגם פרטי ההלכות דשס״ה ל״ת הן הן ענפים מהכללות ויש לכולם שרש למעלה בה״ג דקדושה כמו השס״ה ל״ת עצמן שהן למעלה בחי׳ הדם המחיה האברים דכלים דז״א:

דוד זמירות קרית להו כו׳. הנה בזהר שבחא דאורייתא ורננה כו׳ ולהבין מהו השבח להקב״ה כשזה אסור או מותר הנה הוא ע״ד מה גדלו מעשיך ה׳ מאד עמקו מחשבותיך. כי הנה נודע שכל העולמות עליונים ותחתונים תלוים בדקדוק מצוה א׳ ד״מ אם הקרבן כשר נעשה יחוד עליון ועולים כל העולמות לקבל חיותם ושפעם. ואם שינה שקיבל

הדם

---

place of terror" (Psalm 119:54). This derogation of Torah is the theme of this essay. The opening quotation of this essay is taken from Sotah 35a. Other Chabad references include Rabbi Schneur Zalman's Likutei Torah, *"Va'ehye," and Rabbi Joseph Isaac Schneersohn's* Sefer Hamaamorim *5702, p. 36.* [2] *Psalm 92:10.* [3] *All stages of existence, from the purest spiritual being to the grossly mundane, are called "Worlds" in Kabbala and Chassidic usage. See Tanya I, Glossary. Introduction to Tanya II; Tanya III, ch. 1, note 3; note 3 to the first essay in this Kuntress Acharon; Translator's Explanatory Notes to "On Learning Chassidus," etc.* [4] *Glossary on* Yichud, *defines and lists references.*

(Notes cont. at end of Hebrew Text)

the blood of the offering in his left hand, say, or not in the appropriate vessel, or if some foreign body separates the vessel and the blood it contains, then all the elevations of the world are nullified, as is their life-force and sustenance from the Source of Life, the En Sof,[6] blessed be He.

So, too, through valid tefillin there is revealed the Supernal Intellect of zu'n,[7] the source of life for all worlds. Through the omission of one required detail they are invalidated, and the Intellect departs. This applies as well to the requirements of the prohibitions.

The meditation then may take these lines: Consider "How great are the works" of G–d in the multiplicity of worlds and all their hosts. All of these are literally null when compared to one detail of Torah specification, for Torah requirements are the profundity of the Supreme thought and His wisdom,[8] blessed be He. Through one minor specification all worlds ascend[9] and receive their life-force and sustenance, or the opposite, G–d forbid. From this we may ponder the magnitude of the profundity of His thoughts, blessed be He, that is boundless and endless, and infinitely transcends the vitality of all Creation. The vivifying power of all worlds issues from a minor requirement of it (G–d's thought), for each specification is drawn from its source, namely the depth of His thought, blessed be He. Analogously, man's hair issues from his brain,[10] as is known from Tikunim and Idra Rabba.

This was the delight of King David, may he rest in peace, as he sang to gladden his heart in his Torah study during his time of trouble. However, his extolling ●▲ the praise of Torah with this quality, saying, "Songs were they for me . . ." caused his punishment. G–d reproved him saying, "Do you call them 'songs!' " For indeed, this quality—that all worlds are nothingness compared to one detail of it—is of the hinderpart[11] of the profound thought. This is explained elsewhere in the name of the Ari, of blessed memory, on the passage,[12] "The Torah is (merely) a shade of Supernal *chochmah*."

However the internal aspect of the depth, which is the inner[13] aspect of Torah —*pnimiyut haTorah*—is totally united with the blessed Infinite Light that is clothed within Torah. The unity is a perfect one.[8] In terms of the Infinite, all Worlds are as absolute naught,[14] sheer nothingness, non-existent. For, "You are the same, before the world was created . . ."[15]

Hence,

---

[6] *Their continued existence, their life-force, their vivifying power, would emanate from a plane inferior to the ultimate "Source of Life, the En Sof (Infinite)." In this case, the presence of Creator is concealed behind the façade of nature.* [7] Z'char v'nukva, *masculine and feminine, indicating unity. The mission of man in this universe of the concealment of G–d is to make His presence evident, by living according to His commands and utilising the physical world for the Divine purpose. Each of the names applied to G–d describes a particular aspect of G–d. One name describes His transcendence, G–d before Whom all Creation is naught. Another name indicates power, the creative and sustaining force, G–d Whose hand may be detected in His works. The theme of*

הדם בשמאלו ד"מ או שלא בכלי שרת כשר או שהיתה חציצה אזי נתבטלה עליות העולמות וחיותם ושפעם מחיי החיים א"ס ב"ה וכן בתפילין כשרות מתגלים מוחין עליונים דזו"נ שהם מקור החיים לכל העולמות ובדקדוק אחד נפסלין ומסתלקין המוחין וכה"ג בדקדוקי מצות ל"ת והלכך המתבונן מה גדלו מעשי ה' שבריבוי העולמות וכל צבאם ואיך כולם בטלים במציאות לגבי דקדוק א' מדקדוקי תורה שהוא עומק מחשבה עליונה וחכמתו ית' אשר בדקדוק קל עולים כל העולמות ומקבלים חיותם ושפעם או להיפך ח"ו ומזה נתבונן גדולת עומק מחשבתו ית' שהוא בבחי' בלי גבול ותכלית ומעלתה לאין קץ ותכלית על מעלות חיות כל העולמות שכל חיותם שופע מדקדוק אחד ממנה שהוא נמשך ממקורו הוא עומק מחשבתו ית' כמו שער האדם הנמשך ממוחו עד"מ וכנודע מהתיקונים והאר"י. וזאת היתה שמחת דהע"ה שהיה מזמר ומרנן לשמח לבו בעסק התורה בעת צרתו אך מה שהיה משתבח בתהלת התורה במעלתה זו ואמר זמירות היו לי כו' נענש ע"ז וא"ל הקב"ה זמירות קרית להו משום שבאמת מעלתה זו שכל העולמות בטלים לגבי דקדוק אחד ממנה היא מבחי' אחוריים של עומק המחשבה כמ"ש במ"א בשם האריז"ל על מארז"ל נובלות חכמה שלמעלה תורה. אבל פנימית שבעומק שהוא פנימית התורה היא מיוחדת לגמרי באור א"ס ב"ה המלובש בה בתכלית היחוד ולגבי א"ס ב"ה כל העולמות כלא ממש ואין ואפס ממש כי אתה הוא עד שלא נברא העולם וכו' והלכך גם לפנימיות

---

yichud, *unity, recurrent in Kabbala and Chassidut, is the union of both aspects, that transcendence become immanent, that Creation cease to conceal Him. This unity is effected on different planes, depending on the act which produces that union. Self-immolation, latent or actual, effects one sort of union; Torah study and mitzvah observance causes another. The union called* zu'n *(noted in our text) is of the latter order. The "Supreme Intellect" in the text refers to the first steps of the revelation of G–d culminating in Creation. In its external aspects, the union of the powers of Intellect is constant, for it is the source of Creation, bringing "something" from "nothing." A more profound revelation of G–d, a union more than*

(Notes cont. at end of Hebrew Text)

the internal aspect of Torah too is not to be lauded as being the vivifying force of all Worlds, for they are reckoned as nothingness itself.

In this inward aspect of Torah there can be no mortal joy and delight, but rather, in a manner of speaking, the heart's joy and pleasure of the King, the Holy One, blessed be He, Who delights in it. For "G-d understands its way,"[16] and knows its station and quality, through His self-knowledge,[17] as it were.

This, however, is concealed from the mortal eye, as, "My face cannot be seen"[18] —i.e. the inwardness, as explained there in the name of the Ari, of blessed memory.

Hence the verse, "I was a pleasure to Him,"[19] to *Him* specifically. "Playing before Him," before *Him* specifically, meaning the inwardness. "I was reared with Him," and (the Midrash comments) —"Do not read *amon* (reared) but *uman* (craft) . . ."[20]

In reference to the hinderpart it says, "Playing in the world, His land, and my delights are with mortal men."[21] For the Torah is given in states of inwardness and hinderpart, as written in the "Flying scroll" of Zecharia, "And it was written front and back."[22]

Since David seized upon the hinderpart he was punished with forgetfulness, a product of the state of the hinderpart. Momentarily he was oblivious to the verse, "The sacred service is theirs; on the shoulder shall they carry."[23] The purpose is to combine the "shoulder," the hinderpart, with the sacred service, the Higher Wisdom,[24] in a manner of inwardness.[25] This state is the source of the tablets in the Ark, as we find, "Written on both their sides . . ."[26] Yerushalmi Shekalim explains that they did not have any front and back; study that reference.[27]

Essay 7

●▲"And charity like a mighty (Eitan) river" (Amos, end of ch. 5). The meaning is that charity will be like the river Eitan, issuing from the state of Eitan,[1] the state of "point in its chamber,"[2] and "two comrades . . ."[3] The letters of the word Eitan indicate the future tense, "I am destined to reveal myself," as written, "See, my servant will be wise . . ."[4] This means that at that time the blessed Infinite Light and His Unity will be revealed within the depth of the core of the heart by calling forth the river Eitan, which is a radiance of the supernal wisdom[5] that will illuminate the inwardness

---

[16] *Cf. Job 28:23.* [17] *Rambam, Hilchot Yesodei Hatorah 2:10.* [18] *Exodus 33:23.* Panai, *"My face," also implies* pnimiyut, *inwardness. "Before," in a following quotation, has the same connotation.* [19] *Proverbs 8:30. The verse lauds Wisdom, or Torah, as a delight, but in two contexts. In v. 30 it is G-d's pristine delight; in v. 31 it is man's delight, world's delight. Rabbi Schneur Zalman's thesis is that the first is G-d's exclusively, for it is totally beyond man's ken; mortals can have no comprehension or appreciation of this basic character of Torah. Man's province is the second, as Torah is expressed in terms of the physical world—study and mitzvot. Even this "inferior" aspect of Torah infinitely transcends "world," yet is in turn in-*

לפנימיות התורה אין לשבחה כלל בתהלת חיות כל העולמות מאחר דלא ממש חשיבי ובבחי' פנימיותה אינה שמחת לבב אנוש ושעשועיו אלא כביכול שמחת לב ושעשוע המלך הקב"ה שמשתעשע בה כי אלקים הבין דרכה וידע מקומה ומעלתה בידיעת עצמו כביכול אבל נעלמה מעיני כל חי כמ"ש ופני לא יראו דהיינו בחי' פנימיותה כמש"ש בשם האריז"ל. וזש"ה ואהי' אצלו שעשועים אצלו דוקא. משחקת לפניו לפניו דוקא דהיינו בבחי' פנימיותה וע"ז אמר ואהיה אצלו אמון אל תקרי אמון אלא אומן כו' ועל בחי' אחוריים אמר משחקת בתבל ארצו ושעשועי את בני אדם כי התורה ניתנה בבחי' פנים ואחור כדכתיב במגילה עפה דזכרי' והיא כתובה פנים ואחור ולפי שתפס דוד בבחי' אחוריים לכך נענש בשכחה הבאה מן בחי' אחוריים ונעלם ממנו לפי שעה מ"ש עבודת הקדש עליהם בכתף ישאו לחבר וליחד את הכתפיים שהן בחי' אחוריים אל עבודת הקדש היא ח"ע בבחי' פנים שמשם נמשכו הלוחות שבארון כמ"ש כתובים משני עבריהם כו' וכמ"ש בירושלמי דשקלים שלא היתה בהן בחי' פנים ואחור ע"ש:

וצדקה כנחל איתן (בעמוס ססי' ה'). פי' כמו שנחל איתן הוא המשכה הנמשכת מבחי' איתן שהיא בחי' נקודה בהיכלא ותרין ריעין וכו' ואותיות איתן משמשות לעתיד פי' אנא עתיד לאתגליא כמ"ש הנה ישכיל עבדי וגו' והיינו שיתגלה אז אור א"ס ב"ה ויחודו ית' תוך פנימיות נקודת הלב ע"י המשכת נחל איתן הוא הארת חכמה עילאה שיאיר בפנימיות הלב

---

comparably inferior to what Torah truly is. David lauds Torah in this second aspect, but it is only the "hinderpart" of Torah, and in reality he demeans rather than exalts it. [20] *Tanchuma Bereishit beginning.* [21] *Proverbs 8:31.* [22] *Ezekiel 2:10. The "flying scroll" is found in Zecharia 5:2. Commentators explain that the scrolls are the same.* [23] *Numbers 7:9.* [24] *The initial, highest revelation.* [25] *A thoroughgoing unity, pervasive and penetrating, not superficial or external.* [26] *Exodus 32:15.* [27] *6:1.*

Essay VII

[1] *See "On Learning Chassidus," p. 18.* [2] *Ibid., p. 38 and Trans-*

(Notes cont. at end of Hebrew Text)

of the heart. Then he will be nullified utterly in His unity, blessed be He, from the depths of the heart, after removing the *orla*[6] of physical lusts . . .

At present, during the exile of this folk,[7] counsel is offered to bring a mite of the illumination of the Light of G-d from the state of Eitan into the core of the depth of the heart, in the fashion of the Time to Come.[8] This is through arousing the plenteous mercies above for the G-dly-spark within his soul. For in truth, so long as man does not merit the revelation of the light of G-d of the state of Eitan in the core of the inwardness of his heart, to become nullified in His unity, blessed be He, until the very expiration of the soul, then it is indeed a great pity on the spark within his soul. For that spark is drawn from the state of the Supernal Wisdom itself, and when it cannot illuminate from its own state into the internality of the heart, which is the proper place for the revelation of this Light, then it is actually in exile.

Through the plentiful mercies on high, however, it goes out of exile and imprisonment, and illuminates the core of the inmost of the heart with this great love, as known from the verse, "For Jacob who has redeemed Abraham,"[9] and as noted in Likutei Amarim I, ch. 45.[10]

It is known that the arousal from above[11] is dependent on the arousal from below, meaning that through arousing great mercies in the hearts of the merciful and kindly, to grant a beneficence below physically, gold and silver . . . Therefore the work of charity is actually the work of the river Eitan.

All know the verse, "Skin for skin, but all man possesses he will give for his soul,"[12] his G-dly soul, to illumine it with the light of life, the Infinite, blessed be He.

Essay 8

●▲ I have heard with foreboding and am deeply grieved that G-d's people are preventing him who yearns for the life and longevity of all our brethren,[1] from leading the service in this small sanctuary[2] of our confreres. Our Sages of blessed memory, declare, "Three things prolong the days of man,"[3] and one of these is prolonged worship.

Even one

[6] Based on Deut. 10:16. Orla is the term used for the foreskin removed in the rite of circumcision. [7] Cf. Ovadia 20. [8] The millennium. Essay I, note 10; Translator's Explanatory Notes to "On Learning Chassidus." [9] Isa. 29:22. [10] See also ch. 32. [11] See Tanya III, pg. 345, note 26. [12] Job 2:4.

Essay VIII

[1] I.e., adherents of Chassidut. [2] The synagogue, so-called as distinct from the Sanctuary, the Beit Hamikdash, in Jerusalem. [3] Berachot 32b.

הלב ליבטל ביחודו ית׳ בתכלית מעומקא דלבא אחרי הסרת הערלה מתאוות הגשמיות וכו׳. והנה עתה בגלות החל הזה יש ג״כ עצה יעוצה להאיר קצת אור ה׳ מבחי׳ איתן לתוך נקודה פנימיות הלב כעין לעתיד והיינו ע״י שמעורר על ניצוץ אלקות שבנפשו בחי׳ רחמים רבים העליונים כי באמת כל זמן שאין האדם זוכה שיתגלה אור ה׳ מבחי׳ איתן בנקודת פנימית לבבו ליבטל ביחודו ית׳ מעומקא דלבא עד כלות הנפש ממש אזי באמת יש רחמנות גדולה על הניצוץ שבנפשו כי הניצוץ נמשך מבחי׳ חכמה עילאה ממש וכשאינו יכול להאיר מבחינתו לתוך פנימיות הלב ששם מקום גילוי הארה זו ה״ז בבחי׳ גלות ממש וע״י רחמים רבים העליונים יוצא מהגלות והשביה ומאיר לתוך נקודה פנימיות הלב בחי׳ אהבה רבה זו כנודע ממ״ש ליעקב אשר פדה את אברהם וכמ״ש בלק״א פמ״ה. ומודעת זאת כי אתערותא דלעילא באתעדל״ת דוקא תליא מלתא דהיינו ע״י התעוררות רחמים רבים בלב רחמנים וג״ח להשפיע למטה השפעה גשמיות זהב וכסף וכו׳ ולכן פעולת הצדקה היא פעולת נחל איתן ממש. והנה מודעת זאת מ״ש כי עור בעד עור וכל אשר לאיש יתן בעד נפשו האלקית להאירה באור החיים א״ס ב״ה:

הנה לא טובה השמועה שמעתי ותרגז בטני אשר עם ה׳ מעבירים מלפני התיבה האיש החפץ בחיים ואריכות ימים של כל אנ״ש שבמקדש מעט הזה של אנ״ש כמארז״ל שלשה דברים מאריכים ימיו של אדם ואחד מהם המאריך בתפלתו. ואף גם מי שהשעה

extremely pressed for time, who finds it impossible to tarry until the response of Kedusha in the repetition of the Shmona Esrai—far better is it for him to forego hearing Kedusha and Borchu than to tamper with the lives of those who desire life. Torah does exonerate the compelled.[4] The precentor discharges his obligation for him[5] though he did not hear[6] the precentor, just as though he had heard—and hearing is precisely like responding.[7] The Gemara[8] notes this in reference to those in the fields who are considered under duress. They fulfil their obligation of the Shmona Esrai prayer itself with the precentor's repetition, just as if they had actually heard it. Kedusha and Borchu are also included.

This we have searched out and verified—even in the early generations of the Sages of the Mishnah and Gemara, whose Torah study was constant[9] and their primary service, not worship. It is even more emphatically true at this time, in the period just preceding the advent of Moshiach,[10] when our Torah study is not constant because of the exigencies of our times. The primary service in the period just prior to the coming of Moshiach is worship, as Rabbi Chayim Vital writes in Etz Chayim and Pri Etz Chayim.

Hence, it is fit and proper, beyond any vaguest doubt, to devote ourselves utterly to (worship). It is literally a Torah imperative to those who have knowledge of the efficacy of contemplation, of some profound meditation—each according to his measure—in the presentation of the praises of G-d, blessed be He, in Psukai d'zimra[11] and the two pre-Shema blessings, *Yotzer* and *Ahava*. Through them he can arouse the love latent in the heart of every Jew,[12] that it attain to a state of revelation, in the openness of the heart during Kriat Shema itself.

For this is the commandment of love that is in the verse "and you shall love . . . with all your heart . . ."[13] that is reckoned first among the 613 mitzvot.[14] Rambam, of blessed memory, writes that it is a fundament of Torah and its root, and source of all 248 positive commands.[15] Regarding the love latent in the heart of all Israel by birth and nature there can be no command at all. This is apparent to the understanding. While the love is concealed it is still lodged within the Divine soul alone. Only when it attains to a state of revelation in the animating soul is it

---

[4] *An act performed (or neglected) under compulsion is excused. See Deuteronomy 22:25–27; Nedarim 27a.* [5] *Shulchan Aruch of Rabbi Schneur Zalman 124:1.* [6] *Ibid., 591:2.* [7] *Ibid., 124:2.* [8] *Rosh Hashanah 35a.* [9] *Berachot 35b.* [10] *Lit. "the heels of the Moshiach (Messiah)," a play on Psalm 89:52.* [11] *See Igeret Hateshuvah, ch. 9, footnote 10.* [12] *Likutei Amarim, I, "Ahava—mesuteret."* [13] *Deut. 6:5.* [14] *Cf. Rambam, Yesodei HaTorah II.* [15] *Likutei Amarim I, ch. 4.*

שהשעה דחוקה לו ביותר וא"א לו בשום אופן להמתין עד אחר עניית קדושה של חזרת הש"ץ הזה הלא טוב טוב לו שלא לשמוע קדושה וברכו. מלירד לחייהם של החפצים בחיים ואונס רחמנא פטריה. והש"ץ מוציאו ידי חובתו אף שלא שמע כאילו שמע שהוא כעונה ממש וכדאיתא בגמרא גבי עם שבשדות דאניסי ויוצאים ידי חובת תפלת שמו"ע עצמה בחזרת הש"ץ כאלו שמעו ממש וגם קדושה וברכו בכלל. והנה זאת חקרנוה כן הוא אף גם בדורות הראשונים של חכמי המשנה והגמרא שהיתה תורתם קבע ועיקר עבודתם ולא תפלתם. ומכש"כ עתה הפעם בעקבות משיחא שאין תורתינו קבע מצוק העתים. ועיקר העבודה בעקבות משיחא היא התפלה כמ"ש הרח"ו ז"ל בע"ח ופע"ח. מכש"כ וק"ו שראוי ונכון ליתן נפשינו ממש עליה והיא חובה של תורה ממש למביני מדע תועלת ההתבוננות ועומק הדעת קצת כל חד לפום שיעורא דיליה בסדור שבחו של מקום ב"ה בפסוקי דזמרה ושתי ברכות שלפני ק"ש יוצר ואהבה לעורר בהן האהבה המסותרת בלב כל ישראל לבא לבחי' גילוי בהתגלות הלב בשעת ק"ש עצמה שזאת היא מצות האהבה שבפסוק ואהבת כו' בכל לבבך כו' הנמנית ראשונה בתרי"ג מצות כמ"ש הרמב"ם ז"ל שהיא מיסודי התורה ושרשה ומקור לכל רמ"ח מ"ע כי על אהבה המסותרת בלב כל ישראל בתולדתם וטבעם לא שייך ציווי כלל ודעת לנבון נקל כי כשהאהבה היא מסותרת היא עודינה בנפש האלקית לבדה וכשבאה לבחי' גילוי לנפש החיונית אזי היא

בהתגלות

revealed in the heart in the left ventricle, the abode of the animating soul.[16]

This is the meaning of "elevation of the sparks" mentioned there in Etz Chayim and Pri Etz Chayim in reference to worship, and for this reason is worship the primary service in the period just preceding the coming of Moshiach—to elevate the sparks . . . This may be either the state of transformation[17] or of subjugation of the animal soul to the Divine soul, as is known. For the blood is the soul . . .[18] and the blood is renewed daily through food and drink, and is affected and improved by garments and shelter . . .

On the other hand, in earlier generations when the Divine souls were of a higher order,[19] the purification and elevation were instantaneous in Kriat Shema alone[20] and in the blessings preceding it, and the abridged Psukai d'zimra. . .[21] And this will suffice for the knowing.

Essay 9

●▲ "You shall reprove your comrade"[1]—even one hundred times.[2] Therefore I cannot contain myself and refrain from crying out again, in a voice betraying weakness.[3] I plead with you, out of deep compassion have mercy on your souls. Take care, be painstaking to an extreme concerning Torah and the service of the heart which is worship[4] with kavana, proper intention. All should begin in unison, as one, word by word, not one here and another elsewhere, one mute and the other idly chatting—may G-d protect us. The main cause and instigator of damage comes from those leading the worship. That office is abandoned to whoever wishes to stride forth and seize the honour, or because not even one desires it . . .

For this reason, this is the counsel offered, and an amendment established as law not to be violated further, G-d forbid. That is, select specified people fit for this office, by lot or by consent of the majority of the worshippers. These shall be men who worship word by word, moderately, out loud, neither overly prolonging the prayers nor racing intemperately, G-d forbid. Theirs is the duty to lead the prayers, each on his day as determined. He shall assemble close around him all those who worship at least with some voice,

[16] *Ibid., ch. 9.* [17] *Berachot (54a) explains "With all your heart" (the Hebrew implies a plural) as referring to both the good and evil within man. The evil can be transformed to desire good. Likutei Amarim I, ch. 10, discusses the Tzadik who has wholly or partially achieved this transformation. Subjugation of evil, or the animal soul, leaves it potent and intact, but ineffective.* [18] *Deut. 12:23. The synonymity of (animal or animating) soul and blood. See Likutei Amarim I, ch. 9. The love of G-d is to permeate the heart, the left void filled with blood, the equivalent of the animal soul.* [19] *Cf. Shabbat 112b. "If our predecessors were like angels we are men; if they were men we are donkeys."* [20] *Berachot 13b—Rabbi Judah the Prince "accepted the yoke of*

בהתגלות הלב בחלל שמאלי מקום משכן נפש החיונית וזהו ענין בירור ניצוצות המוזכר שם בע"ח ופע"ח גבי תפלה שלכן היא עיקר העבודה בעקבות משיחא לברר ניצוצות כו' שהוא בחי' אתהפכא או אתכפי' של נפש החיונית לנפש האלקית כנודע כי הדם הוא הנפש כו' והדם מתחדש בכל יום מאוכלין ומשקין וגם מתפעל ונתקן ממלבושים ודירה כו'. משא"כ בדורות הראשונים שהיו נשמות האלקית גדולי הערך היה הבירור נעשה כרגע בק"ש לבד וברכות שלפניה ופסד"ז בקצרה וכו' וד"ל:

הוכח תוכיח את עמיתך אפילו מאה פעמים. ולזאת לא אוכל להתאפק ולהחריש מלזעוק עוד בקול ענות חלושה במטותא מינייכו ברחמין נפישין חוסו נא על נפשותיכם. והשמרו והזהרו מאד מאד על התורה ועל העבודה שבלב זו תפלה בכוונה להתחיל כולם יחד כאחד מלה במלה ולא זה בכה וזה בכה וזה דומם וזה משיח שיחה בטילה ה' ישמרנו ועיקר הסיבה וגרמא בנזקין הוא מהיורדים לפני התיבה שהוא הפקר לכל הרוצה לפשוט רגליו החוטף אפרתי או מחמת שאין גם אחד רוצה וכו'. ואי לזאת זאת העצה היעוצה ותקנה קבועה חוק ולא יעבור עוד ח"ו דהיינו לבחור אנשים קבועים הראוים לזה עפ"י הגורל או בריצוי רוב המנין. דהיינו שמתפללים מלה במלה בדרך המיצוע בקול רם ולא מאריכים יותר מדאי ולא מקצרים וחוטפים ח"ו. ועליהם מוטל חובה לירד לפני התיבה כל אחד ואחד ביומו אשר יגיע לו ולאסוף אליו סביב סמוך כל המתפללים בקול קצת עכ"פ ולא

Heaven" at the moment he passed his hands over his face (at Shema). [21] *Shulchan Aruch Orach Chayim 52.*

Essay IX
[1] *Leviticus 19:17.* [2] *Bava Metzia 31a.* [3] *Exodus 32:18.* [4] *Taanit 2a.*

not whispering nor rushing, G–d forbid. This is amplified in ancient amendments in many cities.

I come now to renew them, to strengthen and invigorate them, never again to be weakened, G–d forbid. (Gevald! Gevald!)[5] How long will this be an obstacle for us![6] Have we not sufficient reproofs and troubles that have overtaken us!—may G–d protect and console us with two-fold salvation,[7] and purify our hearts to serve Him in truth.[8] Strengthen and fortify your hearts, all who hope in G–d.[9]

Also: complete the entire Talmud every single year and in every community by apportioning the tractates by lot or by consent. In a city with numerous synagogues, each congregation shall complete (the Talmud). If a congregation is too small to implement (this programme), they shall join to themselves men of some large congregation. This statute shall not be varied or violated. Each of the participants shall individually conclude Psalm 119 weekly.

Since, due to the frailty of the generation, not every one is capable of fasting as he ought,[10] the counsel offered is the declaration of our Sages, of blessed memory, "Whoever observes Shabbat according to its halacha (law), is forgiven all his sins."[11] Note, according to its law. Therefore it is incumbent upon every individual to master the major laws of Shabbat.[12]

Also, be most careful not to indulge in idle chatter, G–d forbid. For it is known to the initiates in the esoteric science,[13] that in all mitzvot there are the internal and the external aspects. The externality of Shabbat is the cessation of physical labour, just as G–d ceased making physical heaven and earth. The internal aspect of Shabbat is the kavana (intention) in the Shabbat prayers and Torah study, to cleave to the One G–d, as it is said, "It is Shabbat to the Lord your G–d."[14] This is the state of "Remember."[15] The state of "Observe" in the inwardness (of Shabbat) is refraining from speech about material affairs, as G–d ceased from the Ten Utterances[16] through which physical heaven and earth were created. For one parallel to the other . . .[17]

---

[5] *An exclamation of anguish. These two words appeared in the original manuscript written by Rabbi Schneur Zalman.* [6] *Ex. 10:7* [7] *Cf. Job 11:6.* [8] *Prayer-book, Sabbath prayer.* [9] *Based on Psalm 31:25.* [10] *See Igeret Hateshuvah, ch. 2 and 3.* [11] *Shabbat 118b.* [12] *Shabbat 12a. The term is used there in reference to the admonition to examine one's clothing regularly on Shabbat to ensure against unwittingly carrying.* [13] *See "On the Teachings of Chassidus."* [14] *Ex. 20:10; Deut. 5:14.* [15] *"Remember" appears in the Exodus text of the Ten Commandments, and "Observe" in the Deuteronomy text, in the Sabbath commandment.* [16]

ולא בלחש ולא חוטפים ח"ו וכמבואר בתקנות ישנות בכמה עיירות. ועתה באתי לחדשן ולחזקן ולאמצן כל ימותו עוד לעולם ח"ו (בכ"י גוואלד גוואלד) עד מתי יהיה זה לנו למוקש ולא די לנו בכל התוכחות והצרות שעברו עלינו ה' ישמרנו וינחמנו בכפלים לתושיה ויטהר לבנו לעבדו באמת. חזקו ואמצו לבבכם כל המיחלים לה'. גם לגמור כל הש"ס בכל שנה ושנה ובכל עיר ועיר לחלק המסכתות עפ"י הגורל או ברצון. ועיר שיש בה מנינים הרבה יגמרו בכל מנין ומנין. ואם איזה מנין קטן מהכיל יצרפו אליהם אנשים מאיזה מנין גדול בכל ישונה חק ולא יעבור. וכאו"א מהלומדים הנ"ל יגמור לעצמו בכל שבוע התמניא אפי' שבתהלים קי"ט. ולהיות מחמת חלישות הדור אין כח בכל אחד ואחד להתענות כראוי לו. לזאת עצה היעוצה כמארז"ל כל השומר שבת כהלכתו מוחלין לו על כל עוונותיו. כהלכתו דייקא. לכן מוטל על כל אחד ואחד להיות בקי בהלכתא רבתא לשבתא. וגם יזהר מאד שלא לשוח שום שיחה בטילה ח"ו. בהיות מודעת זאת לי"ח כי בכל המצות יש פנימיות וחיצוניות וחיצונית מהשבת הוא שביתה מעשיה גשמיית כמו ששבת ה' מעשות שמים וארץ גשמיים. ופנימית השבת היא הכוונה בתפלת השבת ובת"ת לדבקה בה' אחד כמ"ש שבת לה' אלקיך וזו היא בחי' זכור. ובחי' שמור בפנימיות היא השביתה מדיבורים גשמיים כמו ששבת ה' מיו"ד מאמרות שנבראו בהם שמים וארץ גשמיים כי זה לעומת זה כו':

Avot V; see Tanya II, ch. 11, and Igeret Hateshuvah, ch. 4 ff. [17] *Kohelet 7:14; see Likutei Amarim I, ch. 6, note 1.*

מפתח:

מפתח מכל המאמרים שבאגה"ק

ספרי׳ — אוצר החסידים — ליובאוויטש

מורה שיעור

בלימודי יום יום השווים לכל נפש

שיעורים בתניא

כפי שנחלקו על ידי

כבוד קדושת אדוננו מורנו ורבנו

יוסף יצחק

זצוקללה״ה נבג״מ זי״ע

ש נ י א ו ר ס א ה ן

מליובאוויטש

יוצא לאור על ידי מערכת

„אוצר החסידים״

770 איסטערן פּאַרקוויי ברוקלין, נ.י.

שנת חמשת אלפים שבע מאות ושבעים לבריאה

שנת המאתים וחמשים להסתלקות־הילולא של הבעש״ט ז״ל

ב"ה.

פתח דבר

חוברת זו כוללת את חלוקת השיעורים בתניא — כחלק מהשיעורים השוים לכל נפש — לכל יום מי"ט כסלו עד י"ט כסלו: חלק א — לשנה פשוטה, חלק ב — לשנה מעוברת. השעורים השוים לכל נפש הם:

א) חומש עם רש"י בכל יום פרשה אחת מהסדרה של השבוע עם פירש"י, היינו ביום א' עד שני, ביום ב' עד שלישי וכו'. כאשר אותה הסדרה נמשכת משך ב' או ג' שבועות (משום שחל חג בש"ק) לומדים את השיעורים של חומש עם פירש"י גם במשך השבוע השני והשלישי באותו הסדר כמו שבשבוע הראשון. בשמחת תורה לומדים פרשת ברכה החל מהפרשה של אותו היום מהשבוע עד סיום הסדרה עם פירש"י. באסרו חג דסכות לומדים מהתחלת הסדרה בראשית עד אחר פרשת היום שעומדים בו עם פירש"י.

ב) תהלים בכל יום אחר תפילת שחרית כמו שנחלק כל התהלים לימי החודש. החל מיום שני דר"ח אלול עד יום הכפורים אומרים נוסף על הנ"ל שלשה קאפ' תהלים (ב' דר"ח אלול קאפ' א—ג. ב' אלול קאפ' ד—ו וכו') וביום הכפורים שלשים וששה קאפ': ט' קודם כל נדרי (קטו־קכג). ט קודם השינה (קכד־קלב). ט' אחר מוסף (קלג־קמא). ט' אחר נעילה (קמב־קנ).

ג) תניא: שעורי למוד התניא נחלקו לימי השנה ע"י כ"ק אדמו"ר מוהריי"צ זצוקללה"ה זי"ע וזה לשונו במכתבו המצורף לרשימת חלוקת השעורים:

„שיעורי לימוד בספר ליקוטי אמרים — תניא כפי שנחלק לימי השנה, מראש השנה לחסידות י"ט כסלו עד י"ט כסלו הבא עלינו ועל כל ישראל אחינו לטובה ולברכה בגשמיות וברוחניות".

השעורים האלה הם חוץ מהשעורים דכל חד וחד לפום שיעורא דיליה.

מערכת „אוצר החסידים"

לשנה פשוטה

כסלו

יט ספר לקוטי אמרים הנקרא בשם... וקצרה בעזה"י הסכמת א) הרב... מאניפאלי. ב) הרב... הכהן הסכמת הרבנים... ז"ל נבג"מ.
כ הקדמת המלקט... ־ד־ בעלה וגו'.
כא אך ביודעיי... אמרים הנ"ל.
כב פרק א תניא... ־10־ לתורה).
כג והא דאמרינן... להתייהר כו'.
כד פרק ב ונפש... בראשית.
כה פרק ג והנה... ־14־ ופחדו.
כו כי השכל... וענפי'.
כז פרק ד ועוד... ־ח־ לא תעשה.
כח והנה שלשה... ־16־ ומתלבשת בהן.
כט*) ומאחר שהתורה... חסד ומים.
ל פרק ה ולתוספת... ־18־ צד ופנה.

*) בחודש כסלו של כט יום לומדים ביום כט גם השיעור של יום למ"ד.

טבת

א וזאת מעלה... בפרע"ח).
ב פרק ו והנה... ־20־ שריא לעולם.
ג אבל כל מה... סוף פ"ה.
ד פרק ז אך נפש... ־22־ ובדחי רבנן.
ה אך מי שהוא... ־יב־ לנצח.
ו אך החיות... בשר ודם.
ז פרק ח ועוד... ־יג־ הקדוש.
ח ועל דברים... שעסקו בהן.
ט פרק ט והנה... ־26־ שבמוחין.
י אך הנה כתיב... שבזה"ק.
יא פרק י והנה... ־טו־ שאינו גמור.
יב והנה מדרגה... במ"א].
יג פרק יא וזה... שריא.
יד פרק יב והבינוני... ־32־ ותענוגיו.
טו רק מפני שלא... ־יז־ התורה כנ"ל.
טז ואעפ"כ אינו... ־34־ תפלה כו'.
יז רק שלזה מועיל... עם אחיו.
יח פרק יג ובזה... ־36־ עניני עוה"ז.
יט ואף מי שבתורת ה'... ־יט־ כולו.
כ והנה מדת... כולן].
כא פרק יד והנה... ־כ־ כו' ע"ש.
כב ובזה יובן... צדיק.
כג פרק טו ובזה... ־כא־ מרגילותו.
כד ובזה יובן מ"ש... כלל.
כה פרק טז וזה... ־כב־ בטבעו].
כו וזה רמזו... באריכות.
כז פרק יז ובזה יובן... ־כג־ כלי המעשה.
כח אם לא מי שהוא... במ"א.
כט פרק יח ולתוספת... ־כד־ גלגולים].

שבט

א הנה החכמה... ומובן.
ב פרק יט ולתוספת... ־48־ א"ס ב"ה.
ג וזהו כלל... ־כה־ חוטא כו'.
ד אלא שגלות הזה... כלל.
ה פרק כ והנה... ־כו־ המלובש בהם.
ו ולמשל כמו... העולם.
ז פרק כא והנה... ־כז־ שבלב.
ח וככה ממש... ממש.
ט פרק כב רק... ־54־ העליון ב"ה.
י והנה רצון העליון... תמיד.
יא פרק כג ועם כל... ־56־ ימ"יהם.
יב אך המחשבה... ־כט־ בעליונים].
יג ובזה יובן למה... לקמן.
יד פרק כד וזה... ־ל־ בו וכו'.
טו ולכן אמרו רז"ל... ־60־ וקליפת ע"ז.
טז ומה שפיקוח נפש... כנודע
יז פרק כה וזהו... ־62־ עליו כנודע.
יח והן בבחי' ועשה טוב... ־לב־ לעולמים כו'
יט אלא שלמטה הוא... כנ"ל.
כ פרק כו ברם... ־לג־ פסוק זה.
כא והנה עצה היעוצה... ־לג־ נראית וד"ל.
כב אך העצבות... העצב כנ"ל.
כג פרק כז ואם העצבות... ־לד־ מכולא וכו'.
כד ולכן אל יפול... ־68־ לעילא.
כה ולא עוד אלא... מעט מעט.
כו פרק כח ואפילו... ־לה־ זרה שלה.
כז ולא כטעות העולם... ממש עמו.
כח פרק כט אך... ־לו־ בצדיקים.
כט אבל בבינוני... ־72־ נגדי תמיד.
ל וגם מי שהוא נקי... ־לז־ באריכות.

אדר

א והנה כל מה... -74- כל העבודה.
ב והטעם לפי שבאמת... בזה״ק.
ג פרק ל עוד... -76- באריכות.
ד וכל שלא הגיע... כשגגות.
ה פרק לא והנה... -מ- דעלמא.
ו ואח״כ יבא לידי שמחה... -מ- דכל עלמין.
ז וזאת תהי׳ עבודתו... -80- לפניכם ה׳ וגו׳.
ח ולהיות בחי׳ תשובה... משמחי לב.
ט פרק לב והנה... -מא- באריכות.
י ומ״ש בגמ׳ שמי... דשבת].
יא פרק לג עוד... -מב- נאם ה׳.
יב ועל זה תיקנו... -84- אתו עמו.
יג עוד זאת ישמח... באמונה זו.
יד פרק לד והנה... -86- ה׳ לו.
טו ואם ירחיב ה׳ לו... מסטרא דא.
טז פרק לה והנה... -מד- עכ״ל.
יז והנה ביאור משל... -88- ביחוד גמור.
יח והנה ענין השראת... -מה- וכו׳).
יט והנה כשהאדם עוסק... -מה- וכל הגוף.
כ ואף שמהותה ועצמותה... יבין.
כא פרק לו והנה... -מו- מהאר״י ז״ל).
כב וגם כבר הי׳... ארצך וגו׳.
כג פרק לז והנה... -מז- התפלה.
כד זאת ועוד אחרת... -94- כמו האבות.
כה ומאחר שכללות נפש... -מח- יצירה עשי׳.
כו וכל ניצוץ לא ירד... -96- ניצוצין וכו׳.
כז ובזה יובן מה... -מט- אחרות.
כח ומ״ש רז״ל שת״ת... -מט- כמ״ש לעיל.
כט ואעפ״כ ארז״ל לא... -98- באריכות.

ניסן

א והנה המשכה והארה זו... -98- [פ׳ כ״ג].
ב פרק לח והנה... -נ- כל חי.
ג ואף שבשניהם אור... -100- והתפשטות.
ד כי בגוף הגשמי... -100- בו ית׳.
ה ולא שדביקות המחשבה... -נא- חי ומדבר.
ו כי מי שדעתו יפה... -102- כנז״ל.
ז פרק לט ומפני... -נב- ויקהל.
ח אך היינו דווקא... -104- מצוה עצמה.
ט ועולם האצילות שהוא... -נג- לי״ח].
י והנה שכר מצוה... -106- קדם ה׳.
יא והיינו אפילו אם... -106- לקמן.
יב וכשעוסק שלא לשמה... -נד- בזהר.
יג פרק מ אך... -108- למטה בעו״הז.
יד ואף דאורייתא וקב״ה... -נה- הוא גשמי.
טו אבל בתפלה בכוונה... -נו- בפרע״ח.
טז והנה אף דדחילו... -נו- באריכות
יז פרק מא ברם... -112- ותפילין.
יח וגם יתבונן איך... -נז- ליודעים.
יט והנה אף מי... -114- כנ״ל.
כ אך אמנם אמרו... -נח- החסדים).
כא ואף שלהיות כוונה... -נח- באריכות.
כב אבל יחוד נפשו... -116- אתה וכה״ג.
כג והנה בהכנה זו... -נט- כנ״ל.
כד פרק מב והנה... -118- ידע וגו׳.
כה וכח זה ומדה זו... -ס- שומעת כו׳.
כו וגם כי אין לו... -120- כנ״ל פ״כ.
כז והנה כל אדם... -סא- לי״ח].
כח ועוד זאת יזכור... -122- כמ״ש במ״א.
כט פרק מג והנה... -סב- אין חכמה.
ל והנה באהבה יש... -124- כמ״ש לקמן.

אייר

א׳ והנה בחי׳ אהבה... -124- לי״ח].
ב פרק מד והנה... -סג- צפרא כו׳.
ג ואהבה רבה וגדולה... -126- נעשה טבע
ד ואף אם נדמה... -126- מצרפה כו׳.
ה והנה ב׳ בחי׳ אהבות... -סד- אהבת עולם.
ו רק שאעפ״כ צריך... -סד- וכנודע.
ז פרק מה עוד... -128- טומאתם.
ח וש״ה וישק יעקב... -128- במ״א.
ט פרק מו ויש דרך... -סה- המלך.
י והנה כבל הדברים... -130- וגופא וכו׳.
יא וז״ש אשר קדשנו... -סו- בחייהם.
יב וז״ש אסף ברוח הקדש... -132- האצילות].
יג פרק מז והנה ככל... -סז- כמש״ל.
יד פרק מח והנה כאשר... -134- ויחזרו למקורן.
טו והנה פרטיות הצמצומים... -סח- ותבלית.
טז והמשל בזה... -136- בפועל ממש.
יז למשל כדור הארץ הלזו... -136- במ״א.
יח פרק מט והנה אף... -סט- ובנים.
יט ובזה יובן טוב... -ע- ית׳ כנ״ל.
כ והנה כאשר ישים המשכיל... -ע- ומאודו כנ״ל.
כא פרק נ והנה כל... -140- ח״ו.
כב והנה סדר העבודה... -עא- החיים ב״ה.
כג פרק נא והנה לתוספת... -142- וחיות הללו.
כד והנה על המשכת... -142- כנ״ל].
כה וככה ממש עד״מ... -144- א״ס ב״ה.
כו פרק נב וכמו שבנשמת... -עב- מהשמש.
כז אבל השכינה עצמה... -עג- מצות התורה.
כח ובירידתה בהשתלשלות... -146- כמ״ש בתיקונים.
כט ובהתלבשות מל׳ דאצילות... -עד- שכינה.

סיון

א פרק נג והנה כשהי׳... -148- לי״ח].
ב ובבית שני... -148- יסד ברתא.
ג וז״ש הינוקא... ית׳ וית׳.
ד ליקוטי אמרים... -עו- באריכות.
ה והנה ענין אהבה זו... -עו- שית׳ במקומה.
ו אך הנה ידוע... -עו- יתברך וית׳.
ז שער היחוד והאמונה... -152- ימי בראשית.
ח ואף שלא הוזכר שם... -עז- כולא חד.
ט פרק ב והנה מכאן... -154- הבריאה.
י פרק ג והנה אחרי... -עח- בלעדו באמת.
יא והמשל לזה הוא... -156- להקדים.
יב פרק ד כי הנה... -עט- להטיב.
יג והנה כמו שמדה זו... -158- מאין ליש.
יד [והנה בחי׳ הצמצום... -158- לי״ח.
טו פרק ה והנה על... -פ- פרק ג].
טז פרק ו והנה שם... -160- הכלולה בחסד.
יז והנה מהתכללות המדות... -פא- השמש בשמש.
יח ולכן הוצרך הכתוב... -162- הוא האלקים.
יט פרק ז ובזה יובן... -פב- עליו כלל.
כ והנה גדר ובחי׳... -פב- ולד׳ סטרין.
כא והנה אף על פי... -164- לתחתונים.
כב והנה במ״ש יובן... -פג- מהרמ״ק ז״ל].
כג והנה מכאן יש להבין... -166- דממלא לון.
כד וזהו ג״כ ענין... -פד- גבול ותכלית.
כה כי מקור החיות... -פה- עצמן.
כו פרק ח והנה מ״ש... -170- ולצייר בשכלם.
כז כי המעלה ומדרגה... -פו- ומקור החיות.
כח פרק ט אבל לגבי... -פו- אין קץ.
כט רק מפני שאין... -פז- ידוע למשכילים.
ל הגה״ה (סוד הצמצום... -פז- מן השכל.

תמוז

א פרק י אך מכל מקום... -174- אתכסיאת כו'.
ב עד"מ ביום ראשון... -פח- מדות כלל.
ג פרק יא והנה גם... -176- וסתום בלבו.
ד אבל באמת בחי' אותיות... -פט- כמ"ש במ"א.
ה פרק יב רק שהברואים... -178- מהאותיות עצמן.
ו כי הן ד"מ דוגמת... -צ- יתברך ויתעלה.
ז אגרת התשובה... -צא- עכ"ל הברייתא.
ח והנה מצות התשובה... -182- כ"א מיראה.
ט פרק ב אך כל זה... -צב- יום רצון.
י פרק ג והנה חכמי... -184- ג"פ וכו'.
יא אכן כל זה... -184- תענית.
יב ומ"מ כל בעל... -186- לא תמנו).
יג פרק ד ואולם כל... -186- בנעימים.
יד אך הענין יובן... -צד- האותיות.
טו וביאור הענין... -צה- אלו).
טז וככה ממש... -צה- הוי' וכו'.
יז פרק ה והנה המשכת... -190- כדלקמן).
יח פרק ו אמנם... -צו- כנודע לי"ח.
יט והנה יעקב חבל... -192- נאמר וכו'.
כ פרק ז ואולם דרך... -צז- ונדכה וכו'.
כא והיאך נשבר הלב... -194- כנודע).
כב ואף מי שלא עבר... -צח- כולן.
כג פרק ח והנה אחרי... -צח- מלפפתו וכו'.
כד ומאחר שרוח עברה... -196- למלכא וכו').
כה פרק ט וביאור הענין... -צט- דר"ה.
כו פרק י והנה... -198- כנודע.
כז ומאחר שהתפלה היא... -198- עילאה).
כח פרק יא ואמנם... -ק- לאין קץ.
כט ומה שמשבחים ומברכים... -200- היא מיד.

מנחם אב

א ומ"ש וחטאתי... -קא- פשעיו.
ב פרק יב וטעם השמחה... -202- ימצא טוב.
ג א פותחין בברכה... -204- שבנפש.
ד אך מי הוא הנותן... -204- הנפש כו'.
ה ועתה הפעם הנני... -קג- תורה וכו'.
ו ב קטנתי מכל... -קד- הפנים וגו'.
ז ג וילבש צדקה... -208- [ח"ו].
ח אך מי הוא הגורם... -קה- תדרשנו.
ט ד אין ישראל נגאלין... -קה- נפש מישראל.
י ומה שאין כל אדם... -קו- אלקיך כו'.
יא אך מודעת זאת... -קו- ושבי' בצדקה.
יב וזהו צדק לפניו... -212- אכי"ר.
יג ה ויעש דוד שם... -214 שמבין הכל.
יד אך האותיות הן... -214- נברא בה'.
טו והנה הגם שהיא... -קח- ע"ש)].
טז אך ביאור הענין... -216- בעשיה.
יז והנה באדם התחתון... -קט- ממנה ח"ו.
יח ובזה יובן מ"ש... -218- יבינו.
יט ו זורע צדקה... -220- ישענו כו'.
כ והנה מודעת זאת... -קיא- תכונני.
כא ז אשרינו מה טוב... -222- ועלול וכו'.
כב והנה הארה זו... -222- יספר מרוב.
כג והנה שופרי' דיעקב... -קיב- כמ"ש במ"א.
כד והנה אף שגילוי... -קיב- ממש.
כה ח זורע צדקות... -224- נמוך כו'.
כו והנה מודעת... -קיג- והארת וכו'.
כז אך הענין הוא... -קיג- האריז"ל.
כח וככה ממש עד"מ... -226- בחו"ל וד"ל.
כט ט אהוביי אחיי... -קיד- התורה.
ל ע"כ אהוביי אחיי... -228- ציון כו'.

אלול

א י אד"ש וחיים... -קטו- כו'.
ב והנה לפי שהמצות... -קטו- מצות התורה.
ג אך היינו דוקא... -230- עומדין וכו'.
ד והנה עיקר התשובה... -קטז- נפשו כתיב.
ה והנה מדת חסד... -קטז- בא כו'.
ו יא להשכילך בינה... -232- כל היום.
ז וע"כ ראשית הכל... -קיז- הגנוז.
ח יב והי' מעשה... -234- הקדושות יתברך.
ט והנה אתערותא דלעילא... -קיח- במצרף וכור.
י והנה מודעת זאת... -236- פעמים וכו'.
יא וז"ש והי' מעשה הצדקה... -קיט- כל חטאתם.
יב יג מה רב טובך... -קיט- די כו'.
יג והנה כל איש ישראל... -238- א"א ע"ה.
יד וזהו שאמר דהע"ה... -קכ- בסוכה וגו'.
טו יד לעורר את... -240- ר"ה ור"ה.
טז וז"ש תמיד עיני... -קכא- וד"ל.
יז טו להבין משל ומליצה... -קכא- מהן.
יח אך צריך להקדים... -קכב- במשל ומליצה.
יט והנה כללות הי"ס... -קכג- מדותיהם.
כ והנה כ"ז הוא... -246- באימה וביראה.
כא ומקור ושורש כל... -קכד- במקומו.
כב טז אהוביי אחיי... -248- דף פ'.
כג והנה זהו עפ"י... -קכה- ונפש.
כד יז נודע דבאתערותא... -250- וע"ש היטב.
כה וזהו שארז"ל ועטרותיהם... -קכו- וד"ל.
כו וזהו רחבה מצותך... -קכו- מנוחה כו'.
כז יח כתיב מה יפית... -252- בלק"א.
כח והשגית היא אהבה... -קכז- דעהו.
כט יט עוטה אור... -254- דאצילות.

תשרי

א אך הענין הוא... -קכח- האותיות.
ב והנה בחי' חכמת... -256- מהאריז"ל.
ג האותיות הנגלות לנו... -קכט- כנודע.
ד כ איהו וחיוהי חד... -258- וע"ש.
ה ויש מאין נקרא... -קל- דוקא.
ו והנה ראשית היש... -קל- עילתו.
ז אך נשמות המלאכים... -260- בבי"ע.
ח אמנם מודעת... -קלא- והלידה.
ט ובזה יובן היות... -קלא- וכדלקמן.
י והנה כמו"כ מזיווג... -262- כנ"ל.
יא ועוד זאת יתר... -264- כמ"ש במ"א.
יב ומזה יובן היטב... -קלג- עוה"ב.
יג כא אד"ש כמשפט... -266- בכל יום.
יד אך גם זאת... -קלד- יבא שילה.
טו כב אהוביי אחיי... -קלד- בפרש"י.
טז אך האמת אגיד... -268- ואחור ח"ו.
יז ועצה היעוצה לקבל... -קלה- נס"ו.
יח אהוביי אחיי ורעיי... -קלה- וד"ל.
יט ועוד זאת אדרוש... -270- מלו"נ.
כ כג בגזירת עירין... -קלו- למביני מדע.
כא כי קביעת שכר... -272- לגמרי.
כב וע"כ רע בעיני... -272- בזוה"ק.
כג על כן אהוביי... -קלז- יהי רצון.
כד כד אהוביי אחיי... -קלח- בלבותם.
כה כה להבין אמרי... -276- לו וגו'.
כו וכנודע מ"ש הבעש"ט... -קלט- רוחניות.
כז והנה נודע לי"ח... -278- לארץ.
כח (אלא שבארצות... -קמ- עמהם)).
כט והנה אף כי... -קמ- האר"י ז"ל.
ל והנה נפש האדם... -280- בלא דבור.

חשון

א	והנה זלעו״ז יש... ־280־ המעלות.
ב	ואחר הדברים והאמת... ־קמא־ וכה״ג טובא.
ג	וכמדומה לי שתפיסתם... ־קמב־ אמרי פי.
ד	כו בר״מ פ׳ נשא... ־קמג־ הלכה בלבד.
ה	ועוד יש להפליא... ־286־ בהסתר כו׳.
ו	אך באמת כשתדקדק... ־קמד־ הכל אחד.
ז	ומ״ש האריז״ל... ־קמד־ בבריאה.
ח	והנה כשהמלכות דאצילות... ־288־ מהאריז״ל.
ט	והמשכיל יבין ענין... ־288־ מסטרא דרע.
י	והנה העליונים אין... ־קמה־ עו״ג.
יא	אבל בצאת השכינה... ־290־ בע״ח וד״ל.
יב	כז אהוביי אחיי... ־קמו־ נס״ו.
יג	וז״ש בזוה״ק דצדיקא... ־292־ קודם לברכה.
יד	איתא בזוה״ק... ־292־ ועלול כנודע.
טו	והנה בהיות הצדיק... ־קמז־ תאמין.
טז	והנה יש עוד... ־294־ כוכבים.
יז	כח למה נסמכה... ־קמח־ מנוגה.
יח	והנה מודעת זאת... ־296־ וכו׳.
יט	כט אשת חיל... ־קמט־ ורכ״ט.
כ	והנה אור זה... ־298־ כולא חד.
כא	והנה רצון העליון... ־קנ־ האדם.
כב	וז״ש בזוה״ק פ׳... ־300־ ע״ש.
כג	והנה מודעת זאת... ־קנא־ כנ״ל.
כד	ל מודעת זאת... ־302־ וד״ל.
כה	לא נודע בשערים... ־304־ האברים וכו׳.
כו	לב ברך ה׳ חילם... ־קנג־ תדרשנו.
כז	להבין איך הקורא... ־306־ דוקא.
כח	עיין ע״ח שער... ־קנד־ כנודע.
כט*)	להבין מ״ש בשער... ־308־ יאות כו׳.
ל	אך ההפרש... פקודי).

*) בחדש חשון של כט יום לומדים ביום כט גם השיעור של יום למ״ד.

כסלו

א	ומ״ש בפ׳ פקודי... ־קנה־ האצי׳.
ב	להבין מ״ש בפע״ח... ־310־ דז״א כו׳.
ג	והנה במ״א כתב... ־310־ דוקא.
ד	והנה לקיום מצוה... ־קנו־ אחורי כו׳.
ה	משא״כ מעשה המצות... ־312־ משיג המהות.
ו	משא״כ בסדר ההשתלשלות... ־312־ אשר שם.
ז	ועוד זאת שבאמת... ־קנז־ לא יראו.
ח	ובר מן כל דין... ־314־ הלכותיהן.
ט	אך להבין איך... ־קנח־ וכה״ג.
י	אך עוד זאת... ־316־ אלקות.
יא	והטעם משום דתב״ד... ־316־ וגמרא.
יב	ומ״ש בע״ח (ושער... ־קנט־ וד״ל.
יג	ולהבין פרטי ההלכות... ־קס־ דכלים דז״א.
יד	דוד זמירות... ־320־ צרתו.
טו	אך מה שהי׳... ־קסא־ ע״ש.
טז	וצדקה כנחל איתן... ־322־ א״ס ב״ה.
יז	הנה לא טובה... ־324־ וד״ל.
יח	הוכח תוכיח... ־קסג־ זה כו׳.

גוט יום טוב

לשנה טובה

בלימוד החסידות ודרכי החסידות

תכתבו ותחתמו

מורה שיעור

לשנה מעוברת

כסלו

יט	ספר לקוטי אמרים הנקרא בשם... וקצרה בעזה״י הסכמת א) הרב... מאניפאלי. ב) הרב... הכהן
כ	הסכמת הרבנים... ז״ל נבג״מ.
כא	הקדמת המלקט... בעלה וגו׳.
כב	אך ביודעיי... את ה׳ וגו׳ אכי״ר.
כג	והנה אחר... אמרים הנ״ל.
כד	פרק א. תניא... ושבעים פנים לתורה).
כה	והא דאמרינן... אלא להתייהר כו׳.
כו	פרק ב. ונפש השנית... ובטעמי מצות פ׳ בראשית.
כז	פרק ג. והנה כל... ־14־ ויראתו ופחדו.
כח	כי השכל שבנפש... ויראה וענפי׳.
כט*)	פרק ד. ועוד יש... מצות התורה.
ל	ובפרטות בחי׳... ־ח־ לא תעשה.

*) בחודש כסלו של כט יום לומדים ביום כט גם השיעור של יום למ״ד.

טבת

א	והנה שלשה לבושים... ־16־ בשלשה לבושי׳ אלו.
ב	ולכן נמשלה התורה... ־ט־ המלובשים בתורתו ומצותי׳.
ג	ולכן אמרו יפה... חסד ומים.
ד	פרק ה. ולתוספת... כמ״ש בפרע״ח).
ה	פרק ו. והנה זה... ־20־ תבירו דרוחא כו׳.
ו	וכן כל הדבורים וכל... ־20־ כבתחלה מקודם שנברא.
ז	ולכן נקרא עולם הזה... שם סוף פ״ה.
ח	פרק ז. אך נפש... ־22־ ובדחי רבנן.
ט	אך מי שהוא... ־יב־ שיבולע המות לנצח.
י	אך החיות שבטפות... בגוף בשר ודם.
יא	פרק ח. ועוד זאת... שעסקו בהן.
יב	פרק ט. והנה מקום... ־26־ מחב״ד שבמוחין.
יג	אך הנה כתיב ולאום... ־יד־ אהבה עזה כרשפי אש.
יד	והיא הנקראת בכתוב... כמשל הזונה שבזוה״ק.
טו	פרק י. והנה כשהאדם... ־טו־ ממש כמו השנאה.
טז	וצדיק שאינו גמור... ־30־ לא ייתון הכא וכו׳.
יז	ועוד נקראים... כמ״ש במ״א).
יח	פרק יא. וזה לעומת... שכינתא שריא.
יט	פרק יב. והבינוני... ־32־ אחד כל ימיו.
כ	אך מהות ועצמות... ־32־ עוה״ז ותענוגיו.
כא	רק מפני שלא לו... ־יז־ מצות התורה כנ״ל.
כב	ואעפ״כ אינו נקרא... ־34־ ועיון תפלה כו׳.
כג	רק שלזה מועיל... מיוסף עם אחיו.
כד	פרק יג. ובזה יובן... ־יח־ מן החושך כנ״ל.
כה	אך מאחר שהרע... החיות כנגד כולן).
כו	פרק יד. והנה מדת... ־38־ לכפור האמת.
כז	משא״כ בדבר... צדיקים כו׳ ע״ש.
כח	ובזה יובן... תהי צדיק.
כט	פרק טו. ובזה... ־40־ ולבו חלל בקרבו.

שבט

א ובבינוני יש... ־כא־ יותר מרגילותו.
ב ובזה יובן... עבודתו כלל.
ג פרק טז. וזה כלל... לקמן באריכות
ד פרק יז. ובזה יובן... ־כג־ מצותיו ותורתו.
ה וזה כל האדם... ־כג־ ובפי׳ הרמ״ז שם].
ו והיא בחי׳ תשובה תתאה... כמ״ש במ״א.
ז פרק יח. ולתוספת... גם דחילו.
ח והענין כי האבות... ־כד־ גלגולים].
ט הנה החכמה היא... המושג ומובן.
י פרק יט. ולתוספת... בלב כלל.
יא פרק כ. והנה מודעת... ־כו־ ואפס ממש.
יב כי התהוות כל העולמות... ־כו־ ודקות יותר.
יג אבל עשר בחי׳ חב״ד כו׳... ענייני העולם.
יד פרק כא. והנה... ־52־ במראה נבואתם.
טו והרי דבורו... ־כז־ ולא יתבטלו במציאות.
טז וכל הצמצומים הם... כלא חשיב ממש.
יז פרק כב. רק שהתורה... מאין ליש תמיד.
יח פרק כג. ועם כל הנ״ל... ־כח־ להתלבש בעולמות.
יט ולכן נקרא׳ אברי... ־56־ כגוף לנשמה.
כ וכן הלבוש... ־56־ כל ימיהם.
כא אך המחשבה... ־כט־ לחוד כפיקודין.
כב ומאחר שרצון העליון... בלא״ה].
כג ומזה יוכל המשכיל... כמ״ש לקמן.
כד פרק כד. וזה... כנודע.
כה פרק כה. וזהו שכתוב... ־62־ אח״כ.
כו ואף שהאומר... ־62־ עליו כנודע.
כז והן בבחי׳ ועשה... ־62־ עבודת הצדקה.
כח וכיוצא באלו... ־לב־ ב״ה כנ״ל.
כט ויחוד זה למעלה... ־לב־ כמ״ש במ״א.
ל ובזה יובן למה... ובכל שעה כנ״ל.

אדר ראשון

א פרק כו. ברם... העצב כנ״ל.
ב פרק כז. ואם העצבות... ־לד־ עשה ממש.
ג ואדרבה העצבות... ־לד־ ידים כנ״ל.
ד ובכל דחי׳ ודחי׳... ־לד־ ע״י צדיקים.
ה ושני מיני נחת... ־68־ דקב״ה לעילא.
ו ולא עוד אלא... ־68־ לעילא הרבה.
ז ומקדושה זו נמשכת... מעט מעט.
ח פרק כח. ואפילו... ממש עמו.
ט פרק כט. אך עוד... ־לו־ חומריותן וגסותן.
י והסיבה היא... ־לו־ בשר אדם.
יא וכמאמר הלל הזקן... ־לו־ האדם עצמו.
יב וא״כ הוא... ־72־ ספי״ג).
יג ובפרט כשיזכור... ־72־ נגדי תמיד.
יד וגם מי שהוא נקי... ־לז־ בדבור ומעשה.
טו עוד ישים אל לבו... כמ״ש בזה״ק.
טז פרק ל. עוד זאת... ־76־ כו׳ כמ״ש במ״א.
יז והנה באמת גם מי... ־76־ הלב בתולדתו.
יח והנה באמת שהיא... ־76־ לקמן באריכות.
יט וכל שלא הגיע... ־לט־ הצדקה וכה״ג.
כ ואפילו בבחי׳ סור... ־לט־ שעבר ושנה וכו׳.
כא אבל באמת אם... כשגגות.
כב פרק לא. והנה אף... משמחי לב.
כג פרק לב. והנה... ־מא־ ועד קטן.
כד כי מאחר שגופו... ־מא־ בדבר לבדה.
כה וה״ש הלל הזקן... ־מא־ במ״א באריכות.
כו ומ״ש בגמרא... ־82־ בס׳ חרדים.
כז אבל מי שאינו... ־82־ אהבת ריעים.
כח וגם המקורבים אליו... ט״ו דשבת].
כט פרק לג. עוד זאת... באמונה זו.
ל פרק לד. והנה... ־מג־ כמ״ש לקמן.

אדר שני

א ומשחרב בהמ״ק... ־86־ ה׳ לו.
ב ואם ירחיב ה׳... ־86־ כמ״ש לקמן.
ג והנה בכל פרטי... ־86־ מסטרא דא.
ד פרק לה. והנה... ־מד־ תורתם ועבודתם.
ה והוא בהקדים לשון... ־מד־ בראשו עכ״ל.
ו והנה ביאור... והמשכיל יבין.
ז פרק לו. והנה... ־90־ ואפסי עוד.
ח והנה תכלית... ־מו־ יבטלו במציאות.
ט ולזה נתן הקב״ה... ־מו־ מהאר״י ז״ל).
י וגם כבר הי׳... ־92־ מחייהו כו׳.
יא רק שאח״כ גרם... ארצך וגו׳.
יב פרק לז. והנה תכלית... בעבירה ח״י).
יג ומעות הצדקה... ־מז־ או התפלה.
יד זאת ועוד... ־94־ הגשמי והחומרי.
טו כאשר כל הנשמה... ־94־ כמו האבות.
טז ומאחר שכללות... ־מח־ הממוצעת ביניהן.
יז ונמצא כי כל... ־מח־ שס״ה גידיה.
יח כי כללות ישראל... ־מח־ יצירה עשיה.
יט וכל ניצוץ... ־96־ ניצוצין וכו׳.
כ ובזה יובן... [פ׳ כ״ג].
כא פרק לח. והנה... ־נ־ אברי הגוף.
כב אך אעפ״כ... ־נ־ כל חי.
כג ואף שבשניהם... ־100־ והתפשטות.
כד כי בגוף הגשמי... ־100־ ושכלו בו ית׳.
כה ולא שדביקות המחשבה... ־נא־ חי ומדבר.
כו כי מי שדעתו... בנפשותינו כנז״ל.
כז פרק לט. ומפני... ־104־ היא מצוה עצמה.
כח ועולם האצילות... ־104־ אלקות ממש.
כט והנה צמצום זה... ־נג־ זאת עבודתם.

ניסן

א אך מי ששרש... ־נג־ כידוע לי״ח].
ב והנה שכר מצוה... ־106־ קדם ה׳.
ג והיינו אפילו אם... ־106־ כמ״ש לקמן.
ד וכשעוסק שלא לשמה... ־נד־ כמ״ש בזהר.
ה פרק מ. אך כל זמן... ־נה־ כנ״ל באריכות
ו הגהה [ושם מאיר... ־110־ רצון זו].
ז ובזה יובן... ־110־ כמ״ש בר״מ).
ח כי כמו שכנפי... ־נו־ כמ״ש בפרע״ח).
ט והנה אף דדחילו... במ״א באריכות.
י פרק מא. ברם צריך... ־נו־ עבודת עבד.
יא והנה ה׳ נצב... ־112־ ותפילין.
יב וגם יתבונן... ־112־ הלב והמוח כו׳.
יג ובעטיפת ציצית... ־נז־ לאדונו ומלכו.
יד משא״כ אם לומד... ־נז־ לידע״ם.
טו והנה אף מי... ־114־ ולבושיהן כנ״ל.
טז אך אמנם אמרו... ־116־ ברוך אתה ומה״ג.
יז והנה בהכנה זו... ־116־ בלילה כנודע.
יח והנה כל כוונתו... וכו׳ כנ״ל.
יט פרק מב. והנה במ״ש... ־118־ והאדם ידע וגו׳.
כ וכח זה ומדה זו... ־118־ כמ״ש שם.
כא והשנית היא יגיעת... ־ס־ ואזן שומעת כו׳.
כב וגם כי אין לו... ־120־ כנ״ל פ״כ.
כג והנה כל אדם... ־סא־ כידוע לי״ח].
כד ועוד זאת יזכור... ־סא־ המאמן ידיו וכו׳.
כה וגם להיות לזכרון... כמ״ש במ״א.
כו פרק מג. והנה... ־124־ כמ״ש לקמן.
כז והנה בחי׳ אהבה זו... כידוע לי״ח].
כח פרק מד. והנה כל... ־סג־ צפרא כו׳.
כט ואהבה רבה וגדולה... ־126־ נעשה טבע.
ל ואף אם נדמה לו... ־126־ מצרפה כו׳.

אייר

א והנה ב׳ בחי׳... -סד- אהבת עולם.
ב רק שאעפ״כ... וכו׳ וכנודע.
ג פרק מה. עוד יש... כמ״ש במ״א.
ד פרק מו. ויש דרך... -סה- חבירו אליו.
ה והנה זהו טבע... -סה- לאהבת המלך.
ו והנה ככל הדברים... -130- כנ״ל באריכות.
ז וכולם שואלים... -סו- באור א״ס ב״ה.
ח ולכן המשיל שלמה... -סו- עולמם בחייהם.
ט וז״ש אסף... האצילות].
י פרק מז. והנה בכל דור... כמש״ל.
יא פרק מח. והנה כאשר... -134- ויחזרו למקורן.
יב והנה פרטיות הצמצומים... -134- כלא ממש׳ חשיבי.
יג וככה ממש היא... -סח- גבול ותכלית.
יד והמשל בזה הנה... -סח- האדם ודעתו.
טו אבל הקב״ה... -136- וצומח בלבד.
טז אך ידיעתו ית׳... וכמ״ש במ״א.
יז פרק מט. והנה אף... -138- בשביל אהבת ה׳.
יח ואיך יבא האדם... -138- מרום וקדוש.
יט ואח״כ ברכה שני׳... -ע- ביחודו ית׳ כנ״ל.
כ והנה כאשר ישים... -ע- הדבור בד״ת.
כא כי על מוצא... -ע- ומאודו כנ״ל.
כב פרק נ. והנה כל... -140- מבדילים כו׳ ח״ו.
כג והנה סדר העבודה... חיי החיים ב״ה.
כד פרק נא. והנה לתוספת... בתולדתו כנ״ל].
כה וככה ממש עד״מ... -עב- בתחתונים ממש.
כו וההבדל שבין... -עב- להם להחיותם.
כז וכ״כ עצמו... א״ס ב״ה.
כח פרק נב. וכמו... -עג- האור מהשמש.
כט אבל השכינה... -עג- השמש בלבד.

סיון

א ומהו הלבוש... -עג- מצות התורה.
ב ובירידתה בהשתלשלות... בשם שכינה.
ג פרק נג. והנה כשהיה... -148- כנודע לי״ח].
ד ובבית שני... -148- יסד ברתא.
ה וז״ש הינוקא... ית׳ וית׳.
ו לקוטי אמרים... יתברך ויתעלה.
ז שער היחוד והאמונה... וקב״ה כולא חד.
ח פרק ב. והנה... -154- המים אינו כן.
ט וכ״ש וק״ו בבריאת... -154- בעולם הבריאה.
י פרק ג. והנה... א״כ אפס בלעדו באמת.
יא והמשל לזה... -156- המאיר ואפס בלעדו.
יב וכדברים האלה... -156- צריך להקדים.
יג פרק ד. כי הנה... -עט- הטוב להטיב.
יד והנה כמו שמדה זו... -158- מאין ליש.
טו [והנה בחי׳... כידוע לי״ח.
טז פרק ה. והנה על... פרק ג].
יז פרק ו. והנה... -160- הכלולה בחסד.
יח והנה מהתכללות... -פא- השמש בשמש.
יט ולכן הוצרך הכתוב... הוא האלקים.
כ פרק ז. ובזה... -פב- עליו כלל.
כא והנה גדר ובחי׳... -פב- ולד׳ סטרין.
כב והנה אעפ״י... -164- אפילו לתחתונים
כג והנה במ״ש יובן... -פג- מהרמ״ק ז״ל].
כד והנה מכאן... -166- ודעתו הכל א׳.
כה וז״ש בתקונים... -166- דממלא לון.
כו וזהו ג״כ ענין... -פד- בפועל ממש.
כז וממלא כל עלמין... -פד- גבול ותכלית.
כח כי מקור החיות... -168- שהן מדותיו.
כט והחשבון מורה על... האותיות עצמן.
ל פרק ח. והנה... ומקור החיות.

תמוז

א פרק ט. אבל... -פו- עד אין קץ
ב רק מפני... -פז- ידוע למשכילים.
ג הגהה (סוד... מן השכל.
ד פרק י. אך... -174- דרכיו מדרכנו.
ה ומ״מ לשכך... -174- אתכסיאת כו׳.
ו עד״מ ביום ראשון... מדות כלל.
ז פרק יא. והנה גם... -176- וסתום בלבו.
ח אבל באמת... כמ״ש במ״א.
ט פרק יב. רק... -178- מהאותיות עצמן.
י כי הן ד״מ... יתברך ויתעלה.
יא אגרת התשובה... -צא- עכ״ל הברייתא.
יב והנה מצות... -182- כ״א מיראה.
יג פרק ב. אך כל... יום רצון.
יד פרק ג. והנה... -184- ג״פ וכו׳.
טו אכן כל זה...-184- הלכות תענית.
טז ומ״מ כל... -צג- וחפץ בהצדקה.
יז אכן מספר... כי לא תמנו).
יח פרק ד. ואולם... -186- בנעימים.
יט אך הענין יובן... -צד- החי׳ וכו׳.
כ ככה ממש עד״מ... -צד- מבחי׳ האותיות.
כא וביאור הענין... שם הוי׳ וכו׳.
כב פרק ה. והנה... כדלקמן).
כג פרק ו. אמנם זהו... -צו- כנודע לי״ח.
כד והנה יעקב... נאמר וכו׳.
כה פרק ז. ואולם... -צז- ונדכה וכו׳.
כו והאיך נשבר... -194- בתשובה כנודע).
כז ואף מי שלא עבר... כנגד כולן.
כח פרק ח. והנה... למלכא וכו׳).
כט פרק ט. וביאור... בספ״ק דר״ה.

מנחם אב

א פרק י. והנה תשובה... -198- דזמרה כנודע,
ב ומאחר שהתפלה... עילאה).
ג פרק יא. ואמנם... -ק- לאין קץ.
ד ומה שמשבחים... -200- היא מיד.
ה ומ״ש וחטאתי... על כל פשעיו.
ו פרק יב. וטעם... ימצא טוב.
ז א פותחין... -204- והגוף שבנפש.
ח אך מי הוא... -204- מיצוי הנפש כו׳.
ט ועתה הפעם... אלא תורה וכו׳.
י ב. קטנתי מכל... הפנים וגו׳.
יא ג. וילבש... 208- וגבול [ח״ו].
יב אך מי הוא... תדרשנו.
יג ד. אין ישראל... -קו- ושבי׳ בצדקה.
יד וזהו צדק... סלה אכי״ר.
טו ה. ויעש דוד שם... -214- שמבין הכל.
טז אך האותיות... -קח- וי״ב ע״ש)].
יז אך ביאור הענין... -קח- מבחי׳ ח״ע וכנ״ל.
יח אך העולם הזה... -216- מקננת בעשי׳.
יט והנה באדם... -216- לאברהם כו׳.
כ אך אחר... והמשכילים יבינו.
כא ו. זורע צדקה... -220- ישענו כו׳.
כב והנה מודעת... תכונני.
כג ז. אשרינו... -222- ועלול וכו׳.
כד והנה הארה... -222- יספר מרוב.
כה והנה שופרי׳... -קיב- כמ״ש במ״א.
כו והנה אף... הגורל ממש.
כז ח. זורע צדקות... בחו״ל וד״ל.
כח ט. אהוביי... -קיד- על פי התורה.
כט ע״כ אהוביי אחיי... ה׳ ציון כו׳.
ל י. אד״ש וחיים... נשמתן כו׳.

אלול

א והנה לפי... ־230־ עומדין וכו'.
ב והנה עיקר... ־קטו־ נפשו כתיב.
ג והנה מדת חסד... בא כו'.
ד יא. להשכילך... העליון הגנוז.
ה יב. והי' מעשה... ־קיז־ מדות לבדן.
ו אך הקב"ה... ־234־ הקדושות ית'.
ז והנה אתערותא... ־קיח־ הטוב המחייהו.
ח ובירור זה יהי'... ־קיח־ במצרף וכור.
ט והנה מודעת זאת... ־236־ פעמים וכו'.
י וז"ש והי' מעשה... כל חטאתם.
יא יג. מה רב טובך... בסוכה וגו'.
יב יד. לעורר... ־240־ למעלה מעלה.
יג ובכל שנה ושנה... בעשי"ת וד"ל.
יד טו. להבין משל... ־קכא־ הכלולה מהן.
טו אך צריך להקדים... ־קכב־ במשל ומליצה.
טז והנה כללות הי"ס... ־קכג־ כמו שית').
יז והנה מדות אלו... ־קכג־ שינוי מדותיהם.
יח והנה כ"ז הוא... שיתבאר במקומו.
יט טז. אהוביי... ־248־ בנדרים דף פ'.
כ והנה זהו עפ"י... לב ונפש.
כא יז. גודע דבאתערותא... ־250־ וע"ש היטב.
כב וזהו שארז"ל... מנוחה כו'.
כג יח. כתיב מה יפית... ־252־ כמ"ש בלק"א.
כד ושנית היא אהבה... דרכיך דעהו.
כה יט. עוטה... ־254־ וכתר דאצילות.
כו אך הענין הוא פשוט... ־קכח־ האותיות.
כז והנה בחי' חכמה... ־256־ ושכל.
כח כן עד"ז ממש... ־256־ מהאריז"ל.
כט האותיות הנגלות... וחיות כנודע.

תשרי

א כ. איהו וחיוהי... ־258־ בלה"ק.
ב והגם שהיש הנברא... ־קל־ לגבי עילתו.
ג אך נשמות... ־260־ בבי"ע.
ד אמנם מודעת... ־קלא־ והלידה.
ה ובזה יובן... ־קלא־ וכדלקמן.
ו והנה כמו"כ... ־262־ להחיותם.
ז אמנם מציאותו... ־262־ כנ"ל.
ח ועוד זאת... ־קלב־ דמל' דאצי'.
ט ולפמ"ש בס' הגלגולים... ־264־ כמ"ש במ"א.
י ומזה יובן היטב... חיי עוה"ב.
יא כא. אד"ש... ־266־ בכל יום.
יב אך גם זאת... יבא שילה.
יג כב. אהוביי אחיי... בפרש"י.
יד אך האמת אגיד... יאהב ה' וכו'.
טו וכמו אב רחמן... הדינין נס"ו.
טז אהוביי אחיי... או"נ מלו"נ.
יז כג. בגוירת... ־קלו־ אליהם כלל.
יח וההפרש שבין השראה... ־קלו־ עמלה בה.
יט אבל ההשראה היא... ־272־ ממציאותו לגמרי.
כ וע"כ רע בעיני... ־272־ כמ"ש בזוה"ק.
כא ע"כ אהוביי אחיי... ־קלז־ בפרש"י ז"ל שם.
כב ובשבת קדש בעלות... כן יהי רצון.
כג כד. אהוביי... ־קלח־ לעין כל.
כד וע"כ קבעו חז"ל... בלבותם.
כה כה. להבין... ־276־ לדבר מאומה.
כו (וזהו כי ה'... ־קלט־ וחיות רוחניית.
כז והנה נודע לי"ח... ־278־ מתחת לארץ.
כח (אלא שבארצות... עמהם)).
כט והנה אף כי... האר"י ז"ל.
ל והגה נפש... ־280־ בלא דבור.

חשון

א והנה זלעו"ז... עד רום המעלות.
ב ואחר הדברים... ־קמא־ וכה"ג טובא.
ג וכמדומה לי... ־קמב־ אמרי פי.
ד כו. בר"מ פ' נשא... ־284־ ע"כ בר"מ.
ה והנה המובן... ־קמג־ של הלכה בלבד.
ו ועוד יש להפליא... ־286־ בהסתר כו'.
ז אך באמת כשתדקדק... ־קמד־ הכל אחד.
ח ומ"ש האריז"ל... ־288־ מסטרא דרע.
ט והנה העליונים... ־קמה־ האומות עו"ג.
י אבל בצאת השכינה... כמ"ש בע"ח וד"ל.
יא כז. אהוביי אחיי... ־קמו־ בארחותיו נס"ו.
יב וז"ש בזוה"ק דצדיקא... קודם לברכה.
יג איתא בזוה"ק... ־292־ ועלול כנודע.
יד והנה בהיות הצדיק... ־קמז־ ומצאת תאמין.
טו והנה יש עוד... כוכבים.
טז כח. למה נסמכה... מטה מנוגה.
יז והנה מודעת... מי חטאת וכו'
יח כט. אשת חיל... ־קמט־ דר"י ורכ"ט.
יט והנה אור זה... ־298־ כולא חד.
כ והנה רצון העליון... ־קן־ שבגר"ן האדם.
כא וז"ש בזוה"ק... ־300־ באריכות ע"ש.
כב והנה מודעת זאת... ב"ה כנ"ל.
כג ל. מודעת זאת... ומספר וד"ל.
כד לא. נודע בשערים... האברים וכו'.
כה לב. ברך ה' חילם... כנפש תדרשנו.
כו להבין איך הקורא... קדם ה' דוקא.
כז עיין ע"ח... אפים כנודע.
כח להבין מ"ש בשער... ־308־ פ' פקודי).
כט*) ומ"ש בפ' פקודי... ־קנה־ כמש"ש דר"י.
ל והנה תפלה... עד האצי'.

*) בחדש חשון של כט יום לומדים ביום כט גם השיעור של יום למ"ד.

כסלו

א להבין מ"ש בפע"ח... ־310־ דע"ס דז"א כו'.
ב והנה במ"א כתב... ־310־ שבבי"ע דוקא.
ג והנה לקיום מצוה שא"א... ־קנו־ אחורי כו'.
ד משא"כ מעשה המצות... ־312־ הלומד הסוד.
ה אבל דוקא סודות... ־312־ אשר שם.
ו ועוד זאת שבאמת... ־קנז־ לא יראו.
ז ובר מן כל דין... ־314־ הלכותיהן.
ח אך להבין... ־קנח־ וכה"ג.
ט אך עוד זאת... ־קנח־ מהגברא.
י משא"כ ההלכות... ־316־ אלקות.
יא והטעם משום דחב"ד... ־316־ וגמרא.
יב ומ"ש בע"ח... שוכן וכו' וד"ל.
יג ולהבין פרטי ההלכות... דכלים דז"א.
יד דוד זמירות... ־320־ בעת צרתו.
טו אך מה שהי'... ואחור ע"ש.
טז וצדקה כנחל איתן... א"ס ב"ה.
יז הנה לא טובה... וכו' וד"ל.
יח הוכח תוכיח... לעומת זה כו'.

ג ו ט י ו ם ט ו ב

לשנה טובה

בלימוד החסידות ודרכי החסידות

תכתבו ותחתמו

ספרי׳ — אוצר החסידים — ליובאוויטש

מפתחות

א) מפתח ענינים ב) מפתח שמות ספרים ואנשים

לספר התניא

ונתוסף להם

ג) לוח התיקון. ד) הערות ותיקונים

ה) כתבי יד ודפוסי התניא (רשימה קצרה)

ו) הערות ז) ראשי פרקים מתולדות רבנו הזקן

ח) בראש החוברת פאקסימיליות

•

נערך על ידי

כבוד קדושת

אדמו״ר מנחם מענדל

זצוקללה״ה נבג״מ זי״ע

שניאורסאהן

מליובאוויטש

יוצא לאור על ידי מערכת

״אוצר החסידים״

770 איסטערן פאַרקוויי ברוקלין, נ.י.

שנת חמשת אלפים שבע מאות ושבעים לבריאה

שנת המאתים וחמשים להסתלקות־הילולא של הבעש״ט ז״ל

ב״ה.

פתח דבר

מכ״ק אדמו״ר זי״ע בהוצאה דשנת ה׳תשי״ד *)

בחוברת זו באו: א) מפתח ענינים. ב) מפתח שמות ספרים ואנשים. ג) לוח התיקון. ד) הערות ותיקונים. ה) כתבי יד ודפוסי התניא (רשימה קצרה). ו) הערות. ז) ראשי פרקים מתולדות רבנו הזקן. ח) בראש החוברת — פאקסימיליא של: 1) השער דהוצאה הראשונה של התניא. 2) עמוד מכתב יד התניא מהדורא קמא, אשר קרוב לודאי שזהו גוף כתי״ק רבנו הזקן — ראה רשימת כ״ק מו״ח אדמו״ר זצוקללה״ה נבג״מ זי״ע אודות זה בספר קיצורים והערות לספר לקוטי אמרים.

החוברת נערכה בקשר עם הדפסת התניא בפעם הראשונה בחצי כדור הארץ התחתון[1] — בארצות הברית. בברוקלין, נ. י. שנת תשי״ד.

הוצאה זו היא פוטוגרפיא מ„התוצאה החדשה והמתוקנת״ שנדפסה בווילנא תר״ס, עם התיקונים[2] שנעשו לאחר זה בהאמהות ונכנסו בההוצאות שלאחרי׳.

לוח התיקון הבא בזה ערכתי על פי השוואה לההוצאות הראשונות, ולאלו שנדפסו בסמיכות מקום לרבנו הזקן, אשר קרוב לודאי שהיו שם כת״י התניא מוגהים. ואולי גם מגיהים שקבלו הוראות מרבנו הזקן.

כן נכנסו בו התיקונים המיוחסים להצ״צ, וגם מה שתיקן הרה״ח הוו״ח וכו׳ הר״ר אשר ז״ל שו״ב גראצמאן, הוא שעסק בהגהת והו״ל של התניא הוצאת ווילנא תר״ס, על גליון התניא שלו, וכ״ק מו״ח אדמו״ר אמר לי, אשר, בכלל, יש לסמוך עליו בזה.

ב„הערות ותיקונים״ באו תיקונים על פי השוואה להוצאות אחרות, לבד

---

*) בהוצאה זו נתקנו כמה מטעיות הדפוס שבהוצאות הקודמות, בחלקם נכנסו בפנים ובחלקם — בלוח התיקון ובהערות ותיקונים. כן נדפסו, בפאַקסימיליא כל ארבעת העמודים של הכת״י תניא מהדורא קמא וביאור כ״ק מו״ח אדמו״ר ע״ד כת״י תניא הנ״ל.

1) ראה מכתב כ״ק מו״ח אדמו״ר הנדפס בסוף קונטרס חג השבועות ה׳תש״ח (קונטרס נח).

2) ראה בפנים בהוצאת ווילנא תר״ס ותרס״ט.

הנ״ל, תיקונים במקום שנראה לי טעות המדפיס דמוכח, או על כל פנים קרוב לודאי.

בהוצאת התניא השלימה שמכינים לדפוס –

התניא – באמצע העמוד, ומסביב לו יבואו: מראה מקומות, פירוש קצר, ליקוט מספרי רבותינו נשיאינו וכת״י שלהם המפרשים דברי התניא וכו׳ –

יבואו ג״כ ציוני מקור תיקונים הנ״ל בפרטיות. וזאת למודעי כאן, אשר א) התיקון גו׳ וגו׳ במקום כו׳ וכו׳[3] – באגרת התשובה – הם ע״פ הוצאה הראשונה של אגה״ת מהדורא בתרא (שקלאב. תקס״ו). ב) התיקונים בנוגע להנקודות – הם ע״פ ציוני הרה״ח וכו׳ הר״א שו״ב גראצמאן, והכנסתים בסוג התיקונים בדרך אפשר, כיון שלא הייתי בטוח לגמרי אשר כולם שייכים אליו. ג) תיקוני הביטוי „עו״ג״ „בעוע״ג״ וכיו״ב הם ע״פ הוצאה הראשונה וציוני הנ״ל.

מנחם שניאורסאהן

ג׳ כסלו ה׳תשי״ד, ברוקלין, נ. י.

---

3) ע״פ מש״כ בתשבי ערך גמר „נוהגין רז״ל, כשמביאין פסוק ואינם משלימים אותו כותבין וגומר וכאשר מביאין מאמר מדבריהם ואינם משלימין אותו כותבין וכולי״ – וי״ל הטעם, ע״פ מרז״ל כל פסוקא דלא פסקי׳ משה אנן לא פסקינן לי׳, ולכן אומר שיגמור. – וכנראה שבמכתבים לא דייק בזה רבנו הזקן, ולכן באגה״ק נמצא בכ״מ „כו״ במקום „גו״.

ספר

לקוטי אמרים

חלק ראשון הנקרא בשם ספר
של בינונים

מלוקט מפי ספרים ומפי סופרים קדושי
עליון נ"ע מיוסד על פסוק כי
קרוב אליך הדבר מאוד בפיך ובלבבך
לעשותו לבאר היטב איך הוא קרוב
מאד בדרך ארוכה וקצרה בעזה"י :

נדפס

בסלאוויטא

תחת ממשלת אדונינו המיוחס הגדול החסיד
הדוכס חרייאים סאנגשקי וואייוואדי
וואלינסקי סטארסטי
טשערקסקי ארדערא דיינעגא הרלא
יר"ה :

בשנת כי קרוב אליך הדבר מאוד בפיך ובלבבך
לעשותו לפ"ק

שער התניא דפוס הראשון — פאקסימיליא.

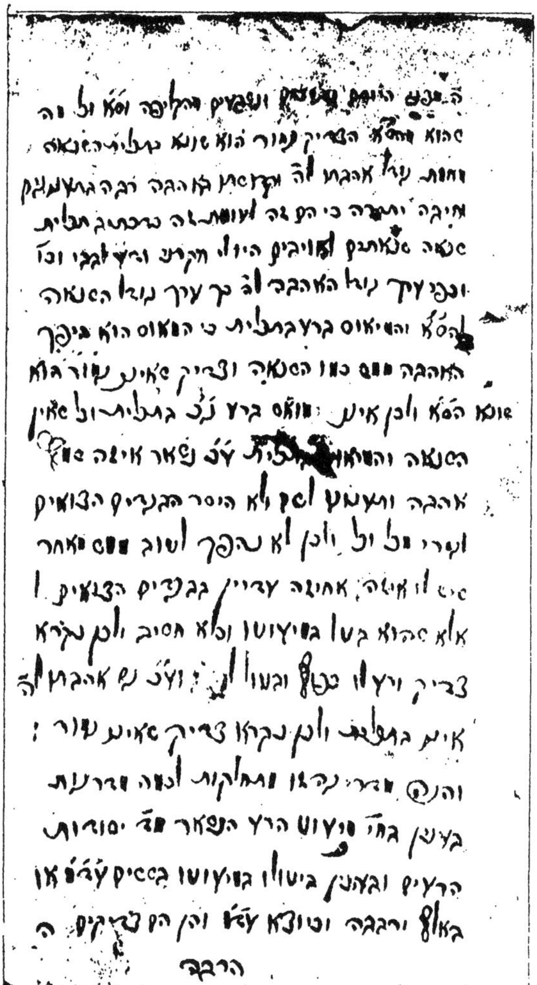

בשורה ס' מתחלת שונא הס"א כנראה יש כאן פליטת הקולמוס ובס' התניא הנדפס אי': שאינו שונא וכו'.

תמונת כתב יד של ספר התניא מהדורא קמא מרבינו הגדול נ"ע זצוקללה"ה נבג"מ זי"ע
(בנדפס: פרק י — דף טו ע"א)

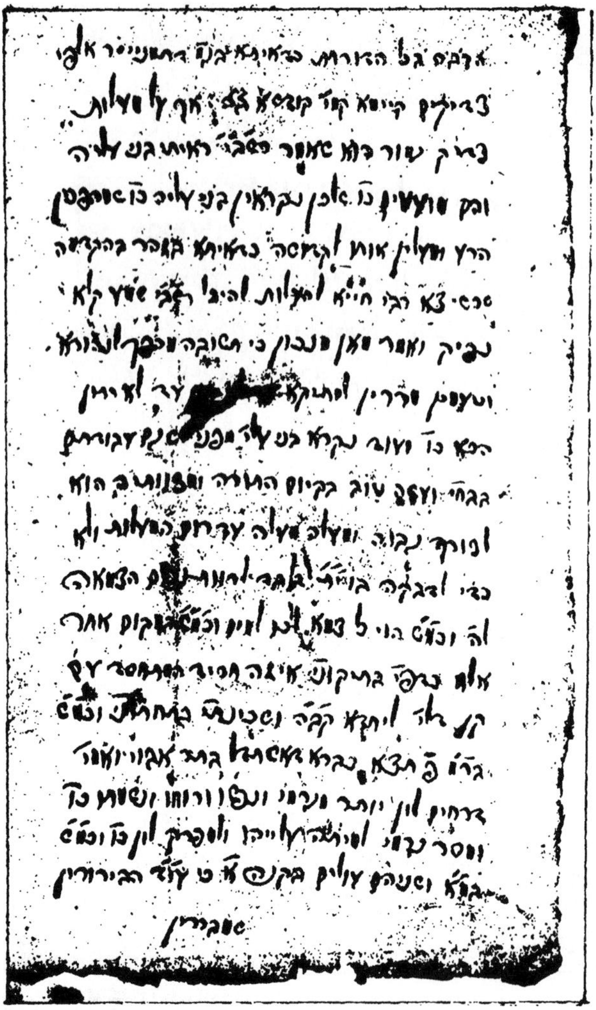

תמונת כתב יד דספר התניא מהדורא קמא מרבינו הגדול נ"ע זצוקללה"ה נבג"מ זי"ע
(בנדפס: פרק י — דף טו ע"א־ב)

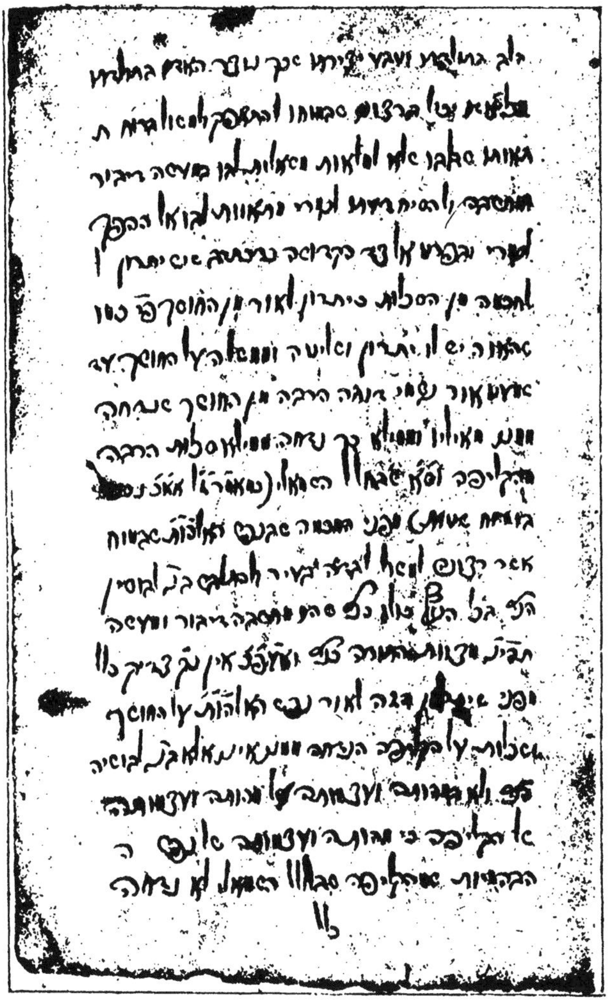

תמונת כתב יד מספר התניא מהדורא קמא מרבינו הגדול נ״ע זצוקללה״ה נבג״מ זי״ע
(בנדפס: פרק יב — דף יז ע״א)

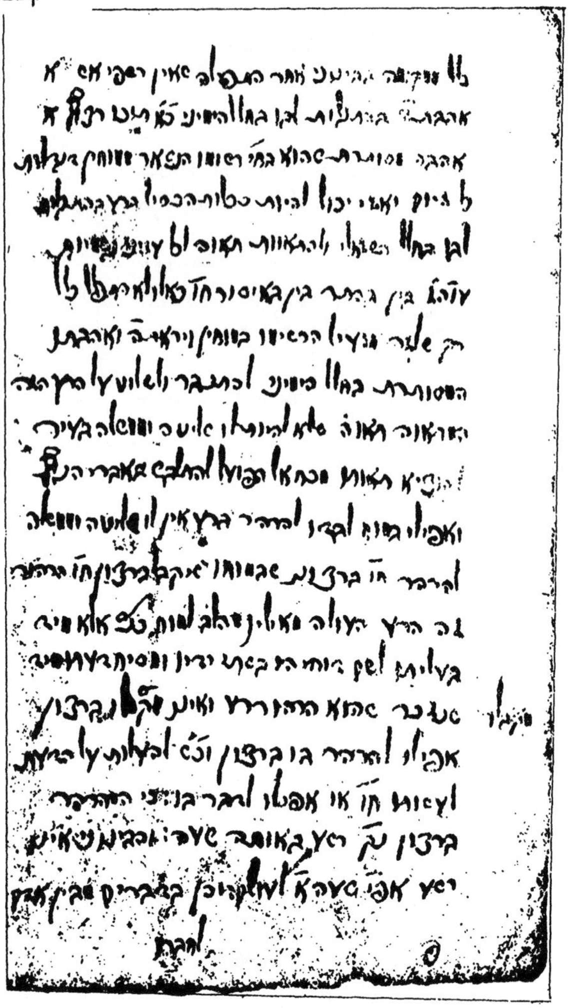

תמונת כתב יד מספר התניא מהדורא קמא מרבינו הגדול נ"ע זצוקללה"ה נבג"מ זי"ע
(בנדפס: פרק יב — דף יז ע"א־ב)

ביאור על אודות הכתב יד. שני עלים
מספר התניא.

הכתב יד הלזה. שנשאר בין הכתבים של הוד
כ"ק אאמו"ר אדמו"ר מהורש"ב זצוקללה"ה נבג"מ זי"ע.

בהשקפה ראשונה בתמונת האותיות עלה אומר
זהו כתב יד קדשו של כ"ק רבינו הגדול. וכן
הסכים לדעת קדשו של כ"ק אאמו"ר הרה"ק.

ר' שמואל שי' כותב אחד בקי בכתבי ידי קודש
כ"ק אבותינו רבותינו הק' - כידוע שאומה
באמונה בנשיאותי הראשונה. שמואל דער שרייבער
העיד אשר זהו כתב יד קדשו של הוד כ"ק
רבינו הגדול בלי שום ספק. ואמר הטעם
בטעמא כי להיותו כתב באמצע שני חיי רבינו
לכן האותיות ברורים בטוב.

אחרי ל"ב או ל"ג שנה. הוד כ"ק אאמו"ר הרה"ק הי' קורא
את שני העלים האלו, בשם דער כתב יד פון תניא
וכאשר הייתי אומר לומר בלשון רבו, הנה אמר לו
הוא קוראו בשם כתב יד.

הוד כ"ק אאמו"ר הרה"ק אמר דגם כי באמצע, אותיות
אין תמונתם בוודאי. ושמעתי לאמר כתוב של כ"ק רבינו
הגדול אבל לפי הנוגע האמת שרי' מצדיקי הוד
כ"ק אאמו"ר אביו. הרה"ק הוא הוסיף לודאי שהוא
כתב יד קדשו של כ"ק רבינו הגדול נ"ע זי"ע.

תמונת כי"ק של
כ"ק אדמו"ר
(מהוריי"צ) נ"ע
מליובאוויטש

מפתח ענינים

— על סדר הא"ב —

מספר לקוטי אמרים (תניא)

אות הראשונה מציינת את החלק. האותיות הבאות אחר זה — הפרק או הסימן (או הפיסקא בקו"א).

ח"א: ספר של בינונים. הקדמה ונ"ג פרקים. **ח"ב**: שער היחוד והאמונה, הקדמה וי"ב פרקים. **ח"ג**: אגרת התשובה. י"ב פרקים. **ח"ד**: אגרת הקדש, ל"ב סימנים. **ח"ה**: קונטרס אחרון ואגה"ק, ט' סימנים.

במהו"ע) דג (י. קובו"ש).
עיי"ע אחד, זווג, נשיקין.
יחו"ע יחו"ת : בז.
יין :
גב (על סתם יינם ע"ג תע־ניות).
ימין, שמאל :
בה (למע') דיג (בעבודה) ד־לב (כל הגוף נכלל בימין).
ינוקא : אלה. אנא. אנג.
יסודות, ד' י', :
אא. אג (האש, המים) אז (המים) אח (הרוח) אט (המים) איט (האש) אכה (העפר) דטו (ד' י.) דך (העפר).
יסורים :
אכו (השמחים בי. עליהם כו')
גא (י. ממרקין) גיב (טעם לשמחה בי. י. דעוה"ז, דגי־הינם) דיא (אין רע יורד מלמע') דכב (יפשפש במ־עשיו).
יעקב :
איג. אלב. אמה. גה. גו. דב. דו. דז. דכז. הז.
יפה שעה א' בתומע"ט בעוה"ז כו' : אד.
יצחק : אמו. דיג.
יצי"מ : אלא. אמז.
יצה"ר :
אז (י. לדברים האסורים, המותרים). עיי"ע לעולם ירגיז.
יראה :
אג (הרוממות) אד (שרש מל"ת) אכג (י. גדולה בעסקו בתורה, אם אין חכ' כו') אמ (בחי' בי.) אמא (כנ"ל) אמב (אטו י. מילתא זוטרתי היא אין כו') אמג (יר"ע יר"ת, קטנות וגדלות בי. אם אין י. אין חכ' אם אין חכ' אין י. אהוי"ר) דיח (י. הרוממות). עיי"ע אהבה, דו"ר.
ירושה : אלג.
ירמי', ר' י' : הה.
יש :
דך (ראשית היש, התהותו).
יש מאין :
בב (ימ"א צ"ל תמיד) בד. דך. דכה (צ"ל תמיד). עיי"ע בריאה.
ישועה : דג. דח.
ישמעאל :
איא (ר"י) דב (חסד דאברהם, דישמעאל).
ישראל :
איט (קרוים אדם) אלז (עולם

ע״י תורה כו׳ ביצירה ברי־
אה כו׳) הד (מ. ונשמות. נק׳
ה״. עבודתם רק הסתלקות).
עיי״ע מט״ט.

מלוכה:
בז. דכד (מ. דרקיע כעין
מ. דארעא).

מלך: בז. גז. דכט.

מלכות:
אטז (מוחין דנוקבא, דז״א)
אנב (מל׳ דאצי׳ ב. י.
ע. נק׳ דבר ה׳. מל׳ מל׳ כל
עולמים) בז (אד׳ שייכות
זמן ומקום) דה (חצו׳ הכלים
דמל׳ דאצי׳ נשמה לעשי׳)
דך (ל׳ כלים דמל׳ דאצי׳ כו׳.
עיקר התהות היש ע״י המל׳.
עלדאת״ג. מל׳ ושאר הספי־
רות. מל׳ וכתר. מל׳ דא״ס)
דכה (דבר מלך שלטון. מל׳
דאצי׳ דבריאה כו׳) דכו (מל׳
פה תושבע״פ. מל׳ דאצי׳. ב.
י. ע. מטרוניתא. אמה. שפחה.
מל׳ ז״א. עה״ד עה״ח. מת־
לבש בק״נ) דל (מקום החש־
בון).

ממכ״ע: אמא. אנא. בז. דג.

מנצפ״ך: בד.

מם״נ:
איח (גם בקשב״ק) אכה (על
קדה״ש) אמא (מ. עסק התו׳
ותפלה) הב (נר״ן נעשים מ״ן
ע״י מ.).

מסך:
איז (קליפות). עיי״ע מחיצה.

מספרים:
ג. אג (ג׳ אמות) גג. גיא.
עיי״ע שלשה.
ז. אג (ז׳ כפולות, ימי הבנין).
י. אג (ע״ס, י׳ בחי׳ בנר״ן)
או (י׳ בחינות בנה״ב). בי.
דכג. עיי״ע עשה״ד. עש״מ.
חי. גג.
כב. ביא.
ק. קא. אטו.
רלא. בא.
רמח. אלז. אנא.
שסה. אלז. אנא.
שע. דג.
ת. דכט (ת׳ עלמין דכסופין).
תרי״ג. אד. אנא. דז. דכט.
תר״ך. אנג. דכט.
ס״ר. אלז. דכז. עיי״ע או־
תיות.

מעשה, עשי׳:
אלה (מעלת מצות מ.)
בט (בחכ׳ עשית) דט (ע. ד־
אלק׳. צדקה) די (צדקה) דיב
(והי׳ מ. הצדקה שלום גו׳
מ. עבודה) דך (מעלת מצות

הו"ע) גד (ע"ס נרמזות בשם
ה') דג (ע"ס, או"מ עליהם.
נק' גופא) דטו (בי' ע"ס
בנה"א. השכלית. ע"ס מאירות
בנשמה) דיט (נהי"ם שבעליון
מתלבשים בתחתון. אחוריים
ופנים דס.) דך (עילה ועלול.
בלי מה. או"כ הס. ל' כלים
דמל' דאצי' כו'. עיגולים ד־
ע"ס. נר"נ דע"ס. מל' ושאר
הס. כתר מל') דכה (ע"ס.
בנפש. י' כתרין דמסאבותא)
הד (כלים דאצי' כו'). עיי"ע
חו"ג. מל'. ת"ת.

כתימו דכל סתימין:
אמ. אנא. בז.

עב, ענן:
גז (ע. ע. עברות חמורות קלות)
דכט (ויבא משה בתוך הענן).

עבודה:
איג (ע. תמה) אטו (עבד.
עובד ואשר ל"ע. ע. תמה ע"י
מלחמה דוקא) אטז (אופן הע.)
אלט (אופנים בע.) אמא (כנ"ל
עבד. בן) אמב (ע. לפי הדעת)
אמג (סדר הע.) דד (ע. שבלב)
דט (עיקר הע. בזה"ז־צדקה)
דיב (מעשה. ע.) דיג (ימין
שמאל בע.) חד (ע. המלאכים
הסתלקות. ע. נשמות גם המ־
שכה) הח (עיקר הע. עתה־
תפלה).

ע"ז: איט. אך. אכד. דכה.

עבירה:
אכד (בתכלית הפירוד. פגם הע.
ענשה) אלז (שס"ה ל"ת) גא
(פגם הע.) גב (תקוני תשובה
לע.) גג (וחטאתך בצדקה פרוק)
גה (עונותיכם מבדילים גו')
גז (ענן עב. ע. השקולות כע"ז
ג"ע וש"ד) גט (פגם הברית)
די (תקון ע. ע"י צדקה בלי
הגבלה) דכה (חטא עה"ד).
עיי"ע שגגה.

עגולים, יושר: דך.

עדן: דה. דיא. דיז.

עוד: בו (ל' טפל. גוף).

עוז:
אלו (תורה) דא (תושבע"פ).
די (תורה).

עול:
אמא (עומ"ש) אמב (קבלת
עומ"ש בק"ש בשמו"ע).

עולה, קרבן ע.:
גב. גג. גד.

עולם:
או (עוה"ז מעשיו קשים כו')
איד (ע. תראה בחייך) אטז
(בריאה יצירה) אך (אינם פו־
עלים שינוי למע') אכג (חיותם
תלוי במעשה המצות. יחוד

תבונה: אב. אטז.

תורה:

אהקדמה (נשמות ות.) **אא** (ביטול ת״ת. ע׳ פנים לת.) **אד** (אורייתא וק׳ כ״ח. חסד ומים). **אה** (ת״ת כנגד כולן. מעלת ידיעת הת. לחם מזון וגם לבוש) **אח** (עונש ביטול ת״ת) **איז** (הת. נצחית) **אכג** (אורייתא וק׳ כ״ח. גדולה מכל המצות וגם מתפלה) **אכה** (ביטול ת. בכ״י. ברכת סלח לנו ע״ז) **אלא** (משיבת נפש) **אלב** (יסוד כל הת.) **אלד** (משחרב ביהמ״ק כו׳ ד״א של הלכה) **אלו** (עוז וכח) **אלז** (ת״ת כנגד כולם. קורא בת. יקראוהו באמת) **אלט** (גלות הת.) **אמ** (תלמודו בידו. מקרא בעשי׳ כו׳ קבלה באצי׳) **אנב** (תלמוד מבריאה משנה מיצירה) **בה** (מימינו אש דת) **גא** (חומר ת״ת) **גט** (תיקון לפגם הברית. תשו״ע) **גי** (ת. תפלה, מלמעלמ״ט מלמטלמ״ע) **דא** (עוז תושבע״פ. מחכ׳ נפקת אבל מקורה כו׳) **דה** (כל האומר אל״א ת. בלי גמ״ח כו׳. בוניך. תמכי אורייתא) **דז** (יעקב מרכבה לת. שלמע׳) **דט** (ת״ת שקול כנגד גמ״ח רק בימיהם כו׳) **די** (מימינו אש דת. מפי הגבורה) **דיט** (נחשל״ת. מחכ׳ נפקת) **דכב** (תושי׳) **דכג** (פנימית הת. מכפרת עונותיו של אדם) **דכו** (לימוד הלכות או״ה. פנימית התורה. עה״ד. עה״ח. ת. ותפלה. מקרא משנה קבלה מלכא שפחה מטרוניתא. מקרא בעשי׳ כו׳ קבלה באצי׳ תושב״כ. שבע״פ. גודל בירור הלכה. ע״י תחתונים דוקא. כל העוסק בת. כו׳ כאלו פדאני כו׳) **דכט** (מעלת תושבע״פ אחעט״ב. מוסר אביך תורת אמך. תושב״כ שבע״פ) **הא** (התקשרות ע״י ת״ת) **הג** (ת. בכונה. שלא בכונה. תפלה בכונה. שלא בכונה. ת. שלא לשמה או סתם) **הד** (ת. ודו״ר) **הה** (הת. נצחית) **הו** (זמירות היו לי חקיך. ת. ועולמות. פנים ואחור דת. ואהי׳ אצלו שעשועים גו׳). עיי״ע כונה. לשמה. מקרא. תומ״צ.

תומ״צ:

אד (מדו״מ דתומ״צ ונר״נ. צמצום אוא״ס בהם) **אה** (מזון. לבוש) **אכג** (איברים או כ״ח). **אכה** (קיומם תלוי בזכרון מס״נ) **אלז** (ת״ת כנגד כולם. לא המדרש עיקר כו׳) **אלט** (תומ״צ ונשמות) **אמא** (עסק

בת. ־ מס״נ.) בה (מזון, לבוש) די (רובם בשיעור מצומצם. שיעור ציצית תפילין לולב סוכה שופר מקוה קרבנות צד־קה) דיג (ימין שמאל בקיום התומ״צ). דך (בז״א, במל׳, ו׳, ה׳, מו״ס, גולגלתא) דכו (בזמה״ז עיקרם בירור ניצו־צות, לע״ל ליחד יחודים) הד (תורה, מצות, תפלה) הה (בזמה״ז עיקרם סו״מ בירור ניצוצות, לע״ל עשה טוב לייחד יחודים) עיי״ע כונה, מצות.

תושי׳ : דכב (תורה).

תחה״מ : אלו. דיז.

תשב״ר : הג.

תכלית :

אלג (ת. הבריאה דירה בתחתו־נים) אלה (ת. בריאת הבינו־נים) אלו (ת. הבריאה דירה בתחתונים׳ אמט (ת. ההשתל׳ יאכפיא כו׳) בז (ת. ברה״ע) דז (ת. ההשתל׳ ־ האדם) הד (ת. ההשתל׳ המשכת העליון ולא עלית התחתון).

תלמיד :

דכז (ב׳ הארות מהצדיק לתלמידיו).

ת״ח :

אב (ת״ח, ע״ה) אכז (שעה ו׳ מאכל ת״ח) דכו (ת״ח, ע״ה).

תמיד, קרבן התמיד :

גיא.

תמיד עיני ה״א גו׳ שנה :

דיד.

תמכי אורייתא : דה.

תענוג : דכט (ת., רצון, שכל).

תענית : גא. גב. גג. גז. הט.

תפארת :

דיב (סתם שם הוי׳. קו ה־מכריע. כלול מאודם ולובן). עיי״ע ספירות.

תפילין : אמא. דכט.

תפיסא : אה (ל׳ ת. כו׳).

תפלה :

איא (שעת מוחין דגדלות) אכג (יחוד עולמות עליונים) אלח (ת. וכונתה) אלט (באצי׳. השתחואות שבשמו״ע) אמא (אלקי נשמה כו׳) גב (על ביטול ת. ס״א תעניות) גי (תורה, ת.) גיא (סלח לנו כו׳ המרבה לסלוח, גואל ישראל. השיבנו כו׳. כנגד תמידין תקנום) דא (עת רצה״ע) דז (זמן הארת כו׳) דח (יהיב פרוטה לעני והדר מצלי. תשו״ע) דיב (גילוי אלקות. בירור. מצרף לכסף גו׳) דכב (להתחזק נגד כל מונע) דכד (שלא לשוח שיחה בטלה) דכו, הג (ת. בכונה, שלא בכ־

מפתח שמות ספרים ואנשים

— שאחר זמן המשנה —

שנזכרו בלקוטי אמרים

בהוספות איזה ביטויים אי רגילים

זח"ב רמה: רא: זח"א רכ"ג: פקודי. ויקהל. זח"ב רנ"ב. רמז. רי. רנ"ה:) הד (ר"מ משפטים. פקודי) הו (אד"ר).

זהר ר"מ־בלי ציון:
אהקדמה. אב. אד. אז. אט. אי. איב. אטז. אכב. אכג. אכד. אכו. אכט. אלא. אלד. אלט. אמ. אמא. אמב. אמד אמו. אמז. אן. אנב. אנג. בהקדמה. בא. בד. בה. בז. בט. גא. גד. גז. גט. גיא. גיב. דג. דה. דו. דח. די. דיב. דטו. דיח. דיט. דכא. דכג. דכד. דכה. דכו. דכז. דכח. דכט. הה. הו. עיי"ע לשון, תיקונים.

זהר חדש: אב.

חיים, רח"ו:
אא. אמ (ב"פ) הח. עיי"ע ע"ח, פרע"ח.

חיל אשר נגע יראת ה' בלי־בם: דל.

חכמים:
בז (ח. בעיניהם) דה (ידוע לכל ח. לב) דכב (ספרי חכמי ישראל). עיי"ע אמת, טבעים, מוסר, קבלה.

חסידים, ס' ח.: אמב. גא.

חרדים, ס' ח.: אלב.

טבעים: אג (וכמ"ש הט).

טועמים מעץ החיים: אמח.

טושו"ע:
אח (הל' ת"ת) אכד (יו"ד סי' ב') אלד (הל' ת"ת) אמא (בש"ע) אמב (ש"ע או"ח ס"א) בהקדמה (א"ח שמ"ג) גא (ח"מ ססי' ל"ד) גג (מ"א הל' תע־נית) דא (ש"ע א"ח) דכג (כנ"ל).

טעמ"צ: אב.

יודא ועוד לקרא:
אהקדמה. בו.

הוי':
בז (ה' יכפר בעדם) דלא (ה"י).

יודעי חן:
אז. אח. איג. אטז. אלח. אלט. אמב. אמג. אנג. בד. גו. דיג. דיד. דיט. דכה (ג"פ) דכט (ב"פ).

יודעים:
אכט (כידוע לי.) אמא (כנ"ל) בהקדמה (ידוע לי.) דכו (לי.).

ילקוט:
דכח (ילקוט פ' שמיני).

יצחק, האריז"ל:
אב (ב"פ) אז. אכו (ב"פ) אלא. אמו. אמח. אן. בא. בב. בז (כתהאריז"ל) גב. גג (ב"פ) גה. גיב (ב"פ) דה (ב"פ) דח (כתהאריז"ל) דיז (לקוטי

שכל:
אמח (ולקרב אל הש.) אמט (לקרב אל ש. הדל) דטו (ולק־רב קצת אל הש.).
שלמה, רשב"א: אמט.
שלמה, רש"י:
בד. גג. גי. גיא. דכב. דכג.
שמעתי: אהקדמה. אלה.
שער היחודים: אמ. הג. הד.
שער הנבואה:
אמ. בב. בה. דיט. הא.
שער הקדושה: אא.
ש"ס — מקום שנסמנה המס':
אא (נדה. אבות. ברכות. ב"ב. יבמות. נדה. שבועות) אב (נדה) איא (אבות) אל (ב"ב) אלב (שבת) אלה (סנה') אלז (תלמוד ירושלמי) אלח (בר־כות) אן (חגיגה) אנג (ברכות) גא (יומא. סנה') גב (זבחים) גג (זבחים. תענית. זבחים. ירו־שלמי) גד (זבחים) גט (ר"ה) גיא (ב"ק. יבמות) דטז (נד־רים. קדושין) דך (ירושלמי) דכב (סנה') דכו (ירוש' פ"ק דברכות) דכט (מגילה. מנחות) הה (חולין) הו (ירוש' שק־לים).

תורה:
אכה (במשנה ת.) דא (כמ"ש בת. משה) דכו (ת. משה).
תנ"ך־מקום שנסמן:
אל (הושע) אמו (שה"ש) בה־קדמה (עקב) גא (נצבים. יואל מג"א) גב (ישעי') גד (ירמי') גה (ישעי'. אמור) גיא (עזרא) דה (קהלת) דו (משלי) דכב (ישעי') דכה (וירא) דכט (דניאל) הו (זכרי') הז (עמוס) הט (תילים).
ת"כ: גב.
תיקונים, ת"ז:
אי. איד. אכג. אכז. אלד. אלו. אלז. אלט (ב"פ) אמ (בתי' מ"ה. ב"פ) אמא. אמד (ב"פ). אנא. אנב (ב"פ) בז (תי' נז'). די. גא (בת"ז) גט. דה (ב"פ) דכו (בריש תי') דכז. דכט. דלא. דלב. הא. הה. הו.
תדב"א: גט.
תנן, תניא:
אא (תניא בספ"ג דנדה) אמ (כדתנן) בי (כדתנן בס' יצי־רה).
תרגום:
דיט (וכתרגום וירא גו').

לוח התיקון[1]

דף	עמוד	שורה המתחל בתיבת	נדפס	צריך להיות
א	א	היטב	מאד	**מאוד**
ג	א	אחר שורה	ימצא. בתניא הוצאת שקלאו תקע״ד: היום יום ה׳ כ״ב אייר תקע״ד לפ״ק	**בתניא הוצאת שקלאו תקע״ד:**
	ב	זה	שכל	**ומתעורר שכל**
		ששים	כללות ישראל ופרטיהם	**נשמות כללות ישראל ופרטיהם ופרטי פרטיהם**
ד	א	שבמדינותינו	שבמדינותינו	**שבמדינתינו**
	ב	מיום	ותבא	**ותבוא עליהם**
ה	ב	ומ״ש	בזוהר	**בזהר**
		אליהו	הפי׳	**פי׳**
		נשמות	דכתיב	**וכדכתיב**
ו	א	משא״כ	עובדי גלולים	**העולם**
		טיבו	עובדי גלולים	מיותר
		וחסד	עובדי גלולים	**העולם**
		נשמת	בזוהר	**בזהר**
		בנשמו׳	על	**מעל**
ז	ב	בשוליו	ועוד	**פרק ד**
ח	א	בשוליו	כו׳	**וכו׳**
יא	א	כל	עובדי גלולים	**העולם**
	ב	עולם	רובו ככולו . . בתוכה [שממנה	**בהוצאה הא׳:** רובו ככולו . . בתוכו * (שממנה. **ועדיין צ״ע**
יב	א	צריך	לקמן מה	**לקמן וכן החיות שבטפות זרע שיצאו ממנו בתאוה בהמית שלא קדש עצמו בשעת תשמיש עם אשתו טהורה מה ****
	ב	היא	עו״ג	**העולם**

---

1) הערה כללית:
מודפס בזה לוח התיקון כללי — אעפ״י שאפשרי שבכמה דפוסים נתקנו כבר בפנים.

הערת המו״ל:

*) **שוב ראיתי שבלוח הטעות שם נתקן שצ״ל** בתוכה.

) **ראה טעמי מצות להרח״ו ס״פ בראשית.

דף	עמוד	שורה המתחלת בתיבת	נדפס	צריך להיות
יג	א	לגמרי	[לבדו]	לקמן בשורה המתחלת כף איתא „לבדו" בלא חצאי מרובע. וכנראה הטעם, כי בהוצאה ה־ראשונה נשמטה תיבה זו רק כאן.
		אומות	עובדי גלולים	העולם
		טומאתה	עובדי גלולים	מיותר
	ב	כן	עובדי גלולים	מיותר
טו	א	לה'	אינו	אינה
טז	א	מלמעלה	כל	אכל
		בשוליו	והבינוני	פרק יב
יז	א	בכל	ומעשה תרי"ג	ומעשה של תרי"ג
	ב	בשוליו	ובזה	פרק יג
כ	א	במ"א	וכו'	כו'
כא	ב	שבמוחו	שבמוחו לשלוט	שבמוח ולשלוט
כג	א	דהיינו	כשהאדם	כשאדם
	ב	מאבותינו	להקדי' ולבאר	לבאר ולהקדי'
		בשוליו	ולפעמים	[ולפעמים
כו	א	עוה"ז	אינן	אינם
		כשמדבר	דבר	דבור
		ללמוד	איזו מאכל	איזה מאכל
	ב	המאכל	נולדה	נולדו
כז	ב	וירידת	נקרא	נקראים
כט	ב	תחתונים	תחתונים	תחתונות
לא	א	נקראים	נקראים	נקראות
	ב	בעבודת	שהוא	שהיא
לב	ב	פרק	לאודעי	לאודועי
לג	א	ומעלה	אין	לאין
		ממילי	לפטר	ליפטר
לה	ב	המתפלל	עו"ג	ערל
לז	ב	אומות	עכו"ם	העולם
לח	ב	ברכת	ברכת	ברכות

דף	עמוד	שורה המתחלת בתיבת	נדפס	צריך להיות
מב	א	ממש וזה	ובריאות	ובריאת
	ב	שהנחילנו	שהנחילנו	שהנחילונו
		ובפרט	ובפרט בארצות עו״ג שאוירם	ובפרט בחו״ל שאויר ארץ העמים
מה	א	הנעשים	הנעשים	הנעשות
		הבהמית	הרעים	הרעות
		בבחי׳	ושכינתא	דשכינתא
	ב	בשוליו	יתברך	ית׳
נא	ב	בשוליו	להוסיף	לבדן
נד	א	בשוליו	להוסיף	אי •
נו	ב	לבדו	ולכלול	ליכלל
נט	א	בשוליו	כופרים	סופרים
סט	ב	סידרו	ברכות	ברכת
עא	ב	שמהותה	אינה	אינו
עב	א	שההשפעה	והמשכות	והמשכת
עד	א	ק״ק	שהיא	שהוא •
עה	א	ומיוחד	ומעשה תרי״ג	ומעשה של תרי״ג
עו	ב	בתוך	השמים	המים •
עז	ב	בשוליו	והנה	פרק ג
פה	ב	בשוליו	צ״ל	אותיות
פח	ב	של	ממדרגות	ממדרגת
צ	ב	בתחלתו	צ״ל: לקוטי אמרים חלק שלישי הנקרא בשם	
		כמ״ש	וכו׳	וגו׳
צא	א	אל	וכו׳	וגו׳
		ושמעת	וכו׳ .. וכו׳	וגו׳ .. וגו׳
		ה׳	וכו׳ .. וכו׳	וגו׳ .. וגו׳
		בשבט	וכו׳	וגו׳
		בעוה״ז	וכו׳	וגו׳
		וכו׳	וכו׳	וגו׳
		כו׳	כו׳	וגו׳
צג	ב	מ״ש	וכו׳	וגו׳
צד	א	וכמ״ש	כו׳	גו׳
		האלקי׳	כו׳ .. כו׳	גו׳ .. גו׳
צה	א	אורך	המורה ההמשכה	המורה על ההמשכה

•) בהוצאה זו נתקן.

דף	עמוד	שורה המתחלת בתיבת	נדפס	צריך להיות
צו	א	וחיות	הנשפעת	הנשפעות
צז	א	וכו׳	וכו׳	וגו׳
		בחי׳	וגם [גרם]	וגרם
	ב	לא	כו׳	וגו׳
		דבר	כו׳	וגו׳
צח	א	רחמיך	וכו׳	וגו׳
		כמ״ש	כמ״ש	וסט״א כמ״ש
	ב	לאהבה	וכו׳	וגו׳
		רוחא	וכו׳	וגו׳
צט	א	וכו׳	וכו׳	וגו׳
		יכופר	וכו׳	וגו׳
		כו׳	כו׳ .. וכו׳	וגו׳ .. וגו׳
		והיו	וכו׳ .. וכו׳	וגו׳ .. וגו׳
ק	א	ל״ד	בזוה״ק	בזה״ק
	ב	כתיב	וכו׳	וגו׳
		תסמכני	וכו׳	וגו׳
קא	א	וכמארז״ל	הנעלבים	הנעלבין
קב	א	חגרה	הם דבר	הם בחי׳ דבר
	ב	מחכמה	הוא	היא
קג	ב	כל	וזו	וזו היא
קיב	א	בשוליו	זורע	ח זורע
	ב	בשוליו	נ״א	[נ״א
קיג	א	שבלב	שהוא	שהיא
קיד	א	דעבדין	כעוע״ג	ככל הגוים
		ובניו	התורה. ע״כ	התורה חוץ מצדיקים שבדור שהן קודמין לבניו וצדיקים שבא״י קודמין לצדיקים ש־בחו״ל לבד מזאת שלא הניחו כמותן בחו״ל וד״ל. ע״כ

דף	עמוד	שורה המתחלת בתיבת	נדפס	צריך להיות
קטו	א	הצדקה	שהוא	שהיא
קטז	ב	מתחת	עו"ג	הגוים
קכב	ב	בבליות	נקרא	נקראים
קכג	ב	לדבוק	לדבוק	לידבק
קכז	א	בבחי'	המלובשת	המתלבשים
	ב	בפנימיות	המלובשת	המלובשים
		נגלה	אליהם הוי' הנעלם ב"ה בבחי'	הגהת הצ"צ: עליהם * הוי' בבחי'
קל	א	שיצאו	נשמת	נשמות
		לומר	דיתבא	דיתבין
קלג	א	העולה	עליהם	אליהם **
קלד	א	לא	אוכל משא	אוכל מלט משא
קלז	א	בשולי הע'	פרק	כד אהוביי
קלח	א	אינה	צוואתו ולא	הגהת הצ"צ: צוואתו כלל ולא
קלט	א	כח	זה	זו
		מבחי'	באפיו	הגהת הצ"צ: באפיו נשמת חיים
	ב	(אלא	שבארצות העו"ג	שבחו"ל
		נשפע	לעו"ג	לאומות
		נשפעי'	העו"ג	האומות
		בארצות	בארצות עו"ג	בחו"ל
		אלקות	העו"ג	הגוים
קמ	ב	נמשכות	העו"ג	האומות
		ולהשליטם	ולהשליטם בזמן	ולהשליטם עתה בזמן
		העו"ג	העו"ג היו שולטין על העו"ג	האומות שולטין עתה על האומות
		והעו"ג	והעו"ג	והאומות
		הזה	לעו"ג	לאומות

*) הערת המו"ל: כן הוא בכת"י המעתיק (גוף כתי"ק הצ"צ אינו). ואולי טעה וצ"ל: אליהם. וכמוש"כ באגה"ק לפני זה: אליו.

**) בהוצאה זו נתקן.

דף	עמוד	שורה המתחילת בתיבת	נדפס	צריך להיות
קמא	א	אבל	עו״ג	נכרי
		ובכוונה	העו״ג	הנכרי
		עו״ג	עו״ג	נכרי
		ובפרט	עו״ג	נכרי
	ב	העו״ג	העו״ג	הנכרים
קמג	א	איסורין	יהי׳	יהיו
	ב	טמא	שהרי .. שדות	הגהת הצ״צ: דהא גם בזמן ב״ש לא היו מתפרנסין מע״ה דאכ־לין פסול אסור ח״ו שהרי ת״ח היו להם שדות
קמה	א	מבין	עו״ג	העולם
	ב	כז מה	אה״ק תובב״א	ט״ס כי נכתב לאנ״ש שבחו״ל.
קמח	א	והנה	כו׳ והוא תיקון ונוצר אותיות רצון והיא ג״כ עת	הוא תיקון נוצר חסד נוצר אותיות רצון והיא עת
קמט	א	בסוף עמוד	אשתאר	דאשתאר
	ב	שהצער	תענוג	התענוג
קנב	א	חיות	זו	זה
		לבריאות	לבריאות	לבריאת
קנג	א	מאור	סובב	הסובב
קנה	ב	גבורה	וברחמים. כו׳	וברחמים כו׳. *
קנו	ב	היא	רבה	רמה **
קנח	ב	ע״י	העולת	העולה
קנט	א	וכו׳	וד״ל	וד״ל: *
קנט	ב	דיצי׳	עשי׳	ועשי׳
קס	א	מתפרטים	מתפרטים	מתפרשים
	כ	מחשבה	עליונה	העליונה

*) בהוצאה זו נתקן.

**) ראה ג״כ מאמרי אדה״ז אתהלך — לאזניא ע׳ קסה ובהערה שם.

לוח התיקון

דף	עמוד	שורה המתחי־לת בתיבת	נדפס	צריך להיות
קסא	**א**	**וזש״ה**	**אצלו**	**אצלו כו׳**
			שעשועים	**שעשועים**
		ויחודו	**פנימיות**	**פנימית**
	ב	**אור**	**נקודה**	**נקודת**
		השפעה	**גשמיות**	**גשמיית**
קסב	**א**	**מִצות**	**כו׳ . . כו׳**	**גו׳ . . גו׳**
קסג	**א**	**שבוע**	**אפי׳**	**אפי**
		בהלכתא	**רבתא**	**רבתי**
		הוא	**הוא**	**היא**

הערות ותיקונים

בדרך אפשר

דף	עמוד	שורה המתחי־לת בתיבת	נדפס	הערה בדרך אפשר
ג	א	**מרנא**	**מרנא**	**כבוד מרנא**
		ונאום משה	**החסיד**	**החסיד מרנא**
	ב	**ואורייתא**	**בזה״ק הרי**	**בזה״ק. הרי**
ד	א	**הנהגתן**	**כנודע וכ״ש**	**כנודע. וכ״ש**
		סופרים	**אצלינו וקצת**	**אצלינו. וקצת**
		ואחד	**מצויה על**	**מצויה. על**
		שיחתו	**יבוננהו ואליהם**	**יבוננהו. ואליהם**
	ב	**שלא**	**הקונטרסים הנ״ל**	**בהוצאת שקלאוו תקס״ו:** הס׳ לק״א וס׳ אגרת התשובה.
		דברי	**ליקוטי**	**לקוטי**
ה	א	**ליקוטי**	**ליקוטי**	**לקוטי —** וכן בכל שאר העמודים **(וכמו שנכתב בשער הספר).**
	ב	**(ומ״ש**	**(ומ״ש .. לתו־רה)**	**לכאורה החצע״ג ותי־בת „הגהה״ — בהגהה זו ובאותן הבאות לק־מן — מיותרות, כי־ון שנדפסו ההגהות מן הצד ובאיתיות שונות. ובכמה מקו־מות בהוצאה זו עצ־מה ההגהות הן בלא חצע״ג. ובדפוסים ה־ראשונים כמה הג־הות הן בלא חצע״ג וגם בלא תיבת „הגהה״.**
		על	**בשער**	**בשערי**
		היא	**מארבע**	**מארבעה**
ח	א	**מלובשים**	**התורה ובפרטות**	**התורה. ובפרטות**
		רמ״ח	**אחר והיראה**	**אחר. והיראה**
		מלכי	**הקב״ה. או**	**הקב״ה או**

דף	עמוד	שורה המתחילה בתיבת	נדפס	הערה בדרך אפשר
		אף	**ונשמה עם**	**ונשמה. עם**
	ב	**מחשבותיכם**	**מחשבותיכם הנה**	**מחשבותיכם. הנה**
		חכמינו	**ז״ל בכדי**	**ז״ל. בכדי**
		ספרים	**וכתובים כדי**	**וכתובים. כדי**
		ממדריגת	**בהן ומאחר**	**בהן. ומאחר**
ט	א	**השכל**	**והשכילו וגם**	**והשכילו. וגם**
		במושכל	**בשכלו ד״מ**	**בשכלו. ד״מ**
	ב	**הערוכות**	**בהם והוא**	**בהם. והוא**
י	א	**המשכלת**	**ולימודה וכל**	**ולימודה. וכל**
		שבע	**מארבע**	**מארבעה**
	ב	**בשעת**	**מחשבה והן**	**מחשבה. והן**
		להיות	**שנברא ולכן**	**שנברא. ולכן**
יא	ב	**שהוא**	**מארבע**	**מארבעה**
יד	ב	**היראה**	**לבדו וכל**	**לבדו. וכל**
		ותורתו	**הגירסא וכח**	**הגירסא. וכח**
		המצות	**האלהית אך**	**האלהית. אך**
טו	א	**כדכתיב**	**חקרני**	**בכתוב תהלים קלט כג:** חקרני א־ל. **אבל בכ״מ בדא״ח לא העתיקו השם כשהובא הכתוב.**
		הרע	**מאחת מארבע**	**מאחד מארבעה**
יז	א	**תאות**	**בר״מ**	**בהגהות המיוחסות להצ״צ מציין לזח״ג רכד סע״א. וא״כ צ״ל כאן:** בזהר
		שמהקליפה	**ממקומו**	**ממקומה**
	ב	**ודומיהן**	**ואדרבה**	**בדפוסים הראשונים — כאן ובעוד מקומות בתניא — ואדרבא. ובש״ס נמצא הן באל״ף והן בה״א.**

דף	עמוד	שורה המחח־לת בתיבת	נדפס	הערה בדרך אפשר
יט	א	שפת ערכה	שקר ואעפ״כ ומדרגת׳ כי	שקר. ואעפ״כ ומדרגת׳. כי
	ב	אופן	מבדילים	היו מבדילים [כן הוא באגה״ת פ״ה מישעי׳ נט, ב]
כ	א	תורה	נביאים כו׳ צדיקים	כנראה הוא ע״פ גירסת הכסא מלך בת״ז — בהקדמה א, ב: מארי תורה נבי־אים חווים צדיקים.
		מואס	חמת מלאה	לקמן חמת מלא — וראה שבת קנב, א. וברש״י שם.
כא	א	פרקו	ואחד	לקמן ואחת. וראה ב׳ הגירסות בש״ס ועין יעקב. ועייג״כ הל׳ ת״ת לאדה״ז פ״ב ס״ג. לקו״ת ראה ביאור לד״ה אחרי ס״ו.
כה	א	חוטא כהמס	כו׳ אלא נמסו והנה	כו׳. אלא נמסו. והנה *
כח	א	כנשר	יאור לי ואני עשיתני	חבור שני כתובים: יחזקאל כט, ט ושם כט, ג. וכן הוא בקונ־טרס ומעין מאמר ג׳ פ״ב — בגכתי״ק. וכן צריך לתקן בהנדפס. — וצ״ע הטעם. אבל בסי׳ בהערה לתקון

*) בהוצאה זו נתקן.

דף	עמוד	שורה המתחלת בתיבת	נדפס	הערה בדרך אפשר
				חצות, בלקו״ת ביאור לד״ה זאת חקת ס״ד. שם שה״ש עוד בי׳ יונתי ס״ב: לי יאורי ואני עשיתני. בהוצאה הא׳: עשיתוני (!).
כט	ב	וז״ש	ה׳ את	צ״ע כי בכתוב (דברים ו, כד) הוא: ה׳ לעשות את.
ל	א	עצמן	באחדותו אבל	באחדותו. אבל
		ממיתה	ישמרנו וההפרש	ישמרנו. וההפרש
	ב	ורמשים	ע״ז ומה	ע״ז. ומה
לא	ב	לעשות	צ״ל: [ואף .. התשובה]	
לב	א	העליון	צ״ל: [והיינו .. לעבודת ה׳]	
לד	א	אין	כאלו כי	כאלו. כי
	ב	אותו	מלמעלה לבד	מלמעלה. לבד
לה	ב	מה	באולתו	כאולתו
לז	א	עולה	ה׳ נקי	דילוג בל׳ הכתוב (תהלים כד, ג־ד).
לח	א	ליכנס	לארץ אלא	לארץ. אלא
		הם	מאמינים ומזה	מאמינים. ומזה
		כאש	להבה וגו׳	צ״ע בתיבה זו, כי הוא סוף פסוק.
	ב	המוח	שהיא	לכאורה צ״ל היא.
לט	ב	ויצה״ר	הדינים נמתקין ... ולא בשרשן	לכאורה צ״ל סיום כולם שוה במ״ם או בנו״ן.
מ	ב	ומנוסי	והוא מנוס לי	צ״ע מקומו.
מא	ב	כנודע	ממ״ש ליעקב	כן הוא ג״כ לקמן ספמ״ה, בקו״א ד״ה וצדקה כנחל ובכ״מ בדא״ח. ועיין לקו״ת

דף	עמוד	שורה המתחי־לת בתיבת	נדפס	הערה בדרך אפשר
				ד״ה מה יפו פ״א. אבל בקרא (ישעי׳ כ״ט, כב): לבית יעקב. ובכמה מדרז״ל (סנה׳ יט, ב. ועוד) מוכח דהכוונה ליעקב עצמו.
מב	א	ודירת	זה אשר ערב לבו	בקרא (ירמי׳ ל, כא) זה ערב את לבו
	ב	כאלו	אינה	אינם
מו	א	כמ״ש	לנו תורת	בשמו״ע: לנו ה׳ אלקינו תורת. וראה הערה לדף טו, א.
	ב	יחדיו	בנקרת .. והדר	בקרא (ישעי׳ ב, כא) בנקרות .. ומהדר
		עוזך	וגו׳	כ״ה בכל הדפוסים אף שאינו פסוק. אבל יודע אשר בכ״מ בזהר ות״ז נמצא „דכתיב״, „שנאמר״ על הנמצא בתפלות וברכות וראה ג״כ תוד״ה נשים (בר־כות כ, א). ואולי לכן גם בזה נאמר וגו׳ ולא וכו׳ אף דאין שייך בזה הטעם דכל פסוקי דלא פסקי׳ משה כו׳
		וכיוצא	בהם ועכשיו	בהם. ועכשיו
מז	א	שם	ית׳ וכן	ית׳. וכן

דף	עמוד	שורה המתחי־לת בתיבת	נדפס	הערה בדרך אפשר
		בכל	איברים משתמרת	בעירובין (נד, א): איברים שלך משתמ־רת
		זאת	המתלבשת	לכאורה: צ״ל: המת־לבש, כיון דקאי על כח, וכדמסיים גידולו וחיותו
מח	א	היא מארבע	ביניהן ונמצא מארבע	ביניהן. ונמצא מארבעה
מט	א	ברבבות	בהארת . . המתלבשות	לכאורה צ״ל: בל׳ יחיד או בל׳ רבים.
נ	א	בו	בו	בהם
	ב	בו	ית׳ ולא	ית׳. ולא
נא	א	מדרגות	מדרגות כי	מדרגות. כי
	ב	בו	סור	סר
נב	א	בדחילו	הנמשכות	בספט״ז ובכ״מ הוא בל׳ זכר.
		ובינתו	הבריאה ומה	הבריאה. ומה
נד	ב	שמקבלים	כבתחתונים	כהתחתונים
נה	א	הכוונה	כו׳	צ״ע מה מוסיף בזה.
	ב	כלל	ניטלו	במשנה (חולין נו, ב): נשתברו גפי׳, דין דניטלו אגפי׳ בב״ח וט״ז שו״ע יו״ד ר״ס נג.
נז	א	תעבודו רבן	וכמ״ש בזהר שיהא	בשינוי ל׳ קצת. בברכות כח, ב: שתהא
נח	ב	נשמה	ואתה נפחתה	אתה נפחתה
נט	א	חפיצה	ילמדו איש	בירמי׳ לא, לג: ילמדו עוד איש. וכ״ה בהק־דמת התניא.

דף	עמוד	שורה המתחי־לת בתיבת	נדפס	הערה בדרך אפשר
ס	א	מחשבתו	ממש	צ״ע הכוונה בזה.
	ב	כמ״ש	בפרד״ס	בפרדס. וכ״ה בהג״ה בפ״ב ובשהיחוה״א פ״ז.
סא	א	המאמן	וכו׳	צ״ע הכוונה בזה.
		עליך	וכו׳	צ״ע הכוונה בזה.
	ב	העולמות	נקרא	בדפוס הא׳: נקר׳, בדפוס השני: נק׳. ונ״ל דצ״ל: נקראת
		התורה	בשת	חסר וא״ו, ע״פ ת״ז (תי׳ ז. כח). ובכ״מ — מלא וא״ו (לעיל פ״מ, מא ועוד).
סג	א	בכל	לאנהרא לון	צ״ע מקומו בתיקונים. וראה זח״ג רטז, ב. רעג, א.
סד	א	השמימה	וכו׳ . . וכו׳	וגו׳ . . וגו׳.
סה	א	מ״ש	אל האדם	כ״ה גם בתו״א צ״ח, ד ובכתוב (משלי כז, יט): לאדם, וכ״כ בלקו״ת נשא (כט, א) שה״ש (לא, ד)
	ב	רבבן	כו׳	גו׳
		דרועין	וכו׳	צ״ע הכוונה בזה.
סו	ב	וסקילה	זו. וגם	זו וגם
סז	ב	ולהחיותם	מאין. כי	מאין כי
		לגבי	ערך	לכאורה מיותר.
		מלמעלה	שהוא	שהיא
סח	א	מתלבש	מתלבש	מתלבשת
		והמשל	הגשמיות	הגשמית

דף	עמוד	שורה המתחלת בתיבת	נדפס	הערה בדרך אפשר
		מתגלית	משפיע	משפיעה
		דכתיב	כו'	גו'
סח	ב	המיוחדת	ועצמותו. כי	ועצמותו כי
		ולא	האדם. כי	האדם כי
		נמצאים	ית'. ודבר	ית' ודבר
		בפרד"ס	בפרד"ס	בפרדס
		פרק	ההסתר וההעלם	ההסתר והעלם
סט	א	רבבות	פרטיים	פרטים
		והחיונית	ולבושיה	ולבושיהן. וכ"ה בפרק מ"א (נז, ב).
		לצד	לצד אחד	לצדדין (כי הסילוק הי' לכל הצדדין בשוה).
		אהבת	דוחקת הבשר	דוחקת את הבשר
		וחפיצה	ומבחוץ	ומחוץ
	ב	כו'	כו'	אולי מרבה גם אותן דערבית.
		כו'	להם	להן
		ק"ש ולמה	דווקא	נמצא בש"ס גם בשני ואוי"ן.
		ק"ש לקיים	לבבך כו'	קאי אמתניתין (ברכות ט, ה) ולכן כו' ולא גו'
		קדוש	מהן .. בהן	מהם .. בהם
		אברהם	דוחקת הבשר	דוחקת את הבשר
		נקרא	נקרא	נקראת
ע	א	לזה	כו' .. כו'	גו' .. גו'
		ולדרים	ולדרים בבחי'	ולדרים עלי' בבחי'

דף	עמוד	שורה המתחלת בתיבת	נדפס	הערה בדרך אפשר
		ולדרים	בשר וכו׳ שזהו	**בשר וגו׳ שזהו. ואולי אפ״ל דהכוונה על מש״כ בפל״ו ולא על סיום הכתוב.**
	ב	חסד	נכספת	**נכספתה**
		אהבה	גם	**וגם**
		שהיא	היוצא	**היוצאה**
עא	א	היא	רגלו	**רגליו**
	ב	לומר	שהיא	**שהוא**
עג	א	ק״ק	שהיא	**שהוא**
עד	ב	המלובשת	דעשי׳. ולכן	**דעשי׳ ולכן**
עה	ב	כל	שיתב׳	**מכאן סמוכות לסיפור חסידים שבתחלה סבר רבנו הזקן לסדר שער היחוד והאמונה קודם לחלק הראשון.**
עו	א	הפנים	אל הפנים	**לפנים**
		ולדבקה	שיתבאר	**ראה לעיל בהערה לע׳ עה, ב.**
		כהונתכם	שיתבאר	**ראה לעיל בהערה לע׳ עה, ב.**
	ב	להבין	כו׳	**גו׳**
		מסתלקת	כרגע	**לרגע**
		ממש	כרגע	**לרגע**
עח	ב	ולמה	אינן	**אינם**
		הבריות	כמארז״ל	**בנדרים ח, ב — בשי־נוי ל׳ קצת.**
עט	ב	כידוע	ל״ח	**לי״ח]**
פג	א	שחוץ	עכ״ל	**אפ״ל גם אם הוא בשי־נוי ל׳ קצת (מובא בשם הרמ״א בד״מ).**

דף	עמוד	שורה המתחילת בתיבת	נדפס	הערה בדרך אפשר
פד	**ב**	**ברואים**	**שמדריגות .. ממדריגות**	**שמדרגת .. ממדריגת**
		ירד	**מועט .. שיוכל**	**מועטת .. שתוכל**
פו	**א**	**שהוא**	**החיות**	**חיות**
פח	**א**	**כולן**	**בתיקונים**	**בשינוי ל' מהנוסחא שהועתקה בסידור.**
צ	**ב**	**פרק**	**בסוף יומא**	**פו, א. בשינוי ל' קצת.**
		המלך	**וכו'**	**צ"ע מה מוסיף.**
		יוכל	**ערבית או**	**בש"ס (ברכות כו, א): ערבית וק"ש**
צא	**א**	**באתערותא**	**וכו'**	**כנראה קאי על הענין (ראה סמ"ו) ולא על הכתוב. ולכן ל"כ** וגו'.
		וכו'	**בצום**	**ביואל (ב, יב): ובצום. וראה ר"ח שער התשובה רפ"ד.**
	ב	**במקום**	**בגמרא**	**ברכות יז, א. בשינוי לשון.**
צב	**ב**	**בעד**	**ג"פ**	**פירושו: גדולים פוליש**
צד	**א**	**וכו'**	**וכו'**	**וגו'**
	א	**וכמ"ש**	**אלקיכם אלקי**	**אלקיכם הוא אלקי (דברים י, יז).**
	ב	**וכו'**	**אנת חכים .. אנת מבין**	**בנוסחא שבסידור אנת הוא חכים .. אנת הוא מבין**
צה	**א**	**בקול**	**וכו'**	**צ"ע למה מרמז.**
צז	**ב**	**פשעיך בעקביו**	**המבדילים המבדילים**	**לכאורה צ"ל: המבדילות. ואולי הוא ע"פ**

דף	עמוד	שורה המתחי־לת בתיבת	נדפס	הערה בדרך אפשר
				ל׳ הכתוב: עונותיכם היו מבדילים.
צח	א	באות	וכו׳	צ״ע למה מרמז.
צט	א	בתורה	בסוף	צע״ק שהוא ד׳ דפים לפני סוף הפרק.
		דחסד	וכו׳	צ״ע מה מוסיף.
		כמ״ש	כמ״ש	לכאורה פי׳ כמו שאומרים, אבל בהוצ־את שקלאו תקס״ו „כמה שכתוב״. וראה לעיל הערה לדף מו, ב.
ק	א	בעזרא	דהיינו	היינו — ועד״ז הוא במהדו״ק.
	ב	חנון	תפלה . . תקנוה	בש״ס (ברכות כו, ב) תפלות . . תקנום
קג	ב	בחי׳	אנכי	ואנכי
קה	א	ממעמקים	(ועד״מ . . כלל) וזלע״ז . . מישר־אל	לכאורה צ״ל: (ועד״מ . . כלל. וזלע״ז . . מישר־אל) — בתניא שקלאוו תקע״ד אין חצע״ג כלל.
		פנימית	פנימית	באגה״ק זו לפעמים חסר וא״ו ולפעמים — מ״ו. וצ״ע אם מדויק הוא.
קז	א	אינן	אינן	אינה
	ב	וביטוי	אחה״ע	לא „אהח״ע״. וי״ל עפמש״כ בזח״ב קכג, א.

דף	עמוד	שורה המתחלת בתיבת	נדפס	הערה בדרך אפשר
קח	א	ממש	שבעה	שבע, וכדמסיים: בונות
		ומלאכים	ונשפע	ונשפע'
קט	ב	ו זורע	זורע	וזורע (כ"ה במשלי יא, יח).
קיא	א	ישראל	כי	לכאורה מיותר.
	ב	הים	מרוב	אינו בהושע ב, א. — ראה בראשית טז, יו"ד.
קיד	א	לגרמייהו	אלקות	אלקה
	ב	לא	וגו'	וכו'
קטז	א	כדכתיב	וכו'	לקמן „וגו'", ושניהם צ"ע כי הוא סוף פסוק.
קיז	א	שבין	כו'	לכאורה מיותר.
		והסתלקות	החיים	החיות
	ב	באורו	מתמזגים ומתמתקים	מתמזגות ומתמתקות
קיח	ב	נתן	וכו'	לכאורה מיותר.
		ובטח	על	בירמי' מח, יא: אל.
קיט	ב	ב"ה	דרך ומדות	הל' צע"ק.
		מזו	הם	הן
		זו	הוא	היא (וכדמסיים: היא מאירה).
קכא	ב	וגרמוהי	חד. משא"כ	חד משא"כ
		בחומר	וגבול. אבל	וגבול אבל
קכב	א	ומדת	לשון	לכאורה מיותר.
		להשפיע	לשון	לכאורה מיותר.
		ולפי	בגדי .. שהוא בגד	צע"ק. בסו"ס חסל"א (לעמברג תר"ך) נדפסה אגרת זו ושם: בגדי .. בגדי'
		בבוא	דהיינו .. בשעת ההשפעה	בד"ה כי ידעתיו סי"ג (אור התורה צח, ב). תיבות אלו אינן.

דף	עמוד	שורה המתחלת בתיבת	נדפס	הערה בדרך אפשר
קכד	א	יראה	יראה בושת	בח״א פ״מ בהגה״ה ופמ״א: ירא בושת. והוא ע״פ ת״ז.
	ב	מלאה	ההכרחיים	ההכרחיות
קכה	ב	בתחייה	וזה	וזהו
		צדיקים	שיאמרו	כ״ה בכ״מ בדא״ח. בב״ב (עה. ב) „שאומרים״.
קכו	א	היא	כו׳	צ״ע מה מרבה.
קכז	ב	בפנימיות	כ״א .. דנהי״מ	צ״ע הכפל.
		צ״ל	ואתגליא	ואתגלי
		וכו׳	אליו הנעלם	אליו הוי׳ הנעלם (וכמו שמסיים).
קכח	ב	(כמ״ש	כמ״ש לעיל	בהעתקה כת״י: כמש״ל. וצ״ע הכוונה.
		[להתלבש]	הם	הוא
		האדם	באיזה .. גשמיות	באיזו .. גשמית
		ומתלבש	גשמיות	גשמיית
קכט	א	דמעשה	תמונת	תמונות
	ב	ומשיג	אצלו	אצלה
קלא	א	ללולב	שנתהפכה	שנהפכה
	ב	דהארה	וכו׳	צ״ע מה מרבה.
		יתר	הנ״ל הארה .. הנ״ל	צע״ק הל׳ והכוונה.
קלב	א	אבל	אבל .. יאמר	לכאורה תיבות אלו מקומם לעיל אחרי תיבת „העשב״. או לקמן אחרי תיבת „פרטיות״.
	ב	יודע	כו׳	לכאורה מיותר.
		ועדיין	ועדיין .. דתורא	בשינוי ל׳ מאשר בש״ס ב״ק עב, א.

דף	עמוד	שורה המתח־לת בתיבת	נדפס	הערה בדרך אפשר
קלג	ב	פרטיות	פרטיות	פרטית
		הנה	פעולת צדקה לחיים	ראה משלי יו״ד טז, יא, יט. וצע״ג.
קלד	א	מנהג	גשמיות	בגשמיות ? גשמיית ?
		דברים	כו׳ ומלכות	„כו״ מיותר (פסחים נד, ב).
		יועץ	כו׳	מיותר.
	ב	מרוב	צואת	את צואת (ישעי׳ ד, ד).
קלה	א	אשר	בתוכחה	בתוכחת
	ב	וע״כ	ולעבדו	לעבדו
קלו	א	שריא	ה׳ עלינו	ה׳ אלקינו עלינו (תהלים צ, יז).
קלז	א	בהל׳	רבתא	רבתי
	ב	לראות	רצונו	ברצונו
קלח	א	ערבית	ערבית ומנחה וכו׳ והעובר	מנחה ערבית*. והעובר
	ב	כאילו	וכו׳	לכאורה מיותר.
		ממש	לו	לכאורה מיותר.
קמ	ב	קיי״ל	לא יצא	דלא יצא. בדפוס תקע״ד: דאינו יוצא.
קמא	א	ובפרט	כו׳. שאז	כו׳ שאז
	ב	כמ״ש	בכהאריז״ל. נמצא	בכהאריז״ל נמצא
		להפשיטן	מגשמיותן כי	מגשמיותן. כי
		ששמעתי	נ״ע אך	נ״ע. אך
קמב	א	ספור	זהרא .. ברחמים ..	בזהר שתח״י: זוהרא .. ברחמי .. שלטא

*) הוספה לאחר זמן:

נ״ל בדא״פ לתרץ הסדר: שחרית ערבית ו(אפילו) מנחה, היינו, אפילו בתפלת מנחה שבאה בהמשך לתפלת שחרית (שלכן אצ״ל אמירת ק״ש עוה״פ), ג״כ כל כך חמורה הפסק שיחה (ואף שמפסיק בפשטות בין ק״ש דשחרית ששייכת גם למנחה — למנחה).

דף	עמוד	שורה המתחלת בתיבת	נדפס	הערה בדרך אפשר
			ישלטו ..	איסור .. לון ..
			אסור .. להון	לון .. וכאלו ..
			.. להון ..	והיתר .. טעמין
			כאלו .. היתר	
			.. טעמי	
	ב	רבותינו	נקרא	נקראת.
קמג	א	ולא	טהרות לנזיקין	לטהרות ונזיקין
		יאיר	אילו לא	בשבת (לג, ב): שאל־מלא לא, אבל ע״פ תוד״ה אלמלא (מגילה כא, א) „לא״ מיותר ע״פ גירסא זו. (וצ״ע בעירובין ק, ב).
	ב	מתפרנסין	אסור	ואסור
		שנעשה	שנעשה	שנעשו
קמד	א	שנפלו	נקרא	נקראת
	ב	דיצירה	צ״ל: (ובריייתות .. שבנוגה)]	
קמה	א	בשבירת	בגמרא	בברכות (ח, א) בשינוי הסדר.
		להמשיך	מהאצילות	שלמעלה מהאצילות
		עליונות	כו׳	לכאורה מיותר.
	ב	שזהו	עבודה	העבודה
		הדברים	והאמת	והאמת האלו
		שהוא	עולם הזה העיקר	„עיקר עוה״ז״ או „עוה״ז בעיקר״, וראה ח״א פל״ז.
קמו	ב	וביראה	וויראת	יראת
		צדקה	ושלשה	ושלש
		האדמה	ושלשה	ושלש
קמז	ב	המאיר	בתיקונים	בזהר *
		לפרה	צ״ל: (הנעשה .. רחמנא)]	

*) לע״ע מצאתי כל הענין בזח״ג רעג, א. וראה ג״כ שם רטז, ב. ובתיקונים (תס״ט קיב, א. קיד, א. ת״ע, קלח, א) מצאתי רק חלק מהמבואר — ואולי טעות המעתיק הוא באגה״ק, ונשתרבב לו ממש״כ בתניא פמ״ד „בתיקונים״.

דף	עמוד	שורה המתחלת בתיבת	נדפס	הערה בדרך אפשר
קמח	א	חסד	עד	ועד
	ב	כללות	כו'	צ"ע מה מוסיף.
		בחי'	כו'	צ"ע מה מוסיף.
קמט	א	בשמש	כו'.	צ"ע מה מוסיף.
		בהון	כו'.	צ"ע מה מוסיף.
	ב	וכו'	וכו'	צ"ע מה מוסיף.
קנ	ב	שבע"פ	תעשה מלאכה	תעשה כל מלאכה
קנא	א	תושבע"פ	אל	ואל
		ל	משארז"ל	ברכות (ו, ב) בשינוי לשון.
קנב	א	תוך	והגידים	ע"י הגידים
		וצור	וצור	צור
	ב	לבבות	כמ"ש	ומ"ש
קנג	א	וזהו	הצדקה	צדקה
	ב	למעלה	וכן	כן
קנד	ב	כמ"ש	פ"ג	פ"ה
קנה	ב	בזוי'	ערך	צ"ע הפי'.
קנו	א	הפרצופים	בנבראים .. בנשמות	לנבראים .. לנשמות
		הגשמיות	והיינו הטעם	והטעם היינו
	ב	מאמרות	העולם) ע"י .. במהות כי	העולם ע"י .. במהות) כי *
		אף	הסוד. אלא מהותה אך	הסוד אלא מהותה. אך
קנז	ב	כלים	מעשיות דוקא ולכן	מעשיות ולכן **
קנח	ב	לבוש	ע"י משנה דיצירה	דיצירה ע"י משנה
קס	א	הבירורין	הנוגעות	הנוגעים
		א"ס	כלא .. דלא	השינוי צ"ע.
קסא	ב	ומאיר	נקודה	נקודת

*) ראה ג"כ מאמרי אדה"ז אתהלך — לאזניא ע' קסד ובהערה שם.
**) ראה שם ע' קסה ובהערה שם.

רשימה קצרה
של כתבי יד ספר התניא*

א. כתב יד ספר התניא מהדורא קמא. ארבעה עמודים. „ה׳ מפני (דף טו ע״א שורה ב)... שמבורריך״ (שם ע״ב שורה יג. ובהוצאתנו שמבוררים). „הלב (יז ע״א שורה ב)... לחבירו״ (שם ע״ב שורה כ. בהוצאתנו לחבירו).
— פאקסימיליא של כת״י זה וביאור אודותו נדפסו לעיל ע׳ 340 ואילך.

ב. מחזיק (9), מו דפים, 16°. „חיים (עו ע״ב שורה יג)... בלבו: (פח ע״ב שורה כד) איתא בר״מ (קמב ע״א שורה יא)... והעבודה שבמקדש: חסר לפענ״ד״ (קמה ע״ב שורה יט. תיבת „שבמקדש״ אינה בנדפס) „קיצור ליקוטי אמרים מלוקט מפי סופרים ומפי ספרים להבין מעט מזעיר מ״ש כי קרוב אליך הדבר מאד וגו׳ איך הוא קרוב מאד בדרך ארוכה וקצרה בעזהי״ת. תניא (בספ״ג דנדה) משביעים (ה ע״א שורה ב)... ב״ה סליק בעזה״י״ (עא ע״א שורה יב. סוף פרק נ בתניא הנדפס).

אח״כ בכת״י אחר וכנראה מאוחר: נכתב בק׳ שקלאב הבירה.

שינוים עיקרים מהתניא הנדפס: חלוק למ״ח פרקים, חסרים כמה קטעים, כל פ״ל ופל״ב שבתניא הנדפס — אינו בכת״י זה, בסוף פמ״ט קטע שאינו בנדפס. ועוד.

ג. 16°. בתחלתו חסר. דפים ב—ז: „בהם (עז ע״א שורה ד)... בלבו: (פח ע״ב שורה כד) מאמר רז״ל אינו דומה שמיעה לראיה (נדפס בס׳ בונה ירושלים סי׳ קי)... יכול כל אדם״ (קרוב לסוף המאמר שם). — הכותרת שעל העמודים — „חנוך״ — חסרים כמה דפים מהכת״י ואח״כ מתחיל דפים ו—לא: „ועל זה (טז ע״א שורה כב. אמצע פי״א בתניא הנדפס)... הגשמיי: סליק״ (עד ע״א שורה כג. פנ״ג קרוב לתחילתו בתניא הנדפס. בהוצאתנו: הגשמי). אח״כ בא דף חלק. דפים א—מז: דרושים מרבנו הזקן. דפים מח—מט חלק.

שינוים עיקרים מהתניא הנדפס, ועל דרך כת״י ב. חלוק לנ״א פרקים.

ד. ספר לקוטי אמרים חלק ראשון הנקרא בשם ספר של בינונים מלוקט .. בעזה״י. לפרט אר״י״ה׳ ש״אג מ״י לא י״רא (תקע״ה).

(2) צה דף (1). 16°.

בסוף אגה״ת: נשלם ח״ג בעד״ה ית׳ ויתברך.

כנראה שהועתק מתניא מודפס!

---

*) ציוני העמודים בתניא אשר ברשימתי זו הם על פי הוצאת ווילנא — תרס״ט ואילך.

הוספה לאחר זמן

ה. **בוך להבין אמרי בינה.** מחזיק רו דפים. בתחלתו מפתח. ג, א: אגה״ק שכתב הרב אדמו״ר ק״ק ווילנע להבין אמרי בינה (קלח ע״א שורה כה)... ומכלל הן כו׳ (קמב ע״א שורה ג). ו, ב: מש״א אדמו״ר שליט״א פ׳ פנחס .. תקנוא״ו לפ״ק להבין ענין תפילה .. ותרגומו ויקטל. ח, א: אגרת התשובה מהדורא קמא. הכותרות שעל העמודים (נכתבו בכתיבה אחרת וכנראה מאוחר) — תניא קטן. טו, א: אליכם אישים אקרא (ג ע״ב שורה ג) .. אמן כן יהי רצון (ד ע״א שורה ל). יו, א: „קיצור לקטי אמרים ..(כנ״ל כת״י ב).. תניא בסוף פ״ג (ה ע״א שורה ב)... ואהבת ג״ שני פעמי״ אור):״ [ובדיו אחר, כנראה מאוחר: כידוע לי״ח] (סב ע״ב שורה יז. ס״פ מג בתניא הנדפס). הכותרות שעל העמודים (בכתיבה אחרת, וכנראה מאוחר) — עד אמצע פרק יוד: „תניא סי׳ ..״, ומשם ואילך — רק הסימון. צג, א: פותחין בברכה (קב ע״א שורה ב) ..ואין טוב וכו׳ (קג סע״א. בהוצאתנו: אלא תורה כו׳). דף צה חלק. דפים צו—קנט דרושים שונים מאדה״ז. דפים קנד—ה קס—קסב חלק. דפים קסג—קעג: פרק א׳ חנוך לנער (עה ע״ב שורה ה) ..ונאצל מרוח פיו ית׳ וית׳: פרק י׳ והנה (פה ע״א שורה ה. בהוצאתנו: „מרוח פיו ואין מעצור כו׳ ...״ ואינו בסיום הפרק). הכותרות שעל העמודים „חנוך פרק ..״. דפים קעד—קפא: דרושים. דפים קפב—רו חלק.

שינוים עיקרים מהתניא הנדפס, ועל דרך כת״י ב. חלוק למ״ב פרקים (אבל החלוקה של פרק מא ופרק מב היא בכתיבה אחרת כמו הכותרות).

ו. (37 דף). על השער: ספר תניא... אכי״ר. בסוף העמוד: „תניא אברהם יצחק יע...״. בדף שלאחריו מתחיל: קיצור לקוטי אמרים .. (כנ״ל כת״י ב) .. תניא (ה ע״א שורה ב) ..רצונו האמיתי (נח ע״א שורה יא. אמצע פמ״א בתניא הנדפס).

אח״כ: (2), פא דפים. דרושים מאדמו״ר הזקן. בתחילתו: מפתח הדרושים ושער מיוחד.

שינוים עיקריים מהתניא הנדפס, ועל דרך כת״י ב. חלוק לל״ט פרקים.

ז. **בוך תניא ברוק.** כולל ספר התניא (ואגה״ק סי׳ ה, יא, יג, יד, כו), דרושי אדמו״ר הזקן. דרושים אחדים מאדמו״ר האמצעי והצ״צ. ועוד. דפים: א—סז, לה—נה, א—טז, (5), נו—קכא (באמצע חסרים איזה דפים בכ״מ. וכנראה שנצטרפו כאן כמה קטעי ביכלאך, בכת״י שונים).

דפים לו—לט (הב׳): „חנוך לנער (עה, ע״ב שורה ה) .. בלבו (פח ע״ב שורה כד) וכמו שכתוב לקמן בפירוש הר״מ דפ׳ נשא ע״ש״. דפים מג—מה (הב׳): אגה״ת מהדו״ק. הכותרת „אור תורה מאדמו״ר הרב הכולל מ׳ שניאור זלמן שילאי״ט״. ועל כל העמודים „אור תורה״. נה, ב: אליכם (ג, ע״ב שורה ג) .. — א״ס כיה״ר (ד, ע״א שורה כג). הכותרת „הקדמת מכתב כולל מאת אדמו״ר מוהרש״ז שלאי״ט״. וחותם „שניאור ז׳ שי״״. א—טז (2): „מכתב כלליות מאת אדומו״ר הרב הכולל מ׳ שניאור זלמן נ״י ויופיע ל׳ [לעד] קיצר לקוטי אמרי .. (כנ״ל כת״י ב) .. מאד: וז״ל אדומו״ר :א: [כ״ז במסגרת בתחלת העמוד] תניא בספ״ג דנדה (ה, ע״א שורה ב) ... רצונו האמיתי סליק״, (נח ע״א

שורה יוד. אמצע פמ״א בתניא הנדפס. בהכת״י — סוף פרק לט). ולאחר זמן (כנראה) ניתוסף עה״ג: הגה״ה והיינו יחוד .. כו׳ כנ״ל [בהנדפס הוא סיום פרק הנ״ל]. לאח״ז: שייך להתניא והנה. ובסוף העמוד: מ. והנה במה שכתבתי. דפים טז, (2): מ והנה (נט, ע״א שורה ו. פמ״ב בתניא הנדפס) .. חיי החיים א״ס ב״ה׳ (עא, א שורה יא. ספ״נ בתניא הנדפס). הכותרת שעל העמודים „קיצר לקוטי אמרים״.

שינויים עקריים מהתניא הנדפס, ועל דרך כת״י ב. אלא שכמה קטעים החסרים בכת״י הנ״ל ניתוספו כאן עה״ג. בסוף פרק כח: סליק חלק ראשון. חלוק לנ׳ פרקים.

ח. **בוך חפר־ווייספיש** דפים: ב—כ, (8), כא—כה, א—ד, (12), א—מט, לה—מג, (9). דפים ב—כא: קיצור לקוטי אמרים .. (כנ״ל כת״י ב) .. תניא בסוף (ה ע״א שורה ב) .. רצונו האמיתי (נח ע״א שורה יא. אמצע פמ״א בתניא הנדפס). דפים כא—כו: חנוך לנער (עה ע״ב שורה ה) .. צפון וסתום בלבו וד״ל (פח ע״ב שורה כד. בהוצאתנו תיבת וד״ל ליתא). בין דף כ ודף כא 8 עמודים (בלי מספרים וכותרות, וכנראה נכתבו אח״כ כשהגיע להמעתיק עוד פרקים מספר התניא): פי׳ יחוד זה (נז ע״ב שורה כ. התחלת דף כא בהכת״י) .. חי החיים א״ס ב״ה (עא ע״א שורה יב. ספ״נ בתניא הנדפס). דפים א—ד (הב׳): אגה״ת מהדורא קמא [בתחילתו במסגרת: סדר התשובה הנק׳ תניא קטון מאדמו״ר הרב א״א מהור״ר שנייאור זלמן נ״י. ובסיומו: היום יום ב׳ ד״ך ימים לחודש מר חשוון שנת תקנ״ו לפ״ק פה ק״ק טשאווס יצ״ו]. אח״כ בכתב אחר (כנראה מאוחר): דרושים מאדמו״ר הזקן (וגם — מאדמו״ר האמצעי והצ״צ).

שינויים עיקרים מהתניא הנדפס, ועל דרך כתב יד ב׳. חלוק לנ׳ פרקים.

ט. מחזיק דפים: (2), א־כח (דף יא נסמן ב׳ פעמים). (13). על השער (ע״ד שער של תניא הנדפס): ספר קיצור ליקוטי אמרים . . בעזרת השם ית׳ בנל״ךי. דפים א־כח: תניא בסוף פ״ג דגדה (ה ע״א שורה ב) . . רצונו האמיתי סליקא לה בעזרת השם יתברך בנל״ך ולאא״ע[1] ירבה (נח ע״א שורה יא, אמצע פמ״א בתניא הנדפס). אח״כ (כח, ב — ע׳ א של דף שלאח״ז) — הקדמת התניא: איגרת מאדוני מו״ אליכם אישים (ג ע״ב שורה ג) . . למקטנם ועד גדולם אמן כן יהי״ר סליק לה בסיעיתא דשמיא (ד ע״א שורה ל). אח״כ (התחלת ע׳ שלאח״ז — עד גמירא): מ והנה במ״ש לעיל (נט ע״א שורה ב, רפמ״ב — בתניא הנדפס) . . חיי החיים א״ס ב״ה (עא ע״א שורה יב, סוף פרק נ — בתניא הנדפס). דפים א־כח נכתב בכתב רש״י, ואח״כ בכתב רגיל. הכותרות על כל העמודים (דפים א־כח) — קיצור ליקוטי אמרים. וכ״ה בהכותרות דפרקים מ־מב (ר׳ עמודים).

שינויים עיקרים מהתניא הנדפס, ועל דרך כתב־יד ב. חלוק למ״ח פרקים.

---

1) ברוך נותן ליעף כח (ע״פ ישעי׳ מ, כט).

2) ולאין אונים עצמה (שם).

י. ל דף (דף יז נסמן פעמיים). תניא פרק א (ה ע״א שורה ב) . . רצונו האמיתי (נח, ע״א שורה יא. אמצע סמ״א בתניא הנדפס).
שינויים עיקריים מהתניא הנדפס, ועל דרך כת״י ב. חלוק לל״ט פרקים.

* * *

תיאור קצר של כתבי יד אגרת התשובה מהדורא קמא

ה. ראה רשימה קצרה של כת״י התניא תיאור כת״י ה. אגרת התשובה נכתבה בו בכתב־יד אחר, ואח״כ הוגהה.

ז. ראה רשימה הנ״ל תיאור כת״י ז.

ח. ראה רשימה הנ״ל תיאור כת״י ח.

ס. כת״י מס׳ 415, כולל דרושי רבינו הזקן. דפים: (3), עא. בכותרות רוב העמודים: „תורת אדמו״ר מהרש״ז שי״ן״. אגה״ת מהדו״ק: סב, א — סח, א.

ע. כת״י מס׳ 294, נכרך מחלקי כמה ביכלאך. דפים: (7), רסח־שעב. הדפים שס־שעב — בכת״י קדום (בחיי אדה״ז) הכולל דרושי רבינו הזקן. אגה״ת מהדו״ק: שסג, א — שסו, ב. שסד, ב בכותרת העמוד: מאדומ״ו לא״ש החדשים מקרוב באו. כת״י זה הוגה באיזה מקומות ע״פ נוסח הדפוס.

פ. (צילום) מס׳ 918. נמסר ע״י י. מונדשיין. כולל דרושי אדה״ז, ונראה ככת״י קדום. דפים: (1), נה. במפתח: „שמעתי מפיו הק׳ תורה . .״. אגה״ת מהדו״ק (במפתח: תניא קטן): דפים א, א — ח, ב. הדפים א, ב, ה — חסרים. המפתח, אגה״ת ודרוש א׳ נכתבו באותיות רש״י.

צ[1]. כת״י מס׳ 789, כולל דרושי הצ״צ, וחידושים בנגלה לא נודע למי. קצה דף. אגה״ת מהד״ק: עה, א — עח, א. בתחלתה בכותרת: סדר התשובה של אדמו״ר מ״מ (!) נבג״מ זי״א.

צ[2]. כת״י אגה״ת מהדו״ק שבתוך ביכל כת״י הנמצא בידי י. מונדשיין. אגה״ת — 19 עמודים. בסופה: סליק בעזה״ת ס׳ אגרת התשובה מאדמו״ר כו׳ (?).

צ[3]. כת״י מס׳ 8°3548 בספרי׳ הלאומית בירושלים. כולל דרושי אדמו״ר האמצעי והצ״צ. „נכתב בליובאוויטש בערך בשנת תקצ״ב״ (פתח־דבר לד״ה אל תצר (כפר חב״ד, תשל״ז) בתיאור כת״י ז). אגה״ת מהדו״ק: קמז, ב — קמח, ב. בתחלתה כותרת: סדר התשובה של אדמו״ר ז״ל נבג״מ זי״א.

צ[4]. כת״י מס׳ 373, כולל דרושי אדמו״ר הזקן, אדמו״ר האמצעי, אדמו״ר הצ״צ ואדמו״ר מהר״ש. דפים: (2), תרסח, (1). אגה״ת מהדו״ק רכד, ב — רכז, א. בתחלתה כותרת: סדר התשובה של אדמו״ר ז״ל נבג״מ זיע״א.

ק. כת״י מס׳ 104, כולל דרושי אדמו״ר האמצעי, אדמו״ר הצ״צ, והר״ה מפאריטש ועוד. ריח דף. אגה״ת מהדו״ק: נא, ב — נה, א. דף נג נכרך (בטעות) בין דפים סד־סה.

ש. כת״י מס׳ 756, כולל דרושי אדמו״ר הצ״צ, אדמו״ר מהר״ש, והר״ה מפאריטש, ועוד. דפים: כג־רפו. אגה״ת מהדו״ק: קכז, א — קלא, א. בתחלתה: מה״ק [=מהדורא קמא] של שעה״ת [=שער התשובה] נדפס בתניא זלקווא. העמוד הראשון נעתק כולו מדפוס זאלקווא. שאר העמודים נעתקו מכת״י אחר (כי אינם זהים עם נוסח הדפ׳), אבל הוגהו בכ״מ ע״פ נוסח הדפ׳. בכותרות העמודים: תניא קטן.

דפוסי תניא*

כל ההוצאות הם 8° ובאותיות מרובעות
מלבד אותן שנרשם בהן אחרת

א. **לקוטי אמרים** חלק ראשון הנקרא בשם ספר של בינונים מלוקט . . . בעזה״י.

נדפס בסלאוויטא . . . בשנת כ״י קרוב אל״יך הדבר׳ מאוד בפיך ובלבבך לעש׳ותו׳ לפ״ק. (בדף עג ע״ב) ליקוטי אמרים חלק שני הנקרא בשם חינוך קטן מלוקט . . . מעבר לשער הסכמות „הקטן משולם זוסיל מאניפאלי״ ו„יהודא ליב הכהן״.

המביאים לדפוס — חתנו של רבנו הזקן „הרבני המופלג הותיק מוהרר שלום שכנא״ — אביו של ה„הצמח צדק״ — ושותפו.

בסוף הספר לוח הטעות.

ההדפסה נשלמה „ביום שהוכפל בו כי טוב יום ג׳ ך׳ ימים לחדש כסלו שנת תקנ״ז לפ״ק. על ידי הפועל העוסק במלאכת הקודש באמונה הפרעסין ציהר נאום אלעזר בהרב מוהר״ר צבי הירש זצ״ל מק״ק סלאוויטא״. פו דף.

נדפסו — טו אלף טופסים. בשנת תקנ״ח — חמשה אלפים. בשנת תקנ״ט — עשרים אלף. ומדי שנה מספר מסוים[1].

ב. **תניא** והוא ספר ליקוטי אמרים . . . והוספנו בו נופך . . . מהות התשובה וענינה. והוא חלק שלישי . . . חלק זה — מהדורא קמא ואינו מחולק לפרקים.

בסופו — לוח הטעות. דברי המתעסק.

הסכמות הראב״ד דזאלקווי ושל אב״ד דקראקא (וחתומים עמו עוד שנים).

הובא לדפוס ע״י יעקב . . . מבראד.

באותיות רש״י — לבד רוב ההגהות והקדמת ח״ב.

זאלקווי — בשנת מבשר טוב משמיע ישועה וגו׳ (תקנ״ט).

צענזירירט פאן האם דען נײנטין אגוסט תשצ״ח. (2) עד דף.

ג[1]. **תניא** והוא . . . זאלקווא תקס״ה. (59) דף.

הקדמת המלקט והקדמת ח״ב — באותיות מרובעות. הפנים — אותיות רש״י.

בסופו דברי המתעסק.

ד. **כנ״ל** זאלקווא תקס״ה. נח, (1) דף.

רק הקדמת ח״ב וההגהות — באותיות מרובעות.

ה[2]. **כנ״ל** זאלקווא תקס״ה. (2), עג, (1) דף.

רק הקדמת ח״ב וההגהות — באותיות מרובעות.

ו[3]. **לקוטי אמרים** חלק ראשון . . . ועתה ניתוסף בו אגרת התשובה . . . (מהד״ת. זו שבהוצאתנו) בשקלאב. בדפוס . . . ברוך . . . בשנת כי קר׳וב אליך הדבר מ׳אוד בפיך ו׳בלבבך לעש׳ותו לפ״ק (תקס״ו).

הסכמות של א — בקיצור — והסכמת הרבנים ברוך ב״ר יהודה מ״מ מק״ק שקלאוו, משה ב״ר ישראל מ״ץ דק״ק קאפוסט צבי הירש ב״ר יעקב מ״ץ דק״ק סמאלייאן.

בההודעה דאגה״ת „האגרת הזאת . . . הנקראת במדינתינו בשם תניא קטן . . .״

בהקדמת המלקט אחר אכי״ר „ארור מסיג . . . שלא להדפיס ה״ס לקו״א וס׳ אגרת התשובה עד . . .״

אחר הקדמת המלקט „וגם אלה לחכמים . . .״ (ע״ד הביטוי עכומ״ז). לאחר ח״ב — לוח הטעות . . . לוח הטעות מאגרת התשובה. מעל״ד: על ידי הפועל . . . ועל ידי . . .

שער מיוחד לאגרת התשובה ומעבר לו הסכמות הרבנים, וגם אלה לחכמים . . . ארור מסיג . . . כ״ד המלקט לקוטי אמרים ואיגרת התשובה הנ״ל. מודעת זאת . . . (ע״ד אגה״ת — מהמו״ל).

אחרי אגה״ת — ד״ה הקל קול יעקב — הנדפס בהקדמת הסידור. אבל הכותרת — אגרת התשובה. בסופו: על ידי המסדר אותיות . . . על ידי . . .

צה. (1), כ דף.

ו (ב)[3]. **כנ״ל.** אבל אגה״ת בלא שער מיוחד ובלא ההסכמות (כבדפוס ז).

ז[3]. **כנ״ל** . . . בדפוס . . . מרדכי . . . לפני אגה״ת: ליקוטי אמרים חלק שלישי הנקרא בשם איגרת התשובה מודעת זאת . . . — אבל בלא שער מיוחד ובלא ההסכמות.

הכותרת שעל ד״ה הקל קול — חתימה. על ידי . . . — הושמט.

שקלאוו תקס״ו. צ״ה, (1), יח דף.

ז (ב)[3]. **כנ״ל.** אבל אגה״ת כבדפוס ו.

ח. **אגרת הקודש** מאדמו״ר נ״ע . . . קוטרס (!) אחרון . . . ג״כ הספ׳ לקוטי אמרים עם אגרת התשוב׳ . . . שניאור זלמן נבג״מ . . . לפרט צד׳ק׳ת׳ ה׳ ע׳שה ומשפטיו עם ישראל . . . (תקע״ד).

הסכמת הרבנים ש׳ בני הגאון המחבר ז״ל נ״ע . . . דוב בער . . . חיים אברהם . . . משה . . .

בהקדמת המלקט חסרות כמה שורות, ומסיימת — אכי״ר. בע׳ שקודם לדף א „השמטה מלוח הטעות״. — אחר הקדמת המלקט „וגם אלה לחכמים״ (וע״ד הביטוי עכומ״ז).

באגה״ק חסרים: סו״ס א — הקטע וכגון דא. סו״ס יט — הקטע אותיות הנגלות. סו״ס כב — הקטע אהוביי אחיי. סו״ס כד — הקטע והעובר ע״ז. סו״ס כה — הקטע ואם משום טומאת. בקו״א: ד״ה ולהבין פרטי ההלכות.

ברשיון הצענזאר אשר באקדעמיא דווילנא, שקלאוו תקע״ד (2), צב (נדפס עט במקום צב) דף.

***ט[4].** **כנ״ל.** שקלאוו תקע״ד. (2), נב, ה, כח, (6) דף.

י. **לקוטי אמרים** . . . ונתוסף בו אגרת התשובה . . . גם אגרת הקדש . . . — חמ״ד תקע״ד.

ברשיון הצענזור אשר באקדעמיא דווילנא. (1), לו, מא־מד, (4), ו, (30) דף.

***יא[5].** **לקוטי אמרים** . . . ברשיון הצענזור אשר באקדעמיא דווילנא. (1), נב, כח, ח, ו דף.

יב. **לקוטי אמרים** . . . אותיות הדפוס — כמו בהוצאה הקודמת. נב, ח, כח, (6) דף.

יג. **תניא** והוא ספר לקוטי אמרים חלק א׳ . . . חלק ד׳ והוא אגרת הקודש עם קונטרס אחרון . . . קאניגסברג . . . בשנת ע׳ב׳ד׳ד׳ את ה׳ ב׳י׳ר׳א׳ה׳ ו׳ג׳י׳ל׳ו׳ ב׳ר׳ע׳ד׳ה׳.

עב דף.

הקדמת המלקט, הקדמת ח״ב וההגהות — באותיות רש״י. בהקדמת המלקט נשמטו כמה ענינים ומסיים אכי״ר.

באגה״ק חסרים: סו״ס א — הקטע וכגון דא. סו״ס יט — הקטע אותיות הנגלות. סו״ס כב — הקטע אהוביי אחיי. סו״ס כד — הקטע והעובר ע״ז. סו״ס כה — הקטע ואם משום טומאת.

הסדר באגה״ק וקו״א: ברך ה׳, הנה לא, הוכח, כל השו״א, דוד זמירות, וצדקה כנחל.

יג (ב)[6]. **תניא** והוא ספר לקוטי אמרים . . . קאניגסבערג בשנת ועבדתם את ה׳ בכל לבבכם.

יד[7]. **תניא** והוא ספר לקוטי אמרים חלק א׳ . . . חלק ד׳ והוא אגרת הקודש עם קונטרס אחרון [בהוצאה זו, בקאניגסברג תקפ״ז ועוד מצאתי אגה״ק נרשם כחלק רביעי של התניא].

---

*) מסומנים בכוכב — אלו ההוצאות אשר הובאו על ידי רושמי ספרים אבל לא ראיתים. — ציוני העמודים בתניא אשר ברשימתי זו הם על פי הוצאת ווילנא — תרס״ט ואילך.

i) רשימת כ״ק מו״ח אדמו״ר בס׳ קיצורים והערות הנ״ל ע׳ קלט. וראה שם ע׳ קיח ואילך.

1) י״א שדפוס זה הוא אחרי דפוס ד.

2) י״א שדפוס זה הוא לפני דפוס ד.

3) י״א שכל אלו הם דפוס אחד בשינוי שערים, ובכמה נכרכה אגרת התשובה שיצאה לאור באותה שנה בפני עצמה.

4) י״א שדפוס זה הוא לפני דפוס ח.

5) י״א שהוא הדפוס שלאח״ז.

6) י״א שהוא דפוס יח דלקמן, ועיי״ש בהערה.

7) י״א שהוא דפוס יט (ב), ופרט השנה „תוקף מ.תרי״י ל.תקפ״ז״.

הסדר באגה״ק וקו״א: ברך ה׳, הנה לא, הוכח, כל הקו״א, דוד זמירות, וצדקה כנחל.

אלטונא תק״ף (1), פ דף.

•טו[8]. לקוטי אמרים (חסר השער).

(84), (3), (92) דף.

טז[9]. תניא והוא ספר לקוטי אמרים . . . והוספנו בו נופך . . . מהות התשובה ועניגה והוא חלק שלישי.

. . . חמו״ד (2), סס, נ־נו — עו דף.

אגה״ת — מהדו״ק.

יז. תניא והוא ספר לקוטי אמרים . . . — הסדר באגה״ק וקו״א — כמו אלטונא, תק״ף.

קאניגסברג שנת „ועצת ה׳ היא תקום״ (תקפ״ז). (2), ע דף.

•יח[10]. תניא והוא ספר לקוטי אמרים . . . חמ״ד. בשנת ועבדתם את ה׳ בכל לבבכם.

עב דף.

יט. תניא והוא ספר ליקוטי אמרים . . . ואגרת הקודש מאדמו״ר נ״ע . . . לכן הדפסנו . . . עם אגרת התשובה [תוכן הקדמת הרבנים בני המחבר ז״ל לאגה״ק]. וכל אלה חוברו . . . בגנזי מרומים.

הובא לבית הדפוס ע״י . . . מהו׳ משה קלאר פיין בדפוס . . . מוה׳ נטע ה׳אסער מאן . . . מהו׳ ישראל אברהם במו׳ יעקב סג״ל.

ביאס, בשנת תר״ג לפ״ק.

מעבר לשער — הסכמות „שנדפס סלאוויטא״ וכן הסכמת „הק׳ יוסף אב״ד דק״ק יאס ואגפי״. אחרי הקדמת המלקט — לוח התקון.

באותיות רש״י, לבד כמה אגרות הקודש. בהקדמת המלקט וכן באגה״ק — חסרים כמה ענינים. בסוף הקונטרס אחרון — מודעא רבה ואם אלה וכו׳.

(2). צב דף.

יט (ב)*. תניא והוא ספר ליקוטי אמרים חלק א . . . חלק ד׳ והוא אגרת הקודש עם קונטרס אחרון. אלטונא, תר״ז. עח דף — הטופס שראיתי — חסר בסופו. ויש להשוותו עם הוצאת אלטונא תק״ף.

בהקדמת המלקט נשמטו כמה ענינים, ומסיימת אכי״ר.

הקדמת המלקט, הקדמת ח״ב וההגהות — באותיות רש״י.

באגה״ק חסרים: סו״ס א — הקטע וכגון דא. סו״ס יט — הקטע אותיות הנגלות. סו״ס כב — הקטע אהוביי אחיי. סו״ס כד — הקטע והעובר ע״ז. סו״ס כה — הקטע ואם משום טומאת.

כ. תניא והוא כולל שלשה חלקים . . . הובא לדפוס ע״י הרבני מוהר״ר יעקב יהודה רייזליר בהמנוח מהור״ר אברהם רייזליר.

לבוב חש״ד. (60) דף.

•כא[11]. תניא והוא ס׳ לקוטי אמרים . . . קאניגסברג, תרי״ב. עב דף.

כב. תניא לקוטי אמרים . . . לעמבערג 1856. מב, (14), טז, (9) דף. הקדמת המלקט — חסרה. ח״ב עד פ״ט — באותיות רש״י. וכן פי״א־יב, פרקי א־ג דאגה״ת, ביאור דאגה״ק סכ״ז.

•כג. תניא . . . לעמבערג 1857. (62) דף.

כג (ב). תניא והוא כולל שלשה חלקים חלק ראשון . . . והשני . . . והשלישי מהות התשובה וענינה מלוקט . . . בעזה״י מהגאון האלקי אספקלריא המאירה הרב שניאור זלמן בעהמ״ח ארבע ש״ע ולכולם בשם יקרא ס׳ ליקוטי אמרים.

הובא לדפוס ע״י האברך מהו׳ אברהם בהרב הקדוש מוהר״ר יהודא גרשון זצ״ל. כתבנית אותיות ביאס.

באותיות רש״י — לבד פרק יח (הסיום), יט־כג, לג־לו, מב (לבד השורה הראשונה), מג, מד.

8) י״א שהוא דפוס י.

9) י״א שנדפס בשנת תקע״ד, ומקומו לע״ל לפני דפוס ח.

10) י״א שהוא דפוס יג בשינוי שער.

*) אף שהוצאה זו היא הוצאה בפני עצמה, אבל מפני סיבות טכניות נשארו המספרים הבאים לאח״ז כמו בהוצאות הקודמות.

11) י״א שהוא דפוס יג.

בהקדמת המלקט נשמטו כמה ענינים ומסיימת אכי״ר.

פרק א מסיים — עץ הדעת טוב ורע.

לעמבערג 1857. (60) דף.

אולי הוא זה המסומן •כג, וא׳ צריך לתקן שם (60) במקום (62).

כד[12]. תניא והוא כולל שלשה חלקים חלק ראשון . . . והשני . . . והשלישי מהות התשובה וענינה מלוקט . . . בעזה״י מהגאון האלקי אספקלריא המאירה הרב שניאור זלמן בעהמ״ח ארבע ש״ע ולכולם בשם יקרא ס׳ ליקוטי אמרים.

הובא לדפוס ע״י האברך מוהר״ר יעקב אריה רייזליר . . . אברהם רייזליר.

מעבר לשער — דברי המדפיס . . . ישכר בהרב המנוח מוהר״ר אברהם בק. הקדמת המלקט — מסיימת אכי״ר.

ההגהות (לבד א׳ — בח״ב פי״ב) — באותיות רש״י.

פרק א מסיים — עץ הדעת טוב ורע.

שנת תרח״י לבוב (60) דף.

כה. תניא והוא כולל ארבעה חלקים . . . ולכולם בשם יקרא ספר ליקוטי אמרים . . . לעמבערג 1860. (98) דף.

אגה״ת — מהדו״ק. לאגה״ק שער בפ״ע: אגרת הקודש . . . נדפס פעם ראשון בק״ק זולצבאך ועתה . . . בשנת כת״ר.

כו. תניא . . . ווין, חש״ד. 4°. מד דף. כל עמוד נסדר בשני טורים.

הקדמת המלקט — חסרה.

כו (ב). כנ״ל.

•כז. לקוטי אמרים תניא והוא ספר לקוטי אמרים . . . חמ״ד. בשנת ובדבר הזה תאריכו ימים. עב דף.

כז (ב). תניא והוא ספר לקוטי אמרים . . . חמ״ד. בשנת ובדבר הזה תאריכו ימים. עב דף.

אולי זה הוא המסומן •כז, ואז צריך לתקן שם תניא והוא . . . (בהשמטת תיבות לקוטי אמרים בתחלה).

כח. לקוטי אמרים חלק . . . לבוב שנת תבר״ך. (2), ע, כח דף.

בהקדמת המלקט — נשמטו כמה ענינים.

כט[13]. כנ״ל. בהשמטת מקום ושנת הדפוס.

ל. תניא לקוטי אמרים . . . (לעמבערג) 1864.

כמה פרקים — באותיות רש״י.

הקדמת המלקט — חסרה. נב, (9), כד, (1) דף.

לא. לקוטי אמרים חלק . . . מלוקט . . . בעזה״י. וניתוסף בו אגרת התשובה . . . גם אגרת הקודש . . . ווילנא, תרל״ב. 146 ע׳.

בהקדמת המלקט נשמטו כמה ענינים ומסיימת — אכי״ר. אחר הקדמת המלקט „אמר המחבר . . .״ (ע״ד הביטוי עכומ״ז).

הקדמת המלקט, הקדמת ח״ב וההגהות — באותיות רש״י.

באגה״ק חסרים: סו״ס א — הקטע וכגון דא. סו״ס יט — הקטע אותיות הנגלות. סו״ס כב — הקטע אהוביי אחיי. סו״ס כד — הקטע והעובר ע״ז. סו״ס כה — הקטע ואם משום טומאת. בקו״א: ד״ה ולהבין פרטי ההלכות.

בשולי השער אשר זוהי הוצאה חדשה מהוצאת שנת 1813!

לב. לקוטי אמרים הנקרא בשם ספר של בינונים . . . ווילנא . . . ראם. תרל״ג. 1872. סה דף.

בשולי השער אשר זוהי הוצאה חדשה מהוצאת שנת 1872!

לג. כנ״ל. ווילנא תרל״ח.

לד. כנ״ל. ווילנא תר״מ.

לה. כנ״ל. ווילנא תרנ״ז.

לג־לה נדפסו מהוצאת שנת 1872.

לו. לקוטי אמרים חלק . . . בתוצאה חדשה ומתוקנת . . . ווילנא בדפוס . . . ראם. שנת בקדוש׳ יש׳ראל׳ יגיל׳ו (תר״ס).

(2), קסג דף.

12) י״א שהוא דפוס כ בשינוי שער.

13) י״א שהוא הדפוס שלפנ״ז בשינוי שער.

. . . הוספנו את ההשלמה מפרק ז׳ (בשער היחוד והאמונה) . . . ההשמטות מהאגה״ק (הרשומות לעיל בהוצאת שקלאב תקע״ד). תיבת פרק שנדפס בתחלת כל אגרת . . . בטעות.

ההסכמות שבדפוס הראשון והסכמת בני המחבר (בהשמטת התאריך שלה).

אגה״ק מסומן, אבל לא הקו״א.

על העטיפה מודעה (בלה״ק ובאידית): אל הקונה הדפים יד, כא, לג, מג, עו, קמ, קמג, קנב יש להחליפם באחרים ולכן הדפסנו מחדש את העלים האלו . . .

מאמהות הוצאה זו (או ע״י פוטוגרפיא) נדפסו כל ההוצאות שבאו אח״ז (פרט להוצאת תל אביב תש״ג; תוניס, ג׳רבה ה׳תשכ״ח) — אחדות מהן בשינוים מועטים. (ראה הוצאה שלאחר זו).

לז. כנ״ל ווילנא תרס״ט (1), קסג דף.

מודעה רבה . . . מכרנו את זכות הדפסת . . . תוצאה חדשה ומתוקנת . . . לכ״ק אדמו״ר הר״ר שלום דובער שליט״א מליובאוויטש . . . לטובת המוסד תומכי תמימים . . .

תיבת פרק שבתחלת כל אגרת — הושמטה (ובטעות נשארה בשולי העמודים קיב, א. קלז, א).

עו, ב שורה יו״ד „תיקנו״ והוא טעות: בשמים (במקום במים).

קלג, א שורה ג׳ נתקן: אליהם — במקום עליהם.

קנא, א שורה ד׳ נשמטו התיבות [אולי צ״ל לבד].

לח. כנ״ל ווילנא תרע״ב.

לט. כנ״ל. ווילנא תרפ״ג.

מ. כנ״ל. ווילנא תר״ץ.

מא. כנ״ל. ווילנא תרצ״ז.

*מב. כנ״ל ווילנא תרצ״ט.

מג. כנ״ל. ווילנא ת״ש.

מד. כנ״ל. מונקאטש תש״ג.

. . . להו״ל מחדש . . . בסוף הס׳ . . . קונטרס . . . מחיי רבנו המחבר . . . המלקט צבי אלימלך קאליש.

נתוספה הסכמה מאת רבני מונקאטש.

(1), קסג דף (פוטוגרפיא מהוצאת ווילנא). קסד־קעו — קונטרס תולדות התניא ה״ה לקוטי סיפורים מתולדות וחיי אדם הגדול . . .

מה. כנ״ל. שנגהאי תש״ג. בהוצאת ועד הדפסת דא״ח אצל ישיבת תומכי תמימים דליובאוויטש שנגהאי.

פוטוגרפיא מהוצאת ווילנא תר״ס.

מו. כנ״ל. תל אביב תש״ג. (1), קסג דף.

סודר מחדש בשורות ובעמודים ע״פ דפוס הנ״ל. הסכמת הרב . . . מאניפאלי והרב . . . הכהן — נדפסו מתוך גלופה.

מז. כנ״ל. יוצא לאור ע״י מערכת אוצר החסידים תש״ז ברוקלין ג. י. נדפס בסביבות מיונכען אשכנז. (1), קסג דף.

מח. לקוטי אמרים . . . יוצא לאור על ידי מערכת אוצר החסידים, ברוקלין, תשי״ד.

בפוטוגרפיא מהוצאת ווילנא. בסוף הספר: מורה שיעור — שיעורי לימוד התניא כפי שנחלק לימי השנה. מפתח ענינים, מפתח שמות ספרים ואנשים. לוח התיקון, הערות ותיקונים, כתבי יד ודפוסי התניא (רשימה קצרה), פאקסימיליא של השער דהוצאה הראשונה, של עמוד מכתב יד התניא. 8°. רג, (2) דף.

מט. כנ״ל. ונתקנו כמה מטעיות הדפוס שבהוצאה שלפני זו.

נר״ן. כנ״ל. הוצאה מוקטנת בפורמט כיס. 16°. ונתקנו כמה מטעיות הדפוס שבהוצאות מח־מט. רטז דף.

נא. כנ״ל אות נר״ן. ונתקנו כמה מטעיות הדפוס שבהוצאה אות נר״ן. כן באו בסוף הספר השמטות והוספות.

ברוקלין, ה׳תשט״ו. ריז דף.

נב. כנ״ל אות מח־מט. ונתקנו כמה מטעיות הדפוס שבהוצאות אות מח־מט. כן נכנסו — בפנים — התיקונים, ההשמטות וההוספות של אות נא וניתוספו עוד תיקונים בהוצאה זו וכן הפאקסימיליא של עוד ג׳ עמודים מכת״י תניא מהדורא קמא.

ברוקלין, ה׳תשט״ז. רו דף.

נג. כנ״ל אות נ־נא. עם התיקונים שנתקנו באות נב וניתוספו עוד תיקונים בהוצאה זו וכן הפאקסימיליא מכ״י כ״ק מו״ח אדמו״ר. ביאור אודות כת״י התניא מהדורא קמא.

ברוקלין, ה׳תשי״ח. ריט דף.

נד. כנ״ל אות נב, עם התיקונים שנתקנו באות נג וניתוספו עוד תיקונים בהוצאה זו. כפר חב״ד באה״ק ת״ו, ה׳תש״כ. רז דף.

נה. כנ״ל אות נד. כפר חב״ד באה״ק ת״ו. ה׳תשכ״ג. רז דף.

נו. כנ״ל אות נג. כפר חב״ד באה״ק ת״ו. ה׳תשכ״ג. ריט דף.

נז. כנ״ל אות נד. כפר חב״ד באה״ק ת״ו. ה׳תשכ״ה. רז דף.

נח. כנ״ל אות נד. כפר חב״ד באה״ק ת״ו. ה׳תשכ״ו. רז דף.

נט. כנ״ל אות נג. כפר חב״ד באה״ק ת״ו. ה׳תשכ״ו. ריט דף.

ס. כנ״ל אות נד. כפר חב״ד באה״ק ת״ו. ה׳תשכ״ז. רז דף.

סא. כנ״ל אות נג. מלבורן, אוסטרליא. ה׳תשכ״ז. ריט דף.

סב. כנ״ל אות נג. כפר חב״ד באה״ק ת״ו. ה׳תשכ״ז. ריט דף.

סג. כנ״ל אות נד. סודר מחדש בשורות ועמודים ע״פ דפוס אות נד. עמודים אחדים נדפסו מתוך גלופה. תוניס, ג׳רבה. ה׳תשכ״ח. רז דף.

סד. כנ״ל אות נד. כפר חב״ד באה״ק ת״ו. ה׳תשכ״ט. רז דף.

סה. כנ״ל אות נג. כפר חב״ד באה״ק ת״ו. ה׳תשכ״ט. ריט דף.

סו. כנ״ל אות נד. כפר חב״ד באה״ק ת״ו. ה׳תש״ל. [נדפס ה׳תשכ״ט]. רז דף.

סז. כנ״ל אות נג. כפר חב״ד באה״ק ת״ו. ה׳תש״ל. [נדפס ה׳תשכ״ט]. ריט דף.

סח. כנ״ל אות נד. מאנטרעאל, קנדה. ה׳תשל״ב. רי דף.

סט. כנ״ל אות נד. לונדון, אנגליא. ה׳תשל״ב. רי דף.

ע״ן. כנ״ל אות נג. כפר חב״ד באה״ק ת״ו. י״א ניסן ה׳תשל״ב. רכב דף.

עא. כנ״ל אות נג. מלבורן, אוסטרליא. ה׳תשל״ב. רכב דף.

עב. כנ״ל אות נד. בצירוף תרגום האנגלי — התרגום סודר מחדש — בגודל סמ. 23.5x16.5 890pp. לונדון אנגלי׳ ה׳תשל״ג.

עג. כנ״ל אות נג. כפר חב״ד באה״ק ת״ו. י״א ניסן ה׳תשל״ב. רכב דף.

עד. כנ״ל אות נד. כפר חב״ד באה״ק ת״ו. ה׳תשל״ג. רז דף.

עה. כנ״ל אות נג. פאיד. מעבר לתעלת סואץ. ה׳תשל״ד. רכב דף.

עו. כנ״ל אות נג. ירושלים עיה״ק, בין החומות. ה׳תשל״ד. רכב דף.

עז. כנ״ל אות נג. חברון באה״ק ת״ו. ה׳תשל״ד. רכב דף.

עח. כנ״ל אות נג. פאיד מעבר לתעלת סואץ. ה׳תשל״ד. רכב דף.

עט. כנ״ל אות נד. כפר חב״ד באה״ק ת״ו. ה׳תשל״ד. רי דף.

פ. כנ״ל אות נד. כפר חב״ד באה״ק ת״ו. ה׳תשל״ז. ריג דף.

פא. כנ״ל אות נג. כפר חב״ד באה״ק ת״ו. ה׳תשל״ז. רכה דף. בסופו — לוח ר״ת.

פב. כנ״ל אות נג. קסבלנקה, מרוקו. ה׳תשל״ח. רכו דף.

פג. כנ״ל אות נג. כפר חב״ד באה״ק ת״ו. ה׳תשל״ח. רכו דף. בסופו — לוח ר״ת.

פד. כנ״ל אות נד. לונדון, אנגליא. ה׳תשל״ח. ריג דף. בסופו — לוח ר״ת.

פה. כנ״ל אות נג עם תיקונים. צפת, באה״ק ת״ו. ה׳תשל״ח. רכז דף. בסופו — לוח ר״ת.

פו. כנ״ל אות פה. נחלת הר חב״ד באה״ק ת״ו. ה׳תשל״ח. רכז דף.

פז. כנ״ל אות פה. בואנס איירס, ארגנטינה. ה׳תשל״ח. רכז דף.

פח. כנ״ל אות פד. אנטורפן, בלגיא. ה׳תשל״ח. רטו דף.

פט. כנ״ל אות פה. פאולא, בראזיל. ה׳תשל״ח. רכז דף.

צ. כנ״ל אות פה. אמשטרדם, הולאנד. ה׳תשל״ח. רכז דף.

צא. כנ״ל אות פד. מילאן, איטליא. ה׳תשל״ח. רכז דף.

צב. כנ״ל אות פה. מקסיקו סיטי, מקסיקו. ה׳תשל״ח. רכז דף.

צג. כנ״ל אות פד. יאהנסבורג, דרום אפריקא. ה׳תשל״ח. ריז דף.

צד. כנ״ל אות פה. ציריך, שווייץ. ה׳תשל״ח. רכז דף.

צה. כנ"ל אות פה. קאראקאס, ווענעזועלא. ה'תשל"ח. רכז דף.

צו. כנ"ל אות פה. המבורג, מערב גרמניא. ה'תשל"ח. רכז דף.

צז. כנ"ל אות פה. קופנהגן, דענמארק. ה'תשל"ח. רכז דף.

צח. כנ"ל אות פה. סטוקהולם, שוועדן. ה'תשל"ח. רכז דף.

צט. כנ"ל אות פה. הלזינקי, פינלאנד. ה'תשל"ח. רכז דף.

ק. כנ"ל אות פד. מאלאגא, ספרד. ה'תשל"ח. רכז דף.

קא. כנ"ל אות פה. פאריז, צרפת. ה'תשל"ח. רכז דף.

קב. כנ"ל אות פה. פורטגאל. ה'תשל"ח. רכז דף.

קג. כנ"ל אות פה. גיבראלטאר. ה'תשל"ח. רכז דף.

קד. כנ"ל אות פה. בודאפעסט, אונגארן. ה'תשל"ט. רכז דף.

קה. כנ"ל אות פה. בעלגראד, יוגאסלאוויע. ה'תשל"ט. רכז דף.

קו. כנ"ל אות פה. אתונא, יון. ה'תשל"ח. רכז דף.

קז. כנ"ל אות פד. אקלאנד, ניו זילאנד. ה'תש"מ. ריז דף.

קח. כנ"ל אות פה. האנג קאנג. ה'תשל"ט. רכז דף.

קט. כנ"ל אות פה. באמביי, הודו. ה'תשל"ח. רכז דף.

קי. כנ"ל אות פה. טאקיא, יאפאן. ה'תשל"ח. רכז דף.

קיא. כנ"ל אות פה. מאנטיוועדעא, אורעגוויי. ה'תשל"ח. רכז דף.

קיב. כנ"ל אות פה. באנקאק, טיילאנד. ה'תשל"ח. רכז דף.

קיג. כנ"ל אות פה. טייפי, טייוואן. ה'תשל"ח. רכז דף.

קיד. כנ"ל אות פה. דובלין, אירלאנד. ה'תשל"ח. רכז דף.

קטו. כנ"ל אות פד. ווין, עסטרייך. ה'תשל"ח. רכז דף.

קטז. כנ"ל אות פה. סאנטיאגא, צ'ילה. ה'תשל"ח. רכז דף.

קיז. כנ"ל אות נז. בוגוטו, קולומביא. ה'תשל"ח. רז דף.

קיח. כנ"ל אות פה. סעאל, קארעא. ה'תשל"ח. רכז דף.

קיט. כנ"ל אות פה. טעהראן, פרס. ה'תשל"ח. רכז דף.

קכ. כנ"ל אות פה. כפר קילייא מארג' עיון, לבנון. ה'תשל"ט. רכז דף.

קכא. כנ"ל אות פה. בית הכנסת ובית המדרש „צמח צדק", רחוב חב"ד 53, ירושלים ת"ו. ה'תשל"ח. רכז דף.

קכב. כנ"ל אות פה. סינגאפאר. ה'תשל"ח. רכז דף.

קכג. כנ"ל אות פה, עם הוספות. ברוקלין, נ. י. עשרת ימי תשובה ה'תשל"ט. רכט דף.

קכד. כנ"ל אות פד, עם הוספות. ברוקלין, נ. י. עשרת ימי תשובה ה'תשל"ט. רטו דף.

קכה. כנ"ל אות קכג. ניקאסיא, קפריסין. ה'תשל"ט. רכז דף.

קכו. כנ"ל אות קכג. אוסלו, נורבגיא. ה'תשל"ט. רכט דף.

קכז. כנ"ל אות קכד. אבא, ניגיריא. ה'תשל"ט. רטו דף.

קכח. כנ"ל אות קכג. ריא דע דזשענירא, בראזיל. רכט דף.

קכט. כנ"ל אות קסה. מאנילא, פיליפינס. ה'תשמ"ב. רלד דף.

קל. כנ"ל אות קכג. טברי', אה"ק ת"ו. ה'תשל"ט. רכט דף.

קלא. כנ"ל אות קכג. עפולה, אה"ק ת"ו. ה'תשל"ט. רכט דף.

קלב. כנ"ל אות קכג. איסטנבול, טורקי'. ה'תשל"ט. רכט דף.

קלג. כנ"ל אות קכג. פאנאמא. ה'תשל"ט. רכט דף.

קלד. כנ"ל אות קכד, עם הוספות. ברוקלין, נ. י. עשי"ת ה'תש"מ שנת השמיטה — שבת להוי'. ריז דף.

קלה. כנ"ל אות קלד. ברוקלין, נ. י. ה'תש"מ. ריז דף.

קלו. כנ"ל אות קלה. כפר חב"ד באה"ק ת"ו. ה'תש"מ. ריז דף.

קלז. כנ"ל אות קלה (בפורמט כיס). פראג, טשכסלובקיע. ה'תש"מ. רכט דף.

קלח. כנ"ל אות קכג (הוצאה מוקטנת — 6x8½ סנטימטר. רשימת הדפוסי תניא הוצא מסיבות טכניות). חיפה, באה"ק, ת"ו. ה'תש"מ. רכט דף.

קלט. כנ"ל אות קכג. בני ברק, באה"ק ת"ו. ה'תש"מ. רכט דף.

קמ. כנ"ל אות עב (בצירוף תרגום האנגלי). עם הוספות שבאות קלד. לונדון, אנגלי'. ה'תש"מ. 899 pp.

קמא. כנ"ל אות קמ — הוצאה מוקטנת. לונדון, אנגלי'. ה'תש"מ.

קמב. כנ"ל אות קלה. תל-אביב-יפו, באה"ק ת"ו. ה'תש"מ. ריז דף.

קמג. כנ"ל אות קכג. עכו, באה"ק ת"ו. ה'תש"מ. רכט דף.

קמד. כנ"ל אות קלה. לוד, באה"ק ת"ו. ה'תש"מ. ריז דף.

קמה. כנ"ל אות קלח (בהוספת רשימת דפוסי התניא ולוח ר"ת). חיפה, באה"ק ת"ו. ה'תשמ"א. רלא דף.

קמו. כנ"ל אות פה. איי טורקס וקעיקאס. ה'תשמ"א. רכט דף.

קמז. כנ"ל אות צג. סידני, אוסטרליא. ה'תשמ"א — שנת הקהל, שנת השמונים לכ"ק אדמו"ר שליט"א. ריז דף.

קמח. כנ"ל אות קלה. כפר חב"ד, באה"ק ת"ו. ה'תשמ"א — שנת השמונים לכ"ק אדמו"ר שליט"א. ריז דף.

קמט. כנ"ל אות קלה. רמלה, באה"ק ת"ו. ה'תשמ"א. ריז דף.

קנ. כנ"ל אות קלה. קרית-גת, באה"ק ת"ו. ה'תשמ"א. ריז דף.

קנא. כנ"ל אות קלז. קרית גן ישראל, נ. י. ה'תשמ"א — שנת הקהל, שנת השמונים לכ"ק אדמו"ר שליט"א. רלא דף.

קנב. כנ"ל אות קלז. בית הכנסת ובית המדרש „צמח צדק", רחוב חב"ד 53, ירושלים ת"ו. ה'תשמ"א רלא דף.

קנג. כנ"ל אות פ. ההוספות כבאות קנא. הוצאה מוקטנת — 5x6 סנטימטר. רעסיפע, בראזיל. ה'תשמ"ב — שנת השמונים לכ"ק אדמו"ר שליט"א. רלא דף.

קנד. כנ"ל אות קנא. ימית, באה"ק ת"ו. כ"ד טבת ה'תשמ"ב — שנת השמונים לכ"ק אדמו"ר שליט"א. רלא דף.

קנה. כנ"ל אות קנא. עצמונה, חבל ימית, באה"ק ת"ו. ה'תשמ"ב — שנת השמונים לכ"ק אדמו"ר שליט"א. רלא דף.

קנו. כנ"ל אות קנא. שארם-א-שיך, אופירה. ה'תשמ"ב — שנת השמונים לכ"ק אדמו"ר שליט"א. רלא דף.

קנז. כנ"ל אות קנא. חצר אדר, חבל ימית, באה"ק ת"ו. כ"ד טבת ה'תשמ"ב — שנת השמונים לכ"ק אדמו"ר שליט"א. רלא דף.

קנח. כנ"ל אות קנא. חולון, באה"ק ת"ו. כ"ד טבת ה'תשמ"ב — שנת השמונים לכ"ק אדמו"ר שליט"א. רלא דף.

קנט. כנ"ל אות קנא. פתח תקוה, באה"ק ת"ו. שנת השמונים לכ"ק אדמו"ר שליט"א. רלא דף.

קס. כנ"ל אות קנא. מגדל העמק, באה"ק ת"ו. ה'תשד"מ. רמ דף.

קסא. כנ"ל אות קנא. הנולולו, האוואיי. ה'תשמ"ב — שנת השמונים לכ"ק אדמו"ר שליט"א. רלא דף.

קסב. כנ"ל אות קנח. חולון באה"ק ת"ו (הוצאה שני') י' שבט ה'תשמ"ב שנת השמונים לכ"ק אדמו"ר שליט"א. רלא דף.

קסג. כנ"ל אות קנא. אילת ת"ו. י"א ניסן ה'תשמ"ב, שמונים שנה לכ"ק אדמו"ר שליט"א. רלא דף.

קסד. כנ"ל אות קלה. ינתקנו כמה מטעויות הדפוס שבכמה מהוצאות הקודמות. ובהוספת: 1) פאקסימיליות של כת"י התניא מהדו"ק (כפי שנדפסו בסוף לקו"א — מהדו"ק). 2) צילומי השערים של כל הוצאות התניא ושל התרגומים כו'. י"א ניסן ה'תשמ"ב, שמונים שנה לכ"ק אדמו"ר שליט"א. ברוקלין, נ. י. שלו דף.

קסה. כנ"ל אות קסא. ונתקנו בה התיקונים שנתקנו בהוצאה קסד. קוסטא ריקא, ה'תשמ"ב — שנת השמונים לכ"ק אדמו"ר שליט"א. רלב דף.

קסו. כנ"ל אות קנג. אסונסאן, פאראגוויי. ה'תשמ"ב — שנת השמונים לכ"ק אדמו"ר שליט"א. רלא דף.

קסז. כנ"ל אות קסה. דאר עס סאלאם, טאנזאניא. תשמ"ג. רלה דף.

קסח. כנ"ל אות קסה. ניירובי, קעניא. ה'תשמ"ג. רלה דף.

קסט. כנ"ל אות קסה. הררי, זימבאבווי. ה'תשמ"ג. רלה דף.

קע. כנ"ל אות קלה. בייזשינג, סין. ה'תשד"מ. רלה דף.

קעא. כנ"ל אות קלה. גאנגזשא, סין. ה'תשד"מ. רלה דף.

קעב. כנ"ל אות קסה. שנגהאי, סין. ה'תשמ"ג, רלה דף.

קעג. כנ"ל אות קסג. צור, לבנון. סיון ה'תשמ"ב. שמונים שנה לכ"ק אדמו"ר שליט"א. רלד דף.

קעד. כנ"ל אות קסג. צידון, לבנון. סיון ה'תשמ"ב. שמונים שנה לכ"ק אדמו"ר שליט"א. רלד דף.

קעה. כנ"ל אות קסג. בירות, לבנון. סיון ה'תשמ"ב. שמונים שנה לכ"ק אדמו"ר שליט"א. רלד דף.

קעו. כנ"ל אות קסג. בקעת הלבנון, לבנון. תמוז ה'תשמ"ב. שמונים שנה לכ"ק אדמו"ר שליט"א. רלד דף.

קעז. כנ"ל אות קסג. חצביא, לבנון. ה'תשמ"ב. שמונים שנה לכ"ק אדמו"ר שליט"א. רלד דף.

קעח. כנ"ל אות קסג. נבטיא, לבנון. ה'תשמ"ב. שמונים שנה לכ"ק אדמו"ר שליט"א. רלד דף.

קעט. כנ"ל אות קסג. מבצר הבופור, לבנון. ה'תשמ"ב. שמונים שנה לכ"ק אדמו"ר שליט"א. רלד דף.

קפ. כנ"ל אות קסג. צור, לבנון (הוצאה שני'). ה'תשמ"ב. שמונים שנה לכ"ק אדמו"ר שליט"א. רלד דף.

קפא. כנ"ל אות קסג. עליי, לבנון. חג הגאולה יב־יג תמוז, ה'תשמ"ב. שמונים שנה לכ"ק אדמו"ר שליט"א. רלד דף.

קפב. כנ"ל אות קסג. דאמור, לבנון. חג הגאולה יב־יג תמוז, ה'תשמ"ב. שמונים שנה לכ"ק אדמו"ר שליט"א. רלד דף.

קפג. כנ"ל אות קסג. גזניה, לבנון. חג הגאולה יב־יג תמוז, ה'תשמ"ב. שמונים שנה לכ"ק אדמו"ר שליט"א. רלד דף.

קפד. כנ"ל אות קסג. בחאמדון, לבנון, אב ה'תשמ"ב. רלב דף.

קפה. כנ"ל אות קסג. דיר אלקמר, לבנון. תמוז ה'תשמ"ב. רלב דף.

קפו. כנ"ל אות קנא. מחנה גן ישראל, לק דזרט, מינרב קוויבק, קנדה. כ' מנחם אב, ה'תשמ"ב. שמונים שנה לכ"ק אדמו"ר שליט"א. רלה דף.

קפז. כנ"ל אות קסג. אלכסנדרי', מצרים. ה'תשד"מ. רג דף.

קפח. כנ"ל אות קסג. קהיר, מצרים. ה'תשד"מ. רג דף.

קפט. כנ"ל אות קסה. פעטראפאליס, בראזיל. ה'תשמ"ב. שמונים שנה לכ"ק אדמו"ר שליט"א. רלה דף.

קצ. כנ"ל אות קסה. רשיא, לבנון. ה'תשמ"ב. שמונים שנה לכ"ק אדמו"ר שליט"א. רלד דף.

קצא. כנ"ל אות קסה. כפר משכי, לבנון. ה'תשמ"ב. שמונים שנה לכ"ק אדמו"ר שליט"א. רלד דף.

קצב. כנ"ל אות קמח. לא פאז, מקסיקו. ה'תשמ"ב. שמונים שנה לכ"ק אדמו"ר שליט"א. רכב דף.

קצג. כנ"ל אות קסה. מאואי, האוואיי. ה'תשמ"ג. שמונים שנה לכ"ק אדמו"ר שליט"א. רלה דף.

קצד. כנ"ל אות קסו. קיטא, עקואדור. ה'תשמ"ג. שמונים שנה לכ"ק אדמו"ר שליט"א. רלב דף.

קצה. כנ"ל אות קסו. לימא, פערו. ה'תשמ"ג. שמונים שנה לכ"ק אדמו"ר שליט"א. רלב דף.

קצו. כנ"ל אות קסה. רחובות, באה"ק. ה'תשד"מ. רמ דף.

קצז. כנ"ל אות קסה. טוקומן, ארגנטינה. ה'תשמ"ג. שמונים שנה לכ"ק אדמו"ר שליט"א. רכ דף.

קצח. כנ"ל אות קסה. קנקורדיא, ענטרה ריוס, ארגנטינה. ה'תשמ"ג. שמונים שנה לכ"ק אדמו"ר שליט"א. רכ דף.

קצט. כנ"ל אות קלה. כפר חב"ד, באה"ק ת"ו. ה'תשמ"ג. רכח דף.

ר. כנ"ל אות קמ. עם תרגום האנגלי (עמוד התרגום מול עמוד התניא) — בגודל סמ. 15x22. פערט, אוסטרליא. תשמ"ג (ההי' שנת גאולת משיח). 936pp.

רא. כנ"ל אות קסה. קאלאמבא, סרי לאנקא. ה'תשמ"ג. רלז דף.

רב. כנ"ל אות קסה. נצרת־עילית, באה"ק ת"ו. ה'תשד"מ. רמ דף.

רג. כנ"ל אות קצט. בת־ים, באה"ק ת"ו. תשד"מ. רכד דף.

רד. כנ"ל אות קסה. ראשון לציון, באה"ק ת"ו. תשד"מ. רלז דף.

רה. כנ"ל אות קסה. קרית מוצקין, באה"ק ת"ו. ה'תשד"מ. רמ דף.

רו. כנ"ל אות קסה. קרית ים, באה"ק ת"ו. תשד"מ. רלז דף.

רז. כנ"ל אות קסה. קרית טבעון, באה"ק ת"ו. תשד"מ. רלז דף.

רח. כנ"ל אות קסה. רייקיאוויק, איסלאנד. ה'תשד"מ. רלז דף.

רט. כנ"ל אות קסה. גרנדה (נדפס ע"י צבא ארצות־הברית). חנוכה, תשד"מ. רלז דף.

רי. כנ"ל אות קסה. גיורג'ס, גרנדה. ה'תשד"מ. רלז דף.

ריא. כנ"ל אות קסה. קרית שמונה, באה"ק ת"ו. תשד"מ. רלז דף.

ריב. כנ"ל אות קסה. המילטון, אנטריא, קנדה. תשד"מ. רלז דף.

ריג. כנ"ל אות ר. עם תרגום האנגלי (עמוד התרגום מול עמוד התניא). עם תיקונים והוספות. בסופו: תמונת כ"ק אדמו"ר הזקן. טאראנטא, אנטעריא, קאנאדא. ה'תשמ"ה. 979 ע'.

ריד. כנ"ל אות קסה. לונדון, אנטריא, קנדה. תשד"מ. רלז דף.

רטו. כנ"ל אות קסה. אטאווע, קנדה. ה'תשד"מ. רלז דף.

רטז. כנ"ל אות קסה. ונקובר, קנדה. תשד"מ. רלז דף.

ריז. כנ"ל אות קסה. ארובא. תשד"מ. רלז דף.

ריח. כנ"ל אות קנג. הוצאה מוקטנת 5x6 סנטימטר. לא פאז, באליוויא. ה'תשד"מ. רלח דף.

ריט. כנ"ל אות קלה. עם תיקונים והוספות. מאריסטאון, מאריס קאונטי, ניו דזשערסי. ה'תשד"מ. רכז דף.

רכ. כנ"ל אות קלה עם הוספות ותיקונים. לאס אנדזשעלעס, קאליפארניא. ה'תשד"מ. רכז דף.

רכא. כנ"ל אות ריג. עם תרגום אנגלי. סינסינעטי, אהייא. תשמ"ה.

רכב. כנ"ל אות קסה. אשקלון, באה"ק ת"ו. ה'תשד"מ. רמ דף.

רכג. כנ"ל אות קסה. באר שבע, באה"ק ת"ו. תשד"מ. רמ דף.

רכד. כנ"ל אות קסה. ברוש, באה"ק ת"ו. ה'תשד"מ. רמ דף.

רכה. כנ"ל אות קסה. מירון, ע"י ציון הרשב"י, באה"ק ת"ו. ה'תשד"מ. רלז דף.

רכו. כנ"ל אות קסה. כרמיאל, באה"ק ת"ו. תשד"מ. רלז דף.

רכז. כנ"ל אות קסה. מטולה, באה"ק ת"ו. ה'תשד"מ. רלז דף.

רכח. כנ"ל אות קסה. קרית חב"ד, צפת, באה"ק ת"ו. ה'תשד"מ. רמ דף.

רכט. כנ"ל אות קסה. קצרין, רמת הגולן, באה"ק ת"ו. ה'תשד"מ. רמ דף.

רל. כנ"ל אות קסה. הר חרמון, באה"ק ת"ו. ה'תשד"מ. רמ דף.

רלא. כנ"ל אות קסה. ראש פינה, באה"ק ת"ו. ה'תשד"מ. רמ דף.

רלב. כנ"ל אות קסה. חצור הגלילית, באה"ק ת"ו. תשד"מ. רמ דף.

רלג. כנ"ל אות קסה. כפר סבא, באה"ק ת"ו. ה'תשד"מ. רמ דף.

רלד. כנ"ל אות קסה. נס ציונה, באה"ק ת"ו. ה'תשד"מ. רמ דף.

רלה. כנ"ל אות קסה. דיעגא, קאליפורניא. תשד"מ. רלז דף.

רלו. כנ"ל אות קסה. טיואוואנא, מעקסיקא. ה'תשד"מ. רלז דף.

רלז. כנ"ל אות קסה. בופולו, נ.י. ה'תשד"מ. רלז דף.

רלח. כנ"ל אות קסה. ראטשעסטער, נ.י. ה'תשד"מ. רלז דף.

רלט. כנ"ל אות קסה. סיראקיוז, נ.י. ה'תשד"מ. רלז דף.

רמ. כנ"ל אות קסה. הארטפארד, קאנעטיקאט. ה'תשד"מ. רלז דף.

רמא. כנ"ל אות קסה. ניו הייווען, קאנעטיקאט. תשד"מ. רלז דף.

רמב. כנ"ל אות קסה. יוסטאן, טעקסאס. ה'תשד"מ. רלז דף.

רמג. כנ"ל אות קסה. מילוואקי, וויסקאנסין. ה'תשד"מ. רלז דף.

רמד. כנ"ל אות רטו. הוצאה מוקטנת — בגודל 6½x10 סנטימטר. מעדיסאן, וויסקאנסין. ה'תשד"מ. רמח דף.

רמה. כנ"ל אות קסה. ניו ארלינס, לויזיאנא. תשד"מ. רלז דף.

רמו. כנ"ל אות קצט. אינדיאנאפאליס, אינדיאנא. תשד"מ. רכג דף.

רמז. כנ"ל אות קסה. קנזס סיטי, מיזורי. תשד"מ. רלז דף.

רמח. כנ"ל אות רכו. מיאמי, פלארידא. ה'תשד"מ. רכו דף.

רמט. כנ"ל אות קסה. סיאטל, וואשינגטאן. ה'תשד"מ. רלט דף.

רנ. כנ"ל אות קסה. אנקארעדזש, אלאסקא. ה'תשד"מ. רלט דף.

רנא. כנ"ל אות קסה. דענווער, קאלאראדא. ה'תשד"מ. רלט דף.

רנב. כנ"ל אות קטה. טרענטאן, נ.ד. (נמצא בדפוס).

רנג. כנ"ל אות קסה (הוצאה מוקטנת — 6½x10 סנטימטר). אייווי היל, נוארק, ניו דזווירסי. תשד"מ. רנב דף.

רנד. כנ"ל אות רנג. מילבורן, נ.ד. ה'תשד"מ. רמח דף.

רנה. כנ"ל אות רנג. יוניאן סיטי, נ.ד. ה'תשד"מ. רמ דף.

רנו. כנ"ל אות קסה. אירווינגטאן, נ. ד. ה'תשד"מ. רמב דף.

רנז. כנ"ל אות קסה. ניו בראנזוויק, נ. ד. ה'תשד"מ. רלח דף.

רנח. כנ"ל אות קסה. אסבורי פארק, נ. ד. ה'תשד"מ. רלח דף.

רנט. כנ"ל אות קסה. שארלאט, נארט קאראליינא. תשד"מ. רמ דף.

רס. כנ"ל אות קסה. טאוזענד אוקס, קאליפארניא. תשד"מ. רלט דף.

רסא. כנ"ל אות קסה. אלבעקורקי, ניו מעקסיקא. תשד"מ. רמ דף.

רסב. כנ"ל אות קסה. תענך, אה"ק ת"ו. ה'תשד"מ. רמ דף.

רסג. כנ"ל אות קסה. אור יהודה, אה"ק ת"ו. ה'תשד"מ. רמ דף.

רסד. כנ"ל אות קסה. אשדוד, אה"ק ת"ו. ה'תשד"מ. רמ דף.

רסה. כנ"ל אות קסה. בית שאן, אה"ק ת"ו. ה'תשד"מ. רמ דף.

רסו. כנ"ל אות קסה. גני תקוה, אה"ק ת"ו. ה'תשד"מ. רמ דף.

רסז. כנ"ל אות קסה. יסוד המעלה, אה"ק ת"ו. ה'תשד"מ. רמ דף.

רסח. כנ"ל אות קסה. נחלת יהודה, אה"ק ת"ו. ה'תשד"מ. רמ דף.

רסט. כנ"ל אות קסה. נתני', אה"ק ת"ו. ה'תשד"מ. רמ דף.

ער. כנ"ל אות קסה. עומר, אה"ק ת"ו. ה'תשד"מ. רמ דף.

רעא. כנ"ל אות קסה. קיבוץ גבים, אה"ק ת"ו. ה'תשד"מ. רמ דף.

ערב. כנ"ל אות קסה. רמת גן, אה"ק ת"ו. ה'תשד"מ. רמ דף.

רעג. כנ"ל אות קסה. רמת ישי, אה"ק ת"ו. ה'תשד"מ. רמ דף.

ערד. כנ"ל אות קסה. ערד, אה"ק ת"ו. ה'תשד"מ. רמ דף.

ערה. כנ"ל אות קמה. פאראמאריבו, סורינאם. ה'תשד"מ. רמז דף.

רעו. כנ"ל אות קסה. קינגסטאן, דזשאמייקא. ה'תשד"מ. רלט דף.

רעז. כנ"ל אות רעו. בארבאדאס. ה'תשד"מ. רלט דף.

רעח. כנ"ל אות קסה. בעווערלי הילס, קאליפארניא. ה'תשד"מ. רלט דף.

רעט. כנ״ל אות קסה. האריסבורג, פענסילווייניא. ה׳תשד״מ. רלח דף.

רפ. כנ״ל אות קסה. ריטשמאנד, ווירדזשיניא. ה׳תשד״מ. רלט דף.

רפא. כנ״ל אות קסה. קליוולאנד, אהייא. ה׳תשד״מ. רלט דף.

רפב. כנ״ל אות ריט. נאשוויל, טענעסי. ה׳תשד״מ. רלו דף.

רפג. כנ״ל אות קסה. אופקים, אה״ק ת״ו. ה׳תשד״מ. רם דף.

רפד. כנ״ל אות קסה. טירת הכרמל, אה״ק ת״ו. ה׳תשד״מ. רם דף.

רפה. כנ״ל אות קסה. נהרי׳, אה״ק ת״ו. ה׳תשד״מ. רם דף.

רפו. כנ״ל אות קסה. רעננה, אה״ק ת״ו. ה׳תשד״מ. רם דף.

רפז. כנ״ל אות קסה. פארט לאודערדייל, פלארידא. ה׳תשד״מ. רלט דף.

רפח. כנ״ל אות רנה. פראנציסקא, קאליפארניא. ה׳תשד״מ. רמח דף.

רפט. כנ״ל אות רנה. בערקלי, קאליפארניא. ה׳תשד״מ. רמח דף.

ת״ו. ה׳תשד״מ. רם דף.

רצ. כנ״ל אות רנה. מניקא, קאליפארניא, ה׳תשד״מ. רמח דף.

רצא. כנ״ל אות קסה. וואוסטער, מאסאטשוסעטס. ה׳תשד״מ. רלט דף.

רצב. כנ״ל אות קסה. נתיבות, אה״ק ת״ו. תשד״מ. רם דף.

רצג. כנ״ל אות קסה. קרית אונו, אה״ק ת״ו. ה׳תשד״מ. רם דף.

רצד. כנ״ל אות קסה. הוצאה מוקטנת — בגודל 6¾x8 סנטימטר. דיטרויט, מישיגען. ה׳תשד״מ. רמח דף.

רצה. כנ״ל אות רצ. פיניקס, אריזאנא. ה׳תשד״מ. רמא דף.

רצו. כנ״ל אות רצ. טוסאן, אריזאנא. ה׳תשד״מ. רמא דף.

רצז. כנ״ל אות רטו. פראווידענץ, ראוד איילאנד. תשד״מ. רמא דף.

רחצ. כנ״ל אות רטו. מזרח בערלין, מזרח גרמניא. תשד״מ. רלט דף.

רצט. כנ״ל אות קסה. פארטלאנד, אריגאן. ה׳תשד״מ. רם דף.

ש. כנ״ל אות קמ. עם תרגום האנגלי (עמוד התרגום מול עמוד התניא) — בגודל סמ. 13½x18½. פריטאריא, דרום אפריקא. ה׳תשד״מ. 979 ע׳.

שא. כנ״ל אות קסה. גואטאמאלא. ה׳תשד״מ. רם דף.

שב. כנ״ל אות שא. אואן, פורטא ריקא. ה׳תשד״מ. רם דף.

שג. כנ״ל אות קסה. בארענקילא, קאלאמביא. תשד״מ. רלט דף.

דש. כנ״ל אות קסה. מעדעלין, קאלאמביא. תשד״מ. רלט דף.

שה. כנ״ל אות קסה. קאלי, קאלאמביא. תשד״מ. רלט דף.

שו. כנ״ל אות קסה. בארבארא, קאליפארניא. ה׳תשד״מ. רלט דף.

שז. כנ״ל אות קסה. שכונים חדשים כפר חב״ד, באה״ק ת״ו. ה׳תשד״מ. רם דף.

שח. כנ״ל אות קסה. נמל תעופה — לוד, באה״ק ת״ו. ה׳תשד״מ. רם דף.

שט. כנ״ל אות קסה. צפרי׳, באה״ק ת״ו. ה׳תשד״מ. רם דף.

שי. כנ״ל אות קסה. ויניציאה, איטאליא. ה׳תשד״מ. רם דף.

שיא. כנ״ל אות קסה. ביהכנ״ס „בית מנחם״, כפר חב״ד (ע״י תושבי הכפר), באה״ק ת״ו. ה׳תשד״מ. רם דף.

שיב. כנ״ל אות קסה. בית רפואה „אסף הרופא״ — סרפנד, באה״ק ת״ו. תשד״מ. רם דף.

שיג. כנ״ל אות קסה. עמנואל, באה״ק ת״ו. ה׳תשד״מ. רם דף.

שיד. כנ״ל אות קצט. הרצלי׳, באה״ק ת״ו. ה׳תשד״מ.

שטו. כנ״ל אות קסה. שכונת רמת אליהו, באה״ק ת״ו. ה׳תשד״מ. רם דף.

שטז. כנ״ל אות רעג. הוצאה שני׳ (ע״י מועצה מקומית). רמת ישי, באה״ק ת״ו. ה׳תשד״מ. רם דף.

שיז. כנ״ל אות קסה. בראזיליא, בראזיל. ה׳תשד״מ. רמא דף.

שיח. כנ״ל אות קסה. פיטסבורג, פענסילווייניא. תשד״מ. רמא דף.

שיט. כנ״ל אות רנה. האליוואוד, פלארידא. ה׳תשד״מ. רמט דף.

שכ. כנ״ל אות רעו. בגודל 10x13 סנטימטר. שיקאגא, אילינאי. ה׳תשד״מ. רלה דף.

שכא. כנ״ל אות קסה. כפר תבור, באה״ק ת״ו. ה׳תשד״מ. רמא דף.

שכב. כנ״ל אות קסה. זשענעוו, שווייץ. ה׳תשד״מ. רמב דף.

שכג. כנ״ל אות קסה. וואדוץ, ליכטענשטיין. ה׳תשד״מ. רמב דף.

שכד. כנ״ל אות קסה. רומא, איטאליע. ה׳תשד״מ. רם דף.

שכה. כנ״ל אות קסה. באלאניא, איטאליע. ה׳תשד״מ. רם דף.

שכו. כנ״ל אות שלה. פירענצא, איטאליע. ה׳תשד״מ. רמב דף.

שכז. כנ״ל אות שלה. טארינא, איטאליע. ה׳תשד״מ. רמב דף.

שכח. כנ״ל אות שלה. טריעסט, איטאליע. ה׳תשד״מ. רמא דף.

שכט. כנ״ל אות שלה. וואלענצא (פא), איטאליע. תשד״מ. רמב דף.

של. כנ״ל אות קסה. וועסט אראנדזש, עסעקס קאונטי, ניו דזשוירסי. ה׳תשד״מ. רלח דף.

שלא. כנ״ל אות קסה. טינעק, בערגען קאונטי, נ.ד. ה׳תשד״מ. רלט דף.

שלב. כנ״ל אות רנג. ליווינגסטאן, נ.ד. ה׳תשד״מ. רנב דף.

שלג. כנ״ל אות קסה. מייפלוואוד, נ.ד. ה׳תשד״מ. רמב דף.

שלד. כנ״ל אות קסה. אטלאנטיק סיטי, אטלאנטיק קאונטי, נ.ד. ה׳תשד״מ. רם דף.

שלה. כנ״ל אות קסה. הוצאה מוקטנת — 6½x10 סנטימטר. דזשערסי סיטי, נ.ד. ה׳תשד״מ. רם דף.

שלו. כנ״ל אות שלה. פאסאייק, נ.ד. ה׳תשד״מ. רמב דף.

שלז. כנ״ל אות שלה. לאנג ביטש, נאסאו קאונטי, לאנג איילאנד, נ.י. ה׳תשד״מ. רמב דף.

שלח. כנ״ל אות שלה. האנטינגטאן, סופאק קאונטי, לאנג איילענד, נ.י. ה׳תשד״מ. רלט דף.

שלט. כנ״ל אות קסה. יודזשין, אריגאן. ה׳תשד״מ. רמב דף.

שמ. כנ״ל אות קסה. מאה שערים, ברחוב בעל התניא, ירות״ו, באה״ק ת״ו. ה׳תשד״מ. רמג דף.

שמא. כנ״ל אות קסה. בית א־ל, באה״ק ת״ו. ה׳תשד״מ. רם דף.

שמב. כנ״ל אות קסה. בית שמש, באה״ק ת״ו. ה׳תשד״מ. רם דף.

שמג. כנ״ל אות קסה. מושב זיתן, באה״ק ת״ו. ה׳תשד״מ. רם דף.

שדמ. כנ״ל אות קכג. עם תיקונים והוספות. קראון הייטס — „כאן צוה ה׳ את הברכה״, ברוקלין, נ.י. נדפס בעליית ביהכנ״ס וביהמ״ד ליובאוויטש שבליובאוויטש — „770״, בדפוס ד„ועד להפצת שיחות״ 788 איסטערן פארקוויי (בהשתתפות תושבי השכונה שיחיו), לקראת יו״ד שבט, ה׳תשד״מ. רמב דף.

שמה. כנ״ל אות קסה. מר״צ/בית הדפוס הצבאי. (ע״י צבא הגנה לישראל). באה״ק ת״ו. ה׳תשד״מ. רמג דף.

שמו. כנ״ל אות קסה. בית רבקה, כפר חב״ד ב׳, באה״ק ת״ו. ה׳תשד״מ. רם דף.

שמז. כנ״ל אות קסה. טגוציגלפא, הנדוראס. ה׳תשד״מ. רמב דף.

שמח. כנ״ל אות שלה. קאממאק, לאנג איילאנד, נ.י. ה׳תשד״מ. רמב דף.

שמט. כנ״ל אות שלה. פאטשאג, לאנג איילאנד, נ.י. ה׳תשד״מ. רמב דף.

שנ. כנ״ל אות שדמ. מכנס, מרוקו. ה׳תשד״מ. רמב דף.

שנא. כנ״ל אות קסה. לאגאס, ניגיריא. ה׳תשד״מ. רמא דף.

שנב. כנ״ל אות קסה. מעלה אדומים, ירות״ו. רמא דף.

שנג. כנ״ל אות קסה. נוה יעקב, ירות״ו. ה׳תשד״מ. רמא דף.

שנד. כנ״ל אות קסה. גבעה הצרפתית, ירות״ו. ה׳תשד״מ. רמא דף.

שנה. כנ״ל אות קסה. ע״י כותל המערבי, שריד בית מקדשנו, ירות״ו. ה׳תשד״מ. רמא דף.

שנו. כנ״ל אות קסה. בית לחם — ע״י קבר רחל אמנו, באה״ק ת״ו. ה׳תשד״מ. רמא דף.

שנז. כנ״ל אות קסה. הר ציון, ע״י קבר דוד המלך, ירות״ו. ה׳תשד״מ. רמא דף.

שנח. כנ״ל אות קסה. כפר רמה — ע״י קבר שמואל הנביא, ירות״ו. ה׳תשד״מ. רמג דף.

שנט. כנ״ל אות קסה. נחלת הר חב״ד, בקרית מלאכי, באה״ק ת״ו. ה׳תשד״מ. רמא דף.

שס. כנ״ל אות קסה. שכם — ע״י קבר יוסף הצדיק, באה״ק ת״ו. ה׳תשד״מ. רמא דף.

שסא. כנ״ל אות קסה. חברון, באה״ק ת״ו. ה׳תשד״מ. רמא דף.

שסב. כנ״ל אות קסה. דימונה, באה״ק ת״ו. ה׳תשד״מ. רמא דף.

שסג. כנ״ל אות שדמ. נאסאו, באהאמאס. ה׳תשד״מ. רמג דף.

שסד. כנ״ל אות שלה. איסט נארטפארט, לאנג איילאנד, נ.י. ה׳תשד״מ. רמג דף.

שסה. כנ"ל אות שלה. מאנטאוק פאינט, לאנג איילאנד, נ.י. ה'תשד"מ. רמג דף.
שסו. כנ"ל אות שלה. ריווערהעד, לאנג איילאנד, נ.י. ה'תשד"מ. רמג דף.
שסז. כנ"ל אות שלה. סעלדען, לאנג איילאנד, נ.י. ה'תשד"מ. רמג דף.
שסח. כנ"ל אות שלה. דיר פארק, לאנג איילאנד, נ.י. ה'תשד"מ. רמג דף.
שסט. כנ"ל אות שלה. סטאני ברוק, לאנג איילאנד, נ.י. ה'תשד"מ. רמג דף.
שע. כנ"ל אות שלה. וואטערטאון, נ.י. ה'תשד"מ. רמג דף.
שעא. כנ"ל אות שלה. דזשיימסטאון, נ.י. ה'תשד"מ. רמג דף.
שעב. כנ"ל אות שלה. קאלעדזש פארק, מערילאנד. ה'תשד"מ. רמט דף.
שעג. כנ"ל אות קסה. גבעת הזיתים — לוד, באה"ק ת"ו. ה'תשד"מ. רמג דף.
שעד. כנ"ל אות קסה. קרית אתא, באה"ק ת"ו. ה'תשד"מ. רמג דף.
שעה. כנ"ל אות קסה. מאנסי נ.י. ה'תשד"מ. רמג דף.
שעו. כנ"ל אות רכ. ליווערפול, אנגלי'. ה'תשד"מ רכג דף.
שעז. כנ"ל אות רכ. שעפילד, אנגלי'. ה'תשד"מ. רכג דף.
שעח. כנ"ל אות קמא. הוצאה מוקטנת 8.2x11 סנטימטר. מנשסתר, אנגלי'. 770 .pp. ה'תשד"מ.
שעט. כנ"ל אות קסה. בירמינגהאם, אנגלי'. ה'תשד"מ. רמא דף.
שפ. כנ"ל אות שלה. ענגעלוואוד, נ.ד. ה'תשד"מ. רמג דף.
שפא. כנ"ל אות שלה. פעיר לאון, נ.ד. ה'תשד"מ. רמג דף.
שפב. כנ"ל אות שלה. טאמאס, ווירדזשין איילאנדס. ה'תשד"מ. רמג דף.
שפג. כנ"ל אות שלה. קוראסאו. ה'תשד"מ. רמג דף.
שפד. כנ"ל אות רעו. סטאטן איילאנד, נ.י. ה'תשד"מ. רמג דף.
שפה. כנ"ל אות שלה. פערט אמבאי, נ.ד. ה'תשד"מ. רמג דף.
שפו. כנ"ל אות קסט. גאיאנא, בראזיל. ה'תשד"מ. רמג דף.
שפז. כנ"ל אות קסט. דזשאזיי דא ריא פרעטא, בראזיל. ה'תשד"מ. רמג דף.
שפח. כנ"ל אות שדמ. קינשאסא, זאיר. ה'תשד"מ. רמג דף.
שפט. כנ"ל אות שדמ. דאמינגא, דומיניקין רעפובליק. ה'תשד"מ. רמג דף.
שצ. כנ"ל אות רעו. לייקוואוד, אושען קאונטי, ניו דזשערסי. ה'תשד"מ. רמה דף.
שצא. כנ"ל אות שלה. וועסטמינסטער, קאליפארניא. ה'תשד"מ. רמח דף.
שצב. כנ"ל אות שלה. לאנג ביטש, קאליפארניא. ה'תשד"מ. רמח דף.
שצג. כנ"ל אות שלה. סיל ביטש, קאליפארניא. ה'תשד"מ. רמח דף.
שצד. כנ"ל אות שלה. האנטינגטאן ביטש, קאליפארניא. ה'תשד"מ. רמח דף.
שצה. כנ"ל אות שלה. ארווייז, קאליפארניא. ה'תשד"מ. רמח דף.
שצו. כנ"ל אות שלה. וויטיאר, קאליפארניא. ה'תשד"מ. רמח דף.
שצז. כנ"ל אות שלה. סאוט קירני, האדסאן קאונטי, נ.ד. ה'תשד"מ. רמג דף.
שצח. כנ"ל אות שלה. אן ארבער, מישיגען. ה'תשד"מ. רמג דף.
שצט. כנ"ל אות שלה. אקראן, אהייא. ה'תשד"מ. רמג דף.
ת. כנ"ל אות שדמ. ישיבת תותי"ל, ברינוא, צרפת. ה'תשד"מ. רמו דף.
תא. כנ"ל אות קסה. ניס, צרפת. ה'תשד"מ. רמו דף.
תב. כנ"ל אות רעו. טרוא, צרפת. ה'תשד"מ. רמו דף.
תג. כנ"ל אות רעו. ראזן, צרפת. ה'תשד"מ. רמו דף.
תד. כנ"ל אות רעו. שטראסבורג, צרפת. ה'תשד"מ. רמו דף.
תה. כנ"ל אות רעו. אבערווילע, צרפת. ה'תשד"מ. רמו דף.
תו. כנ"ל אות רעו. כרטייל, צרפת. ה'תשד"מ. רמו דף.
תז. כנ"ל אות רעו. מאסי, צרפת. ה'תשד"מ. רמו דף.
תח. כנ"ל אות רעו. סרסעל, צרפת. ה'תשד"מ. רמו דף.
תט. כנ"ל אות רעו. גארז', צרפת. ה'תשד"מ. רמו דף.
תי. כנ"ל אות רעו. ווילנעוו לא גארען, צרפת. תשד"מ. רמו דף.
תיא. כנ"ל אות קסה. מושב ברקת, באה"ק ת"ו. ה'תשד"מ. רמג דף.
תיב. כנ"ל אות קסה. קרית היובל, ירות"ו, באה"ק ת"ו. ה'תשד"מ. רמג דף.
תיג. כנ"ל אות קסה. מושב איתן, באה"ק ת"ו. ה'תשד"מ. רמג דף.
תיד. כנ"ל אות קסה. מושב קוממיות, באה"ק ת"ו. ה'תשד"מ. רמג דף.
תטו. כנ"ל אות קסה. מפעל דשנים אורגניים, חירי' — כביש גהה, באה"ק ת"ו. ה'תשד"מ. רמג דף.
תטז. כנ"ל אות רעו. תוניס, תוניסיא. ה'תשד"מ. רמג דף.
תיז. כנ"ל אות רעו. מונטו קרלא, מונקו. ה'תשד"מ. רמט דף.
תיח. כנ"ל אות רעו. בריסל, בעלגיא. ה'תשד"מ. רמג דף.
תיט. כנ"ל אות רעו. מאלמא, שוועדן. ה'תשד"מ. רמג דף.
תכ. כנ"ל אות קסה. עם תיקונים. (הוצאה מוקטנת 6x8½ סנטימטר). אגואס דע בארבארא, בראזיל. ה'תשד"מ. רמה דף.
תכא. כנ"ל אות תכ. אגואס דע לינדאיא, בראזיל. ה'תשד"מ. רמה דף.
תכב. כנ"ל אות תכ. אזאסקא, בראזיל. ה'תשד"מ. רמה דף.
תכג. כנ"ל אות תכ. אטיבאיא, בראזיל. ה'תשד"מ. רמה דף.
תכד. כנ"ל אות תכ. איטו, בראזיל. ה'תשד"מ. רמה דף.
תכה. כנ"ל אות תכ. איטאפירא, בראזיל. ה'תשד"מ. רמה דף.
תכו. כנ"ל אות תכ. איטאפעווי, בראזיל. ה'תשד"מ. רמה דף.
תכז. כנ"ל אות תכ. איטאפעטינינגא, בראזיל. ה'תשד"מ. רמה דף.
תכח. כנ"ל אות תכ. איטאפעסעריקא דא סערא, בראזיל. ה'תשד"מ. רמה דף.
תכט. כנ"ל אות תכ. איטופעווא, בראזיל. ה'תשד"מ. רמה דף.
תל. כנ"ל אות תכ. אמעריקאנא, בראזיל. ה'תשד"מ. רמה דף.
תלא. כנ"ל אות תכ. אנדריי, בראזיל. ה'תשד"מ. רמה דף.
תלב. כנ"ל אות תכ. אראראקוארא, בראזיל. ה'תשד"מ. רמה דף.
תלג. כנ"ל אות תכ. ארוזשא, בראזיל. ה'תשד"מ. רמה דף.
תלד. כנ"ל אות תכ. באורו, בראזיל. ה'תשד"מ. רמה דף.
תלה. כנ"ל אות תכ. באטוקאטו, בראזיל. ה'תשד"מ. רמה דף.
תלו. כנ"ל אות תכ. בארבארא דא אעסטע, בראזיל. ה'תשד"מ. רמה דף.
תלז. כנ"ל אות תכ. בארועri, בראזיל. ה'תשד"מ. רמה דף.
תלח. כנ"ל אות תכ. בערנארדא דא קאמפא, בראזיל. ה'תשד"מ. רמה דף.
תלט. כנ"ל אות תכ. בראגאנסא פאוליסטא, בראזיל. ה'תשד"מ. רמה דף.
תמ. כנ"ל אות תכ. גוארוזשא, בראזיל. ה'תשד"מ. רמה דף.
תמא. כנ"ל אות תכ. גואראטינגועטא, בראזיל. ה'תשד"מ. רמה דף.
תמב. כנ"ל אות תכ. גוארוליאס, בראזיל. ה'תשד"מ. רמה דף.
תמג. כנ"ל אות תכ. דיאדעמא, בראזיל. ה'תשד"מ. רמה דף.
תמד. כנ"ל אות תכ. ואליניאס, בראזיל. ה'תשד"מ. רמה דף.
תמה. כנ"ל אות תכ. ואסאוראס, בראזיל. ה'תשד"מ. רמה דף.
תמו. כנ"ל אות תכ. וויסענטע, בראזיל. ה'תשד"מ. רמה דף.
תמז. כנ"ל אות תכ. זשאזע דאס קאמפאס, בראזיל. ה'תשד"מ. רמה דף.
תמח. כנ"ל אות תכ. זשאנדירא, בראזיל. ה'תשד"מ. רמה דף.
תמט. כנ"ל אות תכ. זשאקארעאי, בראזיל. ה'תשד"מ. רמה דף.
תנ. כנ"ל אות תכ. זשונדיאאי, בראזיל. ה'תשד"מ. רמה דף.
תנא. כנ"ל אות תכ. טאבאאן דא סערא, בראזיל. ה'תשד"מ. רמה דף.
תנב. כנ"ל אות תכ. טאובאטע, בראזיל. ה'תשד"מ. רמה דף.
תנג. כנ"ל אות תכ. לימיירא, בראזיל. ה'תשד"מ. רמה דף.
תנד. כנ"ל אות תכ. מאושי, בראזיל. ה'תשד"מ. רמה דף.
תנה. כנ"ל אות תכ. מייריפארא, בראזיל. ה'תשד"מ. רמה דף.
תנו. כנ"ל אות תכ. נאווא אדעסא, בראזיל. ה'תשד"מ. רמה דף.
תנז. כנ"ל אות תכ. סאנטאנא דא פארנאאיבא, בראזיל. ה'תשד"מ. רמה דף.
תנח. כנ"ל אות תכ. סאנטאס, בראזיל. ה'תשד"מ. רמה דף.

תנט. כנ"ל אות תכ. סאראקאבא, בראזיל. ה'תשד"מ. רמה דף.
תס. כנ"ל אות תכ. סוזאנא, בראזיל. ה'תשד"מ. רמה דף.
תסא. כנ"ל אות תכ. סערא נעגרא, בראזיל. ה'תשד"מ. רמה דף.
תסב. כנ"ל אות תכ. עמבו, בראזיל. ה'תשד"מ. רמה דף.
תסג. כנ"ל אות תכ. עמבו-גואסו, בראזיל. ה'תשד"מ. רמה דף.
תסד. כנ"ל אות תכ. פאוליניא, בראזיל. ה'תשד"מ. רמה דף.
תסה. כנ"ל אות תכ. פיראסונונגא, בראזיל. ה'תשד"מ. רמה דף.
תסו. כנ"ל אות תכ. פיראסיקאבא, בראזיל. ה'תשד"מ. רמה דף.
תסז. כנ"ל אות תכ. פעדרא, בראזיל. ה'תשד"מ. רמה דף.
תסח. כנ"ל אות תכ. פראיא גראנדע, בראזיל. ה'תשד"מ. רמה דף.
תסט. כנ"ל אות תכ. פראנקא דא ראשא, בראזיל. ה'תשד"מ. רמה דף.
תע. כנ"ל אות תכ. קאברעאווא, בראזיל. ה'תשד"מ. רמה דף.
תעא. כנ"ל אות תכ. קאטיא, בראזיל. ה'תשד"מ. רמה דף.
תעב. כנ"ל אות תכ. קאמפאס דא זשארדאן, בראזיל. ה'תשד"מ. רמה דף.
תעג. כנ"ל אות תכ. קאמפינאס, בראזיל. ה'תשד"מ. רמה דף.
תעד. כנ"ל אות תכ. קאראפיקואיבא, בראזיל. ה'תשד"מ. רמה דף.
תעה. כנ"ל אות תכ. קארלאס, בראזיל. ה'תשד"מ. רמה דף.
תעו. כנ"ל אות תכ. קייטאנא דא סול, בראזיל. ה'תשד"מ. רמה דף.
תעז. כנ"ל אות תכ. ראקי, בראזיל. ה'תשד"מ. רמה דף.
תעח. כנ"ל אות תכ. ריא קלארא, בראזיל. ה'תשד"מ. רמה דף.
תעט. כנ"ל אות תכ. ריביירען פירעס, בראזיל. ה'תשד"מ. רמה דף.
תפ. כנ"ל אות תכ. ריביירען פרעטא, בראזיל. ה'תשד"מ. רמה דף.
תפא. כנ"ל אות תכ. אורא פרעטא, בראזיל. ה'תשד"מ. רמה דף.
תפב. כנ"ל אות תכ. בעלא האריזאנטע, בראזיל. ה'תשד"מ. רמה דף.
תפג. כנ"ל אות תכ. זשאאן דעל ריי, בראזיל. ה'תשד"מ. רמה דף.
תפד. כנ"ל אות תכ. זשואיז דע פארא, בראזיל. ה'תשד"מ. רמה דף.
תפה. כנ"ל אות תכ. טרייס קאראסאינס, בראזיל. ה'תשד"מ. רמה דף.
תפו. כנ"ל אות תכ. לאורענסא, בראזיל. ה'תשד"מ. רמה דף.
תפז. כנ"ל אות תכ. נאווא לימא, בראזיל. ה'תשד"מ. רמה דף.
תפח. כנ"ל אות תכ. סאלעדאדע דע מינאס, בראזיל. ה'תשד"מ. רמה דף.
תפט. כנ"ל אות תכ. פאסאס דע קאלדאס, בראזיל. ה'תשד"מ. רמה דף.
תצ. כנ"ל אות תכ. קאנטאושען, בראזיל. ה'תשד"מ. רמה דף.
תצא. כנ"ל אות תכ. קאנסעליירא לאפאיעטע, בראזיל. ה'תשד"מ. רמה דף.
תצב. כנ"ל אות תכ. קאשאמבו, בראזיל. ה'תשד"מ. רמה דף.
תצג. כנ"ל אות תכ. פאנטא גראסא, בראזיל. ה'תשד"מ. רמה דף.
תצד. כנ"ל אות תכ. פאראנאגוא, בראזיל. ה'תשד"מ. רמה דף.
תצה. כנ"ל אות תכ. קאמפא לארגא, בראזיל. ה'תשד"מ. רמה דף.
תצו. כנ"ל אות תכ. קוריטיבא, בראזיל. ה'תשד"מ. רמה דף.
תצז. כנ"ל אות תכ. קריסיאומא, בראזיל. ה'תשד"מ. רמה דף.
תצח. כנ"ל אות תכ. אראראגואמא, בראזיל. ה'תשד"מ. רמה דף.
תצט. כנ"ל אות תכ. בארא מאנסא, בראזיל. ה'תשד"מ. רמה דף.
תק. כנ"ל אות תכ. גאנסאלא, בראזיל. ה'תשד"מ. רמה דף.
תקא. כנ"ל אות תכ. דוקע דע קאשיאס, בראזיל. ה'תשד"מ. רמה דף.
תקב. כנ"ל אות תכ. וואלטא רעדאנדא, בראזיל. ה'תשד"מ. רמה דף.
תקג. כנ"ל אות תכ. פ[illegible] עזאפאליס, בראזיל. ה'תשד"מ. רמה דף.
תקד. כנ"ל אות תכ. פ[illegible]ס ריאס, בראזיל. ה'תשד"מ. רמה דף.
תקה. כנ"ל אות תכ. מיגעל פעריירא, בראזיל. ה'תשד"מ. רמה דף.
תקו. כנ"ל אות תכ. נאווא פריבורגא, בראזיל. ה'תשד"מ. רמה דף.
תקז. כנ"ל אות תכ. נאווא איגואסו, בראזיל. ה'תשד"מ. רמה דף.
תקח. כנ"ל אות תכ. ניטעראי, בראזיל. ה'תשד"מ. רמה דף.
תקט. כנ"ל אות תכ. נילאפאליס, בראזיל. ה'תשד"מ. רמה דף.
תקי. כנ"ל אות תכ. סאקוארעמא, בראזיל. ה'תשד"מ. רמה דף.
תקיא. כנ"ל אות תכ. פעדרא דא אלדייא, בראזיל. ה'תשד"מ. רמה דף.
תקיב. כנ"ל אות תכ. קאבא פריא, בראזיל. ה'תשד"מ. רמה דף.
תקיג. כנ"ל אות תכ. ריא דאס אסטראס, בראזיל. ה'תשד"מ. רמה דף.
תקיד. כנ"ל אות תכ. רעזענדע, בראזיל. ה'תשד"מ. רמה דף.
תקטו. כנ"ל אות תכ. לעאפאלדא, בראזיל. ה'תשד"מ. רמה דף.
תקטז. כנ"ל אות תכ. ערעשין, בראזיל. ה'תשד"מ. רמה דף.
תקיז. כנ"ל אות תכ. פאסא פונדא, בראזיל. ה'תשד"מ. רמה דף.
תקיח. כנ"ל אות תכ. פארטא אלעגרע, בראזיל. ה'תשד"מ. רמה דף.
תקיט. כנ"ל אות תכ. קאנאאס, בראזיל. ה'תשד"מ. רמה דף.
תקכ. כנ"ל אות שדמ. מאנהאטען, נ.י. ה'תשד"מ. רמה דף.
תקכא. כנ"ל אות שדמ. קווינס, נ.י. ה'תשד"מ. רמה דף.
תקכב. כנ"ל אות שסח. שכונת פלעטבוש, ברוקלין, נ.י. ה'תשד"מ. רמה דף.
תקכג. כנ"ל אות ריט. שכונת בארא פארק, ברוקלין, נ.י. ה'תשד"מ. רלו דף.
תקכד. כנ"ל אות שלה. פאר ראקאוויי, נ.י. ה'תשד"מ. רמט דף.
תקכה. כנ"ל אות קסה. עליזאבעט, יוניאן קאונטי, נ.ד. ה'תשד"מ. רמו דף.
תקכו. כנ"ל אות שדמ. על סאלוואדאר. ה'תשד"מ. רמו דף.
תקכז. כנ"ל אות שדמ. מאנאגוא, ניקאראגוא. ה'תשד"מ. רמו דף.
תקכח. כנ"ל אות רצד. (בגודל 8x6¾ סנטימטר). גראנד ראפידס, מישיגען. ה'תשד"מ. רמו דף.
תקכט. כנ"ל אות תקכח. פארמינגטאן הילס, מישיגען. ה'תשד"מ. רמו דף.
תקל. כנ"ל אות תקכח. קאלקאסקא, מישיגען. ה'תשד"מ. רמו דף.
תקלא. כנ"ל אות תקל. קאלאמבוס, אהייא. ה'תשד"מ. רמו דף.
תקלב. כנ"ל אות שלה. אבערלין, אהייא. ה'תשד"מ. רמו דף.
תקלג. כנ"ל אות שלה. וויקליף, אהייא. ה'תשד"מ. רמו דף.
תקלד. כנ"ל אות שסח. בורלינגטאן, ווערמאנט. ה'תשד"מ. רמו דף.
תקלה. כנ"ל אות קסה. טשערי היל, קאמדען קאונטי, נ.ד. ה'תשד"מ. רמו דף.
תקלו. כנ"ל אות שדמ. גלאסגאו, סקאטלאנד. ה'תשד"מ. רמו דף.
תקלז. כנ"ל אות רלח. לאנגמעדא, מאסאטשוסעטס. ה'תשד"מ. רמו דף.
תקלח. כנ"ל אות רלח. ברידזשפארט, קאנעטיקאט. ה'תשד"מ. רמו דף.
תקלט. כנ"ל אות שסח. טשאטאנוגא, טענסעי. ה'תשד"מ. רמח דף.
תקמ. כנ"ל אות ריט. מיניאפאליס, מינעסאטא. ה'תשד"מ. רלה דף.
תקמא. כנ"ל אות שלה. דולוטה, מינעסאטא. ה'תשד"מ. רמח דף.
תקמב. כנ"ל אות שסח. טאנדער ביי, אנטריא, קנדה. ה'תשד"מ. רמו דף.
תקמג. כנ"ל אות שסח. ניאגרא פאלס, אנטריא, קנדה. ה'תשד"מ. רמו דף.
תקמד. כנ"ל אות שסח. גואלף, אנטריא, קנדה. ה'תשד"מ. רמו דף.
תקמה. כנ"ל אות שסח. קינגסטאן, אנטריא, קנדה. ה'תשד"מ. רמו דף.
תקמו כנ"ל אות שסח. קיטשענער — וואטערלו [נדפס בקיטשענער], אנטריא, קנדה. ה'תשד"מ. רמז דף.
תקמז. כנ"ל אות שדמ. מרכז חב"ד טורונטו, 770 חב"ד גייט, וואן אנטריא, קנדה. ה'תשד"מ. רמו דף.
תקמח. כנ"ל אות שסח. פאלם ספרינגס, קאליפארניא. ה'תשד"מ. רמח דף.
תקמט. כנ"ל אות שסח. בורבאנק, קאליפארניא. ה'תשד"מ. רמח דף.
תקנ. כנ"ל אות ר. (עם תרגום האנגלי מול עמוד התניא). האבארט, טאזמייניא. ה'תשד"מ.
תקנא. כנ"ל אות תקנ. וועלינגטאן, ניו זילאנד. ה'תשד"מ.
תקנב. כנ"ל אות תקנ. אדעלייד, אויסטראליא. ה'תשד"מ.
תקנג. כנ"ל אות תקנ. בריסביין, אויסטראליא. ה'תשד"מ.
תקנד. כנ"ל אות תקנ. קאנבערא, אויסטראליא. ה'תשד"מ.
תקנה. כנ"ל אות ריא. ישיבת תומכי תמימים, כפר חב"ד, באה"ק ת"ו. ה'תשד"מ. רמז דף.

תקנו. כנ"ל אות ריא. ישיבת תורת אמת, בעיה"ק ירות"ו. ה'תשד"מ. רמז דף.
תקנז. כנ"ל אות ריא. ביריה, באה"ק ת"ו. ה'תשד"מ. רמז דף.
תקנח. כנ"ל אות ריא. ישוב אבן שמואל, באה"ק ת"ו. ה'תשד"מ. רמז דף.
תקנט. כנ"ל אות ריא. מושב יהונתן, רמת הגולן, באה"ק ת"ו. ה'תשד"מ. רמז דף.
תקס. כנ"ל אות ריא. מושב יערה, באה"ק ת"ו. ה'תשד"מ. רמז דף.
תקסא. כנ"ל אות ריא. מושב רויה, באה"ק ת"ו. ה'תשד"מ. רמז דף.
תקסב. כנ"ל אות ריא. שבי ציון, באה"ק ת"ו. ה'תשד"מ. רמז דף.
תקסג. כנ"ל אות ריא. מעלות, באה"ק ת"ו. ה'תשד"מ. רמז דף.
תקסד. כנ"ל אות ריא. מצפה הרירית, באה"ק ת"ו. ה'תשד"מ. רמז דף.
תקסה. כנ"ל אות רב. נצרת-עילית (הוצאה שני'), באה"ק ת"ו. ה'תשד"מ. רמז דף.
תקסו. כנ"ל אות ריא. פרדס חנה, באה"ק ת"ו. ה'תשד"מ. רמז דף.
תקסז. כנ"ל אות ריא. קיבוץ עין הנצי"ב, באה"ק ת"ו. ה'תשד"מ. רמז דף.
תקסח. כנ"ל אות ריא. קיבוץ עין זיון, רמת הגולן, באה"ק ת"ו. ה'תשד"מ. רמז דף.
תקסט. כנ"ל אות ריא. קרית חיים, באה"ק ת"ו. ה'תשד"מ. רמז דף.
תקע. כנ"ל אות ריא. קרית ביאליק, באה"ק ת"ו. ה'תשד"מ. רמז דף.
תקעא. כנ"ל אות ריא. קרית שמואל, באה"ק ת"ו. ה'תשד"מ. רמז דף.
תקעב. כנ"ל אות ריא. רמות, ירושת"ו. ה'תשד"מ. רמז דף.
תקעג. כנ"ל אות שסח. אושענסייד, קאליפארניא. ה'תשד"מ. רמז דף.
תקעד. כנ"ל אות שסח. אימפיריעל ביטש, קאליפארניא. ה'תשד"מ. רמז דף.
תקעה. כנ"ל אות שסח. בראולי, קאליפארניא. ה'תשד"מ. רמז דף.
תקעו. כנ"ל אות שסח. דעל מאר, קאליפארניא. ה'תשד"מ. רמז דף.
תקעז. כנ"ל אות שסח. וויסטא, קאליפארניא. ה'תשד"מ. רמז דף.
תקעח. כנ"ל אות שסח. טשולא וויסטא, קאליפארניא. ה'תשד"מ. רמז דף.
תקעט. כנ"ל אות רלח. לא האיא, קאליפארניא. ה'תשד"מ. רמז דף.
תקפ. כנ"ל אות שסח. לא מעיסא, קאליפארניא. ה'תשד"מ. רמז דף.
תקפא. כנ"ל אות שסח. לעמאן גראוו, קאליפארניא. ה'תשד"מ. רמז דף.
תקפב. כנ"ל אות שסח. מארקאס, קאליפארניא. ה'תשד"מ. רמז דף.
תקפג. כנ"ל אות שסח. נאשינאל סיטי, קאליפארניא. ה'תשד"מ. רמז דף.
תקפד. כנ"ל אות שסח. על סענטרא, קאליפארניא. ה'תשד"מ. רמז דף.
תקפה. כנ"ל אות שסח. על קאהאן, קאליפארניא. ה'תשד"מ. רמז דף.
תקפו. כנ"ל אות שסח. עסקאנדידאו, קאליפארניא. ה'תשד"מ. רמז דף.
תקפז. כנ"ל אות שסח. פאווי, קאליפארניא. ה'תשד"מ. רמז דף.
תקפח. כנ"ל אות שסח. קאלעקסיקא, קאליפארניא. ה'תשד"מ. רמז דף.
תקפט. כנ"ל אות שסח. קאראנאדא, קאליפארניא. ה'תשד"מ. רמז דף.
תקצ. כנ"ל אות שסח. קארלסבאד, קאליפארניא. ה'תשד"מ. רמז דף.
תקצא. כנ"ל אות שסח. טעקאטי, מעקסיקא. ה'תשד"מ. רמח דף.
תקצב. כנ"ל אות שסח מעקסיקאלי, מעקסיקא. ה'תשד"מ. רמח דף.
תקצג. כנ"ל אות שסח ענסינאדא, מעקסיקא. ה'תשד"מ. רמח דף.
תקצד. כנ"ל אות שסח ראזאריטא, מעקסיקא. ה'תשד"מ. רמח דף.
תקצה. כנ"ל אות שלה. מילטאן, מאסאטשוסעטס. ה'תשד"מ. רמח דף.
תקצו. כנ"ל אות שלה. ראנדאלף, מאסאטשוסעטס. ה'תשד"מ. רמח דף.
תקצז. כנ"ל אות שלה. סטאוטאן, מאסאטשוסעטס. ה'תשד"מ. רמח דף.
תקצח. כנ"ל אות רצא. פריימינגהאם, מאסאטשוסעטס. ה'תשד"מ. רמז דף.
תקצט. כנ"ל אות שדמ. מעמפיס, טענעסי. ה'תשד"מ. רמז דף.
תר. כנ"ל אות שלה. אלבאני, נ.י. ה'תשד"מ. רמח דף.
תרא. כנ"ל אות שלה. איטאקא, נ.י. ה'תשד"מ. רמט דף.
תרב. כנ"ל אות שלה. אליאן, נ.י. ה'תשד"מ. רמט דף.
תרג. כנ"ל אות שלה. באטאוויא, נ.י. ה'תשד"מ. רמט דף.
תרד. כנ"ל אות שלה. בינגהאמטאן, נ.י. ה'תשד"מ. רמט דף.
תרה. כנ"ל אות שלה. דאונקוירק, נ.י. ה'תשד"מ. רמט דף.
תרו. כנ"ל אות שלה. ניאגארא פאלס, נ.י. ה'תשד"מ. רמט דף.
תרז. כנ"ל אות רטו. מנטובה, איטאליא. ה'תשד"מ. רמט דף.
תרח. כנ"ל אות שלה. עלמיירא, נ.י. ה'תשד"מ. רמט דף.
תרט. כנ"ל אות שסח. לאנג בראנטש, נ.ד. ה'תשד"מ. רמט דף.
תרי. כנ"ל אות שלה. פאטערסאן, נ.ד. ה'תשד"מ. רמט דף.
תריא. כנ"ל אות שלה. טענעפלאי, נ.ד. ה'תשד"מ. רמט דף.
תריב. כנ"ל אות שלה. פאראמאס, נ.ד. ה'תשד"מ. רמט דף.
תריג. כנ"ל אות שדמ. מיונכען, מערב גרמניא. ה'תשד"מ. רמט דף.
תריד. כנ"ל אות שדמ. מערב ברלין, מערב גרמניא. ה'תשד"מ. רמט דף.
תרטו. כנ"ל אות שדמ. ברצלונה, ספרד. ה'תשד"מ. רמט דף.
תרטז. כנ"ל אות רטו. בורנמוט, אנגלי'. ה'תשד"מ. רמט דף.
תריז. כנ"ל אות רטו. המפסטד גרדן סאבורב, לונדון, אנגלי'. ה'תשד"מ. רמט דף.
תריח. כנ"ל אות רטו. וואלינגפארד, לונדון, אנגלי'. ה'תשד"מ. רמט דף.
תריט. כנ"ל אות רטו. סאוטענד, לונדון, אנגלי'. ה'תשד"מ. רמט דף.
תרכ. כנ"ל אות שלה. ישיבת אחי תמימים, ברוקליין, מאסאטשוסעטס. ה'תשד"מ. רמח דף.
תרכא. כנ"ל אות שדמ. פרינצטאן, מערסער קאונטי, נ.ד. ה'תשד"מ. רמח דף.
תרכב. כנ"ל אות תקצ. לאס וועגאס, נעוואדא. ה'תשד"מ. רמח דף.
תרכג. כנ"ל אות שלה. אוסטין, טעקסאס. ה'תשד"מ. רמח דף.
תרכד. כנ"ל אות שלה. בראנקס, נ.י. ה'תשד"מ. רמט דף.
תרכה. כנ"ל אות שלה. נמל-תעופה „קנדי", ניו יארק. ה'תשד"מ. רמט דף.
תרכו. כנ"ל אות שלה. ספרינגפילד, מאסאטשוסעטס. ה'תשד"מ. רמט דף.
תרכז. כנ"ל אות שלה. ניו בריטען, קאנעטיקאט. ה'תשד"מ. רמט דף.
תרכח. כנ"ל אות שלה. ניו לאנדאן, קאנעטיקאט. ה'תשד"מ. רמט דף.
תרכט. כנ"ל אות שדמ. רבנות הצבאית דבלגיא. ה'תשד"מ. רמט דף.
תרל. כנ"ל אות שדמ. ארלי, צרפת. ה'תשד"מ. רמח דף.
תרלא. כנ"ל אות שדמ. אלניי, צרפת. ה'תשד"מ. רמח דף.
תרלב. כנ"ל אות שדמ. האוורע, צרפת. ה'תשד"מ. רמח דף.
תרלג. כנ"ל אות שדמ. ליל, צרפת. ה'תשד"מ. רמח דף.
תרלד. כנ"ל אות שדמ. לילא, צרפת ה'תשד"מ. רמח דף.
תרלה. כנ"ל אות שדמ. ויטרי, צרפת. ה'תשד"מ. רמח דף.
תרלו. כנ"ל אות שדמ. פאנטעני, צרפת. ה'תשד"מ. רמח דף.
תרלז. כנ"ל אות שדמ. קרבייל, צרפת. ה'תשד"מ. רמח דף.
תרלח. כנ"ל אות ריט. ליאון, צרפת. ה'תשד"מ. רלח דף.
תרלט. כנ"ל אות קלה. מרסייל, צרפת. ה'תשד"מ. רלו דף.
תרמ. כנ"ל אות ריא. מושב שדה משה, באה"ק ת"ו. ה'תשד"מ רמח דף.
תרמא. כנ"ל אות ריא. שכונת בית וגן, ירות"ו, באה"ק ת"ו. ה'תשד"מ רמח דף.

תרמב. כנ"ל אות ריא. קיבוץ חניתה, רמת הגולן, באה"ק ת"ו. ה'תשד"מ רמח דף.

תרמג. כנ"ל אות ריא. עירית תל אביב — יפו, באה"ק ת"ו. ה'תשד"מ. רמח דף.

תרמד. כנ"ל אות ריא. כפר הנוער הדתי (ע"י כפר חסידים), באה"ק ת"ו. ה'תשד"מ. רמח דף.

תרמה. כנ"ל אות ריא. נתיבות, באה"ק ת"ו (הוצאה שני'). ה'תשד"מ. רמח דף.

תרמו. כנ"ל אות ריא. מושב נוב, רמת הגולן, באה"ק ת"ו. ה'תשד"מ. רמח דף.

תרמז. כנ"ל אות ריא. יבנאל, באה"ק ת"ו. ה'תשד"מ. רמח דף.

תרמח. כנ"ל אות ריא. נהלל, באה"ק ת"ו. ה'תשד"מ. רמח דף.

תרמט. כנ"ל אות שדמ. האוואנא, קיובא. ה'תשד"מ. רמט דף.

תרנ. כנ"ל אות שדמ. אגאדיר, מרוקו. ה'תשד"מ. רמט דף.

תרנא. כנ"ל אות שדמ. טאנשזיר, מרוקו. ה'תשד"מ. רמט דף.

תרנב. כנ"ל אות שדמ. מרקש, מרוקו. ה'תשד"מ. רמט דף.

תרנג. כנ"ל אות שדמ. פאס, מרוקו. ה'תשד"מ. רמט דף.

תרנד. כנ"ל אות שדמ. קניטרא, מרוקו. ה'תשד"מ. רמט דף.

תרנה. כנ"ל אות שדמ. רבט, מרוקו. ה'תשד"מ. רמט דף.

תרנו. כנ"ל אות פז. לא פלאטא ב.א. ארגנטינא. ה'תשד"מ. רמט דף.

תרנז. כנ"ל אות פז. זרטי, ב.א. ארגנטינא. ה'תשד"מ. רמט דף.

תרנח. כנ"ל אות ריא. קאבע, יאפאן. ה'תשד"מ. רמט דף.

תרנט. כנ"ל אות שלה. קארנינג, נ.י. ה'תשד"מ. רמט דף.

תרס. כנ"ל אות שלה. וועין, פאסייק קאונטי, נ.ד. תשד"מ. רמט דף.

תרסא. כנ"ל אות שלה. פארטלאנד, מעין. ה'תשד"מ. רמט דף.

תרסב. כנ"ל אות שדמ. אמיען, צרפת. ה'תשד"מ. רמט דף.

תרסג. כנ"ל אות שדמ. ארזונטייל, צרפת. ה'תשד"מ. רמט דף.

תרסד. כנ"ל אות שדמ. אלפארטוויל, צרפת. ה'תשד"מ. רמט דף.

תרסה. כנ"ל אות שדמ. איוורי סור סען, צרפת. ה'תשד"מ. רמט דף.

תרסו. כנ"ל אות שדמ. באביני, צרפת. ה'תשד"מ. רמט דף.

תרסז. כנ"ל אות שדמ. בולאן, צרפת. ה'תשד"מ. רמט דף.

תרסח. כנ"ל אות שדמ. ווילפענט, צרפת. ה'תשד"מ. רמט דף.

תרסט. כנ"ל אות שדמ. ווילזויף, צרפת. ה'תשד"מ. רמט דף.

עתר. כנ"ל אות שדמ. יערעס (בית רבקה), צרפת. ה'תשד"מ. רמט דף.

תרעא. כנ"ל אות שדמ. כלאמב, צרפת. ה'תשד"מ. רמט דף.

תערב. כנ"ל אות שדמ. כלישי, צרפת. ה'תשד"מ. רמט דף.

תרעג. כנ"ל אות שדמ. כלישי סו בוא, צרפת. ה'תשד"מ. רמט דף.

עדרת. כנ"ל אות שדמ. כשאן, צרפת. ה'תשד"מ. רמט דף.

תרעה. כנ"ל אות שדמ. ליוורי גארגאן, צרפת. ה'תשד"מ. רמט דף.

תרעו. כנ"ל אות שדמ. לא ווארען, צרפת. ה'תשד"מ. רמט דף.

תרעז. כנ"ל אות שדמ. לוואלואס, צרפת. ה'תשד"מ. רמט דף.

תרעח. כנ"ל אות שדמ. מנטרויל, צרפת. ה'תשד"מ. רמט דף.

תרעט. כנ"ל אות שדמ. מעזון אלפארט, צרפת. תשד"מ. רמט דף.

תרפ. כנ"ל אות שדמ. סעווראן, צרפת. ה'תשד"מ. רמט דף.

תרפא. כנ"ל אות שדמ. פנטען, צרפת. ה'תשד"מ. רמט דף.

תרפב. כנ"ל אות שדמ. קרמלין ביסעטר, צרפת. ה'תשד"מ. רמט דף.

תרפג. כנ"ל אות שדמ. שארענטאן, צרפת. ה'תשד"מ. רמט דף.

תרפד. כנ"ל אות שדמ. נאנסי, צרפת. ה'תשד"מ. רנב דף.

תרפה. כנ"ל אות שדמ. מעץ, צרפת. ה'תשד"מ. רנב דף.

תרפו. כנ"ל אות שדמ. אסטענדע, בעלגיא. ה'תשד"מ. רמט דף.

תרפז. כנ"ל אות שדמ. גענט, בעלגיא. ה'תשד"מ. רמט דף.

תרפח. כנ"ל אות שדמ. ליוועו, בעלגיא. ה'תשד"מ. רמט דף.

תרפט. כנ"ל אות שדמ. ליעזש, בעלגיא. ה'תשד"מ. רמט דף.

תרצ. כנ"ל אות שדמ. שארלערוא, בעלגיא. ה'תשד"מ. רמט דף.

תרצא. כנ"ל אות ריא. ביהכנ"ס חב"ד ליובאוויטש, שכונת בית ישראל, ירושת"ו. ה'תשד"מ. רנב דף.

תרצב. כנ"ל אות שלה. אמהורסט, מאסאטשוסעטס. ה'תשד"מ. רמט דף.

תרצג. כנ"ל אות שלה. גרינפילד, מאסאטשוסעטס. ה'תשד"מ. רמט דף.

תרצד. כנ"ל אות שלה. האליאוק, מאסאטשוסעטס. ה'תשד"מ. רמט דף.

תרצה. כנ"ל אות שלה. וועסטפילד, מאסאטשוסעטס. ה'תשד"מ. רמט דף.

תרצו. כנ"ל אות שלה. נארטהאמפטאן, מאסאטשוסעטס. ה'תשד"מ. רמט דף.

תרצז. כנ"ל אות שלה. פיטספילד, מאסאטשוסעטס. ה'תשד"מ. רמט דף.

תרחצ. כנ"ל אות שלה. סטארס, קאנעטיקאט. ה'תשד"מ. רמט דף.

תרצט. כנ"ל אות שלה. סטאפארד ספרינגס, קאנעטיקאט. ה'תשד"מ. רמט דף.

תש. כנ"ל אות שלה. ניו סיטי, נ.י. ה'תשד"מ. רמט דף.

תשא. כנ"ל אות שלה. מאנטיסעלא, נ.י. ה'תשד"מ. רנב דף.

תשב. כנ"ל אות שלה. עלענוויל, נ.י. ה'תשד"מ. רנב דף.

תשג. כנ"ל אות שלה. ספרינג ואלי, נ.י. ה'תשד"מ. רנב דף.

תשד. כנ"ל אות שלה. באלטימאר, מארילאנד. ה'תשד"מ. רמט דף.

תשה. כנ"ל אות שלה. סילווער ספרינג, מארילאנד. ה'תשד"מ. רמט דף.

תשו. כנ"ל אות שסח. עדמאנטאן, אלבערטא, קנדה. ה'תשד"מ. רנב דף.

תשז. כנ"ל אות שסח. קאלגארי, אלבערטא, קנדה. ה'תשד"מ. רנב דף.

תשח. כנ"ל אות שלה. יוריקא, קאליפארניא. ה'תשד"מ. רנב דף.

תשט. כנ"ל אות שלה. סאקראמענטא, קאליפארניא. ה'תשד"מ. רנב דף.

תשי. כנ"ל אות שלה. פאלא אלטא, קאליפארניא. ה'תשד"מ. רנב דף.

תשיא. כנ"ל אות שלה. רפאל, קאליפארניא. ה'תשד"מ. רנב דף.

תשיב. כנ"ל אות שלה. בייאן, ניו דזוירסי. ה'תשד"מ. רנב דף.

תשיג. כנ"ל אות שלה. בלומפילד, ניו דזוירסי. ה'תשד"מ. רנב דף.

תשיד. כנ"ל אות שדמ. הייסטאון, ניו דזוירסי. ה'תשד"מ. רנב דף.

תשטו. כנ"ל אות שלה. רוזוועלט, ניו דזוירסי. ה'תשד"מ. רנב דף.

תשטז. כנ"ל אות שדמ. האקענסאק, ניו דזוירסי. ה'תשד"מ. רנב דף.

תשיז. כנ"ל אות שלה. דאווער, ניו דזוירסי. ה'תשד"מ. רנב דף.

תשיח. כנ"ל אות שלה. נארט בערגן, ניו דזוירסי. ה'תשד"מ. רנב דף.

תשיט. כנ"ל אות שדמ. קינעלאן, ניו דזוירסי. ה'תשד"מ. רנב דף.

תשכ. כנ"ל אות שסח. סאוט האמפטאן, לאנג איילאנד, נ.י. ה'תשד"מ. רנב דף.

תשכא. כנ"ל אות שסח. איסליפ, לאנג איילאנד, נ.י. ה'תשד"מ. רנב דף.

תשכב. כנ"ל אות שסח. באבילאן, לאנג איילאנד, נ.י. ה'תשד"מ. רנב דף.

תשכג. כנ"ל אות שסח. ביי שאר, לאנג איילאנד, נ.י. ה'תשד"מ. רנב דף.

תשכד. כנ"ל אות שסח. סמיטטאון, לאנג איילאנד, נ.י. ה'תשד"מ. רנב דף.

תשכה. כנ"ל אות שסח. פארט דזשעפערסאן, לאנג איילאנד, נ.י. ה'תשד"מ. רנב דף.

תשכו. כנ"ל אות שלה. טאלידא, אהייא. ה'תשד"מ. רנב דף.

תשכז. כנ"ל אות שלה. יונגסטאון, אהייא. ה'תשד"מ. רנב דף.

תשכח. כנ"ל אות שלה. קענטאן, אהייא. ה'תשד"מ. רנב דף.

תשכט. כנ"ל אות שלה. באסטאן, מאסאטשוסעטס. ה'תשד"מ. רנב דף.

תשל. כנ"ל אות שלה. קיימברידזש, מאסאטשוסעטס. ה'תשד"מ. רנב דף.

תשלא. כנ״ל אות שלה. חב״ד־ליובאוויטש קעמפוס, מאריס טאונשיפ, נ.ד. ה׳תשד״מ. רנב דף.
תשלב. כנ״ל אות שלה. סיילעם, אריגאן. ה׳תשד״מ. רנב דף.
תשלג. כנ״ל אות שדמ. דניאלסאן, קאנעטיקאט. ה׳תשד״מ. רנה דף.
תשלד. כנ״ל אות שלה. קואינסי, מאסאטשוסעטס. ה׳תשד״מ. רנב דף.
תשלה. כנ״ל אות שלה. שאראן, מאסאטשוסעטס. ה׳תשד״מ. רנב דף.
תשלו. כנ״ל אות שלה. בראקטאן, מאסאטשוסעטס. ה׳תשד״מ. רנב דף.
תשלז. כנ״ל אות שלה. פאל ריווער, מאסאטשוסעטס. ה׳תשד״מ. רנב דף.
תשלח. כנ״ל אות שלה. ניוטאן, מאסאטשוסעטס. ה׳תשד״מ. רנב דף.
תשלט. כנ״ל אות שלה. פאוטאקעט, ראוד איילאנד. ה׳תשד״מ. רנב דף.
תשמ. כנ״ל אות שלה. ביהכנ״ס טורא דק״ק ישועת ישראל, ניופארט, ראוד איילאנד. ה׳תשד״מ. רנב דף.
תשמא. כנ״ל אות שלה. ווארוויק, ראוד איילאנד. ה׳תשד״מ. רנב דף.
תשמב. כנ״ל אות שלה. קראנסטאן, ראוד איילאנד. ה׳תשד״מ. רנב דף.
תשמג. כנ״ל אות שסח. קאבא לוקאס, מעקסיקא. ה׳תשד״מ. רנב דף.
תשדמ. כנ״ל אות שדמ. וואשינגטאן, דיסטריקט אוו קולומביא — בירת ארה״ב. ה׳תשד״מ. (6) רנב דף.
תשמה. כנ״ל אות ריט. פילאדעלפיא, פענסילוויינע. תשד״מ. רמ דף.
תשמו. כנ״ל אות רמד. או־קלעיר, וויסקאנסין. ה׳תשד״מ. רנב דף.
תשמז. כנ״ל אות רמד. אפעלטאן, וויסקאנסין. ה׳תשד״מ. רנב דף.
תשמח. כנ״ל אות רמד. אקאנאמאוואק, וויסקאנסין. ה׳תשד״מ. רנב דף.
תשמט. כנ״ל אות רמד. אשקאש, וויסקאנסין. ה׳תשד״מ. רנב דף.
תשנ. כנ״ל אות רמד. בילאיט, וויסקאנסין. ה׳תשד״מ. רנב דף.
תשנא. כנ״ל אות רמד. בעראבו, וויסקאנסין. ה׳תשד״מ. רנב דף.
תשנב. כנ״ל אות רמד. בראון דיר, וויסקאנסין. ה׳תשד״מ. רנב דף.
תשנג. כנ״ל אות רמד. ביי־סייד, וויסקאגסין. ה׳תשד״מ. רנב דף.
תשנד. כנ״ל אות רמד. ברוקפילד, וויסקאנסין. ה׳תשד״מ. רנב דף.
תשנה. כנ״ל אות רמד. גלענדייל, וויסקאנסין. ה׳תשד״מ. רנב דף.
תשנו. כנ״ל אות רמד. גראפטאן, וויסקאנסין. ה׳תשד״מ. רנב דף.
תשנז. כנ״ל אות רמד. גרין־ביי, וויסקאנסין. ה׳תשד״מ. רנב דף.
תשנח. כנ״ל אות רמד. דע־פיער, וויסקאנסין. ה׳תשד״מ. רנב דף.
תשנט. כנ״ל אות רמד. וואוואטאוסא, וויסקאנסין. ה׳תשד״מ. רנב דף.
תשס. כנ״ל אות רמד. וואסא, וויסקאנסין. ה׳תשד״מ. רנב דף.
תשסא. כנ״ל אות רמד. וואקעשא, וויסקאנסין. ה׳תשד״מ. רנב דף.
תשסב. כנ״ל אות רמד. וויטפיש־ביי, וויסקאנסין. ה׳תשד״מ. רנב דף.
תשסג. כנ״ל אות רמד. וועסט אליס, וויסקאנסין. ה׳תשד״מ. רנב דף.
תשסד. כנ״ל אות רמד. וועראנא, וויסקאנסין. ה׳תשד״מ. רנב דף.
תשסה. כנ״ל אות רמד. טיענסוויל, וויסקאנסין. ה׳תשד״מ. רנב דף.
תשסו. כנ״ל אות רמד. לא־קרא, וויסקאנסין. ה׳תשד״מ. רנב דף.
תשסז. כנ״ל אות רמד. מאנטיאוואק, וויסקאנסין. ה׳תשד״מ. רנב דף.
תשסח. כנ״ל אות רמד. מארינעט, וויסקאנסין. ה׳תשד״מ. רנב דף.
תשסט. כנ״ל אות רמד. מידעלטאון, וויסקאנסין. תשד״מ. רנב דף.
תשע. כנ״ל אות רמד. מאנאמאני־פאלס, וויסקאנסין. ה׳תשד״מ. רנב דף.
תשעא. כנ״ל אות רמד. מעקוואן, וויסקאנסין. ה׳תשד״מ. רנב דף.
תשעב. כנ״ל אות רמד. ניו בערלין, וויסקאנסין. ה׳תשד״מ. רנב דף.
תשעג. כנ״ל אות רמד. סידארבורג, וויסקאנסין. ה׳תשד״מ. רנב דף.
תשעד. כנ״ל אות רמד. סופיריאר, וויסקאנסין. ה׳תשד״מ. רנב דף.
תשעה. כנ״ל אות רמד. פאנד־דו־לאק, וויסקאנסין. ה׳תשד״מ. רנב דף.
תשעו. כנ״ל אות רמד. פאקס־פאינט, וויסקאנסין. ה׳תשד״מ. רנב דף.
תשעז. כנ״ל אות רמד. קענאשא, וויסקאנסין. ה׳תשד״מ. רנב דף.
תשעח. כנ״ל אות רמד. ריווער הילס, וויסקאנסין. ה׳תשד״מ. רנב דף.
תשעט. כנ״ל אות רמד. רייסין, וויסקאנסין. ה׳תשד״מ. רנב דף.
תשפ. כנ״ל אות רמד. שארוואוד, וויסקאנסין. ה׳תשד״מ. רנב דף.
תשפא. כנ״ל אות רמד. שעבאיגאן, וויסקאנסין. ה׳תשד״מ. רנב דף.
תשפב. כנ״ל אות רמד. מענאמאני, [מישיגען]. ה׳תשד״מ. רנב דף.
תשפג. כנ״ל אות שלה. באיזי, איידעהא. ה׳תשד״מ. רנב דף.
תשפד. כנ״ל אות שלה. ביסמארק, נארט דאקאטא. ה׳תשד״מ. רנב דף.
תשפה. כנ״ל אות שלה. ראפיד סיטי, סאוט דאקאטא. ה׳תשד״מ. רנב דף.
תשפו. כנ״ל אות שלה. ראק ספרינגס, ווייאמינג. ה׳תשד״מ. רנב דף.
תשפז. כנ״ל אות שלה. העלענא, מאנטאנא. ה׳תשד״מ. רנב דף.
תשפח. כנ״ל אות רמח. טאמפא, פלארידא. ה׳תשד״מ. רנב דף.
תשפט. כנ״ל אות שלה. סקראנטאן, פענסילוויניא. ה׳תשד״מ. רנב דף.
תשצ. כנ״ל אות רפו. פייעטוויל, נארט קאראליינא. ה׳תשד״מ. רנב דף.
תשצא. כנ״ל אות שלה. פאקיפסי, נ.י. ה׳תשד״מ. רנה דף.
תשצב. כנ״ל אות שלה. לואיס, מיזורי. ה׳תשד״מ. רנב דף.
תשצג. כנ״ל אות תכ. קאיען, פרענטש גויאנא. ה׳תשד״מ. רנב דף.
תשצד. כנ״ל אות תכ. קאטשאבאמבא, בוליוויא. תשד״מ. רנב דף.
תשצה. כנ״ל אות תכ. דע לא סיערא, בוליוויא. ה׳תשד״מ. רנב דף.
תשצו. כנ״ל אות שכ. סקאקי, אילינאי. ה׳תשד״מ. רלח דף.
תשצז. כנ״ל אות שכ. היילאנד פארק, אילינאי. ה׳תשד״מ. רלח דף.
תשצח. כנ״ל אות שכ. עוועגסטאון, אילינאי. ה׳תשד״מ. רלח דף.
תשצט. כנ״ל אות שדמ. אוען למאן, צרפת. ה׳תשד״מ. רנב דף.
תת. כנ״ל אות שדמ. איסי לע מאלינא, צרפת. ה׳תשד״מ. רנב דף.
תתא. כנ״ל אות שדמ. אטהיס מאנס, צרפת. ה׳תשד״מ. רנב דף.
תתב. כנ״ל אות שדמ. אנטני, צרפת. ה׳תשד״מ. רנב דף.
תתג. כנ״ל אות שדמ. אנגהען, צרפת. ה׳תשד״מ. רנב דף.
תתד. כנ״ל אות שדמ. אנזער, צרפת. ה׳תשד״מ. רנב דף.
תתה. כנ״ל אות שדמ. אסניער, צרפת. ה׳תשד״מ. רנב דף.
תתו. כנ״ל אות שדמ. ארלעאנס, צרפת. ה׳תשד״מ. רנב דף.
תתז. כנ״ל אות שדמ. באנדי, צרפת. ה׳תשד״מ. רנב דף.
תתח. כנ״ל אות שדמ. בלא מעניל, צרפת. ה׳תשד״מ. רנב דף.
תתט. כנ״ל אות שדמ. ברסט, צרפת. ה׳תשד״מ, רנב דף.
תתי. כנ״ל אות שדמ. דראנסי, צרפת. ה׳תשד״מ. רנב דף.
תתיא. כנ״ל אות שדמ. דואי, צרפת. ה׳תשד״מ. רנב דף.
תתיב. כנ״ל אות שדמ. דנקערק, צרפת. ה׳תשד״מ. רנב דף.
תתיג. כנ״ל אות שדמ. דעני, צרפת. ה׳תשד״מ. רנב דף.
תתיד. כנ״ל אות שדמ. ווילורבן, צרפת. ה׳תשד״מ. רנב דף.
תתטו. כנ״ל אות שדמ. ווינע, צרפת. ה׳תשד״מ. רנב דף.
תתטז. כנ״ל אות שדמ. וולנסין, צרפת. ה׳תשד״מ. רנב דף.
תתיז. כנ״ל אות שדמ. וורסאייל, צרפת. ה׳תשד״מ. רנב דף.
תתיח. כנ״ל אות שדמ. טור, צרפת. ה׳תשד״מ. רנב דף.
תתיט. כנ״ל אות שדמ. כאען, צרפת. ה׳תשד״מ. רנב דף.
תתכ. כנ״ל אות שדמ. לא ווארען, צרפת. ה׳תשד״מ. רנב דף.
תתכא. כנ״ל אות שדמ. לא כורנעוו, צרפת. ה׳תשד״מ. רנב דף.
תתכב. כנ״ל אות שדמ. לאריענט, צרפת. ה׳תשד״מ. רנב דף.
תתכג. כנ״ל אות שדמ. לנס, צרפת. ה׳תשד״מ. רנב דף.
תתכד. כנ״ל אות שדמ. לע וועזינעט, צרפת. ה׳תשד״מ. רנב דף.
תתכה. כנ״ל אות שדמ. לע מאנס, צרפת. ה׳תשד״מ. רנב דף.
תתכו. כנ״ל אות שדמ. לע פערע, צרפת. ה׳תשד״מ. רנב דף.
תתכז. כנ״ל אות שדמ. מא, צרפת. ה׳תשד״מ. רנב דף.

תתכח. כנ"ל אות שדמ. מעלען, צרפת. ה'תשד"מ. רנב דף.
תתכט. כנ"ל אות שדמ. נאטו לע סעק, צרפת. ה'תשד"מ. רנב דף.
תתל. כנ"ל אות שדמ. נואזי לע גראנד, צרפת. ה'תשד"מ. רנב דף.
תתלא. כנ"ל אות שדמ. נזאן, צרפת. ה'תשד"מ. רנב דף.
תתלב. כנ"ל אות שדמ. ננט, צרפת. ה'תשד"מ. רנב דף.
תתלג. כנ"ל אות שדמ. נעיי, צרפת. ה'תשד"מ. רנב דף.
תתלד. כנ"ל אות שדמ. סויני סור ארז, צרפת. ה'תשד"מ. רנב דף.
תתלה. כנ"ל אות שדמ. סטען, צרפת. ה'תשד"מ. רנב דף.
תתלו. כנ"ל אות שדמ. סנס, צרפת. ה'תשד"מ. רנב דף.
תתלז. כנ"ל אות שדמ. עוורע, צרפת. ה'תשד"מ. רנב דף.
תתלח. כנ"ל אות שדמ. עלבעף, צרפת. ה'תשד"מ. רנב דף.
תתלט. כנ"ל אות שדמ. מנטרוש, צרפת. ה'תשד"מ. רנב דף.
תתמ. כנ"ל אות שדמ. עפיניי סוסענארט, צרפת. ה'תשד"מ. רנב דף.
תתמא. כנ"ל אות שדמ. פאוילאן סו בוא, צרפת. ה'תשד"מ. רנב דף.
תתמב. כנ"ל אות שדמ. פואטיער, צרפת. ה'תשד"מ. רנב דף.
תתמג. כנ"ל אות שדמ. פוטו, צרפת. ה'תשד"מ. רנב דף.
תתמד. כנ"ל אות שדמ. פנטא קמבא, צרפת. ה'תשד"מ. רנב דף.
תתמה. כנ"ל אות שדמ. פנטעניי רוז, צרפת. ה'תשד"מ. רנב דף.
תתמו. כנ"ל אות שדמ. פנטענבלא, צרפת. ה'תשד"מ. רנב דף.
תתמז. כנ"ל אות שדמ. קלמארט, צרפת. ה'תשד"מ. רנב דף.
תתמח. כנ"ל אות שדמ. קענטי, צרפת. ה'תשד"מ. רנב דף.
תתמט. כנ"ל אות שדמ. ראסני סו בוא, צרפת. ה'תשד"מ. רנב דף.
תתנ. כנ"ל אות שדמ. רען, צרפת. ה'תשד"מ. רנב דף.
תתנא. כנ"ל אות שדמ. שאטארו, צרפת. ה'תשד"מ. רנב דף.
תתנב. כנ"ל אות שדמ. שמפיני, צרפת. ה'תשד"מ. רנב דף.
תתנג. כנ"ל אות שדמ. שעל, צרפת. ה'תשד"מ. רנב דף.
תתנד. כנ"ל אות שדמ. אילפארד, אנגליא. ה'תשד"מ. רנב דף.
תתנה. כנ"ל אות שדמ. אקספארד, אנגליא. ה'תשד"מ. רנב דף.
תתנו. כנ"ל אות שדמ. ברייטאן, אנגליא. ה'תשד"מ. רנב דף.
תתנז. כנ"ל אות שדמ. לעסטער, אנגליא. ה'תשד"מ. רנב דף.
תתנח. כנ"ל אות שדמ. נאטינגהאם, אנגליא. ה'תשד"מ. רנב דף.
תתנט. כנ"ל אות שדמ. קארדיף, אנגליא. ה'תשד"מ. רנב דף.
תתס. כנ"ל אות שדמ. רעדינג, אנגליא. ה'תשד"מ. רנב דף.
תתסא. כנ"ל אות שדמ. קיימברידזש, אנגליא. ה'תשד"מ. רנב דף.
תתסב. כנ"ל אות שדמ. גייטסהעד, אנגליא. ה'תשד"מ. רנב דף.
תתסג. כנ"ל אות שדמ. סאנדערלאנד, אנגליא. ה'תשד"מ. רנב דף.
תתסד. כנ"ל אות שדמ. נארטהאמפטאן, אנגליא. ה'תשד"מ. רנב דף.
תתסה. כנ"ל אות שדמ. בראדפארט, אנגליא. ה'תשד"מ. רנב דף.
תתסו. כנ"ל אות שדמ. בריסטאל, אנגליא. ה'תשד"מ. רנב דף.
תתסז. כנ"ל אות שדמ. לוטאן, אנגליא. ה'תשד"מ. רנב דף.
תתסח. כנ"ל אות שדמ. מיידענהעד, אנגליא. ה'תשד"מ. רנב דף.
תתסט. כנ"ל אות שדמ. אלבאנס, אנגליא. ה'תשד"מ. רנב דף.
תתע. כנ"ל אות שלה. פאינט-א-פירט, גואדאלופ. ה'תשד"מ. רנב דף.
תתעא. כנ"ל אות שלה. פארט-דע-פראנס, מארטיניק. ה'תשד"מ. רנב דף.
תתעב. כנ"ל אות שלה. מארגאריטא, ווענעצועלא. ה'תשד"מ. רנב דף.
תתעג. כנ"ל אות שלה. מאראקייבא, ווענעצועלא.תשד"מ. רנב דף.
תתעד. כנ"ל אות שלה. וואלענציא, ווענעצועלא. ה'תשד"מ. רנב דף.
תתעה. כנ"ל אות שלה. קריסטאבאל, ווענעצועלא. ה'תשד"מ. רנב דף.
תתעו. כנ"ל אות שלה. מאראקיי, ווענעצועלא. ה'תשד"מ. רנב דף.
תתעז. כנ"ל אות פז. בהיא בלנקה, בוינוס איירס, ארגנטינה. ה'תשד"מ. רנב דף.
תתעח. כנ"ל אות פז. בסווילבסו, אנטרה ריוס, ארגנטינה. ה'תשד"מ. רנב דף.
תתעט. כנ"ל אות פז. גואלגואי, אנטרה ריוס, ארגנטינה. ה'תשד"מ. רנב דף.
תתפ. כנ"ל אות פז. גואלגואיטשו, אנטרה ריוס, ארגנטינה. ה'תשד"מ. רנב דף.
תתפא. כנ"ל אות פז. וויליא דומינגוס, אנטרה ריוס, ארגנטינה. ה'תשד"מ. רנב דף.
תתפב. כנ"ל אות פז. וויליא קלרה, אנטרה ריוס, ארגנטינה. ה'תשד"מ. רנב דף.
תתפג. כנ"ל אות פז. וויליאגואי, אנטרה ריוס, ארגנטינה. ה'תשד"מ. רנב דף.
תתפד. כנ"ל אות פז. מוזסוויל, פה, ארגנטינה. ה'תשד"מ. רנב דף.
תתפה. כנ"ל אות פז. מוניגוטיס, פה, ארגנטינה. ה'תשד"מ. רנב דף.
תתפו. כנ"ל אות פז. מרדל פלטה, בוינוס איירס, פה, ארגנטינה. ה'תשד"מ. רנב דף.
תתפז. כנ"ל אות פז. סלוודור, אנטרה ריוס, ארגנטינה. ה'תשד"מ. רנב דף.
תתפח. כנ"ל אות פז. סרס, פה, ארגנטינה. ה'תשד"מ. רנב דף.
תתפט. כנ"ל אות פז. פה, ארגנטינה. ה'תשד"מ. רנב דף.
תתצ. כנ"ל אות פז. פרנה, אנטרה ריוס, ארגנטינה. ה'תשד"מ. רנב דף.
תתצא. כנ"ל אות פז. קונספסיון ד. אורוגואי, אנטרה ריוס, ארגנטינה. ה'תשד"מ. רנב דף.
תתצב. כנ"ל אות פז. קמפנה, בוינוס איירס, ארגנטינה. ה'תשד"מ. רנב דף.
תתצג. כנ"ל אות פז. קריסטובל, פה, ארגנטינה. תשד"מ. רנב דף.
תתצד. כנ"ל אות פז. רוסריו, פה, ארגנטינה. ה'תשד"מ. רנב דף.
תתצה. כנ"ל אות פז. רוסריו ד. טלה, אנטרה ריוס, ארגנטינה. ה'תשד"מ. רנב דף.
תתצו. כנ"ל אות פז. ראפאלה, פה, ארגנטינה. ה'תשד"מ. רנב דף.
תתצז. כנ"ל אות שלה. אבילין, טעקסאס. ה'תשד"מ. רנה דף.
תתצח. כנ"ל אות שלה. אמארילא, טעקסאס. ה'תשד"מ. רנה דף.
תתצט. כנ"ל אות שלה. אנטאניא, טעקסאס. ה'תשד"מ. רנה דף.
תתק. כנ"ל אות שלה. באומאנט, טעקסאס. ה'תשד"מ. רנה דף.
תתקא. כנ"ל אות שלה. בעלייר, טעקסאס. ה'תשד"מ. רנה דף.
תתקב. כנ"ל אות שלה. בראונסוויל, טעקסאס. ה'תשד"מ. רנה דף.
תתקג. כנ"ל אות שלה. ברעקענרידזש, טעקסאס. ה'תשד"מ. רנה דף.
תתקד. כנ"ל אות שלה. קארפאס, טעקסאס. ה'תשד"מ. רנה דף.
תתקה. כנ"ל אות שלה. קאלעדוש סטיישן, טעקסאס. ה'תשד"מ. רנה דף.
תתקו. כנ"ל אות שלה. קארסיקאנא, טעקסאס. ה'תשד"מ. רנה דף.
תתקז. כנ"ל אות שלה. דאלאס, טעקסאס. ה'תשד"מ. רנה דף.
תתקח. כנ"ל אות שלה. על פאסא, טעקסאס. ה'תשד"מ. רנה דף.
תתקט. כנ"ל אות שלה. גאלוועסטאן, טעקסאס. ה'תשד"מ. רנה דף.
תתקי. כנ"ל אות שלה. פארט וואורט, טעקסאס. ה'תשד"מ. רנה דף.
תתקיא. כנ"ל אות שלה. טיילער, טעקסאס. ה'תשד"מ. רנה דף.
תתקיב. כנ"ל אות שלה. וויקא, טעקסאס. ה'תשד"מ. רנה דף.
תתקיג. כנ"ל אות שלה. לארעדא, טעקסאס. ה'תשד"מ. רנה דף.
תתקיד. כנ"ל אות שלה. מק-אלען, טעקסאס. ה'תשד"מ. רנה דף.
תתקטו. כנ"ל אות שלה. לאבאק, טעקסאס. ה'תשד"מ. רנה דף.
תתקטז. כנ"ל אות שלה. פארט ארטור, טעקסאס. ה'תשד"מ. רנה דף.
תתקיז. כנ"ל אות שלה. וויקטאריא, טעקסאס. ה'תשד"מ. רנה דף.
תתקיח. כנ"ל אות שלה. וויטשיטא פאלס, טעקסאס. ה'תשד"מ. רנה דף.
תתקיט. כנ"ל אות שלה. ווארטאן, טעקסאס. ה'תשד"מ. רנה דף.
תתקכ. כנ"ל אות שלה. הארלינדזשען, טעקסאס. ה'תשד"מ. רנה דף.
תתקכא. כנ"ל אות שלה. קילגאר, טעקסאס. ה'תשד"מ. רנה דף.
תתקכב. כנ"ל אות שלה. לאנג וויו, טעקסאס. ה'תשד"מ. רנה דף.
תתקכג. כנ"ל אות שלה. מארשאל, טעקסאס. ה'תשד"מ. רנה דף.
תתקכד. כנ"ל אות שלה. שערמאן, טעקסאס. ה'תשד"מ. רנה דף.
תתקכה. כנ"ל אות שלה. טעקסארקאנא, טעקסאס. ה'תשד"מ. רנה דף.
תתקכו. כנ"ל אות שלה. שוגער לאנד, טעקסאס.תשד"מ. רנה דף.

תתקכז. כנ"ל אות שלה. מיזורי סיטי, טעקסאס. תשד"מ. רנה דף.
תתקכח. כנ"ל אות שלה. ריטשארדסאן, טעקסאס. תשד"מ. רנה דף.
תתקכט. כנ"ל אות שלה. פליינא, טעקסאס. ה'תשד"מ. רנה דף.
תתקל. כנ"ל אות רב. מושב גמזו, באה"ק ת"ו. תשד"מ. רנה ז'ף.
תתקלא. כנ"ל אות רב. מושב נחלים, באה"ק ת"ו. תשד"מ. רנה דף.
תתקלב. כנ"ל אות רב. מצפה רמון, באה"ק ת"ו. תשד"מ. רנה דף.
תתקלג. כנ"ל אות רב. כפר מימון, באה"ק ת"ו. ה'תשד"מ. רנה דף.
תתקלד. כנ"ל אות רב. מצפה יריחו, באה"ק ת"ו. תשד"מ. רנה דף.
תתקלה. כנ"ל אות רב. בית גמליאל, באה"ק ת"ו. תשד"מ. רנה דף.
תתקלו. כנ"ל אות רב. ראש העין, באה"ק ת"ו. ה'תשד"מ. רנה דף.
תתקלז. כנ"ל אות ערב. רמת גן, באה"ק ת"ו. ה'תשד"מ. רנה דף.
תתקלח. כנ"ל אות רב. מגדל, באה"ק ת"ו. ה'תשד"מ. רנה דף.
תתקלט. כנ"ל אות רב. בי"ס חב"ד, יפו, באה"ק ת"ו. ה'תשד"מ. רנה דף.
תתקמ. כנ"ל אות רב. עפולה עלית, באה"ק ת"ו. ה'תשד"מ. רנה דף.
תתקמא. כנ"ל אות רב. באר טובי', באה"ק ת"ו. ה'תשד"מ. רנה דף.
תתקמב. כנ"ל אות שלה. סאוט פאלסבורג, נ. י. ה'תשד"מ. רנה דף.
תתקמג. כנ"ל אות שלה. גלענס פאלס, נ.י. ה'תשד"מ. רנה דף.
תתקמד. כנ"ל אות שלה. טראי, נ.י. ה'תשד"מ. רנה דף.
תתקמה. כנ"ל אות שלה. סאראטאגא ספרינגס, נ.י. תשד"מ. רנה דף.
תתקמו. כנ"ל אות שלה. סקענעקטעדי, נ.י. ה'תשד"מ. רנה דף.
תתקמז. כנ"ל אות שלה. קינגסטאן, נ.י. ה'תשד"מ. רנה דף.
תתקמח. כנ"ל אות שלה. קיטשענער־וואטערלו, אנטריא, קנדה [נדפס בוואטערלו]. ה'תשד"מ. רנה דף.
תתקמט. כנ"ל אות שלה. האליפאקס, קנדה. ה'תשד"מ. רנה דף.
תתקנ. כנ"ל אות שלה. מאנט — רויאל, קוויבעק, קנדה. ה'תשד"מ. רנה דף.
תתקנא. כנ"ל אות שלה. המפסטד, קוויבעק, קנדה. תשד"מ. רנה דף.
תתקנב. כנ"ל אות שלה. וועסטמאונט, קוויבעק, קנדה. תשד"מ. רנה דף.
תתקנג. כנ"ל אות שלה. קוויבעק, קנדה. ה'תשד"מ. רנה דף.
תתקנד. כנ"ל אות שלה. דולארד ד'אורמו, קוויבעק, קנדה. ה'תשד"מ. רנה דף.
תתקנה. כנ"ל אות שלה. אוטרמנט, קוויבעק, קנדה. תשד"מ. רנה דף.
תתקנו. כנ"ל אות שלה. לאוראן, קוויבעק, קנדה. תשד"מ. רנה דף.
תתקנז. כנ"ל אות שלה. שארברוק, קוויבעק, קנדה. תשד"מ. רנה דף.
תתקנח. כנ"ל אות שלה. קוט לוק, קוויבעק, קנדה. תשד"מ. רנה דף.
תתקנט. כנ"ל אות שלה. אגאט, קוויבעק, קנדה. תשד"מ. רנה דף.
תתקס. כנ"ל אות שלה. לאוואל, קוויבעק, קנדה. תשד"מ. רנה דף.
תתקסא. כנ"ל אות שדמ. קאן, צרפת. ה'תשד"מ. רנה דף.
תתקסב. כנ"ל אות שדמ. אנטיב, צרפת. ה'תשד"מ. רנה דף.
תתקסג. כנ"ל אות שדמ. מענטאן, צרפת. ה'תשד"מ. רנה דף.
תתקסד. כנ"ל אות שדמ. בסטי' אי קורסיקא, צרפת. תשד"מ. רנה דף.
תתקסה. כנ"ל אות שדמ. גראס, צרפת. ה'תשד"מ. רנה דף.
תתקסו. כנ"ל אות שדמ. פרעזשוס רפאל, צרפת. תשד"מ. רנה דף.
תתקסז. כנ"ל אות שדמ. וואנס, צרפת. ה'תשד"מ. רנה דף.
תתקסח. כנ"ל אות שדמ. טרופעז מקסים, צרפת. תשד"מ. רנה דף.
תתקסט. כנ"ל אות שדמ. דרגיניאן, צרפת. ה'תשד"מ. רנה דף.
תתקע. כנ"ל אות שדמ. קניא סור מער, צרפת. תשד"מ. רנה דף.
תתקעא. כנ"ל אות שלה. סאנדטאן, סאוט אפריקא. תשד"מ. רנה דף.
תתקעב. כנ"ל אות שלה. ראנדבורג, סאוט אפריקא. תשד"מ. רנה דף.
תתקעג. כנ"ל אות שלה. דזשערמיסטאן, סאוט אפריקא. ה'תשד"מ. רנה דף.
תתקעד. כנ"ל אות שלה. קרוגערסדארף, סאוט אפריקא. ה'תשד"מ. רנה דף.
תתקעה. כנ"ל אות שלה. רודעפארט, סאוט אפריקא. תשד"מ. רנה דף.
תתקעו. כנ"ל אות שלה. ראנדפאנטיין, סאוט אפריקא. ה'תשד"מ. רנה דף.
תתקעז. כנ"ל אות שלה. בענאני, סאוט אפריקא. תשד"מ. רנה דף.
תתקעח. כנ"ל אות שלה. בראקפאן, סאוט אפריקא. תשד"מ. רנה דף.
תתקעט. כנ"ל אות שלה. באקסבורג, סאוט אפריקא. תשד"מ. רנה דף.
תתקפ. כנ"ל אות שלה. ספרינגס, סאוט אפריקא. תשד"מ. רנה דף.

תתקפא. כנ"ל אות שלה. דורבן, סאוט אפריקא. תשד"מ. רנה דף.
תתקפב. כנ"ל אות שלה. פארט עליזאבעט, סאוט אפריקא. ה'תשד"מ. רנה דף.
תתקפג. כנ"ל אות שלה. איסט לאנדאן, סאוט אפריקא. תשד"מ. רנה דף.
תתקפד. כנ"ל אות שלה. בלומפאנטיין, סאוט אפריקא. תשד"מ. רנה דף.
תתקפה. כנ"ל אות שלה. דעלמאס, סאוט אפריקא. תשד"מ. רנה דף.
תתקפו. כנ"ל אות שלה. וויטבאנק, סאוט אפריקא. תשד"מ. רנה דף.
תתקפז. כנ"ל אות שלה. מידעלבורג, סאוט אפריקא. תשד"מ. רנה דף.
תתקפח. כנ"ל אות שלה. וועלקאם, סאוט אפריקא. תשד"מ. רנה דף.
תתקפט. כנ"ל אות שלה. פאטשעפסטרום, סאוט אפריקא. ה'תשד"מ. רנה דף.
תתקצ. כנ"ל אות שלה. קלארקסדארף, סאוט אפריקא. תשד"מ. רנה דף.
תתקצא. כנ"ל אות שלה. פעראייניגינג, סאוט אפריקא. תשד"מ. רנה דף.
תתקצב. כנ"ל אות שלה. וואנדערביילפארק, סאוט אפריקא. ה'תשד"מ. רנה דף.
תתקצג. כנ"ל אות שלה. פיטערסבורג, סאוט אפריקא. תשד"מ. רנה דף.
תתקצד. כנ"ל אות שלה. קימבערלי, סאוט אפריקא. תשד"מ. רנה דף.
תתקצה. כנ"ל אות שלה. אוידסטהארן, סאוט אפריקא. תשד"מ. רנה דף.
תתקצו. כנ"ל אות שלה. גרייהאמסטאן, סאוט אפריקא. תשד"מ. רנה דף.
תתקצז. כנ"ל אות שלה. קרונשטאד, סאוט אפריקא. תשד"מ. רנה דף.
תתקצח. כנ"ל אות שלה. בעטהאל, סאוט אפריקא. תשד"מ. רנה דף.
תתקצט. כנ"ל אות שלה. פארייז, סאוט אפריקא. תשד"מ. רנה דף.
אלף (תתר). כנ"ל אות קסד. ונתקנו (בפנים) עוד כמה מטעויות הדפוס שבכמה מהוצאות הקודמות. ובההוספות — נתוספו השערים של הוצאות התניא והתרגומים כו' שהו"ל מאז. י"א ניסן, תשד"מ. ברוקלין, נ. י. (8), קהת דף.

א'א.[1] כנ"ל אות קמב. בוקרישט, רומעניא. ה'תשד"מ. רמ דף.
א'ב. כנ"ל אות שדמ. אלעסאנדריא, איטאליא. ה'תשד"מ. רנה דף.
א'ג. כנ"ל אות שלה. ליוורנו, איטאליא. ה'תשד"מ. רנה דף.
א'ד. כנ"ל אות שלה. פיזא, איטאליא. ה'תשד"מ. רנה דף.
א'ה. כנ"ל אות שלה. קאלווער סיטי, קאליפארניא. תשד"מ. רנה דף.
א'ו. כנ"ל אות שלה. מאנטפעליער, ווערמאנט. תשד"מ. רנה דף.
א'ז. כנ"ל אות שלה. ליטל ראק, ארקענסא. ה'תשד"מ. רנד דף.
א'ח. כנ"ל אות שלה. ווילמינגטאן, דעלעווער. ה'תשד"מ. רנד דף.
א'ט. כנ"ל אות שלה. אטלאנטא, דזשארדזשיא. ה'תשד"מ. רנד דף.
א'י. כנ"ל אות שלה. אליטה, קנזס. ה'תשד"מ. רנד דף.
א'יא. כנ"ל אות שלה. לואיוויל, קענטאקי. ה'תשד"מ. רנד דף.
א'יב. כנ"ל אות שלה. דזשעקסאן, מיסיסיפי. ה'תשד"מ. רנד דף.
א'יג. כנ"ל אות שלה. אמאהא, נעבראסקא. ה'תשד"מ. רנד דף.
א'יד. כנ"ל אות שלה. טשארלסטאן, וועסט ווירדזשיניא. ה'תשד"מ. רנד דף.
א'טו. כנ"ל אות שלה. פארטסמאוט, ניו האמפשעיר. ה'תשד"מ. רנד דף.
א'טז. כנ"ל אות שלה. טשארלסטאן, סאוט קאראליינא. ה'תשד"מ. רנד דף.
א'יז. כנ"ל אות שלה. טאלסא, אקלאהאמא. ה'תשד"מ. רנד דף.
א'יח. כנ"ל אות שלה. סאלט לייק סיטי, יוטא. ה'תשד"מ. רנה דף.
א'יט. כנ"ל אות שלה. פאול, מינעסאטא. ה'תשד"מ. רנד דף.
א'כ. כנ"ל אות שלה. ראטשעסטער, מינעסאטא. תשד"מ. רנד דף.
א'כא. כנ"ל אות שלה. אלבערט ליא, מינעסאטא. תשד"מ. רנד דף.
א'כב. כנ"ל אות שלה. לואיס פארק, מינעסאטא. ה'תשד"מ. רגד דף.
א'כג. כנ"ל אות שלה. די מאין, אייאווא. ה'תשד"מ. רנד דף.
א'כד. כנ"ל אות שלה. דיביוק, אייאווא. ה'תשד"מ. רנד דף.

---

1) המספרים שאחרי הוצאה האלף יצויינו א'א, א'ב וכו' (ולא תתרא תתרב וכו'). המו"ל.

א'כה. כנ"ל אות שלה. אדעסא, טעקסאס. ה'תשד"מ. רנה דף.

א'כו. כנ"ל אות שלה. ברענהאם, טעקסאס. ה'תשד"מ. רנה דף.

א'כז. כנ"ל אות שלה. אגורא הילס, קאליפארניא. תשד"מ. רנה דף.

א'כח. כנ"ל אות שלה. אוואלאן, קאליפארניא. ה'תשד"מ. רנה דף.

א'כט. כנ"ל אות שלה. אזוסא, קאליפארניא. ה'תשד"מ. רנה דף.

א'ל. כנ"ל אות שלה. אינגלוואוד, קאליפארניא. תשד"מ. רנה דף.

א'לא. כנ"ל אות שלה. אינדאסטרי, קאליפארניא. תשד"מ. רנה דף.

א'לב. כנ"ל אות שלה. אירווינדייל, קאליפארניא. תשד"מ. רנה דף.

א'לג. כנ"ל אות שלה. אלהאמברא, קאליפארניא. תשד"מ. רנה דף.

א'לד. כנ"ל אות שלה. ארקאדיא, קאליפארניא. ה'תשד"מ. רנה דף.

א'לה. כנ"ל אות שלה. באלדווין פארק, קאליפארניא. ה'תשד"מ. רנה דף.

א'לו. כנ"ל אות שלה. בעל, קאליפארניא. ה'תשד"מ. רנה דף.

א'לז. כנ"ל אות שלה. בעל גארדענס, קאליפארניא. תשד"מ. רנה דף.

א'לח. כנ"ל אות שלה. בעלפלאוער, קאליפארניא. תשד"מ. רנה דף.

א'לט. כנ"ל אות שלה. בראדבורי, קאליפארניא. ה'תשד"מ. רנה דף.

א'מ. כנ"ל אות שלה. גאבריעל, קאליפארניא. ה'תשד"מ. רנה דף.

א'מא. כנ"ל אות שלה. גארדענא, קאליפארניא. ה'תשד"מ. רנה דף.

א'מב. כנ"ל אות שלה. גלענדארא, קאליפארניא. תשד"מ. רנה דף.

א'מג. כנ"ל אות שלה. דאוני, קאליפארניא. ה'תשד"מ. רנה דף.

א'מד. כנ"ל אות שלה. דוארטע, קאליפארניא. ה'תשד"מ. רנה דף.

א'מה. כנ"ל אות שלה. דימאס, קאליפארניא. ה'תשד"מ. רנה דף.

א'מו. כנ"ל אות שלה. האווייען גארדענז, קאליפארניא. ה'תשד"מ. רנה דף.

א'מז. כנ"ל אות שלה. האטארן, קאליפארניא. ה'תשד"מ. רנה דף.

א'מח. כנ"ל אות שלה. האנטינגטאן פארק, קאליפארניא. ה'תשד"מ. רנה דף.

א'מט. כנ"ל אות שלה. הידען הילס, קאליפארניא. תשד"מ. רנה דף.

א'נ. כנ"ל אות שלה. הערמאסא ביטש, קאליפארניא. ה'תשד"מ. רנה דף.

א'נא. כנ"ל אות שלה. וואלנאט, קאליפארניא. ה'תשד"מ. רנה דף.

א'נב. כנ"ל אות שלה. וועסט קאווינא, קאליפארניא. תשד"מ. רנה דף.

א'נג. כנ"ל אות שלה. ווערנאן, קאליפארניא. ה'תשד"מ. רנה דף.

א'נד. כנ"ל אות שלה. וועסטלייק ווילידזש, קאליפארניא. ה'תשד"מ. רנה דף.

א'נה. כנ"ל אות שלה. לא האברא הייטס, קאליפארניא. ה'תשד"מ. רנה דף.

א'נו. כנ"ל אות שלה. לא ווערנא, קאליפארניא. תשד"מ. רנה דף.

א'נז. כנ"ל אות שלה. לא מיראדא, קאליפארניא. תשד"מ. רנה דף.

א'נח. כנ"ל אות שלה. לא פוענטע, קאליפארניא. תשד"מ. רנה דף.

א'נט. כנ"ל אות שלה. לאונדייל, קאליפארניא. ה'תשד"מ. רנה דף.

א'ס. כנ"ל אות שלה. לאנקאסטער, קאליפארניא. תשד"מ. רנה דף.

א'סא. כנ"ל אות שלה. לינוואוד, קאליפארניא. ה'תשד"מ. רנה דף.

א'סב. כנ"ל אות שלה. מאנהאטען ביטש, קאליפארניא. ה'תשד"מ. רנה דף.

א'סג. כנ"ל אות שלה. מאנראוויא, קאליפארניא. תשד"מ. רנה דף.

א'סד. כנ"ל אות שלה. מייוואוד, קאליפארניא. ה'תשד"מ. רנה דף.

א'סה. כנ"ל אות שלה. על מאנטע, קאליפארניא. תשד"מ. רנה דף.

א'סו. כנ"ל אות שלה. על סעגונדא, קאליפארניא. תשד"מ. רנה דף.

א'סז. כנ"ל אות שלה. פערנאנדא, קאליפארניא. תשד"מ. רנה דף.

א'סח. כנ"ל אות שלה. קאווינא, קאליפארניא. ה'תשד"מ. רנה דף.

א'סט. כנ"ל אות שלה. קאמערס, קאליפארניא. ה'תשד"מ. רנה דף.

א'ע. כנ"ל אות שלה. קאמפטאן, קאליפארניא. ה'תשד"מ. רנה דף.

א'עא. כנ"ל אות שלה. קארסאן, קאליפארניא. ה'תשד"מ. רנה דף.

א'עב. כנ"ל אות שלה. טעמפל סיטי, קאליפארניא. תשד"מ. רנז דף.

א'עג. כנ"ל אות שלה. לא קאניאדא, קאליפארניא. תשד"מ. רנז דף.

א'עד. כנ"ל אות שלה. מאנטעבעלא, קאליפארניא. תשד"מ. רנז דף.

א'עה. כנ"ל אות שלה. מאנטעריי פארק, קאליפארניא. ה'תשד"מ. רנז דף.

א'עו. כנ"ל אות שלה. מארינא, קאליפארניא. ה'תשד"מ. רנז דף.

א'עז. כנ"ל אות שלה. נארוואק, קאליפארניא. ה'תשד"מ. רנז דף.

א'עח. כנ"ל אות שלה. סאוט גייט, קאליפארניא. ה'תשד"מ. רנז דף.

א'עט. כנ"ל אות שלה. סאוט על מאנטי, קאליפארניא. ה'תשד"מ. רנז דף.

א'פ. כנ"ל אות שלה. סאוט פאסאדינא, קאליפארניא. ה'תשד"מ. רנז דף.

א'פא. כנ"ל אות שלה. סיערא מאדרא, קאליפארניא. תשד"מ. רנז דף.

א'פב. כנ"ל אות שלה. פאלמדייל, קאליפארניא. ה'תשד"מ. רנז דף.

א'פג. כנ"ל אות שלה. פאמאנא, קאליפארניא. ה'תשד"מ. רנז דף.

א'פד. כנ"ל אות שלה. פיקא ריווערא, קאליפארניא. תשד"מ. רנז דף.

א'פה. כנ"ל אות שלה. פע ספרינגס, קאליפארניא. תשד"מ. רנז דף.

א'פו. כנ"ל אות שלה. ראזמעד, קאליפארניא. ה'תשד"מ. רנז דף.

א'פז. כנ"ל אות שלה. ראלינג הילס, קאליפארניא. תשד"מ. רנז דף.

א'פח. כנ"ל אות שלה. ראלינג הילס עסטייטס, קאליפארניא. ה'תשד"מ. רנז דף.

א'פט. כנ"ל אות שלה. רעדאנדא ביטש, קאליפארניא. ה'תשד"מ. רנז דף.

א'צ. כנ"ל אות ריא. עתלית, באה"ק ת"ו. ה'תשד"מ. רנז דף.

א'צא. כנ"ל אות ריא. כפר הרואה, באה"ק ת"ו. ה'תשד"מ. רנז דף.

א'צב. כנ"ל אות ריא. גדרה, באה"ק ת"ו. ה'תשד"מ. רנז דף.

א'צג. כנ"ל אות ריא. חדרה, באה"ק ת"ו. ה'תשד"מ. רנז דף.

א'צד. כנ"ל אות ריא. יקנעם, באה"ק ת"ו. ה'תשד"מ. רנז דף.

א'צה. כנ"ל אות ריא. צה"ל — מחנה „עוצבת השריון", באה"ק ת"ו. ה'תשד"מ. רנז דף.

א'צו. כנ"ל אות ריא. צה"ל — מחנה „עוצבת סיני", באה"ק ת"ו. ה'תשד"מ. רנז דף.

א'צז. כנ"ל אות ריא. מושב רגבה, באה"ק ת"ו. ה'תשד"מ. רנז דף.

א'צח. כנ"ל אות ריא. נוה דקלים, באה"ק ת"ו. ה'תשד"מ. רנז דף.

א'צט. כנ"ל אות ריא. אזור, באה"ק ת"ו. ה'תשד"מ. רנז דף.

א'ק. כנ"ל אות ריא. יבנה, באה"ק ת"ו. ה'תשד"מ. רנז דף.

א'קא. כנ"ל אות ריא. מושב עבדון, באה"ק ת"ו. ה'תשד"מ. רנז דף.

א'קב. כנ"ל אות ריא. מושב גורן, באה"ק ת"ו. ה'תשד"מ. רנז דף.

א'קג. כנ"ל אות ריא. מושב חבת ציון, באה"ק ת"ו. ה'תשד"מ. רנז דף.

א'קד. כנ"ל אות ריא. אמירים, באה"ק ת"ו. תשד"מ. רנז דף.

א'קה. כנ"ל אות ריא. מנחמי', באה"ק ת"ו. תשד"מ. רנח דף.

א'קו. כנ"ל אות ריא. סביון, באה"ק ת"ו. תשד"מ. רנח דף.

א'קז. כנ"ל אות ריא. שלומי, באה"ק ת"ו. תשד"מ. רנח דף.

א'קח. כנ"ל אות ריא. קרית בנימין — קרית אתא, באה"ק ת"ו. תשד"מ. רנח דף.

א'קט. כנ"ל אות ריא. נוה מונוזון, באה"ק ת"ו. תשד"מ. רנח דף.

א'קי. כנ"ל אות ריא. שכון חב"ד, ירושת"ו. תשד"מ. רנח דף.

א'קיא. כנ"ל אות ריא. שכונת קרית ארי', ירושת"ו. ה'תשד"מ. רנז דף.

א'קיב. כנ"ל אות ריא. שכונת עיר גנים, ירושת"ו. ה'תשד"מ. רנז דף.

א'קיג. כנ"ל אות ריא. פקיעין, ע"י מערת הרשב"י, באה"ק ת"ו. ה'תשד"מ. רנז דף.

א'קיד. כנ"ל אות ריא. טברי', ע"י קבר הרמב"ם, באה"ק ת"ו. ה'תשד"מ. רנז דף.

א'קטו. כנ"ל אות ריא. קיבוץ פרוד, באה"ק ת"ו. ה'תשד"מ. רנז דף.

א'קטז. כנ"ל אות ריא. קיבוץ הסוללים, באה"ק ת"ו. תשד"מ. רנז דף.

א'קיז. כנ"ל אות ריא. קיבוץ כפר גלעדי, באה"ק ת"ו. ה'תשד"מ. רנז דף.

א'קיח. כנ"ל אות ריא. קיבוץ גנוסר, באה"ק ת"ו. תשד"מ. רנז דף.

א'קיט. כנ"ל אות ריא. קיבוץ משגב עם, באה"ק ת"ו. תשד"מ. רנז דף.

א'קכ. כנ"ל אות ריא. מושב אבן מנחם, באה"ק ת"ו. תשד"מ. רנז דף.

א'קכא. כנ"ל אות ריא. מושב עין יעקב, באה"ק ת"ו. תשד"מ. רנז דף.

א'קכב. כנ"ל אות ריא. מושב שפר, באה"ק ת"ו. ה'תשד"מ. רנז דף.

א'קכג. כנ"ל אות ריא. בן דור, באה"ק ת"ו. ה'תשד"מ. רנז דף.

א'קכד. כנ"ל אות ריא. ישיבת תו"ת נחלת הר חב"ד — קרית מלאכי, באה"ק ת"ו. ה'תשד"מ. רנז דף.

א'קכה. כנ"ל אות ריא. אלון מורה, גוש עציון, באה"ק ת"ו. ה'תשד"מ. רנז דף.

א'קכו. כנ"ל אות שדמ. מאנט, בעלגיא. ה'תשד"מ. רנז דף.

א'קכז. כנ"ל אות שדמ. אנטווערפן, בעלגיא. ה'תשד"מ. רנז דף.

א'קכח. כנ"ל אות שדמ. קנאקע, בעלגיא. ה'תשד"מ. רנז דף.

א'קכט. כנ"ל אות שלה. וויניא דעל מאר, טשילי. תשד"מ. רנח דף.

א'קל. כנ"ל אות שלה. וואלפאראיסא, טשילי. ה'תשד"מ. רנח דף.

א'קלא. כנ"ל אות שלה. טעמוקא, טשילי. ה'תשד"מ. רנח דף.

א'קלב. כנ"ל אות שלה. קוארנאוואקא, מעקסיקא. ה'תשד"מ. רנח דף.

א'קלג. כנ"ל אות שלה. קארטאגענא, קאלאמביא. ה'תשד"מ. רנח דף.

א'קלד. כנ"ל אות שלה. קוקוטא, קאלאמביא. ה'תשד"מ. רנח דף.

א'קלה. כנ"ל אות שלה. פאלמירא, קאלאמביא. ה'תשד"מ. רנח דף.

א'קלו. כנ"ל אות שלה. פאסטו, קאלאמביא. ה'תשד"מ. רנח דף.

א'קלז. כנ"ל אות שלה. מאניזאלעס, קאלאמביא. ה'תשד"מ. רנח דף.

א'קלח. כנ"ל אות שלה. בריסטאל, קאנעטיקאט. ה'תשד"מ. רנח דף.

א'קלט. כנ"ל אות שלה. דאנבורי, קאנעטיקאט. ה'תשד"מ. רנח דף.

א'קמ. כנ"ל אות שלה. וואטערבורי, קאנעטיקאט. ה'תשד"מ. רנח דף.

א'קמא. כנ"ל אות שלה. מאנטשעסטער, קאנעטיקאט. ה'תשד"מ. רנח דף.

א'קמב. כנ"ל אות שלה. מידלטאון, קאנעטיקאט. ה'תשד"מ. רנח דף.

א'קמג. כנ"ל אות שלה. מערידען, קאנעטיקאט. ה'תשד"מ. רנח דף.

א'קמד. כנ"ל אות שלה. נארוויטש, קאנעטיקאט. ה'תשד"מ. רנח דף.

א'קמה. כנ"ל אות שלה. ווירדזשיניא ביטש, ווירדזשיניא. ה'תשד"מ. רנח דף.

א'קמו. כנ"ל אות שלה. טשעסאפיק, ווירדזשיניא. ה'תשד"מ. רנח דף.

א'קמז. כנ"ל אות שלה. נארפאלק, ווירדזשיניא. תשד"מ. רנח דף.

א'קמח. כנ"ל אות שלה. סאפאולק, ווירדזשיניא. ה'תשד"מ. רנח דף.

א'קמט. כנ"ל אות שלה. פארטסמאוט, ווירדזשיניא. ה'תשד"מ. רנח דף.

א'קנ. כנ"ל אות שלה. פעירפעקס, ווירדזשיניא. ה'תשד"מ. רנח דף.

א'קנא. כנ"ל אות שלה. אליריע, אהייא. ה'תשד"מ. רנח דף.

א'קנב. כנ"ל אות שלה. ביטשוואוד, אהייא. ה'תשד"מ. רנח דף.

א'קנג. כנ"ל אות שלה. פיינזוויל, אהייא. ה'תשד"מ. רנח דף.

א'קנד. כנ"ל אות שלה. לינדהורסט, אהייא. ה'תשד"מ. רנח דף.

א'קנה. כנ"ל אות שלה. קליוולאנד הייטס, אהייא. ה'תשד"מ. רנח דף.

א'קנו. כנ"ל אות שלה. יוניווערסיטי הייטס, אהייא. ה'תשד"מ. רנח דף.

א'קנז. כנ"ל אות שלה. גרייט נעק, לאנג איילאנד, נ.י. ה'תשד"מ. רנח דף.

א'קנח. כנ"ל אות שלה. אירוויין, קאליפארניא. ה'תשד"מ. רנח דף.

א'קנט. כנ"ל אות שלה. וועסט הייווען, קאנעטיקאט. ה'תשד"מ. רנח דף.

א'קס. כנ"ל אות שלה. מאונטיין לייקס, ניו דזוירסי. ה'תשד"מ. רנח דף.

א'קסא. כנ"ל אות שלה. ראנדאלף, ניו דזוירסי. ה'תשד"מ. רנח דף.

א'קסב. כנ"ל אות שלה. חב"ד-ליובאוויטש קעמפוס, מאריס טאונשיפ, נ.ד. (הוצאה שני'). ה'תשד"מ. רנח דף.

א'קסג. כנ"ל אות שלה. פארט לי, ניו דזוירסי. ה'תשד"מ. רנח דף.

א'קסד. כנ"ל אות שדמ. עלקינס פארק, פענסילווייניא. ה'תשד"מ. רנח דף.

א'קסה. כנ"ל אות שדמ. לעקסינגטאן, קענטאקי. ה'תשד"מ. רנח דף.

א'קסו. כנ"ל אות קסט. לאנדרינא, פאראנא, בראזיל. ה'תשד"מ. רנח דף.

א'קסז. כנ"ל אות קסט. פאז דא איגואסו, בראזיל. ה'תשד"מ. רנח דף.

א'קסח. כנ"ל אות ריא. מושב בית יהושע, באה"ק ת"ו. ה'תשד"מ. רנח דף.

א'קסט. כנ"ל אות ריא. ישיבת בני עקיבא נוה הרצוג, ניר גלים, באה"ק ת"ו. ה'תשד"מ. רנח דף.

א'קע. כנ"ל אות ריא. אלוני אבא, באה"ק ת"ו. ה'תשד"מ. רנח דף.

א'קעא. כנ"ל אות ריא. מרכז עיה"ק ירושלים ת"ו. ה'תשד"מ. רנח דף.

א'קעב. כנ"ל אות ריא. קרני שומרון, באה"ק ת"ו. ה'תשד"מ. רנח דף.

א'קעג. כנ"ל אות שדמ. לידז, אנגלי'. ה'תשד"מ. רנח דף.

א'קעד. כנ"ל אות שדמ. ניו קאסעל, אוסטרלי'. ה'תשד"מ. רנח דף.

א'קעה. כנ"ל אות שדמ. שיראז, איראן. ה'תשד"מ. רנח דף.

א'קעו. כנ"ל אות שלה. אמיטיוויל, לאנג איילאנד, נ.י. ה'תשד"מ. רנח דף.

א'קעז. כנ"ל אות שלה. בעלפארט, לאנג איילאנד, נ.י. ה'תשד"מ. רנח דף.

א'קעח. כנ"ל אות שלה. לייק גראוו, לאנג איילאנד, נ.י. ה'תשד"מ. רנח דף.

א'קעט. כנ"ל אות שלה. סאג הארבאר, לאנג איילאנד, נ.י. ה'תשד"מ. רנח דף.

א'קפ. כנ"ל אות שלה. סאוטהאלד, לאנג איילאנד, נ.י. ה'תשד"מ. רנח דף.

א'קפא. כנ"ל אות שלה. סידארהורסט, לאנג איילאנד, נ.י. ה'תשד"מ. רס דף.

א'קפב. כנ"ל אות שלה. פייער איילאנד, לאנג איילאנד, נ.י. ה'תשד"מ. רנח דף.

א'קפג. כנ"ל אות שלה. שעלטער איילאנד, לאנג איילאנד, נ.י. ה'תשד"מ. רנח דף.

א'קפד. כנ"ל אות שדמ. געטעבורג, שוועדן. ה'תשד"מ. רנח דף.

א'קפה. כנ"ל אות שלה. אשאווא, אנטעריא, קנדה. ה'תשד"מ. רנח דף.

א'קפו. כנ"ל אות שלה. בראנטפארד, אנטעריא, קנדה. ה'תשד"מ. רנח דף.

א'קפז. כנ"ל אות שלה. ווינדסאר, אנטעריא, קנדה. ה'תשד"מ. רנח דף.

א'קפח. כנ"ל אות שלה. טימענס, אנטעריא, קנדה. ה'תשד"מ. רנח דף.

א'קפט. כנ"ל אות שלה. יעלאונייף, נארט וועסט טערעטאריס, קנדה. ה'תשד"מ. רנח דף.

א'קצ. כנ"ל אות שלה. מיסיסאגא, אנטעריא, קנדה. ה'תשד"מ. רנח דף.

א'קצא. כנ"ל אות שלה. פיטערבארא, אנטעריא, קנדה. ה'תשד"מ. רנח דף.

א'קצב. כנ"ל אות שלה. קאטערינס, אנטעריא, קנדה. ה'תשד"מ. רנח דף.

א'קצג. כנ"ל אות שלה. קיימברידזש, אנטעריא, קנדה. ה'תשד"מ. רנח דף.

א'קצד. כנ"ל אות שלה. קירקלאנד לייק, אנטעריא, קנדה. ה'תשד"מ. רנח דף.

א'קצה. כנ"ל אות שדמ. אנדאר. ה'תשד"מ. רס דף.

א'קצו. כנ"ל אות שדמ. לוקסעמבורג. ה'תשד"מ. רס דף.

א'קצז. כנ"ל אות שדמ. אוען, צרפת. ה'תשד"מ. רס דף.

א'קצח. כנ"ל אות שדמ. אזשען, צרפת. ה'תשד"מ. רס דף.

א'קצט. כנ"ל אות שדמ. עטיען, צרפת. ה'תשד"מ. רס דף.

א'ר. כנ"ל אות שדמ. אנסי, צרפת. ה'תשד"מ. רס דף.

א'רא. כנ"ל אות שדמ. ארסיי, צרפת. ה'תשד"מ. רס דף.

א'רב. כנ"ל אות שדמ. ארפאזשאן, צרפת. ה'תשד"מ. רס דף.

א'רג. כנ"ל אות שדמ. ארקיי, צרפת. ה'תשד"מ. רס דף.

א'רד. כנ"ל אות שדמ. באניאליי, צרפת. ה'תשד"מ. רס דף.

א'רה. כנ"ל אות שדמ. באניע, צרפת. ה'תשד"מ. רס דף.

א׳רו. כנ״ל אות שדמ. בארדא, צרפת. ה׳תשד״מ. רס דף.

א׳רז. כנ״ל אות שדמ. בוא קאלאמב, צרפת. ה׳תשד״מ. רס דף.

א׳רח. כנ״ל אות שדמ. בואוויי, צרפת. ה׳תשד״מ. רס דף.

א׳רט. כנ״ל אות שדמ. בואסי לעזשיי, צרפת. ה׳תשד״מ. רס דף.

א׳רי. כנ״ל אות שדמ. בורג אן ברעס, צרפת. ה׳תשד״מ. רס דף.

א׳ריא. כנ״ל אות שדמ. בורג לא רען, צרפת. ה׳תשד״מ. רס דף.

א׳ריב. כנ״ל אות שדמ. לע בורזשע, צרפת. ה׳תשד״מ. רס דף.

א׳ריג. כנ״ל אות שדמ. בישיים, צרפת. ה׳תשד״מ. רס דף.

א׳ריד. כנ״ל אות שדמ. בעזאן, צרפת. ה׳תשד״מ. רס דף.

א׳רטו. כנ״ל אות שדמ. בעזאנסא, צרפת. ה׳תשד״מ. רס דף.

א׳רטז. כנ״ל אות שדמ. ברי סור מארן, צרפת. ה׳תשד״מ. רס דף.

א׳ריז. כנ״ל אות שדמ. גארען קאלאמב, צרפת. ה׳תשד״מ. רס דף.

א׳ריח. כנ״ל אות שדמ. גארש, צרפת. ה׳תשד״מ. רס דף.

א׳ריט. כנ״ל אות שדמ. גראסיא, צרפת. ה׳תשד״מ. רס דף.

א׳רכ. כנ״ל אות שדמ. דיזשאן, צרפת. ה׳תשד״מ. רס דף.

א׳רכא. כנ״ל אות שדמ. דיי לא באר, צרפת. ה׳תשד״מ. רס דף.

א׳רכב. כנ״ל אות שדמ. דוני, צרפת. ה׳תשד״מ. רס דף.

א׳רכג. כנ״ל אות שדמ. האגנא, צרפת. ה׳תשד״מ. רס דף.

א׳רכד. כנ״ל אות שדמ. וואלאנס, צרפת. ה׳תשד״מ. רס דף.

א׳רכה. כנ״ל אות שדמ. וואנוו, צרפת. ה׳תשד״מ. רס דף.

א׳רכו. כנ״ל אות שדמ. רואסי אן ברי, צרפת. ה׳תשד״מ. רס דף.

א׳רכז. כנ״ל אות שדמ. ווילמאמבל, צרפת. ה׳תשד״מ. רס דף.

א׳רכח. כנ״ל אות שדמ. ווילטענוו, צרפת. ה׳תשד״מ. רס דף.

א׳רכט. כנ״ל אות שדמ. ווילייר לע בעל, צרפת. ה׳תשד״מ. רס דף.

א׳רל. כנ״ל אות שדמ. ווילנעוו זשארוש, צרפת. ה׳תשד״מ. רס דף.

א׳רלא. כנ״ל אות שדמ. ווישי, צרפת. ה׳תשד״מ. רס דף.

א׳רלב. כנ״ל אות שדמ. וועגסען, צרפת. ה׳תשד״מ. רס דף.

א׳רלג. כנ״ל אות שדמ. ווערניי, צרפת. ה׳תשד״מ. רס דף.

א׳רלד. כנ״ל אות שדמ. זשוויסי, צרפת. ה׳תשד״מ. רס דף.

א׳רלה. כנ״ל אות שדמ. זשענוויל לע פאן, צרפת. תשד״מ. רס דף.

א׳רלו. כנ״ל אות שדמ. זשענעווילליאי, צרפת. ה׳תשד״מ. רס דף.

א׳רלז. כנ״ל אות שדמ. זשערמע אן לייי, צרפת. ה׳תשד״מ. רס דף.

א׳רלח. כנ״ל אות שדמ. טאנאן, צרפת. ה׳תשד״מ. רס דף.

א׳רלט. כנ״ל אות שדמ. טולוז, צרפת. ה׳תשד״מ. רס דף.

א׳רמ. כנ״ל אות שדמ. טיאיי, צרפת. ה׳תשד״מ. רס דף.

א׳רמא. כנ״ל אות שדמ. טראפ, צרפת. ה׳תשד״מ. רס דף.

א׳רמב. כנ״ל אות שדמ. כלו, צרפת. ל״ג בעומר, ה׳תשד״מ. רס דף.

א׳רמג. כנ״ל אות שדמ. לאנס לע סוניע, צרפת. ה׳תשד״מ. רס דף.

א׳רמד. כנ״ל אות שדמ. לא מענא, צרפת. ה׳תשד״מ. רס דף.

א׳רמה. כנ״ל אות שדמ. לאנגזשעמא, צרפת. ה׳תשד״מ. רס דף.

א׳רמו. כנ״ל אות שדמ. לימוזש, צרפת. ה׳תשד״מ. רס דף.

א׳רמז. כנ״ל אות שדמ. לע פעק, צרפת. ה׳תשד״מ. רס דף.

א׳רמח. כנ״ל אות שדמ. מאלאקאף, צרפת. ה׳תשד״מ. רס דף.

א׳רמט. כנ״ל אות שדמ. מאנדיי, צרפת. ה׳תשד״מ. רס דף.

א׳רנ. כנ״ל אות שדמ. מאנזשעראן, צרפת. ה׳תשד״מ. רס דף.

א׳רנא. כנ״ל אות שדמ. נאנטער, צרפת. ה׳תשד״מ. רס דף.

א׳רנב. כנ״ל אות שדמ. מאנמערענסי, צרפת. ה׳תשד״מ. רס דף.

א׳רנג. כנ״ל אות שדמ. מאר דע פאסיי, צרפת. ה׳תשד״מ. רס דף.

א׳רנד. כנ״ל אות שדמ. מאריץ, צרפת. ה׳תשד״מ. רס דף.

א׳רנה. כנ״ל אות שדמ. מונטובון, צרפת. ה׳תשד״מ. רס דף.

א׳רנו. כנ״ל אות שדמ. מולהוז, צרפת. ה׳תשד״מ. רס דף.

א׳רנז. כנ״ל אות שדמ. מעדאן, צרפת. ה׳תשד״מ. רס דף.

א׳רנח. כנ״ל אות שדמ. מאקאן, צרפת. ה׳תשד״מ. רס דף.

א׳רנט. כנ״ל אות שדמ. נאי סור מארן, צרפת. ה׳תשד״מ. רס דף.

א׳רס. כנ״ל אות שדמ. נאי פלעזאנס, צרפת. ה׳תשד״מ. רס דף.

א׳רסא. כנ״ל אות שדמ. נארבאן, צרפת. ה׳תשד״מ. רס דף.

א׳רסב. כנ״ל אות שדמ. סארטרואוויל, צרפת. ה׳תשד״מ. רס דף.

א׳רסג. כנ״ל אות שדמ. סורען, צרפת. ה׳תשד״מ. רס דף.

א׳רסד. כנ״ל אות שדמ. סעל קלו, צרפת. ה׳תשד״מ. רס דף.

א׳רסה. כנ״ל אות שדמ. עבאן, צרפת. ה׳תשד״מ. רס דף.

א׳רסו. כנ״ל אות שדמ. עוויאן, צרפת. ה׳תשד״מ. רס דף.

א׳רסז. כנ״ל אות שדמ. עוורי, צרפת. ה׳תשד״מ. רס דף.

א׳רסח. כנ״ל אות שדמ. עפיניי סור סען, צרפת. ה׳תשד״מ. רס דף.

א׳רסט. כנ״ל אות שדמ. ערמאן, צרפת. ה׳תשד״מ. רס דף.

א׳ער. כנ״ל אות שדמ. פא, צרפת. ה׳תשד״מ. רס דף.

א׳רעא. כנ״ל אות שדמ. פאנטואז, צרפת. ה׳תשד״מ. רס דף.

א׳ערב. כנ״ל אות שדמ. פיערפיט, צרפת. ה׳תשד״מ. רס דף.

א׳רעג. כנ״ל אות שדמ. פערפיניון, צרפת. ה׳תשד״מ. רס דף.

א׳ערד. כנ״ל אות שדמ. פרע זשערוויי, צרפת. ה׳תשד״מ. רס דף.

א׳ערה. כנ״ל אות שדמ. פרען, צרפת. ה׳תשד״מ. רס דף.

א׳רעו. כנ״ל אות שדמ. קאלמאר, צרפת. ה׳תשד״מ. רס דף.

א׳רעז. כנ״ל אות שדמ. קארקאסאן, צרפת. ה׳תשד״מ. רס דף.

א׳רעח. כנ״ל אות שדמ. קורבעוויא, צרפת. ה׳תשד״מ. רס דף.

א׳רעט. כנ״ל אות שדמ. קלערמאן, צרפת. ה׳תשד״מ. רס דף.

א׳רפ. כנ״ל אות שדמ. קראנענבורג, צרפת. ה׳תשד״מ. רס דף.

א׳רפא. כנ״ל אות שדמ. קרייל, צרפת. ה׳תשד״מ. רס דף.

א׳רפב. כנ״ל אות שדמ. ראאן, צרפת. ה׳תשד״מ. רס דף.

א׳רפג. כנ״ל אות שדמ. ראמענוויל, צרפת. ה׳תשד״מ. רס דף.

א׳רפד. כנ״ל אות שדמ. רייי מאלמעזאן, צרפת. ה׳תשד״מ. רס דף.

א׳רפה. כנ״ל אות שדמ. ריס אראנזשיס, צרפת. ה׳תשד״מ. רס דף.

א׳רפו. כנ״ל אות שדמ. שאוויל, צרפת. ה׳תשד״מ. רס דף.

א׳רפז. כנ״ל אות שדמ. שאטיאן, צרפת. ה׳תשד״מ. רס דף.

א׳רפח. כנ״ל אות שדמ. שאטעניי מאלאברי, צרפת. ה׳תשד״מ. רס דף.

א׳רפט. כנ״ל אות שדמ. שאמבערי, צרפת. ה׳תשד״מ. רס דף.

א׳רצ. כנ״ל אות שדמ. שאנטיאי, צרפת. ה׳תשד״מ. רס דף.

א׳רצא. כנ״ל אות שדמ. שואזי-לע-רוא, צרפת. ה׳תשד״מ. רס דף.

א׳רצב. כנ״ל אות שדמ. שעווילי לארו, צרפת. ה׳תשד״מ. רס דף.

א׳רצג. כנ״ל אות שדמ. שעסניי, צרפת. ה׳תשד״מ. רס דף.

א׳רצד. כנ״ל אות שדמ. שערבורג, צרפת. ה׳תשד״מ. רס דף.

א׳רצה. כנ״ל אות שלה. אידענוויל, סאוט אפריקא. ה׳תשד״מ. רס דף.

א׳רצו. כנ״ל אות שלה. בעטלעהיים, סאוט אפריקא. ה׳תשד״מ. רס דף.

א׳רצז. כנ״ל אות שלה. פיטערמאריצבורג, סאוט אפריקא. ה׳תשד״מ. רס דף.

א׳רחצ. כנ״ל אות שלה. פיקסבורג, סאוט אפריקא. ה׳תשד״מ. רס דף.

א׳רצט. כנ״ל אות שלה. קאמפטאן פארק, סאוט אפריקא. ה׳תשד״מ. רס דף.

א׳ש. כנ״ל אות שלה. קארלטאנוויל, סאוט אפריקא. ה׳תשד״מ. רס דף.

א׳שא. כנ״ל אות שלה. ראסטענבורג, סאוט אפריקא. ה׳תשד״מ. רס דף.

א׳שב. כנ״ל אות שלה. ווינדהוק, סאוט-וועסט אפריקא. ה׳תשד״מ. רס דף.

א׳שג. כנ״ל אות שדמ. אמסטלפעהן, האלאנד. ה׳תשד״מ. רס דף.

א׳דש. כנ״ל אות שדמ. אמערספארט, האלאנד. ה׳תשד״מ. רס דף.

א׳שה. כנ״ל אות שדמ. הארלעם, האלאנד. ה׳תשד״מ. רס דף.

א׳שו. כנ״ל אות שדמ. ווערנאן, צרפת. ה׳תשד״מ. רס דף.

א׳שז. כנ״ל אות קפט. פעלאטאס, ריא גראנדע, בראזיל. ה׳תשד״מ. רס דף.

א׳שח. כנ״ל אות שלה. מאנטגאמערי, אלאבאמא. ה׳תשד״מ. רס דף.

א׳שט. כנ״ל אות שלה. מאונט קיסקא, נ.י. ה׳תשד״מ. רס דף.

א׳שי. כנ״ל אות שלה. לאורענס, לאנג איילאנד, נ.י. ה׳תשד״מ. רס דף.

א׳שיא. כנ״ל אות שלה. אסוויגא, נ.י. ה׳תשד״מ. רס דף.

א׳שיב. כנ״ל אות שלה. אשוויל, נ.י. ה׳תשד״מ. רס דף.

א׳שיג. כנ״ל אות שלה. בראקפארט, נ.י. ה׳תשד״מ. רס דף.

א׳שיד. כנ״ל אות שדמ. עליזעבעטוויל, צרפת. ה׳תשד״מ. רס דף.

א׳שטו. כנ״ל אות שלה. גראנד איילאנד, נ.י. ה׳תשד״מ. רס דף.

א׳שטז. כנ״ל אות שלה. דזשענעסיא, נ.י. ה׳תשד״מ. רסב דף.

א׳שיז. כנ״ל אות שלה. הארנעל, נ.י. ה׳תשד״מ. רסב דף.

א'שיח. כנ"ל אות שלה. לואיסטאן, נ.י. ה'תשד"מ. רסב דף.
א'שיט. כנ"ל אות שלה. קארטלאנד, נ.י. ה'תשד"מ. רסב דף.
א'שכ. כנ"ל אות שלה. ספאקיין, וואשינגטאן. ה'תשד"מ. רסב דף.
א'שכא. כנ"ל אות ריא. קיבוץ גבעת ברנר, באה"ק ת"ו. ה'תשד"מ. רסב דף.
א'שכב. כנ"ל אות ריא. רמת השרון, באה"ק ת"ו. ה'תשד"מ. רסב דף.
א'שכג. כנ"ל אות ריא. שכונת סנהדרי' המורחבת, ירושת"ו. ה'תשד"מ. רסב דף.
א'שכד. כנ"ל אות ריא. צה"ל — מחנה רמון, באה"ק ת"ו. ה'תשד"מ. רסב דף.
א'שכה. כנ"ל אות שדמ. מחנה „צבאות השם — ופרצת ליובאוויטש", יפראן, מרוקו. ה'תשד"מ. רסב דף.
א'שכו. כנ"ל אות ריא. ביהכנ"ס האריז"ל, צפת, באה"ק ת"ו. ה'תשד"מ. רסב דף.
א'שכז. כנ"ל אות ריא. קיבוץ נחשולים, באה"ק ת"ו. ה'תשד"מ. רסב דף.
א'שכח. כנ"ל אות שלה. אקאפולקא, מעקסיקא. ה'תשד"מ. רסב דף.
א'שכט. כנ"ל אות שלה. גוואדאלאכארא, מעקסיקא. ה'תשד"מ. רסב דף.
א'של. כנ"ל אות ריא. קיבוץ נען, באה"ק ת"ו. ה'תשד"מ. רסב דף.
א'שלא. כנ"ל אות ריא. קיבוץ אפק, באה"ק ת"ו. ה'תשד"מ. רסב דף.
א'שלב. כנ"ל אות ריא. קיבוץ עינת, באה"ק ת"ו. ה'תשד"מ. רסב דף.
א'שלג. כנ"ל אות ריא. קיבוץ בארות יצחק, באה"ק ת"ו. ה'תשד"מ. רסב דף.
א'שלד. כנ"ל אות ריא. כפר תפוח, באה"ק ת"ו. ה'תשד"מ. רסב דף.
א'שלה. כנ"ל אות ריא. גן יבנה, באה"ק ת"ו. ה'תשד"מ. רסב דף.
א'שלו. כנ"ל אות ריא. ישיבת בנ"ע כרם ביבנה, באה"ק ת"ו. ה'תשד"מ. רסב דף.
א'שלז. כנ"ל אות ריא. קבוצת יבנה, באה"ק ת"ו. ה'תשד"מ. רסב דף.
א'שלח. כנ"ל אות ריא. מרכז שפירא, באה"ק ת"ו. ה'תשד"מ. רסב דף.
א'שלט. כנ"ל אות ריא. גבעת ושינגטון, באה"ק ת"ו. ה'תשד"מ. רסב דף.
א'שמ. כנ"ל אות ריא. שומרה, באה"ק ת"ו. ה'תשד"מ. רסב דף.
א'שמא. כנ"ל אות ריא. מושב אורות, באה"ק ת"ו. ה'תשד"מ. רסב דף.
א'שמב. כנ"ל אות ריא. צוריאל, באה"ק ת"ו. ה'תשד"מ. רסב דף.
א'שמג. כנ"ל אות ריא. מושב גבעתי, באה"ק ת"ו. ה'תשד"מ. רסב דף.
א'שדמ. כנ"ל אות ריא. ברכה, באה"ק ת"ו. ה'תשד"מ. רסב דף.
א'שמה. כנ"ל אות ריא. מחנה צה"ל מרכז תובלה, מלאכי, באה"ק ת"ו. ה'תשד"מ. רסב דף.
א'שמו. כנ"ל אות ריא. מושב שתולים, באה"ק ת"ו. ה'תשד"מ. רסב דף.
א'שמז. כנ"ל אות ריא. מושב תימורים, באה"ק ת"ו. ה'תשד"מ. רסב דף.
א'שמח. כנ"ל אות ריא. מושב בני עייש, באה"ק ת"ו. ה'תשד"מ. רסב דף.
א'שמט. כנ"ל אות ריא. קיבוץ שעלבים, באה"ק ת"ו. תשד"מ. רסב דף.
א'שנ. כנ"ל אות שלה. אראנדזש, ניו דזוירסי. ה'תשד"מ. רסב דף.
א'שנא. כנ"ל אות שלה. איסט אראנדזש, ניו דזוירסי. ה'תשד"מ. רסב דף.
א'שנב. כנ"ל אות שלה. איסט נווארק, ניו דזוירסי. ה'תשד"מ. רסב דף.
א'שנג. כנ"ל אות שלה. איסט בראנזוויק, ניו דזוירסי. ה'תשד"מ. רסב דף.
א'שנד. כנ"ל אות שלה. נארט בראנזוויק, ניו דזוירסי. ה'תשד"מ. רסב דף.

א'שנה. כנ"ל אות שלה. האריסאן, ניו דזוירסי. ה'תשד"מ. רסב דף.
א'שנו. כנ"ל אות שלה. היילאנד פארק, ניו דזוירסי. ה'תשד"מ. רסב דף.
א'שנז. כנ"ל אות שלה. ליאניא, ניו דזוירסי. ה'תשד"מ. רסב דף.
א'שנח. כנ"ל אות שלה. ניו מילפארד, ניו דזוירסי. ה'תשד"מ. רסב דף.
א'שנט. כנ"ל אות שלה. פארלין, ניו דזוירסי. ה'תשד"מ. רסב דף.
א'שס. כנ"ל אות שלה. קליפסייד פארק, ניו דזוירסי. ה'תשד"מ. רסב דף.
א'שסא. כנ"ל אות שלה. קאלאניא, ניו דזוירסי. ה'תשד"מ. רסב דף.
א'שסב. כנ"ל אות שלה. סאמיט, ניו דזוירסי. ה'תשד"מ. רסב דף.
א'שסג. כנ"ל אות שלה. סאמערסעט, ניו דזוירסי. ה'תשד"מ. רסב דף.
א'שסד. כנ"ל אות שלה. רידזשפילד, ניו דזוירסי. ה'תשד"מ. רסב דף.
א'שסה. כנ"ל אות שלה. אנאפאליס, מארילאנד. ה'תשד"מ. רסב דף.
א'שסו. כנ"ל אות שלה. אושען סיטי, מארילאנד. ה'תשד"מ. רסב דף.
א'שסז. כנ"ל אות שלה. הייגערסטאן, מארילאנד. ה'תשד"מ. רסב דף.
א'שסח. כנ"ל אות שלה. סאליסבורי, מארילאנד. ה'תשד"מ. רסב דף.
א'שסט. כנ"ל אות שלה. פרעדריק, מארילאנד. ה'תשד"מ. רסב דף.
א'שע. כנ"ל אות שלה. קאמבערלאנד, מארילאנד. ה'תשד"מ. רסב דף.
א'שעא. כנ"ל אות שלה. ראקוויל, מארילאנד. ה'תשד"מ. רסב דף.
א'שעב. כנ"ל אות שלה. אנטאפאגאסטא, טשילי. ה'תשד"מ. רסב דף.
א'שעג. כנ"ל אות שלה. אריקא, טשילי. ה'תשד"מ. רסב דף.
א'שעד. כנ"ל אות שלה. עקיקי, טשילי. ה'תשד"מ. רסב דף.
א'שעה. כנ"ל אות שלה. קאפיאפא, טשילי. ה'תשד"מ. רסב דף.
א'שעו. כנ"ל אות שלה. יוטיקא, נ.י. ה'תשד"מ. רסב דף.
א'שעז. כנ"ל אות שלה. אושען טאונשיפ, ניו דזוירסי. ה'תשד"מ. רסב דף.
א'שעח. כנ"ל אות שלה. איסט ווינדסאר, ניו דזוירסי. ה'תשד"מ. רסב דף.
א'שעט. כנ"ל אות שלה. וועסט לאנג בראנטש, ניו דזוירסי. ה'תשד"מ. רסב דף.
א'שפ. כנ"ל אות שלה. ווארען, ניו דזוירסי. ה'תשד"מ. רסב דף.
א'שפא. כנ"ל אות שלה. לינקראפט, ניו דזוירסי. ה'תשד"מ. רסב דף.
א'שפב. כנ"ל אות שלה. פיסקאטאווי, ניו דזוירסי. ה'תשד"מ. רסב דף.
א'שפג. כנ"ל אות שלה. קענדאל פארק, ניו דזוירסי. ה'תשד"מ. רסב דף.
א'שפד. כנ"ל אות שלה. רעד באנק, ניו דזוירסי. תשד"מ. רסב דף.
א'שפה. כנ"ל אות שלה. גרייט פאלס, מאנטאנא. ה'תשד"מ. רסב דף.
א'שפו. כנ"ל אות שלה. האלאנדייל, פלארידא. ה'תשד"מ. רסב דף.
א'שפז. כנ"ל אות שלה. האמדען, קאנעטיקאט. ה'תשד"מ. רסב דף.
א'שפח. כנ"ל אות שדמ. ווילרייק, בעלגיא. ה'תשד"מ. רסב דף.
א'שפט. כנ"ל אות שלה. וואלדיוויא, טשילי. ה'תשד"מ. רסב דף.
א'שצ. כנ"ל אות שלה. קאנסעפסיאן, טשילי. ה'תשד"מ. רסב דף.
א'שצא. כנ"ל אות שדמ. בעלפאסט, נארטהערן אירלאנד. ה'תשד"מ. רסב דף.
א'שצב. כנ"ל אות שדמ. איסט גרינסטעד, אנגליא. תשד"מ. רסב דף.
א'שצג. כנ"ל אות שדמ. עדזשווער, אנגליא. ה'תשד"מ. רסב דף.
א'שצד. כנ"ל אות שלה. טינטאן פאלס, ניו דזוירסי. ה'תשד"מ. רסב דף.
א'שצה. כנ"ל אות שלה. ליטל סילווער, ניו דזוירסי. ה'תשד"מ. רסב דף.
א'שצו. כנ"ל אות שלה. פעיר הייווען, ניו דזוירסי. ה'תשד"מ. רסב דף.

א'שצז. כנ"ל אות שלה. ראמסאן, ניו דזוירסי. ה'תשד"מ. רסב דף.

א'שצח. כנ"ל אות שלה. שרוסבורי, ניו דזוירסי. ה'תשד"מ. רסב דף.

א'שצט. כנ"ל אות שלה. בסיסי חל אויר גאנטער — מאקסוועל, מאנטגאמערי, אלאבאמא. ה'תשד"מ. רסה דף.

א'ת. כנ"ל אות שלה. קיאמישא לייק, נ.י. ה'תשד"מ. רסה דף.

א'תא. כנ"ל אות שלה. וואודרידזש, נ.י. ה'תשד"מ. רסה דף.

א'תב. כנ"ל אות שלה. וואודבורן, נ.י. ה'תשד"מ. רסה דף.

א'תג. כנ"ל אות שלה. ברוסטער, נ.י. ה'תשד"מ. רסה דף.

א'תד. כנ"ל אות שלה. טארענס, קאליפארניא. ה'תשד"מ. רסה דף.

א'תה. כנ"ל אות שלה. לומיטא, קאליפארניא. ה'תשד"מ. רסה דף.

א'תו. כנ"ל אות שלה. היילאנד, אינדיאנא. ה'תשד"מ. רסה דף.

א'תז. כנ"ל אות שלה. האמאנד, אינדיאנא. ה'תשד"מ. רסה דף.

א'תח. כנ"ל אות שלה. אספען, קאלאראדא. ה'תשד"מ. רסה דף.

א'תט. כנ"ל אות שלה. באולדער, קאלאראדא. ה'תשד"מ. רסה דף.

א'תי. כנ"ל אות שלה. גראנד דזשאנקשן, קאלאראדא. ה'תשד"מ. רסה דף.

א'תיא. כנ"ל אות שלה. גרילי, קאלאראדא. ה'תשד"מ. רסה דף.

א'תיב. כנ"ל אות שלה. וויל, קאלאראדא. ה'תשד"מ. רסה דף.

א'תיג. כנ"ל אות שלה. עסטעס פארק, קאלאראדא. ה'תשד"מ. רסה דף.

א'תיד. כנ"ל אות שלה. פועבלא, קאלאראדא. ה'תשד"מ. רסה דף.

א'תטו. כנ"ל אות שלה. פארט קאלינס, קאלאראדא. ה'תשד"מ. רסה דף.

א'תטז. כנ"ל אות שלה. קאלאראדא ספרינגס, קאלאראדא. ה'תשד"מ. רסה דף.

א'תיז. כנ"ל אות שלה. אייוואן, קאנעטיקאט. ה'תשד"מ. רסה דף.

א'תיח. כנ"ל אות שלה. איסט הארטפארד, קאנעטיקאט. ה'תשד"מ. רסה דף.

א'תיט. כנ"ל אות שלה. בלומפילד, קאנעטיקאט. ה'תשד"מ. רסה דף.

א'תכ. כנ"ל אות שלה. גלאסטאנבורי, קאנעטיקאט. ה'תשד"מ. רסה דף.

א'תכא. כנ"ל אות שלה. וועטערספילד, קאנעטיקאט. ה'תשד"מ. רסה דף.

א'תכב. כנ"ל אות שלה. ניואינגטאן, קאנעטיקאט. ה'תשד"מ. רסה דף.

א'תכג. כנ"ל אות שלה. סימסבורי, קאנעטיקאט. ה'תשד"מ. רסה דף.

א'תכד. כנ"ל אות שלה. פליינוויל, קאנעטיקאט. ה'תשד"מ. רסה דף.

א'תכה. כנ"ל אות שלה. פארמינגטאן, קאנעטיקאט. ה'תשד"מ. רסה דף.

א'תכו. כנ"ל אות שלה. ראקי היל, קאנעטיקאט. ה'תשד"מ. רסה דף.

א'תכז. כנ"ל אות שלה. גראטאן, קאנעטיקאט. ה'תשד"מ. רסה דף.

א'תכח. כנ"ל אות שלה. העבראן, קאנעטיקאט. ה'תשד"מ. רסה דף.

א'תכט. כנ"ל אות שלה. ווילימאנטיק, קאנעטיקאט. ה'תשד"מ. רסה דף.

א'תל. כנ"ל אות שלה. ווינדסאר, קאנעטיקאט. ה'תשד"מ. רסה דף.

א'תלא. כנ"ל אות שלה. ווינסטעד, קאנעטיקאט. ה'תשד"מ. רסה דף.

א'תלב. כנ"ל אות שלה. טארינגטאן, קאנעטיקאט. ה'תשד"מ. רסה דף.

א'תלג. כנ"ל אות שלה. לעבענאן, קאנעטיקאט. ה'תשד"מ. רסה דף.

א'תלד. כנ"ל אות שלה. סאוט ווינדסאר, קאנעטיקאט. ה'תשד"מ. רסה דף.

א'תלה. כנ"ל אות שלה. קאלטשעסטער, קאנעטיקאט. ה'תשד"מ. רסה דף.

א'תלו. כנ"ל אות שלה. ראקוויל, קאנעטיקאט. ה'תשד"מ. רסה דף.

א'תלז. כנ"ל אות שלה. איווינגוויל, ניו דזוירסי. ה'תשד"מ. רסה דף.

א'תלח. כנ"ל אות שלה. דייטאן, ניו דזוירסי. ה'תשד"מ. רסה דף.

א'תלט. כנ"ל אות שלה. דינס, ניו דזוירסי. ה'תשד"מ. רסה דף.

א'תמ. כנ"ל אות שלה. יארדוויל, ניו דזוירסי. ה'תשד"מ. רסה דף.

א'תמא. כנ"ל אות שלה. מאנמוט דזשאנקשן, ניו דזוירסי. ה'תשד"מ. רסה דף.

א'תמב. כנ"ל אות שלה. פרינצטאן דזשאנקשן, ניו דזוירסי. ה'תשד"מ. רסה דף.

א'תמג. כנ"ל אות שלה. קראנבורי, ניו דזוירסי. ה'תשד"מ. רסה דף.

א'תמד. כנ"ל אות שלה. ביטש הייוועז, ניו דזוירסי. ה'תשד"מ. רסה דף.

א'תמה. כנ"ל אות שלה.ברידזשוואטער, ניו דזוירסי. ה'תשד"מ. רסה דף.

א'תמו. כנ"ל אות שלה. בריק טאון, ניו דזוירסי. ה'תשד"מ. רסה דף.

א'תמז. כנ"ל אות שלה. האלידיי סיטי, ניו דזוירסי. ה'תשד"מ. רסה דף.

א'תמח. כנ"ל אות שלה. וואטשונג, ניו דזוירסי. ה'תשד"מ. רסה דף.

א'תמט. כנ"ל אות שלה. ליזשער ווילעדזש, ניו דזוירסי. ה'תשד"מ. רסה דף.

א'תנ. כנ"ל אות שלה. ניו אידזשעפט, ניו דזוירסי. ה'תשד"מ. רסה דף.

א'תנא. כנ"ל אות שלה. סורף סיטי, ניו דזוירסי. ה'תשד"מ. רסה דף.

א'תנב. כנ"ל אות שלה. פארקד ריווער, ניו דזוירסי. ה'תשד"מ. רסה דף.

א'תנג. כנ"ל אות שלה. פערענעוויל, ניו דזוירסי. ה'תשד"מ. רסה דף.

א'תנד. כנ"ל אות שלה. קרעסטוואוד ווילעדזש, ניו דזוירסי. ה'תשד"מ. רסה דף.

א'תנה. כנ"ל אות שלה. ראסמור, ניו דזוירסי. ה'תשד"מ. רסה דף.

א'תנו. כנ"ל אות שלה. ריווער עדזש, ניו דזוירסי. תשד"מ. רסה דף.

א'תנז. כנ"ל אות שלה. שיפ באטאם, ניו דזוירסי. תשד"מ. רסה דף.

א'תנח. כנ"ל אות שלה. פאלאס ווערדיס עסטייטס, קאליפארניא. ה'תשד"מ. רסה דף.

א'תנט. כנ"ל אות שלה. ראנטשא פאלאס ווערדיס, קאליפארניא. ה'תשד"מ. רסה דף.

א'תס. כנ"ל אות שדמ. טראנדהיים, נארוועגיע. ה'תשד"מ. רסה דף.

א'תסא. כנ"ל אות שלה. הייעטסוויל, מארילאנד. תשד"מ. רסה דף.

א'תסב. כנ"ל אות פז. אזשען, ריא נעגרא, ארגנטינה. ה'תשד"מ. רסו דף.

א'תסג. כנ"ל אות פז. אלטא גראסיא, קאריענטעס, ארגנטינה. ה'תשד"מ. רסו דף.

א'תסד. כנ"ל אות פז. אסול, בוינוס איירס, ארגנטינה. ה'תשד"מ. רסו דף.

א'תסה. כנ"ל אות פז. בארילאטשע, ר. נ., ארגנטינה. ה'תשד"מ. רסו דף.

א'תסו. כנ"ל אות פז. בעריסא, ב. א., ארגנטינה. ה'תשד"מ. רסו דף.

א'תסז. כנ"ל אות פז. בערנאסקאני, לא פאמפא, ארגנטינה. ה'תשד"מ. רסו דף.

א'תסח. כנ"ל אות פז. בראגאדא, ב. א., ארגנטינה. ה'תשד"מ. רסו דף.

א'תסט. כנ"ל אות פז. גאזשא, ק., ארגנטינה. ה'תשד"מ. רסו דף.

א'תע. כנ"ל אות פז. וויזשא אנכעלא, טש., ארגנטינה. ה'תשד"מ. רסו דף.

א'תעא. כנ"ל אות פז. וויזשא מאריא, קאר., ארגנטינה. ה'תשד"מ. רסו דף.

א'תעב. כנ"ל אות פז. טאנדיל, ב. א., ארגנטינה. ה'תשד"מ. רסו דף.

א'תעג. כנ"ל אות פז. טרעלעוו, טשובוט, ארגנטינה. ה'תשד"מ. רסו דף.

א'תעד. כנ"ל אות פז. טרעס אראזשאס, ב. א., ארגנטינה. ה'תשד"מ. רסו דף.

א'תעה. כנ"ל אות פז. כאסע דע מארטין, ב. א., ארגנטינה. ה'תשד"מ. רסו דף.

א'תעו. כנ"ל אות פז. כואז, כ., ארגנטינה. ה'תשד"מ. רסו דף.

א'תעז. כנ"ל אות פז. כוארעס, ב. א., ארגנטינה. ה'תשד"מ. רסו דף.

א'תעח. כנ"ל אות פז. כוכוי, כ., ארגנטינה. ה'תשד"מ. רסו דף.

א'תעט. כנ"ל אות פז. כונין, ב. א., ארגנטינה. ה'תשד"מ. רסו דף.

א'תפ. כנ"ל אות פז. כענעראל ראקא, ר. נ., ארגנטינה. ה'תשד"מ. רסו דף.

א'תפא. כנ"ל אות פז. כענעראל פיניעדא. טש., ארגנטינה. ה'תשד"מ. רסו דף.

א'תפב. כנ"ל אות פז. כענעראל קאמפאס, ענטרה ריוס, ארגנטינה. ה'תשד"מ. רסו דף.

א'תפג. כנ"ל אות פז. לא באנדא, סאנטיאגא דעל עסטערא, ארגנטינה. ה'תשד"מ. רסו דף.

א'תפד. כנ"ל אות פז. לא פאס, ע. ר., ארגנטינה. ה'תשד"מ. רסו דף.

א'תפה. כנ"ל אות פז. לא ריאכא, ל. ר., ארגנטינה. ה'תשד"מ. רסו דף.

א'תפו. כנ"ל אות פז. לויס, ל., ארגנטינה. ה'תשד"מ. רסו דף.

א'תפז. כנ"ל אות פז. מארטין, מ., ארגנטינה. ה'תשד"מ. רסו דף.

א'תפח. כנ"ל אות פז. מענדאסא, מ., ארגנטינה. ה'תשד"מ. רסו דף.

א'תפט. כנ"ל אות פז. מערסעדעס, ב. א., ארגנטינה. ה'תשד"מ. רסו דף.

א'תצ. כנ"ל אות פז. מערסעדעס, לויס, ארגנטינה. ה'תשד"מ. רסו דף.

א'תצא. כנ"ל אות פז. מערסעדעס, קאריענטעס, ארגנטינה. ה'תשד"מ. רסו דף.

א'תצב. כנ"ל אות פז. מריא גראנדע, ע. ר., ארגנטינה. ה'תשד"מ. רסו דף.

א'תצג. כנ"ל אות פז. נועווע דע כוליא, ב. א., ארגנטינה. ה'תשד"מ. רסו דף.

א'תצד. כנ"ל אות פז. נעאוקען, נ., ארגנטינה. ה'תשד"מ. רסו דף.

א'תצה. כנ"ל אות פז. נעקאטשעא, ב. א., ארגנטינה. ה'תשד"מ. רסו דף.

א'תצו. כנ"ל אות פז. סאלטא, ס., ארגנטינה. ה'תשד"מ. רסו דף.

א'תצז. כנ"ל אות פז. סאנטיאגא דעל עסטערא, ס.ד.ע., ארגנטינה. ה'תשד"מ. רסו דף.

א'תצח. כנ"ל אות פז. סאפאלא, נ., ארגנטינה. ה'תשד"מ. רסו דף.

א'תצט. כנ"ל אות פז. סיפאלעטי, ר. נ., ארגנטינה. ה'תשד"מ. רסו דף.

א'תק. כנ"ל אות פז. ענסענאדא, ב. א., ארגנטינה. ה'תשד"מ. רסו דף.

א'תקא. כנ"ל אות פז. פאטאגאנעס, ב. א., ארגנטינה. ה'תשד"מ. רסו דף.

א'תקב. כנ"ל אות פז. פאלאסיאס, פע., ארגנטינה. ה'תשד"מ. רסו דף.

א'תקג. כנ"ל אות פז. פאלמעראס, פע., ארגנטינה. ה'תשד"מ. רסו דף.

א'תקד. כנ"ל אות פז. פאסאדאס, מ., ארגנטינה. ה'תשד"מ. רסו דף.

א'תקה. כנ"ל אות פז. פארמאסא פ., ארגנטינה. ה'תשד"מ. רסו דף.

א'תקו. כנ"ל אות פז. פראנסיסקא, קאר., ארגנטינה. ה'תשד"מ. רסו דף.

א'תקז. כנ"ל אות פז. פ. ראקע ס. פעניא, טש., ארגנטינה. ה'תשד"מ. רסו דף.

א'תקח. כנ"ל אות פז. קאטאמארקא, ק., ארגנטינה. ה'תשד"מ. רסו דף.

א'תקט. כנ"ל אות פז. קאלאן, ע. ר., ארגנטינה. ה'תשד"מ. רסו דף.

א'תקי. כנ"ל אות פז. קאמ. ריוואדאוויא, טשובוט, ארגנטינה. ה'תשד"מ. רסו דף.

א'תקיא. כנ"ל אות פז. קאניועלאס, ב. א., ארגנטינה. ה'תשד"מ. רסו דף.

א'תקיב. כנ"ל אות פז. קאנסעפסיאן, ט., ארגנטינה. ה'תשד"מ. רסו דף.

א'תקיג. כנ"ל אות פז. קארדאבא, קאר., ארגנטינה. ה'תשד"מ. רסו דף.

א'תקיד. כנ"ל אות פז. קאריענטעס, ק., ארגנטינה. ה'תשד"מ. רסו דף.

א'תקטו. כנ"ל אות פז. קוטראל קא, נ., ארגנטינה. ה תשד"מ. רסו דף.

א'תקטז. כנ"ל אות פז. קלארינדא, פ., ארגנטינה. ה'תשד"מ. רסו דף.

א'תקיז. כנ"ל אות פז. ק. סוארעס, ב. א., ארגנטינה. ה'תשד"מ. רסו דף.

א'תקיח. כנ"ל אות פז. ק. פרינגלעס, ב. א., ארגנטינה. ה'תשד"מ. רסו דף.

א'תקיט. כנ"ל אות פז. ראסא, לא פאמפא, ארגנטינה. ה'תשד"מ. רסו דף.

א'תקכ. כנ"ל אות פז. ראפאעל, מ., ארגנטינה. ה'תשד"מ. רסו דף.

א'תקכא. כנ"ל אות פז. ריא גאזשעגאס, ארגנטינה. ה'תשד"מ. רסו דף.

א'ונקכב. כנ"ל אות פז. ריא גראנדע, ט. דעל פועגא, ארגנטינה. ה'תשד"מ. רסו דף.

א'תקכג. כנ"ל אות פז. ריא קוארטא, קאר., ארגנטינה. ה'תשד"מ. רסו דף.

א'תקכד. כנ"ל אות פז. ריווערא, ב. א., ארגנטינה. ה'תשד"מ. רסו דף.

א'תקכה. כנ"ל אות פז. רעסיסטענסיא, טש., ארגנטינה. ה תשד"מ. ריסו דף.

א'תקכו. כנ"ל אות ריא. אבן יהודה, באה"ק ת"ו. ה'תשד"מ. רסט דף.

א'תקכז. כנ"ל אות ריא. מושב אמונים, באה"ק ת"ו. ה'תשד"מ. רסט דף.

א'תקכח. כנ"ל אות ריא. מושב גנות, באה"ק ת"ו. ה'תשד"מ. רסט דף

א'תקכט. כנ"ל אות ריא. כפר זתים, באה"ק ת"ו. ה'תשד"מ. רסט דף.

א'תקל. כנ"ל אות ריא. מושב חמד, באה"ק ת"ו. ה'תשד"מ. רסט דף.

א'תקלא. כנ"ל אות ריא. מושב שדה עוזיה, באה"ק ת"ו. ה'תשד"מ. רסט דף.

א'תקלב. כנ"ל אות ריא. מושב שפיר, באה"ק ת"ו. ה'תשד"מ. רסט דף.

א'תקלג. כנ"ל אות ריא. מושב שרונה, באה"ק ת"ו. ה'תשד"מ. רסט דף.

א'תקלד. כנ"ל אות ריא. כפר קיש, באה"ק ת"ו. ה'תשד"מ. רסט דף.

א'תקלה. כנ"ל אות ריא. שדמות דבורה, באה"ק ת"ו. ה'תשד"מ. רסט דף.

א'תקלו. כנ"ל אות ריא. קיבוץ בית גוברין, באה"ק ת"ו. ה'תשד"מ. רסט דף.

א'תקלז. כנ"ל אות ריא. קיבוץ גליל־ים, באה"ק ת"ו. ה'תשד"מ. רסט דף.

א'תקלח. כנ"ל אות ריא. קיבוץ חפץ חיים, באה"ק ת"ו. ה'תשד"מ. רסט דף.

א'תקלט. כנ"ל אות ריא. קיבוץ מעגן מיכאל, באה"ק ת"ו. ה'תשד"מ. רסט דף.

א'תקמ. כנ"ל אות ריא. צה"ל — מפקדת כוחות שדה, באה"ק ת"ו. ה'תשד"מ. רסט דף.

א'תקמא. כנ"ל אות ריא. קיבוץ אלומות, באה"ק ת"ו. ה'תשד"מ. רסט דף.

א'תקמב. כנ"ל אות ריא. קיבוץ מורן, באה"ק ת"ו. ה'תשד"מ. רסט דף.

א'תקמג. כנ"ל אות ריא. קיבוץ עין צורים, באה"ק ת"ו. ה'תשד"מ. רסט דף.

א'תקמד. כנ"ל אות ריא. יד בנימין, באה"ק ת"ו. ה'תשד"מ. רסט דף.

א׳תקמה. כנ״ל אות ריא. קיבוץ גזר, באה״ק ת״ו. ה׳תשד״מ. רסט דף.

א׳תקמו. כנ״ל אות ריא. קיבוץ מפלסים, באה״ק ת״ו. ה׳תשד״מ. רסט דף.

א׳תקמז. כנ״ל אות ריא. קיבוץ סעד, באה״ק ת״ו. ה׳תשד״מ. רסט דף.

א׳תקמח. כנ״ל אות ריא. רחוב, באה״ק ת״ו. ה׳תשד״מ. רסט דף.

א׳תקמט. כנ״ל אות ריא. שקד, באה״ק ת״ו. ה׳תשד״מ. רסט דף.

א׳תקנ. כנ״ל אות שלה. פארט וויין, אינדיאנא. תשד״מ. רסט דף.

א׳תקנא. כנ״ל אות שלה. לייק טאהא, קאליפארניא. ה׳תשד״מ. רסט דף.

א׳תקנב. כנ״ל אות שלה. ראסא, קאליפארניא. ה׳תשד״מ. רסט דף.

א׳תקנג. כנ״ל אות שלה. רעדינג, קאליפארניא. ה׳תשד״מ. רסט דף.

א׳תקנד. כנ״ל אות ריא. חננית, באה״ק ת״ו. ה׳תשד״מ. רסט דף.

א׳תקנה. כנ״ל אות ריא. כפר גדעון, באה״ק ת״ו. ה׳תשד״מ. רסט דף.

א׳תקנו. כנ״ל אות ריא. כפר הרי״ף, באה״ק ת״ו. ה׳תשד״מ. רסט דף.

א׳תקנז. כנ״ל אות ריא. משואת יצחק, באה״ק ת״ו. ה׳תשד״מ. רסט דף.

א׳תקנח. כנ״ל אות ריא. מרכז חיספית, רמת הגולן, באה״ק ת״ו. ה׳תשד״מ. רסט דף.

א׳תקנט. כנ״ל אות ריא. רמת מגשימים, רמת הגולן, באה״ק ת״ו. ה׳תשד״מ. רסט דף.

א׳תקס. כנ״ל אות ריא. שדרות, באה״ק ת״ו. ה׳תשד״מ. רסט דף.

א׳תקסא. כנ״ל אות שלה. ליבערטי נ.י. נדפס בימים הסמוכים ליום כ״ף במנ״א ה׳תשד״מ — ארבעים שנה ליום הסתלקות הילולא של הרה״ג והרה״ח ומקובל ר׳ לוי יצחק ז״ל — אביו של — יבלח״ט — כ״ק אדמו״ר שליט״א. רסט דף.

א׳תקסב. כנ״ל אות א׳תקסא. בסיס צבאי — פארט לואיס, וואשינגטאן. נדפס בימים הסמוכים לכ׳ במנ״א ה׳תשד״מ — ארבעים שנה (כנ״ל). רסט דף.

א׳תקסג. כנ״ל אות א׳תקסא. אלימפיא, וואשינגטאן. נדפס בימים הסמוכים לכ׳ במנ״א ה׳תשד״מ — ארבעים שנה (כנ״ל). רסט דף.

א׳תקסד. כנ״ל אות א׳תקסא. אורבינו, איטאליע. נדפס בימים הסמוכים לכ׳ במנ״א ה׳תשד״מ — ארבעים שנה (כנ״ל). רסט דף.

א׳תקסה. כנ״ל אות א׳תקסא. אנקונא, איטאליע. נדפס בימים הסמוכים לכ׳ במנ״א ה׳תשד״מ — ארבעים שנה (כנ״ל). רסט דף.

א׳תקסו. כנ״ל אות ריא. קיבוץ אושה, באה״ק ת״ו. נדפס בימים הסמוכים לכ׳ במנ״א ה׳תשד״מ — ארבעים שנה (כנ״ל אות א׳תקסא). רסט דף.

א׳תקסז. כנ״ל אות א׳תקסו. קיבוץ כפר המכבי, באה״ק ת״ו. נדפס בימים הסמוכים לכ׳ במנ״א ה׳תשד״מ — ארבעים שנה (כנ״ל). רסט דף.

א׳תקסח. כנ״ל אות א׳תקסו. קיבוץ לוחמי הגיטאות, באה״ק ת״ו. נדפס בימים הסמוכים לכ׳ במנ״א ה׳תשד״מ — ארבעים שנה (כנ״ל). רסט דף.

א׳תקסט. כנ״ל אות א׳תקסו. קיבוץ רמת יוחנן, באה״ק ת״ו. נדפס בימים הסמוכים לכ׳ במנ״א ה׳תשד״מ — ארבעים שנה (כנ״ל). רסט דף.

א׳תקע. כנ״ל אות א׳תקסו. קיבוץ כפר גליקסון, באה״ק ת״ו. נדפס בימים הסמוכים לכ׳ במנ״א ה׳תשד״מ — ארבעים שנה (כנ״ל). רסט דף.

א׳תקעא. כנ״ל אות א׳תקסו. קיבוץ רגבים, באה״ק ת״ו. נדפס בימים הסמוכים לכ׳ במנ״א ה׳תשד״מ — ארבעים שנה (כנ״ל). רסט דף.

א׳תקעב. כנ״ל אות א׳תקסו. קיבוץ שדות ים, באה״ק ת״ו. נדפס בימים הסמוכים לכ׳ במנ״א ה׳תשד״מ — ארבעים שנה (כנ״ל). רסט דף.

א׳תקעג. כנ״ל אות א׳תקסא. אראדעל, בערגן קאונטי, נ.ד. נדפס בימים הסמוכים לכ׳ במנ״א ה׳תשד״מ — ארבעים שנה (כנ״ל). רסט דף.

א׳תקעד. כנ״ל אות א׳תקסא. בערגנפילד, בערגן קאונטי, נ.ד. נדפס בימים הסמוכים לכ׳ במנ״א ה׳תשד״מ — ארבעים שנה (כנ״ל). רסט דף.

א׳תקעה. כנ״ל אות א׳תקסא. דומאנט, בערגן קאונטי, נ.ד. נדפס בימים הסמוכים לכ׳ במנ״א ה׳תשד״מ — ארבעים שנה (כנ״ל). רסט דף.

א׳תקעו. כנ״ל אות א׳תקסא. קלאסטער, בערגן קאונטי, נ.ד. נדפס בימים הסמוכים לכ׳ במנ״א ה׳תשד״מ — ארבעים שנה (כנ״ל). רסט דף.

א׳תקעז. כנ״ל אות א׳תקסא. קרעסקיל, בערגן קאונטי, נ.ד. נדפס בימים הסמוכים לכ׳ במנ״א ה׳תשד״מ — ארבעים שנה (כנ״ל). רסט דף.

א׳תקעח. כנ״ל אות א׳תקסא. ראטערפארד, בערגן קאונטי, נ.ד. נדפס בימים הסמוכים לכ׳ במנ״א ה׳תשד״מ — ארבעים שנה (כנ״ל). רסט דף.

א׳תקעט. כנ״ל אות א׳תקסו. קיבוץ עין חרוד (מאוחד), באה״ק ת״ו. נדפס בימים הסמוכים לכ׳ במנ״א ה׳תשד״מ — ארבעים שנה (כנ״ל). ערב דף.

א׳תקפ. כנ״ל אות א׳תקסו. קיבוץ תל יוסף, באה״ק ת״ו. נדפס בימים הסמוכים לכ׳ במנ״א ה׳תשד״מ — ארבעים שנה (כנ״ל). ערב דף.

א׳תקפא. כנ״ל אות א׳תקסו. קיבוץ גונן, באה״ק ת״ו. נדפס בימים הסמוכים לכ׳ במנ״א ה׳תשד״מ — ארבעים שנה (כנ״ל). ערב דף.

א׳תקפב. כנ״ל אות א׳תקסו. קיבוץ מצובה, באה״ק ת״ו. נדפס בימים הסמוכים לכ׳ במנ״א ה׳תשד״מ — ארבעים שנה (כנ״ל). ערב דף.

א׳תקפג. כנ״ל אות א׳תקסו. קיבוץ כברי, באה״ק ת״ו. נדפס בימים הסמוכים לכ׳ במנ״א ה׳תשד״מ — ארבעים שנה (כנ״ל). ערב דף.

א׳תקפד. כנ״ל אות א׳תקסו. קיבוץ גשר הזיו, באה״ק ת״ו. נדפס בימים הסמוכים לכ׳ במנ״א ה׳תשד״מ — ארבעים שנה (כנ״ל). ערב דף.

א׳תקפה. כנ״ל אות א׳תקסו. קיבוץ חמדי׳, באה״ק ת״ו. נדפס בימים הסמוכים לכ׳ במנ״א ה׳תשד״מ — ארבעים שנה (כנ״ל). ערב דף.

א׳תקפו. כנ״ל אות א׳תקסו. קיבוץ ירדנה, באה״ק ת״ו. נדפס בימים הסמוכים לכ׳ במנ״א ה׳תשד״מ — ארבעים שנה (כנ״ל). ערב דף.

א׳תקפז. כנ״ל אות א׳תקסו. גדעונה, באה״ק ת״ו. נדפס בימים הסמוכים לכ׳ במנ״א ה׳תשד״מ — ארבעים שנה (כנ״ל). ערב דף.

א׳תקפח. כנ״ל אות א׳תקסו. כפר מחולה, באה״ק ת״ו. נדפס בימים הסמוכים לכ׳ במנ״א ה׳תשד״מ — ארבעים שנה (כנ״ל). ערב דף.

א׳תקפט. כנ״ל אות א׳תקסו. קיבוץ עין חרוד (איחוד), באה״ק ת״ו. נדפס בימים הסמוכים לכ׳ במנ״א ה׳תשד״מ — ארבעים שנה (כנ״ל). ערב דף.

א׳תקצ. כנ״ל אות א׳תקסו. בית חלקי׳, באה״ק ת״ו. נדפס בימים הסמוכים לכ׳ במנ״א ה׳תשד״מ — ארבעים שנה (כנ״ל). ערב דף.

א׳תקצא. כנ״ל אות א׳תקסו. קבוצת שילר, באה״ק ת״ו. נדפס בימים הסמוכים לכ׳ במנ״א ה׳תשד״מ — ארבעים שנה (כנ״ל). ערב דף.

א׳תקצב. כנ״ל אות א׳תקסא. דעלטא, בריטיש קאלאמביא, קאנאדא. נדפס בימים הסמוכים לכ׳ במנ״א ה׳תשד״מ — ארבעים שנה (כנ״ל). ערב דף.

א׳תקצג. כנ״ל אות א׳תקסא. סורי, ב.ק., קאנאדא. נדפס בימים הסמוכים לכ׳ במנ״א ה׳תשד״מ — ארבעים שנה (כנ״ל). ערב דף.

א'תקצד. כנ"ל אות א'תקסא. ריטשמאנד, ב.ק., קאנאדא. נדפס בימים הסמוכים לכ' במנ"א ה'תשד"מ — ארבעים שנה (כנ"ל). ערב דף.

א'תקצה. כנ"ל אות א'תקסא. גוטענבורג, ניו דזוירסי. נדפס בימים הסמוכים לכ' במנ"א ה'תשד"מ — ארבעים שנה (כנ"ל). ערב דף.

א'תקצו. כנ"ל אות א'תקסא. האבאקען, ניו דזוירסי. נדפס בימים הסמוכים לכ' במנ"א ה'תשד"מ — ארבעים שנה (כנ"ל). ערב דף.

א'תקצז. כנ"ל אות א'תקסא. וואשינגטאן טאונשיפ, ניו דזוירסי. נדפס בימים הסמוכים לכ' במנ"א ה'תשד"מ — ארבעים שנה (כנ"ל). ערב דף.

א'תקצח. כנ"ל אות א'תקסא. וועסט ניו יארק, ניו דזוירסי. נדפס בימים הסמוכים לכ' במנ"א ה'תשד"מ — ארבעים שנה (כנ"ל). ערב דף.

א'תקצט. כנ"ל אות א'תקסא. קירני, ניו דזוירסי. נדפס בימים הסמוכים לכ' במנ"א ה'תשד"מ — ארבעים שנה (כנ"ל). ערב דף.

א'תר. כנ"ל אות א'תקסא. וויארעדזא, איטאליע. נדפס בימים הסמוכים לכ' במנ"א ה'תשד"מ — ארבעים שנה (כנ"ל). ערב דף.

א'תרא. כנ"ל אות א'תקסא. פיזרו, איטאליע. נדפס בימים הסמוכים לכ' במנ"א ה'תשד"מ — ארבעים שנה (כנ"ל). ערב דף.

א'תרב. כנ"ל אות א'תקסא. פירודזשא, איטאליע. נדפס בימים הסמוכים לכ' במנ"א ה'תשד"מ — ארבעים שנה (כנ"ל). ערב דף.

א'תרג. כנ"ל אות א'תקסא. קאמאיארע, איטאליע. נדפס בימים הסמוכים לכ' במנ"א ה'תשד"מ — ארבעים שנה (כנ"ל). ערב דף.

א'תרד. כנ"ל אות א'תקסא. ווייט ראק, ב.ק., קאנאדא. נדפס בימים הסמוכים לכ' במנ"א ה'תשד"מ — ארבעים שנה (כנ"ל). ערב דף.

א'תרה. כנ"ל אות א'תקסא. לאנגלי, ב.ק., קאנאדא. נדפס בימים הסמוכים לכ' במנ"א ה'תשד"מ — ארבעים שנה (כנ"ל). ערב דף.

א'תרו. כנ"ל אות שלה. איסט ראטערפארד, ניו דזוירסי. ה'תשד"מ. ערב דף.

א'תרז. כנ"ל אות שלה. וויהאוקען, ניו דזוירסי. ה'תשד"מ. ערב דף.

א'תרח. כנ"ל אות שלה. וועסטפילד, ניו דזוירסי. ה'תשד"מ. ערב דף.

א'תרט. כנ"ל אות שלה. מאונט ארלינגטאן, ניו דזוירסי. ה'תשד"מ. ערב דף.

א'תרי. כנ"ל אות שלה. נאטלי, ניו דזוירסי. ה'תשד"מ. ערב דף.

א'תריא. כנ"ל אות שלה. נארט קאלדוועל, ניו דזוירסי. ה'תשד"מ. ערב דף.

א'תריב. כנ"ל אות שלה. סידאר גראוו, ניו דזוירסי. ה'תשד"מ. ערב דף.

א'תריג. כנ"ל אות שלה. סידאר נאלס, ניו דזוירסי. ה'תשד"מ. ערב דף.

א'תריד. כנ"ל אות שלה. סיקאוקאס, ניו דזוירסי. ה'תשד"מ. ערב דף.

א'תרטו. כנ"ל אות שלה. סעווארען, ניו דזוירסי. ה'תשד"מ. ערב דף.

א'תרטז. כנ"ל אות שלה. פאמפטאן לייקס, ניו דזוירסי. ה'תשד"מ. ערב דף.

א'תריז. כנ"ל אות שלה. קאלדוועל, ניו דזוירסי. ה'תשד"מ. ערב דף.

א'תריח. כנ"ל אות שלה. וועסט קאלדוועל, ניו דזוירסי. ה'תשד"מ. ערב דף.

א'תריט. כנ"ל אות שלה. קליפטאן, ניו דזוירסי. ה'תשד"מ. ערב דף.

א'תרכ. כנ"ל אות שלה. קענילווארט, ניו דזוירסי. ה'תשד"מ. ערב דף.

א'תרכא. כנ"ל אות שלה. בעלוויו, וואשינגטאן. ה'תשד"מ. ערב דף.

א'תרכב. כנ"ל אות שלה. מערסער איילאנד, וואשינגטאן. ה'תשד"מ. ערב דף.

א'תרכג. כנ"ל אות ריא. קיבוץ אייל, באה"ק ת"ו. ה'תשד"מ. ערב דף.

א'תרכד. כנ"ל אות ריא. קיבוץ גבת, באה"ק ת"ו. ה'תשד"מ. ערב דף.

א'תרכה. כנ"ל אות ריא. קיבוץ כפר עזה, באה"ק ת"ו. ה'תשד"מ. ערב דף.

א'תרכו. כנ"ל אות ריא. קיבוץ מעלה הגלבוע, באה"ק ת"ו. ה'תשד"מ. ערב דף.

א'תרכז. כנ"ל אות ריא. קיבוץ ניר עם, באה"ק ת"ו. ה'תשד"מ. ערב דף.

א'תרכח. כנ"ל אות ריא. קיבוץ עלומים, באה"ק ת"ו. ה'תשד"מ. ערב דף.

א'תרכט. כנ"ל אות ריא. קיבוץ שדה אליהו, באה"ק ת"ו. ה'תשד"מ. ערב דף.

א'תרל. כנ"ל אות ריא. קיבוץ שלוחות, באה"ק ת"ו. ה'תשד"מ. ערב דף.

א'תרלא. כנ"ל אות שלה. אוקלאנד, בערגען קאונטי, נ.ד. ה'תשד"מ. ערב דף.

א'תרלב. כנ"ל אות שלה. אלד טאפאן, בערגען קאונטי, נ.ד. ה'תשד"מ. ערב דף.

א'תרלג. כנ"ל אות שלה. אלענדייל, בערגען קאונטי, נ.ד. ה'תשד"מ. ערב דף.

א'תרלד. כנ"ל אות שלה. אלפיין, בערגען קאונטי, נ.ד. ה'תשד"מ. ערב דף.

א'תרלה. כנ"ל אות שלה. באגאטא, בערגען קאונטי, נ.ד. ה'תשד"מ. ערב דף.

א'תרלו. כנ"ל אות שלה. גארפילד, בערגען קאונטי, נ.ד. ה'תשד"מ. ערב דף.

א'תרלז. כנ"ל אות שלה. גלען ראק, בערגען קאונטי, נ.ד. ה'תשד"מ. ערב דף.

א'תרלח. כנ"ל אות שלה. דעמארעסט, בערגען קאונטי, נ.ד. ה'תשד"מ. ערב דף.

א'תרלט. כנ"ל אות שלה. האסברוק הייטס, בערגען קאונטי, נ.ד. ה'תשד"מ. ערב דף.

א'תרמ. כנ"ל אות שלה. וואודקליף לייק, בערגען קאונטי, נ.ד. ה'תשד"מ. ערב דף.

א'תרמא. כנ"ל אות שלה. ווייקאף, בערגען קאונטי, נ.ד. ה'תשד"מ. ערב דף.

א'תרמב. כנ"ל אות שלה. וועסטוואוד, בערגען קאונטי, נ.ד. ה'תשד"מ. ערב דף.

א'תרמג. כנ"ל אות שלה. לאדיי, בערגען קאונטי, נ.ד. ה'תשד"מ. ערב דף.

א'תרמד. כנ"ל אות שלה. לינדהורסט, בערגען קאונטי, נ.ד. ה'תשד"מ. ערב דף.

א'תרמה. כנ"ל אות שלה. מאווא, בערגען קאונטי, נ.ד. ה'תשד"מ. ערב דף.

א'תרמו. כנ"ל אות שלה. מייוואוד, בערגען קאונטי, נ.ד. ה'תשד"מ. ערב דף.

א'תרמז. כנ"ל אות שלה. נארט ארלינגטאן, בערגען קאונטי, נ.ד. ה'תשד"מ. ערב דף.

א'תרמח. כנ"ל אות שלה. סאדלברוק, בערגען קאונטי, נ.ד. ה'תשד"מ. ערב דף.

א'תרמט. כנ"ל אות שלה. עלמוואוד פארק, בערגען קאונטי, נ.ד. ה'תשד"מ. ערב דף.

א'תרנ. כנ"ל אות שלה. עמערסאן, בערגען קאונטי, נ.ד. ה'תשד"מ. ערב דף.

א'תרנא. כנ"ל אות שלה. פאליסיידס פארק, בערגען קאונטי, נ.ד. ה'תשד"מ. ערב דף.

א'תרנב. כנ"ל אות שלה. פארק רידזש, בערגען קאונטי, נ.ד. ה'תשד"מ. ערב דף.

א'תרנג. כנ"ל אות שלה. פעירוויו, בערגען קאונטי, נ.ד. ה'תשד"מ. ערב דף.

א'תרנד. כנ"ל אות שלה. פראנקלין לייקס, בערגען קאונטי, נ.ד. ה'תשד"מ. ערב דף.

א'תרנה. כנ"ל אות שלה. ראמסי, בערגען קאונטי, נ.ד. ה'תשד"מ. ערב דף.

א'תרנו. כנ"ל אות שלה. רידזשוואוד, בערגען קאונטי, נ.ד. ה'תשד"מ. ערב דף.

א'תרנז. כנ"ל אות שלה. רידזשפילד פארק, בערגען קאונטי, נ.ד. ה'תשד"מ. ערב דף.

א'תרנח. כנ"ל אות שלה. באטהורסט, ניו בראנזוויק, קנדה. ה'תשד"מ. ערב דף.

א'תרנט. כנ"ל אות שלה. דזשאן, ניו בראנזוויק, קנדה. ה'תשד"מ. ערב דף.

א'תרס. כנ"ל אות שלה. וואודסטאק, ניו בראנזוויק, קנדה. ה'תשד"מ. ערב דף.

א'תרסא. כנ"ל אות שלה. מאנקטאן, ניו בראנזוויק, קנדה. ה'תשד"מ. ערב דף.

א'תרסב. כנ"ל אות שלה. ניוקאסעל, ניו בראנזוויק, קנדה. ה'תשד"מ. ערב דף.

א'תרסג. כנ"ל אות שלה. סאקוויל, ניו בראנזוויק, קנדה. ה'תשד"מ. ערב דף.

א'תרסד. כנ"ל אות שלה. עדמאנדסטאן, ניו בראנזוויק, קנדה. ה'תשד"מ. ערב דף.

א'תרסה. כנ"ל אות שלה. פרעדריקטאן, ניו בראנזוויק, קנדה. ה'תשד"מ. ערב דף.

א'תרסו. כנ"ל אות שלה. טשארלאטאון, פרינץ עדווארד איילאנד, קנדה. ה'תשד"מ. ערב דף.

א'תרסז. כנ"ל אות שלה. אמהערסט, נאווא סקאשיא, קנדה. ה'תשד"מ. ערב דף.

א'תרסח. כנ"ל אות שלה. אנטיגאניש, נאווא סקאשיא, קנדה. ה'תשד"מ. ערב דף.

א'תרסט. כנ"ל אות שלה. ברידזשוואטער, נאווא סקאשיא, קנדה. ה'תשד"מ. ערב דף.

א'עתר. כנ"ל אות שלה. גלייס ביי, נאווא סקאשיא, קנדה. ה'תשד"מ. ערב דף.

א'תרעא. כנ"ל אות שלה. דארטמוט, נאווא סקאשיא, קנדה. ה'תשד"מ. ערב דף.

א'תערב. כנ"ל אות שלה. טרורא, נאווא סקאשיא, קנדה. ה'תשד"מ. ערב דף.

א'תערג. כנ"ל אות שלה. יארמוט, נאווא סקאשיא, קנדה. ה'תשד"מ. ערב דף.

א'עדרת. כנ"ל אות שלה. נארט סידני, נאווא סקאשיא, קנדה. ה'תשד"מ. ערב דף.

א'תרעה. כנ"ל אות שלה. סידני, נאווא סקאשיא, קנדה. ה'תשד"מ. ערב דף.

א'תרעו. כנ"ל אות שלה. פאינט-קלעיר, קוויבעק, קנדה. ה'תשד"מ. ערב דף.

א'תרעז. כנ"ל אות שלה. קארנער ברוק, ניופאונדלאנד, קנדה. ה'תשד"מ. ערב דף.

א'תרעח. כנ"ל אות שלה. דזשאנ'ס, ניופאונדלאנד, קנדה. ה'תשד"מ. ערב דף.

א'תרעט. כנ"ל אות שלה. ניו גלאסגאו, נאווא סקאשיא, קנדה. ה'תשד"מ. ערב דף.

א'תרפ. כנ"ל אות שלה. טאנערסוויל, נ.י. ה'תשד"מ. ערב דף.

א'תרפא. כנ"ל אות שלה. האוואורט, בערגען קאונטי, נ.ד. ה'תשד"מ. ערב דף.

א'תרפב. כנ"ל אות שלה. מאנטוויל, בערגען קאונטי, נ.ד. ה'תשד"מ. ערב דף.

א'תרפג. כנ"ל אות שלה. נארוואוד, בערגען קאונטי, נ.ד. ה'תשד"מ. ערב דף.

א'תרפד. כנ"ל אות שלה. סאדל ריווער, בערגען קאונטי, נ.ד. ה'תשד"מ. ערב דף.

א'תרפה. כנ"ל אות שלה. אפער סאדל ריווער, בערגען קאונטי, נ.ד. ה'תשד"מ. ערב דף.

א'תרפו. כנ"ל אות שלה. איסט לאנגמעדא, מאסאטשוסעטס. ה'תשד"מ. רעז דף.

א'תרפז. כנ"ל אות שלה. אקאוואם, מאסאטשוסעטס. ה'תשד"מ. רעז דף.

א'תרפח. כנ"ל אות שלה. בעלמאנט, מאסאטשוסעטס. ה'תשד"מ. רעז דף.

א'תרפט. כנ"ל אות שלה. האדלי, מאסאטשוסעטס. ה'תשד"מ. רעז דף.

א'תרצ. כנ"ל אות שלה. וועסט ספרינגפילד, מאסאטשוסעטס. ה'תשד"מ. רעז דף.

א'תרצא. כנ"ל אות שלה. סאוט האדלי, מאסאטשוסעטס. ה'תשד"מ. רעז דף.

א'תרצב. כנ"ל אות שלה. סאוטוויק, מאסאטשוסעטס. ה'תשד"מ. רעז דף.

א'תרצג. כנ"ל אות שלה. סאנדערלאנד, מאסאטשוסעטס. ה'תשד"מ. רעז דף.

א'תרצד. כנ"ל אות שלה. ענפילד, קאנעטיקאט. ה'תשד"מ. רעז דף.

א'תרצה. כנ"ל אות שלה. גרינפילד, ניו האמפשעיר. ה'תשד"מ. רעז דף.

א'תרצו. כנ"ל אות שלה. אבאטספארד, ב.ק. קאנאדא. ה'תשד"מ. רעז דף.

א'תרצז. כנ"ל אות שלה. אוק ביי, ב.ק. קאנאדא. ה'תשד"מ. רעז דף.

א'תרחצ. כנ"ל אות שלה. איאמא, ב.ק. קאנאדא. ה'תשד"מ. רעז דף.

א'תרצט. כנ"ל אות שלה. אינווערמער, ב.ק. קאנאדא. ה'תשד"מ. רעז דף.

א'תש. כנ"ל אות שלה. בורנאבי, ב.ק. קאנאדא. ה'תשד"מ. רעז דף.

א'תשא. כנ"ל אות שלה. גאבריאלא איילאנד, ב.ק. קאנאדא. ה'תשד"מ. רעז דף.

א'תשב. כנ"ל אות שלה. גראנד פארקס, ב.ק. קאנאדא. ה'תשד"מ. רעז דף.

א'תשג. כנ"ל אות שלה. גיבסאנס, ב.ק. קאנאדא. ה'תשד"מ. רעז דף.

א'תשד. כנ"ל אות שלה. ווייטהארס, ב.ק. קאנאדא. ה'תשד"מ. רעז דף.

א'תשה. כנ"ל אות שלה. וויקטאריא, ב.ק. קאנאדא. ה'תשד"מ. רעז דף.

א'תשו. כנ"ל אות שלה. וועסטמינסטער, ב.ק. קאנאדא. ה'תשד"מ. רעז דף.

א'תשז. כנ"ל אות שלה. וועסט וואנקואווער, ב.ק. קאנאדא. ה'תשד"מ. רעז דף.

א'תשח. כנ"ל אות שלה. ווערנאן, ב.ק. קאנאדא. ה'תשד"מ. רעז דף.

א'תשט. כנ"ל אות שלה. טאמבלער רידזש, ב.ק. קאנאדא. ה'תשד"מ. רעז דף.

א'תשי. כנ"ל אות שלה. טיילאר, ב.ק. קאנאדא. ה'תשד"מ. רעז דף.

א'תשיא. כנ"ל אות שלה. טערעס, ב.ק. קאנאדא. ה'תשד"מ. רעז דף.

א'תשיב. כנ"ל אות שלה. טשיליוואק, ב.ק. קאנאדא. ה'תשד"מ. רעז דף.

א'תשיג. כנ"ל אות שלה. לאגאן לייק, ב.ק. קאנאדא. ה'תשד"מ. רעז דף.

א'תשיד. כנ"ל אות שלה. לייאנס ביי, ב.ק. קאנאדא. ה'תשד"מ. רעז דף.

א'תשטו. כנ"ל אות שלה. מאטסקווי, ב.ק. קאנאדא. ה'תשד"מ. רעז דף.

א'תשטז. כנ"ל אות שלה. מייפל רידזש, ב.ק. קאנאדא. ה'תשד"מ. רעז דף.

א׳תשיז. כנ״ל אות שלה. מישאן, ב.ק. קאנאדא. ה׳תשד״מ. רעז דף.

א׳תשיח. כנ״ל אות שלה. נאניימא, ב.ק. קאנאדא. ה׳תשד״מ. רעז דף.

א׳תשיט. כנ״ל אות שלה. נארט וואנקואווער, ב.ק. קאנאדא. ה׳תשד״מ. רעז דף.

א׳תשכ. כנ״ל אות שלה. נעלסאן, ב.ק. קאנאדא. ה׳תשד״מ. רעז דף.

א׳תשכא.כנ״ל אות שלה. סאלט ספרינג איילאנד, ב.ק. קאנאדא. ה׳תשד״מ. רעז דף.

א׳תשכב.כנ״ל אות שלה. סידני, ב.ק. קאנאדא. ה׳תשד״מ. רעז דף.

א׳תשכג. כנ״ל אות שלה. סמיטערס, ב.ק. קאנאדא. ה׳תשד״מ. רעז דף.

א׳תשכד.כנ״ל אות שלה. סעניש, ב.ק. קאנאדא. ה׳תשד״מ. רעז דף.

א׳תשכה.כנ״ל אות שלה. סקוואמיש, ב.ק. קאנאדא. ה׳תשד״מ. רעז דף.

א׳תשכו. כנ״ל אות שלה. פארט מודי, ב.ק. קאנאדא. ה׳תשד״מ. רעז דף.

א׳תשכז. כנ״ל אות שלה. פאועל ריווער, ב.ק. קאנאדא. ה׳תשד״מ. רעז דף.

א׳תשכח.כנ״ל אות שלה. פענטיקטאן, ב.ק. קאנאדא. ה׳תשד״מ. רעז דף.

א׳תשכט.כנ״ל אות שלה. פרינץ דזשארדזש, ב.ק. קאנאדא. ה׳תשד״מ. רעז דף.

א׳תשל. כנ״ל אות שלה. פרינץ רופערט, ב.ק. קאנאדא. ה׳תשד״מ. רעז דף.

א׳תשלא.כנ״ל אות שלה. קאמאקס, ב.ק. קאנאדא. ה׳תשד״מ. רעז דף.

א׳תשלב.כנ״ל אות שלה. קאמבערלאנד, ב.ק. קאנאדא. ה׳תשד״מ. רעז דף.

א׳תשלג.כנ״ל אות שלה. קאמפבעל ריווער, ב.ק. קאנאדא. ה׳תשד״מ. רעז דף.

א׳תשלד.כנ״ל אות שלה. קאסלא, ב.ק. קאנאדא. ה׳תשד״מ. רעז דף.

א׳תשלה.כנ״ל אות שלה. קאקוויטלאם, ב.ק. קאנאדא. ה׳תשד״מ. רעז דף.

א׳תשלו. כנ״ל אות שלה. קעלאונא, ב.ק. קאנאדא. ה׳תשד״מ. רעז דף.

א׳תשלז. כנ״ל אות שלה. קראנברוק, ב.ק. קאנאדא. ה׳תשד״מ. רעז דף.

א׳תשלח.כנ״ל אות שלה. ראסלאנד, ב.ק. קאנאדא. ה׳תשד״מ. רעז דף.

א׳תשלט.כנ״ל אות שדמ. אל דאדידא, מרוקו. ה׳תשד״מ. רעז דף.

א׳תשמ. כנ״ל אות שדמ. אסאווירא, מרוקו. ה׳תשד״מ. רעז דף.

א׳תשמא.כנ״ל אות שדמ. טיטואן, מרוקו. ה׳תשד״מ. רעז דף.

א׳תשמב.כנ״ל אות שדמ. לאראש, מרוקו. ה׳תשד״מ. רעז דף.

א׳תשמג.כנ״ל אות שדמ. סאפי, מרוקו. ה׳תשד״מ. רעז דף.

א׳תשדמ.כנ״ל אות ר. עם תרגום האנגלי (עמוד התרגום מול עמוד התניא). עם תיקונים והוספות. וויניפעג, מאניטאבא, קאנאדא. ה׳תשד״מ.

א׳תשמה.כנ״ל אות ריא. צה״ל — בסיס חיל אויר-צריפין, באה״ק ת״ו. ה׳תשד״מ. רעז דף.

א׳תשמו. כנ״ל אות ריא. טל-אל, באה״ק ת״ו. ה׳תשד״מ. רעז דף.

א׳תשמז. כנ״ל אות ריא. כפר יחזקאל, באה״ק ת״ו. ה׳תשד״מ. רעז דף.

א׳תשמח.כנ״ל אות ריא. קיבוץ אור הנר, באה״ק ת״ו. ה׳תשד״מ. רעז דף.

א׳תשמט.כנ״ל אות ריא. מושב הודי׳, באה״ק ת״ו. ה׳תשד״מ. רעז דף.

א׳תשנ. כנ״ל אות ריא. מושב חזון, באה״ק ת״ו. ה׳תשד״מ. רעז דף.

א׳תשנא. כנ״ל אות ריא. טפחות, באה״ק ת״ו. ה׳תשד״מ. רעז דף.

א׳תשנב. כנ״ל אות ריא. מרחבי׳, באה״ק ת״ו. ה׳תשד״מ. רעז דף.

א׳תשנג. כנ״ל אות ריא. מושב סגולה, באה״ק ת״ו. ה׳תשד״מ. רעז דף.

א׳תשנד. כנ״ל אות ריא. ניר בנים, באה״ק ת״ו. ה׳תשד״מ. רעז דף.

א׳תשנה. כנ״ל אות ריא. ניר ישראל, באה״ק ת״ו. ה׳תשד״מ. רעז דף.

א׳תשנו. כנ״ל אות ריא. ניר עציון, באה״ק ת״ו. ה׳תשד״מ. רעז דף.

א׳תשנז. כנ״ל אות ריא. תמרת, באה״ק ת״ו. ה׳תשד״מ. רעז דף.

א׳תשנח. כנ״ל אות שלה. אביאטע גוואצונע, איטאליע. ה׳תשד״מ. רעז דף.

א׳תשנט. כנ״ל אות שלה. אסטי, איטאליע. ה׳תשד״מ. רעז דף.

א׳תשס. כנ״ל אות שלה. אודינע, איטאליע. ה׳תשד״מ. רעז דף.

א׳תשסא.כנ״ל אות שלה. איווריא, איטאליע. ה׳תשד״מ. רעז דף.

א׳תשסב.כנ״ל אות שלה. בארי, איטאליע. ה׳תשד״מ. רעז דף.

א׳תשסג.כנ״ל אות שלה. בולצאנו, איטאליע. ה׳תשד״מ. רעז דף.

א׳תשסד.כנ״ל אות שלה. ביעללא, איטאליע. ה׳תשד״מ. רעז דף.

א׳תשסה.כנ״ל אות שלה. בירגאמו, איטאליע. ה׳תשד״מ. רעז דף.

א׳תשסו. כנ״ל אות שלה. ברטנורא, איטאליע. ה׳תשד״מ. רעז דף.

א׳תשסז. כנ״ל אות שלה. ברעשיא, איטאליע. ה׳תשד״מ. רעז דף.

א׳תשסח.כנ״ל אות שלה. גוריצי׳, איטאליע. ה׳תשד״מ. רעז דף.

א׳תשסט.כנ״ל אות שלה. ווארעזע, איטאליע. ה׳תשד״מ. רעז דף.

א׳תשע. כנ״ל אות שלה. ווערא{נא, איטאליע. ה׳תשד״מ. רעז דף.

א׳תשעא.כנ״ל אות שלה. ווערצעלי, איטאליע. ה׳תשד״מ. רעז דף.

א׳תשעב.כנ״ל אות שלה. טראני, איטאליע. ה׳תשד״מ. רעז דף.

א׳תשעג.כנ״ל אות שלה. יאנעווע, איטאליע. ה׳תשד״מ. רעז דף.

א׳תשעד.כנ״ל אות שלה. לא ספעצי׳, איטאליע. תשד״מ. רעז דף.

א׳תשעה.כנ״ל אות שלה. לוקא, איטאליע. ה׳תשד״מ. רעז דף.

א׳תשעו. כנ״ל אות שלה. מאסא קאררא, איטאליע. ה׳תשד״מ. רעז דף.

א׳תשעז. כנ״ל אות שלה. מודינה, איטאליע. ה׳תשד״מ. רעז דף.

א׳תשעח.כנ״ל אות שלה. מונצא, איטאליע. ה׳תשד״מ. רעז דף.

א׳תשעט.כנ״ל אות שלה. מיראנו, איטאליע. ה׳תשד״מ. רעז דף.

א׳תשפ. כנ״ל אות שלה. מעסטרע, איטאליע. ה׳תשד״מ. רעז דף.

א׳תשפא.כנ״ל אות שלה. נאפאלי, איטאליע. ה׳תשד״מ. רעז דף.

א׳תשפב.כנ״ל אות שלה. נאווארא, איטאליע. ה׳תשד״מ. רעז דף.

א׳תשפג.כנ״ל אות שלה. סאלוצו, איטאליע. ה׳תשד״מ. רעז דף.

א׳תשפד.כנ״ל אות שלה. סיניגאליא, איטאליע. ה׳תשד״מ. רעז דף.

א׳תשפה.כנ״ל אות שלה. סיענא, איטאליע. ה׳תשד״מ. רעז דף.

א׳תשפו. כנ״ל אות שלה. פאענצא, איטאליע. ה׳תשד״מ. רעז דף.

א׳תשפז. כנ״ל אות שלה. פארמא, איטאליע. ה׳תשד״מ. רעז דף.

א׳תשפח.כנ״ל אות שלה. פאדאווא, איטאליע. ה׳תשד״מ. רעז דף.

א׳תשפט.כנ״ל אות שלה. פאוויא, איטאליע. ה׳תשד״מ. רעז דף.

א׳תשצ. כנ״ל אות שלה. פוסאנו, איטאליע. ה׳תשד״מ. רעז דף.

א׳תשצא.כנ״ל אות שלה. פארלי, איטאליע. ה׳תשד״מ. רעז דף.

א׳תשצב.כנ״ל אות שלה. פיסטויא, איטאליע. ה׳תשד״מ. רעז דף.

א׳תשצג.כנ״ל אות שלה. פירזא, איטאליע. ה׳תשד״מ. רעז דף.

א׳תשצד.כנ״ל אות שלה. קאזאל מונפיראטו, איטאליע. ה׳תשד״מ. רעז דף.

א׳תשצה.כנ״ל אות שלה. קומו, איטאליע. ה׳תשד״מ. רעז דף.

א׳תשצו. כנ״ל אות שלה. קונעאו, איטאליע. ה׳תשד״מ. רעז דף.

א׳תשצז. כנ״ל אות שלה. רעפובליקא די מארינו. ה׳תשד״מ. רעז דף.

א׳תשצח.כנ״ל אות שלה. סאלאניקא, יון. ה׳תשד״מ. רעז דף.

א׳תשצט.כנ״ל אות שלה. ארלאנדא, פלארידא. ה׳תשד״מ. רעז דף.

א׳תת. כנ״ל אות שלה. באל הארבור, פלארידא. ה׳תשד״מ. רעז דף.

א׳תתא. כנ״ל אות שלה. באקא ראטאן, פלארידא. ה׳תשד״מ. רעז דף.

א׳תתב. כנ״ל אות שלה. ביי הארבור איילאנד, פלארידא. ה׳תשד״מ. רעז דף.

א׳תתג. כנ״ל אות שלה. גיינסוויל, פלארידא. ה׳תשד״מ. רעז דף.

א׳תתד. כנ״ל אות שלה. דזשאקסאנוויל, פלארידא. ה׳תשד״מ. רעז דף.

א׳תתה. כנ״ל אות שלה. דייטאנא ביטש, פלארידא. ה׳תשד״מ. רעז דף.

א'תתו. כנ"ל אות שלה. דעלריי ביטש, פלארידא. ה'תשד"מ. רעז דף.

א'תתז. כנ"ל אות שלה. הייאליא, פלארידא. ה'תשד"מ. רעז דף.

א'תתח. כנ"ל אות שלה. טאלאהאסי, פלארידא. ה'תשד"מ. רעז דף.

א'תתט. כנ"ל אות שלה. לייקלאנד, פלארידא. ה'תשד"מ. רעז דף.

א'תתי. כנ"ל אות שלה. נארט מיאמי, פלארידא. ה'תשד"מ. רעז דף.

א'תתיא. כנ"ל אות שלה. נארט מיאמי ביטש, פלארידא. ה'תשד"מ. רעז דף.

א'תתיב. כנ"ל אות שלה. נייפלס, פלארידא. ה'תשד"מ. רעז דף.

א'תתיג. כנ"ל אות שלה. סאוט מיאמי, פלארידא. ה'תשד"מ. רעז דף.

א'תתיד. כנ"ל אות שלה. סאראסאטא, פלארידא. ה'תשד"מ. רעז דף.

א'תתטו. כנ"ל אות שלה. סורפסייד, פלארידא. ה'תשד"מ. רעז דף.

א'תתטז. כנ"ל אות שלה. פאלם ביטש, פלארידא. ה'תשד"מ. רעז דף.

א'תתיז. כנ"ל אות שלה. פאמפאנא ביטש, פלארידא. ה'תשד"מ. רעז דף.

א'תתיח. כנ"ל אות שלה. פארט מייערס, פלארידא. ה'תשד"מ. רעז דף.

א'תתיט. כנ"ל אות שלה. פענסאקאלא, פלארידא. ה'תשד"מ. רעז דף.

א'תתכ. כנ"ל אות שלה. קאראל גייבלס, פלארידא. ה'תשד"מ. רעז דף.

א'תתכא. כנ"ל אות שלה. קאראל ספרינגס, פלארידא. ה'תשד"מ. רעז דף.

א'תתכב. כנ"ל אות שלה. קי וועסט, פלארידא. ה'תשד"מ. רעז דף.

א'תתכג. כנ"ל אות שלה. קייפ קאראל, פלארידא. ה'תשד"מ. רעז דף.

א'תתכד. כנ"ל אות שלה. קלירוואטער, פלארידא. ה'תשד"מ. רעז דף.

א'תתכה. כנ"ל אות שלה. קענדאל, פלארידא. ה'תשד"מ. רעז דף.

א'תתכו. כנ"ל אות ריא. אבני איתן, רמת הגולן, באה"ק ת"ו. ה'תשד"מ. רעז דף.

א'תתכז. כנ"ל אות ריא. אלי־עד, רמת הגולן, באה"ק ת"ו. ה'תשד"מ. רעז דף.

א'תתכח. כנ"ל אות ריא. בני יהודה, רמת הגולן, באה"ק ת"ו. ה'תשד"מ. רעז דף.

א'תתכט. כנ"ל אות ריא. גבעת יואב, רמת הגולן, באה"ק ת"ו. ה'תשד"מ. רעז דף.

א'תתל. כנ"ל אות שלה. ראוויי, ניו דזוירסי. ה'תשד"מ. רעז דף.

א'תתלא. כנ"ל אות שלה. גאלדען, קאלאראדא. ה'תשד"מ. רעז דף.

א'תתלב. כנ"ל אות שלה. וואטקינס, קאלאראדא. ה'תשד"מ. רעז דף.

א'תתלג. כנ"ל אות שלה. לאוולאנד, קאלאראדא. ה'תשד"מ. רעז דף.

א'תתלד. כנ"ל אות שלה. ליטלטאן, קאלאראדא. ה'תשד"מ. רעז דף.

א'תתלה. כנ"ל אות שלה. עווערגרין, קאלאראדא. ה'תשד"מ. רעז דף.

א'תתלו. כנ"ל אות ריא. מושב בן זכאי, באה"ק ת"ו. ה'תשד"מ. רעז דף.

א'תתלז. כנ"ל אות ריא. מושב זרחי', באה"ק ת"ו. ה'תשד"מ. רעז דף.

א'תתלח. כנ"ל אות ריא. מושב מבוא חורון, באה"ק ת"ו. ה'תשד"מ. רעז דף.

א'תתלט. כנ"ל אות ריא. מושב מתתיהו, באה"ק ת"ו. ה'תשד"מ. רעז דף.

א'תתמ. כנ"ל אות ריא. שכונת גילה, ירושת"ו. ה'תשד"מ. רעז דף.

א'תתמא. כנ"ל אות שלה. דיעל, ניו דזוירסי. ה'תשד"מ. רעז דף.

א'תתמב. כנ"ל אות שלה. מעטאטשען, ניו דזוירסי. ה'תשד"מ. רעז דף.

א'תתמג. כנ"ל אות שלה. סאוט פליינפילד, ניו דזוירסי. ה'תשד"מ. רעז דף.

א'תתמד. כנ"ל אות שלה. עדיסאן, ניו דזוירסי. ה'תשד"מ. רעז דף.

א'תתמה. כנ"ל אות שלה. אראנדזש, קאליפארניא. ה'תשד"מ. רעז דף.

א'תתמו. כנ"ל אות שלה. גארדען גראווו, קאליפארניא. ה'תשד"מ. רעז דף.

א'תתמז. כנ"ל אות שלה. לא פאלמא, קאליפארניא. ה'תשד"מ. רעז דף.

א'תתמח. כנ"ל אות שלה. לאגונא ביטש, קאליפארניא. ה'תשד"מ. רעז דף.

א'תתמט. כנ"ל אות שלה. לאגונא הילס, קאליפארניא. ה'תשד"מ. רעז דף.

א'תתנ. כנ"ל אות שלה. לייקוואוד, קאליפארניא. ה'תשד"מ. רעז דף.

א'תתנא. כנ"ל אות שלה. ניופארט ביטש, קאליפארניא. ה'תשד"מ. רעז דף.

א'תתנב. כנ"ל אות שלה. סיגנאל היל, קאליפארניא. ה'תשד"מ. רעז דף.

א'תתנג. כנ"ל אות שלה. סייפרעס, קאליפארניא. ה'תשד"מ. רעז דף.

א'תתנד. כנ"ל אות שלה. סעריטאס, קאליפארניא. ה'תשד"מ. רעז דף.

א'תתנה. כנ"ל אות שלה. פאונטיין וואלי, קאליפארניא. ה'תשד"מ. רעז דף.

א'תתנו. כנ"ל אות שלה. קאסטא מייסא, קאליפארניא. ה'תשד"מ. רעז דף.

א'תתנז. כנ"ל אות שלה. קלערמאנט, קאליפארניא. ה'תשד"מ. רעז דף.

א'תתנח. כנ"ל אות ריא. אלוני בשן, באה"ק ת"ו. ה'תשד"מ. רפ דף.

א'תתנט. כנ"ל אות ריא. אניעם, באה"ק ת"ו. ה'תשד"מ. רפ דף.

א'תתס. כנ"ל אות ריא. גבעת שמואל, באה"ק ת"ו. ה'תשד"מ. רפ דף.

א'תתסא. כנ"ל אות ריא. זכרון יעקב, באה"ק ת"ו. ה'תשד"מ. רפ דף.

א'תתסב. כנ"ל אות ריא. כפר עזריאל, באה"ק ת"ו. ה'תשד"מ. רפ דף.

א'תתסג. כנ"ל אות ריא. מעלה גמלא, רמת הגולן, באה"ק ת"ו. ה'תשד"מ. רפ דף.

א'תתסד. כנ"ל אות ריא. נאות גולן, רמת הגולן, באה"ק ת"ו. ה'תשד"מ. רפ דף.

א'תתסה. כנ"ל אות ריא. קיבוץ אורטל, רמת הגולן, באה"ק ת"ו. ה'תשד"מ. רפ דף.

א'תתסו. כנ"ל אות ריא. קיבוץ אל־רום, רמת הגולן, רמת הגולן, באה"ק ת"ו. ה'תשד"מ. רפ דף.

א'תתסז. כנ"ל אות ריא. קיבוץ אפיק, רמת הגולן, רמת הגולן, באה"ק ת"ו. ה'תשד"מ. רפ דף.

א'תתסח. כנ"ל אות ריא. קיבוץ נחל עוז, באה"ק ת"ו. ה'תשד"מ. רפ דף.

א'תתסט. כנ"ל אות ריא. קשת, רמת הגולן, באה"ק ת"ו. ה'תשד"מ. רפ דף.

א'תתע. כנ"ל אות ריא. רמות, רמת הגולן, באה"ק ת"ו. ה'תשד"מ. רפ דף.

א'תתעא. כנ"ל אות שלה. איסט קואק, לאנג איילאנד, נ.י. ה'תשד"מ. רפ דף.

א'תתעב. כנ"ל אות שלה. בלומינגטאן, אינדיאנא. תשד"מ. רפ דף.

א'תתעג. כנ"ל אות שלה. סאוט בענד, אינדיאנא. ה'תשד"מ. רפ דף.

א'תתעד. כנ"ל אות שלה. קאדאהי, קאליפארניא. ה'תשד"מ. רפ דף.

א'תתעה. כנ"ל אות שלה. ווילמעט, אילינאי. ה'תשד"מ. רפ דף.

א'תתעו. כנ"ל אות שלה. נארטברוק, אילינאי. ה'תשד"מ. רפ דף.

א'תתעז. כנ"ל אות שלה. ספרינגפילד, אילינאי. ה'תשד"מ. רפ דף.

א'תתעח. כנ"ל אות שלה. פיאריא, אילינאי. ה'תשד"מ. רפ דף.

א'תתעט. כנ"ל אות שלה. ראקפארד, אילינאי. ה'תשד"מ. רפ דף.

א'תתפ. כנ"ל אות שלה. קינגסטאן, פענסילווייניא. תשד"מ. רפ דף.

א'תתפא. כנ"ל אות שדמ. אוטרעכט, האלאנד. ה'תשד"מ. רפ דף.

א׳תתפב. כנ״ל אות שדמ. איינדהאווען, האלאנד. ה׳תשד״מ. רפ דף.

א׳תתפג. כנ״ל אות שדמ. אלקמאהר, האלאנד. ה׳תשד״מ. רפ דף.

א׳תתפד. כנ״ל אות שדמ. ארנהעם, האלאנד. ה׳תשד״מ. רפ דף.

א׳תתפה. כנ״ל אות שדמ. בוסום, האלאנד. ה׳תשד״מ. רפ דף.

א׳תתפו. כנ״ל אות שדמ. בוש, האלאנד. ה׳תשד״מ. רפ דף.

א׳תתפז. כנ״ל אות שדמ. ברעדא, האלאנד. ה׳תשד״מ. רפ דף.

א׳תתפח. כנ״ל אות שדמ. גראנינגען, האלאנד. ה׳תשד״מ. רפ דף.

א׳תתפט. כנ״ל אות שדמ. האג, האלאנד. ה׳תשד״מ. רפ דף.

א׳תתצ. כנ״ל אות שדמ. הילווערסאם, האלאנד. תשד״מ. רפ דף.

א׳תתצא. כנ״ל אות שדמ. העלדער, האלאנד. ה׳תשד״מ. רפ דף.

א׳תתצב. כנ״ל אות שדמ. ליידן, האלאנד. ה׳תשד״מ. רפ דף.

א׳תתצג. כנ״ל אות שדמ. ענסכעדע, האלאנד. ה׳תשד״מ. רפ דף.

א׳תתצד. כנ״ל אות שדמ. ראטערדאם, האלאנד. ה׳תשד״מ. רפ דף.

א׳תתצה. כנ״ל אות שדמ. ארמעסאן, צרפת. ה׳תשד״מ. רפ דף.

א׳תתצו. כנ״ל אות שדמ. בוסי אנטואן, צרפת. ה׳תשד״מ. רפ דף.

א׳תתצז. כנ״ל אות שדמ. גאני, צרפת. ה׳תשד״מ. רפ דף.

א׳תתצח. כנ״ל אות שדמ. גוראיי סור מארן, צרפת. ה׳תשד״מ. רפ דף.

א׳תתצט. כנ״ל אות שדמ. וואזורס, צרפת. ה׳תשד״מ. רפ דף.

א׳תתק. כנ״ל אות שדמ. ווילִיער סור מארן, צרפת. ה׳תשד״מ. רפ דף.

א׳תתקא. כנ״ל אות שדמ. טרעמבליי לע גאנעס, צרפת. ה׳תשד״מ. רפ דף.

א׳תתקב. כנ״ל אות שדמ. כובראן, צרפת. ה׳תשד״מ. רפ דף.

א׳תתקג. כנ״ל אות שדמ. מאנט לא זאלי, צרפת. ה׳תשד״מ. רפ דף.

א׳תתקד. כנ״ל אות שדמ. מארעפא, צרפת. ה׳תשד״מ. רפ דף.

א׳תתקה. כנ״ל אות שדמ. מנטפער מייל, צרפת. ה׳תשד״מ. רפ דף.

א׳תתקו. כנ״ל אות שדמ. נואזא, צרפת. ה׳תשד״מ. רפ דף.

א׳תתקז. כנ״ל אות שדמ. סוסי אן ברי, צרפת. ה׳תשד״מ. רפ דף.

א׳תתקח. כנ״ל אות שדמ. עלאנכור, צרפת. ה׳תשד״מ. רפ דף.

א׳תתקט. כנ״ל אות שדמ. פלעזיע טרעוויז, צרפת. ה׳תשד״מ. רפ דף.

א׳תתקי. כנ״ל אות שדמ. שענעוויערס, צרפת. ה׳תשד״מ. רפ דף.

א׳תתקיא. כנ״ל אות ריא. אביטל, באה״ק ת״ו. ה׳תשד״מ. רפ דף.

א׳תתקיב. כנ״ל אות ריא. אחיהוד, באה״ק ת״ו. ה׳תשד״מ. רפ דף.

א׳תתקיג. כנ״ל אות ריא. אילון, באה״ק ת״ו. ה׳תשד״מ. רפ דף.

א׳תתקיד. כנ״ל אות ריא. בית יוסף, באה״ק ת״ו. ה׳תשד״מ. רפ דף.

א׳תתקטו. כנ״ל אות ריא. בית לחם הגלילית, באה״ק ת״ו. ה׳תשד״מ. רפ דף.

א׳תתקטז. כנ״ל אות ריא. בצת, באה״ק ת״ו. ה׳תשד״מ. רפ דף.

א׳תתקיז. כנ״ל אות ריא. גבעת המורה, באה״ק ת״ו. ה׳תשד״מ. רפ דף.

א׳תתקיח. כנ״ל אות ריא. דגני׳ א׳, באה״ק ת״ו. ה׳תשד״מ. רפ דף.

א׳תתקיט. כנ״ל אות ריא. דגני׳ ב׳, באה״ק ת״ו. ה׳תשד״מ. רפ דף.

א׳תתקכ. כנ״ל אות ריא. הזורעים, באה״ק ת״ו. ה׳תשד״מ. רפ דף.

א׳תתקכא. כנ״ל אות ריא. זרעית, באה״ק תו. ה׳תשד״מ. רפ דף.

א׳תתקכב. כנ״ל אות ריא. טירת צבי, באה״ק ת״ו. ה׳תשד״מ. רפ דף.

א׳תתקכג. כנ״ל אות ריא. יהוד, באה״ק ת״ו. ה׳תשד״מ. רפ דף.

א׳תתקכד. כנ״ל אות ריא. כפר וורבורג, באה״ק ת״ו. ה׳תשד״מ. רפ דף.

א׳תתקכה. כנ״ל אות ריא. כפר שמאי, באה״ק ת״ו. ה׳תשד״מ. רפ דף.

א׳תתקכו. כנ״ל אות ריא. לימן, באה״ק ת״ו. ה׳תשד״מ. רפ דף.

א׳תתקכז. כנ״ל אות ריא. מבוא דותן, באה״ק ת״ו. ה׳תשד״מ. רפ דף.

א׳תתקכח. כנ״ל אות ריא. מושב גנים, באה״ק ת״ו. ה׳תשד״מ. רפ דף.

א׳תתקכט. כנ״ל אות ריא. מושב כנרת, באה״ק ת״ו. ה׳תשד״מ. רפ דף.

א׳תתקל. כנ״ל אות ריא. מושב ציפורי, באה״ק ת״ו. ה׳תשד״מ. רפ דף.

א׳תתקלא. כנ״ל אות ריא. מי עמי, באה״ק ת״ו. ה׳תשד״מ. רפ דף.

א׳תתקלב. כנ״ל אות ריא. מלאה, באה״ק תו. ה׳תשד״מ. רפ דף.

א׳תתקלג. כנ״ל אות ריא. מצפה הושעיה, באה״ק ת״ו. ה׳תשד״מ. רפ דף.

א׳תתקלד. כנ״ל אות ריא. נווה זוהר ים המלח, באה״ק ת״ו. ה׳תשד״מ. רפ דף.

א׳תתקלה. כנ״ל אות ריא. ניר יפה, באה״ק ת״ו. ה׳תשד״מ. רפ דף.

א׳תתקלו. כנ״ל אות ריא. נתיב השיירה, באה״ק ת״ו. ה׳תשד״מ. רפ דף.

א׳תתקלז. כנ״ל אות ריא. פורייה נוה עובד, באה״ק ת״ו. ה׳תשד״מ. רפ דף.

א׳תתקלח. כנ״ל אות ריא. קבוץ יזרעאל, באה״ק ת״ו. ה׳תשד״מ. רפ דף.

א׳תתקלט. כנ״ל אות ריא. קבוץ יפעת, באה״ק ת״ו. ה׳תשד״מ. רפ דף.

א׳תתקמ. כנ״ל אות ריא. קבוץ מעגן, באה״ק ת״ו. ה׳תשד״מ. רפ דף.

א׳תתקמא. כנ״ל אות ריא. קבוץ עין גב, באה״ק ת״ו. ה׳תשד״מ. רפ דף.

א׳תתקמב. כנ״ל אות ריא. קבוץ עין גדי, באה״ק ת״ו. ה׳תשד״מ. רפ דף.

א׳תתקמג. כנ״ל אות ריא. קבוץ שדה נחום, באה״ק ת״ו. ה׳תשד״מ. רפ דף.

א׳תתקמד. כנ״ל אות ריא. קבוצת כנרת, באה״ק ת״ו. ה׳תשד״מ. רפ דף.

א׳תתקמה. כנ״ל אות ריא. קדרים, באה״ק ת״ו. ה׳תשד״מ. רפ דף.

א׳תתקמו. כנ״ל אות ריא. ריחן, באה״ק ת״ו. ה׳תשד״מ. רפ דף.

א׳תתקמז. כנ״ל אות ריא. רם און, באה״ק ת״ו. ה׳תשד״מ. רפ דף.

א׳תתקמח. כנ״ל אות ריא. שדה תרומות, באה״ק ת״ו. ה׳תשד״מ. רפ דף.

א׳תתקמט. כנ״ל אות ריא. שדמות מחולה, באה״ק ת״ו. ה׳תשד״מ. רפ דף.

א׳תתקנ. כנ״ל אות ריא. שזור, באה״ק ת״ו. ה׳תשד״מ. רפ דף.

א׳תתקנא. כנ״ל אות ריא. תל עדשים, באה״ק ת״ו. ה׳תשד״מ. רפ דף.

א׳תתקנב. כנ״ל אות ריא. צה״ל, בית דרס עוצבת הבזקה, באה״ק ת״ו. ה׳תשד״מ. רפ דף.

א׳תתקנג. כנ״ל אות ריא. צה״ל, בסיס חצור, באה״ק ת״ו. ה׳תשד״מ. רפ דף.

א׳תתקנד. כנ״ל אות ריא. צה״ל, יחידת רפואה מלאכי, באה״ק ת״ו. ה׳תשד״מ. רפ דף.

א׳תתקנה. כנ״ל אות ריא, גילון — גוש שגב, באה״ק ת״ו. ה׳תשד״מ. רפ דף.

א׳תתקנו. כנ״ל אות ריא. יובלים — גוש שגב, באה״ק ת״ו. ה׳תשד״מ. רפ דף.

א׳תתקנז. כנ״ל אות ריא. יודפת — גוש שגב, באה״ק ת״ו. ה׳תשד״מ. רפ דף.

א׳תתקנח. כנ״ל אות ריא. יעד — גוש שגב, באה״ק ת״ו. ה׳תשד״מ. רפ דף.

א׳תתקנט. כנ״ל אות ריא. כמון — גוש שגב, באה״ק ת״ו. ה׳תשד״מ. רפ דף.

א׳תתקס. כנ״ל אות ריא. מורשת — גוש שגב, באה״ק ת״ו. ה׳תשד״מ. רפ דף.

א׳תתקסא. כנ״ל אות ריא. מכמנים — גוש שגב, באה״ק ת״ו. ה׳תשד״מ. רפ דף.

א׳תתקסב. כנ״ל אות ריא. מצפה אביב — גוש שגב, באה״ק ת״ו. ה׳תשד״מ. רפ דף.

א׳תתקסג. כנ״ל אות ריא. עצמון — גוש שגב, באה״ק ת״ו. ה׳תשד״מ. רפ דף.

א׳תתקסד. כנ״ל אות ריא. צורית — גוש שגב, באה״ק ת״ו. ה׳תשד״מ. רפ דף.

א׳תתקסה. כנ״ל אות ריא. קורנית — גוש שגב, באה״ק ת״ו. ה׳תשד״מ. רפ דף.

א'תתקסו. כנ"ל אות ריא. רקפת — גוש שגב, באה"ק ת"ו. ה'תשד"מ. רפ דף.
א'תתקסז. כנ"ל אות ריא. שכני"ה — גוש שגב, באה"ק ת"ו. ה'תשד"מ. רפ דף.
א'תתקסח. כנ"ל אות שלה. איסט האנאווער, ניו דזווירסי. ה'תשד"מ. רפ דף.
א'תתקסט. כנ"ל אות שלה. בונטאן, ניו דזווירסי. ה'תשד"מ. רפ דף.
א'תתקע. כנ"ל אות שלה. בעלוויל, ניו דזווירסי. ה'תשד"מ. רפ דף.
א'תתקעא. כנ"ל אות שלה. דענוויל, ניו דזווירסי. ה'תשד"מ. רפ דף.
א'תתקעב. כנ"ל אות שלה. האנאווער, ניו דזווירסי. תשד"מ. רפ דף.
א'תתקעג. כנ"ל אות שלה. וויפאני, ניו דזווירסי. ה'תשד"מ. רפ דף.
א'תתקעד. כנ"ל אות שלה. טשאטעם, ניו דזווירסי. תשד"מ. רפ דף.
א'תתקעה. כנ"ל אות שלה. טשעסטער, ניו דזווירסי. ה'תשד"מ. רפ דף.
א'תתקעו. כנ"ל אות שלה. טשעסטער טאונשיפ, ניו דזווירסי. ה'תשד"מ. רפ דף.
א'תתקעז. כנ"ל אות שלה. יוניאן, ניו דזווירסי. ה'תשד"מ. רפ דף.
א'תתקעח. כנ"ל אות שלה. לינדען, ניו דזווירסי. ה'תשד"מ. רפ דף.
א'תתקעט. כנ"ל אות שלה. מאדיסאן, ניו דזווירסי. ה'תשד"מ. רפ דף.
א'תתקפ. כנ"ל אות שלה. מאונט אליוו, ניו דזווירסי. ה'תשד"מ. רפ דף.
א'תתקפא. כנ"ל אות שלה. מאנטקלעיר, ניו דזווירסי. ה'תשד"מ. רפ דף.
א'תתקפב. כנ"ל אות שלה. מאריס פליינס, ניו דזווירסי. ה'תשד"מ. רפ דף.
א'תתקפג. כנ"ל אות שלה. מענדהאם, ניו דזווירסי. ה'תשד"מ. רפ דף.
א'תתקפד. כנ"ל אות שלה. ניו פראווידענס, ניו דזווירסי. ה'תשד"מ. רפ דף.
א'תתקפה. כנ"ל אות שלה. ניוטאן, ניו דזווירסי. ה'תשד"מ. רפ דף.
א'תתקפו. כנ"ל אות שלה. סאוט אראנדזש, ניו דזווירסי. ה'תשד"מ. רפ דף.
א'תתקפז. כנ"ל אות שלה. ספרינגפילד, ניו דזווירסי. ה'תשד"מ. רפ דף.
א'תתקפח. כנ"ל אות שלה. פארסיפאני, ניו דזווירסי. ה'תשד"מ. רפ דף.
א'תתקפט. כנ"ל אות שלה. פיין ברוק, ניו דזווירסי. ה'תשד"מ. רפ דף.
א'תתקצ. כנ"ל אות שלה. פלארהאם פארק, ניו דזווירסי. ה'תשד"מ. רפ דף.
א'תתקצא. כנ"ל אות שלה. קלארק, ניו דזווירסי. ה'תשד"מ. רפ דף.
א'תתקצב. כנ"ל אות שלה. קראנפארד, ניו דזווירסי. ה'תשד"מ. רפ דף.
א'תתקצג. כנ"ל אות שלה. ראסלאנד, ניו דזווירסי. ה'תשד"מ. רפ דף.
א'תתקצד. כנ"ל אות שלה. ראסעל, ניו דזווירסי. ה'תשד"מ. רפ דף.
א'תתקצה. כנ"ל אות שלה. ראסעל פארק, ניו דזווירסי. ה'תשד"מ. רפ דף.
א'תתקצו. כנ"ל אות שלה. ראקאוויי, ניו דזווירסי. ה'תשד"מ. רפ דף.
א'תתקצז. כנ"ל אות שלה. ראקאוויי טאונשיפ, ניו דזווירסי. ה'תשד"מ. רפ דף.
א'תתקצח. כנ"ל אות שלה. סקאטש פליינס, ניו דזווירסי. ה'תשד"מ. רפ דף.
א'תתקצט. כנ"ל אות שלה. פליינפילד, ניו דזווירסי. ה'תשד"מ. רפ דף.
א'תתר (אלפיים). כנ"ל אות שד"מ. קראון הייטס — „כאן צוה ה' את הברכה", ברוקלין, נ.י. נדפס בעליית ביהכנ"ס וביהמ"ד ליובאוויטש שבליובאוויטש — „770", בדפוס ד„ועד להפצת שיחות" 788 איסטערן פארקוויי. כ"ט אלול — אחרית שנה, שנת תהי' שנת דברי משיח. (6), רפב דף.

ב'א. כנ"ל אות שלה. בערקלי הייטס, ניו דזווירסי. ה'תשד"מ. רפ דף.
ב'ב. כנ"ל אות שלה. גארוואוד, ניו דזווירסי. ה'תשד"מ. רפ דף.
ב'ג. כנ"ל אות ריא. מועצה איזורית שער הנגב, באה"ק ת"ו. ה'תשמ"ה. רפב דף.
ב'ד. כנ"ל אות ריא. קבוץ פלמחים, באה"ק ת"ו. ה'תשמ"ה. רפב דף.
ב'ה. כנ"ל אות ריא. קבוץ חצרים, באה"ק ת"ו. ה'תשמ"ה. רפב דף.
ב'ו. כנ"ל אות שלה. באדען, עסטרייך. ה'תשמ"ה. רפב דף.
ב'ז. כנ"ל אות שלה. גראץ, עסטרייך. ה'תשמ"ה. רפב דף.
ב'ח. כנ"ל אות שלה. זאלצבורג, עסטרייך. ה'תשמ"ה. רפב דף.
ב'ט. כנ"ל אות שלה. לינץ, עסטרייך. ה'תשמ"ה. רפב דף.
ב'י. כנ"ל אות שלה. פורקערסדארף, עסטרייך. ה'תשמ"ה. רפב דף.
ב'יא. כנ"ל אות שדמ. וואולאנגאנג, אויסטראליא. ה'תשמ"ה. רפב דף.
ב'יב. כנ"ל אות שלה. וועסט העמפסטעד, לאנג איילאנד, נ.י. ה'תשמ"ה. (6) רפב דף.
ב'יג. כנ"ל אות ריא. אשרת, באה"ק ת"ו. ה'תשמ"ה. רפב דף.
ב'יד. כנ"ל אות ריא. כפר יובל, באה"ק ת"ו. ה'תשמ"ה. רפב דף.
ב'טו. כנ"ל אות ריא. משמר הירדן, באה"ק ת"ו. תשמ"ה. רפב דף.
ב'טז. כנ"ל אות ריא. נתיב העשרה, באה"ק ת"ו. ה'תשמ"ה. רפב דף.
ב'יז. כנ"ל אות ריא. עמקה, באה"ק ת"ו. ה'תשמ"ה. רפב דף.
ב'יח. כנ"ל אות ריא. פוריה כפר עבודה, באה"ק ת"ו. ה'תשמ"ה. רפב דף.
ב'יט. כנ"ל אות ריא. קבוץ דפנה, באה"ק ת"ו. ה'תשמ"ה. רפב דף.
ב'כ. כנ"ל אות ריא. שאר ישוב, באה"ק ת"ו. ה'תשמ"ה. רפב דף.
ב'כא. כנ"ל אות ריא. שדה אליעזר, באה"ק ת"ו. ה'תשמ"ה. רפב דף.
ב'כב. כנ"ל אות קכד. „פוטוגרפיא מהתניא . . שיצא לאור בברוקלין . . תשל"ט . . כאשר כ"ק אדמו"ר שליט"א חילק . . לכל האורחים . . חתם שמו על דף האחרון". „. . . יוצא לאור על ידי מערכת „אוצר החסידים" . . סניף ירושלים עיה"ק תובב"א . . על ידי בית דפוס והוצאת ספרים אשכול . . מהדורא מיוחדת בהדפסה טובה ונאה ע"י שיפוץ . . האותיות". בסופו: „דבר המו"ל־המדפיס של ההוצאה המיוחדת . . ה„מורה שיעור" נסדר מחדש (באותיות יותר גדולות). ה„לוח ראשי תיבות" נערך ונסדר מחדש עם . . הוספות".

תשרי ה'תשמ"ה. (8) רפד דף (דף רפה־רפו דבר המו"ל־המדפיס). בגודל °8 כ 19½X14 סמ.
ב'כג. כנ"ל אות קצט. סניפי נשי ובנות חב"ד, באה"ק ת"ו. ה'תשד"מ. רסט דף.
ב'כד. כנ"ל אות שלה. מאנטעריי, מעקסיקא. ה'תשמ"ה. (6) רפב דף.
ב'כה. כנ"ל אות תכ. קאמענדאנטע סעראו, אנטארקטיקא. ה'תשמ"ה. רפב דף.
ב'כו. כנ"ל אות שלה. דאנקען, אקלאהאמא. ה'תשמ"ה. (6) רפב דף.
ב'כז. כנ"ל אות שדמ. איסטאן, קאנעטיקאט. ה'תשמ"ה. (6) רפב דף.
ב'כח. כנ"ל אות שלה. אנסאניא, קאנעטיקאט. ה'תשמ"ה. (6) רפב דף.
ב'כט. כנ"ל אות שלה. גרענעטש, קאנעטיקאט. ה'תשמ"ה. (6) רפב דף.
ב'ל. כנ"ל אות שלה. דערבי, קאנעטיקאט. ה'תשמ"ה. (6) רפב דף.
ב'לא. כנ"ל אות שלה. וועסטפארט, קאנעטיקאט. ה'תשמ"ה. (6) רפב דף.
ב'לב. כנ"ל אות שלה. מילפארד, קאנעטיקאט. ה'תשמ"ה. (6) רפב דף.
ב'לג. כנ"ל אות שלה. נארוואק, קאנעטיקאט. ה'תשמ"ה. (6) רפב דף.
ב'לד. כנ"ל אות שלה. סטאמפארד, קאנעטיקאט. ה'תשמ"ה. (6) רפב דף.

ב'לה. כנ"ל אות שלה. סטראטפארד, קאנעטיקאט. ה'תשמ"ה. (6) רפב דף.

ב'לו. כנ"ל אות שלה. פעירפילד, קאנעטיקאט. ה'תשמ"ה. (6) רפב דף.

ב'לז. כנ"ל אות שלה. שעלטאן, קאנעטיקאט. ה'תשמ"ה. (6) רפב דף.

ב'לח. כנ"ל אות שלה. טראמבול, קאנעטיקאט. ה'תשמ"ה. (6) רפב דף.

ב'לט. כנ"ל אות שלה. אלעקסאנדריא, ווירדזשיניא. ה'תשמ"ה. (6) רפב דף.

ב'מ. כנ"ל אות שלה. ראענאק, ווירדזשיניא. ה'תשמ"ה. (6) רפב דף.

ב'מא. כנ"ל אות שלה. וואודמיר, לאנג איילאנד, נ.י. ה'תשמ"ה. (6) רפב דף.

ב'מב. כנ"ל אות שלה. פליינוויו, לאנג איילאנד, נ.י. ה'תשמ"ה. (6) רפב דף.

ב'מג. כנ"ל אות שלה. ישיבת אחי תמימים, אראנדוש, קאנעטיקאט. ה'תשמ"ה. (6) רפב דף.

ב'מד. כנ"ל אות שלה. בעטאני, קאנעטיקאט. ה'תשמ"ה. (6) רפב דף.

ב'מה. כנ"ל אות שלה. וואודברידזש, קאנעטיקאט. ה'תשמ"ה. (6) רפב דף.

ב'מו. כנ"ל אות שדמ. אוואלד, צרפת. ה'תשמ"ה. רפד דף.

ב'מז. כנ"ל אות שדמ. אורינאן, צרפת. ה'תשמ"ה. רפד דף.

ב'מח. כנ"ל אות שדמ. אינגווילער, צרפת. ה'תשמ"ה. רפד דף.

ב'מט. כנ"ל אות שדמ. אנגולעם, צרפת. ה'תשמ"ה. רפד דף.

ב'נ. כנ"ל אות שדמ. אבערניי, צרפת. ה'תשמ"ה. רפד דף.

ב'נא. כנ"ל אות שדמ. ארקאשאן, צרפת. ה'תשמ"ה. רפד דף.

ב'נב. כנ"ל אות שדמ. באיאן, צרפת. ה'תשמ"ה. רפד דף.

ב'נג. כנ"ל אות שדמ. בוליי, צרפת. ה'תשמ"ה. רפד דף.

ב'נד. כנ"ל אות שדמ. ביאריטץ, צרפת. ה'תשמ"ה. רפד דף.

ב'נה. כנ"ל אות שדמ. ביטש, צרפת. ה'תשמ"ה. רפד דף.

ב'נו. כנ"ל אות שדמ. בנפעלד, צרפת. ה'תשמ"ה. רפד דף.

ב'נז. כנ"ל אות שדמ. בעזיער, צרפת. ה'תשמ"ה. רפד דף.

ב'נח. כנ"ל אות שדמ. בעלפארד, צרפת. ה'תשמ"ה. רפד דף.

ב'נט. כנ"ל אות שדמ. גרענאבלע, צרפת. ה'תשמ"ה. רפד דף.

ב'ס. כנ"ל אות שדמ. די, צרפת. ה'תשמ"ה. רפד דף.

ב'סא. כנ"ל אות שדמ. דיעז, צרפת. ה'תשמ"ה. רפד דף.

ב'סב. כנ"ל אות שדמ. דעלם, צרפת. ה'תשמ"ה. רפד דף.

ב'סג. כנ"ל אות שדמ. דרע, צרפת. ה'תשמ"ה. רפד דף.

ב'סד. כנ"ל אות שדמ. וואסעלאן, צרפת. ה'תשמ"ה. רפד דף.

ב'סה. כנ"ל אות שדמ. וויטעל, צרפת. ה'תשמ"ה. רפד דף.

ב'סו. כנ"ל אות שדמ. וויטרי לע פרונסוא, צרפת. ה'תשמ"ה. רפד דף.

ב'סז. כנ"ל אות שדמ. וועניסיע, צרפת. ה'תשמ"ה. רפד דף.

ב'סח. כנ"ל אות שדמ. ווערדען, צרפת. ה'תשמ"ה. רפד דף.

ב'סט. כנ"ל אות שדמ. טארבעס, צרפת. ה'תשמ"ה. רפד דף.

ב'ע. כנ"ל אות שדמ. טהיאנוויל, צרפת. ה'תשמ"ה. רפד דף.

ב'עא. כנ"ל אות שדמ. טולאן, צרפת. ה'תשמ"ה. רפד דף.

ב'עב. כנ"ל אות שדמ. לואי, צרפת. ה'תשמ"ה. רפד דף.

ב'עג. כנ"ל אות שדמ. לונעוויל, צרפת. ה'תשמ"ה. רפד דף.

ב'עד. כנ"ל אות שדמ. ליבורן, צרפת. ה'תשמ"ה. רפד דף.

ב'עה. כנ"ל אות שדמ. מאנטבעליארד, צרפת. ה'תשמ"ה. רפד דף.

ב'עו. כנ"ל אות שדמ. מאנטפעליער, צרפת. ה'תשמ"ה. רפד דף.

ב'עז. כנ"ל אות שדמ. מעזאן לאפיט, צרפת. ה'תשמ"ה. רפד דף.

ב'עח. כנ"ל אות שדמ. מרהאנז, צרפת. ה'תשמ"ה. רפד דף.

ב'עט. כנ"ל אות שדמ. נים, צרפת. ה'תשמ"ה. רפד דף.

ב'פ. כנ"ל אות שדמ. סארגעמין, צרפת. ה'תשמ"ה. רפד דף.

ב'פא. כנ"ל אות שדמ. סארעבורג, צרפת. ה'תשמ"ה. רפד דף.

ב'פב. כנ"ל אות שדמ. סעדאן, צרפת. ה'תשמ"ה. רפד דף.

ב'פג. כנ"ל אות שדמ. סעט, צרפת. ה'תשמ"ה. רפד דף.

ב'פד. כנ"ל אות שדמ. סעלעסטא, צרפת. ה'תשמ"ה. רפד דף.

ב'פה. כנ"ל אות שדמ. עפינאל, צרפת. ה'תשמ"ה. רפד דף.

ב'פו. כנ"ל אות שדמ. עפערניי, צרפת. ה'תשמ"ה. רפד דף.

ב'פז. כנ"ל אות שדמ. עקס אן פראוועגס, צרפת. ה'תשמ"ה. רפד דף.

ב'פח. כנ"ל אות שדמ. פאלסבורג, צרפת. ה'תשמ"ה. רפד דף.

ב'פט. כנ"ל אות שדמ. פאלקעמאן, צרפת. ה'תשמ"ה. רפד דף.

ב'צ. כנ"ל אות שדמ. פאן, צרפת. ה'תשמ"ה. רפד דף.

ב'צא. כנ"ל אות שדמ. פארבאש, צרפת. ה'תשמ"ה. רפד דף.

ב'צב. כנ"ל אות שדמ. פעריגע, צרפת. ה'תשמ"ה. רפד דף.

ב'צג. כנ"ל אות שדמ. קאמפיען, צרפת. ה'תשמ"ה. רפד דף.

ב'צד. כנ"ל אות שדמ. קארפענטראס, צרפת. ה'תשמ"ה. רפד דף.

ב'צה. כנ"ל אות שדמ. קלואנז, צרפת. ה'תשמ"ה. רפד דף.

ב'צו. כנ"ל אות שדמ. ראשעל, צרפת. ה'תשמ"ה. רפד דף.

ב'צז. כנ"ל אות שדמ. בוזענוויל, צרפת. ה'תשמ"ה. רפד דף.

ב'צח. כנ"ל אות שדמ. ריימ, צרפת. ה'תשמ"ה. רפד דף.

ב'צט. כנ"ל אות שדמ. שאלאן סור מארן, צרפת. ה'תשמ"ה. רפד דף.

ב'ק. כנ"ל אות שדמ. שאלאן סור סאן, צרפת. ה'תשמ"ה. רפד דף.

ב'קא. כנ"ל אות שדמ. כנס השלוחים — 770 איסטערן פארקוויי, ברוקלין, נ.י. נדפס בעליית ביהכנ"ס וביהמ"ד ליובאוויטש שבליובאוויטש — „770", בדפוס ד„ועד להפצת שיחות", 788 איסטערן פארקוויי. ע"י שלוחי כ"ק אדמו"ר שליט"א בכל מרחבי תבל — כינוס השלוחים דארצה"ב ש"פ תולדות, מבה"ח וער"ח כסלו, חודש הגאולה — ב' פ' ויצא יעקב גר ויעקב הלך לדרכו השנה תהא שנת מלך המשיח.

בסופו: נוסח הפ"נ דהשלוחים ומענה כ"ק אדמו"ר שליט"א, ה'תשמ"ה. (6) רפג דף.

ב'קב. כנ"ל אות שלה. הארטלאנד, וויסקאנסין. ה'תשמ"ה. (6) רפד דף.

ב'קג. כנ"ל אות שדמ. ראודס, יון. ה'תשמ"ה. (6) רפד דף.

ב'קד. כנ"ל אות שדמ. מאנואס, אמאזאנאס, בראזיל. ה'תשמ"ה. (6) רפד דף.

ב'קה. כנ"ל אות שלה. וואטערלו, אייאווא. ה'תשמ"ה. (6) רפד דף.

ב'קו. כנ"ל אות שלה. פעירפילד, אייאווא. ה'תשמ"ה (6) רפד דף.

ב'קז. כנ"ל אות שלה. בעדפארד הייטס, אהייא. ה'תשמ"ה. (6) רפד דף.

ב'קח. כנ"ל אות שלה. גאלדען וועלי, מינעסאטא. ה'תשמ"ה. (6) רפד דף.

ב'קט. כנ"ל אות שלה. ווייט בער לייק, מינעסאטא. ה'תשמ"ה. (6) רפד דף.

ב'קי. כנ"ל אות שלה. מאנקאטא, מינעסאטא. תשמ"ה. (6) רפד דף.

ב'קיא. כנ"ל אות שלה. מינעטאנקא, מינעסאטא. ה'תשמ"ה. (6) רפד דף.

ב'קיב. כנ"ל אות שלה. מענדאטא, מינעסאטא. ה'תשמ"ה. (6) רפד דף.

ב'קיג. כנ"ל אות שלה. נארטפילד, מינעסאטא. ה'תשמ"ה. (6) רפד דף.

ב'קיד. כנ"ל אות שלה. ניו בריטאן, מינעסאטא. ה'תשמ"ה. (6) רפד דף.

ב'קטו. כנ"ל אות שלה. ניופארט, מינעסאטא. ה'תשמ"ה. (6) רפד דף.

ב'קטז. כנ"ל אות שלה. עדיינא, מינעסאטא. ה'תשמ"ה. (6) רפד דף.

ב'קיז. כנ"ל אות שלה. פלימיטה, מינעסאטא. ה'תשמ"ה. (6) רפד דף.

ב'קיח. כנ"ל אות שלה. פארעסט לייק, מינעסאטא. ה'תשמ"ה. (6) רפד דף.

ב'קיט. כנ"ל אות שלה. פרידלי, מינעסאטא. ה'תשמ"ה. (6) רפד דף.

ב'קכ. כנ"ל אות שלה. קלאוד, מינעסאטא. ה'תשמ"ה. (6) רפד דף.

ב'קכא. כנ"ל אות שלה. ראסוויל, מינעסאטא. ה'תשמ"ה. (6) רפד דף.

ב'קכב. כנ"ל אות שלה. רעד ווינג, מינעסאטא. ה'תשמ"ה. (6) רפד דף.

ב׳קכג. כנ״ל אות שלה. בורלינגטאן, מאסאטשוסעטס. ה׳תשמ״ה. (6) רפד דף.

ב׳קכד. כנ״ל אות שלה. בעדפארד, מאסאטשוסעטס. ה׳תשמ״ה. (6) רפד דף.

ב׳קכה. כנ״ל אות שלה. וואלטהאם, מאסאטשוסעטס. ה׳תשמ״ה. (6) רפד דף.

ב׳קכו. כנ״ל אות שלה. וועלעסלי, מאסאטשוסעטס. ה׳תשמ״ה. (6) רפד דף.

ב׳קכז. כנ״ל אות שלה. לאועל, מאסאטשוסעטס. ה׳תשמ״ה. (6) רפד דף.

ב׳קכח. כנ״ל אות שלה. לאורענס, מאסאטשוסעטס. ה׳תשמ״ה. (6) רפד דף.

ב׳קכט. כנ״ל אות שלה. לין, מאסאטשוסעטס. ה׳תשמ״ה. (6) רפד דף.

ב׳קל. כנ״ל אות שלה. לעקסינגטאן, מאסאטשוסעטס. ה׳תשמ״ה. (6) רפד דף.

ב׳קלא. כנ״ל אות שלה. מארבלהעד, מאסאטשוסעטס. ה׳תשמ״ה. (6) רפד דף.

ב׳קלב. כנ״ל אות שלה. סואמפסקאט, מאסאטשוסעטס. ה׳תשמ״ה. (6) רפד דף.

ב׳קלג. כנ״ל אות שלה. ביהכנ״ס נוסח ארי״ — אנשי ליובאוויטש, ברייטאן, מאסאטשוסעטס. ה׳תשמ״ה. (6) רפד דף.

ב׳קלד. כנ״ל אות שלה. אייוואן, מאסאטשוסעטס. ה׳תשמ״ה. (6) רפד דף.

ב׳קלה. כנ״ל אות שלה. בריינטרי, מאסאטשוסעטס. ה׳תשמ״ה. (6) רפד דף.

ב׳קלו. כנ״ל אות שלה. דעדהאם, מאסאטשוסעטס. ה׳תשמ״ה. (6) רפד דף.

ב׳קלז. כנ״ל אות שלה. האל, מאסאטשוסעטס. ה׳תשמ״ה. (6) רפד דף.

ב׳קלח. כנ״ל אות שלה. האלברוק, מאסאטשוסעטס. ה׳תשמ״ה. (6) רפד דף.

ב׳קלט. כנ״ל אות שלה. וויימוטה, מאסאטשוסעטס. ה׳תשמ״ה. (6) רפד דף.

ב׳קמ. כנ״ל אות שלה. וועסטוואוד, מאסאטשוסעטס. ה׳תשמ״ה. (6) רפד דף.

ב׳קמא. כנ״ל אות שלה. נאנטאסקעט, מאסאטשוסעטס. ה׳תשמ״ה. (6) רפד דף.

ב׳קמב. כנ״ל אות שלה. נארוואוד, מאסאטשוסעטס. ה׳תשמ״ה. (6) רפד דף.

ב׳קמג. כנ״ל אות שלה. קאנטאן, מאסאטשוסעטס. ה׳תשמ״ה. (6) רפד דף.

ב׳קמד. כנ״ל אות שלה. איסט הייוען, קאנעטיקאט. ה׳תשמ״ה. (6) רפד דף.

ב׳קמה. כנ״ל אות שלה. נארט הייוען, קאנעטיקאט. ה׳תשמ״ה. (6) רפד דף.

ב׳קמו. כנ״ל אות שלה. בראנפארד, קאנעטיקאט. ה׳תשמ״ה. (6) רפד דף.

ב׳קמז. כנ״ל אות שלה. גילפארד, קאנעטיקאט. ה׳תשמ״ה. (6) רפד דף.

ב׳קמח. כנ״ל אות שלה. וואלינגפארד, קאנעטיקאט. ה׳תשמ״ה. (6) רפד דף.

ב׳קמט. כנ״ל אות שלה. טשעשייר, קאנעטיקאט. ה׳תשמ״ה. (6) רפד דף.

ב׳קנ. כנ״ל אות שלה. ייעלסוויל, קאנעטיקאט. ה׳תשמ״ה. (6) רפד דף.

ב׳קנא. כנ״ל אות שלה. ניוטאון, קאנעטיקאט. ה׳תשמ״ה. (6) רפד דף.

ב׳קנב. כנ״ל אות שלה. אנדרעס, קאלאמביא. ה׳תשמ״ה. (6) רפד דף.

ב׳קנג. כנ״ל אות שלה. ארמעניא, קאלאמביא. ה׳תשמ״ה. (6) רפד דף.

ב׳קנד. כנ״ל אות שלה. בוגא, קאלאמביא. ה׳תשמ״ה. (6) רפד דף.

ב׳קנה. כנ״ל אות שלה. פאפאיאן, קאלאמביא. ה׳תשמ״ה. (6) רפד דף.

ב׳קנו. כנ״ל אות שלה. קארטאגו, קאלאמביא. ה׳תשמ״ה. (6) רפד דף.

ב׳קנז. כנ״ל אות שדמ. אנעמאס, צרפת. ה׳תשמ״ה. (6) רפד דף.

ב׳קנח. כנ״ל אות שדמ. בורז, צרפת. ה׳תשמ״ה. (6) רפד דף.

ב׳קנט. כנ״ל אות שדמ. טול, צרפת. ה׳תשמ״ה. (6) רפד דף.

ב׳קס. כנ״ל אות שדמ. לא סיאטא, צרפת. ה׳תשמ״ה. (6) רפד דף.

ב׳קסא. כנ״ל אות שדמ. לא סעין סור מער, צרפת. ה׳תשמ״ה. (6) רפד דף.

ב׳קסב. כנ״ל אות שדמ. עקס לבען, צרפת. ה׳תשמ״ה. (6) רפד דף.

ב׳קסג. כנ״ל אות שדמ. קלאויר, צרפת. ה׳תשמ״ה. (6) רפד דף.

ב׳קסד. כנ״ל אות שדמ. וורמייזא, גרמניא. ה׳תשמ״ה. (6) רפד דף.

ב׳קסה. כנ״ל אות שדמ. בסיס חיל־אויר דייוויס מאונטיין, אריזאנא. ה׳תשמ״ה. (6) רפד דף.

ב׳קסו. כנ״ל אות שדמ. בענסאן, אריזאנא. ה׳תשמ״ה. (6) רפד דף.

ב׳קסז. כנ״ל אות שדמ. גלענדייל, אריזאנא. ה׳תשמ״ה. (6) רפד דף.

ב׳קסח. כנ״ל אות שדמ. דאגלעס, אריזאנא. ה׳תשמ״ה. (6) רפד דף.

ב׳קסט. כנ״ל אות שדמ. טעמפי, אריזאנא. ה׳תשמ״ה. (6) רפד דף.

ב׳קע. כנ״ל אות שדמ. טשאנדלער, אריזאנא. ה׳תשמ״ה. (6) רפד דף.

ב׳קעא. כנ״ל אות שדמ. יומא, אריזאנא. ה׳תשמ״ה. (6) רפד דף.

ב׳קעב. כנ״ל אות שדמ. לייק האוואסו, אריזאנא. ה׳תשמ״ה. (6) רפד דף.

ב׳קעג. כנ״ל אות שדמ. מייסא, אריזאנא. ה׳תשמ״ה. (6) רפד דף.

ב׳קעד. כנ״ל אות שדמ. נאגאלעס, אריזאנא. ה׳תשמ״ה. (6) רפד דף.

ב׳קעה. כנ״ל אות שדמ. סאן סיטי, אריזאנא. ה׳תשמ״ה. (6) רפד דף.

ב׳קעו. כנ״ל אות שדמ. סיערא וויסטא, אריזאנא. ה׳תשמ״ה. (6) רפד דף.

ב׳קעז. כנ״ל אות שדמ. סעדאנא, אריזאנא. ה׳תשמ״ה. (6) רפד דף.

ב׳קעח. כנ״ל אות שדמ. פרעסקאט, אריזאנא. ה׳תשמ״ה. (6) רפד דף.

ב׳קעט. כנ״ל אות שדמ. פלאגסטאף, אריזאנא. ה׳תשמ״ה. (6) רפד דף.

ב׳קפ. כנ״ל אות שדמ. פלארענס אריזאנא. ה׳תשמ״ה. (6) רפד דף.

ב׳קפא. כנ״ל אות שדמ. קאטאנוואוד, אריזאנא. ה׳תשמ״ה. (6) רפד דף.

ב׳קפב. כנ״ל אות שדמ. קינגמאן, אריזאנא. ה׳תשמ״ה. (6) רפד דף.

ב׳קפג. כנ״ל אות שדמ. קאסא גראנדע, אריזאנא. ה׳תשמ״ה. (6) רפד דף.

ב׳קפד. כנ״ל אות שדמ. וועסט האליוואוד, קאליפארניע. ה׳תשמ״ה. (6) רפד דף.

ב׳קפה. כנ״ל אות שדמ. אחיעזר, באה״ק. ה׳תשמ״ה. (6) רפז דף.

ב׳קפו. כנ״ל אות שדמ. אלי סיני, באה״ק. ה׳תשמ״ה. (6) רפז דף.

ב׳קפז. כנ״ל אות שדמ. אליקים, באה״ק. ה׳תשמ״ה. (6) רפז דף.

ב׳קפח. כנ״ל אות שדמ. באר יעקב, באה״ק. ה׳תשמ״ה. (6) רפז דף.

ב׳קפט. כנ״ל אות שדמ. בית דגן, באה״ק. ה׳תשמ״ה. (6) רפז דף.

ב׳קצ. כנ״ל אות שדמ. בלפוריה, באה״ק ת״ו. ה׳תשמ״ה. (6) רפז דף.

ב׳קצא. כנ״ל אות שדמ. יגל, באה״ק ת״ו. ה׳תשמ״ה. (6) רפז דף.

ב׳קצב. כנ״ל אות שדמ. יקנעם (מושבה), באה״ק ת״ו. ה׳תשמ״ה. (6) רפז דף.

ב׳קצג. כנ״ל אות שדמ. כפר אחים, באה״ק ת״ו. ה׳תשמ״ה. (6) רפז דף.

ב׳קצד. כנ״ל אות שדמ. כפר הנוער קדמה, באה״ק ת״ו. ה׳תשמ״ה. (6) רפז דף.

ב׳קצה. כנ״ל אות שדמ. מושב ינון, באה״ק ת״ו. ה׳תשמ״ה. (6) רפז דף.

ב׳קצו. כנ״ל אות שדמ. מושב יסודות, באה״ק ת״ו. ה׳תשמ״ה. (6) רפז דף.

ב׳קצז. כנ״ל אות שדמ. תלמי יחיאל, באה״ק ת״ו. ה׳תשמ״ה. (6) רפז דף.

ב׳קצח. כנ״ל אות שדמ. מזכרת בתיה, באה״ק ת״ו. ה׳תשמ״ה. (6) רפז דף.

ב׳קצט. כנ״ל אות שדמ. מצפה גיתה, באה״ק ת״ו. ה׳תשמ״ה. (6) רפז דף.

ב׳ר. כנ״ל אות שדמ. מצפה הילה, באה״ק ת״ו. ה׳תשמ״ה. (6) רפז דף.

ב׳רא. כנ״ל אות שדמ. מצפה חרשים, באה״ק ת״ו. ה׳תשמ״ה. (6) רפז דף.

ב׳רב. כנ״ל אות שדמ. מרכז ספיר — כביש הערבה, באה״ק ת״ו. ה׳תשמ״ה. (6) רפז דף.

ב׳רג. כנ״ל אות שדמ. משמר השבעה, באה״ק ת״ו. ה׳תשמ״ה. (6) רפז דף.

ב׳רד. כנ״ל אות שדמ. נאות מרדכי, באה״ק ת״ו. ה׳תשמ״ה. (6) רפז דף.

ב׳רה. כנ״ל אות שדמ. נהורה — מועצה אזורית לכיש, באה״ק ת״ו. ה׳תשמ״ה. (6) רפז דף.

ב׳רו. כנ״ל אות שדמ. ניסנית, באה״ק ת״ו. ה׳תשמ״ה. (6) רפז דף.

ב׳רז. כנ״ל אות שדמ. ניר צבי, באה״ק ת״ו. ה׳תשמ״ה. (6) רפז דף.

ב׳רח. כנ״ל אות שדמ. עדי, באה״ק ת״ו. ה׳תשמ״ה. (6) רפז דף.

ב׳רט. כנ״ל אות שדמ. עין העמק, באה״ק ת״ו. ה׳תשמ״ה. (6) רפז דף.

ב׳רי. כנ״ל אות שדמ. צה״ל — מחנה עובדה, באה״ק ת״ו. ה׳תשמ״ה. (6) רפז דף.

ב׳ריא. כנ״ל אות שדמ. צה״ל פיקוד דרום, באה״ק ת״ו. ה׳תשמ״ה. (6) רפז דף.

ב׳ריב. כנ״ל אות שדמ. צופר — כביש הערבה, באה״ק ת״ו. ה׳תשמ״ה. (6) רפז דף.

ב׳ריג. כנ״ל אות שדמ. קיבוץ אילת השחר, באה״ק ת״ו. ה׳תשמ״ה. (6) רפז דף.

ב׳ריד. כנ״ל אות שדמ. קיבוץ גברעם, באה״ק ת״ו. ה׳תשמ״ה. (6) רפז דף.

ב׳רטו. כנ״ל אות שדמ. קיבוץ הרדוף, באה״ק ת״ו. ה׳תשמ״ה. (6) רפז דף.

ב׳רטז. כנ״ל אות שדמ. קיבוץ חולדה, כאה״ק ת״ו. ה׳תשמ״ה. (6) רפז דף.

ב׳ריז. כנ״ל אות שדמ. קיבוץ יסעור, באה״ק ת״ו. ה׳תשמ״ה. (6) רפז דף.

ב׳ריח. כנ״ל אות שדמ. קיבוץ לוטם, באה״ק ת״ו. ה׳תשמ״ה. (6) רפז דף.

ב׳ריט. כנ״ל אות שדמ. קיבוץ מסילות, באה״ק ת״ו. ה׳תשמ״ה. (6) רפז דף.

ב׳רכ. כנ״ל אות שדמ. קיבוץ מלכיה, באה״ק ת״ו. ה׳תשמ״ה. (6) רפז דף.

ב׳רכא. כנ״ל אות שדמ. קיבוץ נצר סרני, באה״ק ת״ו. ה׳תשמ״ה. (6) רפז דף.

ב׳רכב. כנ״ל אות שדמ. קיבוץ רביבים, באה״ק ת״ו. ה׳תשמ״ה. (6) רפז דף.

ב׳רכג. כנ״ל אות שדמ. קיבוץ רשפים, באה״ק ת״ו. ה׳תשמ״ה. (6) רפז דף.

ב׳רכד. כנ״ל אות שדמ. קדומים, באה״ק ת״ו. ה׳תשמ״ה. (6) רפז דף.

ב׳רכה. כנ״ל אות שדמ. שדה יעקב, באה״ק ת״ו. ה׳תשמ״ה. (6) רפז דף.

ב׳רכו. כנ״ל אות שדמ. תאשור, באה״ק ת״ו. ה׳תשמ״ה. (6) רפז דף.

ב׳רכז. כנ״ל אות שדמ. תדהר, באה״ק ת״ו. ה׳תשמ״ה. (6) רפז דף.

ב׳רכח. כנ״ל אות שדמ. חוצבה — כביש הערבה, באה״ק ת״ו. ה׳תשמ״ה. (6) רפז דף.

ב׳רכט. כנ״ל אות שדמ. עידן — כביש הערבה, באה״ק ת״ו. ה׳תשמ״ה. (6) רפז דף.

ב׳רל. כנ״ל אות שדמ. עין יהב — כביש הערבה, באה״ק ת״ו. ה׳תשמ״ה. (6) רפז דף.

ב׳רלא. כנ״ל אות שדמ. פארן — כביש הערבה, באה״ק ת״ו. ה׳תשמ״ה. (6) רפז דף.

ב׳רלב. כנ״ל אות שדמ. צוקים — כביש הערבה, באה״ק ת״ו. ה׳תשמ״ה. (6) רפז דף.

ב׳רלג. כנ״ל אות שדמ. מגן שאול, באה״ק ת״ו. ה׳תשמ״ה. (6) רפז דף.

ב׳רלד. כנ״ל אות שדמ. פרזון, באה״ק ת״ו. ה׳תשמ״ה. (6) רפז דף.

ב׳רלה. כנ״ל אות שדמ. צה״ל — מחנה יחידות: פרקליטות, מצ״ח, גדנ״ע, בד״צ, משטרה צבאית, מחוז דרום, באה״ק ת״ו. ה׳תשמ״ה. (6) רפז דף.

ב׳רלו. כנ״ל אות שלה. האלברוק, לאנג איילאנד, נ.י. ה׳תשמ״ה. (6) רפז דף.

ב׳רלז. כנ״ל אות שלה. האלצוויל, לאנג איילאנד, נ.י. ה׳תשמ״ה. (6) רפז דף.

ב׳רלח. כנ״ל אות שלה. מאסטיק, לאנג איילאנד, נ.י. ה׳תשמ״ה. (6) רפז דף.

ב׳רלט. כנ״ל אות שלה. מעדפארד, לאנג איילאנד, נ.י. ה׳תשמ״ה. (6) רפז דף.

ב׳רמ. כנ״ל אות שלה. סייוויל, לאנג איילאנד, נ.י. ה׳תשמ״ה. (6) רפז דף.

ב׳רמא. כנ״ל אות שלה. סענטעריטש, לאנג איילאנד, נ.י. ה׳תשמ״ה. (6) רפז דף.

ב׳רמב. כנ״ל אות שלה. קינגס פארק, לאנג איילאנד, נ.י. ה׳תשמ״ה. (6) רפז דף.

ב׳רמג. כנ״ל אות שלה. ראנקאנקאמא, לאנג איילאנד, נ.י. ה׳תשמ״ה. (6) רפז דף.

ב׳רמד. כנ״ל אות שלה. רידוש, לאנג איילאנד, נ.י. ה׳תשמ״ה. (6) רפז דף.

ב׳רמה. כנ״ל אות שלה. שירלי, לאנג איילאנד, נ.י. ה׳תשמ״ה. (6) רפז דף.

ב׳רמו. כנ״ל אות שדמ. אביאל, באה״ק ת״ו. ה׳תשמ״ה. (6) רפט דף.

ב׳רמז. כנ״ל אות שדמ. אביחיל, באה״ק ת״ו. ה׳תשמ״ה. (6) רפט דף.

ב׳רמח. כנ״ל אות שדמ. אחוה, באה״ק ת״ו. ה׳תשמ״ה. (6) רפט דף.

ב׳רמט. כנ״ל אות שדמ. אחוזת שושנה, באה״ק ת״ו. ה׳תשמ״ה. (6) רפט דף.

ב׳רנ. כנ״ל אות שדמ. אמציה, באה״ק ת״ו. ה׳תשמ״ה. (6) רפט דף.

ב׳רנא. כנ״ל אות שדמ. חזון יחזקאל, באה״ק ת״ו. ה׳תשמ״ה. (6) רפט דף.

ב׳רנב. כנ״ל אות שדמ. באר אורה, באה״ק ת״ו. ה׳תשמ״ה. (6) רפט דף.

ב׳רנג. כנ״ל אות שדמ. בניה, באה״ק ת״ו. ה׳תשמ״ה. (6) רפט דף.

ב׳רנד. כנ״ל אות שדמ. גבעתיים, באה״ק ת״ו. ה׳תשמ״ה. (6) רפט דף.

ב׳רנה. כנ״ל אות שדמ. גבעת זיו, באה״ק. ה׳תשמ״ה. (6) רפט דף.

ב׳רנו. כנ״ל אות שדמ. גבעת כח, באה״ק ת״ו. ה׳תשמ״ה. (6) רפט דף.

ב׳רנז. כנ״ל אות שדמ. גבעת עדה, באה״ק ת״ו. ה׳תשמ״ה. (6) רפט דף.

ב׳רנח. כנ״ל אות שדמ. זוהר, באה״ק ת״ו. ה׳תשמ״ה. (6) רפט דף.

ב׳רנט. כנ״ל אות שדמ. טלז סטון, באה״ק ת״ו. ה׳תשמ״ה. (6) רפט דף.

ב׳רס. כנ״ל אות שדמ. יד נתן, באה״ק ת״ו. ה׳תשמ״ה. (6) רפט דף.

ב׳רסא. כנ״ל אות שדמ. כנות, באה״ק ת״ו. ה׳תשמ״ה. (6) רפט דף.

ב׳רסב. כנ״ל אות שדמ. כפר אביב, באה״ק ת״ו. ה׳תשמ״ה. (6) רפט דף.

ב׳רסג. כנ״ל אות שדמ. כפר ברוך, באה״ק ת״ו. ה׳תשמ״ה. (6) רפט דף.

ב׳רסד. כנ״ל אות שדמ. כפר הנוער ניצנים, באה״ק ת״ו. ה׳תשמ״ה. (6) רפט דף.

ב'רסה. כנ"ל אות שדמ. כפר זכריה, באה"ק ת"ו. ה'תשמ"ה. (6) רפט דף.

ב'רסו. כנ"ל אות שדמ. כפר מרדכי, באה"ק ת"ו. ה'תשמ"ה. (6) רפט דף.

ב'רסז. כנ"ל אות שדמ. כפר סילבר, באה"ק ת"ו. ה'תשמ"ה. (6) רפט דף.

ב'רסח. כנ"ל אות שדמ. עלמה, באה"ק ת"ו. ה'תשמ"ה. (6) רפט דף.

ב'רסט. כנ"ל אות שדמ. לכיש, באה"ק ת"ו. ה'תשמ"ה. (6) רפט דף.

ב'ער. כנ"ל אות שדמ. מבשרת ירושלים, באה"ק ת"ו. ה'תשמ"ה. (6) רפט דף.

ב'רעא. כנ"ל אות שדמ. מדרך עוז, באה"ק ת"ו. ה'תשמ"ה. (6) רפט דף.

ב'ערב. כנ"ל אות שדמ. מושב אביגדור, באה"ק ת"ו. ה'תשמ"ה. (6) רפט דף.

ב'רעג. כנ"ל אות שדמ. מושב אחוזם, באה"ק ת"ו. ה'תשמ"ה. (6) רפט דף.

ב'עדר. כנ"ל אות שדמ. מושב אלון הגליל, באה"ק ת"ו. ה'תשמ"ה. (6) רפט דף.

ב'ערה. כנ"ל אות שדמ. מושב בן עמי, באה"ק ת"ו. ה'תשמ"ה. (6) רפט דף.

ב'רעו. כנ"ל אות שדמ. מושב בני דרום, באה"ק ת"ו. ה'תשמ"ה. (6) רפט דף.

ב'רעז. כנ"ל אות שדמ. מושב בני ראם, באה"ק ת"ו. ה'תשמ"ה. (6) רפט דף.

ב'רעח. כנ"ל אות שדמ. מושב בצרון, באה"ק ת"ו. ה'תשמ"ה. (6) רפט דף.

ב'רעט. כנ"ל אות שדמ. מושב גפן, באה"ק ת"ו. ה'תשמ"ה. (6) רפט דף.

ב'רפ. כנ"ל אות שדמ. מושב היוגב, באה"ק ת"ו. ה'תשמ"ה. (6) רפט דף.

ב'רפא. כנ"ל אות שדמ. מושב חצב, באה"ק ת"ו. ה'תשמ"ה. (6) רפט דף.

ב'רפב. כנ"ל אות שדמ. מושב יד רמב"ם, באה"ק ת"ו. ה'תשמ"ה. (6) רפט דף.

ב'רפג. כנ"ל אות שדמ. מושב כרם בן זמרה, באה"ק ת"ו. ה'תשמ"ה. (6) רפט דף.

ב'רפד. כנ"ל אות שדמ. מושב נועם, באה"ק ת"ו. ה'תשמ"ה. (6) רפט דף.

ב'רפה. כנ"ל אות שדמ. מושב ספסופה, באה"ק ת"ו. ה'תשמ"ה. (6) רפט דף.

ב'רפו. כנ"ל אות שדמ. מושב עוזה, באה"ק ת"ו. ה'תשמ"ה. (6) רפט דף.

ב'רפז. כנ"ל אות שדמ. מושב עזריקם, באה"ק ת"ו. ה'תשמ"ה. (6) רפט דף.

ב'רפח. כנ"ל אות שדמ. מושב ערוגות, באה"ק ת"ו. ה'תשמ"ה. (6) רפט דף.

ב'רפט. כנ"ל אות שדמ. מושב דלתון, באה"ק ת"ו. ה'תשמ"ה. (6) רפט דף.

ב'רצ. כנ"ל אות שדמ. מושב שלוה, באה"ק ת"ו. ה'תשמ"ה. (6) רפט דף.

ב'רצא. כנ"ל אות שדמ. מושַב תירוש, באה"ק ת"ו. ה'תשמ"ה. (6) רפט דף.

ב'רצב. כנ"ל אות שדמ. מיטב, באה"ק ת"ו. ה'תשמ"ה. (6) רפט דף.

ב'רצג. כנ"ל אות שדמ. מנוחה, באה"ק. ה'תשמ"ה. (6) רפט דף.

ב'רצד. כנ"ל אות שדמ. מנוף, גוש שגב, באה"ק ת"ו. ה'תשמ"ה. (6) רפט דף.

ב'רצה. כנ"ל אות שדמ. מצפה אבירים, באה"ק ת"ו. ה'תשמ"ה. (6) רפט דף.

ב'רצו. כנ"ל אות שדמ. מצפה דובב, באה"ק ת"ו. ה'תשמ"ה. (6) רפט דף.

ב'רצז. כנ"ל אות שדמ. מרכז אזורי כדורי, באה"ק ת"ו. ה'תשמ"ה. (6) רפט דף.

ב'חצר. כנ"ל אות שדמ. משגב דב, באה"ק ת"ו. ה'תשמ"ה. (6) רפט דף.

ב'רצט. כנ"ל אות שדמ. מתת, באה"ק ת"ו. ה'תשמ"ה. (6) רפט דף.

ב'ש. כנ"ל אות שדמ. נוגה, באה"ק ת"ו. ה'תשמ"ה. (6) רפט דף.

ב'שא. כנ"ל אות שדמ. נוה צוף, באה"ק ת"ו. ה'תשמ"ה. (6) רפט דף.

ב'שב. כנ"ל אות שדמ. ניר חן, באה"ק. ה'תשמ"ה. (6) רפט דף.

ב'שג. כנ"ל אות שדמ. עזה — מימשל צבאי צה"ל, באה"ק ת"ו. ה'תשמ"ה. (6) רפט דף.

ב'דש. כנ"ל אות שדמ. עוצם, באה"ק ת"ו. ה'תשמ"ה. (6) רפט דף.

ב'שה. כנ"ל אות שדמ. עשרת, באה"ק ת"ו. ה'תשמ"ה. (6) רפט דף.

ב'שו. כנ"ל אות שדמ. פרדס כץ, באה"ק ת"ו. ה'תשמ"ה. (6) רפט דף.

ב'שז. כנ"ל אות שדמ. קדרון, באה"ק ת"ו. ה'תשמ"ה. (6) רפט דף.

ב'שח. כנ"ל אות שדמ. קיבוץ אילות, באה"ק ת"ו. ה'תשמ"ה. (6) רפט דף.

ב'שט. כנ"ל אות שדמ. קיבוץ אפיקים, באה"ק ת"ו. ה'תשמ"ה. (6) רפט דף.

ב'שי. כנ"ל אות שדמ. קיבוץ גבעת השלושה, באה"ק ת"ו. ה'תשמ"ה. (6) רפט דף.

ב'שיא. כנ"ל אות שדמ. קיבוץ גרופית, באה"ק ת"ו. ה'תשמ"ה. (6) רפט דף.

ב'שיב. כנ"ל אות שדמ. קיבוץ מעלה צביה, באה"ק ת"ו. ה'תשמ"ה. (6) רפט דף.

ב'שיג. כנ"ל אות שדמ. קיבוץ משמר העמק, באה"ק ת"ו. ה'תשמ"ה. (6) רפט דף.

ב'שיד. כנ"ל אות שדמ. קיבוץ דליה, באה"ק ת"ו. ה'תשמ"ה. (6) רפט דף.

ב'שטו. כנ"ל אות שדמ. קיבוץ רביד, באה"ק ת"ו. ה'תשמ"ה. (6) רפט דף.

ב'שטז. כנ"ל אות שדמ. קיבוץ רמת דוד, באה"ק ת"ו. ה'תשמ"ה. (6) רפט דף.

ב'שיז. כנ"ל אות שדמ. קיבוץ שזפון, באה"ק ת"ו. ה'תשמ"ה. (6) רפט דף.

ב'שיח. כנ"ל אות שדמ. שדה אילן, באה"ק ת"ו. ה'תשמ"ה. (6) רפט דף.

ב'שיט. כנ"ל אות שדמ. שדה דוד, באה"ק ת"ו. ה'תשמ"ה. (6) רפט דף.

ב'שכ. כנ"ל אות שדמ. שדות מיכה, באה"ק ת"ו. ה'תשמ"ה. (6) רפט דף.

ב'שכא. כנ"ל אות שדמ. שדמה, באה"ק ת"ו. ה'תשמ"ה. (6) רפט דף.

ב'שכב. כנ"ל אות שדמ. שחר, באה"ק ת"ו. ה'תשמ"ה. (6) רפט דף.

ב'שכג. כנ"ל אות שדמ. שכונת מטרסדורף — איתרי, ירושת"ו. ה'תשמ"ה. (6) רפט דף.

ב'שכד. כנ"ל אות שדמ. שקף, באה"ק ת"ו. ה'תשמ"ה. (6) רפט דף.

ב'שכה. כנ"ל אות שדמ. תלמים, באה"ק ת"ו. ה'תשמ"ה. (6) רפט דף.

ב'שכו. כנ"ל אות שדמ. צה"ל — בסיס ח"א — נבטים, באה"ק ת"ו. ה'תשמ"ה. (6) רפט דף.

ב'שכז. כנ"ל אות שדמ. אליפלט, באה"ק ת"ו. ה'תשמ"ה. (6) רפט דף.

ב'שכח. כנ"ל אות שדמ. זבדיאל, באה"ק ת"ו. ה'תשמ"ה. (6) רפט דף.

ב'שכט. כנ"ל אות שדמ. כחל, באה"ק ת"ו. ה'תשמ"ה. (6) רפט דף.

ב'של. כנ"ל אות שדמ. כלנית, באה"ק ת"ו. ה'תשמ"ה. (6) רפט דף.

ב'שלא. כנ"ל אות שדמ. נבטים, באה"ק ת"ו. ה'תשמ"ה. (6) רפט דף.

ב'שלב. כנ"ל אות שדמ. קיבוץ משאבי שדה, באה"ק ת"ו. ה'תשמ"ה. (6) רפט דף.

ב'שלג. כנ"ל אות שדמ. מיצד (אספר) — הרי חברון, באה"ק ת"ו. ה'תשמ"ה. (6) רפט דף.

ב'שלד. כנ"ל אות שדמ. קיבוץ אורים, באה"ק ת"ו. ה'תשמ"ה. (6) רפט דף.

ב'שלה. כנ"ל אות שדמ. רמות נפתלי, באה"ק ת"ו. ה'תשמ"ה. (6) רפט דף.

ב'שלו. כנ"ל אות שדמ. טל שחר, באה"ק. ה'תשמ"ה. (6) רפט דף.

ב'שלז. כנ"ל אות שדמ. מישר, באה"ק ת"ו. ה'תשמ"ה. (6) רפט דף.

ב'שלח. כנ"ל אות שדמ. קיבוץ קטורה, באה"ק ת"ו. ה'תשמ"ה. (6) רפט דף.

ב'שלט. כנ"ל אות שלה. אטאל, מאסאטשוסעטס. ה'תשמ"ה. (6) רצה דף.

ב'שמ. כנ"ל אות שלה. וועבסטער, מאסאטשוסעטס. ה'תשמ"ה. (6) רצה דף.

ב'שמא. כנ"ל אות שלה. לעאמינסטער, מאסאטשוסעטס. ה'תשמ"ה. (6) רצה דף.

ב'שמב. כנ"ל אות שלה. פיטשבורג, מאסאטשוסעטס. ה'תשמ"ה. (6) רצה דף.

ב'שמג. כנ"ל אות שלה. קלינטאן, מאסאטשוסעטס. ה'תשמ"ה. (6) רצה דף.

ב'שדמ. כנ"ל אות שלה. אפא-לאקא, פלארידא. ה'תשמ"ה. (6) רצה דף.

ב'שמה. כנ"ל אות שלה. דאניא, פלארידא. ה'תשמ"ה. (6) רצה דף.

ב'שמו. כנ"ל אות שלה. דייווי, פלארידא. ה'תשמ"ה. (6) רצה דף.

ב'שמז. כנ"ל אות שלה. דירפילד ביטש, פלארידא. ה'תשמ"ה. (6) רצה דף.

ב'שמח. כנ"ל אות שלה. האמסטעד, פלארידא. ה'תשמ"ה. (6) רצה דף.

ב'שמט. כנ"ל אות שלה. ווילטאן מאנארס, פלארידא. ה'תשמ"ה. (6) רצה דף.

ב'שנ. כנ"ל אות שלה. וועסטשעסטער, דייד קאונטי, פלארידא. ה'תשמ"ה. (6) רצה דף.

ב'שנא. כנ"ל אות שלה. טאמאראק, פלארידא. ה'תשמ"ה. (6) רצה דף.

ב'שנב. כנ"ל אות שלה. לאנטאנא, פלארידא. ה'תשמ"ה. (6) רצה דף.

ב'שנג. כנ"ל אות שלה. לאודערדייל לייקס, פלארידא. ה'תשמ"ה. (6) רצה דף.

ב'שנד. כנ"ל אות שלה. לאודערהיל, פלארידא. תשמ"ה. (6) רצה דף.

ב'שנה. כנ"ל אות שלה. לייטהאוז פאינט, פלארידא. ה'תשמ"ה. (6) רצה דף.

ב'שנו. כנ"ל אות שלה. לייק וואורט, פלארידא. ה'תשמ"ה. (6) רצה דף.

ב'שנז. כנ"ל אות שלה. מארגייט, פלארידא. ה'תשמ"ה. (6) רצה דף.

ב'שנח. כנ"ל אות שלה. מיאמי ביטש, פלארידא. ה'תשמ"ה. (6) רצה דף.

ב'שנט. כנ"ל אות שלה. מיאמי ספרינגס, פלארידא. ה'תשמ"ה. (6) רצה דף.

ב'שס. כנ"ל אות שלה. מיראמאר, פלארידא. ה'תשמ"ה. (6) רצה דף.

ב'שסא. כנ"ל אות שלה. סאנרייז, פלארידא. ה'תשמ"ה. (6) רצה דף.

ב'שסב. כנ"ל אות שלה. סוויטוואטער, פלארידא. ה'תשמ"ה. (6) רצה דף.

ב'שסג. כנ"ל אות שלה. פלאנטיישען, פלארידא. ה'תשמ"ה. (6) רצה דף.

ב'שסד. כנ"ל אות שלה. פלארידא סיטי, פלארידא. ה'תשמ"ה. (6) רצה דף.

ב'שסה. כנ"ל אות שלה. פעמבראק פיינס, פלארידא. ה'תשמ"ה. (6) רצה דף.

ב'שסו. כנ"ל אות שלה. קאקאנאט קריק, פלארידא. ה'תשמ"ה. (6) רצה דף.

ב'שסז. כנ"ל אות שלה. קופער סיטי, פלארידא. ה'תשמ"ה. (6) רצה דף.

ב'שסח. כנ"ל אות שלה. גרינסבורג, פענסילוויינא. ה'תשמ"ה. (6) רצה דף.

ב'שסט. כנ"ל אות שלה. דזשאנסטאון, פענסילוויינא. ה'תשמ"ה. (6) רצה דף.

ב'שע. כנ"ל אות שלה. וואשינגטאן, פענסילוויינא. ה'תשמ"ה. (6) רצה דף.

ב'שעא. כנ"ל אות שלה. ווילקינסבורג, פענסילוויינא. ה'תשמ"ה. (6) רצה דף.

ב'שעב. כנ"ל אות שלה. יוניאנטאון, פענסילוויינא. ה'תשמ"ה. (6) רצה דף.

ב'שעג. כנ"ל אות שלה. מעקיספארט, פענסילוויינא. ה'תשמ"ה. (6) רצה דף.

ב'שעד. כנ"ל אות שלה. לואיסטאון, פענסילוויינא. ה'תשמ"ה. (6) רצה דף.

ב'שעה. כנ"ל אות שלה. מאנראוויל, פענסילוויינא. ה'תשמ"ה. (6) רצה דף.

ב'שעו. כנ"ל אות שלה. סטייט קאלעדזש, פענסילוויינא. ה'תשמ"ה. (6) רצה דף.

ב'שעז. כנ"ל אות שלה. ניילס, אילינאי. ה'תשמ"ה. (6) רצג דף.

ב'שעח. כנ"ל אות שלה. בעטהיסדא, מארילאנד. ה'תשמ"ה. (6) רצג דף.

ב'שעט. כנ"ל אות שלה. האמילטאן, בערמיודא. ה'תשמ"ה. (6) רצג דף.

ב'שפ. כנ"ל אות שדמ. קאלאמביא, מארילאנד. ה'תשמ"ה. (6) רצג דף.

ב'שפא. כנ"ל אות תכ. מחנה גן ישראל — פרדס חנה, טערא פרעטא, בראזיל. ה'תשמ"ה. (6) רצה דף.

ב'שפב. כנ"ל אות תכ. לואנדא, אנגאלא. ה'תשמ"ה. (6) רצה דף.

ב'שפג. כנ"ל אות תכ. סאפיא, בולגאריא. ה'תשמ"ה. (6) רצה דף.

ב'שפד. כנ"ל אות שלה. אוקדייל, לאנג איילאנד, נ.י. ה'תשמ"ה. (6) רצג דף.

ב'שפה. כנ"ל אות שלה. באהימיא, לאנג איילאנד, נ.י. ה'תשמ"ה. (6) רצג דף.

ב'שפו. כנ"ל אות שלה. גרינלאון, לאנג איילאנד, נ.י. ה'תשמ"ה. (6) רצג דף.

ב'שפז. כנ"ל אות שלה. דזשיימס, לאנג איילאנד, נ.י. ה'תשמ"ה. (6) רצג דף.

ב'שפח. כנ"ל אות שלה. האפאוג, לאנג איילאנד, נ.י. ה'תשמ"ה. (6) רצג דף.

ב'שפט. כנ"ל אות שלה. ווייענדאנטש, לאנג איילאנד, נ.י. ה'תשמ"ה. (6) רצג דף.

ב'שצ. כנ"ל אות שלה. מידל איילאנד, לאנג איילאנד, נ.י. ה'תשמ"ה. (6) רצג דף.

ב'שצא. כנ"ל אות שלה. מעלוויל, לאנג איילאנד, נ.י. ה'תשמ"ה. (6) רצג דף.

ב'שצב. כנ"ל אות שלה. נעסקאנסעט, לאנג איילאנד, נ.י. ה'תשמ"ה. (6) רצג דף.

ב'שצג. כנ"ל אות שלה. סעטאקעט, לאנג איילאנד, נ.י. ה'תשמ"ה. (6) רצג דף.

ב'שצד. כנ"ל אות שלה. גלענוויו, אילינאי. ה'תשמ"ה. (6) רצג דף.

ב'שצה. כנ"ל אות שלה. דירפילד, אילינאי. ה'תשמ"ה. (6) רצג דף.

ב'שצו. כנ"ל אות שלה. פארט מארסבי, פאפאו ניו גיני. ה'תשמ"ה. (6) רצג דף.

ב'שצז. כנ"ל אות שלה. סואווא, פידושי. ה'תשמ"ה. (6) רצג דף.

ב'שצח. כנ"ל אות שלה. וועסט בלומפילד, מישיגען. ה'תשמ"ה. (6) רצג דף.

ב'שצט. כנ"ל אות שלה. סאוטפילד, מישיגען. ה'תשמ"ה. (6) רצג דף.

ב'ת. כנ"ל אות שלה. אריאנט פאינט, לאנג איילאנד, נ.י. ה'תשמ"ה. (6) רצג דף.

ב'תא. כנ"ל אות שלה. ביוויו, לאנג איילאנד, נ.י. ה'תשמ"ה. (6) רצג דף.

ב'תב. כנ"ל אות שלה. בייפארט, לאנג איילאנד, נ.י. ה'תשמ"ה. (6) רצג דף.

ב'תג. כנ"ל אות שלה. בלו פאינט, לאנג איילאנד, נ.י. ה'תשמ"ה. (6) רצג דף.

ב'תד. כנ"ל אות שלה. ברענטוואוד, לאנג איילאנד, נ.י. ה'תשמ"ה. (6) רצג דף.

ב'תה. **כנ"ל** אות שלה. גרינפארט, לאנג איילאנד, נ.י. ה'תשמ"ה. (6) רצג דף.

ב'תו. **כנ"ל** אות שלה. דזשיימספארט, לאנג איילאנד, נ.י. ה'תשמ"ה. (6) רצג דף.

ב'תז. **כנ"ל** אות שלה. דיקס הילס, לאנג איילאנד, נ.י. ה'תשמ"ה. (6) רצג דף.

ב'תח. **כנ"ל** אות שלה. העד או טהא הארבאר, לאנג איילאנד, נ.י. ה'תשמ"ה. (6) רצג דף.

ב'תט. **כנ"ל** אות שלה. וואלי סטרים, לאנג איילאנד, נ.י. ה'תשמ"ה. (6) רצג דף.

ב'תי. **כנ"ל** אות שלה. יאפהאנק, לאנג איילאנד, נ.י. ה'תשמ"ה. (6) רצג דף.

ב'תיא. **כנ"ל** אות שלה. מאונט סיני, לאנג איילאנד, נ.י. ה'תשמ"ה. (6) רצג דף.

ב'תיב. **כנ"ל** אות שלה. סידאר ביטש, לאנג איילאנד, נ.י. ה'תשמ"ה. (6) רצג דף.

ב'תיג. **כנ"ל** אות שלה. סייאסעט, לאנג איילאנד, נ.י. ה'תשמ"ה. (6) רצג דף.

ב'תיד. **כנ"ל** אות שלה. סענטער מאריטשעס, לאנג איילאנד, נ.י. ה'תשמ"ה. (6) רצג דף.

ב'תטו. **כנ"ל** אות שלה. פארט סאלאנגא, לאנג איילאנד, נ.י. ה'תשמ"ה. (6) רצג דף.

ב'תטז. **כנ"ל** אות שלה. פארמינגדייל, לאנג איילאנד, נ.י. ה'תשמ"ה. (6) רצג דף.

ב'תיז. **כנ"ל** אות שלה. קאראם, לאנג איילאנד, נ.י. ה'תשמ"ה. (6) רצג דף.

ב'תיח. **כנ"ל** אות שלה. ראקי פאינט, לאנג איילאנד, נ.י. ה'תשמ"ה. (6) רצג דף.

ב'תיט. **כנ"ל** אות שלה. שארהאם, לאנג איילאנד, נ.י. ה'תשמ"ה. (6) רצג דף.

ב'תכ. **כנ"ל** אות שלה. לאפאיעט, אינדיאנא. ה'תשמ"ה. (6) רצג דף.

ב'תכא. **כנ"ל** אות שלה. וועסט לאפאיעט, אינדיאנא. ה'תשמ"ה. (6) רצג דף.

ב'תכב. **כנ"ל** אות שלה. אוק ביטש, לאנג איילאנד, נ.י. ה'תשמ"ה. (6) רצג דף.

ב'תכג. **כנ"ל** אות שלה. אטלאנטיק, לאנג איילאנד, נ.י. ה'תשמ"ה. (6) רצג דף.

ב'תכד. **כנ"ל** אות שלה. אלד פילד, לאנג איילאנד, נ.י. ה'תשמ"ה. (6) רצג דף.

ב'תכה. **כנ"ל** אות שלה. אקוואבאג, לאנג איילאנד, נ.י. ה'תשמ"ה. (6) רצג דף.

ב'תכו. **כנ"ל** אות שלה. אריגאן, לאנג איילאנד, נ.י. ה'תשמ"ה. (6) רצג דף.

ב'תכז. **כנ"ל** אות שלה. אשראקען, לאנג איילאנד, נ.י. ה'תשמ"ה. (6) רצג דף.

ב'תכח. **כנ"ל** אות שלה. בייקסעדאן, לאנג איילאנד, נ.י. ה'תשמ"ה. (6) רצג דף.

ב'תכט. **כנ"ל** אות שלה. ברוקהייווען, לאנג איילאנד, נ.י. ה'תשמ"ה. (6) רצג דף.

ב'תל. **כנ"ל** אות שלה. דייוויס פארק, לאנג איילאנד, נ.י. ה'תשמ"ה. (6) רצג דף.

ב'תלא. **כנ"ל** אות שלה. וויידינג ריווער, לאנג איילאנד, נ.י. ה'תשמ"ה. (6) רצג דף.

ב'תלב. **כנ"ל** אות שלה. לאורעל, לאנג איילאנד, נ.י. ה'תשמ"ה. (6) רצג דף.

ב'תלג. **כנ"ל** אות שלה. מאטיטאק, לאנג איילאנד, נ.י. ה'תשמ"ה. (6) רצג דף.

ב'תלד. **כנ"ל** אות שלה. מאנארוויל, לאנג איילאנד, נ.י. ה'תשמ"ה. (6) רצג דף.

ב'תלה. **כנ"ל** אות שלה. סענטערפארט, לאנג איילאנד, נ.י. ה'תשמ"ה. (6) רצג דף.

ב'תלו. **כנ"ל** אות שלה. עדזשוואוד, לאנג איילאנד, נ.י. ה'תשמ"ה. (6) רצג דף.

ב'תלז. **כנ"ל** אות שלה. פעקאניק, לאנג איילאנד, נ.י. ה'תשמ"ה. (6) רצג דף.

ב'תלח. **כנ"ל** אות שלה. פארמינגוויל, לאנג איילאנד, נ.י. ה'תשמ"ה. (6) רצג דף.

ב'תלט. **כנ"ל** אות שלה. קאטשאוג, לאנג איילאנד, נ.י. ה'תשמ"ה. (6) רצג דף.

ב'תמ. **כנ"ל** אות שלה. קאלווערטאן, לאנג איילאנד, נ.י. ה'תשמ"ה. (6) רצג דף.

ב'תמא. **כנ"ל** אות שלה. קאפייג, לאנג איילאנד, נ.י. ה'תשמ"ה. (6) רצג דף.

ב'תמב. **כנ"ל** אות שלה. קיסמעט, לאנג איילאנד, נ.י. ה'תשמ"ה. (6) רצג דף.

ב'תמג. **כנ"ל** אות שלה. אנאהיים, קאליפארניא. ה'תשמ"ה. (6) רצה דף.

ב'תמד. **כנ"ל** אות שלה. מאונט יוניאן, פענסילווייניא. ה'תשמ"ה. (6) רצה דף.

ב'תמה. **כנ"ל** אות שלה. פייוואקי, וויסקאנסין. ה'תשמ"ה. (6) רצה דף.

ב'תמו. **כנ"ל** אות שלה. דונדאס, אנטריא, קאנאדא. ה'תשמ"ה. (6) רצה דף.

ב'תמז. **כנ"ל** אות שלה. קאליומעט סיטי, אילינאי. ה'תשמ"ה. (6) רצה דף.

ב'תמח. **כנ"ל** אות שלה. ניו ראשעל, נ.י. ה'תשמ"ה. (6) רצה דף.

ב'תמט. **כנ"ל** אות שלה. גלענברוק, קאנעטיקאט. ה'תשמ"ה. (6) רצה דף.

ב'תנ. **כנ"ל** אות שדמ. אביעזר, באה"ק ת"ו. ה'תשמ"ה. רצה דף.

ב'תנא. **כנ"ל** אות שדמ. אבן ספיר, באה"ק ת"ו. ה'תשמ"ה. רצה דף.

ב'תנב. **כנ"ל** אות שדמ. אדרת, באה"ק ת"ו. ה'תשמ"ה. רצה דף.

ב'תנג. **כנ"ל** אות שדמ. אורה, באה"ק ת"ו. ה'תשמ"ה. רצה דף.

ב'תנד. **כנ"ל** אות שדמ. אילניה, באה"ק ת"ו. ה'תשמ"ה. רצה דף.

ב'תנה. **כנ"ל** אות שדמ. אלעזר, באה"ק ת"ו. ה'תשמ"ה. רצה דף.

ב'תנו. **כנ"ל** אות שדמ. אלקנה, באה"ק ת"ו. ה'תשמ"ה. רצה דף.

ב'תנז. **כנ"ל** אות שדמ. אפרת, באה"ק ת"ו. ה'תשמ"ה. רצה דף.

ב'תנח. **כנ"ל** אות שדמ. ארבל, באה"ק ת"ו. ה'תשמ"ה. רצה דף.

ב'תנט. **כנ"ל** אות שדמ. אריאל, באה"ק ת"ו. ה'תשמ"ה. רצה דף.

ב'תס. **כנ"ל** אות שדמ. אשבול, באה"ק ת"ו. ה'תשמ"ה. רצה דף.

ב'תסא. **כנ"ל** אות שדמ. אשתאול, באה"ק ת"ו. ה'תשמ"ה. רצה דף.

ב'תסב. **כנ"ל** אות שדמ. באר שבע (שכונה ג) (הוצאה שני'), באה"ק ת"ו. ה'תשמ"ה. רצה דף.

ב'תסג. **כנ"ל** אות שדמ. בית ברל, תל־אביב, באה"ק ת"ו. ה'תשמ"ה. רצה דף.

ב'תסד. **כנ"ל** אות שדמ. בית הלוי, באה"ק ת"ו. ה'תשמ"ה. רצה דף.

ב'תסה. **כנ"ל** אות שדמ. בית חשמונאי, באה"ק ת"ו. ה'תשמ"ה. רצה דף.

ב'תסו. **כנ"ל** אות שדמ. בית עוזיאל, באה"ק ת"ו. ה'תשמ"ה. רצה דף.

ב'תסז. **כנ"ל** אות שדמ. בית עריף, באה"ק ת"ו. ה'תשמ"ה. רצה דף.

ב'תסח. **כנ"ל** אות שדמ. בית שערים, באה"ק ת"ו. ה'תשמ"ה. רצה דף.

ב'תסט. **כנ"ל** אות שדמ. בני דרור, באה"ק ת"ו. ה'תשמ"ה. רצה דף.

ב'תע. **כנ"ל** אות שדמ. בני ציון, באה"ק ת"ו. ה'תשמ"ה. רצה דף.

ב'תעא. **כנ"ל** אות שדמ. בצרה, באה"ק ת"ו. ה'תשמ"ה. רצה דף.

ב'תעב. **כנ"ל** אות שדמ. בקוע, באה"ק ת"ו. ה'תשמ"ה. רצה דף.

ב'תעג. **כנ"ל** אות שדמ. בר גיורא, באה"ק ת"ו. ה'תשמ"ה. רצה דף.

ב'תעד. **כנ"ל** אות שדמ. גבעת יערים, באה"ק ת"ו. ה'תשמ"ה. רצה דף.

ב'תעה. **כנ"ל** אות שדמ. גבעת ישעיהו, באה"ק ת"ו. ה'תשמ"ה. רצה דף.

ב'תעו. **כנ"ל** אות שדמ. גן הדרום, באה"ק ת"ו. ה'תשמ"ה. רצה דף.

ב'תעז. **כנ"ל** אות שדמ. גן חיים, באה"ק ת"ו. ה'תשמ"ה. רצה דף.

ב'תעח. **כנ"ל** אות שדמ. גני עם, באה"ק ת"ו. ה'תשמ"ה. רצה דף.

ב'תעט. **כנ"ל** אות שדמ. הוד השרון, באה"ק ת"ו. ה'תשמ"ה. רצה דף.

ב'תפ. כנ"ל אות שדמ. זנוח, באה"ק ת"ו. ה'תשמ"ה. רצה דף.
ב'תפא. כנ"ל אות שדמ. חדיד, באה"ק ת"ו. ה'תשמ"ה. רצה דף.
ב'תפב. כנ"ל אות שדמ. חרוצים, באה"ק ת"ו. ה'תשמ"ה. רצה דף.
ב'תפג. כנ"ל אות שדמ. חרות, באה"ק ת"ו. ה'תשמ"ה. רצה דף.
ב'תפד. כנ"ל אות שדמ. טירת יהודה, באה"ק ת"ו. ה'תשמ"ה. רצה דף.
ב'תפה. כנ"ל אות שדמ. ירקונה, באה"ק ת"ו. ה'תשמ"ה. רצה דף.
ב'תפו. כנ"ל אות שדמ. ישעי, באה"ק ת"ו. ה'תשמ"ה. רצה דף.
ב'תפז. כנ"ל אות שדמ. כוכב יאיר, באה"ק ת"ו. ה'תשמ"ה. רצה דף.
ב'תפח. כנ"ל אות שדמ. כלא שאטה — בית סוהר, עפולה, באה"ק ת"ו. ה'תשמ"ה. רצה דף.
ב'תפט. כנ"ל אות שדמ. כסלון, באה"ק ת"ו. ה'תשמ"ה. רצה דף.
ב'תצ. כנ"ל אות שדמ. כפר אוריה, באה"ק ת"ו. ה'תשמ"ה. רצה דף.
ב'תצא. כנ"ל אות שדמ. כפר בן נון, באה"ק ת"ו. ה'תשמ"ה. רצה דף.
ב'תצב. כנ"ל אות שדמ. כפר הס, באה"ק ת"ו. ה'תשמ"ה. רצה דף.
ב'תצג. כנ"ל אות שדמ. כפר יהושע, באה"ק ת"ו. ה'תשמ"ה. רצה דף.
ב'תצד. כנ"ל אות שדמ. כפר מלל, באה"ק ת"ו. ה'תשמ"ה. רצה דף.
ב'תצה. כנ"ל אות שדמ. כפר סירקין, באה"ק ת"ו. ה'תשמ"ה. רצה דף.
ב'תצו. כנ"ל אות שדמ. כפר שמואל, באה"ק ת"ו. ה'תשמ"ה. רצה דף.
ב'תצז. כנ"ל אות שדמ. כפר שמריהו, באה"ק ת"ו. ה'תשמ"ה. רצה דף.
ב'תצח. כנ"ל אות שדמ. לוזית, באה"ק ת"ו. ה'תשמ"ה. רצה דף.
ב'תצט. כנ"ל אות שדמ. ליאון — שריגים, באה"ק ת"ו. ה'תשמ"ה. רצה דף.
ב'תק. כנ"ל אות שדמ. מבוא ביתר, באה"ק ת"ו. ה'תשמ"ה. רצה דף.
ב'תקא. כנ"ל אות שדמ. מוצא, באה"ק ת"ו. ה'תשמ"ה. רצז דף.
ב'תקב. כנ"ל אות שדמ. מושב בית מאיר, באה"ק ת"ו. ה'תשמ"ה. רצז דף.
ב'תקג. כנ"ל אות שדמ. מחסי', באה"ק ת"ו. ה'תשמ"ה. רצז דף.
ב'תקד. כנ"ל אות שדמ. מטע, באה"ק ת"ו. ה'תשמ"ה. רצז דף.
ב'תקה. כנ"ל אות שדמ. מסילת ציון, באה"ק ת"ו. ה'תשמ"ה. רצז דף.
ב'תקו. כנ"ל אות שדמ. משמר איילון, באה"ק ת"ו. ה'תשמ"ה. רצז דף.
ב'תקז. כנ"ל אות שדמ. משמרת, באה"ק ת"ו. ה'תשמ"ה. רצז דף.
ב'תקח. כנ"ל אות שדמ. נוה ירק, באה"ק ת"ו. ה'תשמ"ה. רצז דף.
ב'תקט. כנ"ל אות שדמ. נחם, באה"ק ת"ו. ה'תשמ"ה. רצז דף.
ב'תקי. כנ"ל אות שדמ. נס הרים, באה"ק ת"ו. ה'תשמ"ה. רצז דף.
ב'תקיא. כנ"ל אות שדמ. סלעית, באה"ק ת"ו. ה'תשמ"ה. רצז דף.
ב'תקיב. כנ"ל אות שדמ. עגור, באה"ק ת"ו. ה'תשמ"ה. רצז דף.
ב'תקיג. כנ"ל אות שדמ. עדנים — נוה נאמן, באה"ק ת"ו. ה'תשמ"ה. רצז דף.
ב'תקיד. כנ"ל אות שדמ. עופרה, באה"ק ת"ו. ה'תשמ"ה. רצז דף.
ב'תקטו. כנ"ל אות שדמ. עזריה, באה"ק ת"ו. ה'תשמ"ה. רצז דף.
ב'תקטז. כנ"ל אות שדמ. עין ורד, באה"ק ת"ו. ה'תשמ"ה. רצז דף.
ב'תקיז. כנ"ל אות שדמ. פדייה, באה"ק ת"ו. ה'תשמ"ה. רצז דף.
ב'תקיח. כנ"ל אות שדמ. פעמי תש"ז, באה"ק ת"ו. ה'תשמ"ה. רצז דף.
ב'תקיט. כנ"ל אות שדמ. פרדסיה, באה"ק ת"ו. ה'תשמ"ה. רצז דף.
ב'תקכ. כנ"ל אות שדמ. פתחיה, באה"ק ת"ו. ה'תשמ"ה. רצז דף.
ב'תקכא. כנ"ל אות שדמ. צה"ל — בית גוברין, באה"ק ת"ו. ה'תשמ"ה. רצז דף.
ב'תקכב. כנ"ל אות שדמ. צה"ל — מחנה צאלים, באה"ק ת"ו. ה'תשמ"ה. רצז דף.
ב'תקכג. כנ"ל אות שדמ. צה"ל — תל נוף, באה"ק ת"ו. ה'תשמ"ה. רצז דף.
ב'תקכד. כנ"ל אות שדמ. צופית, באה"ק ת"ו. ה'תשמ"ה. רצז דף.
ב'תקכה. כנ"ל אות שדמ. צור הדסה, באה"ק ת"ו. ה'תשמ"ה. רצז דף.
ב'תקכו. כנ"ל אות שדמ. צור משא, באה"ק ת"ו. ה'תשמ"ה. רצז דף.
ב'תקכז. כנ"ל אות שדמ. צור נתן, באה"ק ת"ו. ה'תשמ"ה. רצז דף.
ב'תקכח. כנ"ל אות שדמ. צלפון, באה"ק ת"ו. ה'תשמ"ה. רצז דף.
ב'תקכט. כנ"ל אות שדמ. צפרירים, באה"ק ת"ו. ה'תשמ"ה. רצז דף.
ב'תקל. כנ"ל אות שדמ. קיבוץ גבע, באה"ק ת"ו. ה'תשמ"ה. רצז דף.
ב'תקלא. כנ"ל אות שדמ. קיבוץ כפר החורש, באה"ק ת"ו. ה'תשמ"ה. רצז דף.
ב'תקלב. כנ"ל אות שדמ. קיבוץ כפר עציון, באה"ק ת"ו. ה'תשמ"ה. רצז דף.
ב'תקלג. כנ"ל אות שדמ. קיבוץ מסדה, באה"ק ת"ו. תשמ"ה. רצז דף.
ב'תקלד. כנ"ל אות שדמ. קיבוץ משמר דוד, באה"ק ת"ו. ה'תשמ"ה. רצז דף.
ב'תקלה. כנ"ל אות שדמ. קיבוץ משמר השרון, באה"ק ת"ו. ה'תשמ"ה. רצז דף.
ב'תקלו. כנ"ל אות שדמ. קיבוץ נחשון, באה"ק ת"ו. ה'תשמ"ה. רצז דף.
ב'תקלז. כנ"ל אות שדמ. קיבוץ נתיב הל"ה, באה"ק ת"ו. ה'תשמ"ה. רצז דף.
ב'תקלח. כנ"ל אות שדמ. קיבוץ צרעה, באה"ק ת"ו. ה'תשמ"ה. רצז דף.
ב'תקלט. כנ"ל אות שדמ. קיבוץ רמת הכובש, באה"ק ת"ו. ה'תשמ"ה. רצז דף.
ב'תקמ. כנ"ל אות שדמ. קיבוץ שפיים, באה"ק ת"ו. תשמ"ה. רצז דף.
ב'תקמא. כנ"ל אות שדמ. קיבוץ תל קציר, באה"ק ת"ו. ה'תשמ"ה. רצז דף.
ב'תקמב. כנ"ל אות שדמ. רוגלית, באה"ק ת"ו. ה'תשמ"ה. רצז דף.
ב'תקמג. כנ"ל אות שדמ. רמת השבים, באה"ק ת"ו. ה'תשמ"ה. רצז דף.
ב'תקמד. כנ"ל אות שדמ. רמת רזיאל, באה"ק ת"ו. ה'תשמ"ה. רצז דף.
ב'תקמה. כנ"ל אות שדמ. רשפון, באה"ק ת"ו. ה'תשמ"ה. רצז דף.
ב'תקמו. כנ"ל אות שדמ. שדה חמד, באה"ק ת"ו. ה'תשמ"ה. רצז דף.
ב'תקמז. כנ"ל אות שדמ. שדה וורבורג, באה"ק ת"ו. ה'תשמ"ה. רצז דף.
ב'תקמח. כנ"ל אות שדמ. שדה צבי, באה"ק ת"ו. ה'תשמ"ה. רצז דף.
ב'תקמט. כנ"ל אות שדמ. שילה, באה"ק ת"ו. ה'תשמ"ה. רצז דף.
ב'תקנ. כנ"ל אות שדמ. שערי תקוה, באה"ק ת"ו. ה'תשמ"ה. רצז דף.
ב'תקנא. כנ"ל אות שדמ. תלמונד, באה"ק ת"ו. ה'תשמ"ה. רצז דף.
ב'תקנב. כנ"ל אות שדמ. תלמי מנשה, באה"ק ת"ו. ה'תשמ"ה. רצז דף.
ב'תקנג. כנ"ל אות שדמ. תעוז, באה"ק ת"ו. ה'תשמ"ה. רצז דף.
ב'תקנד. כנ"ל אות שדמ. תקוע, באה"ק ת"ו. ה'תשמ"ה. רצז דף.
ב'תקנה. כנ"ל אות שדמ. תרום, באה"ק ת"ו. ה'תשמ"ה. רצז דף.
ב'תקנו. כנ"ל אות שדמ. מאינץ, גרמניא. ה'תשמ"ה. רצז דף.
ב'תקנז. כו"ל אות שדמ. ארלע, צרפת. ה'תשמ"ה. רצז דף.
ב'תקנח. כנ"ל אות שדמ. באניי, צרפת. ה'תשמ"ה. רצז דף.
ב'תקנט. כנ"ל אות שדמ. בישווילער, צרפת. ה'תשמ"ה. רצז דף.
ב'תקס. כנ"ל אות שדמ. ברומאט, צרפת. ה'תשמ"ה. רצז דף.
ב'תקסא. כנ"ל אות שדמ. גאנעס, צרפת. ה'תשמ"ה. רצז דף.
ב'תקסב. כנ"ל אות שדמ. גראסבליעדערסטאף, צרפת. ה'תשמ"ה. רצז דף.
ב'תקסג. כנ"ל אות שדמ. דיעמערינגען, צרפת. ה'תשמ"ה. רצז דף.
ב'תקסד. כנ"ל אות שדמ. דעטווילער, צרפת. ה'תשמ"ה. רצז דף.
ב'תקסה. כנ"ל אות שדמ. האיאנז, צרפת. ה'תשמ"ה. רצז דף.
ב'תקסו. כנ"ל אות שדמ. האשפעלדען, צרפת. ה'תשמ"ה. רצז דף.

ב׳תקסז. כנ״ל אות שדמ. הגאנדאז, צרפת. ה׳תשמ״ה. רצז דף.
ב׳תקסח. כנ״ל אות שדמ. וואלפיסהיים, צרפת. ה׳תשמ״ה. רצז דף.
ב׳תקסט. כנ״ל אות שדמ. ווייסענבורג, צרפת. ה׳תשמ״ה. רצז דף.
ב׳תקע. כנ״ל אות שדמ. ווילע, צרפת. ה׳תשמ״ה. רצז דף.
ב׳תקעא. כנ״ל אות שדמ. וועסטהאפען, צרפת. ה׳תשמ״ה. רצז דף.
ב׳תקעב. כנ״ל אות שדמ. זענטאי, צרפת. ה׳תשמ״ה. רצז דף.
ב׳תקעג. כנ״ל אות שדמ. טרעסערוו, צרפת. ה׳תשמ״ה. רצז דף.
ב׳תקעד. כנ״ל אות שדמ. יסמינג, צרפת. ה׳תשמ״ה. רצז דף.
ב׳תקעה. כנ״ל אות שדמ. לונעל, צרפת. ה׳תשמ״ה. רצז דף.
ב׳תקעו. כנ״ל אות שדמ. לימיי ברעוואן, צרפת. ה׳תשמ״ה. רצז דף.
ב׳תקעז. כנ״ל אות שדמ. לינגאלסהיים, צרפת. ה׳תשמ״ה. רצז דף.
ב׳תקעח. כנ״ל אות שדמ. ליקסהים, צרפת. ה׳תשמ״ה. רצז דף.
ב׳תקעט. כנ״ל אות שדמ. מוטציק, צרפת. ה׳תשמ״ה. רצז דף.
ב׳תקפ. כנ״ל אות שדמ. מלסהיים, צרפת. ה׳תשמ״ה. רצז דף.
ב׳תקפא. כנ״ל אות שדמ. מערלבאך, צרפת. ה׳תשמ״ה. רצז דף.
ב׳תקפב. כנ״ל אות שדמ. מרקאלסעיים, צרפת. ה׳תשמ״ה. רצז דף.
ב׳תקפג. כנ״ל אות שדמ. סאווערן, צרפת. ה׳תשמ״ה. רצז דף.
ב׳תקפד. כנ״ל אות שדמ. סאראוניאן, צרפת. ה׳תשמ״ה. רצז דף.
ב׳תקפה. כנ״ל אות שדמ. סולץ סו פארעט, צרפת. ה׳תשמ״ה. רצז דף.
ב׳תקפו. כנ״ל אות שדמ. עגענהיים, צרפת. ה׳תשמ״ה. רצז דף.
ב׳תקפז. כנ״ל אות שדמ. רייליו, צרפת. ה׳תשמ״ה. רצז דף.
ב׳תקפח. כנ״ל אות שדמ. רמבויעט, צרפת. ה׳תשמ״ה. רצז דף.
ב׳תקפט. כנ״ל אות שדמ. רסהים, צרפת. ה׳תשמ״ה. רצז דף.
ב׳תקצ. כנ״ל אות שדמ. כפר אדומים, באה״ק. ה׳תשמ״ה. רצז דף.
ב׳תקצא. כנ״ל אות שדמ. ניר גלים, באה״ק. ה׳תשמ״ה. רצז דף.
ב׳תקצב. כנ״ל אות שדמ. צה״ל — חיל הים, אשדוד, באה״ק. ה׳תשמ״ה. רצז דף.
ב׳תקצג. כנ״ל אות שדמ. צה״ל — ג׳בליה, באה״ק. ה׳תשמ״ה. רצז דף.
ב׳תקצד. כנ״ל אות שדמ. קדימה, באה״ק. ה׳תשמ״ה. רצז דף.
ב׳תקצה. כנ״ל אות שדמ. תל חנן, באה״ק. ה׳תשמ״ה. רצז דף.
ב׳תקצו. כנ״ל אות שדמ. גאלף מאנאר, אהייא. ה׳תשמ״ה. (6) רצז דף.
ב׳תקצז. כנ״ל אות שלה. שכונת בענסאנהורסט, ברוקלין, נ.י. ה׳תשמ״ה. (6) רצז דף.
ב׳תקצח. כנ״ל אות שלה. סקאטסדייל, אריזאנא. ה׳תשמ״ה. (6) רצז דף.
ב׳תקצט. כנ״ל אות שלה. פועבלא מעקסיקא. ה׳תשמ״ה. (6) רצז דף.
ב׳תר. כנ״ל אות ריג. עם תרגום האנגלי (עמוד התרגום מול עמוד התניא). בסופו: תמונת אדה״ז. קייפ טאון, דרום אפריקא. ה׳תשמ״ה. 1050 pp.
ב׳תרא. כנ״ל אות שלה. אמסטערדאם, נ. י. ה׳תשמ״ה. (6) ש דף.
ב׳תרב. כנ״ל אות שלה. אניאנטא, נ.י. ה׳תשמ״ה. (6) ש דף.
ב׳תרג. כנ״ל אות שלה. גלאווערסוויל, נ. י. ה׳תשמ״ה. (6) ש דף.
ב׳תרד. כנ״ל אות שלה. האנטער, נ. י. ה׳תשמ״ה. (6) ש דף.
ב׳תרה. כנ״ל אות שלה. הערקימער, נ. י. ה׳תשמ״ה. (6) ש דף.
ב׳תרו. כנ״ל אות שלה. וואפינגערס פאלס, נ. י. ה׳תשמ״ה. (6) ש דף.
ב׳תרז. כנ״ל אות שלה. וואודסטאק, נ. י. ה׳תשמ״ה. (6) ש דף.
ב׳תרח. כנ״ל אות שלה. לאק שעלדרייק, נ. י. ה׳תשמ״ה. (6) ש דף.
ב׳תרט. כנ״ל אות שלה. לייק דזשארדזש, נ. י. ה׳תשמ״ה. (6) ש דף.
ב׳תרי. כנ״ל אות שלה. לייק פלאסיד, נ. י. ה׳תשמ״ה. (6) ש דף.
ב׳תריא. כנ״ל אות שלה. מילטאן, נ. י. ה׳תשמ״ה. (6) ש דף.
ב׳תריב. כנ״ל אות שלה. ניו פאלץ, נ. י. ה׳תשמ״ה. (6) ש דף.
ב׳תריג. כנ״ל אות שלה. אהאי, קאליפארניא. ה׳תשמ״ה. (6) ש דף.
ב׳תריד. כנ״ל אות שלה. אקסנארד, קאליפארניא. ה׳תשמ״ה. (6) ש דף.

ב׳תרטו. כנ״ל אות שלה. ווענטורא (בואינא), קאליפארניא. ה׳תשמ״ה. (6) ש דף.
ב׳תרטז. כנ״ל אות שלה. וויינימי, קאליפארניא. ה׳תשמ״ה. (6) ש דף.
ב׳תריז. כנ״ל אות שלה. מורפארק, קאליפארניא. ה׳תשמ״ה. (6) ש דף.
ב׳תריח. כנ״ל אות שלה. סימי וואלי, קאליפארניא. ה׳תשמ״ה. (6) ש דף.
ב׳תריט. כנ״ל אות שלה. פאולא, קאליפארניא. ה׳תשמ״ה. (6) ש דף.
ב׳כתר. כנ״ל אות שלה. קאמאריא, קאליפארניא. ה׳תשמ״ה. (6) ש דף.
ב׳תרכא. כנ״ל אות שלה. אינוואוד, לאנג איילאנד, נ.י. ה׳תשמ״ה. (6) רצט דף.
ב׳תרכב. כנ״ל אות שלה. יולעט, לאנג איילאנד, נ.י. ה׳תשמ״ה. (6) רצט דף.
ב׳תרכג. כנ״ל אות שלה. נארט וואודמיר, לאנג איילאנד, נ.י. ה׳תשמ״ה. (6) רצט דף.
ב׳תרכד. כנ״ל אות שלה. נארט ווייל, ניו דזוירסי. ה׳תשמ״ה. (6) ש דף.
ב׳תרכה. כנ״ל אות ריג. עם תרגום אנגלי. טשעלסי, מישיגען. ה׳תשמ״ה.
ב׳תרכו. כנ״ל אות שלה. מעסינא, דרום אפריקא. ה׳תשמ״ה. (6) רצט דף.
ב׳תרכז. כנ״ל אות שלה. לעיק פארעסט, אילינאי. ה׳תשמ״ה. (6) רצט דף.
ב׳תרכח. כנ״ל אות שלה. דזשאנסאן סיטי, נ.י. ה׳תשמ״ה. (6) רצט דף.
ב׳תרכט. כנ״ל אות שלה. וועסטעל, נ.י. ה׳תשמ״ה. (6) רצט דף.
ב׳תרל. כנ״ל אות שלה. ענדיקאט, נ.י. ה׳תשמ״ה. (6) רצט דף.
ב׳תרלא. כנ״ל אות שלה. אמאגאנסעט, לאנג, איילאנד, נ.י. ה׳תשמ״ה. (6) ש דף.
ב׳תרלב. כנ״ל אות שלה. אפאקואג, לאנג איילאנד, נ.י. ה׳תשמ״ה. (6) ש דף.
ב׳תרלג. כנ״ל אות שלה. בארנס האל, לאנג איילאנד, נ.י. ה׳תשמ״ה. (6) ש דף.
ב׳תרלד. כנ״ל אות שלה. ברידזשהאמפטאן, לאנג איילאנד, נ.י. ה׳תשמ״ה. (6) ש דף.
ב׳תרלה. כנ״ל אות שלה. דזשארדזשיקא, לאנג איילאנד, נ.י. ה׳תשמ״ה. (6) ש דף.
ב׳תרלו. כנ״ל אות שלה. דזשעריקא, לאנג איילאנד, נ.י. ה׳תשמ״ה. (6) ש דף.
ב׳תרלז. כנ״ל אות שלה. דירפילד, לאנג איילאנד, נ.י. ה׳תשמ״ה. (6) ש דף.
ב׳תרלח. כנ״ל אות שלה. דעוואן, לאנג איילאנד, נ.י. ה׳תשמ״ה. (6) ש דף.
ב׳תרלט. כנ״ל אות שלה. האמפטאן בייס, לאנג איילאנד, נ.י. ה׳תשמ״ה. (6) ש דף.
ב׳תרמ. כנ״ל אות שלה. האמפטאן פארק, לאנג איילאנד, נ.י. ה׳תשמ״ה. (6) ש דף.
ב׳תרמא. כנ״ל אות שלה. הארדסקראבל, לאנג איילאנד, נ.י. ה׳תשמ״ה. (6) ש דף.
ב׳תרמב. כנ״ל אות שלה. הייגראונד, לאנג איילאנד, נ.י. ה׳תשמ״ה. (6) ש דף.
ב׳תרמג. כנ״ל אות שלה. וואטער מיל, לאנג איילאנד, נ.י. ה׳תשמ״ה. (6) ש דף.
ב׳תרמד. כנ״ל אות שלה. וויינסקאט, לאנג איילאנד, נ.י. ה׳תשמ״ה. (6) ש דף.
ב׳תרמה. כנ״ל אות שלה. וויקאפואג, לאנג איילאנד, נ.י. ה׳תשמ״ה. (6) ש דף.
ב׳תרמו. כנ״ל אות שלה. אלינדא, בראזיל. ה׳תשמ״ה. (6) ש דף.
ב׳תרמז. כנ״ל אות שלה. ארטיגאס, אורוגוואי. ה׳תשמ״ה. (6) ש דף.

ב׳תרמח. כנ״ל אות שלה. טאקוארעמא, אורוגוואיי. ה׳תשמ״ה. (6) ש דף.
ב׳תרמט. כנ״ל אות שלה. מעלא, אורוגוואיי. ה׳תשמ״ה. (6) ש דף.
ב׳תרן. כנ״ל אות שלה. ריווערא, אורוגוואיי. ה׳תשמ״ה. (6) ש דף.
ב׳תרנא. כנ״ל אות שלה. ליווראמענטא, ריא גראנדע דא סול, בראזיל. ה׳תשמ״ה. (6) ש דף.
ב׳תרנב. כנ״ל אות שדמ. גאלדערס גרין, לאנדאן, אנגליא. ה׳תשמ״ה. (6) ש דף.
ב׳תרנג. כנ״ל אות שלה. פלאריאנאפאליס, בראזיל. ה׳תשמ״ה. (6) ש דף.
ב׳תרנד. כנ״ל אות שלה. קאשיאס דא סול, ר. גראנדע, דא סול, בראזיל. ה׳תשמ״ה. (6) ש דף.
ב׳תרנה. כנ״ל אות שלה. טרימייל הארבאר, לאנג איילאנד, נ.י. ה׳תשמ״ה. (6) ש דף.
ב׳תרנו. כנ״ל אות שלה. מעקאקס, לאנג איילאנד, נ.י. ה׳תשמ״ה. (6) ש דף.
ב׳תרנז. כנ״ל אות שלה. נאיאק, לאנג איילאנד, נ.י. ה׳תשמ״ה. (6) ש דף.
ב׳תרנח. כנ״ל אות שלה. נאפואג, לאנג איילאנד, נ.י. ה׳תשמ״ה. (6) ש דף.
ב׳תרנט. כנ״ל אות שלה. נארט הייווען, לאנג איילאנד, נ.י. ה׳תשמ״ה. (6) ש דף.
ב׳תרס. כנ״ל אות שלה. תיאנא, לאנג איילאנד, נ.י. ה׳תשמ״ה. (6) ש דף.
ב׳תרסא. כנ״ל אות שלה. וועסט תיאנא, לאנג איילאנד, נ.י. ה׳תשמ״ה. (6) ש דף.
ב׳תרסב. כנ״ל אות שלה. ׳פראמיסד לאנד, לאנג איילאנד, נ.י. ה׳תשמ״ה. (6) ש דף.
ב׳תרסג. כנ״ל אות שלה. נארט סי, לאנג איילאנד, נ.י. ה׳תשמ״ה. (6) ש דף.
ב׳תרסד. כנ״ל אות שלה. סאגפאנאק, לאנג איילאנד, נ.י. ה׳תשמ״ה. (6) ש דף.
ב׳תרסה. כנ״ל אות שלה. סאוטפארט, לאנג איילאנד, נ.י. ה׳תשמ״ה. (6) ש דף.
ב׳תרסו. כנ״ל אות שלה. ספרינגוויל, לאנג איילאנד, נ.י. ה׳תשמ״ה. (6) ש דף.
ב׳תרסז. כנ״ל אות שלה. ספרינגס, לאנג איילאנד, נ.י. ה׳תשמ״ה. (6) ש דף.
ב׳תרסח. כנ״ל אות שלה. סקאטלהאל, לאנג איילאנד, נ.י. ה׳תשמ״ה. (6) ש דף.
ב׳תרסט. כנ״ל אות שלה. סקוויירטאון, לאנג איילאנד, נ.י. ה׳תשמ״ה. (6) ש דף.
ב׳עתר. כנ״ל אות שלה. פאנטיגוא, לאנג איילאנד, נ.י. ה׳תשמ״ה. (6) ש דף.
ב׳תרעא. כנ״ל אות שלה. פאנקואג, לאנג איילאנד, נ.י. ה׳תשמ״ה. (6) ש דף.
ב׳תערב. כנ״ל אות שלה. פייערפלייס, לאנג איילאנד, נ.י. ה׳תשמ״ה. (6) ש דף.
ב׳תרעג. כנ״ל אות שלה. פלייאינג פאינט, לאנג איילאנד, נ.י. ה׳תשמ״ה. (6) ש דף.
ב׳עדרת. כנ״ל אות שלה. פריטאון, לאנג איילאנד, נ.י. ה׳תשמ״ה. (6) ש דף.
ב׳תרעה. כנ״ל אות שלה. קאנו פלייס, לאנג איילאנד, נ.י. ה׳תשמ״ה. (6) ש דף.
ב׳תרעו. כנ״ל אות שלה. קינגסטאון, לאנג איילאנד, נ.י. ה׳תשמ״ה. (6) ש דף.
ב׳תרעז. כנ״ל אות שלה. ראוז גראוו, לאנג איילאנד, נ.י. ה׳תשמ״ה. (6) ש דף.
ב׳תרעח. כנ״ל אות שלה. שינעקאק הילס, לאנג איילאנד, נ.י. ה׳תשמ״ה. (6) ש דף.
ב׳תרעט. כנ״ל אות שלה. אושענסייד, לאנג איילאנד, נ.י. ה׳תשמ״ה. (6) ש דף.

ב׳תרפ. כנ״ל אות שלה. ענדוועל, נ.י. ה׳תשמ״ה. (6) ש דף.
ב׳תרפא. כנ״ל אות שלה. ענגלוואוד קליפס, ניו דזוירסי. ה׳תשמ״ה. (6) ש דף.
ב׳תרפב. כנ״ל אות שלה. ריווער ווייל, ניו דזוירסי. ה׳תשמ״ה. (6) ש דף.
ב׳תרפג. כנ״ל אות שלה. פארטאלעזא, סעארא, בראזיל. ה׳תשמ״ה. (6) ש דף.
ב׳תרפד. כנ״ל אות שלה. סאלוואדאר, באיא, בראזיל. ה׳תשמ״ה. (6) ש דף.
ב׳תרפה. כנ״ל אות שלה. פעירבאנקס, אלאסקא. ה׳תשמ״ה. (6) ש דף.
ב׳תרפו. כנ״ל אות שדמ. אנס־אן־סי, אנגליא. ה׳תשמ״ה. (6) ש דף.
ב׳תרפז. כנ״ל אות שדמ. בלאקבורן, אנגליא. ה׳תשמ״ה. (6) ש דף.
ב׳תרפח. כנ״ל אות שדמ. בלאקפול, אנגליא. ה׳תשמ״ה. (6) ש דף.
ב׳תרפט. כנ״ל אות שדמ. סאוטפארט, אנגליא. ה׳תשמ״ה. (6) ש דף.
ב׳תרצ. כנ״ל אות שדמ. סעיל, אנגליא. ה׳תשמ״ה. (6) ש דף.
ב׳תרצא. כנ״ל אות שדמ. פרעסטאן, אנגליא. ה׳תשמ״ה. (6) ש דף.
ב׳תרצב. כנ״ל אות שדמ. אמאדאבעד, אינדיא (הודו). ה׳תשמ״ה. (6) ש דף.
ב׳תרצג. כנ״ל אות שדמ. ניו דעלהי, אינדיא (הודו). ה׳תשמ״ה. (6) ש דף.
ב׳תרצד. כנ״ל אות שדמ. פונא, אינדיא (הודו). ה׳תשמ״ה. (6) ש דף.
ב׳תרצה. כנ״ל אות שדמ. קאראשי, פאקיסטאן. ה׳תשמ״ה. (6) ש דף.
ב׳תרצו. כנ״ל אות שדמ. אוניברסיטת בר־אילן, באה״ק ת״ו. ה׳תשמ״ה. (6) שב דף.
ב׳תרצז. כנ״ל אות שדמ. אלפי מנשה, באה״ק ת״ו. ה׳תשמ״ה. (6) שב דף.
ב׳תרחצ. כנ״ל אות שדמ. בורגתא, באה״ק ת״ו. ה׳תשמ״ה. (6) שב דף.
ב׳תרצט. כנ״ל אות שדמ. ברקן, באה״ק ת״ו. ה׳תשמ״ה. (6) שב דף.
ב׳תש. כנ״ל אות שדמ. בית אגודת חסידי חב״ד אהל יוסף יצחק ליובאוויטש — כפר חב״ד, באה״ק ת״ו. ה׳תשמ״ה. (6) שב דף.
ב׳תשא. כנ״ל אות שדמ. גבעת זאב, באה״ק ת״ו. ה׳תשמ״ה. (6) שב דף.
ב׳תשב. כנ״ל אות שדמ. גבעון החדשה, באה״ק ת״ו. ה׳תשמ״ה. (6) שב דף.
ב׳תשג. כנ״ל אות שלה. אורוגוואייאנא, בראזיל. ה׳תשמ״ה. (6) שב דף.
ב׳תשד. כנ״ל אות שלה. אלטא, בראזיל. ה׳תשמ״ה. (6) ש דף.
ב׳תשה. כנ״ל אות שלה. באזשע, בראזיל. ה׳תשמ״ה. (6) ש דף.
ב׳תשו. כנ״ל אות שלה. מאריא, בראזיל. ה׳תשמ״ה. (6) ש דף.
ב׳תשז. כנ״ל אות שלה. נאווא האמבורג, בראזיל. ה׳תשמ״ה. (6) ש דף.
ב׳תשח. כנ״ל אות שלה. ראזאריא, בראזיל. ה׳תשמ״ה. (6) ש דף.
ב׳תשט. כנ״ל אות שלה. מינאס, אורוגוויי. ה׳תשמ״ה. (6) ש דף.
ב׳תשי. כנ״ל אות שדמ. גדיד — חבל עזה, באה״ק ת״ו. ה׳תשמ״ה. (6) שב דף.
ב׳תשיא. כנ״ל אות שדמ. גינות שומרון, באה״ק ת״ו. ה׳תשמ״ה. (6) שב דף.
ב׳תשיב. כנ״ל אות שדמ. גניטל — חבל עזה, באה״ק ת״ו. ה׳תשמ״ה. (6) שב דף.
ב׳תשיג. כנ״ל אות שדמ. המדפיס הממשלתי — ירושלים ת״ו. ה׳תשמ״ה. (6) שב דף.
ב׳תשיד. כנ״ל אות שדמ. חגור, באה״ק ת״ו. ה׳תשמ״ה. (6) שב דף.
ב׳תשטו. כנ״ל אות שדמ. חניאל, באה״ק ת״ו. ה׳תשמ״ה. (6) שב דף.
ב׳תשטז. כנ״ל אות שדמ. יקיר, באה״ק ת״ו. ה׳תשמ״ה. (6) שב דף.
ב׳תשיז. כנ״ל אות שדמ. ירוחם, באה״ק ת״ו. ה׳תשמ״ה. (6) שב דף.

ב'תשיח. כנ"ל אות שדמ. ירחיב, באה"ק ת"ו. ה'תשמ"ה. (6) שב דף.

ב'תשיט. כנ"ל אות שדמ. כפר דרום — חבל עזה, באה"ק ת"ו. ה'תשמ"ה. (6) שב דף.

ב'תשכ. כנ"ל אות שדמ. כפר הנוער נוה הדסה, באה"ק ת"ו. ה'תשמ"ה. (6) שב דף.

ב'תשכא.כנ"ל אות שדמ. כפר הנוער רזיאל, באה"ק ת"ו. ה'תשמ"ה. (6) שב דף.

ב'תשכב.כנ"ל אות שדמ. כפר יונה, באה"ק ת"ו. ה'תשמ"ה. (6) שב דף.

ב'תשכג.כנ"ל אות שדמ. כפר יעבץ, באה"ק ת"ו. ה'תשמ"ה. (6) שב דף.

ב'תשכד.כנ"ל אות שדמ. מושב שובה, באה"ק ת"ו. ה'תשמ"ה. (6) שב דף.

ב'תשכה.כנ"ל אות שדמ. מעלה שומרון, באה"ק ת"ו. ה'תשמ"ה. (6) שב דף.

ב'תשכו. כנ"ל אות שדמ. נוה ימין, באה"ק ת"ו. ה'תשמ"ה. (6) שב דף.

ב'תשכז. כנ"ל אות שדמ. נצר חזני — חבל עזה, באה"ק ת"ו. ה'תשמ"ה. (6) שב דף.

ב'תשכח.כנ"ל אות שדמ. צה"ל — שבטה, באה"ק ת"ו. ה'תשמ"ה. (6) שב דף.

ב'תשכט.כנ"ל אות שדמ. צה"ל בח"א משאבים, באה"ק ת"ו. ה'תשמ"ה. (6) שב דף.

ב'תשל. כנ"ל אות שדמ. קטיף — חבל עזה, באה"ק ת"ו. ה'תשמ"ה. (6) שב דף.

ב'תשלא.כנ"ל אות שדמ. קיבוץ אלונים, באה"ק ת"ו. ה'תשמ"ה. (6) שב דף.

ב'תשלב.כנ"ל אות שדמ. קיבוץ חולתה, באה"ק ת"ו. ה'תשמ"ה. (6) שב דף.

ב'תשלג. כנ"ל אות שדמ. קיבוץ חפציבה, באה"ק ת"ו. ה'תשמ"ה. (6) שב דף.

ב'תשלד.כנ"ל אות שדמ. קיבוץ יפתח, באה"ק ת"ו. ה'תשמ"ה. (6) שב דף.

ב'תשלה.כנ"ל אות שדמ. קיבוץ לביא, באה"ק ת"ו. ה'תשמ"ה. (6) שב דף.

ב'תשלו. כנ"ל אות שדמ. קיבוץ ניר אליהו, באה"ק ת"ו. ה'תשמ"ה. (6) שב דף.

ב'תשלז. כנ"ל אות שדמ. קיבוץ נצרים — חבל עזה, באה"ק ת"ו. ה'תשמ"ה. (6) שב דף.

ב'תשלח.כנ"ל אות שדמ. קיבוץ צובה, באה"ק ת"ו. ה'תשמ"ה. (6) שב דף.

ב'תשלט.כנ"ל אות שדמ. קרית נטפים, באה"ק ת"ו. ה'תשמ"ה. (6) שב דף.

ב'תשמ. כנ"ל אות שדמ. רפיח ים — חבל עזה, באה"ק ת"ו. ה'תשמ"ה. (6) שב דף.

ב'תשמא.כנ"ל אות שדמ. שער אפרים, באה"ק ת"ו. ה'תשמ"ה. (6) שב דף.

ב'תשמב. כנ"ל אות שלה. פארט־או־פרינץ, האיטי. ה'תשמ"ה (6) שב דף.

ב'תשמג. כנ"ל אות שדמ. אמין, צרפת. ה'תשמ"ה. (6) שה דף.

ב'תשדמ. כנ"ל אות שדמ. פאסטאט, צרפת. ה'תשמ"ה (6) שה דף.

ב'תשמה. כנ"ל אות שדמ. קורדובה, (אנדאלוציא), ספרד — מקום הולדת הרמב"ם. ה'תשמ"ה שב דף.

ב'תשמו. כנ"ל אות שדמ. בספריית אגודת חסידי חב"ד — בית אגודת חסידי חב"ד — אהל יוסף יצחק ליובאוויטש, 770 איסטערן פארקוויי, ברוקלין, נ.י. יום הבהיר — ראש חודש כסלו ה'תשמ"ו. (6) שב דף.

ב'תשמז. כנ"ל אות שלה. מכון חנה, 1367 פרעזידענט סט., קראון הייטס, ברוקלין, נ.י. ה'תשמ"ז. (6) שב דף.

ב'תשמח.כנ"ל אות שלה. מכון חנה, 825 איסטערן פארקוויי, קראון הייטס, ברוקלין, נ.י. ה'תשמ"ז. (6) שב דף.

ב'תשמט.כנ"ל אות שדמ. אבאן, צרפת. ה'תשמ"ה. (6) שה דף.

ב'תשנ. כנ"ל אות שדמ. אולען, צרפת. ה'תשמ"ה. (6) שה דף.

ב'תשנא. כנ"ל אות שדמ. אזאקיא־קארט, צרפת. ה'תשמ"ה. (6) שה דף.

ב'תשנב. כנ"ל אות שדמ. אלאש, צרפת. ה'תשמ"ה. (6) שה דף.

ב'תשנג. כנ"ל אות שדמ. בוק בעלער, צרפת. ה'תשמ"ה. (6) שה דף.

ב'תשנד. כנ"ל אות שדמ. בלויער, צרפת. ה'תשמ"ה. (6) שה דף.

ב'תשנה. כנ"ל אות שדמ. בראן, צרפת. ה'תשמ"ה. (6) שה דף.

ב'תשנו. כנ"ל אות שדמ. געווילער, צרפת. ה'תשמ"ה. (6) שה דף.

ב'תשנז. כנ"ל אות שדמ. דאוויל, צרפת. ה'תשמ"ה. (6) שה דף.

ב'תשנח. כנ"ל אות שדמ. דעסון שארפיע, צרפת. ה'תשמ"ה. (6) שה דף.

ב'תשנט. כנ"ל אות שדמ. דרנאך, צרפת. ה'תשמ"ה. (6) שה דף.

ב'תשס. כנ"ל אות שדמ. הארבורג, צרפת. ה'תשמ"ה. (6) שה דף.

ב'תשסא.כנ"ל אות שדמ. היער, צרפת. ה'תשמ"ה. (6) שה דף.

ב'תשסב.כנ"ל אות שדמ. וואל אן וועלא, צרפת. ה'תשמ"ה. (6) שה דף.

ב'תשסג.כנ"ל אות שדמ. ווילנעוו לובעט, צרפת. ה'תשמ"ה. (6) שה דף.

ב'תשסד.כנ"ל אות שדמ. ווילפראז סור סאן, צרפת. ה'תשמ"ה. (6) שה דף.

ב'תשסה.כנ"ל אות שדמ. ווינגערסיין, צרפת. ה'תשמ"ה. (6) שה דף.

ב'תשסו. כנ"ל אות שדמ. זיוואר, צרפת. ה'תשמ"ה. (6) שה דף.

ב'תשסז. כנ"ל אות שדמ. טהען סערניי, צרפת. ה'תשמ"ה. (6) שה דף.

ב'תשסח.כנ"ל אות שדמ. טסע לא דעמי לון, צרפת. ה'תשמ"ה. (6) שה דף.

ב'תשסט.כנ"ל אות שדמ. לארען דו וואר, צרפת. ה'תשמ"ה. (6) שה דף.

ב'תשע. כנ"ל אות שדמ. מארינען, צרפת. ה'תשמ"ה. (6) שה דף.

ב'תשעא.כנ"ל אות שדמ. ממנהיים, צרפת. ה'תשמ"ה. (6) שה דף.

ב'תשעב.כנ"ל אות שדמ. מעציע, צרפת. ה'תשמ"ה. (6) שה דף.

ב'תשעג.כנ"ל אות שדמ. נידעבראן, צרפת. ה'תשמ"ה. (6) שה דף.

ב'תשעד.כנ"ל אות שדמ. נעף בריזעק, צרפת. ה'תשמ"ה. (6) שה דף.

ב'תשעה.כנ"ל אות שדמ. סולץ, צרפת. ה'תשמ"ה. (6) שה דף.

ב'תשעו. כנ"ל אות שדמ. סלון אן פראוועגס, צרפת. ה'תשמ"ה. (6) שה דף.

ב'תשעז. כנ"ל אות שדמ. עקולוי, צרפת. ה'תשמ"ה. (6) שה דף.

ב'תשעח.כנ"ל אות שדמ. ערשטיין, צרפת. ה'תשמ"ה. (6) שה דף.

ב'תשעט.כנ"ל אות שדמ. פאנטען סור סאן, צרפת. ה'תשמ"ה. (6) שה דף.

ב'תשפ. כנ"ל אות שדמ. פארט דעבוק, צרפת. ה'תשמ"ה. (6) שה דף.

ב'תשפא.כנ"ל אות שדמ. סלאן דע כוק, צרפת. ה'תשמ"ה. (6) שה דף.

ב'תשפב.כנ"ל אות שדמ. סוא לע ליאון, צרפת. ה'תשמ"ה. (6) שה דף.

ב'תשפג.כנ"ל אות שדמ. פריעסט, צרפת. ה'תשמ"ה. (6) שה דף.

ב'תשפד.כנ"ל אות שדמ. קאוויאן, צרפת. ה'תשמ"ה. (6) שה דף.

ב'תשפה.כנ"ל אות שדמ. קאלס קאברי, צרפת. ה'תשמ"ה. (6) שה דף.

ב'תשפו. כנ"ל אות שדמ. קצענהים, צרפת. ה'תשמ"ה. (6) שה דף.

ב'תשפז. כנ"ל אות שדמ. קראפאן, צרפת. ה'תשמ"ה. (6) שה דף.

ב'תשפח.כנ"ל אות שדמ. קרבאס, צרפת. ה'תשמ"ה. (6) שה דף.

ב'תשפט.כנ"ל אות שדמ. שטעלרוט, צרפת. ה'תשמ"ה. (6) שה דף.

ב'תשצ. כנ"ל אות שדמ. שטרוט, צרפת. ה'תשמ"ה. (6) שה דף.

ב'תשצא.כנ"ל אות שדמ. שמפאן מאנט דאר, צרפת. ה'תשמ"ה. (6) שה דף.

ב'תשצב.כנ"ל אות שדמ. אמשטרדם, האלאנד. ה'תשמ"ו. (6) שה דף.

ב׳תשצג. כנ״ל אות שלה. אניסטאון, אלאבאמא. ה׳תשמ״ז. (6) שה דף.
ב׳תשצד. כנ״ל אות שלה. שאמפיין, אילינאי. ה׳תשמ״ז. (6) שז דף.
ב׳תשצה. כנ״ל אות שלה. בית האסורים דזשאליעט, דזשאליעט, אילינאי. חג הגאולה י״ט כסלו, ה׳תשמ״ה. (6) שז דף.
ב׳תשצו. כנ״ל אות שלה. בולאוואיא, זימבאבווי. ה׳תשמ״ז. (6) שה דף.
ב׳תשצז. כנ״ל אות שלה. דזשארדזש, סאוט אפריקא. ה׳תשמ״ז. (6) שה דף.
ב׳תשצח. כנ״ל אות שלה. יוטענהייג, סאוט אפריקא. ה׳תשמ״ו. (6) שה דף.
ב׳תשצט. כנ״ל אות שלה. מאביל, אלאבאמא. ה׳תשמ״ז. (6) שה דף.
ב׳תת. כנ״ל אות שדמ. בי״ס בית רבקה — ע״י בנות חב״ד — 310 קראון סטריט, ברוקלין, נ.י. כ״ף מרחשון, ה׳תשמ״ז. (6) שז דף.
ב׳תתא. כנ״ל אות שדמ. קאטשין, אינדיא (הודו). ה׳תשמ״ז. (6) שז דף.
ב׳תתב. כנ״ל אות שדמ. קאלקאטא, אינדיא (הודו). ה׳תשמ״ז. (6) שז דף.
ב׳תתג. כנ״ל אות שדמ. קאטמאנדו, נעפאל. ה׳תשמ״ז. (6) שז דף.
ב׳תתד. כנ״ל אות שדמ. ראנגון, בורמא. ה׳תשמ״ז. (6) שז דף.
ב׳תתה. כנ״ל אות שלה. גראנד הייווען, מישיגען. ה׳תשמ״ז. (6) שז דף.
ב׳תתו. כנ״ל אות שלה. האלאנד, מישיגען. ה׳תשמ״ז. (6) שז דף.
ב׳תתז. כנ״ל אות שלה. מאונט פלעזענט, מישיגען. ה׳תשמ״ז. (6) שז דף.
ב׳תתח. כנ״ל אות שלה. מאסקיגאן, מישיגען. ה׳תשמ״ז. (6) שז דף.
ב׳תתט. כנ״ל אות שלה. קאלאמאזו, מישיגען. ה׳תשמ״ז. (6) שז דף.
ב׳תתי. כנ״ל אות שלה. ארלינגטאן הייטס, אילינאי. ה׳תשמ״ז. (6) שז דף.
ב׳תתיא. כנ״ל אות שלה. באפאלא גראוו, אילינאי. ה׳תשמ״ז. (6) שז דף.
ב׳תתיב. כנ״ל אות שלה. גלענקאו, אילינאי. ה׳תשמ״ז. (6) שז דף.
ב׳תתיג. כנ״ל אות שלה. די פליינס, אילינאי. ה׳תשמ״ז. (6) שז דף.
ב׳תתיד. כנ״ל אות שלה. דיקאטור, אילינאי. ה׳תשמ״ז. (6) שז דף.
ב׳תתטו. כנ״ל אות שלה. האמוואוד, אילינאי. ה׳תשמ״ז. (6) שז דף.
ב׳תתטז. כנ״ל אות שלה. וואקיגען, אילינאי. ה׳תשמ״ז. (6) שז דף.
ב׳תתיז. כנ״ל אות שלה. ווינעטקא, אילינאי. ה׳תשמ״ז. (6) שז דף.
ב׳תתיח. כנ״ל אות שלה. ליבערטיוויל, אילינאי. ה׳תשמ״ז. (6) שז דף.
ב׳תתיט. כנ״ל אות שלה. מארטאן גראוו, אילינאי. ה׳תשמ״ז. (6) שז דף.
ב׳תתכ. כנ״ל אות שלה. פלאסמור, אילינאי. ה׳תשמ״ז. (6) שז דף.
ב׳תתכא. כנ״ל אות שלה. קאנקאקי, אילינאי. ה׳תשמ״ז. (6) שז דף.
ב׳תתכב. כנ״ל אות שלה. שאומבורג, אילינאי. ה׳תשמ״ז. (6) שז דף.
ב׳תתכג. כנ״ל אות שלה. חדר ליובאוויטש, וועסט ראדזשערס פארק, אילינאי. ה׳תשמ״ז. (6) שז דף.
ב׳תתכד. כנ״ל אות שלה. מישיגען סיטי, אינדיאנא. ה׳תשמ״ז. (6) שז דף.
ב׳תתכה. כנ״ל אות שלה. מונסי, אינדיאנא. ה׳תשמ״ז. (6) שז דף.
ב׳תתכו. כנ״ל אות שלה. אראשידיא, מרוקו. ה׳תשמ״ה. (6) שז דף.
ב׳תתכז. כנ״ל אות שלה. אושזדא, מרוקו. ה׳תשמ״ה. (6) שז דף.
ב׳תתכח. כנ״ל אות שלה. סיפרו, מרוקו. ה׳תשמ״ה. (6) שז דף.
ב׳תתכט. כנ״ל אות שלה. ריש, מרוקו. ה׳תשמ״ה. (6) שז דף.
ב׳תתל. כנ״ל אות שלה. אינזגאן, מרוקו. ה׳תשמ״ז. (6) שז דף.
ב׳תתלא. כנ״ל אות שלה. אל מוחמדיא, מרוקו. ה׳תשמ״ז. (6) שז דף.
ב׳תתלב. כנ״ל אות שלה. באר רשיד, מרוקו. ה׳תשמ״ז. (6) שז דף.
ב׳תתלג. כנ״ל אות שלה. טארודאנט, מרוקו. ה׳תשמ״ז. (6) שז דף.
ב׳תתלד. כנ״ל אות שלה. וואזאן, מרוקו. ה׳תשמ״ה. (6) שז דף.
ב׳תתלה. כנ״ל אות שלה. סוק א־ל ארבע, מרוקו. ה׳תשמ״ה. (6) שז דף.

ב׳תתלו. כנ״ל אות שלה. קסאר א־ל קביר, מרוקו. ה׳תשמ״ה. (6) שז דף.
ב׳תתלז. כנ״ל אות שלה. סאלי, מרוקו. ה׳תשמ״ז. (6) שז דף.
ב׳תתלח. כנ״ל אות שדמ. קואלא לומפור, מאלייזיא. ה׳תשמ״ז. (6) שז דף.
ב׳תתלט. כנ״ל אות שלה. שעפארטאן, אויסטראליא. ה׳תשמ״ז. (6) שז דף.
ב׳תתמ. כנ״ל אות שלה. כולל אברכים — מחנה ישראל — אהל יוסף יצחק ליובאוויטש, ברוקלין, נ.י. ה׳תשמ״ז. (6) שז דף.
ב׳תתמא. כנ״ל אות שלה. בני מילאל, מרוקו. ה׳תשמ״ה. (6) שז דף.
ב׳תתמב. כנ״ל אות שלה. דיבדו, מרוקו. ה׳תשמ״ה. (6) שז דף.
ב׳תתמג. כנ״ל אות שלה. דימנאת, מרוקו. ה׳תשמ״ה. (6) שז דף.
ב׳תתמד. כנ״ל אות שלה. מידלת, מרוקו. ה׳תשמ״ה. (6) שז דף.
ב׳תתמה. כנ״ל אות שלה. סיטאט, מרוקו. ה׳תשמ״ה. (6) שז דף.
ב׳תתמו. כנ״ל אות שלה. ערבאווא, מרוקו. ה׳תשמ״ה. (6) שז דף.
ב׳תתמז. כנ״ל אות שלה. תיזניט, מרוקו. ה׳תשמ״ה. (6) שז דף.
ב׳תתמח. כנ״ל אות שלה. הילקרעסט, נ.י. ה׳תשמ״ז. (6) שז דף.
ב׳תתמט. כנ״ל אות שלה. סאפורן, נ.י. ה׳תשמ״ז. (6) שז דף.
ב׳תתנ. כנ״ל אות שלה. פאמאנא, נ.י. ה׳תשמ״ז. (6) שז דף.
ב׳תתנא. כנ״ל אות שלה. מארקהעם, אנטעריא, קאנאדא. ה׳תשמ״ז. (6) שז דף.
ב׳תתנב. כנ״ל אות שלה. ביהכנ״ס אנ״ש דקראון הייטס, 770 מונטגומרי סט., ברוקלין, נ.י., כ״ד טבת תשמ״ז. (6) שז דף.
ב׳תתנג. כנ״ל אות שדמ. וואלווערהאמפטאן, וועסט מידלאנדס, אנגליא. ה׳תשמ״ז. (6) שז דף.
ב׳תתנד. כנ״ל אות תכ. אבידאס, בראזיל. ה׳תשמ״ז. (6) שז דף.
ב׳תתנה. כנ״ל אות תכ. איזאבעל, בראזיל. ה׳תשמ״ז. (6) שז דף.
ב׳תתנו. כנ״ל אות תכ. בעלעם, בראזיל. ה׳תשמ״ז. (6) שז דף.
ב׳תתנז. כנ״ל אות תכ. סאנטאריין, בראזיל. ה׳תשמ״ז. (6) שז דף.
ב׳תתנח. כנ״ל אות תכ. פארינטינס, בראזיל. ה׳תשמ״ז. (6) שז דף.
ב׳תתנט. כנ״ל אות שדמ. אדמות ישי (תל רומידה), באה״ק ת״ו. ה׳תשמ״ז. (6) שח דף.
ב׳תתס. כנ״ל אות שדמ. בייסינגסטאק, אנגליא. ה׳תשמ״ז. (6) שז דף.
ב׳תתסא. כנ״ל אות שדמ. דזשאנס וואוד, לונדון, אנגליא. ה׳תשמ״ז. (6) שז דף.
ב׳תתסב. כנ״ל אות שדמ. הענדאן, לונדון, אנגליא. ה׳תשמ״ז. (6) שז דף.
ב׳תתסג. כנ״ל אות שדמ. האמפסטעד, לונדון, אנגליא. ה׳תשמ״ז. (6) שז דף.
ב׳תתסד. כנ״ל אות שדמ. ווארטהינג, אנגליא. ה׳תשמ״ז. (6) שז דף.
ב׳תתסה. כנ״ל אות שדמ. וועלווין גארדען סיטי, אנגליא. ה׳תשמ״ז. (6) שז דף.
ב׳תתסו. כנ״ל אות שדמ. טשאטאם, אנגליא. ה׳תשמ״ז. (6) שז דף.
ב׳תתסז. כנ״ל אות שדמ. טשעלטענהאם, אנגליא. ה׳תשמ״ז. (6) שז דף.
ב׳תתסח. כנ״ל אות שדמ. מארגייט, אנגליא. ה׳תשמ״ז. (6) שז דף.
ב׳תתסט. כנ״ל אות שדמ. מייפעיר, לונדון, אנגליא. ה׳תשמ״ז. (6) שז דף.
ב׳תתע. כנ״ל אות שדמ. סטאמפארד היל, לונדון, אנגליא. ה׳תשמ״ז. (6) שז דף.
ב׳תתעא. כנ״ל אות שדמ. סטיינס, אנגליא. ה׳תשמ״ז. (6) שז דף.
ב׳תתעב. כנ״ל אות שדמ. ענפילד, מידלסעקס, אנגליא. ה׳תשמ״ז. (6) שז דף.
ב׳תתעג. כנ״ל אות שדמ. פינטשלי, לונדון, אנגליא. ה׳תשמ״ז. (6) שז דף.
ב׳תתעד. כנ״ל אות שדמ. קאוענטרי, אנגליא. תשמ״ז. (6) שז דף.
ב׳תתעה. כנ״ל אות שדמ. קאלטשעסטער, אנגליא. תשמ״ז. (6) שז דף.
ב׳תתעו. כנ״ל אות שדמ. קאקפאסטערס, אנגליא. ה׳תשמ״ז. (6) שז דף.
ב׳תתעז. כנ״ל אות שדמ. קענסינגטאן, לונדון, אנגליא. ה׳תשמ״ז. (6) שז דף.

ב'תתעח. כנ"ל אות שדמ. האיגייט, לונדון, אנגליא. ה'תשמ"ז. (6) שז דף.

ב'תתעט. כנ"ל אות שדמ. האל, אנגליא. ה'תשמ"ז. (6) שז דף.

ב'תתפ. כנ"ל אות שדמ. העיל, טשעשייר, אנגליא. ה'תשמ"ז. (6) שז דף.

ב'תתפא. כנ"ל אות שדמ. יארק, אנגליא. ה'תשמ"ז. (6) שז דף.

ב'תתפב. כנ"ל אות שדמ. מיל היל, אנגליא. ה'תשמ"ז. (6) שז דף.

ב'תתפג. כנ"ל אות שדמ. ניוקאסעל, אנגליא. ה'תשמ"ז. (6) שז דף.

ב'תתפד. כנ"ל אות שדמ. סאלפארד, אנגליא. ה'תשמ"ז. (6) שז דף.

ב'תתפה. כנ"ל אות שדמ. סטאק־אן־טרענט, אנגליא. ה'תשמ"ז. (6) שז דף.

ב'תתפו. כנ"ל אות שדמ. פרעסטוויטש, מאנשעסטער, אנגליא. ה'תשמ"ז. (6) שז דף.

ב'תתפז. כנ"ל אות שדמ. קינגסבורי, אנגליא. ה'תשמ"ז. (6) שז דף.

ב'תתפח. כנ"ל אות שדמ. וועמבלי, מידלסעקס, אנגליא. ה'תשמ"ז. (6) שז דף.

ב'תתפט. כנ"ל אות שדמ. סאליהאל, וועסט מידלאנד, אנגליא. ה'תשמ"ז. (6) שז דף.

ב'תתצ. כנ"ל אות שדמ. קינגסטאן, אנגליא. ה'תשמ"ז. (6) שז דף.

ב'תתצא. כנ"ל אות שלה. נאקסוויל, טענעסי. ה'תשמ"ז. (6) שז דף.

ב'תתצב. כנ"ל אות שדמ. פינער, אנגליא. ה'תשמ"ז. (6) שז דף.

ב'תתצג. כנ"ל אות שלה. קיסעמי, פלארידא. ה'תשמ"ז. (6) שי דף.

ב'תתצד. כנ"ל אות שלה. פע, ניו מעקסיקא. ה'תשמ"ז. (6) שי דף.

ב'תתצה. כנ"ל אות שדמ. מכון לוי יצחק, קראמפסאל, מאנטשעסטער, אנגליא. ה'תשמ"ז. (6) שי דף.

ב'תתצו. כנ"ל אות שדמ. אלדהאם, מאנטשעסטער, אנגליא. ה'תשמ"ז. (6) שי דף.

ב'תתצז. כנ"ל אות שדמ. עגהאם, סורי, אנגליא. ה'תשמ"ז. (6) שי דף.

ב'תתצח. כנ"ל אות שדמ. ראטשדייל, אנגליא. ה'תשמ"ז. (6) שי דף.

ב'תתצט. כנ"ל אות שדמ. ווילסדען, לונדון, אנגליא. ה'תשמ"ז. (6) שי דף.

ב'תתק. כנ"ל אות שלה. ביהכנ"ס ליובאוויטש, טשעסטנאט היל, מאסאטשוסעטס. ה'תשמ"ז. (6) שי דף.

ב'תתקא. כנ"ל אות שלה. קלאוד, פלארידא. ה'תשמ"ז. (6) שי דף.

ב'תתקב. כנ"ל אות שדמ. לוורע, צרפת. ה'תשמ"ז. (6) שי דף.

ב'תתקג. כנ"ל אות שדמ. מארלי לא וויאל, צרפת. ה'תשמ"ז. (6) שי דף.

ב'תתקד. כנ"ל אות שדמ. פאס, צרפת. ה'תשמ"ז. (6) שי דף.

ב'תתקה. כנ"ל אות שדמ. אדירים, באה"ק ת"ו. ה'תשמ"ז. שי דף.

ב'תתקו. כנ"ל אות שדמ. גדיש, באה"ק ת"ו. ה'תשמ"ז. שי דף.

ב'תתקז. כנ"ל אות שדמ. קבוץ גזית, באה"ק ת"ו. ה'תשמ"ז. שי דף.

ב'תתקח. כנ"ל אות שדמ. קבוץ הזורע, באה"ק ת"ו. ה'תשמ"ז. שי דף.

ב'תתקט. כנ"ל אות שדמ. קבוץ מזרע, באה"ק ת"ו. ה'תשמ"ז. שי דף.

ב'תתקי. כנ"ל אות שדמ. קבוץ מרחבי', באה"ק ת"ו. ה'תשמ"ז. שי דף.

ב'תתקיא. כנ"ל אות שדמ. קבוץ דברת, באה"ק ת"ו, ה'תשמ"ז. שי דף.

ב'תתקיב. כנ"ל אות שדמ. קרית נחום, באה"ק ת"ו. ה'תשמ"ז. שי דף.

ב'תתקיג. כנ"ל אות שדמ. תעשיות לייזר, עתידים, נוה שרת, באה"ק ת"ו. ה'תשמ"ז. שי דף.

ב'תתקיד. כנ"ל אות שלה. העמפסטעד, לאנג איילאנד, נ.י. ה'תשמ"ז. (6) שי דף.

ב'תתקטו. כנ"ל אות שדמ. טברי' — עיר העתיקה, באה"ק ת"ו. ה'תשמ"ז. שי דף.

ב'תתקטז. כנ"ל אות שלה. קייפ טאון, סאוט אפריקא. ה'תשמ"ז. (6) שי דף.

ב'תתקיז. כנ"ל אות שלה. דזשונא, אלאסקא. ה'תשמ"ז. (6) שי דף.

ב'תתקיח. כנ"ל אות שדמ — בהוצאה מוקטנת (6X8 סנטימטר). אולימפיא, פאולא, בראזיל. ה'תשמ"ז. (6) שי דף.

ב'תתקיט. כנ"ל אות ב'תתקיח. איבירובא, ריא גראנדע דו סול, בראזיל. ה'תשמ"ז. (6) שי דף.

ב'תתקכ. כנ"ל אות ב'תתקיח. איזשואי, ריא גראנדע דו סול, בראזיל. ה'תשמ"ז. (6) שי דף.

ב'תתקכא. כנ"ל אות ב'תתקיח. אינדאיאטובא, פאולא, בראזיל. ה'תשמ"ז. (6) שי דף.

ב'תתקכב. כנ"ל אות ב'תתקיח. אלעגרעטע, ריא גראנדע דו סול, בראזיל. ה'תשמ"ז. (6) שי דף.

ב'תתקכג. כנ"ל אות ב'תתקיח. אנזשעלו, ריא גראנדע דו סול, בראזיל. ה'תשמ"ז. (6) שי דף.

ב'תתקכד. כנ"ל אות ב'תתקיח. אסיס, פאולא, בראזיל. ה'תשמ"ז. (6) שי דף.

ב'תתקכה. כנ"ל אות ב'תתקיח. אראסואבא דא סעררא, פאולא, בראזיל. ה'תשמ"ז. (6) שי דף.

ב'תתקכו. כנ"ל אות ב'תתקיח. אראראס, פאולא, בראזיל. ה'תשמ"ז. (6) שי דף.

ב'תתקכז. כנ"ל אות ב'תתקיח. בארונעזא קלארא, ריא גראנדע דו סול, בראזיל. ה'תשמ"ז. (6) שי דף.

ב'תתקכח. כנ"ל אות ב'תתקיח. בורזשא, ריא גראנדע דו סול, בראזיל. ה'תשמ"ז. (6) שי דף.

ב'תתקכט. כנ"ל אות ב'תתקיח. גארסא, פאולא, בראזיל. ה'תשמ"ז. (6) שי דף.

ב'תתקל. כנ"ל אות ב'תתקיח. גבריאל, ריא גראנדע דו סול, בראזיל. ה'תשמ"ז. (6) שי דף.

ב'תתקלא. כנ"ל אות ב'תתקיח. גראוואטאי, ריא גראנדע דו סול, בראזיל. ה'תשמ"ז. (6) שי דף.

ב'תתקלב. כנ"ל אות ב'תתקיח. גראמאדא, ריא גראנדע דו סול, בראזיל. ה'תשמ"ז. (6) שי דף.

ב'תתקלג. כנ"ל אות ב'תתקיח. דום פעדריטו, ריא גראנדע דו סול, בראזיל. ה'תשמ"ז. (6) שי דף.

ב'תתקלד. כנ"ל אות ב'תתקיח. ווארזשעם גראנדע דו סול, פאולא, בראזיל. ה'תשמ"ז. (6) שי דף.

ב'תתקלה. כנ"ל אות ב'תתקיח. וויאמון, ריא גראנדע דו סול, בראזיל. ה'תשמ"ז. (6) שי דף.

ב'תתקלו. כנ"ל אות ב'תתקיח. זשוליוו דע קאסטילייוס, ריא גראנדע דו סול, בראזיל. ה'תשמ"ז. (6) שי דף.

ב'תתקלז. כנ"ל אות ב'תתקיח. טופאנסירעטא, ריא גראנדע דו סול, בראזיל. ה'תשמ"ז. (6) שי דף.

ב'תתקלח. כנ"ל אות ב'תתקיח. לורענסו דא סול, ריא גראנדע דו סול, בראזיל. ה'תשמ"ז. (6) שי דף.

ב'תתקלט. כנ"ל אות ב'תתקיח. מאושי מירים, פאולא, בראזיל. ה'תשמ"ז. (6) שי דף.

ב'תתקמ. כנ"ל אות ב'תתקיח. מאקאץ, ריא דע זשאניירא, בראזיל. ה'תשמ"ז. (6) שי דף.

ב'תתקמא. כנ"ל אות ב'תתקיח. מוקאקא, פאולא, בראזיל. ה'תשמ"ז. (6) שי דף.

ב'תתקמב. כנ"ל אות ב'תתקיח. מיגעל ארקאנזשא, פאולא, בראזיל. ה'תשמ"ז. (6) שי דף.

ב'תתקמג. כנ"ל אות ב'תתקיח. ענקאנטאדו, ריא גראנדע דו סול, בראזיל. ה'תשמ"ז. (6) שי דף.

ב'תתקמד. כנ"ל אות ב'תתקיח. פראנקא, פאולא, בראזיל. ה'תשמ"ז. (6) שי דף.

ב'תתקמה. כנ"ל אות ב'תתקיח. קאמפוס, ריא דע זשאנערא, בראזיל. ה'תשמ"ז. (6) שי דף.

ב'תתקמו. כנ"ל אות ב'תתקיח. קאפון בוניטו, פאולא, בראזיל. ה'תשמ"ז. (6) שי דף.

ב'תתקמז. כנ"ל אות ב'תתקיח. קאראזיניי, ריא גראנדע דא סול, בראזיל. ה'תשמ"ז. (6) שי ז'ף.

ב'תתקמח. כנ"ל אות ב'תתקיח. קואטרי אירמונס, ריא גראנדע דו סול, בראזיל. ה'תשמ"ז. (6) שי דף.

ב׳תתקמט. **כנ״ל** אות ב׳תתקיח. ריא גראנדע, ריא גראנדע דו סול, בראזיל. ה׳תשמ״ו. (6) שי דף.

ב׳תתקנ. **כנ״ל** אות שדמ. „ט״ו בתמוז יום חנוכת „בית אגודת חסידי חב״ד אוהל יוסף יצחק ליובאוויטש״, כפר חב״ד, באה״ק ת״ו. „תניא קדישא זה הודפס במהדורה מצומצמת וממוספרת . . . ביום ט״ו בתמוז יום ג׳ שהוכפל בו כי טוב בשעת חנוכת הבית לעיני אלפי ישראל תוך קריאה ובקשה עמוקה ותפלה משתפכת: ווי וואנט משיח נאו!!״. ה׳תשמ״ו. (6) שי דף.

ב׳תתקנא. **כנ״ל** אות שלה. מעדפארד, אריגאן. ה׳תשמ״ו. (6) שי דף.

ב׳תתקנב. **כנ״ל** אות ב׳תתקיח. בארא וועלהא, קאטארינא, בראזיל. ה׳תשמ״ו. (6) שי דף.

ב׳תתקנג. **כנ״ל** אות ב׳תתקיח. בלומענאו, קאטארינא, בראזיל. ה׳תשמ״ו. (6) שי דף.

ב׳תתקנד. **כנ״ל** אות ב׳תתקיח. זשואיינווילע, קאטארינא, בראזיל. ה׳תשמ״ו. (6) שי דף.

ב׳תתקנה. **כנ״ל** אות ב׳כב. קרית ארבע, ע״י חברון, באה״ק ת״ו. ה׳תשמ״ו. שה דף.

ב׳תתקנו. **כנ״ל** אות שלה. בראקוויל, אנטאריא, קאנאדא. ה׳תשמ״ו. (6) שי דף.

ב׳תתקנז. **כנ״ל** אות שלה. האוקסבורי, אנטאריא, קאנאדא. ה׳תשמ״ו. (6) שי דף.

ב׳תתקנח. **כנ״ל** אות שלה. פרעסקאט, אנטאריא, קאנאדא. ה׳תשמ״ו. (6) שי דף.

ב׳תתקנט. **כנ״ל** אות שלה. קארנוואל, אנטאריא, קאנאדא. ה׳תשמ״ו. (6) שי דף.

ב׳תתקס. **כנ״ל** אות שלה. קעמפטוויל, אנטאריא, קאנאדא. ה׳תשמ״ו. (6) שי דף.

ב׳תתקסא. **כנ״ל** אות שלה. באיסבריאנד, קוויבעק, קאנאדא. ה׳תשמ״ו. (6) שי דף.

ב׳תתקסב. **כנ״ל** אות שלה. ביקאנספילד, קוויבעק, קאנאדא. ה׳תשמ״ו. (6) שי דף.

ב׳תתקסג. **כנ״ל** אות שלה. בראסארד, קוויבעק, קאנאדא. ה׳תשמ״ו. (6) שי דף.

ב׳תתקסד. **כנ״ל** אות שלה. האדסאן, קוויבעק, קאנאדא. ה׳תשמ״ו. (6) שי דף.

ב׳תתקסה. **כנ״ל** אות שלה. האל, קוויבעק, קאנאדא. ה׳תשמ״ו. (6) שי דף.

ב׳תתקסו. **כנ״ל** אות שלה. האנטינגטאן, קוויבעק, קאנאדא. ה׳תשמ״ו. (6) שי דף.

ב׳תתקסז. **כנ״ל** אות שלה. וואל ד׳אר, קוויבעק, קאנאדא. ה׳תשמ״ו. (6) שי דף.

ב׳תתקסח. **כנ״ל** אות שלה. וואל דייוויד, קוויבעק, קאנאדא. ה׳תשמ״ו. (6) שי דף.

ב׳תתקסט. **כנ״ל** אות שלה. וואל מארין, קוויבעק, קאנאדא. ה׳תשמ״ו. (6) שי דף.

ב׳תתקע. **כנ״ל** אות שלה. לאסאל, קוויבעק, קאנאדא. ה׳תשמ״ו. (6) שי דף.

ב׳תתקעא. **כנ״ל** אות שלה. מאנטריאל וועסט, קוויבעק, קאנאדא. ה׳תשמ״ו. (6) שי דף.

ב׳תתקעב. **כנ״ל** אות שלה. מארין הייטס, קוויבעק, קאנאדא. ה׳תשמ״ו. (6) שי דף.

ב׳תתקעג. **כנ״ל** אות שלה. נאנס איילענד, ווערדון, קוויבעק, קאנאדא. ה׳תשמ״ו. (6) שי דף.

ב׳תתקעד. **כנ״ל** אות שלה. ניו גלאסקאו, קוויבעק, קאנאדא. ה׳תשמ״ו. (6) שי דף.

ב׳תתקעה. **כנ״ל** אות שלה. סאטי, קוויבעק, קאנאדא. ה׳תשמ״ו. (6) שי דף.

ב׳תתקעו. **כנ״ל** אות שלה. פיערפאנדס, קוויבעק, קאנאדא. ה׳תשמ״ו. (6) שי דף.

ב׳תתקעז. **כנ״ל** אות שלה. קירקלאנד, קוויבעק, קאנאדא. ה׳תשמ״ו. (6) שי דף.

ב׳תתקעח. **כנ״ל** אות שדמ. שכונת גבעת שאול, ירושת״ו, באה״ק ת״ו. מנ״א ה׳תשמ״ו. שיא דף.

ב׳תתקעט. **כנ״ל** אות שדמ. שכונת הר נוף, ירושת״ו, באה״ק ת״ו. ה׳תשמ״ו. שיא דף.

ב׳תתקפ. **כנ״ל** אות שדמ. קרית קראון הייטס, ווייט לייק, נ.י. י״ב מנ״א — יום הנשואין של כ״ק אדה״ז — ה׳תשמ״ו. (6) שיא דף.

ב׳תתקפא. **כנ״ל** אות ב׳תתקיח. איטענהיים, פאולא, בראזיל. ה׳תשמ״ו. (6) שי דף.

ב׳תתקפב. **כנ״ל** אות ב׳תתקיח. אלפענאס, מינאס זשעראיס, בראזיל. ה׳תשמ״ו. (6) שי דף.

ב׳תתקפג. **כנ״ל** אות ב׳תתקיח. באיטובא, פאולא, בראזיל. ה׳תשמ״ו. (6) שי דף.

ב׳תתקפד. **כנ״ל** אות ב׳תתקיח. בארא דוסיי־סעבאסטיון, פאולא, בראזיל. ה׳תשמ״ו. (6) שי דף.

ב׳תתקפה. **כנ״ל** אות ב׳תתקיח. גובערנאדור וואלאדארעס, מינאס זשעראיס, בראזיל. ה׳תשמ״ו. (6) שי דף.

ב׳תתקפו. **כנ״ל** אות ב׳תתקיח. ווארזעא, בראזיל. ה׳תשמ״ו. (6) שי דף.

ב׳תתקפז. **כנ״ל** אות ב׳תתקיח. זשואן דא באא וויסטא, בראזיל. ה׳תשמ״ו. (6) שי דף.

ב׳תתקפח. **כנ״ל** אות ב׳תתקיח. טערעזינא, פיאאי, בראזיל. ה׳תשמ״ו. (6) שי דף.

ב׳תתקפט. **כנ״ל** אות ב׳תתקיח. לואיס, מאראנייון, בראזיל. ה׳תשמ״ו. (6) שי דף.

ב׳תתקצ. **כנ״ל** אות ב׳תתקיח. לינס, פאולא, בראזיל. ה׳תשמ״ו. (6) שי דף.

ב׳תתקצא. **כנ״ל** אות ב׳תתקיח. מאסייא, אלאגאס בראזיל. ה׳תשמ״ו. (6) שי דף.

ב׳תתקצב. **כנ״ל** אות ב׳תתקיח. פארמאזא, גאיאז, בראזיל. ה׳תשמ״ו. (6) שי דף.

ב׳תתקצג. **כנ״ל** אות ב׳תתקיח. פערואיבע, פאולא, בראזיל. ה׳תשמ״ו. (6) שי דף.

ב׳תתקצד. **כנ״ל** אות ב׳תתקיח. פרעזידענטע פרודענטע, פאולא, בראזיל. ה׳תשמ״ו. (6) שי דף.

ב׳תתקצה. **כנ״ל** אות ב׳תתקיח. קאמפא גראנדע, מאטא גראססא, בראזיל. ה׳תשמ״ו. (6) שי דף.

ב׳תתקצו. **כנ״ל** אות ב׳תתקיח. קאסינא, ריא גראנדע דו סול, בראזיל. ה׳תשמ״ו. (6) שי דף.

ב׳תתקצז. **כנ״ל** אות ב׳תתקיח. קאראגואטאטובא, פאולא, בראזיל. ה׳תשמ״ו. (6) שי דף.

ב׳תתקצח. **כנ״ל** אות ב׳תתקיח. קאשואיירא פאוליסטא, פאולא, בראזיל. ה׳תשמ״ו. (6) שי דף.

ב׳תתקצט. **כנ״ל** אות ב׳תתקיח. קיאבא, מאטא גראססא, בראזיל. ה׳תשמ״ו. (6) שי דף.

ב׳תתר. (שלשת אלפים). **כנ״ל** אות שדמ (בגודל 10x13 סמ.). בחצרות כ״ק אדמו״ר שליט״א, 770 (בגימט׳ „פרצת״) איסטערן פארקוויי, קראון הייטס, ברוקלין, נ.י. „הוספנו בסופה: רשימת המקומות שם נדפס התניא (ע״ס הא״ב), וליד שם המקום בא מספרו ברשימת דפוסי תניא״. נדפס בדפוס דה„לקוטי שיחות״. ח״י אלול, ה׳תשמ״ו. (8) שלח דף.

ג׳א. **כנ״ל** אות ב׳תתקיח. בית הכנסת צא״ח, פאולא, בראזיל. ה׳תשמ״ו. (6) שי דף.

ג׳ב. **כנ״ל** אות ב׳תתקיח. איליאבעלא, פאולא, בראזיל. ה׳תשמ״ו. (6) שי דף.

ג׳ג. **כנ״ל** אות ב׳תתקיח. אראשא, מינאס זשעריים, בראזיל. ה׳תשמ״ו. (6) שי דף.

ג׳ד. **כנ״ל** אות ב׳תתקיח. גוארא 1. ד.פ., בראזיל. ה׳תשמ״ו. (6) שי דף.

ג׳ה. **כנ״ל** אות ב׳תתקיח. זשואון פעסוא. פאראיבא, בראזיל. ה׳תשמ״ו. (6) שי דף.

ג'ו. כנ"ל אות ב'תתקיח. טאגואטינגא, ד. פעדעראל, בראזיל. ה'תשמ"ו. (6) שי דף.

ג'ז. כנ"ל אות ב'תתקיח. לוזיאנא, גאיאז, בראזיל. ה'תשמ"ו. (6) שי דף.

ג'ח. כנ"ל אות ב'תתקיח. סאבראדיניא, ד. פעדעראל, בראזיל. ה'תשמ"ו. (6) שי דף.

ג'ט. כנ"ל אות שלה. בראמאנט, קוויבעק, קאנאדא. ה'תשמ"ו. (6) שי דף.

ג'י. כנ"ל אות שלה. גראנבי, קוויבעק, קאנאדא. ה'תשמ"ו. (6) שי דף.

ג'יא. כנ"ל אות שלה. דזשאליעט, קוויבעק, קאנאדא. ה'תשמ"ו. (6) שי דף.

ג'יב. כנ"ל אות שלה. דראמאנדוויל, קוויבעק, קאנאדא. ה'תשמ"ו. (6) שי דף.

ג'יג. כנ"ל אות שלה. טשארלסבורג, קוויבעק, קאנאדא. ה'תשמ"ו. (6) שי דף.

ג'יד. כנ"ל אות שלה. לענאקסוויל, קוויבעק, קאנאדא. ה'תשמ"ו. (6) שי דף.

ג'טו. כנ"ל אות שלה. נארט האטלי, קוויבעק, קאנאדא. ה'תשמ"ו. (6) שי דף.

ג'טז. כנ"ל אות שלה. סאיערוויל, קוויבעק, קאנאדא. ה'תשמ"ו. (6) שי דף.

ג'יז. כנ"ל אות שלה. מארטין, גואדאלופ. ה'תשמ"ו. (6) שיג דף.

ג'יח. כנ"ל אות שלה. פלינט, מישיגען. ה'תשמ"ו. (6) שיג דף.

ג'יט. כנ"ל אות שלה. וואטערפארד, קאנעטיקאט. ה'תשמ"ז. (6) שיג דף.

ג'כ. כנ"ל אות שלה. אנקאסטער, אנטאריא, קאנאדא. ה'תשמ"ז. (6) שיג דף.

ג'כא. כנ"ל אות שלה. ווינדסאר לאקס, קאנעטיקאט. ה'תשמ"ז. (6) שיג דף.

ג'כב. כנ"ל אות שלה. אלטונא, פענסילוויינא. ה'תשמ"ז. (6) שיג דף.

ג'כג. כנ"ל אות שדמ. כנס השלוחים באמריקא הדרומית, בבית חב"ד המרכזי, בוענאס איירעס, ארגענטינא. עש"ק כ"ף מר־חשון תשמ"ז. (6) שיג דף.

ג'כד. כנ"ל אות שלה. ניופארט ניוס, ווירדזשינא. ה'תשמ"ז. (6) שיג דף.

ג'כה. כנ"ל אות ב'תתקיח. אוהאטובא, פאולא, בראזיל. ה'תשמ"ז. (6) שיג דף.

ג'כו. כנ"ל אות ב'תתקיח. בערטיאגא, פאולא, בראזיל. ה'תשמ"ז. (6) שיג דף.

ג'כז. כנ"ל אות ב'תתקיח. גואראפארי, פאולא, בראזיל. ה'תשמ"ז. (6) שיג דף.

ג'כח. כנ"ל אות ב'תתקיח. וויטאריא, בראזיל. ה'תשמ"ז. (6) שיג דף.

ג'כט. כנ"ל אות ב'תתקיח. נטל, ריא גראנדע די נורטע, בראזיל. ה'תשמ"ז. (6) שיג דף.

ג'ל. כנ"ל אות ב'תתקיח. סעבאסטיאן, פאולא, בראזיל. ה'תשמ"ז. (6) שיג דף.

ג'לא. כנ"ל אות ב'תתקיח. קאשואירא דע איטאפעמירים, בראזיל. ה'תשמ"ז. (6) שיג דף.

ג'לב. כנ"ל אות שלה. קאלאן, פנמה. ה'תשמ"ז. (6) שיג דף.

ג'לג. כנ"ל אות שלה. אל ברוז, מרוקו. ה'תשמ"ז. (6) שיג דף.

ג'לד. כנ"ל אות שלה. גרסיף, מרוקו. ה'תשמ"ז. (6) שיג דף.

ג'לה. כנ"ל אות שלה. וארזזט, מרוקו. ה'תשמ"ז. (6) שיג דף.

ג'לו. כנ"ל אות שלה. אואד זם, מרוקו. ה'תשמ"ז. (6) שיג דף.

ג'לז. כנ"ל אות שלה. בוזד, מרוקו. ה'תשמ"ז. (6) שיג דף.

ג'לח. כנ"ל אות שלה. בזו, מרוקו. ה'תשמ"ז. (6) שיג דף.

ג'לט. כנ"ל אות שלה. טליוין, מרוקו. ה'תשמ"ז. (6) שיג דף.

ג'מ. כנ"ל אות שלה. ערבלו, מרוקו. ה'תשמ"ז. (6) שיג דף.

ג'מא. כנ"ל אות שלה. בית חב"ד, קסבלנקה, מרוקו. ה'תשמ"ז. (6) שיג דף.

ג'מב. כנ"ל אות שלה. גרינוויל, קענטאקי. ה'תשמ"ז. (6) שיג דף.

ג'מג. כנ"ל אות ב'תתקיח. איטאזשאי, קאטארינא, ברזיל. ה'תשמ"ז. (6) שיג דף.

ג'מד. כנ"ל אות ב'תתקיח. אימביטובא, קאטארינא, ברזיל. ה'תשמ"ז. (6) שיג דף.

ג'מה. כנ"ל אות ב'תתקיח. אראקאושו, סערזשיפע, ברזיל. ה'תשמ"ז. (6) שיג דף.

ג'מו. כנ"ל אות ב'תתקיח. לאזשעאדו, ריא גראנדע דו סול, ברזיל. ה'תשמ"ז. (6) שיג דף.

ג'מז. כנ"ל אות ב'תתקיח. לאזשעס, קאטארינא, ברזיל. ה'תשמ"ז. (6) שיג דף.

ג'מח. כנ"ל אות ב'תתקיח. סעבאסטיאן דו סאל, ריא גראנדע דו סול, ברזיל. ה'תשמ"ז. (6) שיג דף.

ג'מט. כנ"ל אות ב'תתקיח. קאשואירא דו סול, ריא גראנדע דו סול, ברזיל. ה'תשמ"ז. (6) שיג דף.

ג'נ. כנ"ל אות תצז. קריסיאומא, קאטארינא, ברזיל. (הוצאה שני") ה'תשמ"ז. (6) שיג דף.

ג'נא. כנ"ל אות ב'תתקיח. שואי, ריא גראנדע דו סול, ברזיל. ה'תשמ"ז. (6) שיג דף.

ג'נב. כנ"ל אות שלה. ביהכנ"ס עץ חיים, ריטשמאנד, ב.ק., קאנאדא. ה'תשמ"ז (6) שיג דף.

ג'נג. כנ"ל אות ב'תתקיח. אטיבאיניא, פאולא, בראזיל. ה'תשמ"ז (6) שיג דף.

ג'נד. כנ"ל אות ב'תתקיח. איטאטיבא, פאולא, בראזיל. ה'תשמ"ז (6) שיג דף.

ג'נה. כנ"ל אות ב'תתקיח. אמפארא, פאולא, בראזיל. ה'תשמ"ז (6) שיג דף.

ג'נו. כנ"ל אות ב'תתקיח. ב. פערדאענס, פאולא, בראזיל. ה'תשמ"ז (6) שיג דף.

ג'נז. כנ"ל אות ב'תתקיח. באיסוגאנגא, פאולא, בראזיל. ה'תשמ"ז (6) שיג דף.

ג'נח. כנ"ל אות ב'תתקיח. ביריטיבא מירים, פאולא, בראזיל. ה'תשמ"ז (6) שיג דף.

ג'נט. כנ"ל אות ב'תתקיח. בערטיאגא, פאולא, בראזיל. ה'תשמ"ז (6) שיג דף.

ג'ס. כנ"ל אות ב'תתקיח. גואראראעמא, פאולא, בראזיל. ה'תשמ"ז (6) שיג דף.

ג'סא. כנ"ל אות ב'תתקיח. זשוקעאי, פאולא, בראזיל. ה'תשמ"ז (6) שיג דף.

ג'סב. כנ"ל אות ב'תתקיח. מארעסיאס, פאולא, בראזיל. ה'תשמ"ז (6) שיג דף.

ג'סג. כנ"ל אות ב'תתקיח. פאובא, פאולא, בראזיל. ה'תשמ"ז (6) שיג דף.

ג'סד. כנ"ל אות ב'תתקיח. פינדאמאניאנגאבא, פאולא, בראזיל. ה'תשמ"ז (6) שיג דף.

ג'סה. כנ"ל אות ב'תתקיח. קאמבורי, פאולא, בראזיל. ה'תשמ"ז (6) שיג דף.

ג'סו. כנ"ל אות ב'תתקיח. קאמפו לומפו, פאולא, בראזיל. ה'תשמ"ז (6) שיג דף.

ג'סז. כנ"ל אות ב'תתקיח. קאשאעירא דא אימאראטא, פאולא, בראזיל. ה'תשמ"ז (6) שיג דף.

ג'סח. כנ"ל אות ב'תתקיח. איטאים פאליסטא, פאולא, בראזיל. ה'תשמ"ז. (6) שיג דף.

ג'סט. כנ"ל אות ב'תתקיח. מאנטע־מאר, פאולא, בראזיל. ה'תשמ"ז. (6) שיג דף.

ג'ע. כנ"ל אות ב'תתקיח. מיגועל פאליסטא, פאולא, בראזיל. ה'תשמ"ז. (6) שיג דף.

ג'עא. כנ"ל אות שלה. בראנדאן, מאניטאבא, קאנאדא. ה'תשמ"ז. (6) שיג דף.

ג'עב. כנ"ל אות שלה. לעטברידזש, אלבערטא, קאנאדא. ה'תשמ"ז. (6) שיג דף.

ג'עג. כנ"ל אות שלה. סאסקאטון, סאסקאטשעוואן, קאנאדא. ה'תשמ"ז. (6) שיג דף.

ג'עד. כנ"ל אות שלה. רעדזשינא, סאסקאטשעוואן, קאנאדא. התשמ"ז. (6) שיג דף.

ג'עה. כנ"ל אות שלה. מבאבאן, סוואזילאנד. התשמ"ח, שנת הקהל. (6) שטו דף.

ג'עו. כנ"ל אות שלה. שכונת איסט ניו יארק, ברוקלין, נ.י. התשמ"ח, שנת הקהל. (6) שטו דף.

ג'עז. כנ"ל אות שדמ. ים סוף — מפרץ אילת. כנס השלוחים מנהלי בתי חב"ד באה"ק ת"ו בעיר אילת, ט"יו כסלו התשמ"ח — שנת הקהל. (6) שטו דף.

ג'עח. כנ"ל אות ב'תתקיח. בראקעסאבא, פאולא, בראזיל. התשמ"ח, שנת הקהל. (6) שטו דף.

ג'עט. כנ"ל אות ב'תתקיח. באררא דו אונא, פאולא, בראזיל. התשמ"ח, שנת הקהל. (6) שטו דף.

ג'פ. כנ"ל אות ב'תתקיח. גואיקא, פאולא, בראזיל. התשמ"ח, שנת הקהל. (6) שטו דף.

ג'פא. כנ"ל אות ב'תתקיח. דורו, פאולא, בראזיל. התשמ"ח, שנת הקהל. (6) שטו דף.

ג'פב. כנ"ל אות ב'תתקיח. זשורייא, פאולא, בראזיל. התשמ"ח, שנת הקהל. (6) שטו דף.

ג'פג. כנ"ל אות ב'תתקיח. טאבאטינגא, פאולא, בראזיל. התשמ"ח, שנת הקהל. (6) שטו דף.

ג'פד. כנ"ל אות ב'תתקיח. טאקע טאקע, פאולא, בראזיל. התשמ"ח, שנת הקהל. (6) שטו דף.

ג'פה. כנ"ל אות ב'תתקיח. טאקע טאקע פעקענא, פאולא, בראזיל. התשמ"ח, שנת הקהל. (6) שטו דף.

ג'פו. כנ"ל אות ב'תתקיח. לאגואיניא, פאולא, בראזיל. התשמ"ח, שנת הקהל. (6) שטו דף.

ג'פז. כנ"ל אות ב'תתקיח. מונגאגוא, פאולא, בראזיל. התשמ"ח, שנת הקהל. (6) שטו דף.

ג'פח. כנ"ל אות ב'תתקיח. סאקו דו הביירא, פאולא, בראזיל. התשמ"ח, שנת הקהל. (6) שטו דף.

ג'פט. כנ"ל אות ב'תתקיח. ס. טיאגא, פאולא, בראזיל. התשמ"ח, שנת הקהל. (6) שטו דף.

ג'צ. כנ"ל אות ב'תתקיח. פאראטי, פאולא, בראזיל. התשמ"ח, שנת הקהל. (6) שטו דף.

ג'צא. כנ"ל אות ב'תתקיח. אסטוריאס, פאולא, בראזיל. התשמ"ח, שנת הקהל. (6) שטו דף.

ג'צב. כנ"ל אות ב'תתקיח. גואאובא, פאולא, בראזיל. התשמ"ח, שנת הקהל. (6) שטו דף.

ג'צג. כנ"ל אות ב'תתקיח. העבראיקא, פאולא, בראזיל. התשמ"ח, שנת הקהל. (6) שטו דף.

ג'צד. כנ"ל אות ב'תתקיח. זשואיין נאווא, קרית גן־ישראל, פאולא, בראזיל. התשמ"ח, שנת הקהל. (6) שטו דף.

ג'צה. כנ"ל אות ב'תתקיח. טאמבו, פאולא, בראזיל. התשמ"ח, שנת הקהל. (6) שטו דף.

ג'צו. כנ"ל אות ב'תתקיח. לאורענסו דא סערא, (מחנה בני עקיבא), פאולא, בראזיל. התשמ"ח, שנת הקהל. (6) שטו דף.

ג'צז. כנ"ל אות ב'תתקיח. נאוועגאנטעס, פאולא, בראזיל. התשמ"ח, שנת הקהל. (6) שטו דף.

ג'צח. כנ"ל אות ב'תתקיח. עדען, פאולא, בראזיל. התשמ"ח, שנת הקהל. (6) שטו דף.

ג'צט. כנ"ל אות ב'תתקיח. ענסעאדא, פאולא, בראזיל. התשמ"ח, שנת הקהל. (6) שטו דף.

ג'ק. כנ"ל אות ב'תתקיח. פיטאנגייראס, פאולא, בראזיל. התשמ"ח, שנת הקהל. (6) שטו דף.

ג'קא. כנ"ל אות ב'תתקיח. פערנאמבוקו, פאולא, בראזיל. התשמ"ח, שנת הקהל (6) שטו דף.

ג'קב. כנ"ל אות ב'תתקיח. פערעקע, פאולא, בראזיל. התשמ"ח, שנת הקהל. (6) שטו דף.

ג'קג. כנ"ל אות שדמ. בארותיים, באה"ק. התשמ"ח. שנת הקהל. (6) שיז דף.

ג'קד. כנ"ל אות שדמ. גאולים, באה"ק. התשמ"ח. שנת הקהל. (6) שיז דף.

ג'קה. כנ"ל אות שדמ. ינוב, באה"ק. התשמ"ח. שנת הקהל. (6) שיז דף.

ג'קו. כנ"ל אות שדמ. כרם מהר"ל, באה"ק. התשמ"ח. שנת הקהל. (6) שיז דף.

ג'קז. כנ"ל אות שדמ. ליבנים, באה"ק. התשמ"ח. שנת הקהל. (6) שיז דף.

ג'קח. כנ"ל אות שדמ. מגדים, באה"ק. התשמ"ח. שנת הקהל. (6) שיז דף.

ג'קט. כנ"ל אות שדמ. מושב ברכי', באה"ק. התשמ"ח. שנת הקהל. (6) שיז דף.

ג'קי. כנ"ל אות שדמ. עינב, באה"ק. התשמ"ח. שנת הקהל. (6) שיז דף.

ג'קיא. כנ"ל אות שדמ. צרופה, באה"ק. התשמ"ח. שנת הקהל. (6) שיז דף.

ג'קיב. כנ"ל אות שדמ. תנובות, באה"ק. התשמ"ח. שנת הקהל. (6) שיז דף.

ג'קיג. כנ"ל אות שדמ. שפרעם — (ציון רבי יהודה בן בבא), באה"ק. התשמ"ח. שנת הקהל. (6) שיז דף.

ג'קיד. כנ"ל אות שדמ. אור עקיבא, באה"ק. התשמ"ח. שנת הקהל. (6) שיז דף.

ג'קטו. כנ"ל אות שדמ. בנימינה, באה"ק. התשמ"ח. שנת הקהל. (6) שיז דף.

ג'קטז. כנ"ל אות שדמ. רמת אביב, באה"ק. התשמ"ח. שנת הקהל. (6) שיז דף.

ג'קיז. כנ"ל אות שלה. סאוט פערי, ניו יארק סיטי, נ.י. התשמ"ח. שנת הקהל. (6) שיז דף.

ג'קיח. כנ"ל אות שלה. בעטערי פארק, ניו יארק סיטי, נ.י. התשמ"ח. שנת הקהל. (6) שיז דף.

ג'קיט. כנ"ל אות שלה. וואל סטריט, ניו יארק סיטי, נ.י. התשמ"ח. שנת הקהל. (6) שיז דף.

ג'קכ. כנ"ל אות שלה. שכונת ברוקלין הייטס, ברוקלין, נ.י. התשמ"ח. שנת הקהל. (6) שיז דף.

ג'קכא. כנ"ל אות שלה. ביהכנ"ס אהבת משה, 612 מייפל סט. ברוקלין, נ.י. התשמ"ח. שנת הקהל. (6) שיז דף.

ג'קכב. כנ"ל אות שלה. שכונת פארק סלאפ, ברוקלין, נ.י. התשמ"ח. שנת הקהל. (6) שיז דף.

ג'קכג. כנ"ל אות שלה. שכונת בראנזוויל, ברוקלין, נ.י. התשמ"ח. שנת הקהל. (6) שיז דף.

ג'קכד. כנ"ל אות שלה. שכונת איסט פלעטבוש, ברוקלין, נ.י. התשמ"ח. שנת הקהל. (6) שיז דף.

ג'קכה. כנ"ל אות שלה. שכונת גרינפאינט, ברוקלין, נ.י. התשמ"ח. שנת הקהל. (6) שיז דף.

ג'קכו. כנ"ל אות שלה. שכונת סטארעט סיטי, ברוקלין, נ.י. התשמ"ח. שנת הקהל. (6) שיז דף.

ג'קכז. כנ"ל אות שלה. שכונת ביי רידוש, ברוקלין, נ.י. התשמ"ח. שנת הקהל. (6) שיז דף.

ג'קכח. כנ"ל אות שלה. לאנג אילאנד סיטי, קווינס נ.י. התשמ"ח. שנת הקהל. (6) שיז דף.

ג'קכט. כנ"ל אות שלה. שכונת סאנסעט פארק, ברוקלין, נ.י. התשמ"ח. שנת הקהל. (6) שיז דף.

ג'קל. כנ"ל אות שלה. מירטל ביטש, סאוט קאראליינא. התשמ"ח. שנת הקהל. (6) שיז דף.

ג'קלא. כנ"ל אות שלה. ווילמינגטאן, נארט קאראליינא. תשמ"ח. שנת הקהל. (6) שיז דף.

ג'קלב. כנ"ל אות שלה. האמפטאן, ווירדזשיניא. התשמ"ח. שנת הקהל. (6) שיז דף.

ג'קלג. כנ"ל אות שלה. וויליאמסבורג, ווירדזשיניא. התשמ"ח. שנת הקהל. (6) שיז דף.

ג'קלד. כנ"ל אות ב'תתקיח. כינוס ב' דשלוחי דרום אמריקא. פאולא, בראזיל. התשמ"ח. שנת הקהל. (6) שיז דף.

ג'קלה. כנ"ל אות ב'תתקיח. קאנטארעירא, פאולא, בראזיל. התשמ"ח. שנת הקהל. (6) שיז דף.

ג׳קלו. כנ״ל אות ב׳תתקיח. רחוב י״א ניסן, אטיבאיא, פאולא, בראזיל. ה׳תשמ״ח. שנת הקהל. (6) שיז דף.

ג׳קלז. כנ״ל אות שלה. בית חב״ד, ברענטוואוד, קאליפארניא. ה׳תשמ״ח. שנת הקהל. (6) שיז דף.

ג׳קלח. כנ״ל אות שלה. בית חב״ד, מארינא דעל ריי, קאליפארניא. ה׳תשמ״ח. שנת הקהל. (6) שיז דף.

ג׳קלט. כנ״ל אות שלה. אואן קאפיסטראנא, קאליפארניא. ה׳תשמ״ח. שנת הקהל. (6) שיז דף.

ג׳קמ. כנ״ל אות שלה. אנא, קאליפארניא. ה׳תשמ״ח. שנת הקהל. (6) שיז דף.

ג׳קמא. כנ״ל אות שלה. אנטאריא, קאליפארניא. ה׳תשמ״ח. שנת הקהל. (6) שיז דף.

ג׳קמב. כנ״ל אות שלה. אפלאנד, קאליפארניא. ה׳תשמ״ח. שנת הקהל. (6) שיז דף.

ג׳קמג. כנ״ל אות שלה. בוענא`פארק, קאליפארניא. ה׳תשמ״ח. שנת הקהל. (6) שיז דף.

ג׳קמד. כנ״ל אות שלה. בּרעא, קאליפארניא. ה׳תשמ״ח. שנת הקהל. (6) שיז דף.

ג׳קמה. כנ״ל אות שלה. גלענדייל, קאליפארניא. ה׳תשמ״ח. שנת הקהל. (6) שיז דף.

ג׳קמו. כנ״ל אות שלה. גראנד טערעס, קאליפארניא. ה׳תשמ״ח. שנת הקהל. (6) שיז דף.

ג׳קמז. כנ״ל אות שלה. ווילא פארק, קאליפארניא. ה׳תשמ״ח. שנת הקהל. (6) שיז דף.

ג׳קמח. כנ״ל אות שלה. טשינא, קאליפארניא. ה׳תשמ״ח. שנת הקהל. (6) שיז דף.

ג׳קמט. כנ״ל אות שלה. פיליפסבורג, מארטען איילאנד (נעדערלאנדס אנטיליס). ה׳תשמ״ח. שנת הקהל. (6) שיז דף.

ג׳קנ. כנ״ל אות ב׳תתקיח. איגואבא, ריא דע זשאניירא, בראזיל. ה׳תשמ״ח. שנת הקהל. (6) שיז דף.

ג׳קנא. כנ״ל אות ב׳תתקיח. איטאבאראי, ריא דע זשאניירא, בראזיל. ה׳תשמ״ח. שנת הקהל. (6) שיז דף.

ג׳קנב. כנ״ל אות ב׳תתקיח. אנגרא דאס רעיס, ריא דע זשאניירא, בראזיל. ה׳תשמ״ח. שנת הקהל. (6) שיז דף.

ג׳קנג. כנ״ל אות ב׳תתקיח. מאא, ריא דע זשאניירא, בראזיל. ה׳תשמ״ח. שנת הקהל. (6) שיז דף.

ג׳קנד. כנ״ל אות ב׳תתקיח. מאושע, ריא דע זשאניירא, בראזיל. ה׳תשמ״ח. שנת הקהל. (6) שיז דף.

ג׳קנה. כנ״ל אות ב׳תתקיח. מירוקו, ריא דע זשאניירא, בראזיל. ה׳תשמ״ח. שנת הקהל. (6) שיז דף.

ג׳קנו. כנ״ל אות ב׳תתקיח. פאקעטא, ריא דע זשאניירא, בראזיל. ה׳תשמ״ח. שנת הקהל. (6) שיז דף.

ג׳קנז. כנ״ל אות ב׳תתקיח. פעדרא דא ריא, ריא דע זשאניירא, בראזיל. ה׳תשמ״ח. שנת הקהל. (6) שיז דף.

ג׳קנח. כנ״ל אות ב׳תתקיח. קאזימירא דע אברעו, ריא דע זשאניירא, בראזיל. ה׳תשמ״ח. שנת הקהל. (6) שיז דף.

ג׳קנט. כנ״ל אות ב׳תתקיח. ישיבה מתנה ישראל, פטרופוליס, בראזיל. ה׳תשמ״ח. שנת הקהל. (6) שיז דף.

ג׳קס. כנ״ל אות ב׳תתקיח. ברוסקע, קאטארינא, בראזיל. ה׳תשמ״ח. שנת הקהל. (6) שיז דף.

ג׳קסא. כנ״ל אות ב׳תתקיח. פראנסיסקא דא סול, קאטארינא, בראזיל. ה׳תשמ״ח. שנת הקהל. (6) שיז דף.

ג׳קסב. כנ״ל אות ב׳תתקיח. קאמבאריו, קאטארינא, בראזיל. ה׳תשמ״ח. שנת הקהל. (6) שיז דף.

ג׳קסג. כנ״ל אות ב׳תתקיח. לאמבארי, מינאס זשעראיס, בראזיל. ה׳תשמ״ח. שנת הקהל. (6) שיז דף.

ג׳קסד. כנ״ל אות ב׳תתקיח. אנטאנינאס, פאראנא, בראזיל. ה׳תשמ״ח. שנת הקהל. (6) שיז דף.

ג׳קסה. כנ״ל אות ב׳תתקיח. גואראטובא, פאראנא, בראזיל. ה׳תשמ״ח. שנת הקהל. (6) שיז דף.

ג׳קסו. כנ״ל אות ב׳תתקיח. טרעס באראס, פאראנא, בראזיל. ה׳תשמ״ח. שנת הקהל. (6) שיז דף.

ג׳קסז. כנ״ל אות ב׳תתקיח. מאטיניאס, פאראנא, בראזיל. ה׳תשמ״ח. שנת הקהל. (6) שיז דף.

ג׳קסח. כנ״ל אות ב׳תתקיח. פאטא בראנקא, פאראנא, בראזיל. ה׳תשמ״ח. שנת הקהל. (6) שיז דף.

ג׳קסט. כנ״ל אות ב׳תתקיח. קאיאבא, פאראנא, בראזיל. ה׳תשמ״ח. שנת הקהל. (6) שיז דף.

ג׳קע. כנ״ל אות שלה. יארבא לינדא, קאליפארניא. ה׳תשמ״ח. שנת הקהל. (6) שיז דף.

ג׳קעא. כנ״ל אות שלה. טאסטין, קאליפארניא. ה׳תשמ״ח. שנת הקהל. (6) שיז דף.

ג׳קעב. כנ״ל אות שלה. לא האברא, קאליפארניא. ה׳תשמ״ח. שנת הקהל. (6) שיז דף.

ג׳קעג. כנ״ל אות שלה. לייק עלסינאר, קאליפארניא. ה׳תשמ״ח. שנת הקהל. (6) שיז דף.

ג׳קעד. כנ״ל אות שלה. לאס אלאמיטאס, קאליפארניא. ה׳תשמ״ח. שנת הקהל. (6) שיז דף.

ג׳קעה. כנ״ל אות שלה. מאנטקלייר, קאליפארניא. ה׳תשמ״ח. שנת הקהל. (6) שיז דף.

ג׳קעו. כנ״ל אות שלה. נארקא, קאליפארניא. ה׳תשמ״ח. שנת הקהל. (6) שיז דף.

ג׳קעז. כנ״ל אות שלה. סאנטי, קאליפארניא. ה׳תשמ״ח. שנת הקהל. (6) שיז דף.

ג׳קעח. כנ״ל אות שלה. סאלאנא ביטש, קאליפארניא. ה׳תשמ״ח. שנת הקהל. (6) שיז דף.

ג׳קעט. כנ״ל אות שלה. סטאנטאן, קאליפארניא. ה׳תשמ״ח. שנת הקהל. (6) שיז דף.

ג׳קפ. כנ״ל אות שלה. ענסינא, קאליפארניא. ה׳תשמ״ח. שנת הקהל. (6) שיז דף.

ג׳קפא. כנ״ל אות שלה. פאנטאנא, קאליפארניא. ה׳תשמ״ח. שנת הקהל. (6) שיז דף.

ג׳קפב. כנ״ל אות שלה. פאסאדינא, קאליפארניא. ה׳תשמ״ח. שנת הקהל. (6) שיז דף.

ג׳קפג. כנ״ל אות שלה. פאראמאונט, קאליפארניא. ה׳תשמ״ח. שנת הקהל. (6) שיז דף.

ג׳קפד. כנ״ל אות שלה. פולערטאן, קאליפארניא. ה׳תשמ״ח. שנת הקהל. (6) שיז דף.

ג׳קפה. כנ״ל אות שלה. פילמאר, קאליפארניא. ה׳תשמ״ח. שנת הקהל. (6) שיז דף.

ג׳קפו. כנ״ל אות שלה. פלאסענטיא, קאליפארניא. ה׳תשמ״ח. שנת הקהל. (6) שיז דף.

ג׳קפז. כנ״ל אות שלה. בית חב״ד, בעל איר, קאליפארניא. ה׳תשמ״ח. שנת הקהל. (6) שיז דף.

ג׳קפח. כנ״ל אות שלה. בית חב״ד, טארזאנא, קאליפארניא. ה׳תשמ״ח. שנת הקהל. (6) שיז דף.

ג׳קפט. כנ״ל אות שלה. בית חב״ד, נארט האליוואוד, קאליפארניא. ה׳תשמ״ח. שנת הקהל. (6) שיז דף.

ג׳קצ. כנ״ל אות שלה. בית חב״ד, שעוויאט הילס, קאליפארניא. ה׳תשמ״ח. שנת הקהל. (6) שיז דף.

ג׳קצא. כנ״ל אות שלה. בית חב״ד, שערמאן אוקס, קאליפארניא. ה׳תשמ״ח. שנת הקהל. (6) שיז דף.

ג׳קצב. כנ״ל אות שלה. קאלסאן, קאליפארניא. ה׳תשמ״ח. שנת הקהל. (6) שיז דף.

ג׳קצג. כנ״ל אות שלה. קאראנא, קאליפארניא. ה׳תשמ״ח. שנת הקהל. (6) שיז דף.

ג׳קצד. כנ״ל אות שלה. קלעמענטע, קאליפארניא. ה׳תשמ״ח. שנת הקהל. (6) שיז דף.

ג׳קצה. כנ״ל אות שלה. ריאלטא, קאליפארניא. ה׳תשמ״ח. שנת הקהל. (6) שיז דף.

ג׳קצו. כנ״ל אות שלה. ריווערסייד, קאליפארניא. ה׳תשמ״ח. שנת הקהל. (6) שיז דף.

ג׳קצז. כנ״ל אות שלה. ראנטשא קוקאמאנגא, קאליפארניא. ה׳תשמ״ח. שנת הקהל. (6) שיז דף.

ג׳קצח. כנ״ל אות ב׳תתקיח. לארענא, פאולא, בראזיל. ה׳תשמ״ח. שנת הקהל. (6) שיז דף.

ג׳קצט. כנ״ל אות שלה. בית משפט העליון דקאליפארניא, לאס אנדזשעלעס קאונטי. נדפס יום ד׳ יוד אייר — נצח שבנצח — ה׳תשמ״ח. שנת הקהל. (6) שיז דף.

ג׳ר. כנ״ל אות שלה. ישיבת אור אלחנן-חב״ד. לאס אנדזשעלעס, קאליפארניא. ה׳תשמ״ח. שנת הקהל. (6) שיז דף.

ג׳רא. כנ״ל אות שדמ. בית חב״ד המרכזי דקאליפארניא, לאס אנדזשעלעס, קאליפארניא. ה׳תשמ״ח. שנת הקהל. (6) שיח דף.

ג׳רב. כנ״ל אות שלה. אקלאהאמא סיטי, אקלאהאמא. ה׳תשמ״ח. שנת הקהל. (6) שיז דף.

ג׳רג. כנ״ל אות שלה. לינקאן, נעבראסקא. ה׳תשמ״ח. שנת הקהל. (6) שיז דף.

ג׳רד. כנ״ל אות שלה. נעבראסקא סיטי, נעבראסקא. ה׳תשמ״ח. שנת הקהל. (6) שיז דף.

ג׳רה. כנ״ל אות שלה. קליר לייק, טעקסאס. ה׳תשמ״ח. שנת הקהל. (6) שיז דף.

ג׳רו. כנ״ל אות ב׳תתקיח. מאקאפא, אמאפא, בראזיל. ה׳תשמ״ח. שנת הקהל. (6) שיז דף.

ג׳רז. כנ״ל אות ב׳תתקיח. מוסקעירו, פארא, בראזיל. ה׳תשמ״ח. שנת הקהל. (6) שיז דף.

ג׳רח. כנ״ל אות ב׳תתקיח. פאטוס, מינאס זשעראיס, בראזיל. ה׳תשמ״ח. שנת הקהל. (6) שיז דף.

ג׳רט. כנ״ל אות ב׳תתקיח. פורנאס, מינאס זשעראיס, בראזיל. ה׳תשמ״ח. שנת הקהל. (6) שיז דף.

ג׳רי. כנ״ל אות ב׳תתקיח. מאנטעס קלאראס, מינאס זשעראיס, בראזיל. ה׳תשמ״ח. שנת הקהל. (6) שיז דף.

ג׳ריא. כנ״ל אות ב׳תתקיח. בארדא דו זשואן, ריא דע זשאנעיא, בראזיל. ה׳תשמ״ח. שנת הקהל. (6) שיז דף.

ג׳ריב. כנ״ל אות ב׳תתקיח. בוזיאוס, ריא דע זשאנעירו, בראזיל. ה׳תשמ״ח. שנת הקהל. (6) שיז דף.

ג׳ריג. כנ״ל אות ב׳תתקיח. פעדרא דא אלדייא, ריא דע זשאנעירו, בראזיל. ה׳תשמ״ח. שנת הקהל. (6) שיז דף.

ג׳ריד. כנ״ל אות ב׳תתקיח. וויסקונדע דע מאוא, ריא דע זשאנעירו, בראזיל. ה׳תשמ״ח. שנת הקהל. (6) שיז דף.

ג׳רטו. כנ״ל אות ב׳תתקיח. כינוס הקהל דישיבה מחנה ישראל, העבראיקא, סאולו, בראזיל. ה׳תשמ״ח. שנת הקהל. (6) שיז דף.

ג׳רטז. כנ״ל אות שדמ. לארענסוויל, ניו דזשערסי. ה׳תשמ״ח. שנת הקהל. (6) שכב דף.

ג׳ריז. כנ״ל אות שלה. אוקלאנד, קאליפארניא. ה׳תשמ״ח. שנת הקהל. (6) שכב דף.

ג׳ריח. כנ״ל אות שלה. בייקערספילד, קאליפארניא. ה׳תשמ״ח. שנת הקהל. (6) שכב דף.

ג׳ריט. כנ״ל אות שלה. דיליינא, קאליפארניא. ה׳תשמ״ח. שנת הקהל. (6) שכב דף.

ג׳רכ. כנ״ל אות שלה. האזע, קאליפארניא. ה׳תשמ״ח. שנת הקהל. (6) שכב דף.

ג׳רכא. כנ״ל אות שלה. וויסיילייא, קאליפארניא. ה׳תשמ״ח. שנת הקהל. (6) שכב דף.

ג׳רכב. כנ״ל אות שלה. טולער, קאליפארניא. ה׳תשמ״ח. שנת הקהל. (6) שכב דף.

ג׳רכג. כנ״ל אות שלה. לאמפאק, קאילפארניא. ה׳תשמ״ח. שנת הקהל. (6) שכב דף.

ג׳רכד. כנ״ל אות שלה. לואיס אביספא, קאליפארניא. ה׳תשמ״ח. שנת הקהל. (6) שכב דף.

ג׳רכה. כנ״ל אות שלה. מאדעסטא, קאליפארניא. ה׳תשמ״ח. שנת הקהל. (6) שכב דף.

ג׳רכו. כנ״ל אות שלה. מאנטעריי, קאליפארניא. ה׳תשמ״ח. שנת הקהל. (6) שכב דף.

ג׳רכז. כנ״ל אות שלה. מאריא, קאליפארניא. ה׳תשמ״ח. שנת הקהל. (6) שכב דף.

ג׳רכח. כנ״ל אות שלה. מערסעד, קאליפארניא. ה׳תשמ״ח. שנת הקהל. (6) שכב דף.

ג׳רכט. כנ״ל אות שלה. סאלינאס, קאליפארניא. ה׳תשמ״ח. שנת הקהל. (6) שכב דף.

ג׳רל. כנ״ל אות שלה. סטאקטאן, קאליפארניא. ה׳תשמ״ח. שנת הקהל. (6) שכב דף.

ג׳רלא. כנ״ל אות שלה. פרעסנא, קאליפארניא. ה׳תשמ״ח. שנת הקהל. (6) שכב דף.

ג׳רלב. כנ״ל אות שלה. בית חב״ד, אוק פארק, קאליפארניא. ה׳תשמ״ח. שנת הקהל. (6) שכב דף.

ג׳רלג. כנ״ל אות שלה. אדעלאנטא, קאליפארניא. ה׳תשמ״ח. שנת הקהל. (6) שכב דף.

ג׳רלד. כנ״ל אות שלה. בארסטא, קאליפארניא. ה׳תשמ״ח. שנת הקהל. (6) שכב דף.

ג׳רלה. כנ״ל אות שלה. ביג בער לייק, קאליפארניא. ה׳תשמ״ח. שנת הקהל. (6) שכב דף.

ג׳רלו. כנ״ל אות שלה. בערנארדינא, קאליפארניא. ה׳תשמ״ח. שנת הקהל. (6) שכב דף.

ג׳רלז. כנ״ל אות שלה. דוארטע, קאליפארניא. ה׳תשמ״ח. שנת הקהל. (6) שכב דף.

ג׳רלח. כנ״ל אות שלה. היילאנד, קאליפארניא. ה׳תשמ״ח. שנת הקהל. (6) שכב דף.

ג׳רלט. כנ״ל אות שלה. לאמא לינדא, קאליפארניא. ה׳תשמ״ח. שנת הקהל. (6) שכב דף.

ג׳רמ. כנ״ל אות שלה. מארינא, קאליפארניא. ה׳תשמ״ח. שנת הקהל. (6) שכב דף.

ג׳רמא. כנ״ל אות שלה. מישאן וויעדזשא, קאליפארניא. ה׳תשמ״ח. שנת הקהל. (6) שכב דף.

ג׳רמב. כנ״ל אות שלה. נידלס, קאליפארניא. ה׳תשמ״ח. שנת הקהל. (6) שכב דף.

ג׳רמג. כנ״ל אות שלה. רעדלאנדס, קאליפארניא. ה׳תשמ״ח. שנת הקהל. (6) שכב דף.

ג׳רמד. כנ״ל אות שלה. טשאטאקוא, נ.י. ה׳תשמ״ח. שנת הקהל. (6) שכב דף.

ג׳רמה. כנ״ל אות ב׳תתקיח. פענינסולא, פאולא, בראזיל. ה׳תשמ״ח. שנת הקהל. (6) שכב דף.

ג׳רמו. כנ״ל אות ב׳תתקיח. אוניאון דא וויטאריא, פאראנא, בראזיל. ה׳תשמ״ח. שנת הקהל. (6) שכב דף.

ג׳רמז. כנ״ל אות ב׳תתקיח. אראקאריא, פאראנא, בראזיל. ה׳תשמ״ח. שנת הקהל. (6) שכב דף.

ג׳רמח. כנ״ל אות ב׳תתקיח. בענטו דו סול, קאטארינא, בראזיל. ה׳תשמ״ח. שנת הקהל. (6) שכב דף.

ג׳רמט. כנ״ל אות ב׳תתקיח. גארוווא, קאטארינא, בראזיל. ה׳תשמ״ח. שנת הקהל. (6) שכב דף.

ג׳רנ. כנ״ל אות ב׳תתקיח. זשאראגוא דו סול, קאטארינא, בראזיל. ה׳תשמ״ח. שנת הקהל. (6) שכב דף.

ג׳רנא. כנ״ל אות ב׳תתקיח. זשוזע דוס פינייאיס, פאראנא, בראזיל. ה׳תשמ״ח. שנת הקהל. (6) שכב דף.

ג׳רנב. כנ״ל אות ב׳תתקיח. לאפא, פאראנא, בראזיל. ה׳תשמ״ח. שנת הקהל. (6) שכב דף.

ג׳רנג. כנ״ל אות ב׳תתקיח. מאטעוס דא סול, פאראנא, בראזיל. ה׳תשמ״ח. שנת הקהל. (6) שכב דף.

ג׳רנד. כנ״ל אות ב׳תתקיח. מאפרא, קאטארינא, בראזיל. ה׳תשמ״ח. שנת הקהל. (6) שכב דף.

ג׳רנה. כנ״ל אות ב׳תתקיח. מורעטעס, פאראנא, בראזיל. ה׳תשמ״ח. שנת הקהל. (6) שכב דף.

ג׳רנו. כנ״ל אות ב׳תתקיח. פורטו אוניאון, קאטארינא, בראזיל. ה׳תשמ״ח. שנת הקהל. (6) שכב דף.

ג׳רנז. כנ״ל אות ב׳תתקיח. קאמפו אלעגרע, קאטארינא, בראזיל. ה׳תשמ״ח. שנת הקהל. (6) שכב דף.

ג׳רנח. כנ״ל אות ב׳תתקיח. קאנואינייאס, קאטארינא, בראזיל. ה׳תשמ״ח. שנת הקהל. (6) שכב דף.

ג׳רנט. כנ״ל אות ב׳תתקיח. ריא נעגריניייו, קאטארינא, בראזיל. ה׳תשמ״ח. שנת הקהל. (6) שכב דף.

ג׳רס. כנ״ל אות שלה. אגודה למען אח״י — קהלת יהודי בוכרא — בארא פארק, ברוקלין, נ.י. ה׳תשמ״ח. שנת הקהל. (6) שכב דף.

ג׳רסא. כנ״ל אות שלה. טעריטאון, נ.י. ה׳תשמ״ח. שנת הקהל. (6) שכב דף.

ג׳רסב. כנ״ל אות שלה. יאנקערס, נ.י. ה׳תשמ״ח. שנת הקהל. (6) שכב דף.

ג׳רסג. כנ״ל אות שלה. מאונט ווערנאן, נ.י. ה׳תשמ״ח. שנת הקהל. (6) שכב דף.

ג׳רסד. כנ״ל אות שלה. סקארסדייל, נ.י. ה׳תשמ״ח. שנת הקהל. (6) שכב דף.

ג׳רסה. כנ״ל אות שלה. ריו׳ערדייל, נ.י. ה׳תשמ״ח. שנת הקהל. (6) שכב דף.

ג׳רסו. כנ״ל אות שלה. בעטהעל, נ.י. ה׳תשמ״ח. שנת הקהל. (6) שכב דף.

ג׳רסז. כנ״ל אות שלה. האריס, נ.י. ה׳תשמ״ח. שנת הקהל. (6) שכב דף.

ג׳רסח. כנ״ל אות שלה. וועסט מאנטיסעלא, נ.י. ה׳תשמ״ח. שנת הקהל. (6) שכב דף.

ג׳רסט. כנ״ל אות שלה. ווייט לייק, נ.י. ה׳תשמ״ח. שנת הקהל. (6) שכב דף.

ג׳ער. כנ״ל אות שלה. קאניאנגא לייק, נ.י. ה׳תשמ״ח. שנת הקהל. (6) שכב דף.

ג׳ערא. כנ״ל אות שלה. סוואן לייק, נ.י. ה׳תשמ״ח. שנת הקהל. (6) שכב דף.

ג׳ערב. כנ״ל אות שלה. שדה תעופה סאליוואן קאונטי, סוואן לייק, נ.י. ה׳תשמ״ח. שנת הקהל. (6) שכב דף.

ג׳רעג. כנ״ל אות שלה. פערנדייל, נ.י. ה׳תשמ״ח. שנת הקהל. (6) שכב דף.

ג׳עדר. כנ״ל אות שלה. מייפלוואוד, נ.י. ה׳תשמ״ח. שנת הקהל. (6) שכב דף.

ג׳ערה. כנ״ל אות שלה. סמאלוואוד, נ.י. ה׳תשמ״ח. שנת הקהל. (6) שכב דף.

ג׳רעו. כנ״ל אות שלה. פאסטערדייל, נ.י. ה׳תשמ״ח. שנת הקהל. (6) שכב דף.

ג׳רעז. כנ״ל אות שלה. ליווינגסטאן מאנאר, נ.י. ה׳תשמ״ח. שנת הקהל. (6) שכב דף.

ג׳רעח. כנ״ל אות שלה. נעווערסינק, נ.י. ה׳תשמ״ח. שנת הקהל. (6) שכב דף.

ג׳רעט. כנ״ל אות שלה. פארקסוויל, נ.י. ה׳תשמ״ח. שנת הקהל. (6) שכב דף.

ג׳רפ. כנ״ל אות שלה. פאלסבורג, נ.י. ה׳תשמ״ח. שנת הקהל. (6) שכב דף.

ג׳רפא. כנ״ל אות שלה. (מחנה שלי״ה), דיירילאנד, נ.י. ה׳תשמ״ח. שנת הקהל. (6) שכב דף.

ג׳רפב. כנ״ל אות שלה. (מחנה אמונה), גרינפילד פארק, נ.י. ה׳תשמ״ח. שנת הקהל. (6) שכב דף.

ג׳רפג. כנ״ל אות שלה. מאנראו, נ.י. ה׳תשמ״ח. שנת הקהל. (6) שכב דף.

ג׳רפד. כנ״ל אות שלה. מאנאלאפאן, ניו דזשערסי. ה׳תשמ״ח. שנת הקהל. (6) שכב דף.

ג׳רפה. כנ״ל אות שלה. מארלבארא, ניו דזשערסי. ה׳תשמ״ח. שנת הקהל. (6) שכב דף.

ג׳רפו. כנ״ל אות שלה. פריהאלד, ניו דזשערסי. ה׳תשמ״ח. שנת הקהל. (6) שכב דף.

ג׳רפז. כנ״ל אות שלה. אלבאנס, ווערמאנט. ה׳תשמ״ח. שנת הקהל. (6) שכב דף.

ג׳רפח. כנ״ל אות שלה. דזשאנסבורי, ווערמאנט. ה׳תשמ״ח. שנת הקהל. (6) שכב דף.

ג׳רפט. כנ״ל אות שלה. מאנטשעסטער, ווערמאנט. ה׳תשמ״ח. שנת הקהל. (6) שכב דף.

ג׳רצ. כנ״ל אות שלה. ראטלאנד, ווערמאנט. ה׳תשמ״ח. שנת הקהל. (6) שכב דף.

ג׳רצא. כנ״ל אות שלה. דאווער, דעלעווער. ה׳תשמ״ח. שנת הקהל. (6) שכב דף.

ג׳רצב. כנ״ל אות שלה. ניוארק, דעלעווער. ה׳תשמ״ח. שנת הקהל. (6) שכב דף.

ג׳רצג. כנ״ל אות שלה. אמבערלי, אהייא. ה׳תשמ״ח. שנת הקהל. (6) שכב דף.

ג׳רצד. כנ״ל אות שלה. בלו אש, אהייא. ה׳תשמ״ח. שנת הקהל. (6) שכב דף.

ג׳רצה. כנ״ל אות שלה. דעיטאן, אהייא. ה׳תשמ״ח. שנת הקהל. (6) שכב דף.

ג׳רצו. כנ״ל אות שלה. מאנטגאמערי, אהייא. ה׳תשמ״ח. שנת הקהל. (6) שכב דף.

ג׳רצז. כנ״ל אות שלה. רעדינג, אהייא. ה׳תשמ״ח. שנת הקהל. (6) שכב דף.

ג׳רחצ. כנ״ל אות שלה. היי פאינט, נארט קאראליינא. ה׳תשמ״ח. שנת הקהל. (6) שכב דף.

ג׳רצט. כנ״ל אות שלה. ווייט פליינס, נ.י. ה׳תשמ״ח. שנת הקהל. (6) שכב דף.

ג׳ש. כנ״ל אות ב׳תתר (ג׳ אלפים). מידלטאון, נ.י. ה׳תשמ״ח. שנת הקהל. (6) שכב דף.

ג׳שא. כנ״ל אות שדמ. חצר ביהכנ״ס וביהמ״ד כ״ק אדמו״ר שליט״א — ע״י מקום הנחת אבן הפינה — ימי הסליחות, ה׳תשמ״ח ותשמ״ח. שנת הקהל. (6) שכב דף.

ג׳שב. כנ״ל אות שלה. פיטערסבורג, פלארידא. ה׳תשמ״ח. שנת הקהל. (6) שכב דף.

ג׳שג. כנ״ל אות שדמ. טבריה, ציון רבי מאיר בעל הנס, באה״ק תובב״א. ה׳תשמ״ח. שנת הקהל. (6) רצה דף.

ג׳דש. כנ״ל אות שדמ. מאסקווא, רוסיא. ה׳תשמ״ט. (6) שכב דף.

ג׳שה. כנ״ל אות שלה. פאפעעטע, טאהיטי. ה׳תשמ״ט. (6) שכב דף.

ג׳שו. כנ״ל אות קצט. כפר חב״ד, באה״ק. ה׳תשמ״ט. (6) שי דף.

ג׳שז. כנ״ל אות רכ עם תיקונים והוספות — **הוצאה מוגדלת 15x22½ ס״מ. בית אגודת חסידי חב״ד, אהל יוסף יצחק ליובאוויטש, 770 איסטערן פארקווי, ברוקלין, נ.י. מוצש״ק וא״ו אדר ראשון ה׳תשמ״ט. שנת המאתיים להולדת כ״ק אדמו״ר הצ״צ. שנת הארבעים לנשיאות כ״ק אדמו״ר שליט״א. (6) שי דף.**

ג׳שח. כנ״ל **אות תקנ (עם תרגום האנגלי מול עמוד התניא — הוצאה מוקטנת) לאקערבי, סקאטלאנד. ה׳תשמ״ט. שנת המאתים להולדת כ״ק אדמו״ר הצ״צ. שנת הארבעים לנשיאות כ״ק אדמו״ר שליט״א.**

ג׳שט. כנ״ל **אות שדמ. עדינגבארא, סקאטלאנד. ה׳תשמ״ט. שנת המאתיים להולדת כ״ק אדמו״ר הצ״צ. שנת הארבעים לנשיאות כ״ק אדמו״ר שליט״א.**

ג׳שי. כנ״ל **אות שדמ. קריקלוואוד, לונדון, אנגליא. ה׳תשמ״ט. שנת המאתיים להולדת כ״ק אדמו״ר הצ״צ. שנת הארבעים לנשיאות כ״ק אדמו״ר שליט״א.**

ג׳שיא. כנ״ל **אות שלה. אלענטאון, פענסילווייניא. ה׳תשמ״ט. שנת המאתיים להולדת כ״ק אדמו״ר הצ״צ. שנת הארבעים לנשיאות כ״ק אדמו״ר שליט״א.**

ג׳שיב. כנ״ל **אות שלה. האנטינגדאן, פענסילווייניא. ה׳תשמ״ט. שנת המאתיים להולדת כ״ק אדמו״ר הצ״צ. שנת הארבעים לנשיאות כ״ק אדמו״ר שליט״א.**

ג׳שיג. כנ״ל **אות שדמ. אליכין, באה״ק. ה׳תשמ״ט. שנת המאתיים להולדת כ״ק אדמו״ר הצ״צ. שנת הארבעים לנשיאות כ״ק אדמו״ר שליט״א.**

ג׳שיד. כנ״ל אות שדמ. הדר עם, באה״ק. ה׳תשמ״ט. שנת המאתיים להולדת כ״ק אדמו״ר הצ״צ. שנת הארבעים לנשיאות כ״ק אדמו״ר שליט״א.

ג׳שטו. כנ״ל אות שדמ. מושב אביבים, באה״ק. ה׳תשמ״ט. שנת המאתיים להולדת כ״ק אדמו״ר הצ״צ. שנת הארבעים לנשיאות כ״ק אדמו״ר שליט״א.

ג׳שטז. כנ״ל אות שדמ. מושב דישון, באה״ק. ה׳תשמ״ט. שנת המאתיים להולדת כ״ק אדמו״ר הצ״צ. שנת הארבעים לנשיאות כ״ק אדמו״ר שליט״א.

ג׳שיז. כנ״ל אות שדמ. פסגת זאב, באה״ק. ה׳תשמ״ט. שנת המאתיים להולדת כ״ק אדמו״ר הצ״צ. שנת הארבעים לנשיאות כ״ק אדמו״ר שליט״א.

ג׳שיח. כנ״ל אות שדמ. פקיעין החדשה, באה״ק. ה׳תשמ״ט. שנת המאתיים להולדת כ״ק אדמו״ר הצ״צ. שנת הארבעים לנשיאות כ״ק אדמו״ר שליט״א.

ג׳שיט. כנ״ל אות ג׳שו. ספריית חב״ד ירושלים ת״ו, ע״ש הרבנית הצדקנית חי׳ מושקא שניאורסאהן ע״ה. הוצאה מיוחדת עם ציוני השיעור היומי על הגליון. ה׳תשמ״ט. שנת המאתיים להולדת כ״ק אדמו״ר הצ״צ. שנת הארבעים לנשיאות כ״ק אדמו״ר שליט״א.

ג׳שכ. כנ״ל אות שלה. ניו הארטפארד, נ.י. ה׳תשמ״ט. שנת המאתיים להולדת כ״ק אדמו״ר הצ״צ. שנת הארבעים לנשיאות כ״ק אדמו״ר שליט״א. (6) שכג דף.

ג׳שכא. כנ״ל אות של״ה. אַסטאָריאַ, קווינס, נ.י. ה׳תשמ״ט. שנת המאתיים . . . הצ״צ. שנת הארבעים לנשיאות כ״ק אדמו״ר שליט״א. (6) שכג דף.

ג׳שכב. כנ״ל אות ג׳שו. טביליסי, גרוזיא, בריה״מ. ה׳תש״נ. הי׳ תהא שנת נסים. מאתיים שנה . . . הצ״צ. שנת הארבעים לנשיאות כ״ק אדמו״ר שליט״א. (6) שיא דף.

ג׳שכג. כנ״ל אות ג׳שז – הוצאה מוגדלת ½ 22x15 סמ. ברוקלין, נ.י. יו״ד שבט, תש״נ. ארבעים שנה לנשיאות כ״ק אדמו״ר שליט״א. (6) רלה דף.

ג׳שכד. כנ״ל אות ג׳שיט. ספריית חב״ד ירושלים, ת״ו. ע״ש הרבנית הצדקנית חי׳ מושקא שניאורסאהן ע״ה, ה׳תש״נ (עם ציוני השיעור היומי על הגליון). מאתיים שנה . . . הצ״צ. ארבעים שנה לנשיאות כ״ק אדמו״ר שליט״א. רלה דף.

ג׳שכה. כנ״ל אות ג׳שכד. הוצאה מוקטנת בפורמט כיס (עם ציוני השיעור היומי על הגליון). ספריית חב״ד ירושלים, ת״ו. ע״ש הרבנית הצדקנית חי׳ מושקא שניאורסאהן ע״ה, ה׳תש״נ. מאתיים שנה . . . הצ״צ. ארבעים שנה לנשיאות כ״ק אדמו״ר שליט״א. רלה דף.

ג׳שכו. כנ״ל אות שדמ. בית חב״ד, קרית ביאליק, באה״ק. ה׳תש״נ. מאתיים שנה . . . הצ״צ. ארבעים שנה לנשיאות כ״ק אדמו״ר שליט״א. רלה דף.

ג׳שכז. כנ״ל אות ב׳תתקיח. אוטינגאַ, פאולא, בראַזיל. ה׳תש״נ. הי׳ תהא שנת נסים. מאתיים שנה . . . הצ״צ. ארבעים שנה לנשיאות כ״ק אדמו״ר שליט״א. (6) שכג דף.

ג׳שכח. כנ״ל אות ב׳תתקיח. טאַמבאַרע, פאולא, בראַזיל. ה׳תש״נ. הי׳ תהא שנת נסים. מאתיים שנה . . . הצ״צ. ארבעים שנה לנשיאות כ״ק אדמו״ר שליט״א. (6) שכג דף.

ג׳שכט. כנ״ל אות ב׳תתקיח. טיעטע, פאולא, בראַזיל. ה׳תש״נ. הי׳ תהא שנת נסים. מאתיים שנה . . . הצ״צ. ארבעים שנה לנשיאות כ״ק אדמו״ר שליט״א. (6) שכג דף.

ג׳של. כנ״ל אות ב׳תתקיח. מאוּאַ, פאולא, בראַזיל. ה׳תש״נ . . . שנת נסים. מאתיים שנה . . . הצ״צ. ארבעים שנה לנשיאות כ״ק אדמו״ר שליט״א. (6) שכג דף.

ג׳שלא. כנ״ל אות ב׳תתקיח. סאַלטאַ, פאולא, בראַזיל. ה׳תש״נ. . . . שנת נסים. מאתיים שנה . . . הצ״צ. ארבעים שנה לנשיאות כ״ק אדמו״ר שליט״א. (6) שכג דף.

ג׳שלב. כנ״ל אות ב׳תתקיח. רודזשע ראַמאָס, פאולא, בראַזיל. ה׳תש״נ. . . . שנת נסים. מאתיים שנה . . . הצ״צ. ארבעים שנה לנשיאות כ״ק אדמו״ר שליט״א. (6) שכג דף.

ג׳שלג. כנ״ל אות שלה. שכונת באָטה ביטש, ברוקלין, נ.י. ה׳תש״נ. . . . שנת נסים. מאתיים שנה . . . הצ״צ. ארבעים שנה לנשיאות כ״ק אדמו״ר שליט״א. (6) שכג דף.

ג׳שלד. כנ״ל אות שלה. וועסט פאלם ביטש, פלארידא. ה׳תש״נ. . . . שנת נסים. מאתיים שנה . . . הצ״צ. ארבעים שנה לנשיאות כ״ק אדמו״ר שליט״א. (6) שכה דף.

ג׳שלה. כנ״ל אות שלה. וועלינגטאן, פלארידא. ה׳תש״נ. . . . שנת נסים. מאתיים שנה . . . הצ״צ. ארבעים שנה לנשיאות כ״ק אדמו״ר שליט״א. (6) שכה דף.

ג׳שלו. כנ״ל אות ג׳שכד. „היכל מנחם״ ירושלים, ת״ו. ה׳ת״נ. . . . שנת נסים. מאתיים שנה . . . הצ״צ. ארבעים שנה לנשיאות כ״ק אדמו״ר שליט״א. (6) רלה דף.

ג׳שלז. כנ״ל אות ג׳שכה. „היכל מנחם״ ירושלים, ת״ו. ה׳תש״נ. . . . שנת נסים. מאתיים שנה . . . הצ״צ. ארבעים שנה לנשיאות כ״ק אדמו״ר שליט״א. (6) רלה דף.

ג׳שלח. כנ״ל אות ג׳שו. מוזיאון ארץ ישראל, תל אביב, באה״ק, ת״ו. ה׳תש״נ. . . . שנת נסים. מאתיים שנה . . . הצ״צ. ארבעים שנה לנשיאות כ״ק אדמו״ר שליט״א. (6) רלה דף.

ג׳שלט. כנ״ל אות ב׳תתקיח. בית חב״ד, מאַרומבי, פאולא, בראזיל. ה׳תש״נ. . . . שנת נסים. מאתיים שנה . . . הצ״צ. ארבעים שנה לנשיאות כ״ק אדמו״ר שליט״א. (6) שכה דף.

ג׳שמ. כנ״ל אות רכ. לענינגראד, בריה״מ. ה׳תש״נ. . . . שנת נסים. מאתיים שנה . . . הצ״צ. ארבעים שנה לנשיאות כ״ק אדמו״ר שליט״א. (6) רלה דף.

ג׳שמא. כנ״ל אות ב׳תתקיח. בית חב״ד, איטאָים, פאולא, בראזיל: ה׳תש״נ. . . . שנת נסים. מאתיים שנה . . . הצ״צ. ארבעים שנה לנשיאות כ״ק אדמו״ר שליט״א. (6) שכה דף.

ג׳שמב. כנ״ל אות ב׳תתקיח. בית חב״ד, זשאזע קאמפאָס, פאולא, בראזיל. ה׳תש״נ. . . . שנת נסים. מאתיים שנה . . . הצ״צ. ארבעים שנה לנשיאות כ״ק אדמו״ר שליט״א. (6) שכה דף.

ג׳שמג. כנ״ל אות ב׳תתקיח. בית חב״ד, פערדיזעס, פאולא, בראזיל. ה׳תש״נ. . . . שנת נסים. מאתיים שנה . . . הצ״צ. ארבעים שנה לנשיאות כ״ק אדמו״ר שליט״א. (6) שכה דף.

ג׳שדמ. כנ״ל אות ב׳תתקיח. בית ליובאוויטש, איפאנעמא, ריא דע זשאניירא, בראזיל. ה׳תש״נ. . . נסים. מאתיים שנה . . . הצ״צ. ארבעים שנה לנשיאות כ״ק אדמו״ר שליט״א. (6) שכה דף.

ג׳שמה. כנ״ל אות ב׳תתקיח. בית ליובאוויטש, טיזשוקא, ריא דע זשאניירא, בראזיל. ה׳תש״נ. . . . שנת נסים. מאתיים שנה . . . הצ״צ. ארבעים שנה לנשיאות כ״ק אדמו״ר שליט״א. (6) שכה דף.

ג׳שמו. כנ״ל אות ב׳תתקיח. העבראַיקא, ריא דע זשאניירא, בראזיל. ה׳תש״נ. . . . שנת נסים. מאתיים שנה . . . הצ״צ. ארבעים שנה לנשיאות כ״ק אדמו״ר שליט״א. (6) שכה דף.

ג׳שמז. כנ״ל אות ב׳תתקיח. באַטאַפאַגאַ, ריא דע זשאניירא, בראזיל. ה׳תש״נ. . . . שנת נסים. מאתיים שנה . . . הצ״צ. ארבעים שנה לנשיאות כ״ק אדמו״ר שליט״א. (6) שכה דף.

ג׳שמח. כנ״ל אות ב׳תתקיח. באַראַ טיזשוקאַ, ריא דע זשאניירא, בראזיל. ה׳תש״נ. . . . שנת נסים. מאתיים שנה . . . הצ״צ. ארבעים שנה לנשיאות כ״ק אדמו״ר שליט״א. (6) שכה דף.

ג׳שמט. כנ״ל אות ב׳תתקיח. וויגאַריאַ זשעראַל, ריא דע זשאניירא, בראזיל. ה׳תש״נ. . . . שנת נסים. מאתיים שנה . . . הצ״צ. ארבעים שנה לנשיאות כ״ק אדמו״ר שליט״א. (6) שכה דף.

ג׳שנ. כנ״ל אות ב׳תתקיח. לאזאנזשייראָס, ריא דע זשאניירא, בראזיל. ה׳תש״נ. . . . שנת נסים. מאתיים שנה . . . הצ״צ. ארבעים שנה לנשיאות כ״ק אדמו״ר שליט״א. (6) שכה דף.

ג׳שנא. כנ״ל אות ב׳תתקיח. לעבלאן, ריא דע זשאניירא, בראזיל. ה׳תש״נ. . . . שנת נסים. מאתיים שנה . . . הצ״צ. ארבעים שנה לנשיאות כ״ק אדמו״ר שליט״א. (6) שכה דף.

ג׳שנב. כנ״ל אות ב׳תתקיח. לעמע, ריא דע זשאניירא, בראזיל. ה׳תש״נ. . . . שנת נסים. מאתיים שנה . . . הצ״צ. ארבעים שנה לנשיאות כ״ק אדמו״ר שליט״א. (6) שכה דף.

ג׳שנג. כנ״ל אות ב׳תתקיח. פלאמענגא, ריא דע זשאניירא, בראזיל. ה׳תש״נ. . . . שנת נסים. מאתיים שנה . . . הצ״צ. ארבעים שנה לנשיאות כ״ק אדמו״ר שליט״א. (6) שכה דף.

ג׳שנד. כנ״ל אות ב׳תתקיח. פעניאַ, ריא דע זשאניירא, בראזיל. ה׳תש״נ. . . . שנת נסים. מאתיים שנה . . . הצ״צ. ארבעים שנה לנשיאות כ״ק אדמו״ר שליט״א. (6) שכה דף.

ג׳שנה. כנ״ל אות ב׳תתקיח. קאַנראַדאַ, ריא דע זשאניירא, בראזיל. ה׳תש״נ. . . . שנת נסים. מאתיים שנה . . . הצ״צ. ארבעים שנה לנשיאות כ״ק אדמו״ר שליט״א. (6) שכה דף.

ג׳שנו. כנ״ל אות ב׳תתקיח. קאָפּאָקאָבּאָנאָ, ריא דע זשאניירא, בראזיל. ה׳תש״נ. . . . שנת נסים. מאתיים שנה . . . הצ״צ. ארבעים שנה לנשיאות כ״ק אדמו״ר שליט״א. (6) שכה דף.

ג׳שנז. כנ״ל אות ב׳תתקיח. קעומאַדאָס עסטאַדאָ, ריא דע זשאניירא, בראזיל. ה׳תש״נ. . . . שנת נסים. מאתיים שנה . . . הצ״צ. ארבעים שנה לנשיאות כ״ק אדמו״ר שליט״א. (6) שכה דף.

ג׳שנח. כנ״ל אות שדמ. ארגמן – בקעת הירדן, באה״ק ת״ו.

„מ״ב ספרי תניא שהודפסו ברחבי ארץ יהודה, שומרון, חבל עזה, רמת הגולן ובקעת הירדן – לרגל שנת הארבעים לנשיאות כ״ק אדמו״ר שליט״א – לחזוק הישובים בגשמיות ורוחניות. בחודש בו עלה ארי׳, במזל ארי׳, והחריב את אריאל על מנת שיבוא ארי׳ ויבנה אריאל״. ה׳תש״נ. היתה תהא שנת נסים. מאתיים שנה . . . הצ״צ. ארבעים שנה לנשיאות כ״ק אדמו״ר שליט״א (6) רמט דף.

ג׳שנט. כנ״ל אות ג׳שנח. בקעות – בקעת הירדן, באה״ק ת״ו. „מ״ב ספרי תניא שהודפסו . . . לשנת הארבעים . . . ויבנה אריאל״. ה׳תש״נ . . . שנת נסים. מאתיים שנה . . . הצ״צ. ארבעים שנה . . . (6) רמט דף.

ג׳שס. כנ״ל אות ג׳שנח. גיתות – בקעת הירדן, באה״ק ת״ו. „מ״ב ספרי תניא שהודפסו . . . לשנת הארבעים . . . ויבנה אריאל״. ה׳תש״נ . . . שנת נסים. מאתיים שנה . . . הצ״צ. ארבעים שנה . . . (6) רמט דף.

ג׳שסא. כנ״ל אות ג׳שנח. יפית – בקעת הירדן, באה״ק ת״ו. „מ״ב ספרי תניא שהודפסו . . . לשנת הארבעים . . . ויבנה אריאל״. ה׳תש״נ . . . שנת נסים. מאתיים שנה . . . הצ״צ. ארבעים שנה . . . (6) רמט דף.

ג׳שסב. כנ״ל אות ג׳שנח. חמרה – בקעת הירדן, באה״ק ת״ו. „מ״ב ספרי תניא שהודפסו . . . לשנת הארבעים . . . ויבנה אריאל״. ה׳תש״נ . . . שנת נסים. מאתיים שנה . . . הצ״צ. ארבעים שנה . . . (6) רמט דף.

ג׳שסג. כנ״ל אות ג׳שנח. מגדלים – בקעת הירדן, באה״ק ת״ו. „מ״ב ספרי תניא שהודפסו . . . לשנת הארבעים . . . ויבנה אריאל״. ה׳תש״נ . . . שנת נסים. מאתיים שנה . . . הצ״צ. ארבעים שנה . . . (6) רמט דף.

ג׳שסד. כנ״ל אות ג׳שנח. מכורה – בקעת הירדן, באה״ק ת״ו. „מ״ב ספרי תניא שהודפסו . . . לשנת הארבעים . . . ויבנה אריאל״. ה׳תש״נ . . . שנת נסים. מאתיים שנה . . . הצ״צ. ארבעים שנה . . . (6) רמט דף.

ג׳שסה. כנ״ל אות ג׳שנח. מעלה אפרים – בקעת הירדן, באה״ק ת״ו. „מ״ב ספרי תניא שהודפסו . . . לשנת הארבעים . . . ויבנה אריאל״. ה׳תש״נ . . . שנת נסים. מאתיים שנה . . . הצ״צ. ארבעים שנה . . . (6) רמט דף.

ג׳שסו. כנ״ל אות ג׳שנח. משואה – בקעת הירדן, באה״ק ת״ו. „מ״ב ספרי תניא שהודפסו . . . לשנת הארבעים . . . ויבנה אריאל״. ה׳תש״נ . . . שנת נסים. מאתיים שנה . . . הצ״צ. ארבעים שנה . . . (6) רמט דף.

ג׳שסז. כנ״ל אות ג׳שנח. נתיב הגדוד – בקעת הירדן, באה״ק ת״ו. „מ״ב ספרי תניא שהודפסו . . . לשנת הארבעים . . . ויבנה אריאל״. ה׳תש״נ . . . שנת נסים. מאתיים שנה . . . הצ״צ. ארבעים שנה . . . (6) רמט דף.

ג׳שסח. כנ״ל אות ג׳שנח. פצאל – בקעת הירדן, באה״ק ת״ו. „מ״ב ספרי תניא שהודפסו . . . לשנת הארבעים . . . ויבנה אריאל״. ה׳תש״נ . . . שנת נסים. מאתיים שנה . . . הצ״צ. ארבעים שנה . . . (6) רמט דף.

ג׳שסט. כנ״ל אות ג׳שנח. קבוץ גלגל – בקעת הירדן, באה״ק ת״ו. „מ״ב ספרי תניא שהודפסו . . . לשנת הארבעים . . . ויבנה אריאל״. ה׳תש״נ . . . שנת נסים. מאתיים שנה . . . הצ״צ. ארבעים שנה . . . (6) רמט דף.

ג׳שע. כנ״ל אות ג׳שנח. קבוץ נערן – בקעת הירדן, באה״ק ת״ו. „מ״ב ספרי תניא שהודפסו . . . לשנת הארבעים . . . ויבנה אריאל״. ה׳תש״נ . . . שנת נסים. מאתיים שנה . . . הצ״צ. ארבעים שנה . . . (6) רמט דף.

ג׳שעא. כנ״ל אות ג׳שנח. רועי – בקעת הירדן, באה״ק ת״ו. „מ״ב ספרי תניא שהודפסו . . . לשנת הארבעים . . . ויבנה אריאל״. ה׳תש״נ . . . שנת נסים. מאתיים שנה . . . הצ״צ. ארבעים שנה . . . (6) רמט דף.

ג׳שעב. כנ״ל אות ג׳שנח. תומר – בקעת הירדן, באה״ק ת״ו. „מ״ב ספרי תניא שהודפסו . . . לשנת הארבעים . . . ויבנה אריאל״. ה׳תש״נ . . . שנת נסים. מאתיים שנה . . . הצ״צ. ארבעים שנה . . . (6) רמט דף.

ג׳שעג. כנ״ל אות ג׳שנח. בדולח – חבל עזה, באה״ק ת״ו. „מ״ב ספרי תניא שהודפסו . . . לשנת הארבעים . . . ויבנה אריאל״. ה׳תש״נ . . . שנת נסים. מאתיים שנה . . . הצ״צ. ארבעים שנה . . . (6) רמט דף.

ג׳שעד. כנ״ל אות ג׳שנח. גן אור – חבל עזה, באה״ק ת״ו. „מ״ב ספרי תניא שהודפסו . . . לשנת הארבעים . . . ויבנה אריאל״. ה׳תש״נ . . . שנת נסים. מאתיים שנה . . . הצ״צ. ארבעים שנה . . . (6) רמט דף.

ג׳שעה. כנ״ל אות ג׳שנח. כפר ים – חבל עזה, באה״ק ת״ו. „מ״ב ספרי תניא שהודפסו . . . לשנת הארבעים . . . ויבנה אריאל״. ה׳תש״נ . . . שנת נסים. מאתיים שנה . . . הצ״צ. ארבעים שנה . . . (6) רמט דף.

ג׳שעו. כנ״ל אות ג׳שנח. מורג – חבל עזה, באה״ק ת״ו. „מ״ב ספרי תניא שהודפסו . . . לשנת הארבעים . . . ויבנה אריאל״. ה׳תש״נ . . . שנת נסים. מאתיים שנה . . . הצ״צ. ארבעים שנה . . . (6) רמט דף.

ג׳שעז. כנ״ל אות ג׳שנח. נאות שדה – חבל עזה, באה״ק ת״ו. „מ״ב ספרי תניא שהודפסו . . . לשנת הארבעים . . . ויבנה אריאל״. ה׳תש״נ . . . שנת נסים. מאתיים שנה . . . הצ״צ. ארבעים שנה . . . (6) רמט דף.

ג׳שעח. כנ״ל אות ג׳שנח. עצמונה – חבל עזה, באה״ק ת״ו. „מ״ב ספרי תניא שהודפסו . . . לשנת הארבעים . . . ויבנה אריאל״. ה׳תש״נ . . . שנת נסים. מאתיים שנה . . . הצ״צ. ארבעים שנה . . . (6) רמט דף.

ג׳שעט. כנ״ל אות ג׳שנח. ארצם – רמת הגולן, באה״ק ת״ו. „מ״ב ספרי תניא שהודפסו . . . לשנת הארבעים . . . ויבנה אריאל״. ה׳תש״נ . . . שנת נסים. מאתיים שנה . . . הצ״צ. ארבעים שנה . . . (6) רמט דף.

ג׳שפ. כנ״ל אות ג׳שנח. חדנ״ס – רמת הגולן, באה״ק ת״ו. „מ״ב ספרי תניא שהודפסו . . . לשנת הארבעים . . . ויבנה אריאל״. ה׳תש״נ . . . שנת נסים. מאתיים שנה . . . הצ״צ. ארבעים שנה . . . (6) רמט דף.

ג׳שפא. כנ״ל אות ג׳שנח. מחנה קרן – רמת הגולן, באה״ק ת״ו. „מ״ב ספרי תניא שהודפסו . . . לשנת הארבעים . . . ויבנה אריאל״. ה׳תש״נ . . . שנת נסים. מאתיים שנה . . . הצ״צ. ארבעים שנה . . . (6) רמט דף.

ג׳שפב. כנ״ל אות ג׳שנח. מרום גולן – רמת הגולן, באה״ק ת״ו. „מ״ב ספרי תניא שהודפסו . . . לשנת הארבעים . . . ויבנה אריאל״. ה׳תש״נ . . . שנת נסים. מאתיים שנה . . . הצ״צ. ארבעים שנה . . . (6) רמט דף.

ג׳שפג. כנ״ל אות ג׳שנח. קבוץ נוה אטי״ב – רמת הגולן, באה״ק ת״ו. „מ״ב ספרי תניא שהודפסו . . . לשנת הארבעים . . . ויבנה אריאל״. ה׳תש״נ . . . שנת נסים. מאתיים שנה . . . הצ״צ. ארבעים שנה . . . (6) רמט דף.

ג׳שפד. כנ״ל אות ג׳שנח. קידמת צבי – רמת הגולן, באה״ק ת״ו. „מ״ב ספרי תניא שהודפסו . . . לשנת הארבעים . . . ויבנה אריאל״. ה׳תש״נ . . . שנת נסים. מאתיים שנה . . . הצ״צ. ארבעים שנה . . . (6) רמט דף.

ג׳שפה. כנ״ל אות ג׳שנח. שעל – רמת הגולן, באה״ק ת״ו. „מ״ב ספרי תניא שהודפסו . . . לשנת הארבעים . . . ויבנה אריאל״. ה׳תש״נ . . . שנת נסים. מאתיים שנה . . . הצ״צ. ארבעים שנה . . . (6) רמט דף.

ג׳שפו. כנ״ל אות ג׳שנח ואות ב׳תנז. אפרת, באה״ק ת״ו. „מ״ב ספרי תניא שהודפסו . . . לשנת הארבעים . . . ויבנה אריאל״. ה׳תש״נ . . . שנת נסים. מאתיים שנה . . . הצ״צ. ארבעים שנה . . . (6) רמט דף.

ג׳שפז. כנ״ל אות ג׳שנח. אריאל – קרית המדע, באה״ק ת״ו. „מ״ב ספרי תניא שהודפסו . . . לשנת הארבעים . . . ויבנה אריאל״. ה׳תש״נ . . . שנת נסים. מאתיים שנה . . . הצ״צ. ארבעים שנה . . . (6) רמט דף.

ג׳שפח. כנ״ל אות ג׳שנח. בית ארי׳, באה״ק ת״ו. „מ״ב ספרי תניא שהודפסו . . . לשנת הארבעים . . . ויבנה אריאל״. ה׳תש״נ

שנת נסים. מאתיים שנה . . . הצ"צ. ארבעים שנה . . . (6) רמט דף.

ג'שפט. כנ"ל אות ג'שנח. ביתר, באה"ק ת"ו. „מ"ב ספרי תניא שהודפסו . . . לשנת הארבעים . . . ויבנה אריאל". ה'תש"נ . . . שנת נסים. מאתיים שנה . . . הצ"צ. ארבעים שנה . . . (6) רמט דף.

ג'שצ. כנ"ל אות ג'שנח. ברקן – אזור תעשי', באה"ק ת"ו. „מ"ב ספרי תניא שהודפסו . . . לשנת הארבעים . . . ויבנה אריאל". ה'תש"נ . . . שנת נסים. מאתיים שנה . . . הצ"צ. ארבעים שנה . . . (6) רמט דף.

ג'שצא. כנ"ל אות ג'שנח. הר אדר, באה"ק ת"ו. „מ"ב ספרי תניא שהודפסו . . . לשנת הארבעים . . . ויבנה אריאל". ה'תש"נ . . . שנת נסים. מאתיים שנה . . . הצ"צ. ארבעים שנה . . . (6) רמט דף.

ג'שצב. כנ"ל אות ג'שנח. חשמונאים, באה"ק ת"ו. „מ"ב ספרי תניא שהודפסו . . . לשנת הארבעים . . . ויבנה אריאל". ה'תש"נ . . . שנת נסים. מאתיים שנה . . . הצ"צ. ארבעים שנה . . . (6) רמט דף.

ג'שצג. כנ"ל אות ג'שנח. כפר רות, באה"ק ת"ו. „מ"ב ספרי תניא שהודפסו . . . לשנת הארבעים . . . ויבנה אריאל". ה'תש"נ . . . שנת נסים. מאתיים שנה . . . הצ"צ. ארבעים שנה . . . (6) רמט דף.

ג'שצד. כנ"ל אות ג'שנח. מבוא מודיעים, באה"ק ת"ו. „מ"ב ספרי תניא שהודפסו . . . לשנת הארבעים . . . ויבנה אריאל". ה'תש"נ . . . שנת נסים. מאתיים שנה . . . הצ"צ. ארבעים שנה . . . (6) רמט דף.

ג'שצה. כנ"ל אות ג'שנח. מגדל עדר – צורף, באה"ק ת"ו. „מ"ב ספרי תניא שהודפסו . . . לשנת הארבעים . . . ויבנה אריאל". ה'תש"נ . . . שנת נסים. מאתיים שנה . . . הצ"צ. ארבעים שנה . . . (6) רמט דף.

ג'שצו. כנ"ל אות ג'שנח. נופים – שומרון, באה"ק ת"ו. „מ"ב ספרי תניא שהודפסו . . . לשנת הארבעים . . . ויבנה אריאל". ה'תש"נ . . . שנת נסים. מאתיים שנה . . . הצ"צ. ארבעים שנה . . . (6) רמט דף.

ג'שצז. כנ"ל אות ג'שנח. נחליאל, באה"ק ת"ו. „מ"ב ספרי תניא שהודפסו . . לשנת הארבעים . . ויבנה אריאל". ה'תש"נ . . . שנת נסים. מאתיים שנה . . . הצ"צ. ארבעים שנה . . . (6) רמט דף.

ג'שצח. כנ"ל אות ג'שנח. עטרת, באה"ק ת"ו. „מ"ב ספרי תניא שהודפסו . . לשנת הארבעים . . ויבנה אריאל". ה'תש"נ . . . שנת נסים. מאתיים שנה . . . הצ"צ. ארבעים שנה . . . (6) רמט דף.

ג'שצט. כנ"ל אות ג'שנח. שבי שומרון, באה"ק ת"ו. „מ"ב ספרי תניא שהודפסו . . לשנת הארבעים . . ויבנה אריאל". ה'תש"נ . . . שנת נסים. מאתיים שנה . . . הצ"צ. ארבעים שנה . . . (6) רמט דף.

ג'ת. כנ"ל אות שדמ. קוריטיבאַ, בראזיל, ה'תנש"א. הי' תהא שנת אראנו נפלאות. ארבעים שנה לנשיאות כ"ק אדמו"ר שליט"א. (6) שכט דף.

ג'תא. כנ"ל אות ב'תתקיח. אוהלי יוסף יצחק ליובאוויטש, פאולא, בראזיל, ה'תנש"א. . . . אראנו נפלאות. ארבעים . . . כ"ק אדמו"ר שליט"א. (6) שכט דף.

ג'תב. כנ"ל אות ב'תתקיח. בית חב"ד, אנדרע, פאולא, בראזיל, ה'תנש"א. . . . אראנו נפלאות. ארבעים . . . כ"ק אדמו"ר שליט"א. (6) שכט דף.

ג'תג. כנ"ל אות ב'תתקיח. בית ספר הרבנית חי' מושקא, פאולא, בראזיל, ה'תנש"א. תהא . . . נפלאות. ארבעים . . . כ"ק אדמו"ר שליט"א. (6) שכט דף.

ג'תד. כנ"ל אות ג'דש. טשקנט, רוסיא. ה'תנש"א. תהא . . . נפלאות. ארבעים . . . כ"ק אדמו"ר שליט"א. (6) שכט דף.

ג'תה. כנ"ל אות שלה. סילוואַ, נארט קאראליינא. ה'תנש"א. תהא . . . נפלאות. ארבעים . . . כ"ק אדמו"ר שליט"א. (6) שכט דף.

ג'תו. כנ"ל אות שלה. פראנקלין, נארט קאראליינא. ה'תנש"א. תהא . . . נפלאות. ארבעים . . . כ"ק אדמו"ר שליט"א. (6) שכט דף.

ג'תז. כנ"ל אות שלה. נאַגס העד, נארט קאראליינא. ה'תנש"א. תהא . . . נפלאות. ארבעים . . . כ"ק אדמו"ר שליט"א. (6) שכט דף.

ג'תח. כנ"ל אות שלה. אָוק רידזש, טענעסי. ה'תנש"א. תהא . . . נפלאות. ארבעים . . . כ"ק אדמו"ר שליט"א. (6) שכט דף.

ג'תט. כנ"ל אות שדמ. בית שניאורסאהן-סלונים, חברון, באה"ק ת"ו. ה'תנש"א. תהא . . . נפלאות. ארבעים . . . כ"ק אדמו"ר שליט"א. (6) רנ דף.

ג'תי. כנ"ל אות שדמ. ישוב מיתר, באה"ק ת"ו. ה'תנש"א. תהא . . . נפלאות. ארבעים . . . כ"ק אדמו"ר שליט"א. (6) רנ דף.

ג'תיא. כנ"ל אות שדמ. ישוב להבים, באה"ק ת"ו. ה'תנש"א. תהא . . . נפלאות. ארבעים . . . כ"ק אדמו"ר שליט"א. (6) רנ דף.

ג'תיב. כנ"ל אות שדמ. ישוב עתניאל, באה"ק ת"ו. ה'תנש"א. תהא . . . נפלאות. ארבעים . . . כ"ק אדמו"ר שליט"א. (6) רנ דף.

ג'תיג. כנ"ל אות ג'שיט ואות שלו. „היכל מנחם" מרכז להפצת מעינות החסידות, ירושלים ת"ו. ה'תנש"א. שנת . . . נפלאות. ארבעים . . . כ"ק אדמו"ר שליט"א. (6) רלה דף.

ג'תיד. כנ"ל אות שדמ. הכנסת, ירושלים ת"ו. נדפס ביום יו"ד כסלו, יום הגאולה של אדמו"ר האמצעי. ה'תנש"א. שנת . . . נפלאות. ארבעים . . . כ"ק אדמו"ר שליט"א. (6) רמט דף.

ג'תטו. כנ"ל אות ג'שכג – הוצאה מוגדלת $22\frac{1}{2}$x15 סמ. ברוקלין, נ.י. חג הגאולה י"ט כסלו – קצב שנה – ה'תקנ"ט-ה'תנש"א. שנת אראנו נפלאות. ארבעים שנה לנשיאות כ"ק אדמו"ר שליט"א. (6) רלז דף.

ג'תטז. כנ"ל אות שדמ. עין אילה, באה"ק, ת"ו. ה'תנש"א. שנת . . . נפלאות. ארבעים שנה לנשיאות כ"ק אדמו"ר שליט"א. (6) רנ דף.

ג'תיז. כנ"ל אות שדמ. N.D.C. (נשוינל דיימנד סנטר) שער דרום ירושלים, באה"ק, ת"ו. י"ט כסלו ה'תנש"א. שנת . . . נפלאות. ארבעים שנה לנשיאות כ"ק אדמו"ר שליט"א. (6) רנ דף.

ג'תיח. כנ"ל אות שדמ. קסרי', באה"ק, ת"ו. ה'תנש"א. שנת . . . נפלאות. ארבעים שנה . . . כ"ק אדמו"ר שליט"א. (6) רנ דף.

ג'תיט. כנ"ל אות ג'שנ. אוועזשאַנעדאַ, פראווינץ, ב. איירעס, ארגענטינא. ה'תנש"א. שנת . . . נפלאות. ארבעים שנה לנשיאות כ"ק אדמו"ר שליט"א. (6) של דף.

ג'תכ. כנ"ל אות ג'שנ. אַליוואַס, פראווינץ, ב. א., ארגענטינא. ה'תנש"א. שנת . . . נפלאות. ארבעים שנה לנשיאות כ"ק אדמו"ר שליט"א. (6) של דף.

ג'תכא. כנ"ל אות ג'שנ. טיגרע, פראווינץ, ב. א., ארגענטינא. ה'תנש"א. שנת . . . נפלאות. ארבעים שנה לנשיאות כ"ק אדמו"ר שליט"א. (6) של דף.

ג'תכב. כנ"ל אות ג'שנ. בית חב"ד המרכזי דבוענאס איירעס, ב. א., ארגענטינא. ה'תנש"א. שנת . . . נפלאות. ארבעים שנה לנשיאות כ"ק אדמו"ר שליט"א. (6) של דף.

ג'תכג. כנ"ל אות ג'שנ. בית חב"ד בעלגראנאָ, ב. א., ארגענטינא. ה'תנש"א. שנת . . . נפלאות. ארבעים שנה לנשיאות כ"ק אדמו"ר שליט"א. (6) של דף.

ג'תכד. כנ"ל אות ג'שנ. בית חב"ד וויזשא דעוואָטאָ, ב. א., ארגענטינא. ה'תנש"א. שנת . . . נפלאות. ארבעים שנה לנשיאות כ"ק אדמו"ר שליט"א. (6) של דף.

ג'תכה. כנ"ל אות ג'שנ. בית חב"ד וויזשא קרעספאָ, ב. א., ארגענטינא. ה'תנש"א. שנת . . . נפלאות. ארבעים שנה לנשיאות כ"ק אדמו"ר שליט"א. (6) של דף.

ג'תכו. כנ"ל אות ג'שנ. מאָראָן, פראווינץ, ב. א., ארגענטינא. ה'תנש"א. שנת . . . נפלאות. ארבעים שנה לנשיאות כ"ק אדמו"ר שליט"א. (6) של דף.

ג'תכז. כנ"ל אות ג'שנ. מארטין, פראווינץ, ב. א., ארגענטינא. ה'תנש"א. שנת . . . נפלאות. ארבעים שנה לנשיאות כ"ק אדמו"ר שליט"א. (6) של דף.

ג'תכח. כנ"ל אות ג'שנ. סיודאַדעלאַ, פראווינץ, ב. א., ארגענטינא. ה'תנש"א. שנת . . . נפלאות. ארבעים שנה לנשיאות כ"ק אדמו"ר שליט"א. (6) של דף.

ג'תכט. כנ"ל אות ג'שנ. פלאַנוס, פראווינץ ב. א., ארגענטינא. ה'תנש"א. שנת . . . נפלאות. ארבעים שנה לנשיאות כ"ק אדמו"ר שליט"א. (6) של דף.

ג'תל. כנ"ל אות ג'שנ. פלאַרעס, פראווינץ, ב. א., ארגענטינא. ה'תנש"א. שנת . . . נפלאות. ארבעים שנה לנשיאות כ"ק אדמו"ר שליט"א. (6) של דף.

ג'תלא. כנ"ל אות ג'שנ. קאַנסטיטוסיאָן, בית ספר לבנות אהלי חינוך, ב. א., ארגענטינא. ה'תנש"א. שנת . . . נפלאות. ארבעים שנה לנשיאות כ"ק אדמו"ר שליט"א. (6) של דף.

ג׳תלב. כנ״ל אות ג׳שנ. קילמעס, פּראווינץ, ב. א., ארגענטינא. ה׳תנש״א. שנת . . . נפלאות. ארבעים שנה לנשיאות כ״ק אדמו״ר שליט״א. (6) של דף.

ג׳תלג. כנ״ל אות ג׳שנ. קרית חב״ד מאָרענאָ, פּראווינץ, ב. א., ארגענטינא. ה׳תנש״א. שנת . . . נפלאות. ארבעים שנה לנשיאות כ״ק אדמו״ר שליט״א. (6) של דף.

ג׳תלד. כנ״ל אות ג׳שנ. ראַמאָס מעחיאַ, פּראווינץ, ב. א., ארגענטינא. ה׳תנש״א. שנת . . . נפלאות. ארבעים שנה לנשיאות כ״ק אדמו״ר שליט״א. (6) של דף.

ג׳תלה. כנ״ל אות ג׳שנ. כפר אורוגוואי, במעמד הדלקת המנורה הבנלאומית, ב. א. ,ארגענטינא. [זאת חנוכה] ה׳תנש״א. שנת . . . נפלאות. ארבעים שנה . . . כ״ק אדמו״ר שליט״א. (6) של דף.

ג׳תלו. כנ״ל אות שלה. דאַנוויל, ווירדזשיניא. ה׳תנש״א. שנת . . . נפלאות. (6) של דף.

ג׳תלז. כנ״ל אות שלה. יאָרקטאָון, ווירדזשיניא. ה׳תנש״א. שנת . . . נפלאות. (6) של דף.

ג׳תלח. כנ״ל אות שלה. לינטשבורג. ווירדזשיניא. ה׳תנש״א. שנת . . . נפלאות. (6) של דף.

ג׳תלט. כנ״ל אות שלה. עקסמאר, ווירדזשיניא. ה׳תנש״א. שנת . . . נפלאות. (6) של דף.

ג׳תמ. כנ״ל אות שלה. אומשליינגא, נארט קאסט, דרום אפריקא. ה׳תנש״א. . . . שנת אראנו נפלאות. (6) של דף.

ג׳תמא. כנ״ל אות שלה. קהלת יהודי גרוזיא. בקווינס, נ.י. ה׳תנש״א. הי׳ תהא שנת אראנו נפלאות. (6) של דף.

ג׳תמב. כנ״ל אות ג׳שנ. אלומיניאַ, פּאולא, בראַזיל. ה׳תנש״א. הי׳ תהא שנת אראנו נפלאות. (6) של דף.

ג׳תמג. כנ״ל אות ג׳שנ. בריגאדעירא טאביאס, פּאולא, בראַזיל. ה׳תנש״א. הי׳ תהא שנת אראנו נפלאות. (6) של דף.

ג׳תמד. כנ״ל אות ג׳שנ. וויניאַדאָ, פּאולא, בראַזיל. ה׳תנש״א. הי׳ תהא שנת אראנו נפלאות. (6) של דף.

ג׳תמה. כנ״ל אות ג׳שנ. לאָוועירא, פּאולא, בראַזיל. ה׳תנש״א. הי׳ תהא שנת אראנו נפלאות. (6) של דף.

ג׳תמו. כנ״ל אות ג׳שנ. מאַרינקע, פּאולא, בראַזיל. ה׳תנש״א. הי׳ תהא שנת אראנו נפלאות. (6) של דף.

ג׳תמז. כנ״ל אות ג׳שנ. סומאַרע, פּאולא, בראַזיל. ה׳תנש״א. הי׳ תהא שנת אראנו נפלאות. (6) של דף.

ג׳תמח. כנ״ל אות ג׳שנ. פּיראַפּאָרא, פּאולא, בראַזיל. ה׳תנש״א. הי׳ תהא שנת אראנו נפלאות. (6) של דף.

ג׳תמט. כנ״ל אות ג׳שנ. פּארטא פעליז, פּאולא, בראַזיל. ה׳תנש״א. הי׳ תהא שנת אראנו נפלאות. (6) של דף.

ג׳תנ. כנ״ל אות ג׳שנ. קאַברעאובא, פּאולא, בראַזיל. ה׳תנש״א. הי׳ תהא שנת אראנו נפלאות. (6) של דף.

ג׳תנא. כנ״ל אות שלה. ליובאַוויטש, בריה״מ. ה׳תנש״א. הי׳ תהא שנת אראנו נפלאות. (6) של דף.

ג׳תנב. כנ״ל אות ג׳דש. ראסטאוו דאן, בריה״מ. הו״ל ע״י קה״ת וחברת „שמי״ר״ שבאה״ק. ה׳תש״נ. בסוף הספר מופיע ה„מורה שיעור״. (8) קעח דף. [שאר ההוספות (שבכל הוצאות התניא) המפתח ענינים, שמות, ספרים וכו׳. לוח התיקון וכו׳. רשימת דפוסי תניא וכו׳ — נשמטו מהוצאה זו. (על כמה שערים נעתקו (ע״פ טעות): סניף: מאסקווא, רוסיא)].

ג׳תנג. כנ״ל אות ג׳תנב. טשיכענוואַלי, גרוזיא. הו״ל ע״י קה״ת וחברת „שמי״ר״ שבאה״ק. ה׳תש״נ. (8) קסג דף. [בסוף הספר נשמטו ה„מורה שיעור״ וכל ההוספות (מפתחות, לוח התיקון, וכו׳. רשימת דפוסי תניא וכו׳) שבכל הוצאות התניא. (על כמה שערים נעתק (ע״פ טעות): סניף: מאסקווא, רוסיא)].

ג׳תנד. כנ״ל אות ג׳תנב. ריגה, לאַטוויאַ. הו״ל ע״י קה״ת וחברת „שמי״ר״ שבאה״ק. ה׳תש״נ. בסוף הספר מופיע ה„מורה שיעור״. (8) קעח דף. [שאר ההוספות נשמטו — כנ״ל אות ג׳תנב. (על כמה שערים נעתקו (ע״פ טעות): סניף: מאסקווא, רוסיא)].

ג׳תנה. כנ״ל אות תנב. ליעפּאַיאַ, לאַטוויאַ. הו״ל ע״י קה״ת וחברת „שמי״ר״ שבאה״ק. ה׳תש״נ. בסוף הספר מופיע ה„מורה שיעור״. (8) קעח דף. [שאר ההוספות נשמטו — כנ״ל אות ג׳תנב. (על כמה שערים נעתקו (ע״פ טעות): סניף: מאסקווא, רוסיא)].

ג׳תנו. כנ״ל אות ג׳שנ. אוזשעינאָ דע מעללאָ, פּאולא, בראַזיל. ה׳תנש״א. שנת . . . נפלאות. שנת הצדי״ק לכ״ק אדמו״ר שליט״א. (6) שלב דף.

ג׳תנז. כנ״ל אות ג׳שנ. איזאבעל, פּאולא, בראַזיל. ה׳תנש״א. שנת . . . נפלאות. שנת הצדי״ק לכ״ק אדמו״ר שליט״א. (6) שלב דף.

ג׳תנח. כנ״ל אות ג׳שנ. אַפּאַרעסידאָ, פּאולא, בראַזיל. ה׳תנש״א. שנת . . . נפלאות. שנת הצדי״ק לכ״ק אדמו״ר שליט״א. (6) שלב דף.

ג׳תנט. כנ״ל אות ג׳שנ. באמסוסעסאָ, פּאולא, בראַזיל. ה׳תנש״א. שנת . . . נפלאות. שנת הצדי״ק לכ״ק אדמו״ר שליט״א. (6) שלב דף.

ג׳תס. כנ״ל אות ג׳שנ. מאָרעירא סעזאַר, פּאולא, בראַזיל. ה׳תנש״א. שנת . . . נפלאות. שנת הצדי״ק לכ״ק אדמו״ר שליט״א. (6) שלב דף.

ג׳תסא. כנ״ל אות ג׳שנ. סילוועיראז, פּאולא, בראַזיל. ה׳תנש״א. שנת . . . נפלאות. שנת הצדי״ק לכ״ק אדמו״ר שליט״א. (6) שלב דף.

ג׳תסב. כנ״ל אות ג׳שנ. פּיקעטע, פּאולא, בראַזיל. ה׳תנש״א. שנת . . . נפלאות. שנת הצדי״ק לכ״ק אדמו״ר שליט״א. (6) שלב דף.

ג׳תסג. כנ״ל אות ג׳שנ. קאַסאַפּאַוואַ, פּאולא, בראַזיל. ה׳תנש״א. שנת . . . נפלאות. שנת הצדי״ק לכ״ק אדמו״ר שליט״א. (6) שלב דף.

ג׳תסד. כנ״ל אות ג׳שנ. קומביקאָ, פּאולא, בראַזיל. ה׳תנש״א. שנת . . . נפלאות. שנת הצדי״ק לכ״ק אדמו״ר שליט״א. (6) שלב דף.

ג׳תסה. כנ״ל אות ג׳שנ. קירים, פּאולא, בראַזיל. ה׳תנש״א. שנת . . . נפלאות. שנת הצדי״ק לכ״ק אדמו״ר שליט״א. (6) שלב דף.

ג׳תסו. כנ״ל אות ג׳שנ. קעלוז, פּאולא, בראַזיל. ה׳תנש״א. שנת . . . נפלאות. שנת הצדי״ק לכ״ק אדמו״ר שליט״א. (6) שלב דף.

ג׳תסז. כנ״ל אות ג׳שנ. קרוזייראָ, פּאולא, בראַזיל. ה׳תנש״א. שנת . . . נפלאות. שנת הצדי״ק לכ״ק אדמו״ר שליט״א. (6) שלב דף.

ג׳תסח. כנ״ל אות ג׳שנ. ראָזעיראַ, פּאולא, בראַזיל. ה׳תנש״א. שנת . . . נפלאות. שנת הצדי״ק לכ״ק אדמו״ר שליט״א. (6) שלב דף.

ג׳תסט. כנ״ל אות ג׳שנ. איליאַ דאָ גאָווערנאַדאָר, ריא דע זשעניירא, בראַזיל. ה׳תנש״א. שנת . . . נפלאות. שנת הצדי״ק לכ״ק אדמו״ר שליט״א. (6) שלב דף.

ג׳תע. כנ״ל אות ג׳שנ. אָלאַריאָ, ריא ד. זש., בראַזיל. ה׳תנש״א. שנת . . . נפלאות. שנת הצדי״ק לכ״ק אדמו״ר שליט״א. (6) שלב דף.

ג׳תעא. כנ״ל אות ג׳שנ. אַנדאַראַי, ריא ד. זש., בראַזיל. ה׳תנש״א. שנת . . . נפלאות. שנת הצדי״ק לכ״ק אדמו״ר שליט״א. (6) שלב דף.

ג׳תעב. כנ״ל אות ג׳שנ. באָנסוסעסאָ, ריא ד. זש., בראַזיל. ה׳תנש״א. שנת. בפלאות. שנת הצדי״ק לכ״ק אדמו״ר שליט״א. (6) שלב דף.

ג׳תעג. כנ״ל אות ג׳שנ. בענפיקאָ, ריא ד. זש., בראַזיל. ה׳תנש״א. שנת . . . נפלאות. שנת הצדי״ק לכ״ק אדמו״ר שליט״א. (6) שלב דף.

ג׳תעד. כנ״ל אות ג׳שנ. ווילאַ יזאַבעל, ריא ד. זש., בראַזיל. ה׳תנש״א. שנת. בפלאות. שנת הצדי״ק לכ״ק אדמו״ר שליט״א. (6) שלב דף.

ג׳תעה. כנ״ל אות ג׳שנ. ווילאַ ראַזאַלי, ריא ד. זש., בראַזיל. ה׳תנש״א. שנת. בפלאות. שנת הצדי״ק לכ״ק אדמו״ר שליט״א. (6) שלב דף.

ג׳תעו. כנ״ל אות ג׳שנ. זשאַקאַרעפּאַגוא, ריא ד. זש., בראַזיל. ה׳תנש״א. שנת . . . נפלאות. שנת הצדי״ק לכ״ק אדמו״ר שליט״א. (6) שלב דף.

ג׳תעז. כנ״ל אות ג׳שנ. מאַדורייפּאַ, ריא ד. זש., בראַזיל. ה׳תנש״א. שנת. בפלאות. שנת הצדי״ק לכ״ק אדמו״ר שליט״א. (6) שלב דף.

ג׳תעח. כנ״ל אות ג׳שנ. מאַראַקאַנאַ, ריא ד. זש., בראַזיל. ה׳תנש״א. שנת. בפלאות. שנת הצדי״ק לכ״ק אדמו״ר שליט״א. (6) שלב דף.

ג׳תעט. כנ״ל אות ג׳שנ. מעיעיר, ריא ד. זש., בראַזיל. ה׳תנש״א. שנת . . . נפלאות. שנת הצדי״ק לכ״ק אדמו״ר שליט״א. (6) שלב דף.

ג׳תפ. כנ״ל אות ג׳שנ. עסטאַסיאָ, ריא ד. זש., בראַזיל. ה׳תנש״א. שנת. בפלאות. שנת הצדי״ק לכ״ק אדמו״ר שליט״א. (6) שלב דף.

ג׳תפא. כנ״ל אות ג׳שנ. ענזשעניאָ דענטראָ, ריא ד. זש., בראַזיל. ה׳תנש״א. שנת . . . נפלאות. שנת הצדי״ק לכ״ק אדמו״ר שליט״א. (6) שלב דף.

ג׳תפב. כנ״ל אות ג׳שנ. פראַנטיסקאָ שאוויעיר, ריא ד. זש., בראַזיל. ה׳תנש״א. שנת . . . נפלאות. שנת הצדי״ק לכ״ק אדמו״ר שליט״א. (6) שלב דף.

ג׳תפג. כנ״ל אות ג׳שנ. פראַסאָ דאָ באנדייראָ, ריא ד. זש., בראַזיל. ה׳תנש״א. שנת . . . נפלאות. שנת הצדי״ק לכ״ק אדמו״ר שליט״א. (6) שלב דף.

ג׳תפד. כנ״ל אות ג׳שנ. קאזשו, ריא ד. זש., בראַזיל. ה׳תנש״א. שנת . . . נפלאות. שנת הצדי״ק לכ״ק אדמו״ר שליט״א. (6) שלב דף.

ג׳תפה. כנ״ל אות ג׳שנ. קאַשאַמבי, ריא ד. זש., בראַזיל. ה׳תנש״א. שנת . . . נפלאות. שנת הצדי״ק לכ״ק אדמו״ר שליט״א. (6) שלב דף.

ג׳תפו. כנ״ל אות ג׳שנ. קריסטאָוואַן, ריא ד. זש., בראַזיל. ה׳תנש״א. שנת. בפלאות. שנת הצדי״ק לכ״ק אדמו״ר שליט״א. (6) שלב דף.

ג׳תפז. כנ״ל אות ג׳שנ. ראמאס, ריא ד. זש., בראזיל. ה׳תנש״א. שנת . . . נפלאות. שנת הצדי״ק לכ״ק אדמו״ר שליט״א. (6) שלב דף.

ג׳תפח. כנ״ל אות ג׳שנ. ריא קאמפרידא, ריא ד. זש., בראזיל. ה׳תנש״א. שנת . . . נפלאות. שנת הצדי״ק לכ״ק אדמו״ר שליט״א. (6) שלב דף.

ג׳תפט. כנ״ל אות ג׳שנ. ריאשועילא, ריא ד. זש., בראזיל. ה׳תנש״א. שנת. נפלאות. שנת הצדי״ק לכ״ק אדמו״ר שליט״א. (6) שלב דף.

ג׳תצ. כנ״ל אות ג׳שנ. ענזשעניא גאווא, ריא ד. זש., בראזיל. ה׳תנש״א. שנת . . . נפלאות. שנת הצדי״ק לכ״ק אדמו״ר שליט״א. (6) שלב דף.

ג׳תצא. כנ״ל אות שלה. אנדאווער, מאסאטשוסעטס. ה׳תנש״א. שנת . . . נפלאות. שנת הצדי״ק לכ״ק אדמו״ר שליט״א. (6) שלב דף.

ג׳תצב. כנ״ל אות שלה. אנאנקאק, ווירדזשיניא. ה׳תנש״א. שנת . . . נפלאות. שנת הצדי״ק לכ״ק אדמו״ר שליט״א. (6) שלב דף.

ג׳תצג. כנ״ל אות שלה. אנאנדייל, ווירדזשיניא. ה׳תנש״א. שנת . . . נפלאות. שנת הצדי״ק לכ״ק אדמו״ר שליט״א. (6) שלב דף.

ג׳תצד. כנ״ל אות שלה. ארלינגטאן, ווירדזשיניא. ה׳תנש״א. שנת . . . נפלאות. שנת הצדי״ק לכ״ק אדמו״ר שליט״א. (6) שלב דף.

ג׳תצה. כנ״ל אות שלה. אשלאנד, ווירדזשיניא. ה׳תנש״א. שנת . . . נפלאות. שנת הצדי״ק לכ״ק אדמו״ר שליט״א. (6) שלב דף.

ג׳תצו. כנ״ל אות שלה. טשאנטילי, ווירדזשיניא. ה׳תנש״א. שנת . . . נפלאות. שנת הצדי״ק לכ״ק אדמו״ר שליט״א. (6) שלב דף.

ג׳תצז. כנ״ל אות שלה. טשעסטער, ווירדזשיניא. ה׳תנש״א. שנת . . . נפלאות. שנת הצדי״ק לכ״ק אדמו״ר שליט״א. (6) שלב דף.

ג׳תצח. כנ״ל אות שלה. טשעסטערפילד, ווירדזשיניא. ה׳תנש״א. שנת. נפלאות. שנת הצדי״ק לכ״ק אדמו״ר שליט״א. (6) שלב דף.

ג׳תצט. כנ״ל אות שלה. מידלאטהיאן, ווירדזשיניא. ה׳תנש״א. שנת . . . נפלאות. שנת הצדי״ק לכ״ק אדמו״ר שליט״א. (6) שלב דף.

ג׳תק. כנ״ל אות שדמ. בהוצאה מוקטנת – 5x8 סנטימטר. ברוקלין, נ.י. ה׳תנש״א. . . . שנת אראנו נפלאות. שנת הצדי״ק לכ״ק אדמו״ר שליט״א. (6) שלג דף.

ג׳תקא. כנ״ל אות ג׳תק. ניקאלאיעוו, אוקראינא, בריה״מ. ה׳תנש״א. שנת. נפלאות. שנת הצדי״ק לכ״ק אדמו״ר שליט״א. (6) שלג דף.

ג׳תקב. כנ״ל אות ג׳תק. דניעפראפעטראווסק, אוקראינא, בריה״מ. ה׳תנש״א. שנת . . . נפלאות. שנת הצדי״ק לכ״ק אדמו״ר שליט״א. (6) שלג דף.

ג׳תקג. כנ״ל אות ג׳תק. מעזשיבוזש, אוק., בריה״מ. ה׳תנש״א. שנת . . . נפלאות. שנת הצדי״ק לכ״ק אדמו״ר שליט״א. (6) שלג דף.

ג׳תקד. כנ״ל אות ג׳תק. מעזריטש, אוק., בריה״מ. ה׳תנש״א. שנת . . . נפלאות. שנת הצדי״ק לכ״ק אדמו״ר שליט״א. (6) שלג דף.

ג׳תקה. כנ״ל אות ג׳תק. האדיטש, אוקראינא, בריה״מ. ה׳תנש״א. שנת . . . נפלאות. שנת הצדי״ק לכ״ק אדמו״ר שליט״א. (6) שלג דף.

ג׳תקו. כנ״ל אות ג׳תק. ציון כ״ק אדמו״ר הזקן, האדיטש, אוקראינא, בריה״מ. ה׳תנש״א. שנת . . . נפלאות. שנת הצדי״ק לכ״ק אדמו״ר שליט״א. (6) שלג דף.

ג׳תקז. כנ״ל אות ג׳תק. אניפאלי, אוקראינא, בריה״מ. ה׳תנש״א. שנת . . . נפלאות. שנת הצדי״ק לכ״ק אדמו״ר שליט״א. (6) שלג דף.

ג׳תקח. כנ״ל אות ג׳תק. ציון הרב המגיד, אניפאלי, אוקראינא, בריה״מ. ה׳תנש״א. שנת . . . נפלאות. שנת הצדי״ק לכ״ק אדמו״ר שליט״א. (6) שלג דף.

ג׳תקט. כנ״ל אות ג׳תק. ניעזשין, אוקראינא, בריה״מ. ה׳תנש״א. שנת . . . נפלאות. שנת הצדי״ק לכ״ק אדמו״ר שליט״א. (6) שלג דף.

ג׳תקי. כנ״ל אות ג׳תק. ציון כ״ק אדמו״ר האמצעי, ניעזשין, בריה״מ. ה׳תנש״א. שנת . . . נפלאות. שנת הצדי״ק לכ״ק אדמו״ר שליט״א. (6) שלג דף.

ג׳תקיא. כנ״ל אות ג׳תק. אבאיאן, רוסיא, בריה״מ. ה׳תנש״א. שנת . . . נפלאות. שנת הצדי״ק לכ״ק אדמו״ר שליט״א. (6) שלג דף.

ג׳תקיב. כנ״ל אות ג׳תק. אריאל, רוסיא, בריה״מ. ה׳תנש״א. שנת . . . נפלאות. שנת הצדי״ק לכ״ק אדמו״ר שליט״א. (6) שלג דף.

ג׳תקיג. כנ״ל אות ג׳תק. טולא, רוסיא, בריה״מ. ה׳תנש״א. שנת . . . נפלאות. שנת הצדי״ק לכ״ק אדמו״ר שליט״א. (6) שלג דף.

ג׳תקיד. כנ״ל אות ג׳תק. טשעכאוו, רוסיא, בריה״מ. ה׳תנש״א. שנת . . . נפלאות. שנת הצדי״ק לכ״ק אדמו״ר שליט״א. (6) שלג דף.

ג׳תקטו. כנ״ל אות ג׳תק. אדעסא, אוק., בריה״מ. ה׳תנש״א. שנת . . . נפלאות. שנת הצדי״ק לכ״ק אדמו״ר שליט״א. (6) שלג דף.

ג׳תקטז. כנ״ל אות ג׳תק. אומאן, אוקראינא, בריה״מ. ה׳תנש״א. שנת . . . נפלאות. שנת הצדי״ק לכ״ק אדמו״ר שליט״א. (6) שלג דף.

ג׳תקיז. כנ״ל אות ג׳תק. בראצלאוו, אוק., בריה״מ. ה׳תנש״א. שנת . . . נפלאות. שנת הצדי״ק לכ״ק אדמו״ר שליט״א. (6) שלג דף.

ג׳תקיח. כנ״ל אות ג׳תק. גייסין, אוקראינא, בוריה״מ. ה׳תנש״א. שנת . . . נפלאות. שנת הצדי״ק לכ״ק אדמו״ר שליט״א. (6) שלג דף.

ג׳תקיט. כנ״ל אות ג׳תק. וויניצא, אוק., בריה״מ. ה׳תנש״א. שנת . . . נפלאות. שנת הצדי״ק לכ״ק אדמו״ר שליט״א. (6) שלג דף.

ג׳תקכ. כנ״ל אות ג׳תק. ציון הבעש״ט, מעזשיבוזש, בריה״מ. ה׳תנש״א. שנת . . . נפלאות. שנת הצדי״ק לכ״ק אדמו״ר שליט״א. (6) שלג דף.

ג׳תקכא. כנ״ל אות ג׳תק. מצענסק, רוסיא, בריה״מ. ה׳תנש״א. שנת . . . נפלאות. שנת הצדי״ק לכ״ק אדמו״ר שליט״א. (6) שלג דף.

ג׳תקכב. כנ״ל אות ג׳תק. סערפוכאוו, רוסיא, בריה״מ. ה׳תנש״א. שנת . . . נפלאות. שנת הצדי״ק לכ״ק אדמו״ר שליט״א. (6) שלג דף.

ג׳תקכג. כנ״ל אות ג׳תק. פאדאלסק, רוסיא, בריה״מ. ה׳תנש״א. שנת . . . נפלאות. שנת הצדי״ק לכ״ק אדמו״ר שליט״א. (6) שלג דף.

ג׳תקכד. כנ״ל אות ג׳תק. פאטעזש, רוסיא, בריה״מ. ה׳תנש״א. שנת . . . נפלאות. שנת הצדי״ק לכ״ק אדמו״ר שליט״א. (6) שלג דף.

ג׳תקכה. כנ״ל אות ג׳תק. פלאווסק, רוסיא, בריה״מ. ה׳תנש״א. שנת . . . נפלאות. שנת הצדי״ק לכ״ק אדמו״ר שליט״א. (6) שלג דף.

ג׳תקכו. כנ״ל אות ג׳תק. כמעלניצקי, אוק., בריה״מ. ה׳תנש״א. שנת . . . נפלאות. שנת הצדי״ק לכ״ק אדמו״ר שליט״א. (6) שלג דף.

ג׳תקכז. כנ״ל אות ג׳תק. נאוואגראד־וואלינסקי, אוקראינא, בריה״מ. ה׳תנש״א. שנת . . . נפלאות. שנת הצדי״ק לכ״ק אדמו״ר שליט״א. (6) שלג דף.

ג׳תקכח. כנ״ל אות ג׳תק. סלאוואטא, אוק., בריה״מ. ה׳תנש״א. שנת . . . נפלאות. שנת הצדי״ק לכ״ק אדמו״ר שליט״א. (6) שלג דף.

ג׳תקכט. כנ״ל אות ג׳תק. קארעץ, אוק., בריה״מ. ה׳תנש״א. שנת . . . נפלאות. שנת הצדי״ק לכ״ק אדמו״ר שליט״א. (6) שלג דף.

ג׳תקל. כנ״ל אות ג׳תק. קיעוו, אוקראינא, בריה״מ. ה׳תנש״א. שנת . . . נפלאות. שנת הצדי״ק לכ״ק אדמו״ר שליט״א. (6) שלג דף.

ג׳תקלא. כנ״ל אות ג׳תק. קריוואי ראג, אוק. בריה״מ. ה׳תנש״א. שנת . . . נפלאות. שנת הצדי״ק לכ״ק אדמו״ר שליט״א. (6) שלג דף.

ג׳תקלב. כנ״ל אות ג׳תק. שעפעטאווקא, אוקראינא, בריה״מ. ה׳תנש״א. שנת . . . נפלאות. שנת הצדי״ק לכ״ק אדמו״ר שליט״א. (6) שלג דף.

ג׳תקלג. כנ״ל אות ג׳תק. קורסק, רוסיא, בריה״מ. ה׳תנש״א. שנת . . . נפלאות. שנת הצדי״ק לכ״ק אדמו״ר שליט״א. (6) שלג דף.

ג׳תקלד. כנ״ל אות ג׳תק. שטשעקינא, רוסיא, בריה״מ. ה׳תנש״א. שנת . . . נפלאות. שנת הצדי״ק לכ״ק אדמו״ר שליט״א. (6) שלג דף.

ג׳תקלה. כנ״ל אות ג׳תק. בעלגאראד, רוסיא, בריה״מ. ה׳תנש״א. שנת . . . נפלאות. שנת הצדי״ק לכ״ק אדמו״ר שליט״א. (6) שלג דף.

ג׳תקלו. כנ״ל אות ג׳תק. כארקאוו, אוקראינא, בריה״מ. ה׳תנש״א. שנת . . . נפלאות. שנת הצדי״ק לכ״ק אדמו״ר שליט״א. (6) שלג דף.

ג׳תקלז. כנ״ל אות ג׳תק. ארשא, בעלארוסיא, בריה״מ. ה׳תנש״א. שנת . . . נפלאות. שנת הצדי״ק לכ״ק אדמו״ר שליט״א. (6) שלג דף.

ג׳תקלח. כנ״ל אות ג׳תק. גאגארין, רוסיא, בריה״מ. ה׳תנש״א. שנת . . . נפלאות. שנת הצדי״ק לכ״ק אדמו״ר שליט״א. (6) שלג דף.

ג׳תקלט. כנ״ל אות ג׳תק. הארדאק, בעלארוסיא, בריה״מ. ה׳תנש״א. שנת . . . נפלאות. שנת הצדי״ק לכ״ק אדמו״ר שליט״א. (6) שלג דף.

ג׳תקמ. כנ״ל אות ג׳תק. וויטעבסק, בעלארוסיא, בריה״מ. ה׳תנש״א. שנת . . . נפלאות. שנת הצדי״ק לכ״ק אדמו״ר שליט״א. (6) שלג דף.

ג׳תקמא. כנ״ל אות ג׳תק. וויאזמא, רוסיא, בריה״מ. ה׳תנש״א. שנת . . . נפלאות. שנת הצדי״ק לכ״ק אדמו״ר שליט״א. (6) שלג דף.

ג׳תקמב. כנ״ל אות ג׳תק. לובני, אוקראינא, בריה״מ. ה׳תנש״א. שנת . . . נפלאות. שנת הצדי״ק לכ״ק אדמו״ר שליט״א. (6) שלג דף.

ג׳תקמג. כנ״ל אות ג׳תק. ליאדי, בריה״מ. ה׳תנש״א. שנת . . . נפלאות. שנת הצדי״ק לכ״ק אדמו״ר שליט״א. (6) שלג דף.

ג׳תקמד. כנ״ל אות ג׳תק. ליאזנע, בריה״מ. ה׳תנש״א. שנת . . . נפלאות. שנת הצדי״ק לכ״ק אדמו״ר שליט״א. (6) שלג דף.

ג׳תקמה. כנ״ל אות ג׳תק. מאזשייסק, רוסיא, בריה״מ. ה׳תנש״א. שנת . . . נפלאות. שנת הצדי״ק לכ״ק אדמו״ר שליט״א. (6) שלג דף.

ג׳תקמו. כנ״ל אות ג׳תק. מירגאָראָד, אוקראַינאַ, בריה״מ. ה׳תנש״א. שנת . . . נפלאות. שנת הצדי״ק לכ״ק אדמו״ר שליט״א. (6) שלג דף.

ג׳תקמז. כנ״ל אות ג׳תק. נעוועל, בריה״מ. ה׳תנש״א. שנת . . . נפלאות. שנת הצדי״ק לכ״ק אדמו״ר שליט״א. (6) שלג דף.

ג׳תקמח. כנ״ל אות ג׳תק. סמאָלענסק, רוסיא, בריה״מ. ה׳תנש״א. שנת . . . נפלאות. שנת הצדי״ק לכ״ק אדמו״ר שליט״א. (6) שלג דף.

ג׳תקמט. כנ״ל אות ג׳תק. פיריאַטין, אוקראַינאַ, בריה״מ. ה׳תנש״א. שנת . . . נפלאות. שנת הצדי״ק לכ״ק אדמו״ר שליט״א. (6) שלג דף.

ג׳תקנ. כנ״ל אות ג׳תק. פרילוקי, אוקראַינאַ, בריה״מ. ה׳תנש״א. שנת . . . נפלאות. שנת הצדי״ק לכ״ק אדמו״ר שליט״א. (6) שלג דף.

ג׳תקנא. כנ״ל אות ג׳תק. רודניאַ, בריה״מ. ה׳תנש״א. שנת . . . נפלאות. שנת הצדי״ק לכ״ק אדמו״ר שליט״א. (6) שלג דף.

ג׳תקנב. כנ״ל אות שלה. האַלמס, נ.י. ה׳תנש״א. שנת . . . נפלאות. שנת הצדי״ק לכ״ק אדמו״ר שליט״א. (6) שלה דף.

ג׳תקנג. כנ״ל אות שלה. דעלמאַר, נ.י. ה׳תנש״א. שנת . . . נפלאות. שנת הצדי״ק לכ״ק אדמו״ר שליט״א. (6) שלה דף.

ג׳תקנד. כנ״ל אות שלה. האַפּוועל דזשאַנקשן, נ.י. ה׳תנש״א. שנת . . . נפלאות. שנת הצדי״ק לכ״ק אדמו״ר שליט״א. (6) שלה דף.

ג׳תקנה. כנ״ל אות שלה. הייד פּאַרק, נ.י. ה׳תנש״א. שנת . . . נפלאות. שנת הצדי״ק לכ״ק אדמו״ר שליט״א. (6) שלה דף.

ג׳תקנו. כנ״ל אות שלה. היילאַנד, נ.י. ה׳תנש״א. שנת . . . נפלאות. שנת הצדי״ק לכ״ק אדמו״ר שליט״א. (6) שלה דף.

ג׳תקנז. כנ״ל אות שלה. וואַסייק, נ.י. ה׳תנש״א. שנת . . . נפלאות. שנת הצדי״ק לכ״ק אדמו״ר שליט״א. (6) שלה דף.

ג׳תקנח. כנ״ל אות שלה. ווינגדייל, נ.י. ה׳תנש״א. שנת . . . נפלאות. שנת הצדי״ק לכ״ק אדמו״ר שליט״א. (6) שלה דף.

ג׳תקנט. כנ״ל אות שלה. ווערבאַנק, נ.י. ה׳תנש״א. שנת . . . נפלאות. שנת הצדי״ק לכ״ק אדמו״ר שליט״א. (6) שלה דף.

ג׳תקס. כנ״ל אות שלה. טיוואָלי, נ.י. ה׳תנש״א. שנת . . . נפלאות. שנת הצדי״ק לכ״ק אדמו״ר שליט״א. (6) שלה דף.

ג׳תקסא. כנ״ל אות שלה. מאדינאַ, נ.י. ה׳תנש״א. שנת . . . נפלאות. שנת הצדי״ק לכ״ק אדמו״ר שליט״א. (6) שלה דף.

ג׳תקסב. כנ״ל אות שלה. מאַרלבאָראָ, נ.י. ה׳תנש״א. שנת . . . נפלאות. שנת הצדי״ק לכ״ק אדמו״ר שליט״א. (6) שלה דף.

ג׳תקסג. כנ״ל אות שלה. מידלהאָפּ, נ.י. ה׳תנש״א. שנת . . . נפלאות. שנת הצדי״ק לכ״ק אדמו״ר שליט״א. (6) שלה דף.

ג׳תקסד. כנ״ל אות שלה. מילברוק, נ.י. ה׳תנש״א. שנת . . . נפלאות. שנת הצדי״ק לכ״ק אדמו״ר שליט״א. (6) שלה דף.

ג׳תקסה. כנ״ל אות שלה. מילערטאָן, נ.י. ה׳תנש״א. שנת . . . נפלאות. שנת הצדי״ק לכ״ק אדמו״ר שליט״א. (6) שלה דף.

ג׳תקסו. כנ״ל אות שלה. ניובורג, נ.י. ה׳תנש״א. שנת . . . נפלאות. שנת הצדי״ק לכ״ק אדמו״ר שליט״א. (6) שלה דף.

ג׳תקסז. כנ״ל אות שלה. ניו האַמבורג, נ.י. ה׳תנש״א. שנת . . . נפלאות. שנת הצדי״ק לכ״ק אדמו״ר שליט״א. (6) שלה דף.

ג׳תקסח. כנ״ל אות שלה. סאָלט פּאָינט, נ.י. ה׳תנש״א. שנת . . . נפלאות. שנת הצדי״ק לכ״ק אדמו״ר שליט״א. (6) שלה דף.

ג׳תקסט. כנ״ל אות שלה. סטאַטסבורג, נ.י. ה׳תנש״א. שנת . . . נפלאות. שנת הצדי״ק לכ״ק אדמו״ר שליט״א. (6) שלה דף.

ג׳תקע. כנ״ל אות שלה. סטאַנפאַרדוויל, נ.י. ה׳תנש״א. שנת . . . נפלאות. שנת הצדי״ק לכ״ק אדמו״ר שליט״א. (6) שלה דף.

ג׳תקעא. כנ״ל אות שלה. סטאָרמוויל, נ.י. ה׳תנש״א. שנת . . . נפלאות. שנת הצדי״ק לכ״ק אדמו״ר שליט״א. (6) שלה דף.

ג׳תקעב. כנ״ל אות שלה. סיילעם, ניו דזשערסי. ה׳תנש״א. שנת . . . נפלאות. שנת הצדי״ק לכ״ק אדמו״ר שליט״א. (6) שמ דף.

ג׳תקעג. כנ״ל אות שלה. נאָרמאַ, ניו דזשערסי. ה׳תנש״א. שנת . . . נפלאות. שנת הצדי״ק לכ״ק אדמו״ר שליט״א. (6) שמ דף.

ג׳תקעד. כנ״ל אות שלה. פּאַטערסאָן, נ.י. ה׳תנש״א. שנת . . . נפלאות. שנת הצדי״ק לכ״ק אדמו״ר שליט״א. (6) שלה דף.

ג׳תקעה. כנ״ל אות שלה. פּיין פּליינס, נ.י. ה׳תנש״א. שנת . . . נפלאות. שנת הצדי״ק לכ״ק אדמו״ר שליט״א. (6) שלה דף.

ג׳תקעו. כנ״ל אות שלה. פּלעזונט וואַלי, נ.י. ה׳תנש״א. שנת . . . נפלאות. שנת הצדי״ק לכ״ק אדמו״ר שליט״א. (6) שלה דף.

ג׳תקעז. כנ״ל אות שלה. ריינבעק, נ.י. ה׳תנש״א. שנת . . . נפלאות. שנת הצדי״ק לכ״ק אדמו״ר שליט״א. (6) שלה דף.

ג׳תקעח. כנ״ל אות שלה. ריינקליף, נ.י. ה׳תנש״א. שנת . . . נפלאות. שנת הצדי״ק לכ״ק אדמו״ר שליט״א. (6) שלה דף.

ג׳תקעט. כנ״ל אות שלה. רעד הוק, נ.י. ה׳תנש״א. שנת . . . נפלאות. שנת הצדי״ק לכ״ק אדמו״ר שליט״א. (6) שלה דף.

ג׳תקפ. כנ״ל אות שלה. פּאָוגואַג, נ.י. ה׳תנש״א. שנת . . . נפלאות. שנת הצדי״ק לכ״ק אדמו״ר שליט״א. (6) שלה דף.

ג׳תקפא. כנ״ל אות שלה. פּאָולינג, נ.י. ה׳תנש״א. שנת . . . נפלאות. שנת הצדי״ק לכ״ק אדמו״ר שליט״א. (6) שלה דף.

ג׳תקפב. כנ״ל אות ג׳תק. כינוס השלוחים האירופאי השלישי, ליובאַוויטש, בריה״מ. ה׳תנש״א. שנת . . . נפלאות. שנת הצדי״ק לכ״ק אדמו״ר שליט״א. (6) שלה דף.

ג׳תקפג. כנ״ל אות שלה. כינוס השלוחים האירופאי השלישי, מאסקווא, בריה״מ. ה׳תנש״א. שנת . . . נפלאות. שנת הצדי״ק לכ״ק אדמו״ר שליט״א. (6) שלה דף.

ג׳תקפד. כנ״ל אות ג׳תק. כינוס השלוחים האירופאי השלישי, אַלמאַ אַטאַ, קאַזאַכסטאַן, בריה״מ. כ׳ מנ״א ה׳תנש״א. שנת . . . נפלאות. שנת הצדי״ק לכ״ק אדמו״ר שליט״א. (6) שלה דף.

ג׳תקפה. כנ״ל אות ג׳תק. ציון כ״ק הרה״ג הרה״ח והמקובל וכו׳ ר׳ לוי יצחק ז״ל, אַלמאַ אַטאַ, קאַזאַכסטאַן, בריה״מ. ה׳תנש״א. . . . שנת אראנו נפלאות. שנת הצדי״ק לכ״ק אדמו״ר שליט״א. (6) שלה דף.

ג׳תקפו. כנ״ל אות שלה. קאַלינינגראַד, בריה״מ. 1991. (הו״ל ע״י קה״ת וחברת „שמי״ר״ שבאה״ק). (8) רו דף

ג׳תקפז. כנ״ל אות שלה. קוסטרומא, מקום גלות של כ״ק אדמו״ר הריי״צ נ״ע בשנת ה׳תרפ״ז. י״ב־י״ג תמוז תשנ״א. הי׳ תהא שנת אראנו נפלאות. הו״ל ע״י קה״ת וחברת „שמי״ר״ שבאה״ק (6) רו דף.

ג׳תקפח. כנ״ל אות שלה. צריציו וולגוגראד, בריה״ם. ה׳תנש״א . . אראנו נפלאות. הו״ל ע״י קה״ת וחברת „שמי״ר״ שבאה״ק (6) רו דף

ג׳תקפט. כנ״ל אות שלה. אַסינינג, נ.י. ה׳תנש״א. שנת . . . נפלאות. שנת הצדי״ק לכ״ק אדמו״ר שליט״א. (6) שלז דף.

ג׳תקצ. כנ״ל אות שלה. בעדפאָרד הילס, נ.י. ה׳תנש״א. שנת . . . נפלאות. שנת הצדי״ק לכ״ק אדמו״ר שליט״א. (6) שלז דף.

ג׳תקצא. כנ״ל אות שלה. ברייערקליף מענאָר, נ.י. ה׳תנש״א. שנת . . . נפלאות. שנת הצדי״ק לכ״ק אדמו״ר שליט״א. (6) שלז דף.

ג׳תקצב. כנ״ל אות שלה. מאונט פלעזענט, נ.י. ה׳תנש״א. שנת . . . נפלאות. שנת הצדי״ק לכ״ק אדמו״ר שליט״א. (6) שלז דף.

ג׳תקצג. כנ״ל אות שלה. נאָרט טאַריטאַון, נ.י. ה׳תנש״א. שנת . . . נפלאות. שנת הצדי״ק לכ״ק אדמו״ר שליט״א. (6) שלז דף.

ג׳תקצד. כנ״ל אות שלה. נאָרט סיילעם, נ.י. ה׳תנש״א. שנת . . . נפלאות. שנת הצדי״ק לכ״ק אדמו״ר שליט״א. (6) שלז דף.

ג׳תקצה. כנ״ל אות שלה. ראָסענהיין, ניו דזשערסי. ה׳תנש״א. שנת . . . נפלאות. שנת הצדי״ק לכ״ק אדמו״ר שליט״א. (6) שלז דף.

ג׳תקצו. כנ״ל אות שלה. פּאַטנאַם לייק, נ.י. ה׳תנש״א. שנת . . . נפלאות. שנת הצדי״ק לכ״ק אדמו״ר שליט״א. (6) שלז דף.

ג׳תקצז. כנ״ל אות שלה. לייק פּורדי, נ.י. ה׳תנש״א. שנת . . . נפלאות. שנת הצדי״ק לכ״ק אדמו״ר שליט״א. (6) שלז דף.

ג׳תקצח. כנ״ל אות שלה. פּורדי סטיישן, נ.י. ה׳תנש״א. שנת . . . נפלאות. שנת הצדי״ק לכ״ק אדמו״ר שליט״א. (6) שלז דף.

ג׳תקצט. כנ״ל אות שלה. פיטש לייק, נ.י. ה׳תנש״א. שנת . . . נפלאות. שנת הצדי״ק לכ״ק אדמו״ר שליט״א. (6) שלז דף.

ג׳תר. כנ״ל אות שלה. קאַטאָנאַ, נ.י. ה׳תנש״א. שנת . . . נפלאות. שנת הצדי״ק לכ״ק אדמו״ר שליט״א. (6) שלז דף.

ג׳תרא. כנ״ל אות שלה. קראָטאָן־אָן־האַדסאָן, נ.י. ה׳תנש״א. שנת . . . נפלאות. שנת הצדי״ק לכ״ק אדמו״ר שליט״א. (6) שלז דף.

ג׳תרב. כנ״ל אות שלה. בעטהעל, קאָנעטיקאָט. ה׳תנש״א. שנת . . . נפלאות. שנת הצדי״ק לכ״ק אדמו״ר שליט״א. (6) שלז דף.

ג׳תרג. כנ״ל אות שלה. ווילטאָן, קאָנעטיקאָט. ה׳תנש״א. שנת . . . נפלאות. שנת הצדי״ק לכ״ק אדמו״ר שליט״א. (6) שלז דף.

ג׳תרד. כנ״ל אות שלה. שילה, ניו דזשערסי. ה׳תנש״א. שנת . . . נפלאות. שנת הצדי״ק לכ״ק אדמו״ר שליט״א. (6) שלז דף.

ג׳תרה. כנ״ל אות שלה. סאוט ווילטאָן, קאָנעטיקאָט. ה׳תנש״א. שנת . . . נפלאות. שנת הצדי״ק לכ״ק אדמו״ר שליט״א. (6) שלז דף.

ג׳תרו. כנ״ל אות שלה. טיטיקאַס, קאָנעטיקאַט. ה׳תנש״א. שנת . . . נפלאות. שנת הצדי״ק לכ״ק אדמו״ר שליט״א. (6) שלז דף.

ג׳תרז. כנ״ל אות שלה. רידזשבורי, קאָנעטיקאַט. ה׳תנש״א. שנת . . . נפלאות. שנת הצדי״ק לכ״ק אדמו״ר שליט״א. (6) שלז דף.

ג׳תרח. כנ״ל אות שלה. רידזשפילד, קאָנעטיקאַט. ה׳תנש״א. שנת . . . נפלאות. שנת הצדי״ק לכ״ק אדמו״ר שליט״א. (6) שלז דף.

ג׳תרט. כנ״ל אות שלה. אַבסיקאָן, ניו דזשערסי. ה׳תנש״א. שנת . . . נפלאות. שנת הצדי״ק לכ״ק אדמו״ר שליט״א. (6) שמ דף.

ג׳תרי. כנ״ל אות שלה. אָושען סיטי, ניו דזשערסי. ה׳תנש״א. שנת . . . נפלאות. שנת הצדי״ק לכ״ק אדמו״ר שליט״א. (6) שמ דף.

ג׳תריא. כנ״ל אות שלה. בריגאַנטין, ניו דזשערסי. ה׳תנש״א. שנת . . . נפלאות. שנת הצדי״ק לכ״ק אדמו״ר שליט״א. (6) שמ דף.

ג׳תריב. כנ״ל אות שלה. דאַראָטהי, ניו דזשערסי. ה׳תנש״א. שנת . . . נפלאות. שנת הצדי״ק לכ״ק אדמו״ר שליט״א. (6) שמ דף.

ג׳תריג. כנ״ל אות שלה. האַמאָנטאָן, ניו דזשערסי. ה׳תנש״א. שנת . . . נפלאות. שנת הצדי״ק לכ״ק אדמו״ר שליט״א. (6) שמ דף.

ג׳תריד. כנ״ל אות שלה. ווענטנאָר, ניו דזשערסי. ה׳תנש״א. שנת . . . נפלאות. שנת הצדי״ק לכ״ק אדמו״ר שליט״א. (6) שמ דף.

ג׳תרטו. כנ״ל אות שלה. לאנגפאָרט, ניו דזשערסי. ה׳תנש״א. שנת . . . נפלאות. שנת הצדי״ק לכ״ק אדמו״ר שליט״א. (6) שמ דף.

ג׳תרטז. כנ״ל אות שלה. לינוואוד, ניו דזשערסי. ה׳תנש״א. שנת . . . נפלאות. שנת הצדי״ק לכ״ק אדמו״ר שליט״א. (6) שמ דף.

ג׳תריז. כנ״ל אות שלה. מאַגנאָליאַ, ניו דזשערסי. ה׳תנש״א. שנת . . . נפלאות. שנת הצדי״ק לכ״ק אדמו״ר שליט״א. (6) שמ דף.

ג׳תריח. כנ״ל אות שלה. מאַרגייט, ניו דזשערסי. ה׳תנש״א. שנת . . . נפלאות. שנת הצדי״ק לכ״ק אדמו״ר שליט״א. (6) שמ דף.

ג׳תריט. כנ״ל אות שלה. מייס לאַנדינג, ניו דזשערסי. ה׳תנש״א. שנת . . . נפלאות. שנת הצדי״ק לכ״ק אדמו״ר שליט״א. (6) שמ דף.

ג׳כתר. כנ״ל אות שלה. מק־קי סיטי, ניו דזשערסי. ה׳תנש״א. שנת . . . נפלאות. שנת הצדי״ק לכ״ק אדמו״ר שליט״א. (6) שמ דף.

ג׳תרכא. כנ״ל אות שלה. מילמיי, ניו דזשערסי. ה׳תנש״א. שנת . . . נפלאות. שנת הצדי״ק לכ״ק אדמו״ר שליט״א. (6) שמ דף.

ג׳תרכב. כנ״ל אות שלה. נאָרטפילד, ניו דזשערסי. ה׳תנש״א. שנת . . . נפלאות. שנת הצדי״ק לכ״ק אדמו״ר שליט״א. (6) שמ דף.

ג׳תרכג. כנ״ל אות שלה. סאָמערס פאָינט, ניו דזשערסי. ה׳תנש״א. שנת .. נפלאות. שנת הצדי״ק לכ״ק אדמו״ר שליט״א. (6) שמ דף.

ג׳תרכד. כנ״ל אות שלה. סמיטוויל, ניו דזשערסי. ה׳תנש״א. שנת . . . נפלאות. שנת הצדי״ק לכ״ק אדמו״ר שליט״א. (6) שמ דף.

ג׳תרכה. כנ״ל אות שלה. עג האַרבאָר סיטי, ניו דזשערסי. ה׳תנש״א. שנת .. נפלאות. שנת הצדי״ק לכ״ק אדמו״ר שליט״א. (6) שמ דף.

ג׳תרכו. כנ״ל אות שלה. עלוואוד, ניו דזשערסי. ה׳תנש״א. שנת . . . נפלאות. שנת הצדי״ק לכ״ק אדמו״ר שליט״א. (6) שמ דף.

ג׳תרכז. כנ״ל אות שלה. עסטעל מאַנאָר, ניו דזשערסי. ה׳תנש״א. שנת .. נפלאות. שנת הצדי״ק לכ״ק אדמו״ר שליט״א. (6) שמ דף.

ג׳תרכח. כנ״ל אות שלה. פלעזענטוויל, ניו דזשערסי. ה׳תנש״א. שנת . . . נפלאות. שנת הצדי״ק לכ״ק אדמו״ר שליט״א. (6) שמ דף.

ג׳תרכט. כנ״ל אות שלה. פאָמאָנאַ, ניו דזשערסי. ה׳תנש״א. שנת . . . נפלאות. שנת הצדי״ק לכ״ק אדמו״ר שליט״א. (6) שמ דף.

ג׳תרל. כנ״ל אות שלה. פאָרט ריפאַבליק, ניו דזשערסי. ה׳תנש״א. שנת ... נפלאות. שנת הצדי״ק לכ״ק אדמו״ר שליט״א. (6) שמ דף.

ג׳תרלא. כנ״ל אות שלה. ריטשלאַנד, ניו דזשערסי. ה׳תנש״א. שנת . . . נפלאות. שנת הצדי״ק לכ״ק אדמו״ר שליט״א. (6) שמ דף.

ג׳תרלב. כנ״ל אות שלה. אַוואַלאָן, ניו דזשערסי. ה׳תנש״א. שנת . . . נפלאות. שנת הצדי״ק לכ״ק אדמו״ר שליט״א. (6) שמ דף.

ג׳תרלג. כנ״ל אות שלה. וואודביין, ניו דזשערסי. ה׳תנש״א. שנת . . . נפלאות. שנת הצדי״ק לכ״ק אדמו״ר שליט״א. (6) שמ דף.

ג׳תרלד. כנ״ל אות שלה. ווילדוואוד, ניו דזשערסי. ה׳תנש״א. שנת . . . נפלאות. שנת הצדי״ק לכ״ק אדמו״ר שליט״א. (6) שמ דף.

ג׳תרלה. כנ״ל אות שלה. ווילדוואוד קרעסט, ניו דזשערסי. ה׳תנש״א. שנת .. נפלאות. שנת הצדי״ק לכ״ק אדמו״ר שליט״א. (6) שמ דף.

ג׳תרלו. כנ״ל אות שלה. וועסט ווילדוואוד, ניו דזשערסי. ה׳תנש״א. שנת .. נפלאות. שנת הצדי״ק לכ״ק אדמו״ר שליט״א. (6) שמ דף.

ג׳תרלז. כנ״ל אות שלה. נאָרט ווילדוואוד, ניו דזשערסי. ה׳תנש״א. שנת .. נפלאות. שנת הצדי״ק לכ״ק אדמו״ר שליט״א. (6) שמ דף.

ג׳תרלח. כנ״ל אות שלה. טאַקעהאָו, ניו דזשערסי. ה׳תנש״א. שנת . . . נפלאות. שנת הצדי״ק לכ״ק אדמו״ר שליט״א. (6) שמ דף.

ג׳תרלט. כנ״ל אות שלה. מאַרמאָראַ, ניו דזשערסי. ה׳תנש״א. שנת . . . נפלאות. שנת הצדי״ק לכ״ק אדמו״ר שליט״א. (6) שמ דף.

ג׳תרמ. כנ״ל אות שלה. סטאָן האַרבאָר, ניו דזשערסי. ה׳תנש״א. שנת . . . נפלאות. שנת הצדי״ק לכ״ק אדמו״ר שליט״א. (6) שמ דף.

ג׳תרמא. כנ״ל אות שלה. סי אייל סיטי, ניו דזשערסי. ה׳תנש״א. שנת . . . נפלאות. שנת הצדי״ק לכ״ק אדמו״ר שליט״א. (6) שמ דף.

ג׳תרמב. כנ״ל אות שלה. עלדאָראַ, ניו דזשערסי. ה׳תנש״א. שנת . . . נפלאות. שנת הצדי״ק לכ״ק אדמו״ר שליט״א. (6) שמ דף.

ג׳תרמג. כנ״ל אות שלה. ריאָ גראַנד, ניו דזשערסי. ה׳תנש״א. שנת . . . נפלאות. שנת הצדי״ק לכ״ק אדמו״ר שליט״א. (6) שמ דף.

ג׳תרמד. כנ״ל אות שלה. קייפ מיי, ניו דזשערסי. ה׳תנש״א. שנת . . . נפלאות. שנת הצדי״ק לכ״ק אדמו״ר שליט״א. (6) שמ דף.

ג׳תרמה. כנ״ל אות שלה. קייפ מיי פאָינט, ניו דזשערסי. ה׳תנש״א. שנת . . נפלאות. שנת הצדי״ק לכ״ק אדמו״ר שליט״א. (6) שמ דף.

ג׳תרמו. כנ״ל אות שלה. קייפ מיי קאָרט האַוז, ניו דזשערסי. ה׳תנש״א. שנת . . . נפלאות. שנת הצדי״ק לכ״ק אדמו״ר שליט״א. (6) שמ דף.

ג׳תרמז. כנ״ל אות שלה. וועסט קייפ מיי, ניו דזשערסי. ה׳תנש״א. שנת . . נפלאות. שנת הצדי״ק לכ״ק אדמו״ר שליט״א. (6) שמ דף.

ג׳תרמח. כנ״ל אות שלה. ברידזשטאָן, ניו דזשערסי. ה׳תנש״א. שנת . . . נפלאות. שנת הצדי״ק לכ״ק אדמו״ר שליט״א. (6) שמ דף.

ג׳תרמט. כנ״ל אות שלה. גרעניטש, ניו דזשערסי. ה׳תנש״א. שנת . . . נפלאות. שנת הצדי״ק לכ״ק אדמו״ר שליט״א. (6) שמ דף.

ג׳תרנ. כנ״ל אות שלה. דאָרטטשעסטער, ניו דזשערסי. ה׳תנש״א. שנת . . . נפלאות. שנת הצדי״ק לכ״ק אדמו״ר שליט״א. (6) שמ דף.

ג׳תרנא. כנ״ל אות שלה. דיוויידינג קריק, ניו דזשערסי. ה׳תנש״א. שנת .. נפלאות. שנת הצדי״ק לכ״ק אדמו״ר שליט״א. (6) שמ דף.

ג׳תרנב. כנ״ל אות שלה. דעלמאַנט, ניו דזשערסי. ה׳תנש״א. שנת . . . נפלאות. שנת הצדי״ק לכ״ק אדמו״ר שליט״א. (6) שמ דף.

ג׳תרנג. כנ״ל אות שלה. הייסלערוויל, ניו דזשערסי. ה׳תנש״א. שנת . . . נפלאות. שנת הצדי״ק לכ״ק אדמו״ר שליט״א. (6) שמ דף.

ג׳תרנד. כנ״ל אות שלה. וויינלאַנד, ניו דזשערסי. ה׳תנש״א. שנת . . . נפלאות. שנת הצדי״ק לכ״ק אדמו״ר שליט״א. (6) שמ דף.

ג׳תרנה. כנ״ל אות שלה. ליסבורג, ניו דזשערסי. ה׳תנש״א. שנת . . . נפלאות. שנת הצדי״ק לכ״ק אדמו״ר שליט״א. (6) שמ דף.

ג׳תרנו. כנ״ל אות שלה. מאָוריסטאָון, ניו דזשערסי. ה׳תנש״א. שנת . . . נפלאות. שנת הצדי״ק לכ״ק אדמו״ר שליט״א. (6) שמ דף.

ג׳תרנז. כנ״ל אות שלה. מילוויל, ניו דזשערסי. ה׳תנש״א. שנת . . . נפלאות. שנת הצדי״ק לכ״ק אדמו״ר שליט״א. (6) שמ דף.

ג׳תרנח. כנ״ל אות שלה. ניופאָרט, ניו דזשערסי. ה׳תנש״א. שנת . . . נפלאות. שנת הצדי״ק לכ״ק אדמו״ר שליט״א. (6) שמ דף.

ג׳תרנט. כנ״ל אות שלה. סידאַרוויל, ניו דזשערסי. ה׳תנש״א. שנת . . . נפלאות. שנת הצדי״ק לכ״ק אדמו״ר שליט״א. (6) שמ דף.

ג׳תרס. כנ״ל אות שלה. סטאָו קריק, ניו דזשערסי. ה׳תנש״א. שנת . . . נפלאות. שנת הצדי״ק לכ״ק אדמו״ר שליט״א. (6) שמ דף.

ג׳תרסא. כנ״ל אות שלה. סיברוק, ניו דזשערסי. ה׳תנש״א. שנת . . . נפלאות. שנת הצדי״ק לכ״ק אדמו״ר שליט״א. (6) שמ דף.

ג׳תרסב. כנ״ל אות שלה. פאָרטעסקיו, ניו דזשערסי. ה׳תנש״א. שנת . . . נפלאות. שנת הצדי״ק לכ״ק אדמו״ר שליט״א. (6) שמ דף.

ג׳תרסג. כנ״ל אות שלה. פאָרט נאָריס, ניו דזשערסי. ה׳תנש״א. שנת . . . נפלאות. שנת הצדי״ק לכ״ק אדמו״ר שליט״א. (6) שמ דף.

ג׳תרסד. כנ״ל אות שלה. פאָרט עליזאַבעט, ניו דזשערסי. ה׳תנש״א. שנת .. נפלאות. שנת הצדי״ק לכ״ק אדמו״ר שליט״א. (6) שמ דף.

ג׳תרסה. כנ״ל אות שלה. פיירטאָן, ניו דזשערסי. ה׳תנש״א. שנת . . . נפלאות. שנת הצדי״ק לכ״ק אדמו״ר שליט״א. (6) שמ דף.

ג׳תרסו. כנ״ל אות שלה. קאַרמעל, ניו דזשערסי. ה׳תנש״א. שנת . . . נפלאות. שנת הצדי״ק לכ״ק אדמו״ר שליט״א. (6) שמ דף.

ג׳תרסז. כנ״ל אות שלה. ביונאַ, ניו דזשערסי. ה׳תנש״א. שנת . . . נפלאות. שנת הצדי״ק לכ״ק אדמו״ר שליט״א. (6) שמ דף.

ג׳תרסח. כנ״ל אות שלה. קאַרבין סיטי, ניו דזשערסי. ה׳תנש״א. שנת . . . נפלאות. שנת הצדי״ק לכ״ק אדמו״ר שליט״א. (6) שמ דף.

ג׳תרסט. כנ״ל אות שלה. טשעסטער, פענסילוויינא. ה׳תנש״א. שנת . . . נפלאות. שנת הצדי״ק לכ״ק אדמו״ר שליט״א. (6) שמ דף.

ג׳עתר. כנ״ל אות שלה. וועסט טשעסטער, פענסילוויינא. ה׳תנש״א. שנת . . נפלאות. שנת הצדי״ק לכ״ק אדמו״ר שליט״א. (6) שמ דף.

ג׳אעתר. כנ״ל אות שלה. אַגלטאָון, דעלעווער. ה׳תנש״א. שנת . . . נפלאות. שנת הצדי״ק לכ״ק אדמו״ר שליט״א. (6) שמ דף.

ג׳תערב. כנ״ל אות שלה. בעיר, דעלעווער. ה׳תנש״א. שנת . . . נפלאות. שנת הצדי״ק לכ״ק אדמו״ר שליט״א. (6) שמ דף.

ג׳תרעג. כנ״ל אות שלה. גלאַסגאָו, דעלעווער. ה׳תנש״א. שנת . . . נפלאות. שנת הצדי״ק לכ״ק אדמו״ר שליט״א. (6) שמ דף.

ג׳עדרת. כנ״ל אות שלה. גרינוויל, דעלעווער. ה׳תנש״א. שנת . . . נפלאות. שנת הצדי״ק לכ״ק אדמו״ר שליט״א. (6) שמ דף.

ג׳תרעה. כנ״ל אות שלה. האָקעסין, דעלעווער. ה׳תנש״א. שנת . . . נפלאות. שנת הצדי״ק לכ״ק אדמו״ר שליט״א. (6) שמ דף.

ג׳תרעו. כנ״ל אות שלה. ניו קאָסל, דעלעווער. ה׳תנש״א. שנת . . . נפלאות. שנת הצדי״ק לכ״ק אדמו״ר שליט״א. (6) שמ דף.

ג׳תרעז. כנ״ל אות שלה. ניופאָרט, דעלעווער. ה׳תנש״א. שנת . . . נפלאות. שנת הצדי״ק לכ״ק אדמו״ר שליט״א. (6) שמ דף.

ג׳תרעח. כנ״ל אות שלה. סטאַנטאָן, דעלעווער. ה׳תנש״א. שנת . . . נפלאות. שנת הצדי״ק לכ״ק אדמו״ר שליט״א. (6) שמ דף.

ג׳תרעט. כנ״ל אות שלה. ברוקלין, מאַרילאַנד. ה׳תנש״א. שנת . . . נפלאות. שנת הצדי״ק לכ״ק אדמו״ר שליט״א. (6) שמ דף.

ג׳תרפ. כנ״ל אות שלה. גרינבעלט, מאַרילאַנד. ה׳תנש״א. שנת . . . נפלאות. שנת הצדי״ק לכ״ק אדמו״ר שליט״א. (6) שמ דף.

ג׳תרפא. כנ״ל אות שלה. דאַבלין, מאַרילאַנד. ה׳תנש״א. שנת . . . נפלאות. שנת הצדי״ק לכ״ק אדמו״ר שליט״א. (6) שמ דף.

ג׳תרפב. כנ״ל אות שלה. דאַרלינגטאָן, מאַרילאַנד. ה׳תנש״א. שנת . . . נפלאות. שנת הצדי״ק לכ״ק אדמו״ר שליט״א. (6) שמ דף.

ג׳תרפג. כנ״ל אות שלה. וואודבּרידוש, מאַרילאַנד. ה׳תנש״א. שנת . . . נפלאות. שנת הצדי״ק לכ״ק אדמו״ר שליט״א. (6) שמ דף.

ג׳תרפד. כנ״ל אות שלה. אובנינסק, בריה״מ. י״ל ע״י קה״ת וחברת „שמי״ר״. ה׳תנש״א. שנת . . . נפלאות. (6) שמ דף.

ג׳תרפה. כנ״ל אות שלה. וואַטערלו, מאַרילאַנד. ה׳תנש״א. שנת . . . נפלאות. שנת הצדי״ק לכ״ק אדמו״ר שליט״א. (6) שמ דף.

ג׳תרפו. כנ״ל אות שלה. טשערי היל, מאַרילאַנד. ה׳תנש״א. שנת . . . נפלאות. שנת הצדי״ק לכ״ק אדמו״ר שליט״א. (6) שמ דף.

ג׳תרפז. כנ״ל אות שלה. לאָורעל, מאַרילאַנד. ה׳תנש״א. שנת . . . נפלאות. שנת הצדי״ק לכ״ק אדמו״ר שליט״א. (6) שמ דף.

ג׳תרפח. כנ״ל אות שלה. מלכּוֹבקא, בריה״מ. ה׳תנש״א. שנת . . . נפלאות. (6) שמ דף.

ג׳תרפט. כנ״ל אות שלה. מאַרילאַנד סיטי, מאַרילאַנד. ה׳תנש״א. שנת..נפלאות. שנת הצדי״ק לכ״ק אדמו״ר שליט״א. (6) שמ דף.

ג׳תרצ. כנ״ל אות שלה. ספרינגפילד, מאַרילאַנד. ה׳תנש״א. שנת . . . נפלאות. שנת הצדי״ק לכ״ק אדמו״ר שליט״א. (6) שמ דף.

ג׳תרצא. כנ״ל אות שלה. עדזשוואוד, מאַרילאַנד. ה׳תנש״א. שנת . . . נפלאות. שנת הצדי״ק לכ״ק אדמו״ר שליט״א. (6) שמ דף.

ג׳תרצב. כנ״ל אות שלה. פאָרעסט היל, מאַרילאַנד. ה׳תנש״א. שנת . . . נפלאות. שנת הצדי״ק לכ״ק אדמו״ר שליט״א. (6) שמ דף.

ג׳תרצג. כנ״ל אות שלה. פלעזענט היל, מאַרילאַנד. ה׳תנש״א. שנת . . . נפלאות. שנת הצדי״ק לכ״ק אדמו״ר שליט״א. (6) שמ דף.

ג׳תרצד. כנ״ל אות שלה. שעווי טשייס, מאַרילאַנד. ה׳תנש״א. שנת . . . נפלאות. שנת הצדי״ק לכ״ק אדמו״ר שליט״א. (6) שמ דף.

ג׳תרצה. כנ״ל אות שלה. גאָלדסבּאָראָ, נאָרט קאַראָליינאַ. ה׳תנש״א. שנת..נפלאות. שנת הצדי״ק לכ״ק אדמו״ר שליט״א. (6) שמ דף.

ג׳תרצו. כנ״ל אות שלה. ווילסאָן, נאָרט קאַראָליינאַ. ה׳תנש״א. שנת . . . נפלאות. שנת הצדי״ק לכ״ק אדמו״ר שליט״א. (6) שמ דף.

ג׳תרצז. כנ״ל אות שלה. לאַמבּערטאָן, נאָרט קאַראָליינאַ. ה׳תנש״א. שנת .. נפלאות. שנת הצדי״ק לכ״ק אדמו״ר שליט״א. (6) שמ דף.

ג׳תרחצ. כנ״ל אות שלה. ראַליי, נאָרט קאַראָליינאַ. ה׳תנש״א. שנת . . . נפלאות. שנת הצדי״ק לכ״ק אדמו״ר שליט״א. (6) שמ דף.

ג׳תרצט. כנ״ל אות שלה. ראַקי מאַונט, נאָרט קאַראָליינאַ. ה׳תנש״א. שנת..נפלאות. שנת הצדי״ק לכ״ק אדמו״ר שליט״א. (6) שמ דף.

ג׳תש. כנ״ל אות שלה. ראָענאָוק ראַפּידס, נאָרט קאַראָליינאַ. ה׳תנש״א. שנת . . . נפלאות. שנת הצדי״ק לכ״ק אדמו״ר שליט״א. (6) שמ דף.

ג׳תשא. כנ״ל אות שלה. יעמאַסי, סאַוט קאַראָליינאַ. ה׳תנש״א. שנת . . . נפלאות. שנת הצדי״ק לכ״ק אדמו״ר שליט״א. (6) שמ דף.

ג׳תשב. כנ״ל אות שלה. וואלטערבּאָראָ, סאַוט קאַראָליינאַ. ה׳תנש״א. שנת .. נפלאות. שנת הצדי״ק לכ״ק אדמו״ר שליט״א. (6) שמ דף.

ג׳תשג. כנ״ל אות שלה. מאַנינג, סאַוט קאַראָליינאַ. ה׳תנש״א. שנת . . . נפלאות. שנת הצדי״ק לכ״ק אדמו״ר שליט״א. (6) שמ דף.

ג׳תשד. כנ״ל אות שלה. סאמטער, סאַוט קאַראָליינאַ. ה׳תנש״א. שנת . . . נפלאות. שנת הצדי״ק לכ״ק אדמו״ר שליט״א. (6) שמ דף.

ג׳תשה. כנ״ל אות שלה. פלארענס, סאַוט קאַראָליינאַ. ה׳תנש״א. שנת . . . נפלאות. שנת הצדי״ק לכ״ק אדמו״ר שליט״א. (6) שמ דף.

ג׳תשו. כנ״ל אות שלה. גלען אַלען, ווירדזשיניאַ. ה׳תנש״א. שנת . . . נפלאות. שנת הצדי״ק לכ״ק אדמו״ר שליט״א. (6) שמ דף.

ג׳תשז. כנ״ל אות שלה. מילערס טאַווערן, ווירדזשיניאַ. ה׳תנש״א. שנת .. נפלאות. שנת הצדי״ק לכ״ק אדמו״ר שליט״א. (6) שמ דף.

ג׳תשח. כנ״ל אות שלה. מעקאַניקסוויל, ווירדזשיניאַ. ה׳תנש״א. שנת . . . נפלאות. שנת הצדי״ק לכ״ק אדמו״ר שליט״א. (6) שמ דף.

ג׳תשט. כנ״ל אות שלה. בּאַלאַקלאַבאַ, בריה״מ. י״ל ע״י קה״ת וחברת „שמי״ר״. ה׳תנש״א. שנת . . . נפלאות. (6) שמ דף.

ג׳תשי. כנ״ל אות שלה. פּראָווידענס פארדוש, ווירדזשיניאַ. ה׳תנש״א. שנת . . נפלאות. שנת הצדי״ק לכ״ק אדמו״ר שליט״א. (6) שמ דף.

ג׳תשיא. כנ״ל אות שלה. בּעקסלי, דזשאָרדזשיאַ. ה׳תנש״א. שנת . . . נפלאות. שנת הצדי״ק לכ״ק אדמו״ר שליט״א. (6) שמ דף.

ג׳תשיב. כנ״ל אות שלה. בּראַנסוויק, דזשאָרדזשיאַ. ה׳תנש״א. שנת . . . נפלאות. שנת הצדי״ק לכ״ק אדמו״ר שליט״א. (6) שמ דף.

ג׳תשיג. כנ״ל אות שלה. גלענוויל, דזשאָרדזשיאַ. ה׳תנש״א. שנת . . . נפלאות. שנת הצדי״ק לכ״ק אדמו״ר שליט״א. (6) שמ דף.

ג׳תשיד. כנ״ל אות שלה. דזשעסאַפּ, דזשאָרדזשיאַ. ה׳תנש״א. שנת . . . נפלאות. שנת הצדי״ק לכ״ק אדמו״ר שליט״א. (6) שמ דף.

ג׳תשטו. כנ״ל אות שלה. הייזלהורסט, דזשאָרדזשיאַ. ה׳תנש״א. שנת . . . נפלאות. שנת הצדי״ק לכ״ק אדמו״ר שליט״א. (6) שמ דף.

ג׳תשטז. כנ״ל אות שלה. וואודבּיין, דזשאָרדזשיאַ. ה׳תנש״א. שנת . . . נפלאות. שנת הצדי״ק לכ״ק אדמו״ר שליט״א. (6) שמ דף.

ג׳תשיז. כנ״ל אות שלה. ווידאַליאַ, דזשאָרדזשיאַ. ה׳תנש״א. שנת . . . נפלאות. שנת הצדי״ק לכ״ק אדמו״ר שליט״א. (6) שמ דף.

ג׳תשיח. כנ״ל אות שלה. לייאָנס, דזשאָרדזשיאַ. ה׳תנש״א. שנת . . . נפלאות. שנת הצדי״ק לכ״ק אדמו״ר שליט״א. (6) שמ דף.

ג׳תשיט. כנ״ל אות שלה. מאונט ווערנאָן, דזשאָרדזשיאַ. ה׳תנש״א. שנת . . . נפלאות. שנת הצדי״ק לכ״ק אדמו״ר שליט״א. (6) שמ דף.

ג׳תשכ. כנ״ל אות שלה. סאַוואַנאַ, דזשאָרדזשיאַ. ה׳תנש״א. שנת . . . נפלאות. שנת הצדי״ק לכ״ק אדמו״ר שליט״א. (6) שמ דף.

ג׳תשכא. כנ״ל אות שלה. קינגסלאַנד, דזשאָרדזשיאַ. ה׳תנש״א. שנת . . . נפלאות. שנת הצדי״ק לכ״ק אדמו״ר שליט״א. (6) שמ דף.

ג׳תשכב. כנ״ל אות שלה. קלאַקסטאָן, דזשאָרדזשיאַ. ה׳תנש״א. שנת . . . נפלאות. שנת הצדי״ק לכ״ק אדמו״ר שליט״א. (6) שמ דף.

ג׳תשכג. כנ״ל אות שלה. ריטשמאַנד היל, דזשאָרדזשיאַ. ה׳תנש״א. שנת . . נפלאות. שנת הצדי״ק לכ״ק אדמו״ר שליט״א. (6) שמ דף.

ג׳תשכד. כנ״ל אות שלה. רידזשלאַנד, סאַוט קאַראָליינאַ. ה׳תנש״א. שנת . . . נפלאות. שנת הצדי״ק לכ״ק אדמו״ר שליט״א. (6) שמ דף.

ג׳תשכה. כנ״ל אות שלה. נארופומינסק, בריה״מ. י״ל ע״י קה״ת וחברת „שמי״ר״. ה׳תנש״א. שנת . . . נפלאות. (6) שמ דף.

ג׳תשכו. כנ״ל אות שלה. סעבאסטופול, בריה״מ. י״ל ע״י קה״ת וחברת „שמי״ר״. ה׳תנש״א. שנת . . . נפלאות. (6) שמ דף.

ג׳תשכז. כנ״ל אות שלה. פעודוסייא, בריה״מ. י״ל ע״י קה״ת וחברת „שמי״ר״. ה׳תנש״א. שנת . . . נפלאות. (6) שמ דף.

ג׳תשכח. כנ״ל אות שלה. פושקינו, מחנה־ישראל, „שמי״ר״. בריה״מ. י״ל ע״י קה״ת וחברת „שמי״ר״. ה׳תנש״א. שנת . . . נפלאות. (6) שמ דף.

ג׳תשכט. כנ״ל אות שלה. קאלוגא, בריה״מ. י״ל ע״י קה״ת וחברת „שמי״ר״ ה׳תנש״א. שנת . . . נפלאות. (6) שמ דף.

ג׳תשל. כנ״ל אות שלה. קאצ׳א, בריה״מ. י״ל ע״י קה״ת וחברת „שמי״ר״ ה׳תנש״א. שנת . . . נפלאות. (6) שמ דף.

ג׳תשלא. כנ״ל אות שלה. מוסקבא, בריה״מ. 9 אלול ה׳תנש״א. שנת . . . נפלאות. הו״ל ע״י קה״ת וחברת „שמי״ר״. (6) שמ דף.

ג׳תשלב. כנ״ל אות שלה. לנינגרד, פיטרבורג, ח״י אלול תשנ״א, יום הולדת שני המאורות הגדולים כ״ק הבעש״ט נ״ע וכ״ק אדמו״ר הזקן נ״ע. שנת . . . נפלאות. י״ל ע״י קה״ת וחברת „שמי״ר״. (6) שמ דף.

ג׳תשלג. כנ״ל אות ג׳תק. כימקי, רוסיא, בריה״מ. ה׳תנש״א. שנת . . . נפלאות. שנת הצדי״ק לכ״ק אדמו״ר שליט״א. (6) שמ דף.

ג׳תשלד. כנ״ל אות ג׳תק. דאָלגאָפרודני, רוסיא, בריה״מ. ה׳תנש״א. שנת..נפלאות. שנת הצדי״ק לכ״ק אדמו״ר שליט״א. (6) שמ דף.

ג׳תשלה. כנ״ל אות ג׳תק. בית חב״ד, פאָרט לאודערדייל, פלאָרידאָ. ה׳תנש״א. שנת . . . נפלאות. שנת הצדי״ק לכ״ק אדמו״ר שליט״א. (6) שמ דף.

ג׳תשלו. כנ״ל אות שלה. אֵיילאָ מאָראַדאַ, פלאָרידאַ. ה׳תנש״א. שנת . . . נפלאות. שנת הצדי״ק לכ״ק אדמו״ר שליט״א. (6) שמ דף.

ג׳תשלז. כנ״ל אות שלה. אַלטעמאָנט, פלאָרידאַ. ה׳תנש״א. שנת . . . נפלאות. שנת הצדי״ק לכ״ק אזמו״ר שליט״א. (6) שמ דף.

ג׳תשלח. כנ״ל אות שלה. אַפאָפקאַ, פלאָרידאַ. ה׳תנש״א. שנת . . . נפלאות. שנת הצדי״ק לכ״ק אדמו״ר שליט״א. (6) שמ דף.

ג׳תשלט. כנ״ל אות שלה. ווינטער ספרינגס, פלאָרידאַ. ה׳תנש״א. שנת . נפלאות. שנת הצדי״ק לכ״ק אדמו״ר שליט״א. (6) שמ דף.

ג׳תשמ. כנ״ל אות שלה. ווינטער פאַרק, פלאָרידאַ. ה׳תגש״א. שנת . . . נפלאות. שנת הצדי״ק לכ״ק אדמו״ר שליט״א. (6) שמ דף.

ג׳תשמא. כנ״ל אות שלה. טאַווינייער, פלאָרידאַ. ה׳תנש״א. שנת . . . נפלאות. שנת הצדי״ק לכ״ק אדמו״ר שליט״א. (6) שמ דף.

ג׳תשמב. כנ״ל אות שלה. יולי, פלאָרידאַ. ה׳תנש״א. שנת . . . נפלאות. שנת הצדי״ק לכ״ק אדמו״ר שליט״א. (6) שמ דף.

ג׳תשמג. כנ״ל אות שלה. לאָנגוואוד, פלאָרידאַ. ה׳תנש״א. שנת . . . נפלאות. שנת הצדי״ק לכ״ק אדמו״ר שליט״א. (6) שמ דף.

ג׳תשדמ. כנ״ל אות שלה. לייק מערי, פלאָרידאַ. ה׳תנש״א. שנת . . . נפלאות. שנת הצדי״ק לכ״ק אדמו״ר שליט״א. (6) שמ דף.

ג׳תשמה. כנ״ל אות שלה. מאַראַטאָן, פלאָרידאַ. ה׳תנש״א. שנת . . . נפלאות. שנת הצדי״ק לכ״ק אדמו״ר שליט״א. (6) שמ דף.

ג׳תשמו. כנ״ל אות שלה. מאַרקאָ איילאַנד, פלאָרידאַ. ה׳תנש״א. שנת . . . נפלאות. שנת הצדי״ק לכ״ק אדמו״ר שליט״א. (6) שמ דף.

ג׳תשמז. כנ״ל אות שלה. מייטלאַנד, פלאָרידאַ. ה׳תנש״א. שנת . . . נפלאות. שנת הצדי״ק לכ״ק אדמו״ר שליט״א. (6) שמ דף.

ג׳תשמח. כנ״ל אות שלה. סוויטוואָטער, פלאָרידאַ. ה׳תנש״א. שנת . . . נפלאות. שנת הצדי״ק לכ״ק אדמו״ר שליט״א. (6) שמ דף.

ג׳תשמט. כנ״ל אות שלה. פערין, פלאָרידאַ. ה׳תנש״א. שנת . . . נפלאות. שנת הצדי״ק לכ״ק אדמו״ר שליט״א. (6) שמ דף.

ג׳תשנ. כנ״ל אות שלה. קאָסעלבעררי, פלאָרידאַ. ה׳תנש״א. שנת . . . נפלאות. שנת הצדי״ק לכ״ק אדמו״ר שליט״א. (6) שמ דף.

ג׳תנשא. כנ״ל אות שלה. קאָקאָנאַט גראָוו, פלאָרידאַ. ה׳תנש״א. שנת . . . נפלאות. שנת הצדי״ק לכ״ק אדמו״ר שליט״א. (6) שמ דף.

ג׳תשנב. כנ״ל אות שלה. ביג פיין קי, פלאָרידאַ. ה׳תנש״א. שנת . . . נפלאות. שנת הצדי״ק לכ״ק אדמו״ר שליט״א. (6) שמ דף.

ג׳תשנג. כנ״ל אות שלה. ליטל פיין קי, פלאָרידאַ. ה׳תנש״א. שנת . . . נפלאות. שנת הצדי״ק לכ״ק אדמו״ר שליט״א. (6) שמ דף.

ג׳תשנד. כנ״ל אות שלה. דאַק קי, פלאָרידאַ. ה׳תנש״א. שנת . . . נפלאות. שנת הצדי״ק לכ״ק אדמו״ר שליט״א. (6) שמ דף.

ג׳תשנה. כנ״ל אות שלה. לאָנג קי, פלאָרידאַ. ה׳תנש״א. שנת . . . נפלאות. שנת הצדי״ק לכ״ק אדמו״ר שליט״א. (6) שמ דף.

ג׳תשנו. כנ״ל אות שלה. פלאַנטיישען קי, פלאָרידאַ. ה׳תנש״א. שנת . . . נפלאות. שנת הצדי״ק לכ״ק אדמו״ר שליט״א. (6) שמ דף.

ג׳תשנז. כנ״ל אות שלה. קי ביסקיין, פלאָרידאַ. ה׳תנש״א. שנת . . . נפלאות. שנת הצדי״ק לכ״ק אדמו״ר שליט״א. (6) שמ דף.

ג׳תשנח. כנ״ל אות שלה. קי לאַרגאָ, פלאָרידאַ. ה׳תנש״א. שנת . . . נפלאות. שנת הצדי״ק לכ״ק אדמו״ר שליט״א. (6) שמ דף.

ג׳תשנט. כנ״ל אות שלה. וולדימיר, בריה״מ. ה׳תנש״א. שנת . . . נפלאות. הו״ל ע״י קה״ת וחברת „שמי״ר״. (6) שמ דף.

ג׳תשס. כנ״ל אות שלה. בוש טערמינאַל, ברוקלין, נ.י. ה׳תשנ״ב. תהא . . . נפלאות בכל. שנת הצדי״ק לכ״ק אדמו״ר שליט״א. (6) שמב דף.

ג׳תשסא. כנ״ל אות שלה. פאָולאָ, בראַזיל. ה׳תשנ״ב. תהא . . . נפלאות בכל. שנת הצדי״ק לכ״ק אדמו״ר שליט״א. (6) שמב דף.

ג׳תשסב. כנ״ל אות שלה. אָלד גרענעטש, קאָנעטיקאַט. ה׳תשנ״ב. תהא . . . נפלאות בכל. שנת הצדי״ק לכ״ק אדמו״ר שליט״א. (6) שמב דף.

ג׳תשסג. כנ״ל אות שלה. בייראַם, קאָנעטיקאַט. ה׳תשנ״ב. תהא . . . נפלאות בכל. שנת הצדי״ק לכ״ק אדמו״ר שליט״א. (6) שמב דף.

ג׳תשסד. כנ״ל אות שלה. בעלטאָון, קאָנעטיקאַט. ה׳תשנ״ב. תהא . . . נפלאות בכל. שנת הצדי״ק לכ״ק אדמו״ר שליט״א. (6) שמב דף.

ג׳תשסה. כנ״ל אות שלה. גלענוויל, קאָנעטיקאַט. ה׳תשנ״ב. תהא . . . נפלאות בכל. שנת הצדי״ק לכ״ק אדמו״ר שליט״א. (6) שמב דף.

ג׳תשסו. כנ״ל אות שלה. גרינפילד היל, קאָנעטיקאַט. ה׳תשנ״ב. תהא . . . נפלאות בכל. שנת הצדי״ק לכ״ק אדמו״ר שליט״א. (6) שמב דף.

ג׳תשסז. כנ״ל אות שלה. דאַריען, קאָנעטיקאַט. ה׳תשנ״ב. תהא . . . נפלאות בכל. שנת הצדי״ק לכ״ק אדמו״ר שליט״א. (6) שמב דף.

ג׳תשסח. כנ״ל אות שלה. וויניפאָוק, קאָנעטיקאַט. ה׳תשנ״ב. תהא . . . נפלאות בכל. שנת הצדי״ק לכ״ק אדמו״ר שליט״א. (6) שמב דף.

ג׳תשסט. כנ״ל אות שלה. וועסטאָן, קאָנעטיקאַט. ה׳תשנ״ב. תהא . . . נפלאות בכל. שנת הצדי״ק לכ״ק אדמו״ר שליט״א. (6) שמב דף.

ג׳תשע. כנ״ל אות שלה. טורן אָוו ריווער, קאָנעטיקאַט. ה׳תשנ״ב. תהא . . . נפלאות בכל. שנת הצדי״ק לכ״ק אדמו״ר שליט״א. (6) שמב דף.

ג׳תשעא. כנ״ל אות שלה. נאָרט סטאַמפאָרד, קאָנעטיקאַט. ה׳תשנ״ב. תהא . . . נפלאות בכל. שנת הצדי״ק לכ״ק אדמו״ר שליט״א. (6) שמב דף.

ג׳תשעב. כנ״ל אות שלה. ניו קיינען, קאָנעטיקאַט. ה׳תשנ״ב. תהא . . . נפלאות בכל. שנת הצדי״ק לכ״ק אדמו״ר שליט״א. (6) שמב דף.

ג׳תשעג. כנ״ל אות שלה. איסט נאָרוואָק, קאָנעטיקאַט. ה׳תשנ״ב. תהא . . . נפלאות בכל. שנת הצדי״ק לכ״ק אדמו״ר שליט״א. (6) שמב דף.

ג׳תשעד. כנ״ל אות שלה. וועסט נאָרוואָק, קאָנעטיקאַט. ה׳תשנ״ב. תהא . . . נפלאות בכל. שנת הצדי״ק לכ״ק אדמו״ר שליט״א. (6) שמב דף.

ג׳תשעה. כנ״ל אות שלה. סאַוט נאָרוואָק, קאָנעטיקאַט. ה׳תשנ״ב. תהא . . . נפלאות בכל. שנת הצדי״ק לכ״ק אדמו״ר שליט״א. (6) שמב דף.

ג׳תשעו. כנ״ל אות שלה. סאַוטפאָרט, קאָנעטיקאַט. ה׳תשנ״ב. תהא . . . נפלאות בכל. שנת הצדי״ק לכ״ק אדמו״ר שליט״א. (6) שמב דף.

ג׳תשעז. כנ״ל אות שלה. ספרינגדייל, קאָנעטיקאַט. ה׳תשנ״ב. תהא . . . נפלאות בכל. שנת הצדי״ק לכ״ק אדמו״ר שליט״א. (6) שמב דף.

ג׳תשעח. כנ״ל אות שלה. סילווערמיין, קאָנעטיקאַט. ה׳תשנ״ב. תהא . . . נפלאות בכל. שנת הצדי״ק לכ״ק אדמו״ר שליט״א. (6) שמב דף.

ג׳תשעט. כנ״ל אות שלה. קראַנבורי, קאָנעטיקאַט. ה׳תשנ״ב. תהא . . . נפלאות בכל. שנת הצדי״ק לכ״ק אדמו״ר שליט״א. (6) שמב דף.

ג׳תשפ. כנ״ל אות שלה. ראַונד היל, קאָנעטיקאַט. ה׳תשנ״ב. תהא . . . נפלאות בכל. שנת הצדי״ק לכ״ק אדמו״ר שליט״א. (6) שמב דף.

ג׳תשפא. כנ״ל אות שלה. ריווערסייד, קאָנעטיקאַט. ה׳תשנ״ב. תהא . . . נפלאות בכל. שנת הצדי״ק לכ״ק אדמו״ר שליט״א. (6) שמב דף.

ג׳תשפב. כנ״ל אות שלה. מוסקוה, ספרית לנין, רוסיא, בריה״מ. ה׳תנש״א. . . . אראנו נפלאות. (6) שמב דף.

ג׳תשפג. כנ״ל אות ג׳תק. אוסאָוואַ, רוסיא, בריה״מ. ה׳תנש״א. . . . נפלאות. שנת הצדי״ק לכ״ק אדמו״ר שליט״א. (6) שמב דף.

ג׳תשפד. כנ״ל אות ג׳תק. אַדינצאָוואַ, רוסיא, בריה״מ. ה׳תנש״א. . . . אראנו נפלאות. שנת הצדי״ק לכ״ק אדמו״ר שליט״א. הו״ל ע״י קה״ת וחברת „שמי״ר״. (6) שמב דף.

ג׳תשפה. כנ״ל אות ג׳תק. אילינקא, רוסיא, בריה״מ. ה׳תנש״א. . . . אראנו נפלאות. שנת הצדי״ק לכ״ק אדמו״ר שליט״א. [ז׳ חשון תשנ״ב]. (6) שמב דף.

ג׳תשפו. כנ״ל אות ג׳תק. באַלאַשיכאַ, רוסיא, בריה״מ. ה׳תנש״א. . . . נפלאות. שנת הצדי״ק לכ״ק אדמו״ר שליט״א. (6) שמב דף.

ג'תשפז. כנ"ל אות ג'תק. טולאַ, רוסיא, בריה"מ. מקום פטירתו של הרב מ. דובין ז"ל. ה'תנש"א. . . . אראנו נפלאות. שנת הצדי"ק לכ"ק אדמו"ר שליט"א. [נדפס כ"ז חשון תשנ"ב]. (6) שמה דף.

ג'תשפח. כנ"ל אות ג'תק. דעדאָווסק, רוסיא, בריה"מ. ה'תנש"א. . . . נפלאות. שנת הצדי"ק לכ"ק אדמו"ר שליט"א. (6) שמב דף.

ג'תשפט. כנ"ל אות ג'תק. וונוקאָווא, רוסיא, בריה"מ. ה'תנש"א. . . . נפלאות. שנת הצדי"ק לכ"ק אדמו"ר שליט"א. (6) שמב דף.

ג'תשצ. כנ"ל אות שלה. טרויצק, רוסיא, בריה"מ. ה'תנש"א. . . . אראנו נפלאות. (6) שמב דף.

ג'תשצא. כנ"ל אות ג'תק. סכאָדניאַ, רוסיא, בריה"מ. ה'תנש"א. . . . נפלאות. שנת הצדי"ק לכ"ק אדמו"ר שליט"א. [נדפס כ"א חשון תשנ"ב]. (6) שמה דף.

ג'תשצב. כנ"ל אות ג'תק. נאראבינאָ, רוסיא, בריה"מ. ה'תנש"א. . . . נפלאות. שנת הצדי"ק לכ"ק אדמו"ר שליט"א. (6) שמב דף.

ג'תשצג. כנ"ל אות ג'תק. ניז'ני, נובגורוד, בריה"מ. כ"ד תשרי, ה'תשנ"ב. שנת הצדי"ק לכ"ק אדמו"ר שליט"א. הו"ל ע"י קה"ת, חברת „שמיר" וחברת „חמ"ה". (6) שמב דף.

ג'תשצד. כנ"ל אות ג'תק. קראַסטנאָגאַרסק, רוסיא, בריה"מ. ה'תנש"א. . . . נפלאות. שנת הצדי"ק לכ"ק אדמו"ר שליט"א. (6) שמב דף.

ג'תשצה. כנ"ל אות ג'תק. רעאוטאָוו, רוסיא, בריה"מ. ה'תנש"א. . . . נפלאות. שנת הצדי"ק לכ"ק אדמו"ר שליט"א. (6) שמב דף.

ג'תשצו. כנ"ל אות שלה. קאַסטיליונצ'עללאַ (ליוורנו), איטאליא. ה'תשנ"ב. תהא . . . נפלאות בכל. שנת הצדי"ק לכ"ק אדמו"ר שליט"א. (6) שמה דף.

ג'תשצז. כנ"ל אות שלה. מאַקאָו. ה'תשנ"ב. תהא . . . נפלאות בכל. שנת הצדי"ק לכ"ק אדמו"ר שליט"א. (6) שמב דף.

ג'תשצח. כנ"ל אות שלה. קאַלון, האָנג קאָנג. ה'תשנ"ב. תהא . . . נפלאות בכל. שנת הצדי"ק לכ"ק אדמו"ר שליט"א. (6) שמב דף.

ג'תשצט. כנ"ל אות שלה. בּיי בּיי, דיסטריקט אָוו טשאנגקינג, סיטשואן פראווענץ, סין. ה'תשנ"ב. תהא . . . נפלאות בכל. שנת הצדי"ק לכ"ק אדמו"ר שליט"א. (6) שמב דף.

ג'תת. כנ"ל אות שלה. טשיינג מאַי, טהיילאַנד. ה'תשנ"ב. תהא . . . נפלאות בכל. שנת הצדי"ק לכ"ק אדמו"ר שליט"א. (6) שמב דף.

ג'תתא. כנ"ל אות שלה. אינאָסבּורג פאָלס, ווערמאָנט. ה'תשנ"ב. תהא . . . נפלאות בכל. שנת הצדי"ק לכ"ק אדמו"ר שליט"א. (6) שמה דף.

ג'תתב. כנ"ל אות שלה. בּאַרטאָן, ווערמאָנט. ה'תשנ"ב. תהא . . . נפלאות בכל. שנת הצדי"ק לכ"ק אדמו"ר שליט"א. (6) שמה דף.

ג'תתג. כנ"ל אות שלה. בּאַרי, ווערמאָנט. ה'תשנ"ב. תהא . . . נפלאות בכל. שנת הצדי"ק לכ"ק אדמו"ר שליט"א. (6) שמה דף.

ג'תתד. כנ"ל אות שלה. בּענינגטאָן, ווערמאָנט. ה'תשנ"ב. תהא . . . נפלאות בכל. שנת הצדי"ק לכ"ק אדמו"ר שליט"א. (6) שמה דף.

ג'תתה. כנ"ל אות שלה. בּראַטלבּאָראָ, ווערמאָנט. ה'תשנ"ב. תהא . . . נפלאות בכל. שנת הצדי"ק לכ"ק אדמו"ר שליט"א. (6) שמה דף.

ג'תתו. כנ"ל אות שלה. דזשאָנסאָן, ווערמאָנט. ה'תשנ"ב. תהא . . . נפלאות בכל. שנת הצדי"ק לכ"ק אדמו"ר שליט"א. (6) שמה דף.

ג'תתז. כנ"ל אות שלה. דזשאָרדזשיאָ סענטער, ווערמאָנט. ה'תשנ"ב. תהא . . . נפלאות בכל. שנת הצדי"ק לכ"ק אדמו"ר שליט"א. (6) שמה דף.

ג'תתח. כנ"ל אות שלה. דזשעפערסאנוויל, ווערמאָנט. ה'תשנ"ב. תהא . . . נפלאות בכל. שנת הצדי"ק לכ"ק אדמו"ר שליט"א. (6) שמה דף.

ג'תתט. כנ"ל אות שלה. האַרדוויק, ווערמאָנט. ה'תשנ"ב. תהא . . . נפלאות בכל. שנת הצדי"ק לכ"ק אדמו"ר שליט"א. (6) שמה דף.

ג'תתי. כנ"ל אות שלה. הייד פּאַרק, ווערמאָנט. ה'תשנ"ב. תהא . . . נפלאות בכל. שנת הצדי"ק לכ"ק אדמו"ר שליט"א. (6) שמה דף.

ג'תתיא. כנ"ל אות שלה. וואודסטאָק, ווערמאָנט. ה'תשנ"ב. תהא . . . נפלאות בכל. שנת הצדי"ק לכ"ק אדמו"ר שליט"א. (6) שמה דף.

ג'תתיב. כנ"ל אות שלה. וואטערבּורי, ווערמאָנט. ה'תשנ"ב. תהא . . . נפלאות בכל. שנת הצדי"ק לכ"ק אדמו"ר שליט"א. (6) שמה דף.

ג'תתיג. כנ"ל אות שלה. ווייט ריווער דזשאַנקשן, ווערמאָנט. ה'תשנ"ב. תהא . . . נפלאות בכל. שנת הצדי"ק לכ"ק אדמו"ר שליט"א. (6) שמה דף.

ג'תתיד. כנ"ל אות שלה. וויליסטאָן, ווערמאָנט. ה'תשנ"ב. תהא . . . נפלאות בכל. שנת הצדי"ק לכ"ק אדמו"ר שליט"א. (6) שמה דף.

ג'תתטו. כנ"ל אות שלה. ווינוסקי, ווערמאָנט. ה'תשנ"ב. תהא . . . נפלאות בכל. שנת הצדי"ק לכ"ק אדמו"ר שליט"א. (6) שמה דף.

ג'תתטז. כנ"ל אות שלה. לאָדלאָו, ווערמאָנט. ה'תשנ"ב. תהא . . . נפלאות בכל. שנת הצדי"ק לכ"ק אדמו"ר שליט"א. (6) שמה דף.

ג'תתיז. כנ"ל אות שלה. לינדאנוויל, ווערמאָנט. ה'תשנ"ב. תהא . . . נפלאות בכל. שנת הצדי"ק לכ"ק אדמו"ר שליט"א. (6) שמה דף.

ג'תתיח. כנ"ל אות שלה. מידלבּורי, ווערמאָנט. ה'תשנ"ב. תהא . . . נפלאות בכל. שנת הצדי"ק לכ"ק אדמו"ר שליט"א. (6) שמה דף.

ג'תתיט. כנ"ל אות שלה. מילטאָן, ווערמאָנט. ה'תשנ"ב. תהא . . . נפלאות בכל. שנת הצדי"ק לכ"ק אדמו"ר שליט"א. (6) שמה דף.

ג'תתכ. כנ"ל אות שלה. ניופּאָרט, ווערמאָנט. ה'תשנ"ב. תהא . . . נפלאות בכל. שנת הצדי"ק לכ"ק אדמו"ר שליט"א. (6) שמה דף.

ג'תתכא. כנ"ל אות שלה. סאָוט בורלינגטאָן, ווערמאָנט. ה'תשנ"ב. תהא . . . נפלאות בכל. שנת הצדי"ק לכ"ק אדמו"ר שליט"א. (6) שמה דף.

ג'תתכב. כנ"ל אות שלה. סואָנטאָן, ווערמאָנט. ה'תשנ"ב. תהא . . . נפלאות בכל. שנת הצדי"ק לכ"ק אדמו"ר שליט"א. (6) שמה דף.

ג'תתכג. כנ"ל אות שלה. סטאָו, ווערמאָנט. ה'תשנ"ב. תהא . . . נפלאות בכל. שנת הצדי"ק לכ"ק אדמו"ר שליט"א. (6) שמה דף.

ג'תתכד. כנ"ל אות שלה. ספרינגפילד, ווערמאָנט. ה'תשנ"ב. תהא . . . נפלאות בכל. שנת הצדי"ק לכ"ק אדמו"ר שליט"א. (6) שמה דף.

ג'תתכה. כנ"ל אות שלה. עסעקס דזשאַנקשן, ווערמאָנט. ה'תשנ"ב. תהא . . . נפלאות בכל. שנת הצדי"ק לכ"ק אדמו"ר שליט"א. (6) שמה דף.

ג'תתכו. כנ"ל אות שלה. פּאָטני, ווערמאָנט. ה'תשנ"ב. תהא . . . נפלאות בכל. שנת הצדי"ק לכ"ק אדמו"ר שליט"א. (6) שמה דף.

ג'תתכז. כנ"ל אות שלה. פליינפילד, ווערמאָנט. ה'תשנ"ב. תהא . . . נפלאות בכל. שנת הצדי"ק לכ"ק אדמו"ר שליט"א. (6) שמה דף.

ג'תתכח. כנ"ל אות שלה. פלימוטה, ווערמאָנט. ה'תשנ"ב. תהא . . . נפלאות בכל. שנת הצדי"ק לכ"ק אדמו"ר שליט"א. (6) שמה דף.

ג'תתכט. כנ"ל אות שלה. קאַבּאָט, ווערמאָנט. ה'תשנ"ב. תהא . . . נפלאות בכל. שנת הצדי"ק לכ"ק אדמו"ר שליט"א. (6) שמה דף.

ג'תתל. כנ"ל אות שלה. קאַלטשעסטער, ווערמאָנט. ה'תשנ"ב. תהא . . . נפלאות בכל. שנת הצדי"ק לכ"ק אדמו"ר שליט"א. (6) שמה דף.

ג'תתלא. כנ"ל אות שלה. קאַלייס, ווערמאָנט. ה'תשנ"ב. תהא . . . נפלאות בכל. שנת הצדי"ק לכ"ק אדמו"ר שליט"א. (6) שמה דף.

ג'תתלב. כנ"ל אות שלה. איסט קאַלייס, ווערמאָנט. ה'תשנ"ב. תהא . . . נפלאות בכל. שנת הצדי"ק לכ"ק אדמו"ר שליט"א. (6) שמה דף.

ג'תתלג. כנ"ל אות שלה. קיממבּרידזש, ווערמאָנט. ה'תשנ"ב. תהא . . . נפלאות בכל. שנת הצדי"ק לכ"ק אדמו"ר שליט"א. (6) שמה דף.

ג'תתלד. כנ"ל אות שלה. קילינגטאָן, ווערמאָנט. ה'תשנ"ב. תהא . . . נפלאות בכל. שנת הצדי"ק לכ"ק אדמו"ר שליט"א. (6) שמה דף.

ג'תתלה. כנ"ל אות שלה. ראַיאַלטאָן, ווערמאָנט. ה'תשנ"ב. תהא . . . נפלאות בכל. שנת הצדי"ק לכ"ק אדמו"ר שליט"א. (6) שמה דף.

ג׳תתלו. כנ״ל אות שלה. ראַנדאָלף, ווערמאָנט. ה׳תשנ״ב. תהא . . . נפלאות בכל. שנת הצדי״ק לכ״ק אדמו״ר שליט״א. (6) שמה דף.

ג׳תתלז. כנ״ל אות שלה. ריטשמאָנד, ווערמאָנט. ה׳תשנ״ב. תהא . . . נפלאות בכל. שנת הצדי״ק לכ״ק אדמו״ר שליט״א. (6) שמה דף.

ג׳תתלח. כנ״ל אות שלה. שאַרלאָט, ווערמאָנט. ה׳תשנ״ב. תהא . . . נפלאות בכל. שנת הצדי״ק לכ״ק אדמו״ר שליט״א. (6) שמה דף.

ג׳תתלט. כנ״ל אות שלה. שעלבורן, ווערמאָנט. ה׳תשנ״ב. תהא . . . נפלאות בכל. שנת הצדי״ק לכ״ק אדמו״ר שליט״א. (6) שמה דף.

ג׳תתמ. כנ״ל אות שלה. בית חב״ד קנאַרסי – בית מרדכי – ברוקלין, נ.י. ה׳תשנ״ב. תהא . . . נפלאות בכל. שנת הצדי״ק לכ״ק אדמו״ר שליט״א. (6) שמה דף.

ג׳תתמא. כנ״ל אות ג׳תק. איוואַנטעיעווקא, רוסיא, בריה״מ. ה׳תנש״א. תהא . . . אראנו נפלאות. שנת הצדי״ק לכ״ק אדמו״ר שליט״א. [נדפס כ״ד חשון תשנ״ב] (6) שמה דף.

ג׳תתמב. כנ״ל אות ג׳תק. פערוואָמייסקי, רוסיא, בריה״מ. ה׳תנש״א. תהא . . . אראנו נפלאות. שנת הצדי״ק לכ״ק אדמו״ר שליט״א. [נדפס כ״ד חשון תשנ״ב] (6) שמה דף.

ג׳תתמג. כנ״ל אות ג׳תק. קליאָזמאָ, רוסיא, בריה״מ. ה׳תנש״א. תהא . . . אראנו נפלאות. שנת הצדי״ק לכ״ק אדמו״ר שליט״א. [נדפס כ״ד חשון תשנ״ב] (6) שמה דף.

ג׳תתמד. כנ״ל אות ג׳תק. שערעמעטיעווסקי, רוסיא, בריה״מ. ה׳תנש״א. תהא . . . אראנו נפלאות. שנת הצדי״ק לכ״ק אדמו״ר שליט״א. [נדפס כ״ג חשון תשנ״ב] (6) שמה דף.

ג׳תתמה. כנ״ל אות שלה. אוסטוזינקא, מוסקבה, בריה״מ. ה׳תשנ״ב.

ג׳תתמו. כנ״ל אות שלה. אלעקסעאסקייא, בריה״מ. ה׳תשנ״ב.

ג׳תתמז. כנ״ל אות שלה. ארבאט, בריה״מ. ה׳תשנ״ב.

ג׳תתמח. כנ״ל אות שלה. האַברינאָ, בריה״מ. ה׳תשנ״ב.

ג׳תתמט. כנ״ל אות שלה. ווידנאיע, רוסיא, בריה״מ. ה׳תשנ״ב.

ג׳תתנ. כנ״ל אות שלה. זזזינו, מוסקבה, בריה״מ. י״ד כסלו, ה׳תשנ״ב.

ג׳תתנא. כנ״ל אות שלה. חרושבקה, בריה״מ. ה׳תשנ״ב.

ג׳תתנב. כנ״ל אות שלה. טברסקאי, בריה״מ. י״ד כסלו, ה׳תשנ״ב.

ג׳תתנג. כנ״ל אות שלה. טושינא, מוסקבה, בריה״מ. ה׳תשנ״ב.

ג׳תתנד. כנ״ל אות שלה. טרובנאיא, מוסקבה, בריה״מ. ה׳תשנ״ב.

ג׳תתנה. כנ״ל אות שלה. טשירטאנובא, בריה״מ. ה׳תשנ״ב.

ג׳תתנו. כנ״ל אות שלה. יסיניבא, מוסקבה, בריה״מ. ה׳תשנ״ב.

ג׳תתנז. כנ״ל אות שלה. ישיבת מקור חיים, קונצבו, בריה״מ. ה׳תשנ״ב.

ג׳תתנח. כנ״ל אות שלה. כוכלובסקי פר„ בריה״מ. ה׳תשנ״ב.

ג׳תתנט. כנ״ל אות שלה. לעפערטאָבאָ, בריה״מ. י״ד כסלו, ה׳תשנ״ב.

ג׳תתס. כנ״ל אות שלה. מוסקבה שיראמושקי, בריה״מ. ה׳תשנ״ב.

ג׳תתסא. כנ״ל אות שלה. מיטישטשי, רוסיא, בריה״מ. ה׳תשנ״ב.

ג׳תתסב. כנ״ל אות שלה. מוסקבורצא, מוסקבה, בריה״מ. י״ד כסלו, ה׳תשנ״ב.

ג׳תתסג. כנ״ל אות שלה. נאגאטינו, מוסקבה, בריה״מ. י״ד כסלו, ה׳תשנ״ב.

ג׳תתסד. כנ״ל אות שלה. נימעצקאיא, סלאבאדא, בריה״מ. ה׳תשנ״ב.

ג׳תתסה. כנ״ל אות שלה. סאקאל, בריה״מ. ה׳תשנ״ב.

ג׳תתסו. כנ״ל אות שלה. סורפוחאבסקאיא, זאכטאבא, בריה״מ. ה׳תשנ״ב.

ג׳תתסז. כנ״ל אות שלה. סטראגינאָ, בריה״מ. ה׳תשנ״ב.

ג׳תתסח. כנ״ל אות שלה. פולו, בריה״מ. י״ד כסלו, ה׳תשנ״ב.

ג׳תתסט. כנ״ל אות שלה. צ׳ייסטי פרודי, בריה״מ. י״ד כסלו, ה׳תשנ״ב.

ג׳תתע. כנ״ל אות שלה. קָנקָבו, בריה״מ. י״ד כסלו, ה׳תשנ״ב.

ג׳תתעא. כנ״ל אות שלה. קולפאטשני פר„ מוסקבה, בריה״מ. ה׳תשנ״ב.

ג׳תתעב. כנ״ל אות שלה. קראסני בורוטאָ, בריה״מ. ה׳תשנ״ב.

ג׳תתעג. כנ״ל אות שלה. קרלאטסקיע, מוסקבה, בריה״מ. י״ד כסלו, ה׳תשנ״ב.

ג׳תתעד. כנ״ל אות ג׳שכה. „היכל מנחם״ מרכז להפצת מעיינות החסידות בעיה״ק ירושלים ת״ו. תשנ״ב. תהא . . . נפלאות בכל. שנת הצדי״ק לכ״ק אדמו״ר שליט״א. (6) רלה דף.

ג׳תתעה. כנ״ל אות ג׳שו. „הסתדרות הכללית באי״י, אה״ק. תשנ״ב. תהא . . נפלאות בכל. שנת הצדי״ק לכ״ק אדמו״ר שליט״א (6) שיז דף.

ג׳תתעו. כנ״ל אות שלה. בעלעיבו, מוסקבא, בריה״מ. ה׳תשנ״ב. (6) שמה דף.

ג׳תתעז. כנ״ל אות ג׳תק. וויחינא, בריה״מ. ה׳תנש״א. שנת . . אראנו נפלאות. . . הצדי״ק לכ״ק אדמו״ר שליט״א. (6) שמה דף.

ג׳תתעח. כנ״ל אות ג׳תק. טעסטילשיקי, מוסקבה, בריה״מ. ה׳תנש״א. שנת . . אראנו נפלאות. . . הצדי״ק לכ״ק אדמו״ר שליט״א. (6) שמה דף.

ג׳תתעט. כנ״ל אות שלה. טפלי סטאן, מוסקבא, בריה״מ. ה׳תשנ״ב. שנת . . נפלאות בכל. . . הצדי״ק לכ״ק אדמו״ר שליט״א. (6) שמה דף.

ג׳תתפ. כנ״ל אות שלה. טרופארבו, מוסקבא, בריה״מ. ה׳תשנ״ב. שנת . . נפלאות בכל. . . הצדי״ק לכ״ק אדמו״ר שליט״א. (6) שמה דף.

ג׳תתפא. כנ״ל אות שלה. כאמובניקי, מוסקבא, בריה״מ. ה׳תשנ״ב. שנת . . נפלאות בכל. . . הצדי״ק לכ״ק אדמו״ר שליט״א. (6) שמה דף.

ג׳תתפב. כנ״ל אות ג׳תק. ליאנוזובו, מוסקבא, בריה״מ. תנש״א. . . שנת . . אראנו נפלאות. . . הצדי״ק לכ״ק אדמו״ר שליט״א. (6) שמה דף.

ג׳תתפג. כנ״ל אות ג׳תק. מדבדקאיא, בריה״מ. ה׳תשנ״ב. (6) שמה

ג׳תתפד. כנ״ל אות שלה. סאדובי־קודרינסקא, מוסקבא, בריה״מ. ה׳תשנ״ב. שנת . . נפלאות בכל. . . הצדי״ק לכ״ק אדמו״ר שליט״א. (6) שמה דף.

ג׳תתפה. כנ״ל אות שלה. ניקולינו, מוסקבא, בריה״מ. ה׳תשנ״ב. (6) שמה דף.

ג׳תתפו. כנ״ל אות שלה. קאליטניקי, מוסקבא, בריה״מ. ה׳תשנ״ב. שנת . . נפלאות בכל. . . הצדי״ק לכ״ק אדמו״ר שליט״א. (6) שמה דף.

ג׳תתפז. כנ״ל אות שלה. קיטאי־גורוד, מוסקבא, בריה״מ. י״ד כסלו, ה׳תשנ״ב. (6) שמה דף.

ג׳תתפח. כנ״ל אות ג׳תק. פעטערבורג, ביה״ס שמ״ר ע״י בית הכנסת, בריה״מ. ה׳תשנ״ב. שמה דף.

ג׳תתפט. כנ״ל אות ג׳תק. פעטערבורג, בדירתו של כ״ק אדמו״ר מהוריי״צ נ״ע [מאָחוואוואָיאַ 22], בריה״מ. תשנ״ב. שנת . . נפלאות בכל. . . הצדי״ק לכ״ק אדמו״ר שליט״א. (6) שמה דף.

ג׳תתצ. כנ״ל אות ג׳תק. פעטראפאוולסקע קרעפאָסט, פעטער־בורג, בריה״מ. תשנ״ב. שנת . . נפלאות בכל. . . הצדי״ק לכ״ק אדמו״ר שליט״א. (6) שמה דף.

ג׳תתצא. כנ״ל אות שלה. בית חב״ד, געטעבורג, שוועדן. תשנ״ב. שנת . . נפלאות בכל. . . הצדי״ק לכ״ק אדמו״ר שליט״א. (6) שמה דף.

ג׳תתצב. כנ״ל אות ג׳תק. אורחאָבאָ באָריסאָבאָ, בריה״מ. תנש״א. שנת . . אראנו נפלאות. . . הצדי״ק לכ״ק אדמו״ר שליט״א. (6) שנ דף.

ג׳תתצג. כנ״ל אות ג׳תק. אָכטירקאָ, אוקראַינאָ, בריה״מ. תשנ״ב. (6) שנ דף.

ג׳תתצד. כנ״ל אות ג׳תק. אָלעקסאַנדריאָ, אוקראַינאָ, בריה״מ. תשנ״ב. (6) שנ דף.

ג׳תתצה. כנ״ל אות ג׳תק. אָסטראָג, אוקראַינאָ, בריה״מ. תשנ״ב. (6) שנ דף.

ג׳תתצו. כנ״ל אות ג׳תק. אָרגעיעוו, מאָלדאָווא, בריה״מ. תשנ״ב. (6) שנ דף.

ג׳תתצז. כנ״ל אות ג׳תק. באַלטאָ, אוקראַינאָ, בריה״מ. תשנ״ב. (6) שנ דף.

ג׳תתצח. כנ״ל אות ג׳תק. בעלצי, מאָלדאָווא, בריה״מ. תשנ״ב. (6) שנ דף.

ג׳תתצט. כנ״ל אות ג׳תק. בענדערי, מאָלדאָווא, בריה״מ. תשנ״ב. (6) שנ דף.

ג׳תתק. כנ״ל אות ג׳תק. בערשאַד, אוקראַינאָ, בריה״מ. תשנ״ב. (6) שנ דף.

ג׳תתקא. כנ״ל אות ג׳תק. בראָדי, אוקראַינאָ, בריה״מ. תשנ״ב. (6) שנ דף.

ג׳תתקב. כנ״ל אות ג׳תק. ברדיטשוב, אוקראַינאַ, בריה״מ. תשנ״ב. (6) שנ דף.

ג׳תתקג. כנ״ל אות ג׳תק. גייוואָראָן, אוקראַינאַ, בריה״מ. תשנ״ב. (6) שנ דף.

ג׳תתקד. כנ״ל אות ג׳תק. דאַראַגאַיי־מילאָוואָ, בריה״מ. תנש״א. שנת . . אראנו נפלאות. . . הצדי״ק לכ״ק אדמו״ר שליט״א. (6) שנ דף.

ג׳תתקה. כנ״ל אות ג׳תק. דובנאָ, אוקראַינאַ, בריה״מ. תשנ״ב. (6) שנ דף.

ג׳תתקו. כנ״ל אות ג׳תק. דנעפּראָדזערזשינסק, אוקראַינאַ, בריה״מ. תשנ״ב. (6) שנ דף.

ג׳תתקז. כנ״ל אות ג׳תק. וואַסילקאָוו, אוקראַינאַ, בריה״מ. תשנ״ב. (6) שנ דף.

ג׳תתקח. כנ״ל אות ג׳תק. זאַלאָטשעוו, אוקראַינאַ, בריה״מ. תשנ״ב. (6) שנ דף.

ג׳תתקט. כנ״ל אות ג׳תק. זאַפּאַראָזשיע, אוקראַינאַ, בריה״מ. תשנ״ב. (6) שנ דף.

ג׳תתקי. כנ״ל אות ג׳תק. זבאַראָוו, אוקראַינאַ, בריה״מ. תשנ״ב. (6) שס דף.

ג׳תתקיא. כנ״ל אות ג׳שיט. „היכל מנחם״, מרכז להפצת מעינות החסידות, ירושלים, ת״ו. תשנ״ב. . . שנת . . נפלאות בכל . . הצדי״ק לכ״ק אדמו״ר שליט״א. (6) רלז דף.

ג׳תתקיב. כנ״ל אות שדמ. כינוס בתי חב״ד, מלון גני שולמית, אשקלון, באה״ק. כ״ד טבת, ה׳תשנ״ב. . . שנת . . נפלאות בכל . . הצדי״ק לכ״ק אדמו״ר שליט״א. (6) רנה דף.

ג׳תתקיג. כנ״ל אות ג׳שנ. אַרקאָ יריס, פּאָולאָ, בראַזיל. תשנ״ב. . . שנת . . נפלאות בכל . . הצדי״ק לכ״ק אדמו״ר שליט״א. (6) שנ דף.

ג׳תתקיד. כנ״ל אות ג׳שנ. ווילאָ זשיגלע, פּאָולאָ, בראַזיל. תשנ״ב. . . שנת . . נפלאות בכל . . הצדי״ק לכ״ק אדמו״ר שליט״א. (6) שנ דף.

ג׳תתקטו. כנ״ל אות ג׳שנ. זשאַרדין דאָ לאַגאָ, פּאָולאָ, בראַזיל. תשנ״ב. . . שנת . . נפלאות בכל . . הצדי״ק לכ״ק אדמו״ר שליט״א. (6) שנ דף.

ג׳תתקטז. כנ״ל אות ג׳שנ. זשאַרדין פּאוליסטא, פּאָולאָ, בראַזיל. תשנ״ב. . . שנת . . נפלאות בכל . . הצדי״ק לכ״ק אדמו״ר שליט״א. (6) שנ דף.

ג׳תתקיז. כנ״ל אות ג׳שנ. מאַריסטעללאָ, פּאָולאָ, בראַזיל. תשנ״ב. . . שנת . . נפלאות בכל . . הצדי״ק לכ״ק אדמו״ר שליט״א. (6) שנ דף.

ג׳תתקיח. כנ״ל אות ג׳שנ. פלאַמבאַיאַנט, פּאָולאָ, בראַזיל. תשנ״ב. . . שנת. . נפלאות בכל . . הצדי״ק לכ״ק אדמו״ר שליט״א. (6) שנ דף.

ג׳תתקיט. כנ״ל אות ג׳תק. טשערניגאָוו, אוקראַינאַ, בריה״מ. תשנ״ב. (6) שס דף.

ג׳תתקכ. כנ״ל אות ג׳תק. טשערקאַסי, אוקראַינאַ, בריה״מ. תשנ״ב. (6) שס דף.

ג׳תתקכא. כנ״ל אות ג׳תק. כמעלניק, אוקראַינאַ, בריה״מ. תשנ״ב. (6) שס דף.

ג׳תתקכב. כנ״ל אות ג׳תק. לאַדיזשין, אוקראַינאַ, בריה״מ. תשנ״ב. (6) שס דף.

ג׳תתקכג. כנ״ל אות ג׳תק. לוואָוו, אוקראַינאַ, בריה״מ. תשנ״ב. (6) שס דף.

ג׳תתקכד. כנ״ל אות ג׳תק. נאָוואָמאָסקאָווסק, אוקראַינאַ, בריה״מ. תשנ״ב. (6) שס דף.

ג׳תתקכה. כנ״ל אות ג׳תק. נארווא, עסטאניא, בריה״מ. תשנ״ב. (6) שס דף.

ג׳תתקכו. כנ״ל אות ג׳תק. סטאַראָקאָנסטאַנטינאָוו, אוקראַינאַ, בריה״מ. תשנ״ב. (6) שס דף.

ג׳תתקכז. כנ״ל אות ג׳תק. סמעלאָ, אוקראַינאַ, בריה״מ. תשנ״ב. (6) שס דף.

ג׳תתקכח. כנ״ל אות ג׳תק. סקווירא, אוקראַינאַ, בריה״מ. תשנ״ב. (6) שס דף.

ג׳תתקכט. כנ״ל אות ג׳תק. פּאָלטאַוואַ, אוקראַינאַ, בריה״מ. תשנ״ב. (6) שס דף.

ג׳תתקל. כנ״ל אות ג׳תק. פּאָפּאָווקאַ, רוסיא, בריה״מ. תשנ״ב. (6) שס דף.

ג׳תתקלא. כנ״ל אות ג׳תק. פוסטשינא נא אקע, בריה״מ. כ״ח אדר א׳, תשנ״ב. (6) שס דף.

ג׳תתקלב. כנ״ל אות ג׳תק. פּיראָבאָ, מוסקבא, בריה״מ. תנש״א. שנת . . אראנו נפלאות. . . הצדי״ק לכ״ק אדמו״ר שליט״א. (6) שס דף.

ג׳תתקלג. כנ״ל אות ג׳תק. פלאָרעשטי, מאָלדאָוואַ, בריה״מ. תשנ״ב. (6) שס דף.

ג׳תתקלד. כנ״ל אות ג׳תק. פּערעמישליאַני, אוקראַינאַ, בריה״מ. תשנ״ב. (6) שס דף.

ג׳תתקלה. כנ״ל אות ג׳תק. קאָוונאַ, בריה״מ. תשנ״ב. (6) שס דף.

ג׳תתקלו. כנ״ל אות ג׳תק. קאָבעליאַקי, אוקראַינאַ, בריה״מ. תשנ״ב. (6) שס דף.

ג׳תתקלז. כנ״ל אות ג׳תק. קאָזאַטין, אוקראַינאַ, בריה״מ. תשנ״ב. (6) שס דף.

ג׳תתקלח. כנ״ל אות ג׳תק. קיראָוואָגראַד, אוקראַינאַ, בריה״מ. תשנ״ב. (6) שס דף.

ג׳תתקלט. כנ״ל אות ג׳תק. קישינעוו, מאָלדאָוואָ, בריה״מ. תשנ״ב. (6) שס דף.

ג׳תתקמ. כנ״ל אות ג׳תק. קרעמענטשוג, אוקראַינאַ, בריה״מ. תשנ״ב. (6) שס דף.

ג׳תתקמא. כנ״ל אות ג׳תק. ראָוונאָ, אוקראַינאַ, בריה״מ. תשנ״ב. (6) שס דף.

ג׳תתקמב. כנ״ל אות ג׳תק. רוזשין, אוקראַינאַ, בריה״מ. תשנ״ב. (6) שס דף.

ג׳תתקמג. כנ״ל אות ג׳תק. ריבניצאַ, מאָלדאָוואַ, בריה״מ. תשנ״ב. (6) שס דף.

ג׳תתקמד. כנ״ל אות ג׳תק. רעזינאַ, מאָלדאָוואַ, בריה״מ. תשנ״ב. (6) שס דף.

ג׳תתקמה. כנ״ל אות ג׳תק. שפּאָלאָ, אוקראַינאַ, בריה״מ. תשנ״ב. (6) שס דף.

ג׳תתקמו. כנ״ל אות ג׳תק. ציון הסבא קדישא, שפּאָלאָ, אוקראַינאַ, בריה״מ. תשנ״ב. (6) שס דף.

ג׳תתקמז. כנ״ל אות ג׳תק. שקלאָוו, בעלאָרוסיא, בריה״מ. תשנ״ב. (6) שס דף.

ג׳תתקמח. כנ״ל אות ג׳תק. אוז׳גאראד, אוקראַינאַ, בריה״מ. תשנ״ב. (6) שס דף.

ג׳תתקמט. כנ״ל אות ג׳תק. אוליאנאווסק, רוסיא, בריה״מ. תשנ״ב. (6) שס דף.

ג׳תתקנ. כנ״ל אות ג׳תק. ארדינקא, רוסיא, בריה״מ. תשנ״ב. (6) שס דף.

ג׳תתקנא. כנ״ל אות ג׳תק. ארינין, בריה״מ. תשנ״ב. (6) שס דף.

ג׳תתקנב. כנ״ל אות ג׳תק. ארשא, אוקראַינאַ, בריה״מ. תשנ״ב. (6) שס דף.

ג׳תתקנג. כנ״ל אות ג׳תק. באר, בריה״מ. תשנ״ב. (6) שס דף.

ג׳תתקנד. כנ״ל אות ג׳תק. באריסאוו, אוקראַינאַ, בריה״מ. תשנ״ב. (6) שס דף.

ג׳תתקנה. כנ״ל אות ג׳תק. באראדינא, רוסיא, בריה״מ. תשנ״ב. (6) שס דף.

ג׳תתקנו. כנ״ל אות ג׳תק. בוטירסקי כוטאר, בריה״מ. תשנ״ב. (6) שס דף.

ג׳תתקנז. כנ״ל אות ג׳תק. בעז׳עצק, רוסיא, בריה״מ. תשנ״ב. (6) שס דף.

ג׳תתקנח. כנ״ל אות ג׳תק. בערדיאנסק, רוסיא, בריה״מ. תשנ״ב. (6) שס דף.

ג׳תתקנט. כנ״ל אות ג׳תק. בערעגאווא, בריה״מ. תשנ״ב. (6) שס דף.

ג׳תתקס. כנ״ל אות ג׳תק. בערעזינא, בריה״מ. תשנ״ב. (6) שס דף.

ג׳תתקסא. כנ״ל אות ג׳תק. בריסק, בריה״מ. תשנ״ב. (6) שס דף.

ג׳תתקסב. כנ״ל אות ג׳תק. גאצ־ינא, רוסיא, בריה״מ. תשנ״ב. (6) שס דף.

ג׳תתקסג. כנ״ל אות ג׳תק. גאליאנאווא, בריה״מ. תשנ״ב. (6) שס דף.

ג׳תתקסד. כנ״ל אות ג׳תק. געניטשעסק, בריה״מ. תשנ״ב. (6) שס דף.

ג׳תתקסה. כנ״ל אות ג׳תק. גראדנא, בעלארוסיא, בריה״מ. תשנ״ב. (6) שס דף.

ג׳תתקסו. כנ״ל אות ג׳תק. דאגאווּפילס (דווינסק), לאטוויא, בריה״מ. תשנ״ב. (6) שס דף.

ג׳תתקסז. כנ״ל אות ג׳תק. דאנעצק, אוקראַינאַ, בריה״מ. תשנ״ב. (6) שס דף.

ג׳תתקסח. כנ״ל אות ג׳תק. דעטסקאעי סעלא, רוסיא, בריה״מ. תשנ״ב. (6) שס דף.

ג׳תתקסט. כנ״ל אות ג׳תק. דז׳אנקאי, קאַזאַכסטאַן, בריה״מ. תשנ״ב. (6) שס דף.

ג׳תתקע. כנ״ל אות ג׳תק. וואלאזין, בריה״מ. תשנ״ב. (6) שס דף.

ג׳תתקעא. כנ״ל אות ג׳תק. וויניגראדאווא, אוקראַינאַ, בריה״מ. כ״ו אדר א׳, תשנ״ב. (6) שס דף.

ג׳תתקעב. כנ״ל אות ג׳תק. וועליז, רוסיא, בריה״מ. תשנ״ב. (6) שס דף.

ג׳תתקעג. כנ״ל אות ג׳תק. ווערעיא, בריה״מ. תשנ״ב. (6) שס דף.

ג׳תתקעד. כנ״ל אות ג׳תק. ז׳אווּאראנקי, בריה״מ. תשנ״ב. (6) שס דף.

ג׳תתקעה. כנ״ל אות ג׳תק. טאגאנקא, רוסיא, בריה״מ. תשנ״ב. (6) שס דף.

ג׳תתקעו. כנ״ל אות ג׳תק. טאגאנראג, רוסיא, בריה״מ. תשנ״ב. (6) שס דף.

ג׳תתקעז. כנ״ל אות ג׳תק. טארוסא, בריה״מ. כ״ח אדר א׳, תשנ״ב. (6) שס דף.

ג׳תתקעח. כנ״ל אות ג׳תק. טוועד, רוסיא, בריה״מ. תשנ״ב. (6) שס דף.

ג׳תתקעט. כנ״ל אות ג׳תק. טשערנאכאווסק, בריה״מ. תשנ״ב. (6) שס דף.

ג׳תתקפ. כנ״ל אות ג׳תק. טשעריקאוו, בריה״מ. תשנ״ב. (6) שס דף.

ג׳תתקפא. כנ״ל אות ג׳תק. טשערקיזאווא, רוסיא, בריה״מ. תשנ״ב. (6) שס דף.

ג׳תתקפב. כנ״ל אות ג׳תק. יאזמאילאווא, רוסיא, בריה״מ. תשנ״ב. (6) שס דף.

ג׳תתקפג. כנ״ל אות ג׳תק. יאלטא, אוקראַינאַ, בריה״מ. תשנ״ב. (6) שס דף.

ג׳תתקפד. כנ״ל אות ג׳תק. יאראסלאוול, רוסיא, בריה״מ. תשנ״ב. (6) שס דף.

ג׳תתקפה. כנ״ל אות ג׳תק. לאָסינקאָ, בריה״מ. תשנ״ב. (6) שס דף.

ג׳תתקפו. כנ״ל אות ג׳תק. לוגאַנסק, אוקראַינאַ, בריה״מ. תשנ״ב. (6) שס דף.

ג׳תתקפז. כנ״ל אות ג׳תק. לידא, בעלארוסיא, בריה״מ. תשנ״ב. (6) שס דף.

ג׳תתקפח. כנ״ל אות ג׳תק. מאגילעוו, בעלארוסיא, בריה״מ. תשנ״ב. (6) שס דף.

ג׳תתקפט. כנ״ל אות ג׳תק. מגא, בריה״מ. תשנ״ב. (6) שס דף.

ג׳תתקצ. כנ״ל אות ג׳תק. מוקאטשעווא, אוקראַינאַ, בריה״מ. תשנ״ב. (6) שס דף.

ג׳תתקצא. כנ״ל אות ג׳תק. מוראם, רוסיא, בריה״מ. תשנ״ב. (6) שס דף.

ג׳תתקצב. כנ״ל אות ג׳תק. נאוואגרודאק, בריה״מ. תשנ״ב. (6) שס דף.

ג׳תתקצג. כנ״ל אות ג׳תק. נאווגאראד, רוסיא, בריה״מ. תשנ״ב. (6) שס דף.

ג׳תתקצד. כנ״ל אות ג׳תק. פאלאצק, בעלארוסיא, בריה״מ. תשנ״ב. (6) שס דף.

ג׳תתקצה. כנ״ל אות ג׳תק. פאוולאבסק, בריה״מ. תשנ״ב. (6) שס דף.

ג׳תתקצו. כנ״ל אות ג׳תק. פושקין, רוסיא, בריה״מ. תשנ״ב. (6) שס דף.

ג׳תתקצז. כנ״ל אות ג׳תק. פינסק, בעלארוסיא, בריה״מ. תשנ״ב. (6) שס דף.

ג׳תתקצח. כנ״ל אות ג׳תק. פסקאוו, רוסיא, בריה״מ. תשנ״ב. (6) שס דף.

ג׳תתקצט. כנ״ל אות ג׳תק. ביהכנ״ס הגדול במאסקווא, בריה״מ. תשנ״ב. (6) שס דף.

ג׳תתר (ד׳ אלפים). כנ״ל אות ג׳תק. ביהכנ״ס מארינה־רוסטשה, מאסקווא, בריה״מ. תשנ״ב. (6) שס דף.

ד׳א. כנ״ל אות ג׳תק. זוועניגאָראָדקאָ, אוקראַינאַ, בריה״מ. תשנ״ב. (6) שס דף.

ד׳ב. כנ״ל אות ג׳תק. זשיטאָמיר, אוקראַינאַ, בריה״מ. תשנ״ב. (6) שס דף.

ד׳ג. כנ״ל אות ג׳תק. טאַלין, עסטאניא, בריה״מ. תשנ״ב. (6) שס דף.

ד׳ד. כנ״ל אות ג׳תק. טאַלנאָיע, אוקראַינאַ, בריה״מ. תשנ״ב. (6) שס דף.

ד׳ה. כנ״ל אות ג׳תק. טארטו, עסטאניא, בריה״מ. תשנ״ב. (6) שס דף.

ד׳ו. כנ״ל אות ג׳תק. טולטשין, אוקראַינאַ, בריה״מ. תשנ״ב. (6) שס דף.

ד׳ז. כנ״ל אות ג׳תק. טיראַספאָל, מאָלדאָוואַ, בריה״מ. תשנ״ב. (6) שס דף.

ד׳ח. כנ״ל אות ג׳תק. טערנאָפּאָל, אוקראַינאַ, בריה״מ. תשנ״ב. (6) שס דף.

ד׳ט. כנ״ל אות ג׳תק. ביקאָוואַ, רוסיא, בריה״מ. כ׳ שבט תשנ״ב. (6) שס דף.

ד׳י. כנ״ל אות ג׳תק. טשערנאגולובקא, בריה״מ. תנש״א. שנת . . או־אנו . . הצדיק. [תשנ״ב]. (6) שס דף.

ד׳יא. כנ״ל אות ג׳תק. ליובערצי, רוסיא, בריה״מ. ז׳ שבט תשנ״ב. (6) שס דף.

ד׳יב. כנ״ל אות ג׳תק. ליטקארינא, רוסיא, בריה״מ. ז׳ שבט תשנ״ב. (6) שס דף.

ד׳יג. כנ״ל אות ג׳תק. מארינא, בריה״מ. ט׳ שבט תשנ״ב. (6) שס דף.

ד׳יד. כנ״ל אות ג׳תק. סאָסענקי, רוסיא, בריה״מ. תנש״א. . . שנת . . אראנו . . הצדיק. (6) שס דף.

ד׳טו. כנ״ל אות ג׳תק. סטשערבינקא, בריה״מ. ט׳ שבט תשנ״ב. (6) שס דף.

ד׳טז. כנ״ל אות ג׳תק. פריאָזינא, בריה״מ. [תשנ״ב]. (6) שס דף.

ד׳יז כנ״ל אות ג׳תק. קאלאָשינא, מאסקבא, בריה״מ. תנש״א. . . שנת אראנו . . הצדיק [תשנ״ב]. שס דף.

ד׳יח. כנ״ל אות ג׳תק. ראָסטאקינאָ, בריה״מ. תשנ״ב. שס דף.

ד׳יט. כנ״ל אות שדמ. אחיטוב, אה״ק. תשנ״ב. . . נפלאות בכל . . הצדי״ק לכ״ק אדמו״ר שליט״א. (6) שס דף.

ד׳כ. כנ״ל אות שדמ. אלוקש, אה״ק. תשנ״ב. . . נפלאות בכל . . הצדי״ק לכ״ק אדמו״ר שליט״א. (6) שנ דף.

ד׳כא. כנ״ל אות שדמ. בורסת היהלומים הישראלית, רמת גן, אה״ק. תשנ״ב. . . נפלאות בכל . . הצדי״ק לכ״ק אדמו״ר שליט״א. (6) שנ דף.

ד׳כב. כנ״ל אות שדמ. ביהכנ״ס אור החיים, עיר העתיקה ירושלים ת״ו, אה״ק. תשנ״ב. . . נפלאות בכל . . הצדי״ק לכ״ק אדמו״ר שליט״א. (6) שנ דף.

ד׳כג. כנ״ל אות שדמ. בי״ס חב״ד גבעת עדה, אה״ק. תשנ״ב. . . נפלאות בכל . . הצדי״ק לכ״ק אדמו״ר שליט״א. (6) שנ דף.

ד׳כד. כנ״ל אות שדמ. מושב אלישמע, אה״ק. תשנ״ב. . . נפלאות בכל . . הצדי״ק לכ״ק אדמו״ר שליט״א. (6) שנ דף.

ד׳כה. כנ״ל אות שדמ. מושב חוסן, אה״ק. תשנ״ב. . . נפלאות בכל . . הצדי״ק לכ״ק אדמו״ר שליט״א. (6) שנ דף.

ד׳כו. כנ״ל אות שדמ. מושב דובב, אה״ק. תשנ״ב. . . נפלאות בכל . . הצדי״ק לכ״ק אדמו״ר שליט״א. (6) שנ דף.

ד׳כז. כנ״ל אות שדמ. מושב תפרח, אה״ק. תשנ״ב. . . נפלאות בכל . . הצדי״ק לכ״ק אדמו״ר שליט״א. (6) שנ דף.

ד׳כח. כנ״ל אות שדמ. צור שלום, אה״ק. תשנ״ב. . . נפלאות בכל . . הצדי״ק לכ״ק אדמו״ר שליט״א. (6) שנ דף.

ד'כט. כנ"ל אות שדמ. קרית עקרון, אה"ק. תשנ"ב. . . נפלאות בכל . . הצדי"ק לכ"ק אדמו"ר שליט"א. (6) שנ דף.

ד'ל. כנ"ל אות שדמ. שכונת בית הכרם, אה"ק. תשנ"ב. . . נפלאות בכל . . הצדי"ק לכ"ק אדמו"ר שליט"א. (6) שנ דף.

ד'לא. כנ"ל אות ג'שנה. אַלטאָ דאָ באָאָ וויסטאָ, פּאָולאָ, בראַזיל. תשנ"ב. . . נפלאות בכל . . הצדי"ק לכ"ק אדמו"ר שליט"א. (6) שנג דף.

ד'לב. כנ"ל אות ג'שנה. אַלטאָ דאָ קאַפּיוואַרי, פּאָולאָ, בראַזיל. תשנ"ב. . . שנת נפלאות בכל . . הצדי"ק לכ"ק אדמו"ר שליט"א. (6) שנג דף.

ד'לג. כנ"ל אות ג'שנה. אַקוּאַרעלאָ, פּאָולאָ, בראַזיל. תשנ"ב. . . שנת נפלאות בכל . . הצדי"ק לכ"ק אדמו"ר שליט"א. (6) שנג דף.

ד'לד. כנ"ל אות ג'שנה. באָסקע לוסיאַדאָס, פּאָולאָ, בראַזיל. תשנ"ב. . . נפלאות בכל . . הצדי"ק לכ"ק אדמו"ר שליט"א. (6) שנג דף.

ד'לה. כנ"ל אות ג'שנה. בעלוועדערע, פּאָולאָ, בראַזיל. תשנ"ב. . . נפלאות בכל . . הצדי"ק לכ"ק אדמו"ר שליט"א. (6) שנג דף.

ד'לו. כנ"ל אות ג'שנה. וואַלע ענקאַנטאַדאָ, פּאָולאָ, בראַזיל. תשנ"ב. . . נפלאות בכל . . הצדי"ק לכ"ק אדמו"ר שליט"א. (6) שנג דף.

ד'לז. כנ"ל אות ג'שנה. ווילאָ אַבערנעזיאָ, פּאָולאָ, בראַזיל. תשנ"ב. . . נפלאות בכל . . הצדי"ק לכ"ק אדמו"ר שליט"א. (6) שנג דף.

ד'לח. כנ"ל אות ג'שנה. ווילאָ אינגלעזאָ, פּאָולאָ, בראַזיל. תשנ"ב. . . נפלאות בכל . . הצדי"ק לכ"ק אדמו"ר שליט"א. (6) שנג דף.

ד'לט. כנ"ל אות ג'שנה. ווילאָ אַלבערטינאָ, פּאָולאָ, בראַזיל. תשנ"ב. . . נפלאות בכל . . הצדי"ק לכ"ק אדמו"ר שליט"א. (6) שנג דף.

ד'מ. כנ"ל אות ג'שנה. ווילאָ בעלאָ, פּאָולאָ, בראַזיל. תשנ"ב. . . נפלאות בכל . . הצדי"ק לכ"ק אדמו"ר שליט"א. (6) שנג דף.

ד'מא. כנ"ל אות ג'שנה. ווילאָ טעלמאָ, פּאָולאָ, בראַזיל. תשנ"ב. . . נפלאות בכל . . הצדי"ק לכ"ק אדמו"ר שליט"א. (6) שנג דף.

ד'מב. כנ"ל אות ג'שנה. ווילאָ לאָלי, פּאָולאָ, בראַזיל. תשנ"ב. . . נפלאות בכל . . הצדי"ק לכ"ק אדמו"ר שליט"א. (6) שנג דף.

ד'מג. כנ"ל אות ג'שנה. ווילאָ מאַריאָ, פּאָולאָ, בראַזיל. תשנ"ב. . . נפלאות בכל . . הצדי"ק לכ"ק אדמו"ר שליט"א. (6) שנג דף.

ד'מד. כנ"ל אות ג'שנה. ווילאָ נאָוואָ סוּאיסאָ, פּאָולאָ, בראַזיל. תשנ"ב. . . נפלאות בכל . . הצדי"ק לכ"ק אדמו"ר שליט"א. (6) שנג דף.

ד'מה. כנ"ל אות ג'שנה. ווילאָ נאָיר, פּאָולאָ, בראַזיל. תשנ"ב. . . נפלאות בכל . . הצדי"ק לכ"ק אדמו"ר שליט"א. (6) שנג דף.

ד'מו. כנ"ל אות ג'שנה. ווילאָ פּאָוליסטאָ, פּאָולאָ, בראַזיל. תשנ"ב. . . נפלאות בכל . . הצדי"ק לכ"ק אדמו"ר שליט"א. (6) שנג דף.

ד'מז. כנ"ל אות ג'שנה. ווילאָ קלאַוּדיאָ, פּאָולאָ, בראַזיל. תשנ"ב. . . נפלאות בכל . . הצדי"ק לכ"ק אדמו"ר שליט"א. (6) שנג דף.

ד'מח. כנ"ל אות ג'שנה. ווילאָ קריסינאָ, פּאָולאָ, בראַזיל. תשנ"ב. . . נפלאות בכל . . הצדי"ק לכ"ק אדמו"ר שליט"א. (6) שנג דף.

ד'מט. כנ"ל אות ג'שנה. זשאַגוּאַריבע, פּאָולאָ, בראַזיל. תשנ"ב. . . נפלאות בכל . . הצדי"ק לכ"ק אדמו"ר שליט"א. (6) שנג דף.

ד'נ. כנ"ל אות ג'שנה. זשאַרדין אימברי, פּאָולאָ, בראַזיל. תשנ"ב. . . נפלאות בכל . . הצדי"ק לכ"ק אדמו"ר שליט"א. (6) שנג דף.

ד'נא. כנ"ל אות ג'שנה. זשאַרדין דאָס פלאָרעס, פּאָולאָ, בראַזיל. תשנ"ב. . . נפלאות בכל . . הצדי"ק לכ"ק אדמו"ר שליט"א. (6) שנג דף.

ד'נב. כנ"ל אות ג'שנה. זשאַרדין דאָס פּעראָלאָס, פּאָולאָ, בראַזיל. תשנ"ב. . . נפלאות בכל . . הצדי"ק לכ"ק אדמו"ר שליט"א. (6) שנג דף.

ד'נג. כנ"ל אות ג'שנה. זשאַרדין סומאַרע, פּאָולאָ, בראַזיל. תשנ"ב. . . נפלאות בכל . . הצדי"ק לכ"ק אדמו"ר שליט"א. (6) שנג דף.

ד'נד. כנ"ל אות ג'שנה. זשאַרדין סיאָמאַראָ, פּאָולאָ, בראַזיל. תשנ"ב. . . נפלאות בכל . . הצדי"ק לכ"ק אדמו"ר שליט"א. (6) שנג דף.

ד'נה. כנ"ל אות ג'שנה. זשאַרדין פּאַנאָראַמאָ, פּאָולאָ, בראַזיל. תשנ"ב. . . נפלאות בכל . . הצדי"ק לכ"ק אדמו"ר שליט"א. (6) שנג דף.

ד'נו. כנ"ל אות ג'שנה. זשאַרדין פּאָר דאָ סאָל, פּאָולאָ, בראַזיל. תשנ"ב. . . נפלאות בכל . . הצדי"ק לכ"ק אדמו"ר שליט"א. (6) שנג דף.

ד'נז. כנ"ל אות ג'שנה. זשאַרדין פּרעזידענטע, פּאָולאָ, בראַזיל. תשנ"ב. . . נפלאות בכל . . הצדי"ק לכ"ק אדמו"ר שליט"א. (6) שנג דף.

ד'נח. כנ"ל אות ג'שנה. טאַקוּאַראַל, פּאָולאָ, בראַזיל. תשנ"ב. . . נפלאות בכל . . הצדי"ק לכ"ק אדמו"ר שליט"א. (6) שנג דף.

ד'נט. כנ"ל אות ג'שנה. מאַטילדע, פּאָולאָ, בראַזיל. תשנ"ב. . . נפלאות בכל . . הצדי"ק לכ"ק אדמו"ר שליט"א. (6) שנג דף.

ד'ס. כנ"ל אות ג'שנה. מאַנאָנסיאַל, פּאָולאָ, בראַזיל. תשנ"ב. . . נפלאות בכל . . הצדי"ק לכ"ק אדמו"ר שליט"א. (6) שנג דף.

ד'סא. כנ"ל אות ג'שנה. מאַנטיקעירא, פּאָולאָ, בראַזיל. תשנ"ב. . . נפלאות בכל . . הצדי"ק לכ"ק אדמו"ר שליט"א. (6) שנג דף.

ד'סב. כנ"ל אות ג'שנה. נאַדיר, פּאָולאָ, בראַזיל. תשנ"ב. . . נפלאות בכל . . הצדי"ק לכ"ק אדמו"ר שליט"א. (6) שגג דף.

ד'סג. כנ"ל אות ג'שנה. סאַנאַטאַריאָס, פּאָולאָ, בראַזיל. תשנ"ב. . . נפלאות בכל . . הצדי"ק לכ"ק אדמו"ר שליט"א. (6) שנג דף.

ד'סד. כנ"ל אות ג'שנה. סידאַדע דאָ סאָל, פּאָולאָ, בראַזיל. תשנ"ב. . . נפלאות בכל . . הצדי"ק לכ"ק אדמו"ר שליט"א. (6) שנג דף.

ד'סה. כנ"ל אות ג'שנה. עוּוערעסט, פּאָולאָ, בראַזיל. תשנ"ב. . . נפלאות בכל . . הצדי"ק לכ"ק אדמו"ר שליט"א. (6) שנג דף.

ד'סו. כנ"ל אות ג'שנה. עמבאַרישאַדאָר, פּאָולאָ, בראַזיל. תשנ"ב. . . נפלאות בכל . . הצדי"ק לכ"ק אדמו"ר שליט"א. (6) שנג דף.

ד'סז. כנ"ל אות ג'שנה. פּאַרקע דאָס פּאָנטעס, פּאָולאָ, בראַזיל. תשנ"ב. . . נפלאות בכל . . הצדי"ק לכ"ק אדמו"ר שליט"א. (6) שנג דף.

ד'סח. כנ"ל אות ג'שנה. פלאָרעסטאָ, פּאָולאָ, בראַזיל. תשנ"ב. . . נפלאות בכל . . הצדי"ק לכ"ק אדמו"ר שליט"א. (6) שנג דף.

ד'סט. כנ"ל אות ג'שנה. פעדראָ דאָ באַו, פּאָולאָ, בראַזיל. תשנ"ב. . . נפלאות בכל . . הצדי"ק לכ"ק אדמו"ר שליט"א. (6) שנג דף.

ד'ע. כנ"ל אות ג'שנה. פעליז, פּאָולאָ, בראַזיל. תשנ"ב. . . נפלאות בכל . . הצדי"ק לכ"ק אדמו"ר שליט"א. (6) שנג דף.

ד'עא. כנ"ל אות ג'שנה. פּראָקאָלאַנזאָ, פּאָולאָ, בראַזיל. תשנ"ב. . . נפלאות בכל . . הצדי"ק לכ"ק אדמו"ר שליט"א. (6) שנג דף.

ד'עב. כנ"ל אות ג'שנה. קאָסקאָטיניאָ, פּאָולאָ, בראַזיל. תשנ"ב. . . נפלאות בכל . . הצדי"ק לכ"ק אדמו"ר שליט"א. (6) שנג דף.

ד'עג. כנ"ל אות ג'שנה. קאַפּיוואַרו, פּאָולאָ, בראַזיל. תשנ"ב. . . נפלאות בכל . . הצדי"ק לכ"ק אדמו"ר שליט"א. (6) שנג דף.

ד'עד. כנ"ל אות שלה. סאָלאָן, אָהייאָ. תשנ"ב. . . שנת נפלאות בכל . . הצדי"ק לכ"ק אדמו"ר שליט"א. (6) שס דף.

ד'עה. כנ"ל אות שלה. בּערנאַרדסוויל, ניו דזשערסי. . . שנת נפלאות בכל . . הצדי"ק לכ"ק אדמו"ר שליט"א. (6) שס דף.

ד'עו. כנ"ל אות שלה. וואַטערטאַון, פלאָרידאָ. תשנ"ב. . . שנת נפלאות בכל . . הצדי"ק לכ"ק אדמו"ר שליט"א. (6) שס דף.

ד'עז. כנ"ל אות שלה. באַלדווין, פלאָרידאָ. תשנ"ב. . . שנת נפלאות בכל . . הצדי"ק לכ"ק אדמו"ר שליט"א. (6) שס דף.

ד'עח. כנ"ל אות שלה. סאַנדערסאָן, פלאָרידאָ. תשנ"ב. . . שנת נפלאות בכל . . הצדי"ק לכ"ק אדמו"ר שליט"א. (6) שס דף.

ד'עט. כנ"ל אות שלה. אָלוסטי, פלאָרידאָ. תשנ"ב. . . שנת נפלאות בכל . . הצדי"ק לכ"ק אדמו"ר שליט"א. (6) שס דף.

ד'פ. כנ"ל אות שלה. לייק סיטי, פלאָרידאָ. תשנ"ב. . . שנת נפלאות בכל . . הצדי"ק לכ"ק אדמו"ר שליט"א. (6) שס דף.

ד'פא. כנ"ל אות שלה. לולו, פלאָרידאָ. תשנ"ב. . . שנת נפלאות בכל . . הצדי"ק לכ"ק אדמו"ר שליט"א. (6) שס דף.

ד'פב. כנ"ל אות שלה. קליפטאַנוויל, פלאָרידאָ. תשנ"ב. . . שנת נפלאות בכל . . הצדי"ק לכ"ק אדמו"ר שליט"א. (6) שס דף.

ד'פג. כנ"ל אות שלה. לייק באַטלער, פלאָרידאָ. תשנ"ב. . . שנת נפלאות בכל . . הצדי"ק לכ"ק אדמו"ר שליט"א. (6) שס דף.

ד'פד. כנ"ל אות שלה. ניו ריווער, פלאָרידאָ. תשנ"ב. . . שנת נפלאות בכל . . הצדי"ק לכ"ק אדמו"ר שליט"א. (6) שס דף.

ד'פה. כנ"ל אות שלה. בּרוקער, פלאָרידאָ. תשנ"ב. . . שנת נפלאות בכל . . הצדי"ק לכ"ק אדמו"ר שליט"א. (6) שס דף.

ד'פו. כנ"ל אות שלה. גראַגאַם, פלאָרידאָ. תשנ"ב. . . שנת נפלאות בכל . . הצדי"ק לכ"ק אדמו"ר שליט"א. (6) שס דף.

ד׳פז. כנ״ל אות שלה. סאַמפּסאַן סיטי, פלאַרידאַ. תשנ״ב. . . שנת נפלאות בכל . . הצדי״ק לכ״ק אדמו״ר שליט״א. (6) שס דף.

ד׳פח. כנ״ל אות שלה. פּאַלאַטקאַ, פלאַרידאַ. תשנ״ב. . . שנת נפלאות בכל . . הצדי״ק לכ״ק אדמו״ר שליט״א. (6) שס דף.

ד׳פט. כנ״ל אות שלה. איסט פּאַלאַטקאַ, פלאַרידאַ. תשנ״ב. . . שנת נפלאות בכל . . הצדי״ק לכ״ק אדמו״ר שליט״א. (6) שס דף.

ד׳צ. כנ״ל אות שלה. אָראַנדזש מילס, פלאַרידאַ. תשנ״ב. . . שנת נפלאות בכל . . הצדי״ק לכ״ק אדמו״ר שליט״א. (6) שס דף.

ד׳צא. כנ״ל אות שלה. סאַטסומאַ, פלאַרידאַ. תשנ״ב. . . שנת נפלאות בכל . . הצדי״ק לכ״ק אדמו״ר שליט״א. (6) שס דף.

ד׳צב. כנ״ל אות שלה. פּאַמאַנאַ פּאַרק, פלאַרידאַ. תשנ״ב. . . שנת נפלאות בכל . . הצדי״ק לכ״ק אדמו״ר שליט״א. (6) שס דף.

ד׳צג. כנ״ל אות שלה. וועלאַקאַ, פלאַרידאַ. תשנ״ב. . . שנת נפלאות בכל . . הצדי״ק לכ״ק אדמו״ר שליט״א. (6) שס דף.

ד׳צד. כנ״ל אות שלה. האַנטינגטאַן, פלאַרידאַ. תשנ״ב. . . שנת נפלאות בכל . . הצדי״ק לכ״ק אדמו״ר שליט״א. (6) שס דף.

ד׳צה. כנ״ל אות שלה. לייק קאַמאַ, פלאַרידאַ. תשנ״ב. . . שנת נפלאות בכל . . הצדי״ק לכ״ק אדמו״ר שליט״א. (6) שס דף.

ד׳צו. כנ״ל אות שלה. סעוויל, פלאַרידאַ. תשנ״ב. . . שנת נפלאות בכל . . הצדי״ק לכ״ק אדמו״ר שליט״א. (6) שס דף.

ד׳צז. כנ״ל אות שלה. פּיערסאַן, פלאַרידאַ. תשנ״ב. . . שנת נפלאות בכל . . הצדי״ק לכ״ק אדמו״ר שליט״א. (6) שס דף.

ד׳צח. כנ״ל אות שלה. פּאַלם סיטי, פלאַרידאַ. תשנ״ב. . . שנת נפלאות בכל . . הצדי״ק לכ״ק אדמו״ר שליט״א. (6) שס דף.

ד׳צט. כנ״ל אות שלה. ווייט סיטי, פלאַרידאַ. תשנ״ב. . . שנת נפלאות בכל . . הצדי״ק לכ״ק אדמו״ר שליט״א. (6) שס דף.

ד׳ק. כנ״ל אות שלה. פּאָרט פּירס, פלאַרידאַ. תשנ״ב. . . שנת נפלאות בכל . . הצדי״ק לכ״ק אדמו״ר שליט״א. (6) שס דף.

ד׳קא. כנ״ל אות שלה. אינדריא, פלאַרידאַ. תשנ״ב. . . שנת נפלאות בכל . . הצדי״ק לכ״ק אדמו״ר שליט״א. (6) שס דף.

ד׳קב. כנ״ל אות שלה. אָסלאָ, פלאַרידאַ. תשנ״ב. . . שנת נפלאות בכל . . הצדי״ק לכ״ק אדמו״ר שליט״א. (6) שס דף.

ד׳קג. כנ״ל אות שלה. וועראָ ביטש, פלאַרידאַ. תשנ״ב. . . שנת נפלאות בכל . . הצדי״ק לכ״ק אדמו״ר שליט״א. (6) שס דף.

ד׳קד. כנ״ל אות שלה. גיפאַרט שארס, פלאַרידאַ. תשנ״ב. . . שנת נפלאות בכל . . הצדי״ק לכ״ק אדמו״ר שליט״א. (6) שס דף.

ד׳קה. כנ״ל אות שלה. ווינטער ביטש, פלאַרידאַ. תשנ״ב. . . שנת נפלאות בכל . . הצדי״ק לכ״ק אדמו״ר שליט״א. (6) שס דף.

ד׳קו. כנ״ל אות שלה. וואַבּאַסאַ, פלאַרידאַ. תשנ״ב. . . שנת נפלאות בכל . . הצדי״ק לכ״ק אדמו״ר שליט״א. (6) שס דף.

ד׳קז. כנ״ל אות שלה. סעבּאַסטיאַן, פלאַרידאַ. תשנ״ב. . . שנת נפלאות בכל . . הצדי״ק לכ״ק אדמו״ר שליט״א. (6) שס דף.

ד׳קח. כנ״ל אות שלה. ראָזלאַנד, פלאַרידאַ. תשנ״ב. . . שנת נפלאות בכל . . הצדי״ק לכ״ק אדמו״ר שליט״א. (6) שס דף.

ד׳קט. כנ״ל אות שלה. בּעירפּוט בּיי, פלאַרידאַ. תשנ״ב. . . שנת נפלאות בכל . . הצדי״ק לכ״ק אדמו״ר שליט״א. (6) שס דף.

ד׳קי. כנ״ל אות שלה. מיקא, פלאַרידאַ. תשנ״ב. . . שנת נפלאות בכל . . הצדי״ק לכ״ק אדמו״ר שליט״א. (6) שס דף.

ד׳קיא. כנ״ל אות שלה. גראַנט, פלאַרידאַ. תשנ״ב. . . שנת נפלאות בכל . . הצדי״ק לכ״ק אדמו״ר שליט״א. (6) שס דף.

ד׳קיב. כנ״ל אות שלה. וואַלקאַריאַ, פלאַרידאַ. תשנ״ב. . . שנת נפלאות בכל . . הצדי״ק לכ״ק אדמו״ר שליט״א. (6) שס דף.

ד׳קיג. כנ״ל אות שלה. מאַלאַבּאַר, פלאַרידאַ. תשנ״ב. . . שנת נפלאות בכל . . הצדי״ק לכ״ק אדמו״ר שליט״א. (6) שס דף.

ד׳קיד. כנ״ל אות שלה. פּאָרט מאַלאַבּאַר, פלאַרידאַ. תשנ״ב. . . שנת נפלאות בכל . . הצדי״ק לכ״ק אדמו״ר שליט״א. (6) שס דף.

ד׳קטו. כנ״ל אות שלה. פּאַלם בּיי, פלאַרידאַ. תשנ״ב. . . שנת נפלאות בכל . . הצדי״ק לכ״ק אדמו״ר שליט״א. (6) שס דף.

ד׳קטז. כנ״ל אות שלה. וועסט מעלבּורן, פלאַרידאַ. תשנ״ב. . . שנת נפלאות בכל . . הצדי״ק לכ״ק אדמו״ר שליט״א. (6) שס דף.

ד׳קיז. כנ״ל אות שלה. מעלבּורן, פלאַרידאַ. תשנ״ב. . . שנת נפלאות בכל . . הצדי״ק לכ״ק אדמו״ר שליט״א. (6) שס דף.

ד׳קיח. כנ״ל אות שלה. קאָוקאָו, פלאַרידאַ. תשנ״ב. . . שנת נפלאות בכל . . הצדי״ק לכ״ק אדמו״ר שליט״א. (6) שס דף.

ד׳קיט. כנ״ל אות שלה. טיטוסוויל, פלאַרידאַ. תשנ״ב. . . שנת נפלאות בכל . . הצדי״ק לכ״ק אדמו״ר שליט״א. (6) שס דף.

ד׳קכ. כנ״ל אות שלה. מימס, פלאַרידאַ. תשנ״ב. . . שנת נפלאות בכל . . הצדי״ק לכ״ק אדמו״ר שליט״א. (6) שס דף.

ד׳קכא. כנ״ל אות שלה. סקאַטסמור, פלאַרידאַ. תשנ״ב. . . שנת נפלאות בכל . . הצדי״ק לכ״ק אדמו״ר שליט״א. (6) שס דף.

ד׳קכב. כנ״ל אות שלה. האַרבּאַר אוקס, פלאַרידאַ. תשנ״ב. . . שנת נפלאות בכל . . הצדי״ק לכ״ק אדמו״ר שליט״א. (6) שס דף.

ד׳קכג. כנ״ל אות שלה. אַלאַנדייל, פלאַרידאַ. תשנ״ב. . . שנת נפלאות בכל . . הצדי״ק לכ״ק אדמו״ר שליט״א. (6) שס דף.

ד׳קכד. כנ״ל אות שלה. האַלי היל, פלאַרידאַ. תשנ״ב. . . שנת נפלאות בכל . . הצדי״ק לכ״ק אדמו״ר שליט״א. (6) שס דף.

ד׳קכה. כנ״ל אות שלה. אָרמאַנד ביטש, פלאַרידאַ. תשנ״ב. . . שנת נפלאות בכל . . הצדי״ק לכ״ק אדמו״ר שליט״א. (6) שס דף.

ד׳קכו. כנ״ל אות שלה. בּאַנעל, פלאַרידאַ. תשנ״ב. . . שנת נפלאות בכל . . הצדי״ק לכ״ק אדמו״ר שליט״א. (6) שס דף.

ד׳קכז. כנ״ל אות שלה. קינגס-פּערי, פלאַרידאַ. תשנ״ב. . . שנת נפלאות בכל . . הצדי״ק לכ״ק אדמו״ר שליט״א. (6) שס דף.

ד׳קכח. כנ״ל אות שלה. היליאַרד, פלאַרידאַ. תשנ״ב. . . שנת נפלאות בכל . . הצדי״ק לכ״ק אדמו״ר שליט״א. (6) שס דף.

ד׳קכט. כנ״ל אות שלה. איטאַליאַ, פלאַרידאַ. תשנ״ב. . . שנת נפלאות בכל . . הצדי״ק לכ״ק אדמו״ר שליט״א. (6) שס דף.

ד׳קל. כנ״ל אות שלה. קאַלאַהאַן, פלאַרידאַ. תשנ״ב. . . שנת נפלאות בכל . . הצדי״ק לכ״ק אדמו״ר שליט״א. (6) שס דף.

ד׳קלא. כנ״ל אות שלה. קענט, פלאַרידאַ. תשנ״ב. . . שנת נפלאות בכל . . הצדי״ק לכ״ק אדמו״ר שליט״א. (6) שס דף.

ד׳קלב. כנ״ל אות שלה. בּרייסוויל, פלאַרידאַ. תשנ״ב. . . שנת נפלאות בכל . . הצדי״ק לכ״ק אדמו״ר שליט״א. (6) שס דף.

ד׳קלג. כנ״ל אות שלה. מעק-קלעני, פלאַרידאַ. תשנ״ב. . . שנת נפלאות בכל . . הצדי״ק לכ״ק אדמו״ר שליט״א. (6) שס דף.

ד׳קלד. כנ״ל אות שלה. גלען מערי, פלאַרידאַ. תשנ״ב. . . שנת נפלאות בכל . . הצדי״ק לכ״ק אדמו״ר שליט״א. (6) שס דף.

ד׳קלה. כנ״ל אות שלה. טיילאַר, פלאַרידאַ. תשנ״ב. . . שנת נפלאות בכל . . הצדי״ק לכ״ק אדמו״ר שליט״א. (6) שס דף.

ד׳קלו. כנ״ל אות שלה. עדי, פלאַרידאַ. תשנ״ב. . . שנת נפלאות בכל . . הצדי״ק לכ״ק אדמו״ר שליט״א. (6) שס דף.

ד׳קלז. כנ״ל אות שלה. בּעלמאַנט, פלאַרידאַ. תשנ״ב. . . שנת נפלאות בכל . . הצדי״ק לכ״ק אדמו״ר שליט״א. (6) שס דף.

ד׳קלח. כנ״ל אות שלה. דזשאַספּער, פלאַרידאַ. תשנ״ב. . . שנת נפלאות בכל . . הצדי״ק לכ״ק אדמו״ר שליט״א. (6) שס דף.

ד׳קלט. כנ״ל אות שלה. גענאַאַ, פלאַרידאַ. תשנ״ב. . . שנת נפלאות בכל . . הצדי״ק לכ״ק אדמו״ר שליט״א. (6) שס דף.

ד׳קמ. כנ״ל אות שלה. ווייט ספּרינגס, פלאַרידאַ. תשנ״ב. . . שנת נפלאות בכל . . הצדי״ק לכ״ק אדמו״ר שליט״א. (6) שס דף.

ד׳קמא. כנ״ל אות שלה. ווינפילד, פלאַרידאַ. תשנ״ב. . . שנת נפלאות בכל . . הצדי״ק לכ״ק אדמו״ר שליט״א. (6) שס דף.

ד׳קמב. כנ״ל אות שלה. דזשאנסטאַון, פלאַרידאַ. תשנ״ב. . . שנת נפלאות בכל . . הצדי״ק לכ״ק אדמו״ר שליט״א. (6) שס דף.

ד׳קמג. כנ״ל אות שלה. ריינפאָרד, פלאַרידאַ. תשנ״ב. . . שנת נפלאות בכל . . הצדי״ק לכ״ק אדמו״ר שליט״א. (6) שס דף.

ד׳קמד. כנ״ל אות שלה. עלערבּי, פלאַרידאַ. תשנ״ב. . . שנת נפלאות בכל . . הצדי״ק לכ״ק אדמו״ר שליט״א. (6) שס דף.

ד׳קמה. כנ״ל אות שלה. סאָפּ, פלאַרידאַ. תשנ״ב. . . שנת נפלאות בכל . . הצדי״ק לכ״ק אדמו״ר שליט״א. (6) שס דף.

ד׳קמו. כנ״ל אות שלה. פראווידענס, פלאַרידאַ. תשנ״ב. . . שנת נפלאות בכל . . הצדי״ק לכ״ק אדמו״ר שליט״א. (6) שס דף.

ד׳קמז. כנ״ל אות שלה. דוקס, פלאַרידאַ. תשנ״ב. . . שנת נפלאות בכל . . הצדי״ק לכ״ק אדמו״ר שליט״א. (6) שס דף.

ד׳קמח. כנ״ל אות שלה. וואורטינגטאַן, פלאַרידאַ. תשנ״ב. . . שנת נפלאות בכל . . הצדי״ק לכ״ק אדמו״ר שליט״א. (6) שס דף.

ד׳קמט. כנ״ל אות שלה. פע, פלאָרידאָ. תשנ״ב. . . שנת נפלאות בכל . . הצדי״ק לכ״ק אדמו״ר שליט״א. (6) שס דף.

ד׳קנ. כנ״ל אות שלה. הייִנסוואורט, פלאָרידאָ. תשנ״ב. . . שנת נפלאות בכל . . הצדי״ק לכ״ק אדמו״ר שליט״א. (6) שס דף.

ד׳קנא. כנ״ל אות שלה. קאַדילאַק, פלאָרידאָ. תשנ״ב. . . שנת נפלאות בכל . . הצדי״ק לכ״ק אדמו״ר שליט״א. (6) שס דף.

ד׳קנב. כנ״ל אות שלה. פאַראַדייס, פלאָרידאָ. תשנ״ב. . . שנת נפלאות בכל . . הצדי״ק לכ״ק אדמו״ר שליט״א. (6) שס דף.

ד׳קנג. כנ״ל אות שלה. פעיר באנקס, פלאָרידאָ. תשנ״ב. . . שנות נפלאות בכל . . הצדי״ק לכ״ק אדמו״ר שליט״א. (6) שס דף.

ד׳קנד. כנ״ל אות שלה. וואָלדאָ, פלאָרידאָ. תשנ״ב. . . שנת נפלאות בכל . . הצדי״ק לכ״ק אדמו״ר שליט״א. (6) שס דף.

ד׳קנה. כנ״ל אות שלה. אָראַנדזש הייטס, פלאָרידאָ. תשנ״ב. . . שנת נפלאות בכל . . הצדי״ק לכ״ק אדמו״ר שליט״א. (6) שס דף.

ד׳קנו. כנ״ל אות שלה. ראַשעל, פלאָרידאָ. תשנ״ב. . . שנת נפלאות בכל . . הצדי״ק לכ״ק אדמו״ר שליט״א. (6) שס דף.

ז׳קנז. כנ״ל אות שלה. ווינדסאָר, פלאָרידאָ. תשנ״ב. . . שנת נפלאות בכל . . הצדי״ק לכ״ק אדמו״ר שליט״א. (6) שס דף.

ד׳קנח. כנ״ל אות שלה. האוטאָרן, פלאָרידאָ. תשנ״ב. . . שנת נפלאות בכל . . הצדי״ק לכ״ק אדמו״ר שליט״א. (6) שס דף.

ד׳קנט. כנ״ל אות שלה. גראָוו פאַרק, פלאָרידאָ. תשנ״ב. . . שנת נפלאות בכל . . הצדי״ק לכ״ק אדמו״ר שליט״א. (6) שס דף.

ד׳קס. כנ״ל אות שלה. מיקאַנאָפי, פלאָרידאָ. תשנ״ב. . . שנת נפלאות בכל . . הצדי״ק לכ״ק אדמו״ר שליט״א. (6) שס דף.

ד׳קסא. כנ״ל אות שלה. עווינסטאָן, פלאָרידאָ. תשנ״ב. . . שנת נפלאות בכל . . הצדי״ק לכ״ק אדמו״ר שליט״א. (6) שס דף.

ד׳קסב. כנ״ל אות שלה. מק־אינטאָש, פלאָרידאָ. תשנ״ב. . . שנת נפלאות בכל . . הצדי״ק לכ״ק אדמו״ר שליט״א. (6) שס דף.

ד׳קסג. כנ״ל אות שלה. אָראַנדזש לייק, פלאָרידאָ. תשנ״ב. . . שנת נפלזות בכל . . הצדי״ק לכ״ק אדמו״ר שליט״א. (6) שס דף.

ד׳קסד. כנ״ל אות שלה. רעדיק, פלאָרידאָ. תשנ״ב. . . שנות נפלאות בכל . . הצדי״ק לכ״ק אדמו״ר שליט״א. (6) שס דף.

ד׳קסה. כנ״ל אות שלה. אַנטהאָני, פלאָרידאָ. תשנ״ב. . . שנת נפלאות בכל . . הצדי״ק לכ״ק אדמו״ר שליט״א. (6) שס דף.

ד׳קסו. כנ״ל אות שלה. ספאַר, פלאָרידאָ. תשנ״ב. . . שנת נפלאות בכל . . הצדי״ק לכ״ק אדמו״ר שליט״א. (6) שס דף.

ד׳קסז. כנ״ל אות שלה. סיטרא, פלאָרידאָ. תשנ״ב. . . שנת נפלאות בכל . . הצדי״ק לכ״ק אדמו״ר שליט״א. (6) שס דף.

ד׳קסח. כנ״ל אות שלה. אייִלאַנד גראָוו, פלאָרידאָ. תשנ״ב. . . שנת נפלאות בכל . . הצדי״ק לכ״ק אדמו״ר שליט״א. (6) שס דף.

ד׳קסט. כנ״ל אות שלה. לאַכלוּסאַ, פלאָרידאָ. תשנ״ב. . . שנת נפלאות בכל . . הצדי״ק לכ״ק אדמו״ר שליט״א. (6) שס דף.

ד׳קע. כנ״ל אות שלה. דזשאַנסאָן, פלאָרידאָ. תשנ״ב. . . שנת נפלאות בכל . . הצדי״ק לכ״ק אדמו״ר שליט״א. (6) שס דף.

ד׳קעא. כנ״ל אות שלה. אינטערלאַכען, פלאָרידאָ. תשנ״ב. . . שנת נפלאות בכל . . הצדי״ק לכ״ק אדמו״ר שליט״א. (6) שס דף.

ד׳קעב. כנ״ל אות שלה. האַליסטער, פלאָרידאָ. תשנ״ב. . . שנת נפלאות בכל . . הצדי״ק לכ״ק אדמו״ר שליט״א. (6) שס דף.

ד׳קעג. כנ״ל אות שלה. מאַנוויל, פלאָרידאָ. תשנ״ב. . . שנת נפלאות בכל . . הצדי״ק לכ״ק אדמו״ר שליט״א. (6) שס דף.

ד׳קעד. כנ״ל אות שלה. אָראַנדזש ספרינגס, פלאָרידאָ. תשנ״ב. . . שנת נפלאות בכל . . הצדי״ק לכ״ק אדמו״ר שליט״א. (6) שס דף.

ד׳קעה. כנ״ל אות שלה. בּיי לייק, פלאָרידאָ. תשנ״ב. . . שנת נפלאות בכל . . הצדי״ק לכ״ק אדמו״ר שליט״א. (6) שס דף.

ד׳קעו. כנ״ל אות שלה. יוּריקאָ, פלאָרידאָ. תשנ״ב. . . שנת נפלאות בכל . . הצדי״ק לכ״ק אדמו״ר שליט״א. (6) שס דף.

ד׳קעז. כנ״ל אות שלה. בּורבּאַנק, פלאָרידאָ. תשנ״ב. . . שנת נפלאות בכל . . הצדי״ק לכ״ק אדמו״ר שליט״א. (6) שס דף.

ד׳קעח. כנ״ל אות שלה. בּלומינגדייל, פלאָרידאָ. תשנ״ב. . . שנת נפלאות בכל . . הצדי״ק לכ״ק אדמו״ר שליט״א. (6) שס דף.

ד׳קעט. כנ״ל אות שלה. ריווערוויו, פלאָרידאָ. תשנ״ב. . . שנת נפלאות בכל . . הצדי״ק לכ״ק אדמו״ר שליט״א. (6) שס דף.

ד׳קפ. כנ״ל אות שלה. בּאָלם, פלאָרידאָ. תשנ״ב. . . שנת נפלאות בכל . . הצדי״ק לכ״ק אדמו״ר שליט״א. (6) שס דף.

ד׳קפא. כנ״ל אות שלה. ווימאַומאַ, פלאָרידאָ. תשנ״ב. . . שנת נפלאות בכל . . הצדי״ק לכ״ק אדמו״ר שליט״א. (6) שס דף.

ד׳קפב. כנ״ל אות שלה. פאָרט לאָנסאָם, פלאָרידאָ. תשנ״ב. . . שנת נפלאות בכל . . הצדי״ק לכ״ק אדמו״ר שליט״א. (6) שס דף.

ד׳קפג. כנ״ל אות שלה. פיקניק, פלאָרידאָ. תשנ״ב. . . שנת נפלאות בכל . . הצדי״ק לכ״ק אדמו״ר שליט״א. (6) שס דף.

ד׳קפד. כנ״ל אות שלה. פירס, פלאָרידאָ. תשנ״ב. . . שנת נפלאות בכל . . הצדי״ק לכ״ק אדמו״ר שליט״א. (6) שס דף.

ד׳קפה. כנ״ל אות שלה. האָמלאַנד, פלאָרידאָ. תשנ״ב. . . שנת נפלאות בכל . . הצדי״ק לכ״ק אדמו״ר שליט״א. (6) שס דף.

ד׳קפו. כנ״ל אות שלה. בּאַרטאָון, פלאָרידאָ. תשנ״ב. . . שנת נפלאות בכל . . הצדי״ק לכ״ק אדמו״ר שליט״א. (6) שס דף.

ד׳קפז. כנ״ל אות שלה. בּייאָנעט פאָינט, פלאָרידאָ. תשנ״ב. . . שנת נפלאות בכל . . הצדי״ק לכ״ק אדמו״ר שליט״א. (6) שס דף.

ד׳קפח. כנ״ל אות שלה. האָדסאָן, פלאָרידאָ. תשנ״ב. . . שנת נפלאות בכל . . הצדי״ק לכ״ק אדמו״ר שליט״א. (6) שס דף.

ד׳קפט. כנ״ל אות שלה. אריפיקאָ, פלאָרידאָ. תשנ״ב. . . שנת נפלאות בכל . . הצדי״ק לכ״ק אדמו״ר שליט״א. (6) שס דף.

ד׳קצ. כנ״ל אות שלה. הערנאַנדאָ בּיטש, פלאָרידאָ. תשנ״ב. . . שנת נפלאות בכל . . הצדי״ק לכ״ק אדמו״ר שליט״א. (6) שס דף.

ד׳קצא. כנ״ל אות שלה. בּייפאָרט, פלאָרידאָ. תשנ״ב. . . שנת נפלאות בכל . . הצדי״ק לכ״ק אדמו״ר שליט״א. (6) שס דף.

ד׳קצב. כנ״ל אות שלה. פיין אָיילאַנד, פלאָרידאָ. תשנ״ב. . . שנת נפלאות בכל . . הצדי״ק לכ״ק אדמו״ר שליט״א. (6) שס דף.

ד׳קצג. כנ״ל אות שלה. בּרוקסוויל, פלאָרידאָ. תשנ״ב. . . שנת נפלאות בכל . . הצדי״ק לכ״ק אדמו״ר שליט״א. (6) שס דף.

ד׳קצד. כנ״ל אות שלה. וויקי וואַשי, פלאָרידאָ. תשנ״ב. . . שנת נפלאות בכל . . הצדי״ק לכ״ק אדמו״ר שליט״א. (6) שס דף.

ד׳קצה. כנ״ל אות שלה. ספרינג היל, פלאָרידאָ. תשנ״ב. . . שנת נפלאות בכל . . הצדי״ק לכ״ק אדמו״ר שליט״א. (6) שס דף.

ד׳קצו. כנ״ל אות שלה. דאַרבּי, פלאָרידאָ. תשנ״ב. . . שנת נפלאות בכל . . הצדי״ק לכ״ק אדמו״ר שליט״א. (6) שס דף.

ד׳קצז. כנ״ל אות שלה. גאַוערס קאָרנער, פלאָרידאָ. תשנ״ב. . . שנת נפלאות בכל . . הצדי״ק לכ״ק אדמו״ר שליט״א. (6) שס דף.

ד׳קצח. כנ״ל אות שלה. אָדעסאַ, פלאָרידאָ. תשנ״ב. . . שנת נפלאות בכל . . הצדי״ק לכ״ק אדמו״ר שליט״א. (6) שס דף.

ד׳קצט. כנ״ל אות ג׳תק. פראַטווינא, בריה״מ. כ״ח אדר א׳, תשנ״ב. (6) שס דף.

ד׳ר. כנ״ל אות ג׳תטו – הוצאה מוגדלת 15x23 סמ. בית חיינו – „בית רבינו שבבבל״, 770 איסטערן פאַרקוויי, ברוקלין, נ. י. י״א ניסן, ה׳תשנ״ב, הי׳ תהא שנת נפלאות בכל. צדי״ק שנה לכ״ק אדמו״ר שליט״א. לזכות כ״ק אדמו״ר שליט״א לרפואה שלימה וקרובה בכל רמ״ח איבריו ושס״ה גידיו הק׳ . . . תיכף ומיד ממש. (6) רמד דף.

ד׳רא. כנ״ל אות שלה. בית הרפואה – קאָני אייִלאַנד, ברוקלין, נ.י. תשנ״ב. . . שנת נפלאות בכל. צדי״ק שנה לכ״ק אדמו״ר שליט״א. (6) שס דף.

ד׳רב. כנ״ל אות שדמ. בית הרפואה – „הדסה״, ירושלים עיה״ק, באה״ק ת״ו. תשנ״ב. . . שנת נפלאות בכל. צדי״ק שנה לכ״ק אדמו״ר שליט״א. (6) רנט דף.

ד׳רג. כנ״ל אות שלה. בית חב״ד – קווינס, נ.י. תשנ״ב. . . שנת נפלאות בכל. צדי״ק שנה לכ״ק אדמו״ר שליט״א. (6) שס דף.

ד׳רד. כנ״ל אות שלה. סאַנדאָמקי, אָהייאָ. תשנ״ב. . . שנת נפלאות בכל . . הצדי״ק לכ״ק אדמו״ר שליט״א. (6) שס דף.

ד׳רה. כנ״ל אות שלה. דזשעסאַמין, פלאָרידאָ. תשנ״ב. . . שנת נפלאות בכל . . הצדי״ק לכ״ק אדמו״ר שליט״א. (6) שס דף.

ד׳רו. כנ״ל אות שלה. פאַסקאָ, פלאָרידאָ. תשנ״ב. . . שנת נפלאות בכל . . הצדי״ק לכ״ק אדמו״ר שליט״א. (6) שס דף.

ד׳רז. כנ״ל אות שלה. אַנטאָניאָ, פלאָרידאָ. תשנ״ב. . . שנת נפלאות בכל . . הצדי״ק לכ״ק אדמו״ר שליט״א. (6) שס דף.

ד׳רח. כנ״ל אות שלה. ספרינג לייק, פלאָרידאַ. תשנ״ב. . . שנת נפלאות בכל . . הצדי״ק לכ״ק אדמו״ר שליט״א. (6) שס דף.

ד׳רט. כנ״ל אות שלה. בושעל, פלאָרידאַ. תשנ״ב. . . שנת נפלאות בכל . . הצדי״ק לכ״ק אדמו״ר שליט״א. (6) שס דף.

ד׳רי. כנ״ל אות שלה. בית חב״ד, טאַמפּאַ, פלאָרידאַ. תשנ״ב. . . שנת נפלאות בכל . . הצדי״ק לכ״ק אדמו״ר שליט״א. (6) שס דף.

ד׳ריא. כנ״ל אות ג׳שנ. בית חב״ד רעסיפע, פערנאַמבוקאָ, בראַזיל. תשנ״ב. . . שנת נפלאות בכל. צדי״ק שנה לכ״ק אדמו״ר שליט״א. (6) שס דף.

ד׳ריב. כנ״ל אות ג׳שנ. אברעו ע לימא, פערנאַמבוקאָ, בראַזיל. תשנ״ב. . . שנת נפלאות בכל. צדי״ק שנה לכ״ק אדמו״ר שליט״א. (6) שס דף.

ד׳ריג. כנ״ל אות ג׳שנ. איגאַראַסו, פערנאַמבוקאָ, בראַזיל. תשנ״ב. . . שנת נפלאות בכל. צדי״ק שנה לכ״ק אדמו״ר שליט״א. (6) שס דף.

ד׳ריד. כנ״ל אות ג׳תק. איטאַמאַראַקאַ, פערנאַמבוקאָ, בראַזיל. תשנ״ב. . . שנת נפלאות בכל. צדי״ק שנה לכ״ק אדמו״ר שליט״א. (6) שס דף.

ד׳רטו. כנ״ל אות ג׳תק. איטאַפּיסומאַ, פערנאַמבוקאָ, בראַזיל. תשנ״ב. . . שנת נפלאות בכל. צדי״ק שנה לכ״ק אדמו״ר שליט״א. (6) שס דף.

ד׳רטז. כנ״ל אות ג׳שנ. איפּאָושוקאַ, פערנאַמבוקאָ, בראַזיל. תשנ״ב. . . שנת נפלאות בכל. צדי״ק שנה לכ״ק אדמו״ר שליט״א. (6) שס דף.

ד׳ריז. כנ״ל אות ג׳שנ. אַלדעיאַ, פערנאַמבוקאָ, בראַזיל. תשנ״ב. . . שנת נפלאות בכל. צדי״ק שנה לכ״ק אדמו״ר שליט״א. (6) שט דף.

ד׳ריח. כנ״ל אות ג׳שנ. אליאַנסאַ, פערנאַמבוקאָ, בראַזיל. תשנ״ב. . . שנת נפלאות בכל. צדי״ק שנה לכ״ק אדמו״ר שליט״א. (6) שס דף.

ד׳ריט. כנ״ל אות ג׳שנ. אַרקאָווערדע, פערנאַמבוקאָ, בראַזיל. תשנ״ב. . . שנת נפלאות בכל. צדי״ק שנה לכ״ק אדמו״ר שליט״א. (6) שס דף.

ד׳רכ. כנ״ל אות ג׳שנ. בעזעררא, פערנאַמבוקאָ, בראַזיל. תשנ״ב. . . שנת נפלאות בכל. צדי״ק שנה לכ״ק אדמו״ר שליט״א. (6) שס דף.

ד׳רכא. כנ״ל אות ג׳שנ. בעלאָ זשאַרדין, פערנאַמבוקאָ, בראַזיל. תשנ״ב. . . שנת נפלאות בכל. צדי״ק שנה לכ״ק אדמו״ר שליט״א. (6) שס דף.

ד׳רכב. כנ״ל אות ג׳שנ. גאַיאַנאַ, פערנאַמבוקאָ, בראַזיל. תשנ״ב. . . שנת נפלאות בכל. צדי״ק שנה לכ״ק אדמו״ר שליט״א. (6) שס דף.

ד׳רכג. כנ״ל אות ג׳שנ. גאַיבו, פערנאַמבוקאָ, בראַזיל. תשנ״ב. . . שנת נפלאות בכל. צדי״ק שנה לכ״ק אדמו״ר שליט״א. (6) שס דף.

ד׳רכד. כנ״ל אות ג׳שנ. גאַראַניוס, פערנאַמבוקאָ, בראַזיל. תשנ״ב. . . שנת נפלאות בכל. צדי״ק שנה לכ״ק אדמו״ר שליט״א. (6) שס דף.

ד׳רכה. כנ״ל אות ג׳שנ. גראַוואַטאַ, פערנאַמבוקאָ, בראַזיל. תשנ״ב. . . שנת נפלאות בכל. צדי״ק שנה לכ״ק אדמו״ר שליט״א. (6) שס דף.

ד׳רכו. כנ״ל אות ג׳שנ. וויטאָריאַ אנטאַו, פערנאַמבוקאָ, בראַזיל. תשנ״ב. . . שנת נפלאות בכל. צדי״ק שנה לכ״ק אדמו״ר שליט״א. (6) שס דף.

ד׳רכז. כנ״ל אות ג׳תק. זשאַבאָאַטאַו, פערנאַמבוקאָ, בראַזיל. תשנ״ב. . . שנת נפלאות בכל. צדי״ק שנה לכ״ק אדמו״ר שליט״א. (6) שס דף.

ד׳רכח. כנ״ל אות ג׳תק. טאַמאַנדאַרע, פערנאַמבוקאָ, בראַזיל. תשנ״ב. . . שנת נפלאות בכל. צדי״ק שנה לכ״ק אדמו״ר שליט״א. (6) שס דף.

ד׳רכט. כנ״ל אות ג׳תק. טימבאַובאַ, פערנאַמבוקאָ, בראַזיל. תשנ״ב. . . שנת נפלאות בכל. צדי״ק שנה לכ״ק אדמו״ר שליט״א. (6) שס דף.

ד׳רל. כנ״ל אות ג׳תק. לאָורענסאָ, פערנאַמבוקאָ, בראַזיל. תשנ״ב. . . שנת נפלאות בכל. צדי״ק שנה לכ״ק אדמו״ר שליט״א. (6) שס דף.

ד׳רלא. כנ״ל אות ג׳שנ. לימאָעירא, פערנאַמבוקאָ, בראַזיל. תשנ״ב. . . שנת נפלאות בכל. צדי״ק שנה לכ״ק אדמו״ר שליט״א. (6) שס דף.

ד׳רלב. כנ״ל אות ג׳שנ. מאַרענאַ, פערנאַמבוקאָ, בראַזיל. תשנ״ב. . . שנת נפלאות בכל. צדי״ק שנה לכ״ק אדמו״ר שליט״א. (6) שס דף.

ד׳רלג. כנ״ל אות ג׳שנ. מאַריאַ פאַריניאַ, פערנאַמבוקאָ, בראַזיל. תשנ״ב. . . שנת נפלאות בכל. צדי״ק שנה לכ״ק אדמו״ר שליט״א. (6) שס דף.

ד׳רלד. כנ״ל אות ג׳שנ. נאַוואָ זשערוזאלעו, פערנאַמבוקאָ, בראַזיל. תשנ״ב. . . שנת נפלאות בכל. צדי״ק שנה לכ״ק אדמו״ר שליט״א. (6) שס דף.

ד׳רלה. כנ״ל אות ג׳שנ. סאַלגאַדיניאַ, פערנאַמבוקאָ, בראַזיל. תשנ״ב. . . שנת נפלאות בכל. צדי״ק שנה לכ״ק אדמו״ר שליט״א. (6) שס דף.

ד׳רלו. כנ״ל אות ג׳שנ. עסקאַדאַ, פערנאַמבוקאָ, בראַזיל. תשנ״ב. . . שנת נפלאות בכל. צדי״ק שנה לכ״ק אדמו״ר שליט״א. (6) שס דף.

ד׳רלז. כנ״ל אות ג׳שנ. פאוליסטאַ, פערנאַמבוקאָ, בראַזיל. תשנ״ב. . . שנת נפלאות בכל. צדי״ק שנה לכ״ק אדמו״ר שליט״א. (6) שס דף.

ד׳רלח. כנ״ל אות ג׳שנ. פאַזוענדאַ נאַוואַ, פערנאַמבוקאָ, בראַזיל. תשנ״ב. . . שנת נפלאות בכל. צדי״ק שנה לכ״ק אדמו״ר שליט״א. (6) שס דף.

ד׳רלט. כנ״ל אות ג׳שנ. פאַלמאַרעס, פערנאַמבוקאָ, בראַזיל. תשנ״ב. . . שנת נפלאות בכל. צדי״ק שנה לכ״ק אדמו״ר שליט״א. (6) שס דף.

ד׳רמ. כנ״ל אות ג׳תק. פאַראַטיבע, פערנאַמבוקאָ, בראַזיל. תשנ״ב. . . שנת נפלאות בכל. צדי״ק שנה לכ״ק אדמו״ר שליט״א. (6) שס דף.

ד׳רמא. כנ״ל אות ג׳תק. פאָרטאָ דע גאַליניאַ, פערנאַמבוקאָ, בראַזיל. תשנ״ב. . . שנת נפלאות בכל. צדי״ק שנה לכ״ק אדמו״ר שליט״א. (6) שס דף.

ד׳רמב. כנ״ל אות ג׳תק. פלאָרעסטאַ, פערנאַמבוקאָ, בראַזיל. תשנ״ב. . . שנת נפלאות בכל. צדי״ק שנה לכ״ק אדמו״ר שליט״א. (6) שס דף.

ד׳רמג. כנ״ל אות ג׳תק. פעסקעירא, פערנאַמבוקאָ, בראַזיל. תשנ״ב. . . שנת נפלאות בכל. צדי״ק שנה לכ״ק אדמו״ר שליט״א. (6) שס דף.

ד׳רמד. כנ״ל אות ג׳תק. קאַבאָ, פערנאַמבוקאָ, בראַזיל. תשנ״ב. . . שנת נפלאות בכל. צדי״ק שנה לכ״ק אדמו״ר שליט״א. (6) שס דף.

ד׳רמה. כנ״ל אות ג׳שנ. קאַעטאַנאַ, פערנאַמבוקאָ, בראַזיל. תשנ״ב. . . שנת נפלאות בכל. צדי״ק שנה לכ״ק אדמו״ר שליט״א. (6) שס דף.

ד׳רמו. כנ״ל אות ג׳תק. קאַמאַראזשיבע, פערנאַמבוקאָ, בראַזיל. תשנ״ב. . . שנת נפלאות בכל. צדי״ק שנה לכ״ק אדמו״ר שליט״א. (6) שס דף.

ד׳רמז. כנ״ל אות ג׳תק. קאַנדאַדאַ, פערנאַמבוקאָ, בראַזיל. תשנ״ב. . . שנת נפלאות בכל. צדי״ק שנה לכ״ק אדמו״ר שליט״א. (6) שס דף.

ד׳רמח. כנ״ל אות ג׳תק. קאַרואַרו, פערנאַמבוקאָ, בראַזיל. תשנ״ב. . . שנת נפלאות בכל. צדי״ק שנה לכ״ק אדמו״ר שליט״א. (6) שס דף.

ד׳רמט. כנ״ל אות ג׳תק. קאַרפינאַ, פערנאַמבוקאָ, בראַזיל. תשנ״ב. . . שנת נפלאות בכל. צדי״ק שנה לכ״ק אדמו״ר שליט״א. (6) שס דף.

ד׳רנ. כנ״ל אות ג׳תק. אַראַסאַיאַבאַ, פערנאַמבוקאָ, בראַזיל. תשנ״ב. . . שנת נפלאות בכל. צדי״ק שנה לכ״ק אדמו״ר שליט״א. (6) שס דף.

ד'רנא. כנ"ל אות ג'תק. טרעס לאַדעיראַס, פערנאַמבוקאָ, בראַזיל. תשנ"ב. . . שנת נפלאות בכל. צדי"ק שנה לכ"ק אדמו"ר שליט"א. (6) שס דף.

ד'רנב. כנ"ל אות שלה. בריטס, דרום אפריקא. תשנ"ב. . . שנת נפלאות בכל. צדי"ק שנה לכ"ק אדמו"ר שליט"א. (6) שס דף.

ד'רנג. כנ"ל אות שלה. אולאַן באַטער, מאָנגאָליא. תשנ"ב. . . שנת נפלאות בכל. צדי"ק שנה לכ"ק אדמו"ר שליט"א. (6) שס דף.

ד'רנד. כנ"ל אות שלה. וועלאַנד, אָנטאַריאָ, קאנאדא. תשנ"ג. הי' תהא שנת נפלאות גדולות. צדי"ק שנה לכ"ק אדמו"ר שליט"א. (6) שס דף.

ד'רנה. כנ"ל אות שלה. בית חב"ד שכונת סלטבוש, ברוקלין, נ.י. תשנ"ג. . . שנת נפלאות גדולות. צדי"ק שנה לכ"ק אדמו"ר שליט"א. (6) שס דף.

ד'רנו. כנ"ל אות שלה. שכונת דזשאַרדזשטאַון, ברוקלין, נ.י. תשנ"ג. . . שנת נפלאות גדולות. צדי"ק שנה לכ"ק אדמו"ר שליט"א. (6) שס דף.

ד'רנז. כנ"ל אות שלה. באַלשאַי מארסקאי, פעטערבורג, רוסיא. תשנ"ג. . . שנת נפלאות גדולות. צדי"ק שנה לכ"ק אדמו"ר שליט"א. (6) שס דף.

ד'רנח. כנ"ל אות שלה. גראז'דאנקא, פעטערבערג, רוסיא. תשנ"ג. . . שנת נפלאות גדולות. צדי"ק שנה לכ"ק אדמו"ר שליט"א. (6) שס דף.

ד'רנט. כנ"ל אות שלה. פאנטאנקא, פעטערבורג, רוסיא. תשנ"ג. . . שנת נפלאות גדולות. צדי"ק שנה לכ"ק אדמו"ר שליט"א. (6) שס דף.

ד'רס. כנ"ל אות א'תשדמ. עם תרגום אנגלי (עמוד התרגום מול עמוד התניא). — בגודל סמ. 22½ x 15½ ברוקלין, נ.י. תשנ"ג. . . שנת נפלאות גדולות. צדי"ק שנה לכ"ק אדמו"ר שליט"א. .1012 pp. (XIII)

ד'רסא. כנ"ל אות שלה. ראַזלין, לאָנג איילאַנד, נ.י. תשנ"ג. . . שנת נפלאות גדולות. צדי"ק שנה לכ"ק אדמו"ר שליט"א. (6) שס דף.

ד'רסב. כנ"ל אות שלה. פרנסה דעל עסטע, ארזענטיי. תשנ"ג. . . שנת נפלאות גדולות. צדי"ק שנה לכ"ק אדמו"ר שליט"א. (6) שס דף.

ד'רסג. כנ"ל אות שלה. אַטקאָ, ניו דזשערסי. תשנ"ג. . . שנת נפלאות גדולות. צדי"ק שנה לכ"ק אדמו"ר שליט"א. (6) שס דף.

ד'רסד. כנ"ל אות שלה. איזזבאַראָ, ניו דזשערסי. תשנ"ג. . . שנת נפלאות גדולות. צדי"ק שנה לכ"ק אדמו"ר שליט"א. (6) שס דף.

ד'רסה. כנ"ל אות שלה. אַשלאַנד, ניו דזשערסי. תשנ"ג. . . שנת נפלאות גדולות. צדי"ק שנה לכ"ק אדמו"ר שליט"א. (6) שס דף.

ד'רסו. כנ"ל אות שלה. באַרינגטאָן, ניו דזשערסי. תשנ"ג. . . שנת נפלאות גדולות. צדי"ק שנה לכ"ק אדמו"ר שליט"א. (6) שס דף.

ד'רסז. כנ"ל אות שלה. בערלין, ניו דזשערסי. תשנ"ג. . . שנת נפלאות גדולות. צדי"ק שנה לכ"ק אדמו"ר שליט"א. (6) שס דף.

ד'רסח. כנ"ל אות שלה. וועסט בערלין, ניו דזשערסי. תשנ"ג. . . שנת נפלאות גדולות. צדי"ק שנה לכ"ק אדמו"ר שליט"א. (6) שס דף.

ד'רסט. כנ"ל אות שלה. ברידזשבאַרא, ניו דזשערסי. תשנ"ג. . . שנת נפלאות גדולות. צדי"ק שנה לכ"ק אדמו"ר שליט"א. (6) שס דף.

ד'רע. כנ"ל אות שלה. גיבסבארא, ניו דזשערסי. תשנ"ג. . . שנת נפלאות גדולות. צדי"ק שנה לכ"ק אדמו"ר שליט"א. (6) שס דף.

ד'רעא. כנ"ל אות שלה. דאַגבערטאָן, ניו דזשערסי. תשנ"ג. . . שנת נפלאות גדולות. צדי"ק שנה לכ"ק אדמו"ר שליט"א. (6) שס דף.

ד'רעב. כנ"ל אות שלה. דזשארדענסאַוו, ניו דזשערסי. תשנ"ג. . . נפלאות גדולות. צדי"ק שנה לכ"ק אדמו"ר שליט"א. (6) שס דף.

ד'רעג. כנ"ל אות שלה. דעלייר, ניו דזשערסי. תשנ"ג. . . שנת נפלאות גדולות. צדי"ק שנה לכ"ק אדמו"ר שליט"א. (6) שס דף.

ד'רעד. כנ"ל אות שלה. דעלראַן, ניו דזשערסי. תשנ"ג. . . שנת נפלאות גדולות. צדי"ק שנה לכ"ק אדמו"ר שליט"א. (6) שס דף.

ד'רעה. כנ"ל אות שלה. האַדאַן הייטס, ניו דזשערסי. תשנ"ג. . . שנת נפלאות גדולות. צדי"ק שנה לכ"ק אדמו"ר שליט"א. (6) שס דף.

ד'רעו. כנ"ל אות שלה. האַדאַנפילד, ניו דזשערסי. תשנ"ג. . . שנת נפלאות גדולות. צדי"ק שנה לכ"ק אדמו"ר שליט"א. (6) שס דף.

ד'רעז. כנ"ל אות שלה. האַרטסאַרד, ניו דזשערסי. תשנ"ג. . . שנת נפלאות גדולות. צדי"ק שנה לכ"ק אדמו"ר שליט"א. (6) שס דף.

ד'רעח. כנ"ל אות שלה. וואָרהיס, ניו דזשערסי. תשנ"ג. . . שנת נפלאות גדולות. צדי"ק שנה לכ"ק אדמו"ר שליט"א. (6) שס דף.

ד'רעט. כנ"ל אות שלה. סטעטסילהורסט. ניו דזשערסי. תשנ"ג. . . נפלאות גדולות. צדי"ק שנה לכ"ק אדמו"ר שליט"א. (6) שס דף.

ד'רפ. כנ"ל אות שלה. לאַנסייד, ניו דזשערסי. תשנ"ג. . . שנת נפלאות גדולות. צדי"ק שנה לכ"ק אדמו"ר שליט"א. (6) שס דף.

ד'רפא. כנ"ל אות שלה. לעגואָלאַ, ניו דזשערסי. תשנ"ג. . . שנת נפלאות גדולות. צדי"ק שנה לכ"ק אדמו"ר שליט"א. (6) שס דף.

ד'רפב. כנ"ל אות שלה. מאַריסוויל, ניו דזשערסי. תשנ"ג. . . שנת נפלאות גדולות. צדי"ק שנה לכ"ק אדמו"ר שליט"א. (6) שס דף.

ד'רפג. כנ"ל אות שלה. מאַרלטאָן, ניו דזשערסי. תשנ"ג. . . שנת נפלאות גדולות. צדי"ק שנה לכ"ק אדמו"ר שליט"א. (6) שס דף.

ד'רפד. כנ"ל אות שלה. מורסטאַון, ניו דזשערסי. תשנ"ג. . . שנת נפלאות גדולות. צדי"ק שנה לכ"ק אדמו"ר שליט"א. (6) שס דף.

ד'רפה. כנ"ל אות שלה. מייסאַוויל, ניו דזשערסי. תשנ"ג. . . שנת נפלאות גדולות. צדי"ק שנה לכ"ק אדמו"ר שליט"א. (6) שס דף.

ד'רפו. כנ"ל אות שלה. מייפל שיה. ניו דזשערסי. תשנ"ג. . . שנת נפלאות גדולות. צדי"ק שנה לכ"ק אדמו"ר שליט"א. (6) שס דף.

ד'רפז. כנ"ל אות שלה. מערטשאַנטוויל. ניו דזשערסי. תשנ"ג. . . נפלאות גדולות. צדי"ק שנה לכ"ק אדמו"ר שליט"א. (6) שס דף.

ד'רפח. כנ"ל אות שלה. סאָמערדייל, ניו דזשערסי. תשנ"ג. . . שנת נפלאות גדולות. צדי"ק שנה לכ"ק אדמו"ר שליט"א. (6) שס דף.

ד'רפט. כנ"ל אות שלה. סאַנדייק, ניו דזשערסי. תשנ"ג. . . שנת נפלאות גדולות. צדי"ק שנה לכ"ק אדמו"ר שליט"א. (6) שס דף.

ד'רצ. כנ"ל אות שלה. סטעטסטאַון, ניו דזשערסי. תשנ"ג. . . שנת נפלאות גדולות. צדי"ק שנה לכ"ק אדמו"ר שליט"א. (6) שס דף.

ד'רצא. כנ"ל אות שלה. ספרינגדייל, ניו דזשערסי. תשנ"ג. . . שנת נפלאות גדולות. צדי"ק שנה לכ"ק אדמו"ר שליט"א. (6) שס דף.

ד'רצב. כנ"ל אות שלה. עדזשאַב, ניו דזשערסי. תשנ"ג. . . שנת נפלאות גדולות. צדי"ק שנה לכ"ק אדמו"ר שליט"א. (6) שס דף.

ד'רצג. כנ"ל אות שלה. פּאַלמיירא, ניו דזשערסי. תשנ"ג. . . שנת נפלאות גדולות. צדי"ק שנה לכ"ק אדמו"ר שליט"א. (6) שס דף.

ד'רצד. כנ"ל אות שלה. פעלאַרשיפ, ניו דזשערסי. תשנ"ג. . . שנת נפלאות גדולות. צדי"ק שנה לכ"ק אדמו"ר שליט"א. (6) שס דף.

ד'רצה. כנ"ל אות שלה. קירסוואוד, ניו דזשערסי. תשנ"ג. . . שנה נפלאות גדולות. צדי"ק שנה לכ"ק אדמו"ר שליט"א. (6) שס דף.

ד'רצו. כנ"ל אות שלה. קרעטאָן, ניו דזשערסי. תשנ"ג. . . שנת נפלאות גדולות. צדי"ק שנה לכ"ק אדמו"ר שליט"א. (6) שס דף.

ד'רצז. כנ"ל אות שלה. ראַנקאָקאַס, ניו דזשערסי. תשנ"ג. . . שנה נפלאות גדולות. צדי"ק שנה לכ"ק אדמו"ר שליט"א. (6) שס דף.

ד'רחצ. כנ"ל אות שלה. ריווערטאָן, ניו דזשערסי. תשנ"ג. . . שנת נפלאות גדולות. צדי"ק שנה לכ"ק אדמו"ר שליט"א. (6) שס דף.

ד'רצט. כנ"ל אות שלה. ריווערסייד, ניו דזשערסי. תשנ"ג. . . שנת נפלאות גדולות. צדי"ק שנה לכ"ק אדמו"ר שליט"א. (6) שס דף.

ד'ש. כנ"ל אות שלה. איסט ריווערטאָן, ניו דזשערסי. תשנ"ג. . . נפלאות גדולות. צדי"ק שנה לכ"ק אדמו"ר שליט"א. (6) שס דף.

ד'שא. כנ"ל אות ג'תק. מוסקבא, בריה"מ. התשנ"א.

ד'שב. כנ"ל אות שדמ. בית הרפואה „בית ישראל", מאַנהאַטען, נ.י. י"א ניסן תשנ"ד. הי' תהא שנת נפלאות דגלית. לזכות כ"ק אדמו"ר שליט"א מלך המשיח . . ויבנה בית המקדש במקומו ותיכף ומיד ממש. (6) רת דף.

ד'שג. כנ"ל אות שלה. טאַססאָן, אַריזאָנאַ. תשנ"ד. (6) שס דף.

ד'שד. כנ"ל אות שלה. קיל דעוויל הילס, נאָרט קאַראָליינאַ. תשנ"ד. (6) שס דף.

ד'שה. כנ"ל אות שלה. קיטי האָק, נאָרט קאַראָליינאַ. תשנ"ד. (6) שס דף.

ד'שו. כנ"ל אות שלה. בית חב"ד מרכז העיר, מילוואָקי, וויסקאָנסין. תשנ"ד. (6) שס דף.

ד'שז. כנ"ל אות שדמ. קיבוץ ניר דוד, באה"ק. ט' כסלו, תשנ"ד.

ד'שח. כנ"ל אות שדמ. ת"ת חב"ד גילה, ירושלים, ת"ו, באה"ק. ט"ז כסלו, תשנ"ד.

ד'שט. כנ"ל אות שדמ. גן נר, באה"ק. י"ז כסלו, תשנ"ד.

ד'שי. כנ"ל אות שדמ. מפעלי תעשי' אוירית בישראל, אה"ק. ח"י כסלו, תשנ"ד.

דפוסי תניא

ד'שיא. כנ"ל את שדמ. סופר־אביב שליד ביהכנ"ס שלום על ישראל, ורד יריחו,־באה"ק. תשנ"ב.
ד'שיב. כנ"ל את שלה. כידנע, [בריה"מ]. תשנ"א.
ד'שיג. כנ"ל את שלה. בירתיכה [בריה"מ]. תשנ"א.
ד'שיד. כנ"ל את שלה. חימקי (ע"י ספרית לנין) [בריה"מ]. תשנ"א.
ד'שטו. כנ"ל את שלה. סאקאלניק, מוסקבא [בריה"מ]. תשנ"א.
ד'שטז. כנ"ל את שלה. פרס [בריה"מ]. תשנ"א.
ד'שיז. כנ"ל את שלה. קלנצובקא, מוסקבא [בריה"מ]. תשנ"א.
ד'שיח. כנ"ל את ג'תק. שערעמעטיעבו. ה'תשנ"ד.
ד'שיט. כנ"ל את שלה. לאָוער מאַנהעטען, נ.י. תשנ"ה. (6) שס דף.
ד'שכ. כנ"ל את ג'תק. מסטיסלאבל. ח' אלול תשנ"ב.
ד'שכא. כנ"ל את ג'תק. סאמארא. ד' אדר ב' תשנ"ב.
ד'שכב. כנ"ל את שלה. פאקראווסקא סטרעשנעווא, מוסקבא. תשנ"ב.
ד'שכג. כנ"ל את שלה. פרעאבראזיענסקא, מוסקבא. א' שבט תשנ"ב.
ד'שכד. כנ"ל את ג'תק. צ'אווראשקי, בריה"מ. תשנ"ב.
ד'שכה. כנ"ל את ג'תק. צ'אסי. ח' אלול תשנ"ב.
ד'שכו. כנ"ל את ג'תק. צ'עריקאב. ט' אלול תשנ"ב.
ד'שכז. כנ"ל את שלה. קאפטעווא, מוסקבא. תשנ"ב.
ד'שכח. כנ"ל את שלה. קוזנעצקי מוסט, מוסקבא. חנוכה תשנ"ב.
ד'שכט. כנ"ל את ג'תק. קאזאן. כ"ט תמוז תשנ"ב.
ד'של. כנ"ל את ג'תק. קריצ'עב. ח' אלול תשנ"ב.
ד'שלא. כנ"ל את ג'תק. ראזאן. ד' אדר ב' תשנ"ב.
ד'שלב. כנ"ל את ג'תק. ראסלאבל. ט' אלול תשנ"ב.
ד'שלג. כנ"ל את ג'תק. רעצ'יצא. י' אלול תשנ"ב.
ד'שלד. כנ"ל את ג'תק. בראווארי. י"ח תמוז תשנ"ג.
ד'שלה. כנ"ל את ג'תק. גלוכאוו. י"ח תמוז תשנ"ג.
ד'שלו. כנ"ל את ג'תתקעא. וינאגראדאבא. י"ח תמוז תשנ"ג.
ד'שלז. כנ"ל את ג'תק. וואלבונאוו. י' תמוז תשנ"ג.
ד'שלח. כנ"ל את ג'תק. טאסנא. כ"ב סיון תשנ"ג.
ד'שלט. כנ"ל את ג'תק. כוסט. י' תמוז תשנ"ג.
ד'שמ. כנ"ל את ג'תק. מאלאדעצנא. י"ב אב תשנ"ג.
ד'שמא. כנ"ל את ג'תק. סאראטוב. כ' חשון תשנ"ג.
ד'שמב. כנ"ל את ג'תק. סבאלאבא. ט' תמוז תשנ"ג.
ד'שמג. כנ"ל את ג'תק. סטאראבין. ט"ז אב תשנ"ג.
ד'שדמ. כנ"ל את ג'תק. סלאנים. י"ד אב תשנ"ג.
ד'שמה. כנ"ל את ג'תק. סעסטראַרעצק. י"ט סיון תשנ"ג.
ד'שמו. כנ"ל את ג'תק. פרוזני. י"ד אב תשנ"ג.
ד'שמז. כנ"ל את ג'תק. קאלפינא. כ"א סיון תשנ"ג.
ד'שמח. כנ"ל את ג'תק. קוברין. ט"ז אב תשנ"ג.
ד'שמט. כנ"ל את ג'תק. אטראדנאע, מוסקבא. ח' סיון תשנ"ג.
ד'שנ. כנ"ל את שדמ. גן מנחם, לאקאוואקסען, פענסילווייניא. תשנ"ז. (6) רנח דף.
ד'שנא. כנ"ל את ג'תק. ביבירעווא, מוסקבא. ח' סיון תשנ"ג.
ד'שנב. כנ"ל את ג'תק. גאראדאק מאסאווטא, מוסקבא. כ"ה אדר תשנ"ג.
ד'שנג. כנ"ל את ג'תק. דיאקאווא, מוסקבא. י"ב אדר תשנ"ג.
ד'שנד. כנ"ל את ג'תק. דמיטראווקא, מוסקבא. ד' ניסן תשנ"ג.
ד'שנה. כנ"ל את ג'תק. זובאווסקאיא, מוסקבא. כ' שבט תשנ"ג.
ד'שנו. כנ"ל את ג'תק. טישינקא, מוסקבא. כ"ב שבט תשנ"ג.
ד'שנז. כנ"ל את ג'תק. כאפילאווקא, מוסקבא. י' שבט תשנ"ג.
ד'שנח. כנ"ל את ג'תק. לובלינא, מוסקבא. כ"ב אדר תשנ"ג.
ד'שנט. כנ"ל את ג'תק. מעשאנסקאיא, מוסקבא. כ"ג אדר תשנ"ג.
ד'שס. כנ"ל את ג'תק. נאוואגירעווא, מוסקבא. י"ז שבט תשנ"ג.
ד'שסא. כנ"ל את ג'תק. ניקיססקאיא, מוסקבא. ד' ניסן תשנ"ג.
ד'שסב. כנ"ל את ג'תק. סאמאטעקא, מוסקבא. כ"ב אייר תשנ"ג.
ד'שסג. כנ"ל את ג'תק. סוכארעווקא, מוסקבא. כ' שבט תשנ"ג.
ד'שסד. כנ"ל את ג'תק. פעטראווסקא ראזומאווסקאיע. מוסקבא. ב' אדר תשנ"ג.
ד'שסה. כנ"ל את ג'תק. פעטראווקא, מוסקבא. כ"ז שבט תשנ"ג.
ד'שסו. כנ"ל את ג'תק. קאדאשי, מוסקבא. י"ח שבט תשנ"ג.

ד'שסז. כנ"ל את ג'תק. קאלוויסקאיא זאסטאווא. מוסקבא. כ"ד אדר תשנ"ג.
ד'שסח. כנ"ל את ג'תק. קאראווינא, מוסקבא. ח' סיון תשנ"ג.
ד'שסט. כנ"ל את ג'תק. קרעסטאווסקאיא זאסטאווא, מוסקבא. ח' סיון תשנ"ג.
ד'שע. כנ"ל את ג'תק. קראסנאיא פלאשאד, מוסקבא. כ"ג אדר תשנ"ג.
ד'שעא. כנ"ל את ג'תק. סאדאוואיא, פטרבורג. ו' שבט תשנ"ג.
ד'שעב. כנ"ל את ג'תק. קאמענדאנטסקי אעראדראמ, פטרבורג. ה' שבט תשנ"ג.
ד'שעג. כנ"ל את ג'תק. שפאלערנאיא. פטרבורג. ה' שבט תשנ"ג.
ד'שעד. כנ"ל את ג'תק. אבאלאן, קיעוו. כ"ח ניסן תשנ"ג.
ד'שעה. כנ"ל את ג'תק. אלעקסאנדראיוסקאיא, קיעוו. כ"ד ניסן תשנ"ג.
ד'שעו. כנ"ל את ג'תק. באבי יאר, קיעוו. כ"ח ניסן תשנ"ג.
ד'שעז. כנ"ל את ג'תק. באלשאיא פאדוואלנאיא. כ"ג ניסן תשנ"ג.
ד'שעח. כנ"ל את ג'תק. בית הכנסת בראדסקיי, קיעוו. כ"ד ניסן תשנ"ג.
ד'שעט. כנ"ל את ג'תק. דארניצא, קיעוו. תשנ"ג.
ד'שפ. כנ"ל את ג'תק. ויגאגראדאר, קיעוו. כ"ט ניסן תשנ"ג.
ד'שפא. כנ"ל את ג'תק. וועטראניע גארי, קיעוו. כ"ט ניסן תשנ"ג.
ד'שפב. כנ"ל את ג'תק. בוטאר אטראדני, קיעוו. כ"ט ניסן תשנ"ג.
ד'שפג. כנ"ל את ג'תק. סוואטאשין, קיעוו. כ"ט ניסן תשנ"ג.
ד'שפד. כנ"ל את ג'תק. סטרעלעצקאיא, קיעוו. כ"ד ניסן תשנ"ג.
ד'שפה. כנ"ל את ג'תק. יעווריעיסקיי באזאר, קיעוו. כ"ג ניסן תשנ"ג.
ד'שפו. כנ"ל את ג'תק. פאדאל, קיעוו. כ"ד ניסן תשנ"ג.
ד'שפז. כנ"ל את ג'תק. סינדוקלעבסקאיא, קיעוו. ז' ניסן תשנ"ג.
ד'שפח. כנ"ל את ג'תק. קאראוואעווסקאיא, קיעוו. ח' ניסן תשנ"ג.
ד'שפט. כנ"ל את ג'תק. סירעגעווקא, קיעוו. כ"ח ניסן תשנ"ג.
ד'שצ. כנ"ל את ג'תק. קרישאטיק, קיעוו. ט' אדר תשנ"ג.
ד'שצא. כנ"ל את ג'תק. בולשעבו. תשנ"ד.
ד'שצב. כנ"ל את ג'תק. מיזסי, מוסקבא. תשנ"ד.
ד'שצג. כנ"ל את ג'תק. בית כנסת מארינא רושצא. מוסקבא. כ"ה שבט תשנ"ד.
ד'שצד. כנ"ל את ג'תק. בלאדיקינו, מוסקבא. תשנ"ד.
ד'שצה. כנ"ל את ג'תק. אנציקלופדיה לתולדות יהודי רוסיה. מוסקבא. תשנ"ד.
ד'שצו. כנ"ל את ג'תק. וסובו (אוסאווא). תשנ"ד.
ד'שצז. כנ"ל את ג'תק. ארחאנגעלסקע. תשנ"ד.
ד'שצח. כנ"ל את ג'תק. בארביחה. תשנ"ד.
ד'שצט. כנ"ל את ג'תק. בוטובו. תשנ"ד.
ד'ת. כנ"ל את ג'תק. בירולובו, מוסקבא. תשנ"ד.
ד'תא. כנ"ל את ג'תק. בוסינובו, מוסקבא. תשנ"ד.
ד'תב. כנ"ל את ג'תק. דאבידקובו, מוסקבא. תשנ"ד.
ד'תג. כנ"ל את ג'תק. וציאקובו, מוסקבא. תשנ"ד.
ד'תד. כנ"ל את ג'תק. בוסטראקובו, מוסקבא. תשנ"ד.
ד'תה. כנ"ל את ג'תק. בראטעבו, מוסקבא. תשנ"ד.
ד'תו. כנ"ל את ג'תק. גילארוכסקוגו, מוסקבא. תשנ"ד.
ד'תז. כנ"ל את ג'תק. וסטאנקינו, מוסקבא. תשנ"ד.
ד'תח. כנ"ל את ג'תק. טאטארובו, מוסקבא. תשנ"ד.
ד'תט. כנ"ל את ג'תק. מנעבניקי, מוסקבא. תשנ"ד.
ד'תי. כנ"ל את ג'תק. עקאטערינובקה, מוסקבא. תשנ"ד.
ד'תיא. כנ"ל את ג'תק. זאגוראנקה. תשנ"ד.
ד'תיב. כנ"ל את ג'תק. טאראסובקה. תשנ"ד.
ד'תיג. כנ"ל את ג'תק. טומילינו. תשנ"ד.
ד'תיד. כנ"ל את ג'תק. ילינסקע. תשנ"ד.
ד'תטו. כנ"ל את ג'תק. מאריופאל. תשנ"ד.
ד'תטז. כנ"ל את ג'תתמג. קליאזמה. ט"ז אייר. תשנ"ד.
ד'תיז. כנ"ל את ג'תק. חלעבניקבו. תשנ"ד.
ד'תיח. כנ"ל את ג'תק. נובומודרעזקבו. תשנ"ד.
ד'תיט. כנ"ל את ג'תק. סולנצעבו, מוסקבא. תשנ"ד.
ד'תכ. כנ"ל את ג'תק. סוסנובי בור, מוסקבא. תשנ"ד.

דפוסי תניא

ד׳תכא. כנ״ל את ג׳תק. סאכורובי, מוסקבא. תשנ״ד.
ד׳תכב. כנ״ל את ג׳תק. פערעדעלקינו. תשנ״ד.
ד׳תכג. כנ״ל את ג׳תק. מעלה חבר, אה״ק. תשנ״ה.
ד׳תכד. כנ״ל את ג׳תק. שני (ליבנה), אה״ק. תשנ״ה.
ד׳תכה. כנ״ל את ג׳תק. בית יתיר גבעת עוז, אה״ק. תשנ״ה.
ד׳תכו. כנ״ל את ג׳תק. אדמות ישי תל רומידה, אה״ק. תשנ״ה.
ד׳תכז. כנ״ל את ג׳תק. מערת המכפלה, אה״ק. תשנ״ה.
ד׳תכח. כנ״ל את ג׳תק. רמת ממרא (חרסינה) גבעת לפיד, אה״ק. תשנ״ה.
ד׳תכט. כנ״ל את ג׳תק. סוסיא, אה״ק. תשנ״ה.
ד׳תל. כנ״ל את ג׳תק. מעון, אה״ק. תשנ״ה.
ד׳תלא. כנ״ל את ג׳תק. כרמל, אה״ק. תשנ״ה.
ד׳תלב. כנ״ל את ג׳תק. תלם, אה״ק. תשנ״ה.
ד׳תלג. כנ״ל את ג׳תק. אדורה, אה״ק. תשנ״ה.
ד׳תלד. כנ״ל את ג׳תק. ביהכנ״ס מנוחה רחל, אה״ק. תשנ״ה.
ד׳תלה. כנ״ל את ג׳תק. גבעת האבות (גיבראן), אה״ק. תשנ״ה.
ד׳תלו. כנ״ל את ג׳תק. בת עין, אה״ק. תשנ״ה.
ד׳תלז. כנ״ל את ג׳תק. ראש צורים, אה״ק. תשנ״ה.
ד׳תלח. כנ״ל את ג׳תק. מעלה עמוס, אה״ק. תשנ״ה.
ד׳תלט. כנ״ל את ג׳תק. אלון שבות, אה״ק. תשנ״ה.
ד׳תמ. כנ״ל את ג׳תק. כרמי צור, אה״ק. תשנ״ה.
ד׳תמא. כנ״ל את ג׳תק. אלעזר, אה״ק. תשנ״ה.
ד׳תמב. כנ״ל את ג׳תק. אל דוד, אה״ק. תשנ״ה.
ד׳תמג. כנ״ל את ג׳תק. כפר אלדד, אה״ק. תשנ״ה.
ד׳תמד. כנ״ל את ג׳תק. תקוע, אה״ק. תשנ״ה.
ד׳תמה. כנ״ל את ג׳תק. אשמורת יצחק, אה״ק. תשנ״ה.
ד׳תמו. כנ״ל את ג׳תק. מגדל עוז, אה״ק. תשנ״ה.
ד׳תמז. כנ״ל את ג׳תק. נוה דניאל, אה״ק. תשנ״ה.
ד׳תמח. כנ״ל את ג׳תק. בית חגי, אה״ק. תשנ״ה.
ד׳תמט. כנ״ל את ג׳תק. עתניאל, אה״ק. תשנ״ה.
ד׳תנ. כנ״ל את ג׳תק. שמעה, אה״ק. תשנ״ה.
ד׳תנא כנ״ל את ג׳תק. מעלה עוטרים, אה״ק. תשנ״ה.
ד׳תנב. כנ״ל את ג׳תק. ישיבה תיכוניה רמת ממרא, אה״ק. תשנ״ה.
ד׳תנג. כנ״ל את ג׳תק. אשכולות, אה״ק. תשנ״ה.
ד׳תנד. כנ״ל את רא. הוטשימין סיטי (סייגון), וויעטנאם. תשנ״ה.
ד׳תנה. כנ״ל את ג׳תק. הר ארטיס, אה״ק. תשנ״ה.
ד׳תנו. כנ״ל את ג׳תק. בית־אל ב׳, אה״ק. תשנ״ה.
ד׳תנז. כנ״ל את ג׳תק. בית־אל א׳, אה״ק. תשנ״ה.
ד׳תנח. כנ״ל את ג׳תק. פסגות, אה״ק. תשנ״ה.
ד׳תנט. כנ״ל את ג׳תק. שילה, אה״ק. תשנ״ה.
ד׳תס. כנ״ל את ג׳תק. עלי, אה״ק. תשנ״ה.
ד׳תסא. כנ״ל את ג׳תק. מעלה לבונה, אה״ק. תשנ״ה.
ד׳תסב. כנ״ל את ג׳תק. עפרה, אה״ק. תשנ״ה.
ד׳תסג. כנ״ל את ג׳תק. כוכב השחר, אה״ק. תשנ״ה.
ד׳תסד. כנ״ל את ג׳תק. רימונים, אה״ק. תשנ״ה.
ד׳תסה. כנ״ל את ג׳תק. כוכב יעקב, אה״ק. תשנ״ה.
ד׳תסו. כנ״ל את ג׳תק. עטרת, אה״ק. תשנ״ה.
ד׳תסז. כנ״ל את ג׳תק. נוה צוף, אה״ק. תשנ״ה.
ד׳תסח. כנ״ל את ג׳תק. בית אריה, אה״ק. תשנ״ה.
ד׳תסט. כנ״ל את ג׳תק. נחליאל, אה״ק. תשנ״ה.
ד׳תע. כנ״ל את ג׳תק. שבות רחל, אה״ק. תשנ״ה.
ד׳תעא. כנ״ל את ג׳תק. רחלים, אה״ק. תשנ״ה.
ד׳תעב. כנ״ל את ג׳תק. כפר תפוח, אה״ק. תשנ״ה.
ד׳תעג. כנ״ל את ג׳תק. עלי זהב, אה״ק. תשנ״ה.
ד׳תעד. כנ״ל את ג׳תק. פדואל, אה״ק. תשנ״ה.
ד׳תעה. כנ״ל את ג׳תק. עופרים, אה״ק. תשנ״ה.
ד׳תעו. כנ״ל את ג׳תק. עמנואל, אה״ק. תשנ״ה.
ד׳תעז. כנ״ל את ג׳תק. אדם, אה״ק. תשנ״ה.
ד׳תעח. כנ״ל את ג׳תק. מעלה מכמש, אה״ק. תשנ״ה.
ד׳תעט. כנ״ל את ג׳תק. אלון, אה״ק. תשנ״ה.
ד׳תפ. כנ״ל את ג׳תק. כפר אדומים, אה״ק. תשנ״ה.
ד׳תפא. כנ״ל את ג׳תק. אלון מורא, אה״ק. תשנ״ה.
ד׳תפב. כנ״ל את ג׳תק. דולב, אה״ק. תשנ״ה.
ד׳תפג. כנ״ל את ג׳תק. כותל המערבי – הכנסת ס״ת הכ״ד של ילדי ישראל, אה״ק. תשנ״ה.
ד׳תפד. כנ״ל את ג׳תק. גבעון החדשה, אה״ק. תשנ״ז.
ד׳תפה. כנ״ל את ג׳תק. טלמון – צפון, אה״ק. תשנ״ז.
ד׳תפו. כנ״ל את ג׳תק. גבעת זאב, אה״ק. תשנ״ז.
ד׳תפז. כנ״ל את ג׳תק. בית חורון, אה״ק. תשנ״ז.
ד׳תפח. כנ״ל את ג׳תק. מבוא חורון, אה״ק. תשנ״ז.
ד׳תפט. כנ״ל את ג׳תק. כוכבים, אה״ק. תשנ״ז.
ד׳תצ. כנ״ל את ג׳תק. רעות, אה״ק. תשנ״ז.
ד׳תצא. כנ״ל את ג׳תק. נעלה, אה״ק. תשנ״ז.
ד׳תצב. כנ״ל את ג׳תק. נילי, אה״ק. תשנ״ז.
ד׳תצג. כנ״ל את ג׳תק. הר אדר, אה״ק. תשנ״ז.
ד׳תצד. כנ״ל את ג׳תק. גינות שומרון, אה״ק. תשנ״ז.
ד׳תצה. כנ״ל את ג׳תק. קרני שומרון, אה״ק. תשנ״ז.
ד׳תצו. כנ״ל את ג׳תק. מצפה צבאים, אה״ק. תשנ״ז.
ד׳תצז. כנ״ל את ג׳תק. קדומים, אה״ק. תשנ״ז.
ד׳תצח. כנ״ל את ג׳תק. מעלה שומרון, אה״ק. תשנ״ז.
ד׳תצט. כנ״ל את ג׳תק. נוה מנחם, אה״ק. תשנ״ז.
ד׳תק. כנ״ל את ג׳תק. יקיר, אה״ק. תשנ״ז.
ד׳תקא. כנ״ל את ג׳תק. נופים, אה״ק. תשנ״ז.
ד׳תקב. כנ״ל את ג׳תק. רבבה, אה״ק. תשנ״ז.
ד׳תקג. כנ״ל את ג׳תק. קרית נטפים, אה״ק. תשנ״ז.
ד׳תקד. כנ״ל את ג׳תק. אריאל, אה״ק. תשנ״ז.
ד׳תקה. כנ״ל את ג׳תק. ברקן, אה״ק. תשנ״ז.
ד׳תקו. כנ״ל את ג׳תק. אלקנה, אה״ק. תשנ״ז.
ד׳תקז. כנ״ל את ג׳תק. שערי תקוה, אה״ק. תשנ״ז.
ד׳תקח. כנ״ל את ג׳תק. אורנית, אה״ק. תשנ״ז.
ד׳תקט. כנ״ל את ג׳תק. צופים, אה״ק. תשנ״ז.
ד׳תקי. כנ״ל את ג׳תק. צור יגאל, אה״ק. תשנ״ז.
ד׳תקיא. כנ״ל את ג׳תק. כוכב יאיר, אה״ק. תשנ״ז.
ד׳תקיב. כנ״ל את ג׳תק. טלמון, אה״ק. תשנ״ז.
ד׳תקיג. כנ״ל את ג׳תק. צור נתן, אה״ק. תשנ״ז.
ד׳תקיד. כנ״ל את ג׳תק. סלעית, אה״ק. תשנ״ז.
ד׳תקטו. כנ״ל את ג׳תק. אבני חפץ, אה״ק. תשנ״ז.
ד׳תקטז. כנ״ל את ג׳תק. שבי שומרון, אה״ק. תשנ״ז.
ד׳תקיז. כנ״ל את ג׳תק. איתמר, אה״ק. תשנ״ז.
ד׳תקיח. כנ״ל את ג׳תק. עינב, אה״ק. תשנ״ז.
ד׳תקיט. כנ״ל את ג׳תק. שקד, אה״ק. תשנ״ז.
ד׳תקכ. כנ״ל את ג׳תק. חומש, אה״ק. תשנ״ז.
ד׳תקכא. כנ״ל את ג׳תק. חרמש, אה״ק. תשנ״ז.
ד׳תקכב. כנ״ל את ג׳תק. מתתיהו, אה״ק. תשנ״ז.
ד׳תקכג. כנ״ל את ג׳תק. קרית ספר, אה״ק. תשנ״ז.
ד׳תקכד. כנ״ל את ג׳תק. אלפי מנשה, אה״ק. תשנ״ז.
ד׳תקכה. כנ״ל את ג׳תק. כפר גנים, פתח תקוה, אה״ק. תשנ״ז.
ד׳תקכו. כנ״ל את ג׳תק. נצרים גוש קטיף, אה״ק. תשנ״ז.
ד׳תקכז. כנ״ל את ג׳תק. גדיד גוש קטיף, אה״ק. תשנ״ז.
ד׳קתכח. כנ״ל את ג׳תק. בדולח גוש קטיף, אה״ק. תשנ״ז.
ד׳תקכט. כנ״ל את ג׳תק. ישיבת „אדרת אליהו״ ביהכנ״ס עתיק „שלום על ישראל״ יריחו, אה״ק. תשנ״ד.
ד׳תקל. כנ״ל את ג׳תק. מושב נעמה יריחו, אה״ק. תשנ״ד.
ד׳תקלא. כנ״ל את ג׳תק. כפר חרוב, אה״ק. תשנ״ז.
ד׳תקלב. כנ״ל את ג׳תק. מבוא חמה, אה״ק. תשנ״ז.
ד׳תקלג. כנ״ל את ג׳תק. מיצר, אה״ק. תשנ״ז.
ד׳תקלד. כנ״ל את ג׳תק. נטור, אה״ק. תשנ״ז.
ד׳תקלה. כנ״ל את ג׳תק. גשור, אה״ק. תשנ״ז.
ד׳תקלו. כנ״ל את ג׳תק. צה״ל מוצב כנף, אה״ק. תשנ״ז.
ד׳תקלז. כנ״ל את ג׳תק. צה״ל מחנה הרעם, אה״ק. תשנ״ז.
ד׳תקלח. כנ״ל את ג׳תק. צה״ל יחש״ם צנובר, אה״ק. תשנ״ז.
ד׳תקלט. כנ״ל את ג׳תק. כינר, אה״ק. תשנ״ז.
ד׳תקמ. כנ״ל את ג׳תק. צה״ל מחנה שגב, אה״ק. תשנ״ז.
ד׳תקמא. כנ״ל את ג׳תק. צה״ל מחנה ארטל, אה״ק. תשנ״ז.
ד׳תקמב. כנ״ל את ג׳תק. צה״ל מחנה יואב, אה״ק. תשנ״ז.
ד׳תקמג. כנ״ל את ג׳תק. צה״ל נח״ל נמרוד, אה״ק. תשנ״ז.

דפוסי תניא

ד'תקמד. כנ"ל את ג'תק. ברוכים, אה"ק. תשנ"ז.
ד'תקמה. כנ"ל את ג'תק. צה"ל קוצבת ברק, אה"ק. תשנ"ז.
ד'תקמו. כנ"ל את ג'תק. צה"ל מחנה סינדיאנה, אה"ק. תשנ"ז.
ד'תקמז. כנ"ל את ג'תק. צה"ל מחנה יצחק, אה"ק. תשנ"ז.
ד'תקמח. כנ"ל את ג'תק. צה"ל מחנה ירדן, אה"ק. תשנ"ז.
ד'תקמט. כנ"ל את ג'תק. עצרת תפלה של ילדי תשב"ר ביהכנ"ס „צמח צדק" עיר העתיקה ירושלים, אה"ק. תשנ"ז.
ד'תקנ. כנ"ל את ג'תק. בית חב"ד קצרין, אה"ק. תשנ"ז.
ד'תקנא. כנ"ל את ג'תק. צומת הרחובות יפו שלומציון, מקום בו דמם של יהודים נשפך וכו' בפיגוע רצחני, הי"ד, ירושלים, אה"ק. תשנ"ז.
ד'תקנב. כנ"ל את ג'תק. צומת הרחובות יפו שרי ישראל, מקום בו דמם של יהודים נשפך וכו' בפיגוע רצחני, הי"ד, ירושלים, אה"ק. תשנ"ז.
ד'תקנג. כנ"ל את ג'תק. דיזינגוף סנטר תל־אביב, בו דמם של יהודים נשפך וכו' בפיגוע רצחני, הי"ד, אה"ק. תשנ"ז.
ד'תקנד. כנ"ל את ג'תק. צומת אשקלון, מקום בו דמם של יהודים נשפך וכו' בפיגוע רצחני, הי"ד, אה"ק. תשנ"ז.
ד'תקנה. כנ"ל את ג'תק. צומת גבעה צרפתית, מקום בו דמם של יהודים נשפך וכו' בפיגוע רצחני, הי"ד, ירושלים, אה"ק. תשנ"ז.
ד'תקנו. כנ"ל את ג'תק. צה"ל ממשל צבאי, חסמ"ר יהודה, עיה"ק חברון, אה"ק. תשנ"ז.
ד'תקנז. כנ"ל את ג'תק. חדר מנחם ברוך, קרית ארבע, עיה"ק חברון, אה"ק. תשנ"ז.
ד'תקנח. כנ"ל את ג'תק. צה"ל מחנה חאוז, חסמ"ר יהודה, אה"ק תשנ"ז.
ד'תקנט. כנ"ל את ג'תק. קיבוץ מנרה, אה"ק. תשנ"ז.
ד'תקס. כנ"ל את ג'תק. קיבוץ מעין ברוך, אה"ק. תשנ"ז.
ד'תקסא. כנ"ל את ג'תק. צה"ל מוצב חממה, אה"ק. תשנ"ז.
ד'תקסב. כנ"ל את ג'תק. צה"ל מוצב ציפורן, אה"ק. תשנ"ז.
ד'תקסג. כנ"ל את ג'תק. צה"ל שער עגל רומת, אה"ק. תשנ"ז.
ד'תקסד. כנ"ל את ג'תק. צה"ל מוצב לילך פלסר 7, אה"ק. תשנ"ז.
ד'תקסה. כנ"ל את ג'תק. צה"ל מחנה גיבור, אה"ק. תשנ"ז.
ד'תקסו. כנ"ל את ג'תק. צה"ל מחנה גשור, אה"ק. תשנ"ז.
ד'תקסז. כנ"ל את ג'תק. צה"ל מוצב סיסן, אה"ק. תשנ"ז.
ד'תקסח. כנ"ל את ג'תק. צה"ל מוצב גמלא, אה"ק. תשנ"ז.
ד'תקסט. כנ"ל את ג'תק. צה"ל מוצב קצביה, אה"ק. תשנ"ז.
ד'תקע. כנ"ל את ג'תק. צה"ל מוצב כירנית, אה"ק. תשנ"ז.
ד'תקעא. כנ"ל את ג'תק. צה"ל מוצב שומרה, אה"ק. תשנ"ז.
ד'תקעב. כנ"ל את ג'תק. צה"ל מוצב תורמוס, אה"ק. תשנ"ז.
ד'תקעג. כנ"ל את ג'תק. צה"ל מוצב אביבים, אה"ק. תשנ"ז.
ד'תקעד. כנ"ל את ג'תק. צה"ל מוצב צבעוני, אה"ק. תשנ"ז.
ד'תקעה. כנ"ל את ג'תק. קרית שמונה (שכונות חדשות), אה"ק. תשנ"ז.
ד'תקעו. כנ"ל את ג'תק. צה"ל מוצב מצפה עדי, אה"ק. תשנ"ז.
ד'תקעז. כנ"ל את ג'תק. צה"ל מחנה נרקיס, אה"ק. תשנ"ז.
ד'תקעח. כנ"ל את ג'תק. צה"ל מחנה פרג, אה"ק. תשנ"ז.
ד'תקעט. כנ"ל את ג'תק. צה"ל מחנה עז 77, אה"ק. תשנ"ז.
ד'תקפ. כנ"ל את ג'תק. אם הדרך על יד מושב גפן, מקום בו דמם של יהודים נשפך וכו' בפיגוע רצחני, הי"ד, אה"ק. תשנ"ז.
ד'תקפא. כנ"ל את שדמ. הודפס על שפת נהר פרת (טורקי'). תשנ"ז.
ד'תקפב. כנ"ל את שדמ. חרן, באר עין אברהם (טורקי'), תשנ"ז.
ד'תקפג. כנ"ל את ג'תתקא. „היכל מנחם", ירושלים ת"ו. תשנ"ז.
ד'תקפד. כנ"ל את שדמ. מערת המכפלה, חברון, באה"ק. לרגל הכינוס השנתי של חסידי חב"ד באה"ק ת"ו. 180 שנה ליסוד קהילת חב"ד בחברון ע"י . . אדמו"ר האמצעי . . אור לט' כסלו . . תשנ"ז. מאתיים שנה להדפסה הראשונה של ס' התניא קדישא.

ד'תקפה. כנ"ל את ג'תק. כולל חב"ד, ירושלים ת"ו. תשנ"ז.
ד'תקפו. כנ"ל את ג'תק. פעצ'אטניק, מוסקבא. התשנ"ד.
ד'תקפז. כנ"ל את ג'תק. פאליחה, מוסקבא. התשנ"ד.
ד'תקפח. כנ"ל את ג'תק. צ'ערעפקובו, מוסקבא. התשנ"ד.
ד'תקפט. כנ"ל את ג'תק. קאפוטנא, מוסקבא. התשנ"ד.
ד'תקצ. כנ"ל את ד'דס. עם תרגום אנגלי (עמוד התרגום מול עמוד התניא). בגודל 22½ x 15½ סמ. ברוקלין, נ.י. תשנ"ז. מאתיים שנה להדפסה ראשונה דס' התניא – תקנ"ז־תשנ"ז (XIII) 1012 pp.
ד'תקצא. כנ"ל את ד'תקצ. עם תרגום אנגלי (עמוד התרגום מול עמוד התניא). הוצאה מוקטנת בגודל 11 x 15 סמ. ברוקלין, נ.י. תשנ"ז. מאתיים שנה להדפסה ראשונה דס' התניא – תקנ"ז־תשנ"ז (XIII) 1012 pp.
ד'תקצב. כנ"ל את ג'תק. קוסינא, מוסקבא. התשנ"ד.
ד'תקצג. כנ"ל את ג'תק. קוסקובא, מוסקבא. התשנ"ד.
ד'תקצד. כנ"ל את ג'תק. קראסקובו. התשנ"ד.
ד'תקצה. כנ"ל את ג'תק. ראזדורי. התשנ"ד.
ד'תקצו. כנ"ל את שדמ. סטמפל פארטיון, לונדון, אנגליא. תשנ"ז. מאתיים שנה להדפסה הראשונה דס' התניא – תקנ"ז־תשנ"ז. (6) רנח דף.
ד'תקצז. כנ"ל את שדמ. ווימלדאן, לונדון, אנגליא. תשנ"ז. מאתיים שנה להדפסה ראשונה דס' התניא – תקנ"ז־תשנ"ז. (6) רנח דף.
ד'תקצח. כנ"ל את שדמ. כלאנדודנא, וויילס. תשנ"ז. מאתיים שנה להדפסה הראשונה דס' התניא – תקנ"ז־תשנ"ז. (6) רנח דף.
ד'תקצט. כנ"ל את שדמ. בית מנחם, מאנטשעסטער, אנגליא. תשנ"ז. מאתיים שנה להדפסה ראשונה דס' התניא. תקנ"ז־תשנ"ז. (6) רנח דף.
ד'תר. כנ"ל את ד'ר. „היכל מנחם", בארא פארק, ברוקלין, נ.י. כ' כסלו, תשנ"ז. הוצאה מיוחדת בקשר למאתיים שנה להדפסה ראשונה דס' התניא – תקנ"ז־תשנ"ז. (6) רמז דף.
ד'תרא. כנ"ל את שדמ. „היכל מנחם", טס־לוק, מאנטרעאל, קנדה. כ' כסלו, תשנ"ז. מאתיים שנה להדפסה ראשונה דס' התניא – תקנ"ז־תשנ"ז. (6) רנח דף.
ד'תרב. כנ"ל את שדמ. מאנטרעאל, קנדה. כ' כסלו, תשנ"ז. מאתיים שנה להדפסה ראשונה דס' התניא – תקנ"ז־תשנ"ז. (6) רנח דף.
ד'תרג. כנ"ל את שדמ. ישיבת תות"ל, מאנטרעאל, קנדה. כ' כסלו, תשנ"ז. מאתיים שנה להדפסה ראשונה דס' התניא – תקנ"ז־תשנ"ז. (6) רנח דף.
ד'תרד. כנ"ל את שדמ. בית רבקה, ליובאוויטש, ברוקלין, נ.י. ימי חנוכה, תשנ"ז. מאתיים שנה להדפסה ראשונה דס' התניא – תקנ"ז־תשנ"ז. (6) רנח דף.
ד'תרה. כנ"ל את ג'תק. ראסטורגועבו. התשנ"ד.
ד'תרו. כנ"ל את שדמ. קניון ירושלים – מלחה, אה"ק. תשנ"ז.
ד'תרז. כנ"ל את שדמ. מכון חנה, ברוקלין, נ.י. כ' כסלו, תשנ"ז. מאתיים שנה להדפסה ראשונה דס' התניא – תקנ"ז־תשנ"ז. (6) רנח דף.
ד'תרח. כנ"ל את שדמ. סמינר בית חי' מושקא, מאנטרעאל, קנדה. ימי חנוכה, תשנ"ז. מאתיים שנה להדפסה ראשונה דס' התניא – תקנ"ז־תשנ"ז. (6) רנח דף.
ד'תרט. כנ"ל את שדמ. בית רבקה, מאנטרעאל, קנדה. כ"ד טבת, תשנ"ז. מאתיים שנה להדפסה ראשונה דס' התניא – תקנ"ז־תשנ"ז. (6) רנח דף.
ד'תרי. כנ"ל את שדמ. ביה"ר סלאון־קעטערינג מעמאריעל, מאנהאטען, נ.י. תשנ"ז. מאתיים שנה להדפסה ראשונה דס' התניא – תקנ"ז־תשנ"ז. (6) רנח דף.
ד'תריא. כנ"ל את שדמ. האטאן גארדען, לונדון, אנגליא. ימי חנוכה, תשנ"ז. מאתיים שנה להדפסה ראשונה דס' התניא – תקנ"ז־תשנ"ז. (6) רנח דף.

ד׳תריב. כנ״ל אות שדמ. קייפטאון [קיימפענג], הענאן פראווינץ, סין. תשנ״ז. מאתיים שנה להדפסה ראשונה דס׳ התניא — תקנ״ז־תשנ״ז. (6) רנח דף.

ד׳תריג. כנ״ל אות שדמ. בעווערלי גארדען פארק, בעווערלי הילס, קאליפארניא. כ״ה אד״ר תשנ״ז. יום הולדת הרבניה הצדקנית מרת חי׳ מושקא נ״ע זי״ע. דידן נצח. מאתיים שנה להדפסה ראשונה דס׳ התניא — תקנ״ז־תשנ״ז. (6) רנח דף.

ד׳תריד. כנ״ל אות שדמ. בי״ס חב״ד, רשת אהלי יוסף יצחק, נס ציונה, באה״ק ת״ו. כ״ד טבת, תשנ״ז. מאתיים שנה להדפסה ראשונה דס׳ התניא — תקנ״ז־תשנ״ז. (6) רנח דף.

ד׳תרטו. כנ״ל אות שדמ. אַגרי פראָסעסאָרס, אלאמאקי קאונטי, אייאווא. מאתיים שנה להדפסה ראשונה דס׳ התניא — תקנ״ז־תשנ״ז. (6) רנח דף.

ד׳תרטז. כנ״ל אות שדמ. סשעליאבינסק, אורל, רוסיא. מאתיים שנה להדפסה ראשונה דס׳ התניא — תקנ״ז־תשנ״ז. (6) רנח דף.

ד׳תריז. כנ״ל אות שדמ. קוזקו, פערו. מאתיים שנה להדפסה ראשונה דס׳ התניא — תקנ״ז־תשנ״ז. (6) רנח דף.

ד׳תריח. כנ״ל אות שדמ. סי־געיט, ברוקלין, נ.י. מאתיים שנה להדפסה ראשונה דס׳ התניא — תקנ״ז־תשנ״ז. (6) רנח דף.

ד׳תריט. כנ״ל אות שדמ. מאריעטא, דזשארדזשיא. מאתיים שנה להדפסה ראשונה דס׳ התניא — תקנ״ז־תשנ״ז. (6) רנח דף.

ד׳כתר. כנ״ל אות שדמ. „כתי״ר״, סעקאנד עוועניו, מאַנהעטאַן, נ.י. חג הגאולה י״ב־י״ג תמוז — שבעים שנה — תרפ״ז־תשנ״ז. מאתיים שנה להדפסה ראשונה דס׳ התניא — תקנ״ז־תשנ״ז. (6) רנח דף.

ד׳תרכא. כנ״ל אות שדמ. בית חב״ד אושען סיטי, מאַרילאַנד. מוצש״ק ח״י אלול תשנ״ז. מאתיים שנה להדפסה ראשונה דס׳ התניא — תקנ״ז־תשנ״ז. (6) רנח דף.

ד׳תרכב. כנ״ל אות שדמ. „בית משיח — 770״, סאַנרייז, פלארידא. לרגלי מוצש״ק ח״י אלול תשנ״ז. מאתיים שנה להדפסה ראשונה דס׳ התניא — תקנ״ז־תשנ״ז. (6) רנח דף.

ד׳תרכג. כנ״ל אות שדמ. אריקיפא, פערו. מאתיים שנה להדפסה ראשונה דס׳ התניא — תקנ״ז־תשנ״ז. (6) רנח דף.

ד׳תרכד. כנ״ל אות שדמ. אנטאנאנאריווא, מאדאגאסקאר. תשנ״ח. (6) רנח דף.

ד׳תרכה. כנ״ל אות ג׳שכה. קריית החינוך „היכל מנחם — סיני״, פאריז, צרפת. עם ציוני השיעור היומי על הגליון. (בגודל 10x14 סמ.). חג הגאולה י״ט כסלו תשנ״ח. (6) רנח דף.

ד׳תרכו. כנ״ל אות ג׳שכה. ישוב נוף אילון, באה״ק. חג הגאולה י״ט כסלו, תשנ״ח. (6) רנח דף.

ד׳תרכז. כנ״ל אות ג׳שכה. שכונת מונטיפיורי, תל־אביב, באה״ק. חג הגאולה י״ט כסלו, תשנ״ח. (6) רנח דף.

ד׳תרכח. כנ״ל אות ג׳שיט. פרעשבורג, בראטיסלאווא, סלאוואקיא. חג הגאולה י״ט כסלו, תשנ״ח. (6) רנח דף.

ד׳תרכט. כנ״ל אות שדמ. בית חב״ד מד״ע (מרכז דוברי עברית), מאנטרעאל, קנדה. חג הגאולה י״ט כסלו, תשנ״ח. (6) רנח דף.

ד׳תרל. כנ״ל אות ד׳תקצא. עם תרגום אנגלי (עמוד התרגום מול עמוד התניא). הוצאה מוקטנת בגודל 15x11 סמ. לונדון, אנגליא. תשנ״ח. 1012pp.

הוספה:

***א. אגרת הקודש** מהרב ... שניאור זלמן ... זולצבאך בשנת יג״ל יעקב׳ ישמח ישראל״ל (תקמ״ז — והוא טעות). לב דף.

***ב. כנ״ל** זולצבאך תקמ״ו (והוא טעות). לב דף.

ג. אגרת הקודש ... השמטה מספר תניא משער היחוד והאמונה ... תרי״ח לעמבערג. (34) דף.

ד. לקוטי אמרים תניא — חלק שלישי הנקרא בשם **אגרת התשובה** — פוטוסטאט מתניא הוצאת „קה״ת״. בסוף הספר: א) הגהות מכ״ק אדמו״ר הצ״צ. ב) לוח התיקון. ג) הערות ותיקונים — שניהם נערכו ע״י כ״ק אדמו״ר שליט״א. ד) ביאורים לאיזה ענינים שבאגה״ת — נלקטו מכתבי כ״ק אדמו״ר שליט״א. 8°. ברוקלין, נ. י. ה׳תשכ״ח. (4) צא-קא דפים. 14 (4) ע׳.

ה. כנ״ל אות ד. בהוצאה מוקטנת 16°. ברוקלין, נ. י. ה׳תשכ״ח. (4) צא-קא דפים.

ו. כנ״ל אות ה. ברוקלין, נ. י. [כפר חב״ד] ה׳תשכ״ח.

ז. כנ״ל אות ד. מלבורן, אויסטראליע. ה׳תשכ״ח.

ח. לקוטי אמרים תניא — חלק שני, שער היחוד והאמונה, עם תרגום ערבי. ראה במדור „תרגומים״ — ערבית.

ט. לקוטי אמרים תניא — חלק שני, שער היחוד והאמונה, עם תרגום רוסי. ראה במדור „תרגומים״ — רוסית.

י. לקוטי אמרים תניא — חלק שלישי, אגרת התשובה, עם תרגום רוסי. ראה במדור „תרגומים״ — רוסית.

יא. לקוטי אמרים — חלק ראשון, פרקים א-יב עם תרגום פורטוגזית. ראה במדור „תרגומים״ — פורטוגזית.

יב. ספר חת״ת [בכרך א׳] ... מכיל חמשה חומשי תורה עם ת״א ופרש״י. ספר תהלים „אהל יוסף יצחק״. ספר תניא עם מורה שיעור ומפתחות. חוברת מיוחדת לקט ... ע״ד חשיבות ומעלת שיעורי חת״ת.

פורמט כיס 16°.

התניא הוא פוטוגרפיא מהנ״ל אות סה. מסיבות טכניות נשמטה רשימת דפוסי התניא. ירושלים, באה״ק ת״ו. ה׳תשמ״א (התניא ריג דף).

יג. ס׳ חת״ת כנ״ל אות יב. 8°.

יד. ס׳ חת״ת כנ״ל אות יג. (בהוספת רשימת דפוסי התניא). ה׳תשמ״א. שנת השמונים לכ״ק אדמו״ר שליט״א, כפר חב״ד באה״ק ת״ו.

טו. לקוטי אמרים תניא. בצירוף מ״מ, ליקוט פירושים, שינויי נוסחאות. נערך ע״י הרה״ת ר׳ אהרן שי׳ חיטריק. יו״ל ע״י מערכת „אוצר החסידים״ ברוקלין, נ.י.

פרק א. ה׳תשל״ג. ע׳ א-סב.
פרקים ב-ג. ה׳תשל״ד. (10) ע׳ סג-קטו.
פרקים ד-ו. ה׳תשל״ד. (14) ע׳ קיז-קנח.
פרקים ז-י. ה׳תשל״ה. (16) ע׳ קנט-ריח.
פרקים יא-יד. ה׳תשל״ה. (16) ע׳ ריט-רסד.
פרקים טו-יז. ה׳תשל״ה. (12) ע׳ רסה-שטז.
פרקים יח-יט. ה׳תשל״ז. (10) ע׳ שיז-שע.
פרקים כ-כג. ה׳תשל״ח. (14) ע׳ שעא-תנב.
פרקים כד-כה. ה׳תשל״ט. ע׳ תנו-תצז.
פרקים כו-כח. ה׳תש״מ. (12) ע׳ תצז-תקלו.
פרקים כט-ל. ה׳תש״מ. (14) ע׳ תקלז-תקפד.
פרקים לא-לב. ה׳תשמ״א. (12) ע׳ תקפה-תרלו.
פרקים לג-לה. ה׳תשמ״א. (12) ע׳ תרלו-תרחצ.
פרקים לו-לז. ה׳תשמ״ב. (14) ע׳ תרצט-תשסח.
פרקים לח-לט. ה׳תשמ״ב. (16) ע׳ תשסט-תתכ.
פרקים מ-מא. ה׳תשמ״ב. (16) ע׳ תתכא-תתפד.
פרקים מב-מג. ה׳תשמ״ג. (16) ע׳ תתפה-תתקמו.
פרקים מד-מה. ה׳תשמ״ג. (12) ע׳ תתקמז-תתקצ.
פרקים מו-נג. ה׳תשד״מ. (28) ע׳ תתקצא-אקלב.

טז. אגרת הקודש. בצירוף מ״מ ליקוט פירושים, שינויי נוסחאות. נערך ע״י הרה״ת ר׳ אהרן שי׳ חיטריק. יו״ל ע״י מערכת „אוצר החסידים״ ברוקלין, נ.י.

סי׳ א. ה׳תשל״ח. ע׳ א-לב.
כנ״ל. עם הוספות בהפתח דבר. ה׳תשל״ח.
סי׳ ב׳. ה׳תשל״ט. ע׳ לג-ע.
סי׳ ג-ה. ה׳תשמ״. (18) ע׳ עא-קמד.
סי׳ ו-י. ה׳תשד״מ. (18) ע׳ קמה-רכ.
סי׳ יא-יד. ה׳תשמ״ו. (20) ע׳ רכא-רצ.

יז. לקוטי אמרים מהדורא קמא (מכתי״), ... ספר התניא (שלשה חלקים הראשונים) כפי שהי׳ נפוץ בכתי״ בין החסידים, לפני הדפסתו ... חלק שלישי נעתק ע״פ דפוס זאלקווא (תקנ״ט) [אות ב׳ ברשימה כללית].

עם שינויי נוסחאות מכמה כתי״: הערות (בחלק ראשון ושני — כלולות בהן השוואות בין המדי״ק ומהד״ב).

בסופו: אגה״ת מהד״ב עם לוח התיקון והערות ותיקונים (צילום מדפוס ברוקלין, נ. י. עשיית ה׳תשל״ט (הנ״ל אות קכד)): רשימה קצרה של כתי״ התניא; פאקסימיליות של הכתי״.

ברוקלין, נ. י. טו, כסלו, ה׳תהי׳ שנת ביאת משיח, שנת השמונים לכ״ק אדמו״ר שליט״א. 16, תרכד ע׳.

יח. כנ״ל אות יז. הוצאה שני׳ — צילום של ההוצאה הראשונה. ברוקלין, נ. י. זאת חנוכה, ה׳תהי׳ שנת ביאת משיח, שנת השמונים לכ״ק אדמו״ר שליט״א. 16, תרכד ע׳.

יט. מילואים לס׳ לקוטי אמרים — מהדו״ק (הנ״ל אות יז-יח). מכיל א) ש״נ מעוד כתי״ שהגיעו ... אחרי הדפסת הספר ... ב) לוח תיקונים והשלמות.

בסופו: תיאור קצר של הכתי״ שבקונטרס, פאקסימיליות, לוח ר״ת.

ברוקלין, נ. י. ערב כד טבת ה׳תהי׳ שנת ביאת משיח. 8, קסד ע׳.

הנ״ל אות יח עם המילואים (הנ״ל אות יט) — כרוכים בכריכה אחת. ברוקלין, נ. י. ה׳תשמ״ב. 16, תרכד, 8, קסד [832] עמודים.

כ. ס׳ שיעורים בספר התניא חלק ראשון (פרקים א-לד) מתורגם ללשון הקודש מס׳ „שיעורים בס׳ התניא״ באידית (ראה לקמן תרגומים — באידית).

לפני השיעור של כל פרק בא צילום דהפרק.

כפר חב״ד, י״א ניסן, שמונים שנה לכ״ק אדמו״ר שליט״א. ה׳תשמ״ב. (6), 456 עמודים.

כא. כנ״ל. הוצאה שני׳. כפר חב״ד. ל״ג בעומר, ה׳תשמ״ב. שמונים שנה לכ״ק אדמו״ר שליט״א.

כב. ס׳ שיעורים בספר התניא (כנ״ל אות כ׳) כרך ב׳ (פרקים לה-נג). ה׳תשמ״ג. שמונים שנה לכ״ק אדמו״ר שליט״א. (8) 457-804.

כג. ס׳ חת״ת. כנ״ל אות יד. כפר חב״ד, באה״ק ת״ו. ה׳תשמ״ג. שמונים שנה לכ״ק אדמו״ר שליט״א.

כד. לקוטי אמרים תניא — חלק ראשון (פרקים א-נג) עם תרגום רוסי, ראה במדור „תרגומים״ — רוסית.

כה. ס׳ שיעורים בספר התניא (הנ״ל אות כ-כב — לקוטי אמרים (פרקים א-נג) בכרך א׳). בהוספת השיעורים להקדמה והסכמות דהתניא בתחלת הס׳. כפר חב״ד, באה״ק ת״ו. ה׳תשד״מ. (8) 808 ע׳.

כו. לקוטי אמרים תניא — (חלק ראשון; חלק שני — שעהיוה״א; חלק שלישי — אגה״ת) — עם תרגום רוסי. ראה במדור „תרגומים״ — רוסית.

כז. לקוטי אמרים תניא — שער היחוד והאמונה. בצירוף מ״מ, ליקוט פירושים, שינויי נוסחאות. נערך ע״י הרה״ת ר׳ אהרן שי׳ חיטריק. יו״ל ע״י מערכת „אוצר החסידים״. ברוקלין, נ.י.

חינוך קטן ופרקים א-ד. ה׳תשד״מ. (14) ע׳ א-קכט.
פרקים ה-ז. ה׳תשד״מ. (18) ע׳ קלא-רה.
פרקים ח-יב. ה׳תשמ״ה. (18) רז-רנח ע׳.

כח. ס' חת"ת (בכרך א') כנ"ל אות יב. „במהדורה שלפנינו . . (חומש] באותיות מאירות . . בפנים החומש, סדר ההפטרות עפ"י מנהג חב"ד . . התניא צולם ממהדורת „אשכול" [הנ"ל ברשימה כללית אות ב'כב] . . לבקשת רבים . . בסוף הספר — עפ"י הסכמת וחוו"ד כ"ק אדמו"ר שליט"א — סידור תהלת ה' לימי חול, שבת, ור"ח".

חוברת מיוחדת . . ע"ד חשיבות שיעורי חת"ת.

יוצא לאור ע"י מערכת „אוצר החסידים" כפר חב"ד. תשמ"ה. בגודל 9½x14½ סנטימטר.

כט. לקוטי אמרים תניא חלק ראשון — עם תרגום ערבי.

ראה במדור „תרגומים" — ערבית.

ל. לקוטי אמרים תניא — פרק א. עם תרגום וביאורים בצרפתית, ראה במדור „תרגומים" — צרפתית.

לא. ס' שיעורים בספר התניא חלק ג — שער היחוה"א. אגרת התשובה. מתורגם ללשון הקודש מס' שיעורים בס' התניא באידית (ראה לקמן תרגומים — באידית).

לפני השיעור של כל פרק בא צילום דהפרק.

כפר חב"ד, באה"ק. ה'תשמ"ו. (XX) (2) 805־1305 עמודים.

לב. לקוטי אמרים — תניא — חלק שלישי הנקרא בשם **אגרת התשובה**

בצירוף מ"מ, ליקוט פירושים, שינויי נוסחאות נערך ע"י הרה"ת ר' אהרן שי' חיטריק. יו"ל ע"י מערכת „אוצר החסידים", ברוקלין, נ.י.

„לאחרונה קיבל כ"ק אדמו"ר שליט"א אגרת התשובה — מהדורא בתרא בגוכתי"ק כ"ק אדמו"ר האמצעי (?) עם תיקונים בגוכתי"ק כ"ק אדמו"ר הזקן.

צילום מכל הגוכתי"ק נדפסה בתחילת הספר במילואה".

פרקים א־יב (פוטו מתניא—אגה"ת הוצאת „קה"ת") [ליקוט פירושים על ריש פ"א].

י"ט כסלו, ה'תשמ"ו. (40) א־מח עמודים.

לג. לקוטי אמרים — תניא — חלק שלישי הנקרא בשם **אגרת התשובה**

בצירוף מ"מ, ליקוט פירושים, שינויי נוסחאות. נערך ע"י הרה"ת ר' אהרן שי' חיטריק. יו"ל ע"י מערכת „אוצר החסידים". ברוקלין, נ.י.

„לאחרונה קיבל כ"ק אדמו"ר שליט"א אגרת התשובה — מהדורא בתרא בגוכתי"ק כ"ק אדמו"ר האמצעי (?) עם תיקונים בגוכתי"ק כ"ק אדמו"ר הזקן.

צילום מכל הגוכתי"ק נדפסה בתחילת הספר במילואה".

פרקים א־יב (פוטו מתניא—אגה"ת הוצאת „קה"ת") בריש הס' „דברים אחדים" ע"ד (כתי' ומהדורות ד)אגה"ת. על כל פרק — ביאורים באגה"ת מכ"ק אדמו"ר שליט"א. בסוף הס' נתוסף: א) „מהדורא קמא" כמו שנדפס ב„לקוטי אמרים — מהדו"ק", ובמילואים (קה"ת, ברוקלין, תשמ"ב (לעיל אות יז־יט)). ב) כמה ממאמרי אדה"ז (שנדפסו בספריו) „שהם יסוד או ביאורים באגה"ת". ג) צילום ממצות וידוי ותשובה מכ"ק אדמו"ר הצ"צ הנדפס בס' דרך מצותיך.

ה'תשמ"ו. (42) א־תרא ע'.

לד. ס' חת"ת (כנ"ל אות כח) עם סידור תהלת ה' השלם (בלי תפלת ר"ה ויוהכ"פ).

כפר חב"ד, אה"ק ת"ו. ה'תשמ"ו.

לה. לקוטי אמרים תניא (עם תרגום אנגלי).

„מייקרא־פיש" על שני כרטיסים. הוצאת „קה"ת" ע"י „ווערדלעד גרופ", מעלבורן, אויסטראליא. עיצוב: שמחה שי' פעטער. תשמ"ה.

(פוטו דהתניא הוצאה אות תקנד — קאנבערא, אויסטראליא תשד"מ. 979 ע').

לו. ס' שיעורים בספר התניא חלק א (פרקים א־לד) מתורגם ללשון הקודש (כנ"ל אות כ' בהוספת השיעורים להקדמה והסכמות דהתניא — בתחלת הס').

(הדפסה רביעית) כפר חב"ד, באה"ק ת"ו (xxxvi) 456 ע'.

לז. ס' שיעורים בספר התניא חלק א' כנ"ל אות לו. הדפסה חמשית. כפר חב"ד, באה"ק ת"ו. ה'תשמ"ו.

לח. ס' שיעורים בספר התניא חלק ב' מתורגם ללשון הקודש — כנ"ל אות כב.

הדפסה שלישית, כפר חב"ד, באה"ק ת"ו. ה'תשמ"ו.

לט. כנ"ל אות לח. הדפסה רביעית. כפר חב"ד, באה"ק ת"ו. תשמ"ו.

מ. ס' שיעורים בספר התניא חלק ג — שער היחוה"א. אגרת התשובה. מתורגם ללשון הקודש — כנ"ל אות לא.

(הדפסה שני') כפר חב"ד, באה"ק ת"ו (xx) (2) 805־1305.

מא. ס' שיעורים בספר התניא חלק ד — אגרת הקודש. קונטרס אחרון. מתורגם ללשון הקודש מס' שיעורים בס' התניא באידית (ראה לקמן תרגומים — באידית).

לפני השיעור של כל סימן בא צילום דהסימן בפנים התניא.

כפר חב"ד, באה"ק. ה'תשמ"ז. (8) 1307־1982 עמודים.

מב. ס' חת"ת (בכרך א') כנ"ל אות לד.

כפר חב"ד, באה"ק, ה'תשמ"ז. בגודל 9½x14½ סנטימטר.

מג. לקוטי אמרים תניא — שער היחוד והאמונה

עם תרגום ספרדית — ראה במדור „תרגומים" — בספרדית (שפאניש).

מד. לקוטי אמרים — תניא — שער היחוד והאמונה — חינוך קטן.

בצירוף מ"מ, ליקוט פירושים, שינויי נוסחאות. נערך ע"י הרה"ת ר' אהרן שי' חיטריק. יו"ל ע"י מערכת „אוצר החסידים". ברוקלין, נ.י.

פרקים א־יב (פוטו מתניא — הוצאת „קה"ת" (הוצאה ג'שז. הוצאה מוגדלת)). — שעהיוה"א בצירוף מ"מ וכו' שי"ל בקונטרסים (ראה לעיל אות כז) — בכרך אחד. בהוספת: א) הוספות והליקוט — שנשמטו מההוצאה הראשונה. ב) תניא מהדו"ק — מכת"י — שיצא לאור בשנת תשמ"ב ומילואים להוצאה הנ"ל [ראה לעיל אות יז־יט].

ה'תשמ"ט (36) א־שסה ע'.

מה. לקוטי אמרים — תניא עם ביאור „משכיל לאיתן".

„השתדלנו לבאר . . בתניא, לסכם באורי רבותינו נשיאינו . . המפוזרים . . ולשלב . . פירושים המקובלים במסורת החסידים . . ע"י זקני המשפיעים . . פעמים מצוטטים ופעמים מתומצתים ומצוינים במ"מ מדוייקים".

„בתחילת כל פרק . . התניא במתכונתו המקורית, כאשר בצידי העמוד מופיע ה„מורה שיעור" . . היום יומי. ובבאור עצמו העתקנו . . קטעי התניא . . פיענוח ר"ת והקיצורים . . „לוח התיקון" וה„הערות בדרך אפשר" אשר לכ"ק אדמו"ר שליט"א".

מאת הרב יקותיאל שי' גרין, כפר חב"ד.

כרך א — פרקים א־יב.

כפר חב"ד. השנה היא שנת נסים. 414 ע'.

כרך ב — פרקים יג־כח (415־420) 421־824 ע'.

מו. ס' חת"ת (בכרך א).

כנ"ל אות מב ובהוספת ספר „היום יום".

כפר חב"ד, באה"ק, ה'תנש"א.

מז. לקוטי אמרים תניא — בכתב „ברייל"

— ראה לקמן במדור „תרגומים" — „ברייל".

מח. לקוטי אמרים תניא. בצירוף מ"מ, ליקוט פירושים, שינויי נוסחאות. נערך ע"י הרה"ת ר' אהרן שי' חיטריק. יו"ל ע"י מערכת „אוצר החסידים". ברוקלין, נ.י.

פוטו מתניא — הוצאה ג'שז. הוצאה מוגדלת. תניא בצירוף מ"מ וכו' שי"ל בקונטרסים (ראה לעיל אות טו) בשני כרכים:

פרקים: א־כח (א'תקלו ע'). ה'תשנ"ב. שנת הצדיי"ק לכ"ק אדמו"ר שליט"א.

כט־נג (תקלז־א'קלב ע'). ה'תשנ"ב. שנת הצדיי"ק לכ"ק אדמו"ר שליט"א.

תרגומים:

א. באידית

לקוטי אמרים תניא.

איבערזעצט אין אידיש, ארויסגעגעבן דורך אוצר החסידים, ברוקלין. (תורגם באידית על ידי הרב אוריאל ז״ל צימער).

כרך ראשון: כולל חלק ראשון, פאקסימיליא של השער דהוצאה הראשונה, של עמוד מכתב יד התניא. 12°, 1־302 ע׳, ה׳תשט״ז.

כרך שני: כולל כל שאר חלקי התניא. פאקסימיליא מג׳ עמודים של כתב־יד התניא. 12°, 304־666 ע׳, ה׳תשי״ח.

שיעורים בספר התניא

אַנטהאַלט אַ טייל פון די שיעורים . . אין ספר „תניא קדישא״, וואָס זיינען געלערנט געוואָרן אין דעם „שיעור תניא אויף דער ראַדיאָ״ . . מיט דער הסכמה און ברכה פון כ״ק אדמו״ר שליט״א . . די שיעורים . . למראה עיני קדשו און כ״ק אדמו״ר שליט״א האָט אין אַ סך ערטער געשריבן באַמערקונגען, ווי אויך צוגעגעבן הערות און ביאורים.

כרך ראשון: כולל חלק ראשון פרקים א־לד. יוצא לאור ע״י מערכת „אוצר החסידים״. ברוקלין, נ. י. ה׳תשמ״א. 8° (8), 406 ע׳.

כרך שני: פרקים לה־נג (כנ״ל). ברוקלין, נ.י. ה׳תשמ״ב. שמונים שנה לכ״ק אדמו״ר שליט״א. (14) 407־744 ע׳.

שיעורים בספר התניא — לקוטי אמרים

פרקים א־נג (הוצאה שני׳ דהנ״ל בכרך א׳) בהוספת: א) הקדמת אדה״ז להתניא, ב) ההסכמות, ג) ציוני השיעורי חת״ת בגליון העמוד, ד) שיחת כ״ק אדמו״ר שליט״א (מש״פ יתרו ה׳תשמ״א) בקשר להופעת כרך הראשון.

ברוקלין, נ.י. ה׳תשמ״ג — שמונים שנה לכ״ק אדמו״ר שליט״א. (14) 1־744 ע׳.

שיעורים בספר התניא — שער היחוד והאמונה. אגרת התשובה.

בריש הס׳: משיחת כ״ק אדמו״ר שליט״א (ש״פ משפטים, מבה״ח אדר תשד״מ —) ע״ד לימוד התניא על הראדיא.

ברוקלין, נ.י. ה׳תשמ״ה. (22) 745־1234 ע׳.

שיעורים בספר התניא — אגרת הקודש. קונטרס אחרון.

בריש הס׳: מכתב כ״ק אדמו״ר שליט״א לימי חנוכה (כ״ף כסלו, ה׳תשמ״ו).

ברוקלין, נ.י. ה׳תשמ״ו. (X) 1235־1896 ע׳.

ב. באנגלית*

חלק ראשון. לקוטי אמרים.

תורגם ע״י הרב ניסן שי׳ מינדל עם הקדמה, הערות ומ״מ מהנ״ל.

בתחלתו — פתח דבר מכ״ק אדמו״ר שליט״א.

פאקסימיליא: א) משער דהוצאה הראשונה של התניא. ב) מעמוד אחד מכתב־יד התניא.

בסופו: מפתח לפסוקי תנ״ך, ש״ס, זהר, רמב״ם ושו״ע ועוד.

הוצאת „קה״ת״, ברוקלין, נ. י. ה׳תשכ״ב. 32, שסח עמודים.

כנ״ל. הוצאה שני׳. ה׳תשכ״ה.

כנ״ל. הוצאה שלישית ומעובדת. ה׳תשכ״ט.

חלק שני. שער היחוד והאמונה.

תורגם ע״י הרב ניסן שי׳ מאנגעל עם הקדמה והערות ומ״מ מהנ״ל. פתח דבר מכ״ק אדמו״ר שליט״א (הנדפס בח״א).

הוצאת „קה״ת״, ברוקלין, נ. י. ה׳תשכ״ה. 20, ג־עח עמודים.

כנ״ל. הוצאה שני׳. ה׳תשכ״ט.

חלק שלישי. אגרת התשובה.

תורגם ע״י הרב יצחק זלמן שי׳ פאזנער עם הקדמה והערות

---

*) ראה גם רשימה כללית אות עב. קמ. קמא. ר. ריג. רכא. ש. שעח. תקנ. תקנא. תקנב. תקנג. תקנד. א׳תשדמ. ב׳תר. ב׳תרכה. ג׳שח. ד׳רס. ד׳תרל.

ומ״מ מהנ״ל. פתח דבר מכ״ק אדמו״ר שליט״א (הנדפס בחלקים הקודמים).

הוצאת „קה״ת״, ברוקלין, נ. י. ה׳תשכ״ו. 16, נט עמודים.

כנ״ל. הוצאה שני׳. ה׳תשכ״ט.

חלק רביעי. אגרת הקודש.

תורגם ע״י הרב יעקב עמנואל שי׳ שוחט עם הקדמה, הערות ומ״מ שלו. פתח דבר — באנגלית — מכ״ק אדמו״ר שליט״א (הנדפס בחלקים הקודמים).

בסופו — מפתח לפסוקי תנ״ך, מאמרי חז״ל בש״ס, זהר, תקו״ז, ז״ח, רמב״ם, שו״ע, כתבי האריז״ל, תניא (חלקים הקודמים). מפתח שמות. מפתח ענינים.

הוצאת „קה״ת״, ברוקלין, נ. י. ה׳תשכ״ח. 22, 358 עמודים.

חלק חמישי. קונטרס אחרון.

תורגם ע״י הרב יצחק זלמן שי׳ פאזנער עם הקדמה, הערות ומ״מ.

הוצאת „קה״ת״, ברוקלין, נ. י. ה׳תשכ״ח. 8, 64 עמודים.

לקוטי אמרים — תניא

עם תרגום אנגלי. עמוד התרגום מול עמוד התניא (נסמן לעיל ברשימה כללית אות עב). התרגום הוא הנ״ל (של הר״ר: נ. מינדעל, נ. מאנגעל, ז. פאזנער, ע. שוחט, שיחיו) שיצאו לאור כל חלק בפ״ע. בהוצאה זו סודר התרגום מחדש. הקדמות המתרגמים בסוף הספר.

עיצוב והכנה לדפוס ע״י „סונסינו פרעס״ עבור „קה״ת״.

בסוף התניא — רשימת ראשי תיבות.

— כרוך בכרך אחד ובב׳ כרכים.

לונדון, אנגליא. ה׳תשל״ג. בגודל 32½x16½ ס״מ. (xii) קןק890.

כנ״ל. עם עמוד התרגום מול עמוד התניא (נסמן לעיל ברשימה כללית אות קמ). בהוצאה זו הוסיפו (בהתרגום) השיעור תניא (משיעורי חת״ת): בפנים התרגום — הציון, ובשולי העמוד התאריך.

יו״ל ע״י „קה״ת״ סניף לונדון, אנגליא. ה׳תש״מ. שנת השמיטה — שבת לה׳. שנת המאה להולדת כ״ק אדמו״ר (מוהריי״צ) נ״ע. (xix) קןק899.

כנ"ל. הוצאה מוקטנת (נסמן ברשימה כללית אות קמא). עם ההוספה הנ"ל דשיעורי התניא. לונדון, אנגליא, ה'תש"מ. שנת השמיטה — שבת לה'. שנת המאה להולדת אדמו"ר (מוהריי"צ) נ"ע. בגודל 11x14¾ סמ. (xix) 899pp.

לקוטי אמרים — תניא

עם תרגום אנגלי. פוטו דהוצאת לונדון, תש"מ.

(נסמן ברשימה כללית אות ר). הוסיפו בסוף הס' רשימה באנגלית דהמקומות שם נדפס התניא בכל העולם. הקדמה באנגלית להוצאה זו, מאת ה„מרכז לעניני חינוך", מלבורן, אויסטרליא. יו"ל ע"י „קה"ת" סניף פערט, אוסטראַליאַ, ה'תשמ"ג. שנת המאה להסתלקות־הילולא של כ"ק אדמו"ר מהר"ש נ"ע בעל הפתגם של „מלכתחילה אַריבער", תהי' שנת גאולת משיח. בגודל 14½x22 סמ. (xix) 899pp [9].

לקוטי אמרים — תניא

עם תרגום אנגלי (כנ"ל). פנים התניא — פוטו דהוצאה האלף. בהוצאה זו נתוספו בחלק האנגלי: תיקונים הרבה בטעויות הדפוס, בהתירגום (להבהיר הענין ולמנוע אי־הבנה). מפתח כללי (באנגלית) בריש הספר. רשימת מקומות שם נדפס התניא על־סדר המדינות. ראשי פרקים מתולדות ימי חיי אדה"ז. והוסיפו, בחלק האנגלי, תמונת אדה"ז בצירוף לר"פ דחייו. וע"ד הו"ל דסידורו. ובסוף הר"פ: ע"ד ההו"ל דהשו"ע. הקדמת כ"ק אדמו"ר שליט"א (באנגלית — להוצאה הראשונה דהתרגום אנגלי) בא בריש הס'.

כל הנ"ל נערך ע"י מערכת „קה"ת" ברוקלין, תמוז תשד"מ. והוצאות התניא שעם תרגום אנגלי, מכאן ואילך נדפסו כולם עם תיקונים והוספות אלו. והם:

אות ריג. טאראנטא, אנטעריא, קאנאדא. ה'תשמ"ה. 979pp.

אות רכא. סינסינעטי, אהייא. ה'תשמ"ה.

אות ש. פריטאריא, דרום אפריקא. בגודל 13½x18½ סמ. ה'תשד"מ. 979pp.

אות תקנ. האַבאַרט, טאַזמייניאַ. ה'תשד"מ.

אות תקנא. וועלינגטאַן, ניו זילאַנד. ה'תשד"מ.

אות תקנב. אַדעלייד, אויסטראַליא. ה'תשד"מ.

אות תקנג. בריסביין, אויסטראַליא. ה'תשד"מ.

אות תקנד. קאַנבעראַ, אויסטראַליא. ה׳תשד״מ.
אות א׳תשד״מ. וויניפעג, מאניטאבא, קאנאדא. ה׳תשד״מ.
אות ג׳שח. לאקערבי, סקאטלנד. ה׳תשמ״ט. (הוצאה מוקטנת).
אות ד׳רס. ברוקלין, נ.י. ה׳תשנ״ג.
אות ד׳תרל. לונדון, אנגליא. ה׳תשנ״ח.

שיעורים בספר התניא

ח״א: פרקים א־לד.
מבואר ע״י הר״ר יוסף שי׳ וויינבערג.
תרגום אנגלי מס׳ שיעורים בספר התניא שהופיע באידית (ראה לעיל תרגומים — אידית).
תורגם ע״י הרב לוי שי׳ וויינבערג, עם הקדמה מהנ״ל. נערך ע״י אורי׳ שי׳ קאַפלון.
הוצאת „קה״ת״, ברוקלין, נ.י. ה׳תשמ״ז. xxviii, 449 עמודים.

ח״ב: פרקים א־לד.
מבואר ע״י הר״ר יוסף שי׳ וויינבערג.
תורגם ע״י הרב לוי שי׳ וויינבערג והרב שלום דובער שי׳ וויינבערג.
נערך ע״י אורי׳ שי׳ קאַפלון.
הקדמת המתרגמים בתחלת הס׳.
הוצאת „קה״ת״, ברוקלין, נ.י. ה׳תשמ״ח. vii, 814־451 ע׳.

ח״ג: שער היחוד והאמונה. אגרת התשובה.
מבואר ע״י הר״ר יוסף שי׳ וויינבערג.
תורגם ע״י הרב שלום דובער שי׳ וויינבערג.
נערך ע״י אורי׳ שי׳ קאַפלון.
הקדמת המתרגם בתחלת הס׳.
הוצאת „קה״ת״, ברוקלין, נ.י. ה׳תשמ״ט. vii, 1122־815 ע׳.

לקוטי אמרים תניא — בכתב „ברייל״ (מהתרגום האנגלי).

יו״ל ע״י קה״ת ומוסד „דזשואיש הערעטידזש פאר דא בליינד״. בג׳ כרכים:
כרך א: ע׳ 1־221.
כרך ב: ע׳ 223־452.
כרך ג: ע׳ 453־577.
ה׳תנש״ב.

ג. באיטלקית

חלק ראשון. לקוטי אמרים.

תורגם בהשגחת הרב גרשון מענדל שי׳ גרליק.

בתחלתו: הקדמת המו״ל: תרגום מפתח דבר כ״ק אדמו״ר שליט״א: מהקדמת הרב ניסן שי׳ מינדל (וכן ההערות ומ״מ שלו — בשולי הגליון).

פאקסימיליות: א) שער דהוצאה הראשונה של התניא. ב) עמוד א׳ מכתב־יד התניא.

בסופו: תרגום מההערות, המפתח שבתרגום האנגלי.

הוצאת „קה״ת״, מילאן, איטאליא. ה׳תשכ״ז. 46, 386 עמודים.

כנ״ל. הוצאה שני׳. אלול, ה׳תשד״מ.

חלק שני. שער היחוד והאמונה.

תורגם בהשגחת הרב גרשון מענדל שי׳ גרליק.

בתחלתו: הקדמת המו״ל: תרגום מפתח דבר כ״ק אדמו״ר שליט״א: מהקדמת הרב ניסן שי׳ מאנגעל (וכן ההערות ומ״מ שלו — בשולי הגליון).

הוצאת „קה״ת״, מילאן, איטאליא. ה׳תשכ״ט. 26, 82 עמודים.

חלק שלישי. אגרת התשובה.

תורגם בהשגחת הרב גרשון מענדל שי׳ גרליק.

בתחלתו: פתח דבר מכ״ק אדמו״ר שליט״א. תרגום מהקדמת הרב יצחק זלמן שי׳ פאזנער (וכן מהערות ומ״מ שלו — בשולי הגליון).

הוצאת „קה״ת״, מילאן, איטאליא. ה׳תש״ל. 18, 66 עמודים.

חלק רביעי. אגרת הקודש.

תורגם בהשגחת הרב גרשון מענדל שי׳ גרליק.

בתחלתו: פתח דבר מכ״ק אדמו״ר שליט״א. תרגום מהקדמת הרב יעקב עמנואל שי׳ שוחט (וכן מהערות ומ״מ שלו — בשולי הגליון).

הוצאת „קה״ת״, מילאן, איטאליא. ה׳תשל״ד. 22, 462 עמודים.

חלק חמישי. קונטרס אחרון.

תורגם בהשגחת הרב גרשון מענדל שי׳ גרליק.

בתחלתו: תרגום מפתח דבר כ״ק אדמו״ר שליט״א, תרגום

מהקדמת הרב יצחק זלמן שי׳ פאזנער (וכן מהערות ומ״מ שלו — בשולי הגליון).

הוצאת „קה״ת״, מילאַן, איטאליא. ה׳תשל״ט. (12), 62 עמודים.

ד. בצרפתית

חלק ראשון. לקוטי אמרים.

תורגם בהשגחת הרב בנימין אליהו שי׳ גורודצקי.

בתחלתו: פאקסימיליא מהשער דהוצאה הראשונה של התניא. פאקסימיליא מעמוד א׳ של כת״י התניא. תרגום מפתח דבר כ״ק אדמו״ר שליט״א. תרגום מהקדמת דר. ניסן שי׳ מינדל (וכן תרגום מהערות ומ״מ שלו — בשולי הגליון). ניו־יארק, ה׳תשל״ה. 34, 370 עמודים.

חלק שני. שער היחוד והאמונה.

תורגם בהשגחת הרב בנימין אלי׳ שי׳ גורודצקי.

בתחלתו: הקדמת המו״ל; תרגום מפתח דבר כ״ק אדמו״ר שליט״א; תרגום מהקדמת הרב ניסן שי׳ מאנגעל (וכן תרגום מהערות ומ״מ שלו — בשולי הגליון).

16, א־סה עמודים.

חלק שלישי. אגרת התשובה.

תורגם בהשגחת הרב בנימין אלי׳ שי׳ גורודצקי.

בתחלתו: תרגום מהקדמת הרב יצחק זלמן שי׳ פאזנער (וכן מהערות ומ״מ שלו — בשולי הגליון).

הוצאת „קה״ת״, פאריז, צרפת. ה׳תשכ״ח.

סט־קכג עמודים.

[בסופו: רשימת הוצאות ספרי קה״ת בצרפתית].

חלק רביעי. אגרת הקודש.

תורגם בהשגחת הרב בנימין אלי׳ שי׳ גורודצקי.

בתחלתו: פתח דבר מכ״ק אדמו״ר שליט״א. תרגום מהקדמת הרב יעקב עמנואל שי׳ שוחט (וכן מההערות והמ״מ שלו — בשולי הגליון).

הוצאת „קה״ת״, ברוקלין, נ. י. ה׳תש״מ.

(6), 9־17, 7־368, (1) עמודים.

[בסופו: רשימת ההוצאות כבאגרת התשובה].

לקוטי אמרים — תניא

פרק א׳.

עם תרגום וביאורים בצרפתית.

הוצאת בית ליובאוויטש, פאריז, צרפת. ה׳תשמ״ה. 97 עמודים.

ה. בספרדית (שפאניש)

חלק שני. שער היחוד והאמונה.

תורגם תחת השגחת הרב דובער ז״ל בוימגארטען.

בתחלתו: הקדמת המו״ל; תרגום מפתח דבר כ״ק אדמו״ר שליט״א: מהקדמת הרב ניסן שי׳ מאנגעל (וכן ההערות ומ״מ שלו — בשולי הגליון).

הוצאת „קה״ת״, בוענאָס איירעס, ארגנטינא. ה׳תשכ״ט. 80 עמודים.

הוצאה שני׳ מהנ״ל עם הוספות ותיקונים. (בהוספת עמוד התניא מול עמוד התרגום).

בהוצאת „קה״ת״, בוענס איירעס, ארגנטינה. ה׳תשד״מ. (11), 68 עמודים.

חלק שלישי. אגרת התשובה.

תורגם תחת השגחת הרב דובער ז״ל בוימגארטען.

בתחלתו: הקדמת הרב יצחק זלמן שי׳ פאזנער (וכן הערות ומ״מ שלו — בשולי הגליון).

הוצאת „קה״ת״, בוענאָס איירעס, ארגנטינא. ה׳תש״ל.

סא עמודים.

[בסופו: רשימת ההוצאות שלהם בספרדית].

ו. בערבית

חלק ראשון. לקוט אמרים.

תורגם בהשגחת הרב יהודה ליב שי׳ רסקין.

המתרגם: הרב דוד שי׳ בוסקילה. המבוא והמ״מ נעשו ע״י

הרב ניסן שי׳ מינדעל.

בתחלת הספר — פתח דבר מהמו״ל.

בסופו: הוספה — משיחת כ״ק אדמו״ר שליט״א מליובאוויטש — ש״פ שמות מבה״ח שבט ה׳תשל״ז בקשר להדפסת התניא בערבית בפעם הראשונה — תרגום חפשי.

הוצאת „קה״ת״, קסבלנקה, מרוקו. כ׳ מנחם אב, ה׳תשד״מ שנת הארבעים להסתלקות והילולא של הרה״ג והרה״ח המקובל רבי לוי יצחק נ״ע שניאורסאהן. 640 עמודים. 8°.

חלק שני. שער היחוד והאמונה.

תורגם ע״י הרב דוד שי׳ בוסקילה. בהשגחת הרב יהודה ליב שי׳ רסקין.

בתחלת הספר — פתח דבר מהמו״ל.

בסופו: הוספה — מענה כ״ק אדמו״ר שליט״א מליובאוויטש על דבר התניא בשפה הערבית.

הוצאת „קה״ת״, קסבלנקה, מרוקו. ה׳תשל״ו. (17), 120 עמודים. 8°.

כנ״ל. הוצאה שני׳, כפר חב״ד ה׳תשל״ט.

חלק שלישי. אגרת התשובה.

תורגם ע״י הרב דוד שי׳ בוסקילו, בהשגחת הרב יהודה לייב שי׳ רסקין.

בהתחלת הספר — פתח דבר מהמו״ל.

בסופו: הוספה־מענה כ״ק אדמו״ר שליט״א מליובאוויטש ע״ד התניא בשפה הערבית.

הוצאת „קה״ת״, קסבלנקה, מרוקו.

יו״ד שבט ה׳תש״מ. שלושים שנה לנשיאות כ״ק אדמו״ר שליט״א.

ז. ברוסית

חלק ראשון. לקוטי אמרים.

תורגם בהשגחת פרופסור ירמי׳ שי׳ ברנובר.

המתרגמת — ג. ליפש.

חוברת א׳: בתחלתה: פתח דבר מהמו״ל. לקוטי אמרים פרקים א־ה.

ירושלים, אה״ק ת״ו. ה׳תשל״ו. 20 עמודים.

חוברת ב׳: פרקים ו־י. ירושלים, אה״ק ת״ו. ה׳תשל״ו. 18 עמודים.

חוברת ג׳: פרקים יא־טו. ירושלים, אה״ק ת״ו. ה׳תשל״ז. 16 עמודים.

לקוטי אמרים — תניא. חלק ראשון (פרקים א־נג).

תרגום — ג. ליפש

יועצי התרגום — הרב ז. לוין

עורך התרגום — פרופ׳ י. ברנובר

עמוד התניא מול עמוד התרגום

הוצאת שמי״ר עיה״ק ירושלים, תובב״א. ה׳תשמ״ב.

פרק לב — אהבת ישראל — . מנוקד ומפורש ע״י הרב יוסף שמחה גינזבורג שי׳.

תורגם ברוסית — ע״י ג. ליפש. באנגלית — ע״י א. קפלן.

בתחת החוברת — מבוא ברוסית ובאנגלית.

ירושלים, אה״ק ת״ו. ה׳תשל״ז. 14 עמודים.

חלק שני. שער היחוד והאמונה.

תורגם בהשגחת פרופסור ירמי׳ שי׳ ברנובר.

המתרגמת — ג. ליפש.

ירושלים, אה״ק ת״ו. ה׳תשל״ז. 42 עמודים.

כנ״ל. הלשון קודש ביחד עם תרגום הרוסי. ירושלים, אה״ק ת״ו. ה׳תשל״ח. 68 עמודים.

חלק שלישי, אגרת התשובה.

תורגם בהשגחת פרופסור ירמיהו שי׳ ברנובר.
המתרגמת — ג. ליפש
יועצי התרגום — הרב ד. אוקניוב, הרב ז. לוין
ירושלים, אה״ק ת״ו. ה׳תשל״ט, 56 עמודים.
הלשון קודש ביחד עם התרגום הרוסי.

לקוטי אמרים — תניא

חלק ראשון (פרקים א־נג).
חלק שני: שער היחוד והאמונה.
חלק שלישי: אגרת התשובה.
עמוד התניא מול עמוד התרגום.
הנ״ל, בכרך אחד.
דזשערזי סיטי, ניו דזשערזי. ה׳תשד״מ. 484 ע׳.

לקוטי אמרים — תניא

הנ״ל, בכרך אחד (פורמט כיס).
לאדיספאלי, איטאליע. ה׳תשד״מ. 484 ע׳.

כנ״ל בכרך אחד (פורמט כיס).
אסטיע, איטאליע. ה׳תשד״מ. 484 ע׳.

כנ״ל בכרך אחד.
ברוקלין, נ.י. ח״י אלול תשמ״ט. שנת המאתיים להולדת כ״ק אדמו״ר הצ״צ. שנת הארבעים לנשיאות כ״ק אדמו״ר שליט״א. 477 ע׳.

ח. פורטוגזית

חלק ראשון. לקוטי אמרים.

פרקים א־יב. הלשון קודש ביחד עם התרגום.

תורגם ע״י משה פיים שי׳. בעריכת: הר״ר צבי ארי׳ שי׳ בעגון, ד״ר ברוך (באריס) קנאפ. בהשגחת הרה״ת ר׳ יעקב ארי׳ ליב שי׳ זאיאנץ. פאלו, בראזיל. ה׳תשמ״א. 72 עמודים.

שער היחוד והאמונה חלק שני.

תורגם ע״י הרב י. דוד שי׳ ווייטמאן ושילה שתחי׳ שמעא.

פאולא, בראזיל.

ה׳תשד״מ. (24), 56 עמודים.

חלק שלישי. אגרת התשובה.

תורגם ע״י הרב יצחק שי׳ מישען ויעקב זאב שי׳ בנדה. בראזיליא, בראזיל. ה׳תשד״מ. 52 עמודים.

לקוטי אמרים — תניא

חלק ראשון (פרקים א־נג).

חלק שני: שער היחוד והאמונה.

חלק שלישי: אגרת התשובה

— בכרך אחד.

פאלו, בראזיל. ה׳תש״נ. הי׳ תהא שנת נסים. מאתיים שנה להולדת כ״ק אדמו״ר הצ״צ. ארבעים שנה לנשיאות כ״ק אדמו״ר שליט״א. xxi, 388. (10) 61 (2).

ט. באשכנזית (גרמנית)

חלק שני. שער היחוד והאמונה (פרקים א־ז).

תורגם ע״י הרב צבי שי׳ צאלער.

בתחלת הספר — פתח דבר מהמו״ל — המתרגם.

זוריך, שווייץ. תפארת שבתפארת, ה׳תשמ״ה. (4), 33 עמודים .8°

יו״ד. בכתב „בריל״

לקוטי אמרים תניא.

בכתב „בריל״ (לשון הקודש), באה״ק, ה׳תנש״א.

בכתב „בריל״ מתרגום האנגלי — ראה לעיל במדור „תרגומים״ — אנגלית בסופה.

הערות:

שם הספר ושם חלקיו:

בשם **לקוטי אמרים** — נקרא ע״י המחבר — רבנו הזקן, ראה הקדמת המלקט, אגרת התשובה פ״ד, יו״ד, יא. הקדמת הסידור, הערה לתיקון חצות (בסידור). בכמה מקומות באגרת הקודש. ועוד.

בשם **תניא:** בהסכמות דהוצאת זאלקווי תקנ״ט („ספר לקוטי אמרים אשר פי השם יקבנו **תניא** קדישא״. „לקו״א ומכונה בשם ספר תניא״). ברוב המקומות בספר תורה אור, ביאור לד״ה ולא תשבית בלקו״ת. בהמאמרים שנדפסו בס׳ בונה ירושלים, שכנראה נכתבו בימי רבנו הזקן.

בשם **ספר של בינונים** או **בינונים** (כל הספר ולא רק חלקו הראשון): ברוב המקומות בלקו״ת.

בשם **קונטרסים:** קודם שנדפס. ראה הערת כ״ק מו״ח אדמו״ר לשיחת י״ט כסלו תרצ״ג אות א, ורשימתו שבסוף ספר קיצורים והערות הנ״ל. — וכן משמע מהקדמת המלקט עצמו.

שער היחוד והאמונה נקרא ג״כ **לקו״א ח״ב, חינוך קטן. סש״ב ח״ב** או **בינונים ח״ב** (לקו״ת ד״ה ראו כי ה׳. ועוד). **תניא ח״ב** (תו״א ביאור לד״ה נ״ח מצוה ס״ב. ועוד).

אגרת התשובה נקרא ג״כ: **לקו״א ח״ג, סש״ב ח״ג** (לקו״ת ביאור לד״ה לבבתיני סוס״ה). **תניא קטן** (בהקדמת המו״ל בהוצאת שקלאב תקס״ו שכן „נקראת במדינתנו״).

קונטרס אחרון נקרא ג״כ אגה״ק — לקו״ת ד״ה ויקרא. ועוד.

השער כמעט בכל ההוצאות — אין נזכר בנוסח השער שער היחוד והאמונה !

וכנראה שנשתרבב מנוסח השער של הוצאה הראשונה, אשר אח״כ לא הוסיפו בשער אלא מה שניתוסף על ההוצאות הקודמות.

לא נזכר שם המחבר — בהוצאות (שראיתי): תקנ״ז. תקס״ה. תקס״ו. תק״ף. תקפ״ז.

בהקדמת המלקט ישנו גם הסיום „והנה אחר שנתפשטו״ — בהוצאות: תקנ״ז. תקס״ו (בקיצור). תר״ס ואילך.

בסוף ח״ב נדפס „חסר״*) בהוצאות: תקנ״ז. תקנ״ט. תקס״ה. תר״ך.

אגרת התשובה במהדורה קמא — בהוצאות: תקנ״ט. תקס״ה. תר״ך.

אגרת הקדש מסומן — בהוצאות: 1856. תרכ״ב. לעמבערג חמו״ד. 1864. ווין חש״ד. תר״ס ואילך.

קונטרס אחרון מסומן)** — בהוצאות: 1856. תרכ״ב. לעמבערג חמו״ד. 1864. ווין חש״ד.

כו׳. בכ״מ — ובפרט באגה״ק — צ״ע מה מרבה בזה. וכמו שציינתי ב„הערות ותיקונים״. ואולי אפ״ל, עכ״פ בחלק מהנ״ל, אשר בהעתקה הקודמת של האגרת הי׳ חסר במקום זה, או שמאיזה סיבה עשה כאן המעתיק השמטה, ורמזה בתיבת „כו׳״, ומי שהשלים אח״כ את החסר — לא שם לבו (או שלא ידע) שמעתה תיבת כו׳ — מיותרת. — לדוגמא ראה (קלח, א שורה טו), אשר הסיום והעובר ע״ז כו׳ — נתוסף רק בהוצאת תר״ס ואילך.

---

*) תלמידו הגדול של רבנו הזקן הרה״ג והרה״ח וכו׳ וכו׳ מוהר״ר אהרן הלוי מסטאראשעלי כותב בהקדמתו לספרו — שלו — שערי היחוד והאמונה: שער היחוד והאמונה . . לא הספיק הזמן בידו להשלימו כפי כוונתו ורצונו הקדוש. — בכל זה בהוצאת תקס״ז שנדפסה בשקלאב בסמיכות מקום רבנו הזקן כבר הושמטה תיבת „חסר״. — מהוצאת תר״ך אין להוכיח, כי הרי גם אגה״ת באה בה במהדו״ק, היינו שקודם תקס״ז.

**) כנראה גם הצ״צ סימן את הקו״א. ד״ה להבין איך הקורא — סימן לג. — (ד״ה עיין ע״ח — נכלל בד״ה הנ״ל בהוצאות שעד שנת תר״ס) — ד״ה להבין מ״ש בשער היחודים — סימן לד. ד״ה להבין מ״ש בפע״ח — סימן לה. — (ד״ה להבין פרטי הלכות — נדפס רק מהוצאת תר״ס ואילך) — ד״ה דוד זמירות — סימן לו, ואילך. — ראה דרך מצותיך, שנדפס מגכי״ק (אלא שצ״ע אם גם המ״מ הם מהצ״צ). — דף מא ע״א. הגהות הצ״צ לתניא פל״ז (נדפסו בס׳ קיצורים והערות ללקו״א)*.

*) הערה לאחר זמן: לאחרונה נתקבלו כמה ביכלאך גכי״ק. ומהם: סהמ״צ (דרך מצותיך) — ואגה״ק לא מסומן בו (היינו שזוהי הוספת המדפיס); ביכל כל המשמח לאגער ובו בד״ה שייך ללק״ת ר״פ ראה (נדפס באוה״ת ראה ע׳ תרסב) ס״א וס״ב מסומן בגכי״ק הצ״צ סי׳ ל״ז (ע״ד קו״א וצדקה כנחל איתן); ביאורי הזהר להצ״צ (ח״ב) ע׳ תתקעג מסומן בגכי״ק הצ״צ סי׳ ל״ו (ע״ד קו״א ד״ה דוד זמירות). רשימות לתהלים (מילואים) ע׳ תרלח — מסומן בגכי״ק הצ״צ כנ״ל (בביאוה״ז).

ראשי פרקים מתולדות רבנו הזקן

כ״ק אדמו״ר מרנא ורבנא שניאור זלמן, נולד חי אלול תק״ה. בחג הבר מצוה — תארוהו גאוני הדור בשם רב תנא הוא ופליג. בשנת תק״ך — חתונתו. עושה תעמולה גדולה — בטרחתו ובממונו — בקרב היהודים להתעסק בעבודת האדמה. תקכ״ד — הולך למעזריטש בפעם הראשונה. תקכ״ז — מקבל את המגידות דליאזנא. תק״ל — התחיל לסדר את השולחן ערוך. תקל״ב — יסד שיטת חסידות חב״ד. מנהל תעמולה אשר היהודים הגרים בגליל וויטעבסק יעתיקו מושבם מעבר לגבול — למדינת רוסיא. תקל״ג־תקל״ח — יסוד הישיבה בליאזנא, וידועה בשם חדר ראשון, חדר ב, חדר ג. תקל״ד — נוסע עם הרה״ק הרמ״מ לווילנא להתראות עם הגר״א, הגר״א אינו מקבלם לראיון. תקל״ז — מלווה את הרה״ק הרמ״מ — בנסיעתו לאה״ק ת״ו — עד עיר מאהליב (שעל נהר דניעסטער). תקמ״ג — ויכוח הגדול במינסק ומנצח בויכוחו. תקנ״א — כתביו בנגלה ובנסתר מתפשטים במרחב גדול. תקנ״ד — מדפיס את ספרו „הלכות ת״ת״. תקנ״ז — מדפיס את ספר התניא. תקנ״ט — א״ח של סוכות נאסר. בי״ט כסלו יצא לחירות. תקס״א — א״ח של סוכות נתבקש לפ״ב, בי״א מנחם אב שנה זו בא מפעטערבורג לליאדי — פלך מאהליב. ערב שבת מברכין אלול תקע״ב עזב את ליאדי, ומטולטל עם ב״ב והרבה מהחסידים עד בואו י״ב טבת תקע״ג לכפר פיענע — פלך קורסק. שם במוצש״ק אור ליום ראשון כ״ד טבת נסתלק, ומ״כ בעיר האדיץ — פלך פאָלטאַווע.

ספריו*: א) הלכות ת״ת. ב) ברכות הנהנין. ג) תניא. ד) סדור. ה) שלחן ערוך. ו) באורי הזהר. ז) תורה אור. ח) לקוטי תורה. ט) בונה ירושלים. י) מאמרי אדמו״ר הזקן — הנחות הר״פ. יא) מאמרי אדמו״ר הזקן — אתהלך ליאזנא. יב) מאמרי אדמו״ר הזקן — תקס״ב. יג) מאמר: כתפוח בעצי היער. יד) מאמר: יסובבנהו. טו) מאמר: בחכמה יבנה בית. טז) מאמר: אני ישנה. יז) מאמר: ציון במשפט תפדה. יח) מאמר: פקודא ליתן מחצית השקל. יט) מאמר: והארץ היתה תהו. כ) מאמר: ומשה נגש אל הערפל. כא) מאמר: אשרי יושבי ביתך. כב) מאמרי אדמו״ר הזקן — תקס״ח. כג) מאמרי אדמו״ר הזקן — תקס״ה. כד) מאמרי אדמו״ר הזקן — תקס״ו. כה) מאמרי אדה״ז — תקס״ז. כו) אגרות קודש. כז) מאמרי אדמו״ר הזקן — תקס״ג (ב׳ כרכים). כח) מאמרי אדמו״ר הזקן — תקס״ד. כט) מאמרי אדמו״ר הזקן — הקצרים. ל) מאמרי אדמו״ר הזקן — תקס״ט. לא) מאמרי אדמו״ר הזקן — תק״ע. לב) מאמרי אדמו״ר הזקן — על פרשיות התורה והמועדים (ב׳ כרכים). לג) מאמרי אדמו״ר הזקן — ענינים.

---

*) ברשימה זו באו הספרים שנדפסו ולא שבכתי״.

לוח ראשי תיבות

רשימה זו היא לפי הראשי תיבות שבס׳ התניא

(כולל הראשי תיבות שבאו בצירוף אותיות השימוש)

א

א:	אחד, אחת
א״א:	אברהם אבינו
א״א:	אדוננו אבינו
א״א:	אי אפשר
א״א:	אריך אנפין
אא״כ:	אלא אם כן
אב״ד:	אב בית דין
אבי״ע:	אצילות בריאה יצירה עשי׳
אדמו״ר:	אדוננו מורנו ורבנו
אד״ש:	אחרי דרישת שלומם
אהוי״ר:	אהבה ויראה
אה״ק:	ארצינו הקדושה, ארץ הקודש
או״א:	אבא ואמא
אוא״ס:	אור אין סוף
או״ה:	איסור והיתר
או״ה:	אומות העולם
או״ח:	אורח חיים
או״נ:	אוהב נפש(ם)
א״ח:	אורח חיים
אח״כ:	אחר כך
א״י:	ארץ ישראל
אי״ה:	אם ירצה ה׳
א״כ:	אם כן
אכי״ר:	אמן כן יהי רצון
א״ל:	אמר ליה
אמ״ר:	אש מים רוח
אנ״ש:	אנשי שלומינו
א״ס:	אין סוף
א״ע:	את עצמו
אע״ג:	אף על גב
אע״ה:	אבינו עליו השלום
אעפ״כ:	אף על פי כן
אפ״ה:	אפילו הכי
אפי׳:	אפילו
א״ק:	אדם קדמון
אקב״ו:	אשר קדשנו במצותיו וצונו
ארז״ל:	אמרו רבותינו זכרונם לברכה
ארמ״ע:	אש רוח מים עפר
א״ת:	אל תקרי
אתדל״ע:	אתערותא דלעילא
אתדל״ת:	אתערותא דלתתא
את״ל:	אם תמצא לומר

ב

ב״א:	בני אדם
בא״א:	בן אדוננו אבינו
באגה״ק:	באגרת הקדש
באדה״ר:	באדם הראשון
באד״ר:	באדרא רבא
בא״ח:	באורח חיים
בא״י:	ברוך אתה ה׳
בא״ס ב״ה:	באין סוף ברוך הוא
ב״ב:	בבא בתרא
בבהמ״ק:	בבית המקדש
בבחי׳:	בבחינה(ות)(ת)
בבי״ע:	בבריאה יצירה עשי׳
בגמ׳:	בגמרא
ב״ד:	בית דין
בדו״ר:	בדחילו ורחימו
בד״מ:	בדרך משל
בד״ת:	בדברי תורה
ב״ה:	בית הלל

ב"ה: ברוך ה'
בה"ח: בחמשה חסדים
בהל': בהלכת (בהלכות)
בהלק"א: בהלקוטי אמרים
בהמ"ק: בית המקדש
ב"ו: בשר ודם
בו"ק: בו' קצוות
בזוה"ק: בזוהר הקדוש
בזח"ב: בזוהר חלק ב'
בזלע"ז: בזה לעומת זה
בחו"ל: בחוץ לארץ
בחי': בחינה(ות)(ת)
בחכ"ע: בחכמה עילאה
ב"י: בני ישראל
בי"ד: ביורה דעה
ביה"כ: ביום הכפורים
בי"ס: בעשר ספירות
בכהאריז"ל: בכתבי הקדוש אלקי רבי יצחק ז"ל
בכ"י: בכתב יד
בכי"ק: בכתב יד קדשו
בכת"י: בכתב ידו
בל"א: בלשון אשכנז
בלא"ה: בלאו הכי
בלה"ק: בלשון הקדש
בלק"א: בלקוטי אמרים
במ"א: במגן אברהם
במ"א: במקום אחר
במדה"ד: במדת הדין
במהור"ר: בן מורינו הרב ורבנו רבי
במו"מ: במשא ומתן
במו"ס: במוחין סתימאה
במחדו"מ: במחשבה דיבור ומעשה
במכש"כ: במכל שכן
בממ"ה: במלך מלכי המלכים
במס"נ: במסירת נפש
במ"ע: במצות עשה
במ"ש: במה שכתוב
במ"ת: במתן תורה

ב"נ: בר נש
בנ"א: בנוסח אחר
בנ"א: בני אדם
בס': בספר
בס"א: בסטרא אחרא
בס"ח: בספר חסידים
בס"י: בספר יצירה
בס"פ: בסוף פרק – פרשה
בספ"ק: בסוף פרק קמא
בעוה"ז: בעולם הזה
בעז"ה: בעזרת ה'
בעזה"י: בעזרת השם יתברך
בע"ח: בעץ חיים
בער"ה: בערב ראש השנה
בע"ת: בעלי תשובה
בעשי"ת: בעשרת ימי תשובה
בפ': בפרק – בפרשת
בפ"מ: בפועל ממש
בפ"ע: בפני עצמו
בפע"ח: בפרי עץ חיים
בפרד"ס: בפשט רמז דרוש סוד
בפרע"ח: בפרי עץ חיים
בקגא"ס: בקנין גמור אגב סודר
בק"נ: בקליפת נוגה
בק"ש: בקריאת שמע
ב"ר: בן רבי
בר"ח: בראשית חכמה
בר"מ: ברעיא מהימנא
ברע"מ: ברעיא מהימנא
בר"פ: בריש פרשת
ברפ"ב: בריש פרק ב'
ב"ש: בית שמאי
בשבה"כ: בשבירת הכֵלים
בשכמל"ו: ברוך שם כבוד מלכותו לעולם ועד
בש"ע: בשלחן ערוך
בתושב"כ: בתורה שבכתב
בתושבע"פ: בתורה שבעל פה
בת"ז: בתיקוני זהר

בת"ח: בתלמיד חכם
בת"כ: בתורת כהנים
בת"ת: בתלמוד תורה

ג

ג"כ: גם כן
ג"ע: גילוי עריות
ג"ע: גן ערן
ג"פ: ג' פעמים
ג"פ: (ח"י ג"פ) 18 גדולים פולניש

ד

ד': דף
ד"א: ד' אמות
דא"א: דאריך אנפין
דאדה"ר: דאדם הראשון
דאו"א: דאבא ואמא
דא"ח: דברי אלקים חיים
דא"י: דארץ ישראל
דאע"ג: דאף על גב
דא"ק: דאדם קדמון
דאר"ש: דאמר רבי שמעון
דב"ב: דבבא בתרא[3]
דבלא"ה: דבלאו הכי
דב"נ: דבר נש
דהע"ה: דוד המלך עליו השלום
דו"מ: דבור ומעשה
דו"ר: דחילו ורחימו
דז"א: דזעיר אנפין
דחב"ד: דחכמה בינה (ו)דעת
ד"ט: ד' טפחים
דטו"ר: דטוב ורע
ד"מ: דרך משל
ד"ס: דברי סופרים
דצ"ל: דצריך להיות
דצח"מ: דומם צומח חי מדבר
דקב"ה: דקודשא בריך הוא

דק"ק: דקהלה קדושה
דר"א: דברי רבי אליעזר, דרבי אליעזר
דר"א: דף ר"א
דר"ה: דראש השנה
דר"ת: דברי תורה

ה

ה': השם, הוי'
האגה"ק: האגרת הקדש
האגה"ת: האגרת התשובה
האר"י: הקדוש אלקי רבי יצחק
הבעש"ט: הבעל שם טוב
הגי': הגירסא
הדו"ש: הדורש שלום(ם)
ה"ה: הרי הוא
ה"ז: הרי זה
החו"ב: החכמה ובינה
הח"מ: החתומים מטה
ה"ט: האי טעמא
הט"ס: הטעותי סופרים
ה"י: ה' ישמרינו
היצה"ר: היצר הרע
הכ"ד: הלא כה דברי
המ"א: המגן אברהם
המע"ט: המעשים טובים
הנ"ל: הנזכר לעיל
הנק': הנקראים
הס"א: הסטרא אחרא
הס': הספר
הסט"א: הסטרא אחרא
העו"ג: העובדי גילולים
העוה"ז: העולם הזה
הע"ס: העשר ספירות
הצ"צ: הצמח צדק
הק': הקדוש
הקב"ה: הקדוש ברוך הוא

הק״ש:	הקריאת שמע
הרח״ו:	הרב חיים ויטאל
הרמב״ם:	הרב משה בן מיימון
הרמב״ן:	הרב משה בן נחמן
הרמ״ז:	הרב משה זכות
הרמ״ק:	הרב משה קורדווארו
הר״ר:	הרב רבי
הרשב״א:	הרב שלמה בן אדרת
השי״ת:	השם יתברך
הש״ס:	הששה סדרים
הש״ץ:	השליח צבור

ו

וא׳:	ואחד
ואגה״ת:	ואגרת התשובה
ואח״כ:	ואחר כך
וא״כ:	ואם כן
וא״ל:	ואם לאו (באגה״ק ה כ״ה בלקו״ת שלח לז, ב)
ואע״ג:	ואף על גב
ואפי׳:	ואפילו
ואעפ״כ:	ואף על פי כן
וא״צ:	ואין צריך
ואצ״ל:	ואין צריך לומר
וב״ה:	ובית הלל
ובהמ״ז:	וברכת המזון
ובחי׳:	ובחינ(ו)ת
ובח״מ:	ובחושן משפט
ובי״ס:	ובעשר ספירות
ובע״ח:	ובעץ חיים
ובע״כ:	ובעל כרחו
ובפ״ק:	ובפרק קמא
ובר״מ:	וברעיא מהימנא
ובשכמל״ו:	וברוך שם כבוד מלכותו לעולם ועד
וגו׳:	וגומר
וגומ״ח:	וגומלי חסדים
וג״ח:	וגמילת חסדים
וגמ״ח:	וגומלי חסדים
וג״ע:	וגילוי עריות
וד׳:	ודף
וד״ל:	ודי למבין
וד״ת:	ודברי תורה
והאגה״ק:	והאגרת הקודש
וה״ג:	וה׳ גבורות
וה״ה:	והרי הוא
והול״ל:	והוה לי׳ למימר
וה״ט:	והאי טעמא
והעו״ג:	והעובדי גילולים
והל״ל:	והוה לי׳ למימר
וה״נ:	והכא נמי
והס״א:	והסטרא אחרא
והסמ״ג:	והספר מצות גדול
והש״ץ:	והשליח ציבור
וז״ש:	וזה שאמר(ו) (שכתוב)
וזש״ה:	וזה (וזהו) שאמר הכתוב
וטע״ס:	וטעות סופרים
ויוה״כ:	ויום הכיפורים
וי״ט:	ויום טוב
וי״ל:	ויש לומר, ויש להבין
ויצה״ר:	ויצר הרע
וי״ש:	ויראת שמים
וית׳:	ויתעלה
וכב״ב:	וכל בני ביתו
וכדפי׳:	וכדפירוש
וכ״ה:	וכן הוא
וכה״ג:	וכהאי גוונא
וכו׳:	וכולי
וכ״ז:	וכל זה
וכ״כ:	וכל כך
וכ״כ:	וכן כתוב[2]
וכמארז״ל:	ומאמר רבותינו
וכמ״ש:	וכמו שכתוב
וכמשארז״ל:	וכמו שאמרו רבותינו זכרונם לברכה
וכמש״ל:	וכמו שנתבאר לעיל
וכמש״ש:	וכמו שכתוב שם

וכ"ש:	וכל שכן
ולז"א:	ולזה אמר
ולפמ"ש:	ולפי מה שכתוב
ומכש"כ:	ומכל שכן
ומע"ט:	ומעשים טובים
ומ"ש:	ומה שכתוב (שאמר)
ומש"ה:	ומשום הכי
ומשו"ה:	ומשום הכי
ונק':	ונקרא
ונ"ל:	ונראה לי
ונר"נ:	ונפש רוח ונשמה
וס':	וספר
וס"א:	וסטרא אחרא
וסד"א:	וסלקא דעתך אמינא
וס"ס:	וספק ספיקא
וס"ת:	וספר תורה
וע"ד:	ועל דא[1]
וע"ה:	ועמי הארץ
וע"ז:	ועל זה
ועז"נ:	ועל זה נאמר
וע"ח:	ועץ חיים
וע"י:	ועל ידי
ועי"ז:	ועל ידי זה
ופסד"ז:	ופסוקי דזמרה
ופע"ח:	ופרי עץ חיים
וקב"ה:	וקודשא בריך הוא
וק"ו:	וקל וחומר
וקי"ל:	וקיימא לן
וק"ש:	וקריאת שמע
ור"ח:	וראש חדש
ור"ח:	וראשית חכמה
ור"מ:	ורבי מאיר
ורמב"ן:	ורבי משה בן נחמן
ור"ר:	ורחמים רבים
וש"ד:	ושפיכת דמים
ות"ת:	ותלמוד תורה

ז

ז"א:	זה אינו
ז"א:	זעיר אנפין
זא"ז:	זה את זה
זו"נ:	ז"א ונוקבא
ז"ט:	ז' טפחים
זי"ע:	זכותו יגן עלינו
ז"ל:	זכרונו(ם) לברכה.
	זרע לבטלה
זלעו(מ)"ז:	זה לעומת זה
זע"ז:	זה על זה. (זה עם זה)
זצוקללה"ה:	זכר צדיק וקדוש לברכה לחיי העולם הבא
זצ"ל:	זכר צדיק לברכה

ח

ח"א:	חלק א'
ח"ב:	חלק ב'
חב"ד:	חכמה בינה דעת
ח"ג:	חלק ג'
חג"ת:	חסד גבורה תפארת
ח"ו:	חס ושלום
חו"ג:	חסד וגבורה
חז"ל:	חכמינו זכרונם לברכה
ח"ע:	חכמה עילאה

ט

טו"ר:	טוב ורע

י

י"ח:	ידי חובתו
י"ח:	יודעי ח"ן (חכמה נסתרה)
י"ח:	שמונה עשרה
י"ל:	יש לומר
ימ"ב:	ימי בראשית
י"ס:	י' (עשר) ספירות
י"ס:	ים סוף
יצה"ט:	יצר הטוב
יצה"ר:	יצר הרע
יצ"ו:	ישמרם צורם ויחזקם

יצ"ט: יצר טוב
יתֹ: יתברך
יתֹ ויתֹ: יתברך ויתעלה
יתבֹ: יתברך
ית"ש: יתברך שמו

כ

כ"א: כי אם
כאו"א: כל אחד ואחד
כביֹ: כביכול
כדאיֹ: כדאיתא
כדפירש"י: כדפירוש רש"י (רבי שלמה יצחקי)
כוֹ: כולי
כ"ז: כל זה
כ"ז: כל זמן
כ"כ: כל כך
כמארז"ל: כמאמר רבותינו זכרונם לברכה
כמו"כ: כמו כן
כמ"ש: כמו שכתוב
כמשארז"ל: כמו שאמרו רז"ל
כמש"ל: כמו שכתוב, שנתבאר, שנזכר לעיל
כנה"ג: כנסת הגדולה
כנז"ל: כנזכר לעיל
כנ"י: כנסת ישראל
כנ"ל: כנזכר לעיל
כ"ע: כולא עלמין
כעועג: כעובדי עבודת גילולים
כע"ז: כעבודה זרה
כ"ק: כבוד קדושת
כרשב"י: כרבי שמעון בן יוחאי
כשא"א: כשאי אפשר
כ"ש: כל שכן
כי"ק: כתב יד קדשו

ל

לאו"א: לאבא ואמא
לבהכ"נ: לבית הכנסת
לבי"ע: לבריאה יצירה עשי
לב"נ: לבר נש
לבנ"י: לבני ישראל
לברע"ה: לבריאת העולם
לג"ע: לגן עדן
להקב"ה: לקדוש ברוך הוא
לה"ק: לשון הקדש
להקדיֹ: להקדים
לה"ר: לשון הרע
לי"ח: לידעי ח"ן (חכמה נסתרה)
למשרע"ה: למשה רבינו עליו השלום
לס"א: לסטרא אחרא
לעבוֹ: לעבוד
לעו"ג: לעובדי גילולים
לעוה"ז: לעולם הזה
לעו"ז: לעומת זה
לע"ז: לעבודה זרה
לע"ל: לעתיד לבא
לפ"ק: לפרט קטן
לק"א: לקוטי אמרים
לק"מ: לא קשיא מידי
לר"ש: לרבי שמעון
לש"ש: לשם שמים
ל"ת: לא תעשה

מ

מאדמו"ר: מאדונינו מורינו ורבינו
מאנ"ש: מאנשי שלומינו
מארז"ל: מאמר רבותינו זכרונם לברכה
מ"ד: מין דוכרין
מדה"ד: מדת הדין

מדה״ר:	מדת הרחמים
מד״ת:	מדברי תורה
מהאגה״ק:	מהאגרת הקדש
מה״ג:	מה׳ גבורות
מהור״ר:	מורנו הרב ורבנו ר׳
מה״מ:	מלכי המלכים
מהסט״א:	מהסטרא אחרא
מהרמ״ק:	מהרב משה קורדווארו
מו״ה:	מורינו ורבנו הרב
מוהר״ר:	מורינו הרב ר׳
מו״ח:	מורי וחמי
מו״ר:	מורינו ורבנו
מ״ז:	מחשבות זרות (זרה)
מזה״ק:	מזוהר הקדוש
מח׳:	מחשבה
מח״ס:	מוחא סתימאה
מחב״ד:	מחכמה בינה דעת
מח״ע:	מחכמה עילאה
מי״ש:	מיראת שמים
מכיה״ק:	מכתב ידו הקדושה
מכ״ק:	מכבוד קדושת
מל׳:	מלכות(ו)
מלה״ר:	מלשון הרע
מלו״נ:	מלב ונפש
מל״ת:	מצות לא תעשה
מ״מ:	מכל מקום
ממ״ה:	מלך מלכי המלכים
ממו״ס:	ממוחין סתימאין
ממחדו״מ:	ממחשבה דיבור ומעשה
ממכ״ע:	ממלא כל עלמין
ממ״ש:	ממה שכתוב
מ״נ:	מין נוקבין
מ״נ:	מסירת נפש
מ״ע:	מצות עשה
מע״ה:	מעמי הארץ
מע״ט:	מעשים טובים
מעוה״ז:	מעולם הזה
מעל״ד:	מעבר לדף
מפ״ב :	מפעטרבורג
מק״מ:	מקדש מלך
מרע״ה:	משה רבינו עליו השלום
מ״ש:	מה שכתוב שאמר(ו)
משא״כ:	מה שאין כן
מש״ש:	מה שכתוב שם
מ״ת:	מתן תורה

נ

נא׳:	נאמר
נ״א:	נוסח אחר
נבג״מ:	נשמתו בגנזי מרומים
נ״ה:	נץ החמה
נה״י:	נצח הוד יסוד
נו״ה:	נצח והוד
נח״ש:	נדוי חרם ושמתא
נ״י:	נר ישראל
נ״ל:	נראה לומר, נראה לבאר
נס״ו:	נצח סלה ועד
נהי״מ:	נצח הוד יסוד מלכות
נק׳:	נקרא
נ״ע:	נשמתו(ם) עדן
נר׳:	נראה
נ״ר:	נחת רוח
נר״נ:	נפש רוח נשמה
נרנח״י:	נפש רוח נשמה חי׳ יחידה

ס

ס״א:	סטרא אחרא
סד״א:	סלקא דעתך אמינא
סוכ״ע:	סובב כל עלמין
סי׳:	סימן
ס״ל:	סבירא לי׳
סס״י:	סוף סימן
ספ״ט:	סוף פרק ט׳
ס״פ:	סוף פרשת (פרק)
ספי׳:	ספירה, ספירות, ספירת

ספי"ג:	סוף פרק יג
ס"ת:	ספר תורה

ע

ע':	עיין
ע"א:	עמוד א'
עאכ"ו:	על אחת כמה וכמה
ע"ב:	עמוד ב'
ע"ג:	על גבי
ע"ד:	על דרך, על דא
עד"ז:	על דרך זה
עד"מ:	על דרך משל
ע"ה:	עליו השלום
ע"ה:	עמוד הימין
ע"ה:	עמי הארץ
עה"ד:	עץ הדעת
עה"ח:	על החתום
עה"ת:	על התורה
עו"ג:	עובדי גילולים
עוה"ב:	עולם הבא
עוה"ז:	עולם הזה
ע"ז:	עבודה זרה
ע"ז:	על זה
ע"ח:	עץ חיים
ע"י:	על ידי
עי"ז:	על ידי זה
ע"כ:	על כרחך
ע"כ:	על כל
ע"כ:	עד כאן
ע"כ:	על כן
עכו"ם:	עבודת כוכבים
עכ"ל:	עד כאן לשונו
עכ"פ:	על כל פנים
ע"ע:	על עצמו
עע"א:	עובדי עבודת אלילים
עע"ז:	עובדי עבודה זרה
ע"פ:	על פי
ע"פ:	על פסוק
ער"ה:	ערב ראש השנה
ע"ש:	עיין שם
ע"ש:	על שם
עש"ב:	עיין שם בארוכה

פ

פ':	פרשת, פרק
פ"א:	פעם אחת, פרק א'
פא"פ:	פנים אל פנים
פב"פ:	פנים בפנים
פ"ה:	פטיש החזק , פרק ה'
פ"ו:	פרק ו'
פ"ט:	פרק ט'
פי':	פירוש
פי"א:	פרק יא
פל"ד:	פרק לד
פנ"א:	פרק נא
פ"ק:	פרק קמא

צ

צ"ל:	צריך להיות
צ"ע:	צריך עיון
צ"צ:	צמח צדק

ק

ק':	קדוש
ק':	קהלת
קב"ה:	קודשא בריך הוא
קטנ':	קטנה
קיי"ל:	קיימא לן
ק"ק:	קודש קדשים
ק"ש:	קריאת שמע

ר

ר':	רב, רבי
ראב"ע:	רבי אלעזר בן עזרי'
רבש"ע:	רבונו של עולם
ר"ה:	ראש השנה
רוה"ק:	רוח הקודש
רז"ל:	רבותינו זכרונם לברכה
ריב"ש:	רבי ישראל בעל שם טוב
ר"ל:	רוצה לומר

ר״ל: רחמנא ליצלן
ר״פ: ריש פרק
רפ״י: ריש פרק י׳
ר״ר: רחמים רבים
ר״ש: רבי שמעון
רשב״י: רבי שמעון בן (בר) יוחאי

ש

שא״א: שאי אפשר
שאח״כ: שאחר כך
שא״כ: שאם כן
שאל״כ: שאם לאו כן
שאע״פ: שאף על פי
שאפי׳: שאפילו
שא״ס: שאין סוף
שא״צ: שאין צריך, שאין צריכים
שארז״ל: שאמרו רבותינו זכרונם לברכה
שאפש׳: שאפשר
שבא״ק: שבאדם קדמון
שבאה״ק: שבארצנו הקדושה
שבעו״ה: שבעונותינו הרבים
שבבהמ״ק: שבבית המקדש
שבג״ע: שבגן עדן
שבזה״ק: שבזהר הקדוש
שבס״ת: שבספר תורה
שבס׳: שבספר
שבע״כ: שבעל כרחו
שבע״פ: שבעל פה
שבע״ת: שבעלי תשובה
שב״ר: של בית רבן
שבתחיה״מ: שבתחית המתים
שו״ב: שוחט ובודק
שז״ל: שכבת זרע לבטלה
ש״ח: שער ח׳
שי׳: שיחי׳
שכ״א: שכל אחד
שכ״ו: שער כ״ו
שליט״א: שיחי׳ לאורך ימים טובים אמן
שמג״ע: שמן גן עדן
שמו״ע: שמונה עשרה
שמס״א: שמסטרא אחרא
שנא׳: שנאמר
שנקר׳: שנקראת
שע״י: שעל ידי
שע״כ: שעל כרחך
שצ״ל: שצריך להיות

ת

ת״ו: תבנה ותכונן
תובב״א: תבנה ותכונן במהרה בימינו אמן
תו״מ: תורה ומצות
ת״ח: תלמיד חכם, תלמידי חכמים
תחה״מ: תחיית המתים
ת״י: תחת יד
תנ״ך: תורה נביאים וכתובים
ת״ר: תנו רבנן
ת״ת: תלמוד תורה

CONTINUATION OF NOTES
FROM FOOT OF
HEBREW PAGES

Notes continued from foot of Hebrew pages

PAGE 284

yearning of the soul can manifest itself only after the soul has freed itself of all the influences of the material body in which it is clothed. This may be attained by relinquishing all tendencies toward the gratification of gross material desires and seeking only the service of G–d. [15] *Sing.* Tzaddik, *"perfectly righteous," one whose innate evil nature has been converted to actual goodness and who is motivated by pure love of G–d. Cf.* Tanya, *ch. 10.* [16] Ps. *97:12.* [17] *The human soul comprises three grades:* Nefesh *(Vitality),* Ruach *(Spirit), and* Neshamah *(Soul).* Nefesh *is the lowest category of the three and is the vitality and life-force of the body.* Ruach *is the spiritual faculty which vivifies man's emotion attributes and is the seat of the moral qualities.* Neshamah *is the most lofty and sublime of the three and is the Divine force which vivifies the human intellect, as it is written, "The* Neshamah *of the Almighty gives them understanding."* (Job *32:8) It is the most refined innermost spark of the soul, and therefore the most divine part of man's being.* Nefesh *is granted to all men;* Ruach *may be acquired through the merit of observing the precepts of the Torah; but to realise* Neshamah, *one must completely purify his physical coarseness. Cf.* Zohar *I, 81a, 206a; II, 141b; III, 70b;* Bereishit Rabbah *14:9;* Shelach *I, 9b.* [18] *A popular ethico-kabbalistic work by Rabbi Eliyahu Devidash.* [19] *Ch. 3.* [20] *There is an innate, hidden love in the heart of every Jew which is an inheritance to us from the Patriarchs. V.* Tanya, *chs. 18, 44.* [21] *Cf.* Deut. *30:20.* [22] *Part III, 67a, 68a. V.* Tanya, *ch. 44.* [23] Isa. *26:9.* [24] Gen. *42:9. See* Yalkut Shimoni, ad locum; Kohellet Rabbah *1:4.* [25] Deut. *4:20; I* Kings. *8:51;* Jer. *11:4. This concept is more fully explained in* Torah Or *by Rabbi Schneur Zalman of Liadi, p. 147.* [26] *Lit., "the other side," the opposite of holiness. A frequent metaphor in Kabbalistic and Chassidic literature to denote the forces of evil.* [27] *With the giving of the Torah on Mount Sinai, for through the Torah the souls of Israel are bound to Him; and the Torah is His Name, as it is stated in* Zohar *II, 90b; III, 73a; etc.* [28] Ibid., *II, 90b.*

PAGE 286

And the basis of Love and Fear is Faith. Thus, ultimately, Faith is the foundation of the observance of the commandments. V. Tanya *I, ch. 33.*

PAGE 288

found in ch. 6. The first five chapters give the reader sufficient background to understand it. [8] Ps. *119:89.* [9] *Rabbi Israel Baal Shem Tov (1698–1760), founder of the Chassidic movement.* [10] Gen. *1:6.* [11] *I.e., the Divine creating forces which bring everything into existence* ex nihilo. *See ch. 11,* infra, *for a full explanation of this concept. See also* Tanya, *chs. 20–22.* [12] Isa. *40:8.* [13] Liturgy, *Morning Prayer.* [14] *Life on our earth is generally classified into four "kingdoms":* Domem—*the "silent," inanimate world, such as water, earth, etc.;* Tzomeach—*vegetable or plant life;* Chai—*living or animal life;* Medaber—*the speaking or human kingdom.* [15] Avot *5:1. "With Ten Utterances was the world created." In the narration of the Creation in the first chapter of Genesis, the words "And G–d said, Let . . ." occur nine times. The first word of the chapter* Bereishit, *"In the beginning," indicates the first Divine Utterance of command which created the heavens, as it is written, "By the* word *of G–d were the* heavens made." *(*Ps. *33:6). Cf.* Rosh Hashanah *32a;* Bereishit Rabbah *17:1; Commentaries on* Avot, ad locum. *See also* Maharsha, Rosh Hashanah, loc. cit. [16] *Rabbi Yitzchak Luria Ashkenazi (1514–72)—in* Etz Chayim, "Shaar Man U'Mad," *Section 3.* [17] *In contrast to the Divine "letters of thought" from which the "hidden" supernal worlds come into being. See ch. 11,* infra. [18] *Phrase used to denote the doctrine of "combination of letters" in all its aspects. Specifically, it refers to the arrangement of the twenty-two letters of the Hebrew alphabet in two-lettered combinations which yield a total of 462 combinations (22×21). Of these, half are the exact reverse of the other half, e.g.,* גד—דג, אב—בא. *Hence, there are 231 two-lettered combinations in direct order and the same number in reverse order. Combinations of groups of three or more letters would, of course, yield a greater number of combinations. Combining the letters in this way involves only the arrangement of the same letters in different order. According to certain systematic rules, the twenty-two letters may be interchanged and substituted one for another (see ch. 7, n. 3,* infra.*), and they may subsequently be arranged in various combinations. Thus, the number of combinations is incalculable, and gives rise to the multitudinous profusion of created beings.* [19] *Ch. 2:4–5.* Sefer Yetzirah *is one of the oldest Kabbalistic works.* [20] *When rearranging the letters of any word into a new combination, the original thought is obscured. Similarly the rearrangements of the supernal letters into a new combination constitutes concealment and diminution of the original vitality and life force. Since the name* even *(like all other things not mentioned in the account of creation) is a new combination of the letters of the Ten Utterances, it is on a lower level than those specifically mentioned in the process of creation. This is what is meant by the "descent" of a combination.*

PAGE 292

HaChazakah, "Hilchot Yesodei Ha-Torah," *ch. 1:7–12;* ibid., "Hilchot Teshuva," *ch. 3:7; Commen-*

tary on Mishnayot, "Sanhedrin," *ch. 10.* [11] *See beginning of ch. 10,* infra. [12] *II* Sam. *23:2.* [13] Ps. *33:6.* [14] *World of Action, our physical world—the lowest of all worlds. It is the final stage in the progressive diminution and concealment of the creative force of the Ten Utterances.* [15] *World of Emanation, the highest spiritual world. It is in a state of unity and proximity with G–d and hence transcends human understanding. It is not a new creation, but only the revelation of the previously concealed.* [16] *World of Creation, the first creation* ex nihilo. *It is finite and receives only a radiance of the Infinite light of* Atzilut, *and may therefore be apprehended by the human mind. Since* Atzilut *is united with G–d, it is above even Prophetic vision until it is veiled and obscured by* Beriah. *This is still infinitely higher than the light of* Beriah *itself.*

PAGE 300

synonym for Tzimtzum *and* Gevurah. [2] Rashi, Gen. *1:1. See* Bereishit Rabbah *12:15;* Sefer Halikutim *by Rabbi Isaac Luria;* Midrash Yelamdenu *quoted in* Talmud Torah.

PAGE 302

(See Deut. *32:2) which symbolises the esoteric aspect of the Torah.* [13] *The soul, being finite and limited, could not comprehend the light of* Atzilut *which is infinite and beyond comprehension. The precepts serve as "garments" of the soul, and veil and screen the Infinite Light so that it can be comprehended and absorbed by the soul; as for example, one looks at a brilliant light through a veil. Cf.* Likutei Amarim, *Part IV,* "Igeret HaKodesh," *ch. 29.* [14] *Brackets are the author's.*

Chapter 6

[1] *The numerical value of each word is 86.* Pardess, "Shaar *12,*" *ch. 2. See also* Shalo, "Shaar HaOtiot," *p. 89a.*

PAGE 330

Chapter 10

[1] Berachot *31b.* [2] Mechilta "Yitro" *19:18;* Tanchumah Yitro *13. I.e., to make it intelligible to man's mind.* [3] *I.e., the scholars of Kabbalah.* [4] Gen. *1:16.* [5] Ibid. *1:5.*

PAGE 344

vah. It will be noted shortly that sin has the opposite effect, both for the transgressing soul and "higher." It is of interest that the beneficial results of good and the deleterious effects of misdeed concern far more than the individual involved. Man's importance is cosmic. All the "worlds" feel the repercussions of man's actions. This concept of man as the ultimate in Creation, the determinant of the fate of the universe, is found frequently. See Rashi on Genesis *1:1 for a typical statement. The word "reflected" is used in the text here for, at most, the revelation is at a far remove from His true being, or even from the Light emanating from Him. The term hints at the unbridgable chasm between finite and what, for want of a better word, we call the Infinite. Some of the terms discussed here are explained more fully in the Translator's Explanatory Notes to "On Learning Chassidus," and in "The Tzemach Tzedek and the Haskalah Movement," p. 110, footnotes 3 and 4. Likutei Amarim I and II are, of course, primary sources.* [4] Tikunei Zohar *30.* [5] *The revelation of G–d effected by performance of mitzvot varies according to each mitzvah, for example a mitzvah of speech (Shema reading, etc.), deed (charity, donning tefillin, etc.), or thought (Torah study, etc.). A different organ of the body performs the mitzvah, and a different "organ of the King" is revealed through the performance, perception of a different aspect of the Creator. (The 613 Biblical commandments are divided into 248 positive and 365 negative commandments.)* [6] *See* Likutei Amarim, *end of chapter 1 and chapter 2, describing "animal" and Divine souls.* [7] *The blessing recited before performing a mitzvah is associated with a positive act rather than with the (passive) restraints exercised in observing a prohibition. Performance brings sanctification with it.* [8] *The* status quo ante, *as it were, is maintained. The beneficence ensuing from performance is not granted, but neither is there any charge of neglect.* [9] Berachot *26a.* [10] Kohelet *1:5.* [11] . . . *the morning reading (*Deuteronomy *6:7) or morning or evening worship.* [12] *The Sefirot are attributes or aspects of G–d, approximating the intellectual and emotive attributes of man, and are indeed the sources of these human attributes. Man reveals himself, he acts, through his attributes (or their "garbs"—thought, speech, and deed). The revelation of G–d, His actions, are similarly through His attributes, the Ten Sefirot. These Sefirot exist on each of the Four Worlds noted above in Note 3. See the Explanatory Notes mentioned there.* [13] *Corporeal man exists on the physical plane of Asiyah, derives from the spiritual Asiyah.* [14] *Opening.* [15] *i.e., the Ten Sefirot.* [16] Leviticus *16:16. "Holy place" refers to atonement for the impure who entered the Sanctuary. See Tractate* Shavuot, *beginning.* [17] *Indicating that purification must attain to that high plane, "before G–d" Himself.* [18] Yerushalmi Chagiga *1:7. The Sage infers from* Jeremiah *9:12, "Because they forsook My Torah" (were the afflictions of exile to be brought upon Israel) that the cause of exile was not idolatry, licentiousness, or bloodshed, but rejection of Torah. These three are cited because of their exceptional gravity (they alone must be kept even at the price of martyrdom) and because the Prophets had denounced these shortcomings in the people.* [19] *See* Exodus *12:19 and 21:21 for examples.* [20] Psalms *89:23.*

PAGE 356

fourth is sod, *the esoteric, mystic interpretation. The simple, literal meaning of teshuvah has been expressed as the abandonment of sin, contrition. Now the* sod *approach will be presented. Ch. 9 offers the* sod *approach to another verse.* [3] *This*

subject will be discussed shortly in the text, but the reader may wish some clarification at this point. The source of the creative power is the Infinite, called by the Ineffable Name, the Tetragrammaton, consisting of four letters: yud, hai, vav, hai. *These letters describe the descent of the Infinite into the corporeal world (among other interpretations). The* yud, *a "point," symbolises seminal wisdom, the flash of intellectual illumination, the first revelation, the start of the process. The first* hai, *in form having dimension, represents* binah, *i.e., understanding, comprehension, and development of the germ-thought into detailed ramification, expansion.* Vav, *in shape extending downward, represents the descent of the Light into lower worlds, those that appear to be "apart" from the Infinite. The final* hai, *again expansion and dimension, is the creative power exercised, manifest in the world created. Through sin, as will be discussed, there is a "dislocation" of the latter* hai, *a diversion of creative power, of vivifying force, into undesirable channels of evil. "Returning the* hai," *both in the lower sense of repudiation of evil and in the superior sense of true unity with G–d (later discussed), are the two types of teshuvah, returning each* hai *to its respective state of unity. (The* Zohar *interpretation in the text is a division of the word teshuvah into two—*tashuv hai, *with the final letter considered an independent word.)* [4] cf. Sanhedrin *99a.* [5] cf. Yerushalmi Peah *1:1.* [6] Moed Katan *28a.* [7] *ch. 28.* [8] Deut. *32:9.* [9] Gen. *2:7.* [10] Zohar. [11] cf. *Rambam,* Yad, Yesodei Hatorah *1;* Yigdal.

PAGE 358

("Thought" in contrast is not revelatory, and can exist in isolation; no other being is needed.) The "utterances" here, the Biblical "And the Lord said, 'Let there be . . .'," and all the Biblical declarations about creating through speech (e.g., Psalm *33:6 and 9, 148:5, etc.)—convey this concept of the new existence of "another" being, the created universe apparently independent. The creative power acts through "speech." Furthermore, speech is of necessity a limitation on thought. It reveals to the listener, true, but one cannot convey all his thought. On the pre-verbalising level one can think briefly and rapidly on ideas that can be articulated only at great length. "Letters" (a variant term for "speech") are instruments, dimensioned, finite. Beings issuing from "speech" bear these speech characteristics—separateness rather than unity, and limitation in their potential. (See "On Learning Chassidus" for a discussion of thought and speech in terms of the origin of man and other beings, and see also "The Tzemach Tzedek and the Haskalah Movement," p. 114, Note 8.)* [16] Gen. *1:26.* [17] Deut. *10:17.* [18] Psalm *136:2.* [19] Job *1:6.* [20] Tikunei Zohar *speaks of the "concealed" and "revealed" worlds. The "concealed" are those united with Him, having no existence apart from Him. (An analogy is the fish of the sea, who cannot exist outside their element.) The "revealed" worlds appear to exist independently of the Creator. The* yud *and* hai *of G–d's name indicate intellect, which is internal, united with the thinker, hence these letters are related to the "concealed" worlds.* Vav *and the latter* hai *are the extension of the process initiated in the first letter; they relate to "speech," separateness, "revealed" worlds.*

PAGE 390

and "strength" (Zohar II:58a and Nitzutze Orot, *by R. Chaim David Azulay,* a.l.; cf. *infra, note 42); see* Tanya *I, ch. 36.* [11] *Proverbs 31:17.* [12] L. H. [13] *Zohar III:225a.—With respect to the terms "permeates" and "encompasses all worlds" (referring to the immanence and transcendence of G–d) see* Tanya *I, ch. 41, 48, and 51;* ibid., *part II: ch. 7.* Cf. infra, *sect. III, note 12.* [14] *Tikunei Zohar 57:91b; 70:122b.* [15] *See below, note 17.* [16] Cf. *Makot 24a: "Habakuk came and based (all commandments) on one belief"; see* Tanya *I, ch. 33. Thus faith is the foundation of all.* [17] *"World," "year," "soul," are crucial concepts in* Sefer Yetzirah *(see there ch. III:3ff,* et passim). *Generally speaking they represent the concepts of* space *(world),* time *(year), and* life, *or vital force (soul). See* Likutei Torah, *III:64d;* ibid., *IV:74d; V:7b.—Above the author mentioned only "year" and "soul," because "world" was already described in the* "above, below, and all four directions." [18] *Psalms 148:14. This passage, literally, may be translated: "the people that is* His relative!" *See Midrash Tehillim IV:3, 4; also* Likutei Torah *IV:19d.* [19] I.e., *"able to cleave unto Him"; see Deut. 11:22, 30:20; Jos 22:5;* (cf. *Deut. 4:4, 10:20, 13:5; Jos. 23:8, Jer. 13:11).* [20] *Avot IV:17. See* Tanya *I, ch. 4.* [21] *The Divine Indwelling.—See Berachot 17a, and Maimonides,* Hilchot Teshuvah *ch. 8.* [22] *Levit. 16:16 —Paradoxically, the Shechinah itself dwells in this material world, while the (spiritual) world-to-come is a mere "reflection," or a "gleam" of the Shechinah. Thus only in this world can one cleave to the Shechinah itself through "repentance and good deeds." In the world-to-come one can attain no more than the "reflection" of the Shechinah.* Cf. infra, *section VIII, note 23.* [23] *Menachot 29b; see* infra, *section V.* [24] *Psalms 148:13, 14;* cf. *Midrash Tehillim IV:3, 4, and* Likutei Torah *IV:19d.* [25] *Text of benedictions uttered before the performance of many precepts. These words emphasise a special relationship between G–d and Israel; see* Tanya *I, ch. 46;* Likutei Torah, *IV:83c;* cf. *Sefer Habahir, 57 (184).* [26] *Proverbs 27:19: "as waters (reflect) face to face, so is the heart of man to man." In other words, there is an equal reflection and response. See Yalkut Shimoni,* a.l. *(vol. II: towards end of 961), and* Tanya *I, ch. 46 and 49.* [27] *See* Tanya *I, ch. 16 and 38, on the concepts (and the distinction between)* intellectual, *and* natural *awe and love.*

PAGE 392

XXIX. [37] *Zohar II: 121a;* ibid., *85a and III: 81a;* cf. *Genesis Rabba 17: 5.* [38] *The Torah stems from* chochmah *while* chochmah *itself derives from the* Supreme keter *which is also referred to as the* Supreme ratzon. *See above, note 37; Tikunei Zohar 70: 127a; and* cf. Tanya *I, ch. 4.* [39] *Psalms 5: 13.* [40] 'Atarah. [41] *The author refers to his exposition appearing* infra, *section XXIX.* [42] Sifre, *Deut., sect. 343 (on Deut. 32: 2); Song Rabba I,* s.v. משכני*: 1;* Tanchuma, Beracha: 4; cf. *above, note 10. See* Likutei Torah, *III: 39d.* [43] *In the Torah (the "body";* tiferet; cf. *Tikunei Zohar 21: 60a, and 70: 131a).* [44] *Brackets appear in the text.* [45] *Proverbs 31: 18.* [46] *Zohar I: 247b; III: 204a. See also* Mechilta *on Exodus 14: 24, and Zohar Chadash 8a.* [47] Par. *Exodus 13: 9.* [48] Cf. *Zohar II: 63b.* [49] Par. *Deut. 4: 29.* [50] Par. *Lament. 2: 19.* [51] Sifre *on Deut. 6: 5.*

PAGE 396

See also Pardess Rimonim *XXV: 1; R. Menachem Mendel,* Reshimot 'al Kohelet, ad loc., *p. 253;* infra, *sect. XXV, note 63.* [17] *As Abraham signifies the attribute of* chesed *in holiness, so Ishmael signifies the attribute of* chesed *in* kelipah; *see Zohar III: 246b (also* ibid., *124a).* Cf. Likutei Torah *IV: 18a.* [18] Cf. *Chulin 89a, and Midrash Tehilim, ed. Buber, 22: 20, in the editor's glosses, note 99.* [19] Par. *Psalms 126: 3.* [20] Par. *Isaiah 11: 11.* [21] Par. *Jer 6: 9; 31: 6; etc.* [22] Cf. *Rosh Hashana 17a.* [23] Or: *to* whistle *at them;* cf. The Arrest and Liberation (op. cit., *in note 1), p. 65.* [24] Par. *Amos 6: 10.* [25] Cf. *Avot 4: 10.* [26] *Micha 7: 20. Jacob signifies the attribute of* truth *(which corresponds to* tiferet*); see Sefer Habahir 49 (137); Zohar II: 267a; Tikunei Zohar, Intr.: 4b; Zohar Chadash 26c.* Cf. *Genesis Rabba 78: 14; and see* infra, *sect. VI.*

PAGE 398

which are not separate from, but absolutely one with the G–dhead. Torah *and* Mitzvot *thus transcend even the level of the "splendour of the Shechinah." When man performs the* Mitzvot *as they are vested in physical objects (*e.g. Tefillin *of leather;* Tzitzit *of wool;* Tzedakah *with money; etc.), he unites his soul with the* Mitzvot *he performs. His soul is vested in the* Mitzvot; *the* Mitzvot *become garments for his soul.* (Cf. *Genesis Rabba 19: 6) These garments serve like channels, or* kelim *(vessels), by means of which the soul, when in Eden, is able to apprehend Divinity,* i.e. *the splendour of the Shechinah. "The principle of this matter is: just as the soul is given a garment in which it vests itself* (i.e., *the body) in order to exist in this world, so it is given also a garment of the supernal splendour wherewith to exist in the world to come and to be able to gaze in the radiant speculum from that Land of Life," Zohar I: 65bf. See* infra, *sect. XXIX;* cf. Etz Chayim *44: 3;* Tanya *I, ch. 5;* Torah Or, *p. 16af.;* Likutei Torah *III: 38d;* infra, *sect. XXIII.* [6] *Encircling (or:* encompassing*) all worlds; denoting the transcendence of G–d.* [7] *Brackets appear in the text.* [8] *Filling (or:* permeating*) all worlds; denoting the immanence of G–d.* [9] *Chapters 48 and 51. See below, note 12.* [10] *That is, by an appropriate action of man;* cf. infra, *section IV, note 45.* [11] *By R. Chaim Vital, containing the principal teachings of R. Isaac Luria. See* Etz Chayim *I: 2f;* et passim. *See Introduction,* s.v. Tzimtzum. [12] *Creation on all its levels is vitalized and sustained by a Divine Force or Emanation. The life-force is called* or pnimi *(inner light). As the soul animates the body, permeating and vitalizing all its organs, precisely so the* or pnimi *is the soul permeating and vitalizing creation on all its levels. However, just as the soul is but a dimmed manifestation of actual Divinity (see* infra, *sect V, note 53), precisely so it is with the* or pnimi. *The* or pnimi *is but a dimmed manifestation, or radiation, of the actual light of the En Sof. The source of the* or pnimi *is the* or makif *(encompassing light). The* or makif *(also called* or sovev*) is the all-inclusive light which not only permeates (in concealed fashion, by way of* tzimtzum*), but also encompasses or transcends creation.* (Cf. *Introduction,* s.v. Tzimtzum.*)*

The or pnimi *denotes the Divine Immanence: G–d as revealed or manifest in creation. The* or makif *denotes the Divine transcendence: the supra-revelatory aspect of G–d. Both these aspects are succinctly adduced in the Midrashic saying: "The Lord is the place of His world, but His world is not His place!" (Gen. Rabba 68: 9; Zohar III: 242a) In terms of the Sefirot the* or makif *corresponds to* keter, *the supreme, transcendent Sefirah; and the* or pnimi *corresponds to* chochmah, *the basic Sefirah which embodies* keter *and is the immanent foundation of all subsequent emanations. See* ref. *cited* supra, *sect. I, note 13;* infra, *sect. XVII;* Likutei Torah *II: 22c.* [13] *See* Tanya *I, ch. 41. This "unification" establishes the essential one-ness between the ranks of G–d the Transcendent, and the Shechinah (G–d as He manifests Himself, and is immanent in His creatures), so that there is complete unity above and below.* [14] *The three general planes in the soul. See* infra, *section V, note 53.* [15] Cf. infra, *sections XVII and XXIX.* [16] *Kiddushin 39b.* [17] *See Zohar II: 123a; Tikunei Zohar, Intr.: 17a. (See Introduction).*

PAGE 400

4: 4. [34] *Zohar I: 4b; III: 133b;* cf. Etz Chayim *XIII: 14.—370 is the numerical equivalent (*gimatriya*) of* ש"ע*, the root letters of* yeshu'ah *and* vayisha'. [35] *Numbers 6: 25.* [36] *Psalms 67: 2.* [37] *That is, "with our participation"; thus, through an act from ourselves. See* Likutei Torah *IV: 43d.*

PAGE 402

brackets at all. [19] *See* supra, *section II, note 16.* [20] I.e. *the worship*

of G–d, as opposed to the pursuit of worldly matters. [21] *The seven (emotive) attributes* chesed, gevurah, tiferet *etc., are the offsprings of the three intellectual faculties of* chochmah, binah, *and* da'at (cf. Tanya *I, ch. 3)*; da'at *in particular exerts a determinative influence upon the attributes (*cf. infra, section *XV). See also* Tanya *II:8.* [22] *The faculty of the* pnimiyut *of the heart.* [23] *Both of which are rooted in* chochmah. [24] *Proverbs 3:19* [25] "*The Lord* by chochmah *founded the earth,*" *or* "*the Lord* in chochmah" *etc.* Chochmah, *the "hyle" of the creation (*cf. *Introduction,* s.v. Chochmah*)* "*embodies*", *as it were, Divinity. Hence the soul contains a spark of Divinity in its faculty of* chochmah—*which ultimately originates in the Supreme* chochmah. *See* Tanya *I, ch. 18*; cf. Etz Chayim *XLII: 3.*

PAGE 404

does it say 'for הוא' *etc? No doubt that the meaning of this passage is intelligible to all, that is, that* 'for הוא your life' *is a reason given*: why *should you love (the L–rd)*? Because 'He is your life.' " (*Beginning of* Kuntress Hahitpa'alut; *see also* Tanya, *part III, ch. 9.)* [37] *The love spoken of in the verse quoted, which follows after the Divine excision of the heart's thin membrane.* [38] היסח הדעת, *lit. removal (or lack) of* da'at. *The interpretation here is that the lack of* da'at *comes through a transcendence of* da'at *rather than the conventional inference of forgetfulness.* [39] *Sanhedrin 97a.* [40] *Prayer is termed* "*momentary life*" *(*חיי שעה*) because it deals with requests for momentary needs (of the momentary life on earth) in opposition to the study of Torah* (חיי עולם, *eternal life), the benefit of which is not for the moment only but for eternity. (Shabbat 10a, see comment by Rashi and R. Samuel Edelis* a.l.; *though* cf. Kuntress Acharon, *sect. 4).*

PAGE 406

supra, *section II, note 16.* [49] *See* Tanya *I, ch. 37.* [50] Par. *Job 33:28.* [51] *Proverbs 4:23.* [52] *See Rashi on Genesis 42:17.* [53] *The forces of evil; see* supra, *sect. III, note 28.* [54] Cf. Mishna, *Bava Batra 10:7, Shevuot 7:7; Bava Batra 174a; etc.* [55] *The word* שביה *may be traced to the root* שוב to return *(thus reading: her repatriates), or to the root* שבה to capture *(thus reading: her captives).* [56] *The active form of the causative stem of the verb* הלך. [57] Tzedek—*righteousness; charity. Psalms 85:14 is now interpreted to read: charity leads the* pnimiyut *of the heart to G–d.*

PAGE 410

256b, and 258a, (commenting on Proverbs 3:19). See Nachmanides on Gen. I:1: "*The word* bereishit *alludes that the universe was created by the ten Sefirot, and indicates the Sefirah which is called* chochmah *(see below, notes 80–82)*—in which is the foundation of everything, *as it is said:* '*The Lord* in chochmah *founded the earth.*' " *Everything thus is founded in* chochmah, *but the most immediate* "*agent*" *to the egression of the universe into substantiality and manifestation is the last Sefirah*—malchut *(which, of course, ultimately originates in* chochmah*)*; cf. infra, *section VIII, note 43; section XX; and* Tanya *I, ch. 52. The earth, therefore, signifies* malchut, *and likewise does* "the word of the Lord," *the letters of speech (the Ten Fiats) wherewith the world was created. See the Introduction on all this. This is* "abba founded barta." *The author proceeds now to elaborate on this theme.* [23] *Larynx, palate, tongue, teeth, and lips.—See* Sefer Yetzirah *II:3; cf.* Zohar *III:227b, 228a, 295b; Tikunei Zohar, 70:132a;* et passim. [24] ב-ו-מ-פ. [25] *The Hebrew terms for these vowels (*komatz, *and* patach*) imply these very actions of the lips.*

PAGE 412

sound). Hence we see that the root of the formation of speech is not from the emotive attributes only, not even from the apprehended intellect—for the child understands everything and is yet unable to speak. Rather, it issues and is formed from the concealed intellect and the primordium of the intellect in the articulate soul (and as explained in Igeret Hakodesh, *section V).*

And this is the meaning of "abba founded barta." *For from* abba—*which is the essence of the Supreme* chochmah, *which transcends* binah *and the apprehended intellect—thence is the root of speech, which is the aspect of* malchut *of Atzilut, referred to as* barta . . .

In fact, the formation of the nature of the letters as they are in speech originates only in the emotive attributes. But, nevertheless, it is by means of a radiation of chochmah—*which issues into the attributes; and without the radiation from* chochmah *into the attributes the letters would not come into being from the attributes . . .*

Accordingly, it is understood that though the foundation of the letters is (ultimately) only from the rank of chochmah, *nevertheless, the letters are not born, and do not issue from* chochmah, *except, when it passes and issues by way of the attributes.*" — Or Hatorah-Shemot *(Kehot: New York, 1960), p. 40. See also* Tanya *II:8, and* Biurei Hazohar, Beshallach: *p. 44d.* [27] *See R. Menachem Mendel of Lubavitch,* Maamarim *(Kehot: New York, 1957), p. 26;* cf. Tanya *III:4.* [28] *See Tikunei Zohar 22:63b.* [29] *The letters follow this order in all the texts (see* supra, *note 23, and also Zohar I:80a; II:123a; Tikunei Zohar 13b; etc.) with the* hai *following upon the* chet, *even though it comes first in the order of the alphabet. In Zohar II:123a and III:295b this particular sequence is interpreted to follow a distinct pattern, see there.* Cf. *also* H. V. *on this passage.* [30] "*The light letter, to which there is no substance*"; Piyut Akdamut, *verse 6. The letter* hai *is called the light letter or the* "easy letter," *because (being a mere aspirate)* "*its pronunciation does not demand any effort*" *(Genesis Rabba XII:10), and, thus, involves less of*

the breath than all other letters. [31] Barta-malchut. [32] Malchut. Cf. Tikunei Zohar 22:63b, and supra, note 16. [33] This name of G-d forms the first half of the Tetragrammaton, thus, the hai wherewith this world was created would appear to be the first, the "upper" hai. [34] The first letter: chochmah. [35] The second letter (the first, or upper hai): binah. [36] Cf. Tikunei Zohar 22:63b, and see Tanya III Ch. 4. [37] The yud: chochmah. [38] Implementing the chochmah expanded by binah (see Introduction; cf. Tanya I, ch. 3; infra, sect. XV). [39] Introd. 17a; cf. ibid., 22:63b. [40] See the Introduction for an explanation of all these terms and concepts. [41] See Tikunei Zohar 22:63b. [42] The fourth letter (of the Tetragrammaton): malchut. [43] Malchut.—Cf. Tanya III:4. [44] Par. Psalms 145:13.

PAGE 414

source of all subsequent levels, though itself inapprehensible. It is the "soul" of all subsequent levels and, therefore, called neshamah l'neshamah (neshamah of the neshamah). Just as in the creative process concrete and apprehensible manifestation begins at the level of Beriah, and we speak mainly of the lower three worlds, so, too, it is with the gradations of the soul. Neshamah corresponds to Beriah, the Sefirah binah (in which the point of chochmah is vested, expanded, and first apprehended; the upper hai). Ruach corresponds to Yetzirah, and the midot (the attributes of chesed to yesod; the letter vav). Nefesh corresponds to Asiyah, the Sefirah malchut, (the latter hai). More specifically, in man, the neshamah denotes the soul's intellect-powers; ruach, the soul's emotion-powers; nefesh, the soul's outer manifestations or garments, viz. the faculties of thought, speech and action. (See Zohar I:79b ff.; ibid., 245a; Zohar Chadash, 34b, and 78c; Etz Chayim 42:1; Torah Or, Miketz, 42b; cf. also infra, sect. XXVIIb.) The higher ranks of the soul are conceived as latently present in man's nefesh, just as the higher worlds and Sefirot are latently present in the lower ones (by means of successive tzimtzum). By the observance of Torah and Mitzvot, i.e., by the service of G-d as behooves, man merits to attain these higher ranks in ever increasing manifestation. (See Zohar I:206a; ibid., II:94b; Biurei Hazohar, Vayigash, p. 26c ff.)

The different gradations in the soul thus denote different levels. These levels are prevalent within the various worlds as well, for "they all are in the likeness of man." (See R. Chayim Vital, Mevoh She'arim, VI: beg. of part 2; Etz Chayim, VI:2; et passim.) [54] Cf. Zohar I:159a; Tikunei Zohar, Intr.: 14b; etc. [55] See Zohar II:151b-152a; cf. Berachot 55a and comment. of Rashi ad loc. (s.v. אותיות); also, Rashi on Job 28:23. [56] See above, note 45. [57] Sefer Yetzirah IV:12. [58] "Seven stones (=letters) build 5040 houses (=words)." Using the formula of factorial (3 letters: 3×2×1 words; 4 letters: 4×3×2×1 words; 5 letters: 5×4×3×2×1 words; etc.) the immense multitude of possible words is easily grasped.—See the commentary attributed to R. Abraham ibn Daud (on this passage), for the phraseology of "stones" and "houses." [59] By the rules of substitution aleph (first letter) can be substituted by tav (last letter), bet (second letter) by shin (second-last letter), etc. See Shabbat 104a, and the comment by R. Samuel Edelis (Maharsha) ad loc. Cf. Shomer Emunim 1:20-23. [60] There are also other schemes of substitution, e.g. of equally sounding letters; letters that have the same source of articulation; letters with certain numerical relationships; etc. [61] Brackets appear in the text. [62] Tanya, part II (Sha'ar Hayichud). [63] I.e. too finite and limited.

PAGE 416

[82] ראשית—the beginning, i.e. the first Sefirah—see Sefer Habahir 3; Zohar I:3b, 31b, and 256b; Zohar Chadash, Medrash Hane'elam, 3a; see also Targum Yerushalmi on Gen. I:1. [83] See Etz Chayim 8: end of ch. 6; cf. Moreh Nevuchim III:53. [84] See Genesis 2:5 (and cf. note 89, below).—There was no man yet to arouse and elicit the Divine chesed by appropriate actions (i.e. the performance of the commandments). [85] Micha 7:18. [86] Psalms 89:3. [87] Genesis Rabba XII:9; cf. Zohar I:230b.—By a slight permutation בהבראם can be changed to באברהם. [88] Micha 7:20.—Abraham signifies chesed (see supra, sect II, note 9), thus "when He created them," He created them "because of (or: by) Abraham," i.e. out of a motive of chesed. Creation is the effect of G-d's chesed, to actualise the "nature of the Benevolent to do good." (See Introduction.) [89] Genesis 2:15 (see Pirke de R. Eliezer, ch. 12; Targum Yerushalmi and Targum Yonatan, ad loc.; Sifre on Deut. XI:13; Genesis Rabba 16:5; Zohar I:27a; Zohar II:165b; Tikunei Zohar 21:62a; Zohar Chadash 18c).—Man was created to carry out G-d's will, i.e. to perform the commandments of the Torah. When doing so, man elicits the Divine chesed. [90] Cf. above, note 83. [91] Yevamot 109b. [92] Cf. Yevamot 105a; Zohar II:119a; [cf. Sefer Hamaamarim—5708 (Kehot: New York, 1958), in the marginal notes by R. Menachem M. Schneerson on p. 266, end of note 7]. See also Massechet Chibut Hakever (Reshit Chochmah, Sha'ar Hayirah, ch. 12), ch 4f, and R. Judah Loewe, Netivot Olam, s.v. גמ"ח, ch. 2.

PAGE 420

made intelligible in all its details. The words uttered are but vessels that contain, and are able to channel and reveal the detailed ideas of the original, germinal thought. Cf. infra, sect. XX, and note 51 a.l.

Section VI

[1] Verse 18.—Brackets appear in the text. [2] See commentaries by R. Abraham Ibn Ezra and R. Levi Gersonides, a.l. [3] Micha 7:20. [4] Zohar III:131b. [5] See supra,

section II, note 26. [6] *Jacob is the "middle bar that bolts from end to end" (Ex. 26:28), that is the bolt mediating between* chesed *and gevurah, thus* rachamim *or* tiferet*; Zohar II: 175b–176a; also Zohar II: 51b,* et passim. *See Introduction, and* infra, *sect. XV.*

PAGE 424

Par. *Job. 33:30, and* cf. *Psalms 56:14.* [43] Par. *Psalms 117:2; see* supra, *note 36.*

PAGE 428

relating the word שופריה *(beauty) to the root* שפר *(to correct, to cleanse)—as in Job 26:13 (see Ibn Ezra* ad loc.*), and in accordance with the Rabbinic interpretation of Exodus I:5 (quoted by Rashi* ad loc.*).*

PAGE 430

Psalms 118:27. [32] Cf. Zohar *passages cited above (note 30):* "E–l *always denotes an abundant radiation from the Supreme* chochmah" *(which derives from* keter, *the Supreme Will, and is the source of* chesed*).* [33] Par. *Genesis 49:3.* [34] Par. *Numbers 15:16.* [35] *Shabbat 118b.* [36] *That is, every soul is more intimately related to one particular precept than to all the others. Inasmuch as the 613 commandments are the 613 general conduits for eliciting the radiation of the Divine light (see above, and* cf. infra *sect. XXIX), there will, thus, be a difference between the various individuals corresponding to the differences in the more intimate relationships to particular precepts.* [37] *Tikunei Zohar 70: 132a (in the light of* ibid., *p. 131), and R. Chaim Vital,* Sha'ar Hamitzvot, *Foreword; see also* Sha'ar Hagilgulim, *XI;* et passim.*—See further on this subject: Sefer Habahir 58 (195); Zohar II: 100a* ff*; Zohar Chadash 59a.* Cf. *also R. Menasseh ben Israel,* Nishmat Chayim, *IV:6* ff. [38] *The following interpretation of this Talmudic passage by the author (which he received from his master, R. Dov Ber, the* Maggid *of Mezeritch, who in turn heard it from the Baal Shem Tov) will clarify this passage: "Every soul has a particular precept and a particular attribute which it needs to perform and develop. That is the meaning of what R. Joseph asked R. Joseph the son of Rabba: 'With what was your father more heedful (*זהיר*)?' For, after all, one is not to sit and evaluate the commandments of the Torah! But R. Joseph asked 'in what was your father more* זהיר*: in what precept did he have an illumination' (taking* זהיר *as an idiom of* זהר*—to shine; to brighten); not that he observed this precept only, but that the fulfillment of the precept of* Tzitzit*—with great care—gave him power and vitality in the observance of the other precepts." See R. Joseph Isaac Schneersohn of Lubavitch,* Sefer HaSichot*—5700, (Kehot: New York, 1956) p. 22b;* idem., Sefer Hamaamarim *5708, p. 240, and the marginal notes by R. Menachem M. Schneerson,* ad loc. Cf. *Maimonides, Commentary on the* Mishna, *Macot 3:16.* Etz Chayim *49:5.* [39] *Which is also beyond reason and knowledge.—(This is not the conclusion of the letter. In the original there were a few more lines pleading for the support of the Torah-scholars in the Holy Land. This conclusion is reproduced in* Igrot Ba'al Hatanya, *p. 93.)*

PAGE 436

Tikunei Zohar, Intr.: 10b; supra, *section VI, note 21.* [35] *See* supra, *end of section III.* [36] *The celestial model of the terrestrial Holy Land (see below, note 44) signifies* malchut, *the Shechinah;* cf. Pardess Rimonim, *23:1,* s.v. ארץ העליונה. [37] *Malachi 3:12* [Eretz chefetz *signifies* Knesset Yisrael; cf. Pardess Rimonim, *23:1,* s.v. ארץ חפץ; Kitzurim Vehe'arot, *p. 99; R. Shmuel of Lubavitch,* Likutei Torah —Torat Shmuel, *vol. III, ch. 99*]. *(See also the commentaries of R. Solomon ben Adret, and R. Samuel Edelis, on* 'Ayin Ya'akov, *Ta'anit 10a, that* eretz *without qualification refers to the Holy Land; and* cf. Pardess Rimonim, *23:1,* s.v. ארץ.*)* [38] Cf. *Targum Yonatan on Malachi 3:12.* [39] *Another term for Shechinah (see above, note 26). See above, note 37.* [40] Malchut, *(synonymous with Shechinah, and* Knesset Yisrael*).* [41] *Psalms 145:13.* [42] Malchut. [43] Malchut *(Shechinah) embodies the supreme* chochmah, *and causes the worlds to egress into manifest substantiality (see Introduction). Though we speak of* malchut *on various levels, relating to the various worlds, it is* malchut *of Atzilut that is vested in them all. This is the meaning of "Your sovereignty* (malchut *of* Atzilut) *is the sovereignty* (malchut) *of all worlds." See* Tanya *I, ch. 52;* Siddur 'im Pirush Hamilot, *p. 53c, and* cf. Etz Chayim *III:1. See also* infra, *section XX, and* Boneh Yerushalayim, *section 43.* [44] *Everything in the celestial spheres has its corresponding model in the terrestrial world (and* vice versa*), with respect to the general, as well as to the particular parts. (See Zohar I: 156a–b; II: 20a; III: 9b). The sages therefore, speak of the* terrestrial *Holy of Holies, and its* celestial *counterpart; the* terrestrial *Temple, and its* celestial *counterpart; the* terrestrial *Jerusalem etc.;* cf. Yerushalmi, *Berachot IV:5; Song Rabba III:19;* Mechilta, *and Midrashim on Exodus XV:17;* Tanchuma, Pekudei *1, 2; Zohar I:128b; etc. The* terrestrial *Holy Land, or Land of Israel, thus corresponds to the* celestial *one; see Zohar III:84a; and see below, notes 45 and 46.* [45] *The terrestrial Land of Israel is referred to as the "Land of Life" (see Jer. 11:19, and Targum Yonatan* ad loc.*; Ezekiel 26:20, and Targum Yonatan, and commentaries* ad loc., *as well as Avot de R. Natan, ch. 34; Ketubot 111a; etc.) and correspondingly the celestial Land of Israel likewise; see Zohar I: 115a;* ibid., *I: 193a, and III: 84a. See* Pardess Rimonim *23:1,* s.v. ארץ החיים. [46] *"The Eternal will bless you out of Zion" (Psalms 128:5), "for it is the Gate of Heaven" (Rashi; see also the other comment.* ad loc.*) See also Genesis 28:17, and Targum, Rashi,* a.l. *(*cf. *note 44,* supra*). "This is none other than the House of G–d, and this is the*

*Gate of Heaven"—the "Gate to G-d" (Zohar 1:149b), the "Gate assuredly through which the blessings pass downwards" etc. (*ibid., *150b.).* Cf. *also Zohar III:123b, and Ibn Ezra on Gen. 28:12.*

Section IX

[1] Par. *Isaiah 42:18.* [2] Par. *Isaiah 38:16 (see Rashi* a.l.*).* [3] Par. *Jeremiah 2:13;* ibid., *17:13.* [4] Lit.: *the Life of life (see* supra, *sect. IV, note 74).* [5] Par. *Isaiah 10:18.*

PAGE 438

in the glossary notes. [27] בעקבות משיחא, lit. *"on the heels," or "in the footsteps of the Messiah." See* Sotah *49:b, and Rashi* a.l., *for this expression and Etz Chayim 3:2 for its mystical implication.* [28] *Amos 9:11.* [29] *The Hut of David,* i.e. *the Shechinah;* cf. *Zohar II:9a.* [30] Cf. infra, *sect. XXX.—See* infra, *sect. XII, on the notion of the* "act *of charity."* [31] *The "other side," the side of evil and impurity.* [32] Cf. *Zohar I:4a.*

PAGE 440

not to be taken as an integral part of the preceeding, but added to support it, and the following interpretation. [14] *Deut. 33:2.* [15] *See Zohar II:115a Tikunei Zohar, Intr.: 11b. See also Zohar II:118b and III:257a, and Berachot 6a (especially in the light of the following note).* [16] *See Zohar I:26b; Tikunei Zohar Intr.: 17a;* et passim. [17] *See Zohar II:118a; Tikunei Zohar 30:74a;* cf. *Zohar II:85b,* ibid., *165b; Tikunei Zohar 70:131a* ff.*—See* Kitzurim Vehe'arot, *pp. 106* f., *and* cf. *R. Joseph Irgass,* Shomer Emunim, *I:24* ff. [18] *Brackets appear in the text.* [19] Cf. Tanya, *part I: ch. 23 and 37;* ibid., *part III, ch. I.* [20] I.e., *though the Torah originates in* chesed, *it was given to man—"from the Mouth of Gevurah," through the attribute of* gevurah; *see Zohar I:48b, and* Derech Emet a.l. Cf. *Zohar I:240a; II:81a; etc. See further: Zohar II:84a, and* cf. *Tikunei Zohar, Intr.: 6a and 11b.* [21] *Zohar III:255a;* ibid., *257a; Tikunei Zohar 69:105a. —Thus, the above-cited verse means:* "From His right"—*from* chesed, "the fire of the Law"—*is the Torah given through* gevurah; cf. *Zohar II:84a, and the commentaries of R. Moses Nachmanides, and R. Chayim ibn Eter* (Or Hachayim), *on Deut. 32:2. See also Zohar II:206b.* [22] *See* infra, *section XV.* [23] *The aspect of* gevurah.

PAGE 446

Section XI

[1] Par. *Daniel 9:22.* [2] *Job 38:19.* [3] *Proverbs 14:30.* [4] *Avot II:4.* [5] *See Mo'ed Katan 28b, [Zohar I:43b;* ibid., *181a;* et passim. *See also* Biurei Hazohar, Vayera, *11b (in comment on Zohar I:115a)].* [6] *Avot IV:22.* [7] Lit.: *the Former of the Beginning. The latter word, which has a cosmological connotation, is often used and translated as "creation," or "universe." It was left untranslated in the text because there is a play on words (*bereishit *here,* reishit *further on), (See also* Pardess Rimonim, *23:10* s.v. יוצר בראשית, *on this term).* [8] Par. *Psalms 112:10, or Prov. 4:7.* Reishit *(the beginning) is another term for* chochmah *(see* supra, *sect. V, notes 80–82).* Chochmah *is the* ayin *(naught) out of which the creation came into being (see further on, and* cf. *the Introduction).* [9] Tanya, Sha'ar Hayichud, *ch. 1* ff. infra, *section XXV; see* Kuzary *III:11, and* cf. *also Hagigah 12b, and Zohar I:207a.* [10] *See* Tanya *I, ch. 18* f., *and Zohar I:207a. See also Intr.*

PAGE 448

here follows "though he is unable." *A gloss inserted in the text, notes the ambiguity of this phrase and states that it does not appear in some manuscripts. There is another version, which reads* "or whether his desire and wish—*though he is unable*—is to live the true life"—*according to which that phrase is but parenthetical.*

PAGE 460

before the children of man. [32] Cf. *Zohar II:120b.* [33] *Brackets appear in the text.*

PAGE 462

Buber, Yitro*:13.) Thus beautiful is unto us the precept of strengthening, and settling in the Holy Land, which is equivalent unto all the commandments, as explained in* Sifre, *sect.* Reey *(Deut. 80), on the verse "and you will dispossess them, and you will dwell in their land.' (Deut. 12:29) And "Israel will not be redeemed except through charity" (see* supra, *sect. X, note 58)—which they perform with the Lord and with His Holy Land, to rectify the basis of the degeneracy and the blemish, (*i.e.*)—"and they scorned the desirable land" etc. (Psalms 106:24)* A fortiori, *then, it is befitting unto us to uphold (this precept) with great joy and an ardent love, as if but this very day did the spirit of the Lord begin to move us, and this very day did the Lord set His spirit upon us . . ."* [5] Par. *Judges 5:2, and I Chron. 29:5.* [6] *Supreme* chochmah *(see* supra, *section X, note 41).* [7] *Deut. 11:12.* [8] *Proverbs 3:19.* [9] *The "upper earth," or "upper land,"* i.e., *the celestial model of the Holy Land;* cf. supra, *sect. VIII, notes 36 and 44.* [10] *"Land of desire" (Malachi 3:12),* cf. supra, *section VIII, note 37.* [11] *Of the* eretz ha'elyonah. [12] *Land of life; see* supra, *end of section VIII, and notes* ad loc. [13] *Eccles. 7:12.* [14] *See* Pardess Rimonim, *XII:1; also,* ibid., *III:5. —*Cf. *Introduction,* s.v. Chochmah. [15] *See Maimonides,* Hilchot Yessodei Hatorah, *2:10;* Tanya *I, beg. of ch. 2.*

PAGE 466

(mother; or imma 'ilaah, *superior mother), the lower Sefirot are the*

"children": da'at, tiferet, *or the* midot *from* chesed *to* yessod *as a whole, correspond to* ben *(son); and* malchut *to* bat *(daughter; or* imma tataah, *the lower mother); see Zohar III: 290a* ff.; Pardess Rimonim, *8:17. The* midot (chesed *to* yesod) *form a configuration* (partzuf) *called* z'eyr anpin. Malchut *is called the configuration of* malchut, nukvah *(the female), or the "feminine aspect of* z'eyr anpin." *(See* supra, *Introduction,* s.v. Partzufim.) *When the* midot *(the masculine aspect of* z'eyr anpin*) are united with* malchut *(the feminine aspect of* z'eyr anpin*), thus forming one complete* partzuf, *this* zivvug *(conjunctio) results in the "birth" of the effects of the Sefirot the realms, levels, or creatures, emanating therefrom). Every creation or derivation from the Sefirot, thus, presupposes a* conjunctio *of the higher levels. Because the potential creation, as it is in the upper Sefirot* (chochmah *and* binah), *becomes realised and manifest through the lower Sefirot (the* midot *and* malchut*) generally we speak simply of the union of the latter, in terms of* zivvug zu"n. *(See more on this subject* infra, *sect. XX, note 62.)* [10] *Their "brains"; the upper Sefirot,* (chochmah, binah, da'at) *from which the lower Sefirot proceed.* [11] *The second and third highest of the soul-gradations, corresponding to* chochmah *and* binah *(see* supra, *sect. V, note 55). The* mochin *(upper Sefirot) are the soul-forces of the* zu'n *(the lower Sefirot).* [12] *Hindersides; as opposed to* pnimiyut, *inwardness. While* pnimiyut *denotes the very essence, the innermost point,* achurayim *denotes extraneity, the point furthest removed from the essence, thus the lowest grade. (See Introduction,* s.v.) [13] *Vessels; as opposed to* 'atzmut *(essence), or* orot *(lights).* 'Atzmut *and* orot *refer to the infinite Divine essence, and the Divine effulgence and emanation. The* kelim, *in turn, signify the qualitatively finitised screening, contraction, and concealment* (tzimtzum) *of the Divine emanation and life-forces, so that they may become vested in, and animate the finite beings. See* Tanya *II: ch. 4. See also* Etz Chayim *2:3. (Introduction,* s.v.) [14] *The Sefirot of Asiyah thus are the lowest and final rank of the sublime Sefirot of Atzilut—which are divine etc.* [15] *The "masculine" and the "feminine"* (i.e. *the* midot *and* malchut) *of Atzilut.* [16] *Tikunei Zohar, Intr.: 3b; see* infra, *beg. of section XX, and the notes* a.l. [17] *See* Tanya *I, ch. 18, and* supra, *sect. IV, note 25.* [18] *R. Dov Ber, the* Maggid *(Preacher) of Mezeritch (disciple of and successor to the Ba'al Shem Tov, and principal master of the author).* [19] *Genesis 18:27.* [20] *I am dust and ashes.* [21] *See* supra, *sect. II, note 9.* [22] *See* supra, *sect. XIII, note 27.* [23] V.L.: *For therewith he loved.*

PAGE 472

the heaven and in the earth). The Zohar *quotes a* Targum *(see* Nitzutzei Orot *on* Zohar *III: 257a) translating: "for it (*i.e. כל, *the Sefirah* yessod*) is united with (or unites) the heaven* (tiferet) *and the earth* (malchut; Knesset Yisrael). *See Zohar I: 31a; II: 116a; III: 257a; Tikunei Zohar, Intr.: 9b. See also Zohar I: 149a–b, and* cf. Pardess Rimonim, *23:11, and 15,* s.v. כי כל, *and* סולם; Likutei Torah—Torat Shmuel, *vol. III, ch. 54.* [52] *Brackets appear in the text.* [53] *These words do not appear in the quotation in* Or Hatorah *(see* supra, *note 38).*

PAGE 476

s.v. הוד).—Hod *has a connotation of majesty and splendour referring to the Divine splendour and majesty inherent in G–d's creation. This innate splendour and beauty makes creation becoming and befitting G–d. The awareness of* hod *as the innate Divine beauty should lead to* hod *in the sense of acknowledging, praising and thanking G–d. And these are the modes of attitude or behaviour utilising the attribute of* hod *in the service of G–d.* [84] *The righteous is the foundation of the world (Proverbs 10:25); the attribute of* yesod. [85] Lit.: *the Life of life (*cf. supra, *sect. IV, note 74).* [86] *See* Likutei Torah—Torat Shmuel, *vol. III, ch. 55.*

PAGE 478

proceed from, and succeed chochmah *and* binah, but keter. *This is the faculty of* da'at 'elyon. *On this level* da'at *unites the point of* chochmah *with* binah, *by a radiation from* keter. *This is the essential, or original union of these Sefirot so that* chochmah *may be externalised in* binah. *That this union may bear offsprings,* i.e. *that the radiation from* chochmah *and* binah *will extend into the lower Sefirot (the* midot*) to irradiate them, this is the function or faculty of* da'at tachton. *See* Etz Chayim *8:3*f.; Torah Or, Toldot, *19a* f., *and* Mishpatim, *75b;* Likutei Torah *V: 30*f.; supra, *Introduction,* s.v. Da'at, and Body of Sefirot. [98] *The widths (or expansions) of the river* (binah); *Zohar III: 142a (on Gen. 36:37). See* Sha'arei Orah, *ch. VIII,* s.v. רחובות הנהר; Boneh Yerushalayim, *sect. 1; and* cf. *Zohar I: 141b.*

Section XVI

[1] Lit.: *the hardships of the times are not concealed from me.*

PAGE 484

cending chochmah *and its apprehension in Eden (*cf. *supra, sect. III, note 12).* [30] *Brackets appear in the text.* [31] *Isaiah 60:21.* [32] *Bava Batra 75b.* [33] *See* supra, *section VII, note 7.* [34] Kadosh, *holy, thus refers to* keter, *the Sefirah which is separate and distinct from the Sefirot transcending them all. (See Introduction.)* Chochmah, *in itself also distinct and inapprehensible* (ibid), *is also referred to as "holy" (see* supra, *sect. X note 41). In that context* keter *is then called* kodesh hakedoshim, *the "holy of holies,"* i.e. *the essential, absolute holiness. See Zohar II: 121a.*

PAGE 486

Tanya *I, for the meaning of this term, esp. ch. 1, 10, 14, 35)*]. [7] *It is the love attained by the* tzadikim *only.— See* Chovot Halevovot, Sha'ar Ahavat Hashem, *ch. 4;* Tanya, *author's Intr. to part II.* [8] *See Zohar III: 39a;* ibid., *88b, and 177b, in the light of Zohar II: 25b.* Cf. *also Zohar II: 57a, and see R. Joseph Isaac Schneersohn,* Sefer Hamaamarim *5710 (New York 1960), pp. 4ff. and 54f.*

PAGE 488

I Samuel 25: 29. See Likutei Torah, *III: 51d (and references* ad loc.*);* infra, *sect. XXIX.* [21] Par. *Psalms 73: 28, and Isaiah 58: 2.* [22] *Forces of evil. The* chitzonim, brought about by sin, separate man from *G–d; see Isaiah 59: 2; Zohar II: 116b, and Tikunei Zohar, 69: 108b.* Cf. *Sefer Habahir 58(196).* [23] *Referring to "the wicked are full of remorse" (*Shevet Mussar, *ch. 25;* cf. *Nedarim 9b); see* Tanya *I, ch 11.* [24] *The realm of evil (*cf. infra, *section XXV, note 39).* [25] *See Sotah 3a.* [26] *Seat of thought.* [27] *Seat of speech.* [28] *Seat of action.* [29] *Isaiah 42: 7*—I.e. *this love, from the dominion of the* kelipah. [30] *Amos 2: 16;* cf. *commentaries by R. Abraham Ibn Ezra, and R. David Kimchi,* ad loc.

PAGE 490

infra*).* [6] *The* partzuf *of* abba. [7] *Text corrected according to* L. H. [8] *The* partzuf *of* imma *(the supreme mother).* [9] Chesed *to* malchut. [10] Microprosopus *(the small, or lesser countenance).—The ten Sefirot form a configuration* (partzuf) *analogous to the image of man (consisting of the ten general categories of the Sefirot; 248 "organs" and 365 "sinews"). The principal, or general* partzuf *subdivides into five configurations: 1.* Keter*—the* partzuf *of* arich anpin *(including the aspect of* atik yomin *(or* atika kadisha*) the very original emanation—see Introd., note 56). 2.* Chochmah*—the* partzuf *of* abba*; 3.* Binah*—the* partzuf *of* imma*; 4. The* Midot *(*chessed *to* yessod*; generally referred to by the all-inclusive principle of* tiferet*)—the* partzuf *of* z'eyr anpin *(sometimes referred to as the masculine aspect of* z'eyr anpin*); 5.* Malchut*—the* partzuf *of* nukva *(the female; sometimes referred to as the feminine aspect of* z'eyr anpin*). Each of these* partzufim *again compounds the levels of the ten Sefirot and the 613 aspects, though the Sefirah by which it is called is the dominant sphere of that configuration. All five proceed from, and succeed each other in this order as different modes of Divine manifestations. Each one has two general aspects:* pnimiyut *(analogous to the relation from soul to body), and* chitzoniyut *(analogous to the relation from body to soul).— See Introduction,* s.v. Partzufim. [11] *The Torah as given to Moses, though originating in the Supreme* chochmah, *is itself on the lower level of* z'eyr anpin, *or* tiferet, Cf. infra, *sect. XX.*

PAGE 496

ibid., *32: 8 and 37: 1.* [53] *The aspects of* Asiyah*—Action, or making.* [54] *Deuteronomy 7: 11; see Eruvin 22a.* [55] *Kidushin 40b,* [56] Yerushalmi *Berachot I: 2;* ibid., *Shabbat I: 2; Levit. Rabba 35: 6;* cf. infra, *section XX.* [57] *See* supra, *section VII, note 37.*

PAGE 500

note 33. [20] *See Ezekiel I: 10. This is the most sublime spiritual aspect, or archetype, which on the manifest level of the material world reflects itself in the form of animal-hood.* [21] *See Zohar III: 240b* ff.*;* cf. Likutei Torah *of R. Isaac Luria, section* Vayikra. [22] Lit.*: the sacred tongue.* [23] *Zohar Chadash Bereishit 17b; Maimonides,* Moreh Nevuchim *III: 10; Nachmanides on Genesis I: 1;* cf. *Sefer Habahir 10 (13)* [*Zohar I: 263a*]. *The word* בריאה *thus denotes an actual creation* ex nihilo. [24] *Zohar I: 11b.* [25] *According to the doctrine of* tzimtzum *(see Introduction) the "void" or primordial space, in which the worlds are created, is illuminated by a* kav *(gleam, or ray) of the light of the En Sof. This* kav *is the essence of the Sefirot and vivifies everything within the primordial space.* [26] *Chapter 3.*

PAGE 502

1 and 2). [30] *The transitionary evolution from one world to the next, the lower one, is always through the lowest stage* (malchut) *of the higher, which becomes the highest stage* ('atik, or keter) *of the lower world (see below, note 46). Thus, implicit in* malchut of Atzilut *are the* kelim *which are the conduits for the vivification from Atzilut to Beriah, Yetzirah, and Asiyah. Generally speaking there are three types of* kelim, *each consisting of ten: the ten* pnimiyim *(the innermost* kelim *of* malchut of Atzilut*) become the soul for Beriah; the ten intermediary* kelim *become the soul for Yetzirah; and the ten* chitzoniyim *(the most outward* kelim *of* malchut of Atzilut*) become the soul for Asiyah. See* Etz Chayim *30: 2, and 44: 2;* Likutei Torah *IV: 69a.* [31] *Shrines.* [32] *Circles.—The Sefirot as they emanate, follow an ordered pattern of gradual evolution, but not a singular scheme only. In the writings of R. Isaac Luria, where their evolution is intricately interwoven with the doctrine of* tzimtzum, *they are explained to egress via the* kav *which irradiates the primordial space of the* tzimtzum, *first as circles (within, throughout, and parallel to the circle of the void), one circle within the other, connected only by the* kav *(which is also their connection with the En Sof). These circles are called the* 'iggulim. *This is the scheme in which the Sefirot proceed from, and succeed each other. The* iggulim *are paired with the subsequent, superior scheme, called* yosher *(the scheme usually referred to in the* Zohar *etc.).* Yosher *(straightness; evenness) is the emanation of the Sefirot in the form of a* partzuf *("*chessed *the right arm;* gevurah *the left arm" etc.; Tik. Zohar, Intr.: 17a), along the* kav, *and culminating in the centre of the primordial space. (See* Etz Chayim, *I: 2ff;* Sha'ar Hahakdamot, hakdamah *4ff). See Introduction,* s.v.

Body of the Sefirot, *and* Partzufim. [33] *R. Schneur Zalman, on the authority of R. Moses Nachmanides (*cf. Sha'ar Hagemul, *in comment on Psalms 104:4), states that the angels are composed of body and soul, matter and form. (See* Torah Or, *4b;* Likutei Torah *IV:98a;* Siddur, Sha'ar Hachanuka, *275d). The angelic body and matter are explained to consist of the root-elements of fire and air, thus extremely subtle and diaphanous and in no way comparable to the cruder forms of matter as we know it. (*Cf. Moreh Nevuchim *II:26, and see below, the quotation from* Sefer Hanikud.*) This view, opposed to that of Maimonides (see* Hilchot Yesodei Hatorah *II:3*ff.*;* Moreh Nevuchim *I:49), finds support in the philosophy of R. Salomon ibn Gabirol (see his* Mekor Chayim, *esp. part IV;* cf. *R. Isaac Abarbanel on II Kings III:3); probably in the thought of R. Judah Halevi (see* Kuzary *IV:3, and the lengthy remarks by R. Judah Muscatto, in his commentary* Kol Yehudah, ad loc.; *see also* Kol Yehudah *on* Kuzary *III:11); Ibn Ezra; with R. Shem Tov ibn Shem Tov (*Sefer Haemunot *IV:1*ff.*, quoted partly by R. Moses Cordovero in his* Pardess Rimonim *VI:6); and generally with the Cabbalists—see* Pardess Rimonim *XXIV:11*f.*, 15, and* Etz Chayim, *50: end of ch. 8. (See also Zohar III:225a,* and cf. *Zohar I:136b.) See also R. Bachya ibn Pakuda,* Chovot Halevavot *I:6; R. Abraham ibn Daud,* Hassagot *on* Hilchot Teshuvah *8:2; R. Isaiah Horowitz,* Shaloh Beassara Maamorot, *ch. 2. From R. Shneur Zalman it would appear that (like Ibn Gabirol) he is of the opinion that all angels are composed thus, inasmuch as he mentions in that category even the angels of Atzilut. From the* Zohar, *Nachmanides and R. Isaac Luria, it would seem that they are of the opinion that not all angels have bodies. In* Zohar Chadash*: 8d, the term separate intelligences (see above, note 18) is used in relation to angels, and as appears from the context, to angels of Beriah (though* cf. *Zohar III:225a). Nachmanides, too, makes frequent use of this term, and sometimes adds "the separate intelligences,* i.e. *the angels,"—see his commentary on the Pentateuch, on Exodus XX:3 (*cf. *also* ibid. *Numbers 22:23); furthermore, in* Sha'ar Hagemul (ad loc. cit.), *he speaks of the angels that are "beneath the Divine throne" (thus beneath Beriah!). R. Isaac Luria, who, in* Etz Chayim *50:8, speaks explicitly of the composite nature of the angels, states elsewhere (*ibid., *26: end of ch. 1) equally explicitly that "there are angels which are not on a rank of corporeality, for they do not become vested in a body, they are a chariot (!) unto the Holy One, blessed is He, and superior to the* neshamah.*" According to the* Zohar (cf. *I:34a; Zohar Chadash: 10a), Nachmanides, and R. Isaac Luria, there are, thus, two general types of angels (a distinction which can be found in Maimonides too,* cf. Moreh Nevuchim *II:6; and* cf. *also* Kuzary *IV:3, and comment.* ad loc.*), the higher one of which is referred to as "abstract intellects." On the other hand, R. Joseph Gikatilla writes that "even among the supernal abstract intelligences that are called angels, there is not one that is simple without any plurality. Though the philosophers called the angels abstract intellects and abstract forms, nevertheless, though they are devoid of such matter as our matter, they also possess a simple, diaphanous supernal form of matter which is incomparable to our matter." (*Sefer Hanikud, *III:3; quoted in* Torah Shelemah, *vol. XVI, pp. 301*f.) *R. Shneur Zalman also uses the term "separate intelligences," and accepts the standard definition thereof as given by Maimonides (see* Likutei Torah *III:46a), but he applies it to the supernal worlds; see* Likutei Torah *III:45a (*cf. *Maim.,* Hilchot Yesodei Hatorah *III;9, and* Moreh Nevuchim *II:5). See further on this subject:* Sefer Yetzirah *I:12, and the comment.* ad loc.; Tanya *I, ch. 39f.;* Biurei Hazohar, Beshallach, *40b–c;* Boneh Yerushalayim, *end of sect. 58, and sect. 59; R. Menachem M. Schneerson of Lubavitch,* Elul-Likut, *(Kehot; 1954), p. 7; etc.* [34] *Job 4:18.* [35] *See* Moreh Nevuchim *III: end of ch. 13, on this verse, (though, unlike Maimonides, R. Shneur Zalman retains the literal sense of "angels").* [36] *The* conjunctio *in a mode of kissing. This most sublime, and highest form of a union, also called the* conjunctio *in a mode of* panim *to* panim, *refers to the* conjunctio *and most absolute union of the essence of the* partzuf *of* abba *with the essence of the* partzuf *of* imma.*—See* Etz Chayim, *15:1; ibid., 39:4, and 9.* [37] *Emended according to* L.H. [38] *The* conjunctio *of the masculine and the feminine. This refers to the union of the* partzuf *of* z'eyr anpin *and the* partzuf *of* malchut. *(See Introduction; and* supra, *sect. XV, note 9.)* [39] *Brackets appear in the text.* [40] *The souls withdrew,* i.e., *the* tzadikim *died before they could sin.* Cf. *Zohar I:56b; II:10b; Zohar Chadash: 19d* ff*; Eccles. Rabba, VII:32 Rashi in his commentaries on Genesis V:24, and Job 4:18.* [41] *See Zohar III:128b.*—Gulgalta, *the skull, refers to the topmost level, the Sefirah* keter. *The passage thus refers to the levels of* keter *of* arich anpin *and* keter *of* z'eyr anpin. [42] *Skull and Beard of the Supernal* Partzuf *(see Zohar III:128b, and 130*ff.*). The Divine light emanates by way of the thirteen general "tufts" (corresponding to the thirteen attributes of the Divine Compassion, Exodus 34:6, 7;* cf. infra, *sect. XXVIII, notes 33*f.*) of the* dikna *(the Beard).* [43] Lit.: *the sort of luminary (*ma-or*).*

PAGE 504

feminine aspect, i.e. malchut.*—See* Etz Chayim, *5:3.* [53] Cf. Tanya *I, ch. 52;* supra, *section V, note 22.* [54] *Of the Sefirot and all spheres.* [55] Sefer Yetzirah *I:7.* [56] *See* supra, section *XVII, note 28.* [57] *Tikunei Zohar, Introd.: 17a.* [58] Keter *thus has two aspects: that of* keter, *the Royal Crown, symbolising the highest level of the lower realm; and that of* malchut, *the lowest level of the superior realm.* [59] *From below Atzilut, towards Atzilut.* [60]

Keter *of Beriah.* [61] *The creation of the souls in Beriah by* malchut of Atzilut. [62] *Before proceeding with this intricate passage, an explanation of the relevant terms and concepts is in place. It has been pointed out (*supra, *sect. XV, note 9) that the Cabbalah makes extensive use of anthropomorphic metaphors and analogies, using terms that describe physical objects or processes to denote spiritual ones. Such is the case in this passage as well. On the terrestrial level there are various terms and concepts related to birth. There are the categories of the* male *and the* female, *the former influencing, or emanating to the latter. The female is impregnated by the male. A* seed *of the male is implanted in the* womb *of the female. This seed originates in the* brain *of the male; originally it is a most subtle, nearly spiritual substance, but as it descends to the point of actual egression it becomes ever more* material. *When the seed is implanted,* conception *takes place, and an embryo develops. During the ensuing period of* pregnancy, *the embryo grows and develops into a foetus, nourished and sustained by the mother's nourishment and sustenance. This development continues until the moment when the foetus is ready for* birth. *With the birth of the foetus, we have the actual revelation and egression into manifest reality of the hitherto concealed foetus. Moreover,* birth *means the actual revelation and egression into manifest reality of the rudimentary plant contained in the seed. One thing more: the perfect health of both parents, the perfect condition of their reproductive organs, is not yet an assurance that conception and reproduction will actually take place. Procreation is dependent on* Divine intervention. *G–d is, as it were, a partner with the parents, and it is the Divine blessing or "participation" which makes possible the birth of the child. (See Kiddushin 30b; Niddah 31a; Zohar III:291b.) Analogous to the process culminating in actual birth is the coming into being of spiritual categories such as the soul. The essence of the soul is its own "soul," the spark of Divinity, the light of the En Sof. This Divine "point" is posited first in* keter *and thence in* chochmah. *It is the highest level of* chochmah; *the* mochin, *the brain. As* chochmah, *the configuration of* abba, *unites with* binah, *the configuration of the supreme* imma, *the seminal point of En Sof is posited in the "womb" of* binah *("the dot in the palace";* cf. supra, *sect. V, note 15), where it develops by way of expansion. In* binah *it is vested with wider dimensions which simultaneously make it more "tangible" by dimming the full force of its radiation. From this* conjunctio *of* abba *and* imma *is born the configuration of* z'eyr anpin, *the* midot chesed *to* yesod. *This progeny, as it is in Atzilut, is still absolute Divinity: En Sof immensely screened and contracted, on a plane of creativity. The original seminal spark of En Sof, which on this plane is successively more contracted than it is on the higher planes, is then "posited" in the configuration of* malchut, *the lower* imma. *The* conjunctio *of* z'eyr anpin *and* malchut *thus leads to a new conception in the "womb" of the lower* imma. *All the creative potentialities of the higher Sefirot, the "rudimentary plant of the seed," the* alma deitkassya *(concealed world), are now posited in* malchut *where they develop in the process of "pregnancy" from their total concealment to the point of their manifestation or "birth". That is why* malchut *is called the "sea into which all the rivers (the Sefirot) stream and pour their potentialities." In* malchut *all the possible creations are still hidden and concealed, just as the waters of the sea cover and conceal all the creatures of the sea. Within the womb of* malchut, *during the period of pregnancy, the potential creatures are "nourished and sustained" by the nourishment and sustenance of* malchut *itself, viz. the lights and emanations of the higher Sefirot that issue into it. Now, when it comes to the point of "birth," the point that the* alma deitkassya *(concealed world) should become an* 'alma deitgalya *(manifest world) that is a finite and distinct entity, this cannot be effected by a simple, progressive and causal development of the Sefirot. Such a development of a gradual descent from higher to lower, is unable to produce so radical an effect. The "intervention" of something more than that, of a much more sublime category, is necessary. Birth, the "opening of the womb" to allow the concealed world to egress into manifestation, is made possible by an issue and radiation into* malchut *from the all-encompassing plane of* atik (keter; or makif), *the transcendent G–dhead. When the* or makif *thus unites with the* or pnimi *as it is in* malchut, *the potentialities of the* or pnimi *become actualised in manifest creation. The birth is referred to as the "splitting of the sea" (as the splitting of the sea that took place on the seventh day after the Exodus from Egypt): the sea,* i.e. malchut, *or the womb of* malchut, *is "split" to allow the egression of the foetal creatures. As the sea is split and a dry passage is produced, the hitherto hidden sea-creatures now become manifest. The conception in the womb of* malchut *alluded to in* Shmini Atzeret, *the Festival of the eighth day of* Succot. *The special liturgy of that day deals with the descent of rain, and from* Shmini Atzeret *until Passover we recite the prayer* morid hageshem *(who causes the rain to descend). The term* Shmini Atzeret *means the Eighth Day of Assembly or Ingathering. The word "eighth" alludes to the eighth Sefirah in reverse order, thus* binah. Atzeret *refers to the ingathering of* binah *(*alma deitkassya*) in* malchut, *alluded to by* morid hageshem. *Moreover, the word* geshem *means not only rain, the Heavenly downpour, but also matter; in the latter sense it alludes to the increasing materialisation of the seminal drop as it descends from the* mochin *of* abba *to the womb of* malchut, *and thence into actual manifestation. Thus* Shmini Atzeret *is referred to as the point of* conception. *The period during which we say the prayer* morid hageshem *(from* Shmini Atzeret *to Passover) is the period of* pregnancy. *The time of the Splitting of the Sea, the Seventh Day of Passover, is the point of* birth. *At that point Atzilut gives birth to Beriah and the creatures therein. All this again indicates the intricate relationship between* keter *and* malchut: *"their beginning is wedged into their*

end, and their end into their beginning." [63] *Zohar II: 52b.* [64] *The* midot, chesed *to* yesod, *and* malchut.

PAGE 506

terial). What is protruding from the seal (lower in the seal), appears engraved (less tangible and material). Likewise, the more sublime the source of origin above, the lower it descends and appears inferior below; and vice versa. *Thus in essence the* Mitzvot *are on a higher plane than the Torah; the Torah merely explains the* Mitzvot. *On the revelatory plane, however, they appear lower (as* malchut*) and the Torah higher (as* tiferet, *or* z'eyr anpin*).* [79] Sefer Yetzirah *I: 7.* [80] *The power of the blessed En Sof vested in* malchut *makes it possible to create* ex nihilo. [81] Lit.*: by means of cause and effect.* [82] Liturgy, *Hymn of* Lecha Dodi. [83] *Berachot I: 2; Shabbat I: 2.* [84] *Study of Torah.* [85] *Observance of a commandment.* [86] *See references, supra,* note *83; and Levit. Rabba 35: 6.* [87] *On the revelatory plane the commandments are related to physical objects and corporeal functions.* [88] I.e., *related to man's mind and intellect.* [89] *The commandments.* [90] *The Torah.—The study of Torah, thus, has a certain advantage over the* Mitzvot; *see references,* infra, *note 91.* [91] Cf. Tanya, Kuntress Acharon, *sect. IV;* Likutei Torah, *II: 33a* ff., *III: 13a* ff. *and 17a* ff.

PAGE 520

7: 8. Cf. *Jeremiah 2: 27;* etc. [41] *Berachot 5a.* [42] *See* ibid., *and Zohar III: 57b.*

PAGE 524

Also: Arachin *15b, and Maimon.,* Hilchot De'ot *VII: 3.* [79] *So much the worse when in thought.* [80] Cf. Tanya *I, ch. 16;* Torah Or, Yitro, *71a;* Likutei Torah *III: 51d-f;* et passim. [81] Par. Liturgy, Amidah *(*par. *Psalms 29: 11).*

Section XXIII

[1] *Daniel 4: 14;* cf. *Pessachim 33a.* [2] *Avot III: 6.* [3] Par. *Eccles. 12: 13.* [4] Par. Liturgy, *prayer of* Alenu *(*cf. *Isaiah 33: 16).* [5] Par. *I Kings 8: 27;* etc. [6] *Numbers 35: 34.*

PAGE 540

side; the realm of evil. [43] Cf. *Isaiah 25: 8. See Zohar I: 54a; also* ibid., *29a, and 34a;* et passim.

PAGE 552

Torah, *IV: 5.* [25] Cf. *Zohar III: 238b.* [26] *The fourth of the six orders of the* Mishnah, *dealing with torts.—Berachot 20a.* [27] *Rosh Hashana 35a.*

PAGE 564

Likutei Torah *III: 32d. And* cf. ibid. *IV: 57c.* [119] H.V.—Par. *2 Chronicles 32: 1.* [120] *See* Etz Chayim, *49.*

Section XXVII

[1] *Emended according to* L.H. *(Text states: "what he wrote to the inhabitants of the Holy Land" etc., but that is an obvious printing-mistake; see* infra, *note 41).* [2] I.e. *doubly and helpfully.—*Par. *Job 11: 6.* [3] Par. *II Kings 4: 9.* [4] *See Berachot 28b.* [5] *Known as R. Mendel of Vitebsk (or Horodoky), of the leading disciples of R. Dov Ber, the* Maggid *of Mezeritch. After the* Maggid's *demise, R. Shneur Zalman accepted his former colleague as his master. In 1777 R. Mendel ascended to the Holy Land, ultimately settling in Tiberias where he founded and led the Chassidic community. There he passed away, and was buried, on the 1st day of Iyar 5548 (1788). His teachings, letters etc., were published under the titles* Pri Haaretz; Likutei Amarim; Pri Ha'etz. [6] V.L. *(see* infra, *note 41) has instead of* etc.—"*who stand on Torah, and worship, and the 'service of* tzedakah, *quietness and surety forever . . .'*" *(*Par. *Avot I: 2; Isaiah 32: 17—*cf. supra, *sect. XII.)* [7] *Isaiah 38: 16.* [8] Par. *Psalms 133: 3.* [9] *As opposed to "seed of falsehood"—Isaiah 57: 4.*

PAGE 566

Isaiah 29: 23.—Disciples are regarded as their master's "children" and the "work of his hands"; see Sanhedrin 19b and 99b. [30] Par. *Isaiah 2: 3 (also: Micha 4: 2).* Cf. *Zohar II: 215a and III: 87b* f. [31] *Part III: 71b;* cf. *Chulin 7b.* [32] *Deut. 7: 11; see Eruvin 22a.* [33] *Psalms 97: 11.* [34] *The Garden of Eden (see Genesis 27: 27, and Rashi* ad loc.; infra, *note 62).—See Chagigah 12a; and* infra, *sect. XXIX, note 20.* [35] Par. *Proverbs 8: 26.* [36] Par. *Isaiah 35: 8.*

PAGE 574

ing to L.H. [32] *The* partzuf *of abba (the Sefirah* chochmah*).* [33] Etz Chayim, Sha'ar Hakelalim: *5; ibid., 14: end of ch. 3, and 8;* et passim.—Abba *draws from the eighth of the thirteen attributes of mercy* (Exodus *34: 6* f.) *Both the eighth (related to* abba*) and the thirteenth of the attributes (related to* imma; binah*) are referred to as* mazal, *because "everything depends and derives* (mazley)" *from them. The eighth attribute is regarded as the most important one and, accordingly, termed the "superior* mazal," *while the thirteenth attribute is termed the "inferior* mazal." *See Zohar II: 177a; III: 134a* f. *and 289a* f. Cf. *Nachmanides on Genesis 24: 1.* [34] *The thirteen attributes are referred to as the "thirteen tufts of the* dikna *(Beard)"; see* ref. *cited* supra, *note 33 (and* cf. *sect. XX, note 42).* Notzer chesed *(He guards* chesed*) is the eighth attribute according to the interpretation of the Zohar and the Cabbalists; see R. Menachem M. Schneerson,* Likutei Sichot, *vol. IV,*

pp. 1348 f., *on the varying enumerations of the thirteen attributes.* [35] *Will; or Favour.* Likutei Torah *of R. Isaac Luria,* Toldot *(on Gen. 25:21), and* Ki Tissa *(on Ex. 34:7);* cf. *Zohar III:289a.—See Responsa by R. Menachem M. Schneerson,* Kovetz Lubavitch *III:1 (New York, 1946), p. 6b.* [36] Lit.: *the Time of Will (or Favour). Auspicious time.* [37] Lit.: *the* tzadikim *of the Most High.* [38] *See Zohar I: 124b;* cf. *Tikunei Zohar, Intr. 10b, and Zohar III:263b; Berachot 61b. See* infra, *sect. XXXII, note 18.* [39] *Brackets appear in the text.* [40] *See Zohar I:124b.* [41] *See* supra, *sect. XIX, note 34.* [42] Par. *Proverbs 16:26* (cf. *Isaiah 53:11); see Sanhedrin 99b.* [43] Cf. supra, *sect. XXVII.* [44] Par. *Psalms 103:17.* [45] Par. *Psalms 74:12.*

PAGE 580

Tik.: 93c. Cf. supra, *sect. V.* [29] *Zohar II:85a; see* supra, *sect. XIX, note 34.* [30] *Zohar II:90b;* supra, *sect. XXIII, note 23.* [31] Lit.: *the savants of the truth.* [32] *The numerical value* (gimatriya) *of keter is 620.* [33] *See* Massechet Atzilut, *near the end; R. Shem Tov ibn Shem Tov,* Sefer Haemunot, *IV:7; R. Moses,* Cordovero, Pardess Rimonim *8:3; and* Shiur Komah, *ch. 93,* s.v. כתר *and* רצון; Tanya, I, *ch. 53.*

PAGE 588

145:13; see supra, *sect. VIII, note 43.* [22] *See* supra, *sect. XX, and note 53* ad loc. [23] Malchut. [24] *Shrines.* [25] Daniel *7:10.* [26] Cf. supra, *end of sect. IV, and sect. XII.* [27] *Great is the Lord and highly to be praised, and to His greatness there is no searching; Psalms 145:3.* [28] *The Shechinah;* malchut.

Section XXXI

[1] Lit.: *well-known in the gates;* par. *Proverbs 31:23.* [2] Cf. *Zohar II:189a–b.* [3] *Between holy and profane;* Liturgy, Havdalah *(*par. *Levit. 10:10). A phrase used to emphasise the essential distinction between the subject, and object of the metaphorical analogy.* [4] Cf. *Levit. 17:11.* [5] Par. *Eccles. 1:6.*

PAGE 594

expression of G–d's will, the concretisation of His thoughts, or wisdom. Mortal intelligence is dimensioned, limited, while G–d's, as infinite as He is, is the Higher Wisdom.. The profound scholarship of Torah would be the obvious means for man's puny intelligence binding itself to G–d's, but how can this be the case with narratives that do not strain even mortal intellect?

PAGE 596

"*Know, that what is Above, is from* you." [3] *An innate love and fear of G–d are endowed to all Israel, concealed in the recesses of heart and mind. These are not products of his efforts, but a heritage. The love is compared to a child's devotion to his father, and the fear to the dread of separation from G–d, as through apostacy. All of Torah and mitzvot, including martyrdom, may be fulfilled with the stimulus of these endowed, latent, unconscious emotions without their ever becoming felt in the heart. Only the mind is aware that a certain act divorces man from G–d, or binds him to G–d. Man's involvement in arousing this degree of intellectual awareness is minimal; his devotion and even readiness for sacrifice are "natural" in that he did not create these latent feelings of love and awe that result in his choice of good and rejection of evil. All he need do is realise the consequences of his actions, and call them to mind. The Torah and mitzvot of this person ascend to Yetzirah, the world of emotion, of innate capacities. (It must be made emphatically plain here, that his choice between self-gratification and devotion to G–d, between "good" and "evil," has been unimpeded. He may as readily choose one as the other. Of his volition he chooses G–d; he chooses to awaken endowed strengths he possesses by inheritance, but* he *chooses.) There is a superior state. With all the resources of mind at his command, he meditates on G–d's greatness and infinitude, on his own insignificance. This entails tremendous intellectual effort, and his mind does eventually comprehend all it is capable of grasping of G–d's greatness. He will even affirm, in his* mind, *that he should be filled with a profound longing, to the point of expiration, with a blazing consuming love of G–d. But this is all in the mind, not a conscious emotion. His* heart *is not filled with love (or awe). He will observe all G–d demands of him, in thought, speech, and deed. His motivation, his stimulus, is intellectual, lodged in the mind only. The emotions are still latent, but his thought is "good," as the Sages say, "G–d joins a good thought to deed." The "good thought" elevates the deed of Torah study and mitzvah observance to Beriah, the realm of intellect. There is a still higher plane of attainment available, Rabbi Schneur Zalman asserts, to all—arousing a conscious tangible love and awe, bringing the latent emotion into a feeling manifest in the heart. What his mind understands, his heart actually feels. These emotions are not mere endowments—they are his works, results of his efforts. Chabad teaches the sequence of intellect and emotion, the latter elicited by the mind. This "intellectual" love and fear is the emotion engendered by the intellect, man's own striving and efforts. Torah and mitzvot resulting from this state ascend to Beriah, but of their "own" accord, because they deserve that exaltation. Love and fear are the "wings" that elevate them, as we shall soon see. Atzilut is unity with G–d. Here, there can be no "felt" emotions, sublime as they might be, for feeling posits one who loves in addition to Him Who is loved. This is not unity. Utter self-abnegation, loss of self-awareness completely, man's becoming a "vehicle" for G–d, with no will but His—this is the province of the Tzadik. Not everyone can attain to this degree, as Tanya I explains at length. Only the rare Tzadik's service of Torah and mitzvot ascends to Atzilut, perfect unity with*

G–d. The Four Worlds are frequently discussed in Chassidut. See Tanya I Glossary, Four Worlds, Translator's Explanatory Notes to "On Learning Chassidus"; Tanya III Ch. 1, note 3; etc. [4] *Tanya I, ch. 40.* [5] *See references end of note 3.* [6] *Performance of action mitzvot involves the physical body. Even speech (in worship, Torah study, etc.) involves physical movement. Through speech and deed the physical world is elevated. However, there is no evident physical involvement in thinking, so the Divine purpose in creating a physical world is unfulfilled.* [7] *Translator's insertion.* [8]—*Even a desirable thought is ineffective in engendering good.* [9] *In the "lower" worlds G–d is concealed. Through mitzvot the Worlds are illuminated with Divine Light. (Cf. Tanya III, ch. 1, and note 5.)* [10] *G–d transcending Creation, time, space, the Infinite for Whom all Creation is naught, becomes united with His Immanent aspect manifest in His works. This Union, resulting from mortal man's physical observance of Torah and Mitzvot, is effected in the Higher Worlds immediately, and will be realised in the mundane world with the coming of the Moshiach.* [11] *See above note 3; Tanya I, chs. 16, 39, 40, etc.* [12] *". . . G–d joins to deed" (Kiddushin 40a).* [13] *Tanya I, ch. 40, note in the text.* [14] *". . . than the measure of retribution" (Sotah 11a).* [15] *In the "likeness" of mortal man Above, Supernal Man has parallels to body and soul, to garments and abode, but of course in non-corporeal terms only. "Garments" of the embodied soul are thought, speech, and deed, and archetypal man has his appropriate "garments." Physical domicile and environment, separate from man but affecting him profoundly, have their counterparts in Supernal Man. The reader will resist forming anthropomorphic representations of Adam Elyon; mortal terminology and analogies are all we possess.* [16] *Tanya I, Glossary. The categories of the human soul are applied to the source of the soul, Adam Elyon.* [17] *The plane immediately superior to the physical world is the spiritual aspect of Asiyah, with Ten Sefirot (divine attributes).* [18] *"Light" refers to the Divine radiance, the revelation, while "vessel" refers to the instrument for the revelation. An analogy—the power of vision is the "light," while the eye proper is the "vessel." See Tanya II, p. 158.* [19] *Torah words uttered without love and awe are, may we say, virtually "earthbound." They can "rise," but not to (as high as) G–d's presence.*

Essay II

[1] *In* Likutei Torah, R'ai, *32b, Rabbi Schneur Zalman interprets the term "face to face" (panim b'fanim) as "internal": the internal aspect of G–d's will shall illuminate the source of the souls of Israel, when man's inner will is directed to G–d.* Panim, *face, also implies "inner."* [2] *I.e., donning Tefillin, giving charity etc., as differentiated from mitzvot performed through speech and thought.*

PAGE 600

[8] *The term "visage," like other anthropomorphic expressions, is common in Kabbala and Chassidut. "Major Visage"* (arich anpin) *refers to the Divine Will, and "Minor Visage" to the revealed emotive attributes. Generally, the latter term refers to the first six emotive attributes, while Malchut, the last, is considered a class unto itself. The "Visages" are on all planes, in all "Worlds," correspondingly higher or lower in accordance with the World in question.* [9] *Essay I, note 15.*

PAGE 602

it progresses in its sensitivity to G–dliness. "They shall go from strength to strength," says the Psalmist (84:8), and the Talmud declares that the righteous have no "rest" in This or the Coming Worlds. In broad terms we may say that there are numerous, if not an infinite number of planes, categorised as the Higher and Lower Gan Eden. We have noted the existence of "Worlds" on different levels of spirituality or corporeality, ranging from virtually total unity and immersion in the Infinite to the point of non-existence, down to our physical universe where the spiritual is subordinate and G–d so concealed that He can be denied. As the presence of G–d is concealed, the independent existence of creatures becomes possible, the ultimate being physical creatures. One step above this mundane World called Asiyah, is its spiritual counterpart and antecedent, the Lower Gan Eden of Asiyah. The soul ascends to the Lower Gan Eden as "reward" for performance of mitzvot, and to the Higher Gan Eden in accordance with its kavana, *intention and dedication.* [11] *The term "under the sun" is found in Kohelet 1:3—"What gain has man of all his striving under the sun." The Talmud (Shabbat 30b) comments that man's labours "under the sun" are vanity, for these are worldly strivings, but there is gain in striving "higher than the sun," meaning study of Torah. In* Likutei Torah, Devarim *13d, Rabbi Schneur Zalman writes, "If one studies Torah for his own glory, wanting to achieve something, to be considered a person of worth, this study is called 'under the sun' where everything is vanity . . ." This sort of Torah study is the first category in note 3 of this Essay.* [12] *Shabbat 119b.*

Essay IV

[1] *Glossary,* Birur. [2] *Glossary* Or; *Essay I and Notes 3 and 9.* [3] Netzach-hod-yesod *are the penultimate attributes. On the Ten Sefirot see glossary. On Minor Visage see Essay III, note 8.* [4] *See references in Essay I, note 3.* [5] *"Garbs" indicate concealment, adaptation. See note 70.* [6] *Essay II, note 1. The Infinite Light does not penetrate to the finite worlds spontaneously.*

PAGE 604

in its state of "Whiteness," is indivisible from the soul. Since soul and its powers are analogous to G–d and the Sefirot, the Divine Will (origin of mitzvot) is a state of unity with Him.

[15] *Tanya III, Ch. 1.* [16] *Essay I, note 3.* [17] *According to* Biblical *Law some agricultural laws (tithes, Sabbatical year, etc.) are operative only in Eretz Israel, for example.* [18] *See Translator's Explanatory Notes to "On Learning Chassidus"; Essay III, note 8.* [19] Moed Katan *9a.* [20] *Ezekiel 1.* [21] *See note 16. In worship one arouses the appropriate emotion, following the preparation of study and contemplation.* [22] *Deut. 11:22 and Rashi;* Nedarim *65a.*

PAGE 606

through the greatest of man's intellectual and emotional resources. The key word in this paragraph is "essence," and in the following contrasting paragraph the opposing term is "existence." [33] *Moses has just been mentioned as one of these. Souls share a common source (see "On Learning Chassidus") in the Creator, but they descend through the Worlds until they enter the body. The Atzilut soul retains its Atzilut character, and is impervious to the "environment" of the lower Worlds. It continues its state of unity. The "Beriah soul" acquires the characteristics of that World, and is immune to influence in the lower, and so on. See note 70.* [34] *The four names of the soul parallel the Four Worlds.* Nefesh *is Asiyah, deed;* ruach *is Yetzirah, emotion, speech;* neshama *is Beriah, intellect, thought;* chaya *is Atzilut. A fifth, highest aspect of the soul, is* yechida. *The lowest three are abbreviated as* nara'n. *See Essay I, note 16; Tanya III, note 1.* [35] *Except for Moses, all the Prophets were granted visions or dreams; theirs was not a conscious revelation—simultaneous revelation and continued awareness by the Prophet of his body and environment. The "trance" was a "divestment of the physical."* [36] *Tanya I, ch. 5.*

PAGE 610

the source, the intellect. [54] *Every thought is of necessity a limitation of the power of intellect. The intellectual powers and the specific idea may be compared to the body of the sun and its rays. Intellect in turn is not the essence of soul, but a mere manifestation of soul. Thus the idea is several removes from the essence of the thinker.* [55] *Tanya I, chs. 45 and 46.* [56] Chochmah-binah-daat, *the "intellectual" attributes of G–d or powers of the human soul.*

PAGE 622

The transcendent and immanent, distinct in the mundane world, are united through the mitzvot. See note 7 below. [5] *The covenant with Noah (Genesis 9:16 and 8:22) assured the simple existence of Creation and the dependability of natural processes quite apart from merit. Chassidut interprets the blessings (Leviticus 26:3, Deuteronomy 11:13) conditional on conduct, as referring to supplemental spiritual benefice—through fulfillment of G–d's wishes even This World is "illumined" with the radiance of the Infinite. Zohar (II:239a; III:26b) describes the "mystery of the offering" as "rising to the mystery of the Infinite." All Creation is "elevated" through the proper sacrificial offerings, and the Consonant Divine response of increaed Light of the Infinite into finite Creation ensues. Each mitzvah elicits the relevant response. Tefillin call forth a revelation of the Divine Intellect, etc.*

PAGE 624

external, is dependent on man's efforts, as in note 5, above. Man's neglect of mitzvot, as the paragraph continues, results in obscuring a particular revelation that should have been manifest. [8] *Tanya I, ch. 4, etc., for a discussion of the origin of Torah.* [9] *I.e. their physical nature is refined, their concealment of the spirit is less pronounced.* [10] *The brain is the instrument of man's supreme faculty. "Hair," insensitive to pain, is symbolic of man's lowest faculty, the least evidently living aspect of man. The physical proximity of the two extremes and their qualitative distance is the point made here. All of Creation, in all its impressiveness and magnitude and complexity, issues from a minor detail of Torah, and is comparable to Torah roughly as a hair is comparable to the brain.* [11] *Indicative of the external aspect, the secondary, as opposed to the "front" or inward, internal aspect, closer to the essential reality.* [12] *Bereishit Rabba 17:7 and 44:19. The Midrash describes several parallels, microcosms to their original: dream to prophecy, Shabbat to the Coming World, the sun to the Light Above, and Torah to the Supreme Wisdom.* [13] *See "On the Teachings of Chassidus," beginning.* [14] *Zohar I 11b.* [15] *Yalkut Shimoni 836; Siddur Daily Shacharit.*

PAGE 626

lator's Explanatory Notes. Chochmah is the "point," Binah, the "chamber." [3] *Zohar III, 4a. Chochmah and binah, the "two comrades who are never separated."* [4] *Isaiah 52:13.* [5] *Tanya I, glossary on* Chochmah

Introductions to the English translation of LIKUTEI AMARIM-TANYA

by the Translators

"KEHOT" PUBLICATION SOCIETY
New York

TABLE OF CONTENTS

INTRODUCTION TO THE BI-LINGUAL EDITION

The purpose of this bi-lingual edition is to aid the novice as well as the savant of Chassidic teachings in the understanding of the one work which is the source of all concepts in ChaBaD philosophy—the TANYA.

It must be noted that whilst the translators have endeavoured to be as accurate and true to the original text as the limitations of the English language permit, it would be self-deceit in thinking that one can *learn* the Tanya by way of a translation. To facilitate the *understanding* of this work, it is hoped that the reader will avail himself of the copious notes provided throughout which explain many of the intricate mystical concepts in Chassidut.

We would like to express our special gratitude to the translators of the five sections. Our thanks are extended to Mr S. M. Bloch of The Soncino Press, London, who was responsible for the design and production of this bi-lingual edition. We also wish to place on record the following names of those who assisted with the proof-reading in devoting so much of their time and energy in the preparation of the work: Rabbi Ch. Farro, Mr F. Hager, Rabbi A. Jaffe, Messrs Z. Jaffe, D. Lipsidge, B. Perrin, R. Rose and M. Salek.

This work is dedicated to the Lubavitcher Rebbe שליט״א in the hope that we have contributed, if minutely, to the spreading of Chassidic Light, and the ultimate goal of לכשיפוצו מעינותיך חוצה

LUBAVITCH FOUNDATION
UNITED KINGDOM

11th of Nissan, 5733

FOREWORD

to the

Second Edition of the Bi-Lingual Tanya

The first printing of the bi-lingual Tanya achieved a world wide success far in excess of the Publishers' expectations. It is with profound joy that we present to the English speaking public the Second Edition of this classic Chassidic work which, in fact, is the embodiment of the sum total of Chassidut.

The translation remains unchanged. However, to facilitate the daily learning of Tanya, we have incorporated within the translation, the dates for the daily study sections, as set out by the Previous Lubavitcher Rebbe, Rabbi J. I. Schneersohn of saintly memory. For a full explanation of the system, the reader is directed to the section entitled Moreh Shiur on page 960.

In addition to the standard edition, the Publishers have complied with the numerous requests to produce the bi-lingual Tanya in a reduced format.

The Publishers dedicate these works to the Lubavitcher Rebbe, Rabbi M. M. Schneerson shlita, in the hope that we have accelerated the coming of the Righteous Moshiach in our days.

KEHOT PUBLICATION SOCIETY
UNITED KINGDOM

11th Nisan 5740

FOREWORD

to the

New Revised Edition

The world-wide interest in Chassidic teachings continues in an ever increasing measure. The Tanya, considered the 'Written Torah' of Chassidism, is now studied by tens of thousands of people, from all walks of life. The Bi-Lingual Tanya has contributed enormously to this global interest, by both stimulating and sating the quest for deeper involvement in *Chassidut*, in those to whom the original Hebrew text remains inaccessible, not only on the intellectual level, but as a *modus vivendi*.

Since its first publication over ten years ago, the Bi-Lingual edition has met with wide acclaim, and is used by both the novice and the more conversant with Chassidic themes, making it a work of classic Judaica.

In this new edition, the publishers have made some important changes. The entire translation has been reviewed, typographical errors have been removed, and many phrases have been reconstructed and retranslated to clarify the subject, and to avoid possible misunderstanding. A comprehensive Table of Contents, a list of Tanya printings by countries, as well as a brief biographical sketch and Portrait of Rabbi Schneur Zalman have also been added.

It is the publishers fervent hope and prayer, together with all those who have assisted in this publication, that we all merit to see the culmination of our aspirations speedily fulfilled—the coming of our righteous Moshiach.

KEHOT PUBLICATION SOCIETY
NEW YORK

Tammuz 5744

FOREWORD
to the
Latest Edition

To commemorate the 300th year since the birth of Rabbi Yisroel Baal Shem Tov, founder of the Chassidic movement and mentor of Chassidic teachings, Kehot Publication Society UK has reprinted the major Chassidic opus — Likutei Amarim Tanya in a third bi-lingual edition.

Since it first appeared in translated format the bi-lingual edition has become the mainstay for countless students of chassidic studies, and was probably the first chassidic work to appear in bi-lingual form.

Many corrections have been made to the translation, and we thank Rabbi S. Lew of London for his painstaking efforts. We have sought to include all the additional material which has become standard since the massive Tanya printing programme was initiated by the late Lubavitcher Rebbe, Rabbi M. M. Schneerson of blessed and sainted memory.

The ever increasing thirst for Jewish scholarship, especially in the field of Jewish mysticism, has resulted in the production of numerous companion volumes, which the student is strongly urged to make use of.

It is our fervent hope that we have contributed to the fulfilment of the response of Moshiach to the Baal Shem Tov's enquiry "when will you come?" that response being "when your wellsprings overflow even to the outside".

KEHOT PUBLICATION SOCIETY
UNITED KINGDOM

18th (Chai) Ellul 5758
300th birthday of the Baal Shem Tov

Part I INTRODUCTION

by Rabbi Nissan Mindel M.A., PH.D.

I. THE BOOK

The author called his work by three distinct names. Each of these names characterises the book in its own way. These names are:

1. *Likutei Amarim*—"Collected Discourses." By this name the author describes his work in his "Compiler's Foreword," thereby humbly disclaiming any originality for his work. In fact the author explicity states that his treatise constitutes a collection of discourses "which have been selected from books and scribes, heavenly saints, who are renowned among us."[1] Under this title the book was first published (Slavita, 1796).[2]

2. *Tanya*, after the initial word of the book, quoting a Baraitic source.[3] The quotation from tannaitic lore serves the author more than a homiletic introduction to his system. Dealing, as it does, with the mystic descent of the soul and its destiny, it provides the author with a starting point, based in the Talmud, from which to unfold his whole system. Under this title the book appeared for the second time (Zolkiev, 1798), with *Likutei Amarim* as subtitle.[4]

3. *Sefer shel Benonim*—"Book of the Intermediates," so called after the type of personality on which the book centers attention, that is, the intermediate type whose moral position is between the *tzaddik* ("righteous man") and *rasha* ("wicked man"). Thus the author pointedly indicates that his primary concern is not with the *tzaddik*, upon whose veneration general *Chasidut* had placed so much emphasis, nor with the *rasha*, upon whose condemnation much has been said in other Jewish ethical works, but with the *benoni*, the "intermediate" man, whose rank is within reach of every person.[5] The name *Sefer shel Benonim* appeared as a subtitle in the first edition ("*Likutei Amarim*, Part One, called *Sefer shel Benonim*"). However, actually the author often refers to the whole book, and not merely its first part, when using the title *Sefer shel Benonim*.[6]

The standard complete editions of this work include the following five parts, each of which is an independent treatise:

Notes will be found at the end of this Introduction

Part I: *Likutei Amarim*, or *Tanya*, or *Sefer shel Benonim*, proper, comprising a Foreword and fifty-three chapters (148 pp.).

Part II: *Sha'ar ha-Yichud veha-Emunah* ("Portal of Unity and Belief"), with a Foreword and twelve chapters (30 pp.).

Part III: *Igeret ha-Teshuvah* ("Epistle of Repentance"), with twelve chapters (22 pp.).

Part IV: *Igeret ha-Kodesh* ("Sacred Epistle"), with thirty-two sections (102 pp.).[6a]

Part V: *Kuntress Acharon* ("Latest Treatise"), 20 pp.

Altogether at least sixty-five editions of the *Likutei Amarim*, or *Tanya*, complete or in part, have appeared to-date,[7] with both names alternating as title and subtitle, respectively. Yet this work, as the other Chabad classics, has never been translated into any European language.[8] Even in its Hebrew original it is not an easy book, because of its construction, almost complete lack of punctuation, and also because some of its basic doctrines are not treated fully therein and must be sought in the author's other works. There seems, therefore, ample reason for presenting to the English-speaking Jewish world a translation of this fundamental work of Chabad, with an introduction and notes, which it is hoped, will facilitate the comprehension of this book and its doctrine. Our present study will confine itself to Part I, to which we shall refer, for the sake of convenience, by its shorter name —*Tanya*.

The author worked on the *Tanya* for twenty years,[9] elaborating its style and form so punctiliously that it came to be regarded by his followers as the "Written Torah" of Chabad, where every word and letter was meaningful. Indeed, the author divided it into fifty-three chapters to correspond to the number of *Sidrot* (weekly portions) in the Pentateuch. It soon became the custom of many Chabad Chasidim to study a chapter of the *Tanya* each week, with the same regularity with which the weekly portions of the Pentateuch were recited.[10]

In his attempt to design the *Tanya* so that it would meet the widest possible need, both of the analytical and searching mind, as well as of the less scholarly, the author has succeeded to a high degree. The former find in it an inexhaustible profundity, and several searching not yet published commentaries have been written on it. This translator has been fortunate in having access to some of the manuscripts in question.[11]

The less scholarly, too, each according to his intellectual capacity, find in it edifying instruction at varying levels. This quality, together with the authority it enjoys, accounts for the widespread recognition which the *Tanya* has commanded from the time of its appearance to the present day.

The *Tanya* was written, as the author indicates in his Foreword, for the "seekers" and the "perplexed." One is tempted to draw a parallel between this author and his book and Maimonides and his *Guide*. Indeed, both men present some striking points in common. Each of them first established his reputation as a Talmudist and Codifier before publishing a work of philosophy; both had written Codes of Jewish Law, which are still authoritative and popular. Each of them created a new lasting school of thought in Jewish philosophy, and the one, like the other, set out to write a work which aimed at helping those who needed guidance in their religious beliefs. Yet both of them evoked sharp opposition from the direction of a part of orthodox Jewry; both were misunderstood and their philosophical treatises were banned.

However, this is as far as the parallel goes. The *Guide* and the *Tanya* represent two widely divergent systems, in essence as well as in form. The two authors were separated by some six centuries in time, and far apart also geographically and in respect of the whole cultural milieu in which they flourished. Maimonides is the rational Jewish philosopher *par excellence;* Rabbi Schneur Zalman is basically a mystic. The "perplexed" for whom they wrote were two entirely different types of people. Maimonides wrote for the man whose perplexity derived from the fact that he desired to retain his traditional beliefs, but was puzzled by the apparent contradiction between tradition and philosophy, yet loath to give up either.[12] The object of the *Guide*, therefore, was to effect a reconciliation between the two.

No such problem confronted Rabbi Schneur Zalman. Philosophy and science hardly had a place among the masses of Eastern European Jewry at that time. The *Haskalah* movement had not yet made any serious inroads upon the minds of the masses. Rabbi Schneur Zalman addressed himself to those "who are in pursuit of righteousness and seek the Lord . . . whose intelligence and mind are confused and they wander about in darkness in the service of G–d, unable to perceive the beneficial light that is buried in books."[13] In other words, he writes for those whose beliefs have not been troubled by doubts, but who merely seek the right path to G–d.

We will, therefore, not find in the *Tanya* the type of scholastic philosophy with which the *Guide* is replete, nor any polemics, nor even an attempt to treat systematically many of the philosophical problems which engaged Maimonides' attention. Such basic beliefs as the Existence of G-d, *creatio ex nihilo*, Revelation, and others, are taken for granted by the author. Others, such as the Divine attributes, Providence, Unity, Messianism, etc., are treated as integral parts of his ethical system, and illuminated by the light of Kabbalah.

The *Tanya* is essentially a work on Jewish religious ethics. The author is primarily concerned with the forces of good and evil in human nature and in the surrounding world, and his objective, as already pointed out, is to pave a new way to the *summum bonum*. He is aware, of course, of the existence of Hebrew literature dealing with the same subject. If he is impelled to write a new book, it is not, as he is careful to note, because of the shortcomings of the available works *per se*, but because the human mind is not equally receptive, nor equally responsive to, the same stimuli. The implication is that many works on Jewish philosophy and ethics were useful for their time and age, or for the specific groups for whom they were written. Now there was a need for a new approach (in the light of the Chasidic doctrine), and for a "guide" that would command a universal appeal. However, the author realises that even this book, in parts at least, cannot be so simple as to be understood by all. Consequently he urges the more learned not to be misled by a sense of misplaced modesty, and not to withhold their knowledge from those who would seek it from them in the understanding of these "Discourses."[14]

R. Schneur Zalman knew his "perplexed" intimately. They flocked to him in great numbers, and they flooded him with written inquiries. Most of them, undoubtedly, were simple folk and laymen. But there were also many students of the Talmud, and philosophically inclined young men, who, like himself in his teens, sought a new way of life and new outlets for their intellectual as well as spiritual drives. The consideration of such a variegated audience largely determined the form and style of the book.

Speaking of form and style, it should also be remembered that long before he committed his teachings and doctrines to writing, he preached them orally.[15] His sermons and discourses, delivered mostly on the Sabbath and on Festivals (which accounts for their homiletic style), were subsequently recorded from memory by his disciples. These

manuscripts had a wide circulation among his followers. Not infrequently Rabbi Schneur Zalman expounded his doctrines in the form of epistles which, being of general interest, were regarded by his followers as pastoral letters, and also copied and recopied for the widest possible circulation. In the course of time, as his community of devotees had greatly increased, Schneur Zalman felt, as he explains in his Foreword, that the time was ripe to present an outline of his teachings in the form of a book, which was to supersede the circulating pamphlets, many of which were replete with errors as a result of repeated copying and transcription, or by the malicious mischief of opponents.[16] This is how the *Likutei Amarim*, or *Tanya*, in its present composition, was born.

2. THE SOURCES

We have already noted that the author of the *Tanya* made no claim to originality for his work. On the contrary, he emphasised his dependence on his predecessors. Among the "books and sages" which influenced his thinking, the Scriptures, Talmud and Lurianic Kabbalah must be given foremost place. This is indicated already in the first chapter, which opens the book with Talmudic quotations, references to the Zoharitic literature and R. Chayyim Vital, the great exponent of Lurianic Kabbalah, and with interspersed quotations from Scripture. Here we already have an indication of the author's cast of mind and his aim to build his system on the combined foundations of Scriptural, Rabbinic and Kabbalistic sources.

Rabbi Schneur Zalman's interpretations and doctrines are based upon the teachings of the Ba'al Shem Tov, the founder of general Chasidut, and his own "masters," Rabbi Dov Ber of Miezricz, the Ba'al Shem Tov's successor, and Rabbi Dov Ber's son Rabbi Abraham, the "Angel."

The author draws abundantly from the *Zohar* and the *Tikunei Zohar*. He mentions by name Maimonides (the *Code*), and Rabbi Moshe Cordovero (*Pardes*). Of other "books and scribes" which influenced him, though he does not mention them by name in the *Tanya*, are R. Isaiah Hurwitz's *Shenei Luchot ha-Berit*, the works of the Maharal (Rabbi Judah Lowe) of Prague, and Bachya ben Asher's *Commentary* on the Bible.[17]

Halevi's *Kuzari* was held in high esteem by Rabbi Schneur Zalman

and his successors. He is known to have studied it ardently with his son and grandson who succeeded him. Similarly Bachya ibn Pakuda's *Duties of the Heart*, which enjoyed great popularity among Talmudic scholars of the day, as it still does.[18] Albo's *Ikarim* was another popular source for the philosophically inclined. It is safe to assume that Rabbi Schneur Zalman was intimately familiar with these, and no doubt also with the whole range of Medieval Jewish philosophy, but there is no evidence of influence by these sources on the composition of the *Tanya*.

It has been wisely said that the proper approach to a problem is in itself half a solution. Quite often it is the approach to the problem, and the method of treating it, that displays the greatest degree of ingenuity and originality, and in themselves constitute the main contribution of the thinker. This is true of R. Schneur Zalman and of the Chabad system which he created. For, while his basic concepts have been gleaned from various sources, his doctrines nevertheless present a complete and unified system, and there is much refreshing originality in its presentation and consistency.

But R. Schneur Zalman did more than that. Very often he has so modified, reinterpreted or remolded the ideas which he had assimilated, as to give them an originality of their own.

To Rabbi Schneur Zalman, as to Kabbalists in general, the Torah, the Jewish Written and Oral Law embodied in the Bible and Talmud (the latter including both the Halachah and Aggadah), was more than a Divinely inspired guide to the *summum bonum*. It constituted the essential law and order of the created universe.[19] The Kabbalah, in its interpretation, was nothing but the inner, esoteric dimension of the Torah, its very "soul." Without this dimension the Torah could not be fully understood. Consequently, when he looked for the "inner," or esoteric, meaning of Biblical and Talmudic texts it was not for the purpose of adding homiletic poignancy to his exposition, but rather to reveal their inner dimension. In his system the esoteric and exoteric, the Kabbalah and the Talmud, are thoroughly blended and unified, just as the physical and metaphysical, the body and soul, emerge under his treatment as two aspects of the same thing. The polarity of things is but external; the underlying reality of everything is unity, reflecting the unity of the Creator. To bring out this unity of the microcosm and macrocosm, as they merge within the mystic unity of the *En Sof* (The Infinite)—that is the ultimate aim of his system.

3. THE COMPOSITION OF THE TANYA

Structurally, the *Tanya* may be divided into a number of sections, each dealing with a major subject and comprising a number of composite topics.

The first section of the work (chapters 1–8) is devoted to an analysis of the psychological structure of the Jewish personality.[20] Here the author discusses the two levels of consciousness (to use modern terminology) on which a person operates. These two levels of consciousness are derived from two sources, which the author terms the "divine soul" and the "animal soul." He examines the essential attributes and practical faculties of each. In dealing with the "animal soul" the author discusses also the nature of evil, both metaphysical and moral. Evil is basically conceived in terms of disunity; good in terms of unity.

Next (chapters 9–17), the author goes on to examine the inevitable conflict ensuing from the two divergent sources of consciousness. He evaluates the relative strength of the two souls and their respective functions, whereby the essential unity of the human personality is strongly upheld. Experientially, however, the conflict produces a variety of personalities, from one extreme to the other, which the author proceeds to define. His attention is focused on the personality of the *Benoni*, which falls mid-way between the extremes. However, in Rabbi Schneur Zalman's definition the *Benoni* is not one whose sins and virtues balance, while the *tzaddik* is a person whose good deeds outweigh his sins, as sometimes defined in the Talmud.[21] The *Benoni* of the *Tanya* is a person who exercises complete self-control and never commits a sin knowingly in any of the three areas of human activity: thought, speech and deed. The *Benoni* of the *Tanya* is thus superior to the *tzaddik* of the Talmud. Nevertheless, our author insists that this ideal personality is within grasp of the average individual, although not without constant effort and vigilance. The underlying doctrine here is that man is essentially and inherently a moral being.

The following chapters (18–25) are designed to support the author's basic theory, namely, that the ideal personality of the *Benoni* is not a mere concept, but one that can actually be realised. To this end he re-examines the functions of the soul, both on the conscious and subconscious level. With regard to the former, the author insists on the supremacy of the intellect. As for the subconscious level, the author draws upon the *Zohar* for certain mystical categories, such as the innate

or "hidden" love and fear (awe) of G–d. The "hidden" love provides a subconscious urge for oneness with G–d; the sense of awe for the Divine Being provides a dread of separateness. Love and awe are therefore not conflicting, but rather complementary categories. The author emphasises the special, and to a considerable extent also hereditary, nature of the Jew, and his attachment to the idea of the unity of G–d, originating with the Patriarchs. This thought is, in some respects, strongly reminiscent of Halevi's concept of the "Divine Influence" (*al'amar al'ilahi*), which Halevi considers germane to the Jewish people.[22]

In this connection the doctrine of Divine Unity comes under discussion.

However, never losing sight of the practical, the author discusses certain states of mind which have a direct bearing on the quest for personal unity as a prelude to unity in the cosmic order, which in turn is *sina qua non* for the realisation of the Divine Unity. He offers a series of practical suggestions to attain mental and emotional stability and inner harmony. The emphasis is on joy, stemming from an intellectually achieved faith, while sadness and dejection are severely censured. All this forms the subject matter of chapters 26–31.

Chapter 32 stands out by itself, as an interpolation not immediately related to the specific discussion. The careful student will note that chapter 31 is more directly continued in chapter 33. It would appear that the author chose to include this particular chapter parenthetically, as it were, in order to give emphasis at this point to one of the cardinal teachings of the Ba'al Shem Tov, which is a corner stone of Chasidut, and which receives special attention in Chabad.[23] We refer to the subject of *ahavat yisrael*, love for fellow Jew (*Lev.* 18:19). In his familiar way, our author gives this precept a mystico-ethical exposition, based on the close soul-relationship within the community of Israel, to which he alluded in his Foreword and chapter 2, and which now receives fuller treatment in this chapter. Hence, some leading Chasidim note the significance of the number of this chapter—32—corresponding to the Hebrew word ל"ב, "heart."[24]

The drama of the inner personal conflict leads the author to an examination of man's destiny, the meaning and purpose of life, and man's place in the cosmic order. These problems are dealt with in chapters 33–37. In the last of these, the author outlines his concept of the Messianic Era and the Resurrection, when the cosmic order will have

attained the acme of perfection and fulfillment as a direct result of man's conscious effort to work towards that goal.

At this point, the author might have concluded his treatise. However, he is not content with leaving us with the impression that life is merely a prelude to after-life. There must be more to life, and to religious experience than serving merely as a means to an end. In the next, and last, fifteen chapters of his work, the author evolves his concept of the Kingdom of Heaven on earth in the *here and now*. In his daily life man is offered a foretaste of the after-life, and in some respects it is of a quality surpassing even the spiritual bliss of the hereafter. The author, therefore, takes up again those categories of man's spiritual phenomena which enable him to transcend his physical limitations and to partake of the supernatural in this life. Here again the mystic is very much in evidence. The author provides new insights into the concept of *kavanah* (the "intention" which must accompany every human act), which is the vehicle of transcendence (chapters 38–40). He discusses the various qualities of *fear* (*awe*) and love, and introduces also the quality of *mercy*, as the basic elements of this transcendency, and as innate qualities in human nature to leap over the gulf that separates the created from the Creator, and to come in direct contact with the *En Sof*, the Limitless (chapters 41–47).

The next two chapters (48–49) are devoted to the all-important Lurianic doctrine of *tzimtzum* which, in the author's system holds the key to both the mystery of creation and the destiny of man. Both man and the world in which he lives are two dimensional creatures of matter and spirit. The tension that inheres in such an order can be relieved only by spiritualising the material. Man has it in his power to achieve personal harmony and unity, by realising his inner nature. In so doing, he becomes the instrument through which the world in which he lives also achieves fulfillment. To be a true master of the world which the Creator had entrusted in his hands, man must first be master of himself. Creation is seen as a process leading from G–d to man; fulfillment is seen as a process leading from man to G–d. The process leading from G–d to man is one of materialising the spiritual; that leading from man to G–d one of spiritualising the material. There is community of interests, as it were, between the Creator and His "counterpart" on earth, a community of interests which is realisable because of a community of "nature," since man partakes in the Divine nature (by reason of the fact that his soul is a

"part" of G-dliness) as G-d concerns Himself with human affairs.

Man's moral acts must be holy acts.[25] The good and the holy are identical; man's duty and purpose in life is to identify himself with his Creator, through identifying his will with that of his Creator. Man is the Divine instrument "to make this world a fitting abode for the *Shechinah* (Divine Presence)," in which both man and G-d can share intimately and fully, in complete harmony and union. On this mystical note the final chapters (50–53) of the treatise conclude.

Notes to Part I Introduction

[1] Hakdamat ha-melaket ("Compiler's Foreword"), Likutei Amarim (*Tanya*), *Kehot Publication Society (Brooklyn, N.Y., 1958), p. 7.* This standard edition will be used for reference in this work.

[2] *See list of 72* Tanya *editions,* Tanya op. cit., *PP. 427 ff.*

[3] *T.B.* Niddah *30b.*

[4] *See n. 2, above.*

[5] Tanya, *beg. ch. 14.*

[6] Ibid., *p. 435.*

[6a] *Parts IV and V, comprising epistles written by the author at different times and on various occasions, were incorporated by the author's sons.*

[7] *See n. 2, above.*

[8] *About other translations see note 5 on page 761.*

[9] Kitzurim VeHaorois LeTanya, *by Rabbi Menachem Mendel of Lubavitch, ed. Rabbi Menachem M. Schneerson, KPS (Brooklyn, N.Y., 1948), p. 121.*

[10] Ibid., *pp. 123, 124.*

[11] *Two are by Rabbi Shmuel Grunem Esterman, first dean of the Yeshiva Tomchei Tmimim, founded in Lubavitch in 1897. A third, extant only in part, is believed to have been written by Rabbi Jacob Kadaner, a disciple of Rabbi Schneur Zalman's son and successor. A fourth commentary is of unknown origin.*

[12] The Guide For the Perplexed, *tr. M. Friedlander (London, 1942),* Introduction, *p. 2.*

[13] Tanya, *beg.* Hakdamat ha-melaket.

[14] Ibid., *p. 7.*

[15] *RSZ is said to have preached his doctrines orally for twelve years before committing them to writing. Cf.* Kitzurim, op. cit., *p. 136.*

[16] Ibid., *pp. 137, 139.*

[17] *The* Zohar *is mentioned in the* Tanya *(part I) forty-nine times; Luria—ten times; Vital and his works—twenty-nine times; Maimonides* (Code)*—five times; Nachmanides—once. Cf. "Index of Books and Persons" in* Tanya, *op. cit., pp. 398 ff.*

[18] *Even where philosophical speculation was frowned upon, Bachya's* Duties of the Heart *enjoyed a unique position. The influential Rabbi Isaiah Hurwitz, for example, severely criticised in his work R. Abraham ibn Ezra, Maimonides* (Guide) *and Gersonides, but held the* Duties of the Heart *in high esteem. See* Shenei Luchot ha-Berit *(Amsterdam, 1698), pp. 2b; 8a; 20b; 47b; 183a; 193b.*

[19] *Comp. "He looked into the Torah and created the world,"* Zohar *("Rom" ed.*

Wilno, 1937), vol. II, 161a; III, 35b, etc. See also Tanchuma, *at the beg. on* Prov. *8:30, to the effect that the Torah was the Divine "tool" in creating the universe.*

[20] *With R. Isaiah Hurwitz and all Kabbalists, RSZ considered the Jewish psychological composition in a category of its own. Judah Halevi made the special destiny of the Jewish people one of the basic doctrines of his* Kuzari. *In the* Tanya *the emphasis is on the individual Jew rather than on the Jewish people as a whole.*

[21] Berachot *7a;* Rosh Hashanah *16b. See discussion of this subject in first ch. of* Tanya.

[22] Kuzari *I:25, 27 ff.*

[23] *See, e.g.* Likutei Torah (*Wilno* ["Rom" *ed.*], *1928*), *Vol. I,* Matot, *pp. 85d ff;* Derech Mitzvoisecho *by R. Menachem Mendel of Lubavitch, KPS* (*Brooklyn, N.Y., 1953*), *pp. 28a ff.*, et al.

[24] *I am indebted to Rabbi Menachem Schneerson, the Lubavitcher Rebbe* שליט"א *for calling my attention to the subject of this chapter.*

[25] *Comp.* Shenei Luchot ha-Berit, *pp. 326b; 380b.*

Part I Glossary

Ahavah, "love" (of G–d), an innate quality of the soul which is the root of obedience to the Divine Law, of the 248 positive commandments (chs. 3, 4). *Ahavah rabbah, ahavah b'taanugim, ahavah mesuteret, ahavat olam*, etc.—various qualities and categories of "love" (chs. 7, 9, 13, 14–18, 40, 43, 44, 46, 49, 50).

Alukah, "leech," in Kabbalah a symbol of the *kelipah (Zohar* III, 80b; 135a [Idra]; also I, 110b [*Medrash ha-Neelam*]; II, 56a). It is based on *Prov.* 30:15, "The leech hath two daughters (crying), 'Give, give!'" It is the embodiment of selfishness (to take, not to give), in contrast to *Kedusha* (v.). Ch. 19; see also *Torah Or, op. cit.*, vol. I *(Maseei)*, *p.* 91b, ff.

Arich anpin, "*long image*"—see *keter.*

Asiyah, fourth of the Four Worlds, generally translated by "Action." But this term is neither definitive nor descriptive, since all Four Worlds are in a sense "action". Asiyah should be understood as the final stage in the creative process. By way of illustration: I have the desire to build a house; the following four stages would be involved from the inception of the idea until its materialisation: (a) A general idea, as yet undefined. (b) A definite idea of the house in my mind. (c) Architectural plan, or design. (d) Actual building of the house. These four stages would generally correspond to the "Four Worlds."

Atzilut, world of "Emanation," highest of the *Four Worlds* (v.), in Chabad etymologically connected with *etzel* ("near"), i.e. nearest to the Source of creation, the *En Sof*, hence still in a state of Infinity. See *Asiyah.*

Av, "father," in the sense of *chochmah* ("wisdom"); *abba v'imma* ("father and mother") are kabbalistic terms of *chochmah* and *binah* (understanding), in that they "give birth" to the *middot* (emotion attributes). In the divine soul they are the source of love and awe of G–d. (Chap. 3).

Avodah, "(Divine) Service." Three general categories are distinguished: out of pure love (that of a "son"), out of awe (that of a "servant"), and out of the combination of both (that of a "servant-son"). The latter is the "perfect" service; service without effort is not perfect. Chaps. 13, 15, 17, 39, 41, 42, 43, see also *Patriarchs.*

Benoni, "Intermediate" category, whose moral character is between *tzaddik* and *rasha*; not in the Halachic definition (one whose good and bad acts balance), but one who never actually commits a wrong, yet evil still inheres in his nature. (Chs. 1, 12, 15, 27, 29, 35, 37, 41). Within reach of everyone (ch. 14).

Benonim, pl. *Sefer shel Benonim*, "Book of Intermediates," another title for *Tanya*.

Beriah, world of "Creation," second of the *Four Worlds* (v.), a definite state, radically different from *Atzilut*. See *Asiyah*.

Binah, "understanding," second of the *Ten Sefirot*; the second stage of intellectual process, developing the original concept (*chochmah*); source of *gevurot* (ch. 13); corresponds to the heart (ch. 44). See also *Av*, *Chabad*.

Birur, "sifting," or "refining." See also *tikun*. The doctrine that every good act contributes to the purification of matter, separating the good from the evil, thus gradually eliminating the latter, since evil in its pristine state cannot exist. The culmination of the process will usher in the Messianic era, all the "sparks" (*nitzotzin*) of holiness which were scattered through the "breaking of the vessels" *(shevirat ha-kelim)* will have been restored. This is one of the basic concepts of Lurianic Kabbalah. (Chs. 24, 37).

Chabad, an acrostic formed of the initial letters of the Hebrew words *chcohmah* ("wisdom"), *binah* ("understanding") and *da'at* ("knowledge"), the first three of Ten *Sefirot*. The terms are defined under their separate headings.
"Chabad" is the name of the intellectual school and movement founded by Rabbi Schneur Zalman of Liadi.

Chesed, "kindness," first of the seven *middot* (emotion attributes); unlimited benevolence; fourth of the Ten *Sefirot*. Corresponds to *chochmah*, "love," "right side," "water." (Foreword, chs. 3, 50). See *Sefirot*, *Mayyim*.

Chochmah, "wisdom," the first of the Ten *Sefirot*, or emanations. "The potentiality of what" (chaps. 3, 18, 19); first of the intellect powers of soul; reason *in potentia*. See also *Av*, *Chabad*.

Chochmah Ila'ah, "Supernal Wisdom," the first of the Ten Supernal *Sefirot* (v.); the attribute of *ch.* in *Atzilut* (v.).

Da'at, "knowledge," the third of the Ten *Sefirot*; with *chochmah* and *binah* belongs to *ChaBaD*, or *Sechel*, completing the intellectual process. Not "knowledge" in the ordinary sense, but in the sense of concentration and attachment, the mental faculty where ideas and concepts mature into corresponding dispositions *(middot)* (chs. 3, 42, 43, 46). See also *Chabad*.

Edom, or "Esau" *(Gen.* 36:1) are symbols of *Kelipah* (v.). The "Kings of Edom" and their deaths *(Gen.* 36:31–39) are mystically linked with the *kelipot*. See *Zohar* III, 135a/b; 142a. Like *Alukah* (v.) Edom and Esau are the embodiment of selfishness ("Feed me" [*Gen.* 25:30]). Ch. 19.

En Sof, the "Endless," "Infinite," the term frequently used in the *Zohar* and later Kabbalistic works to indicate the Unknowable G–d *(Deus)*. Beyond the *En Sof* is the pure G–dhead *(Deitas)* quite undefinable. See *Likutei Torah, op. cit.*, vol. I, p. 7b, quoting Kabbalistic sources on this subject.

Etzem, "essence," the absolute, fundamental, state of a thing, considered apart from its manifestation. Absolute *Etzem* can refer only to G–d (indicated by the Tetragrammaton). The "essence" of the soul refers to the soul itself, not its powers; its *essential* powers are will and delight.

Four Worlds, the four main stages or levels in the creative process resulting from *tzimtzum*: *Atzilut, Beriah, Yetzirah, Asiyah*. See under resp. headings. Within each are innumerable gradations, also described as "worlds," *hechalot*, etc. The Ten *Sefirot* (v.) manifest themselves in each according to its rank and grade; the highest of a lower order is lower than the lowest of a higher order. All are pervaded by *chochmah d'Atzilut*, the first and highest of the Ten Supernal *Sefirot*. (Chaps. 6, 16, 20, 23, 24, 26, 33, 35, 36, 37, 39, 40, 43, 48, 49, 51–53). See also *Tzimtzum*.

Gevurah, "might" or "severity," in the sense of restraint; second of the seven *middot* the antithesis of *chesed*; corresponds to *binah*, "awe," "left side," "fire." Sometimes referred to as *din* ("stern judgment"). (Chaps. 3, 31, 40, 41). See also *Sefirot*.

Ibbur, "pregnancy," the Kabbalistic doctrine, whereby the soul of a person may attach itself to the soul of another person. According to R. Schneur Zalman, when a person makes a consistent effort to transcend his own spiritual limitations, he may, by Divine grace, merit that the spirit of a *tzaddik* should attach itself to, and illuminate, his own soul.

Chap. 14. For other ramifications of this doctrine see also *Likutei Torah, op. cit.*, vol. II, *Devarim*, p. 85c; *Torah Or, op. cit.*, 28a; 55a f., *et al.*

Kabbalah was handed down from generation to generation to a select few, but since the Ba'al Shem Tov, widely disseminated through Chasidut. It is the "inner" dimension of the Torah, corresponding to *sod* (esoteric knowledge) of the four levels of Torah interpretation, known as *pardes* (v.). Also known as *CheN*, *Chochmah Nistarah* ("hidden knowledge") or *Nistar d'Torah*. In Chabad, the "revealed" aspects of the Torah *(Nigleh d'Torah)* are to be found in the plain and homiletic interpretation of the Torah and *Mitzvot*, as well as discussions of G--d and His attributes as expounded in the works of the Talmud, and Early and Later Commentaries. The "hidden" aspects of the Torah are to be found in the interpretation of the Torah, the *Mitzvot*, G–d and His attributes, etc., as contained in the Midrashic literature, the *Zohar* and other works of *Kabbalah* (including Chassidic works) and religious philosophy. (Rabbi Joseph I. Schneersohn, *On the Teachings of Chassidus* [Kuntres Toras Hachassidus], tr. R. Zalman I. Posner, KPS [Brooklyn, N.Y., 1959], p. 17).
According to RSZ knowledge of the Torah is not complete without some knowledge at least also of *Nistar d'Torah*, especially as the higher dimensions of love and awe of G–d lie in this realm. (Compiler's Foreword, beg. ch. 44).

Kedushah, "holiness." The "good" is in the *Tanya* identified with the "holy." Moral acts are those which are entirely consecrated to G–d, without any thought of the self. (Chap. 19). In the sense of "separation" from evil (chaps. 27, 46); "betrothal" *(union with G–d)* by means of the Divine commandments (chap. 46).

Kelipah, "bark," or "shell," the symbol frequently used in Kabbalah to denote "evil" and the source of sensual desires in human nature *(Zohar* I, 19b; II, 69b; 198b; 184a; III, 185a, etc.). Often mentioned together with *Sitra achra* (v.).

Kelipat nogah, "translucent shell," contains some good, and distinguished from the three completely "dark" *kelipot* (v.) containing no good at all. The term is based on an interpretation of the "brightness" *(nogah)* in Ezekiel's vision (1:4). The "animal soul" *(nefesh ha-bahamit)* in the Jew is derived from *kelipat nogah*, by contrast to his "divine soul" (*nefesh elokit*) which is "part" of G–dliness. (Chaps. 1, 7, 37, 40). See *Kelipot*.

Kelipot, pl. of *kelipah.* Three *kelipot* are completely "dark" and evil. A fourth, *kelipat nogah* (v.) contains an admixture of good. (Chaps. 1, 4, 6, 7, 22, 29, 37, 40). See also *Sitra achra.*

Keneset Israel, the "community of Israel," in a spiritual sense, the source from which the individual souls descend and are sustained, sometimes identified with the *Shechinah* itself. (Chaps. 35, 37).

Keter, "crown"—intermediate category between the essence of the *Or En Sof* (the Emanator) and the emanations, hence the source of the Ten *Sefirot* of *Atzilut*; has two categories: *atik yomin* and *arich anpin.* Also identified with *ratzon elyon,* "Supernal Will."

Kuntres (—im, pl.), "treatise." Before the *Likutei Amarim (Tanya)* was printed, the work was referred to by the name of *Kuntresim.* (See *Approbation* and *Compiler's Foreword*).

Makif, "encompassing"; see *Or Makif.* See also *Soul* (powers).

Malchut, "Royalty," the tenth and lowest of the Ten *Sefirot.* Also called the Word of G–d creating and vivifying all existence (as a king rules by edict and command); hence identified with *Shechinah,* the Immanent category of Divine Presence; also the source of all souls. Chap. 52. See also *Shechinah.*

Mayyim, "water," symbol of the Torah (chap. 4); of *chesed* (v.). The G–d-Man relationship in Kabbalah is often symbolised in terms of the meeting of streams of water. G–d's flow of benevolence is termed *mayyim duchrin* ("masculine waters"); man's obedience to G–d and the fulfillment of the Divine commandments are viewed as a stream rising from man to G–d, termed *mayyim nukvin* ("feminine waters"); the former may come as an act of pure grace, but usually in response to the latter. (Chaps. 4, 10, 53).

Merkavah, "chariot" *(Ezek.* 1), the ultimate in submission to G–d, surrender of the will to the Divine Will. The Patriarchs constituted the "chariot" (chs. 18, 23, 34, 39, 46). Every act of obedience to the Divine Law makes one a "chariot" for G–dliness (chs. 23, 29, 34, 37.)

Middot, "attributes," seven in number (corresponding to the 7 days of creation): *chesed, gevurah, tiferet, netzach, hod, yesod, malchut.* (See respective headings). Together with *sechel* (v.) they make up the Ten Supernal *Sefirot* (v.). In the human being the *middot* are affected and

effected by the *sechel*; hence mental states, dispositions and affections. The first three *(ChaGaT)* are the principal attributes; the next three are their *branches*. *Malchut* is the outlet. Only the *ChaGaT* are discussed in the first part of *Tanya* (chaps. 3, 6). See *Igeret ha-Kodesh* (chaps. 13, 15).

Nefashot, pl. of *nefesh*.

Nefesh, "soul." In *Chabad* (v.), based on R. Chayyim Vital (ch. 1), the doctrine of "two" souls is expounded. See also *Neshamah, Soul*.

Nefesh elokit, "divine soul"; "truly a part of G–dliness" (chap. 2). While this doctrine is not new in Chabad (Cf. *Gen. R.* 65:10; *Bachya's Commentary on Gen.* 2:7; *Zohar* III, 165b) it is adopted in the *Tanya* in almost a literal sense and this concept forms a corner stone of the Chabad philosophy.
Contains ten powers, corresponding to the Ten Supernal *Sefirot* (v.), divided into three intellectual faculties *(sechel)* and seven emotion powers *(middot)* and has three external "garments" (thought, speech and deed). Its principal "dwelling place" (organ) in the body is the brain, and the right compartment of the heart. (Chaps. 2, 3, 4, 9, 12, 18, 23, 24, 29, 37, 42, 49).

Nefesh ha-bahamit, "animal soul" in the Jew originates in *kelipat nogah* (v.). Contains same faculties and "garments" as the *nefesh elokit* (v.); its principal "dwelling place" is in the left compartment of the heart (ch. 9); purification *(tikun)* of, by means of "divine" soul (chaps. 37, 38, 39, 53).

Neshamah, "soul," usually refers to the "divine" soul. But all things are said to have a "soul" which is the creative and preserving Divine force ("word") which brought everything into existence *ex nihilo (Sha'ar ha-yichud vehaemunah*, chap. 1). *Neshamah* is the highest of three categories comprising the human soul the other two being *ruach* and *nefesh* (v.). Cf. *Zohar* I, 206a; II, 141b, etc; also R. Isaiah Hurwitz, *Shenei Luchot ha-Berit* I, 9b.

Neshamot, pl. of *neshamah*.

Nitzotzot, "sparks" (see *orot v'kelim*). The divine soul in man is a "spark" of G–dliness, and so all material things have "sparks" of holiness, which is their origin and sustaining quality, their true *reality*, as created beings *ex nihilo*. In performing Divine precepts with material objects, their

"sparks" are "liberated" and returned to their Source and the Divine Unity is reestablished in the midst of the multiplicity of things external. The person performing the precept, together with surrounding Nature are thus reunited with the Creator.

Or, "light," Kabbalistic term for Divine emanation and influence. Because of its special properties (e.g. always attached to source, illuminates all places without itself being affected, can be screened and obscured without affecting source, etc.) it is the favourite kabbalistic metaphor for Divine influence. (Ch. 51).

Or En-Sof, "light of the *En Sof* (Infinite)" (sometimes "Infinite Light") first emanation from the Infinite. (Chs. 6, 18, 35). See *En Sof.*

Or makif, "encompassing light," the Divine influence or creative force of an infinite order which cannot be confined within limited creatures, hence is said to "encompass it" in a pervasive and transcending form (ch. 48). See also *sovev* chs. 23, 41, 46, 48.

Orot v'kelim, "lights and vessels." In the process of creation, the first emanations produced infinite light and finite vessels (the latter being "condensed" light). The light was too "strong" to be contained in the vessels, hence the latter were "shattered" (see *shevirat ha-kelim*) and "sparks" *(nitzotzot)* were scattered and were embedded in the lower forms of existence, down to material creatures. *Kelim* are a part of the *tzimtzum* (v.) process whereby finite beings came into existence.

Patriarchs. The Patriarchs, Abraham Isaac and Jacob, embodied in their natures the three attributes *chesed*, *gevurah* and *tiferet*, respectively, or, what comes to the same thing, love, awe and mercy (*Gen.* 31:53; *Micah* 7:20). They also correspond to right, left and center. Jacob, whose attribute is Truth (*Micah* 7:20), corresponding to *tiferet*, is in the center, hence the "central bolt" locking together (reconciling, or synthesising) the two extremes of *chesed* and *gevurah*. These attributes and their interaction appear on every level of the entire cosmic order, from the primordial source of *Atzilut* down to the physical world. Ch. 13. Cf. *Zohar* II, 175b. They are reflected in three forms of Divine service (in angels as well as in men). See *Avodah Merkavah*.

Ratzon, "will," or "desire." *Ratzon ha-Elyon*, "Supernal Will," i.e. the Divine Will. Where a series of actions are all directed towards an ultimate objective, it is that final objective which constitutes the *innermost* will and desire, while all actions motivated by it are desired only as a

means to that end, and are called "external." Thereby it is emphasised in the *Tanya* that this material world, the last in the series of emanations, is the ultimate objective of Creation; man, the last of the creatures, the ultimate objective (chaps. 22, 23, 36). The Divine commandments in their practical application, are likewise the "innermost" Supernal Will. (Chaps. 23, 35, 40).

Sefirot, Divine "attributes," "emanations," or "manifestations," numbering ten, often referred to as the Ten Supernal *Sefirot*. They are divided into two categories: *sechel* ("intellect") and *middot* ("dispositions"). See respective headings. The *sefirot* manifest themselves in each of the Four Worlds (v.). They are the source of the ten soul powers. (Ch. 3, 6, 18, 39, 51, 53).

Sechel, "intellect," comprising *chochmah, binah, da'at (ChaBaD)*, the first three of the Ten *Sefirot* (v.); sometimes referred to also as *mochin* ("brains"); also as *immot* ("mothers"), being the source of the *middot*. (Chaps. 2, 3, 6, 12, 30, 39, 51).

Shevirat ha-kelim, "breaking of the vessels," one of the most important doctrines of Lurianic Kabbalah is mentioned only in passing in the first part of *Tanya* (ch. 8), more in part IV (*Igeret ha-Kodesh*, chs. 26 28) and other major works, e.g. *Torah Or* (pp. 27c, 56d, 89d, 97b, 103b, etc.), *Likutei Torah* (vol. I, *Bamidbar* 82c; II, *Devarim* 31b, etc.).

Shechinah, Divine Presence, the immanent category of the Divine influence, brought down to earth by the study of the Torah and the practice of good deeds. Identified with *malchut* (v.) and the source of the souls. Corresponds to the second letter *hai* of the *Tetragrammaton* (v.). The sinner, on the other hand, breaks up the unity of the Divine Name, dragging down the *Shechinah* into "exile." (Chaps. 6, 11, 17, 35, 37, 41, 45, 51, 52, 53). See also *Yichud*.

Simchah, "joy." "Service with joy" is a cardinal principle in the philosophy of Chabad, derived from the Lurianic emphasis on joy. (Chaps. 26, 31, 33).

Sitra achra, "the other side," i.e. not the side of holiness; it is another term for "evil" in that it negates the G–dhead. Anything that tends to separate from G–d belongs in the *sitra achra*, the root of evil. See also *Kelipah*.

Sovev, same as *makif*. See *Or makif*.

Soul, see *Nefesh, Neshamah.*

The soul powers *(kochot ha-nefesh)* are divided into two categories: (a) General, or "encompassing" *(makifim)*, so called because they are not confined to any particular organ of the body; and (b) Particular or "immanent." To the first belong *oneg* ("delight") and *ratzon* ("will," or "desire"); to the latter belong *sechel* and *middot*, the senses and other physical manifestation of the body.

Tanya, "it has been taught," referring to a text of a *Baraita*. Popular name of the *Likutei Amarim* by Rabbi Schneur Zalman, after initial word of the work, referring to a Talmudic source (*Niddah* 30b). Although the said source does not indicate it as *Baraita*, it appears as such in *Yevamot* 71a. Furthermore, the author of this source, R. Simlai, is mentioned as a *Tanna* in various sources (e.g. *Vayyikra Rabba* 14:7; *Yalkut Shim'oni, beg. Tazri'a; Talmud Yerushalmi; Pesachim* 5:7, *et al.*).

Tetragrammaton, the Ineffable Divine Name of the four letters *yod-hai-vav-hai*, the creative and preserving force which acts through the other Divine Name *(Elokim)* which is immanent in Nature. In *Kabbalistic* terms the four letters of the *Tetragrammaton* are divided into two combinations: *yod-hai* and *vav-hai*. The former represents the "hidden world" as it was conceived in the Divine Mind (the letter *yod*—a point—symbolising, the Divine *chochmah; hai*—dimensional—symbolising *binah*). The latter combination represents the actually created worlds, the "revealed worlds," including our material world *(vav*—a vertical line—symbolising extension, or emanation, downwards; the second *hai*—the unfolding worlds *after emanation*, including our material world). (Chap. 26). See also *Igeret ha-Teshuvah*, chap. 4; *Torah Or, op. cit.*, 46a; *Likutei Torah*, vol. I, *Emor*, 33b; II, *Tetze*, 39b, *et al.*

Tiferet, "beauty," third of the *middot*, synthesis of *chesed* and *gevurah*, with *chesed* predominating.

Yetzira, world of "Formation," third of the *Four Worlds* (v.). See *Asiyah*.

Yichud, "union," or "unity." Unity and oneness with G-d attainable through knowledge of the Torah and the fulfillment of the Divine commands (chaps. 5, 23, 25, 35, 46). *Yichud Elyon*, "supernal union," the union of the transcedent and immanent categories of Divine influence, unity of the Divine Name, etc. (Chaps. 17, 40, 41).

Tzaddik, "righteous," "perfect." As defined in the Talmud, in connection with Divine Judgment, it refers to a person whose good deeds outweigh

the bad. The two types of *tzaddik, tzaddik gamur* (perfect righteous) and *tzaddik she-eno gamur* (imperfectly righteous) are defined in the *Tanya* in terms of sublimation of innate evil. In the first, his whole nature has been sublimated and harnessed in the service of the good. In the latter there is a residue of evil nature, and there are innumerable gradations, depending on the quality of evil in his nature which has not been sublimated and converted to good. See also *Benoni.*

Ze'er anpin, "small image."

Tzimtzum, "contraction," the most crucial doctrine in Lurianic Kabbalah explaining the creative process by means of the so-called self-limitation of the Infinite Light *(Or En-Sof),* further expounded by rational categories in *Chabad* see *Tanya,* chaps. 21, 38, 48, 49; *Sha'ar ha-Yichud veha-Emunah,* chaps. 6, 7, 9; *Torah Or,* pp. 20, 27, 77; *Likutei Torah,* vol. I, *Behar* 41b; *Hosafot* 51b; *Shelach* 37c; vol. II, *N'tzavim* 49a f.; *Haazinu* 71c; etc.

Part II

INTRODUCTION

by Rabbi Nisen Mangel, M.A.

Rabbi Schneur Zalman, the author of *Shaar HaYichud VeHaemunah*, is the founder of Chabad, the intellectual branch of Chassidism. A major difference between the teachings of Chabad and those of Chassidism in general is that Chabad obligates a knowledge of G–dliness in addition to simple faith. Faith and knowledge, explains Rabbi Schneur Zalman, are each the necessary complement of the other for proper service of G–d. When one dwells upon the greatness of G–d and contemplates His wondrous deeds, he obtains in a small measure a conception of His Infinite power. In conceiving Him, he is aroused to love G–d and to cleave to Him and desires to manifest his love by observing His commandments. In the same way, one who considers the unfathomable essence of the Creator is overcome by a sense of awe and fear of Him and will refrain from acting in opposition to His Will.

Yet, human knowledge is limited and man's intellect cannot visualise what is beyond it. Therefore, human reason cannot conceive the true essence of G–d because of His perfection and the imperfection of man's reason. However, he must believe with pure faith the esoteric aspects of G–d which transcend his intellect. According to Rabbi Schneur Zalman, one must strive to understand Divinity to the limit of his intellectual capacities and beyond that limit he is to believe with simple faith. With the maximum of understanding followed by faith, one will come to serve G–d with warmth and vitality.[1]

In his introduction to *Shaar HaYichud VeHaemunah*, called, "The Education of the Child," the author stresses the importance of educating even the young child to love G–d and have faith in Him. For this will remain with him throughout his life and be a sound basis for the ultimate purpose of his life—the fulfillment of his religious duties.

The twelve chapters forming the body of *Shaar HaYichud VeHaemunah* are a profound exposition of several basic Jewish philosophical concepts. Among them are *creatio ex nihilo*, Divine Providence, His Essence and attributes, His immanence and transcendence, and the doctrine of *Tzimtzum*. The central idea of this work, the pivot around which all the other concepts revolve is the principle of *Yichud HaShem*, Divine Unity.

Notes will be found at the end of this Introduction

Proclamation of this Unity is made daily by Jews in the Scriptural utterance "Sh'ma Yisrael," "Hear O Israel, G-d is our Lord, G-d is One."[2] During the long history of Jewish exile and suffering myriads of Jews have given up their lives rather than renounce their faith in His Unity and Oneness.[3]

The essential meaning of the doctrine of Divine Unity is the belief in absolute monotheism, i.e., there is but one G-d, with none other besides Him. It negates polytheism, the worship of many gods, and paganism, the deification of any finite thing or being or natural force; it excludes dualism, the assumption of two rival powers of good and evil, and pantheism, which equates G-d and nature.

Maimonides' interpretation of G-d's Unity emphasises also that His Essence and Being is a simple and perfect Unity without any plurality, composition or divisibility and free from any physical properties and attributes. In his words:

> G-d is One. He is not two or more than two, but One. None of the things existing in the universe to which the term one is applied is like unto His Unity; neither such a unit as a species which comprises many units, nor such a unit as a physical body which consists of parts. His Unity is such that there is no other unity like it in the world. . . . The knowledge of this truth is a positive precept, as it is written, "Hear O Israel, G-d is our Lord, G-d is One."[4]

The Chassidic interpretation of Unity, based on the Zoharic concepts of "Lower Level Unity" and "Higher Level Unity," gives it a more profound meaning. Rabbi Schneur Zalman explains that Divine Unity does not only exclude the existence of other ruling powers besides the One G-d or of any plurality in Him, but it precludes any existence at all apart from Him. The universe appears to possess an existence independent from its Creator only because we do not perceive the creating force which is its *raison d'etre.* All created things, whether terrestrial or celestial, exist only by virtue of the continuous flow of life and vitality from G-d. The creative process did not cease at the end of the Six Days of Creation, but continues at every moment, constantly renewing all existence. Were this creating power to withdraw even a single moment, all existence would vanish into nothingness, exactly as before the Six Days of Creation. Thus, the true essence and reality of the universe and everything therein is but the Divine power within it.

This aspect of Divine Unity is called in the Zohar *Yichudah Tataah*, Lower Level Unity.

Although everything is Divinity, it does not mean that G–d is identical with the world or limited by it. He is immanent in Creation, yet at the same time He infinitely transcends it. "It is not the essence of the Divine Being," declares Rabbi Schneur Zalman, "that He creates worlds and sustains them."[5] For indeed, the creating power by which all existence is brought into being and sustained is only the Divine *speech*, the words and letters of the Ten Utterances[6] by which the world is created, which is as nothing in relation to His Infinite Being.

Moreover, the Divine speech is united with His Essence in a complete union even after it has become "materialised" in the creation of the worlds. Thus, created beings are always "within" their source, i.e., G–d, and are completely nullified by Him as the rays of the sun are nullified within the sun-globe. It is only from the perspective of the created beings who are incapable of perceiving their source, that they appear as independently existing entities. However, in relation to Him, all creation is naught; there is no existence whatsoever apart from Him. Therefore, the creation of the universe does not effect any change in His Unity and Oneness by its existence, for just as He was alone prior to Creation, so is He One and alone after the Creation. And this constitutes *Yichudah Ilaah*, Higher Level Unity.

This interpretation of Divine Unity is closely related to another fundamental doctrine of Chabad Chassidism—the doctrine of *Tzimtzum*.

Jewish philosophic and Kabbalistic thought has been deeply concerned with the seeming contradiction between the Divine attribute of omnipresence and the existence of the universe. Since G–d is omnipresent and nothing can exist outside of Him, where was there place for the universe to materialise at creation? How could the finite world emerge from G–d the Infinite? How can things which are the antithesis of Divinity exist in His presence?

To solve these problems, Rabbi Yitzchak Luria[7] advanced the doctrine of *Tzimtzum*, the withdrawal and contraction of the Infinite.[8] He explained that before the creation of the worlds, G–d filled all "space"[9] and there was no room (possibility) for the existence of the universe. However, when it arose in His Will to create the worlds, the Infinite withdrew to the sides, as it were, and a vacuum and empty space was formed, thereby making room for their existence. Into this

space there emanated from G–d a ray of light[10] which is the source of all creation. This light and creating force underwent countless *Tzimtzumim* which contracted and diminished it until this corporeal and mundane world, where even things which are in defiance to holiness, were brought into existence.

Thus, according to the Lurianic doctrine of *Tzimtzum*, Creation was preceded by the self-limitation of G–d in order to make room for the material world and everything in it. In post-Lurianic thought, this doctrine received two interpretations. Some held that *Tzimtzum* was to be taken literally, that is to say, G–d actually removed His presence from the space in which the worlds were subsequently created, created them, and retained His connection with them through the exercise of His Providence.

To Rabbi Schneur Zalman, such an interpretation was unthinkable. The doctrine of *Tzimtzum*, he states, cannot be taken literally for several reasons. First, Scripture explicitly declares: "Do I not fill the heavens and the earth, says G–d?"[11] and "The whole earth is full of His glory."[12] The Talmud states, "Just as the soul fills the body so does G–d fill the universe."[13] Our Sages in the Midrash explain that G–d revealed Himself to Moses from a bush in order to teach us that there is no place void of His presence, not even so lowly a thing as a bush.[14] In the Zohar we find, "There is no place devoid of G–d."[15] Such statements abound in Scripture and Rabbinic lore.

Secondly, the literal interpretation of this doctrine implies a change in G–d's omnipresence. Prior to Creation, the Divine presence was ubiquitous; subsequently, through the process of *Tzimtzum*, a vacuum was formed devoid of His presence. Yet, Scripture specifically states, "I, G–d, have not changed."[16] In addition, "withdrawal" is a phenomenon of corporeality which cannot be ascribed to G–d, Who is incorporeal.

Rabbi Schneur Zalman's interpretation of *Tzimtzum*,[17] which has its foundation in Zohar, Kabbalah and the teachings of the Baal Shem Tov, reflects the true spirit and meanings of the Scriptures, Talmud and Midrash. He explained that there are two kinds of Divine *emanations*:[18] a boundless and unlimited effluence, called in Kabbalah *Or En Sof*, the Infinite Light, and a light of a finite order which can give rise to and be confined in finite existence.[19] To say that His power and light can be manifested only in infinity and cannot be revealed in finite existence is to imply a deficiency in His omnipotence and

therefore in His absolute perfection. Both these powers, the infinite as well as the finite, are equal and complementary aspects of His omnipotence; yet His essence transcends them both.

Before Creation, by Divine Will, the infinite power was in ascendancy and the Infinite Light filled all "space" thereby precluding finite existence. The finite light was absorbed and concealed within the boundless and infinite Light as the light of a candle is nullified in the brilliance of the sun. When G-d desired to create the universe, He withdrew His Infinite Light and concealed it within Himself, allowing the revelation of His finite power and light and also making room for the emergence of finite existence. This is the first *Tzimtzum*—not the withdrawal of G-d Himself but only the *concealment* of His Infinite Light. Hence *Tzimtzum* effects no change in His Essence nor in His omnipresence, merely removing the manifestation of His Infinite Light from actuality into latency.

But even this finite power, the source of all Creation, which was revealed as a result of the concealment of the Infinite Light, is itself too abundant and powerful to give rise to finite beings. It is only after innumerable *Tzimtzumim*, which progressively condense and conceal the creative power, that it is possible for finite and physical matter to exist. Unlike the initial *Tzimtzum* which is a complete concealment of the Infinite Light, each of the subsequent *Tzimtzumim* is but a gradual diminution of the Divine light and creative force, and an adaption to the capacity of the endurance of created beings. By this screening and concealment of the power by which all things exist, the world appears to enjoy an independent existence, as if it were apart from G-d. But truly, "The whole earth is full of His Glory" for all things exist only by virtue of the Divine creating power immanent in them and endure only because it is screened from their view. Were permission granted to the eye to see beyond the external physical form, declares Rabbi Schneur Zalman, then we would perceive only the Divine power that pervades and animates every created thing and is its true essence and reality.

It is thought which forms the opening statement of *Shaar HaYichud VeHaemunah*—"*Know* this day and take unto your heart that G-d is the Lord in the heavens above and upon the earth below; there is no other,"[20] i.e., there is nothing apart from Him. This verse enjoins one to meditate upon this and understand it so well that it becomes close to his heart and finds expression in the fulfillment of the Divine precepts.

Notes to Part II Introduction

[1] *See* Likutei Torah *by Rabbi Schneur Zalman of Liadi, Kehot Publication Society (Brooklyn, 1965).* "VaEthchanan," *pp. 7 ff.*

[2] Deut. *6:4. See Ch. 1, note 5.*

[3] *Cf.* Likutei Amarim (Tanya), *Kehot Publication Society (Brooklyn, 1958), Chs. 18–19.*

[4] *Maimonides,* Yad HaChazakah, "Hilchoth Yesodei Hatorah," *1:7. Cf.* Moreh Nevuchim, *I, Chs. 50, 53.*

[5] Torah Or *by Rabbi Schneur Zalman of Liadi, Kehot Publication Society (Brooklyn, 1954), p. 166a. This rules out all pantheistic doctrines which would identify or compound G–d with nature.*

[6] *See Ch. 1, note 15.*

[7] *One of the most famous and influential Kabbalists of the sixteenth century.*

[8] *See* Etz Chaim *1:2; beginning of* Otzroth Chaim, Mavoh Shearim, *and* Emek HaMelech.

[9] *The term "space" is used here in a figurative sense since space itself is a creation* ex nihilo.

[10] *The Divine effluences and emanations are figuratively called "Lights" because light possesses qualities which are characteristic of the Divine emanations. For example, the light which radiates from the sun is as nothing compared to the sun itself and the concealment or revelation of the light reflects no change whatsoever in its source. In the same way, G–d's Essence infinitely transcends His emanations and is not effected by them at all. In addition, similar to the Divine emanations, light is always bound up with its source, and illumines all places without itself being affected.*

[11] Jer. *23:24. Cf.* Likutei Amarim, *Part IV,* "Igeret Hakodesh," *Ch. 25.*

[12] Isa. *6:3.*

[13] Ber. *10a.*

[14] Shemot Rabbah *11:5.*

[15] Tikunim, Tikun *57, p. 91b.*

[16] Mal. *3:6.*

[17] *Cf.* Torah Or, *p. 27a;* Likutei Torah, "Vayikrah," *pp. 101 ff.*

[18] *See Note 10,* supra.

[19] *Even this power is endless and can give rise to innumerable finite worlds and vivify them forever.*

[20] Deut. *4:39.*

Part III INTRODUCTION

by Rabbi Zalman I. Posner

Igeret Hateshuvah, the Epistle on Repentance, is the third section of the Tanya, the basic statement of the Chabad Chassidic system, written by the founder of Chabad, Rabbi Schneur Zalman.

The first section, Likutei Amarim, translated by Nissan Mindel with copious additions, was published in 1962.

The second section, Shaar Hayichud Veha'emunah, The Gate to [the understanding of] G-d's Unity and the Faith, was translated by Nisen Mangel and published in 1965.

Igeret Hateshuvah was originally published in the second edition of Tanya in 1799. That first version differs strikingly from the revised text appearing in the 1806 and all subsequent editions.

These three sections—and the final two following—are not sequential; one may study each independently. However, the author obviously pre-supposed considerable familiarity with the subject. The notes and sources should be of assistance, particularly references to specific material in the first two sections. The Introductions to the first sections will help orient the reader in the Chabad landscape. The Translator's Explanatory Notes to "On Learning Chassidus" (Kehot, 1959) will help the novice understand terms used in the text here. The bibliography on Chabad literature in English is commended to the reader's attention.

Parentheses and brackets appear in the original text. The author frequently used וכו' for an uncompleted quotation or idea. The translator has used three dots (. . .) at these points. Footnotes are by the translator. The translation endeavours to maintain fidelity to the text, with a minimum of transitional words or phrases.

The thread of teshuvah is worked deeply into the fabric of Torah. Teshuvah is as varied as man. It was the anguished awakening of Adam and Cain. Later it was the sobering aftermath of the dismal worship of the Golden Calf. At times it did not come to pass—the stern demands and desperate pleas of the prophets to a wilful and indulgent people to abandon their destructive ways. Teshuvah can be majestic—in the magnitude and power attributed to it by the Talmud sages. From the

dawn of humanity until the age of space, teshuvah is the heartening reverse of the coin of folly and evil.

The word itself is generally rendered "repentance," but "return" is preferable, depicting the soul making its way back to the welcoming G-d from Whom it strayed.

That mortal man has failings is no startling revelation. But the consequence of this commonplace need not be cynicism. Man's faults —even if deliberate or malicious—do not doom or incapacitate him. This doctrine of teshuvah can overcome despair, transform ingrained habit, resist confirmed weakness.

An impressive literature on teshuvah has developed over the centuries. In Talmud, Kabbala, and Musar—for the jurist, the mystic, and the moralist—teshuvah is part of the lexicon. In the early days of Chabad many of these works were part of the required preparation for the aspiring young Chassid.

Teshuvah is a familiar theme in the theoretical literature and in the actual life of the Chassid. Chassidic tradition even has it that there was the possibility of calling adherents of the then new movement *baalei teshuvah*, repentants, before the name Chassid gained universal currency and acceptance.

In 1783, shortly after Rabbi Schneur Zalman assumed leadership of Chassidim in White Russia-Lithuania, he carried on learned debates with the opponents of Chassidut, the formidable Talmud scholars of Vilna and other strongholds of Talmudic learning. A decisive encounter took place in Minsk, where the Rebbe was presented with two objections to Chassidic doctrine. The second, on teshuvah, is of immediate interest here. (The full account is published in Kuntres Bikur Chicago, Kehot, p. 21, written by the late Lubavitcher Rebbe, Rabbi Jospeh I. Schneersohn, of sainted memory.)

The Baal Shem Tov, founder of the Chassidic movement had taught that a scholar and saint must also "do" teshuvah. They charged that this demeans the honour of Torah and scholars by insisting that scholars too must repent. Teshuvah obviously connoted remorse for sin. That this be the divine service of a true saint and "son of Torah" would be a gratuitous insult.

The Rebbe replied in length, repeating the Baal Shem Tov's discussion of the burning bush through which the angel of G-d addressed Moses. The bush is the symbol of the lowly, the humble, the "ordinary" person, in contrast to the lofty productive fruit-bearing

tree that the Talmud describes as the symbol of the scholar. The burning heart, the unrequited longing of the humble, is the means for the revelation of G–d, even to that greatest of prophets, Moses himself.

Moses' reaction was, "I must turn aside," and as Rashi comments, "I must turn from here to approach there." He could recognise now the unique quality of simple folk, their possession of the "heart of fire," and this brought him to teshuvah. But for this unblemished saint teshuvah had a completely different significance. For him teshuvah meant dissatisfaction with what he already was; teshuvah was a driving urge to "turn from here, to approach there."

The Baal Shem Tov taught clearly that the service of the Tzadik, the saint, must be a constant advance. Today must be a higher step in serving G–d than yesterday, and tomorrow must surpass today. This is the mood of teshuvah.

Participants in that debate told of the fiery spirit of the Rebbe as he concluded. "The truth is that the greater the scholar the greater the need for *avodah* (worship or service). And if not, one sins against the Great King . . . Then teshuvah is really necessary, from the depths of the heart, to root out the Amalek that cools (the ardour of) the way of G–d and the ways of serving G–d."

As this narrative indicates and Igeret Hateshuvah explains, teshuvah has meaning on varying levels, from literal regret for palpable evil to the growth of the spirit for the unsullied Tzadik. Chabad in general, and Igeret Hateshuvah in particular, address themselves to the Jew in *his* situation, humble or exalted, illiterate or erudite.

The successors of Rabbi Schneur Zalman, the Rebbes of Chabad for the next six generations until the coming of Moshiach, wrote books and delivered countless discourses (*maamorim*) on the theme of teshuvah. Some of these are profound and recondite; others are in the Yiddish vernacular for the unlettered.

Chassidic motifs characterise their approach to teshuvah as to other subjects treated in Chassidus. The origin of man's soul, the spark of G–dliness within him, his infinite potential, his closeness to G–d, his ability to control his destiny, to remake himself at will—these are grist for the mills of Chassidus, the background for teshuvah. The present Rebbe once described teshuvah as returning to the true "I." Man's undesirable traits and acts are a facade, artificial, a concealment of his true being. Little time is spent dwelling on evil itself; the morbid finds no hospitality in Chassidut.

Another Chabad doctrine is implicit here—that man is a reasoning being, and should not be subject to uncontrolled and erratic caprice, even for a good end. Otherwise man's role would be passive, a helpless plaything of fortuitous emotions. Chabad teaches that emotions must be governed by intellect, and even teshuvah, which might seem to be the least intellectual and reasoned endeavour, is bound up with the mind, particularly advanced forms of teshuvah. Not that Chabad is detached, unemotional, impersonal, but that emotion has its proper place in the spiritual physiognomy of man. Impassioned worship is a Chabad ideal, but it follows study and meditation.

Sublime feeling, Chabad teaches further, and stirring emotions are not sufficient unto themselves. Intense remorse for the past, unshakeable determination for the future, and earnest desire to return to G–d, must be translated into corresponding acts. The test of repentance and its sincerity and depth is its effect on actual life.

The challenge rings, the assurance is firm—teshuvah is within man's grasp.

May the author's sacred purpose in writing this Epistle, expressed in the very title, be brought to fruition in our lives!

ZALMAN I. POSNER

18 Elul 5725
September 1965
Nashville, Tennessee

Part IV INTRODUCTION

by Rabbi Jacob Immanuel Schochet

Igeret Hakodesh (Sacred Epistle) is the fourth of the five parts that make up the celebrated work known as *Tanya*, the classic statement of *Chabad*-Chassidism written by the founder of this school of thought, R. Shneur Zalman of Liadi.

As implied by its title, *Igeret Hakodesh* consists mostly of "epistles sent by (R. Shneur Zalman of Liadi) to teach the people of G–d the way in which they are to walk and the deed which they should do. And inasmuch as he has made references in many places to the *Sefer Likutei Amarim*[1] . . . we have seen fit and proper to join them with the *Sefer Likutei Amarim* and *Igeret Hateshuvah*."[2] The remaining parts consist of discourses on various mystical teachings.

The *Igeret Hakodesh* was first printed in 5574 (1814), a year after the author's passing. It was then, and since,[3] published alongside the *Tanya* speedily coming to be known as the "fourth part of the *Tanya*."[4] In the earlier editions some parts of various sections are missing or were intentionally omitted.[5] The standard edition of the *Tanya* published in Vilna in 1900, upon which all subsequent printings are based, is the first in which the *Igeret Hakodesh* appears in its present near-complete form.[6]

Aside from the original omissions, it should be noted that the author's sons, when authorising publication of the *Igeret Hakodesh*, drew attention to the fact that the publishers had before them merely some of the "copies spread among the disciples," while "to our misfortune the manuscripts written by the (author's) personal saintly hand, which were composed with great punctiliousness . . . have become extinct . . . Should, therefore, an error be discovered . . . the evident error will be indentified as a scribe's error, but the meaning will be clear."[7]

The epistles and discourses were written over a long span of time (*ca.* 1780–1813) but do not follow in any chronological, or otherwise specific order. The earliest datings that I was able to ascertain are for section XXIX as written before 5549 (1788–9),[8] and section XXVII as written in 1788 (late in 5548, or early in 5549).[9] It is reasonable to assume that one or more of the epistles appealing for the support of the

Notes will be found at the end of this Introduction

inhabitants of the Holy Land were written even earlier, at any time after 5537 (1777), the year that R. Mendel Vitebsker[10] ascended to the Holy Land with a large following of Chassidic families. Section XX is no doubt the latest, having been written only a few days before the author's passing on the 24th of Teveth 5573 (1813).[11]

The fifth part of the *Tanya*, also consisting of epistles and discourses (and seemingly a continuation of *Igeret Hakodesh*[12]), appeared together with the original edition of *Igeret Hakodesh*[13] but under the separate title of *Kuntress Acharon* (Latest Discourse).[14]

The contents of *Igeret Hakodesh*, as already implied by the composite nature of this work, are very varied. Most of the epistles are pastoral letters offering guidance and encouragement, and sometimes fatherly admonitions.[15] Some letters touch upon historical aspects of Chassidism[16] and, like the apparent discourses in *Igeret Hakodesh*,[17] most of them contain profound mystical expositions. The precept of *Tzedakah* (charity), and especially *Tzekadah* for the Holy Land, is a dominant theme throughout the *Igeret Hakodesh*.[18] But this book's contents are found to touch upon practically every basic principle and doctrine taught by Chassidism, encompassing the whole of the every day life of the Chassid, with respect to Torah, worship, and social concourse.

Most of the subjects can be found mentioned and elaborated upon in the other parts of the *Tanya*, and in the other works of the author.[19] They are too numerous, and often too intricate to be discussed in detail within the limited confines of this Introduction.[20] There are, however, some subjects appearing in this work, basic and peculiar to Chassidic thought, to which special attention should be drawn:

(a) the doctrine of the *Tzadik*, or *Rebbe*, and the *Rebbe-Chassid* relationship;[21]
(b) the necessity to study the esoteric part of the Torah;[22]
(c) an elaborate and reasoned defense of Chassidic doctrine;[23] and
(d) the attitude of Chassidism to its erstwhile opponents.[24]

The present volume follows the publication of the English translation of the first three parts of the *Tanya: Likutei Amarim*, translated by Dr.

Nissan Mindel; *Sha'ar Hayichud Vehaemunah*, translated by Rabbi Nisen Mangel; and *Igeret Hateshuvah*, translated by Rabbi Zalman I. Posner. The general format of all these publications is similar, but the translations were undertaken separately and individually. Thus the reader may note a number of variations in the rendition of terms, in the transliteration of non-English words, and the general system of translation. Also, this translation was written over a lengthy period of time and under varying conditions; this will explain possible inconsistencies within this work itself. Transliteration, especially, presented a problem. A variety of usages have become common, and these have been a guide more often than strict rules. The more adaptable Sefardi pronunciation is the only principle followed consistently in this matter. However, all these variations will be found to be more formal than essential.

It is needless to emphasise that when the contents of a text are so deeply interwoven with its language and style and involve a highly technical vocabulary, as in the present case, there are so many problems and obstacles as make it nigh to impossible to render a translation that is both faithful to the original and meaningful on its own. Any translation tends to be an interpretation of the text. For any such interpretative renditions in this book, the translator, and he alone, is responsible.

Even so, this translation seeks to remain as close as is practicable to the original, and within the limits of the possible to leave an impression (both in general and in detail) resembling the impression offered by the original.[25] Two significant deviations from this rule are the following: (1) The translator took the liberty to insert transitional words and phrases. These are indicated by round brackets. (2) The translator took the liberty to set off the apparently parenthetical phrases in the text by means of square brackets. It is hoped that this will help clarify the text and make for smoother reading.

Technical terms, a literal translation of which would be meaningless without accompanying explanations, were left untranslated. For all these terms explanation or reference is offered in the footnotes or in the section entitled Mystical Concepts in Chassidism[26] following the Part IV Approbation immediately after this Introduction.

The textual corrections and emendations suggested by the Lubavitcher Rebbe, R. Menachem M. Schneerson שליט"א,[27] are generally incorporated in the body of the translation and noted in the margin.

Also, where textual readings have not been followed too strictly, this has been noted accordingly.

The critical apparatus along the margin of the translation consists of the following:

(a) *variae lectiones;*
(b) note of translator's deviation from the original;
(c) references to the sources of quotations appearing in the text;
(d) references to the sources of paraphrases in the text (usually preceded by the notation *par.*). These references will prove helpful in understanding peculiar phrases and expressions by indicating that they are but paraphrases of a Biblical or Rabbinic text. These references are not included in the Index of References.
(e) References to sources and parallel instances of subjects discussed in the text. These references are a desideratum for research and a proper understanding of the subject-matter.
(f) Explanations of terms and subjects appearing in the text.

Bibliographical information on the texts frequently cited in the notes is given in the bibliography appended to this book.

The *Approbation by the Author's Sons* prefacing the *Tanya*, and already appearing with the translation of the first part of the *Tanya*, is republished here. This was done for the simple reason that having been written for the first edition of *Igeret Hakodesh*, its proper place is here.

In conclusion, may this translation merit to be an effective contribution to the goal of the "*dissemination of the fountains of Chassidism*,"[28] and inspire its readers and students to realise the author, R. Shneur Zalman's aim: "to teach the people of G–d the way in which they are to walk, and the deed which they should do" with respect to *Torah*, *Avodah*, and *Gemilut Chassadim.*

ירושלים עיה"ק ת"ו
בכ"ח מנח"ם א"ב

Notes to Part IV Introduction

[1] *Original name of the* Tanya.

[2] Approbation by the Author's Sons, (*written for the first edition of the* Igeret Hakodesh); *see* infra, *p. 799.*

[3] *With the exception noted by R. Menachem M. Schneerson,* Bibliography of the Tanya-editions (*appended to all* Tanya-*editions since 1954*), s.v. הוספה.

[4] Bibliography, *Introduction to Part IV, KPS* (*Brooklyn, 1968*), *items 8 and 14.*

[5] *See* ibid., *item 8.*

[6] Ibid., *item 36.—"Near-complete," because,*

intentional or not, there still are some relevant omissions; e.g., *see* infra, *sect. XIV, note 2*; sect. XV, note 43; the remark at the end of sect XX; and sect. XXII, note 1.*

[7] Approbation, infra, *pp. 799. This may explain the numerous* variae lectiones. *It would seem, however, that two original manuscripts were available at one time or another,* viz. *of sect. XX and XXV; see the comment affixed to section* XX (infra, *p. 214*), *and the glossary note in the margin of the (Hebrew)* Tanya, *p. 72b.*

[8] *Section I was written in 5549 (1788–9); see R. Menachem M. Schneerson,* Hayom Yom (*Kehot: New York, 1961*), *p. 77. In it appears a reference to section XXIX (see* infra, *p. 13, note 41*). *On the other hand, in sect. XXIX there is a reference to the* Tanya *which was not published until 1796. It is possible, though, that this specific reference (in XXIX) was inserted later.*

[9] *See* infra, *p. 563, and note 5* ad loc.

[10] *See* ibid.—*Section IX, especially, appears to support this assumption; see there, note 19.*

[11] *See* infra, *p. 511, note 122.*

[12] *And, indeed, often quoted as such in later Chassidic literature. See, e.g.,* Torah Or, *p. 49c;* Likute Torah, *II: 1c, III: 16b, IV: 18c, etc.*

[13] *In a few editions some of the sections of the* Igeret Hakodesh *and* Kuntress Acharon *appeared intermingled.*

[14] *An English translation of the* Kuntress Acharon *will appear under separate cover.*

[15] *See especially sections I, II, IX, XI, XXII–XXIV, and XXXI.*

[16] *See sections II and XXV.*

[17] E.g., *sections V, VII, XIII, XV, XVIII–XX, XXVI–XXIX.*

[18] *See sections III–VI, VIII–X, XII, XIV, XVI, XVII, XXI, XXX and XXXII.*

[19] *See especially* Torah Or, *and* Likute Torah, *both works available with detailed* indices.

[20] *See the indices for specific subjects.*

[21] *See sections XXIIa, XXVII, and XXVIII.—[Section XXIIa, as mentioned in the notes, is a mere extract of the original letter. It needs to be viewed in the context of its history and the complete epistle (see* Hatamim *I: 2, (Warsaw, 1935) pp. 32 ff.;* Igroth Ba'al Hatanya Ubnei Doro, ed. *D. Hilman, pp. 58 ff.) to be properly understood and appreciated. Of interest related to XXIIa is the author's Foreword to the* Tanya, *and* Igroth Ba'al Hatanya, *sect. 16.] Cf. also the notion of* Tzadik *as defined in the first part of* Tanya.

[22] *See section XXVI.*

[23] *See section XXV. Of related interest are* Igroth Ba'al Hatanya, *sect. 56 and 57.*

[24] *See sections II and XXV. Of related interest are* Igroth Ba'al Hatanya, *sect. 2–4, 7, 8, 56, 60, 65, and 137; cf. C. M. Hilman,* Beth Rabbi, (*Berdichev, 1903*) *part I: ch. 6, 11–13, and 18.*

[25] *This applies especially to the typical Rabbinic form and style (employing the tool of paraphasing Biblical and Rabbinic expressions) in which most of the letters are written. These paraphrases are retained in their literal sense nearly throughout the translation.*

[26] *The reader will find it helpful to consult also the Introductions and notes to the English translation of the first three parts of the* Tanya *and the essays* On the Teachings of Chassidus, *and* On Learning Chassidus (*Kehot: New York, 1959*).

[27] Luach Hatikun, *and* He'aroth Vetikunim, *both appended to all* Tanya*-editions since 1954.*

[28] *See Preface by the Lubavitcher* Rebbe *to the English translation of the first part of the* Tanya (*p.* vii). *Cf. R. Israel Ba'al Shem Tov's letter appended by R. Jacob Joseph of Polnoy to his* Ben Porath Yossef (*Mefitze Torah: New York, 1954; pp. 254 ff.*), *and prefacing all editions of* Kether Shem Tov. *ed. R. Aaron Hacohen of Apt; cf. also* infra, *sect. XXVI.*

by the Rabbis [long may they live], the sons of the *Gaon* the author [of saintly memory, whose soul is in Eden].

Whereas it has been agreed by us to give authorisation and prerogative to bring to the printing press, for a remembrance unto the children of Israel, the written words of uprightness and truth, the words of the Living G–d, authored by our lord father, teacher and master, of blessed memory, recorded personally in his saintly expression, whose words are all as burning coals to set the hearts aflame to bring them closer to their Father in Heaven; they are entitled *Igeret Hakodesh* (Holy Epistle) being mostly epistles sent by his holy eminence to teach the people of G–d the way by which to walk and the deed which they should do;[1]

And inasmuch as he has made references, in many places, to the *Sefer Likutei Amarim*, since the words of the Torah are scanty in one place and ample in another,[2] especially also as he introduced new material in the *Kuntress Acharon* on certain chapters which he wrote when he composed the *Sefer Likutei Amarim*, profound discussions on passages in the *Zohar*, *Etz Chayim* and *Peri Etz Chayim*, which (passages) appear contradictory to one another, but he, with his inspired perception, has reconciled them, each statement in its own manner, as he has written in the *Likutei Amarim*, we have seen fit and proper to join them with the *Sefer Likutei Amarim* and *Igeret Hateshuvah*[3] of his saintly eminence, our lord father, teacher and master, of blessed memory;

(Therefore), we come to place a great fence and the rabbinic injunction of נח"ש[4] (excommunication) for which there is no remedy, that no man may lift his hand to reprint them in their present form, or in part, for a period of five years from the date below.[5]

However, this should be made known: to our misfortune the manuscripts written by his personal saintly hand which were composed with great punctiliousness, without a superfluous or deficient letter, have become extinct; only this little has remained from the abundance, and it has been carefully collected one by one from the copies spread among the disciples. Should, therefore, an error be discovered [who can understand (and prevent) errors?[6]] the evident error will be identified as a scribe's error, but the meaning will be clear.

Declared by *Dov Ber*, the son of my lord father, teacher and master, *Gaon* and Saint, the Holy of Israel, our teacher and master *Schneur Zalman*, of blessed memory, נבג"מ.[7]

Also declared by *Chayim Abraham*, the son of my lord father, teacher and master, *Gaon* and Saint, our teacher and master *Shneur Zalman*, the memory of the *Tzadik* be blessed. נבג"מ.[7]

Also declared by *Moshe*, the son of my lord father, teacher and master, *Gaon* and Saint, our teacher and master[8] *Shneur Zalman*, of blessed memory, נבג"מ.[7]

Notes to Part IV Approbation

[1] Par. *Exodus 18:20.*

[2] Yerushalmi, *Rosh Hashana 3:5.*

[3] *The* Sha'ar Hayichud Vehaemunah *is not mentioned here, probably because it is the second part proper of the* Likutei Amarim; *it has always been called* Likutei Amarim Part Two, *and printed together with the first part. The* Igeret Hateshuvah, *which came to be called the "third part of the* Tanya," *appeared in its first version in the second edition of the* Tanya *(1798), and in its second, revised version from 1806 onwards (with the exception of the Lemberg 1860 edition); [the first version has been reprinted in* Igroth Ba'al Hatanya, *sect. 52; pp. 82 ff.].*

[4] נדוי חרם שמתא—*three forms of excommunication.*

[5] *In the original edition of 1814 appears the date, 22nd of Iyar '574 (1814), subsequently omitted.* (L.H.)

[6] *Psalms 19:13.*

[7] נשמתו בגנזי מרומים—"*his soul rests in the hidden treasures of heaven.*"

[8] *Emended according to* H.V.

MYSTICAL CONCEPTS IN CHASSIDISM

An Introduction to Kabbalistic Concepts and Doctrines in IGERET HAKODESH-Likutei Amarim-Tanya, Part IV

by Rabbi Jacob Immanuel Schochet

Foreword to First Edition

This volume is a companion to my translation of *Igeret Hakodesh*, the fourth part of R. Schneur Zalman of Liadi's celebrated *Likutei Amarim-Tanya*. It is an introduction serving two purposes: to acquaint the reader with the general nature and contents of *Igeret Hakodesh*, and to introduce the reader to, and acquaint him with, some basic concepts and doctrines which appear throughout that work.

The paragraphs dealing with the nature and contents of *Igeret Hakodesh* appear also alongside the translation, by way of a brief and general Introduction. The explanatory notes, forming the bulk of this volume, appear here on their own, though numerous references have been made to them in the footnotes of the translation. This separate publication was necessitated by technical difficulties but also serves to emphasise the following point.

The Explanatory Notes deal with profoundly intricate subjects, involving very delicate premises and principles of the teachings of Kabbalah and Chassidism. An attempt has been made to offer simplified outlines and explanations to the English-reading novice in this field, but the subject-matter is not as simple as may appear here. In Jewish Mysticism, as in other branches of knowledge, there are different schools of learning and interpretation. These schools differ not only one from another, but sometimes subdivide into further branches within themselves. For example, in the school of R. Isaac Luria which, since shortly after its inception (sixteenth century), dominates the world of Jewish Mysticism, we find, in the very first generation after the passing of its founder, differing interpretations of even so basic a doctrine of that great master as *tzimtzum*.

As the footnotes show, the basic sources of the Explanatory Notes are the writings of R. Schneur Zalman of Liadi, with abundant references to the original writings of the *Zohar* and of R. Isaac Luria. The obvious purpose is to present them in a way that will help clarify the contents of *Igeret Hakodesh*, but it should be noted that the explanations

offered in this volume* represent their author's understanding of the subjects. Though he strove to grasp and offer the views and interpretations of R. Schneur Zalman of Liadi, the reader is reminded that ambition is not necessarily identical with achievement. The involved terminology and subtle phraseology in all the works mentioned often threaten to entrap anyone who cannot claim to belong to the exclusive circle of יודעי ח"ן (adepts in the esoteric science).

Nonetheless, it is hoped that this Introduction will prove successful in its aims, and there remains but to paraphrase the Psalmist with the apology and prayer: "Who can understand (and prevent) errors? Clear Thou me from hidden faults!" (*Psalms* 19:13)

Toronto, 11 Nissan 5728 J.I.S.

* *The same applies to the explanations given in the footnotes of the translation.*

Foreword to Second Revised Edition

The first edition of this introductory tract has been out of print for a long time. The need for a second edition is not only gratifying but also provides an auspicious opportunity to revise and to take into consideration comments and suggestions received since the first printing. This has led to some major changes:

(i) This was written and intended as an Introduction to my translation of *Igeret Hakodesh*. But as many use it for general reference, I have followed the suggestion and have given it a separate title whilst retaining the original one as a sub-title. For this reason I have omitted from the revised edition the technical parts dealing with the nature and contents of *Igeret Hakodesh* (pp. 11–17 in the first edition) which, in any case, appear in the abbreviated Introduction prefacing the translation. On the other hand, the numerous references to *Igeret Hakodesh*, and to the footnotes of its translation, growing out of the original intent and purpose, are retained.

(ii) The first three chapters have been entirely rewritten. The other chapters were expanded, and otherwise underwent only minor revisions.

Technical difficulties prevent me, at this time, from adding a few additional chapters on related concepts and doctrines. But this new edition does afford an opportunity to rectify an omission in the first one, namely, to acknowledge gratefully and to give due credit to my wife שתליט״א for compiling the helpful indices* of both this work and the translation of *Igeret Hakodesh*.

Toronto, 26 Nissan 5731 J.I.S.

* These indices appear together with this work in a separate edition now being prepared for print.

Introduction

This book deals with fundamental concepts and doctrines which appear throughout the writings of Chassidism and are essential for a proper understanding of them. They are concepts and doctrines that have their origins in the basic works of the Kabbalah such as *Sefer Yetzirah* and the *Zohar*-writings. But in these works they appear mostly seminal and rudimentary. They assume their accepted authoritative forms only in the comprehensive expositions of R. Moses Cordovero[1] and R. Isaac Luria.[2] Thus any attempt to explain these concepts and doctrines as they appear in the writings of R. Schneur Zalman of Liadi,[3] can be done only in the context of the works of his predecessors. For this reason the reader will find many references to them throughout this book. Where other works prove helpful, and cross-references enlightening to the serious student seeking to delve further into the subject-matter, these, too, are cited in the footnotes.

It is to be remembered that the concepts and doctrines discussed, deal with profoundly intricate subjects, often involving difficult and delicate premises and principles which touch upon many basic theological problems. They are discussed here because the marginal notes accompanying the translation of *Igeret Hakodesh* (where these concepts and doctrines appear) could not do justice to them. But even the chapters following should be regarded as merely explanatory notes; as an attempt at simplified outlines and explanations, and nothing more. These outlines and explanations neither are, nor claim to be, complete in, and by, themselves. There are many philosophical questions and problems that are related to, and can be raised about, these various concepts and doctrines which are beyond the scope of this book to deal with. Verily, such an objective would require a much larger volume if not several volumes. Those interested in pursuing the subjects further are referred to readily available works devoted to that purpose, often cited in the footnotes, such as the writings of R. Meir ibn Gabbai[4] and R. Joseph Ergas.[5]

NOTES

[1] *Known by the acrostic* REMAK; *1522–1570. Leader of a prominent Kabbalistic school in Safed; author of* Pardess Rimonim, Elima Rabbaty, Shi'ur Komah, Or Ne'erav, *and many other works.* REMAK *is regarded as one of the most important and lucid expositors and systematists of Jewish Mysticism.*

[2] *Known by the acrostic* ARI; *1534–1572. Founder and leader of a Kabbalistic school in Safed that soon became the dominant school in Jewish Mysticism, and exerted a profound influence on the whole Jewish world. The intricate system of the Lurianic Kabbalah, which forms the theoretical basis of Chassidic thought, is authoritatively recorded in the multi-voluminous writings of* ARI*'s principal disciple R. Chayim Vital (1543–1620), such as* Etz Chayim, Mevoh She'arim, Sha'ar Hahakdamot *etc.*

[3] *Known as the* Rav (*Rabbi*), *and amongst Chassidim as the* Alter Rebbe (*Elder Rabbi*); *1745–1813. Founder and leader of* Chabad-*Chassidism; author of* Likutei Amarim (Tanya), *an authoritative revision of* Shulchan Aruch, Torah Or, Likutei Torah, *and so on. (A detailed biography in English is presently available, published by Kehot, New York 1969.)*

[4] *One of the first and foremost systematists of the Kabbalah; originally from Spain and later in Egypt. Author of* Avodat Hakodesh, Derech Emunah, *and* Tola'at Ya'akov. Avodat Hakodesh *is an elaborate introduction to the Kabbalah, dealing with its most important problems and containing profound critical discussions of various philosophical expositions. It should be noted, though, that Ibn Gabbai's works are pre-Lurianic* (Avodat Hakodesh *was completed in 1531, and* Derech Emunah *in 1539*).

[5] *Renowned Talmudist and Kabbalist of the Lurianic school, residing in Livorno and Pisa; 1685–1730. Author of* Minchat Yosef, Shomer Emunim, Teshuvot Divrei Yosef *and so forth.* Shomer Emunim *is written in the form of a dialogue between a mystic (adherent and defender of the Kabbalah) and his rationalist critic, and is a relatively easy philosophical introduction to the main issues and principles of Jewish Mysticism.*

TABLE OF CONTENTS

Chapter 1 ANTHROPOMORPHISM AND METAPHORS

1. *Anthropomorphism*

The terminology of Kabbalah and Chassidism, and thus in the expositions following, is highly anthropomorphic. The terms are borrowed from human concepts and the empirical world. The reason is because these are the only type of words that man can use in any meaningful way. The forms of spatial-temporal concepts are imposed upon the mind of man who lives in a spatial-temporal world. It is for this very reason that the Torah, the Prophets, and our Sages use anthropomorphic language, as it is stated "The Torah speaks in the language of man."[1] For "Had they limited themselves to abstract terms and concepts appropriate to G–d, we would have understood neither the terms nor the concepts. The words and ideas used have accordingly to be such as are adapted to the hearer's mental capacity so that the subject would first sink into his mind in the corporeal sense in which the concrete terms are understood. Then we can proceed to an understanding that the presentation is only approximate and metaphorical, and that the reality is too subtle, too exalted and remote for us to comprehend its subtlety. The wise thinker will endeavour to strip the husk of the terms (i.e., their materialistic meaning) from the kernel, and will raise his conception step by step until he will at last attain to as much knowledge of the truth as his intellect is capable of apprehending."[2]

Thus it is to be kept in mind at all times that the terms and concepts need to be stripped of all and any temporal, spatial and corporeal connotations. All and any anthropomorphic notions and concepts, strictly speaking, are non-ascribable to the Divinity, as Scripture states explicitly: "To whom then will you liken G–d? Or what likeness will you compare to Him? . . . To whom will you liken Me that I should be equal, says the Holy One." (*Isaiah* 40:18, 25). This cardinal premise was adopted by Maimonides as the third in his compilation of the "Thirteen Fundamental Principles of Faith".[3]

At the same time, however, it should also be noted that the anthropomorphic terminology used in Scripture, by the mystics and by others, is not arbitrary just because it is under the protection of the above qualification. Rather, these terms are carefully chosen and possess a profound meaning.

Notes will be found at the end of each Chapter

The Rabbinic-Midrashic and mystical writings abound with references to the idea that the world below in general, and man in particular, are created in the "image" of the "world above".[4] All the categories to be found in the world below and in man are homonymous representations of, and allusions to, certain supernal concepts and notions *to which they correspond*. To be sure, there is no likeness whatever between G–d and the creation, and on the supernal levels of the strictly spiritual realm there are no such things as eyes, ears, hands, and so on, nor such activities and affections as hearing, seeing, walking, talking and so on; however, all these spatial-temporal activities and concepts do symbolise, and, indeed, *for that reason come into being in correspondence to* the original supernal, strictly and purely spiritual, categories.

In a widely-quoted passage, R. Joseph Gikatilla aptly explains this correspondence-relationship by means of the following analogy. When writing the name of a person on a piece of paper, there is surely no likeness, link or relationship between the written letters or words on paper and the physio-mental entity of the person whose name has been recorded. Even so, that writing is a symbol or sign relating to, calling to mind and denoting the full concrete entity of that person. And thus it is with the anthropomorphic and anthropopathic concepts and terms: although there is no concrete or direct link or likeness between them and the meanings they seek to express, nevertheless, they are corresponding signs and symbols relating to, and denoting, specific categories, notions and concepts that are of a strictly spiritual nature, non-spatial and non-temporal.[5]

This, then, is the way the anthropomorphic terminology is to be understood.[6]

2. *The Man-Metaphor*

In discussing Divinity relative to the Universe, the favourite metaphor of the mystics (as of many philosophers) is the analogy to man. Theological concepts and the G–d-world relationship, are often explained in terms of soul-body relationship, and in particular in terms of the various soul-powers, their faculties, functions and manifestations. The "proof-texts" for this usage are the verse "From my flesh I envisage G–d" (Job 19:26) and the Rabbinic analogy "Just as the soul permeates the whole body . . . sees but is not seen . . . sustains the whole body . . . is pure . . . abides in the innermost precincts . . . is unique in the body . . . does not eat and does not drink . . . no man knows where its place is . . .

so the Holy One, Blessed is He, . . .".[7] This, too, in a sense, follows on the above-mentioned principle of a "terrestrial-supernal correspondence."[8]

But even while an understanding of the soul is helpful in understanding matters relating to the Divinity, this is but an anthropomorphic approximation which cannot be carried too far and needs to be qualified. It must be remembered, as R. Schneur Zalman points out, that in some respects the analogy breaks down, and is completely inadequate: "This parallel is only to appease the ear. In truth, however, the analogy has no similarity whatever to the object of comparison. For the human soul . . . is affected by the accidents of the body and its pain . . . while the Holy One, blessed is He, is not, Heaven forfend, affected by the accidents of the world and its changes, nor by the world itself; they do not effect any change in Him . . .".[9] Also, "The soul and the body are actually distinct, one from the other, in their very sources, for the source of the body and its essence does not come into being from the soul . . .".[10] Thus while the body may be fully subordinate to the soul, they are, nevertheless, two distinct entities. In contrast, "in relation to The Holy One, blessed is He, who brings everything into existence *ex nihilo*, everything is absolutely nullified, just as the light of the sun is nullified in the sun itself".[11]

3. *The Light-Metaphor*

Just as the soul provides a favourite metaphor, so we find that the term "light" is favoured by the mystics to describe the various emanations and manifestations of the Divinity.[12] This term is carefully chosen for a number of reasons. R. Joseph Albo sees in it the following advantages that may analogously be related to G–d:

(i) The existence of light cannot be denied. (ii) Light is not a corporeal thing. (iii) Light causes the faculty of sight and the visible colours to pass from potentiality to actuality. (iv) Light delights the soul. (v) One who has never seen a luminous body in his life cannot conceive colours nor the agreeableness and delightfulness of light. (vi) And even he who has seen luminous objects cannot endure to gaze upon an intense light, and if he insists upon gazing beyond his power of endurance his eyes become dim so that he cannot see thereafter even that which is normally visible. By possessing all these qualities, light bears a greater similarity to the things which are free from matter than anything else to

which such things may be compared, and hence they are compared to light so as to make the matter intelligible.[13]

Likewise, R. Joseph Ergas lists the following advantages:[14] (a) Light is the most subtle and tenuous of all sense-perceptions.[15] (b) Light has numerous qualities characteristic of the Divine emanations, as, for example: (i) Light is emitted from the luminary without ever becoming separated from it. Even when its source is concealed or removed, thus no longer emitting perceptible light, the previous rays do not remain entities separate from the luminary but are withdrawn with it. This is a unique quality of light which is not shared with any other substance. (ii) Light spreads itself instantaneously. (iii) Light irradiates all physical objects and is able to penetrate unhindered all transparent objects. (iv) Light does not mix and mingle with another substance. (v) Light *per se* never changes. The perception of more or less intense light, or of differently coloured lights, is not due to any change in the light *per se* but is due to external factors. (vi) Light is essential to life in general. (vii) Light is received and absorbed relative to the capacities of the recipient; and so on.[16]

But here again, this term is only an homonymous approximation, used by way of metaphor and analogy. It is not to be taken in its full, literal sense. R. Joseph Albo already cautions that "No error should be made to the effect that intellectual light is something emanating from a corporeal object like sensible light."[17] R. Moses Cordovero is still more emphatic in warning that this metaphor must not be carried too far "For there is no image whatever that can be imagined that is not corporeal."[18] And R. Menachem Mendel of Lubavitch shows how, in some respects, this analogy, too, evidently breaks down and is inadequate. For example, the emittance of perceptible light from its source is automatic and intrinsically necessary: the luminary cannot withhold the light. Needless to say that this restrictive quality cannot be ascribed to the emanations of the Omnipotent.[19]

In conclusion, then, as the mystics never tire to say, it cannot be mentioned too often or stressed too much that all terms and concepts related to the Divinity must be stripped of all and any temporal, spatial and corporeal connotations and must be understood in a strictly spiritual sense.

Notes to Chapter I

[1] Berachot *31b;* Mechilta, *and* Tanchuma, *on* Exodus *15:7 and 19:18;* Sifra *on* Levit. 20:2.

[2] *R. Bachya ibn Pakuda,* Chovot Halevovot, Sha'ar Hayichud: *ch. 10.* Cf. Otzar Hageonim, Berachot, *Responsa no. 357 (I:p. 131), and Comment. no. 271 (II:p. 92); R. Judah Halevi,* Kuzary *IV:5; Maimonides,* Hilchot Yesodei Hatorah *I:7–12, and* Moreh Nevuchim *I:26, 33, 35* f. *and 46;* Tanya *II:10.*

[3] Commentary on Mishnah, Sanhedrin, *Intr. to ch. 10.* Cf. Hilchot Teshuvah *III:7;* Moreh Nevuchim *I:36 (and the references to Maimonides,* supra, *note 2).*

[4] Midrash Tanchuma, *Pekudei: 3;* Avot de R. Nathan, *ch. 31;* Eccles. Rabba *I:4;* Zohar *I:38a, 140a, 205b;* ibid. *II:20a, 48b, 75b* f.; ibid. *III:35b, 117a;* et passim. *See also* Chovot Halevovot, *I: ch. 10, and II: ch. 2, 3 and 5. (Most of these sources are quoted in the discussion of the "correspondence-theory" in J. I. Schochet,* "The Psychological System of R. Schneur Zalman of Liadi," *parts I and II,* Di Yiddishe Heim, *vol. XI (New York 1970), nos. 3–4.)*

[5] Sha'arei Orah, *Sha'ar I* (ed. *Warsaw 1883, p. 2b).* Cf. *R. Solomon ibn Aderet,* Chidushei Harashba al Agadot Hashass, *on* Bava Batra *74b (Jerusalem 1966, p. 90). For a fuller discussion of the mystics' view of anthropomorphisms see R. Meir ibn Gabbai,* Avodat Hakodesh, *part III, esp. ch. 26* ff. *and ch. 65; R. Moses Cordovero,* Pardess Rimonim, *sect. XXII* (Sha'ar Hakinuyim), *esp. ch. 2; R. Isaiah Horowitz,* Shenei Luchot Habrit, Toldot Adam: Bayit Neeman; *(all of which quote R. Joseph Gikatilla). In addition, the whole of R. Moses Cordovero's* Shi'ur Komah *is devoted to this topic. See also R. Joseph Ergas,* Shomer Emunim *I:24* f. *R. Isaiah Horowitz* (ad loc. cit., *p. 10d) makes the interesting point that strictly speaking it is not that "the Torah speaks in the language of man," but—in accordance with the aforesaid—exactly the other way around because all terrestrial concepts are allusions to supernal ones!*

[6] *This should be remembered with particular regard to the so-called "erotic" concepts and symbolisms, like the frequent occurrence of terms as "masculine" and "feminine", and "conjunctio" and so on. In general these denote the aspects of the active, emanating (influencing) category and the passive, receiving qualities and categories, the mode or form of emanation-reception and so forth (see* Igeret Hakodesh, *sect. XV, note 9). "The whole universe functions according to the principium of masculine and feminine" (R. Chayim Vital,* Etz Chayim *11:6). "There are four principles: masculine and feminine* (זו״ן)*; judgment* (Din) *and compassion* (Rachamim)*; upper and lower; influencer or emanatar* (Mashpia') *and influenced* (Mushpa'; *also called* Mekabel—*recipient). As a rule, the masculine corresponds to compassion, upper and emanator; and the feminine corresponds to judgment, lower and recipient;"* idem., 'Olat Tamid, *beg. of Sha'ar Hatefillah* (ed. *Tel Aviv 1963, p. 2a). Actually, such terminology is not uniquely Kabbalistic. It may be found in the Talmudic writings—*

—(Bava Batra *74b: "All that the Holy One, blessed is He, created in His world, He created male and female;" see the commentaries ad loc., and esp.* Chidushei Harashba al Agadot Hashass, op. cit., *pp. 91* ff., *quoted at length by R. Jacob ibn Chabib in his* Hakotev *on* Ayin Ya'akov)— *as well as in the philosophical literature*

—(e.g., Moreh Nevuchim, *Introduction, and* ibid., *I:17 and III:18). R. Schneur Zalman explains at length why the mystics purposely chose such delicate and seemingly peculiar terminology; see* Likutei Torah *V:9a, and* Biurei Hazohar, ed. *R. Dov Ber of Lubavitch (New York 1955), Noach: pp. 6a* ff. *The earlier mystics, too, elaborate on the usage of these particular concepts; see* Pardess Rimonim *XXII:1;* Shi'ur Komah, *ch. 18;* Shenei Luchot Habrit, ad loc. cit. *(p. 8d* f.); Shomer Emunim *I:26* f.

[7] Berachot *10a;* Midrash Tehillim (ed. *Buber) 103:4, 5 (see notes* ad loc.); Tikunei Zohar *13:28a. See* Shomer Emunim *II:9;* Igeret Hakodesh, *beg. of sect. XV, and sect. XXV and XXIX.*

[8] *See references* supra, *note 4.*

[9] Tanya, *I, ch. 42.*

[10] Ibid., *II:6.*

[11] Ibid., *see at length R. Menachem Mendel of Lubavitch,* Sefer Hachakirah *I:8 (New York 1955, pp. 7b–8b and 26a–b).* Cf. infra, *ch. 2, note 18, and ch. 3, end of section 4.*

[12] *This metaphor, too, like the previous one, abounds in the Talmudic-Midrashic and mediaeval-philosophic writings; see,* e.g., Berachot *17a, 64a and so forth (the concept of* Ziv Hashechinah; *the radiation of the Schechinah);* Sifre, *and* Midrashim, *on* Numbers *6:25;* Pirkei de R. Eliezer, *ch. 3;* Levit. Rabba *ch. 31 (esp. par. 6);* Numbers Rabba *15:5; etc. See further R. Sa'adiah Gaon,* Emunot Vede'ot *III:10;* Kuzary *II:7–8 and III:17, and especially IV:3;* Moreh Nevuchim *I: ends of ch. 5, 19 and 25, and* ibid., *ch. 76; also, R. Moses Narboni,* Commentary on Moreh Nevuchim *I:35; and so on. In general, though, the philosophical works use mostly the term* shefa' *(effluence; emanation) rather than* or; *see more on that in R. Menachem Mendel of Lubavitch,* Derech Mitzvotecha, Haamanat Elokut: *ch. 5 (New York 1956, p. 50b* f.). *The mystics have a special affinity for the term* Or *because its numerical value* (gimatriya) *is equivalent to that of* raz *(mystery):* " *'Let there be light'* (Gen. *1:3)—i.e., let there be* Raz *(Mystery; Concealment); for* Raz *and* Or *are one thing;*" Zohar *I:140a and* Zohar Chadash, *Bereishit:8d; see* Tikunei Zohar *21:56b, and* cf. *R. Moses Cordovero,* Or Ne'erav *(Fuerth, 1701), III: ch. 4.*

[13] Ikkarim *II:29.*

[14] Shomer Emunim *II:11.*

[15] Cf. Kuzary *IV:3: "The noblest and finest of all material things" and so forth.*

[16] Cf. Tanya *I, ch. 52, and* ibid., *II:10. See also R. Schneur Zalman,* Torah Or, Vayakhel: *87a–b, and* Siddur 'im Perush Hamilot, *pp. 48a* ff. *and 164c* ff.*—Obviously this "descriptive analysis" of light is based on the general human perception—the sense-perception—of it, while an exact "scientific analysis" is not really relevant to our purposes. Apart from the fact that this metaphor is qualified in any case (as we shall see), they are the* empirical perceptions *that make the use of this analogy so attractive and helpful in our context.*

[17] Ikkarim, ad loc. cit.; *see there at length.*

[18] *R. Moses Cordovero,* Elima Rabbaty, *I:i:9 (p. 4b). See also* Emunot Vede'ot *I:3 and II:2 with regard to light being an accident (as opposed to substance) and having a limit and boundary.*

[19] Derech Mitzvotecha, ad loc. cit. (supra, *note 12). See also* Shi'ur Komah, *ch. 3–4.*

Chapter 2 TZIMTZUM

One of the basic theological problems is concerned with the seeming enigma of reconciling G–d with the universe: how can there be a transition from the Infinite to the finite, from pure Intelligence to matter, from absolute Unity or Oneness to multifariousness? Moreover, how do we reconcile the Divine creation or bringing about of the universe and its multifarious parts with the eternal and inviolable absolute perfection of G–d, of whom Scripture affirms "I the Eternal, I have not changed" (*Mal.* 3:6)? In essence, the concepts and doctrines discussed in this, and the chapters following, all relate to these issues.

Creation is often explained in terms of a theory of emanationism: by means of a progressive chain of successive emanations from "higher" to "lower" the finite evolved from the Infinite and matter evolved from spirit. But this suggestion as it stands is insufficient. To speak of a causal evolutionary process of successive emanations merely begs the question but does not answer it. For regardless of how long this chain of causal evolutions may be, there always remains some relationship, qualitative as well as quantitative, between the effect and its cause. Just as in a material chain the links are interlocked, connected and interrelated—retaining a basic relationship between the first link and the last one—so, too, would it be in a gradual process of causal evolution. Thus, since the beginning of the chain of emanations is G–d, the Infinite, the aspect of infinity is never really cast off: Had the worlds descended from the light of the Infinite according to a gradual descent from grade to grade by means of cause and effect, this world would not in such a case, have ever been created in its present form—in a finite and limited order—nor, for that matter, even the (spiritual) *Olam Habah* (World-to-Come), the supernal Garden of Eden, or the souls themselves.[1] In a gradual evolution and causal process "The effect is encompassed by the cause, in relation to which it is essentially non-existent . . . Thus, even numerous contractions will not avail to there being matter as dense as earth by way of an evolution from the spirituality of the abstract intelligences, nor even (that most subtle and diaphanous type of "matter") of the angels."[2] Again: "The creation of the worlds is not by way of a development from cause to effect . . . for even myriads upon myriads of occultations and evolutions from grade to grade in a causal process

will not avail the development and coming into being of physical matter—not even the matter of the firmaments—out of an evolution from spirit. Rather, it is the power of the blessed En Sof (Infinite), the Omnipotent, to create . . . *ex nihilo*, and this is not by way of a developmental order but by way of a 'leap'."[3]

Hence, that something non-divine and finite should come about, necessitates there being in the process of emanation a "radical step", a "leap" or "jump" (*dilug; Kefitzah*) which breaks the gradualism and establishes a radical distinction between cause and effect: a radical act of creation.[4] Only after that has occurred, can we speak of an evolutionary process culminating in finite and material entities. And this principle is at the root of the doctrines of *tzimtzum* and the *Sefirot* introduced by the Kabbalah (and elaborated upon in Chassidism) to solve the problem of creation.

The word *tzimtzum* has two meanings: (1) contraction; condensation; and (2) concealment; occultation.[5] Though both these meanings apply in our context, the second one does so, perhaps, more than the first. For the doctrine of *tzimtzum* refers to a refraction and concealment of the radiating emanation from the G–dhead, in a number of stages and in a progressive development of degrees, until finite and physical substances become possible. This intricate theory is first treated in detail by R. Isaac Luria.[6] The basic works of his system all begin with an exposition of *tzimtzum*.[7] R. Schneur Zalman partly deals with it in *Tanya*,[8] more extensively in *Sha'ar Hayichud Vehaemunah*,[9] and above all in *Torah Or* and *Likutei Torah*.[10]

Prior to creation there is but G–d alone. G–d as He is in Himself is called *En Sof*: the Infinite; He that Is Without Limit (End).[11] Of G–d as En Sof nothing can be postulated except that He is *En Sof*: "High above all heights and hidden beyond all concealments, no thought can grasp You at all . . . You have no known Name for You fill all Names and You are the perfection of them all."[12]

In a mystical way, rather difficult to explain, there is a manifestation or Self-revelation of G–d *qua En Sof* even before the act of creation.[13] This manifestation is called *Or En Sof* (the Light of the *En Sof*), and we speak of this Light as equally omnipresent and infinite. This distinction between *En Sof* and *Or En Sof* is extremely important and must be kept in mind. For when speaking of *tzimtzum* and the *Sefirot* we relate these to the *Or En Sof*, the Light and Radiation, rather than to the Luminary and Radiator (*Ma-or*), the *En Sof*.

Now, "when it arose in the Divine Will"[14] to bring about the world and the creatures, the first act in the creative process was to bring about space in which the Divine emanations and, ultimately the evolving, finite world could have a place to exist. This "primordial space" was brought about by a contraction or "withdrawal" and concentration of Divinity into Itself: the omnipresent, infinite Light of the *En Sof* was "withdrawn" into Himself; that is, it was screened, dimmed, hidden and concealed, and where it was dimmed—where this occultation and concealment of the Light occurred—an "empty" place, a "void" (*makom panuy; chalal*) evolved into primordial space. This is the act of the first *tzimtzum*, the radical act of *dilug* and *kefitzah*, as it were: an act of Divine Self-limitation, so to speak, as opposed to revelation. However, this does not mean that the *chalal* is literally empty and void of all Divine radiation, that the Divine Presence is literally and totally withdrawn therefrom. Such interpretation[15] would suggest an illegitimate ascription of spatiality, and hence corporeality, to the Infinite, and violate the principle of omnipresence affirmed in the most literal sense by Scripture[16] and tradition.[17] The *chalal* is *metaphorically* spoken of as a void, in relation to that which is "beyond" or "outside" the *chalal*: "outside" the *chalal* there is a full manifestation of the *Or En Sof* while inside the *chalal* the Light is concealed. The *En Sof*, the Luminary (*Ma-or*) whence the Light issues, Itself is totally unaffected by *tzimtzum*. *Tzimtzum* relates only to the Light of the *En Sof*. Moreover, even in the Light *per se* there is no real change whatever: it is neither reduced nor removed but merely concealed. Even this concealment and occulation is strictly relative: relative to the void and its subsequent contents, without—strictly speaking—affecting the Light itself in any way. Moreover, in relation to the void there is not an absolute and total withdrawal: some residue or vestige (*reshimu*) of the Light remains in the *chalal*.[18]

Despite all these qualifications and the metaphorical interpretation of the withdrawal of the Light, this first act of *tzimtzum* is a radical "leap" (*dilug*) that creates the possibility for a gradual process and evolution of emanations to take place and to culminate in the creation of finite and corporeal entities. The principal purpose of *tzimtzum* is to create a *chalal* in which the Divine creatures would be able to exist and subsist as opposed to becoming dissolved in the Divine Omneity. The infinite radiation of the Divine Light having been dimmed and concealed, as it were, will now no longer consume and nullify the contents of the

chalal in the way, for example, that a spark is totally consumed and nullified in the flame itself, or the way the light of a candle would be totally absorbed and nullified in the very intense light of the sun.

In the second phase of the creative process an overt ray or radiation of the Divine Light is made to beam into the primeval space of the *chalal*. This thin ray or "line" (*kav*) irradiates the *chalal* and is the source of the subsequent emanations: it is both the creative and the *vivifying* force of the creation; it is the immanence of G–d in creation while the concealed Light is the all-encompassing transcendence of G–d taking in all creation. However, the *kav* itself also undergoes a series of numerous, successive contractions and concealments. Each of these contractions and concealments makes it possible for a successively lower stage or creation to take place, ultimately culminating in the lowest stage and creation represented by this finite, material and pluralistic world. It is *via* this *kav* that the process of successive emanations and causal development takes place. Unlike the first *tzimtzum*—which was by way of *dilug* ("leap")—this development and evolution can be spoken of as gradual and causal.[19]

To summarise, *tzimtzum* is "Something in the nature of an occultation and concealment of the flow of the light and life-force so that only an extremely minute portion of the light and life-force should irradiate and flow forth to the lower beings in a manifest way, as it were, to be vested in them and influence and animate them so that they may receive existence *ex nihilo* and be in a state of finitude and limitation."[20] "There is, thus, no change whatever in His blessed Self but only for the created entities which receive their life-force . . . through a process of gradual descent from cause to effect and a downward gradation by means of numerous and various contractions (*tzimtzumim*) so that the created entities can receive their life and existence from it without losing their entity. *These tzimtzumim are all in the nature of a "veiling of the Countenance"* (*Hester Panim*), *to obscure and conceal the light and life-force . . . so that it shall not manifest itself in a greater radiance than the lower worlds are capable of receiving.* Hence it seems to them as if the light and life-force of the Omnipresent, blessed is He . . . were something apart from His blessed Self . . . Yet in regard to the Holy One, blessed is He, there is no *tzimtzum*, concealment and occultation that would conceal and hide before Him and "the darkness is even as the light" (*Psalms* 139:12) as it is written "Even the darkness does not obscure from You . . ." (*ibid.*). For the *tzimtzumim* and "garments"

are not things distinct from His blessed Self, Heaven forfend, but "like the snail whose garment is part of its very self"[21] (*Genesis Rabba* 21:5)."[22]

Notes on Chapter II

[1] Tanya *I: 2. 48.*

[2] Igeret Hakodesh, *sect. XX.*

[3] Likutei Torah *IV:46c; also* ibid., *IV:20d.*

[4] *See* Torah Or, *Esther:90a and 116c;* Likutei Torah *V:40b* f., *41d and 42b* f.

[5] *See R. Nathan ben Yechiel,* Aruch, s.v. צמצם *(and the additional references in* Aruch Hashalem, ad loc.).

[6] *Its roots, though, are to be found in the* Zohar, e.g., *I:15a, and* Zohar Chadash, *Vaetchanan:57a.*

[7] E.g., Etz Chayim, Mevoh She'arim; Sha'ar Hahakdamot; *etc.*

[8] Likutei Amarim, *part I, esp. ch. 21–22 and 48–49.*

[9] Ibid., *part II, esp. ch. 3–4, 6–7 and 9–10.*

[10] *Especially* Torah Or, *Vayera:13c* ff.; Likutei Torah *III:51b* ff., *and V:40b* ff.

[11] *In fact there is a dispute among the Kabbalists whether the term* En Sof *applies to the very Essence and Being of G–d as He is in Himself, or to the Divine Will, i.e., to G–d* qua *First Cause of all beings—while, in turn, there is no term applicable to the very Essence and Being of G–d as He is in Himself (according to the second opinion); see* Pardess Rimonim *III:1* seq., *and R. Menachem Azaryah de Fano,* Pelach Harimon ad loc. *R. Isaac Luria takes a mediating view, that the term* En Sof *does not apply to the very Essence and Being of G–d as He is in Himself, nor to the Divine Will, but to a level of Divinity which exceedingly excels this latter plane. See at length R. Sholom Dov-Ber Schneersohn,* Yom Tov shel Rosh Hashanah *5333, sect. XX (New York 1970, pp. 166* ff.), *and* infra, *ch. 3, note 38. See also* Likutei Torah *I:7b, where R. Schneur Zalman quotes the works of R. Menachem Azaryah de Fano for the choice in terminology of* En Sof *(That Is Without End) rather than the seemingly more comprehensive term* En Lo Techilah *(That Is Without Beginning).*

[12] Tikunei Zohar, *Intr.: 17a–b* (cf. Tanya *I, ch. 48 and 51;* Igeret Hakodesh *sect. XIV and XX).—The term* En Sof *"indicates that there is no grasping Him, neither by apprehension nor by any thought whatever; He is abstracted and separate from all thoughts. He is prior to all those that were emanated, created, formed and fashioned, and no time of start and beginning applies to Him, for He is continually present and exists foreverlasting without any beginning or end whatever;"* Etz Chayim *I:1; see also R. Chayim Vital,* Sha'ar Hahakdamot, *end of Hakdamah III.* En Sof *therefore, is an indication of absolute perfection: "*En Sof *means perfection without any deficiency;"* Likutei Torah *IV:16a (quoting* Avodat Hakodesh *I:8, who in turn is quoting R. Azriel of Geronah,* Perush Eser Sefirot, *Responsum 3).*

[13] *The difficulty in this concept is that revelation or manifestation generally presupposes another existent in, or to whom, this manifestation is directed, while the* En Sof *is the sole omnipresent existent. R. Schneur Zalman offers what he calls a "possible answer" by drawing an analogy to a person speaking to himself: speech is a medium of communication—thus self-revelation—to another outside the self. For man to communicate with himself he need not speak but* thinks *to himself, uses his faculty of thought; in fact, thought is more comprehensive than speech, for some thoughts are difficult to articulate altogether, or would involve a lengthy process before they can be uttered and so on. Speech is merely a form of self-expression and self-revelation, and the lowest form of it at that. Nevertheless, one may still, at times, vest one's thoughts and intellections in distinct and limited letters and words to express them* to oneself. *In some metaphorical sense, analogous*

thereto, there is a mode of self-revelation of the En Sof *even prior to creation. See* Likutei Torah *II:52d* f.; cf. Torah Or, *Vayakhel: 87a–b, and* Siddur im Perush Hamilot, *pp. 48a* ff. *and 164a* ff.

[14] *This phrase is not to be taken in a temporal sense implying a change in the G–dhead, a supposition incompatible with the very idea and concept of the G–dhead and the explicit statement of Scripture that "I, the Eternal, I have not changed"* (Malachi *3:6*). *Change depends on time; it is a relative, temporal-spatial concept. But time and space are themselves creations. From our present, temporal-spatial perspective there is a "before" and "after", but not from the eternal, supra-temporal and supra-spatial perspective. See more on this concept of time (and its relation to creation) in* Etz Chayim *I:1;* Sha'ar Hahakdamot, *Hakd. III;* Shenei Luchot Habrit, *Toldot Adam: Bet Hashem (Glossary Note, p. 4b);* Shomer Emunim *II:14* ff.; Tanya *II:7;* Torah Or, *Miketz: 37a; and so on.* Cf. Moreh Nevuchim *II:13 and 30 (and also* ibid., *I:52), and Responsa of R. Menachem M. Schneerson,* Bitaon Chabad *(Kfar Chabad 1971), no. 33: p. 51* f. *(For a detailed, comprehensive discussion of the problem of time in historio-philosophical context, see* Sefer Hachakirah, *part III (p. 28a* seq.) *and Addenda (p. 108a* seq.).

[15] *There have been some interpretations of this kind. Their inherent difficulties are dealt with critically in* Shomer Emunim *II:34* ff., *and* Tanya *II:7.*

[16] "*The whole earth is full of His glory*" (Isaiah *6:3*); "*Do I not fill the heavens and the earth, says the Eternal*" (Jer. *23:24*)—"I, *indeed, i.e., His very Being and Essence, as it were, and not His glory only!*" (Igeret Hakodesh, *sect. VII; see also* Tanya *I:48, and* Igeret Hakodesh, *sect. XX and XXV*). Cf. Chovot Halevovot *I:10.*

[17] "*There is no place on earth void of the Divine Indwelling Presence* (Shechinah);" Mechilta de Rashby (ed. *D. Hoffman, p. 2) and* Midrash Hagadol-Shemot (ed. *Jerusalem 1956, p. 45), on* Exodus *3:2; see also the other Midrashim on this verse. "There is no place devoid of Him;*" Tikunei Zohar *57:91b and 70:122b* (cf. Igeret Hakodesh, *sect. I and XX*). *See also the references cited in* Midrash Hagadol, op. cit, ad loc. cit., *and in* Torah Shelemah, *vol. VIII, p. 119, note 39, and* ibid., *pp. 248–251;* Igarot Ba'al Hatanya, *no. 56 (Jerusalem 1953, pp. 95–8).* Cf. Shi'ur Komah, *ch. 33–34.*

[18] *To be sure, this outline of* tzimtzum *follows the interpretation of R. Schneur Zalman, and is the most stringent in the preservation of the unaffectedness of G–d. Its key-concepts are that* tzimtzum *relates to the* Or En Sof, *and not to the* En Sof; *and that even in the* Or En Sof *it is but relative to the creation rather than to the Divine Light* per se. *This follows on the general "acosmic" view of R. Schneur Zalman and his predecessors that* vis-à-vis *G–d there is no change whatever. He constantly quotes, throughout all his works, the liturgical phrase "You were prior to the creation of the world, You are after the creation of the world" in the sense that G–d was, is and remains the sole true reality, and creation does not affect Him in any way implying whatever change. (See* Tanya *I: 20;* Igeret Hakodesh, *sect. VI;* et passim; *quoted* infra, *ch. 4, end of section 1.) And thus he follows his ancestor R. Judah Loewe, the* Maharal *of Prague* (Derashot Maharal, *Derushim Naim: Shabbat Hagadol 5349;* ed. *Jerusalem 1968, II: p. 34* f.), *and R. Isaiah Horowitz* (Shenei Luchot Habrit, Beassarah Maamarot: *ch. 1; p. 30a*), *in interpreting* Deut. *4:39 "the Eternal is G–d . . .* there is no other" *in the sense that strictly speaking there is* no other existent *outside G–d. (See* Tanya *II:6.) But, as already mentioned, there have been other interpretations of* tzimtzum *that take a more, or altogether literal view of this doctrine (see* supra, *note 15). For the four types of interpretations that have been suggested at various times see Responsa of R. Menachem M. Schneerson of Lubavitch,* Bitaon Chabad *(Kfar Chabad 1970), no. 31, p. 43.*

[19] *That is, in a very general sense. More specifically, though, the particular aspects of* tzimtzum *are too numerous to count and are of many diverse kinds. In general, however, there are three levels of powerful and comprehensive contractions and condensations which give rise to the lower three Worlds in which there is the appearance of finite and limited creatures distinct from Divinity; see* Tanya, *I, 49, and* infra, *ch. 4. Specifically speaking we*

still make some radical distinctions in the process of tzimtzum *even* after *the* dilug.

[20] Tanya *I, ch. 48.*

[21] *In general, garments are entities separate and distinct from their bearer, but in our context they are not; see commentaries on this* Midrash (*which, incidentally, is much-quoted in mystical works*).

[22] Tanya *I, ch. 21; see also* ibid., *II: 6.*

Chapter 3 SEFIROT

1. *Meaning of Sefirot*

Tzimtzum on its various levels brings about a series of numerous intermediary stages between the infinite Light of the En Sof and the finite universe, making possible the creation of the finite and pluralistic world. These intermediary stages are generally divided into five classes or grades, referred to as the Five Worlds or Realms. The varying radiations of the Divine Light in these Worlds, becoming ever more intensely screened and obscured from one level to the next, are referred to as the *Sefirot.*

There are four principal aspects: (1) *En Sof* (2) *Or En Sof*—the Self-manifestation of G-d; (3) the finite world; and (4) the intermediary levels in the successive development of the creative process brought about by means of *tzimtzum.* Of the *En Sof,* as mentioned before, nothing can be postulated, except that He is *En Sof.*[1] Names or attributes apply only to manifestations, to those aspects of Divinity which are revealed in, and to His creation.[2] These Divine manifestations or attributes are dimmed radiations from the Light of the *En Sof* and they are called the *Sefirot.*[3] The *Sefirot* bridge, as it were, the *Or En Sof* with the ultimate evolving world. That is, in order for finite creations to come about, the Light of the *En Sof* vested Itself in the *Sefirot.*[4] Only by Its prior investment in the *Sefirot* in all the intermediary stages brought about by *tzimtzum* could It be vested in a finite and physical world.[5]

The *Sefirot* are thus Divine emanations, various phases in the manifestation of Divinity. As we speak of them in terms of numerous gradations, extreme care must be taken to avoid any fatal misconception of dualism or a plurality in the G-dhead. There is no suggestion whatever that the *Sefirot* are to be taken as entities distinct and separate from the *En Sof.* On the contrary, there is a basic and intrinsic unity between the *En Sof* and the *Sefirot.* This absolute and intrinsic unity has already been stressed in the ancient *Sefer Yetzirah*: "The ten *Sefirot* are without anything (*beli-mah*).[6] Their end is wedged in their beginning, their beginning is wedged in their end—like a flame bound up in the coal. For the Eternal is One, and there is no second to Him, and prior to One what can you count!"[7]

This simile is re-stated in the *Zohar* with even greater emphasis: "The Holy One, blessed is He, emits ten crowns, supernal holy crowns.

With these He crowns Himself and in these He vests Himself. He is they and they are He, just as the flame is bound up in the coal, and there is no division there."[8] All differentiation is but from *our* perspective and relative to *our* knowledge, while above all is One; all is set in one balance, unvarying and eternal, as it is written "I, the Eternal, I have not changed." (*Malachi* 3:6).[9]

Maimonides' statement that with G–d His Essence, His Being and His Knowledge are absolutely one,[10] a simple unity and not a compound one,[11] applies equally to all the Divine attributes and to all the holy Names ascribed to Him;[12] "It is all an absolute, simple unity which is His very Essence and Being. However, as Maimonides stated,[13] 'This matter is beyond the power of speech to express and beyond the power of the ear to hear and the human heart to understand clearly'."[14] It is beyond apprehension—to apprehend how He unites with them; that is why the attributes of the Holy One, blessed is He, which are the *Sefirot*, are referred to in the sacred *Zohar*[15] as the "Mystery of the Faith" —which is faith that transcends the intellect.[16] The Torah uses human phraseology only to enable the ear to hear what it can understand, therefore permission was granted to the mystics to speak allegorically of *Sefirot*. It is, by way of illustration, like the unity of the light of the sun in its orb with the solar globe—(the solar globe being the luminary, while the radiation and beam that spreads forth and shines from it is called light). When the light is in its source, in the orb of the sun, it is united with it in absolute unity, for there is but one entity: the body of the luminary which emits light. All the attributes of the Holy One, blessed is He, His Will, and His Wisdom, are designated by these names only in relation to the creatures.[17]

This concept of the *Sefirot* or attributes, also explains the very reason for creation. For even while the *Sefirot* or attributes are in absolute unity with the G–dhead, they have actual application in relation to creation only. Thus to actualise, as it were, these Divine potencies, powers or attributes (e.g., wisdom, kindness, compassion, sovereignty and so on) G–d created the universe in which to manifest them (to have subjects upon whom to express or manifest His kindness and compassion, with whom to manifest His majesty and so on).[18] In a similar vein, creation also is a means through which G–d is able to manifest His power or potency in finite entities no less than in the infinite—thereby preserving the principle of absolute omnipotence.[19]

This does not mean that creation implies a change in the G–dhead,

that creation lends the G–dhead a perfection It did not possess before. For all the attributes are eternally of the very Essence and Being of G–d, absolutely one with Him; it is only that they are *manifested* through creation.[20] For the *En Sof*, as stated earlier is "absolute perfection without any deficiency", and " 'You were before the world was created, You are since the world was created'—exactly the same without any change, as it is written 'For I, the Eternal, I have not changed'."[21]

2. *Order of the Sefirot*

The *Sefirot* are ten spheres or classes[22] in the following order: *Keter* (Crown); *Chochmah* (Wisdom); *Binah* (Understanding); *Chesed* (Kindness; Grace; Benevolence); *Gevurah* (Might; Power; Prevalence); *Tiferet* (Beauty); *Netzach* (Endurance; Victory); *Hod* (Splendour; Majesty); *Yesod* (Foundation); *Malchut* (Sovereignty; Kingship). In some schemes *Keter* is omitted from the order of the ten *Sefirot*[23]—for reasons to be explained further on; these schemes take *Chochmah* as the first of the ten and insert *Da'at* (Knowledge) as a *Sefirah* after *Binah*.

The total order of the *Sefirot* is generally divided into two groups referred to as the "three mothers and the seven multiples."[24] That is, the first three are the principal *Sefirot*, the *immot* (mothers)[25] from and through which the other seven *Sefirot* issue forth. When beginning with *Chochmah*, the triad of the first three *Sefirot* is also called *Sechel* (Intellect)[26] while the other seven *Sefirot* are called *Midot* (Attributes; Emotive Faculties).[27] Another distinction is made by calling the first three the "three *Rishonot*" (the three First Ones, or at times the three Upper Ones), and the other seven are called the "seven *Tachtonot*" (seven Lower Ones). The "seven Lower Ones" are subdivided into the two triads of *Chesed-Gevurah-Tiferet* and *Netzach-Hod-Yesod* (all these six together are called the "six *Ketzavot*"—the "six Extremities"), and the singular last one of *Malchut*.[28] While there are a number of other such groupings and distinctions that abound in the mystical writings[29] (and some of these we shall meet up with in the chapters following), the above are the principal or most common ones.

3. *Keter*

Keter is the highest level or sphere of the *Sefirot*. The term itself denotes its significance: as a crown is on top of the head and encompasses it, so *Keter* is on top of all the *Sefirot* and encompasses them all. The analogy

is carried further: just as the crown is not a part of the head nor the body but distinct from it, so *Keter* is essentially distinct from the other *Sefirot.*[30] It is the first emanation, and as such the "lowest level" as it were, of the Emanator.[31] That is why *Keter* is called *Temira dechol Temirin* (the most hidden of all hidden),[32] and is referred to as *Ayin* (naught).[33] These terms signify the total concealment of the rank of *Keter* due to its supreme sublimity.[34] *Keter* is so sublime and concealed that nothing can be said or postulated of it. The *Zohar*, therefore, applies to it Ben Sira's dictum:[35] "Seek not the things that are beyond you and search not out things that are hidden from you."[36] While the other *Sefirot* are sometimes represented by various letters of the alphabet,[37] no letter can describe or represent *Keter.*

That is why *Keter* is sometimes excluded from the scheme of the *Sefirot.* It is too sublime to be included. It is a category and class all in itself.[38] In fact it is called the "intermediary" between the *En Sof* and the *Sefirot*, bridging the gap, as it were: it is the "lowest level" of the Light of the *En Sof* and from it, and through it, issue forth the successive Divine emanations (thus being the very root or soul of the *Sefirot*).[39] *Keter* represents the "lever" of Divine manifestations and as such is called *Ratzon Ha'elyon* (the Supreme or Abysmal Will) of G–d: not a particular will focused on some specific goal but the original Divine Willingness (*Ratzon*) underlying the creative will; it is the "*Will of all wills,*"[40] the "*essence-will*" or the "will to will," as it were, which precedes all powers or attributes (*i.e.*, the *Sefirot*).[41]

4. *Chochmah-Binah-Da'at*

These three *Sefirot* form a triad, in abbreviation called *ChaBaD.* Analogous to them are the three faculties in man's intellect of the same names, i.e., wisdom, understanding and knowledge. *Chochmah* is the root of the succeeding attributes. That is why it is called *Reishit* (Beginning).[42] *Chochmah* represents the first creative activity of G–d;[43] it is the initial Divine instrument of actual creation. The *En Sof*, through the mediation of *Keter*, is "vested" in *Chochmah*, and thence begins creation.[44] Thus it is written:[45] "You have made them all *be-Chochmah*;" and "the Eternal has founded the earth *be-Chochmah*". *Be-Chochmah*[46] may be translated in two interrelated ways, both of which are significant in our context. The first sense is *with*, or *by*, *Chochmah*; thus *Chochmah* is the *instrument* and *hyle* of creation.[47] Everything derives from *Chochmah*; *Chochmah* is immanent in everything (albeit in ever-

increasing concealment) and animates everything, as it is written "*Chochmah* gives life to them that have it" (*Eccles.* 7:12).[48]

The second sense is *in Chochmah*, This means that in *Chochmah* is founded the creation, and the possibilities of all further being exist there *in potentia*.[49] Thus the word *Chochmah* is interpreted to mean כ״ח מ״ה, the "potentiality" of "what is".[50] *Chochmah* is the *seed* of creation, the beginning and first revelation of creation. However, *Chochmah* is so concentrated and compact that it is not apprehensible in itself. In itself *Chochmah* is a state of obscurity (*mocha setima*—the concealed brain). Among the letters of the Tetragrammaton which symbolise all the *Sefirot*, *Chochmah* is represented by the first letter, the *Yud*[51]—a small, simple, non-descriptive point; and is referred to[52] as the "Garden of Eden" of which it is said[53] "no eye has seen it".[54] Thus there is little that can be said of *Chochmah*, for which reason *Chochmah*, too, is referred to as *ayin* (naught).[55] The *potentia* of *Chochmah* is brought out from total obscurity and externalised in *Binah*, the next *Sefirah*.[56] This will be understood by drawing on the analogy to the faculties of the human intellect: *Chochmah* corresponds to an intuitive flash of intellectual illumination: the original idea *per se*. It is the seminal idea, the "inner thought", the details of which are not yet differentiated and externalised; they are not yet processed but intensely concentrated in the intuitive flash. When cogitating on the idea, its details and implications will become revealed; the idea will be understood. The individuations concealed in the original flash are then externalised and become manifest in the mind. The hidden intellect is apprehended by the intellectually cognising subject. This is the faculty and state of *Binah* (understanding).[57]

Binah is really the expansion and elucidation of *Chochmah*. *Chochmah* is informed in *Binah*, and "becomes known solely through *Binah*."[58] The standard definition of the faculty of *Binah* is "To understand or derive one matter out of another matter."[59] Among the letters of the Tetragrammaton *Binah* is represented by the *Hai*.[60] Unlike the simple non-dimensional point of *Yud*, the *Hai* is a more concrete letter: it has dimensions of length and width signifying the dimensions of explanation, understanding and manifestation.[61] Therefore the *Zohar* refers to the *Sefirot* of *Chochmah* and *Binah* as "The dot (*Chochmah*) in the palace (*Binah*)."[62] symbolising the meaning of these categories and their relationship.

However, *Chochmah* and *Binah* by themselves are abstract. The con-

cept is there and it is clear in the mind. But it is only in the mind, internally, while externally it is inaudible and invisible.[63] On its own, when in the mind, it does not lead to any conclusion, it is not fully realised. The concept, wisdom and understanding, are a potential power that needs to be, but has not yet been, actualised.[64] Moreover, strictly speaking, *Chochmah* and *Binah* are two separate faculties: the intuitive flash of intellectual cognition (*Chochmah*) may be there, and so is the power of induction-deduction—(*Binah*), the power of understanding this flash. But how are they joined? How does the "dot" come to, and become externalised and informed in, the "palace"?

These two states—the union of *Chochmah* with *Binah*, and the practical implementation of the informed concept—are effected by the faculty of *Da'at*. However, just as we are speaking of two states, effects or "activities" at two different levels, so we must speak of two categories of *Da'at*—that is, *Da'at* on two planes: *Da'at Elyon* (Upper or Superior *Da'at*) and *Da'at Tachton* (Lower or Inferior *Da'at*).[65]

The etymological meaning of *Da'at* is attachment or union.[66] Thus *Da'at* is the unifying principle that brings together and joins the faculties of *Chochmah* and *Binah*. This unifying principle is called *Da'at Elyon*, for it transcends *Chochmah* and *Binah*; it is a direct derivative or aspect of *Keter*,[67] the Supernal Will that wishes and seeks—and hence is able to effect—the union of *Chochmah* and *Binah*.[68] But to bring about this union is itself but a means towards a further end:[69] to implement or apply and bring to fruition the concept of *Chochmah* that has been informed in *Binah*. To possess wisdom or even understanding does not yet mean that it will actually be implemented and applied in practise.[70] The principle of wisdom need not only be understood but also felt and sensed. It must be channelled to the emotive attributes so that they will act upon it in terms of appropriate dispositions: to seek or pursue that which wisdom dictates should be sought, and to avoid that which wisdom dictates should be avoided. This profound inner concentration on, and devotion to, the *Chochmah* informed in *Binah*, this personal sensing (*Hargashah*), is the faculty of *Da'at Tachton*. It is the full preoccupation in the apprehended and understood concept until an intense union is effected between the intellect and the emotions (*Sechel* and *Midot*)[71] and the idea is brought to its logical conclusion in practical application. This faculty of *Da'at Tachton* is below, and follows upon, *Chochmah* and *Binah*, and of it is said "If there is no *Binah* there can be

no *Da'at*' (*Avot* 3:17).[72] It is this faculty of *Da'at* that is usually referred to when the term *Da'at* appears unqualified.[73]

In the metaphorical terminology of the Kabbalah and Chassidism *Chochmah* is called *Abba* (Father) and *Binah* is called *Imma* (Mother).[74] Metaphorically speaking, the seed of *Abba* is implanted in the womb of *Imma* and there the rudimentary plant of the seed is developed, expanded, externalised and informed. *Da'at* is called *Ben* (Son), i.e., the offspring of this union of *Chochmah* and *Binah*.[75] In *Da'at* the original idea and concept has matured into corresponding dispositions. Therefore *Da'at* is the all-inclusive essence of the *Midot*, of the emotive powers or attributes of the lower *Sefirot*.[76] For the *Midot* express and reveal these dispositions originating in *Sechel* in terms of *Chesed*, *Gevurah*, *Tiferet*, *Netzach*, *Hod*, *Yesod* and *Malchut*.[77]

One final comment in relation to the aforesaid. In explaining these *Sefirot* and their interrelationship as we have done so far (and shall be doing in the chapters following), we did so by analogical reference to the soul-faculties of man: *Keter* (the all-encompassing will) leading to *Chochmah* (the intuitive or seminal intellectual flash) which is joined by *Da'at Elyon* to *Binah* (the faculty of understanding and elucidation) thence to be realised in *Da'at Tachton* and to become enacted in the dispositions of the *Midot*. In man there is, therefore, a temporal sequence, a gradual developing process in temporally distinct stages. Obviously this cannot be said of the Divine process. As R. Isaiah Horowitz has stressed, the analogy is inadequate and breaks down for two basic reasons: Firstly, with G-d there is no temporal sequence; all these "stages" are simultaneous to the extent that as soon as "it arises in G-d's Will" His Will is performed instantaneously and there is no "before" and "after" except in some extremely subtle, *qualitative*, sense. Secondly, with man the *execution* of his will and wisdom is a category distinct, dependent yet separate, from his will and wisdom, while with G-d they are one absolute and inseparable unity.[78]

5. *Chesed-Gevurah-Tiferet*

Chesed means kindness in a sense of absolute, gratuitous and unlimited benevolence.[79] It is the very crystallisation of the disposition to bestow good and kindness for the very sake of kindness, regardless of the merits of the recipient.[80] It is the attribute or disposition that underlies the creation, to bring about recipients for the Divine benevolence, and thus it is written "The world was built by *Chesed*."[81] That is, as it is intrinsic

to the nature of the benevolent to be benevolent *in actu*, G–d brought into being—*ex nihilo*—the world and all the creatures.[82] Creation, therefore, is an act of *Chesed*,[83] and it is from this attribute that the Divine life-force, animating all creation, issues forth. The implication of *Chesed* (creation and its continuous sustenance) is a manifestation of the infinite benevolence (*Chesed*) that is of the essence of G–d.[84]

However, the effulgence of the Divine *Chesed* is as boundless as its Source while the creatures to which it emanates are limited and finite. The finite creatures cannot possibly absorb and endure so abundant and powerful an effulgence as the Divine *Chesed*. If exposed to it they would become nullified in it and cease to exist. *Chesed* needs to be controlled, restrained, and its full force screened, concealed, limited. This is effected through *Gevurah*.

Gevurah means Might or Power in a sense of severity. It is the attribute of *Din* (Law and Judgment).[85] *Din* demands that *Chesed* be justly distributed, i.e., in proportion to the prospective recipient's merit, and not in boundless, gratuitous fashion. Thus it is the principle that seeks to control, limit and restrain.[86]

Gevurah implies *tzimtzum*,[87] contracting, withdrawing, concealing and limiting the Divine emanations. *In themselves*, *Chesed* and *Gevurah* pose an antinomy as principles diametrically opposed to one another,[88] for *Gevurah* seeks to prevent, in whole or in part, the outflow of *Chesed*.[89] Thus from the severity of *Gevurah* is derived also the stern Divine Judgments.[90] But this is not to say that *Gevurah* is a strictly negative concept. On the contrary, being one of the Divine attributes it must be seen as positive and contributory. In fact, the Divine benevolence as channelled through *Gevurah* may have an exclusively distinct advantage.[91] Particularly in the context of the act of creation, *Gevurah*—verily, as expressed by *tzimtzum*—is, in effect, an expression of the Divine Love and Benevolence.[92] For, as we have seen,[93] *tzimtzum* makes it possible for G–d's creatures to exist and subsist. However, this is not the case if *Gevurah* were to be singularly dominant. Just as *Chesed by itself* would make it impossible for creation to subsist so *Gevurah by itself* would prèclude the existence of creation. But as both *Chesed* and *Gevurah* are Divine attributes *in absolute unity with the Divine essence* they are neither separate principles nor do they counter one another.[94] They are able to "operate" successfully by a mediating faculty, the Divine attribute of *Tiferet*.

Tiferet harmonises and blends the free outpouring from *Chesed* with

the severe *tzimtzum* of *Gevurah*. It blends them in such a way so that *Chesed* will still issue forth, limited by *Gevurah* so as to make the *Chesed* endurable, i.e., that the creatures may continue to exist even while benefitting from *Chesed*. *Tiferet*, therefore, is not an equal mixture but tends towards *Chesed*.[95]

This quality accounts for this *Sefirah* being called *Tiferet*, beauty: it blends the differing colours of *Chesed* and *Gevurah*, and the harmonious colourfulness of this attribute makes it beautiful (*Tiferet*).[96]

The relationship between these three *Sefirot* is clearly seen. That is why, together, they form a triad referred to by the acrostic *ChaGaT*. Also, these three are the basic or essential *Midot* in relation to which the others are but derivatives as will be seen in the following section. For all the *Midot* are either an aspect of *Chesed* (of outpouring and effluence) or of *Gevurah* (of withdrawal and restraint) or an aspect of *Tiferet* (of harmonious blending of the former two aspects). Moreover, quite frequently *Tiferet* alone[97] is spoken of as the principle of the *Midot* because it compounds within itself the basic dispositions of the *Midot*.[98]

There are a number of terms that often appear as synonyms for these three *Midot*. Thus *Chesed* is called *Gedulah* (Greatness; Magnificence) because it expresses the infinite Greatness (Benevolence) of G–d;[99] *Gevurah* is synonymous with *Din* (Judgment),[100] and *Tiferet* with *Rachamim* (Compassion; Mercy).[101] *Rachamim*, the Divine Compassion, is the harmonising principle that restrains excessive *Chesed* and mitigates severe *Gevurah*,[102] and thus the Divine plan of creation is made possible and the "disposition of the benevolent to be benevolent" is actualised. In this context *Tiferet* is also called *Emet* (Truth).[103] Similarly, there is frequent reference to various other factors which correspond to these *Midot* as well as to the other *Sefirot*.[104] Thus the seven *Midot* have corresponding entities in the seven dominating figures of Scripture that are referred to as the "fathers of the universe": Abraham, Isaac, Jacob, Joseph, Moses, Aaron and David.[105] Each of these, by his individual position, disposition and mode of service and worship, corresponds to one of the *Midot*. The most frequent reference, and the only one that concerns us in *Igeret Hakodesh*, is made to the three Patriarchs as they correspond to the first three *Midot*. Thus Abraham represents *Chesed* because his inclinations and activities expressed kindness and benevolence to the highest degree.[106] Isaac symbolises *Gevurah* as this attribute was most dominant in him.[107] Jacob represents *Tiferet* because

he compounded the *Chesed* of his grandfather and the *Gevurah* of his father.[108]

6. *Netzach-Hod-Yesod*

These three *Sefirot*, too, form a triad known by the acrostic *NeHY*. Their basic significance, as well as the characteristic of their relationship, is that *Netzach*, *Hod* and *Yesod* are the receptacles for the three Patriarchs,[109]—i.e., for *Chesed*, *Gevurah* and *Tiferet*.[110] In other words, these three "lower" *Midot* serve as tools, vessels, or channels through which the aforementioned "upper" *Midot* effect their purpose and factual application.[111] This does not mean that *NeHY* are identical with *ChaGaT*: *Netzach* is merely a branch and channel of *Chesed*, *Hod* of *Gevurah* and *Yesod* of *Tiferet*.[112]

Chesed-Gevurah-Tiferet are the very essence of the attributes they signify and are directly influenced and directed by *Chochmah*, *Binah* and *Da'at*. Once the attributes of *ChaGaT* are established by *ChaBaD*, they form dispositions to actualise themselves. These dispositions are no longer directly influenced or controlled by *ChaBaD* but are the simple, supra-rational dispositions which seek to carry the attributes of *ChaGaT* to their logical conclusion. These dispositions are *Netzach*, *Hod* and *Yesod*, which act, as it were, on simple faith, or "mechanically," rather than on the stimulus of reason (*Sechel*) the way *ChaGaT* do.[113]

Also, despite their identification as branches or derivatives of their predecessors, *Netzach* is not even proportionally identical with *Chesed*, nor *Gevurah* with *Hod*, nor *Yesod* with *Tiferet*. For since they evolve through the comprehensive attribute of *Tiferet* which includes within it both *Chesed* and *Gevurah*, *Netzach* does not possess the simple intensity of *Chesed* nor *Hod* that of *Gevurah*. Likewise with *Yesod*, though it mediates between *Netzach* and *Hod* as *Tiferet* mediates between *Chesed* and *Gevurah*, for the above-mentioned reason it differs from *Tiferet* not only in intensity, but more significantly because it tends towards *Hod* (the side of *Gevurah*) while *Tiferet*—as we have seen—tends towards *Chesed*.[114] On the other hand, through *Tiferet*, *Netzach* is also able to receive and apply the positive aspects of *Gevurah* while *Hod* is able to receive the flow of *Chesed* thus mitigating its aspect of the severity of *Gevurah*.[115]

Another substantive distinction is the following. Unlike the other *Midot*, *Netzach* and *Hod* usually go paired together. The *Zohar* refers to them as "two halves of one body, like unto twins."[116] And similarly

the terms relating to these two attributes are usually such as are intimately related to one another.[117] In this context, and in light of the aforesaid, *Netzach* and *Hod* are called the "*supports* of the upper *Sefirot*" analogous to the loins, thighs or legs in the body of man which support and uphold the whole body (including the head).[118] Hence they are seen to be outside the body itself, i.e. outside the body of *ChaBaD* and *ChaGaT*—though they support the body—leading it to its destination in general and channelling *Chesed* and *Gevurah* in particular.[119] Thus they are, as said, on the level of activity, directly concerned with the ultimate issuance of *Chesed* and *Gevurah*.

In the metaphor of the man-analogy, *Netzach* and *Hod* are the "kidneys that advise". That is, at the time of the actual emanations from the upper *Midot* it is necessary to deliberate how they are to issue forth in such a way that would be most just and beneficial. For example, when a father seeks to convey some intellectual information to his son, he cannot teach him the simple facts by themselves as they are in his own mind. The father has already contemplated the facts; they are clear in his own mind; he understands them fully. But when he now confronts his son with that information (i.e., the facts as they are in themselves and in their totality) without bringing the reasoning down to the child's level, the latter will be unable to understand and absorb the information. If the information is to be conveyed effectively, the father needs to consider the limited faculties of his son's mind and teach him accordingly.

There are two considerations: on the one hand to teach the child as much as possible (notion of *Chesed*), and on the other hand to withhold that which the child is, as yet, unable to absorb (notion of *Gevurah*). These considerations, the deliberation of the father and the arrangement of the facts and reasoning in such a way that the child will be able to grasp them effectively, are the functions of *Netzach* and *Hod*.[120]

Netzach thus represents the attribute of *Endurance*, of prevailing and standing up against, and *conquering* all that would withhold or interfere (i.e., the aspects of *Gevurah*) with the flow of the Divine Benevolence (*Chesed*).[121] *Hod* seeks to restrain (*Gevurah*) the excess of absorbability, to preserve the Divine Majesty and Splendour from being dissipated in the abundant Benevolence (*Chesed*).[122]

Now, to carry the above metaphor further: If the father's mind is not set on teaching his son, then the son cannot be an efficacious recipient for the father's knowledge. If the conveyance of the information is to be

fully effective, one requires not only an illuminating clarification and presentation of the facts, proportionate to the student's capacities but also, and of no lesser importance, an inner bond between the teacher and the student-recipient. It is not sufficient for the father to place himself momentarily on the son's level, as it were (the deliberation of *Netzach* and *Hod*), but he must create a channel of communication: he must unite himself with the son, create a bond between them. In fact, the very degree of illuminating clarification depends on that bond.

The father's mind needs to be set on teaching his son; he must *want* to teach him. And the greater the father's desire and willingness to teach—stemming from the father's love for his child—the more intense is the bond uniting the two, and the greater and more intense is the efficacy of the father's efforts. If the son were to hear his father pronouncing the facts to himself, he would surely grasp some points of information—especially when he hears his father uttering them clearly and in detail. But this type of newly acquired knowledge is by no means comparable to the more profound knowledge he would have acquired had the father taught him directly, with love and willingness. Now this *bond* uniting Emanator and recipient is the attribute of *Yesod*.[123]

As *Tiferet* mediates between *Chesed* and *Gevurah* so *Yesod* mediates, blends and compounds *Netzach* and *Hod*.[124] Moreover, as the third, the harmonising principle of these *active Sefirot* which compound within them the preceding essential *Sefirot*, *Yesod* is the blending channel of all the preceding *Sefirot*: all the *Sefirot* "pour" their light into *Yesod*,[125] and *Yesod* serves as the all-inclusive principle joining heaven to earth,[126] making it possible for the emanations of the *Sefirot* to issue forth effectively unto the creatures. Thus *Yesod* is the Foundation of the creation.[127]

7. *Malchut*

Malchut is unique among the *Sefirot*. Kingship or Sovereignty is a state of being rather than an activity: when there are subjects subservient to the king one can speak of Kingship and Sovereignty, not so when there are no subjects.[128] Thus *Malchut*, the last and "lowest level" of the *Sefirot*,[129] does not exert any influence of its own: it is a passive sphere which "has nothing of its own except that which the other *Sefirot* pour into it."[130] On the other hand, *Malchut* plays an important rôle. It is the very instrument, as it were, through which the original creative plan is actualised. It is through *Malchut* that the latent and potential creation

emerges into manifest reality and substantiality.[131] Thus *Malchut* is referred to as the "Architect wherewith the whole creation was made"[132] and "Nothing occurs among the lower beings unless it be through *Malchut*."[133]

As *Binah* is the Supernal Mother (*Imma Ilaah*) so *Malchut* is the Nether Mother (*Imma Tataah*).[134] The *potentia* of the world (the seed of *Chochmah*) is externalised and individuated in the womb of *Binah* but remains concealed like a foetus. Therefore *Binah* is called the concealed world (*Alma de-Itkassya*).[135] By way and means of the succeeding *Sefirot* (the *Midot*), *Binah*—the "concealed world"—is implanted in the womb of *Malchut* and thence egresses into manifest being. Thus *Malchut* is called the "manifest world" (*Alma de-Itgalya*).[136] *Malchut* is the "Mouth of G–d":[137] the Word of the Eternal and the Breath of His Mouth by which the world came into actual, manifest being.[138] As *Chochmah* is כ״ח מ״ה, the *potentiality* of what is,[139] so *Malchut* is called מ״ה that *what is*.[140] In *Malchut* the potentiality is finally actualised.[141] Through *Malchut* everything comes into manifest being.[142]

The attribute of *Malchut* actually explains its own term. For it is through *Malchut* that the disposition of the Benevolent to be benevolent can be actualised: a world and creatures come into being. The world and the creatures provide prospective recipients for G–d's benevolence. They make it possible to speak of a Divine Kingdom as "There cannot be a King without a nation" and people distinct from Himself over which to rule.[143] When finite creatures come into being through the *Sefirah* of *Malchut* the Divine attribute of Kingship, Sovereignty, becomes meaningful and real.[144] Thus in *Malchut* is the origin of the revelation of the light of the *En Sof* which extends to, and illuminates, the world and creatures in a "revealed" manner. From this source there extends to each individual entity the particular light and vitality suitable for it: informing, animating and sustaining it. That is why *Malchut* is identical with *Shechinah*, the Divine Indwelling Presence or Immanence.[145]

8. *Iggulim and Yosher;* the "*Body of the Sefirot*"

There are two basic schemes in the emanation of the *Sefirot* or Divine Lights after the concealment of *tzimtzum*.[146] As mentioned above, in the chapter on *Tzimtzum*, the Divine Light was manifested in the sphere of the primordial space (*chalal*) by means of the *kav*, the "line" or ray of light that descended from the *Or En Sof* encompassing the *chalal* to the

very core or midst of the *chalal*.[147] This *kav* did not extend from the circumference to the central point in one immediate and complete manifestation, but gradually. That is, immediately upon "entering" the *chalal* it revolved parallel to the perimeter of the *chalal*, round about the inside of the *chalal*, thus establishing a concentric sphere within it.[148] This concentric sphere of dimmed *Or En Sof* is called *Keter*.

Thereupon the *kav* was extended somewhat further, again only partly, to repeat the same process: a new revolution around the *chalal* to form another concentric sphere immediately below that of *Keter*. This new sphere is *Chochmah*. And in this way the *kav* was extended ever further, gradually descending to the very centre of the *chalal*, expanding and revolving, circles within circles, until the tenth concentric sphere was formed, namely that of *Malchut*, in the very centre of the *chalal*. Thus each of these ten spheres follows out of and succeeds the preceding one, with a successive dimming of the light so that each one is distinct from all the others.[149] This is the scheme of *Iggulim* (circles, or concentric spheres).

In this initial scheme of *Iggulim* the *Sefirot* are like the skins of an onion—one within the other—or like a brain encompassed by many membranes one over the other.[150] The significant point of this scheme is that essentially all the *Sefirot* are related to one another only in terms of a successive process: the one emanating after the other but each one really a *separate, self-contained* sphere or point.

The second, subsequent scheme of emanating *Sefirot* is that of "*Yosher*—like unto the appearance of a man standing upright",[151] that is, "Analogous to man who divides into organs all of which exist level upon level and perfect one another, yet all of them (together) form one body."[152] This analogy serves to point out the full inter-relationship between the *Sefirot* of *Yosher* (just as man's organs are interrelated to one another to form a single body), even while underscoring and retaining the unique characteristics of each one. Thus in the scheme of *Yosher* the *Sefirot* are not simple faculties or principles independent of each other, but they form an essentially unified body. The analogy is carried further to the point of relating the particular *Sefirot* to particular limbs or organs in the Body or Form (*Partzuf*) of Man:[153]

Chochmah, Binah and *Da'at*, in an extended sense, are the three brains in man's head. More specifically, *Chochmah* corresponds to the brain in general, i.e., to the source of thought and intellect. *Binah* corresponds to the heart, the seat of understanding. *Chesed* is the right arm while

Gevurah is the left arm. *Tiferet* is the body, intervening and mediating between, and compounding, the sides of *Chesed* and *Gevurah*.

Netzach is the right leg or thigh while *Hod* is the left leg or thigh,[154] together supporting the whole body and leading it to its destination. *Yesod* is the organ of procreation[155] through which the emanations of the higher *Sefirot* issue forth to *Malchut* to bring about a manifest creation. As *Malchut* is the manifesting aspect, it is said to correspond to the mouth, the organ of speech by means of which the speaker's inner thoughts and emotive dispositions are expressed and revealed. *Keter* is the crown encompassing, thus related to, yet independent of, the body; more specifically, in the context of the man-metaphor, it is often referred to as the skull encompassing (thus transcending) the brain.[156]

As mentioned, the scheme of *Yosher* underscores not only the functions of the *Sefirot* but also their inter-relationship as a unit or Body. Therefore in spite of the locations of the "physical counterparts" in the body of man, the *Sefirot* of *Yosher* are often illustrated by way of three lines—right, left, and centre. This is done by placing *Chochmah* on the right side, in line with but above *Chesed* and *Netzach*, and by placing *Binah* on the left side, in line with but above *Gevurah* and *Hod*. Thus we have three new triads: (1) *Chochmah-Chesed-Netzach*, on the *right* side, the "side of *Chesed*", because there is an innate relationship between these three (*Chesed* is a branch of *Chochmah* and *Netzach* is a branch of *Chesed*); (2) *Binah-Gevurah-Hod* on the *left* side, the "side of *Gevurah*," because there is an innate relationship between these three (*Gevurah* is a branch of *Binah*, and *Hod* is a branch of *Gevurah*); and (3) *Keter-Tiferet-Yesod-Malchut* in the *middle*, symbolic of the central, mediating or all-inclusive harmonising principles they are.[157]

It is also in this scheme of *Yosher* that we speak of the faculty of *Da'at Elyon* the Supernal *Da'at*. This faculty, a branch or derivative of *Keter*, the unifying principle of *Chochmah* and *Binah*, would thus be placed in the middle line as the apex of the triangle *Chochmah-Binah-Da'at*.[158]

The full significance of these two schemes of *Iggulim* and *Yosher* will emerge later on in the context of *Shevirat Hakelim*, *Partzufim* and *Tohu and Tikun*.[159]

9. *The Sefirot as Compounds*

So far we have discussed the *Sefirot* mainly in terms of particular attributes, as specific principles and potencies. At the same time we have also seen the inter-relationship and interaction of the *Sefirot* in a develop-

mental sequence from *Keter* to *Malchut*. But this raises a question: how, in fact, can the *Sefirot* interrelate and interact when they appear to be separate, and in some cases seemingly contradictory principles (*e.g.*, the antimony between *Chesed* and *Gevurah*, and between *Netzach* and *Hod*)? For even when the *Sefirot* do not contradict each other, or some are spoken of as mediating principles, they still are essentially unique powers which, in order to interact, would require some "common denominator."

The mystics solve this problem by stating that, in effect, every *Sefirah* is a compound of ten general levels: every *Sefirah* contains within itself aspects of all the ten *Sefirot*.[160] Thus the *Sefirah* of *Chochmah* divides into *Chochmah* of *Chochmah*, *Binah* of *Chochmah* and so on; the *Sefirah* of *Chesed* is divisible into *Chochmah* of *Chesed*, *Binah* of *Chesed*, and so forth. The differentiation between the *Sefirot* is retained in full so that in every *Sefirah* its own aspect is predominant and determinative: *Chochmah of Chochmah* in *Chochmah*, *Binah of Binah* in *Binah* and so on, so that every *Sefirah* can still be referred to by a specific name and differs radically from all others.[161] This mutual inclusiveness has an important, two-fold significance:

(a) It indicates the integral bond between, and essential unity of, the *Sefirot* (as opposed to regarding each *Sefirah* as independent and non-related, thereby leading to a wrong conception of division in the *Sefirotic* scheme) even while retaining the specific identity of, and differentiation among, the *Sefirot*.

(b) It allows the necessary interaction of all *Sefirot* in everything even though their distinguishing aspects or determinative characteristics may appear to be opposed to each other (*e.g.*, *Chesed* and *Gevurah*). Thus, for example, as the attribute of *Chesed* will express and manifest itself it will involve all other *Sefirot*, including *Gevurah*, by way of the aspect of *Chesed* included in every other *Sefirah*.[162]

This concept of the *Sefirot* as Compounds is intimately related to the concept of the scheme of *Yosher* and, as with the latter, its full significance will emerge in the later chapters on *Shevirat Hakelim*, *Partzufim* and *Tohu and Tikun*.

Notes to Chapter III

[1] *See* supra, *Chapt. 2, notes 11–12.*

[2] Exodus Rabba *3:6: "You wish to know My Name? I am called according to My workings. Sometimes I am called . . .".* Cf. Zohar *III:257b* f., *and see also* Kuzary *II:2;* Moreh Nevuchim *I:61;* Pardess Rimonim *4:10;* Shomer Emunim *II:54* ff.; Torah Shelemah, *vol. VIII, p. 151, note 179. "All the attributes of the Holy One, blessed is He, His Will and His Wisdom, are designated and called by (their) terms relative only to the upper and lower beings alone;"* Tanya *II:10. In a sense, with respect to the* En Sof, R. *Schneur Zalman goes even beyond Maimonides' definition of the attributes as negations* (Moreh Nevuchim *I:58–60*)*: It is even inappropriate to say that "it is impossible to apprehend G–d", because that would be like saying "of a lofty and profound wisdom that it cannot be touched with the hands because of the profundity of the concept. Surely, whoever would hear such a statement will laugh, because the sense of touch relates and applies only to a physical object that can be grasped with the hand. Truly so, the aspect of intellect and apprehension in relation to the Holy One, blessed is He, is considered as an actual physical action . . .";* Tanya *II:9 see also the discussion of attributes in* Torah Or, *Bo:60a, and* Likutei Torah *I:6c, and* ibid., *V:7d*). Cf. Shi'ur Komah, *ch. 57–58.*

[3] Sefirot—*plural form;* Sefirah—*singular form. The doctrine of the* Sefirot *is first mentioned in* Sefer Yetzirah, *and is briefly referred to in the Midrash,* Numbers Rabba *14:12. The word* Sefirah *is variably interpreted as derived from, or related to,* mispar (*number*) *or* sapar (*to number*); Sefer (*book*); siper (*to tell; relate*); sapir (*sapphire; brilliance or luminary; see* Exodus *24:10, and* cf. Ezek. *1:26*); separ (*boundary*); *and* Safra (*scribe*). *See* Zohar *II:136b* f.; Tikunei Zohar, *Intr.: 12b;* Zohar Chadash, Yitro, *33b; commentaries of R. Moses Hagoleh and R. Moses Butril on* Sefer Yetzirah *I:2;* Pardess Rimonim *8:2;* Elima Rabbaty *VI:2 (p. 50d* f.); Shi'ur Komah, *ch. 2;* Etz Chayim *5:5. These interpretations do not conflict with one another, but relate to the various aspects of the* Sefirot *on different levels. As varying manifestations and principles the* Sefirot *are also referred to* (*in* Zohar *and other works*) *by other terms suited to the context* (e.g., *lights, pillars, levels, colours, garments, firmaments, crowns, wreaths, kings, faces, and so on*)*; see* Elima Rabbaty, ibid. *ch. 3–12, and* Shi'ur Komah, *ch. 3–12. The ten sacred Divine Names that one is prohibited to destroy or erase—(see* Shevuot *35a; Maimonides,* Hilchot Yesodei Hatorah *VI:1* f. *Though there are basically only seven such Names, they are "seven that are ten" as some may appear in different forms; see* Zohar *III:11a* f.; cf. Avot de R. Natan, *ch. 34.*)*—are usually identified with the ten* Sefirot*: "the* Sefirot *are the Names, and the Names are the* Sefirot*;" see* Zohar *II:42b, and II:288a;* Shenei Luchot Habrit, *Toldot Adam:* Bet Hashem (*p. 3d*)*;* Shomer Emunim *II:67. However, this identification must be qualified. The* Sefirot *and the Names are not fully identical in the plain sense. For the* Sefirot (*as will be explained* infra, *ch. 5*) *are "divisible" into two aspects:* Orot (*Lights*) *and* Kelim (*Vessels*). *The Divine Names are to be identified only with the* Orot, *the aspect of the Light of the* En Sof *vested in the* Kelim *of the* Sefirot, *thus not with the* Kelim *or with the* Sefirot *as compounds of* Orot *and* Kelim*; see in detail* Likutei Torah *III:51c, and* cf. Shomer Emunim *II:64* ff.; Shenei Luchot Habrit, ad loc. cit.

[4] *See* Igeret Hakodesh, *sect XX.* (*As mentioned in the preceding note, there are two aspects to the* Sefirot*:* Orot *and* Kelim. *Thus the* Sefirot *are to be conceived as "vessels" in which the Divine Light is vested and effects Its workings through them.*)

[5] *See* ibid., *sect. III.—The doctrine of the* Sefirot *is thus essential to an understanding of the principle of creation.* Tzimtzum *and the* Sefirot *explain how it is possible for finite and multifarious creations to come about from an Infinite, Simple* (*as opposed to compound*) *One. In numerous, and at times lengthy, arguments the mystics prove from both traditional and philosophical points of view that the doctrine of* Sefirot *is essential to explain the possibility of the creation of the universe as well as the possibility of a subsequent Divine Providence, or that the transcendent G–dhead also be a "personal" G–d; see, e.g., R. Azriel of Geronah,* Perush Eser

Sefirot, *Responsa 3–5;* Avodat Hakodesh *I:8;* Pardess Rimonim *1:8* f., *and 2:6;* Shomer Emunim *I:41* ff., *and II:13* ff. (*See also further on, and notes 15–20 of this chapter.*)

[6] *See* Igeret Hakodesh, *beginning of sect. XX.* (*The word* beli-mah, *taken from* Job *26:7, denotes that they are not anything substantial and apprehensible;* cf. Pardess Rimonim *1:1;* Shomer Emunim *I:61.*)

[7] Sefer Yetzirah *I:7; see the commentaries* a.l., *especially the one attributed to Nachmanides.*

[8] Zohar *III:70a; see also* ibid., *I:50b* f.

[9] Zohar *II:176a;* cf. Tikunei Zohar, *Intr.: 17a. See also* Avodat Hakodesh *I:11–12;* Pardess Rimonim *5:4;* Shomer Emunim *I:56* ff. *and 67, and* ibid., *II:11 and 57. The* Sefirot, *are therefore not some kind of actual intermediaries or intermediating powers; they are* beli-mah, *abstract concepts of Divine manifestations and nothing more. Hence the mystics emphasise and caution to bear this in mind, in particular at the time of prayer. Man addresses the very G–dhead and not any* Sefirot *or Attributes. Therefore it is written "whensoever we call upon Him"* (Deut. *4:7*) *—upon* Him, *i.e., to exclude His attributes! See R. Bachya ben R. Asher,* Commentary *on* Deut. *4:7 and on* Deut. *11:13;* Pardess Rimonim *32:2* (*where this exclusion is attributed to the* Midrash Sifre). Cf. *also R. Isaac bar Sheshet,* Teshuvot Haribash, *responsum 157; and* Likutei Torah *II:51c and III:30d.*

[10] Hilchot Yesodei Hatorah *II:10;* Shemonah Perakim, *end of ch. VIII.*

[11] Hilchot Yesodei Hatorah *I:7;* cf. Moreh Nevuchim *I:57.*

[12] *See* Moreh Nevuchim *I:57.*

[13] Hilchot Yesodei Hatorah *II:10.*

[14] Tanya *II:8.*

[15] *See* Zohar *I:38a, 39a, 152b, 230b, 231a;* ibid., *II:253a, and III:143a.*

[16] Tanya *II: end of ch. 9; see* Likutei Torah *III:68d.*

[17] Tanya *II:10.* Cf. ibid., *ch. 3, and* Igeret Hakodesh, *sect. XX.*

[18] Zohar *III:69b;* ibid., *257b* f.*;* Pardess Rimonim *2:6;* Shi'ur Komah, s.v. Torah, *sect. XIII: Introd. and ch. 3;* Etz Chayim *1:1, and* Sha'ar Hakelalim, *ch. 1;* Shomer Emunim *II:12* ff.

[19] Perush Eser Sefirot, *Responsa 3 and 7;* Pardess Rimonim *2:6.* Cf. supra, *ch. 3, note 5 and the sources cited there, and* Likutei Torah *III:68d.*

[20] *See* Shomer Emunim *II:12* ff., *where the author also deals with a number of problems related to this concept. See also R. Meir ibn Gabbai,* Derech Emunah (*an exposition and elaboration of R. Azriel's* Perush Eser Sefirot, *dealing with most aspects relating to the doctrine of the* Sefirot), *et* passim.

[21] Tanya *I: ch. 20; see* supra, *ch. 2, note 18.*

[22] *"Ten and not nine; ten and not eleven;"* Sefer Yetzirah *I:4; see commentaries* a.l., *and the references cited* supra, *ch. 3, note 3.*

[23] *See* infra, *this chapter, note 38.*

[24] Tanya *I: ch. 3;* par. Sefer Yetzirah *I:10.*

[25] *Sometimes also called the "three fathers," in the same sense.*

[26] *The faculties of the intellect, at times referred to as the three* Mochin (*Brains*).

[27] *See* Tanya *I: ch. 3. In an extended sense, though, all the* Sefirot *are called* Midot (*Attributes*)*; see* infra, *this chapter, note 149.*

[28] *See* infra, *sections 4–7, and ch. 8.*

[29] *See,* e.g., Derech Emunah, *ch. 9* (*p. 63* f.)*;* Pardess Rimonim *I:1–2 and 8:25.*

[30] Etz Chayim *25:5 and 42:1; see* Igeret Hakodesh, *sect. XVII, XX, and XXIX.*

[31] Ibid., *and see* infra, *this chapter, note 38. —For another interpretation of the term* Keter *see* Derech Emunah, *ch. 9* (*p. 36*).

[32] Zohar *I:147a; see* Pardess Rimonim *5:4 and* Igeret Hakodesh, *sect. XIII.*

[33] Zohar *III:256b;* Igeret Hakodesh, *sect. XVII and note 34* a.l.

[34] *In the same sense it is also called* Atik *or* Atika Kadisha (*the Ancient One, or the Holy Ancient One*), *particularly in the context of the* Partzufim (*see* infra, *ch. 8*). *The origin of this term is* Daniel *7:9, 13 and 22* (cf. Chagigah *14a*), *and it abounds in* Sifra Detzeniyuta *and the* Idrot. *Though* Atik *is essentially a term applied to the* En Sof (*in the sense of being the First Cause, or the Most Ancient Being; also called* Atika dechol Atikin—*the Most Ancient of all Ancients, or* Atik Yomin—*the Ancient of Days; see*, e.g., Zohar *III:288a* ff.), *it is sometimes applied to the highest aspect of* Keter, *i.e., to the very core and essence of this* Sefirah, *because it is the most "ancient" or original emanation from the* En Sof. *See* Avodat Hakodesh *I:3, and R. Chayim Vital,* Mevoh She'arim *III:1:1. See also* Torah Or, *Esther, 98c, on the meaning of* Atik.

[35] *See* Chagigah *13a.*

[36] Zohar *II:42b and 158a.*

[37] *The four letters of the Tetragrammaton represent the ten* Sefirot: Yud—Chochmah; (*the first*) Hai—Binah; Vav—Tiferet, *or the unit of the six* Midot *from* Chesed *to* Yesod; (*the latter*) Hai—Malchut. Keter *is represented by the "thorn" of the* Yud (*thus not by any letter but by a mere dot*). Zohar *III:17a,* *and* ibid. *258a,* et passim.; *see* Tanya *III:4;* Igeret Hakodesh, *sect. V.*

[38] *R. Moses Cordovero always counts* Keter *as part of the ten* Sefirot *and excludes* Da'at *as a separate* Sefirah (*see* Pardess Rimonim *3:1* ff., *and* Or Ne'erav *6:1, par. 5*). *In the system of R. Isaac Luria, followed by Chassidism,* Da'at *is usually counted as one of the* Sefirot *while* Keter *is excluded* (*see* Etz Chayim *23:1, 2, 5 and 8;* ibid., *25:6 and 42:1*). *Their controversy evolves around the interpretation of* Zohar *I: beginning of 31b* (*see* Derech Emet *and other comment.* a.l., *and R. Chayim David Azulay,* Nitzutzei Orot, *on* Zohar *I:31a; see also* Zohar *III: end of 269a and 289b*) *where the* peshat *appears to support the opinion of R. Isaac Luria, though R. Moses Cordovero* (a.l.c., *and see also* ibid., *2:3* ff.) *interprets according to his opinion. In fact this has long been a matter of dispute among the earliest kabbalists. While all are agreed that* Keter *exceedingly excels the* Sefirot (Chochmah *to* Malchut), *some say that* Keter *is identical with the* En Sof (*rather with the* Or En Sof) *and therefore to be excluded from the scheme of* Sefirot, *while others have it that* Keter, *too, is an emanation and effect having a cause just like the other* Sefirot *and, hence, is to be counted among them.* (*See the discussion of these issues in* Pardess Rimonim *3:1* ff., *and* Etz Chayim *42:1.*) *The view of R. Isaac Luria is a third opinion to the effect that* Keter *is somewhere in between* Or En Sof *and the* Sefirot, *part of both, and bridging or linking them: the "lowest" level of the* En Sof *as well as the very root or source of the* Sefirot *following. Thus on the one hand it is an aspect of the* Or En Sof *and excluded, and on the other, it is part of the ten* Sefirot (*see* Etz Chayim a.l.c.; *what appears to be a similar view is that expounded by R. Shem Tov ibn Shem Tov,* Sefer Haemunot *IV: end of ch. 10—discussed in* Pardess Rimonim *3:3, though with the mistaken reference to IV:1—and by R. Meir ibn Gabbai,* Avodat Hakodesh *I:2–3*). *This issue* (*and the related problems as* e.g., *how can one speak of "higher" and "lower" in relation to the* En Sof, *or how can one relate the actual essence of the* En Sof *to* Keter, *and so on*) *relates to the disputed issue whether the term* En Sof *itself has reference to the actual Essence and Being of G–d as He is in Himself or to G–d* qua *First Cause* (*see* supra, *ch. 2, note 11*); *for a wider discussion of all this see* Torah Or, *Vayechi: 105a;* Likutei Torah *V:8a* f., *and also* ibid. *II:53b; and* Yom Tov shel Rosh Hashanah *5333, sect. XX, pp. 666* ff.).

In the context of the aforesaid, R. Isaac Luria adds that when speaking of the essential Sefirot—Keter *is included, but when speaking of their general aspects* (Chitzoniyut *of the* Sefirot) Keter *is omitted and* Da'at *is inserted instead; see* Etz Chayim *23:5 and 8, and* Likutei Torah *III:49c;* cf. Torah Or, a.l.c., *and* Likutei Torah *II:46c and V:8a.*

[39] *See* Igeret Hakodesh, *sect. XVII, XX and XXIX.*

[40] Zohar *III:129a and 288b.*

[41] *See* Igeret Hakodesh, *sect. XXIX. Thus when we speak,* e.g., *of the Torah as the blueprint for the world* (Gen. Rabba *I:1;* Zohar *I:5a*), Keter *would be the Supreme Will underlying this blueprint, the very source*

of origin of the Torah. This is the meaning of the frequent phrase (e.g., Igeret Hakodesh, *sect. I, and notes 37–8* a.l.) "*the Torah derives from* Chochmah *but its source and root surpasses exceedingly the rank of* Chochmah *and is called the Supreme Will.*" *That is, Torah is an expression of Reason or the Divine Wisdom* (Chochmah). *Reason is focused towards achieving a certain goal. But the very purpose of achieving that goal transcends the rational faculty and underlies it. When reason achieves its goal it fulfils a higher aim: the realisation of some deep-seated, innermost desire or will. This innermost desire or will is the Abyssmal or Supreme Will (see* Igeret Hakodesh, *sect. XXIX, note 22*).

[42] Zohar *I:3b*, et passim. *See* Igeret Hakodesh, *sect. V and note 82* a.l. Chochmah *is called* Reishit *regardless of whether* Keter *is counted or not. When* Keter *is included we speak of two spheres that are called* Reishit: Keter *and* Chochmah (*as alluded in the first word of the Torah:* Be-Reishit, *i.e., Two (categories of)* Reishit; *see* Zohar *I:31b*).

[43] *Thus in relation to* Keter, Chochmah *is called* Yesh (*a substance*); *see* Pardess Rimonim *5:4;* Tanya *I, ch. 2 and II:9.*

[44] *See* Tanya *I: ch. 35;* Igeret Hakodesh, *sect. IV, note 25.*

[45] Psalms *104:24;* Proverbs *3:19.*

[46] *The same applies to the first word of the Torah:* Be-Reishit (Reishit *referring to* Chochmah, *as said*); *see* Igeret Hakodesh, *sect. V, notes 22 and 82* ff.

[47] *See* Nachmanides *on* Genesis *I:1, and* cf. Moreh Nevuchim *II:30.—The term* hyle *is applied here to* Chochmah *in the extended sense of* Chochmah *being the basic "substance" of creation that can be referred to as* yesh (cf. supra, *this chapter, note 43*). *Strictly speaking the term* hyle *relates to* Keter; *for* "Keter *is like unto the prime matter that is called* hyle *which contains within it—in potency, though not* in actu*—the root of all four elements;*" Etz Chayim *42:1; see also R. Chayim Vital,* Arba Meot Shekel Kessef (ed. *Tel Aviv 1964*), *p. 94a–b.*

[48] *See* Tanya *I: ch. 18;* Igeret Hakodesh, *sect. XIV and XVII.*

[49] Ibid. (*note 89*), *and* Tanya *I: ch. 19;* Igeret Hakodesh, *sect. V, note 22.* "*All the lower ones are rooted and compounded in* Chochmah, *which is the mystical principle of 'You have made them all in* Chochmah';" Etz Chayim *25:1.*

[50] *The letters of the word* חכמה *make up* כ"ח מ"ה; Zohar *III:235b. See also* Tikunei Zohar, *Intr.:4a and 69:112b;* Zohar Chadash, *34b–c and 100a* ff.; Tanya *II: ch. 3.*

[51] *See* supra, *ch. 3 note 37.*

[52] Zohar *III:290a; see also* ibid., *II:90a.*

[53] *See* Berachot *34b;* Tikunei Zohar, *Intr.: 12a.*

[54] Igeret Hakodesh, *sect. V, and notes 19* ff. a.l.

[55] *See* infra, *this chapter, note 63;* Igeret Hakodesh, *sect. XI.* Cf. Tanya *I: ch. 19. That is, essentially, in itself,* Chochmah *is still called* ayin, *though in relation to* Keter *it is* yesh (supra, *this chapter, note 43*).

[56] Tanya, *I: ch. 3;* cf. Zohar *I:15b.*

[57] Tanya *I: ch. 3;* Igeret Hakodesh, *sect. V.*

[58] Tikunei Zohar *22:63b.*

[59] *The process of induction-deduction;* Chagigah *14a;* Zohar Chadash *4a;* cf. Sifre *on* Deut. *1:13;* Igeret Hakodesh, *sect. XV and note 70* a.l.

[60] *See* supra, *note 37.*

[61] Tanya *III:4;* Igeret Hakodesh, *sect. V.* Cf. Zohar *II:158a.*

[62] Zohar *I:6a;* Igeret Hakodesh, *sect. V, note 15.*

[63] *That is why* Deut. *29:30* ("*the hidden things are unto the Eternal*") *is applied to the* Sefirot, Chochmah *and* Binah; *see* Tikunei Zohar *Intr.: 17a. Thus all three,* Keter-

Chochmah-Binah, *are on a plane* AYiN: A—Keter, Yi—Chochmah, N—Binah; Tikunei Zohar *42:81b;* Igeret Hakodesh, *sect. XI, note 11. See also* Zohar *I:1b, and* Sha'ar Hahakdamot, *Hakd. I.*

[64] *See* Moreh Nevuchim *II:4 that wisdom or reason does not produce motion: the intellect which forms and develops an idea, and the ability to move to act upon this idea, will not produce motion without the existence of a desire (emotive disposition) for the object of which an idea has been formed.* Cf. *also* Shemona Perakim, *ch. 2, to the effect that every action or acting upon, originates in the appetitive faculty of the soul, thus in the emotive dispositions* (Midot) *of man. Hence it is* Da'at, *as essence of the* Midot, *that is the volitive power moving to action, or acting upon that which is proposed by* Chochmah *and* Binah.

[65] *See the detailed discussion of* Da'at *in* Pardess Rimonim *3:8 and 9:5–6;* Etz Chayim, *Sha'ar 24* f.; Sha'ar Hahakdamot, Derush Be'inyan Hada'at *(pp. 270b* ff.*);* Likutei Torah *III:87c* f. *(besides the sources mentioned in the notes following, especially note 72).*

[66] Cf. Genesis *4:1, 17, 25,* et passim. Tikunei Zohar *69:99a;* Etz Chayim *48:2.*

[67] *See* Zohar *III:291a.*

[68] *See* Igeret Hakodesh, *end of sect. XV, and the references in note 79* a.l.; Shenei Luchot Habrit, *Toldot Adam:Bet Hashem (p. 5a* ff.), *especially the glossary notes* a.l., s.v. Inyan Hada'at *and* Veaz Mevuar.

[69] *See* Berachot *17a: "The goal of* Chochmah *is repentance and good deeds;" "Study is greater because it leads to action"* (Kiddushin *40b*)*—"for there is no action without* chochmah" (Zohar *I:266a*).

[70] *For example, a thief may be found to pray for Divine assistance in the very midst of his nefarious activities* (Berachot *63a,* vs. *of* Ayin Ya'akov)*; that is, he has the knowledge of G–d's existence and believes in the Divine ability to help him, but he does not carry this knowledge and understanding to its logical conclusion to apply it consistently with its inherent implications;* cf. Derech Mitzvotecha, Haamanat Elokut: *ch. 2.*

[71] *Thus this faculty of* Da'at Tachton *is the very root and essence, or soul and controlling guide, of the* Midot.

[72] *See* supra, *this chapter, note 65, and* Tanya *I, chs. 3 and 42;* Torah Or, *Mishpatim:74c* ff.*;* Likutei Torah *III:2d and 87c* f.*;* et passim. *See also* Derech Mitzvotecha, a.l.c.—Cf. Zohar *II:123a and III:289b* f.

[73] *See* Etz Chayim *22:1:* "Chochmah *and* Binah *(alone) are to no avail, for* Chochmah *and* Binah *are concealed and become manifest only by means of* Da'at;" Cf. Mevoh She'arim *V:1:12 and 14 ("the principal illumination and manifestation of the brains in man is by means of* Da'at").

[74] Zohar *III:290a* ff.*;* Pardess Rimonim *8:17;* Igeret Hakodesh, *sect. XV, note 9, and* infra, *ch. 8.*

[75] Ibid.

[76] *Thus the* Midot *are called the children of* Chochmah *and* Binah, *or, alternatively,* Tiferet *(or the first six* Midot *in unison) is called the "son" and* Malchut *is called the "daughter". See references in note 74 of this chapter. It is in this context as "soul (essence) of the* Midot" *that* Da'at *is not counted as a separate* Sefirah *to replace* Keter *(see* supra *note 38). For as a mere soul without its own independent vessel or body it cannot be included as one of the ten principles of the* Sefirot*;* Etz Chayim *23:5 and 8; see also* ibid., *40:6. See also R. Joseph Isaac Schneersohn,* Sefer Hamaamarim 5700 *(New York 1955), p. 38.*

[77] *See* Tanya *I: ch. 3, and* Igeret Hakodesh, *sect. XV.*

[78] Shenei Luchot Habrit, a.l.c., s.v. *Inyan Hada'at; see also* Avodat Hakodesh *I:3, and* Pardess Rimonim *11:3.* Cf. supra, *ch. 1, sect. 2.*

[79] Etz Chayim *18:5 (see* infra, *this chapter, note 86); see* Moreh Nevuchim *III:56, and* Igeret Hakodesh, *sect. XV, and note 21* a.l.

[80] *See* Zohar *II:168b, and* Pardess Rimonim *8:1;* cf. infra, *this chapter, note 103.*

[81] Psalms *89:3; see* Tanya *II:4, and* Igeret Hakodesh, *sect. V and X.*

[82] Etz Chayim *I:1*, et passim; Pardess Rimonim *2:6*. Cf. Zohar *III:69b and 257b* f. *See* supra, *section 1, and Chap. 3, note 18.*

[83] Cf. Igeret Hakodesh, *sect. V, and notes 77, 79–82* a.l.

[84] *See* Tanya *II:4;* cf. Igeret Hakodesh, *sect. XIII and XV.—Though this principle and implication is mostly related to* Chesed *and* Malchut, *in fact it is relevant to all the* Sefirot (*as mentioned earlier, see end of section 1, and the references cited there in Chap. 3, note 18*)*: all the* Sefirot, *as Divine attributes, assume actualised manifestation through the process and presence of creation.*

[85] *See* infra, *this chapter, note 100.*

[86] *See* Pardess Rimonim *8:2, and* infra, *this chapter, note 89.*—Etz Chayim *18:5:* "*All fixed measures and limitations are but from the side of* Gevurah. *For* Chesed *indicates an extension in all matters beyond the limit.* Gevurah, *however, does not allow the Supernal Light to extend, but sets to it a limitation and measure to the point of (actual) need—for the light to extend that far but no further;*" cf. Mevoh She'arim *I:1:1, and* infra, *ch. 5, note 6.*

[87] *See* Mevoh She'arim *I:1:1:* "*Every limitation of emanation is from* (Gevurah *and* Din) . . . *Every* tzimtzum *is (a notion of)* Din." *See also* Tanya *II:4 and 6, and* cf. *preceding note.*

[88] Igeret Hakodesh, *sect. XIII.*

[89] *See* Etz Chayim *18:5* (supra, *this chapter, note 86*), *and* Igeret Hakodesh, *sect. VIII, XII, XIII, and XV.*

[90] *See* infra, *this chapter, note 100.*

[91] *See* Torah Or, *Noach: p. 9c, and* cf. infra, *ch. 11, note 9.* Cf. *also* Igeret Hakodesh, *sect. XV, for positive aspects of* Gevurah. *As a general rule, though, the positive effects of* Gevurah *emerge only by prior stimulus or effort.*

[92] *See* Tanya *II:6;* cf. Igeret Hakodesh, *sect. XV.*

[93] *See* supra, *ch. 2.*

[94] *See* Tanya *II:4–6, and* infra, *note 103.*

[95] Pardess Rimonim *8:2, and 9:3;* Igeret Hakodesh, *sect. XII. See R. Levi Yitzchak Schneerson,* Likutei Levi Yitzchak-Zohar (*New York 1971*), *on Zohar I:168a, p. 132.*

[96] Tikunei Zohar *70:133b;* Igeret Hakodesh, *sect. XII and XV.*

[97] *Mostly in the context of the* Partzufim*; see* infra, *ch. 8.*

[98] *In this context, just like* Da'at *is the "soul" of the* Midot (supra, *note 61*), *so* Tiferet *is the "body" of the* Midot.

[99] Zohar *III:302a*, et passim; Tikunei Zohar *22:67b;* Tanya *II:4*; Likutei Torah *IV:17c* ff.; cf. Sifre *on* Numbers *27:12* (*sect. 134, in comment on* Deut. *3:24*). *In the Scriptural reference to the* Midot *in* I Chronicles *29:11, the term* Gedulah *appears, and not* Chesed; *see* Zohar *I:31a and so on. However, strictly speaking, there is a distinct difference between these two terms with* Gedulah *denoting a superior level of Divine Benevolence than* Chesed; *for an extensive discussion of these two terms and their relationship, see R. Menachem Mendel of Lubavitch,* Or Hatorah-Bereishit (*New York 1966*), *vol. I, Vayera: p. 179* ff., *and R. Shemuel Schneersohn,* Likutei Torah-Torat Shemuel (*New York 1946*), *vol. III, ch. 46* ff.

[100] Zohar *II:175b, and also* ibid. *51b;* Tikunei Zohar, *Intr.: 17b;* Igeret Hakodesh, *sect. XII and XIII.*

[101] Zohar Chadash, *Yitro, 31b;* Igeret Hakodesh, *sect. VI and note 6* a.l., *and sect. XII and XV. Obviously it is called* Rachamim *because of the predominance of* Chesed (*see* supra, *note 95*)*;* Chesed per se *would thus be the very core of* Rachamim, *or* "Rachamim *within* Rachamim" (Zohar *III:145b*).

[102] Igeret Hakodesh, *sect. XV.*

[103] Zohar Chadash, *Toldot, 26c;* ibid., *Yitro, 31b. See* Etz Chayim *35:3;* Igeret Hakodesh, *sect. VI, and note 36* a.l., *and* cf. ibid., *sect. II, note 22.—It need be understood that all the* Midot, *as Divine attributes, are* Emet (*truth*), *but they are so only when*

they stand on their own. The quality of Chesed *to dispense benevolence in unlimited fashion, out of absolute, gratuitous and infinite benevolence without regard to the merits of the recipient, is an aspect of truth. For, strictly speaking, nothing is truly fit to receive the Divine benevolence except that from the Divine perspective it is all one ("even the darkness does not darken from You and the night shines as the day—the darkness is even as the light;"* Psalms *139:12), and therefore "in the light of the King's Countenance there is life"* (Prov. *16:15*). *On the other hand, the quality of* Gevurah *to withhold and restrict the Divine effusion is again truthful for the very reason that truth and justice demand distribution in justness and equity, i.e., in proportion to the recipient's merits. Thus, inasmuch as even "the heavens are not pure in His eyes"* (Job *15:15*) *and "His angels He charges with deficiency"* (ibid. *4:18; see* Moreh Nevuchim *III:13, and* Igeret Hakodesh, *sect.* XX *and note 35* a.l.) *from the aspect of* Gevurah, *of law and justice, truth demands the withholding of the Divine Grace. But these aspects of truth are* relative *to these conflicting perspectives: the perspective of* Chesed *on its own and the perspective of* Gevurah *on its own.* Tiferet, *on the other hand, is* absolute *truth in the sense that it reconciles and harmonises* Chesed *and* Gevurah, *that it is not contradicted or opposed by either* Chesed *or* Gevurah *or any other attribute. For* Tiferet *recognises the validity of* Gevurah*—that strictly speaking the recipient is undeserving—but out of a sense of* Rachamim *(Compassion) permits a restrained flow of* Chesed. *Thus, because the motive is strictly one of compassion, even* Gevurah *will agree to this flow, and, therefore,* Tiferet *is a truth recognised from every aspect, without any opposition:* Emet Le-amito, *absolute truth. See* Etz Chayim, *and* Igeret Hakodesh, a.l.c., *and* Yom Tov shel Rosh Hashanah 5666, *sect. 52, p. 434* f.

[104] *As the* Sefirot *are the Divine instruments through which everything comes into being, everything relates directly to one or more of the* Sefirot *in its own individual way, or by way of metaphor and analogy.*

[105] Zohar Chadash, a.l.c. (*note 103*)*; also* Zohar *II:276b, III:302a,* et passim.

[106] Ibid.; Sefer Habahir *48* (*131*); Zohar *I:41a,* et passim; *see* Igeret Hakodesh, *sect. II, note 9, and* ibid., *sect. XIII.*

[107] Supra, *note 105;* Igeret Hakodesh, *sect. XIII, and note 27* a.l.

[108] Supra, *note 105; ref. cited in* Igeret Hakodesh, *sect. II, note 22, and* ibid., *sect. VI. See also* Zohar *I:74a and 146a;* Likutei Levi Yitzchak, a.l.c. (*note 95*).

[109] Tikunei Zohar *70:133b.*

[110] *See* supra, *notes 105–108.*

[111] *See* Tanya *II:5, and* Igeret Hakodesh, *sect. XIX.*

[112] *See* Tikunei Zohar *19:45a, 22:68b, and 30:74a;* Zohar *III:236a;* Igeret Hakodesh, *sect. XV and note 41* a.l. *See further,* Pardess Rimonim *7:2, 8:17 and 24;* Likutei Torah *III:90c–d; (the latter two works being the principal sources for the explanation following).*

[113] Likutei Torah, a.l.c., *and* cf. Igeret Hakodesh, *sect. I.*

[114] *See* Pardess Rimonim *7:2 and 8:24.*

[115] Ibid., *I:4.*

[116] Zohar *III:236a.*

[117] E.g., *the "two hips"* (Tikunei Zohar *13:29a*)*; "two thighs"* (Zohar *I:26b;* Tikunei Zohar, *Intr.: 17a*)*; "two kidneys"* (Zohar *III:296a*)*; and so forth. Just as* ChaGaT *are the three Patriarchs, so* Netzach *and* Hod *are the two brothers Moses and Aaron* (Zohar *I:256b, and II:276b, and ref. cited* supra, *note 105*)*. Also, the Divine Names, and other terms, relating to these two attributes are usually a plural form of one concept; see* Pardess Rimonim a.l.c.

[118] Zohar Chadash, *Vayera, 26d;* Igeret Hakodesh, *sect. I, and* ibid., *sect. V and note 100* a.l.

[119] *See* Igeret Hakodesh, *sect. I, and* Likutei Torah *III:90c–d.*

[120] Igeret Hakodesh, *sect. XV.*

[121] *See* ibid., *note 41 and the ref. cited there.*

[122] Ibid., *notes 64 and 68, and the ref. cited there. While* Hod *is the awe and restraint implicit in the awareness of the* concept *of majesty,* Gevurah *would be the awe and restraint implicit in the awareness of the* confrontation *or presence of majesty, thus much more intense and severe than* Hod; *see* Likutei Torah *III:90c–d.*

[123] Igeret Hakodesh, *sect. XV.*

[124] *See* Pardess Rimonim *8:24, and* Etz Chayim *46:3.* Cf. supra, *notes 112 and 114.*

[125] *See* Tikunei Zohar *21:55b;* ibid., *Addenda, 6:145b. See also next note.*

[126] *In* I Chronicles *29:11, which alludes to the seven* Midot (*see* supra, *note 99*), *the principle of* Yesod *is expressed by the words* כי כל בשמים ובארץ *which the* Zohar (*based on a* Targum) *interprets "for* all (kol, i.e., *the all-comprehensive* Sefirah *of* Yesod) *joins the heaven and the earth;"* Zohar *I:31a, II:116a, III:257a* (*and* Nitzutzei Orot, a.l.) et passim. *See* Igeret Hakodesh, *sect. XV, note 44, and* cf. Tikunei Zohar *21:55b.*

[127] "*The* Tzaddik (*Righteous; symbol of the* Sefirah Yesod) *is the Foundation* (Yesod) *of the world;*" Prov. *10:25.* Zohar, a.l.c. (*note 126*), et passim.

[128] Zohar *III:271b;* cf. Pirkei de R. Eliezer, *ch. 3.* "*When, by His Will was fashioned every thing, His appellation then was that of King;*" Liturgy, *Adon Olam. See also* Tossafot, Berachot *40b,* s.v. אביי אמר; Tanya *II:7, and* Igeret Hakodesh, *sect. XX, and note 44* a.l.

[129] *Hence the lowest level in spiritual categories is usually referred to as the* Malchut (*or more emphatically yet, as* Malchut of Malchut) *of that category.*

[130] Etz Chayim *6:5, 8:5,* et passim: Malchut *is called "a dim speculum because it has no (light) of its own," (like unto "the moon that has no light of its own save that which is given unto it by the sun;"* Zohar *I:249b, and 251b; II:145b;* Tikunei Zohar *44:82b;* et passim. Cf. Shabbat *156a*). *See also* ibid., *36:1. See further* Igeret Hakodesh, *sect. XXXI, note 21, and* cf. Nidah *31b.*

[131] Igeret Hakodesh, *sect. XX; see also* Tanya *II:7.*

[132] Pardess Rimonim *11:2.*

[133] Tikunei Zohar *19:40b, and* Zohar Chadash, *11a.—Probably for this reason did R. Joseph Albo suggest (in the context of identifying the Intelligences with the* Sefirot) *that* Malchut *is identical with the sphere of the Active Intellect (see* Ikkarim *II:11*), *but this has been severely criticised by the Kabbalists; see,* e.g., Avodat Hakodesh *I:7.*

[134] *See* Zohar *I:50a, II:22a, III:290a* ff.; Igeret Hakodesh, *sect. VIII, note 25, and* ibid., *sect. XV, note 9, and sect. XX* (*and note 59* a.l.).

[135] *Also* Alma Ilaah (*the Upper World*); Zohar *I:1b and II:127a.*

[136] (*Also* Alma Tataah (*Lower World*); Zohar *I:1b and II:127a*).—Tanya *I: ch. 52;* Igeret Hakodesh, *sect. XX, and notes 50 and 59* a.l.; ibid., *sect. XXX.*

[137] Tikunei Zohar, *Intr.: 17a.*

[138] Psalms *33:6; see* Igeret Hakodesh, *sect. V, and note 26; sect. XX, and notes 46–50* a.l., *and sect. XXV, and note 22* a.l. *By analogy to human speech, which is but the expression and manifestation or revelation of the speaker's inner thoughts and dispositions,* Malchut *is, as it were, the Divine speech (the ten fiats of* Genesis *I by which the world was created and came into being;* Avot *V:1;* cf. Tanya *II:11–12*).

[139] *See* supra, *note 50.*

[140] *See* Zohar *II:127a* (cf. ibid., *I:1b*); Zohar Chadash, *beg. of Tikunim, 93a.*

[141] Zohar Chadash, *34c.*

[142] *See* Zohar *II:127a;* Tikunei Zohar *70:121a, and* ibid., *Addenda, 3:140a.*

[143] *See* Tanya *II:7, and* supra, *note 128.*

[144] Tanya *II:7;* Igeret Hakodesh, *sect. XX and XXV.* Cf. supra, *notes 18 and 22.*

[145] Tanya, *I, ch. 52;* Igeret Hakodesh, *sect. VIII, and esp. note 25* a.l., *and* ibid., *sect. XXV.*—Imma *and* Shechinah *thus are identical terms. Just as we speak of* Imma *on*

two levels ("higher" and "lower"; Binah and Malchut) *so we speak of* Shechinah *on two levels ("higher" and "lower"; Binah and* Malchut); cf. Igeret Hakodesh, *sect. VIII, note 26. However, any unqualified mention of* Shechinah *usually refers to the lower level of* Malchut. *For a further discussion of* Malchut *see* Pardess Rimonim *7:3–4 and 8, and* ibid., *8: end of ch. 24 and ch. 26.*

[146] *The principal sources for this section are* Etz Chayim *1:2–5, and 2:1;* Sha'ar Hahakdamot, *Hakd. IV and V;* Pardess Rimonim *6:7, and also* ibid., *2:7;* Likutei Torah *III:37c* f. *See also* Igeret Hakodesh, *sect. XX, note 32, and* infra, *note 159.*

[147] *This is how we obtain the relative terms of "above" and "below", "higher" and "lower", and so forth: the periphery of the* chalal *being the highest level, and the centre of the* chalal *being the lowest level.*

[148] *At this stage we thus have (i) the all-encompassing sphere of the* Or En Sof *(manifest outside the* chalal *and concealed within the* chalal*); (ii) the concentric sphere in the upper realm (right adjacent to, but below or inside the perimeter) of the* chalal*; and (iii) the void (below said concentric sphere) of the remainder of the* chalal. *This first concentric sphere is as close to the all-encompassing* Or En Sof *as possible, but not really attached to it except by means of the* kav *from which it evolved. For if the Luminary (*Or En Sof*) and the sphere inside the* chalal *would be truly attached to each other, that part of the* chalal *(the sphere) and its aspect of* tzimtzum *would have been nullified: the inner sphere would have been absorbed by the outer one to revert to the state of one simple light of the* En Sof. *In fact, however, they are fully distinct one from another.*

[149] *Hence also the term* Midot *for the* Sefirot. Midot *means fixed measures and dimensions (and, in an extended sense, garments). For every* Sefirah *has a determined measure and dimension (in a* qualitative *sense), and the* Sefirot *as a whole are also determined in number ("ten and not nine, ten and not eleven"). It is by their individually determined measures that the* Sefirot *are distinguished and differentiated one from another (as we shall see* infra, *ch. 5); see* Zohar *III:257b;* Sefer Yetzirah *I:4–5;* Etz Chayim *1:2;* Sha'ar Hahakdamot, *Hakd, IV.*

[150] *See* Zohar *I:19b* f. *(and* Nitzutzei Orot, a.l.) *and III:9b* f.

[151] *See* Pardess Rimonim *6:3;* Etz Chayim *I:1;* Sha'ar Hahakdamot, *Hakd. IV.—The term* Yosher *(Uprightness; Straightness) is derived from the verse "G–d made man* yashar *(upright)"* (Eccles. *7:29); see* Etz Chayim *8:1. In relation to this scheme of the* Sefirot *it is said "and G–d created man in His image"* (Gen. *1:27)—* Etz Chayim *1:2—for the inherent faculties and powers of man's soul and their interactions are analogous (albeit in a strictly homonymous sense) to the* Sefirot *(see* Igeret Hakodesh, *sect. XV).*

[152] Zohar *I:134b;* Etz Chayim *1:2.—In general, most references to the* Sefirot *in the* Zohar *relate to the scheme of* Yosher, *rather than to that of* Iggulim; *see* Etz Chayim, *and* Sha'ar Hahakdamot, a.l.c.

[153] Tikunei Zohar, *Intr.: 17a, and* cf. supra, *in the explanatory notes for the individual* Sefirot.

[154] *Also called the "kidneys that counsel;" see* supra, *note 117.*

[155] *"The sign of the Holy Covenant," referring to circumcision (the sign or seal of the covenant or* bond *between G–d and Israel).— See* Etz Chayim, *and* Sha'ar Hahakdamot, a.l.c., *with regards to the two aspects of* Yesod *relative to the two types of* Parzufim *(i.e., masculine and feminine).*

[156] *In* Sifra Detzeniyuta, *and in the* Idrot, Keter *is frequently referred to as "skull".—See* Etz Chayim *32:1 and 25:5 on the superiority of the "skull" as* Keter *over the "brains" as* Chochmah-Binah-Da'at.

[157] *See* Zohar *III:153b* (et passim)*;* Etz Chayim *1:2;* Sha'ar Hahakdamot, *Hakd. IV.*

[158] *See* Sefer Hamaamarim 5700, *p. 38, and notes by R. Menachem M. Schneerson* a.l.—Da'at Tachton, *as essence of the* Midot, *obviously does not have a separate organ in this scheme; see* supra, *sect. 4,* s.v. Da'at.

[159] Infra, *ch. 7–9.*

[160] *See* Tikunei Zohar *47:84a, and 69:116b;* cf. *also* Zohar *II:185b, and* Tikunei Zohar *70:125b and 135a.—In referring to every* Sefirah *as a compound of "ten general levels", the word "general" is an intentional qualification; for, in effect, as explained in the sources mentioned, these ten levels subdivide each into ten sub-levels, and so forth.*

[161] *See* Tanya *II:10;* Igeret Hakodesh, *sect. XII and XIII;* Likutei Torah *III:87a* ff., *and 89d* ff.*; references cited* infra, *ch. 9.*

[162] *The issues mentioned here are dealt with in detail by R. Moses Cordovero in* Pardess Rimonim, *Sha'ar 5, especially ch. 5, and Sha'ar 8, esp. ch. 1, 2, 10 and 11.* Cf. *also Maimonides,* Hilchot Yesodei Hatorah *IV: 1–2 (quoted by Cordovero,* ibid., *8:2) which reflects strikingly the argument in* Zohar *II:23b* f. *(quoted at length by Cordovero,* ibid., *ch. 11); see also the glossary note in* Zohar *II:24a* (*and* Nitzutzei Zohar a.l.).

Chapter 4 WORLDS

1. *The Concept of "Worlds"*

Tzimtzum, the process of progressive dimming, occultation and condensation of the light of the *En Sof*, brought about numerous levels, one lower than the other. These numerous levels are divided into five comprehensive categories, referred to as the Five Realms or Worlds. The numerous other levels are the myriads of gradations into which these five worlds subdivide of which each is a microcosm on its own.

Essentially these Worlds are Divine "Garments" in which the *Or En Sof* conceals and clothes Itself, thereby animating and lending them existence.[1] But just as *tzimtzum* and the *Sefirot* are allegorical concepts that assume substantive reality only in relation to man and creation, *i.e.*, from the creature's perspective (looking "from below upwards") but are non-real in essence, *i.e.*, relative to G–d (looking "from above downwards"),[2] so it is with these Worlds. When we speak of different Worlds or Realms, any difference is due to the recipients, and that in two respects: firstly, because the "higher" worlds are those which receive a radiance infinitely greater than the "lower" ones, and secondly, in that the "higher" ones receive this radiance without as many garments and screens as the lower ones.[3] To be sure, the light of the *En Sof* fills all worlds alike and there is no place void of Him.[4] The core and essence of the blessed *En Sof* is identical in the higher and lower worlds, and as He is to be found in the higher worlds so He is to be found in the very lowest. The difference between them is with regard to the stream of vitality from the *En Sof* in terms of "revelation out of concealment." For the higher worlds receive in a more revealed form than do the lower ones, and all creatures therein receive each according to its capacity and nature. The lower worlds, even the spiritual ones, do not receive the light in such a revealed form but only by means of numerous concealing "garments" which hide and screen the Divine Light so that ultimately —on the lowest level, in the physical world—"No light or vitality whatever is visibly revealed, but only corporeal and physical things that appear lifeless."[5] Yet they, too, contain light and vitality from the *En Sof* which lends them existence *ex nihilo*, so that they will not revert to their state of naught and nothingness as they were prior to their creation. In that sense the Holy One, blessed is He, is the "Most Hidden of All Hidden"[6] and is called the "hidden G–d" (*Isaiah* 45:12).[7]

This is analogous to the presence of the soul in the body. The entire soul is a single and simple (as opposed to compound) spiritual entity, without any dimensions of space or size, corporeal shape or physical limitation. Thus one cannot say that it divides into a number of parts corresponding to the number of organs in the body. Rather, the whole soul pervades the entire body equally, from head to foot, and its core and essence is, for example, in the feet no less than in the brain. But from the different kinds of potencies or powers and vitalities contained in the soul's intrinsic essence, each of the body's organs receives the power and vitality appropriate to it according to its capacity and character—the eye for seeing, the ear for hearing, the mouth for speaking and so on. Thus as the different bodily organs express and manifest different powers this is not due to a different soul, or part of the soul, being inherent in them, but it is due to their own different composition and capacity. All powers of the soul are intrinsic to the whole soul and independent of the body, as is evident from the fact that a blind, or otherwise defective, person is able to give birth to a physically normal child.[8]

A similar analogy is to the light of the sun which penetrates the rooms of a house, and even into rooms within rooms. The light does so in accordance with the presence or absence of obstructions; thus there is no change in the light itself, but only in the condition or capacity of the place to be illuminated.[9]

Thus when we speak of "higher" and "lower", in proximity to, or distant from, the *En Sof* and so on, these terms do not refer to any spatial dimensions but to qualitative differences in degree and level.[10]

2. *The Division of the Worlds*

The five comprehensive worlds are:[11]

(1) *Adam Kadmon.* This anthropomorphic term means Primordial Man. *Kadmon* denotes "being primary of all primaries:"[12] This World is also called the Realm of *Keter Elyon* (the Supreme *Keter*), the "lucid and luminous light" (אור צח ומצוחצח) and frequently referred to as *Tzachtzachot*[13]—implying the "pure, lucid *Sefirot* which are concealed and hidden."[14]

(2) *Atzilut*, the World of Emanation. The term is derived from the root אצל, as in *Numbers* 11:17 and *Ecclesiastes* 2:10.

(3) *Beriah*—the World of Creation;

(4) *Yetzirah*—the World of Formation; and

(5) *Asiyah*—the World of Action or Making. These three names are derived from the creative terms in *Isaiah* 43:7.

Adam Kadmon is the most pristine emanation. It is the first and highest stage after *tzimtzum* took place and yet so sublime that in a sense it may be spoken of as completely attached to, and united with the *En Sof*.[15] *Atzilut* is the stage following *Adam Kadmon*, thus further removed from the *En Sof*. This World receives its vivification (the Divine Emanation and Life-force) *via*, or from *Adam Kadmon*, thus in smaller measure and less intense than *Adam Kadmon*.[16] But *Atzilut* is still in such close proximity to the *En Sof* that it, too, is "One with It," being, in effect, Divinity.[17]

Beriah is further removed, and draws its vivification through *Atzilut*,[18] which is smaller in measure yet less intense than *Atzilut*. In fact, the full intensity and effect of *tzimtzum* is first noticeable in this Realm. Although the particular aspects and rungs of *tzimtzum* are too numerous to count and generally are of many diverse kinds, there are, however, three levels of powerful and comprehensive contraction and condensation, which give rise to the three lower Worlds. The World of *Atzilut* (and *a fortiori*, *Adam Kadmon*) is G–dliness Itself.[19] Thus we speak of a *Massach*, or *Prassa* (curtain; covering) separating between *Atzilut* and *Beriah* (and between the subsequent worlds).[20] This denotes the immense separation and distinction between these levels.

Yetzirah is still further removed, and draws its vivification through *Beriah*, and *Asiyah* is the furthest removed having its vivification from *Yetzirah*.[21]

Like the ten *Sefirot*[22] these Five Worlds correspond to the letters of the Tetragrammaton: *Atzilut* corresponds to the *Yud*, *Beriah* to the first *Hai*, *Yetzirah* to the *Vav*, and *Asiyah* to the latter *Hai*. *Adam Kadmon*, for its state of immense sublimity, cannot be represented by any specific letter but by the "thorn" of the *Yud*. Therefore as *Keter* is elevated above all *Sefirot* so *Adam Kadmon* is elevated above all worlds. That is why, generally, only four Worlds are spoken of and referred to.[23]

In fact, the Worlds correspond to the *Sefirot* themselves. Though all ten *Sefirot* emanate and "function" in every World in particular (*Keter* of *Atzilut*, *Chochmah* of *Atzilut*, *Binah* of *Atzilut* and so on),[24] specific *Sefirot* predominate in each of the Worlds. Thus *Adam Kadmon* corresponds to *Keter*; it is the realm of *Keter*, because *Keter* is the predominant *Sefirah* in *Adam Kadmon*. *Atzilut* corresponds to *Chochmah*;

it is the Realm of *Chochmah*, because *Chochmah* is the predominant *Sefirah* in *Atzilut*. *Beriah* corresponds to *Binah*, *Yetzirah* to the *Midot* (*Chesed-Gevurah-Tiferet-Netzach-Yod-Yesod*), and *Asiyah* to *Malchut*, because these are respectively the predominant *Sefirot* in these particular Realms.[25] In terms of the "Man-Image" of the *Sefirot* (the *Partzuf* of *Adam Kadmon*, the original emanation of the Divine Light), the World of *Adam Kadmon* is referred to as the *Atzmut* (the Essence, or soul), *Atzilut* as the Body containing this soul, and *Beriah*, *Yetzirah* and *Asiyah* as the outer Garments in which this Body is clothed.[26] The difference between these worlds is one of degree in concealment of the *Atzmut*, and is, therefore, often compared to four modes of perception referred to as *reshimah* (a mark), *chakikah* (an engraving), *chatzivah* (a carving), and *asiyah* (an enactment):

A *reshimah* is non-substantial; it is a mere sign marked down, barely denoting a distinction between non-marked and marked, thus, between absolute naught and reality (or, rather, the beginning of reality). Its type of reality is so close to naught that there is practically no difference between them. Precisely so, *Atzilut* is the first egression towards substantiality: between absolute naught and infinity and the category of substantiality and finitude. A *chakikah*, on the other hand, is already sensed and perceived in greater measure than the *reshimah*; correspondingly, *Beriah* is the stage of a more perceptible and finite being than *Atzilut*, though still very subtle. A *chatzivah* is more perceptible yet, just as an object hewn and carved is sensed in much greater degree than some engraving. Comparable to that is *Yetzirah*. Full perception, completely in the realm of distinct substantiality and corporeality, is the finished product of an *asiyah*, and corresponding to it is the World which is called by this name—*Asiyah*.[27]

R. Moses Cordovero reads these differences between the Worlds in their very names. He suggests that the term *Atzilut* is also related to the preposition אצל (near-by), thus denoting the close proximity—to the point of unity—of the *Sefirot* of *Atzilut* to their Source. *Beriah* he relates to the verse "But if the Eternal בריאה יברא (*creates* a *creation*)," (*Numbers* 16:30), with the connotation of the coming into being of something new, *ex nihilo*.[28] Therefore *Beriah* is radically different and removed from *Atzilut*. *Yetzirah* he relates to the verse "וייצר—and the Eternal, G-d, *formed* man of the dust of the ground." (*Gen.* 2:7) *Yetzirah* then is related to the "dust of the ground," a lower, much less spiritual, level than *Beriah*. *Asiyah* is self-explicit as the most material

and perceptible of these terms, and this is also suggested by its appearance as the third and last term in the above-mentioned verse of *Isaiah* 43:7.[29]

Now, as has been said, all the *Sefirot* emanate throughout all the Worlds, in general and in particular. All the *Sefirot* manifest themselves in *Atzilut*, as well as in *Beriah*, in *Yetzirah*, and in *Asiyah*. As the *Sefirot* are in *Atzilut* they are still in explicit unity with their Emanator.[30] Through *Malchut* of *Atzilut* (as is the "function" of *Malchut*) the *Sefirot* of *Atzilut* (latently immanent in *Malchut* of *Atzilut*) are projected further to manifest themselves in *Beriah*. *Malchut* of *Atzilut* thus serves as the mediary between *Atzilut* and *Beriah*. In that capacity *Malchut* of *Atzilut* assumes a characteristic of *Keter* which (as stated in ch. 3, section 3) serves as intermediary between a higher stage and the subsequent lower one. Therefore *Malchut* of *Atzilut*, the lowest level of *Atzilut*, re-emerges as *Keter* of *Beriah*, the highest level of Beriah.[31] While the *Sefirot* of *Beriah* are the actual *Sefirot* of *Atzilut*, they are in *Beriah* in a state of great concealment and condensation. For the "downward transition" from *Atzilut* to *Beriah* involves "passage" through the immense *tzimtzum* of the *prassa* that separates these worlds.[32] Therefore, in *Beriah*, the World of Creation, there is the first appearance of finite and limited creatures distinct from Divinity, though still strictly spiritual: the souls of the righteous (*Tzadikim*), and sublime angels.

The same process repeats itself in the next stage of the creative development. Through *Malchut* of *Beriah* the *Sefirot* (all latently present in *Malchut*) are projected further downwards to manifest themselves in *Yetzirah*, emerging there in still greater concealment and condensation. This allows for the appearance of creatures less sublime and more numerous than those of *Beriah*. As this process continues, it culminates in the physical creatures and entities of our physical world in the lowest level of *Asiyah*.[33]

The implications of this creative process are two-fold. On the one hand it allows for the possibility of a finite, physical world with finite, physical creatures to the point that—because of the immense *tzimtzum* involved—they appear distinct and separate from Divinity. On the other hand it implies the Divine Immanence or Indwelling Presence (*Shechinah*) even in the finite and physical. For it is no less than the actual light of the *En Sof* that issues forth from *Malchut* of *Atzilut*, albeit so strongly obscured and condensed that it is not manifest *per se*.[34] For the

En Sof alone is able to create and sustain all beings *ex nihilo*; the *Sefirot* are not to be regarded as "creative agents" separate and distinct from Divinity.[35]

Notes to Chapter IV

[1] Tanya *I: ch. 43.*

[2] *See* supra, *ch. 2, and note 18* a.l., *and ch. 3, section 1.*

[3] Tanya *I: ch. 40.* Cf. Igeret Hakodesh, *sect. XXV.*

[4] Ibid. Cf. supra, *notes 16–17.*

[5] "*Even in completely inanimate matter, such as stones or earth or water, there is a "soul" and spiritual life-force . . . which give life and existence to inanimate matter that it might arise out of the naught and nothingness that preceded the Six Days of Creation;*" Tanya *II:1, based on* Etz Chayim *39:3. See also* Tanya *I: ch. 38;* Igeret Hakodesh, *sect. XXV; and* Etz Chayim *50:* passim.

[6] Tikunei Zohar, *Intr.: 17a.*

[7] Tanya *I: chs. 40 and 51.*

[8] Ibid., *ch. 51; see also* Siddur im Perush Hamilot, *p. 164c–d, as well as* ibid., *pp. 48a* ff.

[9] Ibid. (*sources cited in note 8*).

[10] Cf. *Maimonides,* Hilchot Yesodei Hatorah *II:6;* Etz Chayim *1:2.—In fact this idea may be read in the very term of world in Hebrew; for the word* עולם *is etymologically related to, and itself spelled sometimes as,* עלם *(to be concealed; hidden); see, e.g.,* Exodus *3:15, and the comment in* Pessachim *50b, and* Rashi, a.l.*; also* Eccles. *3:11, and* Midrash Rabba, *and* Rashi, a.l. *The term* Olamot (*Worlds*) *thus denotes the concealment and dimming of the Divine Light. See* Tikunei Zohar *42:82a, and* Sefer Habahir *8 (10).*

[11] *The general sources for the following paragraphs are R. Chayim Vital,* Sha'arei Kedushah *III:1* f.*;* Etz Chayim *1:4, and 43: Intr.;* Mevoh She'arim *VI:2:1;* Pardess Rimonim *5:4;* Shomer Emunim *I:46* ff.

[12] Tikunei Zohar *19:42a, and 70:120a;* cf. Zohar *III:193b. See also* Shomer Emunim *I:62* f.*, and* cf. supra, *ch. 2, note 34.*

[13] *See the responsa by R. Hai Gaon and R. Chamai Gaon in* Pardess Rimonim *11:1 and 3. See also R. Bachya ben R. Asher,* Commentary on Exodus *34:6.*

[14] *See* Tikunei Zohar *69:115b, and 70:135b. See* Pardess Rimonim *11:2* ff.*;* Etz Chayim *1:4, and 12:5;* Igeret Hakodesh, *sect. XXIX;* Torah Or, *Esther, 98b.*

[15] Cf. supra, *note 38.*

[16] *In that sense* Adam Kadmon *is the "soul" of* Atzilut. *In an extended sense, though, it is also the "soul" or spiritual substratum and life-force of all worlds, for the emanation of* Adam Kadmon *extends from the highest level to the very central point of the* chalal (*the world of* Asiyah)*, albeit in ever-increasing concealment; see* Etz Chayim *1:4, and* Igeret Hakodesh, *sect. XX;* infra, *ch. 8, note 2.*

[17] *See* Tanya *I: chs. 39 and 49;* Igeret Hakodesh, *beg. of sect. XX.*

[18] *In that sense* Atzilut *is the "soul" of* Beriah.

[19] Supra, *note 17;* cf. *also,* infra, *ch. 7, note 20.*

[20] *See* Etz Chayim *42:4* (ibid., *ch. 13* f. *of* Klalut ABYA–*I*), ibid *44:1;* Igeret Hakodesh, *sect. XX.*

[21] *Every Realm always being the "soul" of the succeeding one.*

[22] *See* supra, *ch. 3, note 37.*

[23] Sha'arei Kedushah *III:1–2;* Mevoh She'arim *VI:2:1.*

[24] *Moreover, just as the* Sefirot *are compounds dividing into themselves, the Worlds also divide into the general classes of the* Sefirot *as represented by the concept of the Worlds: thus we speak of* Atzilut *of* Atzilut, Beriah *of* Atzilut, Yetzirah *of* Atzilut, *and so on; see* Pardess Rimonim *24:10, and* Igeret Hakodesh, *sect. XIX, note 47 (where this division is explained in detail).*

[25] *See* supra, *note 16; also* Tanya *I: chs. 39 and 52.* Cf. Igeret Hakodesh, *sect. V, note 51.*

[26] Etz Chayim *3:3.*

[27] Pardess Rimonim *16:9;* Shomer Emunim *I:51.*

[28] *See commentary of Nachmanides on this verse, and* cf. Igeret Hakodesh, *sect. XX, note 23.*

[29] Pardess Rimonim *16:1.*

[30] *See* supra, *note 17.*

[31] *See* Igeret Hakodesh, *sect. XX, and notes 29 and 45* a.l.

[32] *See* supra, *note 20.*

[33] *See* Sha'arei Kedushah *III:2;* Tanya *I: ch. 39.*

[34] *See* Tanya *I: chs. 38, 40, and 51 (quoted at the beginning of this chapter), and* Igeret Hakodesh, *sect. VI and XXV.*

[35] Igeret Hakodesh, *sect. XX, and* cf. supra, *ch. 3, note 9.*

Chapter 5 OROT AND KELIM[1]

It has already been explained how the emanations from the *En Sof* are condensed and obscured by means of *tzimtzum*. The numerous grades of condensation presented five comprehensive classes of obscured and concealed *Sefirot*, called the Five Worlds. Now the actual emanations from the *En Sof* are called *Orot* (Lights; sometimes *Atzmut*—Essence). But by definition these *Orot*, the actual emanations, are absolutely bound up with their Source, united with their Emanator, the *En Sof*. Thus, strictly speaking, we cannot really refer to *Orot* (Lights in the plural), as different kinds of emanations or different kinds of *Sefirot*, but only to *Or En Sof*, *the* Light of the *En Sof* (singular). A distinction between *Orot* (a scheme of *Sefirot* that differ from one another) can be made only after *tzimtzum* takes place—relative to *tzimtzum*. Only then, depending on the variations in the degrees of manifestation of the *Or En Sof*, can we speak of *Orot*, of ranks and levels, of different attributes, of the ten *Sefirot*.[2]

For all practical purposes the *Orot* themselves remain unchanged from their origin and Divine Source.[3] A distinction between them is made possible by the *Kelim* (Vessels):

Tzimtzum screened the light of the *En Sof* to such an extent that it produced ten different classes of concealment through each of which the *Or En Sof* manifests itself in a different way. These general types of concealment are called *Kelim*, Vessels. They are the Vessels which contain the Lights, just as, by way of analogy and metaphor, bodies contain souls. Thus the Lights and the *Kelim* together make up the *Sefirot*.[4]

The purpose of *tzimtzum* is for the production of *Kelim*.[5] In fact, *tzimtzum* may be taken as synonymous with *Kelim*, and just as there are various grades of *tzimtzum* so there are various types of *Kelim*.[6]

It is in this context of *Orot* and *Kelim* that R. Moses Cordovero introduces a famous simile to explain the differentiation wrought by the *Kelim*: When pouring water into a number of differently coloured glasses, these waters—though in themselves colourless—will appear coloured according to the hue of the vessels which contain them. So, too, it is with the *Sefirot*. The *Kelim* are the Divine tools that bear different colours corresponding to their individual character or activity (white for *Chesed*, red for *Gevurah* and so on).[7] The Divine Light (the

Orot) that is contained in, and acts through, the *Kelim* is the "colourless" essence like the colourless water that appears coloured only when, and as, vested in the *Kelim*.[8]

Similarly, the Essence (the *Orot*) is analogous to a ray of light radiating through several crystals and thus assuming different colours. Light in itself is simple and colourless but can be divided and coloured, intensified or dimmed and so forth, through the intervening crystals.

A third simile is that of the soul in the body of man. The soul acts through the limbs and organs of the body and manifests itself differently through various activities. Yet the soul is simple and unitary, it is the same soul acting throughout the body, and all differences in manifestations (seeing, hearing, speaking and so on) are due to the differences in the organs.[9]

At the same time it must be kept in mind that when speaking of changes in the manifestations, or of limitations or fixed measures with regard to the *Kelim* of the *Sefirot*, this relates only to the measure and limitation in the activity geared towards the recipients in a set and limited fashion,[10] and not to the *Kelim* (and, *a fortiori*, the *Orot*) themselves![11]

These *Kelim* differ not only from one plane to another (relative to the *Sefirot*) but more so, from one World to another: there are the *Orot* and *Kelim* of *Adam Kadmon*, the *Orot* and *Kelim* of *Atzilut* and so on. On the level of *Adam Kadmon* the *Kelim* (like the state of *tzimtzum* in that Realm) are extremely subtle and diaphanous, hardly distinguishable from the *Orot*.[12] On the level of *Atzilut* the *Kelim* are still very subtle, less so than in *Adam Kadmon* but still totally spiritual. And so, successively the *Kelim* become ever more obstructive until the *Orot* are practically hidden completely in *Asiyah*. Thus when we speak of the different classes of *Sefirot*, i.e. of more or less intense radiations from the *Sefirot* (as the Worlds proceed from, and succeed each other), this difference is not due to any change in the original *Orot* but because of the increasing intensity, concealment and condensation effected by the numerous, successive grades of *Kelim*.[13]

Notes to Chapter V

[1] *The subject of* Orot *and* Kelim *is another controversial topic much discussed since the times of the early mystics; see* Pardess Rimonim *4:1–4. In the paragraphs following, the subject is discussed as it appears in Chassidism, an interpretation generally following the views of R. Moses Cordovero and R. Isaac Luria. For further perusal of this involved theme, in addition to the sources cited in the subsequent notes, see* Zohar *II:42b* f., *and commentaries* a.l.; Pardess Rimonim, Sha'ar *IV;* Etz Chayim *1:3, 40:8, and 47:1;* Sha'ar Hahakdamot, *Derush Keitzad Na'asim Hakelim (pp. 50b* ff.), *and Derushei ABYA: 1 (pp. 376* ff.).

[2] "*Prior to* tzimtzum *all the light was equal in absolute unity and likeness . . . thus there does not apply to it any name or term. For, a name indicates something specific and limited, to recognise a distinction between one* Sefirah *and another. But as everything was a simple light, no name, term, letter or point, nor any image or form whatever, applies to it . . .";* Mevoh She'arim *I:1:1 (see also the sequel* a.l.). Cf. Pardess Rimonim *6:6.*

[3] *This conception is at the core of the controversy mentioned* supra, *note 1.*

[4] *In interpretation of the Creation-account, in the verse "and G-d saw the light that it was good, and He separated"* (Gen. *1:4*), *this separation refers to the formation of the* Kelim *which "set and fashion a separation, limitation, and measure, among the* Orot;" Etz Chayim *4:3. See also* Sha'ar Hahakdamot, *Hakd. IV, and* ibid., *Derush II–Be'olam Hanekudim (p. 59).—The* Kelim *are themselves mixtures of the lowest levels of lights "brought about by a condensation* (hit'abut) *of the light"* (Etz Chayim *47:1*), *and they originate in the* reshimu (*the faint residue*) *of the original light that had remained in the* chalal *after the initial* tzimtzum; *see at length R. Shalom Busaglo,* Hadrat Melech *on* Zohar *I:15a, and* Sha'ar Hahakdamot, a.l.c. supra, *note 1.*

[5] "*The purpose of* tzimtzum *is . . . to fashion the aspect of the* Kelim. *For by means of the condensation and dimming of the light it is possible for the* Kelim *to come into being and to be manifest;*" Etz Chayim *1:3. See* Tanya *II:4.*

[6] Tanya *II:4. Just as* tzimtzum *is synonymous with* Gevurah *and* Din (supra, *ch. 3, note 87*), *so* Kelim *becomes synonymous with* Gevurah *and* Din: "*The attribute of* Din *always restricts* Chesed *so that it will not exceed, just like a vessel restricts the waters so that they will not flow out. And this is the principal meaning of the term* Kelim; *within them the* Atzmut (*the Divine Essence; the Light*) *vests Itself;*" Mevoh She'arim *VI:2:1* Tzimtzum, Gevurah, Din *and* Kelim, *thus have for their purpose to limit and restrain the Divine effulgence from excessive radiation.*

[7] *See* Igeret Hakodesh, *sect. XII, and note 13* a.l.

[8] Pardess Rimonim *4:4; the simile appears already in* Chovot Halevovot, Sha'ar Habechinah, *ch. 1.*

[9] Pardess Rimonim, a.l.c.; *see also* supra, *ch. 4* (*and notes 8 and 9*), *where these two similes are cited in the context of distinguishing between the Worlds.*

[10] Cf. Etz Chayim *6:3:* "*The* Kelim *are to garb the light for the sake of the recipients.*"

[11] Pardess Rimonim a.l.; *see also* Elima Rabbaty, May'an *III:VI: ch. 55* (*pp. 99c* ff.). Cf. supra, *ch. 3, section 1.*

[12] "*Do not err, Heaven forfend, in thinking that in* Adam Kadmon *there are* Kelim *in the literal sense, Heaven forfend . . . When we refer (there) to* Kelim *it is only relative to the Light and* Atzmut *in them. But the* Kelim *themselves are a very pure light, to the very extremity of purity and tenuity. Beware and do not err in this matter!*" Etz Chayim *1:4.*

[13] *See sources mentioned* supra, *note 1.*

Chapter 6 PNIMIYUT AND CHITZONIYUT

Pnimiyut and *Chitzoniyut* are terms which occur frequently in Kabbalistic and Chassidic literature. The terms themselves suggest their meanings. *Pnimiyut* means Inwardness. It refers to the innermost point, the core, the essence or essential-being of the subject to which it is applied.[1]

Opposed to *Pnimiyut* is *Chitzoniyut*, Outwardness, Externality. *Chitzoniyut* is the furthest point from the *Pnimiyut*. It is the most external, the lowest level of the subject to which it is applied.[2]

Synonymous terms are *Panim*, and *Achor* (pl. *Achurayim*), Face, and Back, respectively. *Panim* is an expression of *Pnimiyut*. *Achor* is both literally and conceptually the antonym of *Panim*, and synonymous with the concept of *Chitzoniyut*.[3]

When we speak of the *Pnimiyut* of a *Sefirah*, we refer to the very essence of that *Sefirah*, i.e., the Divine Light. The *Achurayim*, or *Chitzoniyut* of a *Sefirah*, refers to the very lowest and most external rank and level of that *Sefirah*. For example, when we come across a term[4] such as the "aspect of the *Chitzoniyut* of the *Kelim* of *Malchut* of *Atzilut*," this refers to the lowest level of the *Kelim* of the *Sefirah* "*Malchut* of *Atzilut*".

Notes to Chapter VI

[1] *See* Igeret Hakodesh, *sect. IV and XIX.*
[2] Ibid., *sect. XIX.*
[3] Ibid., *sect. IV, VII (see note 27* a.l.), *XIX, XXIIa (see notes 29 and 36* a.l.), *and* cf. Tanya *I:22. See Maimonides,* Shemonah Perakim, *ch. VII, and* Hilchot Yesodei Hatorah *I:10* (cf. *the critique by R. Abraham ibn Daud, cited in* Kessef Mishnah a.l.), *elaborated in* Moreh Nevuchim *I:21 and 37.*
[4] E.g., Igeret Hakodesh, *sect. V.*

Chapter 7 SHEVIRAT HAKELIM

Shevirat Hakelim, and the adjunct concepts to be explained in the chapters following, are central doctrines in the Kabbalah in general, and in the teachings of R. Isaac Luria in particular.[1] Their source is in the Zoharic books *Sifra Detzeniyuta*, *Idra Rabba*, and *Idra Zutta*.[2]

Shevirat Hakelim (the Breaking of the Vessels) is the key-concept in the explanation of the basic problem of multifariousness and the origin of evil. It is based on the Midrashic account of the building and destruction of the primordial worlds,[3] and the mystical account of the eight kings who "reigned in the land of Edom, before there reigned any king over the children of Israel."[4]

The original emission of the *Sefirot* was that of the scheme of *Iggulim*. At first there issued forth a highly concentrated, seminal point of light, compounded of ten gradations, from which the ten *Sefirot* proceeded in gradual order. The most sublime aspect of the original point became *Keter*. It contained within it the successive radiations of *Chochmah* to *Malchut*. From the most sublime aspect of *Keter* issued forth the *Sefirah* of *Chochmah*, containing also the lights of the successive *Sefirot*, *Binah* to *Malchut*. From *Chochmah* emanated the *Sefirah Binah*, containing also the lights of the successive *Sefirot*; and from *Binah* issued forth the *Midot* in unison, and from the latter issued forth *Malchut*. When we speak of successive issuances, it must be remembered that the first issue is that of a *Keli* (Vessel) into which an *Or* (Light) can then emanate and be contained.

Now each *Keli* is commensurate with its respective *Sefirah*. As the *Sefirot* are on successively lower levels, their *Kelim* are also successively smaller. Thus the Vessel of *Chochmah* is smaller than the Vessel of *Keter*; the Vessel of *Binah* is smaller than the Vessel of *Chochmah*, and so forth. When the light of the *En Sof* radiated to the Vessel of *Keter* (including the lights destined for the successive *Sefirot*), the point of *Keter* was able to contain and endure it. Likewise, when the light from *Keter* flowed to *Chochmah*, including the lights destined for the lower *Sefirot*, the Vessel of *Chochmah* was able to absorb practically all of it; the relatively minor excess of light encompassed this Vessel by way of an *Or Makif* (Encompassing, or Transcending Light).[5] The same occurred with the flow from *Chochmah* to *Binah*, though this emanation was already much less intense. The *Kelim* of *Chochmah* and *Binah* could contain these

lights, because of their close proximity to *Keter*, being both "large" and "strong" enough. But as the Divine Light proceeded further, from *Binah* to *Da'at*, the Vessel of *Da'at* could not contain the light and was shattered by the intensity of the radiation. This was so because not only the light meant for *Da'at*, but also the lights meant for the lower *Sefirot* were projected into that Vessel, which were more than it could endure. The unequal proportion of extremely intense *Orot* and extremely subtle *Kelim* precipitated this eventful occurrence.

The total light was then projected to the Vessel of the next *Sefirah*, *Chesed*, and it, too, broke for the same reason. This process continued and repeated itself with the next *Sefirot*, thus all the Vessels broke. The only change occurred on the level of *Yesod*, to which was projected at first only the light destined for the remaining stage, *i.e.*, *Malchut*. The Vessel of *Yesod* was able to contain this light and project it further. But then, as with the other *Sefirot*, the total light emanated from the upper *Sefirot* to *Yesod*, its Vessel also broke. By then the light of *Malchut* was already absorbed in the Vessel of *Malchut*, thereby strengthening the lower and less subtle aspects of that Vessel. Therefore when the total light of the *Midot* was projected to *Malchut*, only the higher and more subtle aspects broke, while the lower ones remained relatively intact. Hence in *Malchut* the breakage was only partial.[6]

The above account of the disproportion between the *Orot* and *Kelim* is the "descriptive" explanation of the "mechanical" event of *Shevirat Hakelim*. At its root, however, the principal "flaw" which precipitated the "breaking of the vessels" and the dissolution of the original scheme of the *Sefirot*, is the fact that these *Sefirot* were separate, independent points (the scheme of *Iggulim*).[7] These *Sefirot* of *Iggulim* were a "*Reshut harabim*" (a domain of pluralism) because there was no unison, bond or unity; they were rather like individuals, each going his own way without any love or affection between them. That is why their *Kelim* were unable to endure the *Orot* and they died. Thus it is written: "Ephraim is united in idolatry, let him alone;" (*Hosea* 4:17).[8] For unity effects preservation and maintenance. A common saying has it that when you take ten reeds separately, they will break; but if you take just three together, they will endure and will not break."[9] For this very reason the first three *Sefirot* were preserved, for they were not separate points but inter-related.[10]

Now, the eight Kings who reigned in the Land of Edom are the Eight *Sefirot* issuing from *Binah: Da'at* to *Malchut*. Of these Kings it is

stated that they reigned and then died; this refers to the breaking of the Vessels. Though, only of the first seven Kings is it stated that they died, but not of the eighth;[11] that is, only seven broke completely, but not the eighth. Now these Kings who died, allude to those Vessels which broke, they are the primordial worlds which were destroyed.[12]

Death means the separation of soul from body: the soul ascends to return to its source, while the body, made of the dust of the earth, is returned to earth. The soul *per se*, therefore, is not affected by death, whereas for the body it is a lowering and degradation from its erstwhile level of being part of man, to the present level of a lifeless corpse. Analogous to this is that which occurred to the Kings: the "soul," the *Orot* of the *Sefirot*, ascended to be re-absorbed in its source, while the remains of the "body", the fragmented *Kelim* of the *Sefirot*, fell to their "grave." However, the analogy does not hold true altogether. For in the case of the "Kings", there was not a real and final death, a real and final separation in totality of the *Orot* and *Kelim*. A residue of the *Orot* remained attached to the fragments. Death is used here in the figurative sense of applying to any degradation;[13] as the broken *Kelim* fell, from a sublime level to lower levels, they are regarded as having died.[14]

As the parts of the vessels were projected downwards, they broke further into an ever increasing number of fragments. Hence, the residue of the Divine Light attached to them was also "fragmented," as it were. Therefore, as the parts fell to the realm of *Atzilut*, we speak of 288 general sparks (*Nitzotzim*);[15] but as they fell further, to *Beriah* and so on, these 288 sparks were subdivided into an ever greater number of smaller sparks, each one attached to a fragment. Also, as these fragments fell progressively deeper, they became not only more numerous but also less tenuous; not so much because the original fragments became cruder themselves, but because the more subtle aspects were gradually assimilated and absorbed among the successive grades and levels. Thus the most subtle aspects of the broken *Kelim* are totally absorbed and assimilated in *Atzilut*; the next grade of aspects is absorbed and assimilated in *Beriah*; the next grade of aspects is absorbed and assimilated in *Yetzirah*; and the lowest grades are in *Asiyah*. The lowest grades which could not be assimilated in the realm of holiness, become the realm of impurity; they are the substance of evil.[16]

The great expositor of the Kabbalah, R. Moses Cordovero, illustrates this process with an analogy to food:[17] Man may select the best of foods in which, chemically speaking, there is no waste or useless matter

whatever; it is totally and absolutely pure. Even so, when he consumes this food and it is digested and assimilated in his body, even the purest food will deliver some refuse that is expelled from the body for being unassimilable. Precisely so, metaphorically speaking, the broken Vessels, though essentially pure mixtures of light, as they are projected down the various levels and assimilated among them, they have some unassimilable parts which, metaphorically speaking, are called their waste and refuse. This waste and refuse is the essence of evil and impurity.[18] Now, because the fragments are deprived of the *Orot* and retain but a spark of holiness, sufficient to sustain their existence, they lead ever more "independent" existences. They become more distinct entities and are, as such, the root-elements of all creations.[19] As they fell to *Beriah*, those aspects that could be assimilated in that World became the creatures of *Beriah*. The unassimilable waste of *Beriah* was projected to *Yetzirah*, where the assimilable aspects became the creatures of *Yetzirah*. The unassimilable waste of *Yetzirah* was projected to *Asiyah*, where the assimilable parts became the creatures of *Asiyah*, while the unassimilable waste of *Asiyah* remained on the lowest levels of this Realm as the elements of evil.[20]

Thus the fragments are responsible for the multifariousness in G–d's creation, and for the existence of evil. And this, indeed, is the very intent and purpose of *Shevirat Hakelim*: it brought about the subjects over which the King can rule in a meaningful way,[21] and provides them with a choice between good and evil so that the King may manifest His attributes of *Chesed* and *Din* and so on.[22]

Notes to Chapter VII

[1] *The concept of* Shevirat Hakelim *appears throughout the various works of the Lurianic system, though see especially* Etz Chayim, Hechal Hanekudim (*Sha'ar 8* ff.); Mevoh She'arim *II:2:1–11;* Sha'ar Hahakdamot, Derush Be'olam Hanekudim (*pp. 81–109*). *In the writings of R. Schneur Zalman this concept is explained in* Torah Or, *Vayeshev, 27c* f.; ibid., *Va'eira, 56d* f., *and Yitro, 110d;* Likutei Torah, *II:37c* ff., *and III:82c.* Cf. *also R. Tzvi Hirsh Horowitz,* Aspaklarya Hameirah *on* Zohar *III:135a* ff.

[2] Zohar *II:176b;* ibid., *III:128a, 135a–b, 142a–b. For R. Moses Cordovero's interpretation of these passages see* Pardess Rimonim *5:4;* Shi'ur Komah, *ch. 60;* Elima Rabbaty, *Eyn Habedolach:I:ch. 6* ff.).

[3] Genesis Rabba *3:7, and 9:2.*

[4] Genesis *36:31* ff.; *see also* I Chronicles *1:43* ff.

[5] *See* Igeret Hakodesh, *sect. III, note 11, for this term.*

[6] *On all the aforementioned see sources mentioned* supra, *note 1, and* Etz Chayim, *Sha'ar Hakelalim, ch. 1;* Limudei Atzilut (*Lemberg 1850*), *p. 1d* f.

[7] *See* supra, *ch. 3, section 8, and* cf. infra, *ch. 9.*

[8] I.e., *Ephraim's unity saved him despite his sinfulness; see* Genesis Rabba *38:6.*

[9] Etz Chayim *11:5; see also* ibid., *9:2 and 19:1.*

[10] Ibid., *and see* Likutei Torah *II:37c* ff., *and III:87a* ff.

[11] *In the first account of the Kings, in* Genesis; *in the second account, in* Chronicles, *it is stated of all eight Kings that they died. Because the breakage was complete in the first seven, the sources speak mostly of the "seven Kings of Edom".*

[12] Zohar a.l.c. (supra, *note 2*).

[13] Cf. Genesis Rabba *96:3.*

[14] Zohar *III:135b;* Etz Chayim *11:4, and 18:1;* Likutei Torah *III:82c.*

[15] *This is adduced in* Genesis *1:2: "And the earth was* tohu *and* vohu *(unformed and unordered);" this refers to the unformed* Sefirot *of the* Iggulim, *as they were not yet ordered and inter-related, but separate principles, thereby causing the "deaths of the Kings". "And the spirit of G-d* מרחפת *(hovered)..."* (ibid.); *the word* מרחפת *divides into two parts:* מ"ת *and* רפ"ח *("died", and the number 288), referring to the death of the Kings and the division of the residue of the Divine Light into 288 sparks (the sparks encumbered in the midst of the word* מת, i.e., *within the "dead" or broken vessels).* Etz Chayim *18:1;* Torah Or, *Vayeshev, 27d.*

[16] *R. Chayim Vital,* Sefer Hagilgulim *(Vilna 1886), ch. 1;* Mevoh She'arim *II:3:8.*

[17] Pardess Rimonim *25:1.*

[18] *The substance of evil thus consists of the waste and remains of the Kings of Edom.* Edom *is the realm of Esau, son of Isaac. The attribute of Isaac is that of* Gevurah *(see* supra, *ch. 3, note 107). The "waste" of Isaac's* Gevurah *extended to Esau, just as the waste of Abraham's* Chesed *extended to Ishmael; hence just as Ishmael is the aspect of impure* Chesed *(see* Igeret Hakodesh, *sect. II, and note 14* a.l.) *so Esau is the aspect of impure* Gevurah (cf. ibid., *note 17, and sect. XXV, note 37*). Edom, *thus, is essentially a place to which* Gevurah *and* Din *are bound to and derive from (see sources cited* supra, *note 12), and* Edom *in its source is the aspect of the original* Kelim (cf. supra, *ch. 5, that* tzimtzum, Gevurah, Din, *and* Kelim *may be taken as synonymous). Hence, the substance of evil is always referred to as the "waste" and "refuse" of the aspects of* Gevurah (*see* Zohar *I:74b;* ibid., *148a*). Cf. *also* infra, *end of ch. 9.*

[19] *That is, the fragments are the origin and substance of matter; they form the four elements. On the higher levels they are the tenuous root-elements of the elements (which are practically spiritual; see* Igeret Hakodesh, *sect. XX, note 30), and the lower they fall the more tangible, material and cruder the elements become until they assume the characteristics of matter as we know it.*

[20] *See* Torah Or, *Vayeshev, 27d. However, on all levels, even on the lowest, there remain sparks of holiness attached to the fragments, which sustain their existence, thus acting as their "animating principles" or "souls"; see* Etz Chayim, *Sha'ar Hakelalim, ch. 2,* and ibid., *19:3.* Cf. infra, *chs. 10 and 11. Because of the multiplicity in them, the lower Worlds of* Beriah, Yetzirah *and* Asiyah *are called the Realm of* Pirud *(Division), while* Atzilut *is called the Realm of* Yichud *(Unity) because the* Orot *and* Kelim *of* Atzilut *are fully absorbed in Divinity and not separated from It; see* Zohar *II:234a* f., *and III:159a* f.; Etz Chayim, *43: Introduction.* Cf. Igeret Hakodesh, *beginning of sect. XX.*

[21] *See* supra, *ch. 3, section 7, and notes 143–144* a.l.

[22] *See* infra, *ch. 11, and note 3* a.l.

Chapter 8 PARTZUFIM

The original scheme of the *Sefirot* was unable to exist, and therefore the *Sefirot* were re-established in a new order in which the *Kelim* would be able to absorb and contain the *Orot* and the emanations could proceed in a gradual manner. The reason for the breakage was that the original *Sefirot* were independent principles, and had not been brought into harmony with each other. The *Kelim* of the *Midot* were for their own *Orot* only, and therefore could not absorb any additional light meant for others. In the new order, the *Sefirot* had to be repaired in such a way that a breakage would not ensue, thus allowing the Divine emanations to proceed in such a way as would make it possible for a world to come into being. This is effected by extending, as it were, the *Sefirot*; by harmonising the *Sefirot*, causing them to function within one another. Thus the *Kelim* would be larger and stronger and able to absorb the *Orot*.

In this new order the *Sefirot* appear as *Partzufim* (Forms; Visages; Configurations), according to the scheme of *Yosher*. *Keter* is no longer a simple point in which the other *Sefirot* are included as latent points, but it is converted into a configuration analogous to the Man-Image (referred to above, ch. 3, section 8) in which every *Sefirah* functions, though *Keter* is the dominant aspect. This *Partzuf* is called *Arich Anpin* (the Long, or Extended Face; *Macroprosopus*). In this Configuration we speak of *Keter* of *Arich Anpin*, *Chochmah* of *Arich Anpin*, *Binah* of *Arich Anpin*, and so forth. *Arich Anpin*, also called the *Yosher* of *Adam Kadmon* (i.e., the basic *Sefirot* scheme of *Yosher* as it is in the Realm of *Adam Kadmon*), is the substratum of everything. Thus it extends from the highest to the lowest level, from *Keter* of *Adam Kadmon* to *Malchut* of *Asiyah* (though in an ever more concealed mode).[2]

Subsequently, the other two *Sefirot* that remained intact were also transmuted. The principle of *Chochmah* is converted to the *Partzuf* of *Abba* (Father), and the principle of *Binah* is converted to the *Partzuf* of *Imma* (Mother; or Supernal Mother). Both *Abba* and *Imma* are complete *Partzufim*, each compounding all ten *Sefirot*; thus we speak of *Keter* of *Abba*, *Chochmah* of *Abba*, *Binah* of *Abba*, and so on; and *Keter* of *Imma*, *Chochmah* of *Imma*, and so forth. These two *Partzufim* are related by *Keter* (the faculty of *Da'at Elyon*), their Configurations issue both from *Arich Anpin* and, so to speak, are parallel to each other (as *Chochmah* and

Binah are in the scheme of *Yosher*, one on the right and the other on the left). Thus they are, as it were, a dual Configuration and are referred to as the "firm friends who never separate".[3]

The six *Midot, Chesed* to *Yesod*, whose *Kelim* had been shattered completely, issue forth from *Imma* as a unit, as the *Partzuf* of *Ben* (the Son), known as *Z'eyr Anpin* (the Small, or Lesser Countenance; *Microprosopus*), again compounding the ten aspects of the *Sefirot.*

Through *Z'eyr Anpin* issues forth *Malchut*, as the *Partzuf* of *Bat* (the Daughter), known as *Nukvah* (the Female), or simply *Malchut*, again compounding all ten aspects of the *Sefirot. Malchut* is essentially related to the *Midot*, but because its Vessel did not break altogether it is a *Partzuf*, or unit, on its own. Nevertheless the relationship remains, and it is called *Nukvah* in terms of the *Z'eyr Anpin*: the *Midot* are the masculine aspect of the *Z'eyr Anpin* while *Malchut* is the feminine aspect of *Z'eyr Anpin*. Hence *Malchut* yearns to be reunited with *Z'eyr Anpin*, to become one with it.[4] To effect this union is the task of man, by means of his worship and service of G–d. This is the concept of the "Unification (*Yichud*) of the Holy One, blessed is He, and His *Shechinah*",[5] to re-establish total unity in the universe.[6]

Again, all these terms, and these concepts of the *Partzufim*, do not imply any pluralism in the G–dhead. The *Partzufim* are *Faces*, i.e., Manifestations of the G–dhead, various aspects under which G–d manifests Himself. Said Rabbi Shimon bar Yochai: "Whatever I said of the Holy Ancient-One,[7] and whatever I said of the *Z'eyr Anpin*, is all One; everything is absolutely One. There is no division in Him, blessed be He and blessed be His Name foreverlasting.[8] The sum of all this is: the Ancient of the Ancient and the *Z'eyr Anpin* are absolutely One. All is, all was, and all shall be; He will not change, He is unchanging, and He has not changed... Should you ask, what then is the difference between one and the other? It is all One, but from (above) His paths divide, and from (below) judgment is found; from *our* perspective they differ one from another."[9]

Notes to Chapter VIII

[1] *This chapter is based essentially on* Etz Chayim *11:7, and* Sha'ar Hakelalim, *ch. 2;* Sha'ar Hahakdamot, *Hakd. I–II;* Mevoh She'arim *II:3:4;* Likutei Torah *II:37d, and V:19d;* Siddur im Perush Hamilot, *p. 179b.* Cf. Igeret Hakodesh, *sect. XIX.*

[2] *See* Igeret Hakodesh, *sect. XX, and note 69* a.l.*;* cf. supra, *ch. 4, note 16.*

[3] Zohar *III:4a.*

[4] *See* Zohar *I:30b* f., *and III:4a.*

[5] *On this concept see R. Shalom Busaglo,* Kissei Melech *on* Tikunei Zohar, *Intr.: 3a;* Tanya *I: ch. 41;* Igeret Hakodesh, *sect. III, and note 13* a.l., *and* ibid., *sect. XXX.*

[6] *See* infra, *ch. 11. Of this final goal it is said: "And the Eternal shall be King over all the earth. In that day shall the Eternal be One and His Name One."* (Zechariah *14:9*).

[7] Atika Kadisha (*see* supra, *ch. 3, note 34*), *the essence of* Arich Anpin.

[8] Zohar *III:290a* f.

[9] Zohar *III:141a* f.

Chapter 9 TOHU AND TIKUN

We now have two schemes of *Sefirot*: the original scheme of *Iggulim* which precipitated *Shevirat Hakelim*, and the subsequent scheme of *Yosher* in which the *Sefirot* were rearranged and the fragments had been assimilated as much as possible.

These two orders are called the worlds of *Tohu* and *Tikun*. *Tohu* refers to the state of the original *Sefirot*, as unformed and unordered points.[1] *Tikun* (Correction; Restitution; Reformation) refers to the state of the *Sefirot* rearranged, mended and reformed as *Partzufim*.[2] Thus among the *Sefirot* of *Tohu* there is no inter-relationship. The *Midot* of *Tohu* are one below the other without any mutual inclusion whatever—each on its own, without relating to its opposite. *Chesed* is simple and absolute *Chesed*, and *Gevurah* is simply and absolutely *Gevurah*. Therefore the *Midot* assert themselves as *Midot per se*, without permitting the guidance of *Sechel* (*Chochmah*, *Binah*, *Da'at*); and, therefore, as simple and absolute *Midot*, they oppose one another, are fully separated and non-related, and precipitate *Shevirat Hakelim*. The *Sefirot* of *Tikun*, on the other hand, compound one another; the *Midot* permit the mitigating influence of *Sechel* and are, therefore, able to inter-relate.[3]

The realm of *Tohu* refers to the primordial worlds that were destroyed, of which G-d said "These do not please Me"; the realm of *Tikun* refers to the new worlds of which it is said: "And G-d saw everything that He had made, and behold it was very good" (*Genesis* 1:31) and G-d said "These please Me".[4] In the same context, *Tohu* is the original world created by the attribute of *Din* (*Gevurah*),[5] and as this world could not subsist, the Creator mitigated the severity of *Din* by blending it with the attributes of *Chesed* and *Rachamim*, bringing into being the world of *Tikun*.[6]

Beside this descriptive connotation, the term *Tikun* has another, an active sense, which will be explained further on in ch. 11 on *Birur* and *Tikun*.

Notes to Chapter IX

[1] *The term* Tohu *is taken from* Genesis *1:2; see* supra, *ch. 7, note 15.*

[2] *In this context R. Isaac Luria reads* Genesis *1:2 as referring to the World of* Tohu, *and* Genesis *1:3 ("Let there be light, and there was light") as referring to the World of* Tikun; Etz Chayim *8:1.*

[3] Likutei Torah *II:37c* ff., *and III:87a* ff.; supra, *ch. 7 (notes 7–10).—In this context man is said to be rooted in the realm of* Tikun *as his soul compounds all ten aspects of the* Sefirot *(see* supra, *ch. 3, note 151), and these themselves in the full inter-relationship of the* Sefirot *as compounds. Hence man is able to control or mitigate his soul-powers of* Chesed *and* Gevurah (e.g., *love and anger, and so on). Animals, on the other hand, are rooted in* Tohu: *they express their natural emotive powers in a simple and extreme manner, unable to control or mitigate them. Though* Tohu, *for being the original emission of* Sefirot, *is said to be rooted higher than* Tikun, Tikun *has an advantage and superiority over* Tohu: *the perfection of the mutual inclusiveness and unity of* Tikun *is the condition drawing forth a manifest indwelling of the* Or En Sof *that is not to be found in* Tohu. *See* Likutei Torah *II:37c* ff.

[4] Genesis Rabba *3:7, and 9:2.—This is not to be understood in a sense of there being some accidental flaw in the original World of* Tohu. *On the contrary, the flaw and defect of* Tohu *were intentionally and purposely formed to allow for the possibility of the effects of* Shevirat Hakelim. *Thus R. Isaac Luria interprets the* Mishnah *of* Avot *V:1 ("By ten sayings the world was created. And why does Scripture teach this? Could it not have been created by a single saying? But this was in order to exact penalty from the wicked . . . and to give good reward to the righteous") to the effect that the Ten Sayings in the opening statement allude to the ten separate* Sefirot *of* Tohu, *and the single saying in the question refers to the unified compound of the* Sefirot *of* Tikun. *The actual order of creation through the stages of* Tohu *and* Tikun *allows for the possibility of evil, providing man with an opportunity to choose between good and evil which, in turn, makes it possible for G–d to manifest His attributes of* Chesed, Gevurah, Tiferet, *and so forth (the principles of reward and punishment spoken of in the* Mishnah). *See* Etz Chayim *11:6, and the discourse on this* Mishnah *in* Sha'ar Hahakdamot *(p. 228* f.); *see also R. Chayim Vital,* Sha'ar Maamarei Rashby Ve-Razal, Avot a.l. *(II: pp. 73a* ff.). Cf. infra, *ch. 11, note 3.*

[5] Cf. supra, *ch. 5, and ch. 7, note 18.*

[6] Genesis Rabba *12:15;* Zohar *III:38a. See* Zohar *I:180b and 280b;* Zohar Chadash, Toldot, *27a.* Cf. Mevoh She'arim *II:3:8.*

Chapter 10 KELIPOT; CHITZONIM; SITRA ACHRA

These terms are synonymous. They are the names for evil and impurity. *Sitra Achra* means the "other side," i.e., the side distinguished from and opposed to holiness and purity. *Chitzonim* means the "external ones," i.e., the most exterior forces, the waste and refuse of holiness that constitutes evil. *Kelipot* means shells, or barks; the outer shells that contain the edible fruit but are themselves inedible.

The substance of the *Kelipot*, as already mentioned earlier, consists of the unassimilable parts of the broken Vessels, thus, their waste and refuse. Each of these subsists by virtue of a spark of holiness attached to them. This holy spark, their vital force without which they would cease to exist,[1] is encumbered and enclosed by the shells as the edible fruit is encumbered and enclosed by its shell, therefore on its own it is unable to make itself felt and to dominate over the shell. Hence the analogous term of *Kelipot.*

There are four basic *Kelipot*, divided into two classes:[2] the three altogether impure and evil *Kelipot*, and *Kelipat Nogah. Kelipat Nogah* is the "skin" immediately covering the spark of holiness. Thus it is in direct contact with holiness, and not altogether evil. It is an intermediary between holy and profane, between absolute good and absolute evil. The other three *Kelipot* are further removed; they are not in direct contact with the spark but cover the *Kelipat Nogah*, one over the other. Their nurture and vitality from holiness comes to them through the medium of *Kelipat Nogah.*[3]

The four *Kelipot*, and the term *Nogah*, are adduced in *Ezekiel* I:14:[4] "*Stormy wind*," "*great cloud*," and "*a fire taking hold of itself*," these denote the three totally impure *Kelipot*; and "*a Brightness* (*Nogah*) *round about it*" denotes the fourth *Kelipah, Kelipat Nogah* (the *Nogah* being a radiation from holiness). The significance of these two classes will be understood by the following:

The Torah, the revealed Word of G–d, is the criterion of absolute good and absolute evil.[5] Whatever man is enjoined to do is absolute good; whatever man is prohibited from doing is absolute evil. Therefore all matters pertaining to the prohibitions of the Torah (the forbidden objects, actions, utterances, thoughts, and so on) flow and

derive from the three altogether impure *Kelipot*. All matters pertaining to the realm of what is essentially permissible, according to the Torah (in distinction from what is commanded, and to the exclusion of what is prohibited), essentially flow and derive from *Kelipat Nogah*.

Kelipat Nogah, being an intermediary category, between pure holiness and absolute impurity, has some relationship to both. This means that all derivations of *Kelipat Nogah* can fall to, and be absorbed in, the three evil *Kelipot*; or, alternatively, they can be elevated to, and be absorbed in, the realm of holiness. When the permitted action (as, for example, simple eating and drinking) is intentionally performed for a higher purpose, for the sake of Heaven (i.e., to have the strength and energy to serve G–d), then the vitality of this action (and the permitted objects it involves) is distilled and absorbed in the realm of holiness. If, on the other hand, the eating and drinking were for purely sensual pleasure, without any more sublime intention, then this vitality is degraded and temporarily absorbed in the three unclean *Kelipot*; *temporarily*, because whereas the food is essentially fit and permitted for consumption (thus not forbidden), its vitality can revert and ascend to holiness along with the consumer when he returns (*Teshuvah*) to the service of G–d.[6]

Therefore, the Hebrew terms for permitted and forbidden are *Muttar* and *Assur*, respectively. *Muttar* literally means "released," "free;" that is, the permitted matter is not tied and bound by the power of the *Chitzonim* preventing it from returning and ascending to holiness. *Assur* literally means "chained," "bound," for the forbidden matter is bound and held captive in the power of the *Chitzonim* preventing it from ascending and becoming absorbed in holiness forever, until the day comes when death (another synonym for evil) will be devoured forever, as is written (*Zechariah* 13:2): "And I will cause the unclean spirit to pass from the earth"; or until the sinner repents to such an extent that his premeditated sins become transmuted into veritable merits,[7] which is achieved through "repentance (*Teshuvah*) out of love," coming from the depths of the heart, with great love and fervour, and from a soul passionately desiring to cleave to the blessed G–d, and thirsting for G–d, like a parched desert soil.[8]

The meaning and intent of the *Kelipot* will be discussed in the next chapter.

Notes to Chapter X

[1] *See* supra, *ch. 7, note 20, and* infra, *ch. 11.*

[2] *On all this see* Etz Chayim *49:2* ff.; Tanya *I: ch. 6* f.; Igeret Hakodesh, *sect. XXV and XXVI.* Cf. Zohar *III: 227a.*

[3] Tanya *I: ch. 37.*

[4] *See* Zohar *II: 203a–b.*

[5] Cf. Mishnat R. Eliezer, *ch. 6; Maimonides,* Hilchot Melachim *VIII: 11;* idem, Shemonah Perakim, *chs. 4 and 6.*

[6] *Though even then a trace of the evil remains in the body, necessitating the purgatory of the grave;* Tanya *I: ch. 8.*

[7] Rosh Hashanah *29a.*

[8] Tanya *I: ch. 7; see also* ibid., *ch. 8, and* Igeret Hakodesh, *sect. XXVI.*

BIRUR AND TIKUN

Man, created last but first in intent,[1] has his abode in this physical world which is also the abode of the *Kelipot*. For it is man's task and mission to subdue the *Kelipot* and prevail over them by means of Torah and the *Mitzvot* in order to realise the Divine Will—the making of this world an abode for Divinity.[2]

It has already been explained that the *Kelipot* are derived from the "Breaking of the Vessels". This significant occurrence was not a catastrophic accident due to some flaw in the cosmogonic process. On the contrary, it was a lawful and purposive development in order to bring about evil. For only where there is an alternative between good and evil can man have freedom of choice. And only where man uses this free choice to perform his tasks and duties can he be rewarded accordingly, and receive his requirements from a perspective of law, righteousness, and equity.[3] Evil therefore serves a Divine purpose.

In fact, the evil inclination in man is an instrument for the love of G–d. Accordingly it is written: "And you shall love the Eternal, your G–d, with all your heart" (*Deuteronomy* 6:5); "with all your heart" means with both your inclinations, the evil inclination as well as the good inclination.[4] The Kabbalah is quite emphatic about this, and states that there can be no greater service done to G–d than to bring into subjection the evil inclination by the power of love for G–d. For when it is subdued and its power broken by man in this way, then he becomes a true lover of G–d, since he has learnt how to make the very evil inclination serve G–d. "All that the Holy One, blessed is He, has made, above and below, is for the purpose of manifesting His glory and for His service. Now who has seen a servant working against his master and laying plans to counteract everything that is of his master's will? It is the will of the Holy One, blessed is He, that men should worship Him and walk in the way of truth, continually, so that man may be rewarded with benefits. As this is the will of the Holy One, blessed is He, how, then, can an evil servant come and counteract the will of his master and tempt man to walk in an evil way, repulsing him from the good way and causing him to disobey the will of the Lord?"

To solve this apparent paradox, the *Zohar* states, that in fact, the intended purpose of evil is merely to execute the Will of G–d, and illustrates it by the famous "parable of the harlot": A king instructed and

cautioned his son to lead an exemplary moral life and not to fall prey to temptation. Then, secretly, the king brought before him a beautiful and clever woman and ordered her to seduce his son, thereby testing his obedience and devotion to his father. She used every blandishment to seduce the prince. But the prince, being good, obeyed the commandment of his father; he refused her allurements and thrust her from himself. Then the father, the king, rejoiced exceedingly, and bestowed upon his son the greatest gifts and highest honours. Now, who caused all that glory to the prince? Surely it was that woman! The *Zohar* concludes "Surely she is to be praised on all counts; for, firstly, she fulfilled the king's command, and secondly, she caused the son to receive all that good, and caused that intense love of the king to his son."[5]

Therefore, it is man's purpose to subdue the *Sitra Achra* and to crush its power, for "When that *Sitra* is subdued, the Holy One, blessed is He, rises upwards[6] and is exalted in His glory. In fact, there is no worship of G–d except when it issues forth from darkness, and no good except when it proceeds from evil . . . The perfection of all things is attained when good and evil are intermingled and then become totally good, for there is no good except if it issues out of evil. By that good His glory rises, and that is the perfect worship".[7]

As man arouses his own attribute of *Gevurah*[8] to subdue and crush the waste of the Supernal *Gevurah* below[9] and prevail over it, he causes a reciprocal effect that the Divine attribute of *Gevurah* will subdue and prevail over the Supernal Judgments (*Hamtakat Hadinim*: the "mitigation of the Judgments") and the Divine *Chesed* and *Rachamim* will manifest themselves below unhindered.[10]

The *Kelipot* thus serve a distinct purpose. There is a spark (*Nitzotz*) of Divinity attached to them which allows them to subsist as a servant to serve the Master's purpose. When this spark is extricated from the *Kelipot* and restored to the realm of Holiness to be absorbed there, the *Kelipot* are deprived of their vitality and cease to exist. And this is the task of man: to extricate that spark of holiness. This is called *Birur*, and this is the concept of *Tikun*.[11]

Birur means Extrication, Disencumbrance. When man relates consciously to the derivatives of the *Kelipot*, actively or passively, in their Divinely intended context, he extricates the spark of Divinity (*Birur*) and restores it to its source, thus causing the Restitution and Reintegration (*Tikun*) of the whole Being. The "shell" is broken, the "fruit" is extracted, and the proper cosmic order is restored.

That is, the potentially holy objects (*Kelipat Nogah*) are sublimated and absorbed in the realm of holiness by the properly performed actions and by safeguarding them from the *Chitzonim*, i.e., by withstanding the temptations of evil. For as *Kelipat Nogah* is fully absorbed in the realm of holiness, the impure *Kelipot* (who receive their vitality through the medium of *Kelipat Nogah*) are deprived of their vitality and are annihilated.[12]

On the other hand, every improper act (sin) causes just the opposite. Sinful acts retain and sustain the *Sitra Achra*;[13] *Kelipat Nogah* is absorbed among the impure *Kelipot*, thus strengthening them and increasing their power, and causing the spark of holiness to be further and increasingly imprisoned and encumbered among the *Kelipot*. This is known as the concept of the *Shechinah-in-exile*:[14] the *Shechinah*, the Divine Indwelling Presence, the spark of Holiness, is exiled among the *Kelipot* to remain there bound up and without escape until the sinner repents intensely, or until the day when G-d will cause the spirit of impurity to pass from the earth.[15]

Every one has his share of sparks that he has to extricate and disencumber. For Adam by his sin, strengthened and increased the power of evil.[16] The many sparks that fell because of his catastrophic act[17] remain for his descendants[18] to extricate.[19] This is the cause and purpose of the *Galut* (Exile, and Diaspora).[20] And when all the sparks shall have been disencumbered, then the *Shechinah* is altogether freed from Its exile and Israel is redeemed: the Messianic Era is ushered in.[21]

Notes to Chapter XI

[1] *See* Tikunei Zohar, *Intr.: 6a, and* Igeret Hakodesh, *sect. VII, note 14.*

[2] "*Clearly the purpose of the evolution of the worlds and their gradual descent is not for the sake of the higher worlds . . . but the ultimate purpose (of creation) is this lowest world. For such was His blessed Will that He delights in the* sitra achra *being subdued and in darkness being turned to light so that the Divine Light of the blessed* En Sof *shall shine forth in the place of darkness and* sitra achra, *throughout the world . . . And for this purpose the Holy One, blessed is He, gave to Israel the Torah . . .*"; Tanya *I: ch. 36, in comment on the Midrashic statement that the purpose of the creation is the Divine wish to have an abode in the nether realms just as in the supernal ones* (Tanchuma, *Bechukotei 3, and Nasso: 13*). *Again: "The purpose of all the contractions* (tzimtzumim) *is the creation of the material human body and the subjugation of the* sitra achra, *to bring about the preeminence of light supplanting darkness . . . as has been explained earlier* (ch. *35–37*) *at length; for this is the purpose for the descent of the world . . . and this is the essence of man's devotion in his Divine service: to elicit the Light of the blessed* En Sof *down below;*" ibid., *ch. 49*. Cf. Igeret Hakodesh, *sect. VII, and see* Emunot

Vede'ot *IV: introd. and ch. 1;* cf. *Maimonides,* Introduction to Commentary on the Mishnah.

[3] Pardess Rimonim *25:3;* Etz Chayim *11:6, 37:2, 39:1, and* Sha'ar Hakelalim, *ch. 2;* supra, *ch. 9, note 4.*

[4] Mishnah, Berachot *IX:5.*

[5] Zohar *II:163a.* Cf. Tanya *I: ch. 9, and end of ch. 29; also* ibid., *ch. 24.—Evil, thus, is not a mere negation or relative concept. In our sense it is quite real. To be sure, the* Kelipot *exist only by virtue of the Divine Will and receive their vitality from the sources of holiness (the "sparks of holiness"), albeit in limited measure, just sufficient for their intended purpose; see* Etz Chayim *31:2. But as man, through his sinful actions, lends additional vitality and strength to the* Kelipot, *they do not suffice with the seduction of man but seek "to conquer and prevail with full force," thus necessitating a severe battle against them; see R. Chayim Vital,* Sha'ar Hapessukim *on* Prov. *9:17 (p. 267), and* idem, Sha'ar Hamitzvot *on* Exodus *22:6 (p. 63);* Etz Chayim *48:2.*

[6] *This apparently paradoxical statement ("rising upwards" rather than a reciprocal manifestation "downwards") really means a most sublime, supernal unification* (Yichud)*: as the* sitra achra *is subdued below, its source in the supernal* Gevurot *is subdued above, thus causing an immense manifestation which then radiates downwards. See the commentaries on this passage, and* Likutei Torah *III:37c* ff.*;* cf. infra, *note 9.*

[7] Zohar *II:184a. See also* ibid., *67b and 128b;* Tanya *I: ch. 27.*

[8] *See* Igeret Hakodesh, *sect. XV.*

[9] *The* Kelipot *deriving from the original* Kelim *which, in turn, originate in the supernal* Gevurah*; see* supra, *ch. 7, note 18.*

[10] *See* Derech Emunah, *section 2 (p. 9a* f.). Cf. Zohar Chadash, *Tik., 94b: "From the side of* Gevurah *they are called 'The valiant ones* (Giborim) *that stand in the breach, that repel the decrees (judgments)'* (Liturgy, *Selichot*)." Cf. *also* supra, *this chapter, note 6, and sources cited there. See also* Siddur im Perush Hamilot, *p. 247a* f., *that precisely this "sweetening of the judgments," the mitigation of* Gevurah, *elicits the most abundant good. This is essentially also the concept of "the righteous turn the attribute of* Din *and* Gevurah *into the attribute of* Rachamim, *while the wicked turn the attribute of* Rachamim *into the attribute of* Gevurah *and* Din*;"* Genesis Rabba *33:3.* Chesed *is free to emanate as the concealment and restraint of* Gevurah *and* Din *are removed, while the limitations of* Gevurah *and the severity of* Din *emerge as the concealment implied by* Gevurah *is increased and strengthened by sin (the notion of* Hesster Panim, *the Concealment or "Hiding" of the Divine Countenance, mentioned in* Deut. *31:17, as opposed to* Heorat Panim*—resp.* Nesiat Panim*—the Shining Illumination or Manifestation of the Divine Countenance as in* Numb. *6:25* f.*;* cf. Igeret Hakodesh, *end of sect. IV, and* supra, *ch. 6,* s.v. Panim). *The implication is that there is no change in G–d but only in, and relative to, man. See* Zohar *III:137b; also* ibid., *II:63a;* Pardess Rimonim *25:3;* Igeret Hakodesh, *sect. XII and XIII.*

[11] *See* Etz Chayim *39:1. Most intimately related to, and practically identical with, this concept of Birur is the theme of* העלאת מ"ן *(the "elevation of* Mayin Nukvin *(feminine waters)"); see* Etz Chayim *39:1;* Tanya *I: chs. 10 and 53;* Igeret Hakodesh, *sect. IV and note 46* a.l. Cf. *also* Igeret Hakodesh, *sect. XXVII and XXVIII.*

[12] Tanya *I: ch. 37;* cf. Etz Chayim *39:1.*

[13] *See* Zohar *II:184a, and* cf. supra, *this chapter, note 10.*

[14] *See* Etz Chayim *47:6.* Cf. Zohar *III:74a* ff.*; also* ibid., *II:189a, and III:79a. See* Tanya *I: chs. 17, 37, and 45;* ibid., *III:3;* Igeret Hakodesh, *sect. IV, XXV, and XXVI.* Cf. *also* Igeret Hakodesh, *sect. XXIII and XXXI.*

[15] Tanya *I: ch. 7, quoted* supra, *end of ch. 10.*

[16] *See* Sha'ar Hapessukim, *Bereishit, on* Gen. *2:17 (pp. 4a* ff.) *for a detailed discussion of the sin of Adam and its implications.*

[17] Ibid., *and see also* Etz Chayim *36:2,*

39:1, et passim; Sha'ar Maamarei Rashby *on* Zohar *II:254b (p. 165b* f.). *See* Igeret Hakodesh, *sect. XII and XXVI.—Relative rectifications in the course of time were reversed and vacated by subsequent national sins of Israel (as in the Desert after the Exodus, and in the periods of the First and Second Temples), thereby prolonging the process of* Birur*; see the sources cited in notes 16–20.*

[18] *The souls of all the descendants of Adam are "sparks" of the original soul of Adam; see* Exodus Rabba *40:2* f., *and* Tanchuma, *Ki Tissa: 12, as interpreted in* Sha'ar Hapessukim a.l.c. (*sect. III; p. 9b* f.). *See* Igeret Hakodesh, *sect. VII.*

[19] Etz Chayim *50:3: "When man is born his soul needs to extricate those sparks that are of his share which had fallen unto* Kelipat Nogah *because of the sin of Adam." See also* ibid., *26:1.*

[20] *See* Sha'ar Hamitzvot, *Re'ey (pp. 111b* ff.), *for a detailed discussion of the concept of* Galut *and its various forms.* Cf. *also* Mevoh She'arim *II:3:8, and* Igeret Hakodesh, *sect. XXVI.*

[21] *See* Etz Chayim *3:6, 19:3, 26:1,* et passim*; sources cited in the preceding notes of this chapter (especially note 14), and* Torah Or, Vayeshev, *27d.* Cf. *also* Tanya *I: ch. 49.*

Part V

INTRODUCTION

by Rabbi Zalman I. Posner

The basic work of Chabad Chassidus, Rabbi Schneur Zalman's *Tanya* or *Likutei Amarim*, has appeared in nearly three-score editions in Hebrew during the past 170 years, in addition to translations. The Fifth Part, *Kuntress Acharon* (Latest Discourse) here translated, was published posthumously by the author's sons with an Introduction to be found on p. X.

It is apparent that the author's intended audience would be conversant with the infinitely complex doctrines of Kabbala, and humility is not a prequisite to the confession that the reader does not fully comprehend the text. Nonetheless Chabad does endeavor to make the arcane accessible so that no field of Torah be beyond reach. The footnotes (by the translator) and references may lighten the burden of the reader. A hasty perusal will probably not be profitable, so it is suggested that the reader acquaint himself with earlier volumes of the translated *Tanya* and the growing library of Chabad in English.

It has become custom among Chabad Chassidim to study a portion of *Tanya* daily, besides the daily portion of Chumash and Tehillim, as outlined by the late Rebbe, Rabbi Joseph I. Schneersohn נבג"מ, and printed in recent editions of the Hebrew *Tanya*. Many Chassidim not fully at ease with the Hebrew-Aramaic frequently employed by the author, and unfamiliar with Chabad and Kabbala terms and doctrines, carefully study the daily *Tanya* portion using the English translations as companion and invaluable aid. It is the hope of the translator that this translation perform that noble function.

May we take the liberty of suggesting that the last two Essays of this work require no previous knowledge, that they are remarkably pertinent to our milieu, that they are the earnest words of a Rebbe calling to his people. May our minds and hearts be open to his call.

Zalman I. Posner

Elul 5728
Nashville, Tennessee

MOREH SHIUR

INTRODUCTION

The *MOREH SHIUR* is a guide to the division of the Tanya into daily study portions, so as to complete reading the entire work in the course of a year, then resuming it again in yearly cycles.

The sections have been apportioned for each day of the year commencing with 19th—*YUD TESS*—Kislev (the 'New Year' for Chassidut), until the following 19th Kislev. The *MOREH SHIUR* is in two parts. The first is for a regular year; the second for a leap year with the added month of Adar II.

The custom of reading the daily portions of Tanya has been introduced as part of the three daily Shiurim—*CHUMASH, TEHILLIM, TANYA ('ChiTaT')*, which are equally significant for all Jews, scholars and laymen alike. These are explained as follows:

CHUMASH WITH RASHI'S COMMENTARY

Every day one reads a section of the Sidra of the week, together with Rashi's commentary: On the first day of the week one reads up to 'sheini'; on the second day up to 'Shlishi', and so forth. When a sidra is extended over two or three weeks (due to a festival coinciding with Shabbat), one covers the sidra in the second and third weeks in the same way as in the first week.

On Simchat Torah one learns the Sidra V'Zos Habracha from the section for the corresponding day of the week on which Simchat Torah occurs, to the end of the Sidra, with Rashi's commentary.

On the day following Simchat Torah (Isru-Chag), one learns the Sidra Bereishit with Rashi's commentary, from the beginning to the appropriate section for the corresponding day of the week (inclusive).

TEHILLIM

To be recited each day after the Morning Prayer, as apportioned for the days of the month, so that the Book of Psalms is concluded each month.

MOREH SHIUR

Commencing on the second day of Rosh Chodesh Elul until Yom Kippur, one recites, in addition to the regular daily portion, three chapters of Tehillim. On the second day of Rosh Chodesh Elul one recites Psalms 1–3; on the 2nd Elul Psalms 4–6; and so forth, until Yom Kippur.

On Yom Kippur, thirty-six chapters are added throughout the day, as follows:
Nine before Kol Nidre (115–123); nine before retiring to sleep (124–132); nine after Musaf (133–141); nine after Ne'ilah (142–150). Thus the entire Book of Psalms is covered during this special period, in addition to the daily recitals.

TANYA

The daily study-sections of the Tanya were introduced by the Previous Lubavitcher Rebbe, Rabbi Yosef Yitzchok Schneersohn, of sainted and blessed memory. The following is an extract from the accompanying letter which he wrote regarding the study of Tanya:

"These are the study-sections of Likutei Amarim—Tanya as divided into daily portions, from the Rosh Hashonno of Chassidut—19th Kislev, until the following 19th Kislev—may it bring us and all Jews goodness and blessing, materially and spiritually."

The above-mentioned study portions are not meant as a substitute for the daily Torah studies required of each Jew according to his ability.

When learning *TANYA*, according to the *MOREH SHIUR*, the reader will encounter some irregularities, these are explained hereunder:

1. Pages vi and vii are not an integral part of the *TANYA* text, they remain untranslated, and do not form part of the *MOREH SHIUR*.

2. The months of Kislev and MarCheshvan sometimes have only 29 days. When this occurs, the portion allotted for the 30th is studied together with the section for the 29th.

3. There are several instances when the daily section ends on a particular page, and the beginning of the next day's portion commences on the page previous. This is due to the layout of the Notes within the Hebrew text being carried forward to the next page. This occurs on the following dates:

In a Regular Year—19th Adar. 16th and 21st Nissan.

In a Leap Year—13th Adar II. 7th and 9th Nissan.

LIST OF TANYA EDITIONS AND PRINTINGS, BY COUNTRIES *

Andorra, 5744-1984
Angola
Luanda, 5745-1985
Antarctica
Commandante Serras, 5745-1985
Argentina
Allen, 5744-1984
Alta Gracia, 5744-1984
Avellaneda, Buenos Aires, 5751-1991
Azul, 5744-1984
Bahia Blanca, Buenos Aires, 5744-1984
Bariloche, Rio Negro, 5744-1984
Basavilbaso, Entre Rios, 5744-1984
Belgrano, Buenos Aires, Ch. H., 5751-1991
Berisso, Buenos Aires, 5744-1984
Bernasconi, La Pampa, 5744-1984
Bragado, Buenos Aires, 5744-1984
Buenos Aires, Central Chabad House, 5751-1991
Buenos Aires, 5738-1978, 5747-1987
Campana, Buenos Aires, 5744-1984
Canuelas, Buenos Aires, 5744-1984
Catamarca, 5744-1984
Ceres, Fe, 5744-1984
Cipolletti, Rio Negro, 5744-1984
Ciudadela, Buenos Aires, 5751-1991
Clorinda, Formosa, 5744-1984
Colon, Entre Rios, 5744-1984
Comodoro Rivadavia, Chubut, 5744-1984
Concepcion, Chubut, 5744-1984
Concepcion del Uruguay, Entre Rios, 5744-1984
Concordia, Entre Rios, 5743-1983
Cordoba, 5744-1984
Coronel Pringles, Buenos Aires, 5744-1984
Coronel Suarez, Buenos Aires, 5744-1984
Corrientes, 5744-1984
Constitucion, Buenos Aires, 5751-1991
Oholei Chinuch Girls School
Cristobal, Fe, 5744-1984
Cutral Co, 5744-1984
Ensenada, Buenos Aires, 5744-1984
Fe, 5744-1984
Formosa, 5744-1984
Francisco, 5744-1984
General Campos, Entre Rios, 5744-1984
General Pineda, Chubut, 5744-1984
General Roca, Rio Negro, 5744-1984
Goya, Corrientes, 5744-1984
Gualeguay, Entre Rios, 5744-1984
Gualeguaychu, Entre Rios, 5744-1984
Jose de Martin, Buenos Aires, 5744-1984
Jujuy, 5744-1984
Juan, 5744-1984
Juarez, Buenos Aires, 5744-1984
Junin, Buenos Aires, 5744-1984
L. Flores, Buenos Aires, 5751-1991
La Banda, Santiago del Estero, 5744-1984
Lanus, Buenos Aires, 5751-1991
La Paz, Entre Rios, 5744-1984
La Plata, Buenos Aires, 5744-1984
La Rioja, 5744-1984
Luis, 5744-1984
Mar del Plata, Buenos Aires, 5744-1984
Maria Grande, Entre Rios, 5744-1984
Martin, Buenos Aires, 5751-1991
Martin, Mendoza, 5744-1984
Mendoza, 5744-1984
Mercedes, Buenos Aires, 5744-1984
Mercedes, Corrientes, 5744-1984
Mercedes, Luis, 5744-1984
Moisesville, Fe, 5744-1984
Monigotes, Fe, 5744-1984
Moron, Buenos Aires, 5751-1991
Moreno, Kiryat Chabad, Buenos Aires, 5751-1991
Necochea, Buenos Aires, 5744-1984
Neuquen, 5744-1984
Nueve de Julio, Buenos Aires, 5744-1984
Olivos, Buenos Aires, 5751-1991

* Only the *first* printing of each city is listed. For a more detailed chronological list - see page 716 (in Hebrew Supplements).

Some cities belonged to different countries in various times. In such instances the most commonly known affiliation is used.

Palacios, 5744-1984
Palmeras, 5744-1984
Patagones, Buenos Aires, 5744-1984
Parana, Entre Rios, 5744-1984
Posadas, Mendoza, 5744-1984
Presidente Roque (Saenz Pena), Chubut, 5744-1984
Quilmes, Buenos Aires, 5751-1991
Rafael, Mendoza, 5744-1984
Rafaela, Fe, 5744-1984
Ramos Mejia, Buenos Aires, 5751-1991
Resistencia, Chubut, 5744-1984
Rio Cuarto, 5744-1984
Rio Gallegos, 5744-1984
Rio Grande, Tierra del Fuego, 5744-1984
Rivera, Buenos Aires, 5744-1984
Rosa, La Pampa, 5744-1984
Rosario, Fe, 5744-1984
Rosario del Tala, Entre Rios, 5744-1984
Salta, 5744-1984
Salvador, Entre Rios, 5744-1984
Santiago del Estero, 5744-1984
Tandil, Buenos Aires, 5744-1984
Tigre, Buenos Aires, 5751-1991
Trelew, Chubut, 5744-1984
Tres Arroyos, Buenos Aires, 5744-1984
Tucuman, 5743-1983
Uruguay Square, Buenos Aires, 5751-1991
Villa Crespo, Buenos Aires, Ch. H., 5751-1991
Villa Devoto, Buenos Aires, Ch. H., 5751-1991
Villa Angela, Chubut, 5744-1984
Villa Clara, Entre Rios, 5744-1984
Villa Domingos, Entre Rios, 5744-1984
Villa Maria, Cordoba, 5744-1984
Villaguay, Entre Rios, 5744-1984
Zapala, Neuquen, 5744-1984
Zarate, Buenos Aires, 5744-1984

Australia

Adelaide, S.A., 5744-1984
Brisbane, Qld., 5744-1984
Canberra, A.C.T., 5744-1984
Hobart, Tas., 5744-1984
Melbourne, Vic., 5727-1967, 5732-1972
Newcastle, N.S.W., 5744-1984
Perth, W.A., 5743-1983
Shepparton, Vic., 5746-1986
Sydney, N.S.W., 5741-1981
Wollongong, N.S.W., 5745-1985

Austria

Baden, 5745-1985
Graz, 5745-1985
Linz, 5745-1985
Purkersdorf, 5745-1985
Salzburg, 5745-1985
Vienna, 5604-1844, 5738-1978

Bahamas

Nassau, 5744-1984

Barbados, 5744-1984

Belgium

Antwerp, 5738-1978, 5744-1984
Brussels, 5744-1984
Charleroi, 5744-1984
Gent, 5744-1984
Knokke, 5744-1984
Leuven, 5744-1984
Liege, 5744-1984
Military Rabbinate, 5744-1984
Mons, 5744-1984
Oostende, 5744-1984
Wilrijk, 5744-1984

Bermuda

Hamilton, 5745-1985

Bolivia

Cochabamba, 5744-1984
De la Sierra, 5744-1984
La Paz, 5744-1984

Brazil

Abreu e Lima, Pernambuco, 5752-1992
Águas de Bárbara, 5744-1984
Águas de Lindóia, 5744-1984
Aldeia, Pernambuco, 5752-1992
Alegrete, Rio Grande do Sul, 5746-1986
Alfenas, Minas Gerais, 5746-1986
Aliança, Pernambuco, 5752-1992
Alta, 5745-1985
Alto da Boa Vista, Paulo, 5752-1992
Alto do Capivarí, Paulo, 5752-1992
Alumínia, Paulo, 5751-1991
Americana, 5744-1984

Amparo, Paulo, 5747-1987
Andaraí, Rio de Janeiro, 5751-1991
André, 5744-1984
André, Paulo, Beit Chabad, 5751-1991
Ângelo, Rio Grande do Sul, 5746-1986
Angra dos Reis, Rio de Janeiro, 5748-1988
Antoninas, Paraná, 5748-1988
Aparecida, Paulo, 5751-1991
Aquarela, Paulo, 5752-1992
Aracajú, Sergipe, 5747-1987
Araçoiaba, Pernambuco, 5752-1992
Araçoiaba da Serra, Paulo, 5746-1986
Araraquara, 5744-1984
Araras, Paulo, 5746-1986
Araruama, 5744-1984
Araucária, Paraná, 5748-1988
Araxá, Minas Gerais, 5746-1986
Arco-Íris, Paulo, 5752-1992
Arcoverde, Pernambuco, 5752-1992
Arujá, 5744-1984
Assis, Paulo, 5746-1986
Astúrias, Paulo, 5748-1988
Atibaia, 5744-1984
Atibaia, Rua Yud-Alef Nissan, Paulo, 5748-1988
Atibainha, Paulo, 5747-1987
B. Perdões, Paulo, 5747-1987
Bagé, 5745-1985
Bárbara do Oeste, 5744-1984
Baronesa Clara, Rio Grande do Sul, 5746-1986
Barra da Tijuca, Rio de Janeiro, 5750-1990
Barra do - Sebastião, Paulo, 5746-1986
Barra do Una, Paulo, 5748-1988
Barra Mansa, 5744-1984
Barra Velha, Catarina, 5746-1986
Barraqueçaba, Paulo, 5748-1988
Barueri, 5744-1984
Baurú, 5744-1984
Belém, 5746-1986
Belo Horizonte, 5744-1984
Belo Jardim, Pernambuco, 5752-1992
Belvedere, Paulo, 5752-1992
Benfica, Rio de Janeiro, 5751-1991
Bento do Sul, Catarina, 5748-1988
Bernardo do Campo, 5744-1984
Bertioga, Paulo, 5747-1987
Bezerra, Pernambuco, 5752-1992
Biritiba Mirim, Paulo, 5747-1987
Blumenau, Catarina, 5746-1986
Boicucanga, Paulo, 5747-1987
Boitúva, Paulo, 5746-1986
Bom Sucesso, Paulo, 5751-1991
Bonsucesso, Rio de Janeiro, 5751-1991
Borda do João, Rio de Janeiro, 5748-1988
Borja, Rio Grande do Sul, 5746-1986
Bosque Lusíadas, Paulo, 5752-1992
Botafogo, Rio de Janeiro, 5750-1990
Botucatú, 5744-1984
Bragança Paulista, 5744-1984
Brasília, 5744-1984
Brigadeiro Tobias, Paulo, 5751-1991
Brusque, Catarina, 5748-1988
Búzios, Rio de Janeiro, 5748-1988
Cabo, Pernambuco, 5752-1992
Cabo Frio, 5744-1984
Cabreúva, Paulo, 5744-1984, 5751-1991
Caçapava, Paulo, 5751-1991
Cachoeira do Imaratá, Paulo, 5747-1987
Cachoeira do Itapemirim, 5747-1987
Cachoeira do Sul, Rio Grande do Sul, 5747-1987
Cachoeira Paulista, Paulo, 5746-1986
Caetano, Pernambuco, 5752-1992
Caetano do Sul, 5744-1984
Caiobá, Paraná, 5748-1988
Cajú, Rio de Janeiro, 5751-1991
Camargibe, Pernambuco, 5752-1992
Camboriú, Catarina, 5748-1988
Camburí, Paulo, 5747-1987
Campinas, 5744-1984
Campo Alegre, Catarina, 5748-1988
Campo Grande, Mato Grosso, 5746-1986
Campo Largo, 5744-1984
Campo Limpo, Paulo, 5747-1987
Campos, Rio de Janeiro, 5746-1986
Campos do Jordão, 5744-1984
Canoas, 5744-1984
Canoinhas, Catarina, 5748-1988
Cantareira, Paulo, 5748-1988
Capão Bonito, Paulo, 5746-1986
Capivari, Paulo, 5752-1992
Caraguatatuba, Paulo, 5746-1986

Carapicuíba, 5744-1984
Carazinho, Rio Grande do Sul, 5746-1986
Carlos, 5744-1984
Carpino, Pernambuco, 5752-1992
Caruarú, Pernambuco, 5752-1992
Cascatinha, Paulo, 5752-1992
Casemiro de Abreu, Rio de Janeiro, 5748-1988
Cassino, Rio Grande do Sul, 5746-1986
Caxambi, Rio de Janeiro, 5751-1991
Caxambú, 5744-1984
Caxias do Sul, Rio Grande do Sul, 5745-1985
Chuí, Rio Grande do Sul, 5747-1987
Cidade do Sol, Paulo, 5752-1992
Condado, Pernambuco, 5752-1992
Conrado, Rio de Janeiro, 5750-1990
Conselheiro Lafaiete, 5744-1984
Contagem, 5744-1984
Copacabana, Rio de Janeiro, 5750-1990
Cotia, 5744-1984
Criciúma, Catarina, 5744-1984, 5747-1987
Cristóvão, Rio de Janeiro, 5751-1991
Cruzeiro, Paulo, 5751-1991
Cuiabá, Mato Grosso, 5746-1986
Cumbica, Paulo, 5751-1991
Curitiba, 5744-1984, 5751-1991
Diadema, 5744-1984
Dom Pedrito, Rio Grande do Sul, 5746-1986
Duque de Caxias, 5744-1984
Duro, Paulo, 5748-1988
Éden, Paulo, 5748-1988
Embaixador, Paulo, 5752-1992
Embú, 5744-1984
Embú-Guaçú, 5744-1984
Encantado, Rio Grande do Sul, 5746-1986
Engenho Dentro, Rio de Janeiro, 5751-1991
Engenho Novo, Rio de Janeiro, 5751-1991
Enseada, Paulo, 5748-1988
Erexim, 5744-1984
Escada, Pernambuco, 5752-1992
Estácio, Rio de Janeiro, 5751-1991
Everest, Paulo, 5752-1992
Fazenda Nova, Pernambuco, 5752-1992
Feliz, Paulo, 5752-1992
Flamboyant, Paulo, 5752-1992
Flamengo, Rio de Janeiro, 5750-1990
Floresta, Pernambuco, 5752-1992
Floresta, Paulo, 5752-1992
Florianópolis. 5745-1985
Formosa, Goias, 5746-1986
Fornos, Minas Gerais, 5748-1988
Fortaleza, Ceará, 5745-1985
Foz do Iguaçú, 5744-1984
Fracalanza, Paulo, 5752-1992
Franca, Paulo, 5746-1986
Francisco do Sul, Catarina, 5748-1988
Francisco Xavier, Rio de Janeiro, 5751-1991
Franco da Rocha, 5744-1984
Gabriel, Rio Grande do Sul, 5746-1986
Gaibú, Pernambuco, 5752-1992
Garanhús, Pernambuco, 5752-1992
Garça, Paulo, 5746-1986
Garuva, Catarina, 5748-1988
Goiana, 5744-1984
Goiana, Pernambuco, 5752-1992
Gonçalo, 5744-1984
Governador Valadares, Minas Gerais, 5746-1986
Gramado, Rio Grande do Sul, 5746-1986
Gravata, Pernambuco, 5752-1992
Gravataí, Rio Grande do Sul, 5746-1986
Guaicá, Paulo, 5748-1988
Guará 1, Distrito Federal, 5746-1986
Guarapari, Paulo, 5747-1987
Guararema, Paulo, 5747-1987
Guaratinguetá, 5744-1984
Guaratuba, Paraná, 5748-1988
Guarujá, 5744-1984
Guarulhos, 5744-1984
Guaúba, Paulo, 5748-1988
Hebraica, Rio de Janeiro, 5750-1990
Hebraica, Paulo, 5748-1988
Ibirubá, Rio Grande do Sul, 5746-1986
Igarassú, Pernambuco, 5752-1992
Iguaba, Rio de Janeiro, 5748-1988
Ijuí, Rio Grande do Sul, 5746-1986
Ilha do Governador, Rio de Janeiro, 5751-1991
Ilhabela, Paulo, 5746-1986
Imbituba, Catarina, 5747-1987
Indaiatuba, Paulo, 5746-1986
Ipanema, Lubavitch House, Rio de Janeiro, 5750-1990
Ipojuca, Pernambuco, 5752-1992

Isabel, 5746-1986
Isabel, Paulo, 5751-1991
Itaboraí, Rio de Janeiro, 5748-1988
Itaim, Chabad House, Paulo, 5750-1990
Itaim Paulista, Paulo, 5747-1987
Itajaí, Catarina, 5747-1987
Itamaracá, Pernambuco, 5752-1992
Itanhaém, Paulo, 5746-1986
Itapecerica da Serra, 5744-1984
Itapetininga, 5744-1984
Itapevi, 5744-1984
Itapira, 5744-1984
Itapissuma, Pernambuco, 5752-1992
Itatiba, Paulo, 5747-1987
Itú, 5744-1984
Itupeva, 5744-1984
Jaboatão, Pernambuco, 5752-1992
Jacareí, 5744-1984
Jacarepaguá, Rio de Janeiro, 5751-1991
Jaguaribe, Paulo, 5752-1992
Jandira, 5744-1984
Jaraguá do Sul, Catarina, 5748-1988
Jardim das Flores, Paulo, 5752-1992
Jardim das Pérolas, Paulo,5752-1992
Jardim do Lago, Paulo, 5752-1992
Jardim Imbirí, Paulo, 5752-1992
Jardim Panorama, Paulo, 5752-1992
Jardim Paulista, Paulo, 5752-1992
Jardim Pôr do Sol, Paulo, 5752-1992
Jardim Presidente, Paulo, 5752-1992
Jardim Siomara, Paulo, 5752-1992
Jardim Sumaré, Paulo, 5752-1992
João da Boa Vista, Paulo, 5746-1986
João del Rei, 5744-1984
João Pessoa, Paraiba, 5746-1986
Joinvile, Catarina, 5746-1986
José do Rio Preto, 5744-1984
José dos Campos, Chabad House, Paulo, 5750-1990
José dos Campos, 5744-1984
José dos Pinhais, Paraná, 5748-1988
Juiz de Fora, 5744-1984
Júlio de Castilhos, Rio Grande do Sul. 5746-1986
Jundiaí, 5744-1984
Juqueí, Paulo, 5747-1987
Juréia, Paulo, 5748-1988
Kiryat Gan Israel, Paulo, 5748-1988
Lagoinha, Paulo, 5748-1988
Lajeado, Rio Grande do Sul, 5747-1987
Lajes, Catarina, 5747-1987
Lambarí, Minas Gerais, 5748-1988
Lapa, Paraná, 5748-1988
Laranjeiras, Rio de Janeiro, 5750-1990
Leblon, Rio de Janeiro, 5750-1990
Leme, Rio de Janeiro, 5750-1990
Leopoldo, 5744-1984
Limeira, 5744-1984
Limoeiro, Pernambuco, 5752-1992
Lins, Paulo, 5746-1986
Livramento, Rio Grande do Sul, 5745-1985
Londrina, Paraná, 5744-1984
Lorena, Paulo, 5748-1988
Lourenço, Pernambuco, 5752-1992
Lourenço, 5744-1984
Lourenço da Serra, Paulo, 5748-1988
Machané B'nei Akiva.
Lourenço do Sul, Rio Grande do Sul, 5746-1986
Louveira, Paulo, 5751-1991
Luís, Maranhão, 5746-1986
Lusiana, Goiás, 5746-1986
Macaé, Rio de Janeiro, 5746-1986
Macapá, Amapá, 5748-1988
Maceió, Alagoas, 5746-1986
Madureira, Rio de Janeiro, 5751-1991
Mafra, Catarina, 5748-1988
Magé, Rio de Janeiro, 5748-1988
Mairiporã, 5744-1984
Manancial, Paulo, 5752-1992
Manaus, Amazonas, 5745-1985
Mantiqueira, Paulo, 5752-1992
Maracanã, Rio de Janeiro, 5751-1991
Maresias, Paulo, 5747-1987
Maria, 5745-1985
Maria Farinha, Pernambuco, 5752-1992
Marinque, Paulo, 5751-1991
Maristela, Paulo, 5752-1992
Mateus do Sul, Paraná, 5748-1988
Matilde, Paulo, 5752-1992
Matinhos, Paraná, 5748-1988
Mauá, Paulo, 5750-1990
Mauá, Rio de Janeiro, 5748-1988

Méier, Rio de Janeiro, 5751-1991
Miguel Arcanjo, Paulo, 5746-1986
Miguel Paulista, Paulo, 5747-1987
Miguel Pereira, 5744-1984
Mocóca, Paulo, 5746-1986
Mogi, 5744-1984
Mogi Mirim, Paulo, 5746-1986
Mongaguá, Paulo, 5748-1988
Monte-Mor, Paulo, 5747-1987
Montes Claros, Minas Gerais, 5748-1988
Moreira César, Paulo, 5751-1991
Moreno, Pernambuco, 5752-1992
Morretes, Paraná, 5748-1988
Morumbi, Paulo, 5750-1990
Mosqueiro, Pará, 5748-1988
Muriquí, Rio de Janeiro, 5748-1988
Nadir, Paulo, 5752-1992
Natal, Rio Grande do Norte, 5747-1987
Navegantes, Paulo, 5748-1988
Nilópolis, 5744-1984
Niterói, 5744-1984
Nova Friburgo, 5744-1984
Nova Hamburgo, 5745-1985
Nova Iguaçú, 5744-1984
Nova Jerusalém, Pernambuco, 5752-1992
Nova Lima, 5744-1984
Nova Odessa, 5744-1984
Óbidos, 5746-1986
Ojeíno de Mello, Paulo, 5751-1991
Olaria, Rio de Janeiro, 5751-1991
Olímpia, Paulo, 5746-1986
Olinda, 5745-1985
Osasco, 5744-1984
Ouro Preto, 5744-1984
Palmares, Pernambuco, 5752-1992
Paquetá, Rio de Janeiro, 5748-1988
Paranaguá, 5744-1984
Parati, Paulo, 5748-1988
Paratibe, Pernambuco, 5752-1992
Parintins, 5746-1986
Parque das Fontes, Paulo, 5752-1992
Passo Fundo, 5744-1984
Passos, Minas Gerais, 5748-1988
Pato Branco, Paraná, 5748-1988
Paubá, Paulo, 5747-1987
Paulínea, 5744-1984
Paulista, Pernambuco, 5752-1992
Paulo, 5738-1978, 5748-1988, 5752-1992
Paulo, Beit HaKnesset Tzach, 5746-1986
Paulo, Oholei Yosef Yitzchác Lubavitch, 5751-1991
Paulo, Rebbetzin Chaya Mushka School, 5751-1991
Pedra do Baú, Paulo, 5752-1992
Pedro, 5744-1984
Pedro da Aldeia, Rio de Janeiro, 5744-1984, 5748-1988
Pedro do Rio, Rio de Janeiro, 5748-1988
Pelotas, Rio Grande, 5744-1984
Penha, Rio de Janeiro, 5750-1990
Península, Paulo, 5748-1988
Perdizes, Beis Chabad, Paulo, 5750-1990
Perequê, Paulo, 5748-1988
Pernambuco, Paulo, 5748-1988
Peruíbe, Paulo, 5746-1986
Pesqueiro, Pernambuco, 5752-1992
Petrópolis, 5742-1982
Petrópolis, Yeshivá Machané Israel, 5748-1988
Pindamonhangaba, Paulo, 5747-1987
Piquete, Paulo, 5751-1991
Piracicaba, 5744-1984
Pirapora, Paulo, 5751-1991
Pirassununga, 5744-1984
Pitangueiras, Paulo, 5748-1988
Poços de Caldas, 5744-1984
Ponta Grossa, 5744-1984
Porto Alegre, 5744-1984
Porto de Galinha, Pernambuco, 5752-1992
Porto Feliz, Paulo, 5751-1991
Porto União, Catarina, 5748-1988
Praça da Bandeira, Rio de Janeiro, 5751-1991
Praia Grande, 5744-1984
Presidente Prudente, Paulo, 5746-1986
Quatro Irmãos, Rio Grande do Sul, 5746-1986
Queimados Estado, Rio de Janeiro, 5750-1990
Queluz, Paulo, 5751-1991
Quirim, Paulo, 5751-1991
Ramos, Rio de Janeiro, 5751-1991
Recife, Beis Chabad, Pernambuco, 5752-1992
Recife, 5742-1982
Resende, 5744-1984
Riachuelo, Rio de Janeiro, 5751-1991
Ribeirão Pires, 5744-1984

Ribeirão Preto, 5744-1984
Rio Claro, 5744-1984
Rio Comprido, Rio de Janeiro, 5751-1991
Rio das Ostras, 5744-1984
Rio de Janeiro, 5739-1979
Rio Grande, Rio Grande do Sul, 5746-1986
Rio Negrinho, Catarina, 5748-1988
Roque, 5744-1984
Rosário, 5745-1985
Roseira, Paulo, 5751-1991
Rudge Ramos, Paulo, 5750-1990
Saco do Ribeira, Paulo, 5748-1988
Salgadinho, Pernambuco, 5752-1992
Salto, Paulo, 5750-1990
Salvador, Bahia, 5745-1985
Sanatórios, Paulo, 5752-1992
Santana do Parnaíba, 5744-1984
Santarém, 5746-1986
Santos, 5744-1984
Saquarema, 5744-1984
Sebastião, Paulo, 5747-1987
Sebastião do Sul, Rio Grande do Sul, 5747-1987
Serra Negra, 5744-1984
Silveiras, Paulo, 5751-1991
Sobradinho, Distrito Federal, 5746-1986
Soledade de Minas, 5744-1984
Sorocaba, 5744-1984
Sumaré, Paulo, 5751-1991
Suzano, 5744-1984
Tabatinga, Paulo, 5748-1988
Taboão da Serra, 5744-1984
Taguatinga, Distrito Federal, 5746-1986
Tamandaré, Pernambuco, 5752-1992
Tambaré, Paulo, 5750-1990
Taquaral, Paulo, 5752-1992
Taubaté, 5744-1984
Teresina, Piauí, 5746-1986
Teresópolis, 5744-1984
Terra Preta, 5745-1985
Machané Gan Israel - Pardes Chana.
Tiago, Paulo, 5748-1988
Tietê, Paulo, 5750-1990
Tijuca, Lubavitch House, Rio de Janeiro, 5750-1990
Timbaúba, Pernambuco, 5752-1992
Tombo, Paulo, 5748-1988
Toque - Toque, Paulo, 5748-1988
Toque - Toque Pequeno, Paulo, 5748-1988
Três Barras, Paraná, 5748-1988
Três Corações, 5744-1984
Três Ladeiras, Pernambuco, 5752-1992
Três Rios, 5744-1984
Tupancireta, Rio Grande do Sul, 5746-1986
Ubatuba, Paulo, 5747-1987
União da Vitória, Paraná, 5748-1988
Uruguaiana, 5745-1985
Utinga, Paulo, 5750-1990
Vale Encantado, Paulo, 5752-1992
Valinhos, 5744-1984
Vargem Grande do Sul, Paulo, 5746-1986
Várzea, Paulo, 5746-1986
Vassouras, 5744-1984
Viamon, Rio Grande do Sul, 5746-1986
Vicente, 5744-1984
Vigório Geral, Rio de Janeiro, 5750-1990
Vila Abernésia, Paulo, 5752-1992
Vila Albertina, Paulo, 5752-1992
Vila Bela, Paulo, 5752-1992
Vila Cláudia, Paulo, 5752-1992
Vila Cris-ina, Paulo, 5752-1992
Vila Inglesa, Paulo, 575 2-1992
Vila Isabel, Rio de Janeiro, 5751-1991
Vila Loli, Paulo, 5752-1992
Vila Maria, Paulo, 5752-1992
Vila Naír, Paulo, 5752-1992
Vila Nova Suiça, Paulo, 5752-1992
Vila Paulista, Paulo, 5752-1992
Vila Rosali, Rio de Janeiro, 5751-1991
Vila Telma, Paulo, 5752-1992
Villa Jigle, Paulo, 5752-1992
Vinhedo, Paulo, 5751-1991
Visconde de Mauá, Rio de Janeiro, 5748-1988
Vitória, 5747-1987
Vitório Antão, Pernambuco, 5752-1992
Volta Redonda, 5744-1984

Bulgaria

Sofia, 5745-1985

Burma

Rangoon, 5746-1986

Canada

Abbottsford, B.C., 5744-1984

Agathe, Que, 5744-1984
Amherst, N.S., 5744-1984
Ancaster, Ont, 5747-1987
Antigonish, N.S., 5744-1984
Bathurst, N.B., 5744-1984
Beaconsfield, Que, 5746-1986
Boisbrand, Que, 5746-1986
Brandon, Man, 5747-1987
Brantford, Ont, 5744-1984
Bridgewater, N.S., 5744-1984
Brockville, Ont, 5746-1986
Bromount, Que, 5746-1986
Brossard, Que, 5746-1986
Burnaby, B.C., 5744-1984
Calgary, Alta, 5744-1984
Cambridge, Ont, 5744-1984
Campbell River, B.C., 5744-1984
Catharines, Ont, 5744-1984
Charlesbourg, Que, 5746-1986
Charlottetown, PEI, 5744-1984
Chilliwack, B.C., 5744-1984
Comox, B.C., 5744-1984
Coquitlam, B.C., 5744-1984
Corner Brook, Nfld, 5744-1984
Cornwall, Ont, 5746-1986
Cote Luc, Que, 5744-1984
Cranbrook, B.C., 5744-1984
Cumberland, B.C., 5744-1984
Dartmouth, N.S., 5744-1984
Delta, B.C., 5744-1984
Dollard des Ormeaux, Que, 5744-1984
Drummondville, Que, 5746-1986
Dundas, Ont, 5745-1985
Edmonton, Alta, 5744-1984
Edmundston, N.B., 5744-1984
Fredericton, N.B., 5744-1984
Gabriola Island, B.C., 5744-1984
Gibsons, B.C., 5744-1984
Glace Bay, N.S., 5744-1984
Grand Forks, B.C., 5744-1984
Grandby, Que, 5746-1986
Guelph, Ont, 5744-1984
Halifax, N.S., 5744-1984
Hamilton, Ont, 5744-1984
Hampstead, Que, 5744-1984
Hawksbury, Ont, 5746-1986
Hudson, Que, 5746-1986
Hull, Que, 5746-1986
Huntington, Que, 5746-1986
Invermere, B.C., 5744-1984
John, N.B., 5744-1984
John's, Nfld, 5744-1984
Joliette, Que, 5746-1986
Kaslo, B.C., 5744-1984
Kelowna, B.C., 5744-1984
Kemptville, Ont, 5746-1986
Kingston, Ont, 5744-1984
Kirkland, Que, 5746-1986
Kirkland Lake, Ont, 5744-1984
Kitchener-Waterloo, Ont, 5744-1984
Printed in Kitchener.
Kitchener-Waterloo, Ont, 5744-1984
Printed in Waterloo.
Lac Desert, Que, Camp Gan Yisroel, 5742-1982
Langley, B.C., 5744-1984
Lassal, Qsue, 5746-1986
Lauran, Que, 5744-1984
Laval, Que, 5744-1984
Lennoxville, Que, 5746-1086
Lethbridge, Alta, 5747-1987
Lions Bay, B.C., 5744-1984
Logan Lake, B.C., 5744-1984
London, Ont, 5744-1984
Maple Ridge, B.C., 5744-1984
Marine Heights, Que, 5746-1986
Markham, Ont, 5746-1986
Matsqui, B.C., 5744-1984
Mission, B.C., 5744-1984
Mississauga, Ont, 5744-1984
Moncton, N.B., 5744-1984
Montreal, 5732-1972
Montreal-Ouest, Que, 5746-1986
Mount Royal, Que, 5744-1984
Nanaimo, B.C., 5744-1984
Nelson, B.C., 5744-1984
New Glasgow, N.S., 5744-1984
New Glasgow, Que, 5746-1986
Newcastle, N.B., 5744-1984
Niagara Falls, Ont, 5744-1984
North Hatley, Que, 5746-1986

North Sydney, N.S., 5744-1984
North Vancouver, B.C., 5744-1984
Nunns Is., Verdun, Que, 5746-1986
Oak Bay, B.C., 5744-1984
Oshawa, Ont, 5744-1984
Ottowa, Ont, 5744-1984
Outremont, Que, 5744-1984
Oyama, B.C., 5744-1984
Penticton, B.C., 5744-1984
Peterborough, Ont, 5744-1984
Pierrefonds, Que, 5746-1986
Pointeclaire, Que, 5744-1984
Port Moody, B.C., 5744-1984
Powell River, B.C., 5744-1984
Prescott, Ont, 5746-1986
Prince George, B.C., 5744-1984
Prince Rupert, B.C., 5744-1984
Quebec City, 5744-1984
Regina, Sask, 5747-1987
Richmond, B.C., 5744-1984
Richmond, Ont, Beis HaKnesset Etz Chaim, 5747-1987
Rossland, B.C., 5744-1984
Saanich, B.C., 5744-1984
Sackville, N.B., 5744-1984
Salt Spring Island, B.C., 5744-1984
Saskatoon, Sask, 5747-1987
Sawyerville, Que, 5746-1986
Sherbrooke, Que, 5744-1984
Sidney, B.C., 5744-1984
Smithers, B.C., 5744-1984
Soffi, Que, 5746-1986
Squamish, B.C., 5744-1984
Surrey, B.C., 5744-1984
Sydney, N.S.W., 5744-1984
Taylor, B.C., 5744-1984
Terrace, B.C., 5744-1984
Thunder Bay, Ont, 5744-1984
Timmins, Ont, 5744-1984
Toronto, Ont, 5744-1984
Toronto, Ont, 5744-1984
Merkaz Chabad, 770 Chabad Gate, Vaughn.
Truro, N.S., 5744-1984
Tumbler Ridge, B.C., 5744-1984
Val d'Or, Que, 5746-1986
Val David, Que, 5746-1986
Val Marine, Que, 5746-1986
Vancouver, B.C., 5744-1984
Vernon, B.C., 5744-1984
Victoria, B.C., 5744-1984
Welland, Ont, 5753-1993
West Vancouver, B.C., 5744-1984
Westminster, B.C., 5744-1984
Westmount, Que, 5744-1984
White Rock, B.C., 5744-1984
Whitehorse, B.C., 5744-1984
Windsor, Ont, 5744-1984
Winnipeg, Man, 5744-1984
Woodstock, N.B., 5744-1984
Yarmouth, N.S., 5744-1984
Yellowknife, NWT, 5744-1984

Chile

Antofagasta, 5744-1984
Arica, 5744-1984
Concepcion, 5744-1984
Copiapo, 5744-1984
Equiqui, 5744-1984
Santiago, 5738-1978
Temuco, 5744-1984
Valdivia, 5744-1984
Valparaiso, 5744-1984
Vina del Mar, 5744-1984

China

Bei Bei, 5752-1992
District of Changqin, Sichuan Province.
Beijing, 5744-1984
Guangzhou, 5744-1984
Shanghai, 5703-1943
Shanghai, 5743-1983

Colombia

Andres, 5745-1985
Armania, 5745-1985
Barranquilla, 5744-1984
Bogota, 5738-1978
Booga, 5745-1985
Cali, 5744-1984
Cartagena, 5744-1984
Cartago, 5745-1985
Cucuta, 5744-1984
Manizales, 5744-1984
Medellin, 5744-1984

Palmira, 5744-1984
Papayan, 5745-1985
Pasto, 5744-1984
Costa Rica
José, 5742-1982
Cuba
Havana, 5744-1984
Cyprus
Nicosia, 5739-1979
Czechoslovakia
Prague, 5740-1980
Denmark
Copenhagen, 5738-1978
Dominican Republic
Domingo, 5744-1984
East Germany
East Berlin, 5744-1984
Ecuador
Quito, 5743-1983
Egypt
Alexandria, 5744-1984
Cairo, 5744-1984
El Salvador, 5744-1984
England
Albans, Herts, 5744-1984
Annes-on-Sea, Lancs, 5745-1985
Basingstoke, Hants, 5746-1986
Birmingham, 5744-1984
Blackburn, Lancs, 5745-1985
Blackpool, Lancs, 5745-1985
Bournemouth, 5744-1984
Bradford, W. Yorks, 5744-1984
Brighton, E. Sussex, 5744-1984
Bristol, Avon, 5744-1984
Cambridge, 5744-1984
Chatham, Kent, 5746-1986
Cheltenham, Glos, 5746-1986
Cockfosters, Herts, 5746-1986
Colchester, Essex, 5746-1986
Coventry, W. Midlands, 5746-1986
Cricklewood, London, 5749-1989
Crumpsal, Manchester, 5746-1986
Machon Levi Yitzchak.
East Grinstead, W. Sussex, 5744-1984
Edgware, Middx, 5744-1984
Egham, Surrey, 5746-1986
Enfield, Middx, 5746-1986
Finchley, London, 5746-1986
Gateshead, Tyne & Wear, 5744-1984
Golders Green, London, 5745-1985
Hale, Cheshire, 5746-1986
Hampstead, London, 5746-1986
Hampstead Garden Suburb, London, 5744-1984
Hendon, London, 5746-1986
Highgate, London, 5746-1986
Hull, Humberside, 5746-1986
Ilford, Essex, 5744-1984
John's Wood, London, 5746-1986
Kensington, London, 5746-1986
Kingsbury, London, 5746-1986
Kingston, Surrey, 5746-1986
Leeds, W. Yorks, 5744-1984
Leicester, 5744-1984
Liverpool, 5744-1984
London, 5732-1972, 5733-1973, 5738-1978 , 5740-1980
Luton, Beds, 5744-1984
Maidenhead, Berks, 5744-1984
Manchester, 5744-1984
Margate, Kent, 5746-1986
Mayfair, London, 5746-1986
Mill Hill, London, 5746-1986
Newcastle, Tyne & Wear, 5746-1986
Northampton, 5744-1984
Nottingham, 5744-1984
Oldham, Manchester, 5746-1986
Oxford, 5744-1984
Pinner, Middx, 5746-1986
Preston, Lancs, 5745-1985
Prestwich, Manchester, 5746-1986
Reading, Berks, 5744-1984
Rochdale, Manchester, 5746-1986
Sale, Cheshire, 5745-1985
Salford, 5746-1986
Sheffield, 5744-1984
Solihull, W. Midlands, 5746-1986
Southend, Essex, 5744-1984
Southport, Merseyside, 5745-1985
Staines, Middx, 5746-1986
Stamford Hill, London, 5746-1986
Stoke-on-Trent, Staffs, 5746-1986

Sunderland, 5744-1984
Wallingford, Oxon, 5744-1984
Welwyn Garden City, Herts, 5746-1986
Wembley, Middx, 5746-1986
Willesden, London, 5746-1986
Wolverhampton, W. Midlands, 5746-1986
Worthing, W. Sussex, 5746-1986
York, 5746-1986

Eretz Yisroel

Achiezer, 5745-1985
Achihud, 5744-1984
Achitov, 5752-1992
Achuzat Shoshana, 5745-1985
Achva, 5745-1985
Adanim-Neve Neeman, 5745-1985
Aderet, 5745-1985
Adi, 5745-1985
Adirim, 5746-1986
Admot Yishai, (Tal Romaida), 5746-1986
Afula, 5739-1979
Afula, Kele Schata Prison, 5745-1985
Afula Ilit, 5744-1984
Ako, 5740-1980
Alfei Menashe, 5745-1985
Alifalt, 5745-1985
Alma, 5745-1985
Alone Aba, 5744-1984
Alone Bashan, 5744-1984
Amatziya, 5745-1985
Ameka, 5745-1985
Amirim, 5744-1984
Ani'am, 5744-1984
Arad, 5744-1984
Arbel, 5745-1985
Argaman, Jordan Valley, 5750-1990
Ariel, 5745-1985
Ariel-Kiriyat Hamada, 5750-1990
Army-South Region Base, 5745-1985
Ashdod, 5744-1984
Ashdod-Army Naval Base, 5745-1985
Ashkelon, Ganei Shulamit Hotel, 5752-1992
Ashkelon, 5744-1984
Ateret, 5750-1990
Atidim, Neve Sharet-Laser Industries, 5746-1986
Atlit, 5744-1984
Atzmon, Gush Segev, 5744-1984
Atzmonah, Gaza Strip, 5750-1990
Avi'el, 5745-1985
Avichaiyl, 5745-1985
Aviezer, 5745-1985
Avital, 5744-1984
Avnei Eitan, Golan Heights, 5744-1984
Azariya, 5745-1985
Badolach, Jordan Valley, 5750-1990
Bakua, 5745-1985
Balfouriya, 5745-1985
Baniya, 5745-1985
Bar Giyora, 5745-1985
Bar-Ilan University, 5745-1985
Barkan, 5745-1985
Barkan Industrial Zone, 5750-1990
Barutiym, 5748-1988
Bat Yam, 5744-1984
Batset, 5744-1984
Batzra, 5745-1985
Be'er Ora, 5745-1985
Be'er Sheva, 5744-1984
Be'er Sheva, Shechuna Gimel (2nd. ed.), 5745-1985
Be'er Tuviya, 5744-1984
Be'er Yaakov, 5745-1985
Bekaot, Jordan Valley, 5750-1990
Ben Dor, 5744-1984
Beracha, 5744-1984
Bet Arif, 5745-1985
Bet Ariyeh, 5750-1990
Bet Berl, Tel Aviv, 5745-1985
Bet Chashmonaiy, 5745-1985
Bet Chilkiya, 5744-1984
Bet Dagan, 5745-1985
Bet Daras Otzvat Havzaka (Army Base), 5744-1984
Bet E-l, 5744-1984
Bet Gamliel, 5744-1984
Bet Guvrin - Army Base, 5745-1985
Bet Halevi, 5745-1985
Bet Lechem, 5744-1984
In proximity to Rachel Imeinu's Tomb
Bet Lechem Haglilit, 5744-1984
Bet Schneerson-Slonim-Chevron, 5751-1991
Bet She'an, 5744-1984
Bet She'arim, 5745-1985

Bet Shemesh, 5744-1984
Bet Uziel, 5745-1985
Bet Yosef, 5744-1984
Betar, 5750-1990
Binyamina, 5748-1988
Biriya, 5744-1984
Bnei Brak, 5740-198C
Bnei Dror, 5745-1985
Bnei Tziyon, 5745-1985
Bnei Yehuda, Golan Heights, 5744-1984
Branches of N'shei u'Bnos Chabad, 5744-1984
Brosh, 5744-1984
Burgata, 5745-1985
Ceasarea (Keysaria), 5751-1991
Chadera, 5744-1984
Chadid, 5745-1985
Chadnas, Golan Heights, 5750-1990
Chagor, 5745-1985
Chamrah, Jordan Valley, 5750-1990
Chananit, 5744-1984
Chaniel, 5745-1985
Charutzim, 5745-1985
Chashmonaiym, 5750-1990
Chatzor Army Base, 5744-1984
Chatzor Haglilit, 5744-1984
Chazon Yechezkel, 5745-1985
Cherut, 5745-1985
Chevron, 5734-1974
Chevron, 5744-1984
Chiriya, , 5744-1984
Organic Vegetables Industry, Gehah Rd.
Chotzvah, Kvish HaArava, 5745-1985
Chulon, 5742-1982
Dganiya Aleph, 5744-1984
Dganiya Bet, 5744-1984
Dimona, 5744-1984
Efrat, 5745-1985, 5750-1990
Egur, 5745-1985
Eilat, 5742-1982
Ein Eylah, 5751-1991
Ein HaEmek, 5745-1985
Ein Vered, 5745-1985
Ein Yahav, Kvish HaArava, 5745-1985
Eiynav, 5748-1988
Elazar, 5745-1985
Eli Ad, Golan Heights, 5744-1984
Eli Sinai, 5745-1985
Eliyachin, 5749-1989
Eliyakim, 5745-1985
Elkana, 5745-1985
Elon, 5744-1984
Elon More - Gush Etzyyon, 5744-1984
Elukesh, 5752-1992
Emanuel, 5744-1984
Eshbol, 5745-1985
Eshtaul, 5745-1985
Even Sapir, 5745-1985
Even Yehuda, 5744-1984
Gadera, 5744-1984
Gadid-Gaza Strip, 5745-1985
Gadish, 5746-1986
Gan Chaiym, 5745-1985
Gan Hadarom, 5745-1985
Gan Or, Gaza Strip, 5750-1990
Gan Yavneh, 5744-1984
Ganei Am, 5745-1985
Ganei Tikva, 5744-1984
Ganital-Gaza Strip, 5745-1985
Gaza - Military Base, 5745-1985
General Histadrut of Eretz Israel, 5752-1992
Geulim, 5748-1988
Gidona, 5744-1984
Gilon, Gush Segev, 5744-1984
Ginot Shomron, 5745-1985
Gitot, Jordan Valley, 5750-1990
Givat Ada, 5745-1985
Givat Eidah, Chabad School, 5752-1992
Givat Hamore, 5744-1984
Givat Hazeitim, Lod, 5744-1984
Givat Koach, 5745-1985
Givat Shapira, Yerushalaim, 5744-1984
Givat Shmuel, 5744-1984
Givat Washington, 5744-1984
Givat Ya'arim, 5745-1985
Givat Yeshaiyahu, 5745-1985
Givat Yoav, Golan Heights, 5744-1984
Givat Zeev, 5745-1985
Givat Ziv, 5745-1985
Givataiym, 5745-1985
Givon Hachadashah (New Givon), 5745-1985

Hadar Am, 5749-1989
Haifa, 5740-1980
Haifa, 5741-1981
Har Adar, 5750-1990
Har Tziyon, 5744-1984
In proximity to Dovid HaMelech's Tomb
Hazor'iym, 5744-1984
Hertzliya, 5744-1984
Hod Hasharon, 5745-1985
Idan, Kvish HaArava, 5745-1985
Ilaniya, 5745-1985
Israeli Army Rabbinate, 5744-1984
By The IDF Printing House
Jebalya-Army Base, 5745-1985
Kachal, 5745-1985
Kadarim, 5744-1984
Kadima, 5745-1985
Kalanit, 5745-1985
Kamon, Gush Segev, 5744-1984
Kanot, 5745-1985
Karmiel, 5744-1984
Karnei Shomron, 5744-1984
Katif-Gaza Strip, 5745-1985
Katzrin, Golan Heights, 5744-1984
Kedumim, 5745-1985
Kerem Maharal, 5748-1988
Keshet, Golan Heights, 5744-1984
Kfar Achim, 5745-1985
Kfar Adumim, 5745-1985
Kfar Aviv, 5745-1985
Kfar Azri'el, 5744-1984
Kfar Baruch, 5745-1985
Kfar Bin Nun, 5745-1985
Kfar Chabad, 5720-1960, 5723-1963, 5725-1965, 5726-1966, 5727-1967, 5729-1969, 5732-1972, 5733-1973, 5734-1974, 5736-1976, 5737-1977, 5738-1978, 5740-1980, 5741-1981. 5743-1983, 5749-1989
Kfar Chabad, 5744-1984
Shikunim Chadashim.
Kfar Chabad, 5744-1984
Beis HaKnesset Beis Menachem.
Kfar Chabad, 5744-1984
Yeshivat Tomchei Tmimim.
Kfar Chabad, 5745-1985
Beis Agudas Chasidei Chabad, Ohel Y. Y. Lubavitch.
Kfar Chabad, 5746-1986
Beis Agudas Chasidei Chabad, Ohel Y. Y. Lubavitch.
Kfar Chabad Bet, 5744-1984
Beis Rivkah.
Kfar Darom-Gaza Strip, 5745-1985
Kfar Gideon, 5744-1984
Kfar Hanoar Hadati, 5744-1984
In proximity to Kfar Chasidim
Kfar Hanoar Kedma, 5745-1985
Kfar Hanoar Neve Hadasa, 5745-1985
Kfar Hanoar Nitzanim, 5745-1985
Kfar Hanoar Raziel, 5745-1985
Kfar HaRif, 5744-1984
Kfar HaRo'e, 5744-1984
Kfar Hes, 5745-1985
Kfar Kish, 5744-1984
Kfar Maimon, 5744-1984
Kfar Malal, 5745-1985
Kfar Mechola, 5744-1984
Kfar Mordechai, 5745-1985
Kfar Ramah, 5744-1984
In proximity to Shmuel HaNavi's Tomb.
Kfar Rut, 5750-1990
Kfar Saba, 5744-1984
Kfar Shamai, 5744-1984
Kfar Shmariyahu, 5745-1985
Kfar Shmuel, 5745-1985
Kfar Silver, 5745-1985
Kfar Sirkin, 5745-1985
Kfar Tapuach, 5744-1984
Kfar Tavor, 5744-1984
Kfar Uriya, 5745-1985
Kfar Warburg, 5744-1984
Kfar Ya'avetz, 5745-1985
Kfar Yam, Gaza Strip, 5750-1990
Kfar Yechezkel, 5744-1984
Kfar Yehoshua, 5745-1985
Kfar Yona, 5745-1985
Kfar Yuval, 5745-1985
Kfar Zechariya, 5745-1985
Kfar Zeitim, 5744-1984
Kibbutz Afik, Golan Heights, 5744-1984
Kibbutz Afikim, 5745-1985

Kibbutz Alonim, 5745-1985
Kibbutz Alumim, 5744-1984
Kibbutz Alumot, 5744-1984
Kibbutz Ayal, 5744-1984
Kibbutz Ayelet Hashachar, 5745-1985
Kibbutz Be'erot Yitzchak, 5744-1984
Kibbutz Bet Guvrin, 5744-1984
Kibbutz Chafetz Chaiym, 5744-1984
Kibbutz Chamadiya, 5744-1984
Kibbutz Chanita, Golan Heights, 5744-1984
Kibbutz Chatzerim, 5745-1985
Kibbutz Cheftziba, 5745-1985
Kibbutz Chulda, 5745-1985
Kibbutz Chulta, 5745-1985
Kibbutz Dafna, 5745-1985
Kibbutz Dalia, 5745-1985
Kibbutz Dovrat, 5746-1986
Kibbutz Eilot, 5745-1985
Kibbutz Ein Charod (Ichud), 5744-1984
Kibbutz Ein Charod (Me'uchad), 5744-1984
Kibbutz Ein Gedi, 5744-1984
Kibbutz Ein Gev, 5744-1984
Kibbutz Ein HaNetziv, 5744-1984
Kibbutz Ein Tzurim, 5744-1984
Kibbutz Ein Zivan, Golan Heights, 5744-1984
Kibbutz El-Rom, Golan Heights, 5744-1984
Kibbutz Enat, 5744-1984
Kibbutz Frud, 5744-1984
Kibbutz Galil-Yam, 5744-1984
Kibbutz Gazit, 5746-1986
Kibbutz Gesher Haziv, 5744-1984
Kibbutz Geva, 5745-1985
Kibbutz Gevar'am, 5745-1985
Kibbutz Gevat, 5744-1984
Kibbutz Gevim, 5744-1984
Kibbutz Gezer, 5744-1984
Kibbutz Gilgal, Jordan Valley, 5750-1990
Kibbutz Ginosar, 5744-1984
Kibbutz Givat Brenner, 5744-1984
Kibbutz Givat Hashlosha, 5745-1985
Kibbutz Gonen, 5744-1984
Kibbutz Grufit, 5745-1985
Kibbutz Hardof, 5745-1985
Kibbutz HaSolelim, 5744-1984
Kibbutz Hazore'a, 5746-1986
Kibbutz Kavri, 5744-1984
Kibbutz Ketura, 5745-1985
Kibbutz Kfar Aza, 5744-1984
Kibbutz Kfar Etziyon, 5745-1985
Kibbutz Kfar Giladi, 5744-1984
Kibbutz Kfar Glickson, 5744-1984
Kibbutz Kfar Hachoresh, 5745-1985
Kibbutz Kfar Hamacabi, 5744-1984
Kibbutz Lavi, 5745-1985
Kibbutz Lochamei Hagetaot, 5744-1984
Kibbutz Lotam, 5745-1985
Kibbutz Ma'agan, 5744-1984
Kibbutz Ma'agan Michael, 5744-1984
Kibbutz Ma'ale HaGilboa, 5744-1984
Kibbutz Ma'ale Tzivia, 5745-1985
Kibbutz Malkiya, 5745-1985
Kibbutz Masada, 5745-1985
Kibbutz Matzuva, 5744-1984
Kibbutz Mazre'a, 5746-1986
Kibbutz Mefalsim, 5744-1984
Kibbutz Merchaviya, 5746-1986
Kibbutz Mesilot, 5745-1985
Kibbutz Misgav Am, 5744-1984
Kibbutz Mishaavei Sadeh, 5745-1985
Kibbutz Mishmar David, 5745-1985
Kibbutz Mishmar Ha'emek, 5745-1985
Kibbutz Mishmar Hasharon, 5745-1985
Kibbutz Moran, 5744-1984
Kibbutz Na'an, 5744-1984
Kibbutz Na'aran, Jordan Valley, 5750-1990
Kibbutz Nachal Oz, 5744-1984
Kibbutz Nachsholim, 5744-1984
Kibbutz Nachshon, 5745-1985
Kibbutz Netzarim-Gaza Strip, 5745-1985
Kibbutz Netzer Sereni, 5745-1985
Kibbutz Netziv Ha-35, 5745-1985
Kibbutz Neve Ativ, Golan Heights, 5750-1990
Kibbutz Nir Am, 5744-1984
Kibbutz Nir Eliyahu, 5745-1985
Kibbutz Ofek, 5744-1984
Kibbutz Or Haner, 5744-1984
Kibbutz Ortal, Golan Heights, 5744-1984
Kibbutz Palmachim, 5745-1985
Kibbutz Ramat David, 5745-1985
Kibbutz Ramat Hakovesh, 5745-1985

Kibbutz Ramat Yochanan, 5744-1984
Kibbutz Ravid, 5745-1985
Kibbutz Regavim, 5744-1984
Kibbutz Reshafim, 5745-1985
Kibbutz Revivim, 5745-1985
Kibbutz Sa'ad, 5744-1984
Kibbutz Sde Eliyyahu, 5744-1984
Kibbutz Sde Nachum, 5744-1984
Kibbutz Sdot Yam, 5744-1984
Kibbutz Sha'albim, 5744-1984
Kibbutz Shfa'iym, 5745-1985
Kibbutz Shizafon, 5745-1985
Kibbutz Shluchot, 5744-1984
Kibbutz Tel Katzir, 5745-1985
Kibbutz Tel Yosef, 5744-1984
Kibbutz Tzira'ah, 5745-1985
Kibbutz Tzova, 5745-1985
Kibbutz Urim, 5745-1985
Kibbutz Usha, 5744-1984
Kibbutz Yardena, 5744-1984
Kibbutz Yasur, 5745-1985
Kibbutz Yazra'el, 5744-1984
Kibbutz Yifat, 5744-1984
Kibbutz Yiftach, 5745-1985
Kidmont Tzvi, Golan Heights, 5750-1990
Kidron, 5745-1985
Kinus Hashluchim, Eilat, 5748-1988
Kiryat Arba-Chevron, 5746-1986
Kiryat Ata, 5744-1984
Kiryat Bialik, 5744-1984
Kiryat Bialik, Chabad House, 5750-1990
Kiryat Binyamin-Kiryat Ata, 5744-1984
Kiryat Chabad, Safed, 5744-1984
Kiryat Chaiym, 5744-1984
Kiryat Ekron, 5752-1992
Kiryat Gat, 5741-1981
Kiryat Haiyovel, Yerushalaim, 5744-1984
Kiryat Malachi, 5744-1984
Yeshivat Tomchei Tmimim Nachalat Har Chabad.
Kiryat Motzkin, 5744-1984
Kiryat Nachum, 5746-1986
Kiryat Netafim, 5745-1985
Kiryat Ono, 5744-1984
Kiryat Shemona, 5744-1984
Kiryat Shmuel, 5744-1984
Kiryat Tibon, 5744-1984
Kiryat Yam, 5744-1984
Kislon, 5745-1985
Kochav Yair, 5745-1985
Kochot Sade Army Base, 5744-1984
Kotel Hama'aravi, Yerushalaim, 5744-1984
Kuranit, Gush Segev, 5744-1984
Kvutzat Kineret , 5744-1984
Kvutzat Shiller, 5744-1984
Kvutzat Yavne, 5744-1984
Lachish, 5745-1985
Liman, 5744-1984
Livnim, 5748-1988
Liyon-Srigim, 5745-1985
Lod, 5740-1980
Lod (Airport), 5744-1984
Luzit, 5745-1985
Ma'ale Efraim, Jordan Valley, 5750-1990
Ma'aleh Adumim, Yerushalaim, 5744-1984
Ma'aleh Gamla, Golan Heights, 5744-1984
Ma'aleh Shomron, 5745-1985
Ma'alot, 5744-1984
Machane Keren, Golan Heights, 5750-1990
Machane Ovdah Army Base, 5745-1985
Machane Rimon Army Base, 5744-1984
Machane Tze'elim Army Base, 5745-1985
Machasiya, 5745-1985
Magen Shaul, 5745-1985
Malachi-Merkaz Tovalah Army Base, 5744-1984
Manof, Gush Segev, 5745-1985
Marom Golan, Golan Heights, 5750-1990
Mass'aot Yitzchak, 5744-1984
Mata, 5745-1985
Matat, 5745-1985
Mavo Betar, 5745-1985
Mavo Dotan, 5744-1984
Mavo Mod'iyn, 5750-1990
Mazkeret Batiya, 5745-1985
Mea Shearim, Yerushalaim, 5744-1984
Rechov Baal HaTanya.
Mechura, Jordan Valley, 5750-1990
Megadim, 5748-1988
Meishar, 5745-1985
Meitav, 5745-1985
Mele'a, 5744-1984

Menachamiya, 5744-1984
Menucha, 5745-1985
Merchaviya, 5744-1984
Merkaz Chispit, Golan Heights, 5744-1984
Merkaz Ezori Kaduri, 5745-1985
Merkaz Sapir, Kvish HaArava, 5745-1985
Merkaz Shapira, 5744-1984
Mesilat Tziyon, 5745-1985
Mesuah, Jordan Valley, 5750-1990
Metula, 5744-1984
Metzad (Asfar)-Harei Chevron, 5745-1985
Mevaseret Yerushalaim, 5745-1985
Mi Ammi, 5744-1984
Michmanim, Gush Segev, 5744-1984
Midrach Oz, 5745-1985
Migdal, 5744-1984
Migdal Eder-Tzoref, 5750-1990
Migdal Haemek, 5742-1982
Migdalim, Jordan Valley, 5750-1990
Miron, 5744-1984
In proximity to RaShBYs' Tomb.
Misgav Dov, 5745-1985
Mishavim-Army Base, 5745-1985
Mishmar Eilon, 5745-1985
Mishmar Hashiv'a, 5745-1985
Mishmar Hayarden, 5745-1985
Mishmeret, 5745-1985
Mitzpe Abirim, 5745-1985
Mitzpe Aviv, Gush Segev, 5744-1984
Mitzpe Charashim, 5745-1985
Mitzpe Dovev, 5745-1985
Mitzpe Gita, 5745-1985
Mitzpe Haririt, 5744-1984
Mitzpe Hila, 5745-1985
Mitzpe Hoshaiya, 5744-1984
Mitzpe Ramon, 5744-1984
Mitzpe Yericho, 5744-1984
Moreg, Gaza Strip, 5750-1990
Moreshet, Gush Segev, 5744-1984
Moshav Achuzam, 5745-1985
Moshav Arugot, 5745-1985
Moshav Avdon, 5744-1984
Moshav Avigdor, 5745-1985
Moshav Avivim, 5749-1989
Moshav Azrikam, 5745-1985
Moshav Bareket, 5744-1984
Moshav Ben Ami, 5745-1985
Moshav Ben Zakai, 5744-1984
Moshav Bet Meiyr, 5745-1985
Moshav Bet Yehoshua, 5744-1984
Moshav Betzaron, 5745-1985
Moshav Bnei Aiysh, 5744-1984
Moshav Bnei Darom, 5745-1985
Moshav Bnei Re'em, 5745-1985
Moshav Brachiya, 5748-1988
Moshav Chatzav, 5745-1985
Moshav Chazon, 5744-1984
Moshav Chemed, 5744-1984
Moshav Chibat Tziyon, 5744-1984
Moshav Chosen, 5752-1992
Moshav Dalton, 5745-1985
Moshav Dishon, 5749-1989
Moshav Dovev, 5752-1992
Moshav Ein Yaakov, 5744-1984
Moshav Eitan, 5744-1984
Moshav Elishama, 5752-1992
Moshav Elon Hagalil, 5745-1985
Moshav Emunim, 5744-1984
Moshav Even Menachem, 5744-1984
Moshav Gamzo, 5744-1984
Moshav Ganim, 5744-1984
Moshav Ganot, 5744-1984
Moshav Gefen, 5745-1985
Moshav Giv'ati, 5744-1984
Moshav Goren, 5744-1984
Moshav Hayogev, 5745-1985
Moshav Hodaiya, 5744-1984
Moshav Kerem Ben Zimra, 5745-1985
Moshav Kineret, 5744-1984
Moshav Komemiyut, 5744-1984
Moshav Matitiyahu, 5744-1984
Moshav Mevo Choron, 5744-1984
Moshav Nechalim, 5744-1984
Moshav Noam, 5745-1985
Moshav Nov, Golan Heights, 5744-1984
Moshav Orot, 5744-1984
Moshav Regva, 5744-1984
Moshav Revaiyah, 5744-1984
Moshav Safsufa, 5745-1985
Moshav Sde Moshe, 5744-1984

Moshav Sde Uziyah, 5744-1984
Moshav Segula, 5744-1984
Moshav Shalva, 5745-1985
Moshav Shapir, 5744-1984
Moshav Sharona, 5744-1984
Moshav Shefer, 5744-1984
Moshav Shetulim, 5744-1984
Moshav Shuva, 5745-1985
Moshav Tifrach, 5752-1992
Moshav Timorim, 5744-1984
Moshav Tirosh, 5745-1985
Moshav Tzipori, 5744-1984
Moshav Uzah, 5745-1985
Moshav Ya'arah, 5744-1984
Moshav Yad Rambam, 5745-1985
Moshav Yehonatan, Golan Heights, 5744-1984
Moshav Yesodot, 5745-1985
Moshav Yinon, 5745-1985
Moshav Zeitan, 5744-1984
Moshav Zerachiya, 5744-1984
Motza, 5745-1985
Mt. Hermon, 5744-1984
N'veh Yaakov, Yerushalaim, 5744-1984
Nacham, 5745-1985
Nachlat Har Chabad, 5738-1978
Nachlat Har Chabad, B'Kiryat Malachi, 5744-1984
Nachlat Yehuda, 5744-1984
Nachliel, 5750-1990
Nahariya, 5744-1984
Natzeret-Ilit, 5744-1984
Ne'ot Golan, Golan Heights, 5744-1984
Ne'ot Mordechai, 5745-1985
Nebatim, 5745-1985
Nebatim Army Base, 5745-1985
Nehalal, 5744-1984
Nehora, 5745-1985
Neot Sadeh, Gaza Strip, 5750-1990
Nes Harim, 5745-1985
Nes Tziyona, 5744-1984
Netaniya, 5744-1984
Netiv Ha'asara, 5745-1985
Netiv Hagedud, Jordan Valley, 5750-1990
Netiv Hashaiyara, 5744-1984
Netivot, 5744-1984
Netzer Chazani-Gaza Strip, 5745-1985
Neve Dkalim, 5744-1984
Neve Monzon, 5744-1984
Neve Tzof, 5745-1985
Neve Yamin, 5745-1985
Neve Yerek, 5745-1985
Neve Zohar-Yam Hamelach, 5744-1984
Nir Banim, 5744-1984
Nir Chen, 5745-1985
Nir Etziyon, 5744-1984
Nir Galim, 5744-1984
Yeshivat Bnei Akiva Neve Hertzog.
Nir Galim, 5744-1984
Nir Israel, 5744-1984
Nir Tzvi, 5745-1985
Nir Yafe, 5744-1984
Nisanit, 5745-1985
Nofim-Shomron, 5750-1990
Nogah, 5745-1985
Ofakim, 5744-1984
Ofara, 5745-1985
Omer, 5744-1984
Or Akiva, 5748-1988
Or Yehuda, 5744-1984
Orah, 5745-1985
Oshrat, 5745-1985
Otzem, 5745-1985
Otzem, Golan Heights, 5750-1990
Otzvat Hashiriyon Army Base, 5744-1984
Otzvat Sinai Army Base, 5744-1984
Pa'amei 5707, 5745-1985
Padiya, 5745-1985
Paran, Kvish HaArava, 5745-1985
Pardes Chana, 5744-1984
Pardes Katz, 5745-1985
Pardesia, 5745-1985
Peki'in, 5744-1984
Peki'in Hachadashah (New Peki'in), 5749-1989
Perzon, 5745-1985
Petach Tikvah, 5742-1982
Petachya, 5745-1985
Pikud Darom Army Base, 5745-1985
Pisgat Ze'ev, 5749-1989
Poriya, Neve Oved, 5744-1984
Poriya, Kfar Avoda, 5745-1985
Ptzael, Jordan Valley, 5750-1990

Ra'anana, 5744-1984
Rafiach Yam-Gaza Strip, 5745-1985
Rakefet, Gush Segev, 5744-1984
Ram On, 5744-1984
Ramat Aviv, 5748-1988
Ramat Eliyahu, 5744-1984
Ramat Gan, 5744-1984
Ramat Gan, Israeli Diamond Exchange, 5752-1992
Ramat Hasharon, 5744-1984
Ramat Hashavim, 5745-1985
Ramat Magshimim, Golan Heights, 5744-1984
Ramat Raziel, 5745-1985
Ramat Yishai, 5744-1984
Ramle, 5741-1981
Ramot, Yerushalaim, 5744-1984
Ramot, Golan Heights, 5744-1984
Ramot Naftali, 5745-1985
Rechov, 5744-1984
Rechovot, 5743-1983
Refuat Malachi Army Base, 5744-1984
Reichan, 5744-1984
Rishfon, 5745-1985
Rishon L'Tziyon, 5743-1983
Roglit, 5745-1985
Roiy, Jordan Valley, 5750-1990
Rosh Ha'aiyn, 5744-1984
Rosh Pina, 5744-1984
Safed, 5738-1978
Safed, 5744-1984
Beis HaKnesset of the Arizal.
Sal'iyt, 5745-1985
Sarafand, 5744-1984
Asof HaRofe Hospital
Sde Chemed, 5745-1985
Sde David, 5745-1985
Sde Eliezer, 5745-1985
Sde Ilan, 5745-1985
Sde Trumot, 5744-1984
Sde Tzvi, 5745-1985
Sde Varburg, 5745-1985
Sde Yaakov, 5745-1985
Sderot, 5744-1984
Sdot Micha, 5745-1985
Seviyon, 5744-1984
Sha'al, Golan Heights, 5750-1990
Sha'ar Efraim, 5745-1985
Sha'ar Hanegev, 5745-1985
Sha'ar Yashuv, 5745-1985
Sha'arei Tikva, 5745-1985
Shachar, 5745-1985
Shadma, 5745-1985
Shadmot Devora, 5744-1984
Shadmot Mechola, 5744-1984
Shaked, 5744-1984
Shavei Shomron, 5750-1990
Shavei Tziyon, 5744-1984
Shchem, 5744-1984
In proximity to Yosef HaTzadik's Tomb.
Shechaniya, Gush Segev, 5744-1984
Shechunat Bait Vagan, Yerushalaim, 5744-1984
Shechunat Bet HaKerem, Yerushalaim, 5752-1992
Shechunat Bet Israel, Yerushalaim, 5744-1984
Beis HaKnesset Chabad Lubavitch.
Shechunat Gila, Yerushalaim, 5744-1984
Shechunat Givat Shaul, Yerushalaim, 5746-1986
Shechunat Har Nof, Yerushalaim, 5746-1986
Shechunat Ir Ganim, Yerushalaim, 5744-1984
Shechunat Kiriyat Ariyeh, Yerushalaim, 5744-1984
Shechunat Matersdorf-Itriy, Yerushalaim, 5745-1985
Shechunat Sanhedria Hamurchevet,
Yerushalaim, 5744-1984
Shekef, 5745-1985
Shfar'am, 5748-1988
Rabbi Yehuda ben Bava's Tomb.
Shikun Chabad, Yerushalaim, 5744-1984
Shilo, 5745-1985
Shivta Army Base, 5745-1985
Shlomi, 5744-1984
Shomera, 5744-1984
Shzur, 5744-1984
Ta'anach, 5744-1984
Ta'oz, 5745-1985
Taku'a, 5745-1985
Tal El, 5744-1984
Tal Shachar, 5745-1985
Talmei Menashe, 5745-1985
Talmei Yechiel, 5745-1985
Tarum, 5745-1985
Tashur, 5745-1985
Tefachot, 5744-1984

Tel Adashim, 5744-1984
Tel Aviv, 5703-1943
Tel Aviv, Israel Museum, 5750-1990
Tel Aviv-Yafo, 5740-1980, 5744-1984
Tel Chanan, 5745-1985
Tel Nof Army Base, 5745-1985
Telmond, 5745-1985
Telz Stone, 5745-1985
Tidhar, 5745-1985
Timrat, 5744-1984
Tirat Hakarmel, 5744-1984
Tirat Tzvi, 5744-1984
Tirat Yehuda, 5745-1985
Tlamim, 5745-1985
Tnuvot, 5748-1988
Tomer, Jordan Valley, 5750-1990
Tveriya, 5739-1979
Tveriya, 5744-1984
In proximity to RaMBaM's Tomb.
Tveriya, Old City, 5746-1986
Tveriya, 5748-1988
Rabbi Meir Baal HaNess' Tomb.
Tzafririm, 5745-1985
Tzalfon, 5745-1985
Tzefariya, 5744-1984
Tzofer, Kvish HaArava, 5745-1985
Tzofit, 5745-1985
Tzrifin Air Force Base, 5744-1984
Tzrufa, 5748-1988
Tzukim, Kvish HaArava, 5745-1985
Tzur Hadasa, 5745-1985
Tzur Masa, 5745-1985
Tzur Natan, 5745-1985
Tzur Shalom, 5752-1992
Tzuriel, 5744-1984
Tzurit, Gush Segev, 5744-1984
Ya'ad, Gush Segev, 5744-1984
Yad Binyamin, 5744-1984
Yad Natan, 5745-1985
Yafit, Jordan Valley, 5750-1990
Yafo, Chabad School, 5744-1984
Yagel, 5745-1985
Yahud, 5744-1984
Yakir, 5745-1985
Yanuv, 5748-1988
Yarchiv, 5745-1985
Yarkona, 5745-1985
Yavne'el, 5744-1984
Yavneh, 5744-1984
Yerucham, 5745-1985
Yerushalaim, 5738-1978, 5741-1981
Beis HaKnesset, Beis HaMedrash Tzemach Tzedek
Rechov Chabad 53
Yerushalaim, Between Walls, 5734-1974
Yerushalaim, Chabad Library, 5749-1989, 5750-1990
Yerushalaim, Downtown, 5744-1984
Yerushalaim, French Hill, 5744-1984
Yerushalaim, Government Printing Office, 5745-1985
Yerushalaim, Hadasa Hospital, 5752-1992
Yerushalaim, Heichal Menachem, 5750-1990,
5751-1991, 5752-1992
Yerushalaim, National Diamond Center, 5751-1991
Yerushalaim, Old City, 5752-1992
Ohr HaChaim Synagogue
Yerushalaim, Printed by Eshkol Publishers, 5745-1984
Yerushalaim, The Kneset, 5751-1991
Yerushalaim, Yeshivat Torat Emet, 5744-1984
Yeshivat Bnei Akiva Kerem B'Yavneh, 5744-1984
Yeshuv Even Shmuel, 5744-1984
Yesod Hama'ala, 5744-1984
Yish'iy, 5745-1985
Yishuv Atniel, 5751-1991
Yishuv Lehavim, 5751-1991
Yishuv Meitar, 5751-1991
Yodfat, Gush Segev, 5744-1984
Yokne'am, 5744-1984
Yokne'am (Moshava), 5745-1985
Yuvlim, Gush Segev, 5744-1984
Zanoach, 5745-1985
Zar'iyt ,5744-1984
Zavdiel, 5745-1985
Zichron Yaakov, 5744-1984
Zohar, 5745-1985

Fiji
Suva, 5745-1985

Finland
Helsinki, 5738-1978

France
Agen, 5744-1984
Aix-en-Provence, 5745-1985

Aix-les-Bains, 5745-1985
Ajaccio (Corse), 5745-1985
Alfortville, 5744-1984
Allauch, 5745-1985
Amiens, 5744-1984
Amin, 5745-1985
Angers, 5744-1984
Angouléme, 5745-1985
Anne-Masse, 5745-1985
Annecy, 5744-1984
Antibes, 5744-1984
Antony, 5744-1984
Arcachon, 5745-1985
Arcay, 5744-1984
Argenteuil, 5744-1984
Arles, 5745-1985
Arpajon, 5744-1984
Asnières, 5744-1984
Athis-Mons, 5744-1984
Aubagne, 5745-1985
Aubervilliers, 5744-1984
Aulnay, 5744-1984
Auvergne, 5745-1985
Avignon, 5745-1985
Avold, 5745-1985
Bagneux, 5744-1984
Bagnolet, 5744-1984
Bastia (Corse), 5744-1984
Bauge, 5745-1985
Bayonne, 5745-1985
Beauvais, 5744-1984
Belfort, 5745-1985
Benfeld, 5745-1985
Besançon, 5744-1984
Béziers, 5745-1985
Bezons, 5744-1984
Biarritz, 5745-1985
Bischeim, 5744-1984
Bischwiller, 5745-1985
Blanc-Mesnil, 5744-1984
Bobigny, 5744-1984
Bois-Colombes, 5744-1984
Boissy-Leger, 5744-1984
Bollwiller, 5745-1985
Bondy, 5744-1984
Bonnet, 5745-1985
Bordeaux, 5744-1984
Bouc Bel-Air, 5745-1985
Boulay, 5745-1985
Boulogne, 5744-1984
Bourg-en-Bresse, 5744-1984
Bourg-la-Reine, 5744-1984
Bourges, 5745-1985
Boussy-Antoine, 5744-1984
Bouzonville, 5745-1985
Brest, 5744-1984
Broons, 5745-1985
Brumath, 5745-1985
Brunoy, 5744-1984
Yeshivat Tomchei Tmimim
Bry-sur-Marne, 5744-1984
Cachan, 5744-1984
Caen, 5744-1984
Cagnes-sur-Mer, 5744-1984
Calas Cabries, 5745-1985
Cannes, 5744-1984
Carcassonne, 5744-1984
Carpentras, 5745-1985
Cavaillon, 5745-1985
Celle Cloud, 5744-1984
Châlon-sur-Saône, 5745-1985
Châlons-sur-Marne, 5745-1985
Chambéry, 5744-1984
Champagne-au-Mont-d'Or, 5745-1985
Champigny, 5744-1984
Chantilly, 5744-1984
Charenton, 5744-1984
Chateauroux, 5744-1984
Chatellrault, 5745-1985
Chatenay-Malabry, 5744-1984
Châtillon, 5744-1984
Chaville, 5744-1984
Chelles, 5744-1984
Chenneviers, 5744-1984
Cherbourg, 5744-1984
Chesnay, 5744-1984
Chevilly-Larue, 5744-1984
Choisy-le-Roi, 5744-1984
Clamart, 5744-1984
Claviers, 5745-1985

Clermont, 5744-1984
Clichy, 5744-1984
Clichy-sous-Bois, 5744-1984
Clouange, 5745-1985
Cloud, 5744-1984
Colmar, 5744-1984
Colombes, 5744-1984
Compiegne, 5745-1985
Corbas, 5745-1985
Corbeille, 5744-1984
Coubron, 5744-1984
Courbevoie, 5744-1984
Crafan, 5745-1985
Creil, 5744-1984
Creteil, 5744-1984
Daville, 5745-1985
Decines-Charpieu, 5745-1985
Delme, 5745-1985
Denis, 5744-1984
Detwiller, 5745-1985
Deuil-la-Barre, 5744-1984
Die, 5745-1985
Diemeringen, 5745-1985
Dieuze, 5745-1985
Dijon, 5744-1984
Dornach, 5745-1985
Douai, 5744-1984
Draguignan, 5744-1984
Drancy, 5744-1984
Dreux, 5745-1985
Dugny, 5744-1984
Dunkerque, 5744-1984
Eaubonne, 5744-1984
Ecueille, 5745-1985
Egenheim, 5745-1985
Elancourt, 5744-1984
Elbeuf, 5744-1984
Elizabethville, 5744-1984
Enghein, 5744-1984
Epernay, 5745-1985
Epinal, 5745-1985
Epinay-sous-Senart, 5744-1984
Epinay-sur-Seine, 5744-1984
Ermont, 5744-1984
Erstein, 5745-1985
Etienne, 5744-1984
Evian, 5744-1984
Evreux, 5744-1984
Evry, 5744-1984
Fastat, 5745-1985
Faulquemont, 5745-1985
Foix-les-Lyon, 5745-1985
Fons, 5745-1985
Fontaine-sur-Saône, 5745-1985
Fontainebleau, 5744-1984
Fontenay, 5744-1984
Fontenay-aux-Roses, 5744-1984
Forbach, 5745-1985
Fosse, 5746-1986
Frejus Raphael, 5744-1984
Fresnes,5744-1984
Gagny, 5744-1984
Garches, 5744-1984
Garenne Colombes, 5744-1984
Garges, 5744-1984
Gennevilliers, 5744-1984
Gentilly, 5745-1985
Germain-en-Laye, 5744-1984
Givors, 5745-1985
Gonesse, 5745-1985
Gournay-sur-Marne, 5744-1984
Grasse, 5744-1984
Gratien, 5744-1984
Grenoble, 5745-1985
Grossbliederstoff, 5745-1985
Guebwiller, 5745-1985
Hagondange, 5745-1985
Hagueneau, 5744-1984
Hayange, 5745-1985
Hochfelden, 5745-1985
Horbourg, 5745-1985
Hyeres, 5745-1985
Ingwiller, 5745-1985
Isming, 5745-1985
Issy-les-Moulineaux, 5744-1984
Ivry-sur-Seine, 5744-1984
Joinville-le-Pont, 5744-1984
Juvisy, 5744-1984
Kremlin-Bicêtre, 5744-1984
Kronenbourg, 5744-1984

La Ciotat, 5745-1985
La Courneuve, 5744-1984
La Meinau, 5744-1984
La Rochelle, 5745-1985
La Seine-sur-Mer, 5745-1985
La Varenne, 5744-1984
Laurent-du-var, 5745-1985
Le Bourget, 5744-1984
Le Havre, 5744-1984
Le Mans, 5744-1984
Le Pecq, 5744-1984
Le Perreux, 5744-1984
Le Vesinet, 5744-1984
Le-Plessis-Trevise, 5744-1984
Lens, 5744-1984
Leurres, 5746-1986
Levallois, 5744-1984
Libourne, 5745-1985
Lillas, 5744-1984
Lille, 5744-1984
Limeil-Brevannes, 5745-1985
Limoges, 5744-1984
Lingolsheim, 5745-1985
Livry-Gargan, 5744-1984
Lixheim, 5745-1985
Long Jumeau, 5744-1984
Lons-le-Saunier, 5744-1984
Lorient, 5744-1984
Louis, 5745-1985
Lunel, 5745-1985
Lunéville, 5745-1985
Lyon, 5744-1984
Macon, 5744-1984
Maison Laffite, 5745-1985
Maisons-Alfort, 5744-1984
Malakoff, 5744-1984
Mande, 5744-1984
Mantes-la-Jolie, 5744-1984
Marckolsheim, 5745-1985
Marhuns, 5745-1985
Marignane, 5745-1985
Marlies-le-Veill, 5746-1986
Marseille, 5744-1984
Massy, 5744-1984
Maur-des-Fosses, 5744-1984
Maurepas, 5744-1984
Maurice, 5744-1984
Meaux, 5744-1984
Melun, 5744-1984
Menton, 5744-1984
Merelbek, 5745-1985
Metz, 5744-1984
Meudon, 5744-1984
Meyzieu, 5745-1985
Molsheim, 5745-1985
Mommenheim, 5745-1985
Montauban, 5744-1984
Montbeliard, 5745-1985
Montfermeuil, 5744-1984
Montgeron, 5744-1984
Montmorency, 5744-1984
Montpellier, 5745-1985
Montreuil, 5744-1984
Montrouge, 5744-1984
Mulhouse, 5744-1984
Mutzig, 5745-1985
Nancy, 5744-1984
Nanterre, 5744-1984
Nantes, 5744-1984
Narbonne, 5744-1984
Neuf-Brisach, 5745-1985
Neuilly, 5744-1984
Neuilly-Plaisance, 5744-1984
Neuilly-sur-Marne, 5744-1984
Nice, 5744-1984
Niederbronn, 5745-1985
Nimes, 5745-1985
Nogent, 5744-1984
Noiseau, 5744-1984
Noisy-le-Grand, 5744-1984
Noisy-le-Sec, 5744-1984
Orléans, 5744-1984
Orly, 5744-1984
Ormesson, 5744-1984
Orsay, 5744-1984
Ouen, 5744-1984
Ouen-l'Aumône, 5744-1984
Oullins, 5745-1985
Pantin, 5744-1984
Paris, 5738-1978

Pau, 5744-1984
Pavillons-sous-Bois, 5744-1984
Perigueux, 5745-1985
Perpignan, 5744-1984
Phalsbourg, 5745-1985
Pierrefitte, 5744-1984
Plan-de-Coques, 5745-1985
Poitiers, 5744-1984
Pontault-Combault, 5744-1984
Pontoise, 5744-1984
Port-de-Bouc, 5745-1985
Pre-Gervais, 5744-1984
Priest, 5745-1985
Puteaux, 5744-1984
Quatzenheim, 5745-1985
Quentin, 5744-1984
Rambouillet, 5745-1985
Reims, 5745-1985
Rennes, 5744-1984
Rillieux, 5745-1985
Ris-Orangis, 5744-1984
Roanne, 5744-1984
Roissy-en-Brie, 5744-1984
Romainville, 5744-1984
Rosheim, 5745-1985
Rosny-sous-Bois, 5744-1984
Rouen, 5744-1984
Rueil-Malmaison, 5744-1984
Salon-en-Provence, 5745-1985
Sarcelles, 5744-1984
Sarre Union, 5745-1985
Sarrebourg, 5745-1985
Sarreguemines, 5745-1985
Sartrouville, 5744-1984
Saverne, 5745-1985
Savigny-sur-Orge, 5744-1984
Sedan, 5745-1985
Selestat, 5745-1985
Sens, 5744-1984
Séte, 5745-1985
Sevran, 5744-1984
Soultz, 5745-1985
Soultz-sous-Forets, 5745-1985
Stains, 5744-1984
Strasbourg, 5744-1984
Struth, 5745-1985
Sucy-en-Brie, 5744-1984
Suresnes, 5744-1984
Tarbes, 5745-1985
Tassin-la-Demi-Lune, 5745-1985
Then-Jerée, 5745-1985
Thiais, 5744 1984
Thionville, 5745-1985
Thônon, 5744-1984
Toul, 5745-1985
Toulon, 5745-1985
Toulouse, 5744-1984
Tours, 5744-1984
Trappes, 5744-1984
Tremblay-les-Gonesses, 5744-1984
Tresserve, 5745-1985
Tropez-Maximes, 5744-1984
Troyes, 5744-1984
Valence, 5744-1984
Valenciennes, 5744-1984
Vanves, 5744-1984
Vaujours, 5744-1984
Vaulx-en-Velin, 5745-1985
Vennissioux, 5745-1985
Verdun, 5745-1985
Verneuil, 5744-1984
Vernon, 5744-1984
Versailles, 5744-1984
Vichy, 5744-1984
Vigneux, 5744-1984
Ville, 5745-1985
Ville-Franche-sur-Saone, 5745-1985
Villejuif, 5744-1984
Villemomble, 5744-1984
Villeneuve-Georges, 5744-1984
Villeneuve-la-Garenne, 5744-1984
Villeneuve-Loubet, 5745-1985
Villepinte, 5744-1984
Villetaneuse, 5744-1984
Villeurbanne, 5744-1984
Villiers-le-Bel, 5744-1984
Villiers-sur-Marne, 5744-1984
Vincennes, 5744-1984
Vitry, 5744-1984
Vitry-le-Francois, 5745-1985

Vittel, 5745-1985
Wallfesheim, 5745-1985
Wasselonne, 5745-1985
Weshofen, 5745-1985
Wingersheim, 5745-1985
Wissembourg, 5745-1985
Yerres, Beit Rivkah, 5744-1984

French Guiana
Cayenne, 5744-1984

Germany
Altona, 5580-1820, 5606-1846
Mainz, 5745-1985
Munich, 5707-1947
Worms, 5745-1985

Gibraltar, 5738-1978

Greece
Athens, 5738-1978
Rhodes, 5745-1985
Salonika, 5744-1984

Grenada
Georges, 5744-1984
U.S.A. Army Base, 5744-1983

Guadeloupe
Martin, 5746-1986
Pointe-a-Pitre, 5744-1984

Guatemala, 5744-1984

Haiti
Port-au-Prince, 5745-1985

Holland
Alkmaar, 5744-1984
Amersfoort, 5744-1984
Amstelveen, 5744-1984
Amsterdam, 5738-1978, 5746-1986
Arnhem, 5744-1984
Breda, 5744-1984
Bussum, 5744-1984
Den Bosch, 5744-1984
Den Haag, 5744-1984
Den Helder, 5744-1984
Eindhoven, 5744-1984
Enschede, 5744-1984
Groningen, 5744-1984
Haarlem, 5744-1984
Hilversum, 5744-1984
Leiden, 5744-1984
Rotterdam, 5744-1984
Utrecht, 5744-1984

Honduras
Tegucigalpa, 5744-1984

Hong Kong
Hong Kong, 5739-1979
Kowloon, 5752-1992

Hungary
Budapest, 5739-1979
Munkacs, 5703-1943

Iceland
Reykjavik, 5744-1984

India
Ahamadabad, 5745-1985
Bombay, 5738-1978
Calcutta, 5746-1986
Cochin, 5746-1986
New Delhi, 5745-1985
Poona, 5745-1985

Iran
Shiraz, 5744-1984
Teheran, 5738-1978

Ireland
Belfast, 5744-1984
Dublin, 5738-1978

Italy
Abbiate Guazzone, 5744-1984
Alessandria, 5744-1984
Ancona, 5744-1984
Asti, 5744-1984
Bari, 5744-1984
Bergamo, 5744-1984
Bertinoro, 5744-1984
Biella, 5744-1984
Bologna, 5744-1984
Bolzano, 5744-1984
Brescia, 5744-1984
Camaiore, 5744-1984
Casale Monferrato, 5744-1984
Castillioncella-Livorno, 5752-1992
Como, 5744-1984
Cuneo, 5744-1984
Faenza, 5744-1984
Ferrara, 5744-1984
Florence, 5744-1984

Forli, 5744-1984
Fossano, 5744-1984
Genova, 5744-1984
Gorizia, 5744-1984
Ivrea, 5744-1984
La Spezia, 5744-1984
Livorno, 5744-1984
Lucca, 5744-1984
Mantova, 5744-1984
Massa Carrara, 5744-1984
Merano, 5744-1984
Mestre, 5744-1984
Milan, 5738-1978
Modena, 5744-1984
Monza, 5744-1984
Napoli, 5744-1984
Novara, 5744-1984
Padova, 5744-1984
Parma, 5744-1984
Pavia, 5744-1984
Perugia, 5744-1984
Pesaro, 5744-1984
Pisa, 5744-1984
Pistoia, 5744-1984
Rome, 5744-1984
Saluzzo, 5744-1984
Senigallia, 5744-1984
Siena, 5744-1984
Trani, 5744-1984
Trieste, 5744-1984
Turin, 5744-1984
Udine, 5744-1984
Urbino, 5744-1984
Valenza, 5744-1984
Varese, 5744-1984
Venice, 5744-1984
Vercelli, 5744-1984
Verona, 5744-1984
Viareggio, 5744-1984

Jamaica
Kingston, 5744-1984

Japan
Kobe, 5744-1984
Tokyo, 5738-1978

Kenya
Nairobi, 5743-1983

Korea
Seoul, 5738-1978

Lebanon
A'leih, 5742-1982
Beaufort Castle, 5742-1982
Beirut, 5742-1982
Bekaa Valley, 5742-1982
Bhamdoun, 5742-1982
Chasabiaya, 5742-1982
Damour, 5742-1982
Deir el Qamar, 5742-1982
Jounieh, 5742-1982
Kfar Kyla Merj U'yun, 5739-1979
Kfar Mechki, 5742-1982
Nabatiye, 5742-1982
Rachaiya, 5742-1982
Sidon, 5742-1982
Tyre,5742-1982

Liechtenstein
Vaduz, 5744-1984

Lithuania
* See *Russia*

Luxembourg, 5744-1984

Macao, 5752-1992

Malaysia
Kuala Lampur, 5746-1986

Marino, Republica di
Marino, 5744-1984

Martinique
Fort de France, 5744-1984

Mexico
Acapulco, 5744-1984
Cabo Lucas, 5744-1984
Cuernavaca, 5744-1984
Encinada, 5744-1984
Guadalajara, 5744-1984
La Paz, 5742-1982
Mexicali, 5744-1984
Mexico City, 5738-1978
Monterrey, 5745-1985
Pueblo, 5745-1985
Rosarita, 5744-1984
Tecate, 5744-1984
Tijuana, 5744-1984

Monaco
Monte Carlo, 5744-1984
Mongolia
Ulaan Baatar, 5753-1993
Morocco
Agadir, 5744-1984
Al Mohammedia, 5746-1986
Arashidia, 5745-1985
Arbalou, 5747-1987
Arbaoua, 5745-1985
Beni Mallal, 5745-1985
Berrechid, 5746-1986
Boujad, 5747-1987
Bzou, 5747-1987
Casablanca, 5738-1978
Casablanca, Beis Chabad, 5747-1987
Debdou, 5745-1985
Dimnas, 5745-1985
El Borouj, 5746-1986
El Jadida, 5744-1984
Essaouira, 5744-1984
Fez, 5744-1984
Guercif, 5746-1986
Ifrane, 5744-1984
Tzivos Hashem-Uforatza Lubavitch Camp.
Inzgan, 5746-1986
Kenitra, 5744-1984
Ksar-el-Kebir, 5745-1985
Larache, 5744-1984
Marrakech, 5744-1984
Meknes, 5744-1984
Midlas, 5745-1985
Ouarzazate, 5746-1986
Oued Zem, 5747-1987
Oujda, 5745-1985
Rabat, 5744-1984
Rhis, 5745-1985
Safi, 5744-1984
Sale, 5746-1986
Sefrou, 5745-1985
Settat, 5745-1985
Souk-el-Arbaa, 5745-1985
Taliouine, 5747-1987
Tangier, 5744-1984
Taroudant, 5746-1986
Tetouan, 5744-1984
Tiznit, 5745-1985
Wazzan, 5745-1985
Nepal
Katmandu, 5746-1986
Netherlands Antilles
Aruba, 5744-1984
Curaçao, 5744-1984
Phillipsburg, Maarten Island, 5748-1988
New Zealand
Auckland, 5740-1980
Wellington, 5744-1984
Nicaragua
Managua, 5744-1984
Nigeria
Abba, 5739-1979
Lagos, 5744-1984
Norway
Oslo, 5739-1979
Trondheim, 5744-1984
Pakistan
Karachi, 5745-1985
Panama
Colon, 5747-1987
Panama City, 5739-1979
Papua New Guinea
Port Moresby, 5745-1985
Paraguay
Asuncion, 5742-1982
Peru
Lima, 5743-1983
Philippines
Manila, 5742-1982
Poland
L'vov, 5604-1843, 5618-1858, 5622-1862
Lemberg, 5616-1856, 5617-1857, 5620-1860, 5624-1864
Zalkiev, 5559-1799
Portugal, 5738-1978
Prussia
Koenigsberg, 5571-1811, 5587-1827, 5591-1831, 5612-1852
Romania
Bucharest, 5744-1984
Yass, 5603-1843

Russia
Bolshay Morskay, 5753-1993
Fontanka, 5753-1993
Grajdanka, 5753-1993
Shklov, 5566-1806, 5574-1814
Slavuta, 5557-1797
Vilna, 5574-1814, 5632-1872, 5633-1872, 5638-1878, 5640-1880, 5656-1896, 5660-1900, 5669-1909, 5672-1912, 5683-1923, 5690-1930, 5697-1937, 5699-1939
Zolkva, 5565-1805
Scotland
Edinburgh, 5749-1989
Glasgow, 5744-1984
Lockerbie, 5749-1989
Sinai Peninsula
Chatzar Adar, 5742-1982
Etzmonah, 5742-1982
Sharm-el-Sheikh, 5742-1982
Yamit, 5742-1982
Singapore, 5738-1978
South Africa
Benoni, 5744-1984
Bethel, 5744-1984
Bethlehem, 5744-1984
Bloemfontein, 5744-1984
Boksburg, 5744-1984
Brakpan, 5744-1984
Brits, 5753-1993
Cape Town, 5745-1985, 5746-1986
Carltonville, 5744-1984
Delmas, 5744-1984
Durban, 5744-1984
East London, 5744-1984
Edenvale, 5744-1984
Ficksburg, 5744-1984
George, 5746-1986
Germiston, 5744-1984
Grahamstown, 5744-1984
Johannesburg, 5738-1978
Kempton Park, 5744-1984
Kimberley, 5744-1984
Klerksdorp, 5744-1984
Kroonstad, 5744-1984
Krugersdorp, 5744-1984
Messina, 5745-1985
Middleburg, 5744-1984
Oudtshoorn, 5744-1984
Parys, 5744-1984
Pietermaritzburg, 5744-1984
Pietersburg, 5744-1984
Port Elizabeth, 5744-1984
Potchefstroom, 5744-1984
Pretoria, 5744-1984
Randburg, 5744-1984
Randfontein, 5744-1984
Roodeport, 5744-1984
Rustenburg, 5744-1984
Sandton, 5744-1984
Springs, 5744-1984
Umshlainga, North Coast, 5751-1991
Vanderbijlpark, 5744-1984
Vereeniging, 5744-1984
Vitenhage, 5746-1986
Welkom, 5744-1984
Windhoek, 5744-1984
Witbank, 5744-1984
Spain
Barcelona, 5744-1984
Cordoba (Andalusia), 5745-1985
Birth Place of RaMBaM
Malaga, 5738-1978
Sri Lanka
Colombo, 5743-1983
Suez Canal
Fayid, 5734-1974
Surinam
Paramaribo, 5744-1984
Swaziland
Mbabane, 5748-1988
Sweden
Goteborg, Bais Chabad, 5752-1992
Goteborg, 5744-1984
Malmo, 5744-1984
Stockholm, 5738-1978
Switzerland
Geneve, 5744-1984
Zurich, 5738-1978
Tahiti
Papeete, 5749-1989

Taiwan
Taipei, 5738-1978
Tanzania
Daar-es-Salaam, 5743-1983
Thailand
Bangkok, 5738-1978
Chiang Mai, 5752-1992
Tunisia
Jerba, 5728-1968
Tunis, 5744-1984
Turkey
Istanbul, 5739-1979
Turks And Caicos Islands, 5741-1981
U.S.S.R.
Adintsova, Russia, 5752-1992
Akhtirka, Ukraine, 5752-1992
Aleksandria, Ukraine, 5752-1992
Alekskaskaya, 5752-1992
Alma Ata, Kazakhstan, 5751-1991
Alma Ata, Kazakhstan, 5751-1991
Tomb of Rabbi L. Y. Schneerson, father of the Rebbe Shlita.
Anipoli, Ukraine, 5751-1991
Anipoli, Ukraine, 5751-1991
Tomb of the Maggid of Meseritch.
Arbat (Irbit), 5752-1992
Ardinka, Russia, 5752-1992
Arinin, 5752-1992
Arsha, Ukraine, 5752-1992
Balaclava, 5751-1991
Balashikha, Russia, 5752-1992
Balta, Ukraine, 5752-1992
Bar, 5752-1992
Baradino, Russia, 5752-1992
Barissov, Ukraine, 5752-1992
Beleybu, Moscow, 5752-1992
Belgorod, Russia, 5751-1991
Beltsy, Moldova, 5752-1992
Bendery, Moldova, 5752-1992
Berdiansk, Russia, 5752-1992
Berdichev, Ukraine, 5752-1992
Beregova, Russia, 5752-1992
Berezniki, Russia, 5752-1992
Bershad, Ukraine, 5752-1992
Bezhetsk, Russia, 5752-1992
Bikovo, Russia, 5752-1992
Breslov, Ukraine, 5751-1991
Brisk, 5752-1992
Brody, Ukraine, 5752-1992
Butirski-Khutar, 5752-1992
Chaisti-Frudy, 5752-1992
Cherkassy, Ukraine, 5752-1992
Cherkizava, Russia, 5752-1992
Chernagulovka, 5752-1992
Chernigov, Ukraine, 5752-1992
Chernyakhavsk, Russia, 5752-1992
Cherykov, 5752-1992
Chirtanova, 5752-1992
Chmelniek, Ukraine, 5752-1992
Dagavfils (Dvinsk), Latvia, 5752-1992
Danetsk, Ukraine, 5752-1992
Daragai-Milovo, 5752-1992
Dedovsk, Russia, 5752-1992
Detskaei Sela, Russia, 5752-1992
Dnepoprotovsk, Ukraine, 5751-1991
Dneprodzerzhinsk, Ukraine, 5752-1992
Dolgoprodni, Russia, 5751-1991
Dubno, Ukraine, 5752-1992
Feodosiya, (Crimea), Ukraine, 5751-1991
Firobo, Moscow, Russia, 5752-1992
Floreshti, Moldova, 5752-1992
Fofovka, Russia, 5752-1992
Folo, 5752-1992
Fushkino, Camp Gan Yisroel-Shamir, 5751-1991
Gachina, Russia, 5752-1992
Gagarin, Russia, 5751-1991
Galianavo, 5752-1992
Geisin, Ukraine, 5751-1991
Genichesk, 5752-1992
Geyvoron, Ukraine, 5752-1992
Gobrino, 5752-1992
Grodna, Belorussia, 5752-1992
Haditch, Ukraine, 5751-1991
Haditch, Ukraine, 5751-1991
Tomb of the Alter Rebbe.
Horodok, Belorussia, 5751-1991
Ilinka, Russia, 5752-1992
Ivanteyevka, Russia, 5752-1992
Jankai, Kazakhstan, 5752-1992
Kabelyaki, Ukraine, 5752-1992

Kacha, Russia, 5751-1991
Kaliningrad, Russia, 5751-1991
Kalitniki, Moscow, 5752-1992
Kalshina, Moscow, Russia, 5752-1992
Kaluga, Russia, 5751-1991
Kazatin, Ukraine, 5752-1992
Khamovniki, Moscow, 5752-1992
Kharkov, Ukraine, 5751-1991
Kharoshovkaya, 5752-1992
Khimki, Russia, 5751-1991
Khmelnitskiy, Ukraine, 5751-1991
Khoklovski, 5752-1992
Kiev, Ukraine, 5751-1991
Kirovograd, Ukraine, 5752-1992
Kishinev, Moldova, 5752-1992
Kliazma, Russia, 5752-1992
Kolpachniy, 5752-1992
Konkovo, 5752-1992
Kontsvo, Yehivat Mekor Chaim, 5752-1992
Koretz, Ukraine, 5751-1991
Kostroma, Russia, 5751-1991
Kovno, C.I.S., 5752-1992
Krasni Buruta, 5752-1992
Krasnogorsk, Russia, 5752-1992
Kremenchug, Ukraine, 5752-1992
Krivoy Rog, Ukraine, 5751-1991
Krlatskiye, Moscow, 5752-1992
Kursk, Russia, 5751-1991
Kutai-Gorod, Moscow, 5752-1992
L'vov, Ukraine, 5752-1992
Ladizhin, Ukraine, 5752-1992
Lefortovo, 5752-1992
Leningrad, Russia, 5750-1990
Leningrad-Peterburg, Russia, 5751-1991
Liadi, 5751-1991
Lianozovo, Moscow, 5752-1992
Liela, Belorussia, 5752-1992
Liepaya, Latvia, 5750-1990
Liozna, 5751-1991
Litkarina, Russia, 5752-1992
Losinka, 5752-1992
Lubavitch, Belorussia, 5751-1991
Lubni, Ukraine, 5751-1991
Lugansk, Ukraine, 5752-1992
Lyubertsi, Russia, 5752-1992
Malakovka, Russia, 5751-1991
Marina, 5752-1992
Medvadkaya, 5752-1992
Meseritch, Ukraine, 5751-1991
Mezhibuzh, Ukraine, 5751-1991
Mezhibuzh, Ukraine, 5751-1991
 Tomb of the Baal Shem Tov.
Mga, 5752-1992
Mirgorod, Ukraine, 5751-1991
Mitishtchi, Russia, 5752-1992
Mogilev, Belorussia, 5752-1992
Moscow, Central Synagogue, Russia, 5752-1992
Moscow, , Russia, 5752-1992
 Marina-Roscha Synagogue
Moscow, Russia, 5749-1989, 5751-1991
Moscow, Russia, Lenin Library, 5752-1992
Moskva Shiramushki, Russia, 5752-1992
Moskvortsa, Moscow, Russia, 5752-1992
Mozsheisk, Russia, 5751-1991
Mtzensk, Russia, 5751-1991
Mukacheva, Ukraine, 5752-1992
Muram, Russia, 5752-1992
Nagatino, Moscow, Russia, 5752-1992
Naravino, Russia, 5752-1992
Naropominsk, 5751-1991
Narva, Estonia, 5752-1992
Nevel, 5751-1991
Nezhin, Ukraine, 5751-1991
Nezhin, Ukraine, 5751-1991
 Tomb of the Mittler Rebbe
Nikolaev, Ukraine, 5751-1991
Nikulini, Moscow, 5752-1992
Nimetskaya-Slavoda, 5752-1992
Nizhne-Novogrod, 5752-1992
Novograd-Valinski, Ukraine, 5751-1991
Novogrod, Russia, 5752-1992
Novogrodak, 5752-1992
Novomoskovsk, Ukraine, 5752-1992
Obinsk, 5751-1991
Oboyan, Russia, 5751-1991
Odessa, Ukraine, 5751-1991
Orgeyev, Moldova, 5752-1992
Orsha, Belorussia, 5751-1991
Oryol, Russia, 5751-1991
Ostozinka, Moscow, Russia, 5752-1992

Ostrog, Ukraine, 5752-1992
Patezh, Russia, 5751-1991
Pavlovsk, 5752-1992
Peremishlani, Ukraine, 5752-1992
Pervomaysy, Russia, 5752-1992
Peterburg, Shamir School, 5752-1992
Peterburg, 5752-1992
22 Makhuavaya.
Petrapovulska-Krepost, Peterburg, 5752-1992
Pinsk, Belorussia, 5752-1992
Piriatin, Ukraine, 5751-1991
Plavsk, Russia, 5751-1991
Podolsk, Russia, 5751-1991
Polotzk, Belorussia, 5752-1992
Poltava, Ukraine, 5752-1992
Pratvina, 5752-1992
Priluki, Ukraine, 5751-1991
Pryazina, 5752-1992
Pskov, Russia, 5752-1992
Puschina Na Oke, 5752-1992
Pushkin, Russia, 5752-1992
Reutov, Russia, 5752-1992
Rezina, Moldova, 5752-1992
Ribnitsa, Moldova, 5752-1992
Riga, Latvia, 5750-1990
Rodnia, Belorussia, 5751-1991
Rostakino, 5752-1992
Rostov Don, 5750-1990
Rovno, Ukraine, 5752-1992
Ruzhin, Ukraine, 5752-1992
Sadovi-Kudrinska, 5752-1992
Scherbinka, 5752-1992
Serpukhov, Russia, 5751-1991
Sevastopol, Ukraine, 5751-1991
Shchekino, Russia, 5751-1991
Shefetovka, Ukraine, 5751-1991
Sheremetiesky, Russia, 5752-1992
Shklov, Belorussia, 5752-1992
Shpola, Ukraine, 5752-1992
Shpola, Ukraine, 5752-1992
Resting place of the "Holy Shpola Zaide."
Skhodnia, Russia, 5752-1992
Skvira, Ukraine, 5752-1992
Slavuta, Ukraine, 5751-1991
Smela, Ukraine, 5752-1992
Smolensk, Russia, 5751-1991
Sokol, 5752-1992
Sorphokhavskaya-Zakhata, 5752-1992
Sossenky, Russia, 5752-1992
Starokonstantioff, Ukraine, 5752-1992
Stragino, 5752-1992
Taganka, Russia, 5752-1992
Taganrag, Russia, 5752-1992
Tallinn, Estonia, 5752-1992
Talnoye, Ukraine, 5752-1992
Tartu, Estonia, 5752-1992
Tarussa, 5752-1992
Tashkent, Russia, 5751-1991
Tbilisi, Georgia, 5750-1990
Tchekov, Russia, 5751-1991
Tepli-Stan, Moscow, 5752-1992
Ternopol, Ukraine, 5752-1992
Testilshiky, Moscow, 5751-1991
Tirosfol, Moldova, 5752-1992
Toshina, Moscow, Russia, 5752-1992
Trobnaya, Moscow, Russia, 5752-1992
Trofarvo, Moscow, 5752-1992
Troitsko, Russia, 5752-1992
Tshichenvali, Georgia, 5750-1990
Tula, Russia, 5751-1991, 5752-1992
Tulshin, Ukraine, 5752-1992
Tver, Russia, 5752-1992
Tverskai, 5752-1992
Tzritziv Volgograd, Russia, 5751-1991
Ulianovsk, Russia, 5752-1992
Uman, Ukraine, 5751-1991
Urkhobo Borisova, 5751-1991
Ussova, Russia, 5752-1992
Uzhgorod, Ukraine, 5752-1992
Vanukovo, Russia, 5752-1992
Vassilkov, Ukraine, 5752-1992
Veliz, Russia, 5752-1992
Vereya, 5752-1992
Viazma, Russia, 5751-1991
Vidnaya, Russia, 5752-1992
Vikhina, 5751-1991
Vinigradova, Ukraine, 5752-1992
Vinnitsa, Ukraine, 5751-1991
Vitebsk, Belorussia, 5751-1991
Vladimir, Russia, 5752-1992

Volozhin, 5752-1992
Yalta, Ukraine, 5752-1992
Yaroslavl, Ukraine, 5752-1992
Yassiniva, Moscow, Russia, 5752-1992
Yazmailava, Russia, 5752-1992
Zabrov, Ukraine, 5752-1992
Zaporozhie, Ukraine, 5752-1992
Zhavaranki, 5752-1992
Zhitomir, Ukraine, 5752-1992
Zhozino, Moscow, Russia, 5752-1992
Zolochev, Ukraine, 5752-1992
Zvenigorodka, Ukraine, 5752-1992

United States of America

Abilene, TX, 5744-1984
Absecon, NJ, 5751-1991
Adelanto, CA, 5748-1988
Agawam, MA, 5744-1984
Agoura Hills, CA, 5744-1984
Akron, OH, 5744-1984
Albans, VT, 5748-1988
Albany, NY, 5744-1984
Albert Lea, MN, 5744-1984
Albuquerque, NM, 5744-1984
Alexandria, VA, 5745-1985
Alhambra, CA, 5744-1984
Allandale, FL, 5752-1992
Allendale, NJ, 5744-1984
Allentown, PA, 5749-1989
Alpine, NJ, 5744-1984
Altamonte Springs, FL, 5751-1991
Altoona, PA, 5747-1987
Amagansett, LI, NY, 5745-1985
Amarillo, TX, 5744-1984
Amberley, OH, 5748-1988
Amherst, MA, 5744-1984
Amityville, LI, NY, 5744-1984
Amsterdam, NY, 5745-1985
Ana, CA, 5748-1988
Anaheim, CA, 5745-1985
Anandale,VA, 5751-1991
Anchorage, AK, 5744-1984
Andover, MA, 5751-1991
Ann Arbor, MI, 5744-1984
Annapolis, MD, 5744-1984
Anniston, AL, 5746-1986
Ansonia, CT, 5745-1985
Anthony, FL, 5752-1992
Antonio, FL, 5752-1992
Antonio, TX, 5744-1984
Apaquogue, LI, NY, 5745-1985
Apopka, FL, 5751-1991
Appleton, WI, 5744-1984
Aquebogue, LI, NY, 5745-1985
Arcadia, CA, 5744-1984
Aripeka, FL, 5752-1992
Arlington, VA, 5751-1991
Arlington Heights, IL, 5746-1986
Artesia, CA, 5744-1984
Asbury Park, NJ, 5744-1984
Asharoken, LI, NY, 5745-1985
Ashland, VA, 5751-1991
Ashville, NY, 5744-1984
Aspen, CO, 5744-1984
Athol, MA, 5745-1985
Atlanta, GA, 5744-1984
Atlantic City, NJ, 5744-1984
Atlantique, LI, NY, 5745-1985
Austin, TX, 5744-1984
Avalon, CA, 5744-1984
Avalon, NJ, 5751-1991
Avon, MA, 5745-1985
Avon, CT, 5744-1984
Azusa, CA, 5744-1984
Babylon, LI, NY, 5744-1984
Bakersfield, CA, 5748-1988
Bal Harbour, FL, 5744-1984
Baldwin, FL, 5752-1992
Baldwin Park, CA, 5744-1984
Balm, FL, 5752-1992
Baltimore, MD, 5744-1984
Baraboo, WI, 5744-1984
Barbara, CA, 5744-1984
Barefoot Bay, FL, 5752-1992
Barnes Hole, LI, NY, 5745-1985
Barre, VT, 5752-1991
Barstow, CA, 5748-1988
Barton, VT, 5752-1991
Bartown, FL, 5752-1992
Batavia, NY, 5744-1984
Baxley, GA, 5751-1991

Bay Harbour Islands, FL, 5744-1984
Bay Lake, 5752-1992
Bay Shore, LI, NY, 5744-1984
Bayonet Point, FL, 5752-1992
Bayonne, NJ, 5744-1984
Bayport, LI, NY, 5745-1985
Bayport, FL, 5752-1992
Bayside, WI, 5744-1984
Bayview, LI, NY, 5745-1985
Beach Haven, NJ, 5744-1984
Beachwood, OH, 5744-1984
Bear, DE, 5751-1991
Beaumont, TX, 5744-1984
Bedford, MA, 5745-1985
Bedford Heights, OH, 5745-1985
Bedford Hills, NY, 5751-1991
Beixedon, LI, NY, 5745-1985
Bel Air, Beis Chabad, CA, 5748-1988
Bell, CA, 5744-1984
Bell Gardens, CA, 5744-1984
Bellaire, TX, 5744-1984
Belleville, NJ, 5744-1984
Bellevue, WA, 5744-1984
Bellflower, CA, 5744-1984
Bellport, LI, NY, 5744-1984
Belltown, CT, 5752-1991
Belmont, MA, 5744-1984
Belmont, FL, 5752-1992
Beloit, WI, 5744-1984
Bennington, VT, 5752-1991
Benson, AZ, 5745-1985
Bensonhurst, Brooklyn, NY, 5745-1985
Bergenfield, NJ, 5744-1984
Berkeley, CA, 5744-1984
Berkeley Heights, NJ, 5744-1984
Bernardino, CA, 5748-1988
Bernardsville, NJ, 5752-1992
Bethany, CT, 5745-1985
Bethel, CT, 5751-1991
Bethel, NY, 5748-1988
Bethesda, MD, 5745-1985
Beverly Hills, CA, 5744-1984
Big Bear Lake, CA, 5748-1988
Big Pine Key, FL, 5751-1991
Binghamton, NY, 5744-1984
Bismarck, ND, 5744-1984
Bloomfield, CT, 5744-1984
Bloomfield, NJ, 5744-1984
Bloomingdale, FL, 5752-1992
Bloomington, IN, 5744-1984
Blue Ash, OH, 5748-1988
Bluepoint, LI, NY, 5745-1985
Boca Raton, FL, 5744-1984
Bogota, NJ, 5744-1984
Bohemia, LI, NY, 5745-1985
Boise, ID, 5744-1984
Boonton, NJ, 5744-1984
Boston, MA, 5744-1984
Boulder, CO, 5744-1984
Bradbury, CA, 5744-1984
Braintree, MA, 5745-1985
Branford, CT, 5745-1985
Brattleboro, VT, 5752-1991
Brawley, CA, 5744-1984
Brea, CA, 5748-1988
Breckenridge, TX, 5744-1984
Brenham, TX, 5744-1984
Brentwood, Beis Chabad, CA, 5748-1988
Brentwood, LI, NY, 5745-1985
Brewster, NY, 5744-1984
Briarcliff Manor, NY, 5751-1991
Brick Town, NJ, 5744-1984
Bridgehampton, LI, NY, 5745-1985
Bridgeport, CT, 5744-1984
Bridgeton, NJ, 5751-1991
Bridgewater, NJ, 5744-1984
Brigantine, NJ, 5751-1991
Brighton, MA, 5745-1985
Beis HaKnesset "Ari" Anshe Lubavitch.
Bristol, CT, 5744-1984
Brockport, NY, 5744-1984
Brockton, MA, 5744-1984
Bronx, NY, 5744-1984
Brooker, FL, 5752-1992
Brookfield, WI, 5744-1984
Brookhaven, LI, NY, 5745-1985
Brookline, MA, 5744-1984
Yeshivat Achei Tmimim.
Brooklyn, MD, 5751-1991

Brooklyn, NY, 5714-1954, 5715-1955, 5716-1956, 5718-1958, 5739-1978, 5740-1979, 5740-1980, 5742-1982, 5744-1984, 5750-1990, 5751-1991, 5752-1992, 5753-1993
Brooklyn, NY, 5744-1984, 5745-1984
Printed by Vaad L'Hafotzas Sichos, above 770 Eastern Parkway
Brooklyn, NY, 5746-1985
Library of Agudas Chasidei Chabad, 770 Eastern Parkway.
Brooklyn, NY, Bath Beach, 5750-1990
Brooklyn, NY, Bay Ridge, 5748-1988
Brooklyn, NY, Boro Park, 5744-1984
Brooklyn, NY, Boro Park, 5748-1988
Bucharian Jewish Center
Brooklyn, NY, Brooklyn Heights, 5748-1988
Brooklyn, NY, Brownsville, 5748-1988
Brooklyn, NY, Canasie,
Bais Chabad "Bais Mordechai", 5752-1991
Brooklyn, NY, Coney Island Hospital, 5752-1992
Brooklyn, NY, Crown Heights, 5749-1989
Brooklyn, NY, Crown Heights, 5746-1986
Courtyard of 770 Eastern Parkway
Brooklyn, NY Crown Heights, 5748-1988
Courtyard of 770 Eastern Parkway, Next to the Even HaPinah.
Brooklyn, NY, Crown Heights, 5748-1988
Next to Ahavat Moshe 612 Maple St.
Brooklyn, NY, Crown Heights, 5746-1986
Next to Kollel Avrachim, Machne Yisroel, Ohel Yosef Yitzchak.
Brooklyn, NY, Crown Heights, 5746-1986
Next to Machon Chana 1367 President St.
Brooklyn, NY, Crown Heights, 5746-1986
Next to Machon Chana 825 Eastern Parkway.
Brooklyn, NY, Crown Heights, 5746-1986
Printed by B'nos Chabad
Next to Beis Rivkah 310 Crown St.
Brooklyn, NY, East Flatbush, 5748-1988
Brooklyn, NY, East New York, 5748-1988
Brooklyn, NY, Flatbush, 5744-1984
Brooklyn, NY, Greenpoint, 5748-1988
Brooklyn, NY, Park Slope, 5748-1988
Brooklyn, NY, Starret City, 5748-1988
Brooklyn, NY, Sunset Park, 5748-1988
Brooksville, FL, 5752-1992
Brown Deer, WI, 5744-1984
Brownsville, TX, 5744-1984
Brunswick, GA, 5751-1991
Bryceville, FL, 5752-1992
Buena, NJ, 5751-1991
Buena Park, CA, 5748-1988
Buffalo, NY, 5744-1984
Buffalo Grove, IL, 5746-1986
Bunnell, FL, 5752-1992
Burbank, CA, 5744-1984
Burbank, FL, 5752-1992
Burlington, MA, 5745-1985
Burlington, VT, 5744-1984
Bushell, FL, 5752-1992
Byram, CT, 5752-1991
Cabot, VT, 5752-1991
Cadillac, FL, 5752-1992
Calais, VT, 5752-1991
Caldwell, NJ, 5744-1984
Calexico, CA, 5744-1984
Callahan, FL, 5752-1992
Calumet City, IL, 5745-1985
Calverton, LI, NY, 5745-1985
Camario, CA, 5745-1985
Cambridge, MA, 5744-1984
Cambridge, VT, 5752-1991
Canoe Place, LI, NY, 5745-1985
Canton, MA, 5745-1985
Canton, OH, 5744-1984
Cape Coral, FL, 5744-1984
Cape May, NJ, 5751-1991
Cape May Court House, NJ, 5751-1991
Cape May Point, NJ, 5751-1991
Carlsbad, CA, 5744-1984
Carmel, NJ, 5751-1991
Carson, CA, 5744-1984
Casa Granda, AZ, 5745-1985
Casselberry, FL, 5751-1991
Cedar Beach, LI, NY, 5745-1985
Cedar Grove, NJ, 5744-1984
Cedar Knolls, NJ, 5744-1984
Cedarburg, WI, 5744-1984

Cedarhurst, LI, NY, 5744-1984
Cedarville, NJ, 5751-1991
Center Moriches, LI, NY, 5745-1985
Centereach, LI, NY, 5745-1985
Centerport, LI, NY, 5745-1985
Cerritos, CA, 5744-1984
Champaign, IL, 5746-1986
Chandler, AZ, 5745-1985
Chantilly, VA, 5751-1991
Charleston, SC, 5744-1984
Charleston, WV, 5744-1984
Charlotte, NC, 5744-1984
Charlotte, VT, 5752-1991
Chatham, NJ, 5744-1984
Chattanooga, TN, 5744-1984
Chautauqua, NY, 5748-1988
Chelsea, MI, 5745-1985
Cherry Hill, NJ, 5744-1984
Cherry Hill, MD, 5751-1991
Chesapeake, VA, 5744-1984
Cheshire, MA, 5745-1985
Chester, VA, 5751-1991
Chester, NJ, 5744-1984
Chester, PA, 5751-1991
Chester Township, NJ, 5744-1984
Chesterfield, VA, 5751-1991
Chestnut Hill, MA, 5746-1986
Beis HaKnesset Lubavitch.
Cheviot Hills, CA, Bais Chabad, 5748-1988
Chevy Chase, MD, 5751-1991
Chicago, IL, 5744-1984
Chino, CA, 5748-1988
Chula Vista, CA, 5744-1984
Cincinnati, OH, 5744-1984
Citra, FL, 5752-1992
Claremont, CA, 5744-1984
Clark, NJ, 5744-1984
Claxton, GA, 5751-1991
Clear Lake, TX, 5748-1988
Clearwater, FL, 5744-1984
Clemente, CA, 5748-1988
Cleveland, OH, 5744-1984
Cleveland Heights, OH, 5744-1984
Cliffside Park, NJ, 5744-1984
Clifton, NJ, 5744-1984
Cliftownville, FL, 5752-1992
Clinton, MA, 5745-1985
Closter, NJ, 5744-1984
Cloud, FL, 5746-1986
Cloud, MN, 5745-1985
Cocoa, FL, 5752-1992
Coconut Creek, FL, 5745-1985
Coconut Grove, FL, 5751-1991
Colchester, CT, 5744-1984
Colchester, VT, 5752-1991
College Park, MD, 5744-1984
College Station, TX, 5744-1984
Colonia, NJ, 5744-1984
Colorado Springs, CO, 5744-1984
Colton, CA, 5748-1988
Columbia, MD, 5745-1985
Columbus, OH, 5744-1984
Commack, LI, NY, 5744-1984
Commerce, CA, 5744-1984
Compton, CA, 5744-1984
Cooper City, FL, 5745-1985
Copiague, LI, NY, 5745-1985
Coral Gables, FL, 5744-1984
Coral Springs, FL, 5744-1984
Coram, LI, NY, 5745-1985
Corbin City, NJ, 5751-1991
Corisicana, TX, 5744-1984
Corning, NY, 5744-1984
Corona, CA, 5748-1988
Coronado, CA, 5744-1984
Corpus, TX, 5744-1984
Cortland, NY, 5744-1984
Costa Mesa, CA, 5744-1984
Cottonwood, AZ, 5745-1985
Covina, CA, 5744-1984
Cranbury, NJ, 5744-1984
Cranbury, CT, 5752-1991
Cranford, NJ, 5744-1984
Cranston, RI, 5744-1984
Cresskill, NJ, 5744-1984
Crestwood Village, NJ, 5744-1984
Croton on Hudson, NY, 5751-1991
Cudahy, CA, 5744-1984
Culver City, CA, 5744-1984
Cumberland, MD, 5744-1984

Cutchogue, LI, NY, 5745-1985
Cypress, CA, 5744-1984
Dairyland, NY, Camp Shaloh, 5748-1988
Dallas, TX, 5744-1984
Danbury, CT, 5744-1984
Dania, FL, 5745-1985
Danielson, CT, 5744-1984
Darby, FL, 5752-1992
Darien, CT, 5752-1991
Darlington, MD, 5751-1991
Davie, FL, 5745-1985
Davis Monthan AFB, AZ, 5745-1985
Davis Park, LI, NY, 5745-1985
Dayton, NJ, 5744-1984
Dayton, OH, 5748-1988
Daytona Beach, FL, 5744-1984
De Pere, WI, 5744-1984
Deal, NJ, 5744-1984
Deans, NJ, 5744-1984
Decatur, IL, 5746-1986
Dedham, MA, 5745-1985
Deer Park, LI, NY, 5744-1984
Deerfield, IL, 5745-1985
Deerfield, LI, NY, 5745-1985
Deerfield Beach, FL, 5745-1985
Del Mar, CA, 5744-1984
Delano, CA, 5748-1988
Delmar, NY, 5751-1991
Delmont, NJ, 5751-1991
Delray Beach, FL, 5744-1984
Demarest, NJ, 5744-1984
Denver, CO, 5744-1984
Denville, VA, 5751-1991
Denville, NJ, 5744-1984
Derby, CT, 5745-1985
Des Moines, IA, 5744-1984
Des Plains, IL, 5746-1986
Detroit, MI, 5744-1984
Devon, LI, NY, 5745-1985
Diego, CA, 5744-1984
Dimas, CA, 5744-1984
Dividing Creek, NJ, 5751-1991
Dix Hills, LI, NY, 5745-1985
Dorchester, NJ, 5751-1991
Dorothy, NJ, 5751-1991
Douglas, AZ, 5745-1985
Dover, DE, 5748-1988
Dover, NJ, 5744-1984
Downey, CA, 5744-1984
Duarte, CA, 5744-1984
Duarte, CA, 5748-1988
Dublin, MD, 5751-1991
Dubuque, IA, 5744-1984
Duck Key, FL, 5751-1991
Dukes, FL, 5752-1992
Duluth, MN, 5744-1984
Dumont, NJ, 5744-1984
Duncan, OK, 5745-1985
Dunkirk, NY, 5744-1984
East Brunswick, NJ, 5744-1984
East Calais, VT, 5752-1991
East Hanover, NJ, 5744-1984
East Hartford, CT, 5744-1984
East Haven, CT, 5745-1985
East Longmeadow, MA, 5744-1984
East Newark, NJ, 5744-1984
East Noralk, CT, 5752-1991
East Northport, LI, NY, 5744-1984
East Orange, NJ, 5744-1984
East Palatka, FL, 5752-1992
East Quogue, LI, NY, 5744-1984
East Rutherford, NJ, 5744-1984
East Windsor, NJ, 5744-1984
Easton, CT, 5745-1985
Eau Claire, WI, 5744-1984
Eddy, FL, 5752-1992
Edgewood, LI, NY, 5745-1985
Edgewood, MD, 5751-1991
Edina, MN, 5745-1985
Edison, NJ, 5744-1984
Egg Harbor City, NJ, 5751-1991
El Cajon, CA, 5744-1984
El Centro, CA, 5744-1984
El Monte, CA, 5744-1984
El Paso, TX, 5744-1984
El Segundo, CA, 5744-1984
Eldora, NJ, 5751-1991
Elizabeth, NJ, 5744-1984
Elkins Park, PA, 5744-1984
Ellenville, NY, 5744-1984

Ellerbee, FL, 5752-1992
Elmira, NY, 5744-1984
Elmwood Park, NJ, 5744-1984
Elwood, NJ, 5751-1991
Elyria, OH, 5744-1984
Emerson, NJ, 5744-1984
Encino, CA, 5748-1988
Endicott, NY, 5745-1985
Endwell, NY, 5745-1985
Enfield, CT, 5744-1984
Englewood, NJ, 5744-1984
Englewood Cliffs, NJ, 5745-1985
Enosburg Falls, VT, 5752-1991
Escondido, CA, 5744-1984
Essex Junction, VT, 5752-1991
Estell Manor, NJ, 5751-1991
Estes Park, CO, 5744-1984
Eugene, OR, 5744-1984
Eureka, CA, 5744-1984
Eureka, FL, 5752-1992
Evanston, IL, 5744-1984
Evergreen, CO, 5744-1984
Evinston, FL, 5752-1992
Ewingville, NJ, 5744-1984
Exmore, VA, 5751-1991
Fair Banks, FL, 5752-1992
Fair Haven, NJ, 5744-1984
Fairbanks, AK, 5745-1985
Fairfax, VA, 5744-1984
Fairfield, CT, 5745-1985
Fairfield, IA, 5745-1985
Fairlawn, NJ, 5744-1984
Fairton, NJ, 5751-1991
Fairview, NJ, 5744-1984
Fall River, MA, 5744-1984
Fallsburg, NY, 5748-1988
Far Rockaway, NY, 5744-1984
Farmingdale, LI, NY, 5745-1985
Farmington, CT, 5744-1984
Farmington Hills, MI, 5744-1984
Farmingville, LI, NY, 5745-1985
Fayetteville, NC, 5744-1984
Fe, NM, 5746-1986
Fe, FL, 5752-1992
Fe Springs, CA, 5744-1984
Fernando, CA, 5744-1984
Ferndale, NY, 5748-1988
Fillmore, CA, 5748-1988
Fire Island, LI, NY, 5744-1984
Fireplace, LI, NY, 5745-1985
Fitchburg, MA, 5745-1985
Flagstaff, AZ, 5745-1985
Flint, MI, 5746-1986
Florence, AZ, 5745-1985
Florence, SC, 5751-1991
Florham Park, NJ, 5744-1984
Florida City, FL, 5745-1985
Flossmoor, IL, 5746-1986
Flying Point, LI, NY, 5745-1985
Fond du Lac, WI, 5744-1984
Fontana, CA, 5748-1988
Forest Hill, MD, 5751-1991
Forest Lake, MN, 5745-1985
Forked River, NJ, 5744-1984
Fort Collins, CO, 5744-1984
Fort Lauderdale, 5744-1984
Fort Lee, NJ, 5744-1984
Fort Lewis (Army Base), WA, 5744-1984
Fort Lonsesome, FL, 5752-1992
Fort Myers, FL, 5744-1984
Fort Pierce, FL, 5752-1992
Fort Salonga, LI, NY, 5745-1985
Fort Wayne, IN, 5744-1984
Fort Worth, TX, 5744-1984
Fortescue, NJ, 5751-1991
Fosterdale, NY, 5748-1988
Fountain Valley, CA, 5744-1984
Fox Point, WI, 5744-1984
Framingham, MA, 5744-1984
Francisco, CA, 5744-1984
Franklin, NC, 5751-1991
Franklin Lakes, NJ, 5744-1984
Frederick, MD, 5744-1984
Freehold, NJ, 5748-1988
Freetown, LI, NY, 5745-1985
Fresno, CA, 5748-1988
Fridley, MN, 5745-1985
Ft. Lauderdale, FL, Bais Chabad, 5751-1991
Fullerton, CA, 5748-1988
Gabriel, CA, 5744-1984

Gainesville, FL, 5744-1984
Galveston, TX, 5744-1984
Garden Grove, CA, 5744-1984
Gardena, CA, 5744-1984
Garfield, NJ, 5744-1984
Garwood, NJ, 5744-1984
Geneseo, NY, 5744-1984
Genoa, FL, 5752-1992
Georgia Center, VT, 5752-1991
Georgica, LI, NY, 5745-1985
Gifford Shores, FL, 5752-1992
Gilford, CT, 5745-1985
Glasgow, DE, 5751-1991
Glastonbury, CT, 5744-1984
Glen Allen, VA, 5751-1991
Glen Mary, FL, 5752-1992
Glen Rock, NJ, 5744-1984
Glenbrook, CT, 5745-1985
Glencoe, IL, 5746-1986
Glendale, AZ, 5745-1985
Glendale, CA, 5748-1988
Glendale, WI, 5744-1984
Glendora, CA, 5744-1984
Glennville, GA, 5751-1991
Glens Falls, NY, 5744-1984
Glenview, IL, 5745-1985
Glenville, CT, 5752-1991
Gloversville, NY, 5745-1985
Golden, CO, 5744-1984
Golden Valley, MN, 5745-1985
Goldsboro, NC, 5751-1991
Golf Manor, OH, 5745-1985
Gowers Corner, FL, 5752-1992
Grafton, WI, 5744-1984
Gragam, FL, 5752-1992
Grand Haven, MI, 5746-1986
Grand Island, NY, 5744-1984
Grand Junction, CO, 5744-1984
Grand Rapids, MI, 5744-1984
Grand Terrace, CA, 5748-1988
Grant, FL, 5752-1992
Great Falls, MT, 5744-1984
Great Neck, LI, NY, 5744-1984
Greeley, CO, 5744-1984
Green Bay, WI, 5744-1984
Greenbelt, MD, 5751-1991
Greenfield, MA, 5744-1984
Greenfield, NH, 5744-1984
Greenfield Hill, CT, 5752-1991
Greenfield Park, NY, Camp Emunah, 5748-1988
Greenlawn, LI, NY, 5745-1985
Greenport, LI, NY, 5745-1985
Greensburg, PA, 5745-1985
Greenville, KY, 5747-1987
Greenville, DE, 5751-1991
Greenwich, CT, 5745-1985
Greenwich, NJ, 5751-1991
Groton, CT, 5744-1984
Grove Park, FL, 5752-1992
Guttenberg, NJ, 5744-1984
Hackensack, NJ, 5744-1984
Hadley, MA, 5744-1984
Hagerstown, MD, 5744-1984
Hall, MA, 5745-1985
Hallandale, FL, 5744-1984
Hamden, CT, 5744-1984
Hammond, IN, 5744-1984
Hammonton, NJ, 5751-1991
Hampton, VA, 5748-1988
Hampton Bays, LI, NY, 5745-1985
Hampton Park, LI, NY, 5745-1985
Hanover, NJ, 5744-1984
Harbor Oaks, FL, 5752-1992
Hardscrabble, LI, NY, 5745-1985
Hardwick, VT, 5752-1991
Harlingen, TX, 5744-1984
Harris, NY, 5748-1988
Harrisburg, PA, 5744-1984
Harrison, NJ, 5744-1984
Hartford, CT, 5744-1984
Hasbrouck Heights, NJ, 5744-1984
Hauppauge, LI, NY, 5745-1985
Hawaiian Gardens, CA, 5744-1984
Haworth, NJ, 5744-1984
Hawthorne, CA, 5744-1984
Hawthorne, FL, 5752-1992
Haynesworth, FL, 5752-1992
Hazelhurst, GA, 5751-1991
Head of the Harbor, LI, NY, 5745-1985
Heampstead, LI, NY, 5746-1986

Heartland, WI, 5745-1985
Hebron, CT, 5744-1984
Heislerville, NJ, 5751-1991
Helena, MT, 5744-1984
Herkimer, NY, 5745-1985
Hermosa Beach, CA, 5744-1984
Hernando Beach, FL, 5752-1992
Hewlett, LI NY, 5745-1985
Hialeah, FL, 5744-1984
Hidden Hills, CA, 5744-1984
High Point, NC, 5748-1988
Highground, LI, NY, 5745-1985
Highland, NY, 5751-1991
Highland, CA, 5748-1988
Highland, IN, 5744-1984
Highland Park, IL, 5744-1984
Highland Park, NJ, 5744-1984
Hightstown, NJ, 5744-1984
Hillcrest, NY, 5746-1986
Hilliard, FL, 5752-1992
Hoboken, NJ, 5744-1984
Hockessin, DE, 5751-1991
Holbrook, LI, NY, 5745-1985
Holbrook, MA, 5745-1985
Holiday City, NJ, 5744-1984
Holland, MI, 5746-1986
Hollister, FL, 5752-1992
Holly Hill, FL, 5752-1992
Hollywood, FL, 5744-1984
Holmes, NY, 5751-1991
Holtsville, LI, NY, 5745-1985
Holyoke, MA, 5744-1984
Homeland, FL, 5752-1992
Homestead, FL, 5745-1985
Homewood, IL, 5746-1986
Honolulu, HI, 5742-1982
Hopewell Jct., NY, 5751-1991
Hornell, NY, 5744-1984
Houston, TX, 5744-1984
Hudson, FL, 5752-1992
Hunter, NY, 5745-1985
Huntigdon, PA, 5749-1989
Huntington, NY, 5744-1984
Huntington, FL, 5752-1992
Huntington Beach, CA, 5744-1984
Huntington Park, CA, 5744-1984
Hyattsville, MD, 5744-1984
Hyde Park, NY, 5751-1991
Hyde Park, VT, 5752-1991
Imperial Beach, CA, 5744-1984
Indianapolis, IN, 5744-1984
Indrio, FL, 5752-1992
Industry, CA, 5744-1984
Inglewood, CA, 5744-1984
Interlachen, FL, 5752-1992
Inwood, LI, NY, 5745-1985
Irvine, CA, 5744-1984
Irvington, NJ, 5744-1984
Irwindale, CA, 5744-1984
Island Grove, FL, 5752-1992
Isle Morada, FL, 5751-1991
Islip, LI, NY, 5744-1984
Italia, FL, 5752-1992.
Ithaca, NY, 5744-1984
Jackson, MS, 5744-1984
Jacksonville, FL, 5744-1984
James, LI, NY, 5745-1985
Jamesport, LI, NY, 5745-1985
Jamestown, NY, 5744-1984
Jasmine, FL, 5752-1992
Jasper, FL, 5752-1992
Jeffersonville, VT, 5752-1991
Jericho, LI, NY, 5745-1985
Jersey City, NJ, 5744-1984
Jesup, GA, 5751-1991
Johnsbury, VT, 5748-1988
Johnson, FL, 5752-1992
Johnson City, NY, 5745-1985
Johnson. VT, 5752-1991
Johnstown, PA, 5745-1985
Johnstown, FL, 5752-1992
Joliet, IL, Joliet Correctional Center, 5745-1985
Jose, CA, 5748-1988
Juan, PR, 5744-1984
Juan Capistrano, CA, 5748-1988
Juna, AK, 5746-1986
Kalamazoo, MI, 5746-1986
Kalkaska, MI, 5744-1984
Kankakee, IL, 5746-1986
Kansas City, MO, 5744-1984

Katonah, NY, 5751-1991
Kauneongo Lake, NY, 5748-1988
Kearny, NJ, 5744-1984
Kendall, FL, 5744-1984
Kendall Park, NJ, 5744-1984
Kenilworth, NJ, 5744-1984
Kennedy Airport, NY, 5744-1984
Kenosha, WI, 5744-1984
Kent, FL, 5752-1992
Key Biscayne, FL, 5751-1991
Key Largo, FL, 5751-1991
Key West, FL, 5744-1984
Kiamesha Lake, NY, 5744-1984
Kilgore, TX, 5744-1984
Killington, VT, 5752-1991
Kingman, AZ, 5745-1985
Kings Park, LI, NY, 5745-1985
Kings-Ferry, FL, 5752-1992
Kingsland, GA, 5751-1991
Kingston, NY, 5744-1984
Kingston, PA, 5744-1984
Kingstown, LI, NY, 5745-1985
Kinnelon, NJ, 5744-1984
Kiryat Gan Israel, NY, 5741-1981
Kismet, LI, NY, 5745-1985
Kissimee, FL, 5746-1986
Knoxville, TN, 5746-1986
La Caniada, CA, 5744-1984
La Cro, WI, 5744-1984
La Habra Heights, CA, 5744-1984
La Havra, CA, 5748-1988
La Jolla, CA, 5744-1984, 5745-1985
La Mesa, CA, 5744-1984
La Mirada, CA, 5744-1984
La Palma, CA, 5744-1984
La Puente, CA, 5744-1984
La Verne, CA, 5744-1984
Lafayette, IN, 5745-1985
Laguna Beach, CA, 5744-1984
Laguna Hills, CA, 5744-1984
Lake Butler, FL, 5752-1992
Lake City, FL, 5752-1992
Lake Como, FL, 5752-1992
Lake Elsinore, CA, 5748-1988
Lake Forest, IL, 5745-1985
Lake George, NY, 5745-1985
Lake Grove, LI, NY, 5744-1984
Lake Hawaso, AZ, 5745-1985
Lake Mary, FL, 5751-1991
Lake Placid, NY, 5745-1985
Lake Purdy, NY, 5751-1991
Lake Tahoe, CA, 5744-1984
Lake Worth, FL, 5745-1985
Lakeland, FL, 5744-1984
Lakewood, CA, 5744-1984
Lakewood, NJ, 5744-1984
Lancaster, CA, 5744-1984
Lantana, FL, 5745-1985
Laredo, TX, 5744-1984
Las Vegas, NV, 5744-1984
Lauderdale Lakes, FL, 5745-1985
Lauderhill, FL, 5745-1985
Laurel, LI, NY, 5745-1985
Laurel, MD, 5751-1991
Lawndale, CA, 5744-1984
Lawrence, MA, 5745-1985
Lawrence, LI, NY, 5744-1984
Lawrenceville, NJ, 5748-1988
Lebanon, CT, 5744-1984
Leesburg, NJ, 5751-1991
Leisure Village, NJ, 5744-1984
Lemon Grove, CA, 5744-1984
Leominster, MA, 5745-1985
Leonia, NJ, 5744-1984
Lewiston, NY, 5744-1984
Lewistown, PA, 5745-1985
Lexington, KY, 5744-1984
Lexington, MA, 5745-1985
Liberty, NY, 5744-1984
Libertyville, IL, 5746-1986
Lighthouse Point, FL, 5745-1985
Lincoln, NB, 5748-1988
Lincroft, NJ, 5744-1984
Linden, NJ, 5744-1984
Linwood, NJ, 5751-1991
Little Pine Key, FL, 5751-1991
Little Rock, AR, 5744-1984
Little Silver, NJ, 5744-1984
Littleton, CO, 5744-1984
Livingston, NJ, 5744-1984

Livingston Manor, NY, 5748-1988
Loch Sheldrake, NY, 5745-1985
Lochloosa, FL, 5752-1992
Lodi, NJ, 5744-1984
Loma Linda, CA, 5748-1988
Lomita, CA, 5744-1984
Lompoc, CA, 5748-1988
Long Beach, CA, 5744-1984
Long Beach, NY, 5744-1984
Long Branch, NJ, 5744-1984
Long Key, FL, 5751-1991
Longmeadow, MA, 5744-1984
Longport, NJ, 5751-1991
Longview, TX, 5744-1984
Longwood, FL, 5751-1991
Los Alamitos, CA, 5748-1988
Los Angeles, CA, 5744-1984
Los Angeles Superior Court, CA, 5748-1988
Los Angeles, CA, Yeshivat Ohr Elchonon, 5748-1988
Los Angeles, CA, Central Bais Chabad, 5748-1988
Louis, MO, 5744-1984
Louis Obispo, CA, 5748-1988
Louis Park, MN, 5744-1984
Louisville, KY, 5744-1984
Loveland, CO, 5744-1984
Lowell, MA, 5745-1985
Lubbock, TX, 5744-1984
Ludlow, VT, 5752-1991
Lulu, FL, 5752-1991
Lumberton, NC, 5751-1991
Lynchburg, VA, 5751-1991
Lyndhurst, NJ, 5744-1984
Lyndhurst, OH, 5744-1984
Lyndonville, VT, 5752-1991
Lynn, MA, 5745-1985
Lynwood, CA, 5744-1984
Lyons, GA, 5751-1991
MacClenny, FL, 5752-1992
Madison, NJ, 5744-1984
Madison, WI, 5744-1984
Magnolia, NJ, 5751-1991
Mahwah, NJ, 5744-1984
Maitland, FL, 5751-1991
Malabar, FL, 5752-1992
Manalapan, NJ, 5748-1988
Mancata, MN, 5745-1985
Manchester, CT, 5744-1984
Manchester, VT, 5748-1988
Manhattan Beach, CA, 5744-1984
Manitowoc, WI, 5744-1984
Manning, SC, 5751-1991
Mannville, FL, 5752-1992
Manorville, LI, NY, 5745-1985
Maplewood, NJ, 5744-1984
Maplewood, NY, 5748-1988
Marathon, FL, 5751-1991
Marblehead, MA, 5745-1985
Marco Island, FL, 5751-1991
Marcos, CA, 5744-1984
Margate, FL, 5745-1985
Margate, NJ, 5751-1991
Maria, CA, 5748-1988
Marina, CA, 5748-1988
Marina del Rey, Beis Chabad, CA, 5748-1988
Marinette, WI, 5744-1984
Marino, CA, 5744-1984
Marlboro, NY, 5751-1991
Marlboro, NJ, 5748-1988
Marmora, NJ, 5751-1991
Marshall, TX, 5744-1984
Maryland City, MD, 5751-1991
Mastic, LI, NY, 5745-1985
Mattituck, LI, NY, 5745-1985
Maui, HI, 5743-1983
Mauricetown, NJ, 5751-1991
Mays Landing, NJ, 5751-1991
Maywood, CA, 5744-1984
Maywood, NJ, 5744-1984
McAllen, TX, 5744-1984
McIntosh, FL, 5752-1992
McKee City, NJ, 5751-1991
McKeesport, PA, 5745-1985
Mechanicsville, VA, 5751-1991
Mecox, LI, NY, 5745-1985
Medford, LI, NY, 5745-1985
Medford, OR, 5746-1986
Melbourne, FL, 5752-1992
Melville, LI, NY, 5745-1985
Memphis, TN, 5744-1984
Mendham, NJ, 5744-1984

Mendota, MN, 5745-1985
Menominee, MI, 5744-1984
Menomonee Falls, WI, 5744-1984
Mequon, WI, 5744-1984
Merced, CA, 5748-1988
Mercer Island, WA, 5744-1984
Meriden, CT, 5744-1984
Mesa, AZ, 5745-1985
Metuchen, NJ, 5744-1984
Miami, FL, 5744-1984
Miami Beach, FL, 5745-1985
Miami Springs, FL, 5745-1985
Micanopy, FL, 5752-1992
Micco, FL, 5752-1992
Michigan City, IN, 5746-1986
Middle Hope, NY, 5751-1991
Middle Island, LI, NY, 5745-1985
Middlebury, VT, 5752-1991
Middleton, WI, 5744-1984
Middletown, CT, 5744-1984
Middletown, NY, 5748-1988
Midlothian, VA, 5751-1991
Milburn, NJ, 5744-1984
Milford, CT, 5745-1985
Millbrook, NY, 5751-1991
Millers Tavern, VA, 5751-1991
Millerton, NY, 5751-1991
Millville, NJ, 5751-1991
Milmay, NJ, 5751-1991
Milton, MA, 5744-1984
Milton, NY, 5745-1985
Milton, VT, 5752-1991
Milwaukee, WI, 5744-1984
Mims, FL, 5752-1992
Minneapolis, MN, 5744-1984
Minnetonka, MN, 5745-1985
Miramar, FL, 5745-1985
Mission Viejo, CA, 5748-1988
Missouri City, TX, 5744-1984
Mobile, AL, 5746-1986
Modena, NY, 5751-1991
Modesto, CA, 5748-1988
Monica, CA, 5744-1984
Monmouth Jct., NJ, 5744-1984
Monroe, NY, 5748-1988
Monroeville, PA, 5745-1985
Monrovia, CA, 5744-1984
Monsey, NY, 5744-1984
Montauk Point, LI, NY, 5744-1984
Montclair, CA, 5748-1988
Montclair, NJ, 5744-1984
Montebello, CA, 5744-1984
Monterey, CA, 5748-1988
Monterey Park, CA, 5744-1984
Montgomery, AL, 5744-1984
Montgomery, AL, 5744-1984
Ganter-Maxwell Air Force Base.
Montgomery, OH, 5748-1988
Monticello, NY, 5744-1984
Montpelier, VT, 5744-1984
Montvale, NJ, 5744-1984
Moorpark, CA, 5745-1985
Morris Plains, NJ, 5744-1984
Morris Township, NJ, 5744-1984
Chabad Lubavitch Campus.
Morristown, NJ, 5744-1984
Morton Grove, IL, 5746-1986
Mount Arlington, NJ, 5744-1984
Mount Kisco, NY, 5744-1984
Mount Olive, NJ, 5744-1984
Mount Pleasant, NY, 5751-1991
Mount Pleasant, MI, 5746-1986
Mount Sinai, LI, NY, 5745-1985
Mount Union, PA, 5745-1985
Mountain Lakes, NJ, 5744-1984
Mt. Vernon, NY, 5748-1988
Mt. Vernon, GA, 5751-1991
Muncie, IN, 5746-1986
Muskegan, MI, 5746-1986
Myrtle Beach, SC, 5748-1988
Nagalas, AZ, 5745-1985
Nags Head, NC, 5751-1991
Nantucket, MA, 5745-1985
Napeague, LI, NY, 5745-1985
Naples, FL, 5744-1984
Nashville, TN, 5744-1984
National City, CA, 5744-1984
Nebraska City, NB, 5748-1988
Needles, CA, 5748-1988
Nesconset, LI, NY, 5745-1985

Neversink, NY, 5748-1988
New Berlin, WI, 5744-1984
New Brighton, MN, 5745-1985
New Britain, CT, 5744-1984
New Brunswick, NJ, 5744-1984
New Canaan, CT, 5752-1991
New Castle, DE, 5751-1991
New City, NY, 5744-1984
New Egypt, NJ, 5744-1984
New Hamburg, NY, 5751-1991
New Hartford, NY 5749-1989
New Haven, CT, 5744-1984
New London, CT, 5744-1984
New Milford, NJ, 5744-1984
New Orleans, LA, 5744-1984
New Paltz, NY, 5745-1985
New Providence, NJ, 5744-1984
New River, FL, 5752-1992
New Rochelle, NY, 5745-1985
New York City, NY, Battery Park, 5748-1988
New York City, NY, Manhattan, 5744-1984
New York City, NY, South Ferry, 5748-1988
New York City, NY, Wall St, 5748-1988
Newark, DE, 5748-1988
Newark-Ivy Hill, NJ, 5744-1984
Newburgh, NY, 5751-1991
Newington, CT, 5744-1984
Newport, MN, 5745-1985
Newport, RI, 5744-1984
Bais HaKnesset Turo, Cong., Yeshuat Yisroel.
Newport, NJ, 5751-1991
Newport, DE, 5751-1991
Newport, VT, 5752-1991
Newport Beach, CA, 5744-1984
Newport News, VA, 5747-1987
Newton, CT, 5745-1985
Newton, MA, 5744-1984
Newton, NJ, 5744-1984
Niagara Falls, NY, 5744-1984
Niles, IL, 5745-1985
Norco, CA, 5748-1988
Norfolk, VA, 5744-1984
Norma, NJ, 5751-1991
North Arlington, NJ, 5744-1984
North Bergen, NJ, 5744-1984
North Brunswick, NJ, 5744-1984
North Caldwell, NJ, 5744-1984
North Hampton, MA, 5744-1984
North Haven, CT, 5745-1985
North Haven, LI, NY, 5745-1985
North Hollywood, Bais Chabad, CA, 5748-1988
North Miami, FL, 5744-1984
North Miami Beach, FL, 5744-1984
North Salem, NY, 5751-1991
North Sea, LI, NY, 5745-1985
North Stamford, CT, 5752-1991
North Tarrytown, NY, 5751-1991
North Wildwood, NJ, 5751-1991
North Woodmere, LI, NY, 5745-1985
Northbrook, IL, 5744-1984
Northfield, MN, 5745-1985
Northfield, NJ, 5751-1991
Northvale, NJ, 5745-1985
Norwalk, CA, 5744-1984
Norwalk, CT, 5745-1985
Norwich, CT, 5744-1984
Norwood, MA, 5745-1985
Norwood, NJ, 5744-1984
Noyack, LI, NY, 5745-1985
Nutley, NJ, 5744-1984
Oak Beach, LI, NY, 5745-1985
Oak Park, Bais Chabad, CA, 5748-1988
Oak Ridge, TN, 5751-1991
Oakdale, LI NY, 5745-1985
Oakland, CA, 5748-1988
Oakland, NJ, 5744-1984
Oberlin, OH, 5744-1984
Ocean City, MD, 5744-1984
Ocean City, NJ, 5751-1991
Ocean Township, NJ, 5744-1984
Oceanside, CA, 5744-1984
Oceanside, LI, NY, 5745-1985
Oconomowoc, WI, 5744-1984
Odessa, TX, 5744-1984
Odessa, FL, 5752-1992
Ogeltown, DE, 5751-1991
Oklahoma City, OK, 5748-1988
Olathe, KS, 5744-1984
Old Field, LI, NY, 5745-1985
Old Greenwich, CT, 5752-1991

Old Tappan, NJ, 5744-1984
Olean, NY, 5744-1984
Olustee, FL, 5752-1992
Olympia, WA, 5744-1984
Omaha, NE, 5744-1984
Onancock,VA, 5751-1991
Oneonta, NY, 5745-1985
Ontario, CA, 5748-1988
Opa-Locka, FL, 5745-1985
Oradell, NJ, 5744-1984
Orange, CA, 5744-1984
Orange, CT, Yeshivat Achei Tmimim, 5745-1985
Orange, NJ, 5744-1984
Orange Heights, FL, 5752-1992
Orange Lake, FL, 5752-1992
Orange Mills, FL, 5752-1992
Orange Springs, FL, 5752-1992
Oregon, LI, NY, 5745-1985
Orient Point, LI, NY, 5745-1985
Orlando, FL, 5744-1984
Ormond Beach, FL, 5752-1992
Oshkosh, WI, 5744-1984
Oslo, FL, 5752-1992
Ossining, NY, 5751-1991
Oswego, NY, 5744-1984
Oxnard, CA, 5745-1985
Palatka, FL, 5752-1992
Palisades Park, NJ, 5744-1984
Palm Bay, FL, 5752-1992
Palm Beach, FL, 5744-1984
Palm City, FL, 5752-1992
Palm Springs, CA, 5744-1984
Palmdale, CA, 5744-1984
Palo Alto, CA, 5744-1984
Palos Verdes Estates, CA, 5744-1984
Pantam Lake, NY, 5751-1991
Pantigo, LI, NY, 5745-1985
Paradise, FL, 5752-1992
Paramount, CA, 5748-1988
Paramus, NJ, 5744-1984
Park Ridge, NJ, 5744-1984
Parksville, NY, 5748-1988
Parlin, NJ, 5744-1984
Parsippany, NJ, 5744-1984
Pasadena, CA, 5748-1988
Passaic, NJ, 5744-1984
Patchogue, LI, NY, 5744-1984
Paterson, NJ, 5744-1984
Patterson, NY, 5751-1991
Paul, MN, 5744-1984
Paula, CA, 5745-1985
Pawguag ,NY, 5751-1991
Pawling, NY, 5751-1991
Pawtucket, RI, 5744-1984
Peconick, LI, NY, 5745-1985
Pembroke Pines, FL, 5745-1985
Pensacola, FL, 5744-1984
Peoria, IL, 5744-1984
Perrine, FL, 5751-1991
Perrineville, NJ, 5744-1984
Perth Amboy, NJ, 5744-1984
Petersburg, FL, 5748-1988
Pewaukee, WI, 5745-1985
Philadelphia, PA, 5744-1984
Phoenix, AZ, 5744-1984
Picnic, FL, 5752-1992
Pico Rivera, CA, 5744-1984
Pierce, FL, 5752-1992
Pierson, FL, 5752-1992
Pine Brook, NJ, 5744-1984
Pine Island, FL, 5752-1992
Pine Plains, NY, 5751-1991
Pinesville, OH, 5744-1984
Piscataway, NJ, 5744-1984
Peach Lake,NY 5751-1991
Pittsburg, PA, 5744-1984
Pittsfield, MA, 5744-1984
Placentia, CA, 5748-1988
Plainfield, NJ, 5744-1984
Plainfield, VT, 5752-1991
Plainview, LI, NY, 5745-1985
Plainville, CT, 5744-1984
Plano, TX, 5744-1984
Plantation, FL, 5745-1985
Plantation Key, FL, 5751-1991
Pleasant Hill, MD, 5751-1991
Pleasant Valley, NY, 5751-1991
Pleasantville, NJ, 5751-1991
Plymouth, MN, 5745-1985
Plymouth, VT, 5752-1991

Pomona, CA, 5744-1984
Pomona, NY, 5746-1986
Pomona, NJ, 5751-1991
Pomona Park, FL, 5752-1992
Pompano Beach, FL, 5744-1984
Pompton Lakes, NJ, 5744-1984
Ponquoque, LI, NY, 5745-1985
Port Arthur, TX, 5744-1984
Port Elizabeth, NJ, 5751-1991
Port Jefferson, NY, 5744-1984
Port Malabar, FL, 5752-1992
Port Norris, NJ, 5751-1991
Port Republic, NJ, 5751-1991
Portland, ME, 5744-1984
Portland, OR, 5744-1984
Portsmouth, NH, 5744-1984
Portsmouth, VA, 5744-1984
Poska, FL, 5752-1992
Poughkeepsie, NY, 5744-1984
Poway, CA, 5744-1984
Prescott, AZ, 5745-1985
Princeton, NJ, 5744-1984
Princeton Junction, NJ, 5744-1984
Promised Land, LI, NY, 5745-1985
Providence, RI, 5744-1984
Providence, FL, 5752-1992
Providence Forge, VA, 5751-1991
Pueblo, CO, 5744-1984
Purdy Station, NY, 5751-1991
Putney, VT, 5752-1991
Queens, NY, Bais Chabad, 5752-1992
Queens, Georgian JCC, 5751-1991
Queens, Astoria, 5749-1989
Queens, Long Island City, NY, 5748-1988
Queens, NY, 5744-1984
Quincy, MA, 5744-1984
Racine, WI, 5744-1984
Rafael, CA, 5744-1984
Rahway, NJ, 5744-1984
Rainford, FL, 5752-1992
Raleigh, NC, 5751-1991
Ramsey, NJ, 5744-1984
Rancho Cucamonga, CA, 5748-1988
Rancho Palos Verdes, CA, 5744-1984
Randolph, MA, 5744-1984
Randolph, NJ, 5744-1984
Randolph, VT, 5752-1991
Rapid City, SD, 5744-1984
Red Bank, NJ, 5744-1984
Red Hook, NY, 5751-1991
Red Wing, MN, 5745-1985
Reddick, FL, 5752-1992
Redding, CA, 5744-1984
Redding, OH, 5748-1988
Redlands, CA, 5748-1988
Redondo Beach, CA, 5744-1984
Rhinebeck, NY, 5751-1991
Rhinecliff, NY, 5751-1991
Rialto, CA, 5748-1988
Richardson, TX, 5744-1984
Richland, NJ, 5751-1991
Richmond, VA, 5744-1984
Richmond, VT, 5752-1991
Richmond Hill, GA, 5751-1991
Ridge, LI, NY, 5745-1985
Ridgebury, CT, 5751-1991
Ridgefield, CT, 5751-1991
Ridgefield, NJ, 5744-1984
Ridgefield Park, NJ, 5744-1984
Ridgeland, SC, 5751-1991
Ridgewood, NJ, 5744-1984
Rio Grande, NJ, 5751-1991
River Edge, NJ, 5744-1984
River Hills, WI, 5744-1984
River Vale, NJ, 5745-1985
Riverdale, NY, 5748-1988
Riverhead, LI, NY, 5744-1984
Riverside, CA, 5748-1988
Riverside, CT, 5752-1991
Riverview, FL, 5752-1992
Roanoke, VA, 5745-1985
Roanoke Rapids, NC, 5751-1991
Rochelle, 5752-1992
Rochester, MN, 5744-1984
Rochester, NY, 5744-1984
Rock Springs, WY, 5744-1984
Rockaway, NJ, 5744-1984
Rockaway Township, NJ, 5744-1984
Rockford, IL, 5744-1984
Rockville, CT, 5744-1984

Rockville, MD, 5744-1984
Rocky Hill, CT, 5744-1984
Rocky Mount, NC, 5751-1991
Rocky Point, LI, NY, 5745-1985
Rolling Hills, CA, 5744-1984
Rolling Hills Estates, CA, 5744-1984
Ronkonkoma, LI, NY, 5745-1985
Roosevelt, NJ, 5744-1984
Rosa, CA, 5744-1984
Rose Grove, LI, NY, 5745-1985
Roseland, FL, 5752-1992
Roseland, NJ, 5744-1984
Roselle, NJ, 5744-1984
Roselle Park, NJ, 5744-1984
Rosemead, CA, 5744-1984
Rosenhayn, NJ, 5751-1991
Rossmoor, NJ, 5744-1984
Roswell, MN, 5745-1985
Round Hill, CT, 5752-1991
Royalton. VT, 5752-1991
Rumson, NJ, 5744-1984
Rutherford, NJ, 5744-1984
Rutland, VT, 5748-1988
Sacramento, CA, 5744-1984
Saddle River, NJ, 5744-1984
Saddlebrook, NJ, 5744-1984
Sag Harbor, LI, NY, 5744-1984
Sagaponack, LI, NY, 5745-1985
Salem, NJ, 5751-1991
Salem, OR, 5744-1984
Salinas, CA, 5748-1988
Salisbury, MD, 5744-1984
Salt Lake City, UT, 5744-1984
Salt Point, NY, 5751-1991
Sampson City, FL, 5752-1992
Sanderson, FL, 5752-1992
Sandusky, OH, 5752-1992
Santee, CA, 5748-1988
Sapp, FL, 5752-1992
Sarasota, FL, 5744-1984
Saratoga Springs, NY, 5744-1984
Satsuma, FL, 5752-1992
Savannah, GA, 5751-1991
Sayville, LI, NY, 5745-1985
Scarsdale, NY, 5748-1988
Schaumburg, IL, 5746-1986
Schenectady, NY, 5744-1984
Scotch Plains, NJ, 5744-1984
Scotsdale, AZ, 5745-1985
Scottsmoor, FL, 5752-1992
Scranton, PA, 5744-1984
Scuttlehole, LI, NY, 5745-1985
Sea Isle City, NJ, 5751-1991
Seabrook, NJ, 5751-1991
Seal Beach, CA, 5744-1984
Seattle, WA, 5744-1984
Sebastian, FL, 5752-1992
Secaucus, NJ, 5744-1984
Sedona, AZ, 5745-1985
Selden, LI, NY, 5744-1984
Setauket, LI, NY, 5745-1985
Seville, FL, 5752-1992
Sewaren, NJ, 5744-1984
Sharon, MA, 5744-1984
Sheboygan, WI, 5744-1984
Shelburne, VT, 5752-1991
Shelter Island, LI, NY, 5744-1984
Shelton, CT, 5745-1985
Sherman, TX, 5744-1984
Sherman Oaks, Bais Chabad, CA, 5748-1988
Sherwood, WI, 5744-1984
Shiloh, NJ, 5751-1991
Shinnecock Hills, LI, NY, 5745-1985
Ship Bottom, NJ, 5744-1984
Shirley, LI, NY, 5745-1985
Shoreham, LI, NY, 5745-1985
Shrewsbury, NJ, 5744-1984
Sierra Madra, CA, 5744-1984
Sierra Vista, AZ, 5745-1985
Signal Hill, CA, 5744-1984
Silver Springs, MD, 5744-1984
Silvermine, CT, 5752-1991
Simmee Valley, CA, 5745-1985
Simsbury, CT, 5744-1984
Skokie, IL, 5744-1984
Smallwood, NY, 5748-1988
Smithtown, LI, NY, 5744-1984
Smithville, NJ, 5751-1991
Solana Beach, CA, 5748-1988
Solon, OH, 5752-1992

Somers Point, NJ, 5751-1991
South Bend, IN, 5744-1984
South Burlington, VT, 5752-1991
South El Monte, CA, 5744-1984
South Fallsburg, NY, 5744-1984
South Gate, CA, 5744-1984
South Hadley, MA, 5744-1984
South Kearny, NJ, 5744-1984
South Miami, FL, 5744-1984
South Norwalk, CT, 5752-1991
South Orange, NJ, 5744-1984
South Pasadena, CA, 5744-1984
South Plainfield, NJ, 5744-1984
South Wilton, CT, 5751-1991
South Windsor, CT, 5744-1984
Southampton, LI, NY, 5744-1984
Southfield, MI, 5745-1985
Southold, LI, NY, 5744-1984
Southport, LI, NY, 5745-1985
Southport, CT, 5752-1991
Southwick, MA, 5744-1984
Sparr, FL, 5752-1992
Spokane, WA, 5744-1984
Spring Hill, FL, 5752-1992
Spring Lake, FL, 5752-1992
Spring Valley, NY, 5744-1984
Springdale, CT, 5752-1991
Springfield, IL, 5744-1984
Springfield, MA, 5744-1984
Springfield, NJ, 5744-1984
Springfield, MD, 5751-1991
Springfield, VT, 5752-1991
Springs, LI, NY, 5745-1985
Springville, LI, NY, 5745-1985
Squiretown, LI, NY, 5745-1985
Stafford Springs, CA, 5744-1984
Stamford, CT, 5745-1985
Stanfordville, NY, 5751-1991
Stanton, CA, 5748-1988
Stanton, DE, 5751-1991
State College, PA, 5745-1985
Staten Island, NY, 5744-1984
Stockton, CA, 5748-1988
Stone Harbor, NJ, 5751-1991
Stony Brook, LI, NY, 5744-1984
Stormville, NY 5751-1991
Storrs, CT, 5744-1984
Stoughton, MA, 5744-1984
Stow Creek, NJ, 5751-1991
Stowe, VT, 5752-1991
Straatsburg, NY, 5751-1991
Stratford, CT, 5745-1985
Suffern, NY, 5746-1986
Suffolk, VA, 5744-1984
Sugar Land, TX, 5744-1984
Sullivan County Airport, Swan Lake, NY, 5748-1988
Summerset, NJ, 5744-1984
Summit, NJ, 5744-1984
Sumter, SC, 5751-1991
Sun City, AZ, 5745-1985
Sunderland, MA, 5744-1984
Sunrise, FL, 5745-1985
Superior, WI, 5744-1984
Surf City, NJ, 5744-1984
Surfside, FL, 5744-1984
Swampscott, MA, 5745-1985
Swan Lake, NY, 5748-1988
Swanton, VT, 5752-1991
Sweetwater, FL, 5745-1985, 5751-1991
Sylva, NC, 5751-1991
Syosset, LI, NY, 5745-1985
Syracuse, NY, 5744-1984
Tallahassee, FL, 5744-1984
Tamarak, FL, 5745-1985
Tampa, FL, 5744-1984, 5752-1992
Tannersville, NY, 5744-1984
Tarrytown, NY, 5748-1988
Tarzana, Bais Chabad, CA, 5748-1988
Tavinier, FL, 5751-1991
Taylor, FL, 5752-1992
Teaneck, NJ, 5744-1984
Tempie, AZ, 5745-1985
Temple City, CA, 5744-1984
Tenafly, NJ, 5744-1984
Texarkana, TX, 5744-1984
Thiensville, WI, 5744-1984
Thousand Oaks, CA, 5744-1984
Threemile Harbor, LI, NY, 5745-1985
Tiana, LI, NY, 5745-1985
Tinton Falls, NJ, 5744-1984

Titusville, FL, 5752-1992
Titycas, CT, 5751-1991
Tivoli, NY, 5751-1991
Toledo, OH, 5744-1984
Torrance, CA, 5744-1984
Torrington, CT, 5744-1984
Trenton, NJ, 5744-1984
Troy, NY, 5744-1984
Trumbull, CT, 5745-1985
Tuckahoe, NJ, 5751-1991
Tucson, AZ, 5744-1984
Tulare, CA, 5748-1988
Tulsa, OK, 5744-1984
Turn Of River, CT, 5751-1991
Tuston, CA, 5748-1988
Tyler, TX, 5744-1984
Union, NJ, 5744-1984
Union City, NJ, 5744-1984
Uniontown, PA, 5745-1985
University Heights, OH, 5744-1984
Upland, CA, 5748-1988
Upper Saddle River, NJ, 5744-1984
Utica, NY, 5744-1984
Vail, CO, 5744-1984
Valkaria, FL, 5752-1992
Valley Stream, LI, NY, 5745-1985
Ventnor, NJ, 5751-1991
Ventura, CA, 5745-1985
Verbank, NY, 5751-1991
Vernon, CA, 5744-1984
Vero Beach, FL, 5752-1992
Verona, WI, 5744-1984
Vestal, NY, 5745-1985
Victoria, TX, 5744-1984
Vidalia, GA, 5751-1991
Villa Park, CA, 5748-1988
Vineland, NJ, 5751-1991
Virginia Beach, VA, 5744-1984
Visalia, CA, 5748-1988
Vista, CA, 5744-1984
Wabasso, FL, 5752-1992
Waco, TX, 5744-1984
Wading River, LI, NY, 5745-1985
Wainscott, LI, NY, 5745-1985
Waldo, FL, 5752-1992
Wallingford, CT, 5745-1985
Walnut, CA, 5744-1984
Walterboro, SC, 5751-1991
Waltham, MA, 5745-1985
Wappingers Falls, NY, 5745-1985
Warren, NJ, 5744-1984
Warwick, RI, 5744-1984
Washington, DC, 5744-1984
Washington, PA, 5745-1985
Washington Township, NJ, 5744-1984
Wassaic, NY, 5751-1991
Watchung, NJ, 5744-1984
Water Mill, LI, NY, 5745-1985
Waterbury, CT, 5744-1984
Waterbury, VT, 5752-1991
Waterford, CT, 5747-1987
Waterloo, IA, 5745-1985
Waterloo, MD, 5751-1991
Watertown, NY, 5744-1984
Watertown, FL, 5752-1992
Watkins, CO, 5744-1984
Waukegan, IL, 5746-1986
Waukesha, WI, 5744-1984
Wausau, WI, 5744-1984
Wauwatosa, WI, 5744-1984
Wayne, NJ, 5744-1984
Webster, MA, 5745-1985
Weehawken, NJ, 5744-1984
Weeki Wachee, FL, 5752-1992
Welaka, FL, 5752-1992
Wellesley, MA, 5745-1985
Wellington, FL, 5750-1990
Wellsville, CT, 5745-1985
West Allis, WI, 5744-1984
West Bloomfield, MI, 5745-1985
West Caldwell, NJ, 5744-1984
West Cape May, NJ, 5751-1991
West Chester, PA, 5751-1991
West Covina, CA, 5744-1984
West Haven, CT, 5744-1984
West Hempstead, LI, NY, 5745-1985
West Hollywood, CA, 5745-1985
West Lafayette, IN, 5745-1985
West Longbranch, NJ, 5744-1984
West Melbourne, FL, 5752-1992

West Monticello, NY, 5748-1988
West New York, NJ, 5744-1984
West Norwalk, CT, 5752-1991
West Orange, NJ, 5744-1984
West Palm Beach, FL, 5750-1990
West Rogers Pk, IL,Cheder Lubavitch, 5746-1986
West Springfield, MA, 5744-1984
West Tiana, LI, NY, 5745-1985
West Wildwood, NJ, 5751-1991
Westchester, Dade County, FL, 5745-1985
Westfield, MA, 5744-1984
Westfield, NJ, 5744-1984
Westlake Village, CA, 5744-1984
Westminster, CA, 5744-1984
Weston, CT, 5752-1991
Westport, CT, 5745-1985
Westwood, MA, 5745-1985
Westwood, NJ, 5744-1984
Wethersfield, CT, 5744-1984
Wharton, TX, 5744-1984
Whippany, NJ, 5744-1984
White Bear Lake, MN, 5745-1985
White City, FL, 5752-1992
White Lake, NY, Kiryat Crown Heights, 5746-1986
White Lake, NY, 5748-1988
White Plains, NY, 5748-1988
White River Junction, VT, 5752-1991
White Springs, FL, 5752-1992
Whitefish Bay, WI, 5744-1984
Whittier, CA, 5744-1984
Wichita Falls, TX, 5744-1984
Wickapoque, LI, NY, 5745-1985
Wickliffe, OH, 5744-1984
Wildwood, NJ, 5751-1991
Wildwood Crest, NJ, 5751-1991
Wilkinsburg, PA, 5745-1985
Williamsburg, VA, 5748-1988
Willimantic, CT, 5744-1984
Williston, VT, 5752-1991
Wilmette, IL, 5744-1984
Wilmington, DE, 5744-1984
Wilmington, NC, 5748-1988
Wilson, NC, 5751-1991
Wilton, CT, 5751-1991
Wilton Manors, FL, 5745-1985
Wimauma, FL, 5752-1992
Windsor, CT, 5744-1984
Windsor, FL, 5752-1992
Windsor Locks, CT, 5747-1987
Winfield, FL, 5752-1992
Wingdale, NY, 5751-1991
Winnetka, IL, 5746-1986
Winnipauk, CT, 5752-1991
Winooski, VT, 5752-1991
Winsted, CT, 5744-1984
Winter Beach, FL, 5752-1992
Winter Park, FL, 5751-1991
Winter Springs, FL, 5751-1991
Woodbine, NJ, 5751-1991
Woodbine, GA, 5751-1991
Woodbourne, NY, 5744-1984
Woodbridge, CT, 5745-1985
Woodbridge, MD, 5751-1991
Woodcliff Lake, NJ, 5744-1984
Woodmere, LI, NY, 5745-1985
Woodridge, NY, 5744-1984
Woodstock, NY, 5745-1985
Woodstock, VT, 5752-1991
Worcester, MA, 5744-1984
Worthington, FL, 5752-1992
Wyandanch, LI, NY, 5745-1985
Wyckoff, NJ, 5744-1984
Wymouth, MA, 5745-1985
Wynimee, CA, 5745-1985
Yaphank, LI, NY, 5745-1985
Yardville, NJ, 5744-1984
Yemassee, SC, 5751-1991
Yoma, AZ, 5745-1985
Yonkers, NY, 5748-1988
Yorba Linda, CA, 5748-1988
Yorktown, VA, 5751-1991
Youngstown, OH, 5744-1984
Yulee, FL, 5751-1991

Uruguay

Artigas, 5745-1985
Mello, 5745-1985
Minas, 5745-1985
Montevideo, 5738-1978
Rivera, 5745-1985
Taquaremba, 5745-1985

Venezuela
Caracas, 5738-1978
Cristobal, 5744-1984
Maracaibo, 5744-1984
Maracay, 5744-1984
Margarita, 5744-1984
Valencia, 5744-1984
Virgin Islands
Thomas, 5744-1984
Wales
Cardiff, 5744-1984
West Germany
Hamburg, 5738-1978
Munich, 5744-1984
West Berlin, 5744-1984
Yugoslavia
Belgrade, 5739-1979
Zaire
Kinshasa, 5744-1984
Zimbabwe
Bulawayo, 5746-1986
Harare, 5743-1983

IMPORTANT DATES IN THE LIFE OF RABBI SCHNEUR ZALMAN

5505 (1745)
18th of Elul, birth of Rabbi Schneur Zalman. Born in Liozna, Russia.
His father: Rabbi Baruch, son of Rabbi Schneur Zalman.
His mother: Rivkah, daughter of Rabbi Abraham.

5518
At the age of thirteen awarded the title of תנא ופליג.

5520
Married Sterna, the daughter of Rabbi Judah Leib Segal, a pious and wealthy man from Vitebsk.

5524
First journey to study under Rabbi Dov Ber, the famous Maggid of Miezricz.

5527
Appointed Maggid (Preacher) of his hometown Liozna.

5530
Starts working on his "Shulchan Aruch."

5532
Works out his system of "ChaBaD" philosphy.

5533-5538
Establishes (in Liozna) an Academy of select disciples known as the First, Second and Third "Cheder"

5543
Successful public debate with leaders of the Mitnagdim in Minsk.

5554
Published his first Halachic work, "Hilchot Talmud Torah."

5557
Publishes his main Chassidic work, the "Tanya."

5559
The day after Simchat Torah arrested and brought to Petersburg.

5559
19th Kislev, released from prison. Day celebrated thereafter as "Chag Hageulo."

5561
Again brought to Petersburg and imprisoned. Subsequently released, but ordered to remain in Petersburg.

5561
On the 11th Av, set free and cleared of all accusations. From Petersburg he leaves immediately for Liadi.

5563
Publishes his "Siddur."

5572
End of Av leaves Liadi, on his flight from the French army, accompanied by family and close disciples.

5573

On the 12th of Tevet, he reaches the village Piena in the District of Kursk.

5573

Passes away on the night of the 24th of Tevet. He was laid to rest in the cemetery of the town of Hadiacz in the District of Poltava.

5574-6

His "Shulchan Aruch" is published posthumously by his sons.

RABBI SCHNEUR ZALMAN OF LIADI

זצוקללה"ה נבג"מ זי"ע

5505-5573 (1745-1812)

לעילוי נשמת אבותינו ואמותינו היקרים

מרת **פראדל לאה מרגליות** בת ר׳ **בנימין** ע״ה **גוטאווסקי**

ר׳ **אברהם חיים אלטר** ב״ר **צבי אליהו הלוי** ע״ה **שטיינברג**

מרת **חי׳ מלכה לכטמן** בת ר׳ **יצחק ארי׳** ע״ה **בורסטין**

ר׳ **יצחק ארי׳** ב״ר **יעקב** ע״ה **לכטמן**

ת. נ. צ. ב. ה.

נדפס על ידי ולזכות

מרת **דבורה שטיינברג**, בנה ובנותי׳, בני ביתם ומשפחתם שיחיו

ר׳ **צבי אליהו** וזוגתו מרת **חי׳ ליאורה** ובניהם **אברהם חיים**

ויצחק ארי׳ ישראל לכטמן שיחיו.

DEDICATED IN LOVING MEMORY OF

FRADLA LEAH MARGULES GUTOWSKI

JAIME STEINBERG PASAZERSKI

ANGELA BURSTIN

LUIS LECHTMAN BURSTIN

LIGIA CORONADO MOYA

may they rest in peace

•

by their children

Dory Steinberg Margules, children and grandchildren

Rabbi Tzvi Eliyahu and Mrs. Chaya Lechtman and children

לזכות

מארא בת דבורה

עזרא בן אסתר רחל שרייבר

מרדכי בן שרה טענענבוים

הרה"ת ר' **מנחם מענדל הומינר**

שיחיו

טשעסטנאט היל,

ברוקליין, מאס.

לעילוי נשמת

ר' שמריהו יצחק

ב"ר **מיכאל** ע"ה

ת.נ.צ.ב.ה.

לזכות

הרה"ח הרה"ת ר' **זלמן יצחק** שי'

ולהבחל"ח זוגתו

הרבנית מרת **ריסיא** ע"ה

פוזנר

על הפצתם אור התורה לקהלתנו

ובכל קצוי תבל

יה"ר שחכמת לבם תשאר בלבנו

נדפס ע"י

משה ושרה רבקה נאש

ראס ואניטה פייסר

דוד ורישא ליאן

עלען וג'ים פרנדרגסט

לואיס וסילבי' ליפשיץ

מייק מילר

סינדי זבדי

מודקש

לעילוי נשמת איש טוב ובעל צדקה וחסד

ר' אברהם יצחק בן ר' ישראל ע"ה

נדפס ע"י ולזכות

אשתו מ' לאה פרידא בת שימא שתליט"א

ובניהם ובנותיהם

ישראל ואשתו איטא בת סאשא וויטא

שימא חנה ובעלה ישעי' בן חנה בערקאוויטש

חיים יעקב וואלף ואשתו הדסה נחמה בת שרה

יהושע ואשתו אריאלה נוה בת חנה פייגא

רבקה צפורה ובעלה ברוך בנימין בן מירל גיטל ראבינאוויטש

אשר ואשתו שרה רינה בת אלישבע

חי' בוניא ובעלה שאול זאב בן פרימד ניומאן

נחמה בתי' ובעלה אהרן מרדכי בן בריינא סאנדלאו

שרה ובעלה דובער בן שרה פרומא יוניק

שפרה דאכל ובעלה יצחק שרגא בן שרה זילבער

וכל משפחתם שיחיו

באסטאמסקי

לאורך ימים ושנים טובות לבריאות נכונה בגו"ר ולהצלחה

רבה ומופלגה בכל עניניהם מתוך רוב שמחה וטוב לבב

לע"נ **מתתיהו** בן **ישעי'** ע"ה
ורחל בת **יהודה** ע"ה
זילאנקא
ובני משפחות **זילאנקא, דיילזמאן,**
שפיגלמאן, וקזאפניק
שנספו בימי מלחמת העולם השני'

ת. נ. צ. ב. ה

יה"ר שהפצת מעיינות החסידות
ושמירת התורה והמצוות יהיו ברכה
לנשמותיהם הקדושות

נדפס ע"י משפחת **זילאנקא** שיחיו

לע"נ הורנו היקרים
ר' **ליאנעל** ומרת **בלאנשא** ע"ה
גאלדמאן

יה"ר שחסדם והתמסרותם
ישפיעו עלינו לנצח

ת. נ. צ. ב. ה.

לזכות
החסיד ר' **זלמן יודא**
ב"ר **שלום ישעי'** ע"ה
דייטש
ת. נ. צ. ב. ה.

נדפס ע"י בנו הרה"ת **נחמי'**
וזוגתו מרת **דבורה**
ובניהם
מנחם מענדל, יוסף חיים, יהושע,
וזלמן יודא
ובתם
מירל
שיחיו
דייטש

לע"נ
ר' **זעליג** - מגיד שיעור בספר התניא
וזוגתו מרת **מאלי**
ובנותיהם
לענא, ריי, רוזא, דורותי, ומרים
ע"ה
שרייבר

ת.נ.צ.ב.ה.

נדפס ע"י נכדתם
גלוריא שתחי' **בנבנשתי-וורטליב**
ונינם
מיכאל שי' **בנבנשתי**

- באהבה -

לזכות
שלוחי כ״ק אדמו״ר זי״ע
בכל מרחבי תבל

נדפס ע״י
א׳ השלוחים שי׳

לזכות **כ״ק אדמו״ר זי״ע**, נשיא דורנו

לחיזוק ההתקשרות **לכ״ק אדמו״ר זי״ע**

לזכות **כ״ק אדמו״ר זי״ע**, ולרפואה שלימה ל**חי׳ מושקא** בת **חנה** שתחי׳

לזכות **כ״ק אדמו״ר זי״ע**, ע״י ר׳ **שמחה** וזוגתו **סענערמאן** ומשפחתם שיחיו

לכבוד יום הגדול והקדוש שלישי לחודש תמוז, יום ההילולא ד**כ״ק אדמו״ר זי״ע**

לזכות כל ממשיכי דרכו הק׳ של **כ״ק אדמו״ר זי״ע**, ע״י **דאמעניקא ואנג׳לא לעפארע**

לזכות הרה״ת ר׳ **מנחם מענדל קפלן וזוגתו** שיחיו, טורנהיל, אנטרריא, שימשיכו להצליח **ושכ״ק אדמו״ר זי״ע** יברכם בכל המצטרך

לזכות ר׳ **אליעזר יעקב** ו**אלאנא קאהן** ומשפחתם שיחיו, ולזכות **כ״ק אדמו״ר זי״ע**, **שלוחיו**, **חסידיו**, **וכלל ישראל**

לכבוד יום הגדול והקדוש שלישי לחודש תמוז, יום ההילולא ד**כ״ק אדמו״ר זי״ע**, ויה״ר שספר זה ימשיך לחנך ולעורר את הדורות הבאים, ויעזור להצית את הניצוץ שבכל איש ישראל, בהוקרה ע״י ר׳ **משה יצחק** ומרת **טובה** שיחיו **פלדמן**

לזכות **אליעזר** שי׳ **ומרים** שתחי׳ **פארקס** וילדיהם ומשפחותיהם וכל יוצאי חלציהם שיחיו
לזכות התמים **אברהם אליהו** שי׳ **פארקס**

לע״נ **רנטו מאיר** ע״ה **מיאהאס**, ע״י בתו **לאה חי׳** ובנו **דוד יוסף** שיחיו

לזכות **חנן** בן **פערל**, **עליזה** בת **ביילא**, **מנחם מענדל** בן **עליזה**, **אסתר חנה** בת **עליזה**, **מנוחה רחל** בת **עליזה** שיחיו
קריביסקי

לזכות הרה״ת ר׳ **ברוך שלום** שיחי׳ **קאנטאר**

לזכות **לייביש, כוכבה, רוזנה, לבנה** ו**יוסף דוד** שיחיו **דזשאקסאן (לוי)**

לע״נ מרת **בריינדל בלימה** בת ר׳ **אליהו** ע״ה

לזכות החינוך החסידותי של כל ילדי ישראל, ע״י משפחת **ברונשטיין**

לזכות הרה״ת ר׳ **שלום** שיחיו **הײדינגספעלד**, שמחה מאניקא, קאליפארניא

לע״נ ר׳ **אברהם נתן** ב״ר **איסאק קאפל** ע״ה ור׳ **איסאק קאפל** ע״ה ב״ר **יצחק** שיחי׳ **ועזיזה** בת **טובה** ע״ה

לע״נ ר׳ **בנציון** ב״ר **יצחק** ע״ה **בולינסקי**, נפטר ד׳ אייר, ע״י ר׳ **משה זאב** בן **אסיא** שי׳ **בולינסקי**

בהוקרה ל**בית חב״ד, שורליין, מאססאטשוסעטס**, ולהרה״ת ר׳ **יוסף וזוגתו** שיחיו **יפה**

לזכות **לוי יצחק** בן **רחל**, **שיינא** בת **ראשא לאה**, **סימא חסיא** בת **שיינא** שיחיו **גארדאן**

לע״נ ר׳ **אליהו** ב״ר **ישעי׳** ע״ה **בוטל**

לזכות ילדי משפחת **גייסינסקי** שיחיו, ע״י הוריהם הרה״ת **יצחק** וזוגתו מרת **יהודית** שיחיו, ל.ב., קאליפארניא

לע״נ ר׳ **משה** בן **נתן** ומרת **עטל** בת ר׳ **זאב** ע״ה, ע״י ר׳ **וויין** ומרת **מערי** ומשפחתם שיחיו **פליישמאן**

לזכות **אחינו בני ישראל** בכל מקום שהם

לזכות הרבנית מרת **אסתר** שתחי׳ **גרויסבוים** לבריאות הנכונה

לע״נ ר׳ **נתן** ומרת **גייל** ע״ה **סלאווטין**

לזכות **בית חב״ד, טולסא, אוקלהומא**, ע״י ר׳ **יואל** ומרת **בטסי** שיחיו **זליגסון**

לזכות הרה״ת **ישעי׳ הלוי** וזוגתו מרת **חנה** שיחיו **סאסקינד**, ולהצלחה במילוי שליחותם ב**אַשוויל, צפון קאראָליינאַ**
לרגל הולדת התאומות **חי׳ מושקא ופעסל** שתחיו ביום י״א טבת תשס״ט
בהוקרה ובידידות ע״י דר. **ליסא לארעלי** ו**ברייען אלען** שיחיו

לזכות **שטערנא שרה** בת **שיינא חי׳**, **פריידא** בת **שיינא חי׳**, **מנחם מענדל הכהן** בן **שיינא חי׳** שיחיו **ווייספיש**

~

לזכות **דזשעניפער סטאקלער ואמאנדא ווארעל** שתחיו, ע״י **רון** שיחי׳ **סטאקלער**

~

לע״נ **אהרן** בן **שלום** ע״ה

~

לע״נ ר׳ **משה דוד** ומרת **שרה כהן** ע״ה, ע״י משפחתם שיחיו

~

לזכות **יהושע**, **גרשום**, **שיינא רינה**, **ואליאנא** שיחיו **סטאנפילד**

~

לזכות **דוד** בן **קיילא חנה**, **עטרה** בת **נוהמי׳**, **נתנאל** בן **עטרה**, **וחוה** בת **עטרה** שיחיו **רעווערע**, טשאפעל הילל, נ.ק.

~

לזכות **יעקב ורבקה טובה** שי׳ **לבנסברגר**, יה״ר שילכו תמיד בדרך התורה, דרך ה׳, ושנזכה לראות בביאת המשיח, אמן

~

לע״נ ר׳ **שרגא פייוויל** ומרת **איידל מרים** ע״ה

~

לע״נ **רבקה** בת **הינדא** ע״ה **קפלן**, ע״י משפחתה, משפחת **מייזר**

~

לע״נ ר׳ **ברוך** ב״ר **זאב** ומרת **לובא** בת ר׳ **יעקב** ע״ה

~

לזכות אבי ר׳ **שלמה** ואמי מרת **סלמא שערטאק** ובני **דניאל** וכלתי **חייקי שערטאק** שיחיו, ע״י ר׳ **יואל שערטאק** שי׳

~

לזכות **עזריאל ויתניאל** שיחיו **אקרמן**, יה״ר שאור התורה ישאר בלבבם ויאיר דרך חייהם

~

לע״נ **יונה**, **בת-שבע**, **אהרן**, **יעקב ושמעון** ע״ה **הארדי**

~

לע״נ ר׳ **שלום דוד** ב״ר **יוסף** ומרת **אסתר פרומא** בר ר׳ **שלום** ע״ה

~

לזכות הרה״ת ר׳ **נח** ומרת **רבקה וחיים יצחק** שיחיו **וואגעל**

~

לע״נ הרה״ח ר׳ **מנחם מענדל** ע״ה **הכהן פלדמן** שהביא אותי לראשונה אל ספר התניא, ע״י מר **רוברט היילנד**

~

לזכות **רחל הודהליה ואהרן אתיאל דוד אונגר** שיחיו. יאיר ה׳ פניו אליהם. ע״י הוריהם גלי ולאה שירה שיחיו **אונגר**

~

בהוקרה לאבי זקני ר׳ **ירוחם פישל** ב״ר **יהודה ליב צייטלין** ולאמי מרת **רבקה רחל רות**, ע״י מרת **בתי׳ לאה מיכלסון**

~

לע״נ הרב **זאב** ומרת **אסתר מרים** ע״ה **קורצמן**, ע״י ילדיהם, **אלון מנחם**, **עקיבא דוד**, **ורניטא** שיחיו **קורצמן**

~

ISBN 978-0-8266-0400-2

9 780826 604002